Jenny Jordan
412 Sage

FUNDAMENTALS OF
FINANCIAL ACCOUNTING

The Robert N. Anthony/Willard J. Graham Series in Accounting

F·O·U·R·T·H
E·D·I·T·I·O·N

FUNDAMENTALS OF
FINANCIAL ACCOUNTING

Glenn A. Welsch
College of Business Administration
The University of Texas at Austin

Robert N. Anthony
Graduate School of Business Administration
Harvard University

Daniel G. Short
College of Business Administration
The University of Texas at Austin

1984

Richard D. Irwin, Inc.
Homewood, Illinois 60430

© RICHARD D. IRWIN, INC., 1974, 1977, 1981, and 1984

ISBN 0-256-02984-9

Library of Congress Catalog Card No. 83–81777

Printed in the United States of America

2 3 4 5 6 7 8 9 0 K 1 0 9 8 7 6 5 4

To
Irma, Katherine, Maryrose,
Jennifer, and Heather

Preface

This Fourth Edition retains all of the features favorably commented upon by numerous faculty members who used the prior editions. It has been updated in all respects, and approximately 80 percent of the assignment material has been replaced or revised. Additional problems/cases contribute a measure of greater depth and analytical substance.

Chapter 17, Financial Reporting and Changing Prices, has been completely rewritten to emphasize the underlying concepts of *FASB Statement No. 33*. The authors present unique illustrations of constant dollar restatement and current cost application especially designed to be understandable to beginning accounting students. Also, a special supplement on income taxes has been added.

To lend an unusual level of flexibility in use and to increase readability, chapters have been divided into two or more separate parts. The objectives of each part are concisely delineated, and the questions for discussion, exercises, and problems/ cases are grouped separately by part (both in the text and the Solutions Manual). A complete list of important terms defined in the chapter, and key words in the definition, with specific page citations, is given at the end of each chapter. The demonstration cases, with solutions, at the end of the various chapters have been carefully selected and written to provide a comprehensive overview of the chapter.

Major portions of each chapter have been rewritten to incorporate the latest developments in financial accounting and to increase comprehension. Numerous illustrations are provided to supplement the written discussions. A unique format has been introduced for many of the exhibits. This format presents the *(a)* illustrative data *(b)* analysis, and *(c)* accounting entries and/or reporting, all in one single exhibit. All of the new features significantly increase the level of flexibility of the text in use.

The prior extensive list of teaching and student aids has been expanded and revised. In addition to the textbook, these aids are:

Available to students:

1. Study Guide (coordinated with the sequence of each chapter; includes comprehensive outlines, illustrations, and sample examination questions with answers).
2. Working Papers (includes all forms, with captions, needed for solving all exercises and problems/cases).
3. Practice Set (application of the complete accounting information processing system as discussed in the textbook).

Available to the instructor:

4. Comprehensive Teachers Manual (includes answers to all questions for class discussion, exercises, and problems/cases; also, includes suggested course plans, assignment schedules, and instructional ideas).
5. List of Check Figures that includes check figures for exercises and problem/cases (available in quantity for distribution to students).
6. Bank of Examination Questions (coordinated by chapter).
7. Teaching Transparencies (as used by the authors for mass sections).

Many accounting instructors prefer to divide the fundamentals course in accounting into two parts—the first semester focusing on financial accounting and the second on management accounting. Many texts, however, are not arranged so that such an approach is feasible with a single text.

This volume and its companion, *Fundamentals of Management Accounting,* are designed to provide material for a fully coordinated fundamentals course. As the titles indicate, this volume deals with the fundamentals of financial accounting, and its companion with the fundamentals of management accounting. Each volume can be used either for a one-semester or a one-quarter course. Both are designed to provide maximum flexibility for the instructor in the selection and order of materials for the classroom. They emphasize those aspects of accounting we believe essential for interpretation and use of accounting information. Mechanical and procedural details are minimized, while the conceptual, measurement, and communication aspects are emphasized.

This book is an introduction to **financial accounting,** which has as its primary subject the communication of relevant financial information to external parties. We strongly believe that a certain level of knowledge of the accounting model, the measuring processes involved, the data classifications, and terminology is essential to the interpretation and effective use of financial statements. We have provided the necessary information in this volume. The key to effective use of financial statements is to understand what they do and do not say, the measuring approaches used, and the standards observed in their development. This is the case both for students who will continue their study of accounting and for those who will not. The materials are arranged to meet the requirements of a wide range of academic institutions and curricula.

This volume represents a significant departure from the traditional financial accounting textbook in several respects. First, it makes possible a high level of *flexibility* for the instructor by presenting separately designated comprehensive discussions of a broad range of subject areas rather than the bare minimum. This approach means that more materials are presented than usually can be covered in the *undergraduate* financial course in accounting (however, it is completely adequate for such a graduate course). Importantly, this coverage gives the instructor a great amount of flexibility to select those topics appropriate to the situation. In contrast, a textbook that provides only the minimum materials imposes on the instructor the unfortunate choice of having to *(a)* present a *de minimus* course or *(b)* devote considerable time developing supplementary textual and homework assignments. Secondly, this text provides additional flexibility because it discusses a number of topics not traditionally included in an elementary textbook. In our judgment, much of the traditional material is essential; however, the recent thrusts and changes in financial accounting make it imperative that certain significant topics be accorded comprehensive treatment. This volume avoids superficial treatment of these new directions by giving special emphasis to concepts, rationale, measurement, and reporting. Certain special issues and traditional procedural topics are presented in chapter *supplements* should coverage of some or all of them be desired.

The primary features of this book and the instructional materials that accompany it are as follows:

- The characteristics of the environment in which the accounting process operates are emphasized in the first chapter and are integrated throughout the other chapters.

- In the first chapter, the student is presented with a comprehensive description of the end products of the financial accounting process—the external financial statements and related disclosures. This emphasis is continued throughout the other chapters.

- This volume presents the maximum amount of material that can ordinarily be covered in a one-semester undergraduate course. Therefore, some choices must be made by the instructor to reduce the coverage of selected topics.

- Accounting is presented as an information processing model designed to enhance communication by the entity to the users of its financial reports.

- The discussions emphasize concepts, standards, and generally accepted accounting principles as the rationale for the way certain things are done in accounting.

- Throughout the chapters, the measuring approaches used in accounting and reporting to decision makers are emphasized.

- Throughout, the focus is on the corporation rather than on the sole proprietorship or the partnership. Actual case examples are utilized. As a consequence, income taxes, dividends, earnings per share, capital stock, the *APB Opinions,* and the *FASB Statements* are discussed.

- Relevant topics, not ordinarily treated in a first course, are discussed. These include cash flow, present value, consolidated statements, purchase versus pooling, statement of changes in financial position (both working capital and cash bases), compensating balances, price level effects, income taxes, and current value.

- One or more *supplements* follow some of the chapters. These supplements focus on special topics including the clerical and mechanical aspects of the accounting process such as special journals, subsidiary ledgers, payrolls, and petty cash. Separation in supplements facilitates their exclusion, or order of selection, without affecting the continuity of the course.

- A special supplement presents an overview of income taxes for the individual taxpayer and for corporations.

• A special supplement presents the 1982 annual report of Johnson & Johnson. Reference to this report is integrated throughout the discussions and problems/ cases in the various chapters.

These features are of particular importance to nonaccounting majors because the first semester usually is their only exposure to the fundamentals of financial accounting. For example, most of the external financial statements coming to the attention of the nonaccounting majors, both in school and in real life, will be consolidated statements. Similarly, an understanding of the effects of general inflation and specific price changes on financial information is essential in these times to the interpretation of reported results.

Answers to questions such as how much time should be spent on each chapter, how much homework should be required, and what materials should be omitted depend on the objectives of the particular course, the time constraints, and the backgrounds of the students. As mentioned above, we have arranged the topical materials to permit maximum flexibility in selecting among various options and in giving varying topical emphasis to fit practically all situations; supplements, parts of chapters, and even entire chapters may be omitted without adversely affecting the continuity of the course. The Solutions Manual includes comments and suggestions that are particularly helpful in selecting among a number of possible options.

The subject matter of the 17 chapters and 17 supplements that comprise this volume has been arranged in what we believe to be a pedagogically sound sequence; nevertheless, considerable rearrangements can be made if the instructor so desires. Each chapter has a summary, and almost all have a demonstration case with a suggested solution. The purpose of the demonstration cases is to tie together the various subtopics discussed in the chapter. Following each chapter are study materials classified as (a) discussion questions, (b) short exercises (suitable for homework, class illustrations, and examinations), and (c) comprehensive problems/cases. Each of these groups of study materials is arranged to follow the topical sequence of the chapter.

The list of students and faculty members to whom the authors feel a sense of gratitude for ideas and suggestions is too long to enumerate here. With respect to this volume, we are particularly grateful to the following individuals who devoted considerable time in discussions, reviewing parts of the manuscript, and testing materials:

The following graduate students at The University of Texas at Austin: Vicky Conway, John Lohman, Ann Lynch, Priscilla Slade, and Leslie Valz. We recognize the valuable editorial suggestions provided by Petria Sandlin, Kathy Springer, and Sherry Stewart, graduate students, University of Texas at Austin, and to Linden Welsch and Thu Nguyen. We are especially grateful to Professors Janet Daniels, University of Hartford, Harry Dickinson, University of Virginia, Ralph Drtina, Lehigh University, and LaVern Krueger, University of Missouri, for their valuable suggestions for this Fourth Edition.

Consultation with Professors Ray Sommerfeld and Sally Jones was especially valuable in preparing the special supplement on income taxes.

Finally, we express our thanks to numerous users of the prior editions for their valuable suggestions.

Our thanks to the American Institute of Certified Public Accountants, American Accounting Association, Financial Accounting Standards Board, and the authors identified by citations for permission to quote from their publications. To Johnson & Johnson, our special thanks for permission to use selected materials from its annual reports. We also appreciate the permission by Commerce Clearing House, Inc. to use selected materials from their 1983 U.S. Master Tax Guide.

Suggestions and comments on the text and the related materials are invited.

Glenn A. Welsch
Robert N. Anthony
Daniel G. Short

Contents

FUNDAMENTALS OF
FINANCIAL ACCOUNTING

Perspectives—Accounting Objectives and Communication

OBJECTIVE OF THIS BOOK

The objective of this book and its companion volume, *Fundamentals of Management Accounting*,[1] is to develop your knowledge of, and your ability to use, accounting information. Accounting often is subdivided into financial accounting and management accounting. This volume on **financial accounting,** focuses on the use of accounting information in the decision-making processes of individuals and groups external to the business, that is, **owners, investors, potential investors, creditors, and the public at large.** The second volume, on management accounting, focuses on the role of accounting information in the decision-making processes of managers with responsibilities inside the organization. Whether you ultimately become an owner, a manager, an investor, or a creditor, or even if your only interest in a business entity is that of a concerned citizen, an understanding of accounting will enhance significantly your effectiveness as a decision maker. Also, as you study these two volumes you will develop an understanding of how accounting information is used in resource-allocation decisions in all types of organizations such as profit-making enterprises, nonprofit endeavors, governmental entities, and social programs. In practically all organizations, long-term success depends in large part on the quality of the resource-allocation decisions that are made. In the broad sense, accounting information is used to aid in the decision-making process and as a measure of the financial results after the decisions are made and implemented.

This book is designed for students who have had no prior academic study of accounting. The chapters usually are divided into parts to facilitate study and to provide flexibility in the selection of materials for emphasis consistent with the time available. Supplements to the chapters are provided to permit additional flexibility; they include (1) more advanced discussion of selected topics and (2) strictly procedural aspects of selected topics.

PURPOSE OF THIS CHAPTER

The purpose of this chapter is to present a broad perspective of the **objectives** of accounting and of the environment in which accounting usually operates. To accomplish this purpose, the chapter is divided into two parts:

Part A—The objectives and environment of accounting
Part B—Communication of accounting information

---

[1] Robert N. Anthony, Glenn A. Welsch, and James S. Reece, Fundamentals of Management Accounting, 4th ed. (Homewood, Ill.: Richard D. Irwin, 1985).

PART A—THE OBJECTIVES AND ENVIRONMENT OF ACCOUNTING

ACCOUNTING DEFINED

Accounting can be defined as the collection of financial data about an organization and the analysis, measurement, recording, and reporting of that information to decision makers. An accounting system processes the *(a)* flows of resources into (inflows) and out (outflows) of the organization; *(b)* resources controlled (i.e., assets) by the organization, and *(c)* claims against those resources (i.e., debts). In addition, accounting requires judgment and interpretation in analyzing, reporting, and using the reported financial results. The accounting flow of economic information of an entity can be summarized as in Exhibit 1–1.

EXHIBIT 1–1
Flow of economic information in accounting

* Financial statements are prepared primarily for investors and creditors and those that advise investors and creditors. Financial statements are prepared under the assumption of reasonably sophisticated and diligent users (FASB, *Statement of Financial Accounting Concepts No. 1*).

If you have studied economics, you will perceive that it has a relationship with accounting. Economics has been defined as the study of how people and society choose to employ scarce productive resources that could have alternative uses to produce various commodities and distribute them for consumption, now or in the future, among various persons and groups in society.[2] This definition suggests a relationship to the definition of accounting. Like economics, accounting has a conceptual foundation that provides guidelines for the collection, measurement, and communication of financial information about the organization. Accounting often is viewed as encompassing the financial planning and controlling process (discussed in *Fundamentals of Management Accounting*) that focus on the future allocations of the scarce resources of the organization. Thus, accounting collects, measures, interprets, and reports information on the same human activities that are the focus of economics. Economics attempts to explain economic relationships primarily on a conceptual level, whereas accounting attempts to report the economic relationships primarily on the practical level. However, accounting measurements must be made as consistent as is possible with economic concepts. Accounting must deal with the very real and complex problems of measuring in monetary terms the economic effects of **exchange transactions** (i.e., resource inflows and outflows), the resources held, and the claims against those resources for each entity. Throughout these two volumes many of the theoretical and practical issues that arise in the measurement process will be discussed from the accounting viewpoint.

---

[2] Paul A. Samuelson, *Economics*, 9th ed. (New York: McGraw-Hill, 1975).

ACCOUNTING OPERATES IN A COMPLEX ENVIRONMENT

The environment in which accounting operates is affected by such broad perva- sive forces as the type of *(a)* government (e.g., democracy versus communism), *(b)* economic system (e.g., free enterprise versus socialism), *(c)* industry (e.g., tech- nological versus agrarian), *(d)* organizations within that society (labor unions), and *(e)* regulatory controls (i.e., private sector versus governmental). Also, account- ing is influenced significantly by the educational level and economic development reflected in the society.

In various ways each of us is associated with social, political, and economic organizations such as businesses, churches, fraternal organizations, political par- ties, states, schools, environmental groups, chambers of commerce, and profes- sional associations. Many of these organizations deal with important resource allocation and societal problems for which decisions must be made. These organi- zations are essential to the workings of a society; indeed, they constitute much of what we call society. Thus, the future quality of our society depends in large measure upon the collective decisions of the managers of such organizations.

Fundamental to a dynamic and successful society is the ability of each organiza- tion to measure and report its accomplishments, to undergo critical self-analysis, and, by means of sound decisions, to renew itself and grow so that individual and societal objectives are served best. Essentially, society, and the various organi- zations that comprise it, thrives in direct proportion to the efficiency with which it allocates scarce resources of human talent, materials, services, and capital. To accomplish this broad goal, organizations and persons interested in those organiza- tions need information about how the resources that the organization controls are obtained and used. Broadly, accounting information is designed to meet this need.

Therefore, accounting is a system designed by members of the society and continuously is undergoing change to meet the evolving needs of society. The environmental characteristics of a society are diverse and complex; therefore, accounting always is facing new challenges. For example, an inflationary spiral necessitates the development of accounting concepts and procedures that will report changes in "real" values separately from purely inflationary effects (see Chapter 17).

Throughout this textbook you will study how accounting is responding to the environment in the United States. In the next few paragraphs we will discuss two environmental characteristics—**measurement in dollars** and the **types of business entities**—because they have pervasive effects on accounting concepts and procedures.

Measurement in dollars

A monetary system provides the primary way to measure and communicate information about the flow of resources in and out of an organization. In a mone- tary system, the unit of exchange (dollars in our case) is the common denominator used to measure value. Thus, the monetary unit provides a means for expressing the available resources and the resource flows of both the society as a whole and the various organizations which comprise that society. Accounting provides monetary measurement of inputs (resources received) and outputs (goods produced and services rendered), and as a consequence, it provides benchmarks for evaluating the efficiency of organizations.

Accounting measures the resources, claims against those resources, and resource flows of organizations within a society in terms of the monetary unit of that society. Accounting uses the monetary system of each country within which it operates. One of the critical problems in accounting is the conversion of financial amounts from one monetary system to another monetary system in measuring resources and resource flows for multinational activities. To deal with this problem, accounting has adopted a **unit-of-measure assumption** (see Exhibit 2–6) which holds that the common denominator or "measuring stick" used for accounting measurements in the United States is the dollar and that the dollar is a useful measuring unit.[3]

Types of business entities

This book will focus primarily on accounting for profit-making entities. In our environment there are three main types of business entities. They will be referred to often throughout this volume; therefore, their primary characteristics are explained below.

A **sole proprietorship** is an unincorporated business that is owned by one person. This type of business entity is common in the fields of services, retailing, and farming. Usually, the owner also is the manager. Legally, the business and the owner are not separate entities—they are one and the same. However, accounting views the business as a **separate entity** to be accounted for separately from its owner.

A **partnership** is an unincorporated business that is owned by two or more persons known as partners. The agreements between the owners are set forth in a partnership contract. This contract specifies such matters as division of profits each period and distribution of resources of the business upon termination of its operations. As in the case of a sole proprietorship, a partnership is not legally separate from its owners. Legally, in a general partnership, each partner is responsible for the debts of the business (i.e., each general partner has what is called unlimited liability). However, accounting views the partnership as a separate business entity to be accounted for separately from its several owners.

A **corporation** is a business that is incorporated under the laws of a particular state; the owners are known as stockholders or shareholders. Ownership is represented by shares of capital stock that usually can be bought and sold freely. When an approved application is filed by the organizers, the state issues a charter that gives the corporation the right to operate legally as a separate legal entity, that is, separate and apart from its owners. The owners enjoy "limited liability," which means that they are liable for the debts of the corporation only to the

---

[3] The exchange unit (dollars) changes in purchasing power due to the effects of inflation and deflation; simply put, the dollar does not always command the same amount of **real** goods. Thus, money does not have the most basic element of any measurement unit (i.e., a meter always is the same length), that is, uniformity in magnitude. During inflation and deflation, the monetary unit is not uniform in magnitude because one unit will command fewer, or more, real goods respectively than before.

extent of their investments therein. The charter specifies the types and amounts of capital stock that can be issued. Most states require a minimum of two or three stockholders and a minimum amount of resources to be contributed at the time of organization. The stockholders **elect** a governing board of directors, which in turn **employs** managers and exercises general supervision of the corporation.[4] Accounting for the business entity focuses on the corporation, not on the directors and managers as individuals.

In terms of economic importance, the corporation is the dominant form of business organization in the United States. The advantages of the corporate form include *(a)* limited liability for the stockholders, *(b)* continuity of life, *(c)* ease in transferring ownership (stock), and *(d)* opportunities to raise large amounts of money by selling shares to a large number of people. Because of these advantages, most large and medium-sized businesses (and many small ones) are organized as corporations. Therefore, we shall emphasize this form of business. Nevertheless, the accounting concepts, standards, and measurement procedures that we will discuss also generally apply to the other types of businesses.

One of the essentials of any measurement process is a precise definition of specifically what is to be measured. Examples of specific things to be measured are the population of California, the rainfall in Michigan, the voter registrations in New York, and the bank deposits in Texas (each for a stipulated time). Similarly, in the measurement of resources and resource flows, accounting requires precise definition of the specific entity for which monetary or financial data are to be collected, measured, and reported. When a specific entity is defined carefully, it is often referred to as an **accounting entity.** The whole nation can be thought of as a specific entity, so can each business unit, and so can each individual person. In any measurement scheme, the definition of that which is to be measured often involves difficult problems. For example, in measuring the population of California should the amount include service personnel? college students? jail inmates? long-term visitors? hotel guests? Similarly, in defining an accounting entity, there are important problems to be resolved. For example, if we are to account for, say, Adams Company, it is defined as a separate and specific accounting entity. Thus, the accounting entity has a specialized definition that is known as the **separate-entity assumption.**[5] **The separate-entity assumption holds that for accounting measurement purposes, the particular entity being accounted for is distinguished carefully from all similar and related entities and persons.** Under this assumption, an accounting entity is held to be separate and distinct from its owner(s). An entity is viewed as **owning the resources** (i.e., **assets**) used by it and as **owing the claims** (i.e., **debts**) against those assets. For measurement purposes, the assets, debts, and activities of the entity are kept completely separate from those of the owners and other entities. For example, in the case

---

[4] There are a number of specialized types of entities that we do not discuss, such as joint ventures, mutual funds, cooperatives, investment trusts, and syndicates. Consideration of these is beyond the scope of this book.

[5] A list of the fundamental assumptions and principles underlying accounting is summarized in Exhibit 2–6.

of Adams Company, the personal assets, debts, and activities of the owners are not included in the accounting measurements of the business itself.

THE USE OF ACCOUNTING INFORMATION BY DECISION MAKERS

Your role as a future decision maker is significant, whether you become a manager, investor, professional person, owner of a business, or simply an interested citizen. Decision makers use various approaches for selecting one alternative solution to a given problem from among a set of several alternative solutions to that problem. Selection of the preferred alternative constitutes the basic decision. In the process of reaching decisions, the decision maker is concerned about the **future** because a decision cannot change the past; however, an effective decision maker does not neglect the past. Knowledge and interpretation of what has happened in the past can aid in making decisions because history may shed considerable light on what the future is likely to hold. Thus, one of the fundamental inputs to decision making is dependable and relevant historical data. A large portion of historical data that are relevant to business decisions are expressed in monetary terms. They include costs (i.e., resources expended), revenues (i.e., resources earned), assets (i.e., things owned), liabilities (i.e., amounts owed), and owners' equity (i.e., total assets less total liabilities of the entity). Thus, accounting provides an important information base for decision making. The information provided by accounting must be understandable and relevant to the decision maker to preclude unwarranted interpretations in the decision-making process. This is a primary reason why measurements in accounting must adhere to certain standards and concepts.

Accounting reports (i.e., financial statements) serve those who use the reported information in three related ways:

1. Accounting provides information that is helpful in making decisions. Most important decisions, regardless of the type of endeavor involved, are based, in part, upon complex financial considerations. Accounting provides an important information base and a particular analytical orientation that help the decision maker assess the potential financial implications and potential outcomes of various alternatives that are being considered. The primary role of accounting is to facilitate decision making by investors, creditors, and others.

2. Accounting reports the economic effects of past decisions on the entity. Once a decision is made and implementation starts, there are important and often subtle financial economic effects on the entity. These economic effects often are critical to the success of the endeavor. Thus, the evolving effects of past decisions must be measured continuously and periodically reported so that the decision maker can be informed of continuing and new problems, and of successes, over time. Thus, accounting provides a continuing **feedback** of the economic effects of a series of decisions already made, the results of which are communicated to the decision maker by means of periodic financial statements.

3. Accounting keeps track of a wide range of items to meet the financial score-keeping and safeguarding responsibilities imposed on all organizations. These

EXHIBIT 1–2
Accounting information flows in a decision and implementation cycle

include how much cash is available for use; how much customers owe the company; what debts are owed by the organization; what items are owned by the company, such as machinery and office equipment; and inventory levels on hand.

Most entities, such as a business or a hospital, engage in activities over an extended period of time during which resources are committed and used with the expectation that there will be desirable results in the form of goods and/or services. During the period of continuing activities, those involved in the organization, be they owners, sponsors, or managers, need information about the continuing amounts of resources committed, resources used, resources on hand, and outputs (goods and services); and this information should be reported, interpreted, and evaluated periodically. The accounting process is designed to provide a continuing flow of such information to all interested parties. A typical flow of accounting information in an entity is diagrammed in Exhibit 1–2. The financial statements constitute the primary source of relevant information on a continuing basis (feedback). This information is important **feedback** concerning the outcome of a particular decision.

A business

First, the objectives of a business are formulated by the organizers. Initially, the owners provide the funds, which often are supplemented by funds provided by creditors. These funds then are used by the managers of the business to acquire machinery, inventory, services, and other resources. Assume you are the manager of the entity and that you develop a "business plan" for operating the business. As the business operates, additional resources flow in from the sale of goods and services. Many other activities occur, many of which involve either the inflow or outflow of resources. As the manager of the business, you need information, on a continuing basis, that tells about the status of the resources. You need to know such things as sources and amounts of funds, revenues (sales and services sold), expenses, the amounts invested in such things as equipment and inventory, the cash situation, the amount spent for research and development, and the amount of money used in the sales efforts.

As the manager, you need information about resources and flows of resources for two fundamental reasons. First, accounting information in response to these and similar questions may aid you in making sound decisions about the entity that can improve its effectiveness and efficiency. Second, accounting information tells you (and other interested parties) what the **score** was during the immediate past periods. This scorekeeping is important to the evaluation and control of performance. In Exhibit 1–2, financial evaluations and interpretations are shown as one of the information inputs to the decision-making process. The exhibit also depicts the accounting processing system which involves **data collection, measurement, evaluation, and reporting of the results.** In the reporting phase, the accounting information is communicated as an aid in making new decisions and in revising prior decisions.

Now, assume instead that you are a stockholder (an owner) who has a substantial amount of money invested in the business but you have little opportunity to directly influence the management. As a stockholder, you must select from among three alternatives: (1) retain your ownership interest, (2) expand or contract it, or (3) dispose of it completely. As a stockholder, you also are interested in decisions that will lead to expansion of the business and raise its level of efficiency. As a consequence of these concerns, you need to have financial information such as the trend of sales, the level of expenses, the amount of earnings, the amount invested by the entity in various assets (such as inventory and machinery), the debts of the business, and the cash balance. In other words, as an investor you need to know how the management is allocating the scarce resources provided by you and the other owners and the creditors. Such information would be necessary to you in selecting one of the three alternatives listed above. The primary objective of the periodic financial statements is to provide, on a continuing basis, information bearing on these alternatives. The accounting information provided should be an important part of the decision-making process of the stockholders in ways similar to those depicted in Exhibit 1–2.

A hospital

Now, assume you are on the board of governors of a local hospital and, as a consequence, share the responsibility for the basic decisions and guidelines for its continued operation at an efficient level. Similar to the owner of a business, you have a wide variety of questions concerning its revenues, expenses, funds tied up in buildings and equipment, cost of charity services, and so on, that are in the scorekeeping category. Also, you are concerned with whether enough resources are being allocated to such activities as emergency care, sanitation, and nursing services. Before any sound decisions in these areas can be made for the future, you must have information about the past and current allocation of resources to them and about the quality and quantity of output or benefits. Thus, as a sponsor, you have many information needs that are important to your decisions for the future.

Now, consider the manager of the hospital. The manager needs accounting information about the operations of the hospital similar to that discussed above for the manager of a business, and for the same reasons. Typically, the manager will need more **detailed** accounting information than the sponsor. In any event, whether one is a sponsor or manager of the hospital, financial measurement and the reporting results should be continuing inputs to the decision-making process. This situation suggests the importance of accounting information which was emphasized in an interesting way in *Forbes* magazine (August 17, 1981) as follows:

> In all of mainland China there are about 30 CPAs. Some might call this a sign of how advanced the Chinese civilization really is, but for the Chinese—who are making an effort to bring their economy into the 20th century—it's a major obstacle. Now the leaders in the Chinese government want modern accounting systems—translation: Western accounting systems—and they want them fast. After all, this is a nation with some 400,000 manufacturing concerns and one accounting firm.

HISTORICAL PERSPECTIVES

Accounting is as old as the exchange processes (whether barter or monetary) that gradually developed with civilization. The earliest written records, including the Scriptures, contain references to what now is called accounting.

Accounting evolved in response to the economic needs of society. Prior to the 15th century it apparently followed no well-defined pattern except that it developed in answer to specific governing and trading needs of the era. The first known treatment of the subject of accounting was written in 1494, two years after the discovery of America. An Italian monk and mathematician, Fr. Luca Paciolo, described an approach that had been developed by the Italian merchants of the time to account for their activities as owner-managers of business ventures. Paciolo laid the foundations of the basic "accounting model" that is used to this day. As economic activity moved from the feudal system to agriculture and then to the Industrial Revolution, accounting adapted to the evolving needs. As business units became more complex and broader in scope, accounting evolved in response to the increased planning and control responsibilities of management. As governments increased in size and became more centralized, accounting was developed to meet the increased accountabilities.

In the 17th and 18th centuries, the Industrial Revolution in England provided the impetus for the development of new approaches in accounting. That impetus was particularly in the direction of management accounting and the accumulation of data concerning the cost of manufacturing each product. In the latter half of the 19th century, English accountants, small in numbers but large in competence, appeared on the American scene. By 1900, the lead in accounting developments, provided earlier by the English, began to shift to America. Since the turn of the century, spearheaded by the accounting profession in the United States, accounting has experienced dynamic, and sometimes controversial, growth.

The accounting profession today

In the period since 1900, accountancy has attained the stature of a profession similar to law, medicine, engineering, and architecture. As with all recognized professions, it is subject to licensing, observes a code of professional ethics, requires a high level of professional competence, is dedicated to service to the public, requires a high level of academic study, and rests on a "common body of knowledge." The accountant, in addition to meeting specified academic requirements, may be licensed by the state to be a **Certified Public Accountant,** or CPA. This designation was first established in 1896. The primary objective was the attainment of high standards of professional competence. It is granted only upon completion of requirements specified by state statutes. Although the CPA requirements vary somewhat among states, generally they include a college degree with a major in accounting, good character, from one to five years specified experience, and successful completion of a three-day examination. The CPA examination, scheduled in each state simultaneously on a semiannual basis, is prepared by the American Institute of Certified Public Accountants and covers accounting theory, auditing, business law, and accounting practice.

As is common with physicians, engineers, lawyers, and architects, accountants (including CPAs) commonly are engaged in professional practice or are employed by businesses, government entities, nonprofit organizations, and so on. Accountants employed in these activities often take and pass a professional examination to become a **Certified Management Accountant,** or CMA.

Practice of public accounting. A CPA can offer professional services to the public for a fee, as does the lawyer and physician. In this posture, the accountant is known appropriately as an independent CPA because certain responsibilities also extend to the general public (third parties) rather than being limited to the specific business or other entity that pays for the services. Independent CPAs, although paid by their clients, are not employees of their clients. This concept of independence from the client is a unique characteristic of the accounting profession. The consequences of this uniqueness are not so widely understood as perhaps they should be. For example, the lawyer and the physician, in case of malpractice or incompetence, generally are subject to potential liability (lawsuits) that may extend only to the client or patient involved (and the family). In contrast, the independent CPA, in case of malpractice or negligence in the audit function, is subject to potential liability that may extend to all parties (whether known to the CPA or not) who have suffered loss or failed to make a profit through reliance on financial statements "approved" by the CPA.

While a single individual may practice public accounting, usually two or more individuals organize an accounting firm in the form of a partnership (in some states incorporation is permitted). Firms vary in size from a one-person office, to regional firms, to the "big-eight" firms, which have hundreds of offices located around the world. Nearly all accounting firms render three types of services: auditing, management advisory services, and tax services.

Auditing. Probably the most important function performed by the CPA in public practice is the audit or attest function. Its purpose is to lend reliability to the financial reports; that is, to assure that they are believable (i.e., relevant, accurate, and not biased). Primarily, this function involves an examination of the financial reports prepared by the management of the entity in order to assure that they are in conformance with **generally accepted accounting concepts and standards** (discussed in Part B). In carrying out this function, the independent CPA examines the underlying transactions, including the collection, classification, and assembly of the financial data incorporated in the financial reports. In performing these tasks, established professional standards must be maintained and the information reported must conform to **generally accepted accounting principles** (often referred to as **GAAP**) appropriate for the entity involved. Additionally, the CPA is responsible for verifying that the financial reports "fairly present" the resource inflows and outflows and the financial position of the entity. The magnitude of these responsibilities may be appreciated when it is realized that the number of transactions involved in a major enterprise such as General Motors runs into the billions each year. The CPA does not examine each one of these transactions; rather, professional approaches are used to ascertain beyond reasonable doubt that they were measured and reported properly.

Occasionally, the auditor may encounter attempts to manipulate accounting reports, for example, to increase reported profit by omitting certain expenses or to overstate financial position by omitting certain debts. There are many intentional and unintentional opportunities for preparing misleading financial reports. The audit function performed by an independent CPA is the best protection available to the public in this respect. Many investors have learned the pitfalls of making investments in enterprises that do not have their financial reports examined by an independent CPA.

At the conclusion of an audit, the independent CPA is required to provide an **auditor's opinion** that indicates whether the financial statements are appropriate and not misleading. For example, a recent auditor's opinion was described in *The Wall Street Journal* (July 27, 1982) as follows: "Price Waterhouse & Co. (an accounting firm) qualified its opinion of Newberry Energy Corp.'s 1982 annual report, noting that the company's Canadian subsidiary may default on its debt and be placed in receivership. The company had a net loss of $4.8 million in fiscal 1982, compared with earnings of $537,000 a year earlier."

Management advisory services. Many independent CPA firms also offer advisory or consulting services. These services usually are accounting based and encompass such activities as the design and installation of accounting, data processing, profit-planning and control (i.e., budget) systems; financial advice; forecasting; inventory controls; cost-effectiveness studies; and operational analyses. This facet of public practice is experiencing rapid growth.

Tax services. CPAs in public practice usually are involved in rendering income tax services to their clients. These services include both tax planning as a part of the decision-making process, tax compliance, and also determination of the income tax liability (reported on the annual tax return). Because of the increasing complexity of state and federal tax laws, particularly income tax laws, a high level of competence in this area is required. CPAs specializing in taxation can provide this competence. The CPA's involvement in tax planning often is quite significant. Virtually every major business decision carries with it significant tax impacts; so much so, in fact, that tax-planning considerations frequently govern the decision.

Employment by organizations

Many accountants, including CPAs and CMAs, are employed by profit-making and nonprofit organizations. A company or other organization, depending upon its size and complexity, may employ from one up to hundreds of accountants. In a business enterprise, the chief financial officer (usually a vice president or controller) is a member of the management team. This responsibility usually entails a wide range of management, financial, and accounting duties. Exhibit 1–3 shows a typical organizational arrangement of the financial function in a business enterprise. In the business entity, accountants typically are engaged in a wide variety of activities, such as general management, general accounting, cost accounting, profit planning and control (i.e., budgeting), internal auditing, and electronic data processing. A common pattern in recent years has been the selection of a "financial expert" as the chief executive or president of the company. One primary function of the accountants in organizations is **management accounting,** that is, to provide data that are useful for **internal** managerial decision making and for controlling operations. In addition, the functions of external reporting, tax planning, control of assets, and a host of related responsibilities normally are performed by accountants in industry. The role of accountants within organizations is emphasized in *Fundamentals of Management Accounting* of this series.

Employment in the public sector

The vast and complex operations of governmental units, from the local to the international level, create a great need for accountants. Accountants employed in the public sector perform functions similar to those performed by their counterparts in private organizations. Additionally, the General Accounting Office (GAO)

EXHIBIT 1–3
Typical organization of the financial function

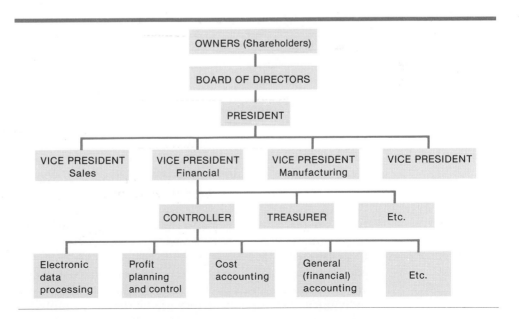

and the regulatory agencies, such as the Securities and Exchange Commission (SEC), Interstate Commerce Commission (ICC), Federal Power Commission (FPC), and Federal Communications Commission (FCC), utilize the services of accountants in carrying out their regulatory duties.

Finally, accountants are involved in varying capacities in the evolving programs of pollution control, health care, minority enterprises, and other socially oriented programs, whether sponsored by private industry or by government.

GROUPS INVOLVED IN ACCOUNTING INNOVATION

At the present time, four important groups in the United States predominate in the development of financial accounting concepts and practice. A general knowledge of their respective historical and continuing roles is important to your understanding of accounting. The groups are the American Institute of Certified Public Accountants, the Financial Accounting Standards Board, the U.S. Securities and Exchange Commission, and the American Accounting Association. The past and present roles of each group are reviewed briefly below.

American Institute of Certified Public Accountants (AICPA)

This institute was organized a few years prior to the turn of the century by a group of accountants engaged in public and industrial accounting. Membership currently is limited to certified public accountants (see pages 11 and 12). In terms of direct impact on financial accounting practice, the AICPA has been the strongest force in accounting in recent decades. It carries on a wide-ranging program encompassing professional development, publications (including the magazine *Journal of Accountancy*), and the development and communication of accounting standards and procedures. During the approximate period 1930–50, the AICPA's Committee on Accounting Procedure issued a number of *Accounting Research Bulletins (ARBs)* that enunciated certain recommended financial accounting principles and procedures. These recommendations were followed by much, but by no means all, of the accounting profession. Realizing the need for a more concentrated effort to develop accounting standards and more adherence to prescribed accounting guidelines, in 1959 the AICPA organized the Accounting Principles Board (APB) to replace the former committee. The APB issued 31 numbered *Opinions* during its existence from 1959 through mid-1973. Basically, accountants are required to follow the provisions of the *Opinions*. The *Opinions* dealt with many of the difficult issues of financial accounting; as a consequence, many of them were highly controversial. Throughout this volume you will encounter a few references to the *ARBs* and numerous references to APB *Opinions*.

Financial Accounting Standards Board (FASB)

This organization began operating June 1, 1973, and continues the development of accounting standards designed to enhance the usefulness and reliability of financial reports. It is appropriate to review its background. Accounting is a complex and frequently controversial professional activity. The intensity of the controversies in recent years is indicated by the fact that a wide range of interested individuals and special interest groups have committed significant amounts of resources and time in attempting to influence the setting of accounting concepts and standards. The controversy on occasion entered the political arena, which generally is viewed as an inappropriate forum in which to establish sound accounting concepts and standards. Accounting issues increasingly have been important in litigation in the courts.

As you study accounting you will realize that the economic results reported in the financial statements, such as asset valuations, profit, and earnings per share, may have impacts on the economy, on the capital markets (including the stock market), and on many major decisions of individuals, groups, and entities. You also may appreciate how the selection of a particular financial accounting approach frequently has a significant effect on the financial results reported through the accounting process (such as profit and earnings per share). In the light of these issues, the AICPA in 1972 decided to reassess the approaches to establishing financial accounting concepts and standards. As a consequence of this reassessment, the APB was discontinued, and in its place the Financial Accounting Standards Board was established and continues to function. The seven FASB members are appointed by an independent board of trustees and serve on a full-time basis (in contrast to the previous groups, each member receives full-time compensation). The FASB was organized to be independent. It has as its sole function the **establishment and improvement of accounting concepts and standards.** The accounting profession, through the FASB, intends to keep the standards-setting function in the **private sector** rather than to have the standards imposed by laws and governmental agencies.

Securities and Exchange Commission (SEC)

This government regulatory agency operates under authority granted by the Securities Acts of 1933 and 1934. These acts were in response to the manipulations, irrational speculation, and lack of credible financial information that existed when the stock market crash occurred in 1929–30. The acts gave the SEC authority to **prescribe accounting guidelines for the financial reports required to be submitted by corporations that sell their securities in interstate commerce** (i.e., registered companies, which primarily are those listed on the stock exchanges). This list includes most of the large, and some medium-sized, corporations. The SEC requires these corporations to submit periodic financial reports, which are maintained in the files of the Commission as a matter of public record. Also, a prospectus, which is a preliminary statement presented to prospective buyers or investors, is required before the sale of securities. From the beginning, the SEC, as a matter of policy, usually has followed the accounting concepts, standards, and procedures established by the accounting profession. The SEC publishes *Regulation S-X* and issues *Accounting Series Releases (ASR),* which prescribe the special guidelines to be followed by registered companies in preparing the financial reports submitted in conformance with the Securities Acts. Throughout its existence, the SEC has exerted a significant impact on accounting. Its staff has worked closely with the accounting profession on the evolution and improvement of accounting standards.

American Accounting Association (AAA)

This association was organized during the World War I period by a group of college accounting professors. The Association sponsors and **encourages the improvement of accounting teaching and accounting research** (primarily on a theoretical plane), and publishes a magazine, *The Accounting Review.* Its committees issue reports that, coupled with the research activities of individual academicians, exert a pervasive influence on the development of accounting theory and standards.

In summary, the prior discussions of the environment in which accounting operates suggest the importance of competitive and successful businesses (from the smallest to the largest) to a free enterprise economy. Economic success in a competitive business economy means earning reasonable profits and providing funds (cash) to meet broad **reinvestment needs.** Adequate reinvestment in businesses means more jobs, better wages, continuing technological advances, expansion of efficient productive capacity, adequate dividends for investors, and more tax revenue to the government (to support socially desirable programs and other governmental activities). The economic dimensions of this success by individual businesses are communicated in accounting reports. For example, the economic information tabulated below was extracted from the annual published **financial statements** of two well-known companies:

Approximate amounts (millions of dollars) of:	General Motors		Westinghouse	
	1981	1982	1981	1982
Total revenue	$62,698.5	$60,025.6	$9,367.5	$9,745.4
Net income	333.4	962.7	438.0	449.3
Total funds provided	8,646.0	11,205.3	208.6	762.0
Total labor cost	19,257.0	17,043.0	?	?
Total plant investment (net).....	18,494.1	19,538.3	2,539.6	2,935.8
Total taxes paid	2,382.4	2,218.1	471.0	438.0
Total cash dividends	730.5	750.2	156.2	153.7

PART B—COMMUNICATION OF ACCOUNTING INFORMATION

This part of the chapter introduces the end product of the accounting processing system—the periodic financial statements. These statements are viewed as an important means of communicating financial information about the entity. Additionally, this part emphasizes the purpose and nature of financial statements. Various approaches are used to derive the dollar amounts; discussion of these approaches will be included in subsequent chapters. In Chapters 1 and 2 we introduce the **basic financial statements** prior to discussion of how they are derived in order to provide an initial overview of how the end product appears. The remaining chapters concentrate on the economic analyses, measurements, and recording of the transactions that necessarily precede financial statement preparation.

COMMUNICATION CONCEPTS AND APPROACHES

Communication consists of a flow of information from one party to one or more other parties. For communication to be effective, the recipient must understand what the sender intends to convey. The process of communication involves numerous problems in understanding precisely the words, symbols, and sounds used by the parties involved. Accounting seeks to communicate by words and symbols financial information that is relevant to the decisions typically made by investors, creditors, and other interested parties. As you make decisions of varying sorts, reliance is placed upon certain information that often is unique to each type of decision. Often, each of us must make decisions without adequate information. Either the needed information is not available in time or the cost and time entailed in developing it is prohibitive when compared to its potential benefits.[6] The nature and form in which information is "packaged" and the avenues used to communicate it sometimes affect the decision. For example, some individuals are more influenced by graphic than by quantitative presentations, others find narrative preferable to tabular expression, some prefer summaries rather than details, and still others are not interested in technical presentations of any sort.

Financial information and the means used to communicate it frequently have strong and pervasive behavioral impacts[7] upon decision makers. The behavioral impacts of accounting extend to both positive and negative motivations of people. The frequency, form, and quality of one's communications with others are often important to motivations.

The terminology and symbols of accounting were developed over a long period of time in the search for ways to communicate financial information effectively. As is common with other professions, such as law and medicine, the terminology and symbols of accounting are somewhat technical. Accounting has developed in direct response to the needs of people. As a consequence, it is continuously evolving new concepts, terminology, procedures, and means of communication. In the chapters to follow, you should pay special attention to the terminology of accounting.

OVERVIEW OF EXTERNAL FINANCIAL STATEMENTS

Financial statements often are classified as (1) internal (i.e., management accounting) statements and (2) external (i.e., financial accounting) statements. Internal financial statements are not distributed to parties outside the entity. They are used exclusively by, and are prepared under the direction of, the **managers** of the entity; therefore, they are prepared to meet specific internal policies and guidelines established by those managers.

In contrast, **external** financial statements are distributed to parties (i.e., external decision makers) outside the entity (which include stockholders and creditors). External parties are unable to specify guidelines for preparation of the statements. The information presented on financial statements is intended to help investors

---

[6] This sentence suggests the concept of **benefit-cost analysis;** that is, a comparison of the cost of pursuing a particular course of action, compared with the economic benefits or advantages derived from that course of action.

[7] A behavioral impact is an individual's response to external forces. An individual may be motivated toward or away from certain courses of action by information or observations that come to his or her attention. For example, one may be motivated to purchase a large automobile rather than a small one for reasons of prestige. However, a financial report showing the relative costs of operating the two automobiles may motivate the individual to purchase the small automobile. Thus, the financial report exerted a significant behavioral impact on the decision maker.

and others make better economic decisions. Thus, financial statements must present information that is relevant to economic decisions; it must be useful for predicting the future successes (and failures) of the business. **Relevance** is an important **qualitative characteristic** of financial statements. To ensure that external parties may understand the information reported in financial statements, the entity is required to conform to specific and well-known **generally accepted accounting principles (GAAP)** that are developed by the accounting profession.

This textbook discusses the development of external financial reports. The next several pages present an **overview** of the external financial statements required by GAAP.

A primary objective of the accounting processing system is the development of financial statements that communicate relevant information to decision makers. An understanding of financial statements at the outset places you in an excellent position to interpret them and to understand how the accounting process operates. The three primary financial statements for a profit-making entity for **external reporting** to owners, potential investors, creditors, and other decision makers are the—

1. Income statement (more descriptively, statement of revenues, expenses, and income).
2. Balance sheet (more descriptively, statement of assets, liabilities, and owners' equity).
3. Statement of changes in financial position (more descriptively, statement of cash inflows and outflows, or of working capital; abbreviated SCFP).

These three required statements summarize the financial activities of the business entity for each specific period of time. They can be produced at any time (such as end of the year, quarter, or month) and can apply to any time span (such as 10 years, 1 year, 1 quarter, or 1 month). The heading of each statement contains a very specific statement of the **time dimension** of the report. Although these three statements directly relate to each other, for convenience, at this point in your study, they will be considered separately. First, we will illustrate them for a simple business situation; the next chapter discusses and illustrates them in a more complex situation.

The income statement

The income statement is designed to report the profit performance of a business entity for a specific period of time, such as a year, quarter, or month. Profit is a word that is used widely in our language, but accountants prefer to use the technical term **net income** which is defined as the difference between revenues and expenses for the specified period. An income statement presents the **results of operations;** that is, it reports, for a **specific period of time** in accordance with the time-period assumption (e.g., "For the Year Ended December 31, 19A"), the items that comprise the total **revenues,** the total **expenses,** and the resulting **net income** (see Exhibit 1–4).

Exhibit 1–4 presents the income statement for the first year of operations of Business Aids, Inc., an enterprise that renders professional secretarial, reproduction, and mailing services for a fee. Business Aids was organized by three individu-

EXHIBIT 1–4
Income statement
(simplified)

BUSINESS AIDS, INC. Income Statement For the Year Ended December 31, 19A	—Name of entity —Title of report —Period of time	} HEADING

Revenues:
Stenographic revenue $30,000
Printing revenue 20,000
Mailing revenue 13,000
    Total revenues $63,000

Expenses:
Salary expense... 30,750
Payroll tax expense 1,100
Rent expense for office space 2,400
Rental payments for copiers 6,600
Utilities expense 400
Advertising expense 960
Supplies expense 90
Interest expense 100
Depreciation expense on office equipment 600
    Total expenses (excluding income tax)   43,000

Pretax income   20,000
Income tax expense ($20,000 × 17%)   3,400

Net income $16,600

Earnings per share (EPS) ($16,600 ÷ 3,000 shares) $5.53

als as a **corporation.** Each owner (called a stockholder or shareholder) received 1,000 shares of capital stock as evidence of ownership. The **heading** of the statement specifically identifies the name of the entity, the title of the report, and the period of time over which the reported net income was earned. Note that the date encompasses a period of time—in this case, one year. There are three major captions: **revenues, expenses,** and **net income.** The detail presented under each caption is intended to be sufficient to meet the needs of decision makers interested in Business Aids, Inc. This latter point is significant because the composition and the detail of a financial statement vary, depending on the characteristics of the business entity and the needs of the users.

Revenues. Revenues represent the sales price of goods sold or services rendered by the entity to others for which the entity will receive (or has received) cash or something else of value. When a business sells goods or renders services, if not on credit, it receives cash immediately. If on credit, it receives an **account receivable** which is collected in cash later. In either case, the business recognizes revenue for the period as the sum of the cash and credit sales for goods sold and of services rendered. Sometimes the cash for a revenue is collected **before** the revenue is earned as in the case of revenue collected in advance of occupancy. Thus, revenue may be thought of as an inflow of resources that results from a profit-making activity. Revenue is measured in dollars as the bargained **cash-equivalent** price agreed on by the two parties to the transaction.[8] Various terms

---

[8] Revenue sometimes is called income, such as rent income, interest income, and royalty income, but this practice tends to cause confusion. Ideally, **income should be used to refer only to the difference between revenues and expenses.**

are used in financial statements to describe revenue, such as sales revenue, service revenue, rental revenue, and interest revenue. Revenues are discussed in more detail in Chapter 4.

Expenses. Expenses represent the dollar amount of resources expended or used up by the entity during a period of time to earn revenues. Expenses may require the immediate payment of cash or some other resource, or the payment of cash or some other resource may occur some time after the expense is incurred. In some cases, cash is paid **before** the expense is incurred, as in the case of the payment of office rent in **advance of occupancy.** For accounting purposes, an expense is reported on the income statement in the period in which it is incurred (i.e., used), which is not necessarily the same as the period in which the cash is paid. **The period in which an expense is deemed to be incurred[9] is the period in which the goods are used or the services are received.**

An expense may represent the cost of **using** equipment or buildings that were purchased for continuing use in operating the business rather than for sale. Such items often have a high initial cost at the date of acquisition, and through use, each one is worn out (or becomes obsolete) over an extended period of time known as **useful life.** As such items are used in operating the business, a portion of their cost becomes an expense. This kind of expense is known as **depreciation expense.** For example, on January 1, 19A, Business Aids purchased office equipment for its own use at a cost of $6,000. It was estimated that the office equipment would have a useful life of 10 years. Therefore, the **depreciation expense** each year for using the equipment is measured as $6,000 ÷ 10 years = $600. The income statement for 19A (Exhibit 1–4) reports this amount as an expense.[10] It also reports interest expense for one year on the $1,000, 10 percent note payable (i.e., $1,000 × 0.10 = $100). Because a corporation has a 17 percent income tax rate on the first $25,000 of income, Business Aids incurred income tax expense of $3,400 (i.e., $20,000 × 0.17 = $3,400). Observe that Business Aids reported both **pretax** and **aftertax** income amounts.[11]

Net income. Net income (often called profit by nonaccountants) is the excess of total revenues over total expenses. If the total expenses exceed the total revenues, a **net loss** is reported. When revenues and expenses are exactly equal for the period, the business is said to have operated at **breakeven.**

Earnings per share (EPS). The amount of earnings per share (EPS) is reported immediately below net income if the business is organized as a corporation. EPS is derived by dividing net income by the number of shares of **common** stock outstanding. Because Business Aids had 3,000 shares of common stock outstanding

---

[9] Incurred, as used in this context, means that the amount involved should be accounted for (i.e., recorded in the accounting system) during the specific period.

[10] Accounting for depreciation is discussed in detail in Chapter 9.

[11] Corporations, except those that qualify under Subchapter S of the Internal Revenue Code, are required to pay income taxes as follows: 17 percent on the first $25,000 of income, 20 percent on the next $25,000, 30 percent on the next $25,000, 40 percent on the next $25,000, and 46 percent on all income in excess of $100,000. Sole proprietorships and partnerships, as business entities, and Subchapter S corporations, are not subject to income taxes. In each of these situations, the owner, or owners, must report the income of the entity on their own individual income tax returns. For illustrative purposes, an average tax rate is used herein to ease the arithmetic.

(i.e., 1,000 shares were owned by each of the three stockholders) and a net income of $16,600, EPS was computed as $16,600 ÷ 3,000 shares = $5.53 per share for the year. Especially in recent years, EPS has been accorded an extensive amount of attention by security analysts and others. As a consequence, the accounting profession has come to accept it as an important information input for investors. Specific accounting guidelines were prescribed by the APB in *Opinion 15* for computing and reporting EPS.

Some people view the income statement as the most important of the three required financial statements because it is designed to report the amount of net income and the details of how that amount was earned. They view the earning of income as the most important factor in a business. The **accounting model** for the income statement is:

$$\text{Revenues} - \text{Expenses} = \text{Net Income (i.e., R} - \text{E} = \text{NI)}$$

The amount of net income for the period represents a net increase in resources (or a net decrease if a loss) that flowed into the business entity during that period as a result of operational activities (i.e., profit-making activities).

The balance sheet

The purpose of the balance sheet is to report the **financial position** of a business at a **particular point** in time. Financial position refers to the amount of resources (i.e., assets) and the liabilities (i.e., debts) of the business on a specific date. As a consequence, this statement frequently is called the statement of financial position. A more descriptive title would be the statement of assets, liabilities, and owners' equity; these are the three major captions on the statement.[12]

Exhibit 1–5 presents the balance sheet at the end of the first year of operations for Business Aids, Inc. Observe that the heading specifically identifies the name of the entity, the title of the report, and the specific date of the statement. Note the specific point in time—in this case, December 31, 19A—is stated clearly on the balance sheet. This contrasts with the dating on the income statement, which indicates a period of time (such as one year). After the statement heading, the **assets** are listed on the left and the **liabilities** and **owners' equity** on the right. The result is that the two sides "balance." The accounting model for the balance sheet specifies this relationship as follows:[13]

$$\text{Assets} = \text{Liabilities} + \text{Owners' Equity (i.e., A} = \text{L} + \text{OE)}$$

As is the case with any equation, its elements may be rearranged. For example, the model frequently is expressed to reflect the fact that owners' equity is a residual (i.e., the difference between the assets and liabilities of the entity), viz:

$$\text{Assets} - \text{Liabilities} = \text{Owners' Equity (i.e., A} - \text{L} = \text{OE)}$$

---

[12] The designation "balance sheet" is unfortunate because it is not descriptive in any sense. It implies that the central fact is that it balances arithmetically, although this actually is an incidental feature. Because of the widespread use of the term, it will be used in this book.

[13] Owners' equity for a corporation usually is called stockholders' or shareholders' equity. Alternative formats for the balance sheet are discussed later.

EXHIBIT 1–5
Balance sheet (simplified)

BUSINESS AIDS, INC.
Balance Sheet
At December 31, 19A

Assets			Liabilities		
Cash		$13,600	Accounts payable	$ 900	
Accounts receivable		13,000	Income taxes payable	500	
Land		20,000	Note payable, short term, 10%	1,000	
Office equipment	$6,000				
Less: Accumulated			Total liabilities		$ 2,400
depreciation	600	5,400	**Stockholders' Equity**		
			Contributed capital:		
			Capital stock (3,000 shares, par value		
			$10 per share)	30,000	
			Contributed capital in excess of par	3,000	
			Retained earnings	16,600	
			Total stockholders' equity		49,600
Total assets		$52,000	Total liabilities and stockholders' equity		$52,000

The accounting model is a basic building block in the total accounting process.[14] Next, we will define and discuss each of the three items in this model.

Assets. Fundamentally, assets are the resources owned by the entity. They may be tangible (physical in character) such as land, buildings, and machinery, or intangible (characterized by legal claims or rights) such as amounts due from customers (legal claims called accounts receivable) and patents (protected rights). In short, assets have present and **future** value, whether physical or not, and are owned by the entity.[15] The FASB, in its **Statement of Financial Accounting Concepts No. 3,** defined assets as "probable future economic benefits obtained or controlled by a particular entity as a result of past transactions or events."

Observe in the balance sheet, given in Exhibit 1–5, that each **asset** listed has an assigned dollar amount. The **cost principle** states that assets generally should be **measured** on the basis of the **total cost incurred to acquire them** (see Exhibit 2–6). To illustrate, the balance sheet for Business Aids reports "Land, $20,000"; this is the amount of resources that was paid for the land when it was acquired. It may well be that because of market changes, the market value of the land at December 31, 19A (date of the balance sheet), actually was more or less than $20,000. Nevertheless, the balance sheet would report the land at its original acquisition cost. It follows that the balance sheet does not necessarily show the current **market value** of the assets listed.

---

[14] The model also may be expressed as Assets = Equities. In this formulation, **equities** is used to denote (1) liabilities, or creditors' equity, which represent claims of creditors; and (2) owners' equity, which represents claims of the owners.

[15] Assets also include prepaid expenses and deferred charges because these represent valid rights or claims in the future for goods and services paid for in advance. These kinds of assets are discussed in later chapters.

It is appropriate to inquire why accountants do not change the measurement of each asset for each subsequent balance sheet to reflect the then market values. This revaluation is not done because the acquisition cost is factually objective (i.e., not an estimate), whereas current market value of the assets owned by the entity would have to be estimated at the end of each year. The estimate would be very subjective because the assets are not sold each year-end. Such subjectivity potentially could reduce the reliability of the financial statements.

Liabilities.   Liabilities are debts or obligations owed by the entity to the creditors. They arise primarily as a result of the purchase of goods or services from others on credit and through cash borrowings to finance the business. The FASB, in **Statement of Financial Accounting Concepts No. 3,** defined liabilities as "future sacrifices arising from present obligations of a particular entity to transfer assets or provide services to other entities in the future as a result of past transactions or events."

If a business fails to pay its creditors, the law may accord the creditors the right to force the sale of assets sufficient to meet their claims.[16]

Business entities frequently borrow money on a **note payable.** In this case, a liability known as notes payable is created. A note payable, which may be short term or long term, specifies a definite maturity or payment date and the rate or amount of interest charged by the lender. Also, many businesses purchase goods and services on open account that does not involve notes, thus creating a liability known as **accounts payable.** Another type of liability arises from the fact that income taxes frequently are paid, at least in part, several months after the end of the year. As a consequence, a liability to the government, **income taxes payable,** must be reported until the taxes are paid fully. You may observe in Exhibit 1–5 that Business Aids listed three liabilities and the amount of each. In respect to amounts, liabilities present few measurement problems because most liabilities are reported at the amount (i.e., the principal) of the debt established by the parties to the transaction.

Owners' equity.   The accounting model (page 21) shows owners' equity to be equal to the total assets minus the total liabilities of the business. Because creditors claims legally come first, the owners' equity represents a **residual interest** or claim of the owners to the assets. Owners' equity sometimes is called net worth, capital, or proprietorship. However, the preferable designations are *(a)* owner's equity for a sole proprietorship; *(b)* partners' equity for a partnership; and *(c)* stockholders' or shareholders' equity for a corporation. Owners' equity in a business is derived from two sources: (1) **contributed capital,** which is the investment of cash or other assets in the business by the owner or owners; and (2) **retained earnings** (or income), which is the amount of accumulated earnings of the business less losses and withdrawals.[17] When the owners receive cash or other assets from the business through withdrawals (defined later), the total

---

[16] In case of dissolution or sale of all the assets of a business, legally the creditors must be paid first and any remainder goes to the owners.

[17] The term *retained earnings* usually is used by businesses organized as corporations. In contrast, sole proprietorships and partnerships usually do not employ this term because it is included in the owners' capital account(s). These distinctions are discussed later.

amount of owners' equity is reduced. When the business incurs a loss, owners' equity also is reduced.

In Exhibit 1–5, the stockholders' equity section reports the following:

1. **Contributed capital**—The three stockholders invested a total of $33,000 in the business and received 3,000 shares of capital stock having a par value of $10 per share (par value will be discussed in Chapter 12). They invested $11 per share, or $1 per share above par value. The 3,000 shares issued are reported at their par value (3,000 × $10) as "Capital stock"; and the remainder, often called a premium (3,000 shares × $1 = $3,000), is reported as "Contributed capital in excess of par value."

2. **Retained earnings**—The accumulated amount of earnings **less** all losses and dividends paid to the stockholders since formation of the corporation is reported as "Retained earnings." During the first year, the business earned $16,600, as shown on the income statement (Exhibit 1–4). This amount is reported as retained earnings on the balance sheet for Business Aids at this date because no dividends were declared or paid to the stockholders during the first year (since organization).

3. **Total stockholders' equity**—The sum of the investment ($33,000) plus the retained earnings ($16,600) = $49,600. This amount may be verified in terms of the basic accounting model: Assets ($52,000) − Liabilities ($2,400) = Stockholders' Equity ($49,600).

If, by contrast, a cash dividend of $6,000 had been declared and paid to the three stockholders during the year, the balance sheet would have reflected cash of $7,600 ($13,600 − $6,000) and retained earnings of $10,600 ($16,600 − $6,000).

Statement of changes in financial position (SCFP)

In recent years, the **financing activities** (i.e., sources of funds) of businesses have become increasingly complex. The business entity of today requires substantial funds for operations and expansion. These funds come from four sources: (1) owner investment, (2) borrowings, and (3) earning a profit and (4) selling noncash assets. In recognition of the need by users of financial statements for information concerning the sources and uses of funds by the business, the APB issued *Opinion* 19 in March 1971. This *Opinion* requires a **Statement of Changes in Financial Position (SCFP)**[18] to accompany the income statement and the balance sheet.

The objective of the SCFP is to communicate to the statement users information about the sources (inflows) and uses (outflows) of cash (or, alternatively, working capital, defined later). Exhibit 1–6 presents a SCFP for Business Aids for a specific period of time (i.e., "For the Year Ended December 31, 19A"). At this point you need not be concerned about the derivation of the amounts illustrated. Rather, your attention is called to the two basic classifications: cash sources (inflows of cash) and cash uses (outflows of cash). The difference between them represents the increase, or decrease, in cash during the period. Because investors and creditors often are interested in future cash flows, this statement provides past information

---

[18] The SCFP is an outgrowth of an earlier "statement of sources and applications of funds," which was optional.

EXHIBIT 1–6
Statement of
changes in financial
position (SCFP)
(simplified)

BUSINESS AIDS, INC.
Statement of Changes in Financial Position, Cash Basis
For the Year Ended December 31, 19A

Sources of cash (inflows):		
From operations:		
From cash revenues	$50,000	
Less: Cash used for expenses	44,400	
Cash inflow from operations		$ 5,600
From other sources:		
Investment by owners (stock issued for cash)	33,000	
Loan—note payable	1,000	
Cash inflow from other sources		34,000
Total cash inflow during the year		39,600
Uses of cash (outflows):		
To purchase office equipment	6,000	
To purchase land	20,000	
Total cash used during the year (outflows)		26,000
Change—increase in cash during the year		$13,600

on cash flows that is useful in projecting the future cash flows of the business. The accounting model for the SCFP is:

Cash Inflows − Cash Outflows = Net Change in Cash (i.e., CI − CO = NC)

The SCFP often is prepared on a working capital basis (discussed later), rather than on the cash basis.

The SCFP is derived from an analysis of the balance sheet and the income statement. For example, total revenue reported on Exhibit 1–4 (the income statement) of $63,000, less $13,000 of the revenue (mailing) extended on credit, equals $50,000, which represents the cash inflow from revenue in Exhibit 1–6. Similarly, total expenses of $46,400 (including income tax expense), shown on Exhibit 1–4, less the **noncash expenses** of $600 for depreciation, $900 for accounts payable, and $500 for income taxes payable, equals the $44,400 reported in Exhibit 1–6 as the cash used for expenses. Thus, the net income earned of $16,600 caused a cash inflow of $5,600. Shares of capital stock were sold that caused a cash inflow of $33,000, and a loan was obtained to secure another $1,000, giving a total cash inflow during the year of $39,600. During the year, $26,000 cash was expended for office equipment and land. Consequently, the statement reports that $13,600 more cash was received than was spent during the year.

A detailed discussion of the SCFP is deferred to Chapter 15 because its preparation requires special procedures that are best understood after your knowledge of accounting is substantial.

DEMONSTRATION CASE

At the end of most chapters, one or more demonstration cases will be presented that provide an overview of the primary issues discussed in the chapter. Each demonstration case is followed by a recommended solution. The case should be

EXHIBIT 1–7
Format of financial
statements—ABC
Service Corporation

ABC Service Corporation
Income Statement

Date _____

Revenues: Computations
  Service revenues . . . . $ 100,500   _____

Expenses:
  ·Various expenses . . . . $ 55500   _____
  Interest expense . . . .   _____
  Depreciation expense   10000   _____
      Total expenses . . . . $ 65500   _____
Pretax income   35000
  Income tax expense   8000
Net income . . . . $ 27000
  Earnings per share . . . . $ 9   _____

10,000
   .15

ABC Service Corporation
Balance Sheet

Date _____

Assets:
  Cash . . . . $ 6000   _____
  Accounts receivable   6000   _____
  Service trucks . . . . $ 20000   _____
      Less: Accumulated depreciation   5000   15000   _____
Total assets . . . . $ 27000

Liabilities:
  Note payable . . . . $ 1500   _____
  Income taxes payable   8000   _____
      Total liabilities . . . . $ 9500   _____

Stockholders' Equity:
  Capital stock, par $_____;
      shares_____   30000   _____
  Contributed capital in excess
      of par value   6000   _____
  Retained earnings   82000   _____
      Total stockholders' equity . . . .   _____
      Total liabilities and
        stockholders' equity . . . . $ _____

read carefully; then you should try to prepare your solution prior to studying
the recommended solution. This form of self-study is highly recommended.

The introductory case presented below is to start you thinking, in monetary
terms, of some of the resource inflows and outflows of a business. It deals with
reporting certain accounting information for the first year of a business entity
that was organized by three individuals. See what you can do with the case

**EXHIBIT 1–8
Suggested
solution—ABC
Service Corporation**

ABC Service Corporation
Income Statement

Date *For the Year Ended December 31, 19A*

		Computations
Revenues:		
Service revenues	$ 100,500	*Given)*
Expenses:		
Various expenses	$ 54,000	*Given)*
Interest expense	1,500	$10,000 × 15%
Depreciation expense	5,000	$20,000 ÷ 4 years)
Total expenses	$ 60,500	
Pretax income	40,000	
Income tax expense	8,000	$40,000 × 20%
Net income	$ 32,000	
Earnings per share	$ 10.67	$32,000 ÷ 3,000 shares)

ABC Service Corporation
Balance Sheet

Date *At December 31, 19A*

Assets:			
Cash		$ 58,000	$36,000 + $10,000 + $94,500 − $55,500 − $7,000 − $20,000
Accounts receivable		6,000	$103,000 − $94,500
Service trucks	$ 20,000		Given, cost of trucks)
Less: Accumulated depreciation	5,000	15,000	$20,000 ÷ 4 years = $5,000
Total assets		$ 79,000	
Liabilities:			
Note payable	$ 10,000		Given, bank loan)
Income taxes payable	1,000		Given, amount unpaid.
Total liabilities		$ 11,000	
Stockholders' Equity:			
Capital stock, par $ 10 ;			
shares 3,000	30,000		3,000 × $10
Contributed capital in excess of par value	6,000		3,000 × ($12 − $10)
Retained earnings	32,000		From income statement*
Total stockholders' equity		68,000	
Total liabilities and stockholders' equity		$ 79,000	

* Beginning RE ($-0-) + Net income ($32,000) − Dividends ($-0-) = Ending RE ($32,000).

before studying the recommended solution. (Note: It will test your comprehension of Part B of the chapter and also your analytical skills.)

ABC Service Corporation was organized by three investors (Able, Baker, and Cain) on January 1, 19A. On that date, as start-up cash, each investor bought 1,000 shares of the corporation's capital stock (par value $10 per share) and paid $12 per share. On the same day, the corporation borrowed $10,000 from a local bank and signed a three-year note payable at 15 percent interest payable each December 31. On January 1, 19A, the corporation purchased two specially designed service trucks for $20,000 cash. Operations were started immediately.

At the end of 19A, the corporation had completed the following business transactions (summarized):

a. Performed services and billed customers for $100,500, of which $94,500 was collected in cash by year-end.
b. Paid $55,500 cash for expenses (including the annual interest on the note owed to the local bank).
c. Paid $7,000 cash to the Internal Revenue Service (IRS) for income taxes, and at the end of the year still owed the IRS $1,000 (the average tax rate was 20 percent).
d. Depreciated the two service trucks on the basis of a four-year useful life (disregard any residual value at the end of the four-year life).

Required:

Complete the two financial statements for 19A by entering the correct amounts (show computations in the space provided) in Exhibit 1–7. The suggested solution is given in Exhibit 1–8.

SUMMARY OF CHAPTER

Accounting interacts with practically all aspects of the environment: social, economic, and political. Any open society is a complex one that is characterized by organizations—businesses, political parties, governmental entities, churches, social institutions, and private groups and associations. Each organization, whether local or international in scope, is an accounting entity. The essence of accounting is the measurement and reporting of financial information for an accounting entity. The measurement and reporting of the inflows and outflows of scarce resources and the financial position of each accounting entity is essential to (1) effective management of each such organization and (2) the understanding and evaluation of it by interested outside parties. Measurement of the financial characteristics of each such organization is essential because each one of you is an important decision maker, both in respect to each of your economic interests and as a concerned citizen in the broader sense. Your decision-making potential is enhanced if you understand the financial impacts of alternative solutions to particular problems.

Part B of the chapter explained and illustrated the basic features of the three required **external** financial reports—the income statement, the balance sheet, and the statement of changes in financial position.

The **income statement,** as the statement of operations, reports revenues, expenses, and the net income for a stated **period of time.** Earnings per share (EPS), which expresses the relationship between net income and the number of shares of common stock outstanding, was illustrated.

The **balance sheet,** as the statement of financial position, reports dollar amounts for the assets, liabilities, and owners' equity at a specific **point in time.**

The **statement of changes in financial position (SCFP),** as the statement of the inflows and outflows of funds, reports those flows for a specific **period of time.**

The fundamental accounting model, **Assets = Liabilities + Owners' Equity,** was introduced as the foundation for the balance sheet and the accounting process in general. The financial statements for a small company were illustrated. In the next chapter you will move one step forward and look at a more complex situation and, at the same time, add more concepts to your knowledge about the characteristics of the external financial statements of a business entity.

IMPORTANT TERMS DEFINED IN THIS CHAPTER

Terms (alphabetically)	Key words in definitions of important terms used in chapter	Page reference
Accounting entity	A business or other organization; for accounting as a unit.	6
AAA	American Accounting Association.	15
AICPA	American Institute of Certified Public Accountants.	14
Assets	Items owned; have value.	22
Auditing	Attest function; reliability; auditors' opinion.	11
Balance sheet	Position statement; Assets = Liabilities + Owners' Equity.	21
Cash inflows	Cash received; increase Cash account.	24
Cash outflows	Cash paid; decrease Cash account.	24
Contributed capital	Total amount invested by stockholders.	24
Corporation	A separate legal entity; shares of stock represent ownership.	5
Depreciation	Allocation of cost of operational asset; based on use.	20
Exchange transaction	An enforceable agreement; resources involved.	3
EPS	Earnings per share; common stock.	20
Expenses	Outflow of assets; for goods and services used.	20
FASB	Financial Accounting Standards Board.	14
GAAP	Generally accepted accounting principles.	12 and 18
Income statement	Required report; operations; income; EPS.	18
Liabilities	Obligations; debts; promise to pay.	23
Management advisory services	Service rendered by CPA firms; consulting; complements audit and tax services.	12
Net income	Revenues − Expenses.	20
Owners' equity	Assets − Liabilities.	23
Partnership	Nonstock; two or more owners.	5
Retained earnings	Accumulated earnings; reduced by dividends.	24
Revenues	Inflow of resources; from sale of goods and services.	19
SEC	Securities and Exchange Commission; government.	15
Separate-entity assumption	Business unit; separate from owners; for accounting and reporting purposes.	6
Sole proprietorship	Nonstock; one owner.	5
SCFP	Statement of changes in financial position.	24
Unit-of-measure assumption	Monetary unit used to account for an entity; the dollar; affected by inflation. The assumption is that the value of the monetary unit is stable.	5

QUESTIONS FOR DISCUSSION

PART A

1. Define accounting briefly and summarize the accounting flow of economic information about an entity.

2. Explain the unit-of-measure assumption including its relationship to accounting.

3. Briefly distinguish among a sole proprietorship, partnership, and corporation.

4. What is meant by an accounting entity? Why is a business treated as a separate entity for accounting purposes? Explain the separate-entity assumption.

5. Briefly explain the three ways that financial statements serve statement users.

6. List and briefly explain the three primary services provided by CPAs in public practice.

7. Briefly explain the role of the:
   a. FASB.
   b. SEC.
   c. AAA.

PART B

8. Financial statements are the end products of the accounting process. Explain.

9. Generally, how would you define communication?

10. The accounting process generates financial reports for both "internal" and "external" audiences. Identify some of the groups in each audience.

11. Complete the following:

Name of statement	A more descriptive name
a. Income statement	a. _____
b. Balance sheet	b. _____
c. Statement of changes in financial position (SCFP)	c. _____

12. What information should be included in the heading of each of the three required financial statements?

13. Explain why the income statement and the SCFP are dated "For the Year Ended December 31, 19X," whereas the balance sheet is dated "At December 31, 19X."

14. Define revenue.

15. Define expense.

16. Briefly define the following: income, loss, and breakeven.

17. What are the purposes of (a) the income statement, (b) the balance sheet, and (c) the SCFP?

18. Explain the accounting model for the income statement. What are the three major items reported on the income statement?

19. Explain the accounting model for the balance sheet. Define the three major components reported on the balance sheet.

20. Explain the accounting model for the SCFP. Explain the three major components reported on the statement.

21. Why is owners' equity referred to frequently as a residual interest?

22. What are the two primary sources of owners' equity in a business?

23. What are the appropriate titles for owners' equity for *(a)* a sole proprietorship, *(b)* a partnership, and *(c)* a corporation?

EXERCISES

PART A

E1–1. Given below is a list of important abbreviations used in Part A of the chapter. These abbreviations also are used widely in business. For each abbreviation give the full designation. The first one is used as an example.

Abbreviation	*Full designation*
1. CPA	Certified Public Accountant
2. APB	
3. GAO	
4. AAA	
5. CMA	
6. AICPA	
7. SEC	
8. FASB	
9. ICC	

PART B

E1–2. Review the chapter explanations of the income statement and the balance sheet models. Apply these models in each independent case below to compute the two missing amounts for each case. Assume it is the end of 19A, the first full year of operations for the company.

Independent Cases	Total Revenues	Total Assets	Total Expenses	Total Liabilities	Net Income (Loss)	Stockholders' Equity
A	$95,000	$150,000	$88,000	$92,000	$	$
B		112,000	61,000		10,000	70,000
C	80,000	92,000	86,000	26,000		
D	65,000			40,000	9,000	77,000
E			81,000	73,000	(6,000)	88,000

E1–3. Rose Corporation was organized by three individuals on January 1, 19A, to render electronic repair services. At the end of 19A, the following income statement was prepared:

Rose Corporation
Income Statement
For the Year Ended December 31, 19A

Revenues:		
Service sales (cash)	$178,000	
Service sales (credit)	12,000	
Total revenues		$190,000
Expenses:		
Salaries	71,000	
Rent	12,000	
Utilities	10,000	
Advertising	11,000	
Supplies	18,000	
Interest	3,000	
Depreciation	5,000	
Total expenses		130,000
Pretax income		60,000
Income tax expense		13,200
Net income		$ 46,800
EPS		$2.34

Required:

a. What was the average monthly revenue amount?
b. What was the monthly rent amount?
c. Explain why "Supplies, $18,000" is an expense.
d. Explain why "Interest, $3,000" is reported as an expense.
e. Explain what is meant by "Depreciation, $5,000."
f. What was the average income tax rate for Rose Corporation?
g. How many shares of capital stock were outstanding?
h. Can you determine how much cash the company had on December 31, 19A?

E1–4. Assume you are the owner of "The College Shop," which specializes in items of special interest to college students. At the end of January 19A you find that (for January only):

a. Sales, per the cash register tapes, totaled $70,000, plus one sale on credit (a special situation) of $300.
b. With the help of a friend (who had majored in accounting), you determined that all of the goods sold during January had cost you $33,000 when they were purchased.
c. During the month, according to the checkbook, you paid $32,000 for salaries, utilities, supplies, advertising, and other expenses; however, you have not yet paid the $500 monthly rent for January on the store and fixtures.

On the basis of the data given, what was the amount of income for January (disregard income taxes)? Show computations. (Hint: A convenient form to use would have the following major side captions: revenue from sales, expenses, and the difference—income.)

E1–5. Small Company, Incorporated, a small service organization, prepared the following report for the month of January 19A:

Service Revenue, Expenses, and Income

Service revenues:
Cash services (per cash register tape)	$75,000	
Credit services (per charge bills; not yet collected by end of January	25,000	$100,000

Expenses:
Salaries and wages (paid by check)	40,000	
Salary for January not yet paid	1,000	
Supplies used (taken from stock, purchased for cash during December)	2,000	
Estimated cost of wear and tear on used delivery truck for the month (depreciation)	400	
Other expenses (paid by check)	16,600	60,000
Pretax income		40,000
Income tax expense (not yet paid)		8,000
Income for January		$ 32,000

Required:

a. You have been asked by the owner (who knows very little about the financial side of business) to compute the "amount that cash increased in January 19A from the operations of the company."

    You decided to prepare a detailed report for the owner with the following major side captions: cash inflows (collections), cash outflows (payments), and the difference—net increase (or decrease) in cash.

b. What was the average income tax rate?

c. See if you can reconcile the "difference—net increase (or decrease) in cash" you computed in *(a)* with the income for January 19A.

E1–6. Libby Corporation was organized by five individuals on January 1, 19A. At the end of January 19A, the following monthly financial data are available:

Total revenues	$90,000
Total expenses (excluding income taxes)	70,000
Cash balance, January 31, 19A	15,000
Receivables from customers (all considered collectible)	10,000
Merchandise inventory (by inventory count at cost)	30,000
Payables to suppliers for merchandise purchased from them (will be paid during February 19A)	9,000
Total stockholders' equity on January 1, 19A	26,000

Assume a 20 percent tax rate on the income of this corporation; the income taxes will be paid during the first quarter of 19B.

Required:

Complete the following two statements for Libby Corporation:

LIBBY CORPORATION
Income Statement
For the Month of January 19A

Total revenues	$ _____
Less: Total expenses (excluding income tax)	_____
Pretax income	_____
Less: Income tax expense	_____
Net income	$ _____

LIBBY CORPORATION
Balance Sheet
At January 31, 19A

Assets:
Cash .... $ _____
Receivables from customers ....   _____
Merchandise inventory ....   _____
Total assets .... $ _____

Liabilities:
Payables to suppliers .... $ _____
Income taxes payable.........................   _____
     Total liabilities ....   _____
Total stockholders' equity ....   _____
Total liabilities and stockholders' equity .... $ _____

E1–7.   Kyle Realty, Incorporated, has been operating for five years and is owned by three investors. S. T. Kyle owns 60 percent of the total outstanding stock of 9,000 shares and is the managing executive in charge. On December 31, 19C, the following financial items for the entire year were determined: commissions earned and collected in cash, $150,000, plus $20,000 uncollected; rental service fees earned and collected, $20,000; salaries expense paid, $60,000; commissions expense paid, $45,000; payroll taxes paid, $4,000; rent paid, $2,200 (not including December rent yet to be paid); utilities expense paid, $700; promotion and advertising paid, $6,400; and miscellaneous expenses paid, $300. There were no other unpaid expenses at December 31. Kyle Realty rents its office space but owns the furniture therein. The furniture cost $5,000 when acquired and has an estimated life of 10 years (depreciate an equal amount each year). The average corporate income tax rate is 30 percent. Also during the year, the company paid the owners "out of profit" cash dividends amounting to $10,000. You have been requested to complete the following income statement:

_____

_____

_____

Revenues:
Commissions earned .... $ _____
Rental service fees ....   _____
     Total revenues .... $ _____
Expenses:
Salaries expense ....   _____
Commission expense ....   _____
Payroll tax expense ....   _____
Rent expense ....   _____
Utilities expense..............................   _____
Promotion and advertising ....   _____
Miscellaneous expenses ....   _____
Depreciation expense ....   _____
     Total expenses (excluding income taxes) .....   _____
Pretax income....................................   _____
Income tax expense ....   _____
Net income .... $ 49,490
Earnings per share (EPS)......................... $ _____

E1–8.   University Bookstore was organized as a corporation by Jane Nash and Roy Opel; each contributed $35,000 cash to start the business and each received 3,000 shares of common stock, par $10 per share. The store completed its first year of operations on December 31, 19A. On that date, the following financial items for the year were determined: December 31, 19A, cash on hand and in the bank, $42,000; December 31, 19A, amounts due from customers from sales of books, $6,100; store and office equipment, purchased January 1, 19A, for $40,000 (estimated useful life 10 years; depreciate an equal amount each year); December 31, 19A, amounts owed to publishers for books purchased, $6,000; and a note payable, 10 percent, one year, dated July 1, 19A, to a local bank for $2,000. No dividends were declared or paid to the stockholders during the year.

Required:

a.   You have been asked to complete the balance sheet at the end of 19A shown below.
b.   What was the amount of net income for the year?
c.   Show how the $100 liability for interest payable was computed. Why is it shown as a liability on this date?

Assets		Liabilities	
Cash	$ ___	Accounts payable	$ ___
Accounts receivable	___	Notes payable	
Store and office equipment	$ ___	Interest payable	100
Less: Accumulated		Total liabilities	$ ___
depreciation to date	___ ___	**Stockholders' Equity**	
		Common stock	___
		Contributed capital in excess	
		of par	___
		Retained earnings	6,000
		Total stockholders' equity	___
		Total liabilities and	
Total assets	$ ___	stockholders' equity	$ ___

E1–9.   Rice Manufacturing Corporation is preparing the annual financial statements for the stockholders. A SCFP, cash basis, must be prepared. The following data on cash flows were developed for the entire year ended December 31, 19D; cash inflow from operating revenues, $270,000; cash expended for operating expenses, $190,000; sale of unissued Rice stock for cash, $30,000; cash dividends declared and paid to stockholders during the year, $20,000; and payments on long-term notes payable, $40,000. During the year, a small tract of land was sold for $10,000 cash (which was the same price that Rice had paid for the land in 19C) and $41,000 cash was expended for two new machines. The machines were used in the factory.

Required:

Prepare a SCFP, cash basis, for 19D. Follow the format illustrated in the chapter.

E1–10.   On June 1, 19F, Rand Corporation prepared a balance sheet just prior to going out of business. The balance sheet totals reflected the following:

	$100,000
Assets (no cash)	$100,000
Liabilities	60,000
Stockholders' equity	40,000

Shortly thereafter, all of the assets were sold for cash.

Required:

a. How would the balance sheet appear immediately after the sale of the assets for cash for each separate case? Use the format given below.

Balances immediately after sale

	Cash received for the assets	Assets	− Liabilities	= Stockholders Equity
Case A	$110,000	$_____	$_____	$_____
Case B	100,000	_____	_____	_____
Case C	90,000	_____	_____	_____

b. How should the cash be distributed in each separate case? (Hint: Creditors have a priority claim over owners upon dissolution.) Use the format given below.

	To creditors	To stockholders	Total
Case A	$_____	$_____	$_____
Case B	_____	_____	_____
Case C	_____	_____	_____

PROBLEMS/CASES

PART A

PC1–1. D. X. Jones owns and operates the DXJ Sporting Goods Company (a sole proprietorship). An employee prepares a financial report for the business at each year-end. This report lists all of the resources (assets) owned by Jones (including such personal items as the home owned and occupied by Jones). It also lists all of the debts of the business (but not the "personal" debts of Jones).

Required:

a. From the accounting point of view, in what ways do you disagree with what is being included and excluded from the report of business assets and liabilities?
b. Upon questioning, Jones responded, "Don't worry about it, we use it only to support a loan from the bank." How would you respond to this comment?

PC1–2. You are one of three partners who own and operate the Triple X Refreshments Company. The company has been operating for seven years, and one of the other partners has prepared the company's annual financial statements. Recently you proposed that "the statements should be audited each year because it would benefit each of us and preclude possible disagreements about the division of profits." The partner that prepares the statements proposed that his "Uncle Ray, who has a lot of financial experience can do the job and at little cost." Your other partner remained silent.

Required:

a. What position would you take on the proposal? Justify your response.
b. Explain what you would strongly recommend and give the basis for your recommendation.

PC1–3.   Below are listed five transactions completed by Ace Company during the year 19A:

a. Sold services for cash, $9,000.
b. Purchased a microcomputer for use in performing the accounting function of the company: cost, $12,000; paid cash.
c. Paid salaries, $20,000 cash.
d. Borrowed cash, $10,000 on a 12 percent interest-bearing note.
e. The owner of Ace Company purchased a special pickup for his personal use; cost, $15,000; paid cash from his personal funds.

Required:

Complete the tabulation given below to indicate the effects (in dollars) of each of the above transactions on the balance sheet, income statement, and SCFP of Ace Company. Consider only the effects on the date the transactions were completed. Provide explanatory comments to support your response for each transaction. Use "+" for increase and "−" for decrease on the income statement and balance sheet.

	Transaction				
Financial statements	*(a)*	*(b)*	*(c)*	*(d)*	*(e)*
Income statement:					
Revenues	$	$	$	$	$
Expenses					
Balance sheet:					
Assets					
Liabilities					
Owners' equity					
SCFP:					
Cash inflow					
Cash outflow					

Explanations:

PC1–4.   On January 1, 19A, three individuals organized TRI Service Company. Each individual invested $5,000 cash in the business. On December 31, 19A, they prepared a list of resources (assets) owned and a list of the debts (liabilities) to support a company loan request of $50,000 to a local bank. None of the three investors had studied accounting. The two lists prepared were as follows:

Company resources:
Cash .... $ 3,000
Service supplies inventory (on hand) 5,000
Service trucks (four practically new) 60,000
Personal residences of organizers (three houses) 190,000
Service equipment used in the business (practically new) 24,000
Bills due from customers (for services already completed) 18,000
    Total $300,000

Obligations of the company:
Unpaid wages to employees $17,000
Unpaid taxes 6,000
Owed to suppliers 7,000
Owed on service trucks and equipment (to a finance company) 41,000
Loan from Organizer T 12,000
    Total .... $ 83,000

Required:

a. If you were advising the local bank with respect to the two lists, what issues would you raise for consideration? Explain the basis for each question and include any recommendations that you have (consider the separate-entity assumption).

b. In view of your response to *(a)*, what do you think the amount of **net resources** (i.e., assets minus liabilities) of the company would be? Show your computations.

PC1–5. Simple Service Company was organized on January 1, 19A. At the end of the first quarter (three months) of operations, the owner prepared a summary of its operations as shown in the first column of the following tabulation:

Summary of Transactions	Computation of	
	Profit	Cash
1. Services performed for customers, $60,000, of which one sixth remained uncollected at the end of the quarter.	$+60,000	$+50,000
2. Cash borrowed from the local bank, $10,000 (one-year note).		
3. Purchased a small service truck for use in the business; cost, $8,000; paid 20 percent down, balance on credit.		
4. Expenses, $40,000, of which one fifth remained unpaid at the end of the quarter.		
5. Purchased service supplies for use in the business, $2,000, of which one fourth remained unpaid (on credit) at the end of the quarter. Also, one fifth of these supplies were unused (still on hand) at the end of the quarter.		
6. Wages earned by employees, $12,000, of which one sixth remained unpaid at the end of the quarter.		
7. Purchased land for future use for $20,000 cash.		
Based only on the above transactions, compute the following for the quarter: Profit (or loss)	$	
Cash inflow (or outflow)		$

Required:

a. For each of the seven transactions given in the tabulation above, enter what you consider the correct amounts. Enter a zero when appropriate. The first transaction is answered by way of illustration.

b. For each transaction, briefly explain the basis for your dollar responses. (Hint: Profit and cash flow totals are not the same.)

PART B

PC1–6. DC Corporation was organized by Donald Dunn and Cynthia Cummings; they had previously operated the company as a partnership. Each owner has 10,000 shares of capital stock of DC Corporation. At the end of the accounting year, 19H, the company bookkeeper prepared the following incomplete balance sheets (amounts simplified for problem purposes):

DC CORPORATION
Balance Sheet

1.	Assets:		
2.	Cash		$28,000
3.	Accounts receivable		15,000
4.	Equipment*	$	
5.	Less: Accumulated depreciation	10,000	40,000
6.	Total _____		$83,000
7.	_____		
8.	Accounts payable	8,000	
9.	Income tax payable	1,000	
10.	Note payable, short term, 15% †	4,000	
11.	_____		
12.	_____		_____
13.	Capital stock, $_____ par value	20,000	
14.	Contributed capital in excess of par	10,000	
15.	Retained earnings	40,000	
16.	_____		70,000
17.	Total liabilities and stockholders' equity		$_____

* Equipment has a 10-year estimated life; equal amounts expensed each year.

† Note dated July 1, 19H, time to maturity, 12 months.

Required (the lines are numbered above for problem reference purposes):

1. Define the term *assets* as used on the balance sheet.
2. What would be DC's cash balance in the bank assuming the company has $500 cash on hand on December 31, 19H?
3. Explain why "Accounts receivable" represents an asset.
4. Compute the amount that the equipment cost when it was acquired by DC Corporation.
5. Explain "Accumulated depreciation." What does the $10,000 indicate?
6. Enter the correct caption here.
7. Enter the correct caption here.
8. Explain why "Accounts payable" is a liability.
9. Explain what this liability represents.
10. What amount of interest expense applies to the year 19H? Note, the amount computed will be shown on the income statement as "Interest expense."
11. Enter the appropriate caption and amount here.
12. Enter the appropriate caption here.
13. Enter the amount of the par value per share of capital stock.
14. What was the total issue price per share of capital stock?
15. Explain what the $40,000 amount means.
16. Enter appropriate caption here.
17. Enter correct amount here.
18. Do you have any suggestions with respect to the heading of the statement?

PC1–7. Davis Corporation was organized on January 1, 19A. At the end of 19A, the company had not yet employed an accountant. However, an employee who was "good with numbers" prepared the following statements at that date:

DAVIS CORPORATION
December 31, 19A

Income from sales of merchandise	$180,000
Total amount paid for goods sold during 19A	(95,000)
Selling costs	(30,000)
Depreciation (on service vehicles used)	(15,000)
Income from services rendered	50,000
Salaries and wages paid	(60,000)
Income taxes (at tax rate of 17%)	(5,100)
Profit for the year 19A	$ 24,900

DAVIS CORPORATION
December 31, 19A

Resources:		
Cash		$ 31,000
Merchandise inventory (held for resale)		44,000
Service vehicles		45,000
Retained earnings (profit earned in 19A)		24,900
Grand total		$144,900
Debts:		
Payables to suppliers		$ 15,000
Note owed to bank		20,000
Due from customers		12,900
Total		47,900
Supplies on hand (to be used in rendering services)	$12,000	
Depreciation (on service vehicles)	15,000	
Capital stock	70,000	
Total		97,000
Grand total		$144,900

Required:

The above statements have some incorrect captions, some items that are under the wrong caption, and the statement headings are incomplete. Prepare a correct income statement and balance sheet. (Hint: All figures [except totals] are correct; the balance sheet total should be $129,900.)

PC1–8. Upon graduation from high school, Jack Kane immediately accepted a job as a plumber's helper for a large local plumbing company. After three years of hard work, Jack received a plumber's license, whereupon he decided to go into business for himself. He had saved $5,000 which he decided to invest in the business. His first step was to transfer this amount from his savings account to a business bank account for "Kane Plumbing Company, Incorporated." His lawyer had advised him to start as a corporation. He then purchased, with cash, a used panel truck for $3,000 and secondhand tools for $800; rented space in a small building; inserted an ad in the local paper; and opened the doors on October 1, 19A. Immediately, Jack found himself very busy and, after one month, employed a helper. Although he knew practically nothing about the financial side of the business, Jack realized from his experience that a number of reports were required and that costs and collections had to be controlled carefully. Accordingly, at the end of the year, prompted in part by concern about his income tax situation (previously he only had to report salary), he recognized the need for financial statements. His wife, Jane, undertook "to develop some financial statements for the business." With the help of a friend, on December 31, 19A, she gathered the following data for the three months just ended: Deposits in the bank account of collections for plumbing services totaled $30,000. The following checks were written: plumber's helper, $7,550; payroll taxes paid, $150; supplies purchased and used on jobs, $9,000; oil, gas, and maintenance on truck, $1,100; insurance, $300; rent, $500; utilities and telephone, $650; and miscellaneous expenses, $400 (including advertising). In addition, there were uncollected bills to customers for plumbing services amounting to $2,000, and the rent for December amounting to $100 had not been paid. The income tax rate on this corporation may be assumed to be 17 percent. Also assume that the "wear and tear on the truck and tools due to use during the three months" was estimated by Jack to be $250.

Required:

a. Prepare an income statement for Kane Plumbing for the three months October–December 19A. Use the following main captions: revenues from services, expenses, pretax income, and net income. (Hint: Expenses, excluding income taxes, totaled $20,000.)

b. Do you visualize that Jack may have a need for one or more additional financial reports for 19A and thereafter? Explain.

PC1–9. During the summer, between her junior and senior years, Mandy Walker was faced with the need to earn sufficient funds for the coming academic year. Unable to obtain a job with reasonable remuneration, she decided to try the lawn-care business for three months. After a survey of the market potential, Mandy acquired a used pickup truck on June 1 for $1,200. On each door she painted "Mandy's Lawn Service, Ph. XX." Additionally, she spent $600 for mowers, trimmers, and tools. To acquire these items she borrowed $2,000 cash on a note (endorsed by a friend) at 15 percent interest per annum, payable at the end of the three months (ending August 31).

At the end of the summer, Mandy realized that she had "done a lot of work and her bank account looked good," which prompted her to become concerned about how much profit the business had earned.

A review of the check stubs showed the following: Deposits in the bank of collections from customers totaled $11,400. The following checks were written: gas, oil, and lubrication, $880; pickup repairs, $150; repair of mowers, $80; miscellaneous supplies used, $100; helpers, $4,725; payroll taxes, $175; payment for assistance in preparing payroll tax forms, $75; insurance, $150; telephone, $90; and $2,075 to pay off the note including interest (on August 31). A notebook kept in the pickup, plus some unpaid bills, reflected that customers still owed her $600 for lawn services rendered and that she owed $100 for gas and oil (credit card charges). She estimated that the "wear and tear" for use of the truck and the other equipment for three months amounted to $400.

Required:

a. Prepare an income statement for Mandy's Lawn Service covering the three months, June, July, and August 19A. Use the following main captions: revenues from services, expenses, and net income. Because this is a sole proprietorship, the company will not be subject to income tax. (Hint: Total revenues amounted to $12,000.)

b. Do you visualize a need for one or more additional financial reports for this company for 19A and thereafter? Explain.

PC1–10. Western Realty Company was organized early in 19A as a corporation by four investors, each of whom invested $5,000 cash. The company has been moderately successful, despite the fact that internal financial controls are inadequate. Although financial reports have been prepared each year (primarily in response to income tax requirements), sound accounting practice has not been followed. As a consequence, the financial performance of the company was known only vaguely by the four stockholders. Recently, one of the stockholders, with the agreement of the others, sold his shares to a local accountant. The new stockholder was amazed when handed the report below, which was prepared by an employee for the last meeting of the board of directors. The accountant could tell at a glance that the reported profit was wrong and quickly observed that no interest expense was shown on a $10,000, 14 percent note payable that had been outstanding throughout the year. Also, no recognition had been given to office equipment that was purchased on January 1, 19D, at a cost of $14,000 with an estimated five-year useful life.

WESTERN REALTY
Profit Statement
December 31, 19D

Commissions earned (all collected)	$130,000
Property management revenue (exclusive of $1,200 not collected)	8,000
Total	138,000
Salaries paid	31,000
Commissions paid	38,000
Payroll taxes paid	3,300
Office supplies expense	120
Rent paid	2,400
Utilities paid	500
Advertising (excluding the December bill for advertising of $4,000 not yet paid)	28,000
Miscellaneous expenses	400
Total	103,720
Profit for the year	$ 34,280

EPS: $34,280 ÷ 10,000 shares = $3.43.

Required:

You have been asked to redraft the income statement, including corrections. Assume an average income tax rate of 20 percent. (Hint: The correct EPS is $2.18.)

PC1–11. Assume you are president of Joy Retailers, Incorporated. At the end of the first year (December 31, 19A) of operations, the following financial data are available for the company:

Cash ....$	16,300
Receivables from customers (all considered collectible)	15,000
Inventory of merchandise (based on physical count and priced at cost)	78,000
Equipment owned, at cost (at year-end, the estimated value to the business for future use was 90% of cost)	20,000
Note payable, one year, 12% annual interest, owed to the bank (dated July 1, 19A)..................................	20,000
Interest on the note through December 31, 19A (due to be paid to the bank on June 30, 19B; $20,000 × 12% × $\frac{6}{12}$)	1,200
Salary payable for 19A (on December 31, 19A, this was owed to an employee who was away because of an emergency; will return around January 10, 19B, at which time the payment will be made)	1,100
Total sales revenue	100,000
Expenses paid, including the cost of the merchandise sold (excluding income taxes at a 17% rate; the taxes will be paid during the first quarter of 19B)	70,700
Capital stock, 1,000 shares outstanding	80,000

Required (show computations):

a. Prepare a summarized income statement for the year 19A. (Hint: EPS is $2.075.)

b. Prepare a balance sheet at December 31, 19A.

PC1–12.　At December 31, 19A, Big J Corporation had been in operation for one year. At the date of organization, each of the 10 investors paid in $10,000 cash and each received 100 shares of capital stock. Due to a need for more cash, on January 1, 19A, the corporation also borrowed $90,000, at 12 percent interest per year, on a note from a local bank. Interest on the note is payable each December 31, and the loan matures December 31, 19D. On December 31, 19A, the income statement and the balance sheet (summarized) were as follows:

Income Statement
For the Year Ended December 31, 19A

Total revenue	$70,000
Total expenses	44,360
Pretax income	25,640
Income tax expense ($25,640 × 20%).....	5,128
Net income	$20,512

Balance Sheet
At December 31, 19A

Assets		Liabilities	
Cash..........................	24,154	Income taxes payable	$ 1,282*
Remaining assets	187,640	Notes payable, long term	90,000
		Stockholders' Equity	
		Capital stock (1,000 shares)	100,000
		Retained earnings	20,512
		Total liabilities and	
Total assets	$211,794	stockholders' equity	$211,794

* Three fourths of the income taxes was paid during the year on a quarterly basis (i.e., $5,128 × 0.25 = $1,282).

An independent CPA audited the above amounts. The CPA found that the bookkeeper had neglected to include two transactions that occurred on December 31, 19A:

1. Payment of a cash dividend of $7.50 per share to each shareholder.
2. Cash payment of interest for one year on the long-term note payable owed to the bank.

Required:

Other than for these two transactions, the amounts were correct. Recast the income statement and the balance sheet to include the effects of these two transactions. Assume a 20 percent tax rate. (Hint: The corrected balance sheet total is $193,494.)

PC1–13.　At the end of 19A, Foster Corporation prepared the following annual income statement and balance sheet:

FOSTER CORPORATION
Income Statement
For the Year Ended December 31, 19A

Revenues	$280,000
Expenses	248,000
Income before taxes	32,000
Income taxes (average rate, 30%).....	9,600
Net income.....................	$ 22,400

FOSTER CORPORATION
Balance Sheet
At December 31, 19A

Assets			Liabilities		
Cash		$ 18,000	Accounts payable		$ 8,000
Accounts receivable		22,000	Income taxes payable		
Inventory (by count)		76,800	(one half unpaid)		4,800
Fixtures	$25,000		Notes payable, 12%		
Less: Accumulated deprecia-			(due June 30, 19B)		20,000
tion	7,000	18,000	Total liabilities		32,800
Total assets		$134,800	**Stockholders' Equity**		
			Common stock, par		
			$10, 5,000 shares	$50,000	
			Contributed capital in		
			excess of par	10,000	
			Retained earnings	42,000	
			Total stockholders' equity		102,000
			Total liabilities and stockholders'		
			equity		$134,800

An independent audit of the above statements and underlying records revealed the following:

1. Depreciation expense included in total expense was $2,000 for 19A; it should have been $2,500.
2. A tentative order was received from a customer on December 31, 19A, for goods having a sales price of $10,000 and was included in sales revenue and accounts receivable. The goods were on hand (and included in the ending inventory), and it is quite likely a sale may not materialize; the customer will decide by January 20, 19B. This tentative order should not have been recognized as a sale in 19A.

Required:

Other than these two items, the amounts on the financial statements were correct. Recast the two statements to take into account the depreciation error and the incorrect recognition of the tentative order. Show computations and assume an average income tax rate of 30 percent. (Hint: Revised EPS is $3.01.)

Financial Reporting and the Fundamental Accounting Concepts

PURPOSE OF THIS CHAPTER

Chapter 1 introduced the primary elements of the income statement, balance sheet, and statement of changes in financial position. This chapter expands that discussion of **external** financial statements to include the classifications used on the statements. Also, it introduces some additional fundamental accounting concepts. Thus, the purpose of this chapter is to expand your background knowledge of financial statements. This knowledge will facilitate your study and understanding of the subsequent chapters. To accomplish this purpose, the chapter is divided into two parts.

Part A—Content of financial statements for external decision makers:

Discusses and illustrates the **subclassifications** of the financial information presented on external financial statements.

Part B—Uses of financial information in decision making and the fundamental concepts of accounting:

Expands the discussion in Chapter 1 of the use of financial information in decision making.

Presents the fundamental concepts that underlie the accounting for, and reporting of, information in the financial statements.

PART A—CONTENT OF FINANCIAL STATEMENTS FOR EXTERNAL DECISION MAKERS

CLASSIFICATION OF ITEMS ON THE FINANCIAL STATEMENTS

External decision makers (that use financial statements) are varied as to background, education, experience, financial interests, and problems because they include investors, creditors, employees, governmental agencies, unions, customers, and other interested parties. Financial statements often are referred to as **general-purpose financial statements** because they are prepared to serve the diverse needs of these groups.

To enhance the clarity and usefulness of financial statements to the wide range of decision makers, **subclassifications** of the economic information presented are included on the financial statements.

In this part of the chapter, the discussions will include a comprehensive illustration of the financial statements of a medium-sized company. We then will briefly discuss a more complicated set of actual financial statements as they were presented by a large, well-known company—Johnson & Johnson (see Special Supplement B immediately preceding the Index).

This part of the chapter continues our introduction to financial statements so you should concentrate on understanding the nature of the classifications and the presentation of accounting information in the financial statements rather than on how the amounts shown were derived. At the conclusion of this chapter, we do not anticipate that you will absorb all aspects of the financial statements that are presented; however, the primary features of each statement should be understood. You also should appreciate the importance of the end product of the accounting process—the financial statements. You will be able to maintain perspective in the chapters that follow when studying the details of information processing, measuring, and reporting in terms of the accounting model. As you study the subsequent chapters, you should return frequently to this one for reference points and further study. Also, the exhibits presented in this chapter will be helpful as a guide in solving some of the assigned problems in subsequent chapters.

To assist the users of financial statements, some standardization of classifications has evolved. When classifications are included on the statements, they sometimes are referred to as **classified financial statements.** Classified financial statements vary in terminology and arrangement from those for Business Aids given in Chapter 1. These differences reflect the fact that financial statements are tailored to the **needs of a wide range of decision makers,** depending upon the type of company and the characteristics of the industry. As a basis for discussion of these classifications, this section presents the financial statements for Diamond, Inc., a large department store that has been in business for more than 40 years.

**The income
statement**

Exhibit 2–1 presents an income statement for Diamond.[1] It follows this basic model: **Revenues — Expenses = Net Income.** Therefore, Exhibit 2–1, stripped of the detailed items, shows the following subclassifications:

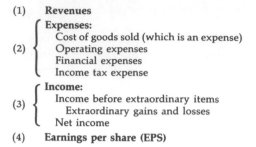

We will discuss the meaning of each of these classifications.

Revenues. Revenues were defined in Chapter 1 (page 19). The revenue of a business that sells services is called **service revenue.** The revenue of a business that sells products or merchandise is called **sales revenue.** Merchandise sold and later returned by the customer represents **returned sales** and reduces revenue. Similarly, allowances granted to customers, say, for a defect in the goods purchased from the store, reduce revenue. Such returns and allowances are **contra revenues** rather than expenses.[2] Therefore, **gross sales** for the period must be reduced by these two amounts to derive the correct net revenue amount, or **net sales revenue,** for the period. Observe the manner of reporting sales revenue in Exhibit 2–1.

Expenses. Expenses were defined in Chapter 1 (page 20). An income statement may be designed to reflect several classifications of expenses. These classifications tend to vary, depending upon the type of business. For a merchandising business, which is one that sells goods manufactured by others, the usual classifications of expenses are as follows:

1. Cost of goods sold. This expense reflects the amount of expense that was incurred for the merchandise (or goods) sold during the period. For example, Diamond sold goods during the period, at selling price, amounting to $3,615,000 net revenue. This merchandise, when purchased by Diamond, cost $2,416,000 as reflected in Exhibit 2–1. The difference between these two amounts, $1,199,000, is known as the **gross margin on sales** (formerly called gross profit on sales). The gross margin indicates the markup on all of the goods sold during the period.[3]

---

[1] The income statement discussed and illustrated in this section sometimes is referred to as a **multiple-step** income statement because it shows several groupings of data and after each group (or step) shows a step difference. Each such difference is appropriately labeled, such as gross margin on sales. In contrast, a single-step income statement would be similar to that illustrated in Exhibit 1–4 because only two major categories (revenues and expenses) were shown and there were no intermediate "step" differences. Many published income statements follow the single-step format. The classifications illustrated for Diamond are used frequently; however, they are not mandatory.

[2] Contra as used in accounting means an offset to, or a reduction of, a basic amount.

[3] Markup is the amount added to the cost of an item to determine its sale price. Markup can be expressed as an amount or as a percent.

EXHIBIT 2–1
Income statement classifications illustrated

DIAMOND, INC.
Income Statement
For the Year Ended December 31, 1984

(1) Rev.		
Gross sales revenue	$3,620,000	
Less: Sales returns and allowances	5,000	
Net sales revenue		$3,615,000
Less: Cost of goods sold		2,416,000
Gross margin on sales		1,199,000
Operating expenses:		
Selling (distribution) expenses:		
Sales salaries	$399,000	
Advertising and promotion	200,000	
Depreciation, store equipment	15,000	
Insurance.............................	18,000	
Taxes (excluding income tax expense)	13,200	
Warranty expense	3,000	
Amortization of trademarks	2,000	
Miscellaneous	9,800	
Total selling expenses		660,000
(2) Exp. General and administrative expenses:		
Administrative salaries	170,000	
Rent expense	9,000	
Office supplies used	8,100	
Estimated losses on doubtful accounts	3,600	
Depreciation, office equipment	1,000	
Insurance.............................	2,000	
Taxes (excluding income tax expense)	400	
Miscellaneous	1,900	
Total general and administrative expenses	196,000	
Total operating expenses		856,000
Pretax income from operations		343,000
Financial expenses and financial revenues:		
Interest expense	56,000	
Revenue from investments and funds	13,000	
Net financial expense		43,000
Pretax income		300,000
Income tax on operations..................		138,000
(3) Inc. Income before extraordinary items............		162,000
Extraordinary items:		
Gain on sale of land held for appreciation*	51,000	
Less: Income tax on the gain	13,000	38,000
Net income..............................		$ 200,000
(4) EPS Earnings per share (EPS) of common stock:		
Income before extraordinary items		$ 9.13
Extraordinary items......................		2.54
Net income..............................		$11.67

* We have assumed that this transaction met the two criteria for an extraordinary item. The land was sold for $56,000 less its very low cost of $5,000, resulting in a pretax gain of $51,000.

To illustrate, the average markup based **on cost** for Diamond was $1,199,000 ÷ $2,416,000 = 49.6 percent; and based **on selling price,** it was $1,199,000 ÷ $3,615,000 = 33.2 percent.

2. Operating expenses.   These are the usual expenses that were incurred in operating the business during the period. Often they are subclassified further, as reflected in Exhibit 2–1, between **selling expenses** and **general and administrative expenses. Selling expenses** (often called distribution expenses) comprise all amounts incurred during the period in performing the sales activities. **General and administrative expenses** include the overall business expenses that are not directly related to selling activities, such as the president's salary and the expenses of the accounting department.

3. Financial expenses.   These are the expenses incurred as a result of borrowing money or for credit extended to the company. The cost of credit usually is referred to as **interest expense.** Interest on debt is a **financing expense** rather than an operating expense; therefore, it is set out in a separate category from cost of goods sold and operating expenses.

Some businesses also **collect** interest for credit they have extended to others which is called **interest revenue** (discussed in a later chapter). When the amount of interest revenue is not substantial, instead of reporting it under the revenue caption along with sales and service revenue, sometimes it is offset against interest expense as shown on Exhibit 2–1. When interest revenue is reported under the revenue classification, "gross margin on sales" cannot be reported because gross margin would include revenues not related to sales. For this reason, and the desire to report both financial expenses and financial revenue under one caption, companies often report these two items as shown in Exhibit 2–1.

Extraordinary items.   This is a special classification used to report nonoperating gains and losses. These items are defined in accounting as being **both** (1) **unusual in nature** and (2) **infrequent in occurrence;** therefore, they are set out separately to aid the user in evaluating the profit performance of the business. To include them in the usual, regular, ongoing revenue or expense categories would lead the user to believe extraordinary items are normal and will occur again in the reasonable future. Observe in Exhibit 2–1 that **extraordinary items** are reported **after** the caption "Income before extraordinary items" and immediately **before** net income.[4]

Income tax expense.   This is the amount of income tax expense incurred for the period encompassed by the income statement. Income tax expense will appear only on the income statements of corporations because other forms of business organization are not subject to federal income tax. The amount of income subject to tax is defined by the Internal Revenue Code and often does not agree

---

[4] AICPA, *APB Opinion No. 30,* "Reporting the Results of Operations" (New York, 1973), mandates that the following format be used at the bottom of the income statement when there are extraordinary items:

Income before extraordinary items.
Extraordinary items (net of any related income tax).
Net income.

with the "accounting" income amount shown on the income statement. Detailed consideration of income taxes is beyond the scope of this book (however, see the overview in Special Supplement A that follows the last chapter). We will use simplified tax rates and computations of income taxes to demonstrate appropriate reporting of the income tax expense and income taxes payable.

Observe in Exhibit 2–1 that total income tax expense is $138,000 + $13,000 = $151,000. When there are extraordinary items, income tax expense must be reported in two parts:

1. Income tax based on normal operations is reported above the caption "Income before extraordinary items" ($138,000 in Exhibit 2–1).
2. Income tax based on the extraordinary items is reported with those items ($13,000 in Exhibit 2–1).

Income amounts. Observe on the income statement (Exhibit 2–1) that three separate "income" amounts are reported; pretax income (an optional step amount), income before extraordinary items (required when there are extraordinary items), and net income. Income before extraordinary items is the difference between "ordinary" revenues and expenses. Net income always is the last item in the body of the income statement; as a result, it often is called the bottom-line figure. It is after extraordinary items and has no qualifications. **Net income is the difference between total revenues and total expenses** (including extraordinary items).

Earnings per share (EPS). A corporation (but not a sole proprietorship or a partnership) is required to report EPS amounts on the income statement. An EPS amount must be reported for income before extraordinary items and for net income.[5] The computation of EPS was illustrated and discussed briefly in Chapter 1. In that chapter, Business Aids, Inc., reported only one EPS amount because there were no extraordinary items. In contrast, Diamond reported three EPS amounts because there was an extraordinary item.[6]

---

[5] AICPA, *APB Opinion No. 15*, "Earnings per Share" (New York, 1969), requires that the two EPS amounts be reported; viz, (1) on income before extraordinary items and (2) on net income. However, many companies also report an EPS amount for the extraordinary category as shown on Exhibit 2–1. *FASB Statement No. 21*, "Suspension of the Reporting of Earnings per Share and Segment Information by Nonpublic Enterprises" (Stamford, Conn., April 1978), suspended the EPS requirement for companies whose shares are not listed on the stock exchanges and for those not sold over the counter. Thus, it is required for most of the larger corporations.

[6] EPS amounts are computed **only for common stock outstanding** (preferred stock is discussed in a later chapter). At this point in your study you need not be concerned about the computation of EPS amounts when both common and nonconvertible preferred stock are outstanding. This topic will be discussed later. However, for those interested, the amounts on Exhibit 2–1 were computed as follows:

Income before extraordinary items:
($162,000 − $25,000, the dividend claim
  of the nonconvertible preferred stock) ÷ 15,000 shares = $ 9.13

Extraordinary gain:
  $38,000 ÷ 15,000 shares =   2.54

Net income:
  ($200,000 − $25,000) ÷ 15,000 shares = $11.67

EXHIBIT 2–2
Balance sheet classifications illustrated

DIAMOND, INC.
Balance Sheet
At December 31, 1984

Assets

Current assets:

Cash		$ 150,000	
Short-term investments		40,000	
Accounts receivable	$425,000		
Less: Allowance for doubtful accounts	15,000	410,000	
Notes receivable, short term		20,000	
Merchandise inventory		1,510,000	
Office supplies inventory		1,000	
Prepaid insurance		4,000	
Total current assets			$2,135,000

Long-term investments and funds:

Stock of X Corporation		10,000	
Sinking fund to pay bonds		150,000	
Total long-term investments and funds			160,000

Operational assets:

Store equipment	150,000		
Less: Accumulated depreciation	60,000	90,000	
Office equipment	16,000		
Less: Accumulated depreciation	4,000	12,000	
Total operational assets			102,000

Intangible assets:

Trademarks			60,000

Other assets:

Land acquired for future store site			68,000
Total assets			$2,525,000

Liabilities

Current liabilities:

Accounts payable	$ 180,000	
Notes payable, short term	100,000	
Wages payable	16,000	
Income tax payable	30,000	
Estimated warranty obligations	24,000	
Total current liabilities		$ 350,000

Long-term liabilities:

Bank notes payable (maturity 1986)	100,000	
Bonds payable (7%, maturity 1994)	500,000	
Total long-term liabilities		600,000
Total liabilities		950,000

Stockholders' Equity

Contributed capital:

Preferred stock, 5%, cumulative, nonconvertible, 5,000 shares outstanding, par $100	500,000	
Common stock, 15,000 shares outstanding, nopar	750,000	
Contributed capital in excess of par, preferred stock	50,000	
Total contributed capital	1,300,000	

Retained earnings (see statement of retained

earnings below)	275,000	
Total stockholders' equity		1,575,000
Total liabilities and stockholders' equity		$2,525,000

The balance sheet

The balance sheet for Diamond, presented in Exhibit 2–2, is based on the accounting model: **Assets − Liabilities = Owners' Equity** (see Chapter 1, page 21). To assist decision makers, each of the three major categories of items—assets, liabilities, and owners' equity—is subclassified on the basis of one of its primary characteristics. The following subclassifications usually are used:[7]

Balance Sheet

Assets **(by order of liquidity)**	**Liabilities** **(by order of time to maturity)**
Current assets	Current liabilities
Long-term investments and funds	Long-term liabilities
Operational (i.e., fixed) assets	
Intangible assets	**Owners' Equity** **(by order of permanency)**
Deferred charges	Contributed capital
Other assets	Retained earnings
	Unrealized capital

Exhibit 2–2 (Diamond's balance sheet) presents the three major categories—assets, liabilities, and owners' equity—in a **vertical** arrangement that is called the **report format.** In contrast, the balance sheet for Business Aids (Exhibit 1–5, page 22) presented the major categories in a **horizontal** arrangement with the assets to the left and the liabilities and owners' equity to the right which is called the **account format.** Both formats are used widely.

We will discuss each of the subclassifications on the balance sheet.

Current assets. Current assets are resources (i.e., assets) owned by the entity that are reasonably expected to be realized in cash or used up within one year from the balance sheet date or during the **normal operating cycle** of the business, whichever is the longer. The normal operating cycle tends to vary for each business because it is the average time required for the normal operating cycle—cash investment in inventory to cash collection from customers. For a merchandising company it may be represented graphically as in Exhibit 2–3.

Observe that Diamond's balance sheet (Exhibit 2–2) reported seven different current assets starting with cash and ending with prepaid insurance. Current assets are listed on the balance sheet essentially in order of decreasing liquidity. **Liquidity** refers to the average period of time required to convert a noncash resource to cash. In addition to cash, current assets include short-term or temporary investments, accounts receivable, notes receivable, inventories, and prepaid expenses.

Short-term investments are current assets because it is expected that they will be sold for cash within the next year or the next operating cycle, whichever is longer. **Accounts receivable** are amounts due the company on "open account" from customers and are current assets because they are expected to be collected in the near future. Observe the **contra amount** (contra because it is an offset), allowance for doubtful accounts. This contra amount will be discussed in Chapter

---

[7] The subclassification titles vary somewhat in actual practice. For example, operational assets often are called property, plant, and equipment.

EXHIBIT 2–3
**Operating cycle for
a retail business**

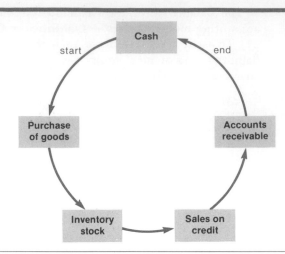

6; it represents an estimate of the amount of accounts receivable that will be uncollectible (i.e., bad debts). **Notes Receivable, Short Term,** is a current asset for essentially the same reason as accounts receivable. **Merchandise inventory** is a current asset because it represents merchandise on hand that will be sold for cash or on short-term credit in the near future. **Office supplies inventory** represents items on hand that will be consumed (i.e., used) in the short term. **Prepaid expenses** are goods or services paid for in advance of their use, such as a two-year insurance premium paid at the beginning of the term of the coverage. As each year of the coverage passes, a portion of the premium paid becomes expense. To illustrate, assume a two-year insurance premium of $600 was paid on January 1, 1984. At the end of 1984, half of the insurance period would have expired. Therefore, **insurance expense** for 1984 would be $300 and the remaining $300 would be reported on the 1984 balance sheet as a current asset because the company still has insurance coverage due for one more year. Similarly, in 1985, insurance expense would be $300 and there would be no prepaid insurance on this policy at December 31, 1985.

Financial institutions and others who lend funds to a company are interested in the current assets of the borrower because such assets provide one indication of the **short-term ability of the business to meet early maturing debts.** For example, a banker making a decision to grant short-term credit to Diamond would consider the amount of each current asset at the date of the loan and throughout its term as important to the lending decision. Such amounts also would be useful in making cash and income projections about the future.

Long-term investments and funds. This noncurrent asset classification reports the investments the company intends to hold for the long run (more than one year, or beyond the operating cycle, whichever is longer). **Long-term investments** include such items as the stocks and bonds of other companies that have been purchased as investments, real estate investments, and so on. This classification also includes cash set aside in **special funds** (such as a savings account) for use in the future for a specified long-term purpose. The "Sinking fund to pay bonds" reported in Exhibit 2–2 represents cash set aside for a special purpose. This fund will be expended at maturity date to retire (i.e., pay off) the bonds payable reported under "Long-term liabilities."[8] While the fund is in existence, it will earn interest revenue that will be reflected on the income statement as revenue from investments and funds (see "Revenue from investments and funds" on Exhibit 2–1).

Operational assets. This classification sometimes is called **property, plant, and equipment** or **fixed assets.** It includes those assets having physical substance (i.e., they are tangible) that were acquired for use in **operating the business** rather than for resale as inventory items or simply held as investments. Typically, they include buildings owned; land on which the buildings reside; and equipment, tools, furniture, and fixtures used in operating the business. They are long-lived and are used in the production and/or sale of other assets or services. Operational assets, with the exception of land, are depreciated over time as they are used (i.e., worn out). Because their productive usefulness decreases as they are used, their initial cost is apportioned to expense over their estimated useful lives. This apportionment of cost over useful life is known as **depreciation.** Land is not depreciated because it does not wear out as do machinery, buildings, and equipment. The amount of depreciation computed for **each period** is reported on the income statement as depreciation **expense,** and the **cumulative,** or accumulated, amount of depreciation expense for all past periods from acquisition date is **deducted** (as a contra amount) on the balance sheet from the cost of the asset to derive **"book or carrying value."** To illustrate, for Diamond, the depreciation for office equipment was determined and reported as follows:

1. **Income statement (Exhibit 2–1)**—Depreciation expense on office equipment for 1984, $1,000, computed as follows:

$$\frac{\text{Cost of the equipment}}{\text{Estimated useful life}} = \frac{\$16,000}{16 \text{ years}}$$
$$= \$1,000 \text{ depreciation expense (each year)}$$

2. **Balance sheet (Exhibit 2–2)**—The amounts shown for office equipment represent the following:

Office equipment, cost when acquired on January 1, 1981 .... $16,000
Accumulated depreciation expense from January 1, 1981, to
December 31, 1984 ($1,000 × 4 years) 4,000
Difference—book value on December 31, 1984; the amount of
equipment cost not yet allocated to depreciation expense $12,000

The difference, $12,000, usually is called the **book value** or **carrying value** of the office equipment. At the end of the 16th year, the book value of the

---

[8] The term *sinking fund,* although widely used in accounting, is not descriptive. It simply refers to a cash fund set aside to pay a long-term debt at the maturity or due date, or for other future needs.

office equipment will be zero because the equipment has no **residual** value at the end of its useful life to the entity. Depreciation expense on store equipment was computed on the basis of a 10-year life (i.e., $150,000 \div 10$ years $= \$15,000$). Depreciation is discussed in detail in Chapter 9.

Intangible assets. This classification includes those long-lived assets that have no **physical existence** (i.e., they are intangible) and have a long life. Their value is derived from the **rights and privileges** that accompany ownership. Examples are patents, trademarks, copyrights, franchises, and goodwill. Intangible assets usually are not acquired for resale but rather are used in the continuing operations of the business. Thus, in this respect, they are similar to operational assets. Diamond reported one intangible asset—trademarks (see Exhibit 2–2). Intangible assets are discussed in detail in Chapter 9.

Deferred charges. This classification represents long-term prepayments for goods and services that are expected to contribute to the earning of revenues in the future. They are the same as the current asset prepaid expenses (defined above), except that the prepayment extends **beyond** one year or the operating cycle, whichever is longer. For example, the prepayment of a five-year insurance premium of $500 on January 1, 19A, theoretically would be reported as follows at December 31, 19A:

```
Income statement:
    Insurance expense for 19A  . . . . . . . . . . .    $100
Balance sheet:
  Current assets:
    Prepaid insurance  . . . . . . . . . . . . . . . .      100
  Deferred charges:
    Prepaid insurance  . . . . . . . . . . . . . . . .      300
```

When the prepaid amounts are relatively small (i.e., not material), the total amount of the long-term prepayment often is reported as a prepaid expense. Observe in Exhibit 2–2 that Diamond did not report any deferred charges.

Other assets. A business may own assets that do not fit reasonably into one of the preceding classifications. Thus, a miscellaneous category called **other assets** may be needed. For example, operational assets retired from service and held for disposal would be reported under this category in a manner similar to the land acquired for future site in Exhibit 2–2.

Current liabilities. Current liabilities are those short-term debts at the balance sheet date that are expected to be paid out of the current assets listed on the same balance sheet. Short-term liabilities are expected to be paid during the coming year or the operating cycle of the business, whichever is longer (see page 53). Diamond's balance sheet (Exhibit 2–2) reports five different current liabilities that sum to $350,000. **Accounts payable** represent amounts owed on open account to suppliers of merchandise purchased for resale. **Short-term notes payable** evidence interest-bearing debt that will mature within the coming year (or operating cycle if it is longer), and **wages payable** represent amounts due employees not yet paid at balance sheet date. **Estimated warranty obligations** represent future amounts that will have to be expended to fulfill guarantees on merchandise already sold or services already rendered.

Working capital is not a separate classification on the balance sheet; however, it is a widely used concept that is based on current assets and current liabilities. It can be expressed as a dollar amount or as a ratio as follows:

As a dollar amount:

Computation: $\left\{\begin{array}{l}\text{Total current} \\ \text{assets}\end{array}\right.$ $-$ $\begin{array}{l}\text{Total current} \\ \text{liabilities}\end{array}$ $=$ $\begin{array}{l}\text{Working capital} \\ \text{dollars}\end{array}$

Example based on Diamond: $2,135,000 \quad - \quad 350,000 \quad = \quad 1,785,000$

As a ratio:

Computation: $\left\{\begin{array}{l}\text{Total current} \\ \text{assets}\end{array}\right.$ $\div$ $\begin{array}{l}\text{Total current} \\ \text{liabilities}\end{array}$ $=$ $\begin{array}{l}\text{Working capital} \\ \text{ratio}\end{array}$

Example: $2,135,000 \quad \div \quad 350,000 \quad = \quad 6.10$

Thus, the working capital of Diamond for 1984 was $1,785,000, and the amount of current assets was 6.10 times the amount of current liabilities. Working capital (in dollars or as a ratio) is a measure of the **liquidity** of the business, that is, its ability to pay its short-term debts and early maturities of its long-term debts. For example, a banker considering a short-term loan may not be impressed by a large amount of current assets; the working capital ratio may be, say, .80, which indicates that current assets are only 80 percent of current liabilities.

Long-term liabilities.   Long-term liabilities represent all of the liabilities that do not qualify as current liabilities. Thus, long-term liabilities are those that will not be paid within one year of the balance sheet date (or within one operating cycle if it is longer). They are different from current liabilities only because of the extended period before maturity. Exhibit 2–2 reports two long-term liabilities for Diamond: "Bank notes payable" (due 2 years hence) which represents amounts borrowed from a bank; and "Bonds payable," (due 10 years from the date of the balance sheet) which represents amounts borrowed from long-term investors.

Owners' equity.   Owners' equity (called stockholders' equity for a corporation) represents the residual claim of the owners (i.e., A − L = OE). This claim results from the initial contributions of the stockholders (usually called **contributed capital**) plus the accumulated earnings of the company less the accumulated dividends declared (usually called **retained earnings**). Exhibit 2–2 reports these two categories of stockholders' equity that are intended to report the **sources** of owners' equity. Often there is more than one class of capital stock, and each is reported separately. Diamond's balance sheet reports two classes of capital stock: (1) preferred stock, 5,000 shares outstanding; and (2) common stock, 15,000 shares outstanding.[9]

---

[9] Preferred stock is designated so because it has certain specified preferences over the common stock. In this particular case, the preferred stock is reported as having two preferences: (1) a dividend preference of 5 percent—this means that dividends on the preferred stock must be paid each year equivalent to 5 percent of the par value per share of the preferred before any dividends can be paid on the common stock; and (2) a cumulative preference—this means that should dividends equiva-

The amount labeled "Contributed capital in excess of par, preferred stock," indicates that the preferred stock initially was sold at an average price of $110 per share. This was $10 per share above its par value of $100 per share because the "excess" was $10 × 5,000 shares = $50,000. The par value is reported as one amount, and the excess is reported separately. The sum of the two amounts represents the amount contributed by the stockholders when the stock was sold initially. The amount of owners' equity ($1,575,000) can be verified as total assets ($2,525,000) minus total liabilities ($950,000). The amount of owners' equity does not represent the amount that the stockholders would receive if the business were sold; simply it is the **"book value"** of their residual claim.

THE STATEMENT OF RETAINED EARNINGS

The balance sheet for Diamond (Exhibit 2–2) is supplemented by the **statement of retained earnings** (Exhibit 2–4). This statement is optional; however, the information presented in it is required to attain "full disclosure." Some companies report the information in the balance sheet. The statement of retained earnings explains the increases and decreases in retained earnings during the period. The

EXHIBIT 2–4
Statement of retained earnings illustrated

DIAMOND, INC.
Statement of Retained Earnings
For the Year Ended December 31, 1984

Beginning balance, retained earnings, January 1, 1984	$220,000
Add net income for 1984	200,000
Total	420,000
Less dividends declared and paid during 1984	145,000
Ending balance, retained earnings, December 31, 1984	$275,000

statement starts with the balance of retained earnings at the beginning of the period. To that balance, net income for the year is added and dividends declared during the year are deducted. Dividends reduce retained earnings on the date they are **declared,** even if they have not yet been paid in cash, because a **legally enforceable obligation** to pay arises on the declaration date. A dividend is **not an expense** on the income statement; rather it is a **distribution** of accumulated earnings. Note that net income for the period ($200,000 for Diamond) is carried from the income statement to the statement of retained earnings, and in that manner it is then carried to stockholders' equity on the balance sheet. Thus, each period net income increases stockholders' equity. After a number of years of operations, retained earnings becomes the primary **source** of stockholders' equity in most corporations.

lent to 5 percent not be paid on the preferred stock for any year, the amount not paid will cumulate and must be paid in subsequent years before any dividends can be paid on the common stock. Capital stock is discussed in detail in Chapter 12.

THE STATEMENT OF CHANGES IN FINANCIAL POSITION (SCFP)

The statement of changes in financial position (SCFP) was discussed briefly in Chapter 1, and a very simple situation was illustrated in Exhibit 1–6. In contrast, a more complex situation (Diamond's) is illustrated in Exhibit 2–5. The SCFP has as its primary purpose the reporting of all inflows (i.e., sources) of cash (or working capital if prepared on that basis) and all outflows (i.e., uses) of cash (or working capital). This information is particularly useful to decision makers (such as stockholders, other potential investors, and creditors of the business) in assessing the probable **future** amounts, timing, and uncertainty of net cash inflows to the business.

The SCFP for Diamond is typical of many retail businesses. For example, the following analytical points may be observed:

1. Total cash inflows amounted to $371,700, and total cash outflows amounted to $263,000, which caused a net increase in cash of $108,700.
2. Of the total cash inflows of $371,700, 62 percent (i.e., $228,700 ÷ $371,700) came from **operations** of the business. This statistic is especially important because it represents the normal operations that are likely to continue into the future. In contrast, the $43,000 cash inflow from **extraordinary items,** because they are by definition unusual and infrequent, cannot be expected to continue into the future.
3. Of the total cash outflows of $263,000, 55 percent was for dividends paid to the owners. This outflow will vary depending upon the decision by the board of directors of the corporation each year as to dividends.

The SCFP illustrations in the first two chapters are presented to facilitate your understanding of what the statement reports and how to interpret it in general. The ways in which the amounts are determined and the more complex issues, including preparation of the SCFP on a working capital (current assets minus current liabilities) basis, are discussed and illustrated in Chapter 15.

An actual, and more complex, set of financial statements are presented for your study in special Supplement B immediately preceding the Index.

PART B—USES OF FINANCIAL INFORMATION IN DECISION MAKING AND THE FUNDAMENTAL CONCEPTS OF ACCOUNTING

FINANCIAL STATEMENTS RELATED TO THE DECISION PROCESSES OF EXTERNAL DECISION MAKERS

Individual external decision makers (see Chapter 1, page 17) do not participate directly in preparation of the financial statements they use nor individually and directly in the development of the accounting guidelines (i.e., GAAP; see page 18) used in the preparation of such statements. Rather, decision makers seek to elicit (select) information from the financial reports that will help them make better decisions than otherwise on specific problems they encounter.

EXHIBIT 2–5
Statement of
changes in financial
position (SCFP),
classifications
illustrated

DIAMOND, INC.
Statement of Changes in Financial Position, Cash Basis
For the Year Ended December 31, 1984

Sources of cash:

From operations:			
Sales revenue		$3,615,000	
Revenue from investments		13,000	
		3,628,000	
Adjustments for **noncash** revenue for this period (deduction)		5,000* (a)	
Cash inflow from sale and investment revenues		3,623,000	
Expenses, including cost of goods sold	$3,466,000* (b)		
Adjustments for **noncash** expenses (deduction)	(71,700)* (c)		
Cash outflow for expenses		3,394,300	
Net cash inflow from continuing operations and investments			$228,700
From extraordinary items (net of income taxes):			
Disposal of land ($56,000–$13,000)			43,000* (d)
From bank note, long term			100,000
Total cash generated (inflows) during the year			371,700

Uses of cash:

To pay dividends during the period:		
On preferred stock	25,000	
On common stock	120,000	
To increase bond sinking fund	50,000	
To purchase land for future store site	68,000	
Total cash used (outflows) during the year		263,000
Increase in cash during the year		$108,700

Explanations:
* At this point in your study, there is no need to be concerned with the derivation of these amounts; however, they may be calculated as follows:

(a) The adjustment of $5,000 to revenue was due to an increase in accounts receivable of that amount during the period, which means that this amount of cash will be collected later.

(b) Expenses from the income statement (Exhibit 2–1):

Cost of goods sold	$2,416,000
Operating expenses	856,000
Interest expense	56,000
Income tax expense	138,000
Total expenses (for this period)	$3,466,000

(c) Noncash expenses from the income statement (Exhibit 2–1):

Depreciation expense, store equipment	$15,000
Amortization of trademarks	2,000
Estimated losses on doubtful accounts	3,600
Depreciation expense, office equipment	1,000
Subtotal	21,600
Net change in accruals, deferrals, and accounts payable (data not given herein)	50,100
Total	$71,700

(The cash outflow related to the noncash expenses occured before, or will occur after, this period.)

(d) The land was sold for $56,000 cash, of which $13,000 was paid for income taxes on the gain, leaving a net cash inflow of $43,000 from this source (also see Exhibit 2–1).

In this part of the chapter, the selection and analysis by decision makers of relevant information from the financial statements is introduced. This part also presents an outline of the **fundamental concepts** that underlie financial accounting and reporting. This outline is presented in this chapter as a point of reference that will be used throughout the chapters to follow.

The broad objective of financial reporting is to provide information that is useful in making decisions. This objective responds to the fact that the investors (i.e., the owners), potential investors, and creditors are concerned primarily with the probable **future cash** returns they can reasonably expect to receive on their investments. The future returns are related to the profits (and losses) of the business and to the resources (assets) it owns and its liabilities. In a similar manner, the creditors of the business are concerned about their future cash returns in the form of interest to be received and collection of the principals of the liabilities at maturity dates.[10] Decision makers are concerned directly with the future rather than with the past; therefore, decision makers must make projections regarding the future. This fact means that the financial information reported in financial statements should have **qualitative characteristics** that focus on their decision-making needs. The information must be **relevant** to their needs, and it must be **reliable.**

Recent past events and trends, if measured and reported appropriately, provide an important basis on which decision makers develop reasonable estimates concerning the future. Financial statements report periodically on the revenues, expenses, incomes, assets, and liabilities of a business; therefore, they provide valuable data for most financial projections made by investors.

In addition to considering the data reported on the financial statements, decision makers must bring to bear in their projections knowledge of such factors as technological changes, environmental influences, competitive forces, behavioral considerations, general economic conditions, and industry characteristics.

Throughout the chapters that follow you will learn more about how financial statements may help decision makers assess the **future prospects** of a business. At this time, only an introduction is possible. For this introduction we will refer to the financial statements of Diamond presented in Part A of this chapter (Exhibits 2–1 through 2–5).

In assessing the probable future cash returns of Diamond, a decision maker probably would want to carefully examine and analyze the company's recent financial statements, say, for the past three to five years. For example, the SCFP (Exhibit 2–5) would reveal trends as to the primary **sources** and **uses** of cash, such as the amount of cash generated by operations (62 percent) or from loans (27 percent), and the primary cash-demanding activities such as the payment of dividends (55 percent) and the purchase of long-lived assets (26 percent). A

---

[10] *FASB Statement of Financial Accounting Concepts No. 1,* "Objectives of Financial Reporting by Business Enterprises" (Stamford, Conn., November 1978), states: "Since investors' and creditors' cash flows are related to enterprise cash flows, financial reporting should provide information to help investors, creditors, and others assess the amounts, timing, and uncertainty of prospective net cash inflows to the related enterprise."

knowledge of each source and each use over several consecutive years would be helpful in projecting future sources and uses of cash.

In a similar manner, a decision maker would make other analyses of the income statement and the balance sheet because they report past financial performance of the company. The income statement reports the normal operational activities that, if continued, would be expected to generate future cash inflows. The performance levels (i.e., efficiency) of the business that can be projected will indicate future cash flows that may be expected reasonably from this primary source. In a similar manner, certain assets reported on the balance sheet provide a basis for projecting other probable cash inflows (such as from the sale of an investment or a tract of land), and the reported liabilities indicate significant future cash demands. These brief comments suggest the importance of understanding **what financial statements say** and what they **do not say** and, just as important, how to analyze them to maximize their usefulness in the decision-making process.

The analysis of financial statements is emphasized in the various chapters that follow with an overall view presented in Chapter 16. By way of introduction, the concept of **proportional relationships** is presented as one phase of such an analysis. Proportional analysis involves the selection of two important amounts from the financial statements that are related in a meaningful way. One, known as the **base amount,** is divided into the other to express the proportional relationship between them. The result may be expressed as a ratio, a percent, or sometimes as a dollar amount. Two examples already have been presented: (1) earnings per share (page 51) and (2) working capital (page 57). Two additional examples based on the financial statements of Diamond, Inc., which focus on **profitability,** are presented below:

1. $$\text{Profit margin} = \frac{\text{Net income}}{\text{Net sales}} = \frac{\$162,000}{\$3,615,000} = 0.045$$

Thus, for the year, Diamond earned 4.5 percent on each dollar of sales.[11]

2. Along with EPS the concept of **return on investment** (ROI) is widely used to measure profitability.

The concept of ROI is especially useful to decision makers. It is particularly significant because it expresses the relationship between **income** and **investment.** The income statement provides the income amount, and the balance sheet provides the investment amount.

The concept of ROI is applied frequently by almost everyone in one way or another. To illustrate, suppose you invested $1,000 on January 1, 19A, and at the end of 19A you received back $1,200. Disregarding income taxes, you may say that you earned $200 during the year on your investment. Based on these amounts, what would be your ROI (i.e., the return on your investment)? You may calculate that your return for the year was $200 ÷ $1,000 = 20 percent on

---

[11] To compute profit margin when there are extraordinary items, income before extraordinary items rather than net income usually should be used to avoid the distortion caused by the unusual and infrequently recurring items.

the investment. Similarly, the ROI for a **business** for a specific period of time may be computed as follows:

$$\frac{\text{Net income}}{\text{Investment (owners' equity)}} = \text{Return on investment (ROI)}$$

The ROI earned by Diamond for 1984 would be computed as follows:[12]

$$\frac{\$162,000 \text{ (from Exhibit 2–1)}}{\$1,575,000 \text{ (from Exhibit 2–2)}} = 10.29\%$$

FUNDAMENTAL CONCEPTS UNDERLYING FINANCIAL ACCOUNTING AND REPORTING

This section presents an overview of the theoretical or conceptual foundation of financial accounting and reporting. This conceptual foundation is presented (in Exhibit 2–6), in overall perspective, to facilitate your study and understanding of the "why" as you study the "how" of accounting in the chapters that follow. Upon completion of this chapter you are not expected to fully understand this conceptual structure, nor to appreciate its full significance (and certainly not to memorize it). Rather, the conceptual foundation is presented here to help you answer questions as they arise during your study of subsequent chapters. By studying both the *how* of accounting and why it is done in specific ways, you will develop a much better understanding of the process of accounting and be able to **interpret** its results in more meaningful and useful ways.

The fundamental concepts underlying financial accounting and reporting that have been specified by the accounting profession may be broadly characterized as follows:[13]

1. **Users** of financial statements identified.
2. **Objectives** of financial statements.
3. **Qualitative characteristics** of financial statements.
4. **Implementation assumptions** of financial statements.
5. **Elements** of financial statements.
6. **Implementation principles** of accounting.
7. **Detailed** accounting practices and procedures.

Each of the above seven characterizations is summarized and illustrated in Exhibit 2–6. For your convenience in subsequent study, Exhibit 2–6 lists the chapter number and text page where each fundamental is **first introduced.**

---

[12] Depending upon the nature of the problem and the preference of the decision maker, the income amount may be either (1) income before extraordinary items or (2) net income. Similarly, the investment amount used may be either (1) owners' equity or (2) total equity (i.e., liabilities plus owners' equity). When total equity is used, interest expense (net of tax) should be added back to income (see Chapter 16).

[13] Financial Accounting Standards Board, *Statement of Financial Accounting Concepts No. 1*, "Objectives of Financial Reporting by Business Enterprises" (November 1978); *No. 2*, "Qualitative Characteristics of Accounting Information" (May 1980); and *No. 3*, "Elements of Financial Statements of Business Enterprises," (December 1980), Stamford Conn.

EXHIBIT 2–6   **Summary of the fundamental concepts underlying financial accounting and reporting (based on *FASB Statements of Concepts Nos. 1, 2,* and *3*)**

Fundamentals	Page	Brief Explanation	Example
USERS of financial statements (persons to whom they are directed—the audience)	3 and 17	Primarily **decision makers** who are "average prudent investors" and are willing to study the information with diligence.	Investors, creditors, including those who advise or represent investors and creditors.
OBJECTIVES of financial statements (decision usefulness)	7	To provide economic information about a business that is useful in projecting the **future cash flows** of that business.	The operations of a business are summarized in **net income** which is the primary long-term source of **cash** generated by a business.
QUALITATIVE characteristics of financial statements (necessary to make the reported information useful to decision makers)	61 17 153	Characteristics that make financial statements useful, viz: 1. Relevance—affects decisions; timely presentation has predictive and feedback value. 2. Reliability (believable)—unbiased, accurate, and verifiable.	1. The financial statements are available soon after their dates have been audited and present complete information. 2. Audited financial statements.
IMPLEMENTATION ASSUMPTIONS of financial statements (imposed by the business environment)	6 405 4 and 783 18 and 150	1. Separate-entity assumption—each business is accounted for separately from its owners and other entities. 2. Continuity (going-concern) assumption—assumes the entity will not liquidate, will continue to pursue its objectives. 3. Unit-of-measure assumption—accounting measurements will be in the monetary unit. 4. Time-period assumption—accounting reports are for short time periods.	1. XYZ Company is a separate entity; its owners and creditors are other entities. 2. Accounting for XYZ Company will assume it will carry on its normal operations. 3. Assets, liabilities, owners' equity, revenues, expenses, etc., are measured in dollars in the United States. 4. Financial statements of XYZ Company are prepared each year.
ELEMENTS of financial statements (basic items reported on the financial statements)	19, 48, 152 20 and 48 425 425	**Income statement:** 1. Revenues—Inflows of net assets, or settlements of liabilities from sale of goods and services that constitute the entity's **ongoing or major operations.** 2. Expenses—Outflows or using up of assets, or incurrence of liabilities for delivery of goods or services, and other activities that constitute the entity's **ongoing or major operations.** 3. Gains—Increases in net assets from **peripheral or incidental transactions,** and all other activities except those from revenues or investments by owners. 4. Losses—Decreases in net assets from **peripheral or incidental transactions** and other events except those from expenses or distributions to owners.	1. Sale of merchandise for cash or on credit. 2. Wages earned by employees paid in cash or owed. 3. Sale of a tract of land for a price **more** than its cost when acquired. 4. Sale of a tract of land for a price **less** than its cost when acquired.

EXHIBIT 2–6 (continued)

Fundamentals	Page	Brief Explanation	Example
ELEMENTS (continued)	22	**Balance sheet:** 5. Assets—Probable future economic benefits, owned by the entity as a result of past transactions.	5. Land, buildings, equipment, patent.
	23	6. Liabilities—Probable future sacrifices of economic benefits as a result of past transactions; involves transfer of assets or services.	6. Note owed to the bank, taxes owed but not yet paid, unpaid wages.
	23	7. Owners' equity—Residual interest of owners after all debts are paid (i.e., Assets − Liabilities = Owners' Equity).	7. Capital stock outstanding, retained earnings.
IMPLEMENTATION PRINCIPLES of accounting (how to apply the concepts)	22 and 397	1. Cost principle—Cost (cash equivalent cost given up) is the appropriate basis for initial recording of assets, liabilities, owners' equity, revenues, expenses, gains, and losses.	1. XYZ Company purchased a machine; record the cash equivalent given up, $10,000 as the cost of the machine.
	152	2. Revenue principle—The cash equivalent amount received for the sale of goods or services is recognized as earned revenue when ownership transfers or as the services are rendered.	2. Sale of merchandise for $2,000, half cash and half on credit—record sale revenue of $2,000 on date of sale.
	67, 154, 402	3. Matching principle—Revenues are recognized in conformity with the revenue principle; then all expenses incurred in earning that revenue must be identified and recorded in the period in which those revenues are recognized.	3. Sales of merchandise during the period of $100,000 is recorded as earned; the cost of those goods, $60,000, is recorded as expense of that period.
	71	4. Reporting principle—The financial statements of an entity should **disclose** (present) all of the **relevant** economic information about that entity.	4. Report inventory on the balance sheet and explain in a note the inventory accounting policies.
	153	5. Reliability principle—The financial statements of an entity should report economic data that are unbiased (neutral), verifiable, and faithfully present what they purport to represent.	5. Report the cash balance on the balance sheet excluding noncash items such as postage stamps and IOUs.
	306	6. Comparability principle—Accounting information reported should be comparable among similar entities, and the accounting principles should be applied in a consistent manner across periods.	6. In accounting for inventories; do not use FIFO one period and LIFO the next period, then back to FIFO.
Exceptions to the above principles (based on practical reasons)	299 and 364	1. Materiality—Amounts of relatively small significance must be recorded; however, they need not be accorded strict theoretical treatment (for cost-benefit reasons).	1. Purchase of a pencil sharpener for $4.98 (an asset) may be recorded as **expense** when purchased.
	365	2. Rational conservatism—Exercise care	2. A loss that is **probable,** but not

EXHIBIT 2–6 *(concluded)*

Fundamentals	Page	Brief Explanation	Example
		not to overstate assets and revenue and not to understate liabilities and expenses.	known for sure, should be recorded.
	365	3. Industry peculiarities—Unique characteristics of an industry may require special accounting approaches.	3. Financial institutions do not use the classification, current assets.
ACCRUAL BASIS	66, 102, 687	Revenues, expenses, assets, liabilities, and owners' equity are accounted for and reported on the basis of when the economic effect occurred rather than when the related cash is received or paid.	XYZ Company sold merchandise for $1,000 on December 20, 19A, on a 30-day credit basis. The cash was collected in full on January 20, 19B. The sale should be recorded and reported in 19A (not 19B).
DETAILED accounting practices and procedures (detailed measurement and recording guidelines)	* * *	1. Those related to asset and income measurement. 2. Those related to reporting accounting information. 3. Other accounting procedures.	1. Straight-line versus accelerated depreciation. 2. Separate reporting of extraordinary items (net of income tax); terminology. 3. Control and subsidiary ledgers; special journals; bank reconciliations, worksheets.

* Throughout most of the chapters.

Financial accounting and reporting to **external** parties must conform to specific **concepts** and guidelines formulated primarily by the accounting profession to protect the interests of the external decision makers by assuring, to the extent practicable, that the external financial statements are reasonably complete, relevant, reliable, and not misleading. These fundamental concepts are in a process of continuing evolution to meet the changing needs of society and to keep the financial accounting measurements and reporting relevant to the current problems of external decision makers. Changes are initiated primarily because of financial reporting problems related to new developments in business, improved ways to measure economic effects, and expansion of international businesses. The evolving problems of financial reporting are the subject of much research by accountants (in academia, practice, and industry) and the groups involved in accounting innovations discussed in Chapter 1 (see page 14).

ACCRUAL BASIS ACCOUNTING

The definition of revenues given on page 19 states that revenue is considered **earned** (i.e., realized) in the period when the revenue **transaction takes place** rather than when the cash is collected. Therefore, the total amount of revenues reported on the income statement for the period should include sales and services of that period collected for in cash plus all sales and services of the period on credit, even though the cash may be collected the next period. Similarly, when rent (for example) is collected in advance, rent revenue should be reported on the income statement for the period in which occupancy occurred, rather in the period of cash collection. Assume rent revenue of $1,200 is collected on December 1, 19A, for 12 months' future occupancy ending November 30, 19B. Rent revenue **earned** in 19A would be $100 and in 19B, $1,100.

In a similar manner, the definition of expenses on page 20 states that expenses are considered **incurred** (i.e., used) in the period when the goods or services are **used or consumed.** Therefore, the total amount of expense **incurred** should be reported on the income statement of the period. In some cases, the expense-incurring services and goods are obtained on credit whereby the cash is paid in a later period; and in other cases, the cash is paid in advance of use of the goods or services (as in the case of prepayment of a three-year insurance premium on a building). In each of these cases, the date of the cash flow is disregarded in determining the period in which the expense should be reported on the income statement.

The approach described above for determining when to report revenues and expenses is necessary to measure revenues properly for the period and to **match** expenses correctly with those revenues. This process is known as the **matching principle** (see Exhibit 2–6). This method of determining when revenues and expenses are to be reported is known as **accrual accounting.** It is required by generally accepted accounting principles (GAAP). In contrast, individuals and very small businesses sometimes use the **cash basis** for their records, which means that all revenues are considered earned only when the cash is collected, and all expenses are considered incurred only when the cash is paid. This method does not conform to GAAP because it incorrectly measures such revenues and expenses due to the fact that the related activities precede or lag the cash-flow dates.

SOME MISCONCEPTIONS

Some people naively confuse a bookkeeper with an accountant and bookkeeping with accounting. In effect, they confuse one of the minor parts with the whole of accounting. Bookkeeping involves the routine and clerical part of accounting and requires only minimal knowledge of the accounting model and its application. A bookkeeper may record the repetitive and uncomplicated transactions in most businesses and may maintain the simple records of a small business. In contrast, the accountant is a highly trained professional competent in the design of information systems, analysis of complex transactions and economic events, interpretation and analysis of financial data, financial reporting, financial advising, auditing, taxation, and management consulting.

A prevalent misconception is that all of the financial affairs of an entity are subject to precise and objective measurement each period and that the accounting results reported in the financial statements, are exactly what happened that period. In contrast, accounting numbers are influenced by estimates in many respects as illustrated in subsequent chapters. Many people believe that accounting should measure and report the market value of the entity (including its assets), but accounting does not attempt to do this. In order to understand financial statements and to interpret them wisely for use in decision making, the user must be aware of their limitations as well as their usefulness. One should understand what the financial statements do and do not attempt to accomplish.

Another misconception related to financial statements is that because of their quantitative nature, they are inflexible in use. As you study accounting you will appreciate that it requires considerable **professional judgment in application** on the part of the accountant in order to capture the economic essense of complex transactions. Thus, accounting is stimulating intellectually; it is not a cut-and-dried subject. Rather, it is one that calls upon your intelligence, analytical ability, creativity, and judgment. Accounting is a communication process involving an audience (users) of a wide diversity of knowledge, interest, and capabilities; therefore, it will call upon your ability as a communicator. The language of accounting encompasses concisely written phrases and symbols used to convey information about the resource flows measured for specific organizations.

As you study accounting and later as a decision maker, you must be wary of these misconceptions. To adequately understand financial statements and to be able to interpret the "figures" wisely, you must have a certain level of knowledge of the concepts and the measurement procedures used in the accounting process. You must learn what accounting "is really like" and appreciate the reasons why certain things are done the way they are. This level of knowledge cannot be gained simply by reading a list of the "concepts" and a list of the misconceptions. Neither can a generalized discussion of the subject matter suffice. A certain amount of involvement, primarily problem solving (similar to the requirement in mathematics courses) is essential in the study of accounting focused on the needs of the user. Therefore, we provide problems aimed at the desirable knowledge level for the user (as well as the preparer) of financial statements.

ACCOUNTING—AN INFORMATION PROCESSING SYSTEM

Accounting records the detailed financial history of the entity and, from that information, derives the financial statements. Thus, the **accounting process** involves the accumulation, analysis, measurement, recording, interpretation, classification, and summarization of the results of each of the many business transactions that affected the entity during the year. After this processing, accounting then transmits messages to decision makers. The messages are in the form of financial statements, and the decision makers are the users. Accounting does not create the basic information (raw financial data); rather, the raw financial data result from the day-to-day transactions initiated, participated in, and completed by the enterprise. The accounting system includes procedures for collecting these data; and as an **information system,** the accounting process is designed to record these data and capture the **economic essence** of each transaction.[14]

An accounting system should be designed to classify financial information

---

[14] The accounting information system should be viewed as a part of the overall information system that necessarily operates in any entity.

on a basis suitable for decision-making purposes and to process the tremendous quantities of data efficiently and accurately. The information system must be designed to report the results periodically, in a realistic and concise format that is understandable to users who often have only a limited technical knowledge of accounting. The information system must be designed to accommodate the special and complex needs of the **internal** management of the entity. These internal needs extend primarily to the planning and control responsibilities of the managers of the enterprise; they are discussed in *Fundamentals of Management Accounting* of this series.

The accountant has the primary responsibility for developing an accounting information system that is essential for most entities, whether operating on a profit or nonprofit basis. In designing an information system, the accountant must consider the factors of (1) cost; (2) benefit; (3) timeliness (i.e., reports must be rendered shortly after the end of the accounting period); and (4) requirements of various outside influences, such as governmental regulatory agencies (examples are the Securities and Exchange Commission and the Internal Revenue Service).

The accounting information processing system will be discussed in Chapters 4–6.

OVERVIEW OF AN ACTUAL ANNUAL REPORT

The preceding discussions illustrated two sets of simplified financial statements that were stripped of many of the surrounding features. To complete our overview of the financial statements of a business, we present the complete **1982 Annual Report** of Johnson & Johnson. This **published** report is presented as **Special Supplement B** at the end of this textbook, just preceding the Index, because it will be referred to throughout the remaining chapters.

A corporation such as Johnson & Johnson is said to "publish" its annual financial report because it is printed and distributed to each stockholder and to others upon request. Companies whose stock is traded on the stock exchanges (and some others) distribute such annual reports. A published annual report typically includes a number of features in addition to the financial statements, such as the president's letter to the stockholders, a list of the principal officers of the company, promotional data on the company's products (including pictures), and other information deemed by the management to be of interest.

The primary components of the annual report presented in Special Supplement B were labeled by Johnson & Johnson as follows:[15]

1. Consolidated Balance Sheet.
2. Consolidated Statement of Earnings and Retained Earnings.

---

[15] The statements are labeled "Consolidated." This word indicates that the parent company owns more than 50 percent of the oustanding voting stock of one or more other companies. This ownership gives the parent company a **controlling interest,** and the other companies are designated as subsidiaries. To prepare the statements on a **consolidated basis,** the financial statements of the subsidiaries are added on a line-by-line basis to those of the parent company. This subject is discussed further in Chapter 14.

3. Consolidated Statement of Common Stock, Additional Capital and Treasury Stock.
4. Consolidated Statement of Changes in Financial Position.
5. Notes to Consolidated Financial Statements.
6. Report of Certified Public Accountants.
7. Supplementary Information.

As recommended by the APB (Accounting Principles Board), **comparative** amounts are presented. That is, most of the items reported show the amount for the current year (e.g., 1982) and the two preceding years (e.g., 1981 and 1980).

On the next few pages we will briefly discuss the seven primary components (listed above) of the Johnson & Johnson Annual Report to relate them to the preceding discussions. A number of items are included in this report that you will not understand at this point of your study; however, you may be surprised to learn how many of those items you understand already. Most of the items that you do not understand will be discussed in subsequent chapters.

We ask you to refer to Special Supplement B at the end of this book (preceding the Index) as you read the brief discussion of the primary components of the 1982 financial statements for Johnson & Johnson that follows.

Consolidated Balance Sheet

The title "Consolidated Statement of Financial Position" often is used. This statement is dated "January 2, 1983" because it is "as of" that specific date, which is referred to as the end of the **accounting period.** You can observe in this balance sheet that Johnson & Johnson follows closely the classifications of assets, liabilities, and owners' equity discussed in the chapter. Although most companies use an accounting period that ends on December 31, Johnson & Johnson uses an accounting year that "ends on the Sunday nearest to the end of the calendar month of December" (refer to the company's note 1). Observe that there are several references to "notes" and that at the bottom of the balance sheet it says "See Notes to Consolidated Financial Statements."

Consolidated Statement of Earnings and Retained Earnings

This statement usually is called the "Income Statement" or "Statement of Income." The Johnson & Johnson income statement is for the **year ended** January 2, 1983, because it covers a period of time, rather than at a specific date. Businesses often use an accounting period that is different from the calendar year because they want to conform to their particular "natural operating year," which ends when the operating activities are the lowest for that business.

Look at the Johnson & Johnson Annual Report and observe that the Consolidated Statement of Earnings starts with **Revenues** and ends with **Net earnings.** Immediately following this caption is the statement of retained earnings (not captioned in this manner), then the earnings per share (EPS) amounts are presented. Observe that Johnson & Johnson does not set out a separate statement of retained earnings as was illustrated for Diamond (Exhibit 2–4). The statement of retained earnings, as such, is not a required statement; however, it usually is considered to be essential in satisfying the **reporting principle** (Exhibit 2–6).

Consolidated Statement of Stockholders' Equity

A consolidated statement of common stock, additional capital, retained earnings, and treasury stock is very useful to satisfy the reporting principle; it reports the detailed changes in each component of stockholders' equity and will be discussed in detail later.

Consolidated Statement of Changes in Financial Position

This statement is dated the same as the income statement because it covers the full accounting period of one year (as opposed to a specific date similar to the balance sheet).

Observe that the SCFP (a short abbreviation for the statement of changes in financial position) tells you where Johnson & Johnson obtained its cash during the year and what the cash was spent for (much more about the SCFP later).

Notes to the Consolidated Financial Statements

One of the broad fundamentals underlying accounting, listed under **implementation principles** in Exhibit 2–6, is the **reporting principle.** This principle relates directly to the financial statements. It specifies that there should be complete and understandable reporting on the financial statements of all relevant economic **information** relating to the economic activities of the entity. To meet the requirements of this principle, the quantitative expressions in the financial statements frequently must be supported by narrative and detailed elaboration. As a consequence, practically all published financial statements will include a section called "Notes to the Financial Statements" or "Financial Review." The notes are considered to be an **integral part** of the financial statements and are important to understanding and interpreting the amounts reported. Take a quick look at the **14** notes presented by Johnson & Johnson; you may find some of them very interesting (e.g., Note 2 about a $50 million loss).

Also, we suggest that you look at **Note 1.** Because of the importance of the **accounting policies** used by a company, *APB Opinion 22,* requires that they be set out separately in the financial report. As you study this book you will learn that there often are two or more acceptable ways to record a particular transaction. Given this fact, financial statement users, may encounter difficulties in interpreting the financial results reported without knowing which alternative was used by the company. The **summary of accounting policies** must be included with the financial statements to meet this need of statement users. Observe that Johnson & Johnson explained its accounting policies in respect to six different items reported on its financial statements.

Report of the Certified Public Accountants (Auditor's Report)

The independent CPA firm, as the outside auditor, is required to express an **independent opinion** on the financial statements or to state that an opinion cannot be expressed. The standard auditor's report contains two paragraphs. The first paragraph, known as the **scope** paragraph, describes the general nature of the audit that was performed. The second paragraph, known as the **opinion** paragraph, reports on the opinion of the auditors in respect to the financial statements after the audit was completed. The opinion paragraph in the auditor's report for Johnson & Johnson states:

> In our opinion, the 1982 consolidated financial statements referred to above present fairly the financial position of Johnson & Johnson and subsidiaries

at January 2, 1983, and January 3, 1982, and the results of their operations and the changes in their financial position for each of the three years in the period ended January 2, 1983, in conformity with generally accepted accounting principles applied on a consistent basis, after giving effect to the adoption in 1981, with which we concur, of FAS No. 52, Foreign Currency Translation, as described in Note 4.

The key words in the above opinion are "present fairly" and "generally accepted accounting principles." If the statements do not meet these two standards, the independent CPA must **qualify** the opinion. When an auditor qualifies an opinion in the auditor's report, a separate paragraph is included between the scope and opinion paragraphs to explain the nature of the qualification. For example, one recent auditor's report read as follows: "Our opinion is qualified only on the basis of inconsistency because the company changed its method of accounting for own engineering costs as described in Note 10 to the financial statements. The new method is in accordance with generally accepted accounting principles."

The auditor's opinion relates to the "fair presentation" of the financial report in its entirety; therefore, the opinion is viewed as a necessary and critically important part of the financial report.

Supplementary Information

Typically, this section reports supplementary information designed to assist the various users of financial statements who need more information about the operations of the business than is presented in the above statements. Johnson & Johnson presents the following supplementary information: *(a)* financial data about the product lines (i.e., segments) of the company, *(b)* operations by geographic areas, *(c)* effects of price changes (e.g., inflation), and *(d)* 10-year summary of financial results and statistical data (e.g., number of employees).

DEMONSTRATION CASE

On January 1, 19A, Baker Retail Corporation was organized by five promoters; each one paid in $10,000 cash and each one received 10,000 shares of Baker stock, par $0.20 per share. At the end of 19A, the following account balances (in alphabetical order) were reported:

Account	Amount	Account	Amount
Accounts payable	$ 45,000	Income taxes payable (none paid)	$?
Accounts receivable	40,000	Interest expense	3,600
Accumulated depreciation, store equipment	?	Investment in stock of Able Corporation	25,000
Administrative expenses*	104,800	Long-term notes payable	30,000
Allowance for doubtful accounts	1,000	Merchandise inventory	101,500
Cash	17,500	Retained earnings	?
Common stock	10,000	Revenue from investments and funds	5,600
Contributed capital in excess of par	?	Sales revenue	997,000
Cost of goods sold	554,400	Sales returns	7,000
Extraordinary gain, pretax	8,000	Selling expenses	265,800
Income tax expense, on operations	?	Store equipment (acquired January 1, 19A)	20,000
Income tax, on extraordinary gain	?	Used equipment held for disposal	1,000

* Includes depreciation expense of $4,000 on store equipment. Excludes income tax expense.

Required (show computations of the six missing amounts):

a. Prepare Baker's income statement for 19A, assuming an income tax rate of 20 percent on all items.
b. Prepare a Baker's classified balance sheet at December 31, 19A, assuming no dividends were declared or paid during 19A.

Suggested solution

Requirement a:

BAKER CORPORATION
Income Statement
For the Year Ended December 31, 19A

Gross sales revenue	$997,000	
Less: Sales returns	7,000	
Net sales revenue		$990,000
Less: Cost of goods sold		554,400
Gross margin on sales		435,600
Operating expenses:		
Selling expenses	265,800	
Administrative expenses	104,800	
Total operating expenses		370,600
Income from operations		65,000
Financial expenses and financial revenues:		
Revenue from investments	5,600	
Interest expense	3,600	
Net financial revenue		2,000
Pretax income		67,000
Income tax on operations ($67,000 × 20%)		13,400
Income before extraordinary items		53,600
Gain, pretax	8,000	
Less: Income tax on the gain ($8,000 × 20%)	1,600	6,400
Net income		$ 60,000
Earnings per share of common stock:		
Income before extraordinary items	$53,600 ÷ 50,000 shares = $1.07	
Extraordinary gain	6,400 ÷ 50,000 shares = 0.13	
Net income	$60,000 ÷ 50,000 shares = $1.20	

Requirement b:

BAKER CORPORATION
Balance Sheet
At December 31, 19A

Assets

Current assets:		
Cash		$ 17,500
Accounts receivable	$40,000	
Less: Allowance for doubtful accounts	1,000	39,000
Merchandise inventory		101,500
Total current assets		158,000
Long-term investments and funds:		
Stock of Able Corporation		25,000
Operational assets:		
Store equipment	20,000	
Less: Accumulated depreciation (Same as depreciation expense in year 19A only)	4,000	16,000
Other assets:		
Used equipment held for disposal		1,000
Total assets		$200,000

Liabilities

Current liabilities:
Accounts payable	45,000	
Income taxes payable ($13,400 + $1,600)	15,000	
Total current liabilities		60,000

Long-term liabilities:
Notes payable	30,000
Total liabilities	

Stockholders' Equity

Contributed capital:
Common stock, par $0.20, 50,000 shares outstanding	10,000	
Contributed capital in excess of par (50,000 × $0.80)	40,000	
Total contributed capital	50,000	
Retained earnings (no dividends, same as net income)	60,000	
Total stockholders' equity		110,000
Total liabilities and stockholders' equity		$200,000

SUMMARY OF CHAPTER

This chapter presented the commonly used subclassifications of financial information on the income statement, balance sheet, and statement of changes in financial position. You learned some of the analytical approaches used by the decision makers when relying on financial reports. You also learned to expect variations in the terminology and format of financial reports.

Financial reports of an existing company were presented to reinforce your understanding and for reference as you study the accounting process in the chapters to follow. The knowledge of financial statements, gained in Chapter 1 and in this chapter, should assure that in studying the details and complexities of accounting, you can maintain a broad view of accounting and keep in mind the nature of the end product—the periodic financial statements. We reemphasize this point because, not infrequently, students soon become immersed in details and lose the broad perspective of the end results—the financial statements and their use.

In Part B of the chapter, a summarization of the fundamentals underlying financial accounting and reporting (i.e., for external decision makers) was presented. In essence, this is a summarization of the major considerations of the chapters that follow. It is presented at this time as a basic foundation to which your attention will be directed in the remaining chapters. It will serve as a basis for understanding much of the "why and how" of financial accounting and reporting. You should return to it often to maintain overall perspective.

IMPORTANT TERMS DEFINED IN THIS CHAPTER

Terms alphabetically	Key words in definitions of important terms used in chapter	Page reference
Accrual accounting	Record revenues and expenses when transaction occurs.	66
Book value	Cost minus any contra amount; carrying value.	55
Classified statements	Subcaptions on financial statements; aids users.	47

Terms alphabetically	Key words in definitions of important terms used in chapter	Page reference
Contra amount	An offset to a major related account.	53
Cost of goods sold	Cost; inventory sold; deduct as an expense.	48
Current assets	Short-term; convert to cash; year or operating cycle.	53
Current liabilities	Short-term; debt; payable from current assets.	56
Deferred charges	Long-term; prepayments of expense.	56
Depreciation	Operational asset cost; expense based on usage.	55
Extraordinary items	Gains or losses; unusual and infrequent.	50
Financial expenses	Interest on debt.	50
Fixed assets	Operational assets; property, plant, and equipment.	55
Gross margin on sales	Sales revenue minus cost of goods sold.	48
Gross sales	Total sales; prior to returned sales.	48
Income tax expense	Expense; based on income; payable to government.	50
Intangible assets	Has value; no physical substance.	56
Liquidity	Nearness of noncash item to cash.	53
Long-term investments	Stock, bonds, other investments; hold beyond current year or operating cycle, if longer.	54
Long-term liabilities	Debt; due beyond current year or operating cycle, if longer.	57
Matching principle	First measure revenue; then determine expenses incurred to earn it.	67
Net sales	Gross sales minus sales returns.	48
Normal operating cycle	Period of time from cash payment back to cash receipt.	53
Operating expenses	Normal expenses of the business; related to normal operations.	50
Operational assets	Property, plant, and equipment; used in normal operations.	55
Other assets	Miscellaneous classification on balance sheet.	56
Prepaid expenses	Expenses paid in advance of usage, short-term.	54
Profit margin	Net sales revenue minus cost of goods sold.	62
ROI	Return on investment; Income ÷ Investment.	62
Returned sales	Goods sold; later returned.	48
Statement of retained earnings	Reports accumulated earnings minus accumulated dividends.	58
Working capital	Current assets minus current liabilities.	57

QUESTIONS FOR DISCUSSION

PART A

1. What is the primary purpose of subclassification of the information presented on financial statements?

2. What are the four major classifications on the income statement?

3. Distinguish between gross sales revenue and net sales revenue.

4. Explain the subclassification "Financial expenses and financial revenues" on a multiple-step income statement.

5. Define extraordinary items. Why should they be reported separately on the income statement?

6. Explain EPS. What EPS amounts should be reported on the income statement?

7. Briefly explain how income tax expense is reported on the income statement when there are extraordinary items.

8. List the six subclassifications of assets reported on a balance sheet.

9. Briefly define (a) current assets, (b) current liabilities, and (c) working capital.

10. What is a prepaid expense?

11. Distinguish between a prepaid expense and a deferred charge.

12. On a balance sheet, investments may be reported under either (a) current assets or (b) long-term investments and funds. Explain.

13. In respect to operational assets, as reported on the balance sheet, briefly explain (a) cost, (b) accumulated depreciation, (c) book value, and (d) carrying value.

14. What are the subclassifications of liabilities on a balance sheet?

15. Briefly explain two major subclassifications of owners' equity for a corporation.

16. What is the purpose of a statement of retained earnings?

17. What are the three major subclassifications on a SCFP?

18. What is meant by a comparative financial statement? Why are comparative financial statements desirable?

19. Briefly, what does the independent auditors' report encompass?

PART B

20. What is proportional analysis? Why is it often useful in interpreting financial statements?

21. Explain (a) profit margin and (b) ROI.

22. What is the basic objective of financial accounting and reporting?

23. What are the two primary qualitative characteristics of financial accounting and reporting?

24. Match the following:

Fundamentals	*Statement*
_____ Users	A. Special journals
_____ Objective	B. Cost, revenue, matching, reporting, reliability, comparability.
_____ Qualitative characteristics	C. Investors, creditors, and other external groups.
_____ Implementation assumptions	D. Relevance and reliability.
_____ Elements of financial statements	E. Materiality, conservatism, industry peculiarities.
_____ Implementation principles	F. Useful in projecting future cash flows.
_____ Exceptions	G. Separate entity, continuity, unit of measure, time period.
_____ Detailed practices and procedures	H. Assets, liabilities, owners' equity, revenues, expenses, gains, and losses.

25. Explain the basic difference between cash basis accounting and accrual basis accounting.

26. Distinguish between accounting and bookkeeping.

27. Explain why a major part of accounting may be viewed as an information system.

EXERCISES

PART A

E2–1. Bill and Marcie Wilson organized the BMW Hardware Company on January 1, 19A, as a corporation. The primary activities involved a hardware store that they bought from the retiring owner. On that date, 20,000 shares of common stock were issued to three shareholders (Bill, Marcie and the former owner of the store); $100,000 cash was received from the shareholders.

At the end of the first year, December 31, 19A, the records maintained by Marcie showed the following:

a. Merchandise sold: for cash, $180,000; on credit, $20,000.
b. Interest on debt: paid in cash, $2,000; owed but not yet paid, $500.
c. Salaries and wages: paid in cash, $40,500, owed but not yet paid, $1,000.
d. Other operating expenses, $5,000.
e. Cost of the merchandise sold, $101,000.
f. Services sold (all for cash), $10,000.
g. Extraordinary (EO) loss, $5,000 (subject to income tax).
h. Average corporate income tax rate on all items, 20 percent.

Required:

a. Complete the following income statement for the year, 19A:

Revenues
Expenses:
   Cost of goods sold
   Operating expenses
   Financial expenses
Pretax income from operations
   Income tax expense
Income before EO item
   EO loss
Net income
EPS

b. What was the total amount of income tax for 19A? Explain.
c. Explain why the $100,000 cash paid by the organizers is not considered to be revenue.

E2–2. The accounting records of Doyle Corporation reflected the following summarized data for the year ended December 31, 19B: sales revenue, $100,000; gross margin rate (markup on selling price), 52 percent; financial (interest) expense, $2,000; extraordinary gain, $5,000; average income tax rate (on all items), 20 percent; operating expenses, $30,000; common stock outstanding, 10,000 shares; and dividends declared and paid, $3,000.

Required:

a. You have been asked to prepare a detailed income statement for 19B. Show your computations. (Hint: EPS on net income is $2 per share.)
b. You also have been asked to compute the amount of retained earnings at the end of 19B (the January 1, 19B, balance was $11,000). Show your computations.

    c. What was the total amount of income taxes for 19B? Explain what the EPS amount on "Income before extraordinary items" means. What is its significance compared to EPS on net income?

E2–3. Below is listed terminology related to the income statement. Match the terms with the brief definitions by entering the appropriate letter to the left for each term.

Terminology	*Brief definition*
_____ Cost of goods sold	A. Defines the amount of income subject to income tax.
_____ Gross sales	
_____ Financial expense	B. Items that are unusual and infrequent.
_____ Interest revenue	C. Sales of services for cash or on credit.
_____ Extraordinary items	D. Revenues + Gains − Expenses − Losses (including EO items).
_____ Service revenue	
_____ Sales returns and allowances	E. Expenses incurred to sell goods.
	F. Total sales prior to returns and allowances.
_____ Income tax expense on operations	G. Amount of income tax excluding EO items.
_____ Income before extraordinary items	H. Time cost of money (borrowing); interest expense.
	I. Overhead expenses of managing the company.
_____ Net sales	J. Sales minus returns and allowances.
_____ Net income	K. Distribution plus general administrative expenses.
_____ Gross margin on sales	L. Return earned by lending money or selling on credit (time cost of money).
_____ EPS	M. Net sales revenue minus cost of goods sold.
_____ Distribution expenses	N. After-tax income from operations (excluding EO items).
_____ Operating expenses	O. Income divided by common shares outstanding.
_____ Pretax income from operations	P. Income from operations before income tax and before EO items.
_____ Internal revenue code	Q. None of the above.
_____ General and administrative expenses	

E2–4. Following is a list of major classification and subclassifications on the balance sheet. Number them in the order in which they normally appear on a balance sheet.

    _____ Current liabilities
    _____ Liabilities
    _____ Owners' equity
    _____ Long-term liabilities
    _____ Long-term investments and funds
    _____ Intangible assets
    _____ Operational assets
    _____ Current assets
    _____ Retained earnings
    _____ Contributed capital
    _____ Assets
    _____ Other assets
    _____ Deferred charges
    _____ Unrealized capital

E2–5. EPS Corporation has just completed the 19C income statement (there were no extraordinary items), except for the EPS computations. Net income has been determined to be $150,000. Common stock outstanding during the year was 30,000 shares, and preferred stock, nonconvertible, 6 percent ($10 par value) outstanding was 10,000 shares. Compute the EPS amount for the income statement. (Hint: First subtract the preferred dividends claim of $100,000 × 6% = $6,000.) Explain why the $6,000 should be subtracted.

E2–6. Fowler Corporation (common stock, 6,000 shares outstanding) is preparing the income statement for the year ended December 31, 19D. The pretax operating income has been determined to be $100,000, and there was a $30,000 pretax loss on earthquake damages to one of the plants properly classified as an extraordinary item. Total income tax expense has been determined correctly to be $28,000 on the basis of a 40 percent tax rate on operations and on the earthquake loss. You have been requested to complete the income statement starting with "pretax operating income." Explain why the income tax amount is separated into two parts in this situation.

E2–7. Candy Corporation was organized in 1970 by 10 investors. Each investor paid in $12 cash per share and received 1,500 shares of $10 par value common stock. In 1980, to raise more capital, Candy Corporation issued 5,000 shares of 7 percent preferred, nonparticipating, cumulative stock, par $20 per share, and received total cash of $125,000. On December 31, 1984, retained earnings amounted to $75,000.

    a. Prepare the stockholders' equity section of the balance sheet at December 31, 1984.
    b. Explain what the $75,000 balance in retained earnings on December 31, 1984, represents.

E2–8. Below is listed terminology related to the balance sheet. Match the terms with the brief definitions by entering appropriate letter to the left for each term.

Terminology	*Brief definition*
_____ Retained earnings	A. A miscellaneous category of assets.
_____ Current liabilities	B. Current assets minus current liabilities.
_____ Liquidity	C. Total assets minus total liabilities.
_____ Contra asset account	D. Balance sheet arranged with assets, liabilities, and
_____ Prepaid expense	owners' equity in descending order (vertical).
_____ Accumulated depreci-	E. Nearness of assets to cash (in time).
ation	F. Assets expected to be realized within one year or
_____ Intangible assets	operating cycle, if longer.
_____ Other assets	G. Same as carrying value; cost less an depreciation
_____ Report format	to date.
_____ Deferred charges	H. Prior period adjustment.
_____ Normal operating	I. Accumulated earnings minus accumulated divi-
cycle	dends.
_____ Book value	J. Current assets divided by current liabilities.
_____ Tangible assets	K. Asset offset account (subtracted from asset).
_____ Working capital	L. Short-term prepayment of an expense prior to its
_____ Liabilities	use or consumption.
_____ Operational assets	M. Assets that do not have physical substance.
_____ Owners' equity	N. Items owned by the business that have future eco-
_____ Working capital ratio	nomic values.
_____ Current assets	O. Liabilities expected to be paid out of current assets
_____ Assets	within the next year or operating cycle, if longer.
_____ Long-term liabilities	P. Liability offset account (deducted from liability).
_____ Contra liability	Q. The average cash-to-cash time involved in the
account	operations of the business.
_____ None of the above	R. Sum of the annual depreciation expense on an asset
	from its acquisition to date.
	S. A long-term prepaid expense.
	T. All liabilities not classified as current liabilities.
	U. Assets that have physical substance.
	V. Obligation to give up (pay) economic benefits in
	the future.

E2–9. On July 1, 19A, Risky Company paid $4,800 cash for a two-year insurance premium. The premium was for a new insurance policy covering all of the assets owned. It is now December 31, 19A, and you are asked to respond to the following questions (show your computations):

    a. How much should be reported for **insurance expense** on the income statement for year ended December 31, 19A?

b. What amount of **prepaid insurance** should be reported on the December 31, 19A, balance sheet? How should it be classified?

E2–10. Investor Manufacturing Corporation is preparing its annual financial statements at December 31, 19B. The company has two investments in shares of other corporations:

a. Common stock of M Corporation: 1,000 shares purchased for $80,000 during 19A. M Corporation is a supplier of parts to Investor Corporation; therefore, the latter "intends to hold the stock indefinitely." The shares acquired represented 2 percent of the total shares outstanding. M stock was selling at $95 at the end of 19B.

b. Common stock of N Corporation: purchased 500 shares at a cost of $60 per share on August 15, 19B. Investor made this investment to "temporarily use some idle cash that probably will be needed next year." N stock was selling at $70 at the end of 19B.

You have been requested to illustrate and explain the basis for the classification and amount that should be reported for each investment on the 19B balance sheet of Investor Corporation.

E2–11. Tabor Company is preparing the balance sheet at December 31, 19X. The following assets are to be reported:

1. Building, purchased 15 years ago (counting 19X); original cost, $330,000; estimated useful life, 20 years from date of purchase; and no residual value.
2. Land, purchased 15 years ago (counting 19X); original cost, $25,000.

Required:

a. You are requested to show how the two assets should be reported on the balance sheet. What is the amount of the book value of these operational assets?

b. What amount of depreciation expense should be reported on the 19X income statement? Show computations.

E2–12. The amounts listed below were selected from the annual financial statements for Lazar Corporation at December 31, 19C (end of the third year of operations):

From the 19C income statement:
Sales revenue	$300,000
Cost of goods sold	(180,000)
All other expenses (including income tax)	(90,000)
Net income	$ 30,000

From the December 31, 19C, balance sheet:
Current assets	$ 90,000
All other assets	275,000
Total assets	$365,000

Current liabilities	$ 50,000
Long-term liabilities	89,000
Capital stock, par $10	150,000
Contributed capital in excess of par	15,000
Retained earnings	61,000
Total liabilities and stockholders' equity	$365,000

Required:

You have been asked to analyze the data on the 19C financial statements of Lazar by responding to the following questions. Show computations.

a. How much was the gross margin on sales?
b. What was the amount of EPS?
c. What was the amount of working capital?
d. What was the working capital ratio?
e. What was the average sales price per share of the capital stock?
f. Assuming no dividends were declared or paid during 19C, what was the beginning balance (January 1, 19C) of retained earnings?

PART B

E2–13. At the end of the accounting year, December 31, 19B, the records of Wilson Corporation reflected the following summarized data:

Revenues for the year (net)	$150,000
Expenses for the year (including $3,000 income taxes)	(138,000)
Net income	$ 12,000
Total assets (including current assets of $48,000).........	$200,000
Liabilities (including current liabilities of $20,000)	$ 90,000
Stockholders' equity (including capital stock, par $10, sold for $80,000, and retained earnings)	110,000
Total liabilties and stockholders' equity	$200,000

Required:

For analytical and interpretative purposes you have been asked to complete the following tabulation:

Item	Computation	Briefly, What Does It Mean?
a. Average income tax rate		
b. Profit margin		
c. EPS		
d. Working capital amount		
e. Working capital ratio		
f. ROI		
g. Amount of long-term liabilities		
h. Amount of retained earnings		

E2–14. The accounting records of Ready Service Company reflected the amounts shown below:

	For the year		
	19A	19B	19C
Service revenue:			
Cash	$40,000	$50,000	
On credit	15,000	11,000	
19C revenue collected in advance of 19C (not			
included in the $50,000)		3,000	
Additional cash collections for:			
19A service revenue	6,000	5,000	
19B service revenue	2,000	7,000	$3,000
Expenses:			
Paid in cash	25,000	30,000	
On credit	5,000	7,000	
19C expenses paid in advance of 19C (not			
included in the $30,000)		1,000	
Additional cash payments for:			
19A expenses	3,000	2,000	
19B expenses	1,000	3,000	3,000

Required:

Complete the following tabulation (show computations):

	For the year	
	19A	*19B*
a. Service revenue that would be reported:		
Accrual basis	$ _____	$ _____
Cash basis	$ _____	$ _____
b. Expenses that would be reported:		
Accrual basis	$ _____	$ _____
Cash basis	$ _____	$ _____

E2–15. Listed below are the fundamental concepts of accounting. You are to match these concepts with the corresponding brief definition. Enter the appropriate letter to the left for each concept.

Fundamental concepts

_____ Primary users of financial statements
_____ Broad objective of financial reporting
_____ Qualitative characteristics of financial statements
_____ Implementation assumptions
_____ Elements of financial statements
_____ Implementation principles
_____ Exceptions to implementation principles
_____ Detailed accounting practices and procedures
_____ None of the above

Brief description

A. To prepare the income tax return of the business.
B. Separate entity, going concern, time periods, and unit of measure.
C. Examples: straight-line versus accelerated depreciation and special journals.
D. To provide financial information that is useful in projecting future cash flows.
E. Relevance and reliability.
F. Investors, creditors, and those who advise and represent them (decision markers).
G. Materiality, industry peculiarities, and rational conservatism.
H. Assets, liabilities, owners' equity, revenues, expenses, gains, and losses.
I. Revenue, cost, matching, reporting, reliability, and comparability.

E2–16. This exercise is designed to aid in your understanding of the contents of actual published financial statements and to observe differences in format and terminology. You are to base your response upon the 1982 Annual Report of Johnson & Johnson (J&J). Refer to **Special Supplement B** at the end of this textbook, immediately preceding the Index. Base your response on the 1982 data.

a. Balance sheet:
   (1) What title was used by J&J?
   (2) Give the following amounts: Assets = Liabilities + Owners' Equity.
   (3) How many shares of common stock had been issued by the end of 1982?
   (4) How much was invested in inventories at the end of 1982?

b. Income statement:
   (5) What title was used by J&J?
   (6) How can you tell that the J&J statements are comparative?
   (7) How much revenue was from sales to customers? How much did the merchandise cost that was sold?
   (8) Were any extraordinary items reported?
   (9) How many EPS amounts were reported?

c. Statement of retained earnings:
   (10) What title was used by J&J?
   (11) What was the amount of dividends paid?
   (12) What amount was carried to the balance sheet?

d. Statement of changes in financial position:
   (13) What was the net cash provided from operations?
   (14) How much cash was spent for property, plant, and equipment?

e. Notes to the financial statements:
   (15) What caused the extraordinary loss of $50 million on the income statement? What was the effect on EPS?
   (16) What was the 1982 effective tax rate (percent) in United States?

f. Supplementary information:
   (17) What line of business (segment) earned the highest operating profit?
   (18) What was the average consumer price index (1967 = 100) for 1982?
   (19) How many dollars would be required in 1982 to purchase the same "market basket of goods" that $1 would purchase in 1967?
   (20) How many people were employed by J&J during 1982?

PROBLEMS/CASES

PART A

PC2–1. Flat Tire Company is developing its annual financial statements for 19D. The following amounts have been determined to be correct: sales, $300,000; distribution expenses, $37,000; interest expense, $3,000; general and administrative expenses, $20,000; extraordinary loss, $15,000; sales returns and allowances, $3,000; cost of goods sold, $160,000; and interest revenue, $1,000.

Required:

a. Prepare a classified income statement for 19D. Assume 20,000 shares of common stock outstanding during the year and an average income tax rate on all items of 20 percent. (Hint: EPS on net income is $2.52 per share.)

   b. Subsequent to preparation of the above income statement you were asked to explain
         some aspects of it, specifically:
         (1)   What is the difference between sales returns and sales allowances?
         (2)   Is gross margin on sales a reliable measure of profitability? Explain.
         (3)   What was the total amount of income tax? Explain.
         (4)   What would be the effect on EPS had the company issued a stock split that
               would have increased the outstanding shares to 40,000?

PC2–2.   (Analytical)
         Below is a partially completed income statement of WRY Corporation for the year ended
         December 31, 19B.

Item	Other data	Amounts	
Gross sales revenue		$	$
Sales returns and allowances	5% of gross sales		
Net sales revenue			200,000
Cost of goods sold			
Gross margin on sales	Average markup on sales, 40%		
Operating expenses:			
Selling expenses			
General and administrative expenses		20,000	
Total operating expenses			
Pretax income from operations			
Financial revenue and expense:			
Interest revenue		3,000	
Interest expense		1,000	
Net financial revenue			
Pretax income			
Income tax on operations			
Income before EO items:			
EO gain		10,000	
Income tax effect			
Net EO gain			
Net income			
EPS (on common stock):			
Income before EO gain			1.00
EO gain			
Net income			

   Required:

       Based upon the data given above, and assuming (1) a 20 percent income tax rate on
   all items and (2) 20,000 common shares outstanding, complete the above income statement.
   Show all computations.

PC2–3.   Ace Jewelers is developing the annual financial statements for 19C. The following amounts
         have been determined to be correct at December 31, 19C: cash, $41,200; accounts receivable,
         $49,000; merchandise inventory, $110,000; prepaid insurance, $600; investment in stock
         of Z Corporation (long term), $31,000; store equipment, $50,000; used store equipment
         held for disposal, $9,000; allowance for doubtful accounts, $800; accumulated depreciation,
         store equipment, $10,000; accounts payable, $43,000; long-term notes payable, $40,000;
         income taxes payable, $7,000; retained earnings, $80,000; and common stock, 100,000 shares
         outstanding, par $1 per share (originally sold and issued at $1.10 per share).

Required:

a. You have been requested to prepare a classified balance sheet at December 31, 19C. (Hint: The balance sheet total is $280,000.)

b. What is the book or carrying value of the:
 (1) Inventory.
 (2) Accounts receivable.
 (3) Store equipment.
 (4) Notes payable (long-term)?
 Explain briefly what these values mean.

c. What is the (1) amount of working capital and (2) working capital ratio? Explain briefly what each of these amounts mean.

d. List any **contra** accounts. What does **contra account** mean?

PC2–4. Acme Trading Corporation is developing the annual financial statements for 19C. The information given below has been verified as correct. The company sells merchandise to retail outlets only. Note that in some instances only totals are provided to shorten the solution.

Financial Data, 19C

Income Statement

Sales revenue	$273,000
Selling expenses	44,700
Interest expense	2,200
Administrative expense*	23,300
Sales returns	3,000
Cost of goods sold	130,000
Extraordinary loss (earth-quake)	10,000
Income tax expense on operations (30%) ... $21,000	
Tax savings on extraor-dinary loss (30%) ... 3,000	18,000
Revenue from divi-dends on stock in-vestment, K Corp.	200

* Includes depreciation expense of $10,000.

Balance Sheet

Cash	$ 31,000
Accounts receivable	30,000
Allowance for doubtful accounts	1,000
Accounts payable	61,000
Retained earnings	72,000
Merchandise inventory	138,000
Investment in stock of K Corp. (long term)	4,000
Income taxes payable	5,000
Accumulated depreciation, store equipment	30,000
Store equipment (acquired January 1, 19A)	90,000
Used equipment held for disposal	38,000
Common stock, par $10 per share	100,000
Long-term notes payable	46,000
Contributed capital in excess of par	16,000

Required:

a. On the basis of the listed data, you have been asked to prepare a classified income statement and a balance sheet for the year ended December 31, 19C. (Hint: EPS on net income is $4.20.)

b. Compute the average markup earned on cost, the amount of working capital, and the working capital ratio. Briefly interpret each.

c. What estimated life is being used to depreciate the store equipment assuming no residual or scrap values? Also, reconcile the balance in the accumulated depreciation account with the related expense on the income statement.

PC2–5. Tasty Bakery is developing its annual financial statements for 19X. The following cash-flow data have been determined to be correct for the year 19X: sales revenue (including $12,000 not collected), $300,000; expenses, $270,000 (including $21,000 of noncash items); cash received from sale of used machine, $1,000; cash received for extraordinary item, $900; cash borrowed on a five-year note payable, $20,000; cash disbursement for dividends,

$12,000; cash expenditure to purchase two new delivery trucks, $9,900; and cash paid on mortgage payable, $5,000.

Required:

a. Prepare a SCFP, cash basis for 19X. (Hint: The cash balance increased by $34,000 during the year.)

b. As a basis for making future cash flow projections, what information on the SCFP for Tasty Bakery would you focus on especially? Explain.

PC2–6. Although Baker's Retail Store has been operating for only four years, the sales volume increase each year has been excellent; apparently it was occasioned by the location, a friendly atmosphere in the store, and a large stock of goods for customer selection. Despite this appearance of success, the company continually has experienced a severe cash shortage, and a recent analysis by a consultant revealed significant inventory overstocking in numerous lines. Baker's Retail Store was organized as a corporation by Samuel Baker (now president) and four additional investors. Each owner invested $41,000 cash and received 4,000 shares of common stock (par value $10 per share). Although Sam Baker is recognized as an excellent retailer, he exhibits very little interest in the financial reports. At a recent meeting of the board of directors, the inadequacy of the financial reports of the company was discussed. The board voted to engage an independent CPA "to examine the accounting system, submit audited financial statements, analyze the financial situation, and make appropriate recommendations to the Board." The independent CPA has just been handed the following financial statements for 19D which were prepared for the last board meeting by the "store bookkeeper" (to simplify this case, assume that all of the amounts are correct; also, only representative amounts have been included):

BAKER'S RETAIL STORE, INC.
Profit Statement
December 31, 19D

Incomes

Sales for the year	$572,000	
Interest collected on charge accounts	1,000	
Dividends received on stock of Y Corporation	200	$573,200

Costs

Salaries, sales	66,500	
Salaries, administrative	36,000	
Depreciation, office equipment	1,200	
Depreciation, store equipment	6,000	
Store rent	18,000	
Office supplies used	800	
Store supplies used	1,900	
Cost of goods sold for the year	340,000	
Bad debt losses (estimated)	300	
Promotion costs	60,000	
Interest on debts	5,000	
Loss on earthquake damage (extraordinary loss)	1,200	
Insurance and taxes (two-thirds selling and one-third administrative)	6,000	
Miscellaneous expenses, sales	2,000	
Miscellaneous expenses, administrative	700	
Sales returns	8,000	
Income taxes on operations $8,000, less tax saving on earthquake loss $400; net taxes	7,600	561,200
Profit		$ 12,000

Balance Sheet
December 31, 19D

Resources		Debts	
Cash	$ 3,500	Accounts payable	$ 20,000
Accounts receivable (offset for allowance for bad		Notes payable, short term	10,000
debts $500)	33,500	Notes payable, long term	80,000
Merchandise inventory (at cost)	269,200	Rent due (for December 19D)	1,500
Office supplies inventory	300	Income taxes owed	4,600
Store supplies inventory	1,600	**Capital**	
Prepaid insurance	1,200		
Stock investment in Y Corporation, long term	5,000	Stock, par $10	200,000
Store equipment (offset for accumulated deprecia-		Excess paid over par	5,000
tion, $25,600)	36,800	Retained earnings	36,000
Office equipment (offset for accumulated deprecia-			
tion, $6,000)	6,000		
	$357,100		$357,100

Required:

a. Recast the income statement and balance sheet using preferred subclassifications and terminology. (Hint: EPS on income before extraordinary items is $0.64.)

b. Compute the amount of working capital and the working capital ratio. Show computations. Explain the meaning of the results. Do they appear to you to be favorable? Explain.

PC2–7.   Ready Repair Company, a successful local automobile repair shop, is preparing its 19E financial statements. On January 1, 19E, the company acquired a substantial quantity of new shop equipment (and the related tools) for use in its testing and repair operations. The equipment involved a cash expenditure of $18,000. On the basis of experience, the owner estimated that the useful life of the new equipment would be five years for the company, at which time the equipment would sell for approximately 20 percent of the original cost.

Your advice is requested on two questions:

a. How much depreciation expense should be reported on the 19E income statement?

b. How should the new equipment be reported on the December 31, 19E, balance sheet? Show your computations and explanations. (Hint: Residual value is 20 percent and should not be depreciated because it will be recovered at the time of disposal. Analyze this situation and try to derive a logical approach for the computation of depreciation expense assuming the equipment will be used approximately the same amount each year.)

PART B

PC2–8.   On December 31, 19D, Friendly Department Store (a corporation) prepared its annual financial statements. The income statement and balance sheet amounts are summarized below:

Income Statement
For the Year Ended December 31, 19D

Sales revenue	$ 200,000
Cost of goods sold	(120,000)
All other operating expenses	(60,000)
Income tax expense	(3,400)
Net income	$ 16,600

Balance Sheet
At December 31, 19D

Current assets		$ 66,000
Operational assets (cost $210,000)		180,000
All other assets		34,000
Total assets		$ 280,000
Current liabilities		$ 30,000
Long-term liabilities		80,000
Total liabilities		110,000
Capital stock, par $10	$100,000	
Contributed capital in excess of par	30,000	
Retained earnings	40,000*	170,000
Total liabilities plus stockholders' equity		$ 280,000

* During 19D, a $5,000 dividend was declared and paid which has been subtracted from this amount.

Required:

For analytical and interpretative purposes you have been asked to compute each of the following amounts. Show computations and briefly explain what each amount communicates to users of this statement.

a. Profit margin.
b. Gross margin.
c. Average income tax rate.
d. EPS.
e. Working capital amount.
f. Working capital ratio.
g. ROI.
h. Average sales price of the capital stock.
i. January 1, 19D, balance (beginning) of retained earnings.
j. Accumulated depreciation at December 31, 19D.

PC2–9. You are considering making a $20,000 investment in the common stock of either X Corporation or Y Corporation. The companies operate in different industries, and their managements have followed different financing policies. In reviewing the latest financial statements you observe the following data:

	X Corporation		Y Corporation	
From the balance sheets:				
Total assets		$240,000		$240,000
Total liabilities		100,000		10,000
Shares outstanding		5,000		10,000
From the income statements:				
Revenues		107,000		107,000
Expenses:				
Interest expense (rate 15%).....	$15,000		$ 1,500	
Income tax expense	29,280*		29,280†	
Remaining expenses	18,800	63,080	32,300	63,080
Net income		$ 43,920		$ 43,920

* ($107,000 − $15,000 − $18,800) × 0.40 = $29,280.
† ($107,000 − $1,500 − $32,300) × 0.40 = $29,280.

From these amounts you observe that the two companies have (1) the same total amount of assets ($240,000), (2) the same amount of revenues ($107,000), and (3) the same net income ($43,920). In respect to these three factors, the two companies appear to be equally attractive. However, as part of your analysis, you decide to investigate further by comparing the following: profit margin, return on stockholders' investment (owners' equity), EPS, and the aftertax, or net, interest rate.

Required:

a. Compute the above amounts for each company. Show computations. (Hint: The pretax interest rate is 15 percent. Interest expense is deductible on the income tax return; therefore, the after-tax rate would be less. Try to determine this lower rate by logical analysis.)

b. Based upon the data given and your analysis, which company would you select for the investment? Explain the basis for your choice.

PC2–10. You are considering investing $50,000 in either A Corporation or B Corporation. Both companies have been operating in the same industry for a number of years. Your decision model calls for an evaluation and interpretation of the financial statements for the last five years; however, you have obtained the statements for last year only. Those statements provided the following data:

	A Corporation	B Corporation
Sales	$500,000	$700,000
Gross margin on sales	210,000	301,000
Income before extraordinary items	60,000	55,000
Net income	20,000	64,000
Total assets	300,000	400,000
Total liabilities (average interest rate 14%)	100,000	100,000
Owners' equity (total)	200,000	300,000
Shares outstanding	10,000	30,000
Income tax rate (average)	40%	40%

Required:

a. Based upon the above data (aside from other factors), what analytical steps would you suggest? Provide computations for each suggestion.

b. On the basis of your analytical results only, which company appears preferable as the investment choice? Explain why.

PC2–11. The financial statements at the end of the fiscal year for Watts Corporation are summarized below at June 30, 19F:

Income Statement

Sales revenue	$800,000
Cost of goods sold	460,000
Gross margin on sales	340,000
Operating expenses and income taxes	292,000
Income before extraordinary items	48,000
Extraordinary gain (net of income taxes)	60,000
Net income	$108,000

Balance Sheet

Current assets	$ 98,000
Investments	90,000
Operational assets (net)	330,000
Other assets	70,000
Total assets	$588,000
Current liabilities	$ 98,000
Long-term liabilities	40,000
Total liabilities	138,000
Capital stock, 8,000 shares	400,000
Contributed capital in excess of par	3,000
Retained earnings	47,000
Total stockholders' equity	450,000
Total liabilities and stockholders' equity	$588,000

Required:

Several important investment decisions are under consideration by a large shareholder. Among the analytical data desired by the investor are certain financial ratios. Accordingly, you have been engaged to provide advice, including the following ratios:

Profit margin:
1. Profit margin based on net income.
2. Profit margin based on income before extraordinary items.

Return on investment (ROI):
3. ROI based on net income and total stockholders' equity.
4. ROI based on income before extraordinary items and total stockholders' equity.

Earnings per share (EPS):
5. EPS based on net income.
6. EPS based on income before extraordinary items.

For each of the three ratio categories given above, select the one that you would deem most relevant and explain the basis for your selection.

PC2–12.   Below are listed the fundamental concepts of accounting. You are to match a "brief description of transaction or event "given to the right with a concept by entering the appropriate letter to the left which *best* matches the description with the concept applied.

Fundamental concept applied	*Brief description of transaction or event*
_____ Users of financial statements	A. Recorded a $1,000 sale of merchandise.
_____ Objective of financial statements	B. Counted (inventoried) the unsold items at the end of the period and valued them in dollars.
Qualitative characteristics:	C. Acquired a vehicle for use in operating the business.
_____ Relevance	D. Reported the amount of depreciation expense because it likely will affect decisions of statement users.
_____ Reliability	
Implementation assumptions:	E. Identified as the investors, creditors, and others interested in the business.
_____ Separate entity	
_____ Continuity	F. Used special accounting approaches because of the uniqueness of the industry.
_____ Unit of measure	
_____ Time period	G. Sold and issued bonds payable of $1 million.
Elements of financial statements:	H. Paid a contractor for an addition to the building with $10,000 cash and $20,000 market value of the stock of the company ($30,000 was deemed to be the cash equivalent price).
_____ Revenues	
_____ Expenses	
_____ Gains	
_____ Losses	I. Engaged an outside independent CPA to audit the financial statements.

Fundamental concept applied	*Brief description of transaction or event*

_____ Assets
_____ Liabilities
_____ Owner's equity
Implementation principles:
_____ Cost
_____ Revenue
_____ Matching
_____ Reporting
_____ Reliability
_____ Comparability
Exceptions to principles:
_____ Materiality
_____ Conservatism
_____ Industry peculiarities

J. Sold merchandise and services for cash and on credit during the year then determined the cost of those goods sold and the cost of rendering those services.

K. Established an accounting policy that revenue shall be recognized only when ownership to the goods sold passes to the customer.

L. Designs and prepares the financial statements to assist the users to project the future cash flows of the business.

M. Established a policy not to include in the financial statements the personal financial affairs of the owners of the business.

N. Sold an asset at a loss that was a peripheral or incidental transaction.

O. Prepared financial statements for 19C that also repeats the statements for 19B.

P. Valued an asset, such as inventory, at less than its purchase cost because the replacement is less.

Q. Prepared reliable financial statements; unbaised and verifiable.

R. Dated the income statement "For the Year Ended December 31, 19B."

S. Used services from outsiders—paid cash for some and the remainder on credit.

T. Acquired an asset (a pencil sharpener which will have a useful life of five years) and recorded as an expense when purchased for $1.99.

U. Disclosed on the financial statements all relevant financial information about the business; necessitated the use of notes to the financial statements.

V. Sold an asset at a gain that was a peripheral or incidental transaction.

W. Assets, $500,000 − Liabilities, $300,000 = $200,000.

X. The accounting and reporting assumes a "going concern."

Y. None of the above.

PC2–13. Art Little Company (not a corporation) prepared the income statement given below including the two footnotes:

ART LITTLE COMPANY
Income Statement, Cash Basis
For the Year Ended December 31, 19B

Sales revenue (does not include $20,000 sales on credit because collection will be in 19C)	$100,000
Expenses (does not include $10,000 expenses on credit because payment will be made in 19C)	75,200
Profit	$ 24,800

Additional data:
    a. Depreciation on operational assets (a company truck) for the year amounted to $15,000. Not included in expenses above.
    b. On January 1, 19B, paid a two-year insurance premium on the truck amounting to $400. This amount is included in the expenses above.

Required:

a. Recast the above income statement on the *accrual basis* in conformity with GAAP. Show computations and explain each change.

b. Explain why the cash basis does not measure as well as the accrual basis on the income statement.

PC2–14. *Forbes* magazine (December 8, 1980, p. 57) reported the following: "One firm sold shares for a new coal mining company. The prospectus stated that the firm had acquired 15,000 acres of land with proven coal deposits. What the 'entreprenuers' who raked in some $20 million didn't mention in the prospectus was that they had only leased surface rights to the land. So the only way they could possibly get any coal out of it was if the black stuff came popping out of its own volition."

Required:

a. What is a prospectus (see Chapter 1, SEC)?
b. In your opinion should the firm referred to above be required to disclose all of the facts cited above (say, in a prospectus)? Why?
c. If the firm referred to above were to prepare a financial statement for external parties, should they be required to disclose the facts cited above, or should disclosure be optional for this situation? Explain.

PC2–15.   Under a caption "Missing Footnotes," *Forbes* magazine (April 26, 1982, page 70), reported the following:

> Here's a footnote U.S. Steel Corp. neglected to include in its recently mailed 1981 annual report: As a result of its $6 billion-plus acquisition of Marathon Oil, U.S. Steel also got as part of the bargain a contingent liability of more than $369 million. That's more than one third of the profits U.S. Steel reported last year.
>
> Here's a footnote Du Pont should be including in its latest annual: As a result of its $7.8 billion purchase last year of Conoco, Du Pont inherited a contingent liability of about $315 million. That's more than one fifth of the combined corporations' reported earnings in 1981.
>
> The reason for both potential liabilities is the Department of Energy's long-standing dispute with the major oil companies over alleged pricing violations and overcharges. Marathon's $369 million liability was calculated from a continuous audit of the company's records by federal energy officials from 1974 to 1980. Conoco's contingent liability is derived from Department of Energy notices alleging probable violation in 1979 and 1980. The $315 million contingent liability appeared in Conoco's last quarterly report issued for the second quarter of last year, just before its accounts were consolidated with Du Pont's. Marathon reported its $369 million potential liability in its last annual report.

Required:

a. In your opinion, how would a contingent liability differ from a full-blown liability? Hint: Consider what the word *contingent* means in the general sense.
b. In your opinion should the two companies (U.S. Steel Corporation and Du Pont be required to disclose (i.e., include a footnote to the financial statements) to present the facts about the respective contingent liabilities? Why?
c. If your answer to *(b)* is yes, who should be the "police person"? Explain.

PC2–16.   This case is designed to help you understand the contents of actual published financial statements and to observe differences in format and terminology. It is based upon the 1982 Annual Report of Johnson & Johnson (J&J) which is presented in Special Supplement B immediately preceding the Index. Respond to the questions based upon the data for the year labeled 1982.

a. Balance sheet:
    (1) What title did J&J use?
    (2) How can you determine that the financial statements are comparative, aside from the title?
    (3) What was the amount of working capital?
    (4) What was the book, or carrying, value of the property, plant, and equipment?

      (5)   How much did customers owe the company?

      (6)   How much did J&J owe for unpaid income taxes on a current basis?

      (7)   How many shares were outstanding of (a) common stock and (b) preferred stock?

b. Income statement:

      (8)   What title did J&J use?

      (9)   What was the primary source of revenues?

     (10) What was the amount of income taxes?

     (11) How much was research expense?

     (12) How much did the goods cost that were sold to customers?

     (13) How much did J&J earn on each share of common stock after the Tylenol loss?

c. Statement of retained earnings:

     (14) What title did J&J use?

     (15) Complete the following:

           Beginning balance of R.E...... $_____

           Net income for 1982 .... _____

           Dividends paid in 1982 .... _____

           Ending balance of R.E. .... $_____

     (16) What amount was carried (a) from the income statement and (b) to the balance sheet?

d. Statement of changes in financial position:

     (17) How was "funds" measured in this statement?

     (18) What was the amount of the net funds from operations?

     (19) How much was the cash from borrowing (on loans, notes and long-term debt)?

     (20) Was the total amount of dividends all paid in cash?

     (21) How much did cash and current marketable securities change?

e. Notes to the financial statements:

     (22) How many notes did J&J present?

     (23) What is the title of Note 1?

     (24) Are the majority of domestic inventories valued on the basis of LIFO or on the basis of FIFO?

     (25) Did J&J have any legal proceedings pending?

     (26) Which quarter of the year had the highest amount of net earnings, worldwide?

f. Auditors' report:

     (27) What title was used for this report?

     (28) Did the auditors' give a "good" or "bad" opinion about the financial statements:

g. Supplementary information:

     (29) What line of business (i.e., segment) had the lowest operating profit? What geographical area had the lowest operating profit?

     (30) What was the average "inflation index" for 1982? How much general inflation occurred in 1982 (over 1981)?

     (31) How many people were: (a) employees and (b) stockholders?

Transaction Analysis

PURPOSE OF THIS CHAPTER

In Chapters 1 and 2 you studied the fundamentals of financial accounting and the financial statements. Your attention now is turned to the accounting process—the way in which the ongoing transactions within a business are recorded, analyzed, and classified in a form from which the periodic financial statements can be developed. In this chapter you will learn the fundamentals of the accounting model and how to analyze business transactions to determine and record quantitatively their economic impacts on that model.

To accomplish these purposes, this chapter is divided into two parts as follows:

Part A—The accounting model and transaction analysis

Part B—The accounting information processing cycle

PART A—THE ACCOUNTING MODEL AND TRANSACTION ANALYSIS

NATURE OF TRANSACTIONS

Accounting focuses on certain events that have an economic impact on the entity. Those particular events are recorded as a part of the accounting process and generally are referred to as **transactions.** A broad definition of transactions includes (1) those events that involve an exchange of resources (assets) and/or obligations (liabilities) between the business (i.e., the accounting entity) and one or more parties other than the entity; and (2) certain events (or economic occurrences) that are not between the entity and one or more parties but yet have a direct and measurable effect on the accounting entity. Examples of the first category of transactions include the purchase of a machine, the sale of merchandise, the borrowing of cash, and the investment in the business by the owners. Examples of the second category of transactions include (1) **economic events,** such as a drop in the replacement cost of an item held in inventory and a flood loss; and (2) **time adjustments,** such as depreciation of an operational asset (as a result of use) and the "using up" of prepaid insurance. Throughout this textbook, the word *transaction* will be used in the broad sense to include both types of events.[1]

Most transactions are evidenced by a **business document** of some sort; in the case of a sale on credit, a charge ticket is prepared, and in the case of a purchase of goods, an invoice is received. In certain other transactions, such as a cash sale, there may be no document other than the cash register tape. The documents that underlie, or support, transactions usually are called **source documents.** The important requirement, from the accounting point of view, is that procedures be established to capture the data on **each transaction as it occurs.** Once this has been done, the data processing characteristics of the accounting system advance the economic impact of each transaction on the entity from initial recording to its final resting place—the periodic financial statements.

The fundamental feature of most transactions with **external parties** is an exchange where the business entity both gives up something and receives something in return. For example, in the case of a sale of merchandise for cash, the entity gives up resources (the goods sold) and receives in return another resource (cash). In the case of a credit sale of merchandise, the resource received at the time of sale is an account receivable (an asset). Later, another transaction occurs when the account receivable is collected; here, the resource relinquished is the receivable and the resource received is cash. As another example, in the purchase of an asset (either merchandise for resale or a truck purchased for use in the business), the entity acquires the asset and gives up cash, or in the case of a credit purchase incurs a liability. Another transaction occurs later when the debt is paid. At that time, the entity gives up a resource (cash) and "receives" satisfaction of the debt. The sale or purchase of services can be analyzed in the same way.

---

[1] A narrow definition of a transaction limits it to the first category, that is, events between the entity and one or more parties other than the entity. This definition is useful in certain circumstances and is conceptually correct. However, accounting recognizes a number of events that are not transactions in the strict sense, therefore, we have defined the term in the broader sense to generalize our terminology.

Thus, transactions have a **dual economic effect** on the accounting entity. We will return to this dual effect when we consider the accounting model in Part B of this chapter.

THE FUNDAMENTAL ACCOUNTING MODEL

The fundamental accounting model expresses in an algebraic format the status of the assets, debts, and owners' claims of an accounting entity at any specific point in time. In Chapters 1 and 2 you learned the **fundamental accounting model** when you studied the balance sheet (the position statement), viz:

$$\text{ASSETS} = \text{LIABILITIES} + \text{OWNERS' EQUITY}$$

You also learned that owners' equity is (1) increased by investments (i.e., contributions) by the owners, (2) decreased by withdrawals by owners (such as dividends), (3) increased by revenues, and (4) decreased by expenses.[2] Thus, we can expand the fundamental accounting model as follows:

$$\text{ASSETS} = \text{LIABILITIES} + \underline{\text{OWNERS' EQUITY}}$$

Decreased by:	Increased by:
Withdrawals	Investments
Expenses	Revenues

The fundamental accounting model is a broad economic description of an accounting entity that accommodates the **recording** of each transaction that directly affects the enterprise. The **dual economic effect** of each transaction (discussed below) is recorded in terms of this expanded accounting model. The dual effect is captured by the same accounting process, whether that processing system is handwritten, mechanized, or computerized.

To illustrate how specific transactions are analyzed and how the dual economic effect is recorded in terms of the fundamental accounting model, let's consider a simple but realistic situation. Throughout the example you should note particularly that (1) each transaction is recorded separately; (2) in recording each transaction, the equality of the fundamental accounting model is maintained (that is, assets will always equal liabilities plus owners' equity); and (3) the **dual effect,** as discussed in the preceding section, is recorded for each transaction.

The
fundamental
accounting
model
illustrated

B. Bass and three friends started a dry cleaning business on January 1, 19A, by investing a total of $20,000 cash from their personal savings accounts. In return for their contribution, each investor was issued 200 shares of the capital stock of the newly organized **corporation**—Bass Cleaners, Inc. Remember that the accounting entity, Bass Cleaners, Inc., is to be distinguished from the four investors in accordance with the separate-entity assumption (Exhibit 2–6). Exhibit

---

[2] Owners' equity sometimes is referred to as equity capital and occasionally as net worth. The latter term is not recommended because it implies that owners' equity on the balance sheet states what the owners' claim is actually worth, which is not the case.

3–1 lists a series of transactions for the year 19A and illustrates the dual effect of each transaction in terms of the accounting model for the business. Also, it provides the information for developing the **income statement** and **balance sheet** shown in Exhibit 3–2. This illustration should be studied carefully as you read the next few paragraphs.

On the balance sheet, because Bass is a corporation, stockholders' equity is represented by the two **sources:** contributed capital and retained earnings.[3] **Retained earnings** represents the accumulated earnings of the corporation to date, less all dividends declared to date. This aspect of the balance sheet was explained and illustrated in Chapter 1 (page 23) and in Chapter 2 (page 57).

From this simple example you can view the broad perspective of the **accounting process.** As transactions occur, they create **raw economic data.** The data from each transaction are subjected to **transaction analysis** to determine the **dual economic effect** of the transaction on the business in terms of the fundamental accounting model. The dual effect then is recorded in the accounting system. Finally, at the end of the accounting period, the financial statements are constructed from the data accumulated in the accounting system.

Bass Cleaners, as reflected in Exhibits 3–1 and 3–2, illustrates two primary data processing problems:

1. An efficient method is needed for **keeping track of (i.e., recording) the amounts** of each kind of asset (cash, accounts receivable, equipment, inventory, etc.); each kind of liability (accounts payable, notes payable, bonds payable, etc.); and each category of owners' equity (capital stock, revenues, and expenses).
2. An efficient and systematic method of continuous **checking** is needed to assure accuracy during the recording process.

The account.   The need to record transactions efficiently and to check the accuracy of the recording led early accountants to develop a series of **accounts.** A separate account is used for each kind of asset, liability, and owners' equity. **An account is a standardized arrangement for recording data by categories.** In most accounting systems, you will find **separate** accounts, individually labeled, for each asset, such as cash, inventory, accounts receivable, equipment, land; for each liability, such as accounts payable, notes payable, taxes payable; and for each element of owners' equity, such as capital stock, sales revenue, service revenue, and various kinds of expenses. For example, the **Cash account** for Bass Cleaners may appear as shown in Exhibit 3–3.

The **balance** in the Cash account of Bass Cleaners is:

Total of increases, \$66,000 — Total of decreases, \$36,700 = \$29,300, balance

---

[3] Owners' equity usually is designated to indicate the kind of ownership arrangement used as follows:

Corporation . . . .   Stockholders' equity
Sole proprietorship . . . . .   Owner's capital
Partnership   . . . .   Partners' capital

EXHIBIT 3–1 Transaction analysis illustrated

BASS CLEANERS INC.
Transaction Analysis—19A

Dual effect of each transaction on the entity

Transactions	Assets	=	Liabilities	+	Stockholders' Equity
a. Bass Cleaners received $20,000 cash invested by owners; 800 shares ($25 par value) of stock issued to the four owners	Cash + $20,000				Capital stock (800 shares) + $20,000
b. Borrowed $5,000 cash on 12% note payable	Cash + 5,000		Note payable + $5,000		
c. Purchased delivery truck for cash at cost of $8,000	Cash − 8,000; Delivery truck + 8,000				
d. Cleaning revenue collected in cash, $40,000	Cash + 40,000				Cleaning revenue + 40,000
e. Cleaning revenue earned in 19A, but the bill is not collected, $4,000	Accounts receivable + 4,000				Cleaning revenue + 4,000
f. Operating expenses paid in cash, $25,800	Cash − 25,800				Operating expenses − 25,800
g. Operating expenses incurred in 19A but not paid, $2,000			Accounts payable + 2,000		Operating expenses − 2,000
h. Paid 12% interest on the $5,000 note payable, (b) above, with cash ($5,000 × 12% = $600)	Cash − 600				Interest expense − 600
i. Depreciation expense for one year on truck ($8,000 ÷ 5 years = $1,600)	Truck − 1,600				Operating expenses, depreciation − 1,600
j. Cash dividend of $1,800 declared and paid to shareholders*	Cash − 1,800				Retained earnings (or dividends paid) − 1,800
k. Collected $1,000 cash on accounts receivable in (e)	Cash + 1,000; Accounts receivable − 1,000				
l. Paid $500 cash on accounts payable in (g)	Cash − 500		Accounts payable − 500		
Totals (end of accounting period)	Total assets $38,700	=	Total liabilities $6,500	+	Total stockholders' equity $32,200

Observe how these items and their respective **ending balances** flow into the **financial statements,** Exhibit 3–2.

* A cash dividend is not an expense; it is a withdrawal of resources by the owners.

EXHIBIT 3–2
Income statement and balance sheet illustrated

Observe that these items and their respective amounts were developed in the **transaction analysis** illustrated in Exhibit 3–1.

BASS CLEANERS, INC.
Income Statement
For the Year Ended December 31, 19A

Cleaning revenue ($40,000 + $4,000)		$44,000
Operating expenses ($25,800 + $2,000 + $1,600)	$29,400	
Interest expense	600	30,000
Net income		$14,000
EPS ($14,000 ÷ 800 shares)		$17.50

Note: To simplify the illustration, income taxes are disregarded.

BASS CLEANERS, INC.
Balance Sheet
At December 31, 19A

Assets

Cash ($20,000 + $5,000 − $8,000 + $40,000 − $25,800 − $600 − $1,800 + $1,000 − $500)		$29,300
Accounts receivable ($4,000 − $1,000)		3,000
Delivery truck	$ 8,000	
Less: Accumulated depreciation	1,600	6,400
Total assets		$38,700

Liabilities

Notes payable	5,000	
Accounts payable ($2,000 − $500)	1,500	
Total liabilities		$ 6,500

Stockholders' Equity

Contributed capital:		
Capital stock (800 shares)	20,000	
Retained earnings (beginning retained earnings, $–0–, plus net income, $14,000, minus dividends declared and paid, $1,800)	12,200	
Total stockholders' equity		32,200
Total liabilities and stockholders' equity		$38,700

EXHIBIT 3–3
Ledger account (T-account format), illustrated

Cash

Left or Debit Side		Right or Credit Side	Acct. No. 101
(Increases)		(Decreases)	
Investment by owners	20,000	To purchase truck	8,000
Loan from bank	5,000	Operating expenses	25,800
Cleaning revenue	40,000	Interest expense	600
Collections on accounts receivable	1,000	Dividends declared and paid	1,800
		Payment on accounts payable	500
	66,000		36,700

Now we will discuss and illustrate how accounts are used to help resolve the two data processing problems listed above.

1. **Keeping track of the amounts for each item**—To do this, a separate **account** is set up for each item that will be reported on the financial statements. Each account is designed so that all increases are entered on one side (e.g., on the left side of the Cash account in Exhibit 3–3) and all decreases are entered on the other side (e.g., on the right side of the Cash account in Exhibit 3–3). To illustrate the increased efficiency possible, compare the list of plus and minus amounts on the cash lines of Exhibit 3–2 with the location arrangement in Exhibit 3–3. Also, imagine thousands or millions of such increases and decreases during the year in a typical business. In contrast, the Cash account shown in Exhibit 3–3 reflects a left side total of $66,000 and a right side total of $36,700; the difference, $29,300, is the ending cash balance (as reported on the balance sheet in Exhibit 3–2). When the total amount on the decrease side of the Cash account is larger than the total amount on the increase side, a cash deficit (bank overdraft) is indicated. The account system is very flexible; for example, instead of being set up in T-account form (as in Exhibit 3–3), it can be set up in other formats such as the columnar form as in Exhibit 3–7. The account system can be used with either (or a combination of) handwritten, mechanical, or computerized approaches.

2. **Providing a systematic method of checking for accuracy during the recording process**—To resolve this problem, the account was designed to provide **dual equalities or balances** that may be summarized as follows:

Equalities	Basis
a. Assets = Liabilities + Owners' Equity	Algebraic relationship in the fundamental accounting model
b. Debits = Credits	Algebraic relationship between account increases and decreases

These two basic equalities may be explained as follows:

a. The fundamental accounting model, **Assets = Liabilities + Owners' Equity,** is an algebraic representation of the economic position of an entity at any point in time. By definition, it always balances and can be rearranged mathematically (e.g., Assets − Liabilities = Owners' Equity). Observe in Exhibit 3–1 that the analysis of each transaction, and the cumulative effects of all transactions, were always in balance in terms of this algebraic model (as shown in the balance sheet in Exhibit 3–2). Thus, the first check for accuracy listed above is applied continuously throughout the accounting process.

b. Now we will consider the second accuracy test listed above, **Debits = Credits.** In this context, it is useful to think of an account as having two sides (i.e., parts), the **left side,** which in accounting is called the **Debit** side, and the **right side,** which in accounting is called the **Credit** side. These designations are shown in Exhibit 3–3.[4]

The Debits = Credits feature in accounting.   To be useful as an accuracy check, the relationships described above, must be systematic, complementary, and flexible. Recall from Chapter 1 that in 1494 a mathematician (Paciolo) first described the fundamental accounting model used today. Perceiving the importance of accuracy, and after designing the T-account (similar to that illustrated in Exhibit 3–3), Paciolo applied an algebraic concept that has proven to be of great significance in minimizing errors in the accounting process. The fundamental accounting model, **Assets = Liabilities + Owners' Equity,** is an algebraic model that has mathematical equality. Paciolo added another algebraic balance feature to the basic model to minimize errors in recording increases and decreases in each account. Let's see how it was done.

Paciolo perceived that having designed the T-account with two sides to reflect increases and decreases, he could add another algebraic **balancing feature** by simply **reversing** the position in the account of the "increases" and "decreases" on the **opposite sides** of the basic accounting model. This second algebraic balance feature is still used to this day; it has the "+" and "−" **in reverse order** on the opposite sides of the accounting model in this way:

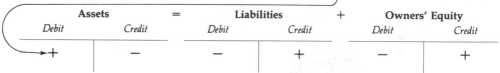

Observe that **debit** always refers to the left side of an account and **credit** always refers to the right side of an account. **Thus, debit and credit positions do not change; only the plus and minus signs change positions.** The addition of this algebraic concept resulted in the second "balancing" feature, that is, **debits always should equal credits.** Thus, the system used for recording increases and decreases in the accounts may be tabulated as follows:[5]

	Increases	Decreases
Assets	Debit	Credit
Liabilities	Credit	Debit
Owners' equity	Credit	Debit

Debits and credits for revenues and expenses.   After some practice you will become comfortable using the words *debit* and *credit* to signify changes in assets, liabilities, and owners' equity accounts. However, some persons are confused about the proper terms to reflect changes in revenue and expense accounts. Remember that owners' equity is increased by credits and decreased by debits. Revenues increase owners' equity; therefore, **revenues are recorded as credits.**

---

[4] Handwritten or manually maintained accounts in the formats shown here are used primarily in small businesses. Highly mechanized and computerized systems retain the concept of the account but not this format. T-accounts are useful primarily for instructional purposes.

[5] Historically, and continuing to the present, accountants refer to the left side as the debit side and to the right side as the credit side. For accounting purposes, the terms **debit** and **credit** have no other meanings. The words **to debit** and **to credit** should not be confused with "increase" or "decrease" as will become clear in the next few paragraphs. Contrary to what some people think, there is no implication of "goodness" attached to credits or "badness" attached to debits (or vice versa). Although rearranged, Exhibit 3–7 still maintains the Debits = Credits feature.

Expenses decrease owners' equity; therefore, **expenses are recorded as debits.** In other words, the debit/credit relationship for owners' equity accounts is applied to revenues and expenses.[6]

In summary, the balancing features of the fundamental accounting model are:

1. **Assets = Liabilities + Owners' Equity**
2. **Debits = Credits**

The next section of this chapter illustrates the use of accounts and emphasizes application of the fundamental accounting model and its dual balancing feature.

TRANSACTION ANALYSIS

Information processing in an accounting system involves collecting raw economic data on each transaction, analyzing the data in terms of the fundamental accounting model (often called **transaction analysis**), **recording** (entering) the results of the analysis in the accounting system (i.e., in the accounts discussed above), and finally, **preparing** the periodic financial statements. This section introduces transaction analysis.

Transaction analysis is a term used frequently to describe the process of studying each transaction to determine its **dual effect** on the entity in terms of the accounting model. In transaction analysis, a careful distinction is made between the cash basis and the accrual basis methods. In Chapter 2, page 66, the distinction between **cash basis accounting** and **accrual basis accounting** was discussed briefly. Recall that the accrual basis is required by GAAP. The concept of **accrual accounting requires that revenues and expenses be measured and reported in the accounting period in which the transactions occur rather than when the related cash is received or paid.**

Now, let's see how **each transaction** is subjected to transaction analysis to determine (1) its dual economic effect on the entity and (2) how that dual effect is recorded in the accounts (i.e., in terms of the fundamental accounting model).

Recall that for each transaction recorded, **two separate balances** must be maintained, viz: (1) Assets = Liabilities + Owners' Equity and (2) Debits = Credits. Bass Cleaners, Inc., will be used to demonstrate transaction analysis and the basic recording process. You should analyze each transaction (listed in Exhibit 3–1) and trace the manner in which the dual effect is recorded in the accounting model by using T-accounts (rather than simple plus and minus as in Exhibit 3–1). The transactions are entered in Exhibit 3–4 in T-accounts and are keyed with letters for ready reference. You should study Exhibit 3–4 intensively (and even restudy it in tandem with the next several chapters) in order to understand clearly *(a)* the fundamental accounting model, *(b)* transaction analysis, *(c)* recording the dual effects of each transaction, and *(d)* the dual-balancing system. Exhibit 3–4 was designed to emphasize these important aspects of the accounting processing system.

---

[6] To "charge an account" is a frequently used expression meaning to **debit** an account. Thus, the word *debit* is used as both a verb and a noun.

EXHIBIT 3–4
Transaction analysis, journal entries, and T-accounts illustrated

Bass Cleaners, Inc.

a. **Received $20,000 cash invested by the four owners and in turn issued 800 shares of capital stock (par value $25 per share).**

Transaction analysis—This transaction increased the company's cash by $20,000, which is recorded in the **Cash** account as a debit (increase); liabilities were unaffected; and owners' equity was increased by $20,000, which is recorded in the **Capital Stock** account as a credit (increase). The entry (recording) in the accounting system may be summarized conveniently as follows (credits are listed last and also are indented for easy identification):

	Debit	Credit
Cash (asset)	20,000	
Capital stock (owners' equity)		20,000

The two **accounts** would appear as follows:

Cash (asset)			**Capital Stock (owners' equity)**		
Debit		*Credit*	*Debit*		*Credit*
(a)	20,000			(a)	20,000

Dual check for accuracy—The entry meets both tests: Assets (+$20,000) = Liabilities (–0–) + Owners' equity (+$20,000), and Debits ($20,000) = Credits ($20,000).

b. **Borrowed $5,000 cash from the bank on a 12 percent note payable.**

Transaction analysis—This transaction increased cash by $5,000, which is recorded in the **Cash** account as a debit (increase); liabilities were increased by $5,000, which is recorded in the **Notes Payable** account as a credit (increase); and owners' equity was unchanged. The entry in the accounting system may be summarized as follows:

	Debit	Credit
Cash (asset)	5,000	
Notes payable (liability)		5,000

The **accounts** affected would appear as follows:

Cash (asset)			**Notes Payable (liability)**		
Debit		*Credit*	*Debit*		*Credit*
(a)	20,000			(b)	5,000
(b)	5,000				

Dual check for accuracy—The entry meets both tests: Assets (+$5,000) = Liabilities (+$5,000) + Owners' Equity (–0–), and Debits ($5,000) = Credits ($5,000).

c. **Purchased a delivery truck for cash at a cost of $8,000.**

Transaction analysis—This transaction increased the asset, **Delivery Truck,** by $8,000, which is recorded in that asset account as a debit (increase); and the cash was decreased by $8,000, which is recorded in the asset account **Cash** as a credit (decrease). Liabilities and owners'

EXHIBIT 3–4
(continued)

equity were not affected. The entry in the accounting system may be summarized conveniently as follows:

Delivery truck (asset)	8,000	
Cash (asset)		8,000

The two **accounts** affected would appear as follows:

Delivery Truck (asset)			**Cash (asset)**		
Debit	*Credit*		*Debit*		*Credit*
(c) 8,000		(a) 20,000	(c) 8,000		
		(b) 5,000			

Dual check for accuracy—The entry meets both tests: Assets (delivery truck, +$8,000 and cash, −$8,000) = Liabilities (–0–) + Owners' Equity (–0–), and Debits ($8,000) = Credits ($8,000).

d. Cleaning revenue earned and collected in cash, $40,000.

Transaction analysis—This transaction increased cash by $40,000, which is recorded in the asset account **Cash** as a debit (increase); liabilities were unaffected; and owners' equity was increased by $40,000 as a result of earning revenue. Owners' equity is credited (increased) for $40,000. A separate owners' equity account, **Cleaning Revenue,** is used to keep track of this particular revenue. The entry may be summarized as follows:

Cash (asset)	40,000	
Cleaning revenue (owners' equity)		40,000

The two **accounts** affected would appear as follows:

Cash (asset)			**Cleaning Revenue (owners' equity)**		
Debit	*Credit*		*Debit*		*Credit*
(a) 20,000	(c) 8,000				(d) 40,000
(b) 5,000					
(d) 40,000					

Dual check for accuracy—The entry meets both tests: Assets (+$40,000) = Liabilities (–0–) + Owners' equity (+$40,000), and Debits ($40,000) = Credits ($40,000).

e. Cleaning revenue earned, but the cash was not yet collected, $4,000.

Transaction analysis—This transaction increased the company's asset, **Accounts Receivable,** by $4,000, which is recorded as a debit (increase) to that account; liabilities were unaffected; and owners' equity was increased by $4,000. Owners' equity is credited (increased) by $4,000 using a separate account, **Cleaning Revenue,** which is used to keep track of this particular revenue. The entry in the accounting system may be summarized as follows:

EXHIBIT 3–4
(continued)

Accounts receivable (asset)	4,000	
Cleaning revenue (owners' equity)		4,000

The effect on the two **accounts** would appear as follows:

Accounts Receivable (asset)		Cleaning Revenue (owners' equity)	
Debit	*Credit*	*Debit*	*Credit*
(e) 4,000		(d) 40,000	
		(e) 4,000	

Dual check for accuracy—The entry meets both tests: Assets (+ $4,000) = Liabilities (–0–) + Owners' Equity (+$4,000), and Debits ($4,000) = Credits ($4,000).

f. **Expenses incurred and paid in cash, $25,800.**

Transaction analysis—This transaction decreased cash by $25,800, which is recorded in the **Cash** account as a credit (decrease); liabilities were unaffected; and owners' equity was decreased by $25,800 as a result of paying expenses. Owners' equity is decreased by debiting a separate account **Operating Expenses,** which is used to keep track of this particular expense. The accounting entry may be summarized as follows:

Operating expense (owners' equity)	25,800	
Cash (asset)		25,800

The effect on the two **accounts** would appear as follows:

Operating Expenses (owners' equity)		Cash (asset)	
Debit	*Credit*	*Debit*	*Credit*
(f) 25,800		(a) 20,000	(c) 8,000
		(b) 5,000	(f) 25,800
		(d) 40,000	

Dual check for accuracy—The entry meets both tests.

g. **Expenses incurred, but the cash not yet paid, $2,000.**

Transaction analysis—This transaction did not affect the company's assets; liabilities were increased by $2,000, which is recorded as a credit (increase) to **Accounts Payable;** and owners' equity was decreased $2,000 by debiting a separate account, **Operating Expenses** which is used to keep track of this particular type of expense. The entry summarized is:

Operating expenses (owners' equity)	2,000	
Accounts payable (liability)		2,000

EXHIBIT 3–4
(continued)

The two **accounts** affected would appear as follows:

Operating Expenses (owners' equity)			Accounts Payable (liability)		
Debit		*Credit*	*Debit*		*Credit*
(f)	25,800			(g)	2,000
(g)	2,000				

Dual check for accuracy—The entry meets both tests.

h. **Paid cash interest incurred on note payable in *(b)* ($5,000 × 12% = $600).**

Transaction analysis—This transaction decreased cash by $600, which is recorded as a credit (decrease) in the **Cash** account; the principal amount of the related liability ($5,000) was unchanged; however, owners' equity was decreased by the amount of the interest ($600) because the payment of interest (but not principal of the note) represents an expense. Owners' equity is decreased by debiting a separate account, **Interest Expense,** which is used to keep track of this particular type of expense. The entry summarized is:

> Interest expense (owners' equity)   600
>   Cash (asset)   600

The two **accounts** affected would appear as follows:

Interest Expense (owners' equity)			Cash (asset)			
Debit		*Credit*	*Debit*		*Credit*	
(h)	600		(a)	20,000	(c)	8,000
			(b)	5,000	(f)	25,800
			(d)	40,000	(h)	600

Dual check for accuracy—The entry meets both tests.

i. **Depreciation expense on the truck for one year ($8,000 ÷ 5 years = $1,600).**

Transaction analysis—This transaction is caused by the **internal** use (wear and tear) of an asset owned for operating purposes. This use is quantified and recorded as depreciation expense. Owners' equity was decreased by this expense, which is recorded as a debit to a separate account for this type of expense, **Operating Expenses** (alternatively, a separate expense account, called depreciation expense, could have been used). Assets (i.e., the delivery truck) was decreased because a part of the cost of the asset was "used up" in operations. Instead of directly crediting (decreasing) the asset account, Delivery Truck, a related **contra account, Accumulated Depreciation, Delivery Truck,** is credited so that the total amount of depreciation can be kept separate from the cost of the asset. This procedure will be explained and illustrated in detail in Chapter 9. The entry summarized is:

> Operating expenses (owners' equity)   1,600
>   Accumulated depreciation, delivery
>   truck (contra account)   1,600

EXHIBIT 3–4
(continued)

The two **accounts** affected would appear as follows:

Operating Expenses (owners' equity)		Accumulated Depreciation, Delivery Truck (contra account)	
Debit	*Credit*	*Debit*	*Credit*
(f) 25,800		(i)	1,600
(g) 2,000			
(i) 1,600			

Dual check for accuracy—The entry meets both tests: Assets (−$1,600) = Liabilities (−0−) + Owners' Equity (−$1,600), and Debits ($1,600) = Credits ($1,600).

j. **Declared and paid cash dividends to stockholders, $1,800.**

Transaction analysis—This transaction decreased the company's cash by $1,800, which is recorded in the **Cash** account as a credit (decrease); liabilities were unaffected; owners' equity was decreased by $1,800 as a result of the resources (cash) paid out of the business to the stockholders. Owners' equity is debited (decreased) by using a separate account, **Retained Earnings,** which is used to keep track of this kind of decrease in owners' equity (and certain increases explained later). Dividends declared and paid decreases owners' equity but it does not represent an expense (which also decreases owners' equity) rather it represents a cash distribution of "earnings" to the owners. The entry summarized is:

> Retained earnings (or dividends paid) 1,800
>   Cash (asset) 1,800

The two **accounts** would appear as follows:

Retained Earnings (owners' equity)		Cash (asset)			
Debit	*Credit*	*Debit*		*Credit*	
(j) 1,800		(a)	20,000	(c)	8,000
		(b)	5,000	(f)	25,800
		(d)	40,000	(h)	600
				(j)	1,800

Dual check for accuracy—The entry meets both tests.

k. **Collected $1,000 cash on accounts receivable in *(e).***

Transaction analysis—This transaction increased the asset cash by $1,000, which is recorded as a debit (increase) in the **Cash** account; another asset, **Accounts Receivable,** was decreased, which is recorded as a credit (decrease) of $1,000. Liabilities and owners' equity were unaffected because there was a change in two assets with no change in total assets. The entry summarized is:

> Cash (asset) 1,000
>   Accounts receivable (asset) 1,000

EXHIBIT 3–4
(concluded)

The two **accounts** would appear as follows:

Cash (asset)				Accounts Receivable (asset)			
Debit		*Credit*		*Debit*		*Credit*	
(a)	20,000	(c)	8,000	(e)	4,000	(k)	1,000
(b)	5,000	(f)	25,800				
(d)	40,000	(h)	600				
(k)	1,000	(j)	1,800				

Dual check for accuracy—The entry meets both tests.

l. **Paid $500 cash on accounts payable in (g).**

Transaction analysis—This transaction decreased cash by $500, which is recorded as a credit (decrease) in the **Cash** account; the $500 decrease in liabilities is recorded as a debit (decrease) to the **Accounts Payable** account. Owners' equity was unaffected because there was no revenue or expense involved in this transaction, merely the payment of a debt. The entry summarized is:

```
Accounts payable (liability) .............................   500
    Cash (asset) .......................................          500
```

The two **accounts** would appear as follows:

Accounts Payable (liability)				Cash (asset)			
Debit		*Credit*		*Debit*		*Credit*	
(l)	500	(g)	2,000	(a)	20,000	(c)	8,000
				(b)	5,000	(f)	25,800
				(d)	40,000	(h)	600
				(k)	1,000	(j)	1,800
						(l)	500

Dual check for accuracy—The entry meets both tests.

For further illustration purposes, each one of the above accounts is repeated in Exhibit 3–6 and their balances (i.e., the total increases minus the total decreases in each account) are shown in Exhibit 3–8.

Observe in Exhibit 3–4 that each transaction affected at least two different accounts because the economic position of the entity, in terms of the fundamental accounting model—Assets = Liabilities + Owners' Equity—always is affected in at least two ways. This dual-effect characteristic of the model is the reason its application often is referred to as a **double-entry** system.

The fundamental accounting model and the mechanics of the debit-credit concept in T-account format can be summarized as follows, where + means increase and − means decrease:

Note particularly that an increase in **revenue** (a credit) represents an **increase** in owners' equity and an increase in **expense** (a debit) represents a **decrease** in owners' equity. When a revenue is earned, the resources (i.e., assets) of the business are increased (or liabilities may be decreased) and, because of the dual effect, owners' equity is increased by the same amount. In contrast, when an expense is incurred, the net resources of the business are decreased (i.e., assets are decreased and/or liabilities increased), and because of the dual effect, the owners' equity is decreased by the same amount.

PART B—THE ACCOUNTING INFORMATION PROCESSING CYCLE

The accounting information processing cycle is **repeated each period.** It involves a series of **sequential** phases (steps), starting with the transactions and extending through the accounting period in the accounting system and finally to the preparation of the required financial statements: income statement, balance sheet, and statement of changes in financial position. In this part, we will consider the primary sequential phases in the information processing cycle in the order in which they usually are accomplished, viz: (1) collecting raw data, (2) analyzing transactions, (3) recording transactions in the **journal,** (4) transferring data from the journal to the **ledger,** (5) preparing a **trial balance,** and (6) preparing the required **financial statements.**

PHASE 1—COLLECTING RAW DATA

The initial phase in the accounting information processing cycle is the collection of raw economic data on each transaction affecting the entity.[7] Such economic data are collected continuously throughout the accounting period as transactions

---

[7] Recall that transactions include *(a)* events that involve an exchange between two or more separate entities (or persons) and *(b)* events that are not between entities but nevertheless have a particular economic impact on the entity being accounted for.

occur. Transactions involving **external** parties usually generate **source documents** that provide essential data. Examples are sales invoices, cash register tapes, purchase invoices, and signed receipts. Documentation must be generated **internally** for certain economic effects such as depreciation and the using up of office supplies already on hand. It is important to realize that most of the raw data (and the supporting documents) entered into an accounting system are not generated by the accounting function but through the various **operating** functions of the business. The quality of the **outputs** of an information processing system is determined primarily by the quality (and timeliness) of the inputs of raw data based on transactions; therefore, a carefully designed and controlled data collection system is essential. Thus, the initial data collection procedure constitutes an integral and important subsystem of an accounting information processing system.

PHASE 2—ANALYZING TRANSACTIONS

This phase in the accounting information processing system was explained and illustrated in Exhibit 3–4. Recall that the objective of this mental process is determination of the **economic effects** on the entity of each transaction in terms of the basic accounting model: Assets = Liabilities + Owners' Equity. When transaction analysis is completed, the economic effects of the transactions analyzed are then entered **formally** into the accounting system.

PHASE 3—RECORDING TRANSACTIONS IN THE JOURNAL

After transaction analysis, the economic effect of each transaction is **formally** entered into the accounting system in a record known as the **journal.**

In a simple situation, the transactions of a business entity could be recorded directly in the separate accounts. However, in more complex situations, it is essential that the economic effects of each transaction on the accounting model be recorded in one place in **chronological order** (i.e., in order of date of occurrence). The accounting record designed for this particular purpose is known as the **journal.** Typically, the dual effects are recorded first in the journal and later are transferred, or posted, to the appropriate accounts (refer to the various "entry summaries" and T-accounts used for Bass Cleaners in Exhibit 3–4).

The journal contains a chronological listing of each entry for all of the transactions. The **format** of the entry in the journal for each transaction is designed to facilitate posting and so that the dual effects on the accounting model and the debit and credit features are linked physically. For example, in Exhibit 3–4, transaction *(a)* for Bass Cleaners would appear in the journal in the following format

		Debit	*Credit*
(Date)	Cash	20,000	
	Capital stock		20,000
	To record investment of cash by owners.		

in which the **debit always is listed first and the credit is listed last and indented** for each identification.

Observe that for instructional purposes, in Exhibit 3–4, this same format was used to summarize the required entry for each transaction. The physical linking of the dual effects of each transaction in the journal is in contrast to the separate accounts, where each transaction is separated physically between two or more accounts. For example, you will recall (Exhibit 3–4) that the dual effect of the above entry for Bass Cleaners would appear in separate accounts as follows:

Cash				Capital Stock	
(Date)	20,000			(Date)	20,000

The **journal,** is the place of original (or first) entry of the dual economic effects of each transaction and, as a result, also it is known as **the book of original entry.** The journal serves three useful purposes:

1. It provides for the initial and orderly listing (by date) of each transaction immediately after the transaction is subjected to transaction analysis.
2. It provides a single place to record the dual economic effects of each transaction without any further subclassifications of the data.
3. It facilitates later tracing; checking for possible errors; and reconstruction of a transaction, its analysis, and its recording.

Knowledge of the approximate date of a transaction very often is used in these activities; the journal is the only place in the accounting system where the dual economic effects of each entry are linked physically and recorded chronologically.

To increase your understanding, let's see how the journal is used in a manually maintained system. The first three transactions for Bass Cleaners have been entered in a typical journal shown in Exhibit 3–5. Recording the transactions in the journal in this manner is known as **journalizing,** and the entries made are called **journal entries.** In summary, you should observe in particular that (1) each transaction and event is first recorded in the journal as a separate entry; (2) each entry in the journal is dated, and entries are recorded in chronological order; (3) for each transaction, the debits (accounts and amounts) are entered first, the credits follow and are indented; and (4) as a consequence, for each transaction, the effects on the accounting model and the debits and credits are linked in one entry. These features provide an "audit or tracing trail" that facilitates subsequent examination of past transactions and assists in the location of errors. The journal also is designed to simplify subsequent accounting (as will be demonstrated later).

PHASE 4—POSTING TO THE LEDGER

In the preceding illustration for Bass Cleaners (pages 102 through 110), a **separate account** was set up for each kind of asset, liability, and owners' equity. An accounting system typically will contain a large number of such accounts. Collectively, the accounts are contained in a record known as the **ledger.** The ledger may be organized in numerous ways. Handwritten accounting systems

EXHIBIT 3–5
Journal illustrated

Date	Account Titles and Explanation	Folio	Debit	Credit
Jan. 1	Cash	101	20,000	
	Capital stock	301		20,000
	Investment of cash by owners			
Jan. 3	Cash	101	5,000	
	Note payable	202		5,000
	Borrowed cash on 12% note			
Jan. 6	Delivery truck	111	8,000	
	Cash	101		8,000
	Purchased delivery			
	truck for use in			
	the business			

Journal — Page 1

may use a loose-leaf ledger—one page for each account. In the case of a "machine" accounting system, a separate machine card is maintained for each account. In the case of a computerized accounting system, the ledger is maintained on magnetic tape or similar electronic storage devices, but there are still separate accounts as in the other systems. Each account also is identified by name as well as by an assigned number.

Exhibit 3–6 shows the ledger for Bass Cleaners in handwritten T-account format. The ledger (i.e., the accounts contained in it) contains information that first was recorded in the journal and then transferred, or **posted,** to the appropriate accounts in the ledger. This transfer from the chronological arrangement in the journal to the account format in the ledger is a very important reclassification of the data because the ledger reflects the data classified (by separate accounts) as assets, liabilities, and owners' equity rather than chronologically.

A business using a manual handwritten system typically will record the transactions in the journal each day and **post** to the ledger less frequently, say, every few days. Of course, the timing of these **information processing activities** varies with the size and complexity of the entity.

The T-account format as illustrated on pages 99 and 101, and in Exhibit 3–6 is useful for instructional purposes. However, the typical account format used is **columnar** as illustrated in Exhibit 3–7. It maintains the debit-credit concept but is arranged to provide columns for date, explanation, folio (F), and running balances.

To post, the debits and credits reflected in the journal entries are transferred

EXHIBIT 3–6
Ledger Illustrated
(T-accounts)

BASS CLEANERS, INC.
LEDGER at December 31, 19A

ASSETS	=	LIABILITIES	+	OWNERS' EQUITY

Cash

(a)	20,000	(c)	8,000
(b)	5,000	(f)	25,800
(d)	40,000	(h)	600
(k)	1,000	(j)	1,800
		(l)	500

(Net debit balance, $29,300)

Notes Payable

	(b)	5,000

Capital Stock

	(a)	20,000

Retained Earnings*
2

(j)	1,800	

Accounts Receivable

(e)	4,000	(k)	1,000

(Net debit balance, $3,000)

Accounts Payable

(l)	500	(g)	2,000

(Net credit balance, $1,500)

Cleaning Revenue

	(d)	40,000
	(e)	4,000

(Net credit balance, $44,000)

Delivery Truck

(c)	8,000

Operating Expenses

(f)	25,800
(g)	2,000
(i)	1,600

(Net debit balance, $29,400)

Accumulated Depreciation Delivery Truck†

	(i)	1,600

Interest Expense

(h)	600

Totals	$38,700	=	$6,500	+	$32,200

Note: The accounting model, Assets = Liabilities + Owner's Equity, given at the top of this exhibit and the totals at the bottom are shown only for your convenience in study; they would not appear in an actual ledger.

* Retained Earnings is an owner's equity account that reports accumulated earnings minus dividends paid to date. Dividends paid reduce cash and owners' equity (see Chapter 12). Dividends paid is a distribution to owners— not an expense because it does not contribute to earning revenue.

† The delivery truck is depreciated over a five-year period because that is its estimated useful life to Bass Cleaners. Depreciation refers to the "wearing out" of the truck due to use. The truck is assumed to wear out at a steady rate each year throughout its life; therefore, the annual depreciation is $8,000 ÷ 5 years = $1,600. This amount is recorded in an account called Accumulated depreciation; it is a negative, or contra, account to the Delivery Truck account. The $1,600 also is an expense for the year. For further explanation of depreciation, see Chapter 9.

EXHIBIT 3–7
Ledger account in columnar format illustrated

Date	Explanation	F	Debit	Credit	Balance
Jan. 1	Investments	1	20,000		20,000
3	Borrowing	3	5,000		25,000
6	Truck purchased	3		8,000	17,000
7	Cleaning revenue	4	40,000		57,000
8	Operating expenses	4		25,800	31,200
10	Interest expense	5		600	30,600
15	Payments to owners	7		1,800	28,800
16	Collections on receivables	8	1,000		29,800
17	Payments on accounts payable	8		500	29,300

Account Title __Cash__   Account Number __101__

directly as debits and credits to the indicated accounts in the ledger. In both the journal (Exhibit 3–5) and ledger (as in the Cash account, in Exhibit 3–6 or as in Exhibit 3–7), you can observe that there is a "folio" column, which is included to provide a numerical **cross-reference** between the journal and the ledger (this cross-reference often is said "to provide an audit trail"). For example, the journal shown in Exhibit 3–5 shows a folio number of 101 for Cash, which indicates the account in the ledger to which that amount was posted. You will recall that this is the account number assigned to cash in Exhibit 3–3. Similarly, if you look at the ledger account for Cash, as shown in Exhibit 3–7, you will observe on the first line of the account the folio number 1, which indicates that the particular amount posted came from page 1 of the journal. Folio numbers are entered during the **posting** process; therefore, the folio numbers indicate whether posting has been accomplished. Transferring amounts from the journal to the ledger is called **posting.** The data ends up in the ledger; therefore, it sometimes is referred to as the **book of final entry.**

PHASE 5—THE TRIAL BALANCE

At the end of the accounting period, in order to verify recording accuracy, and for subsequent processing uses, a **trial balance** is prepared directly from the ledger. A trial balance simply is a listing, in ledger account order, of the ledger **accounts** and their respective net **ending** debit or credit **balances.** The ending balance shown for each account is the difference between the total of the debits and the total of the credits in the account. Exhibit 3–8 shows the

EXHIBIT 3–8
Trial balance
illustrated

BASS CLEANERS, INC.
Trial Balance
December 31, 19A

	Balance	
Account titles	*Debit*	*Credit*
Cash	$29,300	
Accounts receivable	3,000	
Delivery truck	8,000	
Accumulated depreciation, delivery truck.....		$1,600
Notes payable		5,000
Accounts payable		1,500
Capital stock (800 shares)		20,000
Retained earnings (explained later)	1,800	
Cleaning revenues		44,000
Operating expenses.......................	29,400	
Interest expense.........................	600	
Totals...........................	$72,100	$72,100

trial balance of Bass Cleaners at December 31, 19A. It was prepared directly from the ledger accounts given in Exhibit 3–6.

A trial balance serves two purposes in the accounting information processing cycle:

1. It provides a check on the equality of the debits and credits as reflected in the ledger accounts at the end of the period (or whenever taken).
2. It provides financial data in a convenient form for preparation of the financial statements.

PHASE 6—FINANCIAL STATEMENTS

At the end of the accounting period, several phases of the accounting process will be complete, viz: (1) all transactions for the period will have been analyzed and entered in the journal in chronological order, (2) all amounts in the journal will have been posted (transferred) to the ledger accounts, and (3) a trial balance will have been prepared from the ledger.

The next phase is preparation of the three required financial statements that were discussed and illustrated in Chapters 1 and 2. The trial balance provides the basic data needed to prepare the financial statements at the end of the accounting period. The income statement and balance sheet for Bass Cleaners, prepared from the trial balance shown in Exhibit 3–8, were illustrated in Exhibit 3–2.

The demonstration case that follows should be studied carefully because it provides a summary of the six phases of the accounting processes discussed in this chapter. A good understanding of the accounting process is necessary before you study the subsequent chapters.

DEMONSTRATION CASE—THE ACCOUNTING INFORMATION PROCESSING SYSTEM

We have selected this case of a small business to demonstrate the complete **accounting information processing cycle** from the initial capture of the raw economic data to the financial statements developed at the end of the accounting year. Only representative and summary transactions have been selected to keep the length of the case within reason. Small amounts are used to simplify the illustration. You should study each step in the accompanying solution carefully because it reviews the concepts, principles, and procedures introduced in Chapters 1–3.

On January 3, 19A, M. Hall and P. Garza organized a corporation to build and operate an apartment complex called La Paloma. At the start, each one invested $40,000 cash and in turn received 3,000 shares of $10 par value stock. Therefore, on that date the following entry was recorded in the journal:

January 3, 19A:

Cash	80,000	
Capital stock, par $10 (6,000 shares)		60,000
Contributed capital in excess of par		20,000

Shortly thereafter, land was acquired for $30,000 and a construction contract was signed with a builder. The first apartments were rented on July 1, 19B. The owners decided to use a **fiscal year** of July 1 through June 30 for business purposes (instead of a fiscal year which agrees with the calendar year).

It now is July 1, 19C, the beginning of the second year of rental operations; therefore, certain accounts in the ledger will have balances carried over from the prior fiscal year ended June 30, 19C. A complete list of the accounts in the ledger that will be needed for this case, with the balances carried over from the previous fiscal year, is given in Exhibit 3–9. Ledger account (folio) numbers are provided at the left.

Typical transactions (most of them summarized) for the 12-month fiscal year—July 1, 19C, through June 30, 19D—are listed below. To facilitate tracing, instead of using dates, we will use the letter notation to the left of each transaction.

   a. On November 1, 19C, paid $3,000 cash for a two-year casualty insurance policy covering the building, its contents, and liability coverage.

   b. Rental revenue earned: collected in cash, $105,500; and uncollected by June 30, 19D, $2,000.

   c. Paid accounts payable (amount owed from the prior year for expenses), $6,000.

   d. Purchased a tract of land, at a cost of $35,000, as a planned site for another apartment complex to be constructed in "about three years." Cash of $5,000 was paid, and a long-term note payable (12 percent interest per annum, interest payable each six months) was signed for the balance of $30,000.

EXHIBIT 3–9
**Trial balance for
demonstration case**

LA PALOMA APARTMENTS
Ledger Balances
July 1, 19C (start of Year 2 of rental operations)

Account No.	Account titles	Balance Debit	Balance Credit
101	Cash	$ 18,000	
103	Accounts receivable (or rent receivable)		
105	Supplies inventory	2,000	
112	Prepaid insurance		
121	Land (apartment site)...................................	30,000	
122	La Paloma apartment building	200,000	
123	Accumulated depreciation, apartment building...............		$ 10,000
125	Furniture and fixtures	60,000	
126	Accumulated depreciation, furniture and fixtures		12,000
131	Land for future apartment site...........................		
201	Accounts payable		6,000
202	Property taxes payable		
203	Income taxes payable...................................		
204	Mortgage payable, 10% (apartment building)...............		180,000
205	Note payable, long term, 12%		
301	Capital stock (par $10, 6,000 shares)		60,000
302	Contributed capital in excess of par		20,000
303	Retained earnings (accumulated earnings to June 30, 19C).....		22,000
401	Rent revenue..		
521	Utilities and telephone expense		
522	Apartment maintenance expense		
523	Salary and wage expense		
524	Insurance expense		
525	Property tax expense		
526	Depreciation expense		
527	Miscellaneous expenses		
531	Interest expense		
532	Income tax expense		
	Totals	$310,000	$310,000

e. Operating expenses incurred and paid in cash were:

Utilities and telephone expense	$23,360
Apartment maintenance expense	1,200
Salary and wage expense	6,000

f. At the end of the fiscal year (June 30, 19D), the following bills for expenses incurred had not been recorded or paid: June telephone bill, $40; and miscellaneous expense, $100.

g. Paid interest for six months on the long-term note at 12 percent per annum. (Refer to item [d].) (Hint: Interest = Principal × Rate × Time.)

h. An inventory count at the end of the fiscal period, June 30, 19D, showed remaining supplies on hand amounting to $400. Supplies used are considered a miscellaneous expense.

i. By the end of the fiscal period, June 30, 19D, one third (8 months out of 24 months) of the prepaid insurance premium of $3,000 paid in transaction (a) had expired because of passage of time.

j. Depreciation expense for the year was based on an estimated useful life of 20 years for the apartment and 5 years for the furniture and fixtures (assume no residual or salvage value). ·

k. The property taxes for the year ending June 30, 19D, in the amount of $2,700 have not been recorded or paid.

l. Cash payment at year-end on the mortgage on the apartment was:

On principal................	$20,000
Interest ($180,000 × 10%).....	18,000
Total paid	$38,000

m. Income tax expense for the year ending June 30, 19D, was computed to be $5,940 (i.e., a 20 percent average rate). Assume that this obligation will be paid in the next period.

Required:

Complete the accounting information processing cycle by solving each of the following:

1. Set up a ledger with T-accounts that includes all of the accounts listed on the trial balance given in Exhibit 3–9; include the account numbers as given. Enter the July 1, 19C, balances in each account in this manner:

Cash		101
Balance	18,000	

2. Analyze, then **journalize** (i.e., enter in the journal), each transaction listed above for the period July 1, 19C, through June 30, 19D. Number the journal pages consecutively starting with 1.

3. **Post** all entries from the journal to the ledger; use the folio columns for account numbers.

4. **Prepare** a trial balance at June 30, 19D.

5. **Prepare** an income statement for the fiscal year ending June 30, 19D.

6. Prepare a balance sheet at June 30, 19D.

Suggested solution

Requirement 1—Ledger (see pages 121 and 122):

Requirement 2—Journal:

JOURNAL   Page 1

Date	Account Titles and Explanation	Folio	Debit	Credit
a.	Prepaid insurance	112	3,000	
	Cash	101		3,000
	Paid insurance premium for two years in advance.			
	(Explanatory note: An asset account, Prepaid Insurance, is debited because a future service, insurance coverage, is being paid for in advance.)			
b.	Cash	101	105,500	
	Accounts receivable (or rent receivable)	103	2,000	
	Rent revenue	401		107,500
	To record rent revenues earned for the year, of which $2,000 has not yet been collected.			
c.	Accounts payable	201	6,000	
	Cash	101		6,000
	Paid a debt carried over from previous year.			
d.	Land for future apartment site	131	35,000	
	Cash	101		5,000
	Note payable, long term (12%)	205		30,000
	Purchased land as a site for future apartment complex. (This is a second tract of land acquired; the present apartment building was constructed on the first tract.)			
e.	Utilities and telephone expense	521	23,360	
	Apartment maintenance expense	522	1,200	
	Salary and wage expense	523	6,000	
	Cash	101		30,560
	Paid current expenses.			
f.	Utilities and telephone expense	521	40	
	Miscellaneous expenses	527	100	
	Accounts payable	201		140
	Expenses incurred, not yet paid.			

Requirement 2 (continued):

JOURNAL

Page 2

Date	Account Titles and Explanation	Folio	Debit	Credit
g.	Interest expense	531	1,800	
	Cash	101		1,800
	Paid six months' interest on a long-term note ($30,000 × 12% × 6/12 = $1,800).			
h.	Miscellaneous expenses	527	1,600	
	Supplies inventory	105		1,600
	To record as expense supplies used from inventory during the year.			
	(Explanatory note: Supplies are bought in advance of use; hence, at that time they are recorded as an asset, Supplies Inventory. As the supplies are used from inventory, the asset thus used becomes an expense. Refer to Supplies Inventory account [$2,000 − $400 = $1,600].)			
i.	Insurance expense	524	1,000	
	Prepaid insurance	112		1,000
	To record as an expense the cost of the insurance that expired ($3,000 × 8/24 = $1,000).			
j.	Depreciation expense	526	22,000	
	Accumulated depreciation, apartment building	123		10,000
	Accumulated depreciation, furniture and fixtures	126		12,000
	Depreciation expense for one year.			
	Computation: Apartment: $200,000 ÷ 20 years = $10,000. Furniture and fixtures: $60,000 ÷ 5 years = $12,000.			
k.	Property tax expense	525	2,700	
	Property taxes payable	202		2,700
	Property taxes for the current year, not yet paid.			
l.	Mortgage payable (10%)	204	20,000	
	Interest expense	531	18,000	
	Cash	101		38,000
	Payments on principal of mortgage payable plus interest expense.			
m.	Income tax expense	532	5,940	
	Income tax payable	203		5,940
	Income tax for the year; payable later.			

Requirements 1 and 3—Ledger:

LEDGER

Cash					101		Furniture and Fixtures					125
Date	F	Amount	Date	F	Amount	Date	F	Amount	Date	F	Amount
Balance		18,000	(a)	1	3,000	Balance		60,000			
(b)	1	105,500	(c)	1	6,000						
			(d)	1	5,000						
			(e)	1	30,560						
			(g)	2	1,800						
			(l)	2	38,000						

(Net debit balance, $39,140)

Accumulated Depreciation, Furniture and Fixtures					126
			Balance		12,000
			(j)	2	12,000

Accounts Receivable					103
(b)	1	2,000			

Supplies Inventory					105		Land for Future Apartment Site					131
Balance		2,000	(h)	2	1,600	(d)	1	35,000			

Prepaid Insurance					112		Accounts Payable					201
(a)	1	3,000	(i)	2	1,000	(c)	1	6,000	Balance		6,000
									(f)	1	140

Land (Apartment Site)					121		Property Taxes Payable					202
Balance		30,000							(k)	2	2,700

La Paloma Apartment Building					122		Income Taxes Payable					203
Balance		200,000							(m)	2	5,940

Accumulated Depreciation, Apartment Building					123		Mortgage Payable (10%) (apartment building)					204
			Balance		10,000	(l)	2	20,000	Balance		180,000
			(j)	2	10,000						

Requirements 1 and 3 (continued):

Notes Payable, Long Term (12%) 205						
Date	F	Amount	Date		F	Amount
			(d)		1	30,000

Capital Stock 301				
		Balance		60,000

Contributed Capital in Excess of Par 302				
		Balance		20,000

Retained Earnings 303				
		Balance		22,000

Rent Revenue 401				
		(b)	1	107,500

Utilities and Telephone Expense 521		
(e)	1	23,360
(f)	1	40

Apartment Maintenance Expense 522		
(e)	1	1,200

Salary and Wage Expense 523		
(e)	1	6,000

Insurance Expense 524						
Date		F	Amount	Date	F	Amount
(i)		2	1,000			

Property Tax Expense 525		
(k)	2	2,700

Depreciation Expense 526		
(j)	2	22,000

Miscellaneous Expenses 527		
(f)	1	100
(h)	2	1,600

Interest Expense 531		
(g)	2	1,800
(l)	2	18,000

Income Tax Expense 532		
(m)	2	5,940

Requirement 4:

LA PALOMA APARTMENTS
Trial Balance
June 30, 19D

Account No.	Account titles	Debit	Credit
101	Cash	$ 39,140	
103	Accounts receivable (or Rent receivable)	2,000	
105	Supplies inventory	400	
112	Prepaid insurance (16 months)	2,000	
121	Land (apartment site)	30,000	
122	La Paloma apartment building	200,000	
123	Accumulated depreciation, apartment building		$ 20,000
125	Furniture and fixtures	60,000	
126	Accumulated depreciation, furniture and fixtures		24,000
131	Land for future apartment site	35,000	
201	Accounts payable		140
202	Property taxes payable		2,700
203	Income taxes payable		5,940
204	Mortgage payable (10%) (apartment building)		160,000
205	Note payable, long term (12%)		30,000
301	Capital stock (par $10, 6,000 shares)		60,000
302	Contributed capital in excess of par		20,000
303	Retained earnings (accumulated earnings to June 30, 19C)		22,000
401	Rent revenue		107,500
521	Utilities and telephone expense	23,400	
522	Apartment maintenance expense	1,200	
523	Salary and wage expense	6,000	
524	Insurance expense	1,000	
525	Property tax expense	2,700	
526	Depreciation expense	22,000	
527	Miscellaneous expenses	1,700	
531	Interest expense	19,800	
532	Income tax expense	5,940	
	Totals	$452,280	$452,280

Requirement 5:

LA PALOMA APARTMENTS
Income Statement
For the Year Ended June 30, 19D

Revenue:		
Rent revenue		$107,500*
Operating expenses:		
Utilities and telephone expense	$23,400	
Apartment maintenance expense	1,200	
Salary and wage expense	6,000	
Insurance expense	1,000	
Property tax expense	2,700	
Depreciation expense	22,000	
Miscellaneous expenses	1,700	
Total operating expenses		58,000
Income from apartment operations		49,500
Financial expense:		
Interest expense		19,800
Pretax income		29,700
Income tax expense		5,940
Net income		$ 23,760
EPS ($23,760 ÷ 6,000 shares)		$3.96

* Notes:
 a. These amounts were taken directly from Requirement 4, the trial balance.
 b. No products are sold by this business; therefore, gross margin cannot be reported.

Requirement 6:

LA PALOMA APARTMENTS
Balance Sheet
At June 30, 19D

Assets

Current assets:			
Cash		$ 39,140*	
Accounts receivable...................................		2,000	
Supplies inventory		400	
Prepaid insurance		2,000	
Total current assets			$ 43,540
Operational assets:			
Land (apartment site)		30,000	
La Paloma apartment building	$200,000		
Less: Accumulated depreciation, building	20,000	180,000	
Furniture and fixtures.................................	60,000		
Less: Accumulated depreciation, furniture and			
fixtures	24,000	36,000	
Total operational assets			246,000
Other assets:			
Land acquired for future apartment site†			35,000
Total assets			$324,540

Liabilities

Current liabilities:
Accounts payable	140	
Property taxes payable	2,700	
Income taxes payable	5,940	
Total current liabilities		$ 8,780

Long-term liabilities:
Mortgage payable	160,000	
Note payable, long term	30,000	
Total long-term liabilities		190,000
Total liabilities		198,780

Stockholders' Equity

Contributed capital:
Capital stock, par $10 (6,000 shares)	60,000	
Contributed capital in excess of par	20,000	
Total contributed capital	80,000	
Retained earnings (beginning balance $22,000 +		
net income $23,760)	45,760	
Total stockholders' equity		125,760
Total liabilities and stockholders' equity		$324,540

    * These amounts were taken directly from Requirement 4, the trial balance.

    † Classified as "other" rather than "operational" because this land is not being used currently for operating purposes.

SUMMARY OF CHAPTER

This chapter discussed the **fundamental accounting model** and the six phases of the accounting process. You studied the nature of transactions that provide the raw economic data that are entered into the accounting information system. You learned that the fundamental accounting model—Assets = Liabilities + Owners' Equity—provides the basic framework for transaction analysis and the recording of the dual effect of each transaction. The accounting model encompasses two balancing features that must be met with respect to each transaction and event recorded, viz: (1) assets must equal liabilities plus owners' equity and (2) debits must equal credits. After transaction analysis, the dual effects of each transaction are recorded first in the journal and then are posted to the ledger. The journal provides a chronological record of the transactions, and the ledger reflects a **separate** account for each kind of asset, liability, and owners' equity. Normally, asset accounts will have debit balances, whereas liability accounts will have credit balances. Owners' equity accounts normally will show credits for the capital stock and retained earnings accounts—expenses will show debit balances, and revenues will show credit balances. The accounting information processing system accumulates the financial data needed to develop the periodic financial statements: the income statement, balance sheet, and statement of changes in financial position (SCFP).

This chapter also discussed and illustrated the **accounting information processing cycle** for a business entity. It represents a cycle because it is **repeated** each accounting period (usually one year). The sequential phases in the information processing cycle may be outlined as follows:

Phase 1: **Collecting raw data**—Economic data are collected for each transaction at the time of occurrence. Sales invoices, charge tickets, freight bills, notes, signed receipts, and so on, are source documents collected in this step.

Phase 2: **Analyzing transactions**—Each transaction undergoes transaction analysis to determine how it affects the fundamental accounting model: Assets = Liabilities + Owners' Equity.

Phase 3: **Journalizing**—Each transaction is recorded **chronologically** in the journal, which indicates the date, account titles to be debited and credited, the related amounts, and an explanation.

EXHIBIT 3–10
Sequential phases of an accounting information system

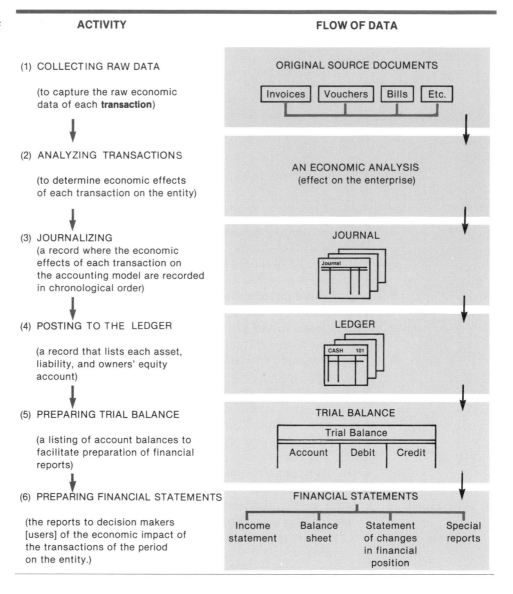

ACTIVITY	FLOW OF DATA
(1) COLLECTING RAW DATA (to capture the raw economic data of each **transaction**)	ORIGINAL SOURCE DOCUMENTS Invoices Vouchers Bills Etc.
(2) ANALYZING TRANSACTIONS (to determine economic effects of each transaction on the entity)	AN ECONOMIC ANALYSIS (effect on the enterprise)
(3) JOURNALIZING (a record where the economic effects of each transaction on the accounting model are recorded in chronological order)	JOURNAL Journal
(4) POSTING TO THE LEDGER (a record that lists each asset, liability, and owners' equity account)	LEDGER CASH 101
(5) PREPARING TRIAL BALANCE (a listing of account balances to facilitate preparation of financial reports)	TRIAL BALANCE Trial Balance Account | Debit | Credit
(6) PREPARING FINANCIAL STATEMENTS (the reports to decision makers [users] of the economic impact of the transactions of the period on the entity.)	FINANCIAL STATEMENTS Income statement Balance sheet Statement of changes in financial position Special reports

Phase 4: **Posting**—Each amount entered in the journal is transferred, or posted, to the appropriate account in the ledger.

Phase 5: **Preparing trial balance**—At the end of the accounting period, the balance in each account (i.e., the net debit or credit balance) in the ledger is determined. The balance of each ledger account then is listed on a trial balance. The equality of debits and credits also is checked.

Phase 6: **Preparing financial statements**—The information on the trial balance is used to develop the periodic financial statements composed of the income statement, balance sheet, and statement of changes in financial position.

The above cycle also is presented in graphic format for study purposes in Exhibit 3–10. As we progress in our study, additions to and elaborations of this information processing cycle will be introduced.

IMPORTANT TERMS DEFINED IN THIS CHAPTER

Terms (alphabetically)	Key words in definitions of important terms used in chapter	Page reference
Accounting information processing cycle	Accounting information; sequential phases (steps); transactions to financial statements.	109
Accrual accounting	Revenues and expenses; measured and reported; on transaction date; not cash basis.	102
Analyzing transactions	Assessment of economic effects of each transaction on the entity.	102
Credit	Algebraic balancing feature; "right side" of T-account; decreases assets; increases liabilities and owners' equity.	101
Debit	"Left side" of T-account; increases assets; decreases liabilities and owners' equity.	101
Fundamental accounting model	Asset = Liabilities + Owners' Equity.	76
Journal	Record transactions; journalizing; chronological order.	110
Journalizing	Recording in the journal; original entry.	111
Ledger	Separate accounts for each revenue, expense, asset, liability, and owners' equity.	111
Posting	Transferring data from journal to ledger.	114
Source documents	Transaction documents; sales invoices.	109
Trial balance	List of accounts; account balances; equality check.	114

QUESTIONS FOR DISCUSSION

PART A

1. Define a business transaction. Why does accounting focus on each business transaction?

2. Give the fundamental accounting model and briefly explain each variable included in it, including revenues, expenses, and investments and withdrawals by owners.

3. Explain why revenues increase and expenses decrease owners' equity.

4. What is the meaning of "to debit" and "to credit"?

5. Complete the following matrix by entering either debit or credit in each cell.

Item	Increases	Decreases
Assets		
Liabilities		
Owners' equity		
Revenues		
Expenses		

6. Complete the following matrix by entering either increase or decrease in each cell.

Item	Debit	Credit
Assets		
Liabilities		
Owners' equity		
Revenues		
Expenses		

PART B

7. Briefly explain what is meant by transaction analysis.

8. Define the journal. What purposes does it serve?

9. Define the ledger. What purpose does it serve?

10. Distinguish between journalizing and posting.

11. What is the purpose of the folio notations in the journal and in the ledger accounts?

12. What is a trial balance? What purposes does it serve?

13. What does the term audit trail imply?

14. Define what is meant by fiscal period as used in accounting.

15. Briefly outline the accounting information processing system for a business.

EXERCISES

PART A

E3–1. Friday Corporation has been operating for one year, 19A. At the end of 19A, the financial statements have been prepared. Below are a series of separate and independent cases based on the 19A financial statements. For each independent case, and the financial relationship it addresses, you are to supply the missing item and its amount.

Case	Data	Missing	
		Item	Amount
Example	Assets, $70,000; owners' equity, $30,000	Liabilities	$40,000
A	Revenues, $100,000; expenses, $62,000		
B	Liabilities, $30,000; owners' equity, $50,000		
C	Cash inflows, $8,000; increase in cash, $20,000		
D	Liabilities, $42,000; assets, $81,000		
E	Net income, $35,000; expenses, $63,000		
F	Net income, $20,000; revenues, $93,000		
G	Expenses, $80,000; revenues, $80,000		
H	Revenues, $80,000; expenses, $90,000		
I	Increase in cash, $18,000; cash outflows, $60,000		
J	Cash outflows, $60,000; cash inflows, $40,000		

E3–2. During its first week of operations, January 1–7, Small Retail Company completed eight transactions, the effects of which are indicated in the dollar amounts given below.

Required:

a. You are to give a brief explanation of each transaction. Assume each transaction stands alone, but may be related to prior transactions unless specifically stated otherwise. Also, if alternate explanations are possible, explain each. Decreases are in parenthesis.

Item	Each Transaction Effect								Ending Balance
	1	2	3	4	5	6	7	8	
Cash	$10,000	$15,000	$(4,000)	$80,000	$(9,000)	$(50,000)	$(11,000)	$ 7,000	$38,000
Accounts receivable				10,000				(7,000)	3,000
Store fixtures					9,000				9,000
Land			12,000						12,000
Accounts payable						20,000	(11,000)		9,000
Notes payable		15,000	8,000						23,000
Capital stock	10,000								10,000
Revenues				90,000					90,000
Expenses						70,000			70,000

b. Based only upon the above tabulation of the effects of each of the eight transactions, provide the following amounts at the end of the week (show computations):

Total assets _____ $ 62,000
Total liabilities _____ $ 32,000
Total owners' equity _____ $ _____
Income _____ $ _____
Proof of owners' equity _____ $ _____

E3–3. For each transaction below indicate the effect upon assets, liabilities, and owners' equity by entering a plus for increase and a minus for decrease.

Transaction	Effect Upon		
	Assets	Liabilities	Owners' Equity
a. Issued stock to organizers for cash.			
b. Borrowed cash from local bank.			
c. Purchased equipment on credit.			
d. Earned revenue, collected cash.			
e. Incurred expenses, on credit.			
f. Earned revenue, on credit.			
g. Paid cash for *(e)*.			
h. Incurred expenses, paid cash.			
i. Earned revenue, collected three fourths cash, balance on credit.			
j. Theft of $100 cash.			
k. Declared and paid cash dividends.			
l. Collected cash for *(f)*.			
m. Depreciated equipment for the period.			
n. Incurred expenses, paid four fifths cash, balance on credit.			
o. Paid income tax expense for the period.			

E3–4. Jiffy Service Company, Inc., was organized by four investors. The following transactions were completed:

a. The investors paid in $40,000 cash to start the business. Each one was issued 1,000 shares of capital stock, par value $10 per share.
b. Equipment for use in the business was purchased at a cost of $8,000, one half was paid in cash and the balance is due in six months.
c. Service fees were earned amounting to $54,000, of which $6,000 was on credit.
d. Operating expenses incurred amounted to $33,000, of which $3,000 was on credit.
e. Cash was collected for $4,000 of the service fees performed on credit in *(c)* above.
f. Paid cash, $2,000, on the operating expenses that were on credit in *(d)* above.
g. Investor A borrowed $10,000 from a local bank and signed a one-year, 10 percent note for that amount.

Required:

Set up a format similar to the following and enter thereon each of the above transactions that should be recorded by Jiffy. Transaction *(a)* is entered as an example.

Transactions	*Assets*	*= Liabilities + Owners' Equity*
a. Investment of cash in the business	Cash + $40,000	Capital stock +$40,000

Also determine the total amounts for assets, liabilities, and owners' equity after completing the recording.

E3–5. The following transactions were completed by Duster Service Company during the year 19X:

1. The organizers paid in cash and in turn received 10,000 shares of capital stock.
2. Duster borrowed cash from the local bank.
3. Duster purchased a delivery truck, paid three fourths cash, and the balance is due in six months.
4. Earned revenues, collected cash in full.
5. Expenses incurred, paid cash in full.

6. Earned revenues, on credit (cash not collected in 19X).
7. Expenses incurred, on credit (cash not paid in 19X).
8. Declared and paid cash dividend to stockholders.
9. Collected half of the amount on credit in 6.
10. Paid all of the credit amount in 7.
11. A spare tire was stolen from the delivery truck (not insured).
12. During the period the delivery truck depreciated ($ amount).

Required:

Below is given a tabulation. For each transaction given above enter in the tabulation a D for debit and a C for credit to reflect the effects on the assets, liabilities, and owners' equity (separate groups are given for owners' equity).

Accounting Model	Transactions											
	1	2	3	4	5	6	7	8	9	10	11	12
a. Assets												
b. Liabilities												
Owners' equity: *c.* Investments												
d. Revenues												
e. Withdrawals												
f. Expenses												

(Note: In some cases there may be both a D and C in the same box.)

E3–6. Snappy Service Company, Inc., was organized and issued 10,000 shares of its capital stock for $30,000 cash. The following transactions occurred during the current accounting period:

a. Received the cash from the organizers.
b. Service fees earned amounted to $35,000, of which $25,000 was collected in cash.
c. Operating expenses incurred amounted to $23,000, of which $17,000 was paid in cash.
d. Bought two machines for operating purposes at the start of the year at a cost of $9,000 each; paid cash.
e. One of the machines was destroyed by fire one week after purchase; it was uninsured. The event to be considered is the fire. (Hint: Set up a fire loss expense account.)
f. The other machine has an estimated useful life to Snappy of 10 years (and no residual value). The event to be considered is the depreciation of the equipment because it was used for one year in rendering services.
g. Stockholder Able bought a vacant lot (land) for $5,000 cash.

Required:

a. Set up appropriate T-accounts and record in them the dual effects on the accounting model of each of the above transactions that should be recorded by Snappy. Key the amounts to the letters starting with (*a*). Number the following accounts consecutively starting with 101 for cash: Cash, Accounts Receivable, Machines, Accumulated

Depreciation, Accounts Payable, Service Fees Earned, Operating Expenses, Fire Loss Expense, Depreciation Expense, and Capital Stock.

b. Complete the following by entering the correct totals:

Assets	$_____
Liabilities	$_____
Owners' equity	$_____
Debits	$_____
Credits	$_____
Net income	$_____

PART B

E3–7. Match the following phases with the brief descriptions of the accounting processing cycle by entering the appropriate letters in the blanks to the left.

Phases of the accounting processing information cycle (sequential order)	*Brief description of phases*
_____ Raw data collection	A. Income statement, balance sheet, SCFP.
_____ Transaction analysis	B. Transfer of amount for each account, affected by the transaction; results in a reclassification of the data.
_____ Journalizing	C. A listing of each account and its debit or credit ending balance; checks debits = credits.
_____ Posting	D. Source documents that underlie each transaction.
_____ Trial balance	E. A chronological record is prepared that reflects the economic effects of each transaction.
_____ Financial statements	F. A careful study of each transaction and determination of its economic effects on the entity.

E3–8. The following T-accounts for Community Service Company, Inc., reflect five different transactions (entries). You are requested to prepare a journal entry for each transaction and write a complete description of each transaction.

Cash				Accounts Payable				Capital Stock, Par $10		
(a)	70,000	(c)	9,000	(e)	1,500	(c)	2,000		(a)	70,000
(b)	20,000	(e)	1,500							
(d)	2,000	(f)	5,000							

Accounts Receivable				Note Payable			Service Revenue		
(b)	4,000	(d)	2,000		(f)	15,000		(b)	24,000

Equipment		Operating Expenses	
(f)	20,000	(c)	11,000

E3–9. On January 1, 19A, Ellen Wood and Hyeok Yi organized the WY Service Company, Inc. The transactions of the company for the first 45 days are summarized below.

Required:

a. You are requested to analyze each transaction and enter it in a journal similar to the one illustrated in Exhibit 3–5.

19A

Jan. 1 Cash invested by the organizers was Wood, $40,000 (for 4,000 shares); and Yi, $30,000 (for 3,000 shares).

3 Paid monthly rent, $1,000.

15 Purchased equipment for use in the business that cost $18,000; paid one third down and signed a 12 percent note payable for the balance. Monthly payments (24) comprised of part principal and part interest are to be paid on the note.

30 Paid cash for operating expenses amounting to $18,000; in addition, operating expenses of $2,000 were incurred on credit.

30 Service fees earned amounted to $40,000, of which $35,000 was collected and the balance was on credit.

Feb. 10 Collected $2,000 on account for service fees previously performed and originally recorded as an account receivable.

12 Paid $1,000 on the operating expenses previously incurred and originally recorded as an account payable.

15 Paid $565 on the equipment note, including $120 interest expense.

b. Compute the amount of income based solely on the above transactions. Also, compute the ending cash balance.

E3–10. Kool Air Conditioning Service Company, Incorporated, has been operating for three years. I. M. Kool, the majority stockholder, built it up from a one-person organization to an operation requiring 10 employees. In the past, few records were maintained; however, Kool now realizes the need for a complete accounting system. The size and complexity of the business is partially indicated by the following selected transactions completed during the first five months of 19E:

Jan. 15 Purchased three new service trucks at $12,000 each; paid a third down and signed a 12 percent one-year, interest-bearing note for the balance. Twelve monthly payments, each including principal and interest, are to be made on the note.

31 Service revenue earned in January amounted to $85,000, which included $5,000 on credit (due in 90 days).

31 Operating expenses incurred in January amounted to $60,000, which included $4,000 on credit (payable in 60 days).

Feb. 5 Dividends declared and paid of $2,000; in cash to the stockholders.

15 Paid $2,132 on the truck note, which included $240 interest.

Apr. 15 Paid 19D taxes on business property, $150; this amount was recorded in 19D as a liability (property taxes payable).

May 1 Collected $4,400 on the services extended on credit in January.

Required:

a. Journalize the above transactions in a form similar to that illustrated in Exhibit 3–5. Number the journal pages consecutively, starting with 51.

b. Post to T-accounts in the ledger; use the folio columns and enter dates. Number the ledger accounts as follows: Cash, 101; Accounts Receivable, 102; Trucks, 103; Accounts Payable, 104; Note Payable, 105; Property Taxes Payable, 106; Retained Earnings, 107; Service Revenue, 108; Operating Expenses, 109; and Interest Expense, 110. As you post, keep in mind that there would be prior amounts carried over from 19D in some of the ledger accounts.

c. Compute the ending balance of cash and the net income, based only on the above transactions.

E3–11. The bookkeeper of Careless Company prepared the following trial balance at December 31, 19B:

Account titles	Debit	Credit
Notes receivable	$ 4,000	
Supplies inventory		$ 200
Accounts payable	800	
Land	16,000	
Capital stock		20,000
Cash	7,045	
Interest revenue	200	
Notes payable		5,000
Operating expenses.....	19,000	
Interest expense		800
Other assets	9,583	
Service revenues		30,583
Total	$56,583	$56,583

An independent CPA (auditor) casually inspected the trial balance and concluded that it contains several errors. You have been requested to draft a correct trial balance and to explain any errors that you discover. All of the amounts are correct except "other assets."

E3–12. Dunn Service Company competes in an industry where the extension of credit to customers is common. For some time after the business was organized by A. D. Dunn and two friends, the only records maintained were for cash receipts and cash payments. Dunn (the company president) stated, "I watched my cash balance to see how I was doing; if cash went up I assumed a profit of that amount, and, to the contrary, if cash went down I assumed a loss." As the company expanded and became involved in more credit, Dunn realized that "I must look at the revenue earned and the expenses incurred on an accrual basis, as well as looking at the cash situation." The following information illustrates the current situation of Dunn Company for the month of January 19B:

Service revenues:
    Cash collected for services performed in January 19B $36,000
    Services performed in January 19B on credit   4,000

Operating expenses:
    Cash paid for expenses incurred in January 19B 17,000
    Expenses incurred in January 19B on credit 25,000

(Disregard income taxes.)

Required:

a. Prepare a special statement to reflect cash inflows, cash outflows, and the change in cash that was caused by the above summarized transactions.
b. Prepare an income statement (accrual basis) to show computation of revenues earned, expenses incurred, and the net income or loss for January 19B.
c. Explain why the cash and accrual results were different.
d. Basically, what does this case suggest as to the inappropriateness of the cash basis to reflect profit performance? Explain and relate to the revenue and matching principles.

PROBLEMS/CASES

PART A

PC3–1. Listed below are the ledger accounts of the AAA Rental Company, Incorporated.

a. Cash.	p. Contributed capital in excess of par.
b. Accounts receivable.	q. Supplies inventory.
c. Common stock.	r. Notes payable, short term.
d. Bonds payable.	s. Retained earnings.
e. Rent revenue.	t. Short-term investments.
f. Prepaid insurance premiums.	u. Other assets.
g. Interest revenue.	v. Operating expenses.
h. Investments, long term.	w. Income taxes payable.
i. Interest expense.	x. Gain on sale of operational assets.
j. Machinery and equipment.	y. Land held for future plant site.
k. Patents.	z. Revenue from investments.
l. Income tax expense.	aa. Wages payable.
m. Property taxes payable.	bb. Accumulated depreciation.
n. Loss on sale of operational assets.	cc. Merchandise inventory.
o. Land, plant site (in use).	

Complete a tabulation similar to the following (enter two check marks for each item above):

			Type of account		Usual balance	
Item	Asset	Liability	Owners' equity (including revenues and expenses)		Debit	Credit
u.	✓		....		✓	
Etc.						

PC3–2. Ready Service Company has been operating for three years. At the end of 19C, the accounting records reflected assets of $320,000 and liabilities of $110,000. During the year 19D, the following summarized transactions were completed:

a. Revenues of $150,000, of which $10,000 was on credit.
b. Issued an additional 1,000 shares of capital stock, par $10 per share, for $10,000 cash.
c. Purchased equipment that cost $15,000, paid cash $10,000, and the balance is due next year.
d. Expenses incurred were $110,500, of which $15,000 was on credit.
e. Collected $8,000 of the credit amount in (a).
f. Declared and paid cash dividends to stockholders of $15,000.
g. Paid $11,000 of the credit amount in (d).
h. Borrowed $10,000 cash, on a 12 percent interest-bearing note, from a local bank (on December 31, 19D), payable June 30, 19E.
i. Cash amounting to $500 was stolen (not covered by insurance).
j. Depreciation on equipment was $1,000 for 19D.

Required:
a. Compute the amounts for assets, liabilities, and owners' equity as of the end of 19D. Use the following format for your response:

	Assets		Liabilities		Owners' Equity	
	Debit	*Credit*	*Debit*	*Credit*	*Debit*	*Credit*
Balances, January 1, 19D						
Transactions:						
a. Revenues						
b. Etc.						
Balances, December 31, 19D						

  b. What was the amount of net income for 19D? Show computations.

  c. What two accounts did you debit for transaction *(a)?* Explain why.

  d. Explain why the dividend declared and paid is not an expense.

PC3–3. Toni Company was organized on January 1, 19A, by J. B. Tory; S. T. Olen; R. R. Neans, and B. T. Irwin. Each organizer invested $8,000 in the company and, in turn, each was issued 8,000 shares of capital stock. To date they are the only stockholders.

During the first quarter (January–March 19A) the company completed the following transactions (summarized and simplified for instructional purposes):

1. Collected a total of $32,000 from the organizers and in turn issued the shares of capital stock.
2. Purchased equipment for use in the business; paid $8,000 cash in full.
3. Purchased land for use in the business; paid $4,000 cash and gave a $6,000, one-year, 12 percent interest-bearing note for the balance.
4. Earned service revenues of $40,000 of which $36,000 was collected in cash, the balance was an open account credit.
5. Incurred $28,000 operating expenses of which $25,000 was paid in cash, the balance was owed on open account credit.
6. In addition, stockholder Tory reported to the company that 500 shares of his Toni stock had been sold and transferred to stockholder Irwin for a cash consideration of $6,000.

Required:

  a. Was Toni Company organized as a sole-proprietorship, a partnership, or a corporation? Explain the basis for your answer.

  b. What was the issue price per share of the capital stock?

  c. The records of the company, during the first quarter, were inadequate. You have been able to prepare the summary of transactions given above. To develop a quick assessment of their economic effects on Toni Company you have decided to complete the tabulation which follows and to use plus (+) for increases and minus (−) for decreases for each transaction.

Item	Transactions—Effects						Ending Amounts
	1	2	3	4	5	6	
Cash	$	$	$	$	$	$	$
Accounts receivable							
Land							
Equipment							
Accounts payable							
Notes payable							
Capital stock							
Service revenues							
Operating expenses							

    d. Did you include the Tory-Irwin transaction in the above tabulation? Why?

    e. Based only upon the completed tabulation above, provide the following amounts (show computations):

        (1) Income for the quarter.

        (2) Total assets at the end of the quarter.

        (3) Total liabilities at the end of the quarter.

        (4) Total owners' equity at the end of the quarter.

        (5) Cash balance at the end of the quarter.

        (6) Net amount of cash inflow from operations, that is, from revenues and expenses combined.

        (7) How much interest must be paid on the note at its maturity date?

PC3–4. SEC Company was organized during January 19A by T. E. Scott, W. D. Evans, and R. L. Cates. On January 20, 19A, the company issued 5,000 shares to each of its organizers. Below is a schedule of the **cumulative** account balances immediately after each of the first 10 transactions.

Accounts	Transactions—Cumulative Balances									
	1	2	3	4	5	6	7	8	9	10
Cash	$75,000	$70,000	$87,000	$77,000	$66,000	$66,000	$70,000	$58,000	$55,000	$54,000
Accounts receivable			8,000	8,000	8,000	11,000	11,000	11,000	11,000	11,000
Office fixtures		20,000	20,000	20,000	20,000	20,000	20,000	20,000	20,000	20,000
Land				14,000	14,000	14,000	14,000	14,000	14,000	14,000
Accounts payable					2,000	2,000	2,000	7,000	4,000	4,000
Notes payable		15,000	15,000	19,000	19,000	19,000	19,000	19,000	19,000	19,000
Capital stock	75,000	75,000	75,000	75,000	75,000	75,000	79,000	79,000	79,000	79,000
Revenues			25,000	25,000	25,000	28,000	28,000	28,000	28,000	28,000
Expenses					13,000	13,000	13,000	30,000	30,000	31,000

Required:

    a. Write a brief explanation of each of the 10 transactions indicated in the above schedule. Assume each transaction stands alone, although some transactions are indirectly related to prior transactions. If alternate transactions are possible explain each.

    b. Based only on the above schedule, provide the following amounts after transaction 10 (show computations):

Income (loss)	$
Total assets	$
Total liabilities	$
Total owners' equity	$
Proof of owners' equity	$
Net cash inflow (outflow) from operations	$

PC3–5. Listed below is a series of accounts for Acme Service Company, Incorporated, which has been operating for three years. These accounts are listed and numbered for identification. Below the accounts is a series of transactions. For each transaction indicate the account(s) to be debited and credited by entering the appropriate account number(s) to the right of each transaction.

1. Cash.
2. Accounts receivable.
3. Supplies inventory.
4. Prepaid insurance.
5. Equipment.
6. Accumulated depreciation, equipment.
7. Patents.
8. Accounts payable.
9. Notes payable.
10. Wages payable.
11. Income tax payable.
12. Capital stock, par $10.
13. Contributed capital in excess of par value.
14. Service revenues.
15. Operating expenses.
16. Income tax expense.
17. Interest expense.
18. None of the above (explain).

Transactions	Debit	Credit
a. Example—Investment by stockholders to start the business; cash was received for stock in excess of the par value.	1	12,13
b. Purchased equipment for use in business; paid half cash and gave note payable for the balance.		
c. Paid cash for salaries and wages.		
d. Collected cash for services performed this period.		
e. Collected cash for services performed last period.		
f. Performed services this period on credit.		
g. Paid operating expenses incurred this period.		
h. Paid cash for operating expenses incurred last period.		
i. Incurred operating expenses this period, to be paid next period.		
j. Purchased supplies for inventory (to be used later); paid cash.		
k. Used some of the supplies from inventory for operations.		
l. Purchased a patent; paid cash.		
m. Made a payment on the equipment note (b) above; the payment was part principal and part interest expense.		
n. Collected cash on accounts receivable for services previously performed.		
o. Paid cash on accounts payable for expenses previously incurred.		
p. Paid three fourths of the income tax expense for the year; the balance to be paid next period.		
q. On last day of current period, paid in cash for an insurance policy covering the next two years.		

PC3–6. Listed below is a series of accounts for Speedo Service Company, Inc. The accounts are numbered for identification.

1. Cash.
2. Accounts receivable.
3. Service supplies inventory.
4. Trucks and equipment.
5. Accumulated depreciation.
10. Accounts payable.
11. Notes payable.
12. Income tax payable.
20. Capital stock, par $10 per share.
21. Contributed capital in excess of par.
25. Service revenues.
26. Operating expenses.

27. Depreciation expense.   29. Income tax expense.
28. Interest expense.   30. None of the above (explain).

During 19X, the company completed the selected transactions given in the tabulation that follows.

Required:

To the right indicate the accounts (by identification number) that should be debited and credited and the respective amounts. The first transaction is used as an example.

Transaction	Debit		Credit	
	Acct. No.	Amount	Acct. No.	Amount
Example: Investment by organizers to start the business, $80,000 cash for 5,000 shares, par $10 per share.	1	80,000	20 21	50,000 30,000
a. Purchased panel truck for use in the business for $12,000; paid one-fourth cash and signed a 10% interest-bearing note for the balance.				
b. Service revenues earned, $120,000 of which $10,000 was on credit.				
c. Operating expenses incurred, $80,000, of which $20,000 was on credit.				
d. Purchased service supplies, $500, paid cash (placed in supplies inventory).				
e. Collected $9,000 of the credit amount in (b).				
f. Paid $13,000 of the credit amount in (c).				
g. Used $300 of the service supplies (taken from inventory) for service operations.				
h. Depreciation on the truck for the year, $2,000.				
i. Paid six months' interest on the note in (a).				
j. Income tax expense for the year, $4,000, paid three-fourths cash, balance payable by April 1 of next year.				

PART B

PC3–7.   The ledger accounts for Mission Real Estate Company, a corporation (organized two years previously), provided the trial balance shown below for the year ended at March 31, 19C (the end of the annual fiscal period).

Trial Balance
At March 31, 19C

Account titles	Debit	Credit
Cash	$ 41,000	
Accounts receivable	53,800	
Office supplies inventory	200	
Automobiles (company cars)	26,000	
Accumulated depreciation, automobiles		$ 12,000
Office equipment	2,000	
Accumulated depreciation, office equipment		1,000
Accounts payable		12,150
Income tax payable		
Salaries and commissions payable		1,000
Notes payable, long term		20,000
Capital stock (par $1; 30,000 shares)		30,000
Contributed capital in excess of par		5,000
Retained earnings (on April 1, 19B)		7,350
Dividends declared and paid during the fiscal year	10,000	
Sales commissions earned		90,000
Management fees earned		8,000
Operating expenses (detail omitted to conserve time)	46,000	
Depreciation expense (on autos and including $333 on office equipment)	6,000	
Interest expense	1,500	
Income tax expense		
Totals	$186,500	$186,500

Required:

a. Prepare an income statement for the year ended March 31, 19C. The above trial balance does not include income taxes. Assume an average tax rate of 30 percent and that the income tax will be paid later. (Hint: EPS is $1.04.)

b. Prepare a balance sheet at March 31, 19C. For both requirements refer to Exhibits 2–1 and 2–2 for examples of the statement formats. (Hint: Total assets, $110,000.)

c. Examine the income statement and develop journal entries that were made for the following:

1. Depreciation expense for the year (automobiles).
2. Income tax expense for the year.
3. Dividends declared and paid during the year.

PC3–8.　Box Home Repair Service was organized two years ago by M. E. Box and three friends. By the end of the second year, three crews were operating and Box (the company president) felt that the business was a success. Although prices charged were high, the customers appeared pleased in view of the quality of the work done and the efficiency with which repairs were completed. The following account balances were reflected by the ledger on January 1, 19B:

Account No.	Account titles	Debit	Credit
101	Cash	$ 6,550	
105	Accounts receivable	3,700	
110	Building supplies inventory (for use on repair jobs)	1,500	
120	Trucks	15,000	
121	Accumulated depreciation on trucks		$ 6,000
200	Accounts payable		3,000
201	Income tax payable		
205	Notes payable, short term		5,000
210	Wages payable		250
220	Note payable, long term		10,000
300	Capital stock, par $1 per share		2,500
400	Service revenue		
501	Operating expenses		
502	Depreciation expense		
503	Interest expense		
504	Income tax expense		
	Totals	$26,750	$26,750

During 19B the following transactions occurred:

a. Paid the $250 wages payable carried over from 19A.

b. Purchased, for cash, additional building supplies for future use, $1,100 (debit the Building Supplies Inventory account).

c. The stockholders' invested an additional $10,000 cash in the business and were issued 10,000 shares of Box capital stock.

d. Purchased an additional truck for $9,500 cash.

e. Collected $2,800 cash on the accounts receivable.

f. Paid the $5,000 short-term note, plus six months' interest at 12 percent per annum.

g. Repair fees earned in 19B, $97,000, which included $7,000 earned in 19B but uncollected (i.e., on credit).

h. Paid operating expenses of $60,000 cash. Additional operating expenses of $4,000 were incurred; the cash will be paid for these in 19C.

i. According to an inventory count of the building supplies at December 31, 19B, unused supplies amounted to $800. (Hint: Supplies used should be debited to Operating Expenses: Supplies used = Amount on hand at start + Additional purchased − Ending inventory.)

j. Depreciation on the three trucks was computed on the basis of an estimated useful life of five years. The new truck will not be depreciated in 19B because it was acquired near the end of the year.

k. Paid $6,000 on the long-term note, plus 12 percent interest on the $10,000 for one year.

l. Paid $5,000 on accounts payable.

m. Income tax expense $5,340 (20 percent rate), all paid in cash.

Required:

1. Set up the ledger accounts listed above and enter the beginning balances; label these as "Balance."

2. Analyze each transaction, then enter it directly in the ledger accounts (you will not need additional accounts). Key your entries with the letter designation (in place of a date). No journal is required; however, it may be helpful to prepare each journal entry on scratch paper before entering it in the ledger.

3. Prepare a trial balance at December 31, 19B. (Hint: Trial balance total, $124,500.)
4. Prepare an income statement. (Hint: EPS, $1.71.)

PC3–9. Fast Stenographic and Mailing Service, Incorporated, was organized by three individuals during January 19A. Each investor paid in $11,000 cash, and each received 1,000 shares of $10 par value stock. During 19A, the transactions listed below occurred. The letters at the left of each item will serve as the date notation.

  a. Received the $33,000 investment of cash by the organizers and issued the shares.
  b. Purchased office equipment which cost $6,000; paid cash.
  c. Paid $400 cash for a two-year insurance policy on the office equipment (debit the asset account, Prepaid Insurance).
  d. Purchased a delivery truck at a cost of $12,000; paid $7,000 down and signed a $5,000, 90-day, 12 percent, interest-bearing note payable for the balance.
  e. Purchased office supplies for cash to be used in the stenographic and mailing operations, $2,000. The supplies are for future use (therefore, debit the asset account, Office Supplies Inventory).
  f. Revenues earned during the year were:

	Cash	On credit
Stenographic fees	$55,000	$6,000
Mailing fees	8,000	2,000

  g. Operating expenses incurred during the year were (excluding transactions [h] through [l]):

Cash	$26,000
On credit	14,000

  h. Paid the $5,000 note on the panel truck. Cash paid out was for the principal plus the interest for three months.
  i. Purchased land for a future building site at a cost of $20,000; paid cash.
  j. Depreciation on the truck for 19A, was computed on the basis of a five-year useful life; on the office equipment, a useful life of 10 years was assumed (compute full-year depreciation on each and assume no residual value).
  k. By December 31, 19A, insurance for one year had expired. Prepaid Insurance should be decreased, and an expense recorded.
  l. An inventory of the office supplies reflected $300 on hand at December 31, 19A. Supplies Inventory should be reduced, and an expense recognized.
  m. Income tax expense, based on a 20 percent rate, was $5,190 (to be paid in 19B).

Required:

1. Analyze and prepare a journal entry for each transaction listed. Use a form similar to Exhibit 3–5 and include a brief explanation after each transaction.
2. Prepare an income statement that reports total revenues, total expenses, pretax income, income taxes, net income, and EPS. No ledger is required; therefore, you can complete this requirement by either (a) selecting and aggregating amounts from the entries made in Requirement 1, or (b) setting up the needed T-accounts on scratch paper. (Hint: Net income, $20,760.)
3. What is the ending balance of cash? Show computations. In general, why is the ending balance of cash different than net income?

PC3–10. (Covers the complete information processing cycle) Able, Baker, and Cain organized ABC Realty as a corporation to conduct a real estate and rental management business. Each contributed $20,000 cash and received 1,500 shares of stock (par value $10 per share).

They commenced business on January 1, 19A. The transactions listed below, representative of those during the first year, were selected from the actual transactions for case purposes.

Assume for case purposes that these transactions comprise all of the transactions for the year. This case demonstrates the complete information processing cycle from the capture of raw economic data to the final output—the financial statements. Use the numbers at the left as the date notation.

1. Received $60,000 cash invested by stockholders and issued 4,500 shares of stock. See the list of accounts given below.
2. On January 1, 19A, purchased office equipment that cost $6,000; paid one-third cash and charged the balance (one third due in 6 months, and the remaining third is due in 12 months). Credit Accounts Payable for the amount not paid in cash.
3. Purchased land for future office site: cost, $20,000; paid cash.
4. Paid office rent in cash, 11 months at $200 per month (debit Rent Expense). Beginning with this transaction, set up separate accounts for each type of expense.
5. Sold nine properties and collected sales commissions of $56,000. Set up an account, "Realty Commissions Revenue."
6. Paid salaries and commissions expense to salespersons amounting to $52,000 and miscellaneous expenses amounting to $1,000.
7. Collected rental management fees, $20,000. Set up an account, "Rental Management Revenue."
8. Paid utilities, $1,400.
9. Paid auto rental fees (auto rented for use in business), $3,600.
10. Paid for advertising, $7,500.
11. At year-end, the December rent had not been paid (credit Rent Payable).
12. The estimated life of the office equipment was 10 years; assume use for the full year in 19A and no residual value.
13. Additional commissions earned during 19A on sale of real estate amounted to $64,000 of which $14,000 was uncollected at year-end.
14. Paid the installment of $2,000 on the office equipment (see 2 above). Assume no interest.
15. Assume an average income tax rate of 30 percent; 19A tax expense of $21,450 will be paid in 19B.

Required:

a. Analyze, then journalize, each of the above transactions in chronological order. Number the journal pages consecutively, starting with 1.
b. Post each transaction from the journal to the ledger; use T-accounts as follows:

Account No.	Account titles	Account No.	Account titles
101	Cash	402	Rental management revenue
102	Accounts receivable	501	Rent expense
103	Office equipment	502	Salary and commission expense
104	Accumulated depreciation, office equipment	503	Miscellaneous expense
105	Land for future office site	504	Utilities expense
201	Accounts payable	505	Auto rental expense
202	Rent payable	506	Advertising expense
203	Income tax payable	507	Depreciation expense
301	Capital stock, par $10	508	Income tax expense
302	Contributed capital in excess of par		
401	Realty commission revenue		

Use folio cross-references when posting.

    c. Prepare a trial balance from the ledger; check the equality of debits and credits. (Hint: Trial balance total is $224,250, including cash of $94,300.)

    d. Use the data on the trial balance to prepare an income statement and balance sheet. Refer to Exhibits 2–1 and 2–2 for the format of these statements. Because of its complexity, preparation of a statement of changes in financial position is deferred to a later chapter. (Hint: EPS, $11.12.)

PC3–11. SD Moving and Storage Company, Inc., was organized four years ago (January 19A) by O. Snow and R. P. Dean. Each contributed $20,000 cash initially and was issued 2,000 shares of capital stock, par $10 per share. Since that time, a good portion of the earnings has been left in the business for growth. SD owns a large warehouse and 11 hauling vans. At the beginning, few financial records were maintained; however, it now has one person who devotes full time to records and reports. Disagreements with the Internal Revenue Service prompted the company to approach an independent CPA for advice. As a consequence, the first audit was performed for 19C. For purposes of this case, we will utilize only representative accounts and transactions to minimize the time requirements. Assume that the accounts for SD showed the following balance on January 1, 19D (the fiscal and calendar years agree):

Account No.	Account titles	Debit	Credit
101	Cash	$ 21,500	
103	Accounts receivable	15,000	
110	Supplies inventory	2,500	
112	Prepaid insurance		
131	Land (on which warehouse is located)	10,000	
133	Warehouse	80,000	
134	Accumulated depreciation, warehouse		$ 16,000
135	Moving vans	75,000	
136	Accumulated depreciation, moving vans		30,000
151	Land for future office building		
201	Accounts payable		10,000
202	Income tax payable		
210	Notes payable, long term (10%)		30,000
301	Capital stock, par $10 (4,000 shares)		40,000
302	Retained earnings		78,000
303	Dividends declared and paid		
401	Trucking revenues		
402	Storage revenues		
501	Operating expenses		
502	Depreciation expense		
505	Interest expense		
506	Income tax expense		
	Totals	$204,000	$204,000

    Representative transactions for 19D follow (use the letter notation at the left for dating purposes):

    a. Purchased land for future office building at a cost of $13,000; paid cash.

    b. Revenues earned:

	Cash	Credit
Trucking	$220,000	$40,000
Storage	30,000	2,000

    c. Paid $1,600 cash for a two-year insurance policy covering the trucks and warehouse. This payment was made on January 2, 19D (debit Prepaid Insurance).

d. Purchased additional supplies for use in operations for cash, $1,600; these supplies are to be used as needed. Debit Account No. 110.

e. At end of 19D paid $10,000 on the principal of the long-term note payable, plus 10 percent interest on the $30,000 for 12 months.

f. Operating expenses incurred:

> Cash $195,000
> On credit   23,000

g. Collections on part of accounts receivable (for trucking and storage services on credit), $38,000 (see [b] above).

h. Payments on part of accounts payable (expenses and services previously incurred on credit), $20,000 cash.

i. Declared and paid cash dividend of $33,000 in December 18D (debit Account No. 303).

j. A full year's depreciation expense for 19D was computed on the basis of the following useful lives: warehouse, 20 years; and moving vans, 5 years (assume no residual values). Debit Account No. 502.

k. On December 31, 19D, an inventory showed supplies remaining on hand (unused) amounting to $1,800. Reduce Supplies Inventory and recognize an expense (Account No. 501).

l. On December 31, 19D, one year of insurance had expired.

m. Income tax expense (30 percent rate), $14,670; paid in cash except for one fourth which will be paid during April 19E.

Required:

1. Set up T-accounts for each account listed above (the above list includes all of the accounts needed) and enter therein the beginning balances given in the following manner.

	Cash	101
Balance	21,500	

2. Set up a journal similar to Exhibit 3–5 and enter each of the transactions. Use the letter designation for dating and include a short explanation after each entry. Number the journal pages consecutively starting with 1.

3. Post each transaction entered in the journal to the ledger accounts; complete the folio columns in both the journal and ledger.

4. Prepare a trial balance from the ledger accounts at December 31, 19D. (Hint: The trial balance total is $511,667, including cash of $21,297).

5. Prepare a classified income statement and balance sheet. See Exhibits 2–1 and 2–2 for the formats for these statements. To support the balance sheet, prepare a statement of retained earnings as follows:

Appropriate Heading

Balance, January 1, 19D	$ _____
Add: Net income for 19D	_____
Total	_____
Deduct: Dividends declared and paid in 19D	_____
Balance, December 31, 19D (reported on balance sheet)	$ _____

(Hint: EPS is $8.56.)

PC3–12. (Note: This is a special case to test your analytical skills.) Simon Lavoie, a local attorney, decided to sell his practice and retire. He has had discussions with an attorney from another state who desires to relocate. The discussions have entered the complex stage of agreeing on a price. Among the important factors have been the financial statements on Lavoie's practice. Lavoie's secretary, under his direction, maintained the records. Each year they developed a "Statement of Profits" on a cash basis from the incomplete records maintained, and no balance sheet was prepared. Upon request, Lavoie provided the other attorney with the following statement for 1984 prepared by his secretary:

S. LAVOIE
Statement of Profits
1984

Legal fees collected		$92,000
Expenses paid:		
Rent for office space	$10,400	
Utilities	360	
Telephone	2,900	
Office salaries	19,000	
Office supplies	900	
Miscellaneous expenses	1,600	
Total expenses		35,160
Profit for the year		$56,840

Upon agreement of the parties, you have been asked to "look into the financial figures for 1984." The other attorney told you that "I question the figures because, among other things, they appear to be on a 100 percent cash basis." Your investigations revealed the following additional data at December 31, 1984:

a. Of the $62,000 legal fees collected in 1984, $28,000 was for services performed prior to 1984.

b. At the end of 1984, legal fees of $7,000 for services performed during the year were uncollected.

c. Office equipment owned and used by Lavoie cost $3,000 and had an estimated remaining useful life of 10 years.

d. An inventory of office supplies at December 31, 1984, reflected $200 worth of items purchased during the year that were still on hand. Also, the records for 1983 indicate that the supplies on hand at the end of that year were approximately $125.

e. At the end of 1984 a secretary, whose salary is $12,000 per year, had not been paid for December because of a long trip that extended to January 15, 1985.

f. The phone bill for December 1984, amounting to $1,500, was not paid until January 11, 1985.

g. The office rent paid of $10,400 was for 13 months (it included the rent for January 1985).

Required:

a. On the basis of the above information, prepare an income statement for 1984 on an accrual basis. Show your computations for any amounts changed from those in the statement prepared by Lavoie's secretary. (Suggested solution format with four column headings: Items; Cash Basis Per Lavoie Statement, $; Explanation of Changes; and Corrected to Accrual Basis Per GAAP, $.)

b. Write a comment to support your schedule prepared in *(a)*. The purpose should be to briefly explain the reasons for your changes and to suggest some other important items that should be considered in the pricing decision.

PC3–13. Refer to the financial statements of Johnson & Johnson given in Special Supplement B immediately preceding the Index. Respond to the following questions for the 1982 annual accounting period.

1. On what date did the 1982 accounting period end?
2. Complete the following fundamental accounting model by providing the amounts Assets, $ _____ = Liabilities, $ _____ + Owners' Equity, $ _____ .
3. How much was the revenue from sales to customers? $ _____ .
4. What was the dual economic effect on the company of the total revenues?
    (a) _____ $ _____
    (b) _____ $ _____
5. What was the dual economic effect on the company of the cost of the products sold?
    (a) _____ $ _____
    (b) _____ $ _____
6. What was the dual economic effect on the company of the cash dividends declared and paid?
    (a) _____ $ _____
    (b) _____ $ _____
7. Interest income was ___debited; ___credited for $ _____, and cash was ___debited; ___credited for $ _____ .
8. Prepare a journal entry to record research expense assuming it was all paid in cash.
9. What amount was shown in the trial balance at the end of the 1982 annual accounting period for (a) long-term debt and (b) cash and cash items?
10. What was the amount of "depreciation and amortization?" Prepare a journal entry to record this amount.

CHAPTER
4

Matching of Expenses with Revenue Each Period

PURPOSE OF THIS CHAPTER

Net income is one of the more significant single amounts developed through the accounting process. In this chapter we will focus on several critical issues involved in the measurement of net income. We will examine some of the complications posed when the lifespan of a business is divided into a series of equal time periods, such as one year. We will consider the problem of realistically identifying revenues within the selected time period and then identifying the expenses that were incurred in order to earn the revenues for that period.

To accomplish these purposes, this chapter is divided into two parts as follows:

Part A—Recognition of revenues and expenses

Part B—Adjusting entries illustrated

PART A—RECOGNITION OF REVENUES AND EXPENSES

RELATIONSHIPS AMONG FINANCIAL STATEMENTS

The three required financial statements—the balance sheet, income statement, and statement of changes in financial position—were discussed in the preceding chapters. In this section we will continue our discussion by emphasizing the relationships among the financial statements. These three financial statements plus the accompanying notes, supporting schedules, and the auditors' opinion should be viewed as the entire financial report for the selected time period. This entire reporting package is necessary to meet the varied needs of a diverse population of financial statement users.

Exhibit 4–1 presents the basic relationships among the three financial statements for a fiscal year, such as January 1 through December 31, 1984. This exhibit emphasizes that the **beginning financial position** of the entity is reported in the balance sheet at the end of the **prior** period and its **ending** financial position is reported in the balance sheet at the end of the **current** year. In addition to information concerning financial position as of specific dates, decision makers (users of the financial report) need information about what happened **during** the current year that **caused** the financial position of the entity to change. The **changes** in financial position between the beginning and ending of the current accounting period are communicated to users in two different "change" statements as follows:

1. **Income statement**—The income statement explains **changes** in owners' equity during the period as a result of **operations.** Net income increases owners' equity, which is shown graphically in Exhibit 4–1, Part 1. The detailed amounts of revenue, expense, and extraordinary items that **caused** this particular change in financial position during the period are reported on the income statement for the period. Therefore, the income statement reports detailed information to explain **one major category of changes** in financial position during the selected time period; this category of changes resulted from **operations** and **extraordinary items.** The accompanying notes and supporting schedules add qualitative elaboration of the income statement.
2. **Statement of changes in financial position (SCFP)**—This statement is designed to report, or explain, all the **causes of changes** in financial position (i.e., assets, liabilities, and owners' equity) during the period that result from the inflow of funds (called financing activities) and outflow of funds (called investing activities). Thus, the SCFP reports all of the entity's **sources** (i.e., inflows) of funds and all of its **uses** (i.e., outflows) of funds during the period. The financial position of the entity was changed as a result of these inflows and outflows of funds. The SCFP may be prepared to measure **funds** as either cash or as working capital (explained later).

The three financial statements are linked together in important ways. This linking together often is referred to as **articulation,** which means that an amount in one statement (e.g., net income on the income statement) is carried to another

EXHIBIT 4–1
**Relationships
among financial
statements**

* This balance sheet also is at the beginning of 1984.

† Funds are measured as either cash or working capital in the SCFP.

statement (e.g., the statement of retained earnings). Similarly, net income is tied to the balance sheet (through retained earnings)—and to the SCFP (discussed later). Decision makers can better interpret the financial statements when they clearly understand these relationships. Your understanding of these relationships will be important as you study both Part B of this chapter and all of the remaining chapters.

TIME-PERIOD ASSUMPTION

Our discussion above of the relationships among the three required financial statements emphasized the timing of financial statements. Each financial statement should specifically identify its **time dimension** (see Chapter 1, pages 18, 21, and 24). Exhibit 4–1 reemphasizes that the time dimension of the balance sheet is at a **specific date** (such as "At December 31, 19X"). In contrast, the two "change" statements cover a **specified period of time** (such as, "For the Year Ended December 31, 19X").

The lifespan of most business entities is indefinite, but decision makers need current information about the entity. Therefore, the lifespan of an entity is divided into a series of short time periods, such as one year, for many measurement financial reporting purposes. This division of the activities of a business into a series of equal time periods is known as the **time-period assumption** (see Exhibit 2–6), which is fundamental to the accounting process and financial reporting.

Because annual periods tend to be dominant throughout our society, the accounting period usually is viewed as being 12 consecutive months. As a consequence, the emphasis in accounting is on **annual** financial statements. Many companies use a year that corresponds to the natural cycle of their business, such as July 1 through June 30, rather than to the calendar year. An accounting year that does not necessarily correspond to the calendar year is known as a **fiscal year.** In addition to the annual financial statements, many businesses prepare and publish quarterly financial reports for external distribution. These usually are called **interim reports.** Also, in addition to annual reports, monthly financial statements frequently are prepared exclusively for **internal management** purposes.

Dividing the lifespan of a business into short time periods, such as a year, for measurement purposes often poses complex accounting problems because some **transactions start in one accounting period and are,** in effect, **concluded in a subsequent period.** This continuity of the effects of a transaction may occur for all classifications; for example:

a. **Assets**—A machine that is purchased in one year may be depreciated over the next 10 years.
b. **Liabilities**—A note payable is signed that requires interest payments each of three years and payment of the principal at the end of the third year.
c. **Owners' equity**—Shares of stock are sold in one year with a cash down payment plus two equal annual installment payments and issuance of the shares at the date of the last installment.
d. **Revenues**—Rent is collected in one year for six months in advance, and two of the occupancy periods (months) extend into the next year.
e. **Expenses**—An insurance premium on property is paid in advance for two years of future coverage.

The time-period assumption has a significant impact on the recognition of periodic revenues and expenses.

PERIODIC RECOGNITION OF REVENUES AND EXPENSES

The process of earning **revenues** through the sale of goods and services and the incurring of **expenses** necessary to earn those revenues is **continuous.** Some revenue and expense transactions cover an extended period of time between their initiation and completion. This causes a problem because financial reports must be made for a specific time period, such as a month, quarter, or year. Therefore, a careful **cutoff** must be made among the selected time periods so that the revenues and expenses for each separate period can be measured reliably.

Frequently, it is difficult to identify a specific revenue and/or expense with a particular accounting period. In response to this problem, the **revenue principle** and the **matching principle** have evolved as two of the broad fundamentals underlying accounting (see Exhibit 2–6). These two principles focus on the measurement of **net income** for each time period. **The revenue principle takes a timing precedence over the matching principle in the measurement process.** First, the revenues earned for the period from the sale of goods and services are measured; next, the matching principle is applied to measure the expenses incurred in earning those particular revenues. To reemphasize, for accounting measurement purposes, the revenue and matching principles require a careful **cutoff** of revenues and expenses at the end of each accounting period and a proper matching of expenses with revenues.

The revenue principle

The revenue principle was defined briefly in Chapter 2, Exhibit 2–6. The revenue principle holds that revenue should be recognized in the period in which it is **earned** (often referred to as realized). Revenue is identified with a specific accounting period by considering **when** the revenue transaction occurrred rather than considering when the related cash is collected. The income statement for each accounting period must report all of the revenues **earned** during the period covered, but must not report any revenues earned in prior or following periods.

To apply the revenue principle, the general guideline is that revenue is considered earned (realized) when the **earning process** is substantially completed. In the case of the sale of **goods,** the earning process is substantially completed when **ownership** of the goods passes from the seller to the buyer. In the case of the sale of **services,** the earning process is substantially completed as the services are performed (rather when the services finally are completed in all respects). This general guideline is applied to most revenue transactions; however, there are a few **exceptions** as follows:

1. **Long-term credit sales coupled with a relatively small down payment—** Such sales often pose the question of **risk** that full collection will not be made ultimately (i.e., a default and repossession may occur). For example, in the case of land development companies, one common practice has been to sell undeveloped land for a down payment of approximately 5 percent coupled with a 10- to 30-year debt payment period. Because of the number of defaults that this industry experienced, the current accounting guideline is that sales revenue should not be recorded as **earned** until the period in which the total cash collected is at least 10 percent of the sale price.

2. **Installment sales—**Often there is a high risk of default when a company sells high-cost items of merchandise with a relatively low cash down payment and liberal credit terms (such as the sale of an expensive TV set). Such situations may require application of **installment-sales accounting.** This method of recognition of revenue is applied when the characteristics of the sale transaction are (1) a relatively small down payment is required; (2) the payment

period is long and calls for monthly payments of principal plus interest; (3) the seller retains conditional ownership of the goods until full payment is made; and (4) bad debt losses cannot be estimated reliably. When all of these characteristics exist in combination, there is a relatively high risk that the merchandise will be repossessed because of nonpayment (default). The installment method of accounting is used in this situation. Under this method, the revenue is considered to be earned as the **cash is collected.** As a consequence, this method is close to cash basis accounting.

3. **Long-term construction contracts**—Revenue and expense recognition problems arise for the **construction contractor** when a construction contract extends across two or more accounting periods. For example, assume a building contractor signs a contract to build a large plant at a cost of $3,500,000 and the construction period is three years, starting January 1, 19A. The contractor estimates a construction cost of $3,200,000; that is, an estimated profit of $300,000. The question is: Should the profit be reported as (1) earned in 19C when the project is completed or (2) allocated on an estimated basis to each of the three years? One accounting method used is called the **completed contract method.** Under this method, all of the profit is recognized as earned in the year of **completion.** This method is conservative because recognition of profit is deferred until completion when the actual profit is known. Another accounting method used for long-term construction contracts is called the **percentage-of-completion method.** It permits **allocation** of profit to each of the three construction periods based on estimates (usually based on the ratio of actual costs incurred during the period to total costs of the project) covering the three-year period. A portion of the estimated $300,000 would be recognized as profit each year during the construction period.

At the present time, a contractor is permitted to select either method of accounting for long-term construction contracts; however, the percentage-of-completion method can be used only if reliable estimates can be made. Many accountants believe that this choice between two **accounting alternatives** for the same set of facts is not sound, but these accountants do not agree on which method is preferable in all cases. Lack of agreement among accountants as to the best measurement apporoach primarily is the reason for the approval of accounting alternatives. Similarly, there are a number of other areas of accounting where measurement and recognition alternatives are permitted for the same set of facts. The accounting profession is striving to eliminate such alternative accounting choices.

The reliability principle

The discussions above of revenue recognition illustrate the **qualitative characteristic of reliability** (see Exhibit 2–6) which holds that all economic data reported on the financial statements must be unbiased, accurate, and verifiable. Thus, the discussion of the percentage-of-completion method of revenue recognition can be used **only if the estimates used in it are reliable,** otherwise the completed contract method must be used. Similarly, the installment-sales method can be used to recognize revenue on credit sales **only if reliable estimates of bad debt losses cannot be made.** The qualitative characteristic of reliability does not permit the reporting of biased or unrealistic estimates of assets, liabilities, revenues, gains, expenses, or losses. Thus, the **reliability** characteristic exerts a significant impact on accounting and reporting.

The matching principle

Expenses are defined on page 20 and in Exhibit 2–6. The matching principle focuses on the measurement of expenses and the matching of them with the periodic revenues **earned** during the period. The matching principle holds that all of the expenses incurred in earning revenues should be identified, or matched, with the revenues earned, period by period.

When applying the matching principle, it is necessary to consider the purposes for which the expenses were incurred. If the expenses are associated with a specific revenue, as is the usual case, the expenses should be identified with the period in which that revenue was earned. In this way, the expenses are matched with the revenues of each period so that income for each period is measured correctly. Expenses incurred in earning the revenues of the period should be reported in that period. Resources expended in one period to earn revenues in other periods should be apportioned to those other periods.

Application of the revenue and matching principles is to identify revenues and expenses among consecutive accounting periods. This identification, or cutoff, by periods often requires that a special type of end-of-period accounting entries be made. Collectively, such entries usually are referred to as **adjusting entries.**

ADJUSTING ENTRIES

Adjusting entries are required by the revenue and matching principles to effect a precise identification, or **cutoff,** of revenues and expenses among consecutive accounting periods because some completed transactions recorded in one accounting period have economic consequences that extend over one or more other accounting periods. As a result, **adjusting entries** may be necessary to change certain account balances at the end of the accounting period, not to correct errors but to reflect these interperiod economic consequences. To illustrate, assume a company purchased a machine for use in the business on January 1, 19A, that cost $50,000 with an estimated useful life of five years (no residual value). On January 1, 19A (the date the transaction was completed), an asset account—machinery—was debited (increased) for $50,000. However, by December 31, 19A (end of the accounting period), the machine has depreciated to $40,000. Therefore, due to a subsequent economic event (use of the machine), an **adjusting entry** must be made to *(a)* decrease the book value of the asset by $10,000 and *(b)* record depreciation expense of $10,000.

Adjusting entries possess four fundamental characteristics as follows:

1. An **income statement** account balance (revenue or expense) is changed.
2. A **balance sheet** account balance (asset or liability) is changed.
3. They usually are recorded at the end of the accounting period.
4. They never directly affect the Cash account.

Adjusting entries are required by four types of transactions as follows:

Revenues (revenue principle applied):

1. **Revenue collected in advance but not yet earned**—Revenue collected in advance of being **earned** must be apportioned (deferred) to the period or periods in which it will be earned. In this situation, cash collection **leads** (precedes) revenue recognition.

    Example: On December 1, 19A, Alpha Company collected $1,000 cash for December 19A and January 19B rent (i.e., $500 per month). On the transaction date, the company debited Cash and credited Rent Revenue for $1,000

    Analysis on December 31, 19A: Rent revenue was earned in 19A for only one month, December; the other monthly rent will be earned in 19B; however, cash was collected in 19A for both months. Therefore, on December 31, 19A, an **adjusting** entry for $500 must be made to *(a)* decrease (debit) rent revenue and *(b)* increase (credit) rent revenue collected in advance. The $500 credit balance in this account must be reported on the 19A balance sheet as a **liability** because the company owes the renter occupancy for one month (January 19B).

2. **Revenue earned but not yet collected or recorded**—Revenue not collected nor recorded but earned in the current accounting period should be recorded as **earned** in the current period, even though the related cash will be collected in a subsequent period. In this case, cash collection **lags** revenue recognition.

    Example: On December 31, 19A, Alpha Company completed two phases of a service job for a customer; the third phase will be done in January 19B. The total contract price was $1,200 (i.e., $400 per phase) cash payable upon completion of all phases.

    Analysis on December 31, 19A: Service revenue of $800 (i.e., $1,200 × ⅔) was earned in 19A, although not yet recorded or collected. Therefore, an **adjusting** entry for $800 must be made on December 31, 19A, to *(a)* increase (debit) accounts receivable and *(b)* increase (credit) service revenue because revenue for the first two phases has been earned in 19A; a receivable must be recorded because the collection of cash will be made in 19B.

Expenses (matching principle applied):

3. **Expense paid in advance**—Expense paid in advance of use of the services or goods must be apportioned (deferred) to the period, or periods, in which such services or goods will be used. In this situation, cash payment **leads** expense recognition.

    Example: On January 1, 19A, Alpha Company paid a two-year premium of $800 for property insurance; the coverage is for 19A and 19B (i.e., $400 per year). The company recorded this transaction on January 1, 19A, as a debit (increase) of $800 to Prepaid Insurance (an asset), and a decrease (credit) to Cash.

Analysis on December 31, 19A: On this date half of the benefit of the insurance coverage has been received. Half of the related insurance premium has expired (i.e., $800 \div 2 = $400); the other half remains prepaid. Therefore, on December 31, 19A, an **adjusting** entry for $400 must be made to *(a)* increase (debit) insurance expense and *(b)* decrease (credit) prepaid insurance. This entry records the $400 expense for 19A and leaves $400 in the asset account, Prepaid Insurance. Prepaid insurance is an asset because Alpha Company has an obligation from the insurance company to provide insurance coverage for 19B (the premium already has been paid).

4. **Expense incurred but not recorded**—Expense incurred (the services or goods have been used) in the current accounting period but not yet recorded or paid (the related cash payment will be in a subsequent period) should be recorded as expense in the current period. In this situation, cash payment **lags** expense recognition.

    Example: On December 31, 19A, Alpha Company employees have earned $1,000 in wages that will be paid in cash on the next payroll date January 6, 19B.

    Analysis on December 31, 19A: The company has incurred wage expense in 19A of $1,000 (the employees were helping to earn 19A revenues), and because the employees have not been paid, the company has a $1,000 liability on December 31, 19A. Therefore, an **adjusting** entry for $1,000 must be made on December 31, 19A, to *(a)* debit (increase) Wage Expense and *(b)* credit (increase) Wages Payable. This liability will be reported on the 19A balance sheet and will be paid on the next payroll date, January 6, 19B.

In summary, adjusting entries are made at the **end** of each accounting period, after the regular entries are completed. At this time, the accountant must make a careful check of the records and supporting documents to determine whether there are any situations such as those listed above for which **adjusting entries** should be made. In practically all situations, one or more such entries invariably will be required at the end of each accounting period. If any required adjusting entries are not made, revenue for the period may be measured incorrectly and/ or expenses may not be matched with the revenues earned during the period. In either instance, the result would be incorrect measurement of amounts on both the income statement and the balance sheet for **both** the current and subsequent period or periods.

Adjusting entries are not unusual. They require no additional competence, only a knowledge and analysis of the actual facts in respect to each item. In Chapter 3, the illustrations, exercises, and problems/cases included several adjusting entries (depreciation expense, prepaid insurance, supplies used, and accrued or unpaid wages) routinely made without special identification or concern.

Terminology

Accountants frequently use two technical terms both in respect to adjusting entries and in a more general sense. Throughout this textbook and in many of your subsequent courses (and in the outside environment) you will encounter the terms **accrued** (or to accrue) and **deferred** (or to defer). Basic and practical definitions for our purposes are: **Accrued,** in the case of expenses, means not yet paid; and in the case of revenues, not yet collected. **Deferred,** in the case of revenues, means collected in advance and, in the case of expenses, paid in advance. To summarize:

	Term	Definition	Example
1.	Accrued expense	An expense incurred, not yet paid	Wages earned by employee but not yet paid
2.	Accrued revenue	A revenue earned, not yet collected	Services performed in advance of collection
3.	Deferred revenue	A revenue not yet earned, collected in advance	Rent collected in advance of occupancy
4.	Deferred expense	An expense not yet incurred, paid in advance	Insurance premium paid in advance

A CASE STUDY

The discussions in this chapter focus on the allocation of revenues and expenses among two or more consecutive accounting periods. Such allocations often have a major impact on the **income statement** and **balance sheet** amounts for the current period. For example, a recent article in *Forbes* ("A Question of Judgment," February 16, 1981) discussed some interesting allocation issues. The article stated, "Tucked away in the middle of an ordinary-looking press release mailed out by ABC (the TV network) in December was a line noting that the method of assigning expenses to each showing of prime-time and movies was being changed. Trivial? Not to an experienced broadcast accountant. That little change could make quite a difference on the bottom line." The "expenses" referred to in this citation often amount to approximately $500 million for "a prime-time series or movie."

The accounting issue discussed in the article was how much of the $500 million should be *(a)* allocated to expense to be matched with the **first** showing and *(b)* how much of the $500 million should be **deferred** as an asset on the balance sheet (and later allocated as expense to subsequent showings). The article continues, "What ABC seems to have done is reduce the first-time charge from 80% to around 75% of the show's cost. That doesn't sound like much until you consider the numbers involved." To illustrate the cited amounts:

	Millions of dollars	
	Expense (80 percent)	Asset (20 percent)
Former Method:		
$500 million allocated, 80%/20%	$400	$100
New Method:		
$500 million allocated, 75%/25%	375	125
Difference: Increase in reported income and assets	$ 25	$ 25

The article explained: "For ABC, that little switch could well turn a loss into a profit in the first quarter of this year and could also boost earnings thereafter. Of course, from the auditors' point of view, there is nothing wrong with doing a little shifting like this—as long as it's within reason. Management is supposed to know better than their CPA firm how much revenue can be expected on these later broadcasts."

The past has shown that "deferring writeoffs of bombs was a common route to high profits in the movie industry until 1973 when practices there were tightened considerably. But the networks may still have a few skeletons in their closets. The point is, networks can change their minds conveniently about the prospects of shows anytime they need an earnings boost—and few shareholders would be the wiser for it."

This case example demonstrates that revenue and expense allocations often (a) involve substantial amounts and (b) significantly affect reported income. As a result, the users of financial statements (and the business press) pay close attention to the allocation decisions made by the managements of the reporting companies.

PART B—ADJUSTING ENTRIES ILLUSTRATED

This part of the chapter continues the discussion of adjusting entries. It provides detailed illustrations and explanations of numerous adjusting entries. Our emphasis will be on the **analysis** of specific examples to determine the appropriate adjusting entry and the related entries that are made in subsequent periods. These illustrations will increase your understanding of the application of the accounting model, measurement of periodic revenues and expenses, and determination of income. Throughout the examples to follow, we will refer to **High-Rise Apartments** (organized as a corporation on January 1, 19A) and will assume that the **current annual accounting period ends December 31, 19B.**

REVENUE COLLECTED IN ADVANCE (DEFERRED REVENUE)

Businesses may collect cash and record it in advance of earning the related revenue from the sale of services or goods. The amount collected in advance is called unearned or deferred revenue. Unearned revenue must be apportioned to the period in which the services are performed or the sale is completed in accordance with the **revenue principle** (see Exhibit 2–6 and page 152). When unearned revenue has been received, an **adjusting entry** usually is required at the end of the period to recognize (1) the correct amount of revenue **earned** during the current period and (2) the remaining obligation in the future to provide the related goods or services. We will analyze one such situation for High-Rise Apartments that occurs because some tenants pay their rent in the middle of each month. (Note: Each **adjusting** entry is letter coded for reference in the illustrations to follow.)

Example: On December 11, 19B, two tenants paid rent for one month from December 11, 19B, through January 10, 19C, in the amount of $1,500. The sequence of entries recorded by High-Rise would be:

December 11, 19B—date of the transaction:

```
Cash ...................................................... 1,500
    Rent revenue ...............................................        1,500
    To record one month's rent for the period December 11, 19B, through
    January 10, 19C.
```

December 31, 19B—end of the accounting period:

> **Analysis:** The $1,500 cash collected included rent revenue for December 19B of $1,500 \times {}^{20}\!/_{30} = \$1,000$, and rent revenue collected in advance for January 19C of $1,500 \times {}^{10}\!/_{30} = \$500$. Therefore, an **adjusting entry** is required on December 31, 19B, to (a) reduce the balance in rent revenue by $500 and (b) record the obligation to furnish occupancy in 19C for one third of a month which was paid in advance of that year. This $500 is a current liability that will be paid in January 19C by providing occupancy rights.

a. December 31, 19B (end of the accounting period)—**adjusting entry:**[1]

```
Rent revenue ................................................. 500
    Rent collected in advance ...................................        500
    To adjust the accounts for revenue collected in advance as of the end
    of the current period.
```

---

[1] Observe that the entry at collection date, December 11, 19B, could have been recorded in a way that would preclude the need for an adjusting entry later, viz:

```
Cash ........................................................ 1,500
    Rent revenue ...............................................        1,000
    Rent collected in advance ..................................          500
```

Alternatively, it could be accounted for as follows with the same end result:

December 11, 19B:

```
Cash ........................................................ 1,500
    Rent collected in advance ..................................        1,500
```

December 31, 19B—adjusting entry:

```
Rent collected in advance ................................... 1,000
    Rent revenue ...............................................        1,000
```

The $1,000 (i.e., $1,500 − $500) rent revenue would be reported on the 19B income statement and the rent revenue collected in advance of $500 would be reported on the 19B balance sheet as a current liability.

January 19C:

Rent revenue collected in advance	500	
Rent revenue		500
To transfer the rent revenue from the liability account to the 19C revenue account because it now has been earned.		

In overall perspective, the three entries above *(a)* recorded the cash transaction and *(b)* allocated the total rent collected between the two periods (19B and 19C) as rent revenue in each period as earned.

REVENUE EARNED PRIOR TO COLLECTION (ACCRUED REVENUE)

At the end of the current accounting period, analysis may reveal that some revenue has been **earned** (in accordance with the revenue principle) but has **not yet been recorded** or collected. Such unrecorded revenue usually is referred to as unrecorded revenue or accrued revenue.

The revenue principle states that if revenue was earned in the current accounting period, it must be recorded and reported in that period along with the asset that has been created (an account receivable). This recording is accomplished by making an **adjusting** entry at the end of the current period to recognize *(a)* a receivable for the amount earned but not yet collected and *(b)* the amount of revenue earned. We will analyze a typical situation for High-Rise Apartments and give the sequence of entries.

Example: On December 31, 19B, the manager of High-Rise Apartments analyzed the rental records and found that one tenant had not paid the December rent amounting to $600. The sequence of entries recorded by High-Rise would be:

b. December 31, 19B (end of the accounting period)—**adjusting entry:**

Rent revenue receivable	600	
Rent revenue		600
To record rent revenue earned in 19B but not collected by year-end.		

January 19C—date of collection:

Cash	600	
Rent revenue receivable		600
To record 19C collection of receivable for 19B rent revenue.		

The adjusting entry at the end of 19B served two measurement purposes: (1) to record rent revenue earned in 19B of $600 and (2) to record a receivable (an asset) for occupancy provided in 19B for which $600 cash will be collected in January 19C. Rent revenue receivable is reported on the December 31, 19B, balance sheet as a current asset.

EXPENSES PAID IN ADVANCE (PREPAID OR DEFERRED EXPENSE)

Frequently a company either pays cash or incurs a liability in one accounting period for assets purchased or services obtained that will be used in one or more future accounting periods to help earn revenues during those future periods. Such transactions create an asset because of the future benefits; that asset usually is called a **prepaid expense** (or a deferred expense). As the future periods pass, the related revenues are earned (in accordance with the revenue principle). Then, as the revenues are earned, period by period, the **prepaid** expense amount must be apportioned to the appropriate periods in accordance with the **matching principle.** For example, if the related revenues are earned over three accounting periods, the prepaid expense must be apportioned to each of those three periods in order to measure net income for each period.

For High-Rise Apartments we will analyze **three** such transactions that occurred in 19B.

Prepaid insurance

On January 1, 19B, High-Rise paid cash of $2,400 in advance for a two-year insurance policy on the apartment building. The sequence of entries by High-Rise for this **prepaid expense** would be:

January 1, 19B—date of the transaction:

Prepaid insurance (an asset account)	2,400	
Cash		2,400
To record prepayment of a two-year premium on building.		

December 31, 19B—end of the accounting period:

    Analysis: The $2,400 cash paid on January 1, 19B, was for insurance coverage for two full years; therefore, insurance **expense** for each of the two years will be $1,200. At the end of 19B, an adjusting entry must be made to *(a)* reduce prepaid insurance by $1,200 and *(b)* record insurance expense of $1,200 for 19B.

c. December 31, 19B (end of the accounting period)—**adjusting entry:**

```
Insurance expense ...............................................   1,200
    Prepaid insurance ...........................................            1,200
    To record 19B insurance expense for 12 months ($2,400 × ¹²⁄₂₄ = $1,200).
```

The adjusting entry serves two measurement purposes: (1) it apportions insurance expense to the current period for **matching** purposes and (2) it adjusts (reduces) the Prepaid Insurance account to the correct asset amount ($1,200) for the **unexpired** insurance remaining at the end of 19B. That is, at the end of 19B, the company was entitled to one more year of insurance protection (with a cost of $1,200) and hence had a current **asset.**

December 31, 19C (end of next accounting period)—**adjusting entry:**

```
Insurance expense ...............................................   1,200
    Prepaid insurance ...........................................            1,200
    To record 19C insurance expense.
```

This entry apportions insurance expense to 19C and reduces the prepaid insurance balance to zero because the policy term ends on December 31, 19C.

Depreciation

On January 1, 19A, a contractor completed an apartment building for High-Rise. The contract price of $360,000 was paid in cash. The building has an estimated **useful life** of 30 years and an estimated $60,000 **residual value** at the end of the 30 years. This transaction involved the acquisition of an asset (building) that may affect the financial statements for the next 30 years (including 19A). At this point, we will consider one continuing effect—depreciation. The sequence of entries by High-Rise is discussed below.

January 1, 19A—date of acquisition of building:

```
Apartment building ..............................................   360,000
    Cash ........................................................            360,000
    To record full payment for construction cost of the building.
```

d. December 31, 19B (end of the accounting period)—**adjusting entry:**

Depreciation expense	10,000	
Accumulated depreciation, building		10,000
To record straight-line depreciation expense for one year		
($360,000 − $60,000) ÷ 30 years = $10,000.		

The adjusting entry for depreciation expense would be repeated at the end of **each year** over the 30-year life of the building. The **estimated** amount expected to be recovered when the asset finally is sold or disposed of is known as the **residual value** (sometimes it is called scrap or salvage value). For computing depreciation, the cost of the asset must be **reduced** by the residual value. The difference ($360,000 − $60,000 = $300,000) is the net amount of cost to be depreciated over the estimated useful life. Thus, the annual depreciation expense on the apartment building would be ($360,000 − $60,000) ÷ 30 years = $10,000.[2] The residual value of $60,000 is deducted because it is the amount of cost that is expected to be recovered at the end of the useful life (of the building) to the company.

In overall perspective, the adjusting entry serves two measurement purposes: (1) it allocates a part of the cost of the building to expense for the current period for matching purposes and (2) it adjusts (reduces) the amount of the asset to represent the undepreciated cost of the asset. The credit to Accumulated Depreciation, Building could have been made directly to the building account with the same effect; however, it is desirable, for reporting purposes, to keep the balance of the asset account Apartment Building at original cost. This is accomplished by setting up an asset **contra,** or **offset,** account titled Accumulated Depreciation, Building. You will recall from Chapters 2 and 3 that on the balance sheet the building would be shown on one line at its acquisition cost and a deduction on the next line for accumulated depreciation (see Exhibit 2–2). The difference between the acquisition cost and accumulated depreciation amounts often is referred to as the **book value,** or **carrying value,** of the asset. The book or carrying value does not represent the current **market** value of the asset because accounting for depreciation is a cost allocation process rather than a market valuation process.

Supplies inventory and expense

On January 1, 19B, the inventory of maintenance supplies was $100; these were **unused** supplies on hand carried over from the previous year. High-Rise purchases maintenance supplies, not for resale but for use as needed, and they are kept in a small storeroom from which supplies are withdrawn as needed. On March 18, 19B, additional supplies were purchased at a cost of $500 and were placed in the storeroom. No accounting entry is made when the supplies are withdrawn for use. To determine the amount of supplies **used** during the

---

[2] This example assumes straight-line depreciation, that is, an equal amount of depreciation expense is apportioned to each period. Other methods of depreciation will be discussed in Chapter 9.

period, an inventory of the supplies remaining on hand is taken at the end of the period. At December 31, 19B, the inventory of the supplies in the storeroom showed $200 in supplies on hand. The sequence of entries by High-Rise would be:

March 18, 19B—date of purchase of supplies:

Inventory of maintenance supplies (an asset)	500	
Cash		500
To record purchase of maintenance supplies for addition to inventory.		
Note: This entry increases the inventory account balance from $100 to $600.		

e. December 31, 19B (end of the accounting period)—**adjusting entry:**

Maintenance expense	400	
Inventory of maintenance supplies		400
To record the amount of supplies used from inventory ($100 + $500 − $200 = $400).		

> **Analysis:** Before the adjusting entry is made, the balance in the Inventory of Maintenance Supplies account is $600 (i.e., beginning inventory, $100, plus the purchase, $500); however, the actual inventory count at this date reflected $200, which means that usage of supplies was $400 (i.e., $100 + $500 − $200 = $400). The above adjusting entry is required to (a) reduce the inventory account by $400 (so that the asset, inventory, will be reflected as $200 per the inventory count) and (b) to record an expense for the amount of supplies used, $400. Therefore, the 19B income statement will report supplies expense of $400, and the 19B balance sheet will report a current asset—inventory of maintenance supplies—of $200.

EXPENSES INCURRED PRIOR TO PAYMENT (ACCRUED EXPENSES)

Most expenses are incurred and paid for during the same period; however, at the end of the accounting period there usually are some expenses that have been **incurred** (i.e., the goods and/or services that already have been used) but are **not yet recorded,** usually because payment has not been made. Such unpaid expenses are referred to as **accrued expenses.** Such expenses must be recorded in the current period because they must be **matched** with the revenues of the current period in accordance with the **matching principle.** Also, the liability for those unpaid expenses must be recorded and reported on the balance sheet of the current period. These effects are recorded by using an adjusting entry. We will analyze and illustrate **three** such transactions each of which required an adjusting entry by High-Rise Apartments.

Salary and wage expense

On December 31, 19B, the manager of High-Rise was on vacation and due to return January 10, 19C. As a consequence, the manager's December salary of $900 was not paid or recorded by December 31, 19B. The sequence of entries by High-Rise for the accrued salary expense (disregard payroll taxes at this time) would be:

f. December 31, 19B (end of the accounting period)—**adjusting entry:**

```
Salary expense ....................................................  900
     Salaries payable (or accrued salaries payable) .........................       900
     To record salary expense and the liability for December salary not yet paid.
```

January 10, 19C—date of payment of the December 19B salary:

```
Salaries payable ...................................................  900
     Cash ............................................................       900
     To record payment of a December 19B salary.
```

The adjusting entry served two measurement purposes: (1) to record an expense incurred in 19B for matching with revenues and (2) to record the liability for the salary owed at the end of 19B for balance sheet purposes. The second entry (in 19C) recorded the payment of that liability.

Property tax expense and liability

On December 28, 19B, a tax bill amounting to $5,700 was received from the city for 19B property taxes. The taxes are due on February 15, 19C; therefore, they were unpaid and unrecorded at the end of 19B. The sequence of entries for High-Rise would be:

g. December 31, 19B (end of the accounting period)—**adjusting entry:**[3]

```
Property tax expense ...............................................  5,700
     Property tax payable ..........................................       5,700
     To record 19B property taxes incurred and the related liability.
```

---

[3] This is an example of a situation where there may or may not be an adjusting entry. For example, assume the tax bill was received on December 5, 19B. At that date, a **current entry** probably would have been made identical to the adjusting entry given above. Under these circumstances, an adjusting entry at December 31, 19B, would not be needed.

This adjusting entry records the incurred, but unpaid, tax expense for 19B, in accordance with the matching principle, and also the tax liability that must be reported on the 19B balance sheet.

February 15, 19C—payment of the 19B liability for property tax:

```
Property tax payable ...........................................  5,700
    Cash ......................................................          5,700
    To record payment of property tax liability.
```

Interest expense

On November 1, 19B, High-Rise borrowed $30,000 cash from a local bank on a 90-day note with an annual interest rate of 12 percent. The principal plus interest is due in three months. The sequence of entries by High-Rise is:

November 1, 19B—date of transaction:

```
Cash .......................................................  30,000
    Note payable, short term ...................................          30,000
    To record a three-month, 12 percent loan from a bank.
```

Analysis: At December 31, 19B, the end of the accounting period, two months have passed since the note was signed; therefore, interest expense for two months has **accrued** on the note because interest legally accrues with the passage of time, notwithstanding the fact that the interest is payable in cash at the maturity date. At year-end, there is a **liability** for interest for the two months at the end of 19B. This expense and the related liability have not yet been recorded; therefore, an **adjusting entry** is necessary to (a) debit interest expense for $600 (i.e., $30,000 \times 12\% \times \frac{2}{12} = \$600$) and (b) credit interest payable for the same amount. The adjusting and payment entries would be:

h. December 31, 19B (end of the accounting period)—**adjusting entry:**

```
Interest expense ...............................................  600
    Interest payable (or accrued interest payable) ..................          600
    To record accrued interest expense for two months on note payable
    ($30,000 \times 12\% \times \frac{2}{12} = \$600).
```

January 31, 19C—maturity date; payment of the principal of the note and interest:

Note payable, short term	30,000	
Interest payable (per adjusting entry)	600	
Interest expense (19C—$30,000 \times 12\% \times \frac{1}{12}$)	300	
Cash		30,900
To record payment of principal plus interest on note payable at maturity date.		

RECORDING ADJUSTING ENTRIES

The preceding examples demonstrated the application of the revenue and matching principles at the **end** of the accounting period by using adjusting entries. In situations when certain economic effects have not been recorded, appropriate adjusting entries are necessary to ensure that both the income statement and balance sheet will be correct. Adjusting entries are made to **allocate** revenue and expense among the current and one or more future periods so that expenses are matched properly with revenues each accounting period.

Basically, adjusting entries relate to transactions that start in one period and, in effect, continue into one or more subsequent periods. Therefore, an analysis to determine whether an adjusting entry is needed, and if so, how it should be made, must be based on the **sequence** of related events covering the periods affected. The demonstration cases at the end of this chapter illustrate how adjusting entries are influenced by particular situations.

Adjusting entries are entered first in the journal (dated the last day of the accounting period) immediately after all of the regular transactions are recorded. The adjusting entries then are **posted** from the journal to the ledger accounts in the usual way. Recording in the journal and posting to the ledger are necessary because adjusting entries reflect economic events, and their effects must be processed through the accounting information system and into the financial statements in the same manner as the regular transactions. These procedures are illustrated in the next chapter within the context of a complete information processing cycle.

In some instances, it is difficult to draw a distinct line between regular and adjusting entries, and there are no real reasons to make the distinction, other than the fact that adjusting entries (a) usually must be made at the **end** of the accounting period and (b) **update** certain income statement and balance sheet accounts. The important point is that adjusting entries (as well as many other entries) are necessary to appropriately measure periodic revenues and to match expenses with those revenues that were earned during the period.

DEMONSTRATION CASE A

(Try to resolve the requirements before proceeding to the suggested solution that follows.)

New Service Corporation is owned by three stockholders and has been in operation for one year, 19A. Cash flow and expenses are critical control problems. Minimal record keeping has been performed to save money. One secretary performs both the secretarial and recordkeeping functions. Because of a loan application made by the corporation, the bank has requested an income statement and balance sheet. Accordingly, the secretary prepared the following (summarized for case purposes):

Profit Statement
Annual—December 31, 19A

Revenues:	
Service	$ 78,500
Expenses:	
Salaries and wages	(43,200)
Utilities	(1,800)
Miscellaneous	(4,000)
Net profit	$ 29,500

Balance Sheet
December 31, 19A

Assets

Cash	$ 4,000
Accounts receivable	85,500
Supplies inventory	8,000
Equipment	40,000
Other assets	16,000
Total assets	$103,500

Liabilities

Accounts payable	$ 9,000
Income taxes payable	
Note payable, one year, 12%	10,000

Net Worth

Capital stock, par $10	50,000
Premium	5,000
Retained profits	29,500
Total liabilities and net worth	$103,500

After reading the two statements, the bank requested that an independent CPA examine them. The CPA found that the secretary used some obsolete captions and terminology and did not include the effects of the following data (i.e., the adjusting entries):

a. Supplies inventory on hand at December 31 amounted to $3,000.
b. Depreciation for 19A. The equipment was acquired during January 19A; estimated useful life, 10 years, and no residual value.

c. The note payable was dated August 1, 19A, and the principal plus interest are payable at the end of one year.

d. Rent expense of $3,600 was included in miscellaneous expense.

e. Income taxes; assume an average tax rate of 17 percent.

Required:

1. Recast the above statements to incorporate the additional data, appropriate captions, preferred terminology, and improved format. Show computations.

2. Prepare the adjusting entries (in journal form) for the additional data at December 31, 19A.

3. Comment on any aspects of this situation that the bank loan officer should note in particular if they appear to be unusual.

Suggested solution

Requirement 1:

NEW SERVICE CORPORATION
Income Statement
For the Year Ended December 31, 19A

	Amounts reported	Effects of adjusting entries*	Corrected amounts
Revenue:			
Service revenue	$ 78,500		$78,500
Expenses:			
Salaries and wages	43,200		43,200
Utilities	1,800		1,800
Supplies expense		(a) + 5,000	5,000
Depreciation expense		(b) + 4,000	4,000
Interest expense		(c) + 500	500
Rent expense		(d) + 3,600	3,600
Miscellaneous expense	4,000	(d) − 3,600	400
Total expenses	49,000		58,500
Pretax income	$ 29,500		20,000
Income tax expense ($20,000 × 17%)		(e) + 3,400	3,400
Net income			$16,600
EPS ($16,600 ÷ 5,000 shares)			$3.32

NEW SERVICE CORPORATION
Balance Sheet
At December 31, 19A

Assets

Cash	$ 4,000		$ 4,000
Accounts receivable	35,500		35,500
Supplies inventory	8,000	(a) − 5,000	3,000
Equipment	40,000		40,000
Accumulated depreciation		(b) − 4,000	(4,000)
Other assets	16,000		16,000
Total assets	$103,500		$94,500

Liabilities

Accounts payable	$ 9,000		$ 9,000
Income taxes payable		(e) + 3,400	3,400
Interest payable		(c) + 500	500
Note payable, one year, 12%	10,000		10,000
Total liabilities	19,000		22,900

Stockholders' Equity

Capital stock, par $10 (5,000 shares)	50,000		50,000
Contributed capital in excess of par	5,000		5,000
Retained earnings	29,500	−29,500 + 16,600	16,600
Total liabilities and stockholders' equity	$103,500		$94,500

Note: Observe changes in captions, terminology, and format.
* The letters identify the adjustments shown under Requirement 2.

Requirement 2:

Adjusting entries at December 31, 19A;

---

a. Supplies expense 5,000

      Supplies inventory 5,000

      To reduce supplies inventory to the amount on hand December 31,
      19A, $3,000, and to record supplies expense, $8,000 −$3,000 = $5,000.

b. Depreciation expense 4,000

      Accumulated depreciation 4,000

      Depreciation for one year, $40,000 ÷ 10 years = $4,000.

c. Interest expense 500

      Interest payable 500

      To record interest expense and the interest accrued (a liability) from
      August 1 to December 31, 19A ($10,000 × 12% × 5/12 = $500).

d. Rent expense 3,600

      Miscellaneous expense 3,600

      To record rent expense in the proper account.

e. Income tax expense 3,400

      Income tax payable 3,400

      To record income tax expense and the liability for unpaid tax as
      computed on the income statement.

Requirement 3:

The loan officer should note particularly the following:

a. The overstatement of net income (by 78 percent; i.e., $29,500 ÷ $16,600) and total assets (by 10 percent; i.e., $103,500 ÷ $94,500), which suggests either (1) an attempt to mislead or (2) the need for better accounting.
b. The very high amount in accounts receivable compared to cash and total assets. This fact suggests inadequate evaluation of credit and/or inefficiency in collections.
c. The small amount of cash compared with accounts payable (a current liability).
d. Inclusion of rent expense in miscellaneous expense.
e. Inapproapriate captions, terminology, and format.

DEMONSTRATION CASE B

(Try to resolve the requirements before proceeding to the suggested solution that follows.)

This case is presented to illustrate **why** and **how** adjusting entries are influenced directly by the manner in which an **initial entry** is made. Determination of whether an **adjusting entry** is needed, and if so, how it should be made, requires a careful **analysis of this situation.**

Situation: On July 1, 19A, Company K paid a two-year insurance premium of $1,200. The annual accounting period ends on December 31.

Required:

1. How much of the premium should be reported as expense in the 19A, 19B, and 19C income statements?
2. What is the amount of prepaid insurance on December 31, 19A? How should this amount be reported on the 19A financial statements?
3. Company K could have recorded the $1,200 payment on July 1, 19A, in one of three ways as follows:

Case A:

Prepaid insurance	1,200	
Cash		1,200

Case B:

Insurance expense	1,200	
Cash		1,200

Case C:

Prepaid insurance	900	
Insurance expense	300	
Cash		1,200

For each case, give the appropriate adjusting entry (at December 31, 19A) in journal form and then post to ledger T-accounts. If no adjusting entry is required, explain why.

Suggested solution

Requirement 1:

Insurance expense: 19A—$1,200 \times$ 6/24 $= $300 (½ year)
                                        19B—$1,200 \times$ 12/24 $=$ 600 (1 year)
                                        19C—$1,200 \times$ 6/24 $=$ 300 (½ year)

Requirement 2:

Prepaid insurance on December 31, 19A—$1,200 \times 18/24 = $900. This amount should be reported on the balance sheet at December 31, 19A, as a current asset. Theoretical strictness suggests that $300 of the $900 should be reported as a deferred charge (a noncurrent asset) because this asset will not be liquidated within the next year; however, this distinction usually is not made in practice when the effect is not material as in this case.

Requirement 3:

Adjusting entry at December 31, 19A:

JOURNAL	LEDGER

CASE A

Adjusting entry:

Insurance expense 300
        Prepaid insurance 300
To reduce prepaid insurance to $900, and to record insurance expense for 19A, $300.

Prepaid Insurance

Initial entry	1,200	Adj. entry	300

Insurance Expense

Adj. entry	300		

CASE B

Adjusting entry:

Prepaid insurance 900
        Insurance expense 900
To record prepaid insurance at the end of 19A, $900, and to reduce insurance expense to $300 for 19A.

Insurance Expense

Initial entry	1,200	Adj. entry	900

Prepaid Insurance

Adj. entry	900		

JOURNAL	LEDGER

CASE C

| Adjusting entry:
No adjusting entry is needed at December 31, 19A, because the correct amounts for both prepaid insurance at December 31, 19A, $900, and insurance expense for 19A, $300 were recorded on the transaction date, July 1, 19A. An adjusting entry would be needed at the end of 19B and also at the end of 19C. | **Prepaid Insurance**
Initial entry   900

Insurance Expense
Initial entry   300 |

SUMMARY OF CHAPTER

This chapter focused on the **revenue** and **matching** principles, and the adjusting entries that are necessary to apply those principles. Matching expenses with revenue for the period is critical because the lifespan of an enterprise, although indefinite in length, must be divided into a series of short time periods (usually one year) for periodic performance measurements. Primary among those performance measurements are the economic effects reported in the periodic financial statements.

In the measurement of net income, the **revenue principle** holds that revenues earned in the period through sale of goods or performance of services must be identified, measured, and reported for that period. The **matching principle** holds that the expenses incurred in earning those revenues must be identified, measured, and matched with revenues earned in the period in order to determine periodic net income. To implement the matching principle, certain transactions and events whose economic effects extend from the current period to one or more future accounting periods must be analyzed at the end of the accounting period. This analysis is the basis for allocating their expense effects to the future periods during which they will aid in the generation of revenues. The allocation of some revenues and expenses to two or more accounting periods requires the use of **adjusting entries**. Adjusting entries follow the same concepts and procedures as entries for the usual transactions except that they are made at the end of the accounting period. At the end of the accounting period they are entered first in the journal and then are posted to the ledger in the same manner as are other entries.

IMPORTANT TERMS DEFINED IN THIS CHAPTER

Terms (alphabetically)	Key words in definitions of terms used in chapter	Page reference
Accrue (accrued)	An expense incurred but not yet paid; a revenue earned but not yet collected.	157
Adjusting entries	End-of-period entries required by the revenue and matching principles to attain a cutoff between periods.	154
Contra account	An account, related to a primary account, that is an offset (or reduction) to the primary account.	163
Defer (deferred)	An expense paid in advance of use; a revenue collected in advance of earning.	157

Terms (alphabetically)	Key words in definitions of terms used in chapter	Page reference
Depreciation	Expense of using (wearing out) a building, machinery, fixtures, etc., each period of useful life.	162
Expenses paid in advance	Cash paid for goods, or services, before those goods or services are used; prepaid expenses.	161
Expenses incurred but not recorded	Expenses actually incurred but not yet paid or recorded.	164
Fiscal year	An accounting period of 12 months that does not necessarily end on December 31.	151
Interest expense	Time value of money; the cost of borrowing money (or other assets acquired).	166
Interim reports	Financial reports for periods of less than one year; quarterly or monthly reports.	151
Matching principle	All costs incurred to earn the revenues of the period must be identified then matched with revenue by recording as expense.	154
Reliability principle	Financial statements must be unbiased, accurate, and verifiable.	153
Residual value	Value (estimated) of an operational asset at the end of its useful life to the business (scrap or salvage value).	163
Revenue collected in advance	Revenue collected in cash before that revenue is earned. Precollected revenue.	158
Revenue earned but not yet collected or recorded	Revenue not yet collected, or recorded, but already earned. Accrued revenue.	160
Revenue principle	Recognize revenue in the period **earned** rather when the cash is received; earning process completed.	152
Supplies inventory	Supplies purchased and still on hand; unused supplies at the end of period.	163
Time-period assumption	Division of the operating activities of a business into a series of equal time periods (usually one year) for accounting purposes.	150

QUESTIONS FOR DISCUSSION

PART A

1. Identify the two **change** statements and briefly explain why they are referred to as change statements.

2. Explain the time-period assumption.

3. What is an interim report?

4. Briefly define natural business year, calendar year, and fiscal year as used in accounting.

5. Identify the *(a)* revenue and *(b)* expense recognition problem related to the time-period assumption.

6. Explain the revenue principle and the matching principle.

7. Contrast the completed contract method with the percentage-of-completion method of recognizing revenues for long-term construction contracts.

8. What is an adjusting entry? Explain why such entries are necessary.

9. What are the three fundamental characteristics of adjusting entries?

10. Briefly define each of the following: accrued expense, accrued revenue, deferred expense, and deferred revenue.

PART B

11. AB Company collected $600 rent for the period December 15, 19A, to January 15, 19B. The $600 was credited to Rent Revenue Collected in Advance on December 15, 19A. Give the adjusting entry required on December 31, 19A (end of the accounting period).

12. On December 31, 19B, Company T recorded the following adjusting entry:

Rent revenue receivable	500	
Rent revenue		500

Explain the situation that caused this entry and give the subsequent related entry.

13. On July 1, 19A, M Company paid a two-year insurance premium of $400 and debited prepaid insurance for that amount. Assuming the accounting period ends in December, give the adjusting entries that should be made at the end of 19A, 19B, and 19C.

14. Explain "estimated residual value." Why is it important in measuring depreciation expense?

15. Explain why adjusting entries are entered in the journal on the last day of the accounting period and then are posted to the ledger.

EXERCISES

PART A

E4–1. Match the following (each letter may be used more than once and each reporting item may be associated with several letters):

Reporting Item	Description
_____ Income statement	A. Reports sources of funds.
_____ Balance sheet	B. Reports EPS.
_____ Statement of changes	C. Reports retained earnings.
in financial position	D. Reports on operations.
_____ Notes to the financial	E. Reports financial position.
statement	F. Reports uses of funds.
	G. Reports extraordinary items.
	H. Reports inflows and outflows of cash or working capital.
	I. Provides qualitative explanations.
	J. Dated: At December 31, 19X.
	K. Dated: For the year ended December 31, 19X.

E4–2. Match the following:

Term	Analysis of the records revealed that—
_____ Deferred revenue	A. At the end of the year wages payable of $2,500 had not been recorded or paid.
_____ Accrued revenue	
_____ Deferred expense	B. Supplies for office use were purchased during the year at a cost of $600 and $100 of the office supplies remained on hand (unused) at year-end.
_____ Accrued expense	
	C. Interest of $300 on a note receivable was earned at year-end, although collection of the interest is not due until the following year.
	D. At the end of the year service revenue of $1,000 was collected in cash but was not yet earned.

E4–3. Tiger Construction Company, Incorporated, specializes in major commercial construction. In 19A, the company signed a contract to build a large warehouse. The contract price was $2,000,000, and the estimated construction cost was $1,400,000. Construction was started on June 1, 19A, and completed March 31, 19B. Actual construction costs were higher than originally estimated; the actual 19A costs were $420,000; and 19B, $1,080,000.

Required:

a. Complete the following tabulation for each separate case. Assume income recognition under percentage of completion is allocated on the basis of actual costs incurred to total estimated costs.

		Pretax income to be recognized	
Case	*Method*	*19A*	*19B*
A	Completed contract	$_____	$_____
B	Percentage of completion	_____	_____

b. Which method would you recommend for Tiger? Explain the basis for your choice.

E4–4. It is December 31, 19B, end of the annual accounting period for TT Service Company. Below are listed six independent transactions (summarized) that affected the company during 19B. The transactions are to be analyzed in terms of their effects on the balance sheet and income statement for 19B.

a. On January 1, 19A, the company purchased a machine that cost $10,000 cash (estimated useful life five years and no residual value).
   (1) Show how the machine should be reported on the 19B balance sheet.
   (2) Show how the 19B income statement should report the effects of the machine usage.

b. On September 1, 19B, the company signed a $10,000, 12 percent, one-year note payable. The principal plus interest is payable on maturity date.
   (1) Show how the liability should be reported on the 19B balance sheet.
   (2) Show how the effects of the note be reported on the 19B income statement.

c. During 19B, service revenues of $90,000 were collected of which $10,000 was collected in advance.
   (1) Show how the $10,000 should be reported on the 19B balance sheet.
   (2) Show how the 19B income statement should report the effects of the transaction.

d. In 19B, expenses paid in cash amounted to $60,000 of which $5,000 was paid for expenses yet to be incurred (prepaid).
   (1) Show how the 19B balance sheet should report the $5,000.
   (2) Show how the income statement should report this situation.

e. In 19B, $85,000 cash revenues were collected and in addition revenues of $5,000 were on credit.
   (1) Show how the $5,000 should be reported on the 19B balance sheet.
   (2) Show how the 19B income statement should report the revenues.

f. In 19B, expenses amounting to $56,000 were paid in cash and in addition expenses of $3,000 were on credit.
   (1) Show how the $3,000 should be reported on the 19B balance sheet.
   (2) Show how the expenses should be reported on the 19B income statement.

E4–5. XT Company started operations on January 1, 19A. It is now December 31, 19A (end of the annual accounting period) and the part-time bookkeeper needs your assistance in analyzing the following three transactions:

a. On January 1, 19A, the company purchased a special machine for a cash cost of $15,000. The machine has an estimated useful life of five years and no residual value.

b. During 19A, the company purchased office supplies that cost $400. At the end of 19A, office supplies of $100 remained on hand.

c. On July 1, 19A, the company paid cash of $300 for a two-year insurance policy on the machine.

Required:

Complete the following schedule as of the end of 19A:

Selected Balance Sheet Amounts

Amount to be reported

Assets:
Machine	$ _____
Accumulated depreciation	_____
Carrying value	_____
Office supplies inventory	_____
Prepaid insurance	_____

Selected Income Statement Amounts

Depreciation expense	$ _____
Office supplies expense	_____
Insurance expense	_____

PART B

E4–6.   Rich Department Store is completing the accounting process for the year just ended, December 31, 19B. The transactions during 19B have been journalized and posted. The following data in respect to adjusting entries are available:

a. Office supplies inventory at January 1, 19B, was $120. Office supplies purchased and debited to Office Supplies Inventory during the year amounted to $360. The year-end inventory showed $80 of supplies on hand.

b. Wages earned during December 19B but unpaid and unrecorded at December 31, 19B, amounted to $1,400. The last payroll was December 28, and the next payroll will be January 6, 19C.

c. Three fourths of the basement of the store is rented for $800 per month to another merchant, J. B. Smith, who sells compatible, but not competitive, merchandise. On November 1, 19B, the store collected six months' rent in advance from Smith amounting to $4,800, which was credited in full to Rent Revenue when collected.

d. The rest of the basement is rented to Spears Specialty; at $360 per month, payable monthly. On December 31, 19B, the rent for November and December 19B was neither collected nor recorded. Collection is expected January 10, 19C.

e. Delivery equipment that cost $21,000 was being used by the store. Estimates in respect to equipment were (1) useful life five years and (2) residual value at the end of five years' use, $1,000. Assume depreciation for a full year for 19B and that the asset will be depreciated evenly over its useful life.

f. On July 1, 19B, a two-year insurance premium amounting to $1,000 was paid in cash and debited in full to Prepaid Insurance.

g. Rich operates an alteration shop to meet its own needs. In addition, the shop does alterations for J. B. Smith. At the end of December 31, 19B, J. B. Smith had not paid for alterations completed amounting to $450, and this amount has not been recorded as Alteration Shop Revenue.

Required:

Give the adjusting entry for each situation that should be entered in the records of Rich Department Store at December 31, 19B.

E4–7.   On April 1, 19B, Davis Corporation received a $4,000, 15 percent note from a customer in settlement of a $4,000 open account receivable. According to the terms, the principal of the note, plus the interest, are payable at the end of 12 months. The annual accounting period for Davis ends on December 31, 19B.

Required:

a.   Give the journal entry for Davis for receipt of the note on April 1, 19B.
b.   Give the adjusting entry required on December 31, 19B.
c.   Give the journal entry on date of collection, March 31, 19C.

On August 1, 19B, to meet a cash shortage, Davis Corporation obtained a $20,000, 12 percent loan from a local bank. The principal of the note, plus interest expense, are payable at the end of 12 months.

Required:

d.   Give the journal entry for Davis on the date of the loan, August 1, 19B.
e.   Give the adjusting entry required on December 31, 19B.
f.   Give the journal entry on date of payment, July 31, 19C.

E4–8.   Kay Company is in the process of making adjusting entries for the year ended December 31, 19B. In developing information for the adjusting entries, the accountant learned that on September 1, 19B, a two-year insurance premium of $2,400 was paid.

Required:

a.   What amount should be reported on the 19B income statement for insurance expense?
b.   What amount should be reported on the December 31, 19B, balance sheet for prepaid insurance?
c.   Give the adjusting entry at December 31, 19B, under each of two cases:

Case 1—Assume that when the premium was paid on September 1, 19B, the book-keeper debited the full amount to Prepaid Insurance.

Case 2—Assume that when the premium was paid September 1, 19B, the bookkeeper debited Insurance Expense for the full amount.

(Hint: In Case 2 be sure that after the adjusting entry, you end with the same amount in the Prepaid Insurance account as in Case 1.)

E4–9.   Wise Manufacturing Company uses a large amount of shipping supplies that are purchased in large volume, stored, and used as needed. At December 31, 19B, the following data relating to shipping supplies were obtained from the records and supporting documents:

Shipping supplies on hand, January 1, 19B	$ 2,000
Purchases of shipping supplies during 19B	13,000
Shipping supplies on hand, per inventory December 31, 19B	4,000

Required:

a.   What amount should be reported on the 19B income statement for shipping supplies expense?

    b. What amount should be reported on the December 31, 19B, balance sheet for shipping supplies inventory?

    c. Give the adjusting entry at December 31, 19B, assuming the purchases of shipping supplies were debited in full to Shipping Supplies Inventory ($13,000).

    d. What adjusting entry would you make assuming the bookkeeper debited Shipping Supplies Expense for the $13,000 supplies? (Hint: In solving *(c)* and *(d),* be sure that each solution ends up with the same amount remaining in the Shipping Supplies Inventory account.)

E4–10. On December 31, 19B, Boston Company prepared an income statement and balance sheet and failed to take into account three adjusting entries. The income statement, prepared on this incorrect basis, reflected a pretax income of $20,000. The balance sheet reflected total assets, $90,000; total liabilities, $30,000; and owners' equity, $60,000. The data for the three adjusting entries were:

1. Depreciation was not recorded for the year on equipment that cost $55,000; estimated useful life, 10 years, and residual value, $5,000.
2. Wages amounting to $8,000 for the last three days of December 19B not paid and not recorded (the next payroll will be on January 10, 19C).
3. Rent revenue of $3,000 was collected on December 1, 19B, for office space for the period December 1, 19B, to February 28, 19C. The $3,000 was credited in full to Rent Revenue when collected.

Required:

Complete the following tabulation (indicate deductions with parentheses):

Item	Pretax income	Total assets	Total liabilties	Owners' equity
Balances reported	$20,000	$90,000	$30,000	$60,000
1. Effects of depreciation	_____	_____	_____	_____
2. Effects of wages	_____	_____	_____	_____
3. Effects of rent revenue	_____	_____	_____	_____
Correct balances	_____	_____	_____	_____

E4–11. Supreme Auto Rentals, Inc., completed its first year of operations on December 31, 19A. Because this is the end of the annual accounting period, the company bookkeeper prepared the following tentative income statement:

Income Statement, 19A

Rental revenue		$102,000
Expenses:		
Salaries and wages	$26,400	
Maintenance expense	10,000	
Rent expense (on location)	8,000	
Utilities expense	3,000	
Gas and oil expense	2,000	
Miscellaneous expense (items not listed above)	400	
Total expenses		49,800
Income		$ 52,200

An independent CPA reviewed the income statement and developed additional data as follows:

1. Wages for the last three days of December amounting to $600 were not recorded or paid (disregard payroll taxes).

2. The telephone bill for December 19A amounting to $200 has not been recorded or paid.
3. Depreciation on rental autos amounting to $20,000 for 19A, was not recorded.
4. Interest on a $20,000, one-year, 12 percent note payable dated November 1, 19A, was not recorded. The 12 percent interest is payable on maturity date of the note.
5. Rental revenue includes $2,000 rental revenue for the month of January 19B.
6. Maintenance expense includes $1,000, which is the cost of maintenance supplies still on hand (per inventory) at December 31, 19A.
7. Assume the income tax rate is 20 percent. Assume payment of income tax will be made in 19B.

Required:

a. Prepare a correct income statement for 19A assuming 10,000 shares of stock are outstanding. Show computations.
b. Give the adjusting entry at December 31, 19A, for each of the additional data items. If none is required explain why.

E4–12. On December 15, 19C, the bookkeeper for Seattle Company prepared the income statement and balance sheet given below (summarized) but neglected to consider three of the adjusting entries.

	As prepared	Effects of adjusting entries	Corrected amounts
Income statement:			
Revenues	$95,000	____	____
Expenses	(83,000)	____	____
Income tax expense		____	____
Income	$12,000		
Balance sheet:			
Assets			
Cash	$18,000	____	____
Accounts receivable	26,000	____	____
Rent receivable		____	____
Equipment*	40,000	____	____
Accumulated depreciation	(8,000)	____	____
	$76,000		
Liabilities			
Accounts payable	$10,000	____	____
Income taxes payable		____	____
Owners' Equity			
Capital stock	50,000	____	____
Retained earnings	16,000	____	____
	$76,000		

* Acquired January 1, 10-year life, no residual value; straight-line depreciation.

Date on the three adjusting entries:

1. Depreciation on the equipment was not recorded for 19C.
2. Rent revenue earned of $1,000 for December 19C was neither collected or recorded.
3. Income taxes for 19C were not paid or recorded; assume an average rate of 20 percent.

Required:

a. Prepare the three adjusting entries (in journal form) that were omitted.

b. Complete the two columns to the right in the above tabulation to reflect the correct amounts on the income statement and balance sheet.

E4–13. (Analytical) TK Company's comparative balance sheets for 19A and 19B reported the following selected amounts:

	19A	19B
Assets:		
Prepaid insurance premium	$500	$700
Liabilities:		
Rent revenue collected in advance	900	500

The 19B income statement reported the following amounts:

	19B
Expenses:	
Insurance expense	$ 750
Revenues:	
Rent revenue	7,200

Required:

a. Compute the total amount of insurance premium that was paid in cash during 19B. Show computations.

b. Compute the total amount of rent revenue that was collected in cash during 19B. Show computations.

PROBLEMS/CASES

PART A

PC4–1. Rust Company, a locally owned corporation, invests in commercial rental properties. Rust's annual accounting period ends on December 31. At the end of each year, numerous adjusting entries must be made because many transactions completed during current and prior years have economic effects on the financial statements of the current and future years. This case is concerned with several such transactions that have been selected for your analysis. Assume the current year is 19D.

Transaction A:

On July 1, 19A, the company purchased office equipment for use in the business at a cash cost of $9,000. The company estimates that the equipment will have a useful life of 10 years and no residual value.

a. Over how many accounting periods will this transaction affect the financial statements of Rust? Explain.

b. Assuming straight-line depreciation, how much depreciation expense should be reported in year 19A and in 19D?

c. What would be the amount of accumulated depreciation immediately after the adjusting entries are made on December 31, 19D?

d. Would an adjusting entry be made at the end of each year during the life of the equipment? Explain why.

Transaction B:

On October 1, 19D, the company collected $12,000 rent on some office space. This amount represented the monthly rent in advance for the six-month period, October 1, 19D, through March 31, 19E. Rent revenue was increased (credited) by $12,000.

a. Over how many accounting periods will this transaction affect the financial statements of Rust? Explain.
b. How much rent revenue on this office space should Rust report in 19D? Explain.
c. Did this transaction create a **liability** as of the end of 19D? Explain.
d. Should an adjusting entry be made on December 31, 19D? Explain why. If your answer is yes, give the adjusting entry.

Transaction C:

On December 31, 19D, the company owed employees unpaid and unrecorded wages of $5,000 because the payroll was paid on December 27 and between this day and year-end employees worked three more days in December 19D.

a. Over how many accounting periods would this transaction affect the financial statements of Rust? Explain.
b. How would this $5,000 affect the 19D income statement and balance sheet of Rust?
c. Should an adjusting entry be made on December 31, 19D? Explain why. If your answer is yes, give the adjusting entry.

Transaction D:

On January 1, 19D, Rust agreed to supervise the planning and subdivision of a large tract of land for a customer—J. Dolan. This service job, to be performed by Rust, involved four separate phases. By December 31, 19D, three phases had been fully completed to the satisfaction of Dolan. The remaining phase will be done during 19E. The total price for the four phases (agreed upon in advance by both parties) was $40,000. Each phase involves approximately the same amount of services. On December 31, 19D, no cash had been collected by Rust for the services already performed.

a. Should Rust record any service revenue on this job for 19D? Explain why. If yes, how much?
b. If your answer to (a) is yes, should Rust make an adjusting entry on December 31, 19D; if yes, give the entry. Explain.

PC4–2. The following information was provided by the records and related documents of Apache Garden Apartments (a corporation) at the end of the annual fiscal period, December 31, 19B:

Revenue:

1. Rental revenue collected in cash during 19B for occupancy in 19B (credited to Rent Revenue)	$497,000
2. Rental revenue earned for occupancy in December 19B but not collected until 19C	8,000
3. In December 19B, collected rent revenue in advance for January 19C	6,000

Salary expense:

4. Cash payment made in January 19B for salaries incurred (earned) in December 19A	3,000
5. Salaries incurred and paid during 19B (debited to Salary Expense)	58,000
6. Salaries earned by employees during December 19B but not to be paid until January 19C	2,000
7. Cash advance to employees in December 19B for salaries to be earned in January 19C	4,000

Supplies used:

   8.   Maintenance supplies on hand (Inventory) on January 1, 19B   2,000
   9.   Maintenance supplies purchased for cash during 19B (debited to Main-
        tenance Supplies Inventory when purchased)   8,000
  10.   Maintenance supplies on hand (Inventory) on December 31, 19B   1,500

Required:

Under the revenue and matching principles, what amounts should be shown on the 19B, income statement for *(a)* rent revenue, *(b)* salary expense, and *(c)* maintenance supplies expense? Show computations with explanations for each numbered item.

PC4–3.   On January 1, 19A, four individuals organized WAS Company. The company has been operating for two years, 19A and 19B. Given below are data relating to six selected transactions that affect both years. The annual accounting period ends December 31.

   a.   On January 1, 19A, the company purchased a computer for use in the business at a cash cost of $14,000. The computer has an estimated useful life of seven years and no residual value. It will be depreciated on a straight-line basis.
   b.   On September 1, 19A, the company borrowed $10,000 cash from City Bank and signed a one-year, 12 percent, interest-bearing note. The interest and principal are payable on August 31, 19B.
   c.   The company owns its office building. On October 1, 19A, the company leased some of its office space to A. B. Smith for $6,000 per year. Smith paid this amount in full on October 1, 19A, and expects to use the space for one year only. The company increased (debited) Cash for $6,000 and increased (credited) Rent Revenue for $6,000 on October 1, 19A.
   d.   Office supplies were purchased for use in the business, Cash was decreased (credited) and Office Supplies Inventory was increased (debited). The unused supplies at each year-end are determined by inventory count. The amounts were:

Year	Purchased	Inventory
19A	$700	$200
19B	500	300

   e.   Wages are paid by the company at the end of each two weeks. The last payroll date in December usually is four days before December 31. Consequently, at each year-end, unpaid wages exist that are paid in cash on the first payroll date in the next year. The wages paid in cash and the wages incurred but not yet paid or recorded at each year end were:

Year	Wages paid in cash during the year	Wages unpaid and unrecorded Dec. 31
19A......	$30,000	$2,000
19B	36,000	3,000

   f.   On July 1, 19A, the company paid a two-year insurance premium (on the computer) of $240. At that date, the company increased (debited) an asset account—Prepaid Insurance—and decreased (credited) Cash, $240.

Required:

Complete the following schedule for 19A and 19B by entering the amounts that should be reported on the financial statements of WAS Company. Show computations.

Balance sheet:

	19A	19B
Assets		
Computer	$____	$____
Less: Accumulated depreciation	____	____
Carrying value	____	____
Office supplies inventory	____	____
Prepaid insurance	____	____
Liabilities		
Note payable, City Bank	____	____
Interest payable	____	____
Rent revenue collected in advance.....	____	____
Wages payable	____	____

Income statement:

	19A	19B
Rent revenue	$____	$____
Depreciation expense	____	____
Interest expense	____	____
Office supplies expense	____	____
Wage expense	____	____
Insurance expense	____	____

PART B

PC4–4. Jackson Service Company is preparing the adjusting entries for the year ended December 31, 19B. On that date, the bookkeeper for the company assembled the following data:

1. On December 31, 19B, salaries earned by employees but not yet paid or recorded amounted to $6,000.
2. Depreciation must be recognized on a service truck that cost $9,000 on July 1, 19B (estimated useful life six years and no residual value).
3. Cash of $1,000 was collected on December 28, 19B, for services to be rendered during 19C (Service Revenue was credited).
4. On December 27, 19B, Jackson received a tax bill of $200 from the city for 19B property taxes (on service equipment) which is payable (and will be paid) during January 19C.
5. On July 1, 19B, the company paid $840 cash for a two-year insurance policy on the service truck (2 above).
6. On October 1, 19B, the company borrowed $10,000 from a local bank and signed a 12 percent note for that amount. The principal and interest are payable on maturity date, September 30, 19C.

Required:

a. The bookkeeper has asked you to assist in preparing the appropriate adjusting entires at December 31, 19B. For each situation above, give the appropriate adjusting entry with a brief explanation. If none is required, explain why.
b. Based on your entries given in Requirement *(a)*, complete the following schedule to reflect the amounts and balance sheet classifications:

| | | | Balance sheet classification (one check on each line) | | |
Item No.	Accounts	19B amount	Assets	Liabilities	Owners' Equity
1	Salaries payable	$_____	_____	_____	_____
2	Accumulated depreciation	_____	_____	_____	_____
3	Revenue collected in advance	_____	_____	_____	_____
4	Property tax payable	_____	_____	_____	_____
5	Prepaid insurance	_____	_____	_____	_____
6	Interest payable	_____	_____	_____	_____

PC4–5 Slow Transportation Company is at the end of its accounting year December 31, 19B. The following data that must be considered to answer the requirements was developed from the company's records and related documents:

1. On July 1, 19B, a three-year insurance premium on equipment was paid amounting to $900 that was debited in full to Prepaid Insurance on that date.
2. During 19B, office supplies amounting to $1,000 were purchased for cash and debited in full to Supplies Inventory. At the end of 19A, the inventory count of supplies remaining on hand (unused) showed $200. The inventory of supplies on hand (unused) at December 31, 19B, showed $300.
3. On December 31, 19B, B&R Garage completed repairs on one of Slow's trucks at a cost of $650; the amount is not yet recorded and, by agreement, will be paid during January 19C.
4. In December 19B, a tax bill, on trucks owned during 19B, amounting to $1,400 was received from the city. The taxes, which have not been recorded, are due and will be paid on February 15, 19C.
5. On December 31, 19B, Slow completed a hauling contract for an out-of-state company. The bill was for $7,500 payable within 30 days. No cash has been collected, and no journal entry has been made for this transaction.
6. On July 1, 19B, Slow purchased a new hauling van at a cash cost of $21,600. The estimated useful life of the van was 10 years, with an estimated residual value of $1,600. No depreciation has been recorded for 19B (compute depreciation for six months in 19B).
7. On October 1, 19B, Slow borrowed $6,000 from the local bank on a one-year, 15 percent note payable. The principal plus interest is payable at the end of 12 months.

Required:

a. Give the adjusting entry required on December 31, 19B, related to each of the above transactions. Give a brief explanation with each entry.
b. Assume Slow Transportation Company had prepared a tentative income statement for 19B that did not include the effect of any of the above items and that the tentative pretax income computed was $30,000. Considering the above items, compute the corrected pretax income for 19B. Show computations.

PC4–6. This case, taken from the experiences of Frindly Department Store, has been selected to give you an opportunity to test your analytical ability in transaction analysis and in developing the adjusting entries where there are both notes receivable and notes payable. The annual fiscal period ends on December 31, 19B. Each of the two situations otherwise is independent.

Situation A—Frindly arranged a line of credit whereby a local bank will loan Frindly cash for short-term working capital needs. Repayment will vary from 60 to 90 days. Occasionally, the company also borrows a substantial amount on a long-term basis. On October 1, 19B, Frindly borrowed $40,000 on a one-year, 12 percent note. The principal plus interest is payable at the end of 12 months.

Situation B—Frindly sells approximately 40 percent of its goods on credit; accounts are due at the end of the month in which the sale is made. From time to time, special efforts must be made to collect an account. J. Doe was such a case. Doe owed $1,000 on an account and was unable to pay. After lengthy negotiations, on November 1, 19B, Doe gave Frindly a 15 percent note for the $1,000 coupled with a mortgage on two personal automobiles. The note matures at the end of two years. At the end of the first full year, Doe agreed to pay half of the principal ($500) plus interest on the amount of principal outstanding during the year. The remaining principal plus interest is payable at the end of the second year.

Required:

a. What amount should be shown on income statement for 19B for each situation?
b. What items and amount(s) should be shown on Frindly's balance sheet at December 31, 19B, for each situation?
c. Give the adjusting journal entry required for each situation at December 31, 19B. Show computations.
d. What would be the amount of error in 19B pretax income if the adjusting entries given in *(c)* were omitted? Explain.

PC4–7.   Rapid Service Company has completed its annual financial statements for the year ended December 31, 19C. The income statement (summarized) reflected the following:

Revenues:		
	Service	$95,600
	Rental (office space)	2,400
	Total revenues	98,000
Expenses:		
	Salaries and wages	44,000
	Service supplies used	2,600
	Depreciation expense	2,000
	Maintenance of equipment	2,000
	Rent expense (service building)	8,400
	Oil and gas for equipment	1,800
	Insurance expense	200
	Utilities expense.....................	800
	Other expenses	6,200
	Total expenses	68,000
Pretax income........................		$30,000

An audit of the records and financial statements by a CPA revealed that the following items were not considered:

1. Service revenue of $700 earned yet not collected on December 31, 19C, was not included in the $95,600 on the income statement.
2. The $2,600 of service supplies used included $600 of service supplies still on hand in the supplies storeroom on December 31, 19C.
3. Rent revenue of $100 that was collected in advance and not yet earned by December 31, 19C, was included in the $2,400 on the income statement.

4. Property tax for 19C of $400 was billed during December 19C, but will be due and paid during Janauary 19D (not included in the above amounts on the income statement).
5. A two-year insurance premium of $400 was paid on July 1, 19B; no premiums were paid in 19C.

Required:

a. Recast the above income statement to include, exclude, or omit each of the items identified by the CPA. Use a format similar to the following:

Items	Amounts as reported	Corrections	Amounts that should be reported

b. The owner of the company asked you to explain the following:
   (1) The insurance premium was paid in 19B; therefore, why was insurance expense reported in 19C?
   (2) Although the company paid no cash for depreciation expense, $2,000 was included in 19C as expense. Why was this so?

PC4–8. (Analytical) Sims Service Company has completed its financial statements for the year ended December 31, 19A. The balance sheet correctly reported the following selected items and amounts:

Assets
1. Prepaid insurance (one-year policy was purchased and paid for on May 1, 19A; debited Prepaid Insurance) .... $ 480
2. Service truck (purchased on January 1, 19A) $7,700
   Accumulated depreciation (no residual value) 1,100   6,600

Liabilities:
3. Rent collected in advance (cash collected for annual rent on October 1, 19A; credited Rent Revenue) 600
4. Salaries payable (monthly salary for J. Doe was not yet paid) 1,500

Required:

a. What amount of insurance premium was paid on May 1, 19A? Assuming the premium paid originally was recorded as a debit to Prepaid Insurance and a credit to Cash, give the adjusting entry that was made on December 31, 19A.
b. What was used as the estimated useful life of the service truck? Give the adjusting entry that was made on December 31, 19A.
c. What was the amount of cash collected for rent on October 1, 19A? Give the adjusting entry that was made on December 31, 19A.
d. What was J. Doe's total annual salary? How much of it was paid in cash during 19A? Give the adjusting entry that was made on December 31, 19A.

PC4–9. Modern Service Company is completing the information processing cycle at the end of its fiscal year, December 31, 19B. Below is listed the correct balance for each account at December 31, 19B *(a)* before the adjusting entries for 19B and *(b)* after the adjusting entries for 19B.

		Account balance, December 31, 19B			
		Before adjusting entries		*After adjusting entries*	
		Debit	Credit	Debit	Credit
a.	Cash	$ 8,000		$ 8,000	
b.	Service revenue receivable			400	
c.	Prepaid insurance	300		200	
d.	Operational assets	120,200		120,200	
e.	Accumulated depreciation, equipment		$ 21,500		$ 25,000
f.	Income taxes payable				5,500
g.	Capital stock		70,000		70,000
h.	Retained earnings, January 1, 19B		14,000		14,000
i.	Service revenue		60,000		60,400
j.	Salary expense	37,000		37,000	
k.	Depreciation expense			3,500	
l.	Insurance expense			100	
m.	Income tax expense			5,500	
		$165,500	$165,500	$174,900	$174,900

Required:

a. Compare the amounts in the columns before and after the adjusting entries in order to reconstruct the four adjusting entries that were made in 19B. Provide a brief explanation of each.

b. Compute the amount of income assuming (1) it is based on the amounts, "before adjusting entries" and (2) it is based on the amounts, "after adjusting entries." Which income amount is correct? Explain why.

PC4–10.   This is a case to test your ability to analyze a specific situation and to determine whether an adjusting entry is required and, if so, what the entry should be.

General situation: On December 1, 19A, Voss collected cash, $4,000, which was for office space rented to an outsider. The rent collected was for the period December 1, 19A, through March 31, 19B. The annual accounting period ends on December 31.

Required:

a. How much of the $4,000 should Voss report as revenue on the 19A annual income statement? How much of it should be reported as revenue on the 19B income statement?

b. What is the amount of rent revenue collected in advance as of December 31, 19A? How should Voss report this amount on the 19A financial statements?

c. On December 1, 19A, Voss could have recorded the $4,000 collection in one of three different ways as follows:

Case A:

Cash	4,000	
Rent revenue		4,000

Case B:

Cash	4,000	
Rent revenue collected in advance		4,000

Case C:

Cash	4,000	
Rent revenue		1,000
Rent revenue collected in advance		3,000

For each case, give the appropriate adjusting entry (in journal form) at December 31, 19A. If no adjusting entry is required, explain why.

d. Do you believe one of the approaches shown above is better than the other two? Which one? Explain.

PC4–11. (Comprehensive) Morris Transportation Corporation has been in operation since January 1, 19A. It is now December 31, 19A, the end of the annual accounting period. The company has not done well financially during the first year, although transportation revenue has been fairly good. The three stockholders manage the company but they have not given much attention to recordkeeping. In view of a serious cash shortage, they asked a local bank for a $10,000 loan. The bank requested a complete set of financial statements. The 19D annual financial statements given below were prepared by a clerk and then were given to the bank.

MORRIS TRANSPORTATION CORPORATION
December 31, 19A

Income Statement

Transportation revenue	$90,000
Expenses:	
Salaries	20,000
Maintenance	15,000
Other expenses	25,000
Total expenses	60,000
Net income	$30,000

Balance Sheet

Assets

Cash	$ 1,000
Receivables	4,000
Inventory of maintenance supplies	5,000
Equipment	30,000
Remaining assets	37,000
Total assets	$77,000

Liabilities

Accounts payable	$ 7,000

Capital

Capital stock	40,000
Retained earnings	30,000
Total liabilities and capital	$77,000

After briefly reviewing the statements and "looking into the situation," the bank requested that the statements be redone (with some expert help) to "incorporate depreciation, accruals, inventory counts, income taxes, and so on." As a consequence of a review of the records and supporting documents, the following additional information was developed:

1. The inventory of maintenance supplies of $5,000 shown on the balance sheet has not been adjusted for supplies used during 19A. An inventory count of the maintenance

supplies on hand (unused) on December 31, 19A, showed $2,000. Supplies used are debited to Maintenance Expense.

2. The insurance premium paid in 19A was for years 19A and 19B; therefore, the prepaid insurance at December 31, 19A, amounted to $1,000. The total insurance premium was debited in full to Other Expenses when paid in 19A.

3. The equipment cost $30,000 when purchased January 1, 19A, and has an estimated useful life of five years (no residual value). No depreciation has been recorded for 19A.

4. Unpaid (and unrecorded) salaries at December 31, 19A, amounted to $1,500.

5. At December 31, 19A, hauling revenue collected in advance amounted to $3,000. This amount was credited in full to Transportation Revenue when the cash was collected earlier during 19A.

6. Assume an income tax rate of 20 percent.

Required:

a. Give the six adjusting entries (in journal form) required by the above additional information for December 31, 19A.

b. Recast the above statements after taking into account the adjusting entries. You do not need to use subclassifications on the statements. Suggested form for the solution:

	Amounts reported	Changes		Correct amounts
Items		Plus	Minus	
(List here each item from the two statements)				

(Hint: The correct balance sheet total is $69,000.)

c. Compute the amount of the error in (1) net income and (2) total assets due to the omission of the adjusting entries. Draft a brief nontechnical report for the bank explaining causes of the differences.

PC4–12. (Comprehensive)   Small Company is completing the information processing cycle for its annual accounting period that ended on December 31, 19D. All of the current entries for 19D were entered correctly in the accounting system. A list of all of the ledger accounts and their respective balances (i.e., an unadjusted trial balance) was prepared immediately after the last current entry was journalized and posted.

The accountant was away from work for a few days. During this time, a new assistant to the president requested that the bookkeeper prepare an income statement and balance sheet immediately "for our use" despite a suggestion by the bookkeeper that "the adjustments have to be determined by the accountant." Consequently, the following statements (summarized for case purposes) were prepared by the bookkeeper and given to the assistant.

Income Statement
For the Year Ended
December 31, 19D

Revenues:

Sales	$240,000
Services	50,000
Total revenues	290,000

Expenses:

Cost of goods sold	150,000
Salaries and wages	65,000
Utilities	18,000
Other expenses	7,000
Total expenses	240,000
Net income	$ 50,000

Balance Sheet
At December 31, 19D

Assets

Cash	$ 23,000
Accounts receivable	61,000
Inventory	130,000
Prepaid insurance	6,000
Equipment*	100,000
Accumulated depreciation, equipment	(30,000)
Remaining assets	10,000
Total assets	$300,000

Liabilities

Accounts payable	$ 41,000
Income taxes payable	
Notes payable, one year, 15%	20,000

Stockholders Equity

Capital stock, par $10	150,000
Contributed capital in excess of par	15,000
Retained earnings	74,000
Total liabilities and stockholders' equity	$300,000

* Acquired January 1, 19A; estimated life, 10 years, and no residual value.

After returning, the accountant immediately prepared another set of statements which included the following additional data:

a. The inventory at the end of December 19D should have been $120,000 instead of $130,000.

b. The prepaid insurance amount of $6,000 was the total premium paid on July 1, 19D, which covered a two-year period from payment date. (The $6,000 was debited to Prepaid Insurance.)

c. Depreciation for 19D was not recorded. (Hint: Refer to the balance sheet.)

d. Interest on the note payable was not recorded. The note was dated November 1, 19D, and the principal plus interest is payable at the end of one year.

e. Assume an average income tax rate of 20 percent.

Required:

a. Prepare the appropriate adjusting entry, in journal form, for each item of additional data.

b. Recast the income statement and balance sheet to incorporate the additional data. Suggested format:

| | | Changes | | |
Items	Amounts reported	Plus	Minus	Correct amounts
Income statement:				
Balance sheet:				

c. Draft a brief nontechnical explanation for the management to adequately explain why the second set of financial statements should replace the first set. (Hint: Correct EPS is $1.49.)

PC4–13. Refer to the Johnson & Johnson financial statements given at the end of this textbook immediately preceding the Index. Respond to the following questions for the 1982 annual accounting period.

1. On what date did the 1982 accounting year end?

2. What was the name of the firm of independent CPAs?

3. Reconcile the beginning and ending balances of retained earnings.

4. Explain how (use amounts as well as words) the revenue item "royalties and miscellaneous" affects the 1982 balance sheet; assume all cash transactions.

5. Explain how J&J applied the time-period assumption.

6. Explain how J&J applies the revenue and matching principles. Use "Sales to customers" and "Cost of products sold" as examples.

7. What is the primary indicator in the financial statements that the company applied the reliability principle?

8. What amount was recorded in the adjusting entry for "depreciation and amortization"? Give the journal entry to record that amount.

9. How much was the accrued expenses related to salaries, wages, and commissions? Prepare the journal entry to record that amount.

10. How much did owners' equity increase due to the sale and issuance of preferred stock during 1982?

Information Processing in an Accounting System

PURPOSE OF THIS CHAPTER

In Chapter 3, Part B, we discussed the accounting information processing cycle and in Chapter 4 we discussed one important phase of that cycle—adjusting entries. The purpose of this chapter is to expand those discussions to include all of the phases and procedures in the accounting information processing cycle. This cycle is a systematic approach to periodic recording, measuring, and classifying of financial data, and preparing periodic financial statements, and as such is repeated each accounting period.

Students who plan to major in accounting need a solid understanding of accounting information processing from the professional and technical points of view. Other students, particularly those interested in careers in management, need a general understanding of the information processing cycle because, as managers, they will have to assess such things as (1) the capabilities and limitations of such a system, (2) the basic adaptations that should be expected for different types and sizes of entities, (3) cost-benefit relationships (i.e., the benefit of financial information versus the cost of providing the information), (4) the internal control implications of the system, and (5) the relationship of the accounting information processing system to the overall information system of the entity.

In addition to the discussions of information processing in this chapter, the following supplement is provided:

Supplement 5A—Reversing entries

MANUAL, MECHANICAL, AND ELECTRONIC DATA PROCESSING

Information processing refers to the sequence and approaches used in accounting to accomplish the following: (1) collecting economic data about the activities of the company (by means of business documents), (2) recording the effects of the activities of the company in the accounting system in terms of the accounting model, (3) classifying and recording the data collected, and (4) preparing the periodic financial statements. In most entities, an extremely large amount of accounting data must be handled. Although information processing can be time consuming and costly to the enterprise, a well-designed processing system provides a smooth, uninterrupted, and efficient flow of data from the points of occurrence of the transactions from day to day to the financial statements at the end of the accounting period. The processing of accounting data may be performed in one of three ways, or, as is the usual case, by a combination of them. The three approaches may be described briefly as follows:

1. **Manual data processing**—With this approach, the accounting work is performed by hand (i.e., manually). Manual processing of accounting data has been employed in our discussions in the previous chapters. The manual approach is used extensively in small entities. Also, in large and medium-sized businesses, certain parts of the information process often are performed manually. The manual approach is useful for discussing and illustrating the application of accounting concepts, principles, and measurement procedures. Also, it is convenient for explaining and illustrating the accounting process because you can readily see what is being done. You cannot see what is going on inside a computer.

2. **Mechanical data processing**—Mechanical data processing often is used in accounting to record repetitive transactions that occur in large numbers. Mechanical processing of accounting data employs accounting machines that vary widely in type and application. They encompass mechanical devices, some of which display a combination typewriter-adding machine keyboard. Mechanical processing encompasses not only the strictly mechanical devices, such as posting machines, but also punched-card equipment. The latter consists of (1) keypunch machines, on which cards are punched to record the transactions; (2) sorting machines, which sort the cards in a predetermined order; and (3) tabulating machines, which print the output, such as a listing of the expenses for the period. Although mechanical data processing is used today, it is being superseded rapidly by electronic data processing.

3. **Electronic data processing**—Electronic processing of accounting data uses electronic computers of varying size and sophistication. When electronic data processing is employed, the use of manual and mechanical activities in an accounting system is reduced to a minimum. Because of the large capability to store data and the speed with which such data can be manipulated and recalled, electronic data processing is widely used in accounting. Electronic data processing involves the use of "hardware" and "software." The computer and equipment related to it (usually called peripheral equipment) constitute the **hardware. Software** includes *(a)* the computer programs that must be

designed as instructions to the computer and *(b)* other items related to the operation of the system. Other items include materials used in operating the system, training materials, and studies of various sorts. Electronic data processing is applied widely to such accounting problems as payrolls, billings for goods and services, accounts receivable, accounts payable, inventories,[1] and even to the preparation of detailed financial statements. The rapid development of microcomputers and software "packages" for them has made it technically and economically feasible for even the smallest businesses (and individuals) to maintain their accounting system electronically.

EXPANDING THE ACCOUNTING INFORMATION PROCESSING CYCLE

The discussions in this chapter expand the accounting information processing cycle introduced in Chapter 3, Part B. You should review that introductory material (particularly Exhibit 3–10) before proceeding further. Our discussion of the accounting information processing cycle is expanded in this chapter to encompass **four additional phases** indicated by an **asterisk** in Exhibit 5–1. Each phase in a complete accounting information processing cycle is outlined in that exhibit in the chronological (timing) order in which each phase usually is implemented.

The four phases added (6, 8, 9, and 10) are information processing phases only and involve no new accounting concepts or principles beyond those that you have already learned in the first four chapters. These four added phases are designed to provide an orderly flow of the data processing work **at the end of the accounting period** and usually are helpful in completion of the financial statements with minimum effort. Also, they tend to decrease errors and omissions. The phases discussed in Chapter 3 will be reviewed, and the four added phases will be discussed and illustrated in detail in the remainder of this chapter. These illustrations use a manual system for instructional purposes.

Phase 1— Collecting raw economic data from completed transactions

This phase is a necessary continuing activity that collects **source documents** (such as sales invoices) from all of the transactions as they occur. The collection process involves all operations of the entity and a large number of employees (including nonaccountants). Source documents provide data to be analyzed and recorded in the accounting system. The source documents must be collected in a timely manner and must provide complete and accurate data about each transaction.

Phase 2— Analyzing transactions

Primarily this is a mental activity performed by accountants in order to identify and measure the economic impact of each transaction on the entity in terms of the basic accounting model: Assets = Liabilities + Owners' Equity. The analysis of each transaction involves determination of the specific asset, liability, and owners' equity accounts that should be increased and/or decreased to properly reflect the economic consequences of each transaction. Analysis of transactions

---

[1] These terms are discussed in more depth in Robert N. Anthony, Glenn A. Welsch, and James S. Reece, *Fundamentals of Management Accounting,* 4th ed. (Homewood, Ill.: Richard D. Irwin, 1985).

EXHIBIT 5–1
Outline of all phases of the accounting information processing cycle

Phases Completed during the Accounting Period

1. **Collection of raw economic data** generated by the transactions of the entity; supported with business documents.
2. **Transaction analysis** of all current transactions (as they occur) to determine the economic effects on the entity in terms of the accounting model.
3. **Journalizing** the results of the analysis of the current transactions. This phase encompasses recording the entries in chronological order in the journal.
4. **Posting** the current entries from the journal to the respective accounts in the ledger.

Phases Completed Only at the End of the Accounting Period

5. Preparation of an unadjusted trial balance from the ledger.
*6. Preparation of an accounting worksheet:
   a. Collection of data for adjusting entries and analysis of the data in the context of the accounting model.
   b. Separation of the adjusted data among the income statement, balance sheet, and statement of changes in financial position.
7. Preparation of financial statements:
   a. Income statement.
   b. Balance sheet.
   c. Statement of changes in financial position (SCFP; discussed in Chapter 15).
*8. Adjusting entries (at the end of the period):
   a. Recorded in the journal.
   b. Posted to the ledger.
*9. Closing the revenue and expense accounts in the ledger:
   a. Recorded in the journal.
   b. Posted to the ledger.
*10. Preparation of a post-closing trial balance.

Phase Completed Only at the Start of the Next Accounting Period

11. Optional *reversing entries* (see Supplement 5A).

* Phases added in this chapter to complete the entire cycle

requires, for each transaction, the supporting source document(s) and often other related information.

Phase 3— Journalizing

Journalizing is the process of recording the results of the **transaction analysis** of each completed transaction in the **journal** in the debit-credit format. Thus, the economic impacts of each transaction on the entity are recorded first in the journal in chronological order.

Phase 4— Posting

Accounting data first are recorded in the journal (Phase 3), next these data are transferred or **posted** to the **ledger** to reclassify and aggregate the information in terms of the fundamental accounting model: Assets = Liabilities + Owners' Equity. The ledger is composed of a number of separate accounts; one for each kind of asset, liability, and owners' equity. Thus, posting to the ledger reorders the data from the chronological order in the journal to the classifications explicit within the fundamental accounting model. The ledger is viewed as the basic accounting record because it provides appropriately classified economic data about the entity that will be used to complete the remaining phases of the accounting information processing cycle (including preparation of the periodic financial statements).

Chapter 3 illustrated the use of a **trial balance** to prepare the periodic financial statements. However, the **remaining phases** of the accounting information processing cycle were not discussed or illustrated. Phases 5 through 10 are known as **end-of-period** phases. We will now discuss the specific procedures associated with the remaining phases.

Phase 5—Preparation of an unadjusted trial balance

At the **end of the accounting period,** after all current transactions have been recorded in the journal (journalized) and then posted to the ledger, a listing of all **ledger** accounts and their balances is prepared. This listing is called an **unadjusted trial balance** because it serves to check the equalities of the accounting model (A = L + OE and Debits = Credits) but does **not** include the effects of the particular group of end-of-period entries called **adjusting entries** which were discussed and illustrated in Chapter 4, Part B.

Phase 6—The worksheet

The outline presented in Exhibit 5–1 lists six different phases that are completed at the end of the accounting period, including a **worksheet.** The end-of-period phases involve numerous related details and the possibility of errors. Preparation of the worksheet that precedes the journalizing and posting of the adjusting and closing entries (Phases 8 and 9) is designed to minimize the possibility of errors. Once completed, the worksheet provides all of the data needed to complete the remaining end-of-period phases in the accounting information processing cycle. It accomplishes this broad purpose by bringing together in one place, in an orderly way, the (1) unadjusted trial balance, (2) adjusting entries, (3) income statement, (4) statement of retained earnings, (5) balance sheet, and (6) the closing entries (explained later).[2]

Preparation of a worksheet. The simplified case used in Chapter 4 (pages 158–167) for High-Rise Apartments will be used to illustrate the preparation of a typical worksheet at the end of the accounting year, December 31, 19B. To facilitate explanation, two exhibits are presented:

Exhibit 5–2—Worksheet format with **unadjusted** trial balance and adjusting entries.

Exhibit 5–3—Worksheet completed; reflects the **income statement, statement of retained earnings,** and **balance sheet.**

The sequential steps involved in developing the worksheet are:

Step 1—Set up the worksheet **format** by entering the appropriate column headings. This step is illustrated in Exhibit 5–2, which includes in the left column the account titles (taken directly from the ledger) and six separate pairs of debit/credit money columns. Each pair of the six money columns represents

---

[2] This entire section on the worksheet can be omitted without affecting the remaining chapters.

one of the end-of-period phases of the accounting information processing cycle.

Step 2—Enter the **unadjusted** trial balance as of the end of the accounting period directly from the ledger into the first pair of debit/credit columns. When all of the current entries for the period, **excluding** the adjusting entries, have been recorded in the journal and posted to the ledger, the amounts for the **unadjusted** trial balance are the balances of the respective ledger accounts. Before proceeding to the next step, the equality of the debits and credits in the unadjusted trial balance should be assured by totaling each column (totals $481,460). When a worksheet is used, there is no real need to develop a **separate** unadjusted trial balance (Phase 5).

Step 3—The second pair of debit/credit columns, headed "Adjusting Entries," is completed by developing and then entering the adjusting entries **directly** on the worksheet. The adjusting entries for High-Rise Apartments shown in Exhibit 5–2 were illustrated (with the same letter codes) and discussed in detail in Chapter 4, Part B. To facilitate examination (for potential errors), future reference, and study, the adjusting entries usually are coded on the worksheet as illustrated in Exhibit 5–2. Some of the adjusting entries may require the addition of one or more account titles in addition to those of the original trial balance listing (see last four account titles in Exhibit 5–2). After the adjusting entries are completed on the worksheet, the equality of debits and credits for those entries is checked (totals $19,900).

The remaining steps to complete the worksheet are reflected by the shaded area in Exhibit 5–3; these steps are:

Step 4—The pair of debit/credit columns headed "Adjusted Trial Balance" is completed. Although not essential, this pair of columns helps to assure accuracy. Simply, the adjusted trial balance is the line-by-line combined amounts of the unadjusted trial balance, plus or minus the amounts entered as adjusting entries in the second pair of columns. For example, the Rent Revenue account reflects a $128,463 credit balance under Unadjusted Trial Balance. To this amount is **added** the **credit** amount, $600, and **minus** the **debit** amount, $500, giving a combined amount of $128,563, which is entered as a **credit** under Adjusted Trial Balance. For those accounts that were unaffected by the adjusting entries, the unadjusted trial balance amount is carried directly across to the Adjusted Trial Balance column. After each line has been completed, the equality of the debits and credits under Adjusted Trial Balance is checked (total $499,260).

Step 5—The amount of each line, under Adjusted Trial Balance, is extended horizontally across the worksheet and entered *(a)* as a debit, if it is a debit under Adjusted Trial Balance, or as a credit, if it is a credit under Adjusted Trial Balance; and *(b)* under the financial statement heading (income statement, retained earnings, or balance sheet) on which it must be reported. You can see that each amount extended across (1) was entered under **only one** of the six remaining columns, and (2) that debits remain debits and credits remain credits in the extending process.

EXHIBIT 5-2 Worksheet format with unadjusted trial balance and adjusting entries

HIGH-RISE APARTMENTS, INC.
Worksheet for the Year Ended December 31, 19B

Account Titles	Unadjusted Trial Balance Debit	Unadjusted Trial Balance Credit	Adjusting Entries Debit	Adjusting Entries Credit	Adjusted Trial Balance Debit	Adjusted Trial Balance Credit	Income Statement Debit	Income Statement Credit	Retained Earnings Debit	Retained Earnings Credit	Balance Sheet Debit	Balance Sheet Credit
Cash	2,297											
Prepaid insurance	2,400			(c) 1,200								
Inventory of maintenance supplies	600			(e) 400								
Land	25,000											
Apartment building	360,000											
Accumulated depreciation, building		10,000		(d) 10,000								
Notes payable		30,000										
Rent collected in advance				(a) 500								
Mortgage payable		238,037										
Capital stock, 500 shares		50,000										
Retained earnings, Jan. 1, 19B		24,960										
Dividends declared and paid	12,000											
Rent revenue		128,463	(a) 500	(b) 600								
Advertising expense	500											
Maintenance expense	3,000		(e) 400									
Salary expense	17,400		(f) 900									
Interest expense	19,563		(h) 600									
Utilities	34,500											
Miscellaneous expenses	4,200											
Insurance expense			(c) 1,200									
Depreciation expense			(d) 10,000									
Salaries payable				(f) 900								
Property tax expense			(g) 5,700									
Property tax payable				(g) 5,700								
Interest payable				(h) 600								
Rent revenue receivable			(b) 600									
	481,460	481,460	19,900	19,900								

EXHIBIT 5–3 Worksheet completed

HIGH-RISE APARTMENTS, INC.
Worksheet for the Year Ended December 31, 19B

Account Titles	Unadjusted Trial Balance Debit	Credit	Adjusting Entries Debit	Credit	Adjusted Trial Balance Debit	Credit	Income Statement Debit	Credit	Retained Earnings Debit	Credit	Balance Sheet Debit	Credit
Cash	2,297				2,297						2,297	
Prepaid insurance	2,400			(c) 1,200	1,200						1,200	
Inventory of maintenance supplies	600			(e) 400	200						200	
Land	25,000				25,000						25,000	
Apartment building	360,000				360,000						360,000	
Accumulated depreciation, building		10,000		(d) 10,000		20,000						20,000
Notes payable		30,000				30,000						30,000
Rent collected in advance				(a) 500		500						500
Mortgage payable		238,037				238,037						238,037
Capital stock, 500 shares		50,000				50,000						50,000
Retained earnings, Jan. 1, 19B		24,960				24,960				24,960		
Dividends declared and paid	12,000				12,000				12,000			
Rent revenue		128,463	(a) 500	(b) 600		128,563		128,563				
Advertising expense	500				500		500					
Maintenance expense	3,000		(e) 400		3,400		3,400					
Salary expense	17,400		(f) 900		18,300		18,300					
Interest expense	19,563		(h) 600		20,163		20,163					
Utilities expense	34,500				34,500		34,500					
Miscellaneous expenses	4,200				4,200		4,200					
Insurance expense			(c) 1,200		1,200		1,200					
Depreciation expense			(d) 10,000		10,000		10,000					
Salaries payable				(f) 900		900						900
Property tax expense			(g) 5,700		5,700		5,700					
Property tax payable				(g) 5,700		5,700						5,700
Interest payable				(h) 600		600						600
Rent revenue receivable			(b) 600		600						600	
	481,460	481,460	19,900	19,900	499,260	499,260	97,963	128,563				
Income tax expense†			(i) 6,120		6,120		6,120					
Income tax payable‡				(i) 6,120								6,120
Net income‡							24,480			24,480		
			6,120	6,120			128,563	128,563		49,440		
									12,000	49,440		
Retained earnings, Dec. 31, 19B§									37,440			37,440
									49,440	49,440	389,297	389,297

* Explanation of adjusting entries is provided in Exhibit 5–4.
† Revenues, $128,563 − Pretax expenses, $97,963 = $30,600; $30,600 × tax rate, 20% = $6,120.
‡ Pretax income, $30,600 − Income tax, $6,120 = $24,480.
§ $49,440 − $12,000 = $37,440.

Step 6—At this point, the two Income Statement columns are summed (subtotals). The difference between these two subtotals represents the **pretax income (or loss).** Income tax expense then is computed by multiplying this difference by the tax rate. In Exhibit 5–3, the computation was (pretax revenues, $128,563 − pretax expenses, $97,963) × tax rate, 20% = $6,120. The **adjusting entry** for income tax then was entered at the bottom of the worksheet (a "loopback"). Income tax expense and income tax payable now can be extended horizontally to the Income Statement and Balance Sheet columns. Net income is entered as a **balancing debit** amount in the Income Statement column and as a credit (i.e., increase) in Retained Earnings.

Step 7—The two Retained Earnings columns are summed, and the difference is the ending balance of retained earnings. This balance amount is entered as a balancing debit amount (under Retained Earnings) and also as a balancing credit amount (i.e., an addition to owners' equity). At this point, the two Balance Sheet columns should sum to equal amounts. The continuous checking of equality of debits and credits in each pair of debit/credit columns helps to assure the correctness of the worksheet. However, the balancing feature alone does not assure that the worksheet contains no errors. For example, if an expense amount (a debit) were extended to either the Retained Earnings debit column or to the Balance Sheet debit column, the worksheet would balance in all respects; however, at least two money columns would be in error. Therefore, special care must be exercised in selecting the appropriate debit/credit columns during the horizontal extension process.[3]

The completed worksheet, Exhibit 5–3, provides the data needed to complete the remaining phases of the accounting information processing cycle as follows (summarized from Exhibit 5–1):

Phase	Phase description	Source on worksheet
7	Prepare income statement	Income Statement columns
	Prepare balance sheet	Balance Sheet columns
	Prepare statement of retained earnings	Retained Earnings columns
8	Record adjusting entries in journal and post to ledger	Adjusting Entries columns
9	Record closing entries in journal and post to ledger	Income Statement and Retained Earnings columns
10	Post-closing trial balance	Prepare from ledger and check with Balance Sheet columns.

**Phase 7—
Preparing
financial
statements from
the worksheet**

The completed worksheet provides in one place the amounts needed to prepare the income statement, balance sheet, and statement of retained earnings. The statement of retained earnings, although not a required statement, usually is prepared by corporations (see Exhibits 2–4 and 2–7 for examples). This statement ties together the income statement and the stockholders' equity section of the

---

[3] The number of paired columns on a worksheet can be reduced by omitting both, or either, the Adjusted Trial Balance columns and the Retained Earnings columns. Also, the number of columns can be reduced further by using only one money column for each set instead of separate debit and credit columns (for example, the credits can be indicated by parentheses).

balance sheet. For example, the statement of retained earnings for High-Rise Apartments would be as follows:

HIGH-RISE APARTMENTS, INC.
Statement of Retained Earnings
For the Year Ended December 31, 19B

Retained earnings balance January 1, 19B	$24,960
Add net income of 19B	24,480
Total	49,440
Less dividends declared and paid in 19B	12,000
Retained earnings balance, December 31, 19B	$37,440

The task of preparing the income statement and balance sheet is simply one of properly **classifying** the data provided by the worksheet. Classified financial statements were illustrated in Exhibit 3–2; therefore, they will not be repeated here.

The worksheet described above does not provide data for the statement of changes in financial position (SCFP). This statement requires special analytical procedures; as a consequence, a special worksheet must be used to develop it. The special worksheet will be discussed and illustrated in Chapter 15.

Phase 8— Recording adjusting entries in the accounts

Immediately after completion of the worksheet, the financial statements are prepared and distributed to the interested users. Observe that by using the worksheet, preparation and distribution of the financial statements are not delayed by the remaining phases of the accounting cycle. After the financial statements have been prepared, the **adjusting entries** reflected on the completed worksheet are entered in the journal and then posted to the ledger. These entries are "dated" as of the last day of the accounting period. This task is a clerical one because the entries merely are copied from the worksheet into the journal. The adjusting entries for High-Rise Apartments, with a **folio** notation to indicate that posting is completed, are illustrated in Exhibit 5–4. The ledger, with the adjusting entries posted (in color to facilitate identification), is shown in Exhibit 5–6. This phase is required to enter the economic effects of the adjusting entries into the accounting system.

Phase 9— Closing the revenue and expense accounts

In our study of the fundamental accounting model, we have emphasized that the **revenue** and **expense** accounts are subdivisions of retained earnings which itself is a part of **owners' equity.** The revenue, gain, expense, and loss accounts can be thought of as "income statement accounts," whereas the remainder of the accounts can be viewed as "balance sheet accounts." The revenue, gain, expense, and loss accounts are often called **temporary** (or nominal) accounts because data temporarily are collected in them for the **current accounting period only.** At the end of each period, their balances are transferred, or **closed,** to the Retained Earnings account. This periodic clearing out or closing of the balances of the income statement accounts into Retained Earnings serves two purposes: (1) it transfers net income (or loss) to retained earnings (i.e., owners' equity), and (2) it establishes a zero balance in the revenue and expense accounts to start the

EXHIBIT 5–4
Adjusting entries illustrated

	JOURNAL			Page 6
Date 19B	Account Titles and Explanation	Folio	Debit	Credit
Dec. 31	*a.* Rent revenue	340	500	
	Rent collected in advance	204		500
	To adjust the accounts for revenue collected in advance (see pages 159 and 160).			
31	*b.* Rent revenue receivable	102	600	
	Rent revenue	340		600
	To adjust for rent revenue earned in 19B, but not yet collected (see pages 160–161).			
31	*c.* Insurance expense	356	1,200	
	Prepaid insurance	103		1,200
	To adjust for insurance expired during 19B (see pages 161–162).			
31	*d.* Depreciation expense	360	10,000	
	Accumulated depreciation, building	113		10,000
	To adjust for depreciation expense for 19B (see pages 162–163).			
31	*e.* Maintenance expense	351	400	
	Inventory of maintenance supplies	104		400
	To adjust for supplies used from inventory during 19B (see page 164).			
31	*f.* Salary expense	352	900	
	Salaries payable	206		900
	To adjust for salaries earned but not yet recorded or paid (see page 165).			
31	*g.* Property tax expense	361	5,700	
	Property tax payable	207		5,700
	To adjust for 19B property tax incurred, but not yet recorded or paid (see pages 165–166).			
31	*h.* Interest expense	353	600	
	Interest payable	209		600
	To adjust for accrued interest expense for two months on note payable ($30,000 $\times$ 12% $\times$ 2/12 = $600) (see pages 166–167).			
31	*i.* An adjusting entry for income tax expense will be computed on the worksheet when the pretax income is computed thereon (see page 170 and 202). The entry will be:			
	Income tax expense	370	6,120	
	Income tax payable	208		6,120

next accounting period. In this way, the **income statement accounts** again are ready to serve their **temporary** periodic collection function for the next period. The journal entries that clear out the temporary accounts are called **closing entries.**

In contrast, the **balance sheet accounts** (assets, liabilities, and owners' equity) are not closed periodically; therefore, they are often called **permanent** (or real) accounts. To illustrate, the ending cash balance of one accounting period must be in the Cash account at the start of the next accounting period. The only time a permanent account has a zero balance is when the item represented (such as machinery or notes payable) is no longer owned (or is fully depreciated) or owed. The balance at the end of the period in each balance sheet account is carried forward in the ledger as the **beginning** balance for the next period.

In summary, the **closing entries,** made at the end of the accounting period to transfer the balances of all revenue and expense accounts, simply represent a mechanical phase. To close an account means to transfer its balance to another designated account by means of an entry. For example, an account that has a credit balance (such as a revenue account) would be closed by **debiting** that account for an amount equal to its balance and crediting the account to which the balance is to be transferred. In the closing process, a credit balance is always transferred to another account as a credit, and similarly a debit is always transferred as a debit for the same amount. The closing entries are **dated** the last day of the accounting period and are entered in the journal in the usual debit-credit format and are immediately posted to the ledger.

Another temporary account, called Income Summary, sometimes is used to facilitate the closing procedure. It is a clearance account used to "clear" the revenues and expenses to retained earnings. To illustrate the closing procedure, assume the following summarized data from the accounts of Alpha Corporation at December 31, 19E, the end of the accounting period:

Stockholders' Equity Accounts

Capital stock, 5,000 shares, par $10	$ 50,000
Retained earnings beginning balance January 1, 19E.....	15,000
Total revenues earned during 19E	100,000
Total expenses incurred during 19E	80,000
Total dividends declared and paid during 19E	10,000

The four required closing entries, assuming an **income summary account** is used, would be dated December 31, 19E, and would appear in the journal as follows:

a.	Revenue	100,000	
	Income summary		100,000
	To close the revenue amount into Income Summary.		
b.	Income summary	80,000	
	Expenses		80,000
	To close the expense amount into Income Summary.		

c. Income summary 20,000
        Retained earnings   20,000
            To close the Income Summary amount (i.e., net income) into
            Retained Earnings.

d. Retained earnings... 10,000
        Dividends declared and paid   10,000
            To close the dividends paid amount into Retained Earnings.

After the above closing entries are posted to the ledger accounts, the temporary
accounts—revenue, expenses, and income summary—will reflect zero balances.
Similarly, the dividends account will reflect a zero balance. The Retained Earnings
account (a permanent account) will reflect an ending balance calculated as follows:
$15,000 + $20,000 − $10,000 = $25,000.

Posting each of the above closing entries is diagrammed, and their effects on
the **temporary and permanent ledger** accounts are shown below for instructional
purposes only:

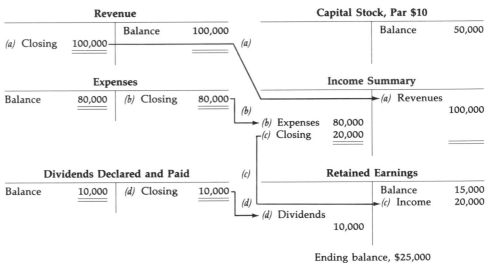

ALPHA CORPORATION

Ending balance, $25,000

In the above example of Alpha Corporation, only one revenue and one expense
account were used for illustrative purposes. However, **all** income statement accounts must be closed at the end of the accounting period using the closing
procedure illustrated above. In the above example, we assumed that dividends
declared and paid were recorded previously as a debit to a **temporary** account,
Dividends Declared and Paid, rather than as a direct debit to Retained Earnings.
Therefore, the temporary account, Dividends Declared and Paid, was closed into
Retained Earnings. When this temporary account is not used, a closing entry
for it obviously is not needed.

Closing entries illustrated, High-Rise Apartments, Inc.　Now, let's return to High-Rise Apartments and apply the closing procedure. The closing entries in the journal are shown in Exhibit 5–5; the posting notation (folio) to the ledger also is indicated. Observe that **all** of the revenue and expense accounts are closed, and in the process their balances are transferred into Retained Earnings. Also, the Dividends Declared and Paid account is closed into Retained Earnings.

For instructional purposes, the ledger accounts with (1) the trial balance totals, (2) the adjusting entries posted (in color), and (3) the closing entries posted (in black boxes) are shown in Exhibit 5–6 in T-account format. The colors and boxes are used to facilitate your study of the mechanics of each step. You should observe that **all** of the adjusting and closing amounts are verifiable or traceable directly to the completed worksheet (Exhibit 5–3).

One additional point should be emphasized. The closing entry in the journal for expenses (and for revenues when there is more than one) is a **compound** entry, which saves closing time and space (of course, a separate closing entry

EXHIBIT 5–5
Closing entries illustrated (High-Rise Apartments, Inc.)

	JOURNAL			Page 7
Date 19B	Account Titles and Explanation	Folio	Debit	Credit
Dec. 31	Rent revenue	340	128,563	
	Income summary	330		128,563
	To transfer revenues into Income Summary.			
31	Income summary ($97,963 + $6,120)	330	104,083	
	Advertising expense	350		500
	Maintenance expense	351		3,400
	Salary expense	352		18,300
	Interest expense	353		20,163
	Utilities expense	354		34,500
	Miscellaneous expenses	355		4,200
	Insurance expense	356		1,200
	Depreciation expense	360		10,000
	Property tax expense	361		5,700
	Income tax expense	370		6,120
	To transfer expense amounts into Income Summary.			
31	Income summary	330	24,480	
	Retained earnings	305		24,480
	To transfer Net Income into Retained Earnings.			
31	Retained earnings	305	12,000	
	Dividends declared and paid	306		12,000
	To transfer Dividends Declared and Paid into Retained Earnings.			

could be made for each separate expense account). Notice that the total debit to Income Summary in each entry can be taken from the worksheet.

After the closing process is completed, observe that all of the temporary (i.e., the income statement) accounts are closed to a zero balance and are ready for reuse during the next accounting period for accumulating the revenues and expenses of that period. The Retained Earnings account now has an ending balance

EXHIBIT 5–6
Ledger accounts illustrated (High-Rise Apartments, Inc.)

LEDGER—19B

Cash	101
2,297	

Property Tax Payable	207
	(g) 5,700

Maintenance Expense	351
3,000	(7) 3,400
(e)	

Rent Revenue Receivable	102
(b) 600	

Income Tax Payable	208
	(i) 6,120

Salary Expense	352
17,400	(7) 18,300
(f) 900	

Prepaid Insurance	103
2,400	(c) 1,200

Interest Payable	209
	(h) 600

Interest Expense	353
19,563	(7) 20,163
(h) 600	

Inventory of Maintenance Supplies	104
600	(e) 400

Mortgage Payable	251
	238,037

Utilities Expense	354
34,500	(7) 34,500

Land	110
25,000	

Capital Stock	301
	50,000

Miscellaneous Expenses	355
4,200	(7) 4,200

Apartment Building	111
360,000	

Retained Earnings	305
(7) 12,000	24,960
	(7) 24,480

Insurance Expense	356
(c) 1,200	(7) 1,200

Accumulated Depreciation, Building	113
	10,000
	(d) 10,000

Dividends Declared and Paid	306
12,000	(7) 12,000

Depreciation Expense	360
(d) 10,000	(7) 10,000

EXHIBIT 5-6
(concluded)

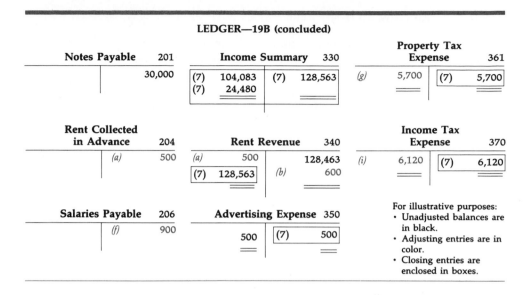

LEDGER—19B (concluded)

Notes Payable 201

	30,000

Income Summary 330

| (7) | 104,083 | (7) | 128,563 |
| (7) | 24,480 | | |

Property Tax Expense 361

| (g) | 5,700 | (7) | 5,700 |

Rent Collected in Advance 204

| | | (a) | 500 |

Rent Revenue 340

| (a) | 500 | | 128,463 |
| (7) | 128,563 | (b) | 600 |

Income Tax Expense 370

| (i) | 6,120 | (7) | 6,120 |

Salaries Payable 206

| | | (f) | 900 |

Advertising Expense 350

| | 500 | (7) | 500 |

For illustrative purposes:
- Unadjusted balances are in black.
- Adjusting entries are in color.
- Closing entries are enclosed in boxes.

of $37,440, which will be reported on the December 31, 19B, balance sheet as a part of stockholders' equity.[4]

Phase 10—Post-closing trial balance

Despite guidance provided by the worksheet, occasional errors may be made in the adjusting and closing mechanics. After the completion of those two phases, it is desirable to verify the equality of the ledger account balances. This verification in computerized accounting systems can be practically automatic. In other systems it may be done by using a printing calculator or an adding machine. Instead, some accountants prefer to prepare another formal trial balance, called a **post-closing trial balance,** before starting a new period. All of the income statement accounts have been closed to retained earnings, therefore, the post-closing trial balance will reflect balances **only** for the permanent accounts classified as assets, liabilities, and owners' equity. These balances should be identical with those shown in the last two columns of the worksheet (Exhibit 5–3). The ending balances reflected in the ledger accounts, after the closing process, will be the beginning balances for the next period.

---

[4] A common bookkeeping approach to "ruling a permanent T-account" with a carry-forward balance is as follows:

Retained Earnings 305

Dividends (19B)	12,000	Jan. 1, 19B, balance	24,960
Balance carried forward to 19C	37,440	Net income (19B)	24,480
	49,440		49,440
		Jan. 1, 19C, balance	37,440

REVERSING ENTRIES

Some accountants add an **optional phase** to the accounting information processing cycle, which is known as **reversing entries.** This phase is dated as of the **first day of the next accounting period** and is used for the sole purpose of **facilitating** certain subsequent entries in the accounts. Reversing entries are related specifically to certain adjusting entries that already have been journalized and posted to the accounts. When appropriate, such adjusting entries are reversed on the first day of the next period (i.e., the debits and credits simply are reversed). This reversal process requires what are called reversing entries. Reversing entries are **strictly optional** and involve only bookkeeping mechanics rather than accounting concepts and principles. Supplement 5A, at the end of this chapter, discusses and illustrates reversing entries for those who desire to become familiar with this optional facilitating technique.

INTERIM FINANCIAL STATEMENTS

Many companies prepare interim financial statements **during** the accounting year for each month or each quarter. **Monthly** financial statements, when prepared, almost always are for **internal** management uses only. In contrast, many larger companies prepare **quarterly** financial statements for internal management use and also present summarized versions of them to their stockholders and other external parties.

When monthly or quarterly interim financial statements are prepared, the company usually does not go through the phases of **interim adjusting and closing entries.** The formal phases of journalizing and posting adjusting entries typically are performed **only** at the end of the annual accounting period. Instead, the company prepares a worksheet to facilitate preparation of the interim financial statements. Therefore, the worksheet serves another very useful purpose when interim monthly or quarterly financial statements are prepared. At the end of each interim period, an **unadjusted** trial balance is taken from the ledger accounts and entered directly on an interim (say, monthly) worksheet. The interim worksheet then is completed by entering the interim adjusting entries thereon and extending the adjusted amounts to the Retained Earnings, Income Statement, and Balance Sheet columns. The interim statements (say, monthly) are prepared on the basis of the worksheet. In such situations, the remaining phases of the accounting information processing cycle (adjusting entries recorded, closing entries recorded, and post-closing trial balance) need not be completed at the end of each interim period.

SUMMARY OF CHAPTER

This chapter focused on the **accounting information processing cycle** that must be completed in situations where periodic financial statements are developed for both external and internal users. The cycle captures raw economic data on transactions as they occur, then records and processes their economic effects on the entity and communicates these effects by means of the periodic financial statements. The information system must be designed to measure net income, financial position, and funds flow accurately and effectively. Such an information system also must be designed to fit the specific characteristics of the entity.

We cannot overemphasize that the worksheet, the closing entries, and the post-closing trial balance phases are mechanical data processing procedures and do not involve any new accounting principles or measurement approaches.

The 10 phases discussed in this chapter constitute the accounting information processing cycle that is repeated each accounting period in all accounting systems. The information processing system captures the economic essence of all transactions at their points of incurrence and carries those effects to the end result— the periodic financial statements. Numerous adaptations of the procedures used to implement the cycle are observed in actual situations because entities have different characteristics such as size, type of industry, complexity, accounting expertise, and sophistication of the management.

The information processing activities in a particular entity can be efficient, effective, and timely in terms of the outputs (the financial statements), but unfortunately, the opposite may be true. The quality of the system depends on the competence of those performing the data processing tasks and the importance attached by the management and owners to the financial measurement of operating results and financial position. In this context, the information processing system of an entity is significant to all parties interested in the entity because the end results—the financial statements—are important in their decision-making models.

SUPPLEMENT 5A—REVERSING ENTRIES

After completion of Phase 10 of the accounting information processing cycle (i.e., the post closing trial balance), an **optional facilitating phase** may be added as Phase 11 (see Exhibit 5–1). This optional phase involves **reversing entries.** Reversing entries are **dated at the beginning of the next period** and relate **only to certain adjusting entries** made at the end of the immediate prior period. Certain adjusting entries may be reversed on the first day of the next period **solely to facilitate recording subsequent related entries.** Unlike most of the prior phases in the accounting information processing cycle, reversing entries are strictly optional and involve only bookkeeping mechanics rather than accounting principles or concepts.

The reversing entry phase is presented because (1) it introduces a common data processing technique used in most companies, whether the system is manual, mechanical, or computerized; and (2) a knowledge of the circumstances under which this phase may be used gives some additional insight into certain relationships in the efficient processing of accounting information.[5]

Reversing entries are given this name because they reverse, at the start of the next accounting period, the effects of certain adjusting entries made at the

---

[5] Knowledge of reversing entries is important primarily to students who plan to study accounting at the advanced level. This knowledge is not significant for study of the remaining chapters in this book.

EXHIBIT 5–7
Purpose of reversing
entries illustrated

DAY COMPANY

Situation: The payroll was paid on December 28, 19B; the next payroll will be on January 13, 19C. At December 31, 19B, wages of $3,000 were earned for the last three days of the year that had not been paid or recorded.

| With reversing entry | Without reversing entry |

a. **The preceding adjusting entry:**

December 31, 19B, adjusting entry to record the $3,000 accrued (unpaid) wages:

Wage expense	3,000		Wage expense	3,000	
Wages payable			Wages payable		
(a liability)		3,000	(a liability)		3,000

b. **The closing entry:** The revenue and expense accounts are closed to Income Summary after the adjusting entries are completed and posted to the ledger.

December 31, 19B, closing entry:

Income summary	3,000		Income summary	3,000	
Wage expense		3,000	Wage expense		3,000

c. **The reversing entry:** The information processing cycle in 19B is complete. All closing entries have been posted, and the post-closing trial balance has been verified. At this point in time, January 1, 19C, the accountant should decide whether it is desirable to reverse any of the 19B adjusting entries (i.e., any reversing entries) to simplify the **subsequent related entries.** Question: Would a reversing entry on January 1, 19C, simplify the entry to be made on January 13, 19C, when the wages are paid?

January 1, 19C, reversing entry.

Wages payable			No reversing entry assumed.
(a liability)	3,000		
Wage expense		3,000	

d. **The subsequent entry that was facilitated:** The payroll of $25,000 was completed and paid on January 13, 19C. This subsequent payment entry is to be recorded. Question: Did the reversing entry facilitate or simplify this entry?

January 13, 19C, payroll entry:

Wage expense	25,000		Wages payable	3,000	
Cash		25,000	Wage expense	22,000	
			Cash		25,000

* Explanation: Observe that when the reversing entry was used, this last entry required only one debit, contrasted with two debits when no reversing entry was made. This difference was due to the fact that the reversing entry served to (1) clear out the liability account, Wages Payable, and (2) set up a temporary **credit** in the Wage Expense account. After the last entry, to record the payment of the payroll, both accounts affected—Wage Expense and Wages Payable—are identical in balance under both approaches. If the reversing entry is not made, the company must go to the trouble of identifying how much of the $25,000 paid on January 13, 19C, was expense and how much of it was to pay the liability set up in the adjusting entry at the end of the prior period ([*a*] above).

EXHIBIT 5–8   **Reversing entries illustrated, journal and ledger**

Situation: On September 1, 19A, Company X loaned $1,200 on a one-year, 10 percent, interest-bearing note. On August 31, 19B, the company will collect the $1,200 principal plus $120 interest revenue. The annual accounting period ends December 31.

JOURNAL

a. September 1, 19A—To record the loan:

Note receivable	1,200	
Cash		1,200

b. December 31, 19A (end of the accounting period)— Adjusting entry for four months' interest revenue earned but not collected ($1,200 × 10% × 4/12 = $40):

Interest receivable	40	
Interest revenue		40

c. December 31, 19A—To close interest revenue:

Interest revenue	40	
Income summary		40

d. January 1, 19B—To reverse adjusting entry of December 31, 19A:

Interest revenue	40	
Interest receivable		40

Observe that after this entry, the Interest Receivable account reflects a zero balance and Interest Revenue reflects a **debit** balance of $40 (four months' interest).

e. August 31, 19B—Subsequent entry; to record collection of note plus interest for one year:*

Cash	1,320	
Note receivable		1,200
Interest revenue		120

LEDGER

Cash

	x,xxx	(a) 9/1/19A		1,200
(e) 8/31/19B	1,320			

Note Receivable

(a) 9/1/19A	1,200	(e) 8/31/19B		1,200

Interest Receivable

(b) 12/31/19A	40	(d) 1/1/19B		40

Interest Revenue

(c) 12/31/19A	40	(b) 12/31/19A		40
(d) 1/1/19B	40	(e) 8/31/19B		120

Income Summary

		(c) 12/31/19A		40

Note: To demonstrate the facilitating feature, assume the reversing entry (d) was not made. The August 31, 19B, entry would be more complex, viz:

Cash	1,320	
Note receivable		1,200
Interest receivable		40
Interest revenue		80

* Observe that after this entry the Note Receivable account has a zero balance and the Interest Revenue an $80 balance which represents eight months' interest revenue earned in 19B.

end of the previous period. **Reversing entries are always the opposite of the related adjusting entry.** It may be desirable to "reverse" certain adjusting entries; the other adjusting entries should not be reversed.

To illustrate reversing entries and the type of situation where a reversing entry will simplify the subsequent accounting entry, assume that Day Company is in the process of completing the information processing cycle at the end of its accounting period, December 31, 19B. To place the reversing entry in context, Exhibit 5–7 presents a situation that shows (1) an adjusting entry on December 31, 19B; (2) the reversing entry that could be made on January 1, 19C; and (3) the subsequent entry on January 13, 19C, that was facilitated or simplified. To demonstrate the facilitating effect of a reversing entry, we also have presented entries in the tabulation reflecting the same situation assuming no reversing entry. You should study carefully the two sets of entries and the explanatory comments in Exhibit 5–7. The reversing entry is shown in color for emphasis.

Exhibit 5–8 presents another illustration of the effects of reversing entries. It is presented to emphasize the facilitating feature of reversing entries as reflected in both the journal and ledger. The **reversing entry** is shown in color to facilitate your study.

In the above discussion we explained that certain adjusting entries could be reversed to facilitate or simplify subsequent related entries and that certain adjusting entries would **not** be reversed. How does one decide which entries may be reversed to advantage? There is no inflexible rule that can be provided. The accountant must analyze each situation and make a rational choice. In general, it can be said that short-term accruals and deferrals are candidates for reversal.

The adjusting entry to record depreciation and other entries of this type should never be reversed. In these situations, the adjusting entry is not followed by a subsequent "collection or payment" entry; therefore, it would be not only pointless to reverse the adjusting entry for depreciation but would introduce an error into the accounts because the accumulated depreciation account would reflect a zero balance throughout the period. Thus, many adjusting entries are not candidates for reversal, and those that are candidates are easily identified if one considers the nature of the subsequent related entry (i.e., whether there is a subsequent collection or payment).

Perhaps the most compelling reason for reversing entries is to increase the likelihood that the effects of certain adjusting entries will not be overlooked when recording the next related transaction in the following period.

IMPORTANT TERMS DEFINED IN THIS CHAPTER

Terms (alphabetically)	Key words in definitions of terms used in chapter	Page reference
Accounting information processing cycle	Accounting phases (steps) from the time a transaction is completed to the financial statements.	196
Closing entries	End-of-period entries to close all revenue and expense accounts to retained earnings (through income summary).	195
Computer hardware	Computer and other equipment used with it.	195

Terms (alphabetically)	Key words in definitions of terms used in chapter	Page reference
Computer software	Computer programs and instructions for using an electronic computer.	195
Electronic data processing	Accounting process performed (in whole or in part) using electronic computers.	195
Manual data processing	Accounting process performed (in whole or in part) in handwriting; manually.	195
Mechanical data processing	Accounting process performed (in whole or in part) using machines.	195
Permanent (real) accounts	Permanent (or real) accounts are the balance sheet accounts; no closing entries.	205
Post-closing trial balance	Trial balance prepared after all of the closing entries have been posted.	209
Reversing entries	Recorded at beginning of next accounting period; backs out certain adjusting entries; facilitates subsequent entries.	210
Temporary (nominal) accounts	Income statement accounts; closed at the end of the accounting period.	203
Worksheet	A "spread sheet" designed to minimize errors and to provide data for the financial statements.	198

QUESTIONS FOR DISCUSSION

1. Briefly explain the nature of an accounting information processing system.

2. Distinguish among manual, mechanical, and electronic data processing. How does each relate to accounting information processing?

3. Briefly identify, in sequence, the 11 phases of the accounting information processing cycle.

4. Contrast transaction analysis with journalizing.

5. Compare journalizing with posting.

6. Explain in what way posting reflects a change in classification of the data.

7. Contrast an unadjusted trial balance with an adjusted trial balance. What is the basic purpose of each?

8. What is the basic purpose of the worksheet?

9. Why are adjusting entries entered on the worksheet?

10. Why are adjusting entries recorded in the journal and posted to the ledger even though they are entered on the worksheet?

11. What are the purposes of closing entries? Why are they recorded in the journal and posted to the ledger?

12. Distinguish among (a) permanent, (b) temporary, (c) real, and (d) nominal accounts.

13. Explain why the income statement accounts are closed but the balance sheet accounts are not.

14. What is a post-closing trial balance? Is it a useful part of the accounting information processing cycle? Explain.

15. What are reversing entries? When are reversing entries useful? Give one example of an

adjusting entry that *(a)* should be reversed and *(b)* another one that should not be reversed (based on Supplement 5A).

EXERCISES ——

E5–1. Small Company prepared the unadjusted trial balance given below at the end of the accounting year, December 31, 19B. To simplify the case, the amounts given are in thousands of dollars.

Account title	*Debit*	*Credit*
Cash	$ 19	
Accounts receivable	22	
Prepaid insurance	3	
Machinery (10-year life, no residual value)	30	
Accumulated depreciation, machinery		$ 3
Accounts payable		2
Wages payable		
Income tax payable		
Capital stock, nopar (1,000 shares)		40
Retained earnings		5
Dividends declared and paid during 19B	2	
Revenues (not detailed)		56
Expenses (not detailed)	30	
Totals	$106	$106

Other data not yet recorded at December 31, 19B:

1. Insurance expired during 19B, $1.
2. Depreciation expense for 19B, $3.
3. Wages payable, $2.
4. Income tax rate, 30 percent.

Required:

(Note: A worksheet may be used but is not required.)

a. Complete the income statement and balance sheet given below for 19B.
b. Give the adjusting entries for 19B.
c. Give the closing entries for 19B.

Income Statement, 19B

Revenues (not detailed)	$ _____
Expenses (not detailed)	_____
Pretax income	_____
Income tax expense	_____
Net income	$ _____
EPS	$ _____

Balance Sheet, 19B

Assets		Liabilities	
Cash .... $ _____		Accounts payable .... $ _____	
Accounts receivable ...... _____		Wages payable .... _____	
Prepaid insurance .... _____		Income tax payable .... _____	
Machinery .... _____		**Owners' Equity**	
Accumulated depreciation . _____		Capital stock .... _____	
		Retained earnings .... _____	
Total .... $ _____		Total .... $ _____	

E5–2. Assume that the worksheet at December 31, 19B, for Boise Realty Corporation has been completed through "Adjusted Trial Balance" and you are ready to extend each amount to the several columns to the right. The columns that will be used are listed below with code letters:

Code	Columns
A	Income Statement, debit
B	Income Statement, credit
C	Retained Earnings, debit
D	Retained Earnings, credit
E	Balance Sheet, debit
F	Balance Sheet, credit

Below are listed representative accounts to be extended on the worksheet. You are to give, for each account, the code letter that indicates the proper worksheet column to the right of "Adjusted Trial Balance" to which the amount in each account should be extended. Assume normal debit and credit balances.

Account titles	Code
1. Cash	
2. Inventory of office supplies	
3. Interest payable	
4. Capital stock	
5. Commissions earned	
6. Rent revenue collected in advance	
7. Salary expense	
8. Sales return	
9. Retained earnings, beginning balance (a credit)	
10. Building	
11. Mortgage payable	
12. Income tax payable	
13. Sales commissions receivable	
14. Accumulated depreciation on building	
15. Contributed capital in excess of par	
16. Dividends declared and paid	
17. Income tax expense	
18. Prepaid insurance	
19. Net income amount (indicate both the debit and credit on the worksheet)	
20. Net loss amount (indicate both the debit and credit on the worksheet)	
21. Retained earnings, ending balance amount (indicate both the debit and credit on the worksheet)	

E5–3. Miller Company is completing the annual accounting information processing cycle at December 31, 19B. The worksheet, as shown below, has been started (to simplify, amounts given are in thousands of dollars).

		Unadjusted trial balance	
Account No.	Account	Debit	Credit
101	Cash	$ 20	$
102	Accounts receivable	38	
103	Inventory	22	
104	Prepaid insurance	3	
110	Equipment (10-year life, no residual value)	70	
111	Accumulated depreciation, equipment		7
119	Accounts payable		11
120	Wages payable		
121	Income tax payable		
122	Revenue collected in advance		
123	Note payable, long term (10% each December 31)		20
130	Capital stock, par $10		60
131	Contributed capital in excess of par		10
140	Retained earnings		15
141	Dividends declared and paid	8	
145	Revenues		99
146	Expenses	61	
147	Income tax expense		
	Totals	$222	$222

Data not yet recorded for 19B:

a. Insurance expense, $1.
b. Depreciation expense, $7.
c. Wages earned by employees not yet paid, $2.
d. Revenue collected by Miller not yet earned, $3.
e. Income tax rate, 20 percent. (Note: No accrued interest is recorded because interest is paid on each December 31.)

Required:

Complete the worksheet in every respect (you may use account numbers instead of account titles). Set up additional column headings for Adjusting Entries, Adjusted Trial Balance, Income Statement, Retained Earnings, and Balance Sheet. Record all revenues and expenses (except income tax) in the two accounts given (145 and 146).

E5–4.   West corporation, a small company, is completing the annual accounting information processing cycle at December 31, 19B. The worksheet has been started as reflected below.

Account Titles	Unadjusted Trial Balance	
	Debit	Credit
Cash	$ 17,000	
Accounts receivable	15,000	
Equipment	20,000	
Accumulated depreciation		$ 6,000
Other assets	54,500	
Accounts payable		9,000
Long-term note payable		15,000
Capital stock, par $10		30,000
Contributed capital in excess of par		1,500
Retained earnings		15,000
Revenues		80,000
Expenses	50,000	
	$156,500	$156,500
Income tax expense		
Income tax payable		
Net income		

Data not yet recorded for 19B:

a. Depreciation expense, $2,000.
b. Income tax rate, 30 percent.

Required:

Complete the worksheet in all respects. Set up additional column headings for Adjusting Entries, Adjusted Trial Balance, Income Statement, Retained Earnings, and Balance Sheet.

E5–5. Moline Service Company is in the process of completing the information processing cycle at the end of the fiscal year, December 31, 19B. The worksheet and financial statements have been prepared, and the next step is to journalize the adjusting entries. The two trial balances given below were taken directly from the completed worksheet.

		December 31, 19B			
Account Titles		Unadjusted Trial Balance		Adjusted Trial Balance	
		Debit	Credit	Debit	Credit
a.	Cash	$ 8,000		$ 8,000	
b.	Accounts receivable			700	
c.	Prepaid insurance	300		250	
d.	Equipment	120,200		120,200	
e.	Accumulated depreciation, equipment		$ 21,500		$ 25,500
f.	Income tax payable				4,000
g.	Capital stock, par $10		50,000		50,000
h.	Retained earnings, January 1, 19B		14,000		14,000
i.	Service revenues		60,000		60,700
j.	Salary expense	17,000		17,000	
k.	Depreciation expense			4,000	
l.	Insurance expense			50	
m.	Income tax expense			4,000	
		$145,500	$145,500	$154,200	$154,200

Required:

By examining the amounts in each trial balance, reconstruct the four adjusting entries that were made between the unadjusted trial balance and the adjusted trial balance. Give a brief explanation of each adjusting entry.

E5–6.   The accountant for Rocky Corporation has just completed the following worksheet for the year ended December 31, 19D (note the shortcuts used by the accountant to reduce the number of vertical columns on the worksheet):

Account Titles	Unadjusted Trial Balance (credits)	Adjusting Entries		Income Statement (credits)	Balance Sheet (credits)
		Debit	Credit		
Cash	15,000				15,000
Prepaid insurance	300		100		200
Accounts receivable	20,000				20,000
Machinery	80,000				80,000
Accumulated depreciation	(24,000)		8,000		(32,000)
Other assets	13,700				13,700
Accounts payable	(7,000)				(7,000)
Rent collected in advance			200		(200)
Interest payable			450		(450)
Income tax payable			3,375		(3,375)
Notes payable, long term	(10,000)				(10,000)
Capital stock, par $10	(50,000)				(50,000)
Retained earnings	(18,000)				(18,000)
Revenues	(80,000)	200		(79,800)	
Expenses (not detailed)	60,000	100		60,100	
Depreciation expense		8,000		8,000	
Interest expense		450		450	
Income tax expense		3,375		3,375	
Net income				7,875	(7,875)
Totals	–0–	12,125	12,125	–0–	–0–

Required:

a. Prepare the adjusting entries in journal form required on December 31, 19D. Write a brief explanation with each entry.

b. Prepare the closing entries at December 31, 19D.

E5–7. For each of the 10 independent situations, give the journal entry by entering the appropriate code(s) and amounts.

Code	Account	Code	Account
A	Cash	K	Interest revenue
B	Office supplies inventory	L	Wage expense
C	Revenue receivable	M	Depreciation expense
D	Office equipment	N	Interest expense
E	Accumulated depreciation	O	Supplies expense
F	Note payable	P	Capital stock
G	Wages payable	Q	Retained earnings
H	Interest payable	R	Dividends declared and paid
I	Rent revenue collected in advance	S	Income summary
J	Service revenues	X	None of the above

Independent Situations	Debit		Credit	
	Code	Amount	Code	Amount
a. Accrued wages, unrecorded and unpaid at year-end, $400.				
b. Service revenue collected and recorded as revenue, but not yet earned, $700.				
c. Dividends declared and paid during year and debited to Dividends account, $900. Give entry at year-end.				
d. Depreciation expense for year not yet recorded, $650.				
e. Balance at year-end in Service Revenue account, $59,000. Give entry at year-end.				
f. Service revenue earned but not yet collected at year-end, $300.				
g. Balance at year-end in Interest Revenue account, $360. Give entry at year-end.				
h. Office Supplies Inventory account at year-end, $550; inventory of supplies on hand at year-end, $100.				
i. At year-end interest on note payable not yet recorded or paid, $180.				
j. Balance at year-end in Income Summary account after all revenue and expense accounts have been closed, $9,900 (credit).				

E5–8. (Based on the Supplement 5A)   Dover Company has completed the accounting information processing cycle for the year ended December 31, 19A. Reversing entries are under consideration (for January 1, 19B) for two different adjusting entries (of December 31, 19A). For case purposes, the relevant data are given in T-accounts, viz:

Prepaid Insurance

1/1/19A Balance	600	(a) 12/31/19A Adj. entry	400

Insurance Expense

(a) 12/31/19A Adj. entry	400	(c) 12/31/19A Closing entry	400

Accrued Wages Payable

		(b) 12/31/19A Adj. entry	1,000

Wage Expense

Paid during 19A	18,000	(d) 12/31/19A Closing entry	19,000
(b) 12/31/19A Adj. entry	1,000		

Income Summary

12/31/19A Closing entries		12/31/19A	
(c)	400	Closed to Retained	
(d)	19,000	Earnings	19,400

Required:

Would a reversing entry on January 1, 19B, facilitate the next related entry for *(a)* Prepaid Insurance and *(b)* Accrued Wages Payable? Explain why.

PROBLEMS/CASES

PC5–1. Rye Company was very careless about its financial records during its first year of operations, 19A. It is December 31, 19A, end of the accounting period. An outside CPA examined the records and discovered numerous errors. Five of those errors are described in the tabulation below. Assume each error is independent of the others. Analyze each error and indicate its effect on 19A and 19B income, assets, and liabilities *if not corrected.* Use these codes to indicate the effect of each dollar amount: O = overstated; U = understated, and N = no effect. Write an explanation of your analysis of each transaction to support your response. The first error is used as an example.

	Effect on					
Independent Errors	**Pretax Income**		**Assets**		**Liabilities**	
	19A	19B	19A	19B	19A	19B
a. Depreciation expense for 19A, not recorded in 19A, $800.	O–800	N	O–800	O–800	N	N
b. Wages earned by employees during 19A, not recorded or paid in 19A, but will be paid in 19B, $600.						
c. Revenue earned during 19A, but not collected or recorded until 19B, $400.						
d. Amount paid in 19A and recorded as expense in 19A, but not an expense until 19B, $700.						
e. Revenue collected in 19A and recorded as revenue in 19A, but not earned until 19B, $500.						
f. Sale of services and cash collected in 19A. Recorded as a debit to Cash and as a credit to Accounts Receivable, $900.						

Explanation of analysis of errors if not corrected:

    a. Failure to record depreciation in 19A caused depreciation expense to be too low; hence, income was overstated by $800. Also, accumulated depreciation is too low by $800, which causes assets to be overstated by $800 until the error is corrected.

PC5–2. General Services Company, Inc., a small service company, maintains its records without the help of an accountant. After considerable effort, an outside accountant prepared the following trial balance as of the end of the annual accounting period, December 31, 19C:

Account titles	*Debit*	*Credit*
Cash	$ 24,900	
Accounts receivable	33,000	
Service supplies inventory	500	
Prepaid insurance	600	
Service trucks (5-year life, no residual value)	20,000	
Accumulated depreciation, service trucks		$ 8,000
Other assets	10,000	
Accounts payable		1,000
Wages payable		
Income tax payable		
Note payable (3 years, 10% each December 31)		10,000
Capital stock, par $10		30,000
Contributed capital in excess of par		3,000
Retained earnings		8,000
Dividends declared and paid	1,000	
Service revenues		70,000
Expenses (not detailed)*	40,000	
Income tax expense		
	$130,000	$130,000

*Excludes income tax expense.

Data not yet recorded at December 31, 19C:

1. The supplies inventory count on December 31, 19C, reflected $200.
2. Insurance expired during 19C, $200.
3. Depreciation expense for 19C, $4,000.
4. Wages earned by employees not yet paid on December 31, 19C, $500.
5. Income tax rate, 20 percent.

Required:

    Note: A worksheet may be used but is not required.

    a. You have been asked to complete the statements given below (show computations) for 19C.
    b. Give the 19C adjusting entries.
    c. Give the 19C closing entries.

Income Statement, 19C

Service revenues		$ _____
Expenses (not detailed)	$ _____	
Supplies expense	_____	
Insurance expense	_____	
Depreciation expense	_____	
Wage expense	_____	
Total expenses		_____
Pretax income		_____
Income tax expense		_____
Net income		$ _____
EPS		$ _____

Balance Sheet, 19C

Assets

Cash	$ _____
Accounts receivable	_____
Service supplies inventory	_____
Prepaid insurance	_____
Service trucks	_____
Accumulated depreciation, trucks	_____
Other assets	_____
Total assets	$ _____

Liabilities

Accounts payable	$ _____
Wages payable	_____
Income tax payable	_____
Note payable, long term	_____
Total liabilities	_____

Stockholders' Equity

Capital stock, par $10	_____
Contributed capital in excess of par	_____
Retained earnings	_____
Total stockholders' equity	_____
Total liabilities and stockholders' equity	$ _____

PC5–3. Delta Company was organized on January 1, 19A. At the end of the first year of operations, December 31, 19A, the bookkeeper prepared the following two trial balances (amounts in thousands of dollars):

Account titles	Unadjusted trial balance Debit	Unadjusted trial balance Credit	Adjusted trial balance Debit	Adjusted trial balance Credit
Cash	$ 30	$	$ 30	$
Accounts receivable.........................	25		25	
Prepaid insurance	3		2	
Rent receivable.............................			1	
Operational assets	48		48	
Accumulated depreciation, operational assets				6
Other assets	4		4	
Accounts payable		11		11
Wages payable				2
Income tax payable				2
Rent revenue collected in advance				3
Note payable, 10% (dated January 1, 19A)		30		30
Capital stock, par $10 per share		50		50
Retained earnings				
Dividends declared and paid	2		2	
Revenues (total)		92		90
Expenses (total including interest)	71		80	
Income tax expense			2	
Totals	$183	$183	$194	$194

Required:

Note: A worksheet may be completed, but is not required.

a. Based upon inspection of the two trial balances, give the 19A adjusting entries developed by the bookkeeper (provide brief explanations).
b. Based upon the above data, give the 19A closing entries with brief explanations.
c. Respond to the following questions (show computations):
   (1) How many shares of stock were outstanding at year-end?
   (2) What was the estimated useful life of the operational assets assuming no residual value?
   (3) What was the amount of interest expense that was included in the total expenses?
   (4) What was the balance of Retained Earnings on December 31, 19A?
   (5) What was the average income tax rate?
   (6) How would the two accounts (a) Rent Receivable and (b) Rent Revenue Collected in Advance be reported on the balance sheet?
   (7) In general, explain why cash increased by $30,000 during the year despite the fact that net income was very low comparatively.
   (8) What was the amount of EPS for 19A?
   (9) What was the selling price of the shares?
   (10) When was the insurance premium paid and over what period of time did the coverage extend?

PC5–4. The ledger accounts of Home Service Company at the end of the second year of operations, December 31, 19B (prior to the closing entries), were as shown below. The 19B adjusting entries are identified by letters, and account numbers are given to the right of the account name.

Cash	101
Bal. 20,000	

Note Payable, 10 Percent	201
	Jan 3, 19B 10,000

Capital Stock, Par $10	301
	Bal. 50,000

Inventory, Maintenance Supplies	102
Bal. 500	(a) 400

Wages Payable	202
	(e) 600

Cont. Capital in Excess of Par	302
	Bal. 6,000

Service Equipment	103
Jan. 1, 19A 90,000	

Interest Payable	203
	(b) 1,000

Retained Earnings	303
	Bal. 9,000

Accumulated Depreciation, Service Equipment	104
	Bal. 18,000
	(d) 18,000

Revenue Collected in Advance	204
(c) 7,000	

Service Revenues	304
(c) 7,000	Bal. 220,000

Remaining Assets	105
Bal. 42,500	

	Income Tax Payable	205
	(f)	6,600

Expenses		305
Bal.	160,000	
(a)	400	
(b)	1,000	
(d)	18,000	
(e)	600	
(f)	6,600	

Required:

a. Develop three 19B trial balances of Home Service Company using the following format:

Account No.	Unadjusted Trial Balance		Adjusted Trial Balance		Post-Closing Trial Balance	
	Debit	Credit	Debit	Credit	Debit	Credit
101						

b. Write an explanation of each adjusting entry for 19B.
c. Give the closing journal entries (do not use Income Summary).
d. What was the apparent useful life of the service equipment? What assumptions must you make to answer this question?
e. What was the average income tax rate for 19B?
f. What was the issue (sale) price per share of the capital stock?

PC5–5. Stimson Corporation has partially completed the following worksheet for the year ended December 31, 19E:

Account Titles	Unadjusted Trial Balance		Adjusting Entries	
	Debit	Credit	Debit	Credit
Cash	18,770			
Accounts receivable	25,680			
Supplies inventory	180			(a) 110
Interest receivable			(b) 300	
Long-term note receivable, 10%	6,000			
Equipment	75,000			
Accumulated depreciation		30,000		(c) 7,500
Accounts payable		11,000		
Short-term notes payable, 12%		8,000		
Interest payable				(d) 320
Income tax payable				(e) 4,000
Capital stock, par $10		40,000		
Contributed capital in excess of par		2,000		
Retained earnings		7,000		
Service revenue		67,680		
Interest revenue				(b) 300
Expenses (not detailed)	40,050		(a) 110	
Depreciation expense			(c) 7,500	
Interest expense			(d) 320	
Income tax expense			(e) 4,000	
Totals	165,680	165,680	12,230	12,230

Required:

a. Add additional columns for Adjusted Trial Balance, Income Statement, Retained Earnings, and Balance Sheet; and complete the worksheet.

b. Give the 19E closing entries.

c. Explain why the adjusting and closing entries must be journalized and posted.

PC5–6. Virginia Corporation is completing the accounting information processing cycle for the year ended December 31, 19C. The unadjusted trial balance, taken from the ledger, was as follows:

		Unadjusted trial balance	
Account No.	Account titles	Debit	Credit
101	Cash	$ 43,550	
103	Accounts receivable (net)	17,000	
105	Prepaid insurance	450	
107	Interest receivable		
120	Long-term note receivable, 12%	6,000	
150	Equipment	90,000	
151	Accumulated depreciation		$ 20,000
170	Other assets	30,000	
201	Accounts payable		14,000
203	Wages payable		
205	Interest payable		
210	Long-term note payable, 15%		10,000
300	Capital stock, par $10		80,000
301	Contributed capital in excess of par		12,000
310	Retained earnings		24,000
311	Dividends declared and paid during 19C	8,000	
320	Service revenue		150,000
322	Interest revenue		
350	Expenses (not detailed)*	115,000	
351	Depreciation expense		
360	Interest expense		
207	Income tax payable		
		$310,000	$310,000

* Includes wage expense and insurance expense.

Additional data for adjusting entries:

a. Expired insurance during 19C was $150.
b. Interest on the long-term note receivable (dated September 1, 19C) is collected annually each August 31.
c. The equipment was acquired on January 1, 19A (assume no estimated residual value).
d. At December 31, 19C, wages earned but not yet paid or recorded, amounted to $3,000.
e. Interest on the long-term note payable (dated May 1, 19C) is paid annually each April 30.
f. Assume a 20 percent average income tax rate.

Required:

a. Complete a worksheet for the year ended December 31, 19C. Key the adjusting entries with letters. (Hint: Net income is $16,872.)
b. Prepare a single-step income statement, a statement of retained earnings, and an unclassified balance sheet.
c. Write a brief explanation of each adjusting entry reflected on the worksheet.
d. Give the closing entries in journal form. Explain why they must be journalized and posted to the ledger.

PC5–7. (Note: This is an extended case selected to review Chapters 2, 3, 4, and 5.) W&P Moving and Storage Service, Incorporated, has been in operation for several years. Revenues have increased gradually from both the moving and storage services. The **annual** financial statements prepared in the past have not conformed to GAAP. The newly employed president decided that starting at the end of 1984, accurate and complete balance sheet, income and cash-flow statements would be prepared. The first step was to employ a full-time bookkeeper and engage a local CPA firm for assistance. It is now December 31, 1984, the end of the current fiscal year. The bookkeeper has developed a trial balance. A member of the staff of the CPA firm will advise and assist the bookkeeper in completing the accounting information processing cycle for the first time. The unadjusted trial balance at December 31, 1984, is shown below.

Unadjusted Trial Balance, December 31, 1984

Debits		*Credits*	
Cash	$ 25,880	Accumulated depreciation	$ 18,000
Accounts receivable	2,030	Accounts payable	6,000
Office supplies inventory	150	Wages payable	
Prepaid insurance	600	Interest payable	
Land for future building		Revenue collected in	
site	6,000	advance	
Equipment	68,000	Income tax payable	
Remaining assets (not		Note payable (12%)	30,000
detailed)	27,000	Capital stock, par $10	20,000
Salary expense	74,000	Retained earnings,	
Advertising expense	1,000	January 1, 1984	21,600
Utilities expense	1,270	Hauling revenue	106,400
Maintenance expense	6,500	Storage revenue	14,000
Miscellaneous expenses	570		
Insurance expense			
Wage expense			
Depreciation expense			
Interest expense			
Income tax expense			
Dividends declared and			
paid	3,000		
	$216,000		$216,000

Examination of the records and related documents provided the following additional information that should be considered for adjusting entries:

a. A physical count of office supplies inventory at December 31, 1984, reflected $40 on hand. Office supplies used are considered to be a miscellaneous expense. No office supplies were purchased during the year.

b. On July 1, 1984, a two-year insurance premium was paid amounting to $600.

c. The equipment cost $68,000 when acquired. It is estimated to have a 10-year useful life to the company and an $8,000 residual value.

d. Unpaid and unrecorded wages earned by employees at December 31, 1984, amounted to $1,200.

e. The $30,000 note payable was signed on October 1, 1984, for a 12 percent bank loan, principal and interest are due at the end of 12 months from that date.

f. Storage revenue collected and recorded as earned before December 31, 1984, included $400 collected in advance from one customer for storage time in 1985. (Hint: Reduce storage revenue.)

g. Gasoline, oil, and fuel purchased for the vehicles and used during the last two weeks of December 1984 amounting to $300 have not been paid for nor recorded (this is considered maintenance expense).

h. The average income tax rate is 20 percent which produces income tax expense of $5,600.

Required:

a. Enter the unadjusted trial balance on a worksheet; then, based on the above data, enter the adjusting entries. Complete the worksheet. (Hint: The adjusted trial balance total is $230,000.)

b. Using the worksheet, prepare a single-step income statement, statement of retained earnings, and balance sheet. (Hint: The balance sheet total is $105,400.)

c. Using the worksheet, prepare the 1984 adjusting entries in journal form.

d. Using the worksheet, prepare 1984 closing entries in journal form.

PC5–8. (Note: This is an extended case selected to review Chapters 2, 3, 4, and 5.) Charter Air Service, Incorporated, was organized to operate a charter service in a city of approximately 350,000 population. The 10 organizers were issued 7,500 shares of $10 par-value stock for a total of $75,000 cash. To obtain facilities to operate the charter services, the company rents from the city hangar and office space at the city airport for a flat monthly rental. The business has prospered because of the excellent service and the high level of maintenance on the planes. It is now December 31, 1984, end of the annual accounting period, and the accounting information processing cycle is in the final phase. Following are representative accounts and unadjusted amounts selected from the ledger at December 31, 1984, for case purposes:

Unadjusted Trial Balance, December 31, 1984

Debits		*Credits*	
Cash	$ 24,600	Accumulated depreciation,	
Prepaid insurance	6,000	aircraft	$ 60,000
Maintenance parts inventory	18,000	Notes payable, 12%	100,000
Aircraft	260,000	Capital stock, par $10	75,000
Salary expense	90,000	Retained earnings, January	
Maintenance expense	24,000	1, 1984	20,600
Fuel expense	63,000	Charter revenue	262,400
Advertising expense	2,000		
Utilities expense	1,400		
Rent expense	14,000		
Dividends declared and			
paid	15,000		
	$518,000		$518,000

For the adjusting entries, the following additional data were developed from the records and supporting documents:

a. On January 1, 1984, the company paid a three-year insurance premium amounting to $6,000.

b. The aircraft, when purchased on January 1, 1981, cost $260,000; and the estimated useful life to the company is approximately 10 years. The equipment has an estimated residual value of $60,000.

c. On July 1, 1984, the company borrowed $100,000 from the bank on a five-year, 12 percent loan. Interest is payable annually starting on June 30, 1985.

d. Charter revenue, on occasion, is collected in advance. On December 31, 1984, collections in advance amounted to $1,000; when collected, this amount was recorded as Charter Revenue.

e. Rent amounting to $14,000 on hangar and office space was paid during the year and recorded as Rent Expense. This included rent paid in advance amounting to $2,000 for January and February 1985. The total amount was recorded as Rent Expense in 1984.

f. The inventory of maintenance parts at December 31, 1984, showed $7,000. All parts purchased are debited to Maintenance Parts Inventory when purchased.

g. For case purposes, assume an average income tax rate of 20 percent which results in income tax expense of $6,000.

Required:

a. Enter the above accounts and unadjusted balances from the ledger on a worksheet. (The following accounts should be added at the bottom of the worksheet because they will be needed for the adjusting entries: Insurance Expense, Depreciation Expense, Interest Expense, Interest Payable, Revenue Collected in Advance, Prepaid Rent Expense, Income Tax Expense, and Income Tax Payable.)

b. Based on the additional data given above, enter the 1984 adjusting entries on the worksheet.

c. Complete the worksheet. (Hint: The adjusted trial balance total is $550,000.)

d. Based on the worksheet, prepare a single-step income statement, a statement of retained earnings, and a classified balance sheet. (Hint: The total on the balance sheet is $217,-600.)

e. Journalize the 1984 adjusting entries.

f. Journalize the 1984 closing entries.

PC5–9. (Based on the Supplement 5A) Alvin Corporation has completed all information processing including the annual financial statements at December 31, 19D. The adjusting entries recorded at that date were as follows:

a. Insurance expense 150
        Prepaid insurance   150

b. Interest receivable 200
        Interest revenue   200

c. Supplies expense   80
        Supplies inventory   80

d. Depreciation expense 2,000
        Accumulated depreciation   2,000

e. Wage expense 500
        Wages payable   500

f. Interest expense 300
        Interest payable   300

g. Income tax expense 4,000
        Income tax payable   4,000

Required:

For each of the above adjusting entries indicate whether it usually would be reversed. Give the reversing entry in each instance (if none, so state) and explain the basis for your response.

PC5–10. Refer to the financial statements of Johnson & Johnson given immediately preceding the Index. Respond to the following for the 1982 annual accounting year, which ended on January 2, 1983.

1. Below are seven T-accounts; each account has the abbreviation "Bal." for balance. You are to *(a)* enter the correct balance, and *(b)* diagram all of the closing entries (and show the transferred amounts).

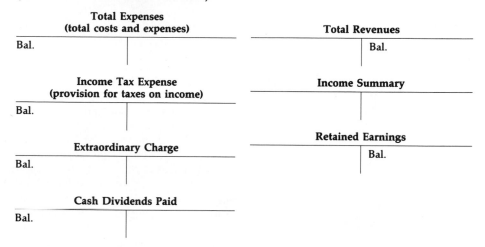

2. Journalize each of the closing entries and provide an explanation of the purpose of each one.
3. From among the above accounts, list the accounts and their balances that would appear on a post-closing trial balance.
4. From among the above accounts, list the accounts and their balances that would be reported on the 1982 balance sheet.
5. Were there any income tax effects not included in the income tax expense amount that you entered above? Explain.

C·H·A·P·T·E·R 6

Accounting for Sales Revenue and Cost of Goods Sold

PURPOSE OF THIS CHAPTER

The purchasing and selling functions are important activities for most businesses involved in retail, wholesale, or manufacturing operations. Retail and wholesale merchandising businesses devote much of their energies to buying and selling goods. Practically all manufacturing businesses also devote significant efforts and resources to purchasing and selling activities. Usually, a manufacturing business purchases raw materials for conversion into finished products, which then are sold. It is not uncommon for a service business also to be involved in purchasing and selling activities. Because of the importance of the purchasing and selling functions, decision makers who use financial statements devote considerable attention to analysis of the marketing successes and failures of a business.

Our discussions in the preceding chapters relating to the measurement of assets, liabilities, income, and cash flows usually were limited to service businesses, but those discussions are as appropriate for merchandising and manufacturing companies as for service businesses. Recall that Business Aids, Inc., was a service business (Exhibit 1–4). However, Diamond, Inc. (Exhibit 2–1) was a merchandising business.

Two distinguishing features on the income statements of retail, wholesale, and manufacturing businesses (as opposed to service businesses) are (1) **sales revenue** and (2) **cost of goods sold**.[1] For example, Diamond's income statement (Exhibit 2–1) reported cost of goods sold of $2,416,000 (which was 67 percent of net sales revenue).

This chapter will discuss and illustrate the measuring, recording, and reporting of sales revenue and cost of goods sold for retail, wholesale, and manufacturing businesses as follows:

Part A—Accounting for sales revenue (including credit sales and bad debts)

Part B—Accounting for cost of goods sold (including accounting for inventories)

This chapter also includes the following supplements:

Supplement 6A—Data processing; control accounts and subsidiary ledgers

Supplement 6B—Aging accounts receivable

Aside from these two directly related problems, this chapter will not consider other manufacturing activities. That topic is discussed in the other volume of this series, *Fundamentals of Management Accounting*.

---

[1] Similar titles sometimes used are "cost of sales" and "cost of products sold." Regardless of title, it is an **expense**.

PART A—ACCOUNTING FOR SALES REVENUE

Accounting for sales revenue requires careful measurement of the economic effects of each sale of goods in accordance with the revenue principle (Exhibit 2–6). Sales may be for cash or on credit and also may involve the trade-in of noncash assets. Determination of the correct amount of sales revenue to be recorded and the appropriate period in which sales revenue should be recognized sometimes poses special problems. The **revenue principle** holds that sales revenue is (a) measured as the **market value** of the considerations received, or the market value of the item sold, whichever is the more clearly determinable; and (b) usually recognized in the accounting period when ownership of the goods passes from the seller to the buyer. Problems in implementing this principle will be discussed and illustrated in this part of the chapter.

For illustrative purposes, the income statement for Campus Corner (Exhibit 6–1) will be used to emphasize the selling and purchasing activities of a small business.[2]

In Exhibit 6–1 observe that cost of goods sold (an expense) is set out separately from the remaining expenses which makes it possible to report a step difference called **gross margin on sales**.[3] This difference between net sales revenue and cost of goods sold reflects the total amount of **markup** on all goods sold during the period. It is expressed in dollars on the income statement ($40,000) and often is reported as the gross margin ratio (Cost of goods sold, $40,000 ÷ Net sales revenue, $100,000 = .40, or 40 percent). For Campus Corner, it can be said that

EXHIBIT 6–1
Income statement

CAMPUS CORNER
Income Statement (multiple-step format)
For the Year Ended December 31, 19F

	Amount	Percentage analysis
Gross sales	$108,333	
Less: Sales returns and allowances	8,333	
Net sales revenue	100,000	100
Cost of goods sold	60,000	60
Gross margin on sales	40,000	40
Operating expenses:		
Selling expenses (detailed) ... $15,000		
Administrative expenses (detailed) ... 10,000	25,000	25
Pretax income	15,000	15
Income tax expense	3,000	3
Net income	$ 12,000	12
EPS ($12,000 ÷ 10,000 shares)	$1.20	

[2] In this chapter, to simplify the illustrations, we ordinarily shall not show the detailed operating expenses. In the single step format for the income statement, revenues would be reported as above under a major caption "Revenues." However, all expenses, including cost of goods sold, would be reported under a major caption "Expenses." Therefore, in the single step format, gross margin on sales is not reported.

[3] This often is called gross profit on sales or simply gross margin or gross profit. In the *Accounting Terminology Bulletins* the AICPA recommended against use of the term *profit* in this context.

(a) for each $1 of net sales the average gross margin was $0.40, or *(b)* the average markup maintained on sales was 40 percent of sales.[4]

RECORDING SALES REVENUE

When ownership of goods passes from the seller to the buyer, the seller must record revenue for the sale transaction. Under the revenue principle, the sales price (net of any discounts) is the measure of the amount of revenue realized. If the sale is for cash, the amount of revenue to be recorded simply is the amount of cash that was received. If the sale is on credit, the revenue is the **cash equivalent** of the assets to be received **excluding** any financing charges (i.e., interest). If the sale is for noncash items (such as the sale of goods for other goods), the amount of revenue to recognize is the cash equivalent of the goods received or given up, whichever is the more clearly determinable. Thus, under the revenue principle, Campus Corner would recognize a sale in 19F (i.e, when ownership passes) as follows:

a. Cash sales for the day per the cash register tapes:

```
Jan. 2  Cash ................................................ 2,000
            Sales revenue ........................................        2,000
```

b. Credit sales for the day per all charge tickets:

```
Jan. 2  Accounts receivable .................................. 1,000
            Sales revenue ........................................        1,000
```

Alternatively, if it is desired to maintain a **separate sales revenue** account in the ledger for the sales of each department, the two entries above could be as follows:[5]

```
Jan. 2  Cash ................................................ 2,000
        Accounts receivable .................................. 1,000
            Sales, Department 1 ..............................        1,000
            Sales, Department 2 ..............................        1,500
            Sales, Department 3 ..............................          500
```

---

[4] This percent is based on sales revenue rather than cost. The markup percent on **cost** would be $40,000 ÷ $60,000 = 66⅔ percent.

[5] See Supplement 6A for an applicable data processing procedure.

Credit sales and sales discounts

A substantial portion of the sales made by many businesses is on credit. When merchandise is sold on credit, the terms of payment should be definite so there will be no misunderstanding as to the amounts and due dates. In fact, credit terms usually are printed on each credit document. Frequently, credit terms are abbreviated by symbols such as, "n/10, EOM," which means the net amount (i.e., the sales amount less any sales returns) is due not later than 10 days after the end of the month (EOM) in which the sale was made. In other cases, the terms may be "n/30," which means that the net amount is due 30 days after the date of the invoice (i.e., after date of sale). In still other cases, **sales discounts** (often called cash discounts) are granted to the purchaser to encourage early payment. For example, the credit terms may be "2/10, n/30," which means that if cash payment is made within 10 days from the date of sale, the customer may deduct 2 percent from the invoice price; however, if not paid within the 10-day discount period, the full sales price (less any returns) is due in 30 days from date of sale.

When a cash discount is granted, a customer is motivated to pay within the discount period because by doing so the savings are substantial. For example, with terms 2/10, n/30, 2 percent is saved by paying 20 days early, which equates to approximately 37 percent annual interest. As a consequence, credit customers usually will take advantage of the sales discount. Credit customers conceivably may borrow cash from a bank (at a lower interest rate) in order to take advantage of cash discounts, and thus avoid paying a high interest rate that would result from not taking cash discounts. Because the cash discount on sales almost always will be taken, the Sales Revenue account should be credited (i.e., increased) for the cash that probably will be received rather than for the gross sales amount. To do otherwise would be inconsistent with the **revenue principle** which holds that sales revenue should be measured as the cash or cash equivalent received for the goods sold. To illustrate the proper procedure, assume a sale by Campus Corner of $1,000 with terms 2/10, n/30. The sequence of entries would be as follows:

a. January 18, date of sale on credit:

Accounts receivable	980	
Sales revenue		980
Terms: 2/10, n/30 ($1,000 × 0.98 = $980).		

b. January 27, date of collection if payment is made **within** the discount period (the usual case):

Cash	980	
Accounts receivable		980

January 31, date of collection if payment is made **after** the discount period (the unusual case):

```
Cash ......................................................... 1,000
    Sales discount revenue* ...................................              20
    Accounts receivable ........................................             980
    * Interest revenue sometimes is used because conceptually it is in the nature
of interest revenue earned.
```

The preferred method for recording sales revenues, which was illustrated, is known as the **net method.** As an alternative, some companies use the **gross method of recording sales revenues.** Under the gross method, sales revenue is recorded without deducting the amount of the cash discount. Thus, the following entries would be made by Campus Corner if the gross method were used instead of the net method (as was the case in the previous illustration):

a. January 18, date of sale on credit:

```
Accounts receivable ........................................... 1,000
    Sales revenue ..............................................          1,000
```

b. January 27, date of collection if payment is made **within** the discount period (the usual case):

```
Cash ......................................................... 980
Sales discounts ...............................................  20
    Accounts receivable ........................................         1,000
    Terms 2/10, n/30 ($1,000 × .98 = $980).
```

c. January 31, date of collection if payment is made **after** the discount period (the unusual case):

```
Cash ......................................................... 1,000
    Accounts receivable ........................................         1,000
```

The Sales Discounts account (used with the gross method) can be reported as *(a)* a contra revenue account, *(b)* an addition to selling expense, or *(c)* an interest expense. The gross method overstates both accounts receivable and sales revenue.

While the net method is theoretically preferable, most companies will select the method that they believe involves the most bookkeeping convenience. However, the convenience differences are not significant.

Cash discounts should be distinguished from **trade discounts.** A cash discount is a price concession given to encourage early payment of an account. A trade discount is a device sometimes used by vendors for quoting sales prices; the amount **after** the trade discount is the sales price. For example, an item may be quoted at $10 per unit subject to a 20 percent trade discount on orders of 100 units or more; thus, the price for the large order would be $8 per unit.

In recent years there has been a trend toward more credit sales, particularly at the retail level. However, the use of cash discounts appears to be declining. In some jurisdictions, they are not legal in certain situations because the effect is to charge the cash customers more than the credit customers who pay within the discount period. Also, the discount not taken by credit customers is a hidden financing charge that may be governed by legislation dealing with credit practices.

Extending credit usually entails a significant increase in the amount of record-keeping required because detailed records must be maintained for each credit customer. Some businesses have their credit sales handled by a credit card company (such as Mastercard or Visa) that charges a fee for this service. The fee paid to the credit card company is recorded as a collection expense (and not a sales discount). Supplement 6A discusses some aspects of the detailed records maintained for credit customers.

MEASURING BAD DEBT EXPENSE

Despite careful credit investigation, there will be a few credit customers who do not pay their obligations. When an account receivable proves uncollectible, the business incurs a **bad debt loss.** Businesses that extend credit do so with the expectation that there will be a certain amount of bad debt losses on credit sales. As a matter of fact, an extremely low rate of bad debt losses may be evidence of too tight a credit policy. If the credit policy is too restrictive, many credit customers who would pay their bills on a timely basis may be turned away. Thus, bad debt losses can be thought of as a necessary expense associated with generating credit sales.

To account for bad debt losses, the matching principle requires that bad debt expense be matched with the period's sale revenues that gave rise to those losses. This requirement is difficult to implement because it may be one or more years after the particular sale was made before the business will be aware of the fact that the customer will be unable to pay.

To satisfy the matching principle in credit situations, the **bad debt allowance method** was developed to measure bad debt expense. The allowance method recognizes that bad debt losses are incurred in the year in which the sales that generated those losses were made rather than in the year that the customer is unable to pay. There is no way of telling in advance which individual accounts ultimately will prove worthless; therefore, the allowance method is based upon the concept of **estimating** in each accounting period what the probable amount of bad debt losses due to uncollectible accounts will be during the collection period. The estimate is made on the basis of total credit sales for the period because the individual accounts that will be bad are not known in the period of sale.

Estimating the probable amount of expense due to uncollectible accounts is neither complex nor fraught with major uncertainties. For a company that has been operating for some years, experience provides a sound basis for projecting probable future bad debt losses related to credit sales, and new companies often rely on the experience of similar companies that have been operating for a number of years, if such information is available. To illustrate, an analysis of accounting data on total credit sales and total uncollectible accounts for the past five years by Campus Corner indicated an average bad debt loss of .9 percent of total credit sales, viz:

Year	Bad debt losses	Credit sales
19A	$ 440	$ 54,000
19B	480	57,000
19C	620	53,000
19D	500	66,000
19E	660	70,000
	$2,700	$300,000

Aggregate: $2,700 ÷ $300,000 = .9 percent average loss rate for the five-year period 19A–E

Usually a company will adjust the average loss rate of the past to reflect future expectations. Campus Corner expects a small increase in uncollectible accounts from 19F sales; therefore, it increased the expected loss rate to 1.0 percent.

Now let's see how the allowance method would be applied to the above example. Assuming net credit sales in 19F of $40,000, we would record bad debt expense of $40,000 × 1% = $400 in 19F. This estimate would require the following **adjusting entry** at the end of the accounting period, December 31, 19F:

Bad debt expense	400	
Allowance for doubtful accounts (or bad debts)		400

To adjust for the estimated bad debt loss based on credit sales with an average expected loss rate of 1 percent ($40,000 × 1% = $400).

Bad debt expense of $400 would be reported on the 19F income statement, and it would be matched with the related sales revenue for 19F, the year in which the credit was granted. The Bad Debt Expense account is closed at the end of each accounting period along with the other expense accounts. Rather than crediting the Accounts Receivable account, the credit in the above entry was made to a **contra account** descriptively titled "Allowance for Doubtful Accounts" because there is no way of knowing which account receivable is involved.

Other acceptable titles for this contra account are "Allowance for Bad Debts" and "Allowance for Uncollectible Accounts." The balance in Allowance for Doubtful Accounts **always** is considered as a subtraction from the balance of Accounts Receivable. Thus, the two accounts would be reported in the current asset section of the balance sheet as follows:

CAMPUS CORNER
Balance Sheet (partial)
At December 31, 19F

Current assets:
Cash $34,000
Accounts receivable $100,000
    Less: Allowance for doubtful accounts 2,400*   97,600

* This amount assumes a balance of $2,000 carried forward prior to the above entry.

Allowance for Doubtful Accounts carries a cumulative credit balance; it is not closed because it is a balance sheet account. It sometimes is described as a contra account, an asset reduction account, or an offset account, but more frequently as a **valuation account.** These descriptions derive from the fact that the balance of the allowance account is the total amount of the accounts receivable that is estimated to be uncollectible. Thus, the difference between the balances of Accounts Receivable and the allowance account measures the estimated net realizable value of accounts receivable. In the above example, the difference between the two accounts—$97,600—represents the **estimated net realizable value** of accounts receivable (also called the book value of accounts receivable).

In the above illustration, the bad debt estimate was based only on credit sales. Occasionally, a company bases the estimate on total sales (i.e., cash plus credit sales). This practice is illogical because (1) it is impossible to have a bad debt loss on a cash sale (except in the case of a "hot" check which is uncollectible), and (2) a shift in the relative proportion between cash and credit sales would affect the accuracy of the estimate. The total amount of credit sales for each period can be determined (because these transactions are recorded in Accounts Receivable as debits); therefore, there is no reason for not using credit sales as the base for the estimate. Another method of estimating bad debt losses (known as aging accounts receivable) is explained and illustrated in Supplement 6B.

Writing off a bad debt

When an individual customer's account receivable ultimately is determined to be uncollectible (i.e., bad), the amount should be removed from the Accounts Receivable account with an offsetting debit to the allowance account. This entry does not record a bad debt loss (expense) because the estimated expense was recorded with an adjusting entry in the period of sale (one or more years earlier), and the related allowance account was established to absorb the later write-off. To illustrate, assume Campus Corner sold J. Doe merchandise on credit in 19D amounting to $100 (which was properly credited to 19D Sales Revenue and debited to Accounts Receivable). At the end of 19F, Campus Corner decided that it would never collect the $100; accordingly, they made the following entry:

December 31, 19F:

Allowance for doubtful accounts 100
        Accounts receivable (J. Doe) 100
        To write off a receivable from J. Doe determined to be uncollectible.

Observe that the above entry did not affect the income statement because the expense already had been recorded (when the adjusting entry was made at the end of 19D). Also, the entry did not change the **net realizable value** (i.e., the book value) of Accounts receivable. The difference between Accounts Receivable and the allowance account remains the same as before the entry, viz:

	Before write-off	After write-off
Accounts receivable	$100,000	$99,900
Less: Allowance for doubtful accounts	2,400	2,300
Difference—estimated net realizable value.....	$ 97,600	$97,600

Actual write-offs compared with estimates. The uncollectible accounts actually written off seldom will equal the estimated amounts previously recorded. If the accounts actually written off are less than the estimated amount, the Allowance for Doubtful Accounts will continue with a credit balance.[6] If an account is written off as bad and the customer subsequently pays it, the write-off entry should be reversed and the collection should be recorded in the usual way.

Terminology. The caption "Accounts receivable" often appears on the balance sheet under current assets without additional descriptive terms; however, a more descriptive designation such as "Receivables from trade customers" is preferable. Receivables from other than the regular trade customers, such as loans to officers or employees, should not be included in the accounts receivable category. Rather, such nontrade receivables should be reported as separate items.

SALES RETURNS AND ALLOWANCES

Many businesses permit customers to return unsatisfactory or damaged merchandise and receive a cash or credit refund. In some cases, rather than taking back such merchandise, a cash or credit adjustment may be given to the customer. To measure correctly sales revenue, such transactions must be recorded by, in effect, reversing the sales entry. Although the Sales account could be debited (i.e., reduced) to record these reductions in sales, a separate account entitled "Sales Returns and Allowances" often is used. This account serves an important control

---

[6] On the other hand, if the amount written off is more than the allowance balance, there will be a temporary debit balance in the allowance account. This situation will be resolved when the next adjusting entry is made. It indicates that the estimated loss rate used may be too low.

objective by informing the management of the volume of returns and allowances. If cash is refunded, the Cash account is credited. Alternatively, if a credit adjustment is given, accounts receivable of the customer must be credited. The Sales Returns and Allowances account is a contra revenue account; therefore, it is a deduction from gross sales revenue (as shown in Exhibit 6–1). To illustrate, assume a customer, F. Fox, bought five new lamps from Campus Corner for $500. Fifteen days after payment, Fox returned one lamp that was damaged. The sequence of entries by Campus Corner would be:

Date of sale:

Accounts receivable (F. Fox)	500	
Sales revenue		500
To record sale.		

Date of sale return:

Sales returns and allowances	100	
Cash*		100
To record sale return, 1 unit.		
* If payment had not been made this credit would be to Accounts Receivable.		

PART B—ACCOUNTING FOR COST OF GOODS SOLD

NATURE OF COST OF GOODS SOLD

The income statement shown in Exhibit 6–1 (Campus Corner) reported an expense called cost of goods sold, which is unique to nonservice types of businesses. Cost of goods sold (CGS) is a relatively simple concept. Sales revenue represents the merchandise sold during the accounting period valued at **sales price,** whereas cost of goods sold is the same merchandise valued at **cost.** Thus, revenue and expense are matched on the income statement in conformity with the **matching principle** (see Exhibit 2–6). Cost of goods sold includes the cost of all merchandise sold during the period, but it excludes the cost of all merchandise remaining on hand at the end of the accounting period (i.e., the ending merchandise inventory).

Typically, a business will start each accounting period with a stock of merchandise on hand for resale which is called the **beginning** (or initial) **inventory (BI).** The merchandise on hand at the end of an accounting period is called the **ending** (or final) **inventory (EI)** for that period, which automatically becomes the beginning inventory for the next period.

During the accounting period, the beginning inventory usually is increased by the purchase or manufacture of additional merchandise. The sum of the beginning inventory and the **purchases (P)** during the period represents the **goods available for sale** during that period. If all of the goods available for sale were sold during the period, there would be no ending inventory. Typically, not all of the goods available for sale are sold; therefore, a quantity of goods remains on hand which is the ending inventory for the period. From these facts we can state the cost of goods sold (CGS) model as follows:

$$BI + P - EI = CGS$$

To illustrate, Campus Corner reported cost of goods sold of $60,000 (Exhibit 6–1), which was determined as follows:

Beginning inventory (January 1, 19F)	$40,000
Add purchases of merchandise during 19F	55,000
Goods available for sale	95,000
Deduct ending inventory (December 31, 19F)	35,000
Cost of goods sold	$60,000

INVENTORY SYSTEMS

To compute cost of goods sold, three amounts must be known: (1) beginning inventory, (2) purchases of merchandise during the period, and (3) ending inventory. The ending inventory of one accounting period is the beginning inventory of the succeeding period. Therefore, the beginning inventory amount always will be available from the preceding period. The amount of purchases for the period will be accumulated in the accounting system. The amount of the **ending** inventory can be determined by using one of two distinctly different inventory systems:

1. **Periodic inventory system**—Under this system, no up-to-date record of inventory is maintained during the year. An actual physical count (i.e., an inventory count) of the goods remaining on hand is required at the **end of each period.** The number of units of each type of merchandise on hand then is multiplied by the purchase cost per unit to compute the dollar amount of the ending inventory. Thus, the amount of goods on hand at any point during the year is not known until the last day of the period when the inventory count is completed. Also, the amount of cost of goods sold cannot be determined until the inventory count is completed.

2. **Perpetual inventory system**—This system involves the maintenance of up-to-date inventory records in the accounting system throughout the period. For each type of goods stocked, a detailed record is maintained that shows (a) units and cost of the beginning inventory, (b) units and cost of each purchase, (c) units and cost of the goods for each sale, and (d) the units and amount on hand at any point in time. This up-to-date record is maintained on a transaction-by-transaction basis throughout the period. **Thus, the inventory record provides both the amount of ending inventory and the cost of goods sold amount at any point in time.**

Periodic inventory system

The periodic inventory system requires an actual count of the goods on hand at the end of the period and valuation of the units at their purchase cost. The primary reasons for using the periodic inventory system are low cost and convenience. Consider the cost and difficulty associated with a grocery store attempting to keep track of the number of units sold and the cost of each purchase and sales of the thousands of low-priced items that usually are stocked. When small items are sold for cash (as in a grocery store), usually no record is made at the cash register of the cost and quantity of each item (rather the total sales price is entered into the cash register). The primary disadvantage of a periodic inventory system is the lack of inventory control (for purchasing purposes and detection of theft).[7] Nevertheless, many companies use the periodic system either for all items offered for sale or for only the small, low-cost items.

A periodic inventory system applies the cost of goods sold model given on page 244 as follows:

A periodic inventory system may be outlined sequentially as follows:

1. **Record all purchases**—During the period, the purchase cost of all goods bought is recorded in an account called Purchases (or Merchandise Purchases). Thus, a credit or cash purchase would be recorded as follows:

January 14, 19F:

Purchases	9,000	
Accounts payable (or Cash)		9,000

2. **Record all sales**—During the period, the sales price received for all goods sold is recorded in a Sales Revenue account. Thus, a credit or cash sale would be recorded as follows:

January 30, 19F:

Accounts receivable (or Cash)	8,000	
Sales revenue		8,000

---

[7] Because of this important disadvantage, large chain stores now have computerized perpetual inventory systems tied in directly to the cash registers.

3. **Count the number of units on hand**—At the end of the current period, the Inventory account balance still reflects the inventory amount carried over from the prior period because **no entries** are made to the Inventory account during the current period. Thus, to measure the ending inventory for the current period, a physical inventory count must be made on all goods on hand. A physical count is necessary because, under the periodic inventory system, a transaction-by-transaction unit and cost record is not maintained for purchases, cost of goods sold, and the inventory balance. This count must be made at the end of each period for which financial statements are to be prepared. Taking a physical inventory count is discussed later.

4. **Compute the dollar valuation of the ending inventory**—The dollar amount of the ending inventory quantities is computed by multiplying the number of units on hand (determined in 3 above) by their unit purchase cost. The dollar amounts of all of the types of goods stocked are summed to measure the total ending inventory valuation for the company.

5. **Compute cost of goods sold**—After the ending inventory valuation is measured (as in 4 above), cost of goods sold for the period was computed as follows for Campus Corner:

CAMPUS CORNER
Schedule of Cost of Goods Sold
For the Year Ended December 31, 19F

Beginning inventory (carried over from the last period in the Inventory account)	$40,000
Add purchases for the period (accumulated balance in the Purchases account)	55,000
Goods available for sale	95,000
Less ending inventory (determined by physical count, per above)	35,000
Cost of goods sold (as shown in Exhibit 6–1)	$60,000

       * Based on the data given on page 244.

Perpetual inventory system

A perpetual inventory system typically involves a considerable amount of clerical effort; however, it is effective in measuring inventory and cost of goods sold and in maintaining inventory control. The maintenance of a separate inventory record for each type of goods stocked on a transaction-by-transaction basis usually is desirable, particularly for control purposes. To minimize bookkeeping difficulties, most perpetual inventory systems are computerized. Whether the accounting system is manual, mechanical, or computerized, the data that are recorded and reported are the same. For instructional purposes, let's look at a manual approach. Assume, for this illustration only, that Campus Corner stocks and sells only one item, called Super X. The following events apply to 19F:

Jan.   1   Beginning inventory—8 units, at unit cost of $5,000.
July 14   Purchased—11 additional units, at unit cost of $5,000.
Nov. 30   Sold—13 units, at unit sales price of $8,333.
Dec. 31   Return sale—1 unit (returned to stock and refunded sales price).

EXHIBIT 6–2
Perpetual inventory record

		Goods Purchased			Goods Sold			Balance on Hand		
PERPETUAL INVENTORY RECORD										
Item Super X			Code No. 33					Minimum stock 10		
Location Storage No. 4			Valuation basis Cost					Maximum stock 20		
Date	Explanation	Units Rec'd	Unit Cost	Total Cost	Units Sold	Unit Cost	Total Cost	Units	Unit Cost	Total Cost
Jan. 1	Beginning inventory							8	5,000	40,000
July 14	Purchase	11	5,000	55,000				19	5,000	95,000
Nov. 30	Sale				13	5,000	65,000	6	5,000	30,000
Dec. 31	Return sale				(1)	5,000	(5,000)	7	5,000	35,000
Recap: Total purchases		11		55,000						
Total cost of goods sold					12		60,000			
Ending inventory								7		35,000

The perpetual inventory record for this single item stocked is shown in Exhibit 6–2.[8]

The beginning inventory, purchases, cost of goods sold, and ending inventory amounts on the above perpetual inventory record agree with the amounts computed on page 244 using the periodic inventory system. In this situation, the two systems will produce the same end results unless an error has been made. However, each of the two systems will serve the company in different ways because the periodic system provides no details regarding the inventory changes whereas the perpetual system provides all of the details on a day-to-day basis.

When the perpetual inventory system is computerized, the computer does exactly what was done manually in Exhibit 6–2; however, a computerized system does it with tremendous speed and accuracy. Computerization effectively overcomes many of the difficulties associated with the perpetual system, which permits large, medium, and even small companies to use the perpetual system.

A perpetual inventory system may be outlined sequentially as follows:

1. **Record all purchases**—During the period, the purchase cost of each type of goods bought is entered in the **Inventory** ledger account as an increase

---

[8] Measuring inventories and cost of goods sold when there are different unit purchase costs is deferred to Chapter 7.

and in a detailed perpetual inventory record (Exhibit 6–2). Thus, a cash or credit purchase of goods for resale would be recorded as follows (refer to Exhibit 6–2):

July 14, 19F:

> Inventory* (Super X, code 33) 55,000
>   Accounts payable (or Cash)   55,000
>   * Also entered in the perpetual inventory record as shown in Exhibit 6–2.

2. **Record all sales**—During the period, each sale is recorded by means of **two companion entries.** One entry is to record the sales revenue at **sales price,** and the other entry is to record the **cost of goods sold at purchase cost.** The sales revenue is recorded in the Sales Revenue account, and the cost of goods sold is recorded in the Cost of Goods Sold account. Thus, a credit or cash sale would be recorded as follows (refer to data presented in Exhibit 6–2):

November 30, 19F:

a. To record the sales revenue at the sales price of $8,333 per unit:

> Accounts receivable (or Cash) 108,329
>   Sales revenue (13 units @ $8,333)   108,329

b. To record the cost of goods sold (at cost per the perpetual inventory record—Exhibit 6–2):

> Cost of goods sold* 65,000
>   Inventory (13 units @ $5,000)   65,000
>   * Also entered in the perpetual inventory record as shown in Exhibit 6–2.

3. **Record all returns**—During the period, both **purchase returns and sales returns** are recorded in the Inventory account and on the perpetual inventory record at cost. For example, the return by a customer of one unit of Super X on December 30 requires companion entries to reverse the two entries made on the date of sale, shown above (only for the number of units returned). The return would be recorded as follows (refer to Exhibit 6–2):

a. To record the sales return at sale price (one unit):

> Sales returns and allowances (1 unit @ $8,333) 8,333
>   Accounts receivable (or Cash) 8,333

b. To record the return of the unit to inventory:

> Inventory (1 unit @ $5,000) 5,000*
>   Cost of goods sold 5,000
>   * This amount was provided by the perpetual inventory record; also it is restored to the
>   perpetual inventory record as shown in Exhibit 6–2.

4. **Use cost of goods sold and inventory amounts**—At the end of the accounting period, the balance in the Cost of Goods Sold account provides the total amount of that expense that is reported on the income statement. It is not necessary to use the cost of goods sold model to compute the expense (shown on page 244) because under the perpetual inventory system the Cost of Goods Sold account in the ledger always is up-to-date. Similarly, the Inventory account would reflect the ending inventory amount that would be reported on the balance sheet. The sum of all the inventory balances in the various perpetual inventory records should equal the balance in the Inventory account in the ledger at any point in time.

This illustration demonstrates that when a perpetual inventory system is used, it is not necessary to take a physical inventory count of the merchandise remaining on hand at the end of the accounting period in order to measure the inventory amount and cost of goods sold. However, because clerical errors, theft, and spoilage may occur, a physical inventory should be taken from time to time to check upon the accuracy of the perpetual inventory records. If an error is found, the perpetual inventory records and the Inventory account must be changed to agree with the physical count.

To summarize, there are two basic accounting differences between periodic and perpetual systems:

1. Inventory account:
   a. Periodic—During the period, the balance in the Inventory account is not changed; thus, it reflects the beginning inventory amount. During the period, each purchase is recorded in the Purchases account. As a consequence, the ending inventory for each accounting period must be measured by physical count, then valued (or "costed") at unit purchase cost.
   b. Perpetual—During the period, the Inventory account is increased for each purchase and decreased (at cost) for each sale. Thus, at the end of the period, it measures the correct amount of ending inventory.

2. Cost of Goods Sold account:
   a. Periodic—During the period, no entry is made for cost of goods sold. At the end of the period, after the physical inventory count, cost of goods sold is measured as:

$$\frac{\text{Beginning}}{\text{inventory}} + \text{Purchases} - \frac{\text{Ending}}{\text{inventory}} = \frac{\text{Cost of}}{\text{goods sold}}$$

   b. Perpetual—During the period, cost of goods sold is recorded at the time of each sale and the Inventory account is reduced (at cost). Thus, the system measures the amount of cost of goods sold for the period.

The perpetual inventory system is used widely because of the following advantages over the periodic inventory system:

1. It provides up-to-date inventory amounts (units and dollar cost for each item).
2. It provides the cost of goods sold amount without the necessity of taking a periodic inventory count.
3. It provides continuing information necessary to maintain minimum and maximum inventory levels by appropriate timing of purchases.
4. It provides continuing information about the quantity of goods on hand at various locations.
5. It provides a basis for measuring the amount of theft.
6. It provides cost of goods sold information needed to record sales at both selling price and cost.
7. It is readily adaptable for use by computers that quickly process large quantities of inventory data.

For these reasons there has been an increase in the use of the perpetual inventory system and a decrease in use of the periodic inventory system.

ADDITIONAL ISSUES IN MEASURING PURCHASES

In accordance with generally accepted accounting principles (GAAP), goods purchased for resale are recorded as a purchase at the date that **ownership** passes from the seller to the buyer. Normally, ownership is considered to pass when the goods are received and not when the purchase order is placed. Goods purchased should be recorded at their **cash equivalent cost** in accordance with the cost principle. Cost includes the cash equivalent price paid to the vendor (seller) plus other amounts paid for transportation and handling in order to get the goods into location and condition for intended use. Cost does not include expenditures such as interest paid on cash borrowed to make the purchase. In accounting for purchases, several measurement problems frequently are encountered. Many of these problems are similar to those discussed in Part A of this chapter from the perspective of the seller.

Purchase returns and allowances

Goods purchased may be returned to the vendor (seller) because they do not meet specifications, arrive in unsatisfactory condition, or otherwise are unsatisfactory. When the goods are returned or when the vendor makes an allowance because of the circumstances, the effect on the cost of purchases must be measured.

The purchaser will receive a cash refund or a reduction in the liability to the vendor for the purchase. To illustrate, assume Campus Corner returned to Company B, for credit, unsatisfactory goods that cost $1,000. The return would be recorded by Campus Corner (which uses the periodic system) as follows:

Accounts payable (or cash)	1,000	
Purchase returns and allowances*		1,000
* Inventory is credited when the perpetual inventory system is used.		

Purchase returns and allowances are accounted for as a deduction from the cost of purchases.

Transportation-in

Under the cost principle, assets should be measured and recorded at their **cash equivalent cost.** Thus, the **purchase cost** of goods acquired for resale should include all freight and other transportation-in costs incurred by the purchaser. When a perpetual inventory system is used, transportation costs paid on goods purchased should be apportioned to each inventory item and included in the inventory cost amount entered in the perpetual inventory. When a periodic inventory system is used, such costs should be entered as a debit (i.e., increase) to the Purchases account. However, because of the problems associated with apportioning a freight bill to the several items it may cover, often it is more practical to use a separate ledger account entitled "Transportation-in," or "Freight-in." Also, for control purposes it is often useful to separately classify this significant cost. Thus, in this situation the journal entry to record a payment for transportation charges upon delivery of merchandise acquired for resale would be:

Jan. 17	Transportation-in	3,000	
	Cash		3,000

At the end of the period, the balance in the Transportation-in account would be reported as an addition to the cost of purchases.

Assuming freight-in and purchase returns, cost of goods sold may be reflected as follows on the income statement when periodic inventory procedures are used (refer to Campus Corner, page 246):

Cost of goods sold:			
Beginning inventory		$40,000	
Purchases	$53,000		
Add: Freight-in	3,000		
Deduct: Purchase returns and allowances	(1,000)		
Net purchases		55,000	
Goods available for sale		95,000	
Less: Ending inventory		35,000	
Cost of goods sold			$60,000

Purchase discounts

A situation that corresponds to cash discounts on sales (page 237) occurs when merchandise is purchased for resale—except that the cash discount is received rather than given. When merchandise is purchased on credit, terms such as 2/10, n/30 sometimes are specified. This means that if payment of the purchase invoice cost is made within 10 days from date of purchase, a 2 percent purchase discount is granted. If payment is not made within the discount period, then the full purchase invoice cost is due 30 days after purchase. To illustrate, assume Campus Corner purchases goods from a number of suppliers. On January 17, the company purchased goods from Vendor B that had a $1,000 invoice price with terms, 2/10, n/30. On January 26, Campus Corner will pay $980 for the goods. Therefore, the purchase should be recorded on the net basis by Campus Corner as follows:[9]

January 17—date of purchase:

Purchases*	980	
Accounts payable		980
* Inventory is debited when a perpetual inventory system is used.		

January 26—date of payment, within the discount period:

Accounts payable	980	
Cash		980

If for any reason Campus Corner did not pay within the 10-day discount period, the following entry would result:

Feb. 1	Accounts payable	980	
	Purchase discounts lost (or Interest expense)	20	
	Cash		1,000

---

[9] Some persons prefer to record the transaction at the date of purchase at the gross amount, that is, at $1,000. In this instance, payment within the discount period would result in credit to an account called Purchase Discounts, $20. The purchase discount credit would then be reported as a revenue, or as a deduction from purchases. This credit is not revenue and if deducted in full from purchases on the income statement would tend to misstate both inventory and purchases. In contrast, the net basis has the distinct advantage in that recording the **purchase discount lost** calls direct attention to inefficiency—failure to take the discount. The gross approach conceptually and practically is deficient for reasons similar to those cited with respect to sales discounts.

Purchase discounts lost should be reported on the income statement as a **financial expense** along with interest expense on debts.

TAKING A PHYSICAL INVENTORY

We explained earlier in the chapter that whether a periodic or perpetual inventory system is used, a physical inventory count must be taken from time to time. When a **periodic** inventory system is used, the inventory must be counted (and costed) at the **end of each period** because the financial statements cannot be prepared without this key amount. When a perpetual inventory system is used, the inventory count may be scheduled at various times to verify the perpetual inventory records. The two steps in taking a **physical inventory count** are:

1. **Quantity count**—The **count** of merchandise is made after the close of business on the inventory date. Normally, it would be difficult to count the goods accurately during business hours when sales activities are taking place. A physical count is made of all items of merchandise on hand and entered on an appropriate form. An inventory form, such as the one shown in Exhibit 6–3, may be used. Special care must be exercised in the quantity count to be sure that all of the merchandise owned by the business is included, wherever located, and that all items for which the entity does not have legal ownership

EXHIBIT 6–3
Physical inventory form

Campus Corner
PHYSICAL INVENTORY SHEET

Date of Inventory _12/31/81_ Department _Hand. Inel._ Taken by _M. K._

Location	Identification of Merchandise	Quantity on Hand	Date Purchased	Unit Cost	Unit Market Price*	Unit Cost (LCM)	Inventory Amount
1	Headsets #8-16	20	12/2/81	$ 20	$ 21	$ 20	$ 400
2	Television sets #17-961	7	11/5/81	.300	.300	.300	2,100
2	Radios #23-72	4	10/26/81	.52	.50	.50	200
	Total Department Inventory						6,000
	TOTAL INVENTORY VALUE—ALL DEPARTMENTS	12/31/81					$35,000

* Replacement cost that would have to be paid if the item were being purchased on the inventory date (see lower of cost or market discussion in Chapter 7).

are excluded. Occasionally, a business will have possession of goods it does not own (see discussion of consignments in Chapter 7).

2. **Inventory costing**—After the physical count of goods on hand has been completed, each kind of merchandise must be assigned a **unit cost.** The quantity of each kind of merchandise is multiplied by the unit cost to derive the inventory amount (as illustrated in Exhibit 6–3). The sum of the inventory amounts for all merchandise on hand measures the total ending inventory amount for the business. Exhibit 6–3 reflects computation of the ending inventory shown on the income statement for Campus Corner (see page 235). In determining the value of inventory, the cost principle must be applied; therefore, unit purchase cost, as defined above, must be used. A problem arises if there are different unit costs for inventory items that otherwise are exactly the same. When this situation occurs, there are several ways to identify unit purchase cost for inventory purposes such as the first-in, first-out (FIFO), last-in, first-out (LIFO), or average cost approaches. These alernative approaches to costing inventories are discussed in detail in Chapter 7.

Management must deal with complex problems associated with planning and control of inventories. An excessive amount of inventory may tie up resources (i.e., cash) that could be employed more economically in other ways in the business. Insufficient inventory often results in lost sales. Decisions must be made concerning maximum and minimum levels of inventory that should be maintained; when to reorder; how much to reorder; and the characteristics of the items to stock, such as size, color, style, and specifications. Many of these issues are discussed in *Fundamentals of Management Accounting.* From the viewpoint of the investor, creditor, and other interested parties, information concerning the investment in inventory frequently is important in decision making. Therefore, explanatory footnotes related to inventories frequently are included in the financial reports.

DATA PROCESSING—CLOSING ENTRIES FOR SALES REVENUE, COST OF GOODS SOLD, AND MERCHANDISE INVENTORY

Closing the sales revenue and bad debt expense accounts

This chapter introduced some new revenue and expense accounts related to the selling and purchasing functions. Because these accounts are **temporary** accounts, they must be closed at the end of the accounting period.

Sales Revenue is closed by recording a debit in that account and a credit in the Income Summary. Sales Discount Revenue is closed in the same way. Bad Debt Expense is closed by recording a credit in that account and a debit to the Income Summary. Sales Returns and Allowance (a contra revenue account) is closed by recording a credit to that account and a debit to the Income Summary. The closing entries for cost of goods sold (an expense) and the merchandise inventory amounts depend upon the inventory system (periodic versus perpetual) used.

Closing entries when a periodic inventory system is used

When a periodic inventory system is used, there is no Cost of Goods Sold account in the ledger. The merchandise inventory account requires two directly related closing entries: (1) an entry to close the **beginning inventory** amount to the Income Summary account and (2) an entry to transfer the **ending inventory** amount from the Income Summary account to the Inventory account. Campus Corner (see page 246) would make two closing entries for the merchandise inventories as follows:

December 31, 19F.

a. To close (transfer) the **beginning** merchandise inventory amount into Income Summary:

Income summary	40,000	
Merchandise inventory (beginning)		40,000

b. To transfer the **ending** merchandise inventory amount from the Income Summary account to the Merchandise Inventory account:

Merchandise inventory (ending)	35,000	
Income summary		35,000

The effects of these two entries are (a) to replace the beginning inventory amount in the Merchandise Inventory account with the ending inventory amount and (b) to enter the beginning inventory amount in the Income Summary account as an **expense** (a debit) and to remove the ending inventory amount from the Income Summary account (a credit) as a cost transfer to the asset account Merchandise Inventory.

In addition, the Purchases account is closed to Income Summary as follows:

Income summary	55,000	
Purchases		55,000

The reason for the two closing entries for merchandise inventories under the **periodic inventory system** can be understood if you recall that under this system the ending inventory of the prior year (say, 1984) automatically is the beginning inventory for the current year (say, 1985) and that the Inventory account balance is unchanged throughout the year (because all purchases of merchandise are debited to the Purchases account rather than to the Inventory account). Therefore, at the end of the current year, the beginning inventory amount ($40,000 for Campus Corner) is still in the Inventory account at December 31, 19F. Simply, it must be transferred out as an expense and be replaced with the December 31, 19F, ending inventory amount ($35,000 for Campus Corner). The credit (i.e., $35,000) in entry *(b)* above is made to Income Summary because the beginning inventory and purchases have been closed to the Income Summary. When the ending inventory amount is transferred out of the Income Summary, the end result is that the Income Summary has been decreased by the amount of cost of goods sold (beginning inventory plus purchases minus ending inventory equals cost of goods sold). After completion of these closing entries, the Merchandise Inventory, Purchases, and Income Summary accounts for Campus Corner would appear as follows:

PERIODIC INVENTORY SYSTEM

Merchandise Inventory

12/31/19E (beginning)	40,000	*(a)* To close	40,000
(b) 12/31/19F (ending)	35,000		

Purchases

12/31/19F (balance)	55,000	*(c)* To close	55,000

Income Summary

Operating expenses (not shown)		Revenues (not shown)	
(a) 12/31/19E (beginning inventory)	40,000	*(b)* 12/31/19F (ending inventory)	35,000
(c) (purchases)	55,000		

(Note that these three amounts net to $60,000, the amount of cost of goods sold.)

These closing entries, along with all the other closing entries, are illustrated in the demonstration case (Rote Appliance Store) at the end of this chapter.[10] This demonstration case should be studied carefully because it ties together all of the parts discussed in this chapter.

Closing entries when a perpetual inventory system is used

When a perpetual inventory system is used, the Merchandise Inventory account and Cost of Goods Sold account are affected by day-to-day transactions. Therefore, at the end of the accounting period, each of these accounts will reflect the correct up-to-date balance. Consequently, no adjusting or closing entries are needed for the Merchandise Inventory account; it reflects the ending inventory

---

[10] There are several mechanical variations in how the closing entries can be made; all of them give the same end results. For example, some persons prefer to record the two inventory entries as adjusting, rather than closing, entries. Also, some persons prefer to use a temporary Cost of Goods Sold account in the closing process under a periodic inventory system; in this approach the two inventory amounts and purchases are first transferred to the Cost of Goods Sold account, which is then closed to Income Summary.

amount that will be reported on the balance sheet. Because the Cost of Goods Sold account is an expense account, it will be closed. For example, Campus Corner would record the following closing entry under the perpetual inventory system:

December 31, 19F:

Income summary	60,000	
Cost of goods sold		60,000

Inventory shrinkage

Inventory shrinkage occurs as a result of theft, breakage, spoilage, and incorrect measurements. The measurement of inventory shrinkage is important for internal management purposes and, if large, is a major issue to investors and creditors. The dollar amount of shrinkage is reported on **internal** financial statements, but seldom, if ever, are such amounts significant enough to be reported **separately** on **external** financial statements. Accurate measurement of this loss is related directly to the inventory system used.

When a **periodic inventory** system is used, measurement of shrinkage loss often is difficult, and may be impossible. The inventory, as counted at the end of the period, does not, in itself, provide a basis for measurement of shrinkage. An implicit assumption underlying the periodic inventory model (i.e., Beginning inventory + Purchases − Ending inventory = Cost of goods sold) is that if an item is not in ending inventory, it must have been sold. Therefore, cost of goods sold includes inventory shrinkage.

Alternatively, a perpetual inventory system will provide data on shrinkage loss. The inventory record provides both cost of goods sold and the ending inventory. These data make it possible to measure shrinkage loss. To illustrate, assume the perpetual inventory records show cost of goods sold for the period, 12 units, $60,000 (Exhibit 6–2), and ending inventory of 7 units, $35,000. An inventory count at the end of the period showed 6 units on hand. In the absence of clerical error, an inventory shrinkage (probably due to theft) would be reported as 1 unit, and the loss amount would be $5,000 (assuming no insurance recovery). The entry to record the shrinkage, assuming a perpetual inventory system, would be:

Inventory shrinkage*	5,000	
Inventory		5,000
* Closed to Income Summary.		

DEMONSTRATION CASE

(Try to resolve the requirements before proceeding to the suggested solution that follows.)

Rote Appliance Store has been operating for a number of years. It is a relatively small but profitable retail outlet for major appliances, such as refrigerators and air conditioners. Approximately 40 percent of the sales are on short-term credit. This case has been selected and simplified to demonstrate information processing when there are significant selling activities (the service activities have been deleted). The case has been structured to illustrate the application of both perpetual and periodic inventory systems with the same data. The annual accounting period ends December 31, 19D. Two independent cases will be assumed:

Case A—Perpetual inventory system is assumed.

Case B—Periodic inventory system is assumed.

The trial balance derived from the ledger at December 31, 19D, was:

| | Unadjusted trial balance | | | |
| | Case A—Perpetual inventory system used | | Case B—Periodic inventory system used | |
Account titles	Debit	Credit	Debit	Credit
Cash	$ 34,100		$ 34,100	
Accounts receivable	5,000		5,000	
Allowance for doubtful accounts		$ 1,000		$ 1,000
*Merchandise inventory:				
January 1, 19D			20,000	
December 31, 19D	16,000			
Store equipment	30,000		30,000	
Accumulated depreciation, equipment		9,000		9,000
Accounts payable		8,000		8,000
Income tax payable				
Capital stock, par $10		40,000		40,000
Retained earnings, January 1, 19D		9,000		9,000
Sales revenue		102,000		102,000
Sales returns and allowances	2,000		2,000	
*Cost of goods sold	60,000			
*Purchases			57,000	
*Purchase returns and allowances				1,000
Expenses (not detailed)	21,900		21,900	
Depreciation expense				
Income tax expense				
	$169,000	$169,000	$170,000	$170,000

* These account balances are different between the two cases because of the effects of the two inventory systems used.

Data developed by Rote as a basis for the adjusting entries at December 31, 19D, were:

a. Credit sales in 19D amounted to $40,000; the average loss rate for bad debts is estimated to be 0.25 percent of credit sales.

b. The store equipment is depreciated on the basis of an estimated 10-year useful life with no residual value.

c. On December 31, 19D, the periodic inventory count of goods remaining on hand reflected $16,000.

d. The average income tax rate is 20 percent.

e. The beginning inventory, January 1, 19D, was as shown on the trial balance (Case B).

Required:

a. Based upon the above data, complete a worksheet at December 31, 19D, similar to that shown in Exhibit 5–3. If you prefer, you may omit the columns for Adjusted Trial Balance. **Prepare a separate worksheet for each separate case.**

b. Based upon the completed worksheets, present an income statement for each case. Use a single-step format for Case A and a multiple-step format for Case B.

c. Based upon the two worksheets, present, in parallel columns, the adjusting entries for each case at December 31, 19D.

d. Based upon the two worksheets, present, in parallel columns, the closing entries for each situation at December 31, 19D.

In preparing the worksheet when a **perpetual inventory** system is used, no new complications are presented. The inventory amount is extended across the worksheet as an asset because the balance in the Inventory account reflects the ending inventory when a perpetual inventory system is used. The expense—cost of goods sold—is extended to the Income Summary debit column along with the other expenses. See Exhibit 6–4.

In preparing the worksheet with a **periodic inventory system,** both the beginning and ending inventory amounts must be used. First, the beginning inventory amount must be extended horizontally as a debit to the Income Statement column (because it now is an expense). A special line, "Merchandise inventory, ending" is added to the bottom of the worksheet, and the ending inventory amount is entered on this line under Income Statement, credit. This amount also is listed on the same line under Balance Sheet, debit.[11]

---

[11] There are several mechanical ways of handling the inventories on the worksheet when a periodic inventory system is used. Some accountants view the inventory entries as closing rather than adjusting entries. The various approaches arrive at the same net result, and each has its particular mechanical advantages and disadvantages.

Suggested solution

Requirement a:

EXHIBIT 6–4   Worksheets compared for perpetual and periodic inventory systems

ROTE APPLIANCE STORE
Worksheet, December 31, 19D
Case A—Assuming Perpetual Inventory System Is Used

Account Titles	Trial Balance		Adjusting Entries*		Income Statement		Retained Earnings		Balance Sheet	
	Debit	Credit	Debit	Credit	Debit	Credit	Debit	Credit	Debit	Credit
Cash	34,100								34,100	
Accounts receivable	5,000								5,000	
Allowance for doubt-ful accounts		1,000		(a) 100						1,100
Merchandise inven-tory Dec. 31, 19D	16,000								16,000	
Store equipment	30,000								30,000	
Accumulated depre-ciation, equipment		9,000		(b) 3,000						12,000
Accounts payable		8,000								8,000
Income tax payable				(c) 3,000						3,000
Capital stock, par $10		40,000								40,000
Retained earnings, Jan. 1, 19D		9,000						9,000		
Sales revenue		102,000				102,000				
Sales returns and allowances	2,000				2,000					
Cost of goods sold	60,000				60,000					
Expenses (not de-tailed)	21,900		(a) 100 (b) 3,000		22,000					
Depreciation expense					3,000					
	169,000	169,000			87,000	102,000				
Income tax expense†			(c) 3,000		3,000					
Net income					12,000			12,000		
			6,100	6,100	102,000	102,000	–0–	21,000		
Retained earnings, Dec. 31, 19D							21,000			21,000
							21,000	21,000	85,100	85,100

* Note that a **simplifying mechanical change** is used—the "Adjusting Entries" total is not entered until **after** the income tax is computed and entered.
 † ($102,000 − $87,000) × 20% = $3,000 income tax expense.

Accounting for Sales Revenue and Cost of Goods Sold

Requirement a (concluded):

EXHIBIT 6–4 (concluded)

ROTE APPLIANCE STORE
Worksheet, December 31, 19D
Case B—Assuming Periodic Inventory System Is Used

Account titles	Trial Balance		Adjusting Entries*		Income Statement		Retained Earnings		Balance Sheet	
	Debit	Credit	Debit	Credit	Debit	Credit	Debit	Credit	Debit	Credit
Cash	34,100								34,100	
Accounts receivable	5,000								5,000	
Allowance for doubtful accounts		1,000		(a) 100						1,100
Merchandise inventory, Dec. 31, 19C	20,000				20,000					
Store equipment	30,000								30,000	
Accumulated depreciation, equipment		9,000		(b) 3,000						12,000
Accounts payable		8,000								8,000
Income tax payable				(c) 3,000						3,000
Capital stock, par $10		40,000								40,000
Retained earnings, Jan. 1, 19D		9,000						9,000		
Sales revenue		102,000				102,000				
Sales returns and allowances	2,000				2,000					
Purchases	57,000				57,000					
Purchase returns and allowances		1,000				1,000				
Expenses (not detailed)	21,900		(a) 100		22,000					
Depreciation expense			(b) 3,000		3,000					
Merchandise inventory, Dec. 31, 19D						16,000			16,000	
	170,000	170,000			104,000	119,000				
Income tax expense†			(c) 3,000		3,000					
Net income					12,000			12,000		
			6,100	6,100	119,000	119,000	–0–	21,000		
							21,000			21,000
							21,000	21,000	85,100	85,100

* Note that a **simplifying mechanical change** is used—the "Adjusting Entries" total is not entered until after the income tax is computed and entered.

† ($119,000 − $104,00) × 20% = $3,000 income tax expense.

Requirement b:

ROTE APPLIANCE STORE
Income Statement
For the Year Ended December 31, 19D
Case A—Perpetual Inventory System and Single-Step Format

Revenues:		
Sales	$102,000	
Less: Sales returns and allowances	2,000	
Net sales revenue		$100,000
Expenses:		
Cost of goods sold	60,000	
Expenses (not detailed for case purposes)	22,000	
Depreciation expense	3,000	85,000
Pretax income		15,000
Income tax expense ($15,000 × 20%)		3,000
Net income		$ 12,000
EPS ($12,000 ÷ 4,000 shares)		$3.00

ROTE APPLIANCE STORE
Income Statement
For the Year Ended December 31, 19D
Case B—Periodic Inventory System and Multiple-Step Format

Gross sales revenue		$102,000
Less: Sales returns and allowances		2,000
Net sales revenues		100,000
Cost of goods sold:		
Inventory, January 1, 19D	$ 20,000	
Purchases	57,000	
Purchase returns and allowances	(1,000)	
Goods available for sale	76,000	
Less: Inventory, December 31, 19D	16,000	
Cost of goods sold		60,000
Gross margin on sales		40,000
Operating expenses:		
Expenses (not detailed for case purposes)	22,000	
Depreciation expense	3,000	25,000
Pretax income		15,000
Income tax expense ($15,000 × 20%)		3,000
Net income		$ 12,000
EPS ($12,000 ÷ 4,000 shares)		$3.00

Requirement c:

Adjusting Entries
December 31, 19D

		Case A		Case B	
		Perpetual inventory		*Periodic inventory*	
a.	Expenses (estimated bad debt loss)	100		100	
	Allowance for doubtful accounts		100		100
	Bad debt loss estimated, $40,000 × 0.25% = $100.				
b.	Depreciation expense	3,000		3,000	
	Accumulated depreciation, equipment		3,000		3,000
	Depreciation for one year, $30,000 ÷ 10 years = $3,000.				
c.	Income tax expense	3,000		3,000	
	Income tax payable		3,000		3,000
	Income tax for year, $15,000 × 20% = $3,000				

Requirement d:

Closing Entries
December 31, 19D

		Case A		Case B	
		Perpetual inventory		*Periodic inventory*	
1.	Sales revenue	102,000		102,000	
	Sales returns and allowances		2,000		2,000
	Income summary		100,000		100,000
	To transfer the revenue amounts to Income Summary.				
2.	Income summary	(Not applicable)		56,000	
	Purchase returns and allowances			1,000	
	Purchases				57,000
	To transfer purchase amounts to Income Summary.				
3.	Income summary	(Not applicable)		20,000	
	Merchandise inventory (beginning)				20,000
	To transfer beginning inventory to Income Summary.				
4.	Merchandise inventory (ending)	(Not applicable)		16,000	
	Income summary				16,000
	To transfer ending inventory from Income Summary.				
5.	Income summary	60,000		(Not applicable)	
	Cost of goods sold		60,000		
6.	Income summary	28,000		28,000	
	Expenses (not detailed)		22,000		22,000
	Depreciation expense		3,000		3,000
	Income tax expense		3,000		3,000
	To transfer expense amounts to Income Summary.				
7.	Income summary	12,000		12,000	
	Retained earnings		12,000		12,000
	To transfer net income to Retained Earnings.				

SUMMARY OF CHAPTER

This chapter discussed the measuring, recording, and reporting of the effects on income of the selling and purchasing activities of various types of business.

An important expense, cost of goods sold, was discussed. In conformity with the matching principle, the total cost of the goods sold during the period must be matched with the sales revenue earned during the period. The Cost of Goods Sold account measures the **cost** of merchandise that was sold while the Sales Revenue account measures the **selling price** of the same merchandise. When cost of goods sold is deducted from sales revenue for the period, the difference is called gross margin on sales. From this amount, the remaining expenses must be deducted to derive income.

The chapter also discussed and illustrated the effect on cost of goods sold of the beginning and ending inventory amounts. We observed that the ending inventory of one period is the beginning inventory of the next period. Two inventory systems were discussed for measuring the merchandise remaining on hand at the end of the period (ending inventory) and cost of goods sold for the period: (1) the perpetual inventory system, which is based on the maintenance of detailed and continuous inventory records for each kind of merchandise stocked; and (2) the periodic inventory system, which is based upon a physical inventory count of ending inventory and the costing of those goods in order to determine the proper amounts for cost of goods sold and ending inventory.

SUPPLEMENT 6A—DATA PROCESSING; CONTROL ACCOUNTS AND SUBSIDIARY LEDGERS

This supplement explains the use of control accounts and subsidiary ledgers that facilitate recordkeeping in situations where a large number of similar transactions occur. Their use does not involve accounting theory, principles, or standards but instead involves only the mechanics of processing. The use of control accounts and subsidiary ledgers will be explained and illustrated for accounts receivable; however, the procedure also is applicable in any situation that involves numerous transactions that are similar and require detailed recordkeeping, such as accounts payable and operational assets.

In the preceding discussions and illustrations, charge sales and services were credited to a revenue account with the corresponding debit to an account designated **Accounts Receivable.** Subsequently, upon payment, the Accounts Receivable account was decreased (a credit). Some businesses carry thousands of individual customers on a credit status. If a separate Accounts Receivable account was maintained in the general ledger for each customer, there would be thousands of receivable accounts in the general ledger. Instead, in most large businesses, the Accounts Receivable account is an aggregation of all of the individual customer

GENERAL LEDGER

Date 19A	Cash #101	Folio	Debit	Credit	Balance
Jan. 12		3	1 000		

	Accounts Receivable Control #102				
Jan 5		1	2 400		2 400
7		2		140	2 260
12		3		1 000	1 260

	Sales #610				
Jan 5		1		2 400	2 400

	Sales Returns #620				
Jan 7		2	140		140

accounts. However, to attain adequate control, and for billing purposes, a business also must maintain detailed records concerning each customer's account.

Most large businesses maintain a **single control account** in the general ledger for Accounts Receivable and a **separate subsidiary ledger** that carries an individual account for each credit customer. Thus, in the above example, the **general ledger** would include Accounts Receivable as a **single control account** and the **subsidiary ledger** may include several thousand **individual receivable accounts.** At any given point, the **sum** of the individual account balances in the receivable subsidiary ledger should equal the single balance in the Accounts Receivable control account in the general ledger. The Accounts Receivable account in the general ledger is called a control account because it "controls" the subsidiary ledger. The individual customer accounts, as subdivisions of the control account,

SUBSIDIARY LEDGER

Adams, J. K. 102.1

Date		Description	Ref	Debit	Credit	Balance
Jan.	5		1	740		740
	7	Return	2		140	600
	12		3		400	200

Baker, B. B. 102.2

Date		Description	Ref	Debit	Credit	Balance
Jan.	5		1	120		120

Ford, C. E. 102.3

Date		Description	Ref	Debit	Credit	Balance
Jan.	5		1	340		340
	12		3		340	-0-

Moore, W.E. 102.4

Date		Description	Ref	Debit	Credit	Balance
Jan.	5		1	320		320
	12		3		220	100

Price, V. T. 102.5

Date		Description	Ref	Debit	Credit	Balance
Jan.	5		1	430		430
	12		3		40	390

Ward, B. L. 102.6

Date		Description	Ref	Debit	Credit	Balance
Jan.	5		1	450		450

are subsidiary to the control account; thus the designation, subsidiary ledger.

To illustrate the use of a control account with a subsidiary ledger for Accounts Receivable, we will assume several transactions for the Mayo Department Store. We will illustrate a manual system for instructional purposes, but control accounts and subsidiary ledgers also are used extensively with computerized systems. First, assume that on January 5, 19A, credit sales were made to six different customers. These sales could be recorded in the general journal as follows:

GENERAL JOURNAL   Page 1

Date	Account Titles and Explanation	Folio	Debit	Credit
Jan. 5	Accounts receivable	102	2,400	
	Sales revenue	610		2,400
	To record the following credit sales:			
	Adams, J. K. .... $ 740	102.1		
	Baker, B. B. 120	102.2		
	Ford, C. E. 340	102.3		
	Moore, W. E. 320	102.4		
	Price, V. T. 430	102.5		
	Ward, B. L. 450	102.6		
	Total $2,400			

Posting of the above journal entry to the control account in the general ledger is indicated by entering the Accounts Receivable and Sales Revenue **account numbers** in the folio column in the usual manner. Posting to the individual customer accounts in the subsidiary ledger is indicated by entering an individual customer's account number in the folio column of the journal. Thus, the total amount was posted to the control account, Accounts Receivable (a debit total of $2,400), and the several single amounts were posted to the subsidiary ledger as illustrated on page 267. Note that the debit-credit-balance form is used in our example of a subsidiary ledger rather than the T-account form that often is used for instructional purposes.

Now, assume that on January 7 one customer, J. K. Adams, returned some unsatisfactory merchandise purchased on January 5. Mayo accepted the goods and gave Adams credit on his account. The resultant journal entry was:

GENERAL JOURNAL   Page 2

Jan. 7	Sales returns	620	140	
	Accounts receivable	102		140
	To record the return of goods:			
	Adams, J. K. $140	102.1		

The folio column reveals that the above entry has been posted in total to the control account in the general ledger and that the single amount has been posted to the individual customer account in the subsidiary ledger.

Now, let's complete the example by assuming subsequent collections on accounts from some of the customers. The collections are recorded in the journal entry given below. The folio column indicates that the entry has been posted in total to the control account and each single amount to the individual customer accounts in the subsidiary ledger.

GENERAL JOURNAL   Page 3

Jan. 12	Cash	101	1,000	
	Accounts receivable	102		1,000
	To record collections on accounts as follows:			
	Adams, J. K. .... $ 400	102.1		
	Ford, C. E. 340	102.3		
	Moore, W. E. 220	102.4		
	Price, V. T. 40	102.5		
	Total $1,000			

The subsidiary ledger should be reconciled frequently with the control account in order to determine whether errors were made in posting. This reconciliation is accomplished by summing the balances in the subsidiary ledger to determine whether that total agrees with the total shown by the control account in the general ledger. This check can be done simply by running an adding machine tape from the subsidiary ledger or by preparing a schedule or listing of the individual customer account balances. A reconciliation schedule for Mayo follows:

MAYO DEPARTMENT STORE
Schedule of Accounts Receivable
January 28, 19A

Account		Amount
No.	Customer	(per subsidiary)
102.1	Adams, J. K.	$ 200
102.2	Baker, B. B.	120
102.4	Moore, W. E.	100
102.5	Price, V. T.	390
102.6	Ward, B. L.	450
102	Total accounts receivable (per control account)	$1,260

In this instance, the subsidiary ledger total agrees with the balance in the control account. If there is disagreement, one or more errors are indicated; however, the mere fact of agreement does not necessarily mean there are no errors. A transaction could be posted to the wrong customer's account, and the two ledgers would still reconcile in total.

In the above situation, the **Sales Revenue** account also could have been established as a control account supported by a subsidiary ledger that would contain separate accounts for the sales of **each department** or for **each product.** Another common application of control accounts relates to **accounts payable** when there are numerous purchases on credit.

Control accounts are also useful when accounting for **operational assets.** For example, the Office Equipment account usually is included in the general ledger as a control account. In such instances, the control account is supported by a subsidiary ledger of office equipment that includes an account for each different kind of office equipment, such as copiers, typewriters, calculators, and furniture. These examples illustrate that the control account/subsidiary ledger procedure is an important element of the accounting information processing system of most enterprises.

A particular advantage of the use of subsidiary ledgers in a manual system is that it facilitates the subdivision of work. A person can be trained in a short time to maintain a subsidiary ledger because a knowledge of the broad field of accounting is not required for such routine recordkeeping tasks.

In the journal entries given above, the individual amounts relating to each individual customer accounts were listed in the Explanation column of the journal and then were posted to the subsidiary ledger. There are two approaches to simplifying this particular phase of the recordkeeping. Obviously, amounts could be transferred directly from the charge tickets to the subsidiary ledger accounts and thus avoid the detailed listing in the journal entry. This approach is used sometimes by small companies. Another simplifying approach involves the use of a related procedure known as **special journals.** This procedure is explained and illustrated in Supplement 8B.

Although our illustration used a manual approach to illustrate subsidiary ledgers, most companies of any size apply the procedure by means of electronic computers. The computer can be programmed to process credit sales, returns, collections on account, reconciliation of account balances, and a printout of monthly bills to be mailed to the customers.

SUPPLEMENT 6B—AGING ACCOUNTS RECEIVABLE

Usually as an account receivable gets older there is an increase in the probability that the account will be uncollectible. Therefore, an analysis of the age of accounts receivable provides management with valuable information concerning probable cash inflows, losses due to uncollectible accounts, and the general effectiveness of the credit and collection activities of the entity. Aging analysis of accounts receivable also is used by some companies to provide information needed to make the **adjusting entry** at the end of each period for estimated bad debt expense.

An aging analysis of the individual accounts receivable balances is done to **estimate** the amount of bad debts instead of estimating bad debt expense on the basis of credit sales for the period, as illustrated on page 240. The amount estimated to be uncollectible under the aging method is the balance that should be in the account "Allowance for Doubtful Accounts" at the end of the period. The **difference** between the **actual balance** in that account and the **estimated balance** is the amount recorded as bad debt expense in the adjusting entry at the end of the period.

To illustrate, assume the general ledger for Macon Appliance Store, whose fiscal year ended December 31, 19B, reflected the following account balances:

```
Accounts receivable  ...............  $ 40,000 (debit balance)
Allowance for doubtful accounts .....       900 (credit balance)
Sales on credit for 19B .............    200,000
```

The adjusting entry for bad debt **expense** must be made at December 31, 19B. The company uses the **aging method** for determining the amount of the adjusting entry to record estimated bad debt expense. Consequently, the following aging analysis of accounts receivable was completed:

Aging Analysis of Accounts Receivable, December 31, 19B						
Customer	Total	Not Yet Due	1–30 Days Past Due	31–60 Days Past Due	61–90 Days Past Due	Over 90 Days Past Due
Adams, A. K.	$ 600	$ 600				
Baker, B. B.	1,300	300	$ 900	$ 100		
Cox, R. E.	1,400			400	$ 900	$ 100
Day, W. T.	3,000	2,000	600	400		
Zoe, A. B.	900					900
Total	$40,000	$17,200	$12,000	$8,000	$1,200	$1,600
Percent	100%	43%	30%	20%	3%	4%

The management, on the basis of experience and knowledge of specific situations, can use the above analysis as a basis for realistically estimating the probable **rates of uncollectibility for each age group.** Assume the management **estimated** the following probable bad debt loss rates: not yet due, 1 percent; 1–30 days past due, 3 percent; 31–60 days, 6 percent; 61–90 days, 10 percent; over 90 days, 25 percent. The following estimating schedule can be prepared:

Estimate of Probable Uncollectible Accounts, December 31, 19B			
Age	Amount of Receivable	Percent Estimated to Be Uncollectible	Balance Needed in Allowance for Doubtful Accounts
Not yet due	$17,200	1	$ 172
1–30 days past due	12,000	3	360
31–60 days past due	8,000	6	480
61–90 days past due	1,200	10	120
Over 90 days past due	1,600	25	400
Total	$40,000		$1,532

The resultant adjusting entry on December 31, 19B, would be:

```
Dec. 31  Bad debt expense ............................................. 632
             Allowance for doubtful accounts ..........................       632
         To adjust Allowance for Doubtful Accounts to the estimated bal-
         ance needed.

         Computations
             Balance needed (per schedule above) ...................... $1,532
             Balance before adjustment (page 271) .....................     900
             Difference—adjustment needed (increase) ..............  $  632
```

Some persons argue that the aging method approach to estimate the amount of bad debt expense does not apply the **matching principle** as effectively as the percent-of-credit-sales method discussed in the chapter. When the estimate is based on the amount of credit sales for the period from which uncollectible accounts ultimately will occur, bad debt expense is best matched with the current period's sales revenues.

In contrast, the aging method, because it is based on the ending balance in Accounts Receivable, tends to match bad debt expense with credit sales for a number of periods; hence, the matching principle may not be served well each period. However, the aging method produces a good measurement of the net realizable value of accounts receivable because it takes into account probable losses by actual age distribution of the amounts in each account.

In practice, the percent-of-credit-sales method appears to be used more widely.

IMPORTANT TERMS DEFINED IN THIS CHAPTER

Terms (alphabetically)	Key words in definitions of important terms used in chapter	Page reference
Aging accounts receivable	Method to estimate uncollectible accounts based on the age of each account receivable.	270
Bad debt allowance method	Method that bases bad debt expense on an estimate of uncollectible accounts.	239
Bad debt loss	Expense associated with estimated uncollectible accounts receivable.	239
Gross margin on sales	As a dollar amount, net sales minus cost of goods sold; as a ratio, gross margin divided by net sales revenue.	235
Gross method to record revenue	Sales revenue is recorded without deducting the authorized cash discount.	238
Inventory shrinkage	Missing inventory caused by theft, breakage, spoilage, and incorrect measurements.	257
Markup	The difference between net sales revenue and cost of goods sold.	235
Net method to record revenue	Sales revenue is recorded after deducting the amount of any authorized cash discount.	238
Periodic inventory system	Ending inventory and cost of goods sold are determined at the end of the accounting period.	244
Perpetual inventory system	A detailed inventory record is maintained continuously during the accounting period.	244
Physical inventory count	Actual count of units in inventory.	253

Terms (alphabetically)	Key words in definitions of important terms used in chapter	Page reference
Purchase discount	Cash discount received for prompt payment of an account payable.	252
Purchase returns and allowances	A deduction from the cost of purchases associated with unsatisfactory goods.	250
Sales discount	Cash discount offered to encourage prompt payment of an account receivable.	237
Sales returns and allowances	A contra revenue account which is associated with unsatisfactory goods.	242
Subsidiary ledgers	A group of sub-accounts that provides more detail than the general ledger control account.	266
Trade discount	A discount that is deducted from list price to derive the actual sales price.	239

QUESTIONS FOR DISCUSSION

PART A

1. In a company characterized by extensive selling and purchasing activities, the **quantity** of goods included in sales revenue also must be included in a particular **expense** amount. Explain the basis for this statement.

2. Explain the difference between gross sales and net sales.

3. What is gross margin on sales? How is the gross margin ratio computed (in your explanation, assume that net sales revenue was $100,000 and cost of goods sold was $60,000)?

4. Explain what is meant by sales discount. Use 1/10, n/30 in your explanation.

5. When merchandise, invoiced at $1,000, is sold on terms, 2/10, n/30, the vendor must make the following entry:

   Accounts receivable . . . .
       Sales revenue . . . .

   What amounts should be used in this entry under the net method of recording sales discounts? Why is the net method preferred over the gross method?

6. A sale is made for $500; terms are 2/10, n/30. At what amount should the sale be recorded under the net method of recording sales discounts? Give the required entry with an explanation. Also, give the collection entry assuming it is after the discount period.

7. Because the actual time of cash collection is not relevant in determining the date on which a sale should be given accounting recognition, what factor is relevant?

8. Why is an estimate, instead of the actual amount of bad debts, used as the measure of periodic bad debt expense?

9. What is a contra account? Give two examples.

10. Define the book value of accounts receivable.

11. Why should estimated bad debt losses be based on credit sales rather than on total sales for the period?

12. What is the distinction between sales allowances and sales discounts?

PART B

13. Define goods available for sale. How does it differ from cost of goods sold?

14. Define beginning inventory and ending inventory.

15. Briefly distinguish between the perpetual and periodic inventory systems. Basically, how does each measure (a) inventory and (b) cost of goods sold?

16. Describe the periodic inventory model. Explain the **source** of each variable in the model.

17. Why is it necessary to take an actual physical inventory count at the end of the period when the periodic inventory system is used?

18. Under the cost principle, at what amount should a purchase be recorded? Be specific.

19. What is the purpose of a perpetual inventory record for each item stocked?

20. What accounts are debited and credited for a purchase of goods for resale (a) when a perpetual inventory system is used and (b) when a periodic inventory system is used?

21. What accounts are debited and credited for a sale of goods on credit (a) when a perpetual inventory system is used and (b) when a periodic inventory system is used?

22. Why is there no purchases account when the perpetual inventory system is used?

23. Why is transportation-in considered to be a cost of purchasing merchandise?

EXERCISES

PART A

E6–1. Supply the missing dollar amounts for the 19B income statement of Better Retail Company for each of the following independent cases:

	Case A	Case B	Case C	Case D	Case E
Sales revenue	$800	$800	$800	$?	$?
Selling expenses	?	190	80	120	180
Cost of goods sold	?	480	?	500	610
Income tax expense	?	30	30	20	40
Gross margin	400	?	?	?	390
Pretax income	100	40	?	80	?
Administrative expenses	100	?	60	100	90
Net income	80	?	120	?	80

E6–2. The following data were taken from the records of Reliable Appliances, Incorporated, at December 31, 19D:

Sales revenue $150,000
Administrative expenses 15,000
Distribution (selling) expenses 20,000
Income tax rate 20%
Gross margin ratio 30%
Shares of stock outstanding 4,000

Required:

Prepare a complete income statement for Reliable. Show all computations. (Hint: Set up side captions starting with sales revenue and ending with earnings per share; rely on the percents given.)

E6–3. The following data were taken from the records of Fun Center, Incorporated, at December 31, 19B:

Gross margin (40% ratio)	$24,000
Selling (distribution) expenses	9,000
Administrative expenses	?
Pretax income	10,000
Income tax rate, 17%	
Shares of stock outstanding	2,000

Required:

Prepare a complete multiple-step income statement for Fun Center. Show all computations. (Hint: Set up the side captions starting with sales revenue and ending with earnings per share; rely on the percents given.)

E6–4. The following data were taken from the records of Leo Corporation on December 31, 19B:

Sales of merchandise for cash	$145,000
Sales of merchandise for credit	257,000
Sales returns and allowances	2,000
Selling expenses	100,000
Cost of goods sold	242,000
Administrative expenses	40,500

Items not included in above amounts:
  Estimated bad debt loss, 1% of net credit sales.
  Average income tax rate, 20 percent.
  Number of shares of common stock outstanding, 20,000.

Required:

a. Based on the above data, prepare a multiple-step income statement. There were no extraordinary items. Include a column for percentage analysis.
b. How much was the gross margin? What was the gross margin ratio? Explain what these two amounts mean.

E6–5. The following summarized data were provided by the records of Melody's Music Store, Incorporated, for the year ended December 31, 19B:

Sales of merchandise for cash	$124,000
Sales of merchandise on credit	80,000
Cost of goods sold	120,000
Distribution expenses	30,800
Administrative expenses	20,000
Sales returns and allowances	4,000

Items not included in above amounts:
  Estimated bad debt loss, 1½% of credit sales.
  Average income tax rate, 20 percent.
  Number of shares of common stock outstanding, 10,000.

Required:

a. Based upon the above data, prepare a multiple-step income statement. Include a Percentage Analysis column.
b. What was the amount of gross margin? What was the gross margin ratio? Explain.

E6–6. During the months of January and February, the WZH Corporation sold goods to three customers. The sequence of events was as follows:

Jan. 6 Sold goods for $800 to J. Doe and billed that amount subject to terms, 3/10, n/30.

6 Sold goods to R. Roe for $600 and billed that amount subject to terms, 2/10, n/30.

14 Collected cash due from J. Doe.

Feb. 2 Collected cash due from R. Roe.

28 Sold goods for $1,000 to B. Moe, and billed that amount subject to terms, 2/10, n/45.

Required:

a. Give the appropriate journal entry for each date. Assume a periodic inventory system is used and that the net method is used to record sales revenue.

b. Explain how each account balance as of February 28 should be reported, assuming that this is the end of the accounting period.

E6–7. The following transactions were selected from among those completed by Richard Retailers:

19B

Nov.25 Sold 20 items of merchandise to Customer A at an invoice price of $2,000 (total); terms 3/10, n/30.

28 Sold 10 items of merchandise to Customer B at an invoice price of $4,000 (total); terms, 3/10, n/30.

30 Customer B returned one of the items purchased on the 28th; the item was defective and credit was given to the customer.

Dec. 6 Customer B paid the account balance in full.

30 Customer A paid in full for the invoice of November 25, 19B.

Required:

a. Give the appropriate journal entry for each of the above transactions assuming Richard Retailers uses the periodic inventory system and records sales revenue under the net method.

b. Assume it is December 31, 19B, end of the accounting period. Show how the various account balances would be reported on the balance sheet and the income statement.

E6–8. MK Company started business on January 1, 19A. During the year, 19A, the company's records indicated the following:

Sales on cash basis	$200,000
Sales on credit basis	100,000
Collections on accounts receivable	70,000

The manager of MK Company is concerned about accounting for the bad debts. At December 31, 19A, although no accounts were considered bad, several customers were considerably overdue in paying their accounts. A friend of the manager suggested a 1 percent bad debt rate on sales, which the manager decided to use at the start.

Required:

a. Assume you have been employed, on a part-time basis, to assist with the recordkeeping for MK Company. The manager told you to set up bad debt expense of $3,000. Give the required entry.

b. Assume you were concerned about how the $3,000 was determined and the manager told you it was from another manager "who knew his business" and used 1 percent of sales. Do you agree with the $3,000? If you disagree, give the correct entry and explain the basis for your choice.

c. Show how the various accounts related to credit sales should be shown on the December 31, 19A, income statement and balance sheet.

E6–9. During 19G, West Ready-to-Wear Shop had sales revenue of $110,000, of which $40,000 was on credit. At the start of 19G, Accounts Receivable reflected a debit balance of $8,000 and the Allowance for Doubtful Accounts, a $500 credit balance. Collections on accounts receivable during 19G amounted to $33,000.

Data during 19G:

1. December 31, 19G, an account receivable (J. Doe) of $700 from a prior year was determined to be uncollectible; therefore, it was written off immediately as a bad debt.

2. December 31, 19G, on the basis of experience, a decision was made to continue the accounting policy of basing estimated bad debt losses on 2 percent of credit sales for the year.

Required:

a. Give the required journal entries for the two items on December 31, 19G (end of the accounting period).

b. Show how the amounts related to accounts receivable and bad debt expense would be reported on the income statement and balance sheet for 19G. Disregard income tax considerations.

c. On the basis of the data available does the 2 percent rate appear to be reasonable? Explain.

PART B

E6–10. Supply the missing dollar amounts for the 19B income statement of Joplin Retailers for each of the following independent cases:

Case	Sales Revenue	Beginning Inventory	Purchases	Total Available	Ending Inventory	Cost of Goods Sold	Gross Margin	Expenses	Pretax Income or (Loss)
A	900	100	700	?	200	?	?	200	?
B	900	180	750	?	?	?	?	100	0
C	900	140	?	?	300	650	?	100	?
D	900	?	600	?	210	?	?	150	50
E	900	?	650	?	100	?	100	?	(50)

E6–11. Supply the missing dollar amounts for the 19D income statement of Sweeney Company for each of the following independent cases:

	Case A	Case B	Case C
Sales revenue	6,000	6,000	6,000
Sales returns and allowances	150	?	?
Net sales revenue	?	?	?
Beginning inventory	9,000	9,500	8,000
Purchases	5,000	?	5,300
Freight-in	?	120	120
Purchase returns	40	30	?
Goods available for sale	?	14,790	13,370
Ending inventory	10,000	9,000	?
Cost of goods sold	?	?	5,400
Gross margin	?	110	?
Expenses	690	?	520
Pretax income	1,000	(500)	—0—

E6–12. The following list of transactions involving University Book Store were selected from the records of January 19B:

1. Sales: cash, $130,000; and on credit, $40,000 (terms, n/30).
2. Some of the merchandise sold on credit in 1 and subsequently returned for credit, $800.
3. Purchases: cash, $80,000; and on credit, $15,000 (terms, n/60).
4. Some of the merchandise purchased and subsequently returned for credit, $700.
5. Shipping costs paid in cash on the merchandise purchased, $400 (debit Freight-in).
6. Bad debt losses, on the basis of experience, are estimated to be 1 percent of credit sales net of sales returns and allowances.
7. An account receivable amounting to $150 was written off as uncollectible. The sale was made two years earlier.

Required:

a. Give the journal entry that would be made for each transaction, assuming the company uses a periodic inventory system.
b. Prepare an income statement for January 19B, through the caption "Gross margin on sales" and show the details of cost of goods sold. The December 31, 19A, inventory of merchandise was $75,000; and the physical inventory count of merchandise taken on January 31, 19B, amounted to $90,000.

E6–13. L & L Sport Shop sells merchandise on credit terms of 2/10, n/30. A sale invoiced at $800 was made to K. Williams on February 1, 19B. The full amount of the account was paid on time. L & L uses the net method of recording sales discounts.

Required:

a. Give the journal entry to record the credit sale.
b. Give the journal entry assuming the account was collected in full on February 9, 19B.
c. Give the entry assuming, instead, the account was collected in full on March 2, 19B.

On March 4, 19B, L & L purchased sporting goods from a supplier, on credit, invoiced at $6,000; the terms were 1/15, n/30. L & L uses the net method to record purchases.

Required:

d. Give the journal entry to record the purchase on credit. Assume periodic inventory system.

e. Give the journal entry assuming the account was paid in full on March 12, 19B.

f. Give the journal entry assuming, instead, the account was paid in full on March 28, 19B.

E6–14. Arnold Company uses a perpetual inventory system. Because it is a small business and sells only five different high-cost items, a perpetual inventory record is maintained for each item. The following selected data relate to Item A for the month of January:

1. Beginning inventory—quantity 5, cost $77 each.
2. Purchased—quantity 4, cost $72 each; paid $20 total freight.
3. Sold—quantity 6, sales price $150 each.
4. Returns—one sold in (3) was returned for full credit.

Required:

a. Give the journal entries for the above transactions assuming a perpetual inventory system and cash transactions.

b. Prepare the perpetual inventory record for Item A.

c. For January, give the following amounts for Item A:

    a. Sales revenue .... $ _____
    b. Cost of goods sold .... $ _____
    c. Gross margin on sales ..... $ _____
    d. Ending inventory .... $ _____

d. Is it possible to determine if there was any inventory shrinkage? Explain.

E6–15. Flower Company uses a perpetual inventory system that provides amounts for the period for (a) cost of goods sold and (b) ending inventory. Physical inventory counts are made from time to time to verify the perpetual inventory records. On December 31, 19B, the end of the accounting year, the perpetual inventory record for Item No. 18 showed the following (summarized):

	Units	Unit cost	Total cost
Beginning inventory	500	$2	$1,000
Purchases during the period	900	2	1,800
Sales during the period (sales price $3.50)	800		

Required:

a. Give the journal entry to record the purchase of 900 units for cash during the period.

b. Give the journal entry to record the sales for cash during the period.

c. Assume a physical inventory count was made after the above transactions and it reflected 590 units of Item No. 18 on hand. Give any journal entry required.

d. Give the following amounts for 19B related to Item No. 18:

    1. Ending inventory ...... units ____ $ ____
    2. Cost of goods sold ..... units ____ $ ____
    3. Shrinkage loss .... units ____ $ ____

e. As a manager, would you investigate in this situation? How?

E6–16. During 19B, Iota Corporation's records reflected the following for one product stocked:

1. Beginning inventory ..... 1,000 units, unit cost $2
2. Purchases .... 8,000 units, unit cost $2
3. Sales .... 7,000 units, unit sales price $3
4. Purchase returns .... 10 units, for $2 per unit refund from the supplier
5. Sales returns .... 5 units, for $3 per unit refund to the customer

Required:

a. All transactions were in cash; give the journal entries for the above transactions assuming:

> Case A—A perpetual inventory system.
>
> Case B—A periodic inventory system.

b. How would the amount of cost of goods sold be determined in each case?
c. Would you expect the cost of goods sold amount to be the same for Case A as for Case B? Why?

E6–17. The trial balance for Valley Store, Incorporated, at December 31, 19B (the end of the accounting year), is given below. Only selected accounts are given to shorten the case. The company uses a periodic inventory system. With the exception of the ending inventory, all of the accounts (before adjusting and closing entries) that you will need are listed in the trial balance.

Data developed as a basis for the adjusting entries at December 31, 19B, were:

a. Estimated bad debt expense for 19B was 1 percent of net credit sales of $12,000.
b. An inventory of store supplies on hand taken at December 31, 19B, reflected $50.
c. Depreciation on the store equipment is based on an estimated useful life of ten years and no residual value.
d. Wages earned through December 31, 19B, not yet paid or recorded amounted to $500.
e. The beginning inventory is shown in the trial balance. A physical inventory count of merchandise on hand and unsold, at December 31, 19B, reflected $2,000.
f. Assume an average income tax rate of 20 percent.

Required:

Prepare a worksheet similar to the one in the demonstration case. If desired, you may omit columns for Adjusted Trial Balance and Retained Earnings. Enter the trial balance, adjusting entries, ending inventory, and complete the worksheet.

Debits		*Credits*	
Cash	$ 7,600	Allowance for doubtful	
Accounts receivable	3,000	accounts	$ 150
Merchandise inventory,		Accumulated depreciation	900
January 1, 19B	4,000	Accounts payable	5,000
Store supplies inventory	250	Wages payable	
Store equipment	3,000	Income tax payable	
Sales returns	150	Capital stock, par $10	6,000
Purchases	6,000	Retained earnings	1,870
Bad debt expense		Sales revenue	13,000
Depreciation expense		Purchase returns	80
Freight-in (on purchases)	100		
Income tax expense			
Other operating expenses	2,900		
	$27,000		$27,000

E6–18. The trial balance for Home Appliances, Incorporated, at December 31, 19B (end of the accounting year), is given below. Only selected items have been used in order to shorten the case. The company uses a perpetual inventory system. All of the accounts you will need are listed in the trial balance.

Trial Balance
December 31, 19B

Account titles	Debit	Credit
Cash	$ 6,800	
Accounts receivable	12,000	
Allowance for doubtful accounts		$ 700
Merchandise inventory, ending	64,000	
Operational assets	40,000	
Accumulated depreciation		12,000
Accounts payable		8,000
Income tax payable		
Capital stock, par $10		60,000
Retained earnings, January 1, 19B		14,300
Sales revenue		105,000
Sales returns and allowances	1,200	
Cost of goods sold	56,000	
Expenses (not detailed)	20,000	
Bad debt expense		
Depreciation expense		
Income tax expense		
	$200,000	$200,000

Additional data developed for the adjusting entries:

a. Estimated bad debt expense is 2 percent of net credit sales. Net credit sales for 19B amounted to $35,000.
b. The operational assets are being depreciated $4,000 each year.
c. The average income tax rate is 20 percent.

Required:

Prepare a worksheet similar to the one in the demonstration case. If desired, you may omit columns for Adjusted Trial Balance and Retained Earnings. Enter the trial balance, adjusting entries, and complete the worksheet.

PROBLEMS/CASES

PART A

PC6–1. The following data were taken from the year-end records of Tip Top Company. You are to fill in all of the missing amounts. Show computations.

Income statement items		Case A		Case B
Gross sales revenue		$110,000		$212,000
Sales returns and allowances		?		12,000
Net sales revenue		?		?
Cost of goods sold	(62%)	?		?
Gross margin on sales		?	(40%)	?
Operating expenses		18,000		?
Pretax income		?		35,000
Income tax expense (20%)		?		?
Income before extraordinary items		?		?
Extraordinary items	(gain)	5,000	(loss)	10,000
Less: Income tax (20%)		?		?
Net income		?		?
EPS (5,000 shares)		4.00		?

PC6–2. Adaire Equipment Company, Inc., sells heavy construction equipment. There are 10,000 shares of capital stock outstanding. The annual fiscal period ends on December 31. The

following condensed trial balance was taken from the general ledger on December 31, 19D:

Account titles	Debit	Credit
Cash	$ 11,000	
Accounts receivable	20,000	
Allowance for doubtful accounts		$ 1,000
Inventory (ending)	90,000	
Operational assets	40,000	
Accumulated depreciation		8,000
Liabilities		17,000
Capital stock		100,000
Retained earnings, January 1, 19D		20,000
Sales revenue		208,000
Sales returns and allowances	8,000	
Cost of goods sold	110,000	
Selling expenses	37,000	
Administrative expenses	20,000	
Interest expense	3,000	
Extraordinary loss, unusual and infrequent storm damage	5,000	
Income tax expense*	10,000	
	$354,000	$354,000

* Assume a 40 percent average tax rate on both operations and the extraordinary loss.

Required:

a. Prepare a multiple-step income statement similar to the format in Exhibit 2–1. (Hint: Reflect the income tax effect of the extraordinary loss as is done with the extraordinary item in Exhibit 2–1.)

b. Prepare the following ratio analyses:
   1. Gross margin on sales ratio.
   2. Profit margin ratio (see Chapter 2).
   3. Return on investment; use owners' equity (see Chapter 2).

c. To compute *(b)* 2 and *(b)* 3, what amount did you use as the numerator? Explain why.

d. Briefly explain the meaning of each of the three ratios computed in *(b)*.

PC6–3. Gnu Corporation is a local grocery store organized seven years ago as a corporation. At that time, a total of 10,000 shares of common stock was issued to the three organizers. The store is in an excellent location, and sales have increased each year. At the end of 19G, the bookkeeper prepared the following statement (assume all amounts are correct; also note the inappropriate terminology and format):

GNU CORPORATION
Profit and Loss
December 31, 19G

	Debit	Credit
Sales		$305,000
Cost of goods sold	$169,500	
Sales returns and allowances	5,000	
Selling expenses	60,000	
Administrative and general expenses	30,000	
Interest expense	500	
Extraordinary loss	4,000	
Income tax expense (on operations, $12,000 less $1,200 saved on the extraordinary loss)	10,800	
Net profit	25,200	
	$305,000	$305,000

Required:

a. Prepare a multiple-step income statement similar to Exhibit 2–1. Assume an average 30 percent income tax rate.

b. Prepare the following ratio analyses:
   1. Profit margin on sales ratio (see Chapter 2).
   2. Gross margin on sales ratio.
   3. Return on investment; use owners' equity of $150,000 (see Chapter 2).

c. In computing ratios *(b)* 1 and *(b)* 3, what amount did you use for income? Explain why.

d. Generally, it is conceded that of the three ratios in *(b)*, return on investment has the highest information content for the typical investor. Why?

PC6–4. The data below were selected from the records of Baldwin Company for the year ended December 31, 19C.

Balances January 1, 19C:
Accounts receivable (various customers) $80,000
Allowance for doubtful accounts 6,000

Transactions during 19C:

1. Sold merchandise for cash, $200,000. Sold merchandise and made collections, on credit terms, 2/10, n/30, in the order given below (assume a unit sales price of $1,000 in all transactions and use the net method to record sales revenue):
2. Sold merchandise to T. Smith; invoice price, $18,000.
3. Sold merchandise to K. Jones; invoice price, $30,000.
4. T. Smith returned one of the units purchased in 2 above, two days after purchase date and received account credit.
5. Sold merchandise to B. Sears; invoice price, $20,000.
6. T. Smith paid his account in full within the discount period.
7. Collected $72,000 cash from customer sales on credit in prior year, all within the discount periods.
8. K. Jones paid the invoice in 3 above within the discount period.
9. Sold merchandise to R. Roy; invoice price, $10,000.
10. Three days after paying the account in full, K. Jones returned one defective unit and received a cash refund.
11. Collected $5,000 cash on an account receivable on sales in a prior year, after the discount period.
12. Baldwin wrote off a 19A account of $2,500 after deciding that the amount would never be collected.
13. The estimated bad debt rate used by Baldwin is 1 percent of *net* credit sales.

Required:

a. Give the journal entries for the above transactions, including the write-off of the uncollectible account and the adjusting entry for estimated bad debts. Assume a periodic inventory system. Show computations for each entry. (Hint: Set up T-accounts on scratch paper for Cash, Accounts Receivable by customer, Allowance for Doubtful Accounts, Sales Revenue, Sales Returns, Sales Discount Revenue, and Bad Debt Expense (this will provide the data needed for the next requirement).

b. Show how the accounts related to the above sale and collection activities should be reported on the 19C income statement and balance sheet.

PC6–5. The following transactions were selected from the records of Emerson Company:

July 15   Sold merchandise to Customer A at an invoice price of $4,000; terms 2/10, n/30.
      20   Sold merchandise to Customer B at an invoice price of $3,000; terms 2/10, n/30.
      21   Purchased inventory from Alpha Supply Company at an invoice price of $500; terms 3/10, n/45.
      22   Purchased inventory from Beta Supply Company at an invoice price of $1,000; terms 1/10, n/30.
      23   Received payment from Customer A, within the discount period.
      25   Paid invoice from Alpha Supply Company, within the discount period.
Aug. 25   Received payment from Customer B, after the discount period.
      26   Paid invoice from Beta Supply Company, after the discount period.

Required:

a.   Give the appropriate journal entry for each of the above transactions. Assume that Emerson uses the periodic inventory system and records sales and purchases using the net method.

b.   Give the appropriate journal entry for each of the above transactions. Assume that Emerson uses the periodic inventory system and records sales and purchases using the gross method.

PC6–6.   (Based on Supplement 6B)   Ready Equipment Company uses the aging approach to estimate bad debt expense at the end of each accounting year. Credit sales occur frequently on terms, n/60. The balance of each account receivable is aged on the basis of three time periods as follows: *(a)* not yet due; *(b)* up to one year past due; and *(c)* more than one year past due. Experience has shown that for each age group the average loss rate on the amount of the receivable at year-end due to uncollectibility is *(a)* 1 percent, *(b)* 5 percent, and *(c)* 30 percent.

At December 31, 19F (end of the current accounting year), the Accounts Receivable balance was $50,500, and the Allowance for Doubtful Accounts balance was $2,000. To simplify, only five customer accounts are used; the details of each on December 31, 19F, follow:

A. Able—Account Receivable

Date	Explanation	Debit	Credit	Balance
3/11/19E	Sale	15,000		15,000
6/30/19E	Collection		5,000	10,000
1/31/19F	Collection		3,000	7,000

C. Carson—Account Receivable

2/28/19F	Sale	21,000		21,000
4/15/19F	Collection		10,000	11,000
11/30/19F	Collection		3,000	8,000

M. May—Account Receivable

11/30/19F	Sale	18,000		18,000
12/15/19F	Collection		8,000	10,000

T. Tyler—Account Receivable

3/2/19D	Sale	5,000		5,000
4/15/19D	Collection		5,000	–0–
9/1/19E	Sale	12,000		12,000
10/15/19E	Collection		10,000	2,000
2/1/19F	Sale	19,000		21,000
3/1/19F	Collection		1,000	20,000
12/31/19F	Sale	1,500		21,500

Z. Ziltch—Account Receivable

12/30/19F	Sale	4,000		4,000

Required:

a. Set up an aging analysis schedule and complete it; follow the illustration given in Supplement 6B.
b. Compute the estimated uncollectible amount for each age category and in total.
c. Give the adjusting entry for bad debt expense at December 31, 19F.
d. Show how the amounts related to accounts receivable should be presented on the 19F income statement and balance sheet.

PART B

PC6–7.   This problem is designed to demonstrate the accounting for cash discounts by both the vendor and purchaser. Observe the consistency between both parties to the same transactions—one party's sales discount is another party's purchase discount.

Assume the following summarized transactions between Company A, the vendor, and Company B, the purchaser. Use the letters to the left as the date notations. Assume each company uses a periodic inventory system and each uses the net method to record sales revenue and purchases.

1. Company A sold Company B merchandise for $10,000; terms, 2/10, n/30.
2. Prior to payment, Company B returned $1,000 (one tenth) of the merchandise for credit because it did not meet B's specifications.

Required:

Give the following journal entries in parallel columns for each party:

a. The sale/purchase transaction.
b. The return transaction.
c. Payment in full assuming it was made within the discount period.
d. Payment in full assuming, instead, it was made after the discount period.

Use a form similar to the following:

		Co. A—Vendor		Co. B—Purchaser	
Date	*Accounts*	*Debit*	*Credit*	*Debit*	*Credit*

PC6–8.   College Shop, Incorporated, is a student co-op. It has been operating successfully for a number of years. The board of directors is composed of faculty and students. On January

1, 19X, when this case starts, the beginning inventory was $200,000; the Accounts Receivable balance was $3,000; and the Allowance for Doubtful Accounts had a credit balance of $400. A periodic inventory system is used and purchases are recorded using the net method.

The following transactions (summarized) have been selected from 19X for case purposes:

1.	Merchandise sales for cash	$340,000
2.	Merchandise returned by customers as unsatisfactory, for cash refund	1,400
	Merchandise purchased from vendors on credit; terms, 2/10, n/30:	
3.	May Supply Company invoice price, before deduction of cash discount	4,000
4.	Other vendors, invoice price, before deduction of cash discount	115,000
5.	Purchased equipment for use in the store; paid cash	1,800
6.	Purchased office supplies for future use in the store; paid cash	600
7.	Freight on merchandise purchased; paid cash (set up a separate account for this item)	500
	Accounts payable paid in full during the period as follows:	
8.	May Supply Company, paid after the discount period	4,000
9.	Other vendors, paid within the discount period	98,000

Required:

a. Prepare journal entries for each of the above transactions.
b. Give the closing entry required at December 31, 19X, for:
   1. Beginning inventory.
   2. Ending inventory (assume $130,000).
c. Prepare a partial income statement through gross margin on sales.
d. Explain why it was preferable to record purchases using the net method.

PC6–9. The transactions listed below were selected from those occurring during the month of January 19D for Ranch Department Store, Incorporated. A wide line of goods is offered for sale. Credit sales are extended to a few select customers; however, the usual credit terms are n/EOM.

1.	Sales to customers:	
	Cash	$350,000
	On credit	20,000
2.	Unsatisfactory merchandise returned by customers:	
	Cash	4,000
	Credit	1,000
	Merchandise purchased from vendors on credit; terms, 1/20, n/30:	
3.	AB Supply Company, amount billed, before deduction of cash discount	1,000
4.	From other vendors, amount billed, before deduction of cash discount	120,000
5.	Freight paid on merchandise purchased; paid cash (set up a separate account for this item)	2,000
6.	Collections on accounts receivable	17,000
	The accounts payable were paid in full during the period as follows:	
7.	AB Supply Company, paid after the discount period	1,000
8.	Other vendors, paid within the discount period	118,800
9.	Purchased two new typewriters for the office; paid cash	900
10.	An account receivable from a customer from a prior year amounting to $300 was determined to be uncollectible and was written off.	
11.	At the end of January the adjusting entry for estimated bad debts is to be made. The loss rate, based on experience, is 1% of net credit sales for the period (i.e., on credit sales less credit returns).	

Relevant account balances on January 1, 19D, were Accounts Receivable, $3,200 (debit); and Allowance for Doubtful Accounts, $900 (credit). Total assets at the end of the period, $250,000.

Required:

a. Prepare journal entries for the above transactions assuming a periodic inventory system is in use and record purchases using the net method.

b. Show how the following amounts should be reported on the January 19D income statement and balance sheet. Show computations.

(1) Bad debt expense.

(2) Balance in accounts receivable.

(3) Balance in allowance for doubtful accounts.

c. Explain why bad debt expense should not be debited for the $300 uncollectible account written off in January.

PC6–10. Quick Distributing Company uses a perpetual inventory system for the items it sells. The following selected data relate to Item 10, a small but high-cost item stocked during the month of January 19B.

1. Beginning inventory—quantity, 70; cost, $50 each.
2. Purchases—quantity, 90; cost, $48 each plus $180 for transportation on the purchases.
3. Sales—quantity, 120; sale price, $95 each.
4. Returns—Quick accepted a return of two of the items sold in 3 because they were not needed by the customer and they had not been used.
5. At the end of January 19B a physical inventory count showed 37 items remaining on hand.

Required (assume all transactions were cash):

a. Prepare the perpetual inventory record for Item 10.

b. Give journal entries for each of the above transactions.

c. Prepare the income statement for January 19B through gross margin on sales as it related to Item 10. What was the gross margin ratio?

d. As the responsible manager, would you investigate the inventory shrinkage? How?

e. Assume that you observe quite often that the required items are out of stock. How can a perpetual inventory system be helpful in avoiding this problem?

PC6–11. Ditmore Company uses a perpetual inventory system. During the month of January 19D, the perpetual inventory record for Item A, which is one of the 23 items stocked, is shown below (summarized):

PERPETUAL INVENTORY RECORD

Date	Explanation	Goods Purchased		Goods Sold		Balance	
		Units	Total Cost	Units	Total Cost	Units	Total Cost
1	Beginning inventory					40	3,200
2	Purchase (at $80 each)	20					
3	Sale (sales price $150 each)			31			
4	Purchase return (one unit)						
5	Purchase (at $80 each)	30					
6	Sale return (one unit)						
7	Sale (sales price $150 each)			29			
8	Inventory shortage (two units)						

Required:

a. Complete the perpetual inventory record.
b. Give the journal entry for each transaction reflected in the perpetual inventory record (assume transactions are cash).
c. Complete the following tabulation:

> Income statement:
> Sales ....$_____
> Cost of goods sold .... _____
> Gross margin on sales .... _____
> Gross margin ratio .... _____
>
> Balance sheet:
> Inventory .... _____

d. Explain how the inventory shortage should be reported.
e. As the responsible manager, would you investigate this situation? How?
f. Assume "stockout" has been a problem. What would you recommend?

PC6–12. The following transactions, relating to one product sold by Robertson Company, were completed in the order given during January:

a. Purchased—quantity, 120; cost, $20 each.
b. Sold—quantity, 100; $30 each.
c. Purchase return—returned one of the units purchased in *(a)* because it was the wrong size.
d. Sales return—accepted two units from a customer that were sold in *(b)*. The customer did not need them, and they were not damaged.
e. Inventories:
   Beginning inventory, January 1—30 units at total cost of $600.
   Ending inventory, January 31—per periodic inventory count, 51 units @ $20 = $1,020.
f. Cost of goods sold for January—98 units @ $20 = $1,960.

Required:

Give the journal entries that would be made for the above transactions assuming: Case A—a perpetual inventory system is used, and Case B—a periodic inventory system is used. To do this, set up the following form (assume cash transactions):

| | | Perpetual | | Periodic | |
		Debit	Credit	Debit	Credit
Date	Explanation				
a.	To record the purchase				
b.	To record the sale				
c.	To record the purchase return				
d.	To record the sales return				
e.	To record the closing entries for inventories				
f.	To record the closing entry for cost of goods sold				
g.	To close purchases and purchase returns				

PC6–13. Roberta Retailers Inc., is completing the accounting information processing cycle for the year ended December 31, 19D. The worksheet given below has been completed through

the adjusting entries. (An optional column "Adjusted Trial Balance," may be helpful in completing the requirements.)

Required:

a. Complete the following worksheet (periodic inventory system is used). Assume an average income tax rate of 20 percent.

b. Give the closing journal entries at December 31, 19D. Close all revenue and expense accounts to Income Summary.

ROBERTA RETAILERS, INC.
Worksheet—December 31, 19D

Account Titles	Trial Balance		Adjusting Entries		Income Statement		Retained Earnings		Balance Sheet	
	Debit	Credit	Debit	Credit	Debit	Credit	Debit	Credit	Debit	Credit
Cash	25,700									
Accounts receivable	12,000									
Allowance for doubtful accounts		300		*(a)* 400						
Merchandise inventory Jan. 1, 19D	30,000									
Equipment	22,500									
Accumulated depreciation, equipment		7,500		*(b)* 1,500						
Other assets	20,000									
Accounts payable		8,000								
Interest payable				*(c)* 300						
Note payable, long term, 12%		10,000								
Capital stock, par $10		50,000								
Contributed capital in excess of par		7,500								
Retained earnings, Jan. 1, 19D		13,000								
Dividends declared and paid (19D)	6,000									
Sales revenue		95,000								
Sales returns and allowances	1,000									
Purchases	52,000									
Freight-in	2,000									
Purchase returns and allowances		1,100								
Operating expenses (not detailed)	20,300									
Bad debt expense			*(a)* 400							
Depreciation expense			*(b)* 1,500							
Interest expense	900		*(c)* 300							
Merchandise inventory, Dec. 31, 19D ($32,000)										
	192,400	192,400								
Income tax expense										
Income tax payable										
Net income										
Retained earnings, Dec. 31, 19D										

PC6–14. A recent annual report for Sears Roebuck & Company contained the following information at the end of their fiscal year:

	Year 1	Year 2
Accounts receivable	$7,022,075,000	$7,336,308,000
Allowance for doubtful accounts	(86,605,000)	(96,989,000)
	$6,935,470,000	$7,239,319,000

A footnote to the financial statements disclosed that uncollectible accounts amounting to $55,000,000 were written off as bad during Year 1 and $69,000,000 during Year 2. Assume that the tax rate for Sears was 40 percent.

Required:

a. Determine the bad debt expense for Year 2 based on the facts given above.
b. Working capital is defined as current assets minus current liabilities. How was Sears' working capital affected by the write-off of $69,000,000 in uncollectible accounts during Year 2? What impact did the recording of bad debt expense have on working capital in Year 2?
c. How was net income affected by the $69,000,000 write-off during Year 2? What impact did the recording of bad debt expense have on net income for Year 2?

PC6–15. (Note: This is an extended problem designed to review Chapters 3, 4, 5, and 6.) Quality Furniture Store, Inc., has been in operation for a number of years and has been quite profitable. The losses on uncollectible accounts and on merchandise returns are about the same as for other furniture stores. The company uses a perpetual inventory system. The annual fiscal period ended December 31, 19B, and the end-of-period accounting information processing cycle has been started. The following trial balance was derived from the general ledger at December 31, 19B.

Account titles	Debit	Credit
Cash	$ 28,880	
Accounts receivable	36,000	
Allowance for doubtful accounts		$ 4,600
Merchandise inventory (ending)	110,000	
Store equipment	20,000	
Accumulated depreciation		8,000
Accounts payable		10,000
Income tax payable		
Interest payable		
Notes payable, long term (12%)		50,000
Capital stock, par $10		70,000
Retained earnings, January 1, 19B		11,400
Sales revenue		441,000
Sales returns and allowances	25,000	
Cost of goods sold	223,350	
Selling expenses	102,700	
Administrative expenses	49,070	
Bad debt expense		
Depreciation expense		
Interest expense		
	$595,000	$595,000
Income tax expense		
Net income		

Data for adjusting entries:

a. The bad debt losses due to uncollectible accounts are estimated to be $6,000.
b. The store equipment is being depreciated over an estimated useful life of 10 years with no residual value.
c. The long-term note of $50,000 was for a two-year loan from a local bank. The interest rate is 12 percent, payable at the end of each 12-month period. The note was dated April 1, 19B. (Hint: Accrue interest for nine months.)
d. Assume an average 20 percent corporate income tax rate.

Required:

a. Based upon the above data, complete a worksheet similar to the one illustrated in the chapter for the demonstration case. If you prefer, you may omit columns for Adjusted Trial Balance and Retained Earnings. (Hint: Net income is $22,704.)
b. Based upon the completed worksheet, prepare a multiple-step income statement and classified balance sheet.
c. Based upon the completed worksheet, prepare the adjusting and closing journal entries for December 31, 19B. Close all revenue and expense accounts to Income Summary.

PC6–16. (Note: This is an extended problem designed to review the materials discussed in Chapters 3, 4, 5, and 6.) Northwest Appliances, Incorporated, is owned by six local investors. It has been operating for four years and is at the end of the 19D fiscal year. For case purposes, certain accounts have been selected to demonstrate the information processing activities at the end of the year for a corporation that sells merchandise rather than services. The following trial balance, assumed to be correct, was taken from the ledger on December 31, 19D. The company uses a periodic inventory system.

Debits		*Credits*	
Cash	$ 18,000	Allowance for doubtful	
Accounts receivable	28,000	accounts	$ 600
Merchandise inventory,		Accumulated depreciation	12,000
January 1, 19D	80,000	Accounts payable	15,000
Prepaid insurance	300	Notes payable,	
Store equipment	40,000	long term (12%)	30,000
Sales returns and		Capital stock, par $10	40,000
allowances	3,000	Retained earnings,	
Purchases	250,000	January 1, 19D	2,000
Freight-in	11,000	Sales revenue	400,000
Operating expenses	76,300	Purchase returns	7,000
	$506,600		$506,600

Additional data for adjusting entries:

a. Credit sales during the year were $100,000; based on experience a 1 percent loss rate on credit sales has been established.
b. Insurance amounting to $100 expired during the year.
c. The store equipment is being depreciated over a 10-year estimated useful life with no residual value.
d. The long-term note payable for $30,000 was dated May 1, 19D, and carries a 12 percent interest rate per annum. The note is for three years and interest is payable on April 30 each year.
e. Assume an average income tax rate of 30 percent.
f. Inventories:
   Beginning inventory, January 1, 19D (per above trial balance), $80,000.
   Ending inventory, December 31, 19D (per physical inventory count), $75,000.

Required:

a. Prepare a worksheet at December 31, 19D, similar to the one shown in the demonstration problem in the chapter. If you prefer, you may omit columns for Adjusted Trial Balance and Retained Earnings. To save time and space, all operating expenses have been summarized. However, you should set up additional expense accounts for depreciation, bad debts, interest, and income tax. Also, you will need additional liability accounts for interest payable and income tax payable. (Hint: Net income is $37,940.)

b. Based upon the completed worksheet, prepare a multiple-step income statement and classified balance sheet.

c. Based upon the completed worksheet, prepare the adjusting and closing journal entries at December 31, 19D. Close all revenue and expense accounts to Income Summary.

PC6–17. (Related to Supplement 6A) City Department Store, Incorporated, is a large department store located in a midwestern city with a population of approximately 200,000 persons. The store carries top brands and attempts to appeal to "quality customers." Approximately 80 percent of the sales are on credit. As a consequence, there is a significant amount of detailed recordkeeping related to credit sales, returns, collections, and billings. The accounts receivable records are maintained manually; however, the store is considering computerizing this phase of the accounting information system. Included in the general ledger is a control account for Accounts Receivable. Supporting the control account is an accounts receivable subsidiary ledger which has individual accounts for more than 20,000 customers. For case purposes, a few accounts and transactions with simplified amounts have been selected. The case requirement is intended to indicate the nature of the data processing work that City Store plans to computerize; however, here it will be completed manually.

On January 1, 19F, the Accounts Receivable control account (No. 52), in the general ledger, reflected a debit balance of $4,000 and the subsidiary ledger reflected the following balances:

52.1	Akins, A. K.	$400
52.2	Blue, V. R.	700
52.3	Daley, U. T.	900
52.4	Evans, T. V.	300
52.5	May, O. W.	800
52.6	Nash, G. A.	100
52.7	Roth, I. W.	600
52.8	Winn, W. W.	200

During the month of January, the following transactions and events relating to sales activities occurred (use the notation at the left for date):

a. Sales of merchandise on credit.

Akins, A. K.	$300
Blue, V. R.	250
Winn, W. W.	730
May, O. W.	140
Daley, U. T.	70
Roth, I. W.	370
Evans, T. V.	410

b. Unsatisfactory merchandise returned by customers:

Roth, I. W.	$ 30
Winn, W. W.	70
Akins, A. K.	20

c. Collections on accounts receivable:

Winn, W. W.	$800
May, O. W.	940
Akins, A. K.	200
Roth, I. W.	700
Blue, V. R.	750
Daley, U. T.	600

d. The account for G. A. Nash has been inactive for several years. After an investigation, the management decided that it was uncollectible; therefore, it is to be written off immediately.

e. The estimated loss rate is 2 percent of net credit sales (i.e., on credit sales less returns for credit).

Required:

a. Set up the general ledger control account for Accounts Receivable. Also, set up the general ledger account for Allowance for Doubtful Accounts (No. 53) with a credit balance of $600. Indicate the beginning balance as "Bal." and for convenience use T-accounts for these two accounts.

b. Set up an accounts receivable subsidiary ledger; use three columns—Debit, Credit, and Balance. Enter the beginning balances with the notation "Bal."

c. Prepare journal entries for each of the above transactions.

d. Post the entries prepared in (c) to the Accounts Receivable control account, Allowance for Doubtful Accounts, and the subsidiary ledger. Use folio numbers.

e. Prepare a schedule of accounts receivable to show how much each customer owed at the end of January.

f. Show how accounts receivable and the related allowance amounts would be reported in the January balance sheet.

C·H·A·P·T·E·R 7

Costing Methods for Measuring Inventory and Cost of Goods Sold

PURPOSE OF THIS CHAPTER

In the previous chapters, we assumed that the unit cost of items that were purchased for inventory remained stable. In reality, however, the unit cost of inventory items often will change each time a new purchase order is placed. When unit cost changes in this manner, the accountant must answer two difficult questions at the end of the accounting period: (1) What quantity (units) of goods and what cost (dollars) should be assigned to **ending inventory?** (2) What quantity of goods and what cost should be assigned to **cost of goods sold?**

This chapter discusses the generally accepted accounting answers to these two questions and their implementation in an information processing system. The discussions and illustrations will be presented in two parts as follows:

Part A—Measuring ending inventory and cost of goods sold with a periodic inventory system

Part B—Application of a perpetual inventory system and selected inventory costing problems

PART A—MEASURING ENDING INVENTORY AND COST OF GOODS SOLD WITH A PERIODIC INVENTORY SYSTEM

INVENTORY EFFECTS ON THE MEASUREMENT OF INCOME

A close relationship exists between ending inventory and cost of goods sold. When the periodic inventory system (Chapter 6) is used, inventory items not in the ending inventory are assumed to have been sold. Thus, the measurement of ending inventory affects both the balance sheet (assets) and the income statement (cost of goods sold and net income). The amount of inventory, measured at the end of the accounting period, affects not only the accounting income for that period but also the amount of income for the **following accounting period.** This two-period effect is due to the fact that the ending inventory for one period is the beginning inventory for the next accounting period. To illustrate these effects, assume that the 19A and 19B income statements for Company X reflected pretax incomes of $5,000 and $6,500, respectively, measured as follows:

	19A		19B	
Sales revenue		$100,000		$110,000
Cost of goods sold:*				
Beginning inventory	$ –0–		$10,000	
Purchases	70,000		58,000	
Goods available for sale	70,000		68,000	
Ending inventory	10,000		–0–	
Cost of goods sold		60,000		68,000
Gross margin		40,000		42,000
Expenses		35,000		35,500
Pretax income		$ 5,000		$ 6,500

    * See Chapter 6: BI + P − EI = CGS.

Observe that the ending inventory, as measured and reported at December 31, 19A, amounted to $10,000. This amount also is reported as the beginning inventory of 19B.

To illustrate inventory effects on **pretax** income, assume that an error was made in measuring the ending inventory at December 31, 19A, because the recorded amount should have been $11,000 (i.e., $1,000 more than shown above). The $1,000 understatement of the ending inventory could have been due to either one or a combination of the following factors:

1. In physically counting the inventory items, some items were left out incorrectly. They had a cost of $1,000.
2. Although the physical count of items was correct, in determining the total cost of inventory, a higher unit cost should have been used. This higher cost would have increased the amount of the inventory by $1,000.

We now will see how this $1,000 understatement of the 19A ending inventory affected the pretax income amounts for each of the two years. The income statements may be restated to reflect the correct inventory amount as follows:

	19A		19B	
Sales revenue		$100,000		$110,000
Cost of goods sold:				
Beginning inventory	$ –0–		$11,000	
Purchases	70,000		58,000	
Goods available for sale	70,000		69,000	
Ending inventory	11,000		–0–	
Cost of goods sold		59,000		69,000
Gross margin		41,000		41,000
Expenses		35,000		35,500
Pretax income		$ 6,000		$ 5,500

Observe that in comparison with the preceding income statements, pretax income for 19A is more by $1,000 and less by the same amount for 19B. Thus, a comparison of the two sets of income statements demonstrates the following generalizations:

1. **In the period of the change**—An increase in the amount of the ending inventory for a period decreases cost of goods sold by the same amount, which in turn increases pretax income for that period by the same amount. To the contrary, a decrease in the amount of ending inventory increases cost of goods sold which in turn decreases pretax income for that period by the same amount.
2. **In the next period**—An increase in the amount of the ending inventory for a period increases the beginning inventory for the next period. The increase in beginning inventory increases cost of goods sold which decreases the pretax income of the **next period** by the same amount. To the contrary, a decrease in the amount of the ending inventory for a period decreases cost of goods sold of the next period which increases pretax income of the **next period** by the same amount.

There is a direct relationship between ending inventory and pretax income. Conversely, there is an inverse relationship between beginning inventory and pretax income.

The above illustration was presented to indicate the importance of careful measurement of inventory. Care must be exercised in (1) measuring the **quantity** of items that should be included in the inventory and (2) applying the dollar **unit cost** to the units included in the ending inventory.

ITEMS TO BE INCLUDED IN INVENTORY

Inventory usually includes tangible property that is: (1) held for sale in the normal course of business or (2) to be consumed in producing goods or services for sale. Inventory is reported on the balance sheet as a current asset because it normally will be consumed or converted into cash within one year or within the next operating cycle of the business, whichever is the longer. Inventory is less liquid (i.e., less readily convertible to cash) than accounts receivable, therefore, inventory usually is listed below accounts receivable on the balance sheet.

The kinds of inventory normally held depend upon the characteristics of the business:[1]

Retail or wholesale business:

Merchandise inventory—goods (or merchandise) held for resale in the normal course of business. The goods usually are acquired through purchase in a completely manufactured condition and are ready for sale without further processing.

Manufacturing business:[2]

Finished goods inventory—goods manufactured by the business, completed and ready for sale.

Work in process inventory—work (or goods) in the process of being fabricated or manufactured but not yet completed as finished goods. Work in process inventory, when completed, becomes finished goods inventory.

Raw materials inventory—items acquired by purchase, growth (such as food products), or extraction of natural resources for the purpose of processing into finished goods. Such items are accounted for as raw materials inventory until used. When used, their cost is included in the work in process inventory (along with direct labor and factory overhead costs). The flow of inventory costs in a manufacturing environment can be diagrammed as follows:

The work in process inventory includes the cost of raw materials used and the **direct** labor incurred in the manufacturing process and the factory overhead costs. Direct labor cost represents the earnings of employees who work directly on the products being manufactured. Factory overhead costs include all manufacturing costs that are not direct material or direct labor costs. For example, the salary of the plant supervisor would be included in factory overhead.

The discussions that follow focus on merchandise and finished goods inventories.

In measuring the **physical quantity** of goods in the inventory, a company should include all items to which it has **ownership,** regardless of their locations. In business transactions involving purchase and sale, accounting focuses on the passage of ownership. Usually when ownership passes, one party records a sale

---

[1] Supplies on hand usually are reported as prepaid expenses.

[2] *Fundamentals of Management Accounting* presents a complete discussion of inventory measurement and accounting in a manufacturing environment.

and the other party records a purchase. In a purchase/sale transaction, the basic guideline is that ownership to the goods passes at the **time intended by the parties** to the transaction. Usually, ownership passes when the goods are delivered by the seller to the buyer; however, there are situations in which this is not the case.

The intentions of the parties concerning the time of passage of ownership are not always clear. In such situations, all of the circumstances must be assessed and judgment applied as to when the buyer and seller intended ownership to pass. For example, goods may be sold on credit and the buyer may request the vendor (seller) to hold the goods pending shipping instructions. In this instance, ownership appears to have passed, regardless of the delivery date. A similar question arises when a third party has physical possession of the goods for a period of time. For example, an independent transportation company may have possession of the goods as they are moved from the seller's location to the buyer's location. If the terms of the sale provide that the buyer must pay the transportation charges (known as FOB shipping point), then ownership usually is assumed to pass when the vendor delivers the goods to the transportation agent. In contrast, if the terms of the sale are FOB destination (i.e., the seller must pay the freight), ownership usually is assumed to pass when the goods are delivered to the buyer at destination.[3]

The passage-of-ownership guideline is a facet of the revenue principle, previously discussed (Exhibit 2–6). The passage-of-ownership guideline has a legal basis and prevails in the accounting process with respect to both the sale and purchase of goods. In the absence of the passage-of-ownership guideline, the financial statements could be manipulated to overstate revenue by entering all **sales orders** received up through the last day of the period, regardless of the fact that ownership to the goods ordered may not have passed to the buyer. Conversely, costs could be manipulated by not recording purchases even though ownership to the goods has passed.

When a company has possession of goods that it does not own, those goods should be excluded from the inventory. This situation often occurs when goods are on **consignment** for sale on a commission basis. The supplier (known as the consignor) legally retains ownership to the goods on consignment, although the goods are in the physical possession of the party that will sell them (known as the consignee). The consignor, although the goods are not in his or her physical possession, should include them in the ending inventory. The consignee, although having possession of the goods, should exclude them from the ending inventory because ownership still resides with the consignor.

In summary, in identifying the individual items to be included in the ending inventory at a specific date, ownership, rather than physical possession is the controlling consideration. The inventory should include all of the goods to which the entity has legal ownership.

---

[3] FOB stands for "free on board"; it is used in business to indicate who is responsible for paying the transportation charges: FOB destination, seller pays the freight; FOB shipping point, buyer pays the freight.

MEASURING INVENTORY COST

In Chapter 6 we discussed the application of the cost principle to the purchase of goods for resale. Goods in inventory are recorded in accordance with the **cost principle** as follows:

> The primary basis of accounting for inventory is cost, which has been defined generally as the price paid or consideration given to acquire an asset. As applied to inventories, cost means, in principle, the sum of the applicable expenditures and charges directly or indirectly incurred in bringing an article to its existing condition and location.[4]

In accordance with the cost principle, indirect expenditures related to the purchase of goods, such as freight, insurance, and storage, theoretically should be included in measuring the purchase cost of the goods acquired. However, because these incidental amounts frequently are not **material in amount** (see the materiality concept, Exhibit 2–6) when related to the total purchase cost, and because there often is no convenient method of apportioning such costs to each item of goods, they may not be assigned to the inventory cost. Thus, for practical reasons, some companies use the **net invoice price** when assigning a unit cost to goods included in the ending inventory and record the indirect purchase expenditures as a separate cost which is added to cost of goods sold.

Chapter 6 discussed the assignment of **dollar cost** to (a) the ending inventory and (b) cost of goods sold in situations in which there were no changes in unit purchase (or manufacturing) cost during the period (including the beginning inventory). This chapter expands those discussions to the typical situation in which the cost per unit of the goods stocked changes during the annual accounting period. To illustrate the typical situation, assume Summer Retail Store stocks a product that reflected the beginning inventory, merchandise purchases, and sales data given in Exhibit 7–1.

When there is a change in the unit cost of items purchased for inventory, an accounting allocation problem must be resolved before the financial statements can be prepared. In the case of Summer Retail Store, the accounting problem is: of the $3,630 total cost of **goods available for sale,** how much should be apportioned to cost of goods sold (i.e., for the 320 units sold) and how much should be apportioned to the ending inventory (i.e., 470 units − 320 units = 150 units). The answer to this problem necessarily involves assignment of the four unit cost amounts ($6, $7, $8, and $9), or some combination of them, to the ending inventory and to cost of goods sold. This part of the chapter discusses the alternative methods used for making this allocation (assignment) of costs.

Chapter 6 presented two alternative inventory systems used to accumulate data to facilitate determination of (a) the ending inventory and (b) cost of goods sold. To review, the two alternative inventory systems are:[5]

---

[4] AICPA, *Accounting Research Bulletin No. 43* (New York, 1961), chap. 4, statement 3.

[5] Often a single company will use one of the systems for certain items stocked and the other system for the remaining items. The choice usually depends upon such factors as the nature of the item (size), unit cost, number of units stocked, and cost to implement the system.

EXHIBIT 7–1
Illustrative
inventory data

SUMMER RETAIL STORE
19A Illustrative Data—Beginning Inventory, Purchases, and Sales

Transactions	Symbol	Number of units	Unit cost	Total cost
Beginning inventory January 1, 19A (carried over from last period)	BI	100	$6	$ 600
Purchases during 19A:				
January 3, first purchase	P	50	7	$ 350
June 12, second purchase	P	200	8	1,600
December 20, third purchase	P	120	9	1,080
Total purchases during 19A		370		3,030
Goods available for sale during the year		470		3,630
Goods sold during 19A:				
January 6 (unit sales price, $10)	S	40		
June 18 (unit sales price, $12)	S	220		
December 24 (unit sales price, $14)	S	60		
Total sales during 19A		320		?
Ending inventory December 31, 19A (units 470 − 320)	EI	150		?

1. **Periodic inventory system**—This system accumulates total merchandise acquisition cost (including the beginning inventory), and at the **end of the accounting period,** the ending inventory is measured by means of a physical inventory count of all goods remaining on hand. The units counted on hand then are valued (costed) in dollars by using appropriate unit purchase cost amounts (for example, from above, some combination of $6, $7, $8, and $9). The periodic inventory system measures **cost of goods sold** as a residual amount; that is:

$$BI + P - EI = CGS$$

2. **Perpetual inventory system**—This system maintains a detailed daily inventory record throughout the period for each item stocked. This record includes (a) the beginning inventory, (b) each purchase, (c) each issue (i.e., sales), and (d) a continuous (perpetual or running) balance of the inventory. Thus, this system measures cost of goods sold and ending inventory without a physical inventory count at the end of each accounting period. Under this system, the **ending inventory** can be viewed as a residual amount; that is:

$$BI + P - CGS = EI$$

The discussions that follow in Part A of this chapter present several alternative inventory costing methods under the assumption that the **periodic inventory system** is used. Part B of this chapter discusses these methods with a perpetual inventory system. The four generally accepted **inventory costing methods** commonly used are:

1. Weighted average.
2. First-in, first-out (FIFO).
3. Last-in, first-out (LIFO).
4. Specific identification.

The primary objective of the inventory costing methods is not limited to measurement of the amount of goods on hand in order to obtain the balance sheet amount, but the objective also is to measure cost of goods sold, which is important in the measurement of income.

APPLICATION OF THE INVENTORY COSTING METHODS WITH THE PERIODIC INVENTORY SYSTEM

The four inventory costing methods listed above are **alternative allocation methods** for assigning the total amount of goods available for sale (BI + P) between (a) ending inventory (reported as an asset at the end of the period) and (b) cost of goods sold (reported as an expense of the period). For illustration, refer to the data for Summer Retail Store given in Exhibit 7–1. These two allocated amounts are given below. They were calculated using the weighted-average inventory costing method. At this point you need not be concerned about how the two amounts were calculated.

	Units	Amount
Goods available for sale (total amount to be allocated)	470	$3,630
Cost allocation:		
Ending inventory (determined by inventory count and then costed at weighted-average unit cost)	150	1,158
Cost of goods sold (residual amount)	320	$2,472

The amount of **goods available for sale** ($3,630) was allocated between **ending inventory** ($1,158) and **cost of goods sold** ($2,472), and the sum of these two amounts (and the related units as well) necessarily must be the same as goods available for sale. This cost allocation procedure also is portrayed graphically in Exhibit 7–2.

Each of the four inventory costing methods listed above will be discussed and illustrated using the data for Summer Retail Store given in Exhibit 7–1.

The total amount of cost to be allocated (cost of goods available for sale) is provided directly by the accounting records under either the periodic inventory system or the perpetual inventory system. The **periodic inventory system** requires computation of the ending inventory by means of a physical count of the goods remaining on hand (which then are costed in dollars by applying one of the inventory costing methods), and cost of goods sold is computed as a residual amount; the amount that remains after ending inventory is subtracted from cost of goods available for sale.

EXHIBIT 7–2
Graphic illustration of cost allocation

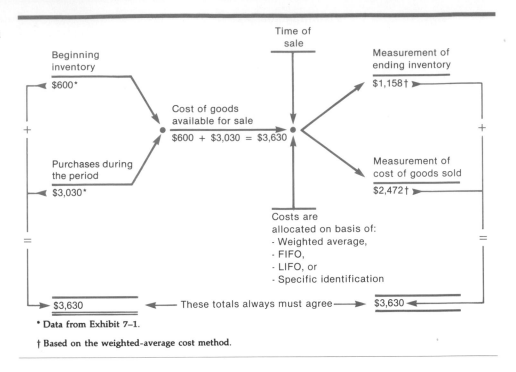

* Data from Exhibit 7–1.

† Based on the weighted-average cost method.

INVENTORY COSTING METHODS ILLUSTRATED

A choice among the inventory costing methods is necessary only when there are different unit costs in the beginning inventory and/or purchases during the current period. (If unit costs are stable, all of the methods provide exactly the same amounts.) The choice among the inventory costing methods is not based on the physical flow of goods on and off the shelves. Although the actual **physical flow** of goods usually is first-in, first-out (FIFO), a company can use any of the four inventory costing methods. Generally accepted accounting principles only require that the inventory costing method used be rational and systematic.

A company is not required to use the same inventory costing method for all inventory items, and no particular justification is required for the selection of one or more of the acceptable methods. However, a change in method is viewed as significant and requires special disclosures in the footnotes to the financial statements.

Weighted-average inventory costing method

The weighted-average method requires computation of the weighted-average unit cost of the goods available for sale. In a periodic inventory system, the computed unit cost is applied to the **number of units** in inventory determined by the physical inventory count to derive the total cost of ending inventory. Cost of goods sold is determined by subtracting the ending inventory amount from the amount of goods available for sale. To illustrate, the weighted-average method would be applied by Summer Retail Store (Exhibit 7–1) as follows under a **periodic** inventory system.[6]

Step 1—Computation of the weighted-average unit cost for the period:

$$\frac{\text{Total goods available for sale—at cost}}{\text{Total goods available for sale—units}} = \frac{\$3,630}{470} = \$7.72 \quad \left\{ \begin{array}{l} \text{Weighted-} \\ \text{average} \\ \text{cost per} \\ \text{unit for} \\ \text{the period} \end{array} \right.$$

Step 2—Allocation of the cost of goods available for sale under the periodic inventory system:

	Units	Amount
Goods available for sale (Exhibit 7–1)	470	$3,630
Ending inventory (150 units × $7.72)......	150	1,158*
Cost of goods sold (residual amount)......	320	$2,472†

* Reported on the balance sheet.
† Reported as an expense on the income statement. This amount can be verified as 320 units × $7.72 = $2,470 (a $2 rounding error).

The weighted-average cost method is rational, systematic, easy to apply, and not subject to manipulation. It weights the number of units purchased and unit costs that prevailed during the period (including the beginning inventory). Thus, it is representative of costs during the entire period (including the beginning inventory) rather than of the cost only at the beginning, end, or at one point during the period.[7] Representative costs are reported on both the balance sheet (ending inventory) and the income statement (cost of goods sold).

First-in, first-out inventory costing method

The first-in, first-out method, frequently referred to as **FIFO,** assumes that the oldest units (i.e., the first costs in) are the first units sold (i.e., the first costs out). In other words, the units in the beginning inventory are treated as if they were sold first, the units from the first purchase sold next, and so on until the units left in the ending inventory all come from the most recent purchases. FIFO allocates the oldest unit costs to cost of goods sold and the most recent unit costs to the ending inventory.

Frequently, FIFO is justified on the basis that it is consistent with the actual physical flow of the goods. In most businesses, the first goods placed in stock tend to be the first goods sold. However, FIFO can be applied regardless of the actual physical flow of goods because the objective of FIFO is to allocate costs to ending inventory and to cost of goods sold in a systematic and rational manner.

[6] When an average cost is used, uneven unit cost amounts usually are rounded to the nearest cent. The rounded unit cost amount is used to compute the ending inventory amount which allocates any rounding error to cost of goods sold. Under the perpetual inventory system, a moving average unit cost (rather than the weighted-average unit cost) usually is used (see Part B).

[7] A weighted-average unit cost rather than a simple average of the unit costs must be used. For example, ($6 + $7 + $8 + 9) ÷ 4 = $7.50 would be incorrect because it does not consider the number of units at each unit cost.

To illustrate, the FIFO method would be applied by Summer Retail Store (Exhibit 7–1) as follows under a **periodic** inventory system:

	Units	Unit cost	Total cost
Goods available for sale (Exhibit 7–1)	470		$3,630
Valuation of ending inventory (FIFO):			
At latest unit costs, 150 units:			
From December 20 purchase (latest)	120	$9	$1,080
From June 12 purchase (next latest)	30	8	240
Valuation, FIFO basis	150		1,320*
Cost of goods sold (residual FIFO amount)	320		$2,310†

* Report on balance sheet.
† Report as an expense on income statement. This amount can be verified as follows: Units sold at oldest costs—100 units @ $6 = $600, plus 50 units @ $7 = $350, plus 170 units @ $8 = $1,360, which sum to $2,310.

The FIFO method is rational, systematic, easy to apply, and not subject to manipulation. On the balance sheet, the FIFO ending inventory amount is costed on the basis of the most recent unit costs and, therefore, it is likely to be a realistic valuation prevailing at the balance sheet date. In contrast, on the income statement, cost of goods sold is at the oldest unit costs, which may not reflect the current cost of items which were sold. The significance of the impact of FIFO, on the income statement (i.e., cost of goods sold and income) and the balance sheet (i.e., the ending inventory amount under current assets) depends on the extent to which unit costs increase or decrease during the period. Comparative effects are illustrated later.

Last-in, first-out inventory costing method

The last-in, last-out method, frequently referred to as **LIFO,** assumes that the most recently acquired goods are sold first. Regardless of the physical flow of goods, LIFO treats the costs of the most recent units purchased as cost of goods sold, which leaves the unit costs of the beginning inventory and the earlier purchase cost in the ending inventory. The LIFO flow assumption is the exact opposite of the FIFO flow assumption.

That is, under LIFO, the total ending inventory cost is measured at the oldest unit costs and cost of goods sold is measured at the newest unit costs.

To illustrate, the LIFO method would be applied by Summer Retail Store (Exhibit 7–1) as follows under a **periodic** inventory system.

	Units	Unit cost	Total cost
Goods available for sale (Exhibit 7–1)	470		$3,630
Valuation of ending inventory (LIFO):			
At older unit costs, 150 units:			
From beginning inventory (oldest)	100	$6	$600
From January 3 purchase (next oldest)	50	7	350
Valuation, LIFO basis	150		950*
Cost of goods sold (residual LIFO amount)	320		$2,680†

* Report on balance sheet.
† Report as an expense on the income statement. This amount can be verified as follows: Units sold at latest costs—120 units @ $9 = $1,080, plus 200 units @ $8 = $1,600, which sum to $2,680.

The LIFO method is rational and systematic. However, it is subject to manipulation by buying (or not buying) goods at the end of a period when unit costs have changed, which makes it possible to manipulate cost of goods sold and, hence, reported income. On the income statement, LIFO cost of goods sold is based on the latest unit costs, which is a realistic measurement of the current cost of items which were sold. In contrast, on the balance sheet, the ending inventory amount is based on the oldest unit costs which may be an unrealistic valuation. The comparative impact of LIFO will be discussed later.[8]

Specific identification inventory costing method

Specific identification is another method of allocating the cost of goods available for sale to cost of goods sold and the ending inventory is to keep track of the purchase cost of each item; this is done either by coding the purchase cost on each unit before placing it in stock or by keeping a separate record of the unit and identifying it with a serial number. When a sale is made, the cost of that specific unit is identified and recorded. For example, using the data given in Exhibit 7–1, if the 40 units sold on January 6 were selected specifically from the units that were purchased at $6 each (i.e., from the beginning inventory), the cost of goods sold amount for that particular sale would be measured as 40 units $\times$ $6 = $240. Alternatively, if 20 of the units were selected from those that cost $6 each (from the beginning inventory) and the other 20 from those that cost $7 each (from the January 3 purchase), cost of goods sold would be measured as (20 units $\times$ $6) + (20 units $\times$ $7) = $260.

The specific identification method would be rather tedious and impractical where (1) unit costs are low, (2) unit costs change frequently, or (3) a large number of different items are stocked. On the other hand, where there are "big-ticket" items such as automobiles and expensive jewelry, it is especially appropriate because each item tends to be different from the other items. In such situations, it is rational because the **selling price** usually is based on a markup over specific cost. However, the method may be manipulated when the units are identical because one can affect the cost of goods sold and the ending inventory accounts by "picking and choosing" from among the several available unit costs, even though the goods are identical in other respects. To illustrate, in the above example, cost of goods sold was either $240 or $260, depending on the choices made. In that example, income would be different by $20, depending on an arbitrary selection from a group of identical items.

COMPARISON OF THE INVENTORY COSTING METHODS

Each of the four alternative inventory costing methods is in accordance with generally accepted accounting principles, although each may produce significantly

---

[8] This discussion assumes an item-by-item application of LIFO and costing of goods sold currently throughout the period. For income tax purposes LIFO costing must be done at the end of the taxable year. Although the concepts are the same, many companies use an application known as dollar-value LIFO, and the costing is at the end of the year. These complexities are beyond the scope of this book. See Welsch, Zlatkovich, and Harrison, *Intermediate Accounting*, 6th ed. (Homewood, Ill.: Richard D. Irwin, 1982).

different income and asset (i.e., ending inventory) amounts. To illustrate this difference, the comparative results for Summer Retail Store are as follows:

	Sales revenue	Cost of goods sold	Gross margin	Balance sheet (inventory)
Weighted average	$3,880	$2,472	$1,408	$1,158
FIFO	3,880	2,310	1,570	1,320
LIFO (end of period)	3,880	2,680	1,200	950

From the above results, we see that when unit costs are changing, each method tends to give different income and different inventory amounts. Observe that the difference in **pretax income** among each of the methods is the same as the difference in the inventory amounts. The method that provides the highest ending inventory amount also provides the highest income amount and vice versa. The weighted-average cost method tends to give income and inventory amounts that fall between the FIFO and LIFO extremes.

We will focus now on a comparison of the FIFO and LIFO methods because they usually represent the extreme, and opposite, effects. Note in the comparison above that unit costs were **increasing** and that LIFO provided the lower income and inventory amounts, whereas FIFO provided the higher income and inventory amounts. In comparing the effects of LIFO with FIFO, it is important to note that the comparative effects will depend upon the direction of change in unit cost. **When unit costs are rising, LIFO will result in lower income and a lower inventory valuation than will FIFO. Conversely, when unit costs are declining, LIFO will result in higher income and higher inventory valuation than will FIFO.** These effects occur because LIFO will cause the newer unit costs to be reflected on the income statement whereas FIFO will cause the older unit costs to be reflected on the income statement.

INCOME TAX EFFECTS

The selection of an inventory costing method often will have a significant impact on income taxes to be paid in particular years. We have seen that the various inventory costing methods allocate different amounts of income among accounting periods. Thus, when prices are rising, **LIFO** often is preferred for income tax purposes because an early tax deduction is to be preferred to a later tax deduction. The shifting of tax liability to later years becomes important because the company can earn interest on money that otherwise would be paid as taxes.

In recent years, a large number of businesses have adopted LIFO because it tends to minimize early income tax payments. Prices have been rising, and with rising prices, LIFO allocates higher costs to cost of goods sold. This in turn reduces pretax income so the income tax bill is lower. Of course, the inventory effect suggests that should prices decline at some future date, those businesses may want to change from LIFO to FIFO to minimize income taxes on the downward trend of prices. Under many circumstances, it is difficult to obtain permission from the Internal Revenue Service to change the inventory costing method.

EXHIBIT 7–3
Income tax effects illustrated

A. Fact situation for 19B (when prices increased rapidly):

a.	Sales revenue	$900,000
b.	Cost of goods sold:	
	FIFO basis	400,000
	LIFO basis	600,000
c.	Remaining expenses (excluding income taxes)	250,000
d.	Average income tax rate	30%

B. Effect on income tax expense:

	Inventory costing method	
	FIFO	*LIFO*
Sales revenue	$900,000	$900,000
Cost of goods sold	400,000	600,000
Gross margin	500,000	300,000
Less: Remaining expenses (except income taxes)	250,000	250,000
Pretax income	250,000	50,000
Income tax expense (30% rate)	75,000	15,000
Net income	$175,000	$ 35,000
EPS (100,000 shares common stock outstanding)	$1.75	$.35

Reduction in income tax expense ($75,000 − $15,000) = $60,000.
Cash saved ($75,000 − $15,000) = $60,000.

The income tax effects associated with LIFO and FIFO are illustrated in Exhibit 7–3.

In this situation, ending inventory, cost of goods sold, and pretax income all were different by $200,000 which was caused by the divergence between the FIFO and LIFO methods. Costs were rising, and there was a significant difference between the "old" and "new" unit costs. The $200,000 difference, when multiplied by the 30 percent income tax rate, indicates a cash saving of $60,000 in 19B. The internal revenue code specifies a LIFO conformity rule: if LIFO is used on the income tax return, it also must be used on the financial reports. It is well to keep in mind that LIFO cannot provide permanent tax savings because (a) when inventory levels drop or (b) costs drop, the income effect reverses and the income taxes deferred will have to be paid. The only advantage of deferring income taxes in such situations is due to the fact that interest can be earned on the money that otherwise would be paid as taxes for the current year.

EVALUATION OF ALTERNATIVE INVENTORY COSTING METHODS

No one method of inventory costing can be considered as the "best." It would be unreasonable to assume that the tax consequences are not important in the choice of method. Many observers believe that businesses set selling prices within a "LIFO assumption" because the goods sold must be replaced on the shelf at the latest cost rather than at earlier cost.

Many accountants believe that the best inventory costing method is the one that best reflects the sales pricing policy of the company, and many companies do price units for sale in each of the ways implied by these four costing methods. Other accountants believe that the choice of method should be based upon whether the measurement emphasis should be on the income statement or on the balance sheet. Those who believe that the income statement should be accorded primary emphasis tend to defend LIFO because it matches the most recent purchase cost with current sales revenue. To the contrary, those who prefer to emphasize the balance sheet tend to prefer FIFO because it reports the ending inventory on the balance sheet at the most current cost price. Because of these considerations, it is not difficult to understand why the accounting profession, and the income tax laws, have accepted several alternative inventory costing methods.

COMPARABILITY PRINCIPLE

The previous section (page 307) emphasized that different income statement and balance sheet amounts result from the use of different inventory costing methods. These differences in reported financial data cause problems for statement users in comparing companies that use different accounting methods. Problems are also created when an individual business changes accounting methods over time. The **comparability principle** (Exhibit 2–6) is applied to maximize comparability when accounting alternatives are permitted. The comparability principle holds that in the accounting process all concepts, principles, and measurement approaches should be applied in a similar or consistent way from one period to the next in order to assure that the data reported in the financial statements are reasonably comparable over time. This principle prevents arbitrary changes from one accounting or measurement approach to another. The comparability principle is not inflexible. It permits changes in accounting when the changes tend to improve the measurement of financial results and financial position. Comparability is a difficult concept to define precisely and poses troublesome problems in application.

In respect to inventories, a business is not permitted to change from one inventory costing method to another from period to period. Changing from one inventory costing method to another is a major event, and such a change requires full disclosure as to the reason for the change and the accounting effects.

PART B—APPLICATION OF A PERPETUAL INVENTORY SYSTEM AND SELECTED INVENTORY COSTING PROBLEMS

Recall that in Chapter 6, Part B, the periodic and perpetual inventory systems were discussed and illustrated. Regardless of which of the two alternative inventory systems is used, one or more of the inventory costing methods (discussed in Part A) must be applied. The discussions and illustrations in Part A of this chapter assumed a periodic inventory system (i.e., in this system the units in the ending inventory are determined by a physical inventory count, and then the units found to be on hand are valued in dollars by applying one of the inventory costing methods).

This part of the chapter discusses and illustrates **application of each of the inventory costing methods with a perpetual inventory system.** Separate discussion of the two systems is essential because:

a. The timing of the application of the inventory costing methods between the two systems causes some differences in the allocated amounts. The periodic inventory system costs inventory units at the end of the period, whereas the perpetual inventory system costs units on a day-to-day basis.
b. The accounting entries vary between the two systems.
c. The inventory controls that are available with the two systems vary.
d. Recent developments of computers of various capabilities have encouraged a high percent of large, medium, and even small businesses to change to the perpetual inventory system for numerous items in their inventories.

APPLICATION OF THE INVENTORY COSTING METHODS WITH A PERPETUAL INVENTORY SYSTEM

A perpetual inventory system requires the maintenance of a day-to-day **perpetual inventory record** for each kind of goods or merchandise stocked and sold. This record is designed to show units, unit costs, and dollar amounts, at all times, for (a) beginning inventory, (b) goods received (purchases), (c) goods sold (issues), and (d) balance of goods on hand (ending inventory). Each purchase and each sale transaction is entered in the perpetual inventory record when it occurs. The perpetual inventory record is designed so that cost of goods sold and the ending inventory are measured on a perpetual or continuous basis.

In the discussions to follow, a **perpetual inventory record** will be illustrated for each of the four inventory costing methods. To illustrate each application, we will use the data for Summer Retail Store given in Exhibit 7–1. The manual system is used for instructional purposes. The beginning inventory of 100 units at a unit cost of $6 would have been carried over in the records from the prior period. Recall from Chapter 6 that each purchase would be recorded as follows and, at the same time, entered on the perpetual inventory record (see Exhibit 7–4):

```
Jan. 3   Inventory (50 units @ $7) .....................................   350
              Cash (or accounts payable) ...............................          350
```

A sale generates two companion entries when a perpetual inventory system is used; one at sale price and one at cost:

Jan. 6	Cash	400	
	Sales revenue (40 units @ $10)		400
	Cost of goods sold (FIFO basis)	240	
	Inventory (40 units @ $6)		240

Weighted-average inventory costing method

When the weighted-average cost method is applied with a perpetual inventory system, a **moving weighted-average** unit cost is used because the cost of goods sold amount is measured and recorded at the **time of each sale.** Instead, if one were to apply the concept of an **annual** weighted average, the recording of cost of goods sold would be delayed until year-end, which is the only time an annual average unit cost can be computed.

In applying a moving weighted average, a **new** average unit cost is computed at the time of **each purchase.** Cost of goods sold and the remaining inventory are measured at the then prevailing moving average unit cost. An illustration of a perpetual inventory record on a moving weighted-average basis for the data

EXHIBIT 7–4
Moving weighted-average method—perpetual inventory system

PERPETUAL INVENTORY RECORD

Item	Item A						Cost Basis	Moving average	
Location	320						Minimum Level	100	
Code	13						Maximum Level	300	

Date	Received (purchases)			Issued (sales)			Inventory Balance		
	Units	Unit Cost	Total Cost	Units	Unit Cost	Total Cost	Units	Unit Cost	Total Cost
1/1 bal.							100	6.00	600
1/3	50	7.00	350				150	6.33	950
1/6				40	6.33	253	110	6.33	697
6/12	200	8.00	1,600				310	7.41*	2,297
6/18				220	7.41	1,630	90	7.41	667
12/20	120	9.00	1,080				210	8.32*	1,747
12/24				60	8.32	499	150	8.32	1,248
Total cost of goods sold						2,382			
Total ending inventory									1,248

* New moving weighted-average unit cost computed.

given in Exhibit 7–1 is shown in Exhibit 7–4. The moving weighted-average unit cost was recomputed three times during the period because there were three purchases. Units sold are removed from the inventory record at the then moving average unit cost. For example, the moving weighted-average unit cost was computed on the date of the first purchase as follows:

	Units	Cost
Beginning inventory	100	$600
Purchase, January 3	50	350
Totals	150	$950

Moving average unit cost:
$950 ÷ 150 units = $6.33 per unit.

The companion entries for the sale on January 6 would reflect sales revenue of $400 and cost of goods sold of $253 (from the perpetual inventory record) as follows:

```
Jan. 6   Cash ...................................................................   400
             Sales revenue (40 units @ $10) .............................          400

         Cost of goods sold (moving average basis) ........................   253
             Inventory ...........................................................          253
         From Exhibit 7–4.
```

FIFO inventory costing method

When the FIFO method is applied with a perpetual inventory system, after each issue the remaining units on hand must be "layered" by the different unit costs which frequently are referred to as "inventory cost layers." The identification of inventory cost layers is necessary because goods are removed from the perpetual inventory record in FIFO order; that is, the oldest unit cost is taken off first. An illustration of a perpetual inventory record on a FIFO basis is shown in Exhibit 7–5. Each purchase and each sale of goods is entered in the inventory record at the time of the transaction. At each transaction date, the balance column on the perpetual inventory record is restated to show the units and amount on hand for each different unit cost. At the same time, each transaction would be recorded in the journal. For example, the two companion journal entries to record the sales of June 18 are:

```
June 18   Cash .................................................................   2,640
              Sales revenue (220 units @ $12) .......................          2,640

          Cost of goods sold (FIFO basis) ............................   1,590
              Inventory ...........................................................          1,590
          From Exhibit 7–5, $360 + $350 + $880 = $1,590.
```

EXHIBIT 7–5
FIFO method—
perpetual inventory
system

PERPETUAL INVENTORY RECORD

(heading—same as in Exhibit 7–4, except cost basis—FIFO)

Date	Received (purchases)			Issued (sales)			Inventory Balance*		
	Units	Unit Cost	Total Cost	Units	Unit Cost	Total Cost	Units	Unit Cost	Total Cost
1/1 bal.							100	6	600
1/3	50	7	350				100	6	600
							50	7	350
1/6				40	6	240	60	6	360
							50	7	350
6/12	200	8	1,600				60	6	360
							50	7	350
							200	8	1,600
6/18				60	6	360			
				50	7	350			
				110	8	880	90	8	720
12/20	120	9	1,080				90	8	720
							120	9	1,080
1/24				60	8	480	30	8	240
							120	9	1,080
Total cost of goods sold						2,310			
Total ending inventory									1,320

* Maintained by FIFO unit cost inventory layers.

LIFO inventory costing method

When the LIFO method is applied with a perpetual inventory system, the inventory cost layers must be identified separately on the perpetual inventory record, as was the case with FIFO. This identification is necessary so that the units (and their unit costs) can be removed at the time of sale from the inventory record in the inverse order that they came in. Unit costs are removed from the perpetual inventory record at the time of each issue which means that the **timing of costing is during the period rather than at the end of the period.** A perpetual inventory record on a LIFO basis is illustrated in Exhibit 7–6.

**EXHIBIT 7–6
LIFO method,
costed currently—
perpetual inventory
system**

PERPETUAL INVENTORY RECORD

(heading—same as in Exhibit 7–4, except cost basis—LIFO)

Date	Received (purchases)			Issued (sales)			Inventory Balance*		
	Units	Unit Cost	Total Cost	Units	Unit Cost	Total Cost	Units	Unit Cost	Total Cost
1/1 bal.							100	6	600
1/3	50	7	350				100	6	600
							50	7	350
1/6				40	7	280	100	6	600
							10	7	70
6/12	200	8	1,600				100	6	600
							10	7	70
							200	8	1,600
6/18				200	8	1,600			
				10	7	70			
				10	6	60	90	6	540
12/20	120	9	1,080				90	6	540
							120	9	1,080
12/24				60	9	540	90	6	540
							60	9	540
Total cost of goods sold						2,550			
Ending inventory									1,080

* Maintained by LIFO unit cost inventory layers.

**Specific
identification
inventory
costing method**

When the specific identification method is applied with a perpetual inventory system, the item-by-item choice (for entry in the perpetual inventory record and in the accounts) should be made at the time of sale rather than later (which is possible under the periodic inventory system). Application of the specific identification costing method in a perpetual inventory system is accomplished in a manner similar to the preceding illustrations.

COMPARISON OF PERIODIC AND PERPETUAL INVENTORY SYSTEMS

There are two important implementation differences between the periodic inventory system and the perpetual inventory system, viz:

a. The perpetual system requires more clerical effort than the periodic system.

b. The periodic system requires a year-end physical inventory whereas the perpetual system does not.

In the past, most businesses used the periodic inventory system because of its relative low cost and convenience, but recent advances in computer technology have produced a significant reduction in the cost of maintaining a perpetual inventory system. As a result, many businesses have adopted the perpetual system. The perpetual system offers the advantage of providing management with inventory information which is always up-to-date and the status of the inventory is readily available.

The periodic and perpetual inventory systems may produce different valuations of cost of goods sold and ending inventory because of differences with respect to the timing of the costing of cost of goods sold and inventory. The **periodic** inventory system costs ending inventory and cost of goods sold at the **end** of the accounting period. In contrast, the **perpetual** inventory system costs inventory and cost of goods sold **throughout** the accounting period.

The FIFO inventory method results in identical valuations of ending inventory and cost of goods sold under both the periodic and perpetual inventory systems. The results are identical because of the basic FIFO assumption that the first goods into inventory are the first goods taken out of inventory, and that order always is maintained. To illustrate, compare the following FIFO results for Summer Retail Store:

FIFO	*Perpetual inventory system*	*Periodic inventory system*
Source	Exhibit 7–5	Page 304
Ending inventory	$1,320	$1,320
Cost of goods sold	2,310	2,310
Total goods available	$3,630	$3,630

In contrast, results typically will be different under periodic and perpetual systems when either the LIFO or the average inventory costing method is used. The results will be different under the **average cost** method because the **periodic** inventory system applies an **annual** weighted average for cost allocation whereas the **perpetual** inventory applies a series of **moving** averages throughout the accounting period.

Results will be different under the **LIFO** method because **at the end** of the accounting period the **periodic** inventory system allocates the most recent purchase cost to cost of goods sold. In contrast, the **perpetual** system allocates the most recent purchase costs to cost of goods sold **during** the accounting period on the data that each sales transaction occurs.

To illustrate the differences that can occur between LIFO and weighted average, compare the following results for Summer Retail Store:

LIFO	Perpetual inventory system	Periodic inventory system
Source	Exhibit 7–6	Page 304
Ending inventory	$1,080	$ 950
Cost of goods sold	2,550	2,680
Total goods available	$3,630	$3,630
Weighted Average		
Source	Exhibit 7–4	Page 303
Ending inventory	$1,248	$1,158
Cost of goods sold	2,382	2,472
Total goods available	$3,630	$3,630

To summarize, the four **inventory costing methods** (weighted average, FIFO, LIFO, and specific identification) are alternative methods of measuring the valuation of ending inventory and cost of goods sold. Each method assumes a different flow of unit costs during the accounting period; therefore, each method tends to produce different results. The **periodic** and **perpetual inventory systems** are two different accounting approaches for applying the inventory costing methods to measure cost of goods sold and ending inventory. The periodic inventory system assumes **cost allocation at the end of the accounting period** (using one of the four inventory costing methods), while the perpetual inventory system assumes **cost allocation currently during the accounting period** (again, using one of the inventory costing methods). Because of these two different timing assumptions, the two systems tend to give different valuations of ending inventory and cost of goods sold under the weighted average, LIFO, and specific identification costing methods, but valuations are always the same under FIFO.

SELECTED INVENTORY PROBLEMS

The remaining discussions in this chapter relate to three issues that may directly affect the valuation of the ending inventory reported on the balance sheet and the amount of income reported on the income statement; they are (a) lower of cost or market (LCM) valuation, (b) damaged items, and (c) estimating the ending inventory.

Inventories at lower of cost or market (LCM)

We have emphasized that inventories should be measured at their unit purchase cost in accordance with the cost principle. However, when the goods remaining in the ending inventory can be replaced with identical goods at a lower cost, the lower unit cost should be used as the inventory valuation. This rule is known as measuring inventories on a **lower of cost or market (LCM) basis.** It is a departure from the cost principle in favor of conservatism (see Exhibit 2–6). The LCM basis recognizes a "holding" loss in the period in which the replacement cost of an item dropped, rather than in the period in which the item actually is sold. The holding loss is the difference between purchase cost and the subsequent lower replacement cost. To illustrate, assume that an office equipment dealer

EXHIBIT 7–7
Effect of inventory measurement at LCM

	Inventory measured at—	
	Cost (FIFO)	LCM
Sales revenue..............................	$41,500	$41,500
Cost of goods sold:		
Beginning inventory.....................	$ 5,000	$ 5,000
Add purchases	20,000	20,000
Goods available for sale	25,000	25,000
Less ending inventory (10 calculators):		
At purchase cost of $450	4,500	
At LCM of $400		4,000
Cost of goods sold	20,500	21,000
Gross margin on sales	21,000	20,500
Expenses	15,000	15,000
Pretax income	$ 6,000	$ 5,500

has 10 new electronic calculators remaining in the 19B ending inventory. The calculators were purchased for $450 each and were marked to sell at $499.95. At the date of the ending inventory, however, the same new calculators can be purchased for $400 and will be marked to sell for $429.95. The 10 calculators should be costed in the ending inventory at the lower of cost ($450) or current market ($400). The LCM basis costs the ending inventory at $400 per unit. There are several effects associated with using a replacement cost of $400 against using the original purchase cost of $450 for the 10 calculators included in the ending inventory. By costing them at $50 per unit below their purchase cost, 19B pretax income will be $500 (i.e., 10 × $50), less than it would have been had they been costed in the inventory at $450 per unit. This $500 loss in the economic value of the inventory (i.e., the holding loss) was due to a decline in the replacement cost. Because the loss is included in the cost of goods sold, 19B pretax income will be reduced by $500 in the period in which the replacement cost dropped (19B) rather than in the later period when the goods actually are sold. The $500 loss also reduces the amount of inventory that is reported on the 19B balance sheet. These effects are demonstrated in Exhibit 7–7. LCM usually is applied to all inventories on an item-by-item basis rather than on the aggregate inventory as a whole.[9]

Damaged and deteriorated goods

Merchandise on hand that is damaged, obsolete, or shopworn should not be measured and reported at original cost but at present **net realizable value** when it is below cost.

Net realizable value is the **estimated amount** that will be realized when the goods actually are sold in their deteriorated condition, less all repair and sale costs.

To illustrate net realizable value, assume a retail store has on hand two television

---

[9] In contrast, if the replacement cost had increased to, say, $500 each, there would have been a **holding gain** of 100 units × $50 = $500. Generally accepted accounting principles do not permit recognition of holding gains because revenue is recognized only at date of sale of the goods. Because of the unfavorable connotations, holding gains are called windfall profits in the political arena.

sets that have been used as demonstrators and cannot be sold as new sets (i.e., they are shopworn). When purchased, the sets cost $300 each. In the light of their present condition, realistic estimates are:

	Per set
Estimated sales price in present condition	$175
Estimated repair costs of $20 and sales costs of $15	35
Estimated net realizable value	$140

On the basis of these estimates, the two television sets would be included in the inventory at $140 each, rather than at the original cost of $300 each. Net realizable value is used, rather than cost, because it records the loss in the period in which it occurred rather than in the period of sale and does not overstate the asset.

If a **periodic** inventory system is used, the item is included in the ending inventory of **damaged goods** at its estimated net realizable value, and the loss is reflected in cost of goods sold. However, if a **perpetual** system is used, the following entry would be made:

Inventory of damaged goods (2 × $140)	280	
Loss on damaged goods (an expense) ($600 − $280)	320	
Inventory (2 × $300)		600

The perpetual inventory record also would be changed to reflect this entry.[10]

Estimating ending inventory and cost of goods sold

When a periodic **inventory system** is used, a physical inventory count must be taken to determine the amount of the ending inventory. Taking a physical inventory is a time-consuming task in many businesses. As a consequence, physical inventories may be taken only once a year. Nevertheless, managers often desire financial statements for internal use on a monthly or, at least, a quarterly basis. When a periodic inventory system is used, some businesses **estimate** the ending inventory for the monthly or quarterly financial statements rather than taking a physical inventory. The **gross margin method** is used for this purpose. The method uses an **estimated gross margin ratio** as the basis for the computation. The gross margin ratio is derived by dividing the gross margin amount by

---

[10] The subsequent entries may be as follows:

a. To record actual repair costs of $25:

Inventory of damaged goods	25	
Cash		25

b. To record sale of the two sets for $360 (less actual selling costs of $15):

Cash ($360 − $15)	345	
Selling expense	15	
Inventory ($280 + $25)		305
Gain on sale of damaged goods		55

net sales revenue. The gross margin method assumes that the **gross margin ratio** for the current period should be essentially the same as it was in the recent past. Therefore, the average gross margin ratio from one or more prior periods is used as an estimate of the ratio for the current period. This estimated ratio then can be used to compute **estimated amounts** for (1) gross margin on sales, (2) cost of goods sold, and (3) ending inventory.

To <u>illustrate</u> the gross margin method, assume Patz Company uses the periodic inventory system and is preparing **monthly** financial statements at January 31, 19D. The accounting records provide the sales revenue, beginning inventory, purchases, and expense amounts listed below.

PATZ COMPANY
Income Statement
For the Month Ended January 31, 19D

Sales revenue		$100,000*
Cost of goods sold:		
Beginning inventory	$15,000*	
Add purchases	65,000*	
Goods available for sale	80,000	
Less ending inventory	?	
Cost of goods sold		?
Gross margin on sales		?
Expenses		30,000*
Pretax income		$?

     * Provided by the accounts.

The amount of the ending inventory at the end of January is to be **estimated** rather than determined by physical count. Assume that the yearly net sales for 19C amounted to $1,000,000 and gross margin was $400,000; therefore, the actual gross margin ratio for 19C was $400,000 ÷ $1,000,000 = .40. Management has decided that this ratio is a realistic estimate for use during 19D. Using the .40 as our estimate for 19D, we can compute an **estimated** inventory valuation. The computational steps, in lettered sequence, are shown below to estimate the ending inventory for January and to complete the estimated income statement.

PATZ COMPANY
Income Statement
For the Month Ended January 31, 19D (estimated)

			Computations (sequence a, b, c)
Sales revenue		$100,000	Per accounts
Cost of goods sold:			
Beginning inventory	$15,000		Per accounts
Add purchases	65,000		Per accounts
Goods available for sale	80,000		
Less ending inventory	20,000		*c.* $ 80,000 − $60,000 = $20,000
Cost of goods sold		60,000	*b.* $100,000 − $40,000 = $60,000*
Gross margin on sales		40,000	*a.* $100,000 × .40 = $40,000
Expenses		30,000	Per accounts
Pretax income		$ 10,000	

     * Or alternatively, $100,000 × (1.00 − .40) = $60,000.

The balance sheet can be completed by reporting the $20,000 estimated ending inventory amount as a current asset.

The gross margin method (sometimes called gross profit method) has several other uses apart from making possible preparation of the monthly or quarterly financial statements without a physical count of the ending inventory. Auditors and accountants may use this method to test the reasonableness of the amount of the inventory determined by other means. If the current gross margin ratio has changed materially from the recent past, it may suggest an error in the ending inventory. The method also is used in the case of a casualty loss (i.e., when an inventory of goods is destroyed or stolen and its valuation must be estimated for settlement purposes with an insurance company).[11]

DEMONSTRATION CASE A

(Try to resolve the requirements before proceeding to the suggested solution that follows.)

This case focuses on the effects of an error in the amount of the ending inventory. It does not introduce any new accounting concepts or procedures.

Metal Products, Incorporated, has been operating for eight years as a distributor of a line of metal products. It is now the end of 19C, and for the first time the company will undergo an audit by an independent CPA. The company uses a **periodic** inventory system. The annual income statements, prepared by the company, were:

	For the year ended December 31	
	19C	19B
Sales revenue	$800,000	$750,000
Cost of goods sold:		
Beginning inventory	40,000	45,000
Add purchases	484,000	460,000
Goods available for sale	524,000	505,000
Less ending inventory	60,000	40,000
Cost of goods sold	464,000	465,000
Gross margin on sales	336,000	285,000
Operating expenses	306,000	275,000
Pretax income	30,000	10,000
Income tax expense (20%)	6,000	2,000
Net income	$ 24,000	$ 8,000

During the early stages of the audit, the independent CPA discovered that the ending inventory for 19B was understated by $15,000.

---

[11] Another method, known as the retail inventory method, is used widely to estimate the ending inventory by department stores. It is essentially the same as the gross margin method, but differs in detail. Discussion of it is deferred to more advanced courses.

Required:

a. Based on the above income statement amounts, compute the gross margin ratio on sales for each year. Do the results suggest an inventory error? Explain.
b. Reconstruct the two income statements on a correct basis.
c. Answer the following questions.
    (1) What are the correct gross margin ratios?
    (2) What effect did the $15,000 understatement of the ending inventory have on 19B pretax income? Explain.
    (3) What effect did the inventory error have on 19C pretax income? Explain.
    (4) How did the inventory error affect income tax expense?

Suggested solution

Requirement a. Gross margin ratios as reported:

$$19B: \$285,000 \div \$750,000 = .38$$
$$19C: \$336,000 \div \$800,000 = .42$$

The change in the gross margin ratio from .38 to .42 suggests the possibility of an inventory error in the absence of any other explanation.

Requirement b. Income statements corrected:

	For the year ended December 31	
	19C	*19B*
Sales revenue	$800,000	$750,000
Cost of goods sold:		
Beginning inventory	55,000*	45,000
Add purchases	484,000	460,000
Goods available for sale	539,000	505,000
Less ending inventory	60,000	55,000*
Cost of goods sold	479,000	450,000
Gross margin on sales	321,000	300,000
Operating expenses	306,000	275,000
Pretax income	15,000	25,000
Income tax expense (20%)	3,000	5,000
Net income	$ 12,000	$ 20,000

* Increased by $15,000.

Requirement c:

1. Correct gross margin ratios:

$$19B: \$300,000 \div \$750,000 = .400$$
$$19C: \$321,000 \div \$800,000 = .401$$

The inventory error of $15,000 was responsible for the difference in the gross margin ratios reflected in Requirement *(a)*. The error in the 19B ending inventory affected gross margin for both 19B and 19C, in the opposite direction, but by the same amount ($15,000).

2. Effect on pretax income in 19B: **Ending income understatement** ($15,000) caused an **understatement of pretax income** by the **same amount.**

3. Effect on pretax income in 19C: Beginning inventory **understatement** (by the same $15,000 since the inventory amount is carried over from the prior period) caused an **overstatement** of pretax income by the same amount.

4. Total income tax expense for 19B and 19C combined was the same ($8,000) regardless of the error. However, there was a shift of $3,000 ($15,000 × 20 percent) income tax expense from 19B to 19C.

> **Observation**—An ending inventory error in one year affects pretax ending income by the amount of the error and in the next year affects pretax income again by the same amount but in the opposite direction.

DEMONSTRATION CASE B

(Try to resolve the requirements before proceeding to the suggested solution that follows.)

This case presents the effects on ending inventory, cost of goods sold, and the related accounting entries of a **periodic** inventory system compared with a **perpetual** inventory system assuming the LIFO inventory costing method is applied in each system.

Balent Appliances distributes a number of high-cost household appliances. One product, microwave ovens, has been selected for case purposes. Assume the following summarized transactions were completed during the accounting period in the order given below (assume all transactions are cash).

		Units	Unit cost
a.	Beginning inventory	11	$200
b.	Sales (selling price $420)	8	?
c.	Sales returns (can be resold as new)	1	200
d.	Purchases	9	220
e.	Purchase returns (damaged in shipment)	1	220

Required:

a. Compute the following amounts assuming application of the LIFO inventory costing method:

	Ending inventory		Cost of goods sold	
	Units	Dollars	Units	Dollars
(1) Periodic inventory system (costed at end of period)	____	____	____	____
(2) Perpetual inventory system (costed during period)	____	____	____	____

b. Give the indicated journal entries for transactions *(b)* through *(e)* assuming:
   (1) Periodic inventory system.
   (2) Perpetual inventory system.

Suggested solution

Requirement a:

	Ending inventory		Cost of goods sold	
	Units	Dollars	Units	Dollars
1. Periodic inventory system (costed at end of the period)	12	$2,420	7	$1,540
2. Perpetual inventory system (costed during the period)	12	2,560	7	1,400

Computations:

Goods available for sale: (11 units @ $200 = $2,200) + (8 units @ $220 = $1,760) = $3,960.

1. Periodic LIFO inventory (costed at end):

Ending inventory: (11 units @ $200 = $2,200) + (1 unit @ $220 = $220) = $2,420.

Cost of goods sold: (Goods available, $3,960) − (Ending inventory, $2,420) = $1,540.

2. Perpetual LIFO inventory (costed during period):

Ending inventory: (8 units @ $220 = $1,760) + (4 units @ $200 = $800) = $2,560.

Cost of goods sold: 7 units @ $200 = $1,400.

Requirement b. Journal entries:

	1. Periodic Inventory System			2. Perpetual Inventory System		
b.	Sales:			Sales:		
	Cash (8 × $420)	3,360		Cash	3,360	
	Sales revenue		3,360	Sales revenue		3,360
				Cost of goods sold	1,600	
				Inventory (8 × $200) ..		1,600
c.	Sales returns:			Sales returns:		
	Sales returns	420		Sales returns	420	
	Cash (1 × $420) ..		420	Cash		420
				Inventory (1 × $200)	200	
				Cost of goods sold ...		200
d.	Purchases:			Purchases:		
	Purchases	1,980		Inventory	1,980	
	Cash (9 × $220) ..		1,980	Cash		1,980
e.	Purchase return:			Purchase return:		
	Cash	220		Cash	220	
	Purchase returns ..		220	Inventory		220

SUMMARY OF CHAPTER

This chapter focused on the problem of measuring cost of goods sold and ending inventory when unit costs change during the period. Inventory should include all the items remaining on hand for resale to which the entity has owner-ship. Costs flow into inventory when goods are purchased (or manufactured) and flow out (as expense) when the goods are sold or disposed of otherwise. When there are several unit cost amounts representing the inflow of goods for the period, a rational and systematic method must be used to allocate unit cost amounts to the units remaining in inventory and to the units sold (cost of goods sold). The chapter discussed and illustrated four different inventory costing meth-ods and their applications in both a perpetual inventory system and a periodic inventory system. The methods discussed were weighted-average cost, FIFO, LIFO, and specific identification. Each of the inventory costing methods is in accordance with generally accepted accounting principles. The selection of a method of inventory costing is particularly important because it will affect reported income, income tax expense (and hence cash flow), and the inventory valuation reported on the balance sheet. In a period of rising prices, FIFO gives a higher income than does LIFO; in a period of falling prices, the opposite result occurs.

Damaged, obsolete, and deteriorated items in inventory should be assigned a unit cost that represents their current estimated net realizable value. Also, the ending inventory of new items (not damaged, deteriorated, or obsolete) should be measured on the basis of the lower of actual cost or replacement cost (i.e., LCM basis).

This chapter explained another fundamental accounting principle (Exhibit 2–6) known as the comparability principle which holds that all accounting concepts, principles, and measurement approaches should be applied in a consistent manner from period to period.

IMPORTANT TERMS DEFINED IN THIS CHAPTER

Terms (alphabetically)	Key words in definitions of important terms used in chapter	Page reference
Comparability principle	Accounting methods should be consistently applied from one period to the next.	308
Consignments	Goods in possession of a seller but legal title is retained by the supplier.	298
Finished goods inventory	Manufactured goods that are completed and ready for sale.	297
First-in, first-out	Inventory costing method that assumes the oldest units are the first units sold.	303
Gross margin method	Method to estimate ending inventory based on the gross margin ratio.	317
Last-in, first-out	Inventory costing method that assumes the newest units are the first units sold.	304
Lower of cost or market	Departure from cost principle that serves to recognize a "holding" loss when replacement cost drops below cost.	315
Merchandise inventory	Goods held for resale in the ordinary course of business.	297
Moving weighted average	Weighted-average inventory costing method applied in the perpetual inventory system.	310
Net realizable value	Estimated amount to be realized when goods are sold, less repair and disposal costs.	316
Periodic inventory system	Ending inventory and cost of goods sold are determined at the end of the accounting period; a physical inventory count must be taken.	300

Terms (alphabetically)	Key words in definitions of important terms used in chapter	Page reference
Perpetual inventory system	A detailed daily inventory record is updated continuously during the accounting period; provides ending inventory and cost of goods sold.	300
Raw materials inventory	Items acquired for the purpose of processing into finished goods.	297
Specific identification	Inventory costing method that identifies the cost of the specific item that was sold.	305
Weighted average	Inventory costing method used with a periodic inventory system that averages all purchase costs to calculate a weighted-average unit cost on an annual basis.	302
Work in process inventory	Goods in the process of being manufactured that are not yet complete.	297

QUESTIONS FOR DISCUSSION

PART A

1. Assume the 19A ending inventory was understated by $100,000. Explain how this error would affect the 19A and 19B pretax income amounts. What would be the effects if the 19A ending inventory were overstated by $100,000 instead of understated?

2. Match the type of inventory with the type of business in the following matrix:

Type of Inventory	Type of Business	
	Trading	Manufacturing
Merchandise		
Finished goods		
Work in process		
Raw materials		

3. Why is inventory an important item to both internal management and external users of financial statements?

4. What are the general guidelines for deciding which items should be included in inventory?

5. In measuring cost of goods sold and inventory, why is passage of ownership an important issue? When does ownership to goods usually pass? Explain.

6. Identify the two parties to a consignment. Which party should include the goods on consignment in inventory? Explain.

7. Explain the application of the cost principle to an item in the ending inventory.

8. When a perpetual inventory system is used, unit costs of the items sold are known at the date of each sale. In contrast, when a periodic inventory system is used, unit costs

are known only at the end of the accounting period. Explain why these statements are correct.

9. The periodic inventory model is $BI + P - EI = CGS$, and the perpetual inventory model is $BI + P - CGS = EI$. Explain the significance of the difference between these two models.

10. The chapter discussed four inventory costing methods. List the four methods and briefly explain each.

11. The four inventory costing methods may be applied with either a periodic inventory system or a perpetual inventory system. Briefly explain how the methods are applied in each system.

12. Explain how income can be manipulated when the specific identification inventory costing method is used.

13. Contrast the effects of LIFO versus FIFO on reported assets (i.e., the ending inventory) when (a) prices are rising and (b) prices are falling.

14. Contrast the income statement effect of LIFO versus FIFO (i.e., on pretax income) when (a) prices are rising and (b) prices are falling.

15. Contrast the effects of LIFO versus FIFO on cash outflow and inflow.

PART B

16. What is the purpose of a perpetual inventory record? List the four main column headings and briefly explain the purpose of each.

17. When a perpetual inventory system is used, a **moving weighted average** is used. In contrast, when a periodic inventory system is used, an **annual weighted average** is used. Explain why the different averages are used.

18. The weighted-average inventory costing method usually produces different results when a perpetual inventory system is used rather than a periodic inventory system. Explain why.

19. Explain briefly application of the LCM concept to the ending inventory and its effect on the income statement and balance sheet when market is lower than cost.

20. When should net realizable value be used in costing an item in the ending inventory?

21. The chapter discussed the gross margin method to estimate inventories. Briefly explain this method and indicate why it is used.

22. Briefly explain the comparability principle. How might it relate to the inventory costing methods?

EXERCISES

PART A

E7–1. Handy Corporation prepared the two income statements given that follows (simplified for illustrative purposes):

	First quarter 19B		Second quarter 19B	
Sales revenue		$10,000		$13,000
Cost of goods sold:				
Beginning inventory	$ 2,000		$ 3,000	
Purchases	9,000		10,000	
Goods available for sale	11,000		13,000	
Ending inventory	3,000		4,000	
Cost of goods sold		8,000		9,000
Gross margin		2,000		4,000
Expenses		1,000		1,000
Pretax income		$ 1,000		$ 3,000

During the third quarter it was discovered that the ending inventory for the first quarter should have been $3,500.

Required:

a. What effect did this error have on the combined pretax income of the two quarters? Explain.
b. Did this error affect the EPS amounts for each quarter? Explain.
c. Prepare corrected income statements for each quarter.
d. Set up a schedule which reflects the comparative effects of the correct and incorrect amounts.

E7–2. Fashion Clothing Store purchased 100 new shirts and recorded a total cost of $2,940 determined as follows:

Invoice cost	$2,000
Less: Cash discount 2%	
Shipping charges	530
Import taxes and duties	110
Interest paid in advance (15%) on $2,000	
borrowed to finance the purchase	300
	$2,940

Give the journal entry(s) to record this purchase assuming a periodic inventory system. Show computations.

E7–3. The records at the end of January 19B for Newman Company showed the following for a particular kind of merchandise:

Transactions	Units	Total cost
Inventory, December 31, 19A	30	$390
Purchase, January 9, 19B	60	900
Sale, January 11, 19B (at $35 per unit)	50	
Purchase, January 20, 19B	35	490
Sale, January 27, 19B (at $36 per unit)	41	

Required:

Assuming a periodic inventory system, compute the amount of (1) goods available for sale, (2) ending inventory, and (3) cost of goods sold at January 31, 19B, under each of the following inventory costing methods (show computations and round to the nearest dollar):

     a. Weighted-average cost.

     b. First-in, first-out.

     c. Last-in, first-out.

     d. Specific identification (assume the sale on Janaury 11 was "identified" with the purchase of January 9, the sale of January 27 was "identified" with the purchase of January 20, and any excess identified with the beginning inventory).

E7–4. Dean Company uses a periodic inventory system. At the end of the annual accounting period, December 31, 19B, the accounting records provided the following information for Product Z:

Transaction	Units	Unit cost
1. Inventory, December 31, 19A	2,000	$20
For the year 19B:		
2. Purchase, April 11	2,000	22
3. Sale, May 1 (@ $50 each)	3,000	
4. Purchase, June 1	6,000	24
5. Sale, July 3 (@ $53 each)	4,000	
6. Operating expenses (excluding income tax expense), $140,000.		

Required:

     a. Prepare a separate income statement through pretax income that details cost of goods sold for:

          Case A—Annual weighted average.

          Case B—FIFO.

          Case C—LIFO.

          Case D—Specific identification assuming two thirds of the first sale was "selected" from the beginning inventory and one third was "selected" from the items purchased on April 11, 19B. The second sale was "selected" from the purchase of June 1, 19B.

          For each case, show the computation of the ending inventory. (Hint: Set up adjacent columns for each case.)

     b. For each case, compare the pretax income and the ending inventory amounts. Explain the similarities and differences.

E7–5. Use the data given in Exercise 7–3 for this exercise (assume cash transactions and a periodic inventory system).

Required:

     a. Compute (1) goods available for sale, (2) cost of goods sold, and (3) ending inventory for Case A—FIFO, and Case B—LIFO.

     b. In parallel columns, give the journal entries for each purchase and sale transaction, assuming a periodic inventory system is used for each case. Set up captions as follows:

	FIFO		LIFO	
Accounts	Debit	Credit	Debit	Credit

     c. Prepare an income statement through gross margin and explain why the FIFO and LIFO ending inventory, cost of goods sold, and gross margin amounts are different.

     d. Which inventory costing method may be preferred for income tax purposes? Explain.

E7–6. During January 19B, Nixon Company reported sales revenue of $400,000 for the one item stocked. The inventory for December 31, 19A, showed 7,500 units on hand with a cost of $165,000. During January 19B, two purchases of the item were made: the first was for 1,500 units at $24 per unit; and the second was for 7,600 units at $25 each. The periodic inventory count reflected 8,600 units remaining on hand on January 31, 19B. Total operating expense for the month was $84,900.

Required:

a. On the basis of the above information, complete the 19B summary income statements under FIFO and LIFO. Use a single list of side captions including computation of cost of goods sold. Set up three separate column headings as follows: Units, FIFO, and LIFO. Show your computations of the ending inventory.
b. Which method gives the higher pretax income? Why?
c. Which method gives the more favorable cash flow effects? By how much, assuming a 20 percent tax rate?

E7–7. King Company uses a periodic inventory system. Data for 19B were: beginning merchandise inventory (December 31, 19A), 1,600 units @ $15; purchases, 6,000 units @ $18; expenses (excluding income taxes), $51,800; ending inventory per physical count at December 31, 19B, 1,500 units; sales price per unit, $33; and average income tax rate of 20 percent.

Required:

a. Prepare income statements under the FIFO, LIFO, and weighted-average costing methods. Use a format similar to the following:

Income statement	Units	FIFO	LIFO	Weighted average
Sales revenue	____	$____	$____	$____
Cost of goods sold:				
Beginning inventory	____	____	____	____
Purchases	____	____	____	____
Goods available for sale	____	____	____	____
Ending inventory	____	____	____	____
Cost of goods sold	____	____	____	____
Gross margin	____	____	____	____
Expenses		____	____	____
Pretax income		____	____	____
Income tax expense		____	____	____
Net income		____	____	____

Inventory costing method

b. Comparing FIFO and LIFO, which method is preferable in terms of (1) net income and (2) cash flow? Explain.
c. What would be your answer to Requirement *(b)* assuming prices were falling? Explain.

E7–8. Following is partial information for the income statement of Prelim Company under three different inventory costing methods assuming a periodic inventory system:

	FIFO	LIFO	Weighted average
Unit sales price, $30.			
Cost of goods sold:			
Beginning inventory (480 units)	$ 9,600	$ 9,600	$ 9,600
Purchases (520 units)	13,000	13,000	13,000
Goods available for sale			
Ending inventory (530 units)			
Cost of goods sold			
Expenses, $1,500			

Required:

a. Compute cost of goods sold under the FIFO, LIFO, and weighted-average inventory costing methods.

b. Prepare an income statement through pretax income for each method.

c. Rank the three methods in order of favorable cash flow and explain the basis for your ranking.

PART B

E7–9. Eastern Company uses a perpetual inventory system and FIFO. The inventory records reflected the following for January 19B:

Transactions	Units	Unit cost
Beginning inventory, January 1	100	$1.00
Purchase, January 6	200	1.10
Sale, January 10 (at $2.40 per unit)	110	
Purchase, January 14	100	1.30
Sale, January 29 (at $2.60 per unit)	160	

Required:

a. Prepare the perpetual inventory record for January. See Exhibit 7–4 for an example of a perpetual inventory record.

b. Give journal entries indicated by the above data for January (assume cash transactions).

c. Prepare a summary income statement for January through gross margin.

E7–10. At the end of the accounting period, the inventory records of Cain Company reflected the following:

Transactions (in order of date)	Units	Unit cost
Beginning inventory	500	$10
1. Purchase No. 1	600	12
2. Sale No. 1 (@ $23 per unit).....	(700)	
3. Purchase No. 2	800	14
4. Sale No. 2 (@ $25 per unit).....	(500)	
Ending inventory	(700)	

Required:

a. Compute goods available for sale in units and dollars.

b. Compute the (1) ending inventory valuation and (2) cost of goods sold assuming a **periodic** inventory system under the LIFO inventory costing method.

c. For comparative purposes compute the (1) ending inventory valuation and (2) cost of goods sold assuming a **perpetual** inventory system under the LIFO inventory costing method. To do this prepare a perpetual inventory record and cost each sale when made. See Exhibit 7–4 for an example of a perpetual inventory record.

d. Compare the results of (b) and (c) and explain why the valuations of ending inventory and cost of goods sold are different as between the periodic and perpetual inventory systems.

E7–11. Use the data given in Exercise 7–3 for this exercise (assume cash transactions, a perpetual inventory system, and moving average cost).

Required:

a. Prepare the perpetual inventory record for January on a moving average basis. Round to the nearest cent on unit costs and the nearest dollar on total cost. See Exhibit 7–4 for an example of a perpetual inventory record.
b. Give the journal entry to record the purchase of January 9.
c. Give the journal entries to record the sale on January 11.
d. Prepare a summarized income statement through gross margin for January.
e. Explain why a moving average rather than a weighted average for the period was used.
f. When the average cost method is used, would the ending inventory and cost of goods sold amounts usually be different between periodic and perpetual inventory systems? Explain why.

E7–12. Garden Company uses a perpetual inventory system and applies FIFO inventory costing. The data below were provided by the accounting records for 19B:

Transactions (in order of date)	Units	Unit cost	Total cost
Beginning inventory	100	$10	$1,000
1. Purchase No. 1	300	12	3,600
2. Sale No. 1 (@ $21 each)	(200)		
3. Purchase No. 2	400	14	5,600
4. Sale No. 2 (@ $23 each)	(200)		
Ending inventory	400		

Required:

a. Compute the valuation of (1) cost of goods sold and (2) ending inventory assuming a perpetual inventory system and application of the FIFO inventory costing method.
b. Give the entries to record transactions 1 and 2 assuming FIFO:

Case A—A perpetual inventory system.
Case B—A periodic inventory system.

Use adjacent amount columns for each system and assume cash transactions.
c. Explain why the entries are different between the perpetual and periodic inventory systems.

E7–13. Contemporary Sound Company is preparing the annual financial statements at December 31, 19D. Two different types of tape recorders that were used as demonstrators remained on hand at year-end. These items will be sold as damaged (used) merchandise; therefore, they must be removed from the ending inventory of new merchandise. The company uses a perpetual inventory system. These items will be included in the inventory of damaged goods. Data on the tape recorder models are:

	Model 2–206	Model 112A
Quantity damaged	1	2
Actual unit cost	$400	$300
Regular sales price	700	500
Estimated unit market value in present condition	380	250
Estimated unit cost to sell	60	35

Required

a. Compute the valuation of each item that should be used for 19D inventory purposes. Show computations.
b. Give the required entry(s) to reflect the appropriate inventory valuations in the accounts.

E7–14. Arthur Company is preparing the annual financial statements dated December 31, 19B. Ending inventory information about the five major items stocked for regular sale is:

Ending inventory, 19B

Item	Quantity on hand	Unit cost when acquired (FIFO)	Replacement cost (market) at year-end
A......	50	$20	$18
B......	100	45	45
C......	20	60	62
D......	40	40	40
E......	1,000	10	8

Required:

a. Compute the valuation that should be used for the 19B ending inventory using the LCM rule applied on an item-by-item basis. (Hint: Set up columns for Item, Quantity, Total Cost, Total Market, and LCM Valuation.

b. Compute the valuation of ending inventory using the LCM rule applied to total cost and total market value of the inventory.

c. Which method (a) or (b) is preferable? Why?

E7–15. Rocky Retail Company prepares annual financial statements each December 31. The company uses a periodic inventory system. This system requires an annual detailed inventory count of all items on the store shelves and items stored in a separate warehouse. However, the management also desires quarterly financial statements but will not take a physical inventory count four times during the year. Accordingly, they use the gross margin method to estimate the ending inventory for the first three quarters.

At the end of the first quarter, March 31, 19D, the accounting records provided the following information:

1.	Beginning inventory, January 1, 19D	$ 60,000
Data for the first quarter of 19D:		
2.	Sales revenue	305,000
3.	Return sales	5,000
4.	Purchases...	196,000
5.	Freight-in	4,000
6.	Operating expenses (excluding income tax expense).....	50,000
7.	Estimated average income tax rate, 20%.	
8.	Estimated gross margin ratio, 40%.	

Required:

Based on the above information prepare a detailed income statement for the first quarter of 19D. Show all computations.

E7–16. On November 2, 19C, a fire destroyed the inventory of Dixon Retail Store. The accounting records were not destroyed; therefore, they provided the following information:

	19A	19B	19C to date of fire
Sales revenue	$120,000	$142,000	$120,000
Cost of goods sold	73,200	85,200	?
Gross margin on sales.....	46,800	56,800	?
Expenses	34,800	42,800	37,000
Pretax income	$ 12,000	$ 14,000	?
Ending inventory	$ 20,000	$ 22,000	?
Purchases during year.....	70,000	87,200	68,000

Required:

a. Based on the data available, prepare an estimated income statement for 19C up to the date of the fire. Show details for the cost of goods sold. Disregard income taxes and show computations.

b. What amount of loss on the inventory should be submitted to the insurance company (a casualty loss insurance policy is in effect)? Write a brief statement in support of the amount of indemnity claimed.

PROBLEMS/CASES

PART A

PC7–1. The income statement for Mellon Company summarized for a four-year period shows the following:

	19A	19B	19C	19D
Sales revenue	$1,000,000	$1,200,000	$1,300,000	$1,100,000
Cost of goods sold	600,000	610,000	870,000	650,000
Gross margin	400,000	590,000	430,000	450,000
Expenses	300,000	328,000	362,000	317,000
Pretax income	100,000	262,000	68,000	133,000
Income tax expense (30%)	30,000	78,600	20,400	39,900
Net income	$ 70,000	$ 183,400	$ 47,600	$ 93,100

An audit revealed that in determining the above amounts, the ending inventory for 19B was overstated by $50,000. The company uses a periodic inventory system.

Required:

a. Recast the above income statements on a correct basis.
b. Did the error affect cumulative net income for the four-year period? Explain.
c. Did the error affect cash inflows or outflows? Explain.

PC7–2. Arch Company has just completed a physical inventory count at year-end, December 31, 19B. Only the items on the shelves, in storage, and in the receiving area were counted and costed on a FIFO basis. The inventory amounted to $90,000. During the audit, the independent CPA developed the following additional information:

a. Goods costing $400 were being used by a customer on a trial basis and were excluded from the inventory count at December 31, 19B.

b. Goods in transit on December 31, 19B, from a supplier, with terms FOB destination, cost, $700. Because these goods had not arrived, they were excluded from the physical inventory count.

c. On December 31, 19B, goods in transit to customers, with terms FOB shipping point, amounted to $900 (expected delivery date January 10, 19C). Because the goods had been shipped, they were excluded from the physical inventory count.

d. On December 28, 19B, a customer purchased goods for cash amounting to $1,500 and left them "for pickup on January 3, 19C." Arch Company had paid $800 for the goods and, because they were on hand, included the latter amount in the physical inventory count.

e. Arch Company, on the date of the inventory, received notice from a supplier that goods ordered earlier, at a cost of $2,400, had been delivered to the transportation company on December 27, 19B; the terms were FOB shipping point. Because the shipment had not arrived by December 31, 19B, it was excluded from the physical inventory.

f. On December 31, 19B, Arch Company shipped $750 worth of goods to a customer, FOB destination. The goods are expected to arrive at their destination no earlier than January 8, 19C. Because the goods were not on hand, they were not included in the physical inventory count.

g. One of the items sold by Arch Company has such a low volume that the management planned to drop it last year. In order to induce Arch Company to continue carrying the item, the manufacturer-supplier provided the item on a consignment basis. At the end of each month, Arch Company (the consignee) renders a report to the manufacturer on the number sold and remits cash for the cost. At the end of December 19B, Arch Company had five of these items on hand; therefore, they were included in the physical inventory count at $2,000 each.

Required:

Begin with the $90,000 inventory amount and compute the correct amount for the ending inventory. Explain the basis for your treatment of each of the above items. (Hint: The correct amount is $82,750. Set up three columns: Item, Amount, and Explanation.)

PC7–3. Wyman Company uses a periodic inventory system. At the end of the annual accounting period, December 31, 19E, the accounting records for the most popular item in inventory showed:

Transaction	Units	Unit cost
Beginning inventory, January 1, 19E	300	$20
Transactions during 19E:		
1. Purchase, February 20	500	22
2. Sale, April 1 (@ $40 each)	(600)	
3. Purchase, June 30	400	24
4. Sale, August 1 (@ $42 each)	(200)	
5. Return sale, August 5, (related to transaction 4)	10	

Required:

Compute the amount of (1) goods available for sale, (2) ending inventory, and (3) cost of goods sold at December 31, 19E, under each of the following inventory costing methods (show computations and round to the nearest dollar):

a. Weighted-average cost.
b. First-in, first-out.
c. Last-in, first-out.
d. Specific identification, assuming the April 1, 19E, sale was "selected" one third from the beginning inventory and two thirds from the purchase of February 20, 19E. Assume the sale of August 1, 19E, was "selected" from the purchase of June 30, 19E.

PC7–4. At the end of January 19B, the records at Chicago Company showed the following for a particular item that sold at $20 per unit:

Transactions	Units	Amount
Inventory, January 1, 19B	500	$3,000
Sale, January 10	(400)	
Purchase, January 12	600	4,200
Sale, January 17	(550)	
Purchase, January 26	310	2,790
Purchase return, January 28	(10)	Out of Jan. 26 purchase

Required:

a. Assuming a periodic inventory system, prepare a summarized income statement through gross margin on sales under each method of inventory: (1) weighted-average cost, (2) FIFO, (3) LIFO, and (4) specific identification. For specific identification, assume the first sale was out of the beginning inventory and the second sale was out of the January 12 purchase. Show the inventory computations in detail.

b. Between FIFO and LIFO, which method will derive the higher pretax income? Which would derive the higher EPS?

c. Between FIFO and LIFO, which method will derive the lower income tax expense? Explain, assuming a 20 percent average tax rate.

d. Between FIFO and LIFO, which method will produce the more favorable cash flow? Explain.

PC7–5. Speculative Company sells large computers that it acquires from a foreign source. During the year 19W, the inventory records reflected the following:

	Units	Unit cost	Total cost
Beginning inventory	10	$25,000	$250,000
Purchases	30	20,000	600,000
Sales (35 units @ $45,000).			

The company uses the LIFO inventory costing method. On December 28, 19W, the unit cost of the computer was decreased to $18,000. The cost will be decreased again during the first quarter of the next year.

Required:

a. Complete the following income statement summary using the LIFO method and the periodic inventory system (show computations):

Sales revenue	$ _____
Cost of goods sold	_____
Gross margin	_____
Expenses	400,000
Pretax income	$ _____
Ending inventory	$ _____

b. The management, for various reasons, is considering buying 20 additional units before December 31, 19W, at $18,000 each. Restate the above income statement (and ending inventory) assuming this purchase is made on December 31, 19W.

c. How much did pretax income change because of the decision on December 31, 19W? Is there any evidence of income manipulation? Explain.

PC7–6. Big Top Corporation reported the following summarized annual data at the end of 19X:

	(millions)
Sales revenue	$950
Cost of goods sold*	540
Gross margin	410
Expenses	200
Pretax income	$210

* Based on ending FIFO inventory of $150 million. On a LIFO basis this ending inventory would have been $80 million.

Before issuing the preceding statement the company decided to change from FIFO to LIFO for 19X because "it better reflects our operating results." The company has always used FIFO.

Required:

a. Restate the summary income statement on a LIFO basis.
b. How much did pretax income change due to the LIFO decision for 19X? What caused the change in pretax income?
c. If you were a shareholder, what would be your reaction to this change? Explain.

PC7–7. This case demonstrates the effect on income of (a) rising prices and (b) falling prices in comparing FIFO with LIFO. Income is to be evaluated under four different situations as follows:

Prices are rising:
  Situation A—FIFO is used.
  Situation B—LIFO is used.
Prices are falling:
  Situation C—FIFO is used.
  Situation D—LIFO is used.

The basic data common to all four situations are sales, 600 units for $5,600; beginning inventory, 500 units; purchases, 500 units; ending inventory, 400 units; and operating expenses, $3,000. The following tabulated income statements for each situation have been set up for analytical purposes:

	Prices rising		Prices falling	
	Situation A FIFO	Situation B LIFO	Situation C FIFO	Situation D LIFO
Sales revenue..................	$5,600	$5,600	$5,600	$5,600
Cost of goods sold:				
Beginning inventory.............	1,000	?	?	?
Purchases.....................	1,500	?	?	?
Goods available for sale	2,500	?	?	?
Ending inventory	1,200	?	?	?
Cost of goods sold	1,300	?	?	?
Gross margin	4,300	?	?	?
Expenses......................	3,000	3,000	3,000	3,000
Pretax income	1,300	?	?	?
Income tax expense (20%)	260	?	?	?
Net income	$1,040	?	?	?

Required:

a. Complete the above tabulation for each situation. In Situations A and B (prices rising), assume the following: beginning inventory, 500 units @ $2 = $1,000; and purchases, 500 units @ $3 = $1,500. In Situations C and D (prices falling), assume the opposite; that is, beginning inventory, 500 units @ $3 = $1,500; and purchases, 500 units @ $2 = $1,000. Use periodic inventory procedures.
b. Analyze the relative effects on pretax income and on net income as demonstrated by Requirement (a) when prices are rising and when prices are falling.
c. Analyze the relative effects on the cash position for each situation.
d. Would you recommend FIFO or LIFO? Explain.

PART B

PC7–8. The income statements for four consecutive years for Clean Company reflected the following summarized amounts:

	19A	19B	19C	19D
Sales revenue	$60,000	$70,000	$80,000	$65,000
Cost of goods sold	36,000	38,300	50,100	39,000
Gross margin	24,000	31,700	29,900	26,000
Expenses	15,000	16,700	19,100	15,800
Pretax income	$ 9,000	$15,000	$10,800	$10,200

Subsequent to development of the above amounts, it has been determined that the physical inventory taken on December 31, 19B, was overstated by $4,000.

Required:

a. Recast the above income statements to reflect the correct amounts, taking into consideration the inventory error.
b. Compute the gross margin ratio for each year (1) before the correction and (2) after the correction. Do the results lend confidence to your corrected amounts? Explain.
c. What effect would the error have had on the income tax expense assuming a 20 percent average rate?

PC7–9. Michigan Company has completed taking the periodic inventory count of merchandise remaining on hand at the end of the fiscal year, December 31, 19D. Questions have arisen concerning inventory costing for five different items. The inventory reflected the following:

	Units	Original unit cost
Item A—The two units on hand are damaged because they were used as demonstrators. The company estimated that they may be sold at 20 percent below cost and that disposal costs will amount to $60 each.	2	$260
Item B—Because of a drop in the market, this item can be replaced from the original supplier at 10 percent below the original cost. The sale price also was reduced.	20	70
Item C—Because of style change, it is highly doubtful that the four units can be sold; they have no scrap value.	4	20
Item D—This item no longer will be stocked; as a consequence it will be marked down from the regular sale price of $110 to $50. Cost of selling is estimated to be 20 percent of the original cost.	3	80
Item E—Because of high demand and quality, the cost of this item has been raised from $120 to $144; hence, all replacements for inventory in the foreseeable future will be at the latter price.	15	120

The remaining items in inventory pose no valuation problems: their costs sum to $50,000.

Required:

Compute the total amount of the ending inventory including the damaged goods. List each of the above items separately and explain the basis for your decision with respect to each item.

PC7–10. Pepper Hardware Store uses a perpetual inventory system. This problem will focus on one item stocked, designated as Item A. The beginning inventory was 2,000 units @ $4. During January, the following transactions occurred that affected Item A:

Jan. 5 Sold 500 units at $10 per unit.
       10 Purchased 1,000 units at $5 per unit.
       16 Sold 1,800 units at $10 per unit.
       18 Purchased 2,300 units for $13,800.
       24 Sold 600 units at $12 per unit.

Required (assume cash transactions):

a. Prepare a perpetual inventory record for January on (1) a FIFO basis and (2) a LIFO basis.
b. Give the entry for each basis for the purchase on January 10.
c. Give the entries for each basis for the sale on January 16.
d. Complete the following financial statement amounts for each basis:

		January	
		FIFO	LIFO
Income statement:			
	Sales revenue	$?	$?
	Cost of goods sold	?	?
	Gross margin	?	?
	Expenses	12,000	12,000
	Pretax income	?	?
Balance sheet:			
	Current assets:		
	Merchandise inventory	?	?

e. Which method derives the higher pretax income? Under what conditions would this comparative effect be the opposite?
f. Assuming a 20 percent average tax rate, which method would provide the more favorable cash position? By how much? Explain.
g. Which basis would you recommend for Pepper? Why?

PC7–11. Carbo Company uses a perpetual inventory system. Below is a perpetual inventory record for the period for one product sold at $6 per unit.

PERPETUAL INVENTORY RECORD

Date								
a.						400		1,200
b.	800	3.30				12,000		
c.				500	1,600	700		2,240
d.	300		1,050					3,290
e.				200		800		2,632
f.				300	987	500		
g.	100	3.65				600		

Required:

1. Complete the column captions for the perpetual inventory record.
2. What inventory costing method is being used?
3. Enter all of the missing amounts on the perpetual inventory record.
4. Complete the following tabulation:

		Units	Per unit	Amount
a.	Beginning inventory	_____	_____	_____
b.	Ending inventory	_____	_____	_____
c.	Total purchases	_____	_____	_____
d.	Total cost of goods sold	_____	_____	_____

5. Give the entry(s) for date *(b)*.
6. Give the entry(s) for date *(c)*.
7. Complete the following tabulation:

	Assumption	Cost of goods sold	Ending inventory
a.	FIFO	_____	_____
b.	LIFO (end of period)	_____	_____
c.	Annual weighted average (for the period)	_____	_____

8. Assume a periodic inventory taken at the end of the period reflected 590 units on hand. Give any entry(s) required. (Disregard Requirement 7.)
9. Disregard Requirements 7 and 8 and assume that on date *(h)* 10 units of the beginning inventory were returned to the supplier and a cash refund of $2.90 per unit was recovered. Give the required entry.

PC7–12. Kent Company executives are considering their inventory policies. They have been using the moving average method with a perpetual inventory system. They have requested an "analysis of the effects of using FIFO versus LIFO." Selected financial statement amounts (rounded) for the month of January 19B based upon the moving average method are as follows:

	Units	Amounts
Income statement:		
Sales revenue	180	$10,600
Cost of goods sold	180	5,710
Gross margin on sales		4,890
Less: Expenses		1,700
Pretax income		$3,190
Balance sheet:		
Merchandise inventory		$2,620

Transactions during the month were:

Beginning inventory 50 units @ $30.

Jan. 6 Sold 40 units @ $55.
    9 Purchased 100 units @ $32.
    16 Sold 80 units @ $60.
    20 Purchased 110 units @ $33.
    28 Sold 60 units @ $60.

Required:

a. Copy the above statement data and extend each item to the right by adding columns for FIFO and LIFO (costed currently) using perpetual inventory system. This statement will provide one basis for analyzing the different results among the three inventory costing methods.
b. Which inventory costing method produces the highest pretax income? Explain.
c. Between FIFO and LIFO, which inventory costing method provides the more favorable cash position for 19B? Explain.

PC7–13. Vista Company prepared their annual financial statements dated December 31, 19B. The company uses a periodic inventory system and applies the FIFO inventory costing method; however, the company neglected to apply LCM to the ending inventory. The preliminary 19B income statement is summarized below:

Sales revenue		$310,000
Cost of goods sold:		
Beginning inventory	$ 40,000	
Purchases	206,000	
Goods available for sale	246,000	
Ending inventory (FIFO cost)	50,000	
Cost of goods sold		196,000
Gross margin		114,000
Operating expenses		58,000
Pretax income		56,000
Income tax expense (25%)		14,000
Net income		$42,000

Assume you have been asked to restate the 19B financial statements to incorporate LCM. You have developed the following data relating to the 19B ending inventory:

				Current replacement
		Acquisition cost		*unit cost*
Item	*Quantity*	*Unit*	*Total*	*(market)*
A	2,000	$ 2	$ 4,000	$ 2
B	3,000	6	18,000	5
C	4,000	4	16,000	5
D	1,000	12	12,000	10
			$50,000	

Required:

a. Restate the above income statement to reflect LCM valuation of the 19B ending inventory. Apply LCM on an item-by-item basis and show computations.
b. Compare and explain the LCM effect on each amount that was changed in (a).
c. What is the conceptual basis for applying LCM to merchandise inventories?
d. Thought question: What effect did LCM have on the cash flow of 19B? What will be the long-term effect on cash flow?

PC7–14. On April 15, 19B, Lowlands Company suffered a major flood that damaged their entire merchandise inventory. Fortunately, Lowlands carried a casualty insurance policy that covered floods. The accounting records were not damaged; therefore, they provided the following information for the period January 1 through April 14, 19B:

Merchandise inventory, December 31, 19A	$ 21,000
Transactions through April 14, 19B:	
Purchases	70,000
Purchase returns	2,000
Freight-in	1,000
Sales	103,000
Sales returns	3,000

Required:

For insurance indemnity purposes you have been asked to estimate the amount of the inventory loss. Your analysis to date indicates that (a) a 35 percent gross margin rate is reasonable and (b) the damaged merchandise can be sold to a local salvage company for approximately $2,000 cash.

What amount should be presented to the insurance company as a claim for insurance indemnity? Show computations.

PC7–15. The president of ET Company has been presented with the March 19B financial statements. They reflect data for three months as summarized below:

Income statements

	January	February	March	Quarter
Sales revenue	$100,000	$106,000	$90,000	$296,000
Cost of goods sold	61,000	59,360	?	?
Gross margin on sales.....	39,000	46,640	?	?
Expenses	32,000	33,500	32,000	97,500
Pretax income	$ 7,000	$ 13,140	$?	$?
Gross margin ratio	.39	.44	.40 (estimated)	
Ending inventory	$ 14,000	$ 16,000		

The company uses a periodic inventory system. Although monthly statements are prepared, a monthly inventory count is not made. Instead, the company uses the gross margin method for monthly inventory purposes.

Required:

a. Complete computations in the following tabulation to estimate the results for March.

	Amounts	*Computations*
Cost of goods sold:		
Beginning inventory	$16,000	From records
Purchases	51,000	From records
Goods available for sale	?	?
Ending inventory	?	?
Cost of goods sold	?	

b. Complete the income statements given above (March and Quarter). Disregard income tax.
c. What level of confidence do you think can be attributed to the results for March? Explain.
d. Would you recommend continued use of the method for the company? Explain.

PC7–16. The 1981 annual report of Standard Oil Company (Indiana) contained the following footnote:

During both 1981 and 1980, the company reduced certain inventory quantities which were valued at lower LIFO costs prevailing in prior years. The effect of these reductions was to increase aftertax earnings by $71 million, or $.24 per share, and $74 million, or $.25 per share, in 1981 and 1980, respectively.

Required:

a. Explain why the reduction in inventory quantity increased aftertax earnings (net income) for Standard Oil.

b. If Standard Oil had used FIFO, would the reductions in inventory quantity in 1980 and 1981 have increased aftertax earnings? Explain.

PC7–17. Several years ago, the financial statements of Lafayette Radio Electronics Corporation contained the following footnote:

> Subsequent to the issuance of its financial statements, the company discovered a computational error in the amount of $1,046,000 in the calculation of its year-end inventory which resulted in an overstatement of ending inventory.

Assume that Lafayette reported an incorrect net income amount of $3,101,000 for the year in which the error occurred and that the income tax rate is 40 percent.

Required:

a. Compute the amount of net income that Lafayette should report after correcting the inventory error. Show computations.

b. Assume that the inventory error had not been discovered. Identify the financial statement accounts that would have been incorrect for the year the error occurred and for the subsequent year. State whether each account was understated or overstated.

PC7–18. The 1981 annual report for General Motors Corporation included the following footnote:

> Inventories are stated generally at cost, which is not in excess of market. The cost of substantially all domestic inventories was determined by the last-in, first-out (LIFO) method. If the first-in, first-out (FIFO) method of inventory valuation had been used by the Corporation for U.S. inventories, it is estimated they would be $2,077.1 million higher at December 31, 1981, compared with $1,784.5 million higher at December 31, 1980.

In 1981, GM reported net income (after taxes) of $320.5 million. On December 31, 1981, the balance of the GM retained earnings account was $15,340 million.

Required:

a. Determine the amount of net income that GM would have reported in 1981 if the FIFO method had been used (assume a 48 percent tax rate).

b. Determine the amount of retained earnings that GM would have reported on December 31, 1981, if the FIFO method had always been used (assume a 48 percent tax rate).

c. Use of the LIFO method reduced the amount of taxes that GM had to pay for 1981 compared with the amount that would have been paid if FIFO had been used. Calculate the amount of this reduction (assume a 48 percent tax rate).

PC7–19. Refer to the financial statements of Johnson & Johnson given in Special Supplement B immediately preceding the Index. Respond to the following questions:

1. What inventory costing method was used by Johnson & Johnson?
2. The total amount of inventories at the end of 1982 was $957.5. Determine the following inventory amounts: *(a)* raw materials and supplies, *(b)* goods in process, and *(c)* finished goods.
3. If all inventories had been costed under FIFO, what amount of total inventories would have been reported on the 1982 balance sheet?
4. If all inventories had been costed under FIFO, what amount of earnings before taxes and extraordinary items would have been reported on the 1982 income statement?
5. What is the "current cost" of the inventory on the 1982 balance sheet?

C·H·A·P·T·E·R 8

Cash, Short-Term Investments in Securities, and Receivables

PURPOSE OF THIS CHAPTER

This chapter discusses the measurement and reporting of a group of assets known as **liquid assets:** cash, short-term investments in securities, and receivables. They are designated as liquid assets because of a primary characteristic: they are either cash or close to conversion to cash. Thus, they meet the definition of a current asset.

To explain the features and accounting problems peculiar to liquid assets, this chapter is divided into three parts as follows:

Part A—Safeguarding and reporting cash

Part B—Measuring and reporting short-term investments

Part C—Measuring and reporting receivables

This chapter also includes the following Supplements:

Supplement 8A—Petty cash

Supplement 8B—Special journals

PART A—SAFEGUARDING AND REPORTING CASH

CASH DEFINED

Cash is defined as money and any instrument that banks normally will accept for deposit and immediate credit to the depositor's account, such as a check, money order, or bank draft. Following this definition, cash **excludes** such items as notes receivable, IOUs, and postage stamps (a prepaid expense). Cash usually is divided into three categories: cash on hand, cash deposited in banks, and other instruments that meet the definition of cash. It is not unusual for a business to have several bank accounts. Even though a separate cash account may be maintained for each bank account, all cash accounts are combined as one amount for financial reporting purposes.

Because cash is the most liquid asset and is received and used continuously, it imposes heavy responsibilities on the management of an entity. These cash management responsibilities may be summarized as follows:

1. Safeguarding to prevent theft, fraud, loss through miscounting, and so on.
2. Accurate accounting so that relevant reports of cash inflows, outflows, and balances may be prepared periodically.
3. Control to assure that a sufficient amount of cash is on hand to meet *(a)* current operating needs, *(b)* maturing liabilities, and *(c)* unexpected emergencies.
4. Planning to prevent excess amounts of idle cash from accumulating. Idle cash produces no revenue; therefore, it often is invested in securities to derive a return (i.e., revenue) pending future need for the cash.

INTERNAL CONTROL OF CASH

Internal control refers to those policies and procedures of an entity designed primarily to safeguard all of the **assets** of the enterprise. Internal control procedures should extend to all assets: cash, receivables, investments, operational assets, and so on. An important phase of internal control focuses on cash. Effective internal control of cash normally should include:

Separation of functions and routines:

1. Complete separation of the **functions** of receiving cash from disbursing cash.
2. Complete separation of the **procedures** for cash receipts from cash disbursements.
3. Complete separation of *(a)* the **physical** handling of cash from *(b)* all phases of the **accounting** function.
4. Require that all cash receipts be deposited in a bank daily. Keep any cash held on hand (for making change) under strict control.
5. Require that all cash payments be made by prenumbered checks with a separate approval of the expenditures and separate approval of the checks in payment.

Responsibilities assigned to individuals:

6. Assign the cash receiving and cash paying responsibilities to different individuals.
7. Assign the cash handling and cash recordkeeping responsibilities to different individuals.
8. Assign the cash payment approval and check signing responsibilities to different individuals.
9. Assign responsibilities for the cash function and the accounting function to different individuals.

The separation of individual responsibilities and the use of prescribed policies and procedures are particularly important phases in the control of cash. A clear-cut separation of duties and responsibilities among persons would deter theft because collusion would be required among two or more persons to steal cash and then conceal the theft in the accounting records. Prescribed procedures are designed so that the work done by one individual automatically is checked by the results reported by other individuals.

To indicate how easy it is to conceal cash theft when internal control is lacking, two examples are provided:

Example 1—An employee handles both cash receipts and the recordkeeping. Cash amounting to $100 was collected from J. Doe in payment of an account receivable. An employee pocketed the cash and made an entry for $100 crediting Accounts Receivable (J. Doe) and debiting Allowance for Doubtful Accounts.

Example 2—Occasionally an employee with cash payment authority would send a fictitious purchase invoice through the system. The check, payable to a fictitious person, was not mailed, but instead was cashed by the employee.

In each example, the accounting records would not reveal the theft, and the financial statements would not provide any evidence that theft had occurred. The theft in Example 2 could have been prevented with simple internal control procedures.

All cash disbursements should be made with prenumbered checks. Ideally for cash payments there should be separate routines and responsibilities specified for (1) payment approvals, (2) check preparation, and (3) check signing. When procedures similar to these are followed, it is difficult to conceal a fraudulent cash disbursement without the collusion of two or more persons. The level of internal control, which is subject to close scrutiny by the outside independent auditor, increases the reliability that users can accord the financial statements of the business.

BANK STATEMENTS TO DEPOSITORS

When a depositor opens a bank account, a **signature card** must be completed that lists the names and signatures of persons authorized to sign checks drawn against the account. When a deposit is to be made, the depositor must fill out a **deposit slip** that includes the name of the account, the account number, and a listing of the coins, currency, and checks deposited. In recent years, most banks have converted almost exclusively to personalized checks; that is, the name, address, and bank account number of the depositor are preprinted on each check. Obviously, the use of personalized checks is an important safety feature for all parties concerned.

Each month, the bank provides the depositor with a **bank statement** that lists (1) each deposit recorded by the bank during the period, (2) each check cleared by the bank during the period, and (3) a running balance of the depositor's account. The bank statement also will reflect any bank charges or deductions (such as service charges) made directly to the depositor's account by the bank. Also included with the bank statement are copies of the deposit slips and all checks that cleared through the bank during the period covered by the statement. A typical bank statement (excluding the deposit slips and canceled checks) is shown in Exhibit 8–1.

Exhibit 8–1 lists three items that need explanation. First, observe that on June 20, listed under "Checks and Debits," is a deduction for $18 coded with "NC."[1] This code indicates an "NSF check charge" (in slang, a "hot" or "rubber" check); NSF stands for Not Sufficient Funds. A check for $18 was received from a customer, R. Roe, which then was deposited by J. Doe Company with its bank, the Texas Commerce Bank. The Bank processed the check through banking channels to Roe's bank. Roe's account did not have sufficient funds to cover it; therefore, Roe's bank returned it to the Texas Commerce Bank which then charged it back to J. Doe Company. The NSF check is now a receivable; consequently, J. Doe Company must make an entry debiting Receivables (R. Roe) and crediting Cash for the $18.

The second item on Exhibit 8–1 that requires explanation is the $6 listed on June 30 under "Checks and Debits" and coded "SC." This is the code for **bank service charges.** The bank statement included a memo by the bank explaining this service charge (which was not supported by a check). J. Doe Company must make an entry to reflect this $6 decrease in the bank balance as a debit to an appropriate expense account, such as Bank Service Expense, and a credit to Cash.

The third item that needs explanation is the $100 listed on June 12 under "Deposits" and coded "CM" for "credit memo." J. Doe Company had asked the bank to collect a note receivable held by Doe that had been received from a customer. The bank collected the note and increased the depositor account of J. Doe Company. The bank service charge (SC) included the collection service cost. J. Doe Company must record the collection by making an entry to debit Cash and credit Note Receivable for the $100.

---

[1] These codes vary among banks.

EXHIBIT 8–1 **Example of a bank statement**

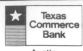

Texas Commerce Bank
Austin
NATIONAL ASSOCIATION

7TH & LAVACA
AUSTIN, TEXAS 78789
PHONE: 512/476-6611

ACCOUNT NUMBER	STATEMENT DATE	PAGE NO.
877–95861	6–30–84	1

J. Doe Company
1000 Blank Road
Austin, Texas 78703

STATEMENT OF ACCOUNT

Please examine statement and checks promptly. If no error is reported within ten days, the account will be considered correct. Please report change of address.
For questions or problems call TCB-Austin's Hotline - 476-6100

ON THIS DATE	YOUR BALANCE WAS	DEPOSITS ADDED		CHECKS AND DEBITS SUBTRACTED		SERVICE COST	RESULTING BALANCE
		NO.	AMOUNT	NO.	AMOUNT		
6-1-84	7 562 40	5	4 050 00	23	3 490 20	6 00	122 20

CHECKS AND DEBITS			DEPOSITS	DATE	DAILY BALANCE
			3 000 00	6-1-84	7 562 40
				6-2-84	10 562 40
500 00				6-4-84	10 062 40
55 00	5 00	40 00		6-5-84	9 962 40
100 00			500 00	6-8-84	10 362 40
8 20	16 50	160 00		6-10-84	10 177 70
2 150 00	10 00		*100 00CM	6-12-84	8 117 70
7 50	15 30			6-16-84	8 094 90
35 00	1 50		150 00	6-17-84	8 208 40
40 20	15 00	6 00		6-18-84	8 147 20
*18 00NC				6-20-84	8 129 20
125 50	80 00	2 00		6-21-84	7 921 70
18 90			300 00	6-24-84	8 202 80
7 52	19 60			6-27-84	8 175 68
15 00	32 48			6-28-84	8 128 20
*6 00SC				6-30-84	8 122 20

Code:
CM–Credit Memo–Customer note collected
NC–Not sufficient funds
SC–Service charge

MEMBER F.D.I.C.   IMPORTANT: SEE REVERSE SIDE OF STATEMENT.

CASH ACCOUNTS IN THE LEDGER

Typically, a balance sheet reports **cash** as the first current asset because it is the most liquid of all assets. The amount of cash reported on a balance sheet is the **total amount** of cash at the end of the last day of the accounting period. The total amount of cash reported (as defined on page 343) is the end-of-period total of—

1. Cash on deposit in all checking accounts subject to current checking privileges (offset by any overdrafts).[2]
2. Cash on hand (not yet transmitted to a bank for deposit).
3. Cash held in all petty cash funds.

Typically, a company will have a separate account in the **ledger** for each separate bank account.[3] Often companies maintain a daily minimum amount of **cash on hand.** Although such amounts are included in debits to the **regular Cash account,** those amounts have not yet been deposited because they represent *(a)* amounts of cash received since the last deposit was made and/or *(b)* a stable amount of cash needed for making change to start the next day.

Frequently, a **petty cash system** is maintained for the purpose of making separate **small cash payments** (not making change) in lieu of writing a separate check for each such item. This system necessitates the use of another separate cash account, usually called Petty Cash (discussed later).

EXHIBIT 8–2
Sample form and instructions for a bank reconciliation

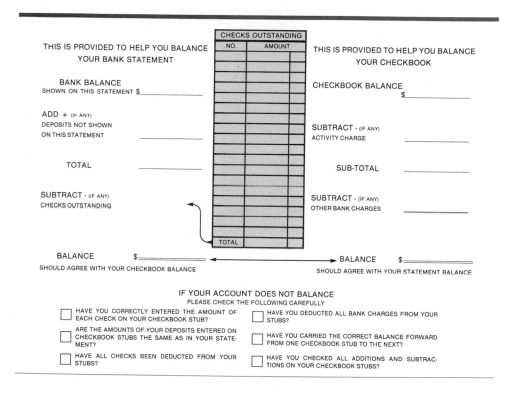

---

[2] Adjusted for deposits in transit and outstanding checks (discussed later).

[3] Larger companies often carry one Cash control account in the ledger which is supplemented with a series of separate cash subsidiary accounts for the depository banks. Refer to Supplement 6A.

BANK RECONCILIATION

Bank reconciliation is a term usually used to identify the process of comparing (reconciling) the **ending** cash balance reflected in a **company's Cash account** and the **ending** cash balance reported by the bank on the monthly **bank statement.** A bank reconciliation serves two primary accounting purposes:

a. Checks on the accuracy of both the ending balance of the company's Cash account and ending balance reported on the bank statement, which also involves development of the true cash balance.

b. Identifies certain transactions that have not been recorded in the company's accounts, although they appear on the bank statement (and vice versa).

A bank reconciliation should be completed for each separate checking account (i.e., for each bank statement received from each bank) at the end of each month.

Usually, the ending cash balance in the bank as shown on the bank statement will not agree with the ending cash balance shown by the related Cash ledger account on the books of the depositor. For example, assume the Cash ledger account at the end of June 1984 of J. Doe Company reflected the following (Doe has only one checking account):

Cash

June 1	Balance	7,010.00*	June	Checks written	3,800.00
June	Deposits	5,750.00			

(Ending balance, $8,960.00)

* Including $200 undeposited cash held for change.

The $8,122.20 **ending cash balance** shown on the **bank statement** (Exhibit 8–1) is different from the $8,960.00 **ending book balance** of cash shown on the **books of the J. Doe Company** because (1) some transactions affecting cash were recorded in the books of depositor Doe but were not reflected on the bank statement, and (2) some transactions were reflected on the bank statement but had not been recorded in the books of the depositor, Doe. The most common causes of a difference between the ending bank balance and the ending book balance of cash are:

1. **Outstanding checks**—checks written by the depositor and recorded in the depositor's ledger as credits to the Cash account that have not cleared the bank (hence they are not listed on the bank statement as a deduction from the bank balance). The outstanding checks are identified by comparing the canceled checks returned with the bank statement and with the record of checks (such as the check stubs) maintained by the depositor.

2. **Deposits in transit**—deposits taken or mailed to the bank by the depositor and recorded in the depositor's ledger as debits to the Cash account that have not been recorded by the bank (hence they are not reflected on the bank statement as an increase in the bank balance). Deposits in transit usually happens when deposits are made one or two days before the close of the period covered by the bank statement. These are known as deposits in transit

and are determined by comparing the deposits listed on the bank statement with the copies of the deposit slips retained by the depositor.

3. **Bank service charges**—explained on page 345.
4. **NSF checks**—explained on page 345.
5. **Errors**—both the bank and the depositor may make errors, especially when the volume of cash transactions is large.

In view of these factors, a **bank reconciliation** should be made by the depositor (whether for a business or a personal account) immediately after each bank statement is received. A bank reconciliation is an important element of internal control and is needed for accounting purposes. To encourage bank reconciliation by depositors, many banks provide a format on the back of the bank statement for such purposes. Instructions for completing a bank reconciliation also may be given. A typical form is shown in Exhibit 8–2.

Bank reconciliation illustrated

The bank reconciliation for the month of June prepared by J. Doe Company to reconcile the **ending bank balance** (Exhibit 8–1, $8,122.20) with the **ending book balance** (page 347, $8,960) is shown in Exhibit 8–3. On the completed reconciliation, Exhibit 8–3, the **true** (correct) cash balance is $9,045, which is different from both the reported bank and book balances before the reconciliation.

Although the layout of a bank reconciliation can vary, the most simple and flexible one follows a balancing format with the "Depositor's Books" and the "Bank Statement" identified separately. This format starts with two different amounts: (1) the reported **ending balance per books** and (2) the reported **ending balance per bank statement.** Provision then is made for additions to, and subtractions from, each balance so that the last line reflects the same correct cash balance (for the bank and the books). This correct balance represents the amount that **should be** reflected in the Cash account **after the reconciliation.** In this example it is also the amount of cash that should be reported on the balance sheet because J. Doe Company has only one checking account and no petty cash system (see

EXHIBIT 8–3
Bank reconciliation illustrated

J. DOE COMPANY				
Bank Reconciliation				
For the Month Ending June 30, 1984				
Depositor's Books			**Bank Statement**	
Ending cash balance per books		$8,960.00	Ending cash balance per bank statement	$ 8,122.20
Additions:			Additions:	
Proceeds of customer note collected by bank		100.00	Deposit in transit	1,800.00
Error in recording check No. 137		9.00	Cash on hand	200.00
		9,069.00		10,122.20
Deductions:			Deductions:	
NSF check of R. Roe	$18.00		Outstanding checks	1,077.20
Bank service charges	6.00	24.00		
Ending true cash balance		$9,045.00	Ending true cash balance	$ 9,045.00

page 347). J. Doe Company followed these steps in completing the bank reconciliation:

1. **Identification of the outstanding checks**—A comparison of the canceled checks returned by the bank with the records of the company of all checks drawn revealed the following checks still outstanding (not cleared) at the end of June:

Check No.	Amount
101	$ 145.00
123	815.00
131	117.20
Total	$1,077.20

This total was entered on the reconciliation as a **deduction** from the bank account because the checks will be deducted by the bank when they clear the bank.

2. **Identification of the deposits in transit**—A comparison of the deposit slips on hand with those listed on the bank statement revealed that a deposit made on June 30 for $1,800 was not listed on the bank statement. This amount was entered on the reconciliation as an **addition** to the bank account because it will be added by the bank when the deposit is recorded by the bank.

3. **Cash on hand**—On the date of the bank statement, cash on hand (i.e., undeposited cash held for making change) amounted to $200. This amount is included in the company's Cash account but was not included in the bank statement balance (it was not deposited); therefore, it must be entered on the reconciliation as an addition to the bank balance (as it would be, if deposited).

4. Items on bank statement not yet recorded in the books of J. Doe Company; refer to Exhibit 8–4.

    a. Proceeds of note collected, $100 (explained on page 345)—entered on the bank reconciliation as an **addition** to the book balance; it already has been included in the bank balance. A journal entry is required to increase the Cash account balance and decrease the Note Receivable balance for this item.

    b. NSF check of R. Roe, $18 (explained on page 345)—entered on the bank reconciliation as a **deduction** from the book balance; it already has been deducted from the bank statement balance. A journal entry is required to reduce the Cash account balance for this item and to increase the receivable account.

    c. Bank service charges, $6 (see page 345)—entered on the bank reconciliation as a **deduction** from the book balance; it already has been deducted from the bank balance. A journal entry is required to reduce the Cash account balance for this item and to increase an expense account.

5. **Error**—At this point J. Doe Company found that the reconciliation did not balance by $9. Because this amount is divisible by 9, they suspected a transposition. (A transposition, such as writing 27 for 72, always will cause an error

EXHIBIT 8–4
**Entries from bank
reconciliation
(Exhibit 8–3)**

Accounts of J. Doe Company:

a. Cash 100
      Note receivable 100
    To record note collected by bank.

b. Accounts receivable 18
      Cash 18
    To record NSF check.

c. Bank service expense 6
      Cash 6
    To record service fees charged by bank.

d. Cash 9
      Accounts payable (name) 9
    To correct error made in recording a check payable to a creditor.

Cash account of J. Doe Company:

    The Cash account prior to reconciliation was given on page 347. After the above journal entries are posted, the Cash account is as follows:

Cash (after recording results of bank reconciliation)

June 1	Balance	7,010.00	June	Checks written	3,800.00
June	Deposits	5,750.00	June 30	NSF check*	18.00
June 30	Note collected*	100.00	June 30	Bank service charge*	6.00
June 30	Correcting entry*	9.00			

(True cash balance, $9,045.00)

* Based on the bank reconciliation.

that is exactly divisible by 9.) Upon checking the journal entries made during the month, they found that a check was written by J. Doe Company for $56 to pay an account payable for that amount. The check was recorded in the company's accounts as $65. The incorrect entry made was a debit to Accounts Payable and a credit to Cash for $65 (instead of $56). Therefore, $9 (i.e., $65 — $56) must be **added** to the book cash balance on the reconciliation; the bank cleared the check for the correct amount, $56. The following correcting entry must be made in the accounts: Cash, debit $9; and Accounts Payable, credit $9.

Note in Exhibit 8–3 that the "Depositor's Books" and the "Bank Statement" parts of the bank reconciliation now agree at a **true cash balance** of $9,045. This is the amount that will be included in the cash amount reported on a balance sheet prepared at the end of the period.

A bank reconciliation as illustrated in Exhibit 8–3 accomplishes two major objectives outlined on page 347 viz:

1. Checks the accuracy of the bank balance and the company cash records which involves development of the **true cash balance.** The true cash balance is the amount of cash that must be in the Cash account for financial reporting

purposes (i.e., the balance sheet) and the amount that would be in the bank if all cash items were recognized by the bank.

2. Identifies any previously unrecorded transactions or changes that are necessary to cause the company's Cash account(s) to reflect the **true cash balance.** These transactions or changes require journal entries. The explanations given above of the development of the bank reconciliation of J. Doe Company cite such transactions and changes. Therefore, the entries shown in Exhibit 8–4, taken directly from the "Depositor's Books," part of the bank reconciliation, (Exhibit 8–3) must be entered into the company's records.

Observe that all of the additions and deductions on the "Depositor's Books" ✳ side of the reconciliation require journal entries to update the Cash account. The additions and deductions on the "Bank Statement" side do **not** require journal entries because they will work out automatically when they clear the bank. The cash amount reported on the balance sheet and reflected in the Cash account will be the **true cash balance** only if the proper journal entries are made after the bank reconciliation is completed.

The importance of the bank reconciliation procedure in generating entries to **update** the Cash account should not be overlooked. This feature is important in measuring the true cash balance that should be reported on the balance sheet.

CASH OVER AND SHORT

Regardless of the care exercised, errors in handling cash inevitably occur when a large number of cash transactions is involved. These errors cause cash shortages or cash overages at the end of the day when the cash is counted and compared with the cash records for the day. Cash overages and shortages must be recorded in the accounts. To illustrate, assume that at the end of a particular day the count of cash from sales amounted to $1,347.19 but the cash register tapes for sales totaled $1,357.19—a **cash shortage** of $10 is indicated. The sales for the day should be recorded as follows:

Cash	1,347.19	
Cash over and short	10.00	
Sales		1,357.19
To record cash sales and cash shortage.		

In the case of a cash **overage,** the Cash Over and Short account would be credited. Sales revenue should be recorded for the correct amount reflected on the register tapes regardless of any cash overage or shortage. Sometimes the bank reconciliation will divulge a cash shortage or overage that must be reflected under the "books" portion of the reconciliation and recorded in an accounting entry. At the end of the period, the Cash Over and Short account, in the case of a cumulative debit balance, usually is reported as miscellaneous expense. If a credit balance exists, it is reported as miscellaneous revenue.

PETTY CASH

The discussion of internal control explained that all major disbursements of cash should be made by **prenumbered checks.** Many businesses find it inconvenient and expensive in terms of paperwork and employee time to write checks for small payments for items such as taxi fares, newspapers, and small amounts of supplies. To avoid this inconvenience and expense, businesses frequently establish a **petty cash fund** to handle small miscellaneous cash payments. To establish a petty cash fund, a check should be drawn "Pay to the order of Petty Cash" for the amount needed in the fund and cashed. Small cash payments, supported by written receipts, are made from this fund, and no journal entry is made at the time of payment. When the petty cash fund runs low and at the end of each accounting period, the expenditures from the fund are summarized and an accounting entry is made to reflect the payments from the fund (as a debit to expenses) and to record the check written to reimburse the fund for the total amount spent. For balance sheet reporting, the amount in the Petty Cash account must be added to the other cash balances. The details of accounting for a petty cash fund are discussed and illustrated in Supplement 8A to this chapter.

COMPENSATING BALANCES

A **compensating balance** exists when the bank requires the business to maintain a minimum amount in its bank account. A compensating balance, may be required by the bank explicitly (by a loan agreement), or implicitly (by informal understanding), as part of a credit-granting arrangement. Often, it is difficult for the independent auditor to know whether or not an informal understanding exists. Information on compensating balances is important to statement users because there are two major effects on the business: (1) a compensating balance requirement imposes a restriction on the amount of cash readily available in the checking account; and (2) if it arises in connection with a loan, the compensating balance increases the real rate of interest on the loan because not all of the cash borrowed can be used (i.e., the minimum must remain on deposit).

Information concerning a compensating balance must be reported in the notes to the financial statements because of its importance to statement users.

DATA PROCESSING OF CASH

Small businesses usually process cash transactions manually. In contrast, large businesses often process cash information by means of electronic computers. However, the recent development of microcomputers, and the software needed for processing accounting information, has brought computer processing of cash information within the cost-benefit range of small and medium-sized businesses. The basic data activities of accounting broadly are the same whether manual, mechanical, or electronic approaches are used. For most instructional situations, the basic characteristics of accounting information processing are best viewed in terms of a manual system.

Supplement 8B to this chapter presents one information processing procedure known as **special journals.** Two of these special journals relate to information processing of cash inflows (i.e., cash receipts journal) and cash outflows (i.e., cash payments journal). Supplement B illustrates the manual system for the special journals; however, computerized systems for these cash activities follow in essentially the same manner.

PART B—MEASURING AND REPORTING SHORT-TERM INVESTMENTS

To employ idle cash, primarily to earn investment revenue, a company may invest in commercial paper (such as certificates of deposit), or in the capital stocks (equity securities) or bonds (debt securities) of another company. Such investments are facilitated because commercial paper is sold by local banks, and the stocks and bonds of most of the large corporations are "listed" on the New York or American stock exchanges. Capital stock of smaller unlisted companies frequently can be bought and sold "over the counter" or between individuals and companies directly.

When bonds of another company are acquired, the purchaser has become a creditor of the issuing company because bonds represent debt owed by the other company similar to a long-term note payable. As the holder of a bond, the investor is entitled to receive interest on the principal of the bond and the principal if held to maturity. In contrast, when shares of capital stock are purchased as an investment, the purchaser becomes one of the owners (frequently called stockholders, shareholders, or equityholders) of the company that issued the stock. As an owner, the stockholder receives dividends when they are declared and paid by the board of directors of the other company. Most capital stock confers voting rights, which means the stockholder is provided an opportunity to exercise some **control** over the issuing company. The amount of control depends upon the number of voting shares owned by the stockholder in relation to the total number of such shares of stock outstanding.

Investments made by one company in the stocks or bonds of another company may be either (1) short-term investments (sometimes called temporary investments) or (2) long-term investments (sometimes called permanent investments). This chapter discusses the measurement and reporting of short-term investments; long-term investments are discussed in Chapter 13.

SHORT-TERM INVESTMENTS DEFINED

To be classified as a short-term (or temporary) investment, a security (e.g., a stock or bond) must meet a twofold test of (1) marketability and (2) an expected short-term holding period. **Marketability** means that the security must be traded regularly on the market so that there is a continuous market available and a determinable market price. Therefore, short-term investments usually are listed stocks and bonds, or short-term government securities. A **short-term holding period** means that it must be the **intention** of the management to convert the securities into cash in the near future for normal operating purposes.[4] Short term refers to the longer of the normal operating cycle of the business or one year as specified in the definition of current assets (Chapter 2, page 53). The distinction between short-term and long-term investments is important because (1) there are accounting differences that must be observed and (2) short-term investments must be classified as a current asset, whereas the long-term investments are reported under a noncurrent caption, "Investments and funds."

MEASUREMENT OF SHORT-TERM INVESTMENTS

In accordance with the **cost principle,** short-term investments, when acquired, are measured and recorded at their cost. Cost includes the market price paid plus all additional costs incurred to purchase the security. To illustrate, assume Brown Corporation had approximately $50,000 in cash that would not be needed for operations for six or more months. In December, Brown purchased 1,000 shares of American Telephone and Telegraph (AT&T) stock for $56,000, including all broker's fees, transfer costs, and taxes related to the purchase. This transaction would be recorded as shown in Exhibit 8–5.

Short-term investments held at the end of the accounting period are reported, at the **lower of cost or market** (LCM) on the balance sheet as a current asset (lower of cost or market is discussed in the next section). The **current market value** at the date of the balance sheet should be shown parenthetically. For example, at the end of the accounting period, December 31, 19A, Brown Corporation would report the short-term investment of AT&T stock, assuming a market value **above** cost of $57 per share, as shown in Exhibit 8–5.

When a cash dividend is received on capital stock (an equity security), or interest is received on a debt security held as a short-term investment, Cash is debited for the amount received, and a revenue account, such as Investment Revenue, is credited for the same amount. To illustrate, assume Brown Corporation received a cash dividend of $.70 per share on the AT&T stock on February 2, 19B. This transaction would be recorded by Brown as shown in Exhibit 8–5.

When a short-term investment is sold, the difference between the sale price and the cost of the security is recorded as a gain, or loss, as illustrated in Exhibit 8–5.

When a company owns short-term equity securities in several other companies, the securities held are referred to collectively as a **short-term portfolio of equity securities.** If debt securities also are held, they are considered to be a separate **portfolio** of <u>debt securities.</u> Each portfolio of short-term investments is managed (i.e., acquired, held, and sold) with the objective of maximizing the return while

---

[4] We shall see later that long-term investments also include marketable securites. Thus, the basic distinction between short-term and long-term investments hinges primarily on the intention of management in respect to their expected disposal date. As a result, the same kind of security may be a short-term investment in one company and a long-term investment in another company, depending upon the intentions of the respective managements.

EXHIBIT 8–5
Accounting for
short-term
investments
illustrated

December 1, 19A—Purchase of 1,000 shares of AT&T common stock for $56,000 including
  all transfer costs:

Short-term investments (1,000 shares @ $56) 56,000
    Cash   56,000

December 31, 19A (end of the accounting period)—on this date the AT&T stock was selling
  at $57 (i.e., **above** acquisition cost)*

Balance sheet at December 31, 19A:
  Current assets:
    Cash (assumed amount) $62,000
    Short-term investments at cost (current market value, $57,000) 56,000

February 2, 19B—Received a quarterly cash dividend on the AT&T stock of $.70 per share:

Cash (1,000 shares @ $.70 per share) 700
    Investment revenue   700

April 5, 19B—Sold 250 shares of the AT&T stock at $58 per share (cash).

Cash (250 shares @ $58) 14,500
    Short-term investments (250 shares @ $56)   14,000
    Gain on sale of investments   500
    * See next section on LCM when the market price is **less** than the acquisition price.

minimizing the risk. Thus, each **investment portfolio** is accounted for as a whole rather than as a number of separate investments.

Short-term
investments
valued at lower
of cost or market
(LCM)

Although short-term investments are measured and recorded at cost when acquired and are measured thereafter in conformity with the cost principle, there is an important exception related **only** to equity securities. The exception occurs when the **current** market value of the **short-term portfolio of equity securities** drops below the recorded acquisition cost.[5]

Chapter 7, relating to inventories of merchandise, explained that items of merchandise in the inventory for which the **current replacement cost** had dropped below acquisition cost should be measured on a lower of cost or market (LCM) basis. The same principle applies to the **short-term portfolio of equity securities.** Because of a drop in market value, the short-term portfolio of equity securities has lost a part of its value as a short-term source of **cash.** The drop in value is viewed as a **holding or unrealized loss** that should be recognized in the period in which the drop occurred. However, a holding gain is **not** recorded when the current market value is **above** the acquisition cost. The LCM basis is an exception to both the **cost principle** and the **comparability principle.** The LCM basis is applied because the **conservatism exception** (see Exhibit 2–6) is permitted to

---

[5] FASB, *Statement of Accounting Standards No. 12,* "Accounting for Certain Marketable Securities" (Stamford, Conn. December 1975). The procedures and accounting entries in this section specifically follow the **requirements** of *FASB Statement 12.* This statement **does not apply LCM to investments in debt securities.**

override the cost and comparability principles. The LCM rule of equity securities is not required to be applied to short-term investments in **debt** securities; they are accounted for at cost (with parenthetical disclosure of their current market value).

For short-term investments in equity securities, at the end of the accounting period, any difference between their cost and a **lower** end-of-period market value is recorded as a debit to an **expense** account called Unrealized Loss on Short-Term Investments and a credit to an **asset contra** account called Allowance to Reduce Short-Term Investments to Market. Thus, this entry records the holding (market) loss as an expense in the period in which the market dropped and revalues the short-term investment on an LCM basis.

To illustrate a situation where market is **lower** than cost at the end of the accounting period, we return to Brown Corporation (and continue the situation in Exhibit 8–5). Recall that at the end of 19B, Brown Corporation still owned 750 shares of the AT&T common stock acquired at $56 per share (i.e., total cost is, $42,000). At the end of 19B, the AT&T stock was selling on the stock exchange at $55 per share, which was $1 per share less than cost. Therefore, the LCM valuation must be applied to it. This means that an **unrealized** loss of $750 must be recorded and reported as shown in Exhibit 8–6.

The illustration presented in Exhibit 8–6 involved only one stock investment (AT&T) in the investment portfolio. Often the portfolio includes several different equity securities. In such cases, LCM is based upon the **total portfolio cost versus total portfolio market** amount rather than on an item-by-item basis. To illustrate, assume Cox Company has three separate stocks, A, B, and C (rather than one)

EXHIBIT 8–6
Recording and reporting short-term equity investments at LCM

Entries:
December 31, 19B (end of accounting period)—AT&T common stock held as a short-term investment; 750 shares, cost $56, current market, $55 per share.

Unrealized loss on short-term investments	750*	
Allowance to reduce short-term investments to market		750

Computation:

Cost (750 shares @ $56)	$42,000	
Market (750 shares @ $55)	41,250	
Unrealized loss	$ 750	

Financial statements:
Balance sheet at December 31, 19B:
Current assets:

Short-term investments (at cost)	$42,000	
Less: Allowance to reduce short-term investments to market	750	$41,250

or alternatively:

Current assets:

Short-term investment, at LCM (cost $42,000)	$41,250

Income statement for year ended December 31, 19B:
Expenses:

Unrealized loss on short-term investments	$750

in its short-term **investment portfolio.** The measurement at the end of the accounting period would be derived as follows:

	Portfolio	
Security	Acquisition cost	Current market
A Company common stock	$10,000	$ 9,000
B Company preferred stock	23,000	22,000
C Company common stock	7,000	8,000
Total portfolio	$40,000	$39,000

Under the LCM basis, the Short-Term Investments account of Cox Company would be written down to $39,000 by recognizing a $1,000 unrealized loss as follows:[6]

Unrealized loss on short-term investments	1,000	
Allowance to reduce short-term investments to market		1,000

When investments are **sold** that previously have been written down to a lower market (i.e., LCM), the gain or loss is measured as the difference between the sale price and the original purchase cost regardless of any balance in the allowance account. Any balance in the allowance account at the end of the accounting period is adjusted (up or down) to reflect any difference between total portfolio cost and a lower total portfolio market of the short-term investments held at the end of the accounting period.

To illustrate, assume that Cox Company sold all of the portfolio on January 15, 19C, for $39,400 cash. This transaction would be recorded as follows:[7]

Cash	39,400	
Loss on sale of short-term investments	600	
Short-term investments (at cost)		40,000

---

[6] In contrast, when the LCM rule is applied to merchandise inventories, the item-by-item basis usually is used because merchandise is not viewed "as a single item" but as separate items.

[7] Assuming no short-term investments were held at the end of 19C, the following entry would be made:

December 31, 19C:

Allowance to reduce short-term investments to market	1,000	
Recovery of unrealized loss on short-term investments*		1,000

  * Some accountants prefer the title: "Unrealized Gain on Short-Term Investments."

Note that the LCM effect is to record a holding loss in the period that the market dropped below cost and to record an offset (a holding gain) in the period of sale. This anomalous effect occurs because LCM is not consistent with either cost basis accounting or market value accounting for Investments.

CERTIFICATES OF DEPOSIT

In recent years, a common short-term investment strategy to employ idle cash has been to purchase debt securities called **certificates of deposit** (CDs). A "CD" is an investment contract (a certificate is received) an investor may purchase from a bank for cash. The contract specifies (1) a limited period of time for the investment, such as 90 days, 6 months, 1 year, and so on; and (2) a guaranteed interest rate. Generally, the larger the amount of the certificate (the amount invested), the higher the interest rate. The interest rate also tends to be higher for longer time periods to maturity. Certificates of deposit and similar commercial paper often are used for the short-term employment of idle cash because of the relatively high interest return and the liquidity factor.

Certificates of deposit are measured and accounted for on the cost basis (not LCM) because they are **debt** securities. At the end of the accounting period, an **adjusting entry** is made for any accrued interest earned but not yet collected. CDs are accounted for separately from cash. The interest earned is reported on the income statement as **investment revenue.** For external reporting purposes, certificates of deposit are reported on the balance sheet as a current asset as shown here:

```
Current assets:
    Cash  . . . . . . . . . . . . . . . . . . .    $200,000
    Certificates of deposit . . . . .      300,000
```

ADJUSTING ENTRIES FOR INVESTMENT REVENUE

At the end of the accounting period, **no adjusting entry is made for dividend revenue** on capital stock held as an investment because dividends (1) do not accrue on the basis of time and (2) are not paid unless formally declared by the board of directors of the issuing corporation. In contrast, when CDs, bonds, or other **debt securities are held, an adjusting entry is required** for accrued interest revenue as for each debt security because interest is a legal liability that increases in amount with the passage of time. Accrual of interest is illustrated in Chapter 4 and in Part C of this chapter.

PART C—MEASURING AND REPORTING RECEIVABLES

RECEIVABLES DEFINED

Broadly, **receivables encompass all claims of the entity against other entities or persons for money, goods, or services.** In most businesses there are two types of receivables: trade receivables and special (nontrade) receivables. Either type may include both short-term receivables (i.e., classified as current assets) and long-term receivables (i.e., classified as long-term investments or other assets). For example, a balance sheet may report the following receivables:

Current assets:
Trade accounts receivable $40,000
       Less: Allowance for doubtful accounts 3,000 $37,000
Trade notes receivable, short term   5,000
Special receivables:
     Due from employees   400
     Equipment note receivable, short term   600

Long-term investments:
Note receivable, long term   10,000
Special receivable, long term   8,000

Other assets:
Utility deposits   2,000
Due from company officers   1,000

TRADE RECEIVABLES

Trade receivables include trade accounts receivable, usually called **accounts receivable,** and trade notes receivable. Either may be short term or long term, although the latter is relatively rare in most situations. Trade receivables arise from the regular operating activities of the business; that is, from the sale of merchandise and/or services.

Trade accounts receivable and the contra account, Allowance for Doubtful Accounts, were discussed in detail in Chapter 6.

Many businesses **factor** their accounts receivable instead of holding them until due date for collection. "Factoring" is a term used for the **sale** of accounts receivable to a financial institution, which usually occurs on the date that the goods and/or services are sold. Factoring is used widely because the company immediately receives the cash for sales; however, the rate of interest for factoring arrangements tends to be high. A discussion of the detailed accounting involved for factoring is beyond the objectives of this book.

SPECIAL RECEIVABLES

Special (or nontrade) receivables arise from transactions other than the sale of merchandise and/or services. Special receivables may be short term or long term and should be given descriptive titles similar to those illustrated above. They should not be included in the caption "Accounts receivable." Other than for appropriate classification on the balance sheet, special receivables seldom involve unusual measurement or reporting problems.

NOTES RECEIVABLE

Notes receivable may be either **trade** notes receivable or **special** notes receivable, depending upon the source of the note. A promissory note is an unconditional promise in writing (i.e., a formal document) to pay (1) a specified sum of money on demand or at a definite future date known as the maturity or due date and (2) specified interest at one or more future dates. The person who signs a promissory note is known as the **maker,** and the person to whom payment is to be made is known as the **payee.** The maker views the note as a "note payable," whereas the payee views the note as a "note receivable." A note receivable involves two distinctly different amounts: (1) **principal,** which is the amount that the interest amount is based upon and (2) **interest,** which is the specified amount charged for use of the principal. The **face amount** of a note is the amount specified on the note that is payable at maturity.

Interest calculations on notes

Interest represents the time value of money; that is, the cost of using money over time. To the payee of a promissory note, interest is **revenue;** while to the maker it is **expense.** The formula for computing interest is:

$$\text{Principal} \times \frac{\text{Annual rate}}{\text{of interest}} \times \frac{\text{Fraction of}}{\text{year}} = \frac{\text{Interest}}{\text{amount}}$$

It is important to remember that **interest rates** are quoted on an **annual basis** and, therefore, must be restated for time periods of less than one year. Thus, the interest on a $10,000, 12 percent, 90-day promissory note would be calculated as follows:

$$\$10,000 \times .12 \times 90/360 = \$300$$

When a note specifies a number of days, the exact days must be counted on the calendar to determine the due date and then related to the number of days in the year. For computing interest, sometimes it is assumed that the year encompasses 360 days, so that each day's interest is $\frac{1}{360}$ of a year rather than $\frac{1}{365}$. This simplification has the effect of making the actual interest cost for a short-term loan slightly higher than the stated amount of interest.[8]

All commercial notes involve interest, either explicitly or implicitly, because money borrowed, or loaned, has a time value that cannot be avoided.[9]

Accounting for notes receivable

Notes receivable usually arise as a result of a business selling merchandise or services. Although most businesses use open accounts (i.e., accounts receivable), those selling high-priced items on credit frequently require notes from their customers. To illustrate, assume Jackson Company received a $10,000, 12 percent, interest-bearing note from a customer as a result of the sale of goods; the payee would record it on the date of the sale as follows:

Notes receivable (trade)	10,000	
Sales revenue		10,000

To record 90-day, 12 percent, interest-bearing note received from customer.

Note: Assuming the note was in settlement of an open account receivable, which frequently happens, the credit would have been to Accounts Receivable instead of to Sales Revenue.

---

[8] For simplicity throughout this book, interest dates are given in a manner that avoids the needless counting of exact days on a calendar. Most lending institutions use 365 days in the calculations.

[9] An **interest-bearing note** explicitly specifies a stated rate of interest (such as 12 percent) on the face of the note, and the interest is to be paid in addition to the **face amount** of the note. In contrast, a **noninterest-bearing note** does not explicitly state an interest rate on the note because the interest charge is included in the face amount of the note (i.e., the interest is implicit).

When **collection** is made at **maturity date** 90 days later, the entry to record the principal amount and the interest would be:

Cash 10,300
    Notes receivable (trade) 10,000
    Interest revenue 300
    To record collection of a 90-day, 12 percent, interest-bearing note receivable of $10,000 plus interest ($10,000 × .12 × 90/360 = $300).

Default of a note receivable

A note receivable that is not collected at maturity is said to be **dishonored** or **defaulted** by the maker. Immediately after default, an entry should be made by the payee transferring the amount due from the Notes Receivable account to a special account such as Special Receivable—Defaulted Trade Notes. The maker is responsible for both the unpaid principal and the unpaid interest; therefore, the receivable account should reflect the full amount owed to the payee. To illustrate, assuming the above note receivable was defaulted by the maker, the entry in the accounts of Jackson Company (the holder or payee) would be:[10]

Special receivable—defaulted trade notes 10,300
    Notes receivable (trade) 10,000
    Interest revenue 300
    To record the principal and interest earned on defaulted note.

Special Receivable—Defaulted Trade Notes is reported as a current or noncurrent asset depending upon the probable collection date.

Discounting a note receivable

Many businesses prefer a note receivable rather than an open account receivable from customers involved in large amounts of credit. The primary reasons are (1) the note provides formal evidence of the receivable and (2) notes, if negotiable, often can be sold to a financial institution, such as a bank, or to individuals to obtain needed cash **before** the maturity date. Selling a note receivable to a financial institution frequently is referred to as **discounting** a note receivable.

Promissory notes almost always are negotiable. **A negotiable instrument** is one that can be transferred by endorsement (there are other technical legal requisites for negotiability). The most common negotiable instrument is a check. Notes and a number of other instruments can be transferred by endorsement. An en-

---

[10] From date of default, the amount due at that date (principal plus interest) continues to draw interest either at the stipulated rate or the legal rate as specified by the law of the state. There may be a question about the propriety of recognizing the interest revenue until collection is made when there is a reasonable probability that collection will not be made.

dorsement may be made simply by signature of the holder, in which case it is said to be "with recourse." **With recourse** means that in case of default, as in the case of a "hot" check (i.e., one that the depositor's bank has turned down because of insufficient funds in the depositor's account), the endorser is liable for repayment. In contrast, an endorsement may be made "without recourse" by writing this phrase on the instrument before the endorsement signature. **Without recourse** means that the endorser cannot be held liable contractually in the case of default by the maker. Entities and individuals seldom will accept endorsements without recourse; that is, a discounted note receivable usually is endorsed with recourse and, as a result, the financial institution can rely on both the maker and the endorser. An endorsement with recourse makes the endorser **contingently liable;** that is, if the maker does not pay the note at maturity, the endorser must do so. The **reporting principle** (Exhibit 2–6) requires that such contingent liabilities be reported on the financial statements. Reporting usually requires a note to the financial statements, as illustrated on page 364.

The sale of a note receivable provides the payee with immediate cash and causes the transfer of the asset (note receivable) to the lender. A difference between the interest specified on the note and the interest charged by the purchaser of the note must be recorded as interest by the payee.

To illustrate the discounting of a note receivable, assume that Jackson Company held the $10,000, 12 percent, 90-day interest-bearing note receivable (page 361) for 30 days, then sold it to the Texas Commerce Bank at a **discount rate** of 15 percent per annum. The discount rate is the annual rate of interest required by the bank and may be more or less than the interest rate specified on the note. The discount rate is applied to the **maturity value** of the note, that is, the principal amount of the note **plus** the amount of interest due at maturity. The discount rate of interest is applied to the number of days the bank will hold the note (in this case, 60 days). Computation of the amount of cash the bank will pay for the note is:

Discounting a note receivable:

Note: Principal, $10,000; annual interest rate, 12%; term, 90 days.
Discounted: Thirty days after date; discount rate, 15% per year.

Principal amount	$10,000.00
Plus: Interest due at maturity ($10,000 × .12 × 90/360)	300.000
Maturity value—amount subject to discount rate	10,300.00
Less: Discount—interest charged by bank ($10,300 × .15 × 60/360)	257.50
Cash proceeds—amount the bank pays for the note	$10,042.50

The discounting or sale of the above note receivable would be recorded by the payee (Jackson Company) as follows:[11]

---

[11] The credit of $42.50 to Interest Revenue may be explained as follows: Had the note been held to maturity, the payee would have earned $300 interest revenue; however, the bank charged interest amounting to $257.50. The difference is $42.50, which is the net interest earned by the payee for holding it 30 of the 90 days. The discount rate is applied to the maturity value of the note because that is the amount the bank will advance, less the interest required by the bank.

Cash 10,042.50	
Notes receivable (trade)	10,000.00
Interest revenue	42.50
To record discounting of note receivable.	

Even though the note was sold, the financial institution has recourse against the endorser in case of default by the maker. Therefore, in accordance with the reporting principle, the endorser (Jackson Company) must disclose the **contingent liability** related to the note by means of a footnote to the financial statements similar to the following:

Note: At December 31, 19B, the company was contingently liable for notes receivable discounted in the amount of $10,300.

EXCEPTIONS TO ACCOUNTING PRINCIPLES

In the preceding chapters, the terms **materiality** (or material amount) and **conservatism** were used often. The conservatism exception was cited earlier as the reason for using the LCM basis in measuring inventory (page 315) and short-term investments (page 356). The terms materiality and conservatism modify the **implementation principles** listed in Exhibit 2–6. In that exhibit, three exceptions to the implementation principles were identified and outlined; they are: (1) materiality, (2) rational conservatism, and (3) industry peculiarities.

Although accounting recognizes that measurement and compliance with the fundamental accounting concepts, assumptions, and principles (Exhibit 2–6) are essential, from a practical point of view the benefits of extremely high accuracy in measurement and absolute compliance with concepts sometimes are offset by purely practical considerations. Under certain **limited conditions,** an exception may be permitted to override one or more of the other principles. These conditions are specified for the following three exceptions:

1. **Materiality**—The fundamental accounting principles must be followed without exception for each transaction when the amount involved in the transaction is **material** (i.e., significant) in relationship to its overall effect on the financial statements. Although amounts **not** material must be accounted for, they **need not be accorded theoretically correct treatment.** For example, a pencil sharpener that cost $7.99 and has a five-year estimated life need not be depreciated under the matching principle; rather the $7.99 may be expensed in the period of acquisition because the amount involved is not material. The clerical cost alone of recording depreciation over the five-year period would exceed, by far, the cost of the asset. Additionally, the $1.60 annual depreciation amount would not affect any important decisions by statement users.

2. **Rational conservatism**—This concept holds that where more than one accounting or measurement alternative is permissible for a transaction, the one having the **least favorable immediate effect on income or owners' equity usually should be selected.** For example the LCM basis is used in measuring the amount of short-term investments and merchandise inventory. In this case, conservatism overrides the cost principle so that a holding loss (but not a gain) that occurs before the asset is sold is recorded and reported.

3. **Industry peculiarities**—This concept holds that the **unique characteristics of an industry may require use of special accounting approaches and measurement procedures in order to produce realistic financial reporting.** For example, in the insurance and mutual fund industries, investment portfolios are accounted for and reported at market value (rather than at LCM or at cost).

DEMONSTRATION CASE

(Try to resolve the requirements before proceeding to the suggested solution that follows.)

Dotter Equipment Company has been selling farm machinery for more than 30 years. The company has been quite successful in both sales and repair services. A wide range of farm equipment, including trucks, is sold. The company policy is to seek "high volume and quality service, at the right price." Credit terms with varying conditions are typical. Although most of the credit granted is carried by several financial institutions, Dotter will carry the credit in special circumstances. As a result, the company occasionally accepts a promissory note and keeps it to maturity. However, if a cash need arises, some of these notes may be sold (i.e., discounted) to the local bank with which Dotter has its checking account. This case focuses on two farm equipment notes that were received during 19D. By following these notes from date of sale of farm equipment to final collection, we can see the various measurement problems posed and the accounting for them. The accounting period ends December 31, 19D.

The series of transactions in respect to the two notes follows:

Equipment Note No. 1:

19D

Jan. 15   Sold a farm tractor to S. Scott for $20,000 and received a 25 percent cash down payment plus a $15,000 equipment note receivable for the balance. The note was due in nine months and was interest bearing at 12 percent per annum. A mortgage on the tractor was executed as a part of the agreement.

Apr. 15   The Scott equipment note was sold to the local bank at a 13 percent per annum discount rate. Dotter endorsed the note, with recourse, and the proceeds were deposited in Dotter's checking account.

Oct. 15   Scott paid the bank the face amount of the note plus the interest, $15,000 + ($15,000 × .12 × $\frac{9}{12}$) = $16,350.

Required:

a. Give appropriate journal entries for Dotter Equipment Company on each of the three dates. Show the interest computations and give an explanation for each entry.

b. Assume that instead of payment on October 15, 19D, S. Scott defaulted on the note. When notified by the bank, Dotter paid the note and interest in full. Give the appropriate entry for this assumption and one for the further assumption that Scott later paid Dotter in full on December 1, 19D.

Equipment Note No. 2:

19D

Oct.   1   Sold a farm truck to B. Day for $7,000; received a down payment of $1,000 and set up an account receivable for the balance; terms, n/30.

Nov. 1   Day came in and wanted an extension on the account receivable "until he sold some equipment." After some discussion it was agreed to settle the account receivable with a six-month, 12 percent, interest-bearing note. Day signed the $6,000 note and a mortgage on this date.

Dec. 31   End of the accounting period. An adjusting entry is required.

19E

Jan.   1   Start of the new accounting period.

May   1   On this due date, Day paid the face amount of the note plus interest in full. The note was marked paid, and the mortgage was canceled by Dotter.

Required:

c. Give appropriate journal entries on each date, including any adjusting entries at year-end and the entry on maturity date. Omit closing entries at year-end. Explain what could be done on January 1, 19E, to simplify subsequent accounting. Provide a brief explanation with each entry.

Suggested Solution   The solutions for Requirements *(a)*, *(b)*, and *(c)* are given in Exhibits 8–7 and 8–8.

SUMMARY OF CHAPTER

This chapter discussed the measurement and reporting of cash, short-term investments, and receivables. Because cash is the most liquid of all assets and is flowing continually into and out of a business, it can be one of the most critical control problems facing the managers. Also, it may be of critical importance to decision makers who rely on financial statements for relevant information. The measurement and reporting of cash includes such problems as controlling and safeguarding cash, reconciling bank balances, petty cash, and recording the cash inflows and outflows.

The use of short-term investments to employ idle cash was discussed. Marketability and the intention of management in respect to the holding period are

EXHIBIT 8–7
Accounting for discounted and defaulted notes receivable illustrated

Requirement *a*. Equipment Note No. 1:
January 15, 19D—Note executed:

Cash	5,000.00	
Equipment notes receivable	15,000.00	
Sales revenue		20,000.00

Sale of tractor to S. Scott for cash and equipment note; terms of note, nine months, 12 percent interest, including a mortgage.

April 15, 19D—Note discounted:

Cash	15,287.25	
Equipment notes receivable		15,000.00
Interest revenue		287.25

Discounted Scott equipment note receivable at bank discount rate of 13 percent.

Proceeds computed:

Principal amount	$15,000.00
Interest to maturity ($15,000 × .12 × 9⁄12)	1,350.00
Maturity value	16,350.00
Discount ($16,350 × .13 × 6⁄12)	(1,062.75)
Cash proceeds.............................	$15,287.25

October 15, 19D—Maturity date of note:
No entry required; Scott paid the bank that owned the note. During the period from April 15, 19D, until the note was paid, Dotter was contingently liable for the note because of the possibility that Scott would default.

Requirement *b*. Note defaulted:
October 15, 19D—Under the assumption that Scott defaulted on the note on due date, Dotter would have to pay the principal plus interest in full.

Special receivable (defaulted note—S. Scott)	16,350.00	
Cash		16,350.00

Scott note defaulted; payment to bank of the $15,000 principal plus interest ($15,000 × .12 × 9⁄12 = $1,350).

December 1, 19D—Scott paid Dotter the full amount of the note plus interest.

Cash	16,350.00	
Special receivable (defaulted note, S. Scott)		16,350.00

Payment received in full on Scott note in default.

Note: In most states, Dotter could also have assessed Scott interest at the **legal** rate on the $16,350 amount overdue; in this case, there would be a credit to Interest Revenue.

fundamental in the classification of an investment as short term as opposed to long term. Short-term investments are accounted for in accordance with the **cost principle;** however, in accordance with the conservatism exception, the LCM basis is applied to the short-term investment portfolio of **equity securities** at the end of each accounting period. **Debt securities** held as short-term investments are accounted for at **cost** (not LCM). Long-term investments are discussed in Chapter 13.

Receivables include trade receivables (usually called accounts receivable), spe-

EXHIBIT 8–8
**Accounting for
interest accrual on
notes receivable
illustrated**

Requirement *c*. Equipment Note No. 2:

October 1, 19D—Sale and account receivable:

Cash	1,000	
Accounts receivable	6,000	
Sales revenue		7,000
Sold truck to B. Day; terms of the receivable, n/30.		

November 1, 19D—Note executed:

Equipment notes receivable	6,000	
Accounts receivable		6,000
Settled account receivable with a six-month, 12 percent interest-bearing note.		

December 31, 19D—Accrual (end of accounting period):

Interest receivable	120	
Interest revenue		120
Adjusting entry for two month's interest accrued at 12 percent on Day equipment note ($6,000 \times .12 \times \frac{2}{12} = \$120$).		

January 1, 19E—Start of next accounting period:
  No entry is required on this date; however, a **reversal** of the adjusting entry could be made to facilitate the subsequent entry when the interest is collected on April 30, 19E. The **optional reversing entry** would be (see Supplement 5A).

Interest revenue	120	
Interest receivable		120
Reversing entry on Day note.		

April 30, 19E—Maturity date (assuming **no** reversing entry was made on January 1, 19E):

Cash $6,000 + ($6,000 \times .12 \times \frac{6}{12}$)	6,360	
Note receivable (principal amount)		6,000
Interest revenue ($6,000 \times .12 \times \frac{4}{12}$)		240
Interest receivable		120

cial receivables, and notes receivable. Each of these should be accounted for separately. Interest calculations and discounting of notes receivable were discussed and illustrated.

The chapter emphasized the importance of careful measurement of these liquid assets and the importance of examining their characteristics before classifying them as current assets for reporting purposes. Financial statement users often are faced with decisions in which these liquid assets are critical; therefore, they should be measured properly and reported adequately.

SUPPLEMENT 8A—PETTY CASH

A petty cash fund is established to avoid the inconvenience and cost of writing checks for the many small payments that occur daily in some businesses. This

Supplement discusses and illustrates the detailed accounting and recordkeeping for a petty cash fund (also called an imprest fund).

Establishing the petty cash fund.   To establish a petty cash fund, a check should be written for the estimated amount needed to meet the expected payments, say, for an average month. The check, made payable to "Petty Cash," is cashed, and the money kept in a safe place under the direct control of a **designated individual** known as the **custodian.** The entry to set up a **separate Cash account** and to record the initial check would be:

Petty cash	100	
Cash		100
To record establishment of a petty cash fund.		

Disbursements from the petty cash fund.   The policies of the petty cash fund should require that the custodian maintain a perpetual record of all disbursements and the amount of cash on hand. No entry is made in the regular ledger accounts at the time each payment is made from the petty cash fund by the custodian. Instead, the custodian maintains a separate **petty cash record** in which each disbursement is recorded when made. This record is supported by documentation, such as a signed bill, voucher, or receipt for each payment made. As an internal control feature, occasional surprise audits of the fund, and the records of disbursements should be conducted. "Borrowing" from the fund by the custodian or others should not be allowed. Careless handling of petty cash often leads to theft.

Replenishment of the petty cash fund.   When the amount of cash held by the custodian gets low, and at the end of each accounting period, the fund should be reimbursed (or replenished) with an amount of cash sufficient to restore it to the original amount (to $100 in the example). Reimbursement is accomplished by having the custodian turn in the petty cash record and the supporting documents to the accountants. On the basis of these records, a check to "Petty Cash" is written for the amount of cash needed for replenishment which is the same as the sum of the expenditures reported by the custodian. The check is cashed, and the money is given to the custodian, which increases the cash held by the custodian to the original amount ($100 in the example). A journal entry is made to credit Cash for the amount of the check and to debit expenses. The petty cash documents turned in by the custodian provide the underlying support for this journal entry.

To illustrate, assume that by the end of the month, there remained $8.50 petty cash on hand of the $100. This means that cash expenditures by the custodian amounted to $91.50 for the month. Assuming no shortage or overage, the bills, vouchers, and receipts accumulated by the custodian should sum to this amount. These documents provide support for the additional check to petty cash for $91.50.

The detailed data for recording the replenishment check in the following journal entry are based on the supporting documents:

Telephone expense	....	12.40
Office supplies expense	....	6.32
Postage expense	....	21.45
Delivery expense	....	6.33
Taxi fare expense	....	14.87
Repair expense, office equipment	....	15.00
Coffee expense	....	10.04
Miscellaneous expense	....	5.09
Cash	....	91.50

It should be emphasized that the Petty Cash account is debited **only** when the petty cash fund is first established and when the fund amount is increased on a permanent basis. The Petty Cash account carries a stable balance at all times ($100 in the above example). Expense accounts, not Petty Cash, are debited, and the **regular** Cash account is credited when the fund is replenished. Therefore, there will be no further entries in the petty cash fund once it is established unless it is decided by management to discontinue the fund or to increase or decrease the original amount on a permanent basis. The fund must be replenished (a) when the balance of cash in the fund is low, and (b) always at the end of the accounting period, whether low or not. Replenishment at the end of the accounting period is necessary in order to (a) record the expenses incurred by the fund up to the date of the financial statements and (b) have the same amount of cash on hand that is shown in the Petty Cash account and included on the balance sheet (see page 346). The petty cash fund should be subject to rigid internal control procedures to remove all temptations to misuse it.

SUPPLEMENT 8B—SPECIAL JOURNALS

In the preceding chapters we have used the **general journal** to record all transactions in chronological order (i.e., by order of date). The general journal is flexible in that any transaction can be recorded in it. However, it is inefficient if used for recording transactions that have a high rate of occurrence, such as credit sales, credit purchases, cash receipts, and cash payments. The **general** journal is inefficient in three ways: (1) the same journal entry must be recorded repeatedly (except for changed amounts), (2) a large number of journal entries must be posted to the ledger, and (3) division of labor is difficult with a single journal. Special journals are designed to reduce these inefficiencies as demonstrated below.

In discussing and illustrating special journals, we emphasize that no accounting principles or concepts are involved—we are dealing simply with the **mechanics** of data processing. Although special journals can, and should, be designed to meet a special need when a particular type of data processing problem arises, we will limit this discussion to the four special journals that often are used: credit sales, credit purchases, cash receipts, and cash payments.

Credit sales journal.   This journal is designed to accommodate **only credit sales.** Cash sales are entered in the cash receipts journal as explained below. You will recall that the journal entry to record a credit sale (assuming a periodic inventory system) is:[12]

Jan. 3   Accounts receivable (customer's name) 100
    Sales   100
    To record credit sale; Invoice No. 324; terms, n/30.

The credit sales journal is designed specifically to simplify (1) recording only this kind of entry and (2) subsequent posting to the ledger. The design of a credit sales journal is shown in Exhibit 8–9. Observe the **saving** in space, time, and accounting expertise required to journalize a credit sale (all of these are minimized).

Posting the credit sales journal.   Posting the special credit sales journal involves two distinct phases. First, the **individual charges** (i.e., debits) must be posted daily to the customers' individual accounts in the **accounts receivable subsidiary ledger** (see Chapter 6, Supplement 6A). This task may be divided among several employees. Second, periodically (usually weekly or monthly), the **totals** are posted to the **general ledger** accounts: Accounts Receivable (debit) and Sales Revenue (credit). In this activity, there is a significant saving in time compared with posting each transaction to the general ledger.

Posting on a daily basis to the **subsidiary ledger,** as shown in Exhibit 8–9, is indicated in the folio column by entering the account number for each individual customer. Daily posting to the subsidiary ledger is necessary because the customer may, on any day, want to pay the current balance then owed.

The second phase in posting the sales journal is to transfer to the general ledger the total credit sales for the month. Thus, the $1,200 total will be posted to the general ledger as (1) a debit to the Accounts Receivable **control account** and (2) as a credit to the Sales Revenue account. This posting is shown in Exhibit 8–9; note in the credit sales journal that two ledger account numbers were entered for the $1,200 total to indicate the posting procedure.

The credit sales journal can be adapted readily to fill special needs. For example, sales taxes could be recorded by adding a column headed "Sales Taxes Payable," and separate sales columns can be added to accumulate sales by department or product. You should observe the following efficiencies attained: (1) recording in the credit sales journal is much less time consuming than separately entering each credit sale in the general journal; (2) posting is reduced significantly by

---

[12] For instructional purposes, we will utilize simplified amounts, a limited number of transactions and customers, T-accounts, and a manual system. In many companies these procedures are computerized.

EXHIBIT 8–9
Credit sales journal
and accounts
receivable
subsidiary ledger
illustrated

		CREDIT SALES JOURNAL				Page 9
Date		Customer	Terms	Invoice Number	Folio	Amount
Jan.	3	Adams, K. L.	n/30	324	34.1	100
	4	Small, C. C.	n/30	325	34.6	60
	6	Baker, C. B.	n/30	326	34.2	110
	10	Roe, R. R.	n/30	327	34.5	20
	11	Mays, O. L.	n/30	328	34.3	200
	16	Roe, R. R.	n/30	329	34.5	90
	18	Null, O. E.	n/30	330	34.4	30
	20	Baker, C. B.	n/30	331	34.2	180
	21	Small, C. C.	n/30	332	34.6	150
	31	Null, O. E.	n/30	333	34.4	260
		Total				1,200
		Posting				(34) (81)

ACCOUNTS RECEIVABLE SUBSIDIARY LEDGER

Adams, K. L.   34.1

Jan.	3		9	100	

Baker, C. B.   34.2

Jan.	6		9	110	
	20		9	180	290

Mays, O. L.   34.3

Jan.	11		9	200	

Null, O. E.   34.4

Jan.	18		9	30	
	31		9	260	290

Roe, R. R.   34.5

Jan.	10		9	20	
	16		9	90	110

Small, C. C.   34.6

Jan.	4		9	60	
	27		9	150	210

GENERAL LEDGER

Accounts Receivable (control)   34

Jan. 31	9	1,200	

Sales Revenue   81

	Jan. 31	9	1,200

transferring the **total** to the general ledger as opposed to posting separate debits and credits for each sales transaction; (3) the opportunity for division of labor; and (4) additional information (such as sales revenue by department) can be recorded easily.

Credit purchases journal. Following exactly the same pattern as described above, a credit purchases journal may be designed as shown below to accommodate the entry common to all purchases on credit, viz:

> Jan. 8   Purchases* 392
>   Accounts payable, C. B. Smith 392
> To record purchase on credit from C. B. Smith, Purchase Order No.
> 139; invoice dated January 5, 19B; terms 2/10, n/30. Recorded net
> of discount, $400 × .98 = $392.
>
> * This debit assumes a periodic inventory system; if a perpetual system is used this account
> would be Merchandise Inventory.

Only credit purchases are recorded in the credit purchases journal. Cash purchases are entered in the cash payments journal as illustrated later. The design of a purchases journal generally is as shown in Exhibit 8–10.

EXHIBIT 8–10
Credit purchases journal illustrated

	CREDIT PURCHASES JOURNAL					Page 4
Date	Creditor's Account	Purchase Order No.	Date of Invoice	Terms	Folio	Amount
Jan. 8	Smith, C. B. Etc.	139	Jan. 5	2/10, n/30	51.8	392
	Total					784
	Posting					(6) (51)

Observe that purchases are recorded net of the purchase discount as explained in Chapter 6, page 237. The cash payments journal will be used to record the subsequent payment of cash for the purchase including situations where the purchase discount is lost.

Exhibit 8–10 was not completed in detail for illustrative purposes because it follows essentially the same pattern already illustrated for the sales journal, both in respect to entries therein and the two phases in posting. Daily posting would involve transfer to the creditors' individual accounts in the **accounts payable subsidiary ledger.** Periodically, the total would be posted to the **general ledger** as (1) a debit to the Purchases account and (2) a credit to the Accounts Payable control account. The efficiencies cited for the sales journal also are realized by a purchases journal.

Cash receipts journal. The design of a special journal to accommodate **all, and only, cash receipts** is more complex because there are a number of different accounts that are **credited individually** when the Cash account is debited. To resolve this problem, more than one **credit** column is necessary to accommodate

EXHIBIT 8–11   **Cash receipts journal illustrated**

			DEBITS	CREDITS				
Date		Explanation	Cash	Account Title	Folio	Accounts Receivable	Sundry Accounts	Cash Sales
Jan.	2	Cash sales	1,237					1,237
	3	Cash sales	1,482					1,482
	4	Sale of land	2,500	Land	43		2,000	
				Gain on sale of land	91		500	
	4	Cash sales	992					992
	6	Invoice #324	100	Adams, K.L.	34.1	100		
	6	Cash sales	1,570					1,570
	10	Bank loan, 12%	1,000	Notes payable	54		1,000	
	15	Invoice #328	200	Mays, O.L.	34.3	200		
	26	Cash sales	1,360					1,360
	31	Invoice #326	110	Baker, C.B.	34.2	110		
	31	Cash sales	1,810					1,810
		Totals	12,361			410	3,500	8,451
		Posting	(12)			(34)	(NP)	(81)

CASH RECEIPTS JOURNAL   Page 14

the various credits. The number and designation of the debit and credit columns will depend upon the character of the repetitive cash receipts transactions in the particular business.

A typical cash receipts journal with some usual transactions recorded is shown in Exhibit 8–11. Notice in particular that there are separate debit and credit sections. Each column illustrated is used as follows:

1. **Cash debit**—This column is used for **each** debit to cash. The column is totaled at the end of the month and posted as one debit amount to the Cash account in the general ledger. The posting number at the bottom indicates the total was posted to account number "12," which is the Cash account.[13]
2. **Accounts Receivable credit**—This column is used to enter the individual amounts collected on trade accounts which must be posted to the individual customer accounts in the **accounts receivable subsidiary ledger** (as indicated by the posting numbers in the folio columns). The **total** of this column is posted at the end of the month as a credit to the Accounts Receivable **control** account in the general ledger as indicated by the posting number "34."

---

[13] This design assumes that the company correctly records credit sales at net of discounts. If credit sales are recorded at "gross," then a Sales Discount debit column also would be needed in this special journal.

3. **Sundry Accounts credit**—This column is used for recording credits to all accounts other than those for which special credit columns are provided (in this example Accounts Receivable and Sales Revenue). The titles of the accounts to be credited are entered under the column "Account Title." Because the Sundry Accounts column represents a number of **accounts,** the **total** is not posted; rather, each individual amount must be posted as a credit directly to the indicated general ledger account. Account numbers entered in the related folio column indicate the posting.

4. **Cash Sales credit**—This column is used to record **all cash sales.** The total at the end of the month is posted as a credit to the Sales Revenue account in the general ledger.

Jan. 2	Cash	1,237	
	Sales revenue		1,237
	To record total cash sales for the day.		
3	Cash	1,482	
	Sales revenue		1,482
	To record total cash sales for the day.		
4	Cash	2,500	
	Land		2,000
	Gain on sale of land		500
	To record sale of land for $2,500 that originally cost $2,000.		
4	Cash	992	
	Sales revenue		992
	To record total cash sales for the day.		
6	Cash	100	
	Accounts receivable		100
	To record total collection of K. L. Adams account for Invoice No. 324 (no discount).		
6	Cash	1,570	
	Sales revenue		1,570
	To record total cash sales for the day.		
10	Cash	1,000	
	Notes payable		1,000
	To record bank loan, 90-day, 12 percent.		
15	Cash	200	
	Accounts receivable		200
	To record collection of O. L. Mays account for Invoice No. 328 (no discount).		
26	Cash	1,360	
	Sales revenue		1,360
	To record total cash sales for the day.		
31	Cash	110	
	Accounts receivable		110
	To record total collection of C. B. Baker account for Invoice No. 326 (no discount).		
31	Cash	1,810	
	Sales revenue		1,810
	To record total cash sales for the day.		

Posting the cash receipts journal involves the same two phases explained previously for the credit sales and credit purchases journals. The **daily posting** phase encompasses posting the individual credits to the accounts receivable subsidiary ledger. The **second phase** involves posting the totals periodically to the accounts in the general ledger, with the exception of the column total for "Sundry Accounts," as explained above.

The individual accounts shown in the "Sundry Accounts" column can be posted daily or at the end of the month. Posting through January is indicated by account code numbers in the illustrated cash receipts journal.

The representative entries shown in the illustrated cash receipts journal are summarized in Exhibit 8–11, in **general journal form,** for convenience in assessing the increased efficiencies of the cash receipts journal approach in journalizing and posting a large number of individual cash transactions.

Other debit and credit columns can be added to the cash receipts journal to accommodate repetitive transactions that also involve cash receipts.

Cash payments journal. The special cash payments journal (often called the check register) is designed to accommodate efficiently the recording of **all (and only) cash payments.** The basic credit column is for Cash; columns for debits are incorporated into the format to accommodate repetitive transactions that involve cash payments. The cash payments journal also must include a column

EXHIBIT 8–12   **Cash payments journal illustrated**

CASH PAYMENTS JOURNAL							Page 16
Date	Check No.	Explanation	CREDITS	DEBITS			
			Cash	Account Title	Folio	Accounts Payable	Sundry Accounts	Cash Purchases

Date	Check No.	Explanation	Cash	Account Title	Folio	Accounts Payable	Sundry Accounts	Cash Purchases
Jan 2	101	Purchased mdse.	1,880					1,880
4	102	Invoice #37	2,970	Ray Mfg. Co.	51.3	2,970		
5	103	Jan. rent	1,200	Rent expense	71		1,200	
8	104	Purchased mdse.	250					250
10	105	Freight on mdse.	15	Freight in	63		15	
14	106	Invoice #42	980	Bowe Supply Co.	51.1	980		
15	107	Paid note, plus	2,200	Notes payable	54		2,000	
		interest		Interest expense	79		200	
20	108	Insurance premium	600	Prepaid insurance	19		600	
26	109	Purchased mdse.	2,160					2,160
29	110	Invoice #91 - after	500	Myar Corp.	51.2	490		
		discount period		Discount lost	80		10	
31	111	Wages	1,000	Wage expense	76		1,000	
		Totals	13,755			4,440	5,025	4,290
		Posting	(12)			(51)	(NP)	(61)
Feb. 1		Etc.						

for "Sundry Accounts, Debits" to accommodate the nonrecurring transactions involving cash payments for which a special debit column is not provided.

A typical cash payments journal with some usual transactions recorded is shown in Exhibit 8–12. Observe that in common with the cash receipts journal, there are separate debit and credit sections. Each column illustrated is used as follows:

1. **Cash credit**—This column is for **every credit** to the Cash account. The column is totaled at the end of the month and posted as a credit to the Cash account in the general ledger.
2. **Accounts Payable debit**—This column is used to enter the individual amounts paid on accounts payable. The individual amounts are posted as debits to the **accounts payable subsidiary ledger** (as indicated by the account numbers under folio), and the total at the end of the month is posted as a debit to the Accounts Payable control account in the general ledger.
3. **Sundry Accounts debit**—This column is used to record all accounts debited for which special columns are not provided (in this example Accounts Payable and Purchases are provided). The titles of the accounts to be debited are entered under the column "Account Titles." Because this column represents a number of accounts, the total cannot be posted; rather, each individual amount is posted as a debit directly to the indicated general ledger account.
4. **Cash Purchases debit**—All cash purchases are entered in this column. The total at the end of the month is posted as a debit to the Purchases account in the ledger.

Posting the cash payments journal involves two phases: (1) **daily posting** of the individual credit amounts to the **accounts payable subsidiary ledger;** and (2) **periodic posting** of the totals to the **general ledger,** with the exception of the total of "Sundry Accounts." The posting of the individual amounts in the "Sundry Accounts" column can be done during the period, say, daily.

The illustrative transactions entered in the cash payments journal (Exhibit 8–12) were:

Jan. 2   Issued Check No. 101 for cash purchase of merchandise costing $1,880.
    4   Issued Check No. 102 to pay account payable owed to Ray Manufacturing Company within the discount period. Discount allowed, 1 percent; Invoice No. 37, $3,000.
    5   Issued Check No. 103 to pay January rent, $1,200.
    8   Issued Check No. 104 for cash purchase of merchandise costing $250.
   10   Issued Check No. 105 for freight-in on merchandise purchased, $15.
   14   Issued Check No. 106 to pay account payable owed to Bows Supply Company within the discount period. Discount allowed, 2 percent; Invoice No. 42, $1,000.
   15   Issued Check No. 107 to pay $2,000 note payable plus 10 percent interest for one year.
   20   Issued Check No. 108 to pay three-year insurance premium, $600.
   26   Issued Check No. 109 for cash purchase of merchandise costing $2,160.
   29   Issued Check No. 110 to pay account payable to Myar Corporation;

terms, 2/10, n/30; Invoice No. 91, $500. Therefore, accounts payable to Myar was credited for $490 at the purchase date (see Chapter 6, page 252). The payment was made after the discount period; hence, the full invoice price of $500 was paid and purchase discount lost of $10 was recorded.

31 Issued Check No. 111 to pay wages amounting to $1,000.

Additional debit and credit columns can be added to the cash payments journal to accommodate other repetitive transactions involving cash disbursements.

Many companies control expenditures with a **voucher system** for controlling expenditures rather than with the credit purchases and the cash payments journals. A voucher system is particularly adaptable to computerized accounting and provides tight control mechanisms on the sequence of events for each transaction from incurrence until final cash payment. The voucher system is explained and illustrated in Chapter 10.

In summary, special journals do not involve new accounting principles or concepts. Rather, they represent a mechanical technique designed to increase efficiency in the data processing cycle. Special journals are not standardized; they should be designed especially to fit each particular situation. Although a manual approach has been illustrated for instructional purposes, many companies have computerized the procedures represented by special journals. In computerized systems, essentially the same mechanics illustrated for the manual system are accomplished by the computer.

IMPORTANT TERMS DEFINED IN THIS CHAPTER

Term (alphabetically)	Key words in definitions of terms used in chapter	Page reference
Bank reconciliation	Process of verifying the accuracy of both the bank statement and the cash accounts of the business.	347
Bank statement	Monthly report from a bank that shows deposits recorded, checks cleared, and a running bank balance.	344
Cash	Money and any instrument that banks will accept for immediate increase in depositor's checking account.	343
Cash over and short	Difference between the amount of cash held at a particular time and the amount the cash records call for.	352
Certificates of deposit	A CD; an investment contract that can be purchased from banks; specifies amount, time, and interest rate.	359
Compensating balances	Exists when a bank requires that a specified minimum cash balance must be maintained in the depositor's account.	353
Conservatism in accounting	When more than one alternative is acceptable in accounting, use the one that has the least short-term favorable effect on income and owners' equity.	365
Contingent liability	An endorser (on a negotiable instrument) is liable for its payment if the maker defaults; a contingent liability exists for the endorser.	363
Default of note receivable	Failure of the maker (payor) of a note to pay it by its maturity date.	362

Term (alphabetically)	Key words in definitions of terms used in chapter	Page reference
Deposits in transit	Deposits made by a depositor that have not yet been reported on the bank statement.	348
Discounting a note receivable	Sale of a note receivable to another party prior to its maturity date.	362
Exceptions to accounting principles	Implementation principles may be modified in application for *(a)* immaterial amounts, *(b)* conservatism, and *(c)* industry peculiarities.	364
Holding (unrealized) loss	Difference between original purchase cost of an investment and its current market value; if market value is **lower,** there is an unrealized loss (if not sold).	356
Internal control	Policies and procedures of a business designed to safeguard the assets of the business.	343
Investment portfolio	A group of securities (stock or bonds) held as an investment; grouped to be accounted for as one unit.	355
Lower of cost or market	Valuation of an investment at either *(a)* original cost or *(b)* current market whichever is lower.	355
Materiality	Small amounts involved in transactions must be recorded; however, the theoretically correct way may, but need not, be followed; use a simple accounting approach.	364
Negotiable instrument	A formal (written) instrument that specifies the terms of a debt; it is **transferable by endorsement.**	362
Notes receivable	A written promise that requires another party to pay the business under specified conditions (amount, time, interest).	360
Outstanding checks	Checks written by a depositor that have not yet been cleared (cashed) by the depositor's bank.	348
Petty cash	A small amount of cash set aside for making small cash payments instead of writing checks.	347
Receivables, short-term	Short-term notes and accounts owed to the business by regular trade customers.	359
Short-term investment	An investment that *(a)* is marketable and *(b)* will have a short-term holding period.	354
Special receivables	Receivables that arise from transactions other than merchandise and services sold.	360
Trade receivables	Another name for accounts receivable; open accounts owed to the business by trade customers.	360

QUESTIONS FOR DISCUSSION

PART A

1. Define cash in the context of accounting and indicate the types of items that should be included and excluded. Identify typical categories of cash.

2. Outline the primary characteristics of an effective internal control system for cash.

3. Why should cash-handling and cash-recording activities be separated? Generally, how is this separation accomplished?

4. What are the purposes and nature of a bank reconciliation? Specifically, what balances are reconciled?

5. Briefly explain how the **total** amount of cash reported on the balance sheet is determined.

6. What is the purpose of petty cash? How is it related to the regular Cash account?

PART B

7. Define a short-term investment. What is the twofold test for classification of an investment as short term?

8. Is a marketable security always classified as a short-term investment? Explain.

9. How does the cost principle apply in accounting for short-term investments in *(a)* debt securities and *(b)* equity securities?

10. What is the rationale for application of the LCM basis to the short-term investment portfolio of equity securities?

11. Explain the purpose and nature of the account, Allowance to Reduce Short-Term Investments to Market.

PART C

12. Distinguish between accounts receivable and special receivables.

13. Define a promissory note indicating the designation of the parties and explain what is meant by principal, maturity date, face amount, and interest rate.

14. Distinguish between an interest-bearing and noninterest-bearing note.

15. What is a negotiable note?

16. What is a defaulted note? Who is responsible for its payment? Explain.

17. What is meant by discounting a note receivable?

18. What is a contingent liability? How does one arise in respect to a note receivable?

19. Identify and briefly explain the three recognized exceptions to the implementing accounting principles.

EXERCISES

PART A

E8–1. National Company operates several branches and, as a consequence, has cash on hand at several locations as well as several bank accounts. The general ledger at the end of 19A showed the following accounts: Petty Cash—Home Office, $500; City Bank—Home Office, $57,300; Cash Held for Making Change, $1,000 (included in the regular Cash Account balance); Petty Cash—Branch A, $100; National Bank—Branch A, $4,458; Petty Cash—Branch B, $200; Southwest Bank—Branch B, $864; Petty Cash—Branch C, $100; State Bank—Branch C, $965; and Metropolitan Bank—Savings account, $7,500; and post-dated checks held that were received from two regular customers, $600.

The four bank balances given represent the true cash balances as reflected on the bank reconciliations.

Required:

What cash amount should be reported on National's 19A balance sheet? Explain the basis for your decisions on any questionable items.

E8–2. Bye Service Company prepared a December 31, 19B, balance sheet that reported cash, $5,849. The following items were found to have been included in the reported cash balance:

	Balance per bank statement at City Bank	$4,934*
a.	A deposit made to the local electric utility	600
b.	Postage stamps on hand	40
c.	Check signed by a customer, returned NSF	30
d.	Petty cash on hand	150
e.	IOUs signed by employees	80
f.	Check signed by the company president for an advance to him; to be held until he "gives the word to cash it."	1,000
g.	Money orders on hand (received from customers)	45
h.	A signed receipt from a freight company that involved a $10 overpayment to them. They have indicated "a check will be mailed shortly."	10
i.	A money order obtained from the post office to be used to pay for a special purchase upon delivery; expected within the next five days	160
	Total cash shown on the 19B balance sheet	$7,049

* Items not considered: deposit in transit, $300; checks outstanding, $175; and cash held for making change, $100 (all included in the regular Cash account).

Required:

a. The reported cash balance has been questioned. Compute the correct cash amount that should be reported on the balance sheet. Give appropriate reporting for any items that you exclude. (Hint: Set up a form similar to the above.)

b. Assume the company carries two cash accounts in the general ledger—Cash and Petty Cash. What is the correct balance that should be reflected in each cash account at December 31, 19B (end of the accounting period)? Show computations.

E8–3. Baker Company has just received the June 30, 19B, bank statement and the June ledger accounts for cash, which are summarized below:

Bank Statement

	Checks	Deposits	Balance
Balance, June 1, 19B			$ 4,900
Deposits during June		$17,000	21,900
Checks cleared through June	$17,700		4,200
Bank service charges	20		4,180
Balance, June 30, 19B			4,180

Cash

June 1	Balance	4,500	June	Checks written	18,100
June	Deposits	19,000			

Petty Cash

June 30	Balance	200	

Required:

a. Reconcile the bank account, assuming that a comparison of the checks written with the checks that have cleared the bank show outstanding checks of $900 and that cash on hand (for making change) on June 30 is $100 (included in the Cash account). Some of the checks that cleared in June were written prior to June; there were no deposits in transit carried over from May, but there is a deposit in transit at the end of June.

b. Give any journal entries that would be made as a result of the bank reconciliation.
c. What is the balance in the Cash account after the reconciliation entries?
d. What total amount of cash should be reported on the balance sheet at June 30?

E8–4.   The September 30, 19D, bank statement for Dotson Company and the completed September ledger accounts for cash are summarized below:

Bank Statement

	Checks	Deposits	Balance
Balance, September 1, 19D			$ 5,100
Deposits recorded during September		$27,000	32,100
Checks cleared during September	$27,300		4,800
NSF check—J. J. Jones	80		4,720
Bank service charges	23		4,597
Balance, September 30, 19D			4,597

Cash

Sept. 1	Balance	5,300	Sept.	Checks written	27,800
Sept.	Deposits	29,500			

Petty Cash

Sept. 30	Balance	100	

Cash on hand for making change (included in the Cash account) on September 1 and September 30 amounted to $200. There were no outstanding checks and no deposits in transit carried over from August; however, there are deposits in transit and checks outstanding at the end of September.

Required:

a. Reconcile the bank account. (Hint: Audit carefully because you may find an error made by either the bank or the company.)
b. Give any journal entries that would be made as a result of the bank reconciliation.
c. What should be the balance in the Cash account after the reconciliation entries?
d. What total amount of cash should Dotson report on the September 30 balance sheet?

E8–5.   The March 31, 19C, bank statement for Diamond Company and the March ledger accounts for cash are summarized below:

Bank Statement

	Checks	Deposits	Balance
Balance, March 1, 19C			$ 8,600
Deposits during March		$28,000	36,600
Note collected for depositor			
(including $60 interest)		1,060	37,660
Checks cleared during March	$32,200		5,460
Bank service charges	35		5,425
Balance, March 31, 19C			5,425

Cash

Mar. 1	Balance	8,320	Mar.	Checks written	32,500
Mar.	Deposits	31,000			

Petty Cash

Mar. 31	Balance	200

A comparison of March deposits recorded with deposits on the bank statement showed deposits in transit of $3,000. Similarly, outstanding checks at the end of March were determined to be $900. Cash on hand (not petty cash) for making change (included in the Cash account) was $300 at March 31.

Required:

a. Prepare a bank reconciliation for March. (Hint: A cash overage or shortage is involved; however, the bank figures have been verified as correct.)

b. Give any journal entries that should be made by Diamond based on the reconciliation.

c. What amount should be reflected as the ending balance in the Cash account after the reconciliation entries? What total amount of cash should be reflected on Diamond's balance sheet at the end of March?

PART B

E8–6. Perry Company, in July 19B, had accumulated excess cash that would not be needed for 10 to 15 months. To employ the idle cash profitably, the management decided to purchase some shares of stock as a short-term investment. The following related transactions occurred:

19B

July 30   Purchased 5,000 shares of the common stock of Sharp Corporation on the American stock exchange. The cash price, including fees and transfer costs related to the acquisition, amounted to $20,000.

Dec. 15   Received a cash dividend of $.30 per share on the Sharp shares.

30   Sold 1,000 of the Sharp shares at $5 per share for cash.

Required:

a. Give appropriate journal entries for Perry Company on each date for this short-term investment. The accounting period of Perry Company ends on December 31.

b. Show how this short-term investment should be reported on the balance sheet at December 31, 19B. Assume the same market value as on December 30.

E8–7. Darby Company, to put some idle cash to work, decided to purchase some common stock in Bay Corporation as a short-term investment. The following related transactions reflect what happened after this decision:

19B

Feb.   1   Purchased 7,000 shares of Bay Corporation common stock at a cash cost of $42,000.

Aug. 15   Received a cash dividend on the Bay stock of $.30 per share.

Dec. 30   Sold 3,000 shares of the Bay stock at $5.80 per share.

31   End of the accounting year. Bay stock was selling at $5.75 per share.

Required:

a. Give appropriate journal entries for Darby Company on each date (including December 31) for the investment in Bay stock. Darby Company had no other short-term investments.

b. Show how the effects of this short-term investment should be reported on the financial statements at December 31, 19B.

c. Give the entry on January 15, 19C, assuming the remaining shares were sold at $5.50 per share.

d. Explain what Darby Company should do about the allowance account on December 31, 19C, assuming no short-term investments are held on that date.

E8–8. White Company, to use some idle cash in March 19B, acquired 200 shares of common stock in each of three corporations at the following costs: Corporation A, $8,000; Corporation B, $6,000; and Corporation C, $12,000. At the end of the annual accounting period, December 31, 19B, the quoted market prices per share were: Corporation A, $40; Corporation B, $25; and Corporation C, $61.

Required:

a. Give the journal entry by White Company to record the acquisition of these short-term investments in equity securities.

b. Give the entry to record cash dividends of $1,200 received on the short-term investments in November 19B.

c. Give the entry to reflect the investments at LCM at December 31, 19B. Show computations.

d. Show how the investments would be reported on the financial statements at December 31, 19B.

e. Give the entry on January 5, 19C, assuming all of the shares were sold for $25,000 cash.

f. Give any entry required at December 31, 19C, assuming no short-term equity investments are held at that time (disregard any closing entries).

E8–9. Cable Company, to put some idle cash to work, purchased a debt security as a short-term investment at a cash cost of $20,000 on August 1, 19B. The security (due in 12 months) earns 9 percent annual interest on its principal amount of $20,000, payable on the date of maturity. At the end of the annual accounting period (December 31), the same security could be purchased for $19,600 cash.

a. Give all of the journal entries for Cable Company that are indicated on the following dates and provide an explanation for each date:
  (1) August 1, 19B.
  (2) December 31, 19B.
  (3) July 31, 19C.

b. Show how the security would affect the 19B financial statements.

PART C

E8–10. Approximately 40 percent of the merchandise sold by Gordon Company is sold on credit. Accounts receivable that are overdue, if material in amount, are "converted" to notes receivable when possible. This case traces one sale through accounts receivable, to notes receivable, and to final collection. The related transactions during 19B were:

Jan. 10 Sold merchandise on account to B. A. Cable for $10,000; terms, n/30.

Mar. 1 The account was unpaid; therefore, Gordon Company asked Cable to sign a six-month 12 percent, interest-bearing note for the account. Cable executed the note on this date.

Aug. 31 Cable paid the principal of the note plus interest.

Required:

a. Give the journal entry that Gordon should make on each of the three dates.

b. Give the journal entry that would have been made on September 1, 19B, assuming Cable defaulted.

c. Give the journal entry assuming the default in *(b)* and also that Cable paid the note in full on September 15, 19B (no additional interest was paid).

E8–11.   Hoosier Company sells a line of products that has a high unit sales price. Credit terms are traditional in the industry; accordingly, Hoosier frequently takes a promissory note for the sale price. This exercise follows one promissory note, taken at date of sale, through final collection. The accounting year ends December 31. The transactions and events were:

19B

Dec. 1 Sold merchandise to B. T. Hamm on a three-month, 12 percent, interest-bearing note for $3,000.

     31 End of accounting year, adjusting entry.

19C

Jan. 1 Start of new accounting period.

Mar. 1 Collected the note plus interest.

Required:

a. Give appropriate journal entries for Hoosier Company at each of the four dates; if none, so state.

b. With respect to the note, what item(s) and amount(s) would be reported on the 19B income statement?

c. With respect to the note, what item(s) and amount(s) would be reported on the balance sheet at December 31, 19B?

E8–12.   Jones Company frequently sells merchandise on a promissory note, which later is sold (i.e., discounted) to the local bank to obtain cash needed before maturity date. The following transactions relate to one note that followed this pattern:

19B

Apr. 1 Sold merchandise for $9,000 to R. C. Day; took a six-month, 12 percent, interest-bearing note.

June 1 Discounted the note at the local bank at an 11 percent discount rate; received the cash proceeds upon endorsement of the note to the bank.

Oct. 1 Due date of the note plus interest.

Required:

a. Give appropriate journal entries at each of the three dates, assuming Day paid the bank for the note on due date.

b. Give the appropriate journal entry on October 1, 19B, assuming Day defaulted on the note and Jones Company had to make payment plus a $20 protest fee. This protest fee will be charged to Day.

c. Give the appropriate journal entry assuming Day paid Jones in full on October 5, 19B (no additional interest was paid).

E8–13. (Based on Supplement 8A)   On January 1, 19B, Boston Company established a petty cash fund amounting to $200 by writing a check to "Petty Cash." The fund was assigned to J. Wright, an employee, to administer as custodian. At the end of January there was $10 cash remaining in the fund. Signed receipts for expenditures during January were summarized as follows: postage, $63; office supplies, $28; transportation, $51; newspapers, $34; and miscellaneous (coffee for the office), $14.

Required:

a. Give the journal entry to establish the petty cash fund on January 1, 19B.
b. Give the journal entry to replenish the fund on January 31, 19B.
c. What balance would be reflected in the Petty Cash account in the ledger at January 31? Explain.
d. How would petty cash be reported on the balance sheet at January 31, 19B?
e. What effect did the petty cash fund activities have on the January 19B income statement?
f. Assume it is January 5, 19C, and the management has decided to increase the petty cash fund to $250. Give the required journal entry.

PROBLEMS/CASES

PART A

PC8–1. Careless Company has one trusted employee who, as the owner said, "handles all of the bookkeeping and paperwork for the company." This employee also is responsible for counting, verifying, and recording cash receipts and payments, such as making the weekly bank deposit, preparing checks for major expenditures (signed by the owner), making small expenditures from the cash register for daily expenses, and collecting accounts receivable. The owner asked the local bank for a $25,000 loan, whereupon the bank asked that an audit be performed covering the year just ended. The independent auditor (a local CPA), in a private conference with the owner, presented some evidence of the following activities of the trusted employee during the past year:

1. Cash sales sometimes were not entered in the cash register, and the trusted employee pocketed approximately $40 per month.
2. Cash taken from the cash register (and pocketed by the trusted employee) was replaced with **expense memos** with fictitious signatures (approximately $10 per day).
3. A $500 collection on an account receivable of a valued out-of-town customer was pocketed by the trusted employee and was covered by making a $500 entry as a debit to Return Sales and a credit to Accounts Receivable.
4. A $700 collection on an account receivable from a local customer was pocketed by the trusted employee and was covered by making a $700 entry as a debit to Allowance for Doubtful Accounts and a credit to Accounts Receivable.

Required:

a. What was the approximate amount stolen during the past year?
b. What would be your recommendations to the owner?

PC8–2. Hall Manufacturing Company is a relatively small local business that specializes in the repair and renovation of antique jewelry, brass objects, and silverware. The owner is an expert craftsman. Although a number of skilled workers are employed, there is always a large backlog of work to be done. A long-time employee, who serves as clerk-bookkeeper, handles cash receipts, keeps the records, and writes checks for disbursements. The checks are signed by the owner. Small amounts are paid in cash by the clerk-bookkeeper, subject to a month-end review by the owner. Approximately 100 regular customers regularly are extended credit, that typically amount to less than $500. Although credit losses are small, in recent years the bookkeeper had established an Allowance for Doubtful Accounts, and all write-offs were made at year-end. During January 19E (the current year), the owner decided to start construction as soon as possible of a building for the business that would provide many advantages over the presently rented space and would have space usable for expansion of facilities. As a part of the considerations in financing, the financing institution asked for "19D audited financial statements." The company records never had been audited. Early in the audit, the independent CPA found numerous errors and one combination of amounts, in particular, that caused concern.

There was some evidence that a $1,500 job completed by Hall had been recorded as a receivable (from a new customer) on July 15, 19D. The receivable was credited for a $1,500 cash collection a few days later. The new account never was active again. The auditor also observed that shortly thereafter three write-offs of Accounts Receivable balances had been made to Allowance for Doubtful Accounts as follows: Jones, $250; Adams, $750; and Coster, $500; all of whom were known as regular customers. These write-offs drew the attention of the auditor.

Required:

a. Can you determine what caused the CPA to be concerned? Explain. Should the CPA report his suspicions to the owner?

b. What recommendations would you make in respect to internal control procedures for this company?

PC8–3. The bookkeeper at Laizee Company has not reconciled the bank statement with the Cash account, saying, "I don't have time." You have been asked to prepare a reconciliation and review the procedures with the bookkeeper.

The April 30, 19D, bank statement and the April ledger accounts for cash showed the following (summarized):

Bank Statement

	Checks	Deposits	Balance
Balance, April 1, 19D.................			$23,550
Deposits during April		$38,000	61,550
Note collected for depositor			
(including $90 interest)		1,090	62,640
Checks cleared during April	$44,700		17,940
NSF check—A. B. Cage	140		17,800
Bank service charges	30		17,770
Balance, April 30, 19D................			17,770

Cash

Apr.	1	Balance	22,850	Apr.	Checks written	44,500
Apr.		Deposits	42,000			

Petty Cash

Apr. 30 Balance	200	

A comparison of checks written before and during April with the checks cleared through the bank reflected outstanding checks at the end of April of $600. No deposits in transit were carried over from March, but there was a deposit in transit at the end of April. Cash on hand, held for change, at the end of April was $100 (included in the regular Cash account).

Required:

a. Prepare a detailed bank reconciliation for April.
b. Give any required journal entries as a result of the reconciliation. Why are they necessary?
c. What were the balances in the cash accounts in the ledger on May 1, 19D?
d. What total amount of cash should be reported on the balance sheet at the end of April?

PC8–4. The August 19B bank statement for Western Company and the August 19B ledger accounts for cash are given below:

Bank Statement

	Checks	Deposits	Balance
Aug. 1			$16,000
2	$ 300		15,700
3		$7,000	22,700
4	400		22,300
5	200		22,100
9	900		21,200
10	300		20,900
15		9,000	29,900
21	700		29,200
24	21,000		8,200
25		8,000	16,200
30	800		15,400
31		2,180*	17,580
31	30†		17,550

* $2,000 note collected plus interest.
† Bank service charge.

Cash

		Checks written:	
Aug. 1 Balance	15,250	Aug. 2	300
Deposits:		4	900
Aug. 2	7,000	15	600
12	9,000	17	550
24	8,000	18	800
31	6,000	18	700
		23	21,000

Petty Cash

Aug. 31 Balance	100	

Cash on hand for making change at the end of August amounted to $150 (included in the regular Cash account). There were three outstanding checks at the end of July: $200, $400, and $300. There were no deposits in transit at the end of July.

Required:

a. Determine the deposits in transit at the end of August.
b. Determine the outstanding checks at the end of August.
c. Prepare a bank reconciliation for August.
d. Give any journal entries that should be made as a result of the bank reconciliation by Western Company. Why are they necessary?
e. After the reconciliation journal entries are posted, what balances would be reflected in the cash accounts in the ledger?
f. What total amount of cash should be reported on the August 31, 19B, balance sheet?

PC8–5. The December 31, 19B, bank statement for Never-out Company and the December 19B ledger accounts for cash are given below.

Bank Statement

Date	Checks	Deposits	Balance
Dec. 1			$41,000
2	400, 150	16,000	56,450
4	7,000, 80		49,370
6	120, 180, 1,500		47,570
11	900, 1,200, 90	21,000	66,380
13	450, 700, 1,900		63,330
17	17,000, 2,000		44,330
23	40, 23,500	36,000	56,790
26	1,800, 2,650		52,340
28	2,200, 4,800		45,340
30	13,000, 1,890, 200*	19,000	49,250
31	1,650, 1,200, 28‡	6,360†	52,732

* NSF check, J. Doe, a customer.
† Note collected, principal, $6,000 plus interest.
‡ Bank service charge.

Cash

Dec. 1 Balance	55,850	Checks written during December:		
Deposits:		40	5,000	2,650
Dec. 11	21,000	13,000	4,800	1,650
23	36,000	700	1,890	2,200
30	19,000	4,400	1,500	7,000
31	17,000	1,200	120	150
		180	80	450
		17,000	23,500	2,000
		90	900	1,900
		1,800	1,200	

Petty Cash

Dec. 31 Balance	150	

The November 19B, bank reconciliation showed the following: True cash balance at November 30, $55,700; deposits in transit on November 30, $16,000; and outstanding checks on November 30, $400 + $900 = $1,300. At the end of December 19B, cash held on hand for making change amounted to $150 (included in the regular Cash account).

Required:

a. Determine the deposits in transit December 31, 19B.
b. Determine the outstanding checks at December 31, 19B.
c. Prepare a bank reconciliation at December 31, 19B.
d. Give any journal entries that should be made as a result of the bank reconciliation made by Never-out Company. Why are they necessary?
e. After the reconciliation journal entries, what balances would be reflected in the cash accounts in the ledger?
f. What total amount of cash should be reported on the December 31, 19B, balance sheet?

PART B

PC8–6.   Davis Company, to use idle cash, usually acquires common stocks as a short-term investment. This case focuses on the purchase of three different common stocks during 19B. The annual accounting period ends December 31. The sequence of transactions was:

19B
Apr.   2   Purchased (with cash) the following common stocks as a short-term investment:

Corporation	Number of shares	Total price per share
X	300	$50
Y	400	70
Z	500	90

Sept. 8   Received a cash dividend of $2 per share on Corporation Z stock.
Dec. 30   Sold the stock of Corporation Y for $76 per share.
Dec. 31   Quoted market prices on this date were: Corporation X stock, $53; Corporation Y stock, $75; and Corporation Z stock, $86.

Required:

a. Give the journal entry for Davis Company on each date.
b. Illustrate how the effects of these investments would be reflected on the 19B income statement and the balance sheet at December 31, 19B.
c. What was the amount of the 19B holding loss? Explain what this means.
d. Assume it is December 31, 19C, and that all of the X and Z shares still are held and that their market values per share are X, $51; and Z, $88. Give the required LCM entry. (Hint: Leave the correct balance in the Allowance account.)

PC8–7.   On July 1, 19D, CAL Corporation purchased, as a short-term investment, ten $1,000, 10 percent bonds of Lowe Corporation at par (i.e., at $1,000 each). The bonds mature on June 30, 19G. Annual interest is payable on June 30 each year. The accounting period for CAL Corporation ends on December 31.

Required:

a. Give the journal entries required for CAL Corporation on the following dates (if no entry is required, explain why): July 1, 19D, and December 31, 19D (adjusting entry).
b. At the end of 19D, the bonds were quoted on the market at $990 each. Give any LCM basis journal entry required on December 31, 19D. If none is required, explain why.

c. Show how this investment would be reported on the 19D balance sheet and income statement.

d. Give the journal entry required on June 30, 19E.

PC8–8. Superior Manufacturing Company produces and sells one main product. Demand is seasonal, and the unit sales price is high. Superior's accounting year ends December 31. Typically, in the busy months of the demand cycle, the company collects large amounts of cash, which is idle during the slow months. As a consequence, the company consistently acquires short-term investments to earn a return on what otherwise would be idle cash. Recently, the company purchased 1,000 shares of common stock in each of two other corporations—Corporations A and B. The prices per share, including fees and related costs, were A, $30; and B, $70. In addition, Superior purchased a $10,000 bond of James Corporation. The bond pays 9 percent annual interest on each March 31. The bond was purchased on April 1, 19B, for $10,000 cash (i.e., at par).

The sequence of transactions was:

19B

Apr. 1 Purchased the 2,000 shares of common stocks and the $10,000 bond. (Hint: Account for the stock and bond portfolios separately.)

Oct. 3 Received a cash dividend of $.60 per share on the stock of Corporation B.

Nov. 30 Sold 600 shares of the stock of Corporation A at $26 per share and 600 shares of the stock of Corporation B at $75 per share.

Dec. 31 End of the accounting period. The market prices on this date were A stock, $29; B stock, $68; and James bonds, 100 (i.e., at par). (Hint: Do not overlook accrued interest.)

Required:

a. Give the journal entries for Superior at each of the four dates given above. Omit any closing entries.

b. Show how the effects of the investment would be reported on the balance sheet at December 31, 19B.

c. What items and amounts would be reported on the 19B income statement?

PART C

PC8–9. Doan Company sells approximately 60 percent of its merchandise on credit; terms, n/30. Occasionally, a promissory note will be received as a part of the collection process of a delinquent account. This case focuses on two different sales that ended with promissory notes. The annual accounting period ends December 31. The sequence of transactions was:

Note No. 1:

19B

Feb. 15 Sold merchandise for $3,000 to A. B. Lee; received $1,000 cash, and the balance was debited to Accounts Receivable.

Apr. 1 Received an interest-bearing note in settlement of the overdue account of Lee. Terms of the note were four months, 12 percent interest.

July 31 Due date for note; Lee defaulted.

Oct. 1 Lee paid the defaulted note plus interest, plus 8 percent interest on the defaulted amount for the period July 31–October 1. The 8 percent is the legal rate of interest on overdue obligations.

Note No. 2:

19B

Oct. 1 Sold merchandise for $3,600 to J. K. Pope, received $600 cash, and the balance was charged to Accounts Receivable (terms, n/EOM).

Nov. 1 Received an interest-bearing note in settlement of the overdue account from Pope. The terms of the note were three months, 12 percent interest.

Dec. 31 End of fiscal period.

19C

Jan. 1 Start of new accounting period.

     30 Maturity date of the note. Pope paid the principal plus interest.

Required:

a. Note No. 1—Give the required journal entries for Doan Company on each date. Show interest calculations. Omit any closing entries.

b. Note No. 2—Give the required journal entries for Doan Company on each date. Show interest calculations. Omit any closing entries.

c. Note No. 2—How much interest revenue will be reported on the 19B income statement of Doan Company?

d. Note No. 2—How will this note affect the 19B balance sheet of Doan Company?

PC8–10. Farmer Company sells heavy machinery. Credit terms are customary and usually involve promissory notes and a mortgage on the machinery sold. Down payments of 20 percent to $33\frac{1}{3}$ percent are required. The annual accounting period ends December 31. This problem focuses on two different promissory notes that were received in 19B. The transactions were:

Note No. 1:

19B

Feb. 1 Sold equipment to W. D. Fort for $30,000; received a 20 percent cash down payment and a four-month, 12 percent, interest-bearing note for the balance.

Mar. 1 Sold the note to the local bank at a 10 percent discount rate; endorsed the note to the bank and received the cash proceeds.

June 1 Due date of the note plus interest; Fort paid the note and interest in full.

Required:

a. Give the journal entry for Farmer Company on each of the three dates. Show interest computations. Assume that Fort paid the bank the principal plus interest on the due date.

b. Give the journal entry on the due date, June 1, 19B, assuming instead that Fort defaulted on the note and Farmer paid the local bank the face amount of the note plus interest, and plus a $25 protest fee.

c. How much interest revenue will be reported on the 19B income statement for Note No. 1?

Note No. 2:

19B

Dec. 1 Sold equipment to W. T. Owens for $20,000; received $5,000 cash down payment and a three-month, 12 percent, interest-bearing note for the balance.

  31 End of accounting period.

19C

Jan. 1 Start of new accounting period.

Mar. 1 Due date of the principal plus interest; Owens paid the note plus interest in full.

Required:

d. Give the journal entry for Farmer Company on each of the four dates (omit any closing entries). State any assumptions you make.

e. How much interest revenue (Note No. 2) will be reported on the 19B income statement?

f. Show how Note No. 2 should be reported on the balance sheet at December 31, 19B.

PC8–11. (Based on Supplement 8B) York Company completes a variety of transactions each year. A number of them are repetitive in nature; therefore, the company maintains five different journals: general, credit sales, credit purchases, cash receipts, and cash payments. Selected transactions are listed below that are to be appropriately entered in these journals. To shorten this case amounts have been simplified and the number of transactions limited. All credit sales and credit purchases are recorded net of discount.

Selected transactions are listed below (use the letter to the left in lieu of the date and use the letter *v* for the last day of the period):

a. Sold merchandise to K. K. May at invoice cost of $250; terms, 2/10, n/20; Invoice No. 38.

b. Received merchandise from Sable Company at invoice cost of $300; credit terms, 1/10, n/20; Purchase Order No. 17.

c. Sold merchandise to B. B. Wise for $200 on credit; terms, 2/10, n/20; Invoice No. 39.

d. Received merchandise from Rex Supply Company at an invoice cost of $200 on credit; terms, 1/10, n/20; Purchase Order No. 18.

e. Sold merchandise to A. B. Cox for $150.

f. Received merchandise from Baker Manufacturing Company at a cost of $360; paid cash (number the checks consecutively starting with No. 81).

g. Purchased an operational asset (machinery) at a cost of $3,000; gave a 90-day, 12 percent, interest-bearing note payable for the purchase price.

h. Sold a tract of land for $9,000 which previously was used by the company as a parking lot and originally cost $3,000; collected cash.

i. Collected the account receivable from B. B. Wise within the discount period; Invoice No. 39.

j. Paid $600 for a three-year insurance policy on operational assets.

k. Obtained a $5,000 bank loan; signed a one-year, 12 percent, interest-bearing note payable.

l. Paid the account payable to Rex Supply Company within the discount period.

m. Paid monthly rent, $650.

n. Sold merchandise for cash, $1,400.

o. Purchased merchandise for cash, $980.

p. Sold merchandise on credit to C. C. Coe for $700; terms, 2/10, n/20; Invoice No. 40.

q. Received merchandise on credit from Stubbs Company at an invoice cost of $400; terms, 2/10, n/30; Purchase Order No. 19.

r. Collected the account receivable from K. K. May after the discount period.

s. Paid the account payable to Sable Company after the discount period.

t. Paid monthly salaries, $2,400.

u. By year-end, six months of the prepaid insurance had expired.

Use the following general ledger account code numbers for posting: Cash, 11; Accounts Receivable, 14; Prepaid Insurance, 16; Machinery, 17; Land, 19; Accounts Payable, 21; Notes Payable, 22; Purchases, 31; Purchase Discounts Lost, 33; Sales Revenue, 41; Sales Discount Revenue, 43; Expenses, 51; and Gain on Sale of Operational Assets, 53. For journals, use the following page numbers: General, 15; Credit Sales, 18; Credit Purchases, 14; Cash Receipts, 21; and Cash Payments, 34.

Required:

1. Draft a format for each of the five journals, including a general journal, following the illustrations included in Supplement 8B. Include folio columns.

2. Set up separate T-accounts for each of the general ledger accounts listed above.

3. Set up separate T-accounts (with account numbers) for the subsidiary ledgers as follows:

Accounts receivable (14)	*Accounts payable (21)*
Coe—14.1	Stable—21.1
May—14.2	Stubbs—21.2
Wise—14.3	Rex—21.3

4. Enter each transaction in the appropriate journal.

5. Indicate all postings to the **subsidiary ledgers** by entering appropriate account numbers in the folio columns.

6. Total each money column in the special journals and indicate all postings to the **general ledger** accounts by entering the account code numbers in the folio columns and below total amounts posted. Use the account code numbers given above.

PC8–12. Refer to the financial statements of Johnson & Johnson in Special Supplement B immediately preceding the Index. Respond to the following questions using the 1982 financial statements:

1. How much did cash and marketable securities change during 1982?

2. How much cash was invested in additions to property, plant, and equipment during 1982?

3. How much did the company have invested in marketable securities? Explain the basis for the classification of these securities.

4. Did the company make a journal entry for lower of cost or market on the marketable securities? Explain.

5. Complete the following schedule:

	1982	1981
Accounts receivable	_____	_____
Less: Allowance for doubtful accounts	_____	_____
Accounts receivable expected to be collected	_____	_____

6. What was the book value of accounts receivable at the end of 1982?

7. Assume bad debts of $1.1 million were written-off during 1982. Give the journal entry that J&J would have made.

8. How much did the allowance for doubtful accounts increase during 1982?

9. Using your response to Question 8 and assuming the write-off of $1.1 million of bad debts during 1982, give the journal entry that J&J would have made for bad debt expense for 1982.

10. What was the percent of the balance in the allowance for doubtful accounts to sales to customers for 1982? Was the percent for 1981 higher or lower than 1982?

Operational Assets—Plant and Equipment, Natural Resources, and Intangibles

PURPOSE OF THIS CHAPTER

Operational assets are the **noncurrent assets** that a business retains more or less permanently (not for sale) for use (physical substance or in terms of rights) in the course of **normal ongoing operations.** Operational assets include land in use, plant and equipment, furniture and fixtures, natural resources, and certain intangibles (such as a patent) used in operating the business. Operational assets also are referred to as "fixed" assets, "long-lived" assets, or "property, plant, and equipment." The degree of efficiency in the utilization of the operational assets influences the earnings of the business. The types and costs of the operational assets, their ages and states of repair, and the future demands for funds needed to replace them influence many important decisions. The expense of maintaining and operating these assets often has a major effect on income.

An operational asset is acquired by a business because of the future services potentially available from the asset to create future revenue through use by the entity. Thus, such an asset can be viewed as a bundle of services that is purchased in **advance of usage** for creating revenue. As those services are used, as in the use of a machine, the **prepaid cost** of the services, in part, is allocated as an **expense** of each of the periods of utilization. To illustrate, assume a truck is purchased at a cost of $10,000 for use in the business. The cost is debited to an asset account and, assuming a five-year useful life, each year a part of the cost of the asset is apportioned to expense. This periodic apportionment of the prepaid costs of operational assets to expense is known as **depreciation, depletion, or amortization,** depending upon the characteristics of the particular asset.

The financial statements report information in respect to operational assets. The economic impact of operational assets on the balance sheet, income statement, and statement of changes in financial position is useful information for decision makers.

The purpose of this chapter is to discuss and illustrate the measuring, accounting, and reporting of operational assets *(a)* at acquisition, *(b)* during subsequent use, and *(c)* at disposition. To accomplish this purpose the chapter is subdivided as follows:

Part A—Property, plant and equipment, and depreciation

Part B—Repairs and maintenance, natural resources, and intangible operational assets

Supplement 9A—Trading in assets

CLASSIFICATION OF OPERATIONAL ASSETS

Typical business operations require a combination of assets with different characteristics and purposes. Each type of asset—be it current, long-term investments, or operational—serves a particular purpose not served by the other types of assets. The optimum combination of assets varies with each business, and its determination is a major responsibility of the management. An objective of the financial statements is to report the different assets classified by types and the amount of resources committed to each type. For measuring and reporting purposes, operational assets may be classified broadly as:

1. **Tangible operational assets**—the long-lived tangible assets (i.e., having physical substance) acquired for continued use in carrying on the normal operations of the business and not intended for resale. Examples are land, buildings, equipment, furniture, tools, vehicles, and mineral deposits. There are three kinds of tangible operational assets: *(a)* land—not subject to depreciation; *(b)* plant, equipment, and fixtures—subject to periodic **depreciation;** and *(c)* natural resources—the wasting assets used in the operation of the business, such as coal mines, gravel pits, oil wells, and timber tracts. Natural resources are subject to **depletion.**
2. **Intangible operational assets**—the assets that do not have physical substance that are held by the business because of the **special rights** they confer. Examples are patents, copyrights, franchises, licenses, and trademarks. Intangible assets are subject to periodic **amortization.**

PRINCIPLES UNDERLYING ACCOUNTING FOR OPERATIONAL ASSETS

The primary phases of accounting for operational assets are:

1. Measuring and recording the cost of the asset at **acquisition** date.
2. After acquisition, measuring the expense of **using** the asset during its useful life.
3. Recording **disposals** of operational assets.

At the date of acquisition, an operational asset is measured and recorded in conformity with the **cost principle.** After acquisition, a portion of the cost of an operational asset (except land) is matched periodically with the revenues earned during its useful life in accordance with the **matching principle.**

PART A—PROPERTY, PLANT AND EQUIPMENT, AND DEPRECIATION

MEASURING AND RECORDING ACQUISITION COST

Under the **cost principle** (Exhibit 2–6), all reasonable and necessary costs incurred in acquiring an operational asset, placing it in its operational setting and preparing it for use, less any cash discounts, should be recorded in an appropriately designated asset account. Cost is measured as the **net cash equivalent** paid or to be paid. **Acquisition cost** can be determined readily when an operational asset is purchased for cash. For example, the acquisition cost of a machine on January 1, 19A, may be measured as follows:

Invoice price of the machine......................	$10,000
Less: Cash discount allowed ($10,000 × .02).......	200
Net cash invoice price	9,800
Add: Transportation charges paid by purchaser	150
Installation costs paid by purchaser	200
Sales tax paid ($10,000 × .02)	200
Cost—amount debited to the Machinery account.....	$10,350

The acquisition of this operational asset would be recorded as follows:

January 1, 19A:

Machinery	10,350	
Cash		10,350

The $10,350 cost of the machine is unaffected by whether the cash discount ($200) actually is taken by the purchaser. If it is not taken, the discount is **interest expense.**

When an operational asset is purchased and a **noncash** consideration is included in part, or in full, payment for it, the cash equivalent cost is measured as any cash paid plus the **market value** of the noncash consideration given. Alternatively, if the market value of the noncash consideration cannot be reasonably determined, the market value of the asset purchased is used for measurement purposes. To illustrate, assume a tract of timber (a natural resource) was acquired by Fast Corporation. Payment in full was made as follows: $28,000 cash plus 2,000 shares of Fast Corporation capital stock (nopar).[1] At the date of the purchase, Fast stock was selling at $12 per share. The cost of the tract would be measured as follows:

Cash paid	$28,000
Market value, noncash consideration given	
(2,000 shares nopar stock @ $12)................	24,000
	52,000
Title fees, legal fees, and other costs paid in cash	
(incidental to the acquisition)	1,000
Cost—amount debited to the asset account	$53,000

---

[1] See Chapter 12 for discussion of capital stock.

The journal entry to record the acquisition of this natural resource would be:

January 1, 19A:

Timber tract (#20)	53,000	
Cash		29,000
Capital stock, nopar (2,000 shares @ $12)		24,000

When land is purchased, all of the incidental costs paid by the purchaser, such as title fees, sales commissions, legal fees, title insurance, delinquent taxes, and surveying fees, should be included in the cost of the land. Because land is not subject to depreciation, it must be recorded and reported as a separate operational asset.

Not infrequently, an old building or used machinery is purchased for operational use in the business. Renovation and repair costs incurred by the purchaser **prior to use** should be debited to the asset account as a part of the cost of the asset. Repair costs incurred **after** the asset is placed in use usually are normal operating expenses.

Basket purchases

When two or more kinds of operational assets are acquired in a single transaction and for a single lump sum, the cost of each kind of asset acquired must be **measured and recorded separately.** For example, when a building and the land on which it is located are purchased for a lump sum at least two separate accounts must be established: one for the building (which is subject to depreciation) and one for the land (which is not subject to depreciation). This means that the single sum must be apportioned between the land and the building on a **rational** basis.

Relative market value of the several assets at the date of acquisition is the most logical basis on which to allocate the single lump sum. Appraisals or tax assessments often have to be used as indications of the market values. To illustrate, assume Fox Company paid a total of $300,000 cash to purchase a building suitable for an additional plant and the land on which the building is located. The separate, true market values of the building and land were not known; therefore, a professional appraisal was obtained that showed the following **estimated** market values: building, $189,000; and land, $126,000 (apparently the buyer got a good deal). The apportionment of the $300,000 purchase price and the journal entry to record the acquisition are illustrated in Exhibit 9–1.

Capitalization of interest as a cost of operational assets

In the preceding paragraphs we have discussed application of the **cost principle** in determining the acquisition cost of an operational asset. *FASB Statement 34* provides for the inclusion of **interest cost** as a part of the acquisition cost of an operational asset under very limited conditions. A basic concept of accounting is that interest on borrowed funds must be recorded and reported as interest

EXHIBIT 9–1
recording a basket
purchase of an
operational asset

Situation:

Fox Company purchased a building and the related land for $300,000 cash. Estimated current market values: building, $189,000; and land, $126,000.

Allocation of acquisition cost:

| Asset | Appraised value | | Apportionment of lump-sum acquisition cost | |
	Amount	Ratio	Computation	Apportioned cost
Building	$189,000	.60*	$300,000 × .60 =	$180,000
Land	126,000	.40†	300,000 × .40 =	120,000
	$315,000	1.00		$300,000

* $189,000 ÷ $315,000 = .60.
† $126,000 ÷ $315,000 = .40.

Entry to record the acquisition:

Plant building	180,000	
Land—plant site	120,000	
Cash		300,000

expense on the income statement when incurred. Interest is incurred on funds borrowed because of the **passage of time** (rather than when the related cash is paid); that is, interest is the **time cost of money**.

When an operational asset is purchased and a loan is incurred as all, or part, of the payment, periodic interest on the debt is recorded and reported as interest **expense** over the term of the loan. However, *FASB Statement 34* provides an exception to this principle. The exception is that interest cost must be capitalized as a part of the cost of acquiring assets that require a period of time to get them ready for their intended use. **In such situations, interest on the average expenditures incurred during the construction or acquisition period is recorded as a part of the cost of the operational asset.** Interest is included in the cost of the asset *(a)* **only** during the construction or acquisition period and *(b)* not in excess of total interest cost incurred by the entity during the period. It is not necessary that the debts of the company be related to the construction of the operational asset.[2]

To illustrate capitalization of interest during construction, assume that on January 1, 19A, Byers Corporation signed a contract that required Dow Construction Company to build a new plant building at a contract price of $1,000,000. The construction period started March 1, 19A, and the building was substantially

---

[2] FASB, *Statement of Financial Accounting Standards No. 34*, "Capitalization of Interest Cost" (Stamford, Conn., October 1979). Under this *Statement*, interest cannot be capitalized for assets that are (1) in use or ready for their intended use, or (2) not used in the earnings activities of the entity. *Statement 34* specifies the qualifying assets as follows: "Assets that are constructed or otherwise produced for an enterprise's own use (including assets constructed or produced for the enterprise by others for which deposits or progress payments have been made)."

complete and ready for its intended use on December 31, 19A (end of the 10-month construction period). Byers Corporation was required to make the following quarterly cash progress payments on the contract during 19A:

	Date of payment	Amount
a.	March 31, 19A	$ 120,000
b.	June 30, 19A	220,000
c.	September 30, 19A	480,000
d.	December 31, 19A	180,000
	Total	$1,000,000

To make the progress payments, Byers Corporation borrowed 60 percent of each payment from a financial institution at 10 percent annual interest; the remaining cash needed was from within Byers Corporation. Total interest cost incurred by Byers during the period was $70,000 (at an average rate of 10 percent).

Upon completion, December 31, 19A, Byers Corporation should reflect the following acquisition cost in the operational asset account, Plant Building:

Contract price (paid in full)		$1,000,000
Add interest during the construction period:		
a. $120,000 \times .10 \times 9/12 =$	$ 9,000	
b. $220,000 \times .10 \times 6/12 =$	11,000	
c. $480,000 \times .10 \times 3/12 =$	12,000	
d. $180,000$—no interest	–0–	32,000*
Total acquisition cost		$1,032,000

* Note that this amount was not based on the specific borrowings of 60 percent but on the expenditures. The amount cannot exceed the $70,000 total interest cost for the period (19A).

FASB Statement 34 provides the following guidelines that must be observed:

1. Interest is capitalized **only** during the construction period.
2. Interest is computed on the average **expenditures** during the construction period.
3. The applicable **borrowing interest rate** for the company is used.
4. Interest is computed **regardless of the source** of the funds (borrowed or obtained from normal operations of the entity).
5. Interest added to the cost of the operational assets **cannot** exceed the total amount of total interest cost incurred by the entity in that period (for all purposes).

MATCHING THE COST OF AN OPERATIONAL ASSET WITH FUTURE REVENUES

The acquisition cost of an operational asset that has a limited useful life represents the **prepaid cost** of a bundle of **future** services or benefits (i.e., future economic usefulness to the entity). The **matching principle** (Exhibit 2–6) requires that the acquisition cost of operational assets (other than land) be apportioned as expense to the periods in which revenue is earned as a result of using those assets. Thus, the acquisition cost of this kind of operational asset is matched in a systematic and rational manner in the future with the future revenues to which it contributes by way of services and benefits.

We should make clear the distinction among three different terms that are used to describe the cost apportionment required by the matching principle as follows:

1. **Depreciation**—the systematic and rational apportionment of the acquisition cost of **tangible operational assets** (other than natural resources) to future periods in which the services or benefits contribute to revenue. Example—depreciation of the $10,350 cost of a machine over its estimated useful life of 10 years and no residual value (see page 398):

   December 31, 19B:

Depreciation expense ($10,350 ÷ 10 years)	1,035	
Accumulated depreciation, machinery		1,035

2. **Depletion**—the systematic and rational apportionment of the acquisition cost of **natural resources** to future periods in which the use of those natural resources contributes to revenue. Example—depletion of the $53,000 cost of a timber tract over the estimated period of cutting based on "cutting" rate of approximately 20 percent per year (see page 399):

   December 31, 19B:

Depletion expense ($53,000 × .20)	10,600	
Timber tract (No. 20)		10,600
Note: A contra account could be used such as Accumulated Depletion.		

3. **Amortization**—the systematic and rational apportionment of the acquisition cost of **intangible operational assets** to future periods in which the benefits contribute to revenue. Example—amortization of the $8,500 cost of a patent over its estimated economic useful life to the entity of 17 years:

December 31, 19B:

Patent expense ($8,500 ÷ 17 years) 500
    Patents 500
Note: A contra account could be used such as Accumulated Patent Amortization.

The three terms—depreciation, depletion, and amortization—relate to the same basic objective; namely, the apportionment of the acquisition cost of an operational asset to the future periods in which the benefits of its use contribute to earning revenue.

The amounts of depreciation, depletion, and amortization measured and recorded during each period are reported as expenses or costs for the period. The amounts of depreciation, depletion, and amortization **accumulated since acquisition date** are reported on the balance sheet as deductions from the assets to which they pertain. To illustrate, an operational asset, such as the machine illustrated above, would be reported on the balance sheet (at the end of the second year in the example) as follows:

Balance Sheet
At December 31, 19B

Property, plant, and equipment:
Machinery $10,350
    Less: Accumulated depreciation 2,070 $8,280*

or

Machinery (less accumulated depreciation, $2,070) $8,280*
   * Called book value or carrying value.

We emphasize that the amounts for operational assets reported on the balance sheet do not represent their market values at the balance sheet date, rather, the amounts are book, or carrying, values. The **book,** or **carrying value** of an operational asset is its acquisition cost, less the accumulated apportionments to expense of that cost from acquisition date to the date of the balance sheet. Recording and reporting depreciation is a process of **cost allocation;** it is not a process of determining the current market value of the asset. Under the **cost principle,** the cost of an operational asset is measured and recorded at acquisition date at its current market value. The cost is not remeasured on a market value basis at subsequent balance sheet dates, rather the acquistion cost is reduced by the accumulated expense allocation for depreciation, depletion, or amortization.

OPERATIONAL ASSETS SUBJECT TO DEPRECIATION

Two classifications of operational assets were identified on page 397. In this section, the discussion will be limited to those tangible operational assets subject to depreciation. The classification, **tangible operational assets,** includes all kinds of buildings, machinery, furniture, and other equipment used in the operation of the business. Although the term **fixed** asset is used sometimes, more descriptive terms such as **property, plant, and equipment** and **land, plant, and equipment** are used in most published financial statements.

Buildings, machinery, furniture, and other tangible operational assets (except land) decrease in economic utility to the user because of a number of causative factors, such as wear and tear, the passage of time, effects of the elements (such as the weather), obsolescence (i.e., becoming out-of-date), technological changes, and inadequacy. These causative factors always impact on such assets during the periods in which the assets are being used to generate revenues. Thus, under the **matching principle,** at the end of each accounting period an **adjusting entry** is needed to record these expense-causing factors. In developing the adjusting entry, accounting principles require that a **rational and systematic** measurement approach be used to match the acquisition cost of tangible operational assets with periodic revenues.[3]

Because of the wide diversity of operational assets subject to depreciation and the varying effects of the causative factors listed above, a number of **depreciation methods** have been developed that are acceptable for both accounting and income tax purposes. In the paragraphs to follow, we will discuss and illustrate the methods of measuring and recording depreciation that usually are used.

Each of the depreciation methods requires three amounts for each asset: (1) **actual acquisition cost,** (2) **estimated net residual value,** and (3) **estimated useful life.** It is important to observe that of these three amounts, two are **estimates** (residual value and useful or service life); thus, the periodic amount of depreciation expense that is recorded and reported is an **estimate.** To illustrate, depreciation expense may be measured as follows:

Acquisition cost	$625
Less: Estimated residual value	25
Amount to be depreciated over useful life	$600
Estimated useful life	3 years
Annual depreciation expense: $600 ÷ 3 = ...	$200

Estimated residual value[4] must be deducted from acquisition cost because it represents that part of the acquisition cost that is expected to be recovered by the user upon disposal of the asset at the end of its estimated useful life to the entity. **Residual value** is the total estimated amount to be recovered **less** any estimated costs of dismantling, disposal, and selling. Because disposal costs may

---

[3] AICPA, *Accounting Research Bulletin No. 43* (New York, 1961), chap. C, par. 5, defines depreciation accounting as "a system of accounting which aims to distribute the cost or other basic value of tangible capital assets, less salvage value (if any), over the estimated useful life of the unit (which may be a group of assets) in a systematic and rational manner. It is a process of allocation, not of valuation."

[4] Residual value also is called scrap value or salvage value; however, "residual value" is a more descriptive term because the asset may not be scrapped or sold as salvage upon disposition—a subsequent buyer may renovate it and reuse it for many years.

approximately equal the gross residual amount recovered, many depreciable assets are assumed to have no residual value. It is important to realize that the estimated net residual value is not necessarily the value of the asset as salvage or scrap, rather, it may be the value to another user at the date on which the **current owner** intends to dispose of it. For example, a company whose policy is to replace all trucks at the end of three years normally would use a higher estimated residual value than would a user of the same kind of truck whose policy is to replace the trucks at the end of five years.

Estimated useful or service life should be viewed as the useful **economic** life to the **present owner** rather than as the total economic life to all potential users. In the truck example above, for accounting purposes, one owner would use a three-year estimated useful life, whereas the other owner would use a five-year estimated useful life.

Estimates are necessary to allocate a known cost amount (the acquisition cost of an operational asset) over a number of future periods during which the asset will contribute to the earning of revenues. The allocation must be made at the end of each period because it would not be very useful in the measurement of periodic income to defer all cost allocations until the date of disposal of an operational asset which is "used up."

The determination of estimated useful life of an operational asset must conform to the **continuity assumption** (see Exhibit 2–6). This assumption holds that the business will continue as a going concern; that is, that the business will continue indefinitely to pursue its commercial objectives (it will not liquidate in the foreseeable future). This assumption prevents a business from estimating the life of an operational asset to be less than its potential life because of some conjecture that the business will liquidate in the near future.

DEPRECIATION METHODS

Several **methods of depreciation** will be discussed and illustrated in this section. For this purpose we will use the common set of facts and notations shown in Exhibit 9–2.

The several depreciation methods commonly used are identical in basic concept; that is, each method allocates a portion of the cost of a depreciable asset to

EXHIBIT 9–2
Illustrative data for depreciation

	Symbols	Illustrative amounts
Acquisition cost of a particular operational asset (a productive machine)	C	$625
Estimated net residual value at end of useful life	RV	$ 25
Estimated service life:		
Life in years	N^*	3
Life in units of productive output	P^*	10,000
Depreciation rate	R	
Dollar amount of depreciation expense per period	D	
* Lowercase letters will be used for the current period.		

each of a number of future periods in a systematic and rational manner. The methods vary among themselves as to the allocation pattern to each of the future periods.

The discussions to follow will define, illustrate, and evaluate the following commonly used depreciation methods:[5]

1. Straight line.
2. Productive output (units of production).
3. Sum-of-the-years' digits.
4. Declining balance.

Straight-line depreciation method

The straight-line method has been used widely because of its simplicity and apparent relationship to the pattern of use of the **utility** of many kinds of depreciable assets. Under this method, an **equal portion** of the acquisition cost less the estimated residual value is allocated to each accounting period during the estimated useful life. Thus, the annual depreciation expense is measured as follows (refer to Exhibit 9–2):

$$D = \frac{C - RV}{N} \quad \text{or} \quad D = \frac{\$625 - \$25}{3 \text{ years}} = \$200 \text{ depreciation expense per year}$$

A **depreciation schedule** covering the entire useful life of the machine can be developed as follows:

Depreciation Schedule—Straight-Line Method

		End of year	
Year	Periodic depreciation expense	Balance in accumulated depreciation	Book value
At acquisition			$625
1	$200	$200	425
2	200	400	225
3	200	600	25
	$600		

The adjusting entry for depreciation expense on this machine would be the same for each of the three years of the useful life, viz:

Adjusting entry	Year 1	Year 2	Year 3
Depreciation expense	200	200	200
Accumulated depreciation, machinery	200	200	200

[5] AICPA, *Accounting Trends and Techniques* (Annual Survey of Accounting Practices Followed in 600 Stockholders' Reports), 4th ed. (New York, 1981), p. 249, reports on the use of the various depreciation methods used by the 600 companies surveyed (some companies use more than one method): straight line, 565; declining balance, 57; sum-of-the-years' digits, 25; accelerated method—not specified, 68; and the units of production, 52.

Observe that (a) **depreciation expense** is a constant amount for each year (often called a fixed expense), (b) **accumulated** depreciation increases by an equal amount each year, and (c) **book value** decreases by the same amount each year. This is the reason for the designation, straight line.

The straight-line method is simple, rational, and systematic (i.e., logical, stable, consistent, and realistically predictable from period to period). It is especially appropriate where the asset is used essentially at the same rate each period. It implies an approximately equal decline in the economic usefulness of the asset each period. For these reasons, it is used far more often than all of the other methods combined (see footnote 5).

Productive-output method

The productive-output method, sometimes called the units-of-production method, is based upon the assumption that the revenue-generating benefits derived each period from a depreciable asset are related directly to the periodic **output** of the asset. For example, many accountants believe that certain equipment, such as a machine, should be depreciated on the basis of units produced each period (i.e., based on a measure of output) rather than on the mere passage of time as is assumed by the straight-line method. These accountants believe that many productive assets contribute to the earning of revenues only when they are used productively, not merely because time has passed.

The productive-output method relates acquisition cost less estimated residual value to the estimated productive output; therefore, a depreciation rate per unit of output is computed as follows (refer to Exhibit 9–2):

$$R = \frac{C - RV}{P} \quad \text{or} \quad R = \frac{\$625 - \$25}{10,000 \text{ units}} = \$.06 \text{ depreciation rate per unit of output}$$

Assuming 3,000 units of actual output from the illustrative machine in Year 1, depreciation expense for Year 1 would be:

$$D = R \times p \quad \text{or} \quad D = \$.06 \times 3,000 = \$180 \text{ depreciation expense}$$

Assuming actual output to be 5,000 units in Year 2 and 2,000 units in Year 3, a depreciation schedule could be developed as follows:

Depreciation Schedule—Productive-Output Method

Year	Periodic depreciation expense		End of year Balance in accumulated depreciation	Book value
At acquisition				$625
1	(3,000 × $.06)	$180	$180	445
2	(5,000 × .06)	300	480	145
3	(2,000 × .06)	120	600	25
		$600		

The **adjusting entry** for depreciation at the end of each year would be:

Adjusting entry	Year 1	Year 2	Year 3
Depreciation expense	180	300	120
Accumulated depreciation, machinery	180	300	120

Observe that depreciation expense, accumulated depreciation, and book value vary from period to period directly with the periodic outputs; thus, when the productive-output method is used, depreciation expense is said to be a **variable** expense.

The productive-output method is simple, rational, and systematic. It is appropriate where output of the asset can be measured realistically and where the economic utility of the asset to the entity tends to decrease with productive use rather than with the passage of time. Also, when the productive use varies significantly from period to period, a more realistic **matching** of expense with revenue is attained. Despite these conceptual and practical advantages, it is not used widely (see footnote 5).

Accelerated depreciation methods

Accelerated depreciation is based upon the notion that there should be relatively large amounts of depreciation expense reported in the early years of the useful life of the asset and correspondingly reduced amounts of depreciation expense in the later years. The basis for this conclusion is that a depreciable asset is more efficient in earning revenue in the early years than in the later years of its life. Also, repair expense tends to be lower in the early years and higher in the later years. Therefore, it is contended that the **combined effect** of decreasing depreciation expense and increasing repair expense is relatively constant from period to period over the life of the asset as illustrated below:

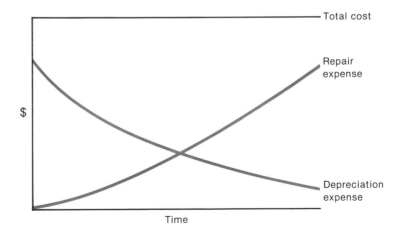

Accelerated depreciation has considerable appeal from the **income tax** viewpoint. Higher depreciation expense means lower reported periodic income amounts in the early years which causes income tax expense to be less. Of course, the effect reverses in the later years; however, an early tax deduction is to be preferred over a later tax deduction because of the **time value of money.**[6] There are several variations of accelerated depreciation; however, the two accelerated methods usually used are the sum-of-the-years'-digits method and the declining balance method.

Sum-of-the-years'-digits method. The sum-of-the-years'-digits method, sometimes abbreviated as the SYD method, is used primarily because it is simple and produces a significantly accelerated effect when compared with straight-line depreciation. Depreciation expense each year is computed by multiplying the acquisition cost, **less** estimated residual value, by a fraction that is successively **smaller** each year. Each of the decreasing fractions is determined by using the sum of the digits comprising the estimated useful life as the denominator and the specific year of life in **inverse order** as the numerator. The computations may be demonstrated as follows using the illustrative data given in Exhibit 9–2.

To compute the denominator:[7]
Sum of digits (comprising the useful life): $1 + 2 + 3 = 6$.
Numerators:
Digits (specific year of life) in inverse order: 3, 2, 1.

To compute the depreciation fraction:
Year 1, ³⁄₆; Year 2, ²⁄₆; Year 3, ¹⁄₆ (total ⁶⁄₆).

The accelerated effects of the SYD method can be observed in the following depreciation schedule:

Depreciation Schedule—Sum-of-the-Years'-Digits Method

Year	Computations	Periodic depreciation expense	Balance in accumulated depreciation (End of year)	Book value (End of year)
At acquisition.....				$625
1................	$600 × ³⁄₆ =	$300	$300	325
2................	600 × ²⁄₆ =	200	500	125
3................	600 × ¹⁄₆ =	100	600	25
Total		$600		

---

[6] The time value of money refers to interest that can be earned on money invested or used in the business.

[7] The denominator (i.e., sum of the digits) can be computed by using the formula:

$$SYD = n\left(\frac{n+1}{2}\right)$$

For example, a five-year life would be:

$$SYD = 5\left(\frac{5+1}{2}\right) = 15$$

The **adjusting entry** for depreciation expense by year would be:

Adjusting entry	Year 1	Year 2	Year 3
Depreciation expense	300	200	100
Accumulated depreciation, machinery	300	200	100

Observe that, compared to straight-line results (page 406), depreciation expense under the SYD method is higher in the earlier years and lower in the later years. The total amounts of depreciation expense over the entire life of the asset are the same under both methods.

The SYD method is relatively simple to apply and is considered to be "rational and systematic"; therefore, it is acceptable under generally accepted accounting principles. Reference to footnote 5 indicates that it is not used widely.

Declining balance method. The declining balance (DB) method of depreciation is based upon the income tax laws and regulations. Under current income tax regulations the DB rate of depreciation is determined by computing the straight-line (SL) rate ignoring residual value; the SL rate determined in this manner then is multiplied by the **income tax acceleration percentage** permitted for income tax purposes.[8] This acceleration rate varies at the current time from a high of 200 percent to a low of 150 percent depending upon the type of property and the date of acquisition. To illustrate, DB depreciation would be computed as follows assuming an estimated useful life of five years (see Exhibit 9–2):

1. Compute SL rate exclusive of residual value:

$$\text{1 period of life} \div \text{5 total periods} = 20\%$$

2. Computation of the DB rate for three different income tax acceleration rates (for illustrative purposes):

SL rate (excluding RV)	×	Income tax acceleration rate	=	DB depreciation rate
Case A 20%	×	200% or 2.00	=	40% or .40
Case B 20%	×	175% or 1.75	=	35% or .35
Case C 20%	×	150% or 1.50	=	30% or .30

Because DB depreciation is permitted for income tax purposes, and because it gives a significantly accelerated amount of depreciation expense (similar to SYD), it is used often on income tax returns. DB depreciation is considered by

---

[8] Accelerated depreciation is limited for tax purposes to assets having a useful life of three years or more (short periods are used in this textbook to simplify the computations). The Congress often changes the *income tax acceleration percentages* for various types of property. There are numerous other tax provisions which affect depreciation that are too detailed to be considered in this book.

many accountants to be unsound because it only incidentally conforms to the matching principle. Nevertheless, about 5 percent of a sample of companies use DB for financial accounting purposes, presumably because they use it for income tax purposes (see footnote 5). The DB method is the only method that ignores residual value.

Depreciation expense is computed by multiplying the **DB depreciation rate** (computed as illustrated above) by the **undepreciated cost of the asset** (i.e., its current book value) ignoring residual value. Because the estimated residual value is ignored in developing the DB rate, the undepreciated balance of the asset at the end of the last year of its life will tend to be **higher** than the residual value. However, it cannot be less because the income tax regulations specify that an asset cannot be depreciated below its estimated residual value.

Computation of DB depreciation expense is illustrated below using the data given in Exhibit 9–2 and assuming an **income tax acceleration percentage** of 150 percent:

To compute the DB rate:
SL rate (ignoring residual value) = 1 year ÷ 3 years = 33.3% or .333.
150% acceleration DB rate = 33.3% × 1.50 = 50%, or .50.
To compute annual depreciation expense (Year 1):
Current carrying value of the asset, $625 × .50 = $313.

The effects of the DB method are illustrated in the following schedule:

Depreciation Schedule—Declining Balance (DB) Method

Year	Computations	Periodic depreciation expense	Balance in accumulated depreciation	Book value
At acquisition				$625
1	.50 × $625	$313	$313	312
2	.50 × 312	156	469	156
3	.50 × 156	78	547	78*

End of year spans the "Balance in accumulated depreciation" and "Book value" columns.

* This must be the computed amount, but it cannot be less than the estimated residual value (in this illustration, not less than $25).

The adjusting entry for depreciation at each year-end would be:

Adjusting entry	Year 1	Year 2	Year 3
Depreciation expense	313	156	78
Accumulated depreciation, machinery	313	156	78

To date, the accounting profession has not provided officially definitive guidelines for selection of a depreciation method that would be preferable for each type of depreciable asset. Therefore, each one of the several methods can be

EXHIBIT 9–3
Depreciation
methods compared
graphically
(including a typical
repair curve)

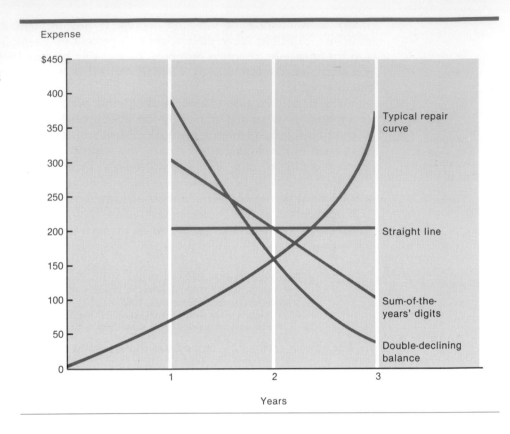

characterized as an acceptable alternative for financial reporting purposes, which means that any of the above depreciation methods may be used regardless of the characteristics of the operational asset and the way it is used. Exhibit 9–3 further illustrates the significant differences among the three most commonly used depreciation methods.

GAAP requires that the depreciation method selected must be "rational and systematic" and that it should reliably measure net income of the company considering the circumstances in which the asset is used. Thus, it is usual for a company to use more than one depreciation method.

DEPRECIATION EFFECTS ON INCOME AND CASH FLOW

Although each of the four depreciation methods produces different amounts of depreciation expense each accounting period of the life of an asset, the **total** amount of depreciation expense recorded over the life of the asset is the same (i.e., its acquisition cost less any residual value), except for the DB method in some cases. Because each method produces a different pattern of depreciation expense, during the life of the asset each one will cause different periodic amounts to be reported for *(a)* pretax income, *(b)* income tax expense, *(c)* net income, *(d)* retained earnings, and *(e)* book value of the asset. Depreciation often is confusing

EXHIBIT 9–4 Illustration of depreciation effects on net income and cash flow

Panel A—Data assumed (refer to Exhibit 9–2):

Revenues (all cash): Year 1, $5,000; Year 2, $6,000; Year 3, $7,000.

	Year 1	Year 2	Year 3
Depreciation expense:			
SL (straight line) (refer to page 406)	$ 200	$ 200	$ 200
SYD (refer to page 410)	300	200	100
Remaining expenses (all cash)	2,800	3,300	3,800
Income tax rate, 20%.			

Panel B—Income statements comparing SL and SYD:

	Year 1		Year 2		Year 3	
Accrual basis	SL	SYD	SL	SYD	SL	SYD
Revenues (cash)	$ 5,000	$ 5,000	$ 6,000	$ 6,000	$ 7,000	$ 7,000
Depreciation expense (noncash)	(200)	(300)	(200)	(200)	(200)	(100)
Remaining expenses (cash)	(2,800)	(2,800)	(3,300)	(3,300)	(3,800)	(3,800)
*Pretax income	2,000	1,900	2,500	2,500	3,000	3,100
Income tax expense (20%)	(400)	(380)	(500)	(500)	(600)	(620)
†Net income	$ 1,600	$ 1,520	$ 2,000	$ 2,000	$ 2,400	$ 2,480

  * Different between SL and SYD by the amount of depreciation expense.
  † Different between SL and SYD by the amount of depreciation expense *less* the reduction in income tax expense.

Panel C—Depreciation effects on cash flow comparing SL and SYD:

	Year 1		Year 2		Year 3	
Cash flow basis	SL	SYD	SL	SYD	SL	SYD
Revenues (all cash)	$ 5,000	$ 5,000	$ 6,000	$ 6,000	$ 7,000	$ 7,000
Depreciation expense (noncash)	–0–	–0–	–0–	–0–	–0–	–0–
Remaining expenses (all cash)	(2,800)	(2,800)	(3,300)	(3,300)	(3,800)	(3,800)
*Pretax cash inflow	2,200	2,200	2,700	2,700	3,200	3,200
Income tax expense (all cash)	(400)	(380)	(500)	(500)	(600)	(620)
†Aftertax cash inflow	$ 1,800	$ 1,820	$ 2,000	$ 2,000	$ 2,600	$ 2,580

  * Same regardless of depreciation method used.
  † Different between SL and SYD by the difference in income tax.

to users of financial statements because of these varied effects, particularly as they relate to net income and cash flows (i.e., the receipts and payments of cash). Exhibit 9–4 illustrates the effects of depreciation on (a) the income statement and (b) cash flows under the SL and SYD methods.

Effects of depreciation on the income statement

Depreciation is an expense on the income statement, thus **pretax** income is reduced by the amount of depreciation expense for the period (refer to Exhibit 9–4, Panel B). However, because depreciation is tax deductible, it reduces net income each period only by its **aftertax** amount; that is, by the amount of depreciation expense less the tax reduction, or tax savings, it created. For example, in Exhibit 9–4, Panel A, straight-line depreciation expense in Year 1 of $200 reduced **pretax** income by $200 and also reduced income tax expense by $40. The net effect was to reduce net income by \$160 [i.e., \$200 − (\$200 × .20) = \$160]. In contrast, the **higher** SYD depreciation expense in Year 1 reduced net income by \$240 [i.e., \$300 − (\$300 × .20) = \$240].

Exhibit 9–4, Panel A, also compares the effects of straight-line (SL) depreciation with sum-of-the-years'-digits (SYD) depreciation over the entire life of a depreciable operational asset. Observe that in Year 1, SL produces a **higher** net income than does SYD; in Year 2 (the crossover year) both produce the same net income, and in Year 3, SL produces a **lower** net income than does SYD. In all cases, net income is changed by the **aftertax** amount of depreciation expense. Observe that the total net income for the three years was \$6,000, regardless of the depreciation method used.

Effects of depreciation on cash flow

When an operational asset is acquired, there is a cash **outflow** (i.e., payment) for its acquisition (and/or later cash outflows for any related debt). Subsequent journal entries for depreciation do not involve cash outflows because the expense lags the cash outflow already made. Therefore, depreciation expense does not represent a current cash outflow; it is a noncash expense on the income statement. However, depreciation expense does affect cash flow each period because it **reduces** the amount of income tax that otherwise would be paid. In this way it reduces the amount of cash outflow for income tax (this reduction often is called a "tax saving"). Thus, if depreciation expense is increased for the period the cash outflow for income tax is decreased. This cash flow effect is illustrated in Exhibit 9–4, Panel C. Observe in Panel C, for Year 1, that the **aftertax cash inflow is higher** under SYD than under SL even though Panel B shows **net income to be lower** under SYD than under SL. In Year 1, net income (Panel B) is \$80 **less** under SYD than under SL, which is caused by the **aftertax** effect of depreciation expense [i.e., (\$300 − \$200) − (\$400 − \$380) = \$80]. In contrast, cash inflow (Panel C) is \$20 more under SYD than under SL, which is caused by the "tax saving" of depreciation expense [i.e., (\$300 − \$200) × .20 = \$20]. In summary, as the amount of depreciation expense is increased net income is decreased and cash inflow is increased (i.e., tax saving).

Finally, let's consider some misleading terminology that often is used. Analysts and others often say that "cash is provided by depreciation." Depreciation is not a source of cash, and the accumulated depreciation amount does not represent cash or a fund of cash available to replace the operational asset when it is disposed of. Accumulated depreciation is a contra asset account (not cash). Exhibit 9–4, Panel C, demonstrates that *(a)* the aftertax cash inflow (bottom line) is the result of sales to customers, less cash expenses, and *(b)* depreciation expense reduces cash outflow because less income taxes are paid. A significant long-term effect of depreciation expense is a reduction of the cumulative balance of retained earnings. A lower balance in retained earnings in some situations possibly could reduce cash dividends. If cash dividends were reduced there would be a decrease in cash outflows.[9]

---

[9] The discussion in this section assumes the same depreciation method is used for financial reporting and income tax purposes. Chapter 10 discusses the reporting implications of the use of different depreciation methods for financial reporting and tax purposes.

DEPRECIATION FOR INTERIM PERIODS

The preceding illustrations assumed that depreciation expense for a full year is recorded at the end of each year by means of an adjusting entry. Some businesses record depreciation for interim periods, such as monthly, quarterly, or semiannually. Also, a depreciable asset may be acquired or disposed of during the year which requires that depreciation expense be recorded for periods of less than one year. It is customary to compute depreciation on a proportional basis to either the nearest month, quarter, or six-month period. For example, depreciation for a full month may be assumed to start or end at the nearest first of the month. For all of the methods illustrated, except productive output, monthly depreciation usually is determined by computing the annual amount of depreciation as illustrated, then dividing by 12 to obtain the monthly amount.[10] To illustrate, in Exhibit 9–4, sum-of-the-years'-digits (SYD) depreciation for the first year was determined to be $300. Assume the asset was acquired on August 12, 19A, with a December 31 fiscal year ending. The depreciation expense for 19A would be (nearest-month basis):

$$\frac{\$300}{12} \times 5 \text{ months} = \$125$$

Depreciation expense is an estimate; therefore, one never should record depreciation amounts below one dollar because this would suggest a higher degree of accuracy than is warranted. For this reason, depreciation amounts always should be rounded to the nearest amount—one, ten, or hundred dollars—depending upon the cost of the depreciable asset compared with total depreciable assets in accordance with the **materiality exception** (see Exhibit 2–6).

CHANGES IN DEPRECIATION ESTIMATES

Recall that depreciation is based on two estimates—useful life and residual value—which are made at the time a depreciable asset is acquired. Sometimes it is necessary to revise one, or both, of these initial estimates as experience with the asset accumulates. When it becomes clear that either estimate should be revised (to a material degree), the undepreciated balance, less any residual value, at that date should be apportioned, based on the new estimate, over the remaining estimated life. In accounting this is called a "change in estimate."

To illustrate, assume the following for a particular machine:

Cost of machine when acquired	$33,000
Estimated life	10 years
Estimated residual value	$ 3,000
Accumulated depreciation through Year 6	
(assuming the straight-line method is used)	$18,000

---

[10] Under the productive-output method, monthly depreciation is derived by multiplying the unit depreciation rate by the output for the particular month.

Shortly after the start of Year 7, the initial estimates were changed to the following:

Revised estimated total life .... 14 years
Revised estimated residual value $1,000

No entry is required when this decision is reached. However, the **adjusting entry at the end of Year 7** would be:

Depreciation expense	1,750	
Accumulated depreciation		1,750
Computations:		
Acquisition cost	$33,000	
Accumulated depreciation, Years 1–6	18,000	
Undepreciated balance..	15,000	
Less: Revised residual value	1,000	
Balance to be depreciated	$14,000	
Annual depreciation:		
$14,000 ÷ (14 years − 6 years) = ...	$ 1,750	

Under GAAP, changes in accounting estimates and depreciation methods should be made only when the new estimate or accounting method "better measures" the periodic income of the business. The **comparability principle** (Exhibit 2–6) requires that accounting information reported in the financial statements should be comparable across accounting periods and among similar entities. This principle exerts a significant constraint on changing depreciation estimates and methods unless the effect is to improve the measurement of depreciation expense and, hence, net income.

PART B—REPAIRS AND MAINTENANCE, NATURAL RESOURCES, AND INTANGIBLE OPERATIONAL ASSETS

REPAIRS AND MAINTENANCE

Subsequent to the acquisition of a tangible operational asset, related cost outlays often must be made for such items as ordinary repairs and maintenance, major repairs, replacements, and additions. The central measurement problem is determination of which expenditures should be recorded as expenses of the period when incurred, and which should be recorded as assets (i.e., as a prepayment) to be matched with **future** revenues. The term **expenditure** means the payment of cash or the incurrence of a debt for an asset or service received. The purchase of a machine or a service, such as repairs on a truck, may be for cash or on credit. In either case, there is an expenditure.

In measuring the cost of using operational assets, **two** basic types of expenditures are involved. The two types of expenditures are called capital expenditures and revenue expenditures.

Capital expenditures

Capital expenditures for the acquisition of an asset or for the expansion or improvement of an asset already owned. A capital expenditure benefits one or more accounting periods **beyond the current period;** therefore, capital expenditures are recorded in appropriate asset accounts. For example, a plant **addition** that cost $90,000 would be recorded as follows:

Plant	90,000	
Cash		90,000

Revenue expenditures

Revenue expenditures for **normal operating** items such as ordinary repairs, maintenance, and salaries that benefit **only** the current period; therefore, when revenue expenditures are incurred, they are debited directly to appropriate expense accounts.[11] For example, the payment of $600 for ordinary repairs to the plant would be recorded in the current period as follows:

Repair expense	600	
Cash		600

Each expenditure made subsequent to the acquisition of an operational asset must be evaluated carefully to classify it as either a capital or revenue expenditure. The distinction between capital and revenue expenditures is essential to conform with the matching principle. The expenditures must be matched with the periodic revenues to which they relate. The purpose and nature of the expenditure is the controlling factor in its classification. In the next few paragraphs we will discuss the usual types of outlays subsequent to acquisition of a tangible operational asset.

Extraordinary repairs

Extraordinary repairs are classified as **capital expenditures;** therefore, an extraordinary repair is debited to the related **asset** account and depreciated over the **remaining** life of that asset. **Extraordinary repairs** occur infrequently, involve relatively large amounts of money, and tend to increase the economic usefulness of the asset in the future because of either greater efficiency or longer life, or both. They are represented by major overhauls, complete reconditioning, and major replacements and betterments. For example, the complete replacement of a roof on the factory building would constitute an extraordinary repair, whereas patching the old roof would constitute an ordinary repair.

To illustrate the accounting for extraordinary repairs, assume a machine that originally cost $40,000 is being depreciated on a straight-line basis over 10 years

---

[11] The term *revenue* expenditure is widely used. It suggests that the expenditure is to be deducted in the current period from revenue in deriving income. However, a term such as expense expenditure would be more descriptive.

with no estimated residual value. At the beginning of the seventh year, a major reconditioning was completed at a cost of $12,700. The estimated useful life was changed from 10 years to 13 years (i.e., a change in estimate). A typical sequence of entries would be:

At acquisition of the asset:

Machinery	40,000	
Cash...		40,000
Purchase of machinery.		

Depreciation—annually at end of Years 1 through 6:

Depreciation expense	4,000	
Accumulated depreciation, machinery		4,000
Adjusting entry to record annual depreciation ($40,000 ÷ 10).		

Extraordinary repair—at start of seventh year:[12]

Machinery	12,700	
Cash...		12,700
Expenditure for major repair.		

Revised depreciation—annually at end of Years 7 through 13:

Depreciation expense	4,100	
Accumulated depreciation, machinery		4,100
Adjusting entry to record annual depreciation.		

Computation:
Original cost	$40,000	
Depreciation, Years 1–6	24,000	
Book value remaining		$16,000
Extraordinary repair		12,700
Balance to be depreciated over remaining life		$28,700
Annual depreciation: $28,700 ÷ (13 − 6) years = $4,100		

---

[12] Some accountants prefer to debit the related asset account, as illustrated above, only when the major repair increases the efficiency above normal. In contrast, when it is estimated that only the useful life is extended, those accountants instead would debit the related accumulated depreciation

Additions

Additions are extensions to, or enlargements of, existing assets, such as the addition of a wing to a present building. These represent **capital expenditures;** therefore, the cost of such additions should be debited to the existing account for the asset and depreciated over the remaining life of the asset to which the cost is related. However, if the life of the addition is shorter than the life of the related asset, the addition should be depreciated over its remaining life (less any residual value).

Ordinary repairs and maintenance

Ordinary repairs and maintenance always are classified as **revenue expenditures** and debited to an appropriate **expense** account in the period in which incurred. **Ordinary repairs and maintenance** are those relatively small recurring outlays essential to keep a tangible operating asset in **normal** operating condition. Ordinary repairs do not add materially to the economic value of the asset or to its estimated useful life. Rather, they tend to restore and repair the effects of normal wear and tear that occur with usage. As a consequence, normal repair and maintenance tend to assure that the expected useful life and operating efficiency of the asset will be maintained. These reasons justify the matching of current repair and maintenance expenditures (i.e., expense) with revenues of the current period.

NATURAL RESOURCES

Natural resources, such as a mineral deposit, oil well, or timber tract, often are referred to as "wasting assets" because they are consumed physically, or **depleted,** as used. When acquired or developed, a natural resource is measured and recorded in the accounts in accordance with the **cost principle.** As the natural resource is consumed or used up, the acquisition cost, in accordance with the **matching principle,** must be apportioned among the various periods in which the resulting revenues are recognized. The term **depletion** is used to describe this process of periodic cost allocation over the period of use of a natural resource. A **depletion rate** per unit of the resource produced is computed by dividing the total acquisition and development cost (less any estimated residual value, which is rare) by the **estimated** units that can be withdrawn economically from the resource. The depletion rate, thus computed, is multiplied each period by the **actual** number of units withdrawn. This procedure is the same as the productive-output method of calculating depreciation (see page 407).

To illustrate accounting for a natural resource, assume that a gravel pit was developed at a cost of $80,000 and that a reliable estimate was made that 100,000 cubic yards of gravel could be withdrawn economically from the pit. The **depletion rate per unit** would be computed as follows (assuming no residual value):

$$\$80,000 \div 100,000 \text{ cubic yards} = \$.80 \text{ per cubic yard (depletion rate per unit)}$$

account. This distinction usually is not made because it is difficult to apply practically. Also, subsequent book value and depreciation expense would be the same regardless of which account is debited because the remaining book value to be depreciated would be the same in either instance.

Depletion expense for the first year, assuming 5,000 cubic yards of gravel were withdrawn during the year, would be recorded by means of the following adjusting entry.[13]

Depletion expense 4,000
    Gravel pit   4,000
  Depletion for the year, 5,000 cubic yards × $.80 = $4,000.

At the end of the first year, this natural resource should be reported as follows:

Balance Sheet

Operational assets:
    Gravel pit (cost, $80,000 − $4,000 accumulated depletion) $76,000

Because it is difficult to estimate the recoverable units from a natural resource, the depletion rate often must be revised. This is a "change in estimate"; therefore, the undepleted acquisition cost is spread over the estimated remaining recoverable units by computing a new depletion rate. For example, assume in Year 2 that the estimate of recoverable units remaining was changed from 95,000 to 150,000 cubic yards. The depletion rate to be applied to the cubic yards of gravel withdrawn in Year 2 would be:

($80,000 − $4,000) ÷ 150,000 cubic yards = $.51 per cubic yard

When buildings and similar improvements are constructed in connection with the development and exploitation of a natural resource, they should be recorded in separate asset accounts and **depreciated**—not depleted. Their estimated useful lives cannot be longer than the time required to exploit the natural resource unless they have a significant use-value after the resource is depleted.

INTANGIBLE OPERATIONAL ASSETS

An intangible operational asset, like any other asset, has value because of certain rights and privileges conferred by law upon the owner of the asset. However, an intangible asset has no material or physical substance as do tangible assets such as land and buildings. Thus, intangible assets are characterized by their lack of physical substance and the special rights that ownership confers. Examples of intangible operational assets are patents, copyrights, franchises, licenses, trademarks, and goodwill. The acquisition of an intangible asset usually requires the expenditure of resources. For example, an entity may purchase a

---

[13] Consistent with the procedure for recording depreciation, an Accumulated Depletion account may be used. However, as a matter of precedent, the asset account itself usually is credited directly for the periodic depletion. Either procedure is acceptable. The same is true for intangible operational assets, discussed in the next section.

patent from the inventor. The cost of an intangible asset should be measured and recorded in the accounts and reported on the financial statements of the entity in the same way as a tangible asset.[14]

At acquisition, an intangible operational asset is recorded at its cash equivalent cost in accordance with the **cost principle.** Cost is defined as the sum of all expenditures made to acquire the rights or privileges.

Each type of intangible operational asset should be recorded in a separate asset account when acquired. To illustrate, assume that on January 1, 19A, Mason Company purchased a patent from its developer, J. Doe, at a cash price of $17,000. The acquisition of this intangible asset would be recorded as follows:

January 1, 19A:

Patents	17,000	
Cash		17,000
Purchase of patent rights from J. Doe.		

Under the cost principle, an intangible right or privilege, although it may have value, is not recorded unless there has been an identifiable expenditure of resources to acquire or develop it. For example, the demise of a competitor's patent may cause the company's patent to be more valuable. This increase in value would not be recorded because there was no expenditure of resources incident to the increase in value.

Research and development (R&D) costs are recorded as expenses in the period incurred, even though they sometimes result in the development of a patent which has future value.

Amortization of intangible operational assets

Intangible operational assets normally have limited lives; however, they seldom, if ever, have a residual value. Intangible assets have a limited life because the **rights or privileges** that give them value terminate or simply disappear. Therefore, the acquisition cost of an intangible operational asset must be written off over its estimated economic life. This systematic write-off usually is called **amortization.**

APB Opinion 17, requires that each intangible asset be amortized over its estimated economic life. The *Opinion* specifies that, for accounting purposes, the estimated useful life of an intangible asset cannot exceed 40 years. The *Opinion* does not permit an arbitrary and immediate write-off of an intangible asset. Prior to *Opinion 17,* this write-down sometimes was done under the guise of conservatism.

Although an intangible asset may be amortized by using any "systematic and rational" method that reflects the actual expiration of its economic usefulness, the **straight-line** method is used almost exclusively.

---

[14] Intangible operational assets often are referred to as intangible assets.

Patents.   A patent, when acquired, is recorded at its cash equivalent cost in accordance with the **cost principle.** Subsequent to acquisition, a patent is **amortized,** in accordance with the **matching principle,** over the shorter of its economic life or its remaining legal life (of the 17 years from date of grant). To illustrate, assume the patent acquired by Mason Company, recorded above, had an estimated 10-year remaining economic life. At the end of 19A, the **adjusting entry** to record amortization for one year would be (see footnote 12):

December 31, 19A:

Patent expense	1,700	
Patents		1,700

Adjusting entry to record amortization of patent over the estimated economic life of 10 years ($17,000 ÷ 10 years = $1,700).

The amount of patent amortization expense recorded for 19A is reported on the income statement as an operating expense. The patent would be reported on the December 31, 19A, balance sheet as follows:

Intangible assets:
Patents (cost, $17,000, less amortization) $15,300

Copyrights.   A copyright is similar to a patent. A copyright gives the owner the exclusive right to publish, use, and sell a literary, musical, or artistic piece of work for a period not exceeding 50 years beyond the author's death. The same principles, guidelines, and procedures used in accounting for and reporting the cost of patents also are appropriate for copyrights.

Franchises and licenses.   Franchises and licenses frequently are granted by governmental and other units for a specified period and purpose. For example, a city may grant one company a franchise to distribute gas to homes for heating purposes, or a company may sell franchises, such as the right for a local outlet to operate a Kentucky Fried Chicken local restaurant. Franchises and licenses usually require the expenditure of resources by the franchisee to acquire them; therefore, they represent intangible operational assets that should be accounted for as illustrated earlier for patents.

Leaseholds.   Leasing is a common type of business contract whereby the owner (or lessor) for a consideration known as rent, extends to another party (the lessee) certain rights to use specified property. Leases may vary from simple arrangements, such as the month-to-month lease of an office or the daily rental of an automobile, to long-term leases having complex contractual arrangements. The rights granted to a lessee frequently are referred to as a **leasehold.**

Long-term leases sometimes require a lump-sum advance rental payment by the lessee. In such cases, the lessee should record the advance payment as a debit to an intangible asset account (frequently called Leaseholds) and amortize it to expense over the contractual life of the lease. The true amount of annual rent expense includes the amortization of the leasehold; therefore, the annual amortization is debited to Rent Expense. To illustrate, assume that Favor Company leased a building for its own use on January 1, 19A, under a five-year contract that required, in addition to the monthly rental payments of $2,000, a single payment in advance of $20,000. The advance payment would be recorded as follows:

January 1, 19A:

```
    Leasehold (or Rent paid in advance) ............................... 20,000
        Cash .....................................................               20,000
    Rent paid in advance.
```

At the end of 19A, and at the end of each of the remaining four years, the following **adjusting** entry would be made to reflect amortization of this intangible asset:[15]

December 31, 19A:

```
    Rent expense ................................................... 4,000
        Leasehold .....................................................        4,000
    Adjusting entry to record amortization of leasehold over five years
    ($20,000 ÷ 5 years = $4,000).
```

The $2,000 monthly rental payments would be debited to Rent Expense when paid each month. Thus, the 19A income statement would report rent expense of $28,000 [i.e., ($2,000 × 12) + $4,000 = $28,000]. The December 31, 19A, balance sheet would report an asset, Leasehold, of $16,000 (i.e., Cost, $20,000 − Amortization, $4,000 = $16,000).

Leasehold improvements.   In most instances, when buildings, improvements, or alterations are constructed by the **lessee** on leased property, such assets legally revert to the owner of the property at the end of the lease. The lessee has full use of such improvements during the term of the lease, therefore, they should be recorded as an intangible operating asset, "Leasehold Improvements." These expenditures should be amortized over the estimated useful life of the related improvement or the remaining life of the lease, whichever is shorter.

---

[15] This discussion presumes the normal or **operating** type of lease. In some instances, a lease is in effect a sale/purchase agreement. Such leases, known as financing leases, involve complex accounting problems that are deferred to more advanced accounting books.

Goodwill.   Usually, when a successful business is sold as a unit, the price will be somewhat in excess of the sum of the market values of its recorded assets less its liabilities. A business may command an excess price because an intangible operational asset called goodwill attaches to a successful business.

Goodwill represents the potential of a business to earn above a normal rate of return on the recorded assets less the liabilities. Goodwill arises from such factors as customer confidence, reputation for dependability, efficiency and internal competencies, quality of goods and services, and financial standing. From the date of organization, a successful business continually builds goodwill. In this context, the goodwill is said to be "generated internally at no identifiable cost." On the other hand, when a business is purchased as an entity, the purchase price will include a payment for any goodwill that exists at that time. **In conformance with the cost principle, goodwill is recorded as an intangible operational asset only when it actually is purchased.**

To illustrate, assume Richard Roe purchased the College Men's Store on January 1, 19A, for $200,000 cash. At the date of purchase, it was determined that the recorded assets had a total **market value** of $160,000, comprised of the market values of inventory, $110,000; fixtures, $35,000; prepaid rent, $1,000; and other assets, $14,000. Roe did not accept any of the store's liabilities. The purchase would be recorded by Roe as follows:

January 1, 19A:

Inventory	110,000	
Furniture and fixtures	35,000	
Prepaid rent	1,000	
Other assets	14,000	
Goodwill	40,000	
Cash		200,000
Purchase of College Men's Store.		

The intangible asset—goodwill—must be amortized to expense over its estimated economic life not to exceed 40 years *(APB Opinion 17)*. Assuming a 40-year economic life, the amortization for 19A would be recorded in an **adjusting entry** as follows:

December 31, 19A:

Goodwill amortization (expense)	1,000	
Goodwill		1,000
Adjusting entry to record goodwill amortization for one year based on 40-year economic life ($40,000 ÷ 40 years = $1,000).		

Many other types of intangible assets may be observed in financial statements. Examples are formulas, processes, and film rights. These types are accounted for, and reported, in a manner similar to that illustrated above.

DEFERRED CHARGES

An asset category called **deferred charges** is reported occasionally on balance sheets. A deferred charge, like a prepaid expense, is an **expense paid in advance;** that is, goods or services were acquired that will be used to earn future revenues. A deferred charge is a **long-term** prepaid expense and, therefore, cannot be classified as a current asset. A prepaid expense is a short-term prepayment and, for this reason, is classifed as a current asset. Thus, the only difference between the two is time. For example, a $1,000 insurance premium for five years' coverage paid at the start of Year 1 would be reported as follows at the end of Year 1:

Income statement:
Insurance expense $200

Balance sheet:
Current assets:
    Prepaid insurance..................... 200
Deferred charges:
    Insurance premium paid in advance 600

Common examples of deferred charges are bond issuance costs (Chapter 11), start-up costs, organization costs, and plant rearrangement costs. In conformance with the matching principle, deferred charges are amortized to expense each period over the future periods benefited.

DISPOSAL OF OPERATIONAL ASSETS

Operational assets may be disposed of in two ways: voluntarily by sale, trade-in, or retirement; or involuntarily as a result of a casualty, such as a storm, fire, or accident. Whatever the nature of the disposal, the cost of the asset and any accumulated depreciation, depletion, or amortization must be removed from the accounts at the date of disposal. The difference between any resources received upon disposal of an operational asset and the **book value** of the asset at the date of disposal represents a "gain or loss on disposal of operational assets." This gain (or loss) is not revenue (or expense) because it is from "peripheral or incidental" activities rather than from normal operations (see Exhibit 2–6). To illustrate, assume a machine is sold for $3,500 cash when the account balances showed: Machine, $10,000; and Accumulated Depreciation, Machine, $7,000 (i.e., a book value of $3,000). The entry to record this **voluntary** disposal would be:

Cash	3,500	
Accumulated depreciation, machine	7,000	
Machine		10,000
Gain on disposal of operational asset		500

Gain computed:
Sale price	$3,500	
Book value at date of sale ($10,000 — $7,000)	3,000	
Difference — gain	$ 500	

When an operational asset is disposed of at any date other than the end of the accounting period, it may be necessary to record depreciation, depletion, or amortization for the fraction of the year to the date of disposal. After this entry is made, the entry to record the disposal must be recorded. A gain or loss on involuntary disposals of operational assets is reported on the income statement; the asset and the related accumulated depreciation would no longer be reported

EXHIBIT 9–5
Involuntary disposal of an operational asset

Situation of Bye Company:

January 1, 19A—Purchased a heavy-duty truck for $38,000 cash; estimated useful life eight years and $6,000 residual value (straight-line depreciation).

December 31—End of accounting year.

June 30, 19D—The truck was wrecked and the insurance company paid a claim of $21,000 (i.e., the replacement cost of the truck at the date of the wreck).

Entries during the life of the truck:

January 1, 19A—To record purchase of the truck:

Truck	38,000	
Cash		38,000

December 31—To record annual depreciation 19A–19C:

	19A		19B		19C	
Depreciation expense	4,000		4,000		4,000	
Accumulated depreciation		4,000		4,000		4,000

Computation: ($38,000 — $6,000) ÷ 8 years = $4,000.

June 30, 19D—Entries on date of disposal (wreck):

1. To record depreciation for six months (to date of wreck):

Depreciation expense	2,000	
Accumulated depreciation		2,000

    Computation: $4,000 × $\frac{6}{12}$ = $2,000.

2. To record the involunary disposal of the asset and the insurance indemnity:

Cash (insurance indemnity)	21,000	
Accumulated depreciation ($4,000 × 3) + $2,000	14,000	
Casualty loss on operational assets	3,000	
Truck		38,000

on the balance sheet. Exhibit 9–5 illustrates the acquisition, depreciation, and **involuntary disposal** of an operational asset (a heavy-duty truck).

DEMONSTRATION CASE

(Try to resolve the requirements before proceeding to the suggested solution that follows.)

Diversified Industries has been in operation for a number of years. It started as a construction company, and in recent years it has expanded into a number of related activities, including heavy construction, ready-mix concrete, sand and gravel, construction supplies, and earth-moving services.

The transactions given below were selected from those completed during 19D. They focus on the primary issues discussed in this chapter. Amounts have been simplified for case purposes.

19D

Jan. 1 The management decided to purchase a building that was approximately 10 years old. The location was excellent, and there was adequate parking space. The company bought the building and the land on which it was situated for $305,000 cash. A reliable appraiser appraised the property at the following market values: land, $126,000; and building, $174,000.

Jan. 12 Paid renovation costs on the building amounting to $38,100.

June 19 Purchased a third location for a gravel pit (designated No. 3) at a cost of $50,000 cash. The location had been carefully surveyed, and it was estimated that 100,000 cubic yards of gravel could be removed from the deposit.

July 10 Paid $1,200 ordinary repairs on the building.

Aug. 1 Paid $10,000 for costs of preparing the gravel pit, acquired in June 19D, for exploitation.

December 31, 19D (end of the annual accounting period)—the following data were developed as a basis for the adjusting entries:

a. The building will be depreciated on a straight-line basis over an estimated useful life of 30 years. The estimated residual value is $35,000.

b. During 19D, 12,000 square yards of gravel were removed from gravel pit No. 3. Use an Accumulated Depletion account.

c. The company owns a patent right that is used in operations. The Patent account on January 1, 19D, reflected a balance of $3,300. The patent has an estimated remaining life of six years (including 19D).

Required:

1. Give the journal entries for the five transactions completed during 19D.
2. Give the adjusting entries on December 31, 19D.
3. Show the December 31, 19D, balance sheet classification and amount for each of the following items: land, building, gravel pit, and patent.

Suggested solution

Requirement 1. Entries during 19D:

January 1, 19D:

Land (building site)	128,100	
Building	176,900	
Cash		305,000

Allocation of purchase price based on appraisal:

Item	Appraisal value	Percent	Computation	Allocation
Land	$126,000	42	× $305,000 =	$128,100
Building	174,000	58	× 305,000 =	176,900
Totals	$300,000	100		$305,000

January 12, 19D:

Building	38,100	
Cash...		38,100
Renovation costs on building prior to use.		

June 19, 19D:

Gravel pit (No. 3)	50,000	
Cash...		50,000
Purchased gravel pit; estimated production, 100,000 cubic yards.		

July 10, 19D:

Repair expense	1,200	
Cash...		1,200
Ordinary repairs.		

August 1, 19D:

Gravel pit (No. 3)	10,000	
Cash		10,000
Preparation costs.		

Requirement 2. Adjusting entries, December 31, 19D:

a. Depreciation expense, building 6,000

　　Accumulated depreciation 6,000

Computations:

Cost ($176,900 + $38,100)	$215,000
Less: Residual value	35,000
Cost to be depreciated	$180,000

Annual depreciation: $180,000 ÷ 30 years = $6,000.

b. Depletion expense 7,200

　　Accumulated depletion, gravel pit (No. 3) 7,200

Computations:

Cost ($50,000 + $10,000)	$60,000

Depletion rate:
　$60,000 ÷ 100,000 cubic yards = $.60
Depletion expense:
　$.60 × 12,000 cubic yards = $7,200

c. Patent expense 550

　　Patent 550

Computation:
　$3,300 ÷ 6 years = $550

Requirement 3. Balance sheet, December 31, 19D:

Assets

Operational assets:		
Land		$128,100
Building	$215,000	
Less: Accumulated depreciation	6,000	209,000
Gravel pit	60,000	
Less: Accumulated depletion	7,200	52,800
Total operational assets		$389,900
Intangible assets:		
Patent ($3,300 − $550)		2,750

SUMMARY OF CHAPTER

This chapter discussed accounting for operational assets, which are the noncurrent assets that a business retains for long periods of time for use in the course of normal operations rather than for sale. They include tangible assets and intangible assets. At acquisition, operational assets are measured and recorded in the accounts at cost, in conformity with the cost principle. Cost includes the cash equivalent purchase price plus all reasonable and necessary expenditures made to acquire and prepare the asset for its intended use.

An operational asset represents a bundle of future services and benefits that has been paid for in advance. As an operational asset is used, this bundle of future services gradually is used to earn revenue. Therefore, in accordance with the matching principle, the asset cost (less any estimated residual value) is allocated to periodic expense over the periods benefited. In this way, the expense associated with the use of operational assets is matched with the revenues earned. This allocation process is known as depreciation in the case of property, plant, and equipment; as depletion in the case of natural resources; and as amortization in the case of intangibles.

Four methods of depreciation are used widely: straight line, productive output, sum-of-the-years'-digits, and declining balance.

Expenditures related to operational assets are classified either as:

1. **Capital expenditures**—those expenditures that provide benefits for one or more accounting periods beyond the current period; consequently, they are debited to appropriate asset accounts and depreciated, depleted, or amortized over their useful lives; or
2. **Revenue expenditures**—those expenditures that provide benefits during the current accounting period only; consequently, they are debited to appropriate current expense accounts when incurred.

Ordinary repairs and maintenance costs are revenue expenditures, whereas extraordinary repairs and additions are capital expenditures.

Operational assets may be disposed of voluntarily by sale or retirement, or involuntarily through casualty, such as storm, fire, or accident. Upon disposal, such assets must be depreciated, depleted, or amortized up to the date of disposal. The disposal transaction is recorded by removing the cost of the old asset and the related accumulated depreciation, depletion, or amortization amount from the accounts. A gain or loss on disposal of an operational asset will result when the disposal price is different from the book value of the old asset. Special rules apply to the trade in of an asset as all, or part, of the consideration given for another asset (trade-ins are discussed in Supplement 9A).

SUPPLEMENT 9A—TRADING IN ASSETS

It is not unusual when acquiring an asset to trade in another asset. Although there may be a direct trade of two assets, the typical case involves the trading in of an old asset plus the payment of cash for the difference (often called boot). In such transactions, the asset acquired must be recorded in the accounts and the old asset removed from the accounts.

Accounting for the exchange of one asset for another asset depends on two factors:[16]

1. Whether the two assets are similar or dissimilar.
2. Whether cash for the difference (boot) is paid or received.

The trading in of an old truck for another truck would involve similar assets. In contrast, the trading in of a plot of land for a new truck would involve dissimilar assets.

The basic principle for recording the exchange of assets can be stated as follows: If the assets exchanged are **similar,** the exchange should be recorded on a "book value" basis because there is no completed earning process.[17] If the assets exchanged are **dissimilar,** the exchange should be recorded on a "market value" basis because there is a completed earning process.

Exhibit 9–6 illustrates accounting for the acquisition of an asset when another asset is given as a trade-in. Four independent cases are illustrated as follows:

Case	Situation
A	**Similar** assets are exchanged; **no cash boot** is paid.
B	**Dissimilar** assets are exchanged; **no cash boot** is paid.
C	**Similar** assets are exchanged; **cash boot** is paid.
D	**Dissimilar** assets are exchanged; **cash boot** is paid.

The four cases illustrated in Exhibit 9–6 are sufficient for our objective to explain the exchange of assets. Sometimes the terms of the transaction involving a trade-in also includes the **receipt** of cash boot, in which case the recording becomes more complex.

Under fundamental accounting principles *(APB Opinion 29)* an asset, when acquired, never should be recorded at an amount greater than its market value (i.e., its cash equivalent price). In some instances, this constraint will serve to reduce a gain (or increase a loss) on disposal.

In the illustration in Exhibit 9–6, the market value of old Asset O was $200 in excess of its book value [i.e., $2,200 − ($5,000 − $3,000)]. Therefore, in Cases B and D (relating to dissimilar assets), this amount was recorded as a gain. In contrast, if the market value of old Asset O were $1,900 (i.e., $100 below book value), a loss of $100 would be reported in Cases B and D. A loss would be recorded for Cases A and C (similar assets) when the market value of either asset is below book value because it indicates an impairment of value.

---

[16] *APB Opinion 29,* "Accounting for Nonmonetary Transactions" (New York, May 1973), specifies the appropriate accounting for transactions that involve the exchange of assets when either or both of these factors are present.

[17] In the case of an exchange of similar productive assets, because the asset acquired performs essentially the same productive function as the asset given up, the exchange is only one step in the earning process. The earning process in these situations is completed when the goods or services are sold that the similar productive assets helped to produce. In contrast, in the case of an exchange of dissimilar productive assets, the earning process is completed because the productive function of the productive asset given up is terminated. The asset acquired serves a different economic purpose for the entity and begins a new earning process of its own.

EXHIBIT 9–6
Trading in used
assets illustrated

Situation of Company T:

Transaction: Company T acquired Asset N, and traded in Asset O. At the date of the transaction, the accounts of Company T reflected the following:

Asset O:
Cost when acquired	$5,000
Accumulated depreciation	3,000
Estimated market value	2,200

Asset N:
Market value	2,250

Case A—Similar assets are exchanged; **no** cash boot paid.

Principle applied: The asset acquired is recorded at the **book value** of the asset traded in.

Asset N	2,000	
Accumulated depreciation, Asset O	3,000	
Asset O		5,000

Case B—Dissimilar assets are exchanged; **no** cash boot paid.

Principle applied: The asset acquired is recorded at the **market value** of the asset traded in.

Asset N	2,200	
Accumulated depreciation, Asset O	3,000	
Asset O		5,000
Gain on disposal of operational asset		200

Case C—Similar assets are exchanged; **$50 cash boot** is **paid.**

Principle applied: The asset acquired is recorded at the **book value** of the asset traded in **plus the cash boot** paid.

Asset N ($2,000 + $50)	2,050*	
Accumulated depreciation, Asset O	3,000	
Asset O		5,000
Cash		50

* This amount cannot exceed the market value of the asset acquired.

Case D—Dissimilar assets are exchanged; **$50 cash boot** is **paid.**

Principle applied: The asset acquired is recorded at the **market value** of the asset traded in **plus the cash boot** paid.

Asset N ($2,200 + $50)	2,250*	
Accumulated depreciation, Asset O	3,000	
Asset O		5,000
Cash		50
Gain on disposal of operational asset		200

* This amount cannot exceed the market value of the asset acquired.

IMPORTANT TERMS DEFINED IN THIS CHAPTER

Terms (alphabetically)	Key words in definitions of important terms used in chapter	Page reference
Acquisition cost	Net cash equivalent amount paid for an asset.	397
Amortization	Systematic and rational apportionment of the cost of an intangible operational asset over its useful life.	402

Terms (alphabetically)	Key words in definitions of important terms used in chapter	Page reference
Basket purchase	Acquisition of two or more assets in a single transaction for a single lump sum.	399
Book (or carrying) value	Acquisition cost of an operational asset less accumulated depreciation, depletion or amortization.	403
Capital expenditures	Expenditures that are debited to an asset account; the acquisition of an asset.	417
Capitalization of interest	Interest expenditures included in the cost of an operational asset; interest capitalized during construction period.	399
Copyrights	Exclusive right to publish, use, and sell a literary, musical or artistic work.	422
Deferred charges	An expense paid in advance of usage of the goods or services; long-term prepayment.	425
Depletion	Systematic and rational apportionment of the cost of a natural resource over the period of exploitation.	402
Depreciation	Systematic and rational apportionment of the cost of a tangible operational asset over its useful life.	402
Declining depreciation	An accelerated depreciation method based upon a multiple of the straight-line rate; it disregards residual value.	404
Estimated residual value	Estimated amount to be recovered, less disposal costs, at the end of the estimated useful life of an operational asset.	404
Estimated useful life	Estimated service life of an operational asset to the present owner.	405
Extraordinary repairs	Major, high cost, and long-term repairs; debited to an asset account (or accumulated depreciation); a capital expenditure.	417
Goodwill	Acquisition cost of the purchase of a business that is in excess of the market value of the net assets of the business purchased.	424
Intangible operational assets	Assets used in the operations of a business that have special rights but not physical substance.	397
Leaseholds	Rights granted to a lessee under a lease contract.	422
Leasehold improvements	Expenditures by the lessee on leased property that have use value beyond the current accounting period.	423
Operational assets	Tangible and intangible assets owned by a business and used in its operations.	397
Productive-output depreciation	Cost of an operational asset is allocated over its useful life based upon the periodic output related to total estimated output.	407
Repairs and maintenance	Expenditures for normal operating upkeep of operational assets; debit expense for ordinary repairs.	416
Residual value	Estimated amount to be recovered, less disposal costs, at the end of the estimated useful life of an operational asset.	404
Revenue expenditures	Expenditures that are debited to an expense account; the incurrence of an expense.	417
Straight-line depreciation	Cost of an operational asset is allocated over its useful life in equal periodic amounts.	406
Sum-of-years'-digits depreciation	Cost of an operational asset is allocated over its useful life based upon a fraction where the denominator is the total of all of the useful years and the numerator is the year of life in inverse order.	409
Tangible operational assets	Assets used in the operations of a business that have physical substance.	397

QUESTIONS FOR DISCUSSION

PART A

1. Define operational assets. Explain how they may be considered as a "bundle of future services."

2. What are the classifications of operational assets? Briefly explain each.

3. Relate the cost principle to accounting for operational assets.

4. Describe the relationship between the matching principle and accounting for operational assets.

5. Define and illustrate the book value of a three-year-old operational asset that cost $11,500, has an estimated residual value of $1,500 and an estimated useful life of five years. Relate book value to market value.

6. Under the cost principle, what amounts usually should be included in the acquisition cost of an operational asset?

7. What is a "basket purchase"? What measurement problem does it pose?

8. Briefly explain the circumstances under which interest cost must be included in the acquisition cost of an operational asset.

9. Briefly distinguish among depreciation, depletion, and amortization.

10. In computing depreciation, three values must be known or estimated; identify and explain the nature of each.

11. Estimated useful life and residual value of an operational asset relate to the current owner or user rather than to all users. Explain this statement.

12. What kind of a depreciation-expense pattern is provided under the straight-line method? When would its use be particularly appropriate?

13. What kind of depreciation-expense pattern emerges under the productive-output method? When would its use be particularly appropriate?

14. What are the arguments in favor of accelerated depreciation?

15. Explain how monthly depreciation should be computed when the sum-of-the-years'-digits method is used for an asset having a 10-year life.

PART B

16. Distinguish between capital expenditures and revenue expenditures.

17. Distinguish between ordinary and extraordinary repairs. How is each accounted for?

18. Over what period should an addition to an existing operational asset be depreciated? Explain.

19. Define an intangible operational asset.

20. What period should be used to amortize an intangible operational asset?

21. Define goodwill. When is it appropriate to record goodwill as an intangible operational asset?

22. Distinguish between a leasehold and a leasehold improvement.

23. Over what period should a leasehold improvement be amortized? Explain.

24. Compare the accounting for a prepaid expense with a deferred charge.

25. When an operational asset is disposed of **during** the accounting period, two separate entries usually must be made. Explain this statement.

EXERCISES

PART A

E9–1. For each asset listed below, enter a code letter to the left to indicate the allocation procedure for each asset. Use the following letter codes:

	A—Amortization		P—Depletion
	D—Depreciation		N—None of these

_____	1.	Land	_____	11.	Copyright
_____	2.	Patent	_____	12.	Investment in common stock
_____	3.	Building	_____	13.	Mineral deposit
_____	4.	Cash	_____	14.	Machinery
_____	5.	Oil well	_____	15.	License right
_____	6.	Trademark	_____	16.	Deferred charge
_____	7.	Goodwill	_____	17.	Inventory of goods
_____	8.	Stamps	_____	18.	Timber tract
_____	9.	Franchise	_____	19.	Tools
_____	10.	Plant site in use	_____	20.	Gravel pit

E9–2. A machine was purchased by Ryan Company on March 1, 19A, at an invoice price of $20,000. On date of delivery, March 2, 19A, Ryan Company paid $10,000 on the machine and the balance was an open account at 12 percent interest. On March 3, 19A, $200 was paid for freight on the machine, and on March 5 installation costs relating to the machine were paid amounting to $600. On October 1, 19A, Ryan Company paid the balance due on the machine plus the interest.

Required:

a. Give the journal entries on each of the above dates through October 19A.
b. Give the adjusting entry for straight-line depreciation at the end of 19A, assuming an estimated useful life of 10 years and an estimated residual value of $2,800. Depreciate to the nearest month. The accounting period ends December 31, 19A.
c. What would be the book value of the machine at the end of 19B?

E9–3. Raul Company purchased a building and the land on which it is located for a total cash price of $480,000. In addition, they paid transfer costs of $1,000. Renovation costs on the building amounted to $9,250. An independent appraiser provided market values of building, $363,750; and land, $121,250.

Required:

a. Apportion the cost of the property on the basis of the appraised values. Show computations.

    b. Give the journal entry to record the purchase of the property, including all expenditures. Assume that all transactions were for cash and that <u>all purchases</u> occurred at the start of Year 1.

    c. Give the journal entry to record straight-line depreciation at the end of one year assuming an estimated 20-year useful life and a $20,000 estimated residual value.

    d. What would be the book value of the property at the end of Year 2?

E9–4. On January 1, 19A, Stonewall Corporation purchased land at a cost of $120,000 and paid transfer fees of $6,000. Clearing the land, and planning for the building construction was started immediately. Construction of an office building for company use was started on April 1, 19A. The company borrowed approximately 80 percent of the funds to purchase the land and construct the office building at a 12 percent interest rate. The remaining cash needed was paid from company funds. Total interest cost for 19A was $36,000. The company made the following cash expenditures at the dates indicated:

January 1, 19A, down payment on the land (20%).............	$ 24,000
January 1, 19A, transfer costs on the land	6,000
March 1, 19A, fees for preliminary surveys and work prior to start of construction	12,000
Progress payments to contractor for construction costs:	
May 31, 19A, No. 1	200,000
August 31, 19A, No. 2	300,000
November 30, 19A, No. 3 (end of the construction period).....	200,000

Required:

    a. Compute the cost of the tangible operational asset with separate amounts for the land and building. Assume the construction period started on April 1, 19A. Show computations.

    b. How much interest expense should be reported on the 19A income statement?

E9–5. Astro Corporation purchased a machine at a cost of $1,350. The estimated useful life was four years, and the residual value, $150. Assume that the estimated productive life of the machine is 50,000 units and each year's production was Year 1, 20,000 units; Year 2, 15,000 units; Year 3, 9,000 units; and Year 4, 6,000 units.

Required:

    a. Determine the amount for each cell in the following table. Show your computations and round to the nearest dollar.

Year	Depreciation Expense			
	Straight Line	Productive Output	Sum-of-the-Years'-Digits	150 Percent Declining Balance
1				
2				
3				
4				
Total				

b. Assuming the machine was used directly in the production of one of the products manufactured and sold by the company, what factors might be considered in selecting a preferable depreciation method in terms of the matching principle?

E9–6. Vance Company purchased a machine that cost $18,000. The estimated useful life was five years, and the estimated residual value, $3,000. Assume the estimated useful life in productive units is 50,000. Units actually produced were Year 1, 9,000; and Year 2, 11,000.

Required:

a. Determine the appropriate amounts to complete the table below. Show computations.

	Depreciation expense		Book value at end of	
Method of depreciation	Year 1	Year 2	Year 1	Year 2
Straight line	_____	_____	_____	_____
Productive output	_____	_____	_____	_____
Sum-of-the-years'-digits	_____	_____	_____	_____
150% declining balance	_____	_____	_____	_____

b. Which method would result in the lowest EPS for Year 1? for Year 2?

E9–7. East Company acquired, and paid for, a machine that cost $5,300 on July 1, 19B. The estimated useful life is four years, and the estimated residual value is $500. The accounting period ends December 31.

Required:

a. Compute monthly depreciation expense for July 19B and July 19C assuming *(a)* the straight-line method and *(b)* the SYD method.
b. Assume cash revenues of $40,000 and cash expenses of $30,000 for the year 19B and an income tax rate of 20 percent. Complete the following tabulation for 19B:

	Straight Line	Sum-of-the-Years'-Digits
Revenues		
Expenses		
Depreciation expense		
Pretax income		
Income tax expense		
Net income		

c. Which method produced the higher net income? By how much? Explain why the net incomes differ (use amounts).

E9–8. Belt Company owns the office building occupied by its administrative office. The office building was reflected in the accounts on the December 31, 19D, balance sheet as follows:

Cost when acquired $250,000
Accumulated depreciation (based on straight-line
  depreciation, an estimated life of 30 years,
  and a $40,000 residual value) 105,000

During January 19P, on the basis of a careful study, the management decided that the total estimated useful life should be changed to 25 years (instead of 30) and the residual value reduced to $35,000 (from $40,000).

Required:

a. Give the adjusting entry for straight-line depreciation at the end of 19P. Show computations.
b. Explain the rationale for your response to *(a)*.

PART B

E9–9.   For each item listed below, enter the appropriate letter to the left to indicate the type of expenditure. Use the following:

A—Capital expenditure
B—Revenue expenditure
C—Neither

    _____   1. Paid $500 for ordinary repairs.
    _____   2. Paid $6,000 for extraordinary repairs.
    _____   3. Addition to old building; paid cash, $10,000.
    _____   4. Routine maintenance; cost, $300; on credit.
    _____   5. Purchased a machine, $6,000; gave long-term note.
    _____   6. Paid $2,000 for organization costs.
    _____   7. Paid three-year insurance premium, $600.
    _____   8. Purchased a patent, $3,400 cash.
    _____   9. Paid $10,000 for monthly salaries.
    _____ 10. Paid cash dividends, $15,000.

E9–10.   Florida Company operates a small manufacturing facility as a supplement to its regular service activities. At the beginning of 19L, an operational asset account for the company showed the following balances:

Manufacturing equipment $70,000
Accumulated depreciation through 19K   48,400

During 19L, the following expenditures were incurred for repairs and maintenance:

    1. Routine maintenance and repairs on the equipment $1,000
    2. Major overhaul of the equipment   6,400

The equipment is being depreciated on a straight-line basis over an estimated life of 15 years and a $4,000 estimated residual value. The annual accounting period ends on December 31.

Required:

a. Give the adjusting entry for depreciation on the manufacturing equipment that was made at the end of 19K. Starting with 19L, what is the remaining estimated life?
b. Give the journal entries to record appropriately the two expenditures for repairs and maintenance during 19L.
c. Give the adjusting entry that should be made at the end of 19L for depreciation of the manufacturing equipment assuming no change in the estimated life or residual value. Show computations.

E9–11.   At the end of the annual accounting period, December 31, 19C, the records of Wang Company reflected the following:

Machine A:
Cost when acquired $34,000
Accumulated depreciation   12,000

During January 19D, the machine was renovated extensively including several major improvements at a cost of $8,000. As a result, the estimated life was increased from 8 years to 10 years, and the residual value was increased from $2,000 to $5,500.

Required:

a. Give the journal entry to record the renovation. How old was the machine at the end of 19C?
b. Give the adjusting journal entry at the end of 19D to record straight-line depreciation for the year.
c. Explain the rationale for your entries given in *(a)* and *(b)*.

E9–12.   In February 19A, Rapid Extractive Industries paid $450,000 for a mineral deposit. During March, $150,000 was spent in preparing the deposit for exploitation. It was estimated that 800,000 total cubic yards could be extracted economically. During 19A, 40,000 cubic yards were extracted. During January 19B, another $90,000 was spent for additional developmental work. After conclusion of the latest work, the estimated remaining recovery was increased to one million cubic yards over the remaining life. During 19B, 35,000 cubic yards were extracted.

Required:

Give the appropriate journal entry on each of the following dates:

a. February 19A, for acquisition of the deposit.
b. March 19A, for developmental costs.
c. Year 19A, for annual depletion assuming the company uses a contra account (show computations).
d. January 19B, for developmental costs.
e. Year 19B, for annual depletion (show computations).

E9–13.   Reo Manufacturing Company had three intangible operational assets at the end of 19F (end of the fiscal year):

1. Patent—Purchased from J. Ray on January 1, 19F, for a cash cost of $4,260. Ray had registered the patent with the U.S. Patent Office five years earlier on January 1, 19A. Amortize over the remaining legal life.
2. A franchise acquired from the local community to provide certain services for 10 years starting on January 1, 19F. The franchise cost $26,000 cash.
3. On January 1, 19F, the company leased some property for a five-year term. Reo immediately spent $4,800 cash for long-term improvements (estimated useful life, eight years, and no residual value). At the termination of the lease, there will be no recovery of these improvements.

Required:

a. Give the journal entry to record the acquisition of each intangible. Provide a brief explanation with the entries.
b. Give adjusting journal entry at December 31, 19F, for amortization of each intangible. Show computations. The company does not use contra accounts.
c. Show how these assets, and any related expenses, should be reported on the financial statements for 19F.

E9–14.   MB Company acquired three intangible operational assets during 19C. The relevant facts were:

1.   On January 1, 19C, the company purchased a patent from C. Cox for $2,550 cash. Cox had developed the patent and registered it with the Patent Office on January 1, 19A. Amortize over the remaining legal life.

2.   On January 1, 19C, the company purchased a copyright for a total cash cost of $9,500 and the remaining legal life was 25 years. The company executives estimated that the copyright would be of no value by the end of 20 years.

3.   MB Company purchased a small company in January 19C at a cash cost of $100,000. Included in the purchase price was $16,400 for goodwill; the balance was for plant, equipment, and fixtures (no liabilities were assumed). Amortize the goodwill over the maximum period permitted.

Required:

a.   Give the journal entry to record the acquisition of each intangible.

b.   Give the adjusting journal entry that would be required at the end of the annual accounting period, December 31, 19C, for each intangible. The company uses contra accounts. Include a brief explanation and show computations.

c.   What would be the book (carrying) value of each intangible at the end of 19D?

E9–15.   Vol Company conducts operations in several different localities. In order to expand into still another city, the company obtained a 10-year lease, starting January 1, 19D, on a very good downtown location. Although there was a serviceable building on the property, the company had to construct an additional structure to be used for storage purposes. The 10-year lease required a $12,000 cash advance rental payment, plus cash payments of $1,000 per month during occupancy. During January 19D, the company spent $30,000 cash constructing the additional structure. The new structure has an estimated life of 12 years with no residual value (straight-line depreciation).

Required:

a.   Give the journal entries for Vol Company to record the payment of the $12,000 advance on January 1, 19D, and the first monthly rental.

b.   Give the journal entry to record the construction of the new structure.

c.   Give any adjusting entries required at the end of the annual accounting period for Vol Company on December 31, 19D, in respect to (1) the advance payment and (2) the new structure. Show computations.

d.   What is the total amount of expense resulting from the lease for 19D?

E9–16.   Rye Company is in the process of preparing the balance sheet at December 31, 19B. The following are to be included:

Prepaid insurance	$ 450
Long-term investment in common stock of	
X Corporation, at cost (market $6,200)	6,000
Patent (at cost)	3,400
Accumulated amortization, patent	3,400
Accounts receivable	20,000
Allowance for doubtful accounts	600
Franchise (at cost)	1,000
Accumulated amortization, franchise	300
Land—site of building	10,000
Building	280,000
Accumulated depreciation building	150,000

Required:

Show how each of the above assets would be reflected on the Rye Company balance sheet at December 31, 19B. Use the following subcaptions: Current assets, Investments and funds, Tangible operational assets, and Intangible operational assets. The company uses the "accumulated" accounts as listed above. (Hint: Intangible operational assets sum to $3,300 on the balance sheet.)

E9–17. Stanley Company sold a small truck that had been used in the business for three years. The records of the company reflected the following:

Delivery truck	$12,000
Accumulated depreciation	10,000

Required:

a. Give the journal entry for disposal of the truck assuming the sales price was $2,000.
b. Give the journal entry for the disposal of the truck assuming the sales price was $2,200.
c. Give the journal entry for the disposal of the truck assuming the sales price was $1,800.
d. Summarize any underlying principles that can be observed from the three different situations above.

E9–18. The records of the Phoenix Company on December 31, 19D, reflected the following data in respect to a particular machine:

Machine, original cost	$27,000
Accumulated depreciation	16,000*

* Based on a six-year estimated useful life, a $3,000 residual value, and straight-line depreciation.

On April 1, 19E, the machine was sold for $10,700 cash. The accounting period ends on December 31.

Required:

a. How old was the machine on January 1, 19E? Show computations.
b. Give the journal entry, or entries, incident to the sale of the machine.

E9–19. On August 31, 19C, a delivery truck owned by Prince Corporation was a total loss as the result of an accident. On January 1, 19C, the records reflected the following:

Truck (estimated residual value, 10% of cost)	$10,000
Accumulated depreciation (straight line, two years)	3,000

The truck was insured; therefore, Prince Corporation collected $6,300 cash from the insurance company on October 5, 19C.

Required:

a. Based on the data given, compute the estimated useful life and the estimated residual value of the truck.
b. Give all of the journal entries with respect to the truck from January 1 through October 5, 19C. Show computations.

E9–20. (Based on Supplement 9A) Mason Company owned a particular machine (designated Machine O for case purposes) which no longer met the needs of the company. On December 31, 19F, the records reflected the following:

Machine O:
    Original cost $30,000
    Accumulated depreciation   17,000

On January 3, 19G, the company acquired another machine (Machine N) and traded in Machine O. On this date, a reliable estimate of the market value of Machine O was $15,000.

Required:

a. Give the journal entry by Mason to record the transaction completed on January 3, 19G, for each of the following independent cases:

    Case A—The machines were similar, and no cash difference was paid or received by Mason.

    Case B—The machines were dissimilar, and no cash difference was paid or received by Mason.

b. For each case, explain the underlying reason for the amount that you recorded as the cost of Machine N.

E9–21. (Based on Supplement 9A) Use the facts and requirements given in Exercise 9–20 except that for each case assume Mason paid a $1,000 cash difference (boot). The market value of Machine N was $16,100.

PROBLEMS/CASES

PART A

PC9–1. White Company purchased three used machines from J. Evers for a cash price of $39,000. Transportation costs on the machines amounted to $1,000. The machines immediately were overhauled, installed, and started operating. The machines were essentially different; therefore, each had to be recorded separately in the accounts. An appraiser was employed to estimate their market values at date of purchase (prior to the overhaul and installation). The book values reflected on Evers' books also are available. The book values, appraisal results, installation costs, and renovation expenditures were:

	Machine A	Machine B	Machine C
Book value—Evers	$5,000	$ 9,000	$6,000
Property tax appraisal	6,000	15,000	9,000
Installation costs	200	400	100
Renovation costs prior to use	800	500	600

Required:

a. Compute the cost of each machine by making a realistic allocation. Explain the rationale for the allocated basis used.

b. Give the journal entry to record the purchase of the three machines assuming all payments were cash. Set up a separate asset account for each machine.

c. Give the entry to record depreciation expense at the end of Year 1, assuming:

Estimates

Machine	Life	Residual value	Depreciation method
A	6	$ 300 ...	Straight line
B	4	2,900 ...	SYD
C	5	1,700 ...	200% DB

PC9-2. Bye Company purchased a machine that cost $34,375. The estimated useful life is 10 years, and the estimated residual value is 4 percent of cost. The machine has an estimated useful life in productive output of 110,000 units. Actual output was Year 1, 15,000; and Year 2, 12,000.

Required:

a. Determine the appropriate amounts for the table below. Show your computations.

Depreciation method	Depreciation expense Year 1	Year 2	Book value at end of Year 1	Year 2
Straight line ....$	$_____	$_____	$_____	$_____
Productive output	_____	_____	_____	_____
Sum-of-the-years'-digits	_____	_____	_____	_____
200% declining balance	_____	_____	_____	_____

b. Give the adjusting entries for Years 1 and 2 under each method.
c. In selecting a depreciation method, some companies assess the comparative effect on **cash flow** and EPS. Briefly comment on the depreciation methods in terms of cash flow and EPS effects.

PC9-3. Stable Corporation purchased an operational asset on January 1, 19A, at a cash cost of $34,000. The estimated useful life is five years, and the estimated residual value is $4,000. Assume a constant 30 percent income tax rate; all paid in cash.

The company is deciding to use either straight-line (SL) depreciation or declining balance (DB) depreciation. The 5-year projected all-cash incomes (before depreciation and income tax) are shown in the second column below.

Schedule to Compare Projected SL and DB Results

Year	Income (all-cash) before Depreciation and Income Tax	Depreciation Expense (dollars) SL	200% DDB	Income Tax Expense (dollars) SL	200% DB	Net Income (dollars) SL	200% DB	Net Cash Inflow (dollars) SL	200% DB
1	$ 40,000	6,000	13,600	10,200	7,920	23,800	18,480	29,800	32,080
2	40,000								
3	40,000								
4	40,000								
5	40,000								
Total	200,000	30,000		51,000		119,000		149,000	

Required:

a. Complete the above schedule. Round to nearest dollars. (Hint: Use total line to prove your computations.)
b. Briefly explain two ways to compute the last two columns (cash flow).
c. Identify and briefly explain any generalizations that can be made from the columns for (1) depreciation, (2) income tax, (3) net income, and (4) cash flow.
d. Which method would you recommend in this particular situation? Explain the basis for your recommendation.

PC9–4. (This PC is comprehensive and challenging.)   Slick Corporation acquired a large machine for use in its productive activities at a cash cost of $189,000. The machine was acquired on January 1, 19A, at which time its estimated useful life was 500,000 units of output over a period of 10 years. The estimated residual value was $24,000. Assume a 40 percent income tax rate for Slick.

The top management of Slick is considering using either straight-line (SL), productive-output (PO), or SYD depreciation. The management also is developing a 10-year profit plan. The 10-year projected all-cash incomes (before depreciation and income tax) are shown in the first column below.

Required:

a. Complete the following tabulation (round to nearest $1):

Year	Income (all-cash) before Depreciation and Income Tax		Depreciation Expense (dollars)			Income Tax Expense (dollars)			Net Income (loss) (dollars)		
	Units	Dollars	SL	PO	SYD	SL	PO	SYD	SL	PO	SYD
1	70,000	96,500	16,500	23,100	30,000	32,000	29,360	26,600	48,000	44,040	39,900
2	75,000	103,400									
3	80,000	102,300									
4	75,000	103,400									
5	60,000	82,700	16,500	19,800	18,000	26,480	25,160	25,880	39,720	37,740	38,820
6	60,000	82,700									
7	50,000	69,000									
8	20,000	27,600	16,500	6,600	9,000	4,440	8,400	7,440	6,660	12,600	11,160
9	8,000	11,000									
10	2,000	2,400	16,500	660	3,000	(5,640)	696	(240)	(8,460)	1,044	(360)
Σ	500,000	681,000	165,000	165,000	165,000	206,400	206,400	206,400	309,600	309,600	309,600

b. List, and briefly explain any generalizations that you can make from the columns for (1) depreciation expense, (2) income tax expense, and (3) net income.

c. Which method would you recommend in this situation? Explain the basis for your recommendation.

PC9–5. (This PC is comprehensive and challenging.) On January 1, 19A, Brown Corporation purchased a special machine for use in the business that cost $33,000. The machine has a three-year useful life and a residual value of $3,000. The company is considering using either the straight-line method (SL) or the 200 percent declining balance method (DB) of depreciation. Assume an average income tax rate of 30 percent and that it is paid in full in cash.

Required:

a. You have been asked to prepare an analysis of the effects of SL versus 200 percent DB depreciation on the projected financial statements and cash flows over the life of the machine (19A–19C). Accordingly, you have decided to complete the following schedules—one set based on straight-line depreciation and another set based on 200 percent declining balance depreciation:

	Year 1	Year 2	Year 3
Income statements:			
Revenues (all-cash)	$90,000	$95,000	$99,000
Expenses (all-cash)	(60,000)	(62,000)	(63,000)
Depreciation expense			
Pretax income			
Income tax expense			
Net income			
EPS (5,000 shares)			
Balance sheets:			
Operational assets:			
Machine			
Accumulated depreciation			
Book value			
Cash flows:			
Revenues			
Expenses			
Depreciation expense			
Income tax			
Net cash inflow			

Requirement b.

Complete the following summary based upon your answer to Requirement *(a):*

Items Compared	Year 1		Year 2		Year 3		Total (both methods)
	SL	200% DB	SL	200% DB	SL	200% DB	
1. Net income							
2. Machine, book value							
3. Net cash inflow							

Requirement c.

List, and briefly explain, any generalizations that you can make about the three items summarized in Requirement *(b):* (1) net income, (2) machine book value, and (3) net cash inflow.

Requirement d.

Which method would you recommend? Explain the basis for your recommendation.

Instructional note: This problem assumes a constant income tax rate in order to focus on the different effects of SL versus DB depreciation. Also, the time period is limited to a three-year useful life only to reduce the computational burden.

PC9–6. Erie Company owns an existing building that was constructed at an original cost of $300,000. It is being depreciated on a straight-line basis over a 20-year estimated useful life and has a $60,000 estimated residual value. At the end of 19H, the building had been depreciated for a full eight years. In January 19I, a decision was made, on the basis of new information, that a total estimated useful life of 30 years, and a residual value of $39,000 would be more realistic. The accounting period ends December 31.

Required:

a. Compute the amount of depreciation expense recorded in 19H and the book value of the building at the end of 19H.
b. Compute the amount of depreciation that should be recorded in 19I. Show computations. Give the adjusting entry for depreciation at December 31, 19I.

PART B

PC9–7. Rice Company found it necessary to make extensive repairs on its existing building and to add a new wing. The existing building originally cost $300,000; and by the end of 19J, it was half depreciated on the basis of a 20-year estimated useful life and no residual value. During 19K, the following expenditures were made that were related to the building:

1. Ordinary repairs and maintenance expenditures for the year, $9,000 cash.
2. Extensive and major repairs to the roof of the building, $20,000 cash. These repairs were completed on June 30, 19K.
3. The new wing was completed on June 30, 19K, at a cash cost of $170,000. The wing had an estimated useful life of 10 years and no residual value.

Required:

a. Give the journal entry to record each of the 19K transactions.
b. Give the adjusting entry that would be required at the end of the annual accounting period, December 31, 19K, for the building after taking into account your entries in *(a)* above. Assume straight-line depreciation. The company computes depreciation based on the nearest month.
c. Show how the assets would be reported on the December 31, 19K, balance sheet. (Hint: Depreciation expense for 19K is $25,000.)

PC9–8. Dakota Company has five different intangible operational assets to be accounted for and reported on the financial statements. The management is concerned about the amortization of the cost of each of these intangibles. Facts concerning each intangible are:

1. Patent—The company purchased a patent at a cash cost of $26,000 on January 1, 19E. The patent had a legal life of 17 years from date of registration with the U.S. Patent Office, which was January 1, 19A. Amortize over the remaining legal life.
2. Copyright—On January 1, 19E, the company purchased a copyright at a cash cost of $15,000. The legal life remaining from that date is 30 years. It is estimated that the copyrighted item will have little or no value by the end of 25 years.

3. Franchise—The company obtained a franchise from X Company to make and distribute a special item. The franchise was obtained on January 1, 19E, at a cash cost of $10,000 and was for a 10-year period.

4. License—On January 1, 19D, the company secured a license from the city to operate a special service for a period of five years. Total cash expended in obtaining the license was $8,000.

5. Goodwill—The company started business in January 19C by purchasing another business for a cash lump sum of $400,000. Included in the purchase price was the item "Goodwill, $80,000." Dakota executives stated that "the goodwill is an important long-term asset to us." Amortize over the maximum period permitted.

Required:

a. You have been asked to analyze each intangible and give the journal entry to record each of the five acquisitions.

b. Give the adjusting entry for each intangible asset that would be necessary at the end of the annual accounting period, December 31, 19E. Provide a brief explanation and show computations. If no entry is required for a particular item, explain the basis for your conclusion.

c. Determine the book value of each intangible on January 1, 19G. (Hint: The total book value for the five intangibles is $119,000.)

PC9–9. On January 1, 19A, Investor Corporation was organized by five individuals for the purpose of purchasing and operating a successful business known as Kampus Korner. The name was retained, and all of the assets, except cash, were purchased for $300,000 cash. The liabilities were not assumed by Investor Corporation. The transaction was closed on January 5, 19A, at which time the balance sheet of Kampus Korner reflected the book values shown below:

KAMPUS KORNER
January 5, 19A

	Book value	Market value*
Accounts receivable (net)	$ 30,000	$ 30,000
Inventory	180,000	175,000
Operational assets (net)	19,000	50,000
Other assets	1,000	5,000
Total assets	$230,000	
Liabilities	$ 80,000	
Owners' equity	150,000	
Total liabilities and owners' equity	$230,000	

* These values for the assets purchased were provided to Investor Corporation by an independent appraiser.

As a part of the negotiations, the former owners of Kampus Korner agreed not to engage in the same or similar line of business in the same general region.

Required:

a. Give the journal entry by Investor Corporation to record the purchase of the assets of Kampus Korner. Include goodwill.

b. Give the adjusting journal entries that would be made by Investor Corporation at the end of the annual accounting period, December 31, 19A, for:

(1) Depreciation of the operational assets (straight line) assuming an estimated remaining useful life of 20 years and no residual value.

(2) Amortization of goodwill assuming the maximum amortization period is used.

PC9–10. During 19A, Wilson Company disposed of three different assets. On January 1, 19K, prior to their disposal, the accounts reflected the following:

Assets	Original cost	Residual value	Estimated life	Accumulated depreciation (straight line)
Machine A	$20,000	$2,000	10 years	$12,600 (7 years)
Machine B.....	35,400	3,000	9 years	21,600 (6 years)
Machine C.....	65,200	6,400	14 years	46,200 (11 years)

The machines were disposed of in the following ways:

Machine A—Sold on January 1, 19K, for $6,400 cash.

Machine B—Sold on May 1, 19K, for $13,200; received cash, $3,200, and a $10,000 interest-bearing (12 percent) note receivable due at the end of 12 months.

Machine C—On July 2, 19K, this machine suffered irreparable damage from an accident. On July 10, 19K, it was given to a salvage company at no cost. The salvage company agreed to remove the machine immediately at no cost. The machine was insured, and $18,000 cash was collected from the insurance company.

Required:

Give all journal entries incident to the disposal of each machine. Explain the accounting rationale for the way that you recorded each disposal.

PC9–11. (Note: This is a comprehensive PC to test your analytical ability.)

It is the end of the annual fiscal period, December 31, 19F, for Modern Company. The following items must be resolved before the financial statements can be prepared:

1. On January 1, 19F, a used machine was purchased for $5,000 cash. This amount was debited to an operational asset account, Machinery. Prior to use, cash was expended for (a) overhauling the machine, $600, and (b) for installation, $150; both of these amounts were debited to Expense. The machine has an estimated remaining useful life of five years and a 10 percent residual value. Straight-line depreciation will be used.

2. A small warehouse (and the land on which it is located) was purchased on January 1, 19F, at a cash cost of $40,000 which was debited to an operational asset account, Warehouse. The property was appraised for tax purposes near the end of 198E as follows: warehouse, $21,250; and land, $8,250. The warehouse has an estimated remaining useful life of 10 years and a 10 percent residual value. 200%—declining balance depreciation will be used.

3. During the year 19F, usual recurring repair costs of $1,200 were paid. During January 19F, major repairs (on the warehouse purchased in 2 above) of $1,000 were paid. Repair expense was debited $2,200, and Cash was credited.

4. On June 30, 19F, the company purchased a patent for use in the business at a cash cost of $2,040. The patent was dated July 1, 19A. The Patent account was debited.

5. On December 31, 19F, the company acquired a new truck that had a list price of $15,000 (estimated life, five years; residual value, $2,000). The company paid for the

truck with cash, $7,000, and issued to the seller 600 shares of its own capital stock, par $10, and market value $12 per share.

Required:

a. Give the journal entry or entries that should be made to correct the accounts at December 31, 19F, before the adjusting entries are made. If none is required, so state.

b. Give the adjusting journal entry at December 31, 19F, after the corrections in Requirement (a) have been made.

PC9–12. (Special case for discussion) The quotation below was taken directly from *Forbes* magazine (November 22, 1982, p. 178). You are to study it carefully and identify at least two primary accounting issues. Be prepared to discuss all aspects of this article.

One of the old standbys for financial officers when times got tough has always been to try to pick up earnings by slowing depreciation charges.

Last year's Accelerated Cost Recovery System only made that easier by effectively permitting companies to depreciate plant and equipment at different rates for tax and accounting purposes. Says Ronald Murray, Coopers & Lybrand's director of accounting and SEC technical services: "Now you can have a slower book depreciation schedule, which helps financial statements, and yet still stay with fast depreciation for tax purposes, which helps cash flow."

Changing depreciation schedules can make quite a difference for a company. Inland Steel, which recently slowed down its depreciation, will reduce this year's losses by $43 million, or $1.20 per share (Inland made only $57 million last year).

"We realized that, compared to our competitors, our conservative method of depreciation might have hurt us with investors because of its negative impact on net earnings," comments RTE Controller Douglas Haag. Says Duane Borst, Inland Steel's comptroller: "Why should we put ourselves at a disadvantage by depreciating more conservatively than other steel companies do?"

Up until recently, of course, most corporations were pushing for faster depreciation to escape the ravages of inflation. Now, by dragging out their depreciation schedules, firms may run the risk of repeating the errors of the automobile and steel industries, which found themselves hard pressed to replace assets because of years of underdepreciation.

The easiest way to lower depreciation charges is to switch from accelerated depreciation to straight line, where the same sum gets written off every year.

Those companies who want to lower their depreciation even further in hard times can switch to the units of production method, where charges are tied not to time but to production volume. In this way a plant running at 40% of capacity generates 60% lower depreciation charges. Ernst & Whinney's Denny Beresford, partner in charge of accounting standards, expects that more companies will follow the lead of Inland Steel and Asarco by switching to units-of-production depreciation.

For the investor, several questions remain so far unresolved. What about the problem of technological obsolescence, for example? Any slow method of depreciation might well encourage management to keep a piece of machinery in operation long after far superior replacements become available. The risk is great with units of production, especially in slow times.

Beresford raises a related issue: quality of earnings. "Some people would view a company that uses accelerated depreciation as being more conservative in its financial reporting and thus having a higher quality of earnings," he comments. IBM, for example, is still using the so-called sum-of-the-years method, which raises depreciation charges dramatically in the early years of an asset's life and then slows down as time goes on. As Beresford puts it: "A company changing away from accelerated to straight line might be viewed by some people as reporting at that time lower quality earnings." It's worth watching.

Slowdown				
Below, a look at nine companies that switched some or all depreciation schedules and the effect of earnings.				
Company	Switch	Year	Addition to net income (per share)	Earnings per share
Asarco	s.l. to u.o.p.	1980	$0.38	$8.02
Bell & Howell	acc. to s.l.	1981	0.04	3.83
Burlington Industries	acc. to s.l.	1981	0.15	3.98
Chrysler	acc. to s.l.	1981	0.52	−7.18
Cone Mills	acc. to s.l.	1981	0.10	5.87
Harsco	acc. to s.l.	1981	0.08	3.15
Inland Steel	s.l. to u.o.p.	1982	1.20	NA
McGraw-Edison	acc. to s.l.	1981	0.13	5.11
JP Stevens	acc. to s.l.	1980	0.06	1.43

Abbreviations: s.l. stands for straight line; acc. for accelerated; u.o.p. for units of production. NA Not available.

PC9–13. Refer to the financial statements of Johnson & Johnson in Special Supplement B immediately preceding the Index. Respond to the following questions for 1982.

1. What amount was reported in 1982 for "accumulated depreciation and amortization"?
2. Generally what methods of depreciation are used?
3. What total amount of "depreciation and amortization" expense was reported for 1982?
4. Give your explanation of why depreciation and amortization expense was added to net income in the computation of "Total funds provided from operations" on the SCFP.
5. Were any deferred charges reported on the balance sheet? If deferred charges are not reported separately, what amount on the balance sheet would include them?
6. How much interest did the company capitalize?
7. What were the amounts of *(a)* total interest and *(b)* interest expense reflected on the income statement?
8. What segment (line of business) of the company had the highest amount of identifiable assets at year-end 1982?
9. What segment (line of business) of the company had the highest amount of "depreciation and amortization" in 1982?
10. Of the total "Identifiable assets at year-end," what percent was outside the United States?

PC9–14. (Based on Supplement 9A) Quick Manufacturing Company operates a number of machines. One particular bank of machines consists of five identical machines acquired on the same date. At the beginning of 19G the operational asset account for the five machines showed the following:

Machinery (Type A, five machines). $200,000
Accumulated depreciation (Type A machines). 108,000*

* Based on 10-year estimated useful life and $4,000 residual value
per machine and straight-line depreciation.

One of the machines (Type A) was disposed of on September 1, 19G.

Required:

a. How old were the Type A machines at January 1, 19G? Show computations.
b. What was the book value of the machine at date of disposal? Show computations. The company computes depreciation to the nearest full month.
c. Give all journal entries to record the disposal of the machine under two independent assumptions:
   (1) It was sold outright for $14,000 cash.
   (2) It was exchanged for a new machine having a "quoted" price of $47,000; however, it was determined that it could be purchased for $44,000 cash. The old machine was traded in, and $30,000 was paid in cash. Assume the machines were similar. No reasonable market value was determinable for the old machine.

C·H·A·P·T·E·R
10

Measuring and Reporting Liabilities

PURPOSE OF THIS CHAPTER

A business generates or receives resources from three distinct sources: *(a)* capital contributions by owners, *(b)* sale of goods and services, and *(c)* extension of credit by creditors. Creditors provide resources to the business through cash loans and by providing property, goods, and services to the entity on credit. The borrowing activities of the entity create **liabilities** that are defined as probable future sacrifices of economic benefits arising from present obligations of a particular enterprise to transfer assets or provide services to other entities in the future as a result of past transactions or events.[1]

From the point of view of the user of the financial statements, the liabilities reported on the balance sheet, and the related expense incurred from borrowing (i.e., interest expense), reported on the income statement, often are important factors in evaluating the financial performance of an entity. Usually there are a number of different kinds of liabilities and a wide range of creditors; therefore, those interested in the business necessarily must rely on the financial statements for relevant information on these important financial activities of an entity. The accounting model, coupled with the audit made by an independent accountant, provides the user with reliable evidence that all liabilities are identified, properly measured, and fully reported.

This chapter discusses the measurement and reporting problems associated with the various classifications of liabilities. Throughout this chapter, the discussions emphasize (1) identification of liabilities, (2) measurement of the amount of each liability, (3) accounting for the various types of liabilities, and (4) appropriate reporting. To accomplish this purpose, the chapter is divided into two parts:

Part A—Accounting for, and reporting, liabilities

Part B—Present value and future value concepts

This chapter includes the following supplements:

Supplement 10A—Payroll accounting

Supplement 10B—The voucher system

---

[1] FASB, *Statement of Financial Concepts No. 3*, "Elements of Financial Statements of Business Enterprises" (Stamford, Conn., December 1980).

PART A—ACCOUNTING FOR, AND REPORTING, LIABILITIES

Although there are various ways to classify liabilities, for accounting and reporting purposes the following classifications typically are used:

1. Current liabilities:
   a. Accounts payable.
   b. Short-term notes payable.
   c. Other short-term obligations.
2. Long-term liabilities:
   a. Long-term notes payable and mortgages.
   b. Bonds payable.
   c. Other long-term obligations.

Bonds payable will be discussed in Chapter 11. Each of the other classifications will be discussed and illustrated in this chapter.

MEASURING LIABILITIES

Usually a liability involves the payment of the two distinctly different amounts; *(a)* the **principal** of the debt and *(b)* the **interest** on the principal. To illustrate, assume that you borrowed $1,000 cash on January 1, 19A, and signed a $1,000 note payable that specified 10 percent interest and a time to maturity (repayment) of one year. You would receive $1,000 cash and repay $1,100 ($1,000 principal plus $100 interest). In this situation, this liability would be measured and recorded on January 1, 19A, at its principal amount. The transaction would be recorded as follows:

January 1, 19A:

Cash	1,000	
Note payable		1,000

Fundamentally, liabilities are measured in accordance with the **cost principle.** The amount of a liability, when initially incurred, is equivalent to the current market value of the resources received when the transaction occurred. In most cases, liabilities are measured, recorded, and reported at their **principal** amounts, which is usually the same as the face amount or maturity value. However, there are two important exceptions to the general case:

1. Noninterest-bearing notes—some notes do not specify a rate of interest but nevertheless there is **implicit** interest. To illustrate, assume you borrow $1,000 cash on January 1, 19A, and agree to repay $1,100 in one year. You sign a $1,100 note that does not specify an interest rate (this is a noninterest-bearing note). The difference between the cash you borrow and the amount you repay ($1,100 − $1,000 = $100) is implicit interest.

2. Liabilities with a **stated** interest rate that is either higher or lower than the **going** or **market** rate for the transaction. To illustrate, the stated rate on the above note may be six percent and the going or market rate 10 percent. Measuring liabilities with an effective interest rate that is different than the stated interest rate requires application of present value concepts (discussed in Part B of this chapter). In most situations, the stated and effective interest rates for liabilities will be the same; in these situations, the liabilities are measured at their **principal** amounts.

CURRENT LIABILITIES

Current liabilities are defined as short-term obligations that will be paid within the **current operating cycle** of the business or within one year of the balance sheet date, whichever is the longer. This definition presumes that current liabilities will be paid with assets that are classified as current assets on the same balance sheet.[2]

An important financial relationship is the dollar difference between total current assets and total current liabilities. This difference is called **working capital.** The relationship between current assets and current liabilities also is measured as a ratio known as the current ratio (or the working capital ratio). The current ratio is computed by dividing total current assets by total current liabilities. To illustrate, assume the balance sheet for State Company on December 31, 19B, reported total current assets of $900,000 and total current liabilities of $300,000. The amount of working capital would be $900,000 − $300,000 = $600,000. The current ratio would be $900,000 ÷ $300,000 = 3.00, or 3 to 1. A current ratio of 3 to 1 means that, at the balance sheet date, there were $3 of current assets for each $1 of current liabilities. These relationships often assist creditors and others in assessing the ability of a company to meet its short-term obligations.[3]

Current liabilities commonly include trade accounts payable, short-term notes payable, accrued expenses (such as wages payable, taxes payable, and interest payable), cash dividends payable, and revenues collected in advance (also called deferred or unearned revenues).

Accounts payable

Trade accounts payable are created by purchases of goods for resale and services made in the normal course of business. The term **accounts payable** is used in accounting to mean **trade** accounts payable. Typical journal entries associated with creating and paying an account payable are:

---

[2] Current assets and current liabilities were defined and discussed in Chapter 2. Current assets are defined as cash and other resources reasonably expected to be realized in cash or sold or consumed within one year from the date of the balance sheet or during the **normal operating cycle,** whichever is the longer.

The AICPA Committee on Accounting Procedure defined current liabilities as follows: The term *current liabilities* is used principally to designate obligations whose liquidation is reasonably expected to require the use of existing resources properly classifiable as current assets, or the creation of other current liabilities.

[3] Interpretation of financial ratios is discussed in Chapter 16.

March 6, 19B (purchase on credit, periodic inventory system):

Purchases	980	
Accounts payable...		980
Purchase of merchandise on credit; terms, 2/10, n/30. (Invoice price, $1,000		
$\times$ .98 = $980.)		

March 11, 19B (payment of liability):[4]

Accounts payable	980	
Cash		980
Payment of account payable within the discount period.		

Accrued expenses

    Accrued expenses (also called accrued liabilities) arise when there are expenses that have been incurred but have not yet been paid or recorded at the end of the accounting period. These liabilities are recorded as adjusting entries. To illustrate a typical accrued expense, assume that on December 31, 19B, the annual amount of property taxes for 19B was determined to be $1,600, which had not been paid or recorded. At the end of the accounting period, December 31, 19B, the expense and related liability must be recorded and reported, although the amount will not be paid until January 15, 19C.[5] Therefore, the following **adjusting entry** must be made:

December 31, 19B (adjusting entry):

Property tax expense	1,600	
Property taxes payable		1,600
Adjusting entry to record property taxes incurred in 19B yet not recorded		
or paid.		

---

[4] In case of payment after the discount period, the entry would be:

Accounts payable	980	
Purchase discounts lost (or Interest expense)	20	
Cash		1,000

[5] If these taxes already had **been paid** (i.e., Expense debited and Cash credited), there would be no accrued liability to record at year-end. Similarly, if these taxes **already had been recorded but not paid** (i.e., Expense debited and Taxes Payable credited), there would be no need to make an adjusting entry at year-end.

The entry in 19C for payment of the above liability would be:

January 15, 19C:

```
Property taxes payable ...........................................    1,600
    Cash  ....................................................                 1,600
    Payment of liability for property taxes accrued in 19B.
```

Payroll liabilities   When employees perform services, the employer incurs an obligation that is not satisfied until the employees are paid on a weekly or monthly payroll basis. In previous chapters, accounting for wage and salary expense was simplified by disregarding payroll taxes and payroll deductions; we will now discuss these additional complications.

In addition to the obligation to the employee for salary or wages, the employer incurs other liabilities that are related directly to the payment of salaries and wages. These additional liabilities usually arise as a result of federal and state laws (social security taxes), and contractual obligations (such as pension plans and union dues). Some of these liabilities are paid by the **employees** through the employer (as payroll deductions); others must be paid by the **employer** and thus are additional expenses to the business.

The take-home pay of most employees is considerably less than the gross salary or wages because of **payroll deductions** for such items as employee income taxes withheld, social security taxes (known as FICA taxes) that must be paid by the employee, and other employee deductions such as insurance and union dues. The employer is required to pay the amounts, deducted from the wages, to the designated governmental agencies and other organizations such as the union. From the date of the payroll deduction until the date of payment to the agencies or organizations, the employer must record and report the **current liabilities** that are owed to the designated taxing agencies and other parties. A typical journal entry for a $100,000 payroll would be as follows:

January 31, 19B:

```
Salaries expense .................................................   60,000
Wages expense ...................................................   40,000
    Liability for income taxes withheld—employees ................            21,000
    Liability for union dues withheld—employees ..................               400
    FICA taxes payable—employees ...............................             6,000
    Cash (take-home pay) .......................................            72,600
    To record the payroll including employee deductions (see Supplement
    10A).
```

In addition to the payroll taxes that the **employees** must pay through the employer, the **employer** is required by law to pay additional specified payroll taxes, such as the employer's share of social security taxes (FICA) and Federal Unemployment Compensation (FUTA). These taxes constitute an operating expense for the business. Therefore, a second entry related to the payroll is needed to record the payroll taxes to be paid by the employer. A typical entry, related to the above payroll, would be as follows:

January 31, 19B:

Payroll tax expense	9,400*	
FICA taxes payable—employer (matching)		6,000
FUTA taxes payable—employer		700
State unemployment taxes payable—employer		2,700
Employer payroll taxes for January payroll.		
* Total payroll expense: $100,000 + $9,400 = $109,400.		

The six current liabilities recorded in the two entries immediately above will be paid in the near future when the company remits the requisite amounts of cash to the appropriate taxing agencies and other parties. Details involved in payroll accounting are discussed and illustrated in Supplement 10A to this chapter. Payroll accounting does not entail any new accounting concepts or principles; however, a significant amount of clerical detail is involved.

Deferred revenues

Deferred revenues (frequently called unearned revenues or revenues collected in advance) arise when revenues are collected during the current period that will not be earned until a later accounting period (see Chapter 4).

Deferred revenues create a liability because cash has been collected but the related revenue has not been earned by the end of the accounting period; therefore, there is a **current obligation** to render the services or to provide the goods in the future. To illustrate, assume that on November 15, 19B, rent revenue collected amounted to $6,000, which was recorded as a debit to Cash and a credit to Rent Revenue. Assume further that at the end of 19B it was determined that $2,000 of this amount was for January 19C rent. Thus, there is a current liability of $2,000 for deferred rent revenue that must be recognized. The sequence of entries for this situation would be as follows:

November 15, 19B (collection of rent revenue):

Cash	6,000	
Rent revenue		6,000
Collection of rent revenue.[6]		

_____

[6] On November 15, 19B, the credit could have been made to Rent Revenue Collected in Advance, in which case the adjusting entry to give the same results on December 31, 19B, would be:

Rent revenue collected in advance	4,000	
Rent revenue		4,000

December 31, 19B (adjusting entry for unearned rent revenue):

```
Rent revenue ...................................................... 2,000
    Rent revenue collected in advance (deferred revenue) .............        2,000
    Adjusting entry to record unearned rent revenue at the end of the account-
    ing period.
```

LONG-TERM LIABILITIES

Long-term liabilities encompass all obligations of the entity not properly classi-fied as current liabilities. Long-term liabilities often are incurred in conjunction with the purchase of operational assets or the borrowing of large amounts of cash for asset replacements and major expansions of the business. Long-term liabilities usually are represented by long-term notes payable or bonds payable. A long-term liability often is supported by a mortgage on specified assets of the borrower **pledged** as security for the liability. A mortgage involves a separate document that is appended to the note payable. A liability supported by a mortgage is said to be a "**secured** debt." An **unsecured** debt is one for which the creditor relies primarily on the integrity and general earning power of the borrower.

Long-term liabilities are reported on the balance sheet under a separate caption below "Current liabilities." As a long-term debt approaches the maturity date, the portion of it that is to be paid in the next current period is reclassified as a current liability. To illustrate, assume a five-year note payable of $50,000 was signed on January 1, 19A. Repayment is to be in two installments as follows: December 31, 19D, $25,000; and December 31, 19E, $25,000. The December 31, 19B, 19C, and 19D balance sheets would report the following:

```
December 31, 19B:
  Long-term liabilities:
    Note payable ....................... $50,000
December 31, 19C:
  Current liabilities:
    Maturing portion of long-term note ..... 25,000
  Long-term liabilities:
    Long-term note ..................... 25,000
December 31, 19D:
  Current liabilities:
    Maturing portion of long-term note ..... 25,000
```

Notes payable may be either short term or long term. A short-term note payable usually has a maturity date within one year from the balance sheet date and often arises as a result of borrowing cash or from purchasing merchandise or services on credit. Bonds payable (see Chapter 11) always are long-term liabilities, except for any currently maturing portion as illustrated above for the long-term note payable.

Notes payable

A note payable (short term or long term) is a written promise to pay a stated sum at one or more specified dates in the future. A note payable may require a single-sum repayment at the due or maturity date or it may call for installment payments (known as an annuity). To illustrate installment payments, consider the purchase of a sailboat for $3,000, with a $1,000 cash down payment and a note payable for the balance which specifies 12 equal monthly payments that include principal and interest.

Notes payable require the payment of interest and, hence, the recording of interest expense. Interest expense is incurred on liabilities because of the **time value of money.** The word **time** is significant because the longer borrowed money is held, the larger the total dollar amount of interest expense. Thus, one must pay more interest for a two-year loan of a given amount, at a given **interest rate,** than for a one-year loan. To the borrower, interest is an **expense;** whereas to the lender (creditor), interest is a **revenue.** In calculating interest, three variables must be considered: (1) the principal, (2) the interest rate, and (3) the duration of time. Therefore the interest formula is:

$$\text{Interest} = \text{Principal} \times \text{Rate} \times \text{Time}$$

To illustrate, assume $10,000 cash was borrowed by Baker Company on November 1, 19A, and a six-month, 12 percent, interest-bearing note payable was given. The interest is payable at the due date of the note. The computation of interest expense would be: $10,000 \times .12 \times 6/12 = $600. This note would be recorded in the accounts as follows:

November 1, 19A:

Cash	10,000	
Note payable, short term		10,000
Borrowed on short-term note; terms, six months at 12 percent per annum; interest is payable at maturity.		

Interest is an expense of the period when the money is used (unpaid); therefore it is measured, recorded, and reported on a **time basis** rather than when the cash actually is paid or borrowed. This concept is based on legal as well as on economic considerations. For example, were the $10,000 loan cited above to be paid off in two months instead of in six months, interest amounting to $10,000 $\times .12 \times 2/12 = $200 would have to be paid.

The **adjusting entry** for accrued interest payable would be made at the end of the accounting period on the basis of time expired from the last interest date or from the date of the note. To illustrate, assume the accounting period ends

December 31, 19A. Although the $600 interest for the six months will not be paid until April 30, 19B, two months' unpaid interest (i.e., November and December 19A) must be accrued by means of the following adjusting entry by Baker Company:

December 31, 19B:

```
Interest expense .........................................................    200
    Interest payable .....................................................              200
    Adjusting entry to accrue two months' interest ($10,000 × .12 × 2/12 =
    $200).
```

At maturity date the payment of principal plus interest for six months would be recorded as follows:[7]

April 30, 19C:

```
Notes payable, short term ...........................................    10,000
Interest payable (per prior entry) ..................................       200
Interest expense ($10,000 × .12 × 4/12) ...........................       400
    Cash ($10,000 + $600 interest) ................................            10,600
    To record payment of note payable including interest.
```

Accounting for a note payable is the same whether it is classified as a current or as a long-term liability. Accounting for a note payable also is the same regardless of the purpose for which the note was executed.

Lease liabilities   Leases are classified for accounting purposes as operating leases and capital leases.

1. **Operating lease**—a short-term lease in which the owner (called the lessor), for a stated rental, grants the user (called the lessee) the right to use property under specified conditions. The lessor is responsible for the cost of ownership (such as taxes, insurance, and major maintenance), and the lessee pays a monthly rental (and usually the utilities). The lease of an automobile on a daily basis and office space on a monthly basis are typical of operating leases.

---

[7] This journal entry assumes no reversing entry was made on January 1, 19C. (See Supplement 5A.) If a reversing entry of the accrual had been made on January 1, 19C, the payment entry would have been:

```
Notes payable, short term .........................................    10,000
Interest expense ..................................................       600
    Cash ..........................................................            10,600
```

When the monthly rent is paid, the lessor records rent revenue and the lessee records rent expense. Any unpaid rentals constitute a current liability.

2. **Capital lease**—a long-term, noncancelable lease contract in which the lessor transfers most of the **risks and rewards of ownership** to the lessee during the lease term. Thus, the lessee assumes most of the costs of ownership (such as taxes, insurance, and maintenance) and, in addition, pays a periodic rental. For accounting purposes this type of lease is viewed as a **sale** of the leased property by the lessor and a **purchase** of it by the lessee. Therefore, when a capital lease is signed, the lessor records a sale of the property (on the installment basis) and the lessor records a purchase of it (on long-term financing) that involves recognition of a long-term liability. Accounting for capital leases requires the use of present value concepts (discussed in Part B of this chapter).

Deferred income tax

Throughout the preceding chapters, we discussed and illustrated income taxes paid by corporations. In those illustrations, income tax expense was reflected on the income statement and income tax payable was reflected as a liability on the balance sheet. In addition to income tax payable, most corporate balance sheets report another tax item called **deferred income tax.**

The concept of deferred income tax is that **income tax expense** should be based on the **taxable** income reported on the income statement, while **income tax payable** necessarily must be based on the taxable income per the **tax return** (i.e., as specified in the tax laws). Often there is a difference between the time when certain revenues or expenses (which affect income taxes) appear on the income statement and when they appear on the tax return. Thus, a deferred income tax amount will result whenever there is a **timing difference** between when a taxable revenue or tax-deductible expense appears on the income statement and when it appears on the tax return. Deferred taxes are created only by timing differences; therefore, deferred taxes always will "reverse" or "turnaround." To illustrate a deferred tax reversal, consider a $10,000 taxable revenue that is reported on the 19A income statement but not on the 19A tax return. This timing difference will result in the recording of a deferred tax liability in 19A. In 19B, when the $10,000 taxable revenue is reported on the tax return (but not on the income statement), the deferred tax amount is reduced to zero (i.e., it "reverses"). In a similar manner, when a tax-deductible expense is on the income statement and the tax return in different periods, a timing difference must be accounted for. Accounting for deferred income taxes is illustrated in Exhibit 10–1.

Observe in Exhibit 10–1 that income tax expense for Web Corporation (on the income statement) does not agree with income tax payable on the balance sheet in years 19A and 19C. However, the totals for the three years agree ($27,000).

The difference between "Income tax expense" on the income statement and "Income tax payable" on the balance sheet in Exhibit 10–1 was due to a single expense—depreciation. Web Corporation purchased a depreciable asset at the beginning of 19A that cost $12,000 and had a useful life of three years with no residual value. The company used straight-line depreciation in its accounts (and on its income statement) and accelerated depreciation on its tax return. This timing

EXHIBIT 10–1   **Deferred income taxes illustrated**

Situation—Web Corporation:

a. Depreciation—Straight-line depreciation on income statement and accelerated depreciation on income tax return:

	19A	19B	19C
Income statement:			
Income before depreciation expense and before income tax expense	$34,000	$34,000	$34,000
Depreciation expense	4,000	4,000	4,000
Pretax income	30,000	30,000	30,000
Income tax expense (30%)	9,000	9,000	9,000
Net income	$21,000	$21,000	$21,000
Balance sheet (December 31):			
Liabilities:			
Income tax payable	$ 8,400	$ 9,000	$ 9,600
Deferred income tax	600	600*	

    * Cumulative balance.

Computation of income tax and income tax payable as reported above:

a. Depreciation expense computed:

Year	Straight-line depreciation (for income statement)	Accelerated depreciation (for tax purposes)
19A	$4,000	$6,000
19B	4,000	4,000
19C	4,000	2,000

b. Computation of tax **expense** as reported on the income statement:

	19A	19B	19C	
Income before depreciation expense and before income tax expense	$34,000	$34,000	$34,000	
Less: Depreciation expense (straight line)	4,000	4,000	4,000	
Amount subject to tax	30,000	30,000	30,000	
Income tax **expense** (30%)	$ 9,000	$ 9,000	$ 9,000 ←	

c. Computation of income tax **payable** as reported on the tax return:

	19A	19B	19C	
Income before depreciation expense and before income taxes	$34,000	$34,000	$34,000	Compare these amounts
Less: Depreciation expense (accelerated)	6,000	4,000	2,000	
Amount subject to tax	28,000	30,000	32,000	
Income tax **payable** (30%)	$ 8,400	$ 9,000	$ 9,600 ←	

Entries to record income taxes:

	19A		19B		19C	
Income tax expense (from income statement)	9,000		9,000		9,000	
Income tax payable (from tax return)		8,400		9,000		9,600
Deferred income tax (the difference)		600				600

difference caused a difference between income tax expense and income tax payable as shown in Exhibit 10–1.

Deferred income tax is recorded when a difference exists between income tax expense and income tax payable. Web Corporation would record deferred tax each year as shown in Exhibit 10–1.

The $600 deferred income tax amount would be reported as a liability on the balance sheet of Web Corporation in 19A and 19B, and no deferred income tax liability would be reported in 19C because the deferred tax amount "reversed" during 19C. This effect occurred because the advantage of the increased depreciation deduction in early years using accelerated depreciation for tax purposes was offset in 19C. Recall that regardless of the method of depreciation used, only the cost of the asset (less any residual value) can be depreciated for both accounting and tax return purposes ($12,000 in the example above). Also, this illustration demonstrates what has been noted before—the economic advantage of accelerated depreciation over straight line is only the time value of money. That is, the tax savings resulting from use of accelerated depreciation in early years can be invested to earn a certain return during 19B and 19C.

Deferred tax amounts often are very large. For example, Exxon Corporation recently reported a deferred income tax liability of $6,218,015,000 which represented 20 percent of total liabilities. This amount is, in effect, an interest free loan to Exxon from the government.

It is possible to have a debit balance in deferred income taxes, but such a situation is not typical because the tax law usually does not require "early" tax payments. The result of a debit balance would be, in effect, an interest free loan to the government from the corporation. If the deferred income tax account has a debit balance, it would be reported under assets on the balance sheet as a prepaid expense (if short term) or deferred charge (if long term).

APB Opinion 11, "Accounting for Income Taxes" (December 1967), specifies that deferred income tax shall be recorded **only** when there is a timing difference between the income statement and the tax return. A timing difference occurs only when an item of revenue or expense will be included on **both** the income statement and the tax return in different years so that the deferred tax effect automatically will reverse (as illustrated in Exhibit 10–1). Another type of difference between the income statement and tax return amounts is called a **permanent difference.** A permanent difference does not create deferred income tax because the revenue or expense appears on either the income statement or the tax return but not both. For example, interest revenue on tax-free municipal bonds is included on the income statement of the recipient, but is not reported on the recipient's federal income tax return.

On the balance sheet, the total amount of deferred income tax must be reported in part as a current liability (or asset) and in part as a long-term liability (or asset) depending upon the classification of the specific asset that gave rise to the deferred tax amount. Thus, the deferred income tax amount for Web Corporation would be classified as noncurrent because it was related to a noncurrent asset.

This discussion of deferred income taxes was presented so that you will understand the nature of deferred income tax reported on the balance sheets of most medium and large corporations. Income tax payable (as a liability) is easy to comprehend; however, many statement users have difficulty understanding the other tax item—deferred income tax.[8]

CONTINGENT LIABILITIES

A contingent liability is defined as a potential liability that has arisen as a result of an event or transaction that **already has occurred,** but its conversion to an effective liability is dependent upon the occurrence of one or more **future** events or transactions (i.e., a future contingency). To illustrate, assume that in 19B Baker Company was sued for $100,000 damages arising from an accident involving one of the trucks owned by the company. The suit is scheduled for trial during March 19C. Whether an effective liability is created will depend upon the decision of the court at the termination of the trial. When financial statements are prepared at December 31, 19B, a contingent liability must be disclosed. Because of the accident, the company is contingently liable for the payment of damages.

A contingent liability is **not** recorded in the accounts unless a loss is probable. Rather, it is reported in a note to the financial statements. For example, the contingent future liability arising from the Baker Company lawsuit may be disclosed by a note to the 19B balance sheet similar to the following:

> The company is contingently liable for $100,000 because of a lawsuit based on an accident involving a company vehicle. Legal counsel believes that the suit is lacking in merit. Trial is scheduled for March 19C.

CONTROLLING EXPENDITURES

The purchase of merchandise, services, and operational assets often requires that either a short-term or long-term liability be recorded. As a consequence, a large number of cash payments on liabilities typically are made in a business. In most companies, control over cash expenditures is essential to prevent the misapplication of cash in the cash-disbursement process. In a very small business it is often possible for the owner to give personal attention to each transaction when it is incurred and to make each cash payment. This personal attention may assure that the business is getting what it pays for, that cash is not being disbursed carelessly, and that there is no theft or fraud involving cash.

As a business grows and becomes more complex, the owner or top executive cannot devote personal attention to each transaction involving the processing

---

[8] It is unfortunate that the accounting profession adopted the term deferred income taxes because it is not descriptive of an item that may be reported as either a liability or an asset. More descriptive (but less succinct) titles are:

Liabilities:
Estimated future income taxes payable due to tax timing differences.

Assets:
Estimated future income tax savings due to tax timing differences.

of cash disbursements. In such situations these activities must be assigned to various employees. The assignment of these responsibilities to others creates a need for systematic and effective procedures for the control of cash expenditures. This is an important facet of the internal control of a well-designed accounting system.

In Chapter 8, the essential features of effective **internal control** were discussed, with emphasis on the control of cash receipts. Similar internal control procedures were discusssed in respect to cash disbursements: the separation of duties, disbursement of cash by check, petty cash, and the two special journals—the purchases journal and the cash disbursements journal. In larger companies and in computerized accounting systems, the method usually used for maintaining control over cash expenditures is known as the **voucher system.** This system replaces the cash disbursements journal procedures that were explained in Supplement 8B.

The voucher system

The voucher system is designed to establish strict control over transactions that create a legal obligation to make an expenditure of cash. The system requires that a **written authorization,** called a **voucher,** be approved by one or more designated managers at the time each such transaction occurs. An approved voucher is required regardless of whether the transaction involves the purchase of merchandise or services, the acquisition of operational assets, the payment of a liability, or an investment. The system permits checks to be issued only in payment of properly prepared and approved vouchers. Check writing is kept completely separate from the voucher-approval, check-approval, and check-distribution procedures.

The voucher system requires that every obligation be supported by a previously approved voucher and that each transaction be recorded when incurred. The incurrence of each obligation is treated as an independent transaction, and each payment of cash is treated as another independent transaction. This sequence of voucher approval, followed by payment by check, is required even in strictly cash-disbursement transactions. To illustrate, the **cash** purchase of merchandise for resale would be recorded under the voucher system as follows:

1. To record the incurrence of an obligation (with a periodic inventory system):

Purchases	1,000	
Vouchers payable		1,000

2. To record payment of the obligation by check (immediately thereafter):

Vouchers payable	1,000	
Cash		1,000

In a voucher system, the account designated **Vouchers Payable** replaces the account entitled Accounts Payable; but "Accounts payable," as the designation on the balance sheet, continues to be used. Entries of the first type are entered in a voucher register, and entries of the second type are entered in a check register.

The primary objective of the voucher system is to attain continuous control over each step in an expenditure from the incurrence of an obligation to the final disbursement of cash to satisfy the obligation. Thus, every single transaction leading to a cash payment, and the cash payment itself, is reviewed systematically, then subjected to an approval system based on separately designated responsibilities. Supplement 10B discusses and illustrates the **mechanics** of the voucher system.

PART B—PRESENT VALUE AND FUTURE VALUE CONCEPTS

CALCULATION OF PRESENT VALUE AND FUTURE VALUE AMOUNTS

The measuring and reporting of liabilities, when they are first recorded in the accounts and during the periods they are outstanding, often involve application of the concepts of present value and future value. These concepts also are used in measuring the effects of long-term investments in bonds, leases, pension plans, and sinking funds. Most of these applications in accounting involve either measurement of a liability or a receivable, or the establishment of a fund of cash to be used in the future for some special purpose (such as the retirement of debt).

The concepts of present value and future value focus on the time value of money, which is another name for interest. The time value of money refers to the fact that a dollar received today is worth more than a dollar to be received one year from today (or at any other later date) because a dollar received today can be invested say at 10 percent, so that it grows to $1.10 in one year. In contrast, if the dollar is to be received one year from today, one is denied the opportunity to earn the $.10 interest revenue for the year. The difference between the $1 and $1.10 is due to interest that can be earned during the year. Interest is the cost of the use of money for a specific period of time, just as rent represents the cost for use of a tangible asset for a period of time. Interest may be specified (i.e., stated explicitly), as in the case of an interest-bearing note, or it may be unspecified, as in a noninterest-bearing note (but interest is paid nonetheless; i.e., it is implicitly there).

For many years, the time value of money often was overlooked in accounting for some transactions. In recent years, several *Opinions* issued by the APB have required the application of present value determinations. Of particular significance was *Opinion 21* entitled "Interest on Receivables and Payables." This *Opinion* requires the application of present value determinations to a number of transactions. For example, the *Opinion* states: "In the absence of established exchange prices for the related property, goods, or service or evidence of the market value of the note, the present value of a note that stipulates either no interest or a rate of interest that is clearly unreasonable should be determined by **discounting** all future payments on the notes using an imputed rate of interest." To illustrate, assume a machine is purchased for $20,000. The purchaser is allowed to pay the $20,000 at the end of two years, and there is an implied interest rate of 12 percent (which is the market rate of interest). The $20,000 to be paid represents the current cash equivalent amount of the debt **plus** the interest that will be paid during the two years. Under the cost principle, the machine account should be debited for the present value (current cash equivalent) of the debt, or $15,944 (see pages 474 and 475).

There are four different types of problems related to the time value of money; they are identified in Exhibit 10–2. Each type of problem is based on the interest formula that was discussed in Part A of this chapter, viz:

$$\text{Interest} = \text{Principal} \times \text{Rate} \times \text{Time}$$

EXHIBIT 10–2
Symbols representing the four types of present value and future value problems

Payment or Receipt	Symbol	
	Present value	Future value
Single amount	p	f
Annuity (equal payments or receipts for a series of equal time periods)	P	F

In **future value** problems, you will be given the amount of cash (principal) to be invested and you will be asked to use the basic interest formula to calculate the amount of principal plus interest that will be available at some future date. In contrast, **present value** problems involve a simple rearrangement of the basic interest formula. In present value problems, you will be given the amount that will be available at some future date (principal plus interest) and you will be asked to calculate the current cash equivalent of that amount.

Tables have been developed to avoid the detailed arithmetic calculations that are required in present value and future value computations. These tables (pages 468 to 469) provide values for each of the four types of problems for different periods of time *(n)* and at different rates of interest *(i)*. The values given in the tables are based on payments of $1, so if a problem involves payments other than $1, it is necessary to multiply the value from the table by the amount of the payment.[9] To illustrate these concepts, we will examine each of the four types of present value and future value problems.

---

[9] Present value and future value problems assume cash flows. The basic concepts are the same for cash inflows (receipts) and cash outflows (payments). Thus, there are no fundamental differences between present value and future value calculations for cash payments versus cash receipts.

Future value of a single amount
(f)

The future value is the sum to which an amount will increase at *i* interest rate for *n* periods. The future sum will be the **principal plus compound interest.** The future value concept is based upon compound interest so that the amount of interest for each period is calculated by multiplying the interest rate by the principal plus any interest that accrued in prior years but was not paid out.

To illustrate, assume that on January 1, 19A, $1,000 was deposited in a savings account at 10 percent annual interest, compounded annually. At the end of three years, that is, on December 31, 19C, the $1,000 that was deposited would increase to $1,331 as follows:

	Amount at start of year	+ Interest during the year	= Amount at end of year
Year 1	$1,000	+ $1,000 × .10 = $100 =	$1,100
Year 2	1,100	+ 1,100 × .10 = 110 =	1,210
Year 3	1,210	+ 1,210 × .10 = 121 =	1,331

However, we can avoid the detailed arithmetic by referring to Table 10–1, **Future value of $1.** For $i = 10$ percent, $n = 3$, we find the value 1.331; therefore, we can compute the balance at the end of Year 3 as $1,000 × 1.331 = $1,331. The increase of $331 was due to the time value of money; it would be interest revenue to you and interest expense to the savings institution. With any positive interest rate, the future value of $1 always will be greater than $1. Exhibit 10–3 presents a summary of this future value concept.

Present value of a single amount
(p)

Present value of a single amount is the value now (i.e., the present) of an amount to be received at some date in the future. It can be said to be the inverse of the future value concept. To compute the present value of a sum to be received in the future, the future sum is subjected to compound discounting at *i* interest rate for *n* periods. In compound discounting, the interest is subtracted rather than added, as in compounding (as was demonstrated in the discussion of the future value concept). To illustrate discounting, assume that today is January 1, 19A, and that you will receive $1,000 cash on December 31, 19C; that is, three years from now. Assuming an interest rate of 10 percent per year, how much would the $1,000 be worth today; that is, what is its present value (today, on January 1, 19A)? We could set up a discounting computation, year by year, that would be the inverse to the tabulation shown on page 470. However, to facilitate the computation, we can refer to the **Present value of $1 table,** Table 10–2. For $i = 10$ percent; $n = 3$, we find the present value of $1 is .7513. The $1,000, to be received three years hence, has a present value of $1,000 × .7513 = $751.30. The difference (i.e., the discount) of $248.70 is due to the time value of money; it is the interest. The concept of the present value of $1 is summarized in Exhibit 10–3.

Future value of an annuity *(F)*

Basically, the future value of an **annuity** is the same as the future value of a single amount, except for the addition of the concept of an annuity. The word

EXHIBIT 10–3
Time value of money determinations

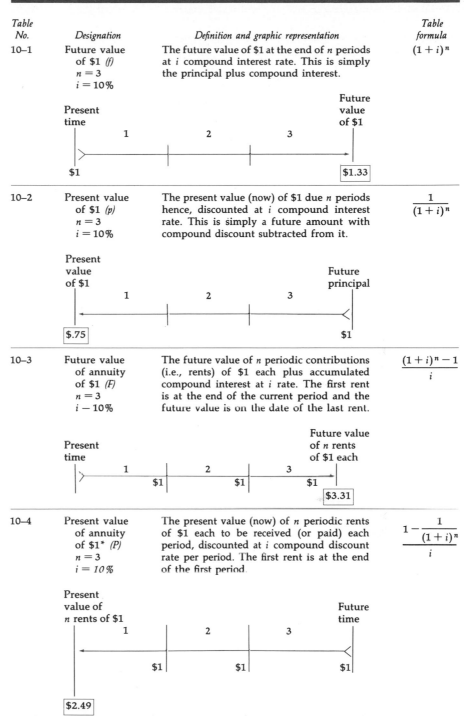

Table No.	Designation	Definition and graphic representation	Table formula
10–1	Future value of $1 (f) $n = 3$ $i = 10\%$	The future value of $1 at the end of n periods at i compound interest rate. This is simply the principal plus compound interest.	$(1 + i)^n$

Present time — Future value of $1

1   2   3

$1 .... $1.33

| 10–2 | Present value of $1 (p) $n = 3$ $i = 10\%$ | The present value (now) of $1 due n periods hence, discounted at i compound interest rate. This is simply a future amount with compound discount subtracted from it. | $\dfrac{1}{(1 + i)^n}$ |

Present value of $1 — Future principal

1   2   3

$.75 .... $1

| 10–3 | Future value of annuity of $1 (F) $n = 3$ $i - 10\%$ | The future value of n periodic contributions (i.e., rents) of $1 each plus accumulated compound interest at i rate. The first rent is at the end of the current period and the future value is on the date of the last rent. | $\dfrac{(1 + i)^n - 1}{i}$ |

Present time — Future value of n rents of $1 each

1   2   3

$1 $1 $1

$3.31

| 10–4 | Present value of annuity of $1* (P) $n = 3$ $i = 10\%$ | The present value (now) of n periodic rents of $1 each to be received (or paid) each period, discounted at i compound discount rate per period. The first rent is at the end of the first period. | $\dfrac{1 - \dfrac{1}{(1 + i)^n}}{i}$ |

Present value of n rents of $1 — Future time

1   2   3

$1 $1 $1

$2.49

* Observe that these are **ordinary** annuities; that is, they are often called end-of-period annuities. Thus, for F, the future amount is on the date of the last rent; and for P, the present value is at the beginning of the period of the first rent. Annuities **due** assume the opposite; that is, they are "beginning-of-period" annuities. Ordinary annuity values can be converted to annuities due simply by multiplication of $(1 + i)$. Annuities due are discussed at the next level of accounting sophistication, intermediate accounting.

TABLE 10–1
Future value of $1,
$f = (1 + i)^n$

Periods	2 %	3 %	3.75 %	4 %	4.25 %	5 %	6 %	7 %	8 %
0	1.	1.	1.	1.	1.	1.	1.	1.	1.
1	1.02	1.03	1.0375	1.04	1.0425	1.05	1.06	1.07	1.08
2	1.0404	1.0609	1.0764	1.0816	1.0868	1.1025	1.1236	1.1449	1.1664
3	1.0612	1.0927	1.1168	1.1249	1.1330	1.1576	1.1910	1.2250	1.2597
4	1.0824	1.1255	1.1587	1.1699	1.1811	1.2155	1.2625	1.3108	1.3605
5	1.1041	1.1593	1.2021	1.2167	1.2313	1.2763	1.3382	1.4026	1.4693
6	1.1262	1.1941	1.2472	1.2653	1.2837	1.3401	1.4185	1.5007	1.5869
7	1.1487	1.2299	1.2939	1.3159	1.3382	1.4071	1.5036	1.6058	1.7138
8	1.1717	1.2668	1.3425	1.3686	1.3951	1.4775	1.5938	1.7182	1.8509
9	1.1951	1.3048	1.3928	1.4233	1.4544	1.5513	1.6895	1.8385	1.9990
10	1.2190	1.3439	1.4450	1.4802	1.5162	1.6289	1.7908	1.9672	2.1589
20	1.4859	1.8061	2.0882	2.1911	2.2989	2.6533	3.2071	3.8697	4.6610

Periods	9 %	10 %	11 %	12 %	13 %	14 %	15 %	20 %	25 %
0	1.	1.	1.	1.	1.	1.	1.	1.	1.
1	1.09	1.10	1.11	1.12	1.13	1.14	1.15	1.20	1.25
2	1.1881	1.2100	1.2321	1.2544	1.2769	1.2996	1.3225	1.4400	1.5625
3	1.2950	1.3310	1.3676	1.4049	1.4429	1.4815	1.5209	1.7280	1.9531
4	1.4116	1.4641	1.5181	1.5735	1.6305	1.6890	1.7490	2.0736	2.4414
5	1.5386	1.6105	1.6851	1.7623	1.8424	1.9254	2.0114	2.4883	3.0518
6	1.6771	1.7716	1.8704	1.9738	2.0820	2.1950	2.3131	2.9860	3.8147
7	1.8280	1.9487	2.0762	2.2107	2.3526	2.5023	2.6600	3.5832	4.7684
8	1.9926	2.1436	2.3045	2.4760	2.6584	2.8526	3.0590	4.2998	5.9605
9	2.1719	2.3579	2.5580	2.7731	3.0040	3.2519	3.5179	5.1598	7.4506
10	2.3674	2.5937	2.8394	3.1058	3.3946	3.7072	4.0456	6.1917	9.3132
20	5.6044	6.7275	8.0623	9.6463	11.5231	13.7435	16.3665	38.3376	86.7362

TABLE 10–2
Present value of $1,
$p = \dfrac{1}{(1 + i)^n}$

Periods	2 %	3 %	3.75 %	4 %	4.25 %	5 %	6 %	7 %	8 %
1	0.9804	0.9709	0.9639	0.9615	0.9592	0.9524	0.9434	0.9346	0.9259
2	0.9612	0.9426	0.9290	0.9246	0.9201	0.9070	0.8900	0.8734	0.8573
3	0.9423	0.9151	0.8954	0.8890	0.8826	0.8638	0.8396	0.8163	0.7938
4	0.9238	0.8885	0.8631	0.8548	0.8466	0.8227	0.7921	0.7629	0.7350
5	0.9057	0.8626	0.8319	0.8219	0.8121	0.7835	0.7473	0.7130	0.6806
6	0.8880	0.8375	0.8018	0.7903	0.7790	0.7462	0.7050	0.6663	0.6302
7	0.8706	0.8131	0.7728	0.7599	0.7473	0.7107	0.6651	0.6227	0.5835
8	0.8535	0.7894	0.7449	0.7307	0.7168	0.6768	0.6274	0.5820	0.5403
9	0.8368	0.7664	0.7180	0.7026	0.6876	0.6446	0.5919	0.5439	0.5002
10	0.8203	0.7441	0.6920	0.6756	0.6595	0.6139	0.5584	0.5083	0.4632
20	0.6730	0.5534	0.4789	0.4564	0.4350	0.3769	0.3118	0.2584	0.2145

Periods	9 %	10 %	11 %	12 %	13 %	14 %	15 %	20 %	25 %
1	0.9174	0.9091	0.9009	0.8929	0.8850	0.8772	0.8696	0.8333	0.8000
2	0.8417	0.8264	0.8116	0.7972	0.7831	0.7695	0.7561	0.6944	0.6400
3	0.7722	0.7513	0.7312	0.7118	0.6931	0.6750	0.6575	0.5787	0.5120
4	0.7084	0.6830	0.6587	0.6355	0.6133	0.5921	0.5718	0.4823	0.4096
5	0.6499	0.6209	0.5935	0.5674	0.5428	0.5194	0.4972	0.4019	0.3277
6	0.5963	0.5645	0.5346	0.5066	0.4803	0.4556	0.4323	0.3349	0.2621
7	0.5470	0.5132	0.4817	0.4523	0.4251	0.3996	0.3759	0.2791	0.2097
8	0.5019	0.4665	0.4339	0.4039	0.3762	0.3506	0.3269	0.2326	0.1678
9	0.4604	0.4241	0.3909	0.3606	0.3329	0.3075	0.2843	0.1938	0.1342
10	0.4224	0.3855	0.3522	0.3220	0.2946	0.2697	0.2472	0.1615	0.1074
20	0.1784	0.1486	0.1240	0.1037	0.0868	0.0728	0.0611	0.0261	0.0115

TABLE 10–3
Future value of annuity of $1 (ordinary),

$$F = \frac{(1+i)^n - 1}{i}$$

Period rents*	2%	3%	3.75%	4%	4.25%	5%	6%	7%	8%
1	1.	1.	1.	1.	1.	1.	1.	1.	1.
2	2.02	2.03	2.0375	2.04	2.0425	2.05	2.06	2.07	2.08
3	3.0604	3.0909	3.1139	3.1216	3.1293	3.1525	3.1836	3.2149	3.2464
4	4.1216	4.1836	4.2307	4.2465	4.2623	4.3101	4.3746	4.4399	4.5061
5	5.2040	5.3091	5.3893	5.4163	5.4434	5.5256	5.6371	5.7507	5.8666
6	6.3081	6.4684	6.5914	6.6330	6.6748	6.8019	6.9753	7.1533	7.3359
7	7.4343	7.6625	7.8386	7.8983	7.9585	8.1420	8.3938	8.6540	8.9228
8	8.5830	8.8923	9.1326	9.2142	9.2967	9.5491	9.8975	10.2598	10.6366
9	9.7546	10.1591	10.4750	10.5828	10.6918	11.0266	11.4913	11.9780	12.4876
10	10.9497	11.4639	11.8678	12.0061	12.1462	12.5779	13.1808	13.8164	14.4866
20	24.2974	26.8704	29.0174	29.7781	30.5625	33.0660	36.7856	40.9955	45.7620

Period rents*	9%	10%	11%	12%	13%	14%	15%	20%	25%
1	1.	1.	1.	1.	1.	1.	1.	1.	1.
2	2.09	2.10	2.11	2.12	2.13	2.14	2.15	2.20	2.25
3	3.2781	3.3100	3.3421	3.3744	3.4069	3.4396	3.4725	3.6400	3.8125
4	4.5731	4.6410	4.7097	4.7793	4.8498	4.9211	4.9934	5.3680	5.7656
5	5.9847	6.1051	6.2278	6.3528	6.4803	6.6101	6.7424	7.4416	8.2070
6	7.5233	7.7156	7.9129	8.1152	8.3227	8.5355	8.7537	9.9299	11.2588
7	9.2004	9.4872	9.7833	10.0890	10.4047	10.7305	11.0668	12.9159	15.0735
8	11.0285	11.4359	11.8594	12.2997	12.7573	13.2328	13.7268	16.4991	19.8419
9	13.0210	13.5795	14.1640	14.7757	15.4157	16.0853	16.7858	20.7989	25.8023
10	15.1929	15.9374	16.7220	17.5487	18.4197	19.3373	20.3037	25.9587	33.2529
20	51.1601	57.2750	64.2028	72.0524	80.9468	91.0249	102.4436	186.6880	342.9447

* There is one rent each period.

TABLE 10–4
Present value of annuity of $1 (ordinary),

$$P = \frac{1 - \frac{1}{(1+i)^n}}{i}$$

Period rents*	2%	3%	3.75%	4%	4.25%	5%	6%	7%	8%
1	0.9804	0.9709	0.9639	0.9615	0.9592	0.9524	0.9434	0.9346	0.9259
2	1.9416	1.9135	1.8929	1.8861	1.8794	1.8594	1.8334	1.8080	1.7833
3	2.8839	2.8286	2.7883	2.7751	2.7620	2.7232	2.6730	2.6243	2.5771
4	3.8077	3.7171	3.6514	3.6299	3.6086	3.5460	3.4651	3.3872	3.3121
5	4.7135	4.5797	4.4833	4.4518	4.4207	4.3295	4.2124	4.1002	3.9927
6	5.6014	5.4172	5.2851	5.2421	5.1997	5.0757	4.9173	4.7665	4.6229
7	6.4720	6.2303	6.0579	6.0021	5.9470	5.7864	5.5824	5.3893	5.2064
8	7.3255	7.0197	6.8028	6.7327	6.6638	6.4632	6.2098	5.9713	5.7466
9	8.1622	7.7861	7.5208	7.4353	7.3513	7.1078	6.8017	6.5152	6.2469
10	8.9826	8.5302	8.2128	8.1109	8.0109	7.7217	7.3601	7.0236	6.7101
20	16.3514	14.8775	13.8962	13.5903	13.2944	12.4622	11.4699	10.5940	9.8181

Period rents*	9%	10%	11%	12%	13%	14%	15%	20%	25%
1	0.9174	0.9091	0.9009	0.8929	0.8850	0.8772	0.8696	0.8333	0.8000
2	1.7591	1.7355	1.7125	1.6901	1.6681	1.6467	1.6257	1.5278	1.4400
3	2.5313	2.4869	2.4437	2.4018	2.3612	2.3216	2.2832	2.1065	1.9520
4	3.2397	3.1699	3.1024	3.0373	2.9745	2.9137	2.8550	2.5887	2.3616
5	3.8897	3.7908	3.6959	3.6048	3.5172	3.4331	3.3522	2.9906	2.6893
6	4.4859	4.3553	4.2305	4.1114	3.9975	3.8887	3.7845	3.3255	2.9514
7	5.0330	4.8684	4.7122	4.5638	4.4226	4.2883	4.1604	3.6046	3.1611
8	5.5348	5.3349	5.1461	4.9676	4.7988	4.6389	4.4873	3.8372	3.3289
9	5.9952	5.7590	5.5370	5.3282	5.1317	4.9464	4.7716	4.0310	3.4631
10	6.4177	6.1446	5.8892	5.6502	5.4262	5.2161	5.0188	4.1925	3.5705
20	9.1285	8.5136	7.9633	7.4694	7.0248	6.6231	6.2593	4.8696	3.9539

* There is one rent each period.

annuity refers to a series of periodic payments characterized by (1) an **equal** amount each period (for two or more future consecutive periods), (2) **equal** length of each consecutive period, and (3) and **equal** interest rate each period. The future value of an annuity involves **compound interest** on each periodic amount. To illustrate, assume that you decide to deposit (i.e., contribute) $1,000 cash in a savings account each year for three years at 10 percent interest per year (i.e., a total of $3,000). The first $1,000 deposit is made on December 31, 19A; the second one on December 31, 19B; and the third and last one on December 31, 19C. How much would you have in the savings account at the end of Year 3, that is, immediately after the third (and last) deposit on December 31, 19C? In this situation, the first $1,000 deposit would draw compound interest for two years (for a total principal and interest of $1,210); the second deposit would draw interest for one year (for a total principal and interest of $1,100); and the third deposit would draw no interest because it was made on the last day of the final year in the savings plan. Thus, the total amount in the savings account, at the end of three years would be $3,310 ($1,210 + $1,100 + $1,000). We could compute separately the interest on each deposit to derive the future value of this annuity. However, we can refer to Table 10–3, **Future value of annuity of $1.** For $i =$ 10 percent, $n = 3$, we find the value 3.31.[10] Therefore, the total of your three deposits (of $1,000 each) would have increased to $1,000 × 3.31 = $3,310 on December 31, 19C. The increase of $310 was due to the time value of money; it is interest revenue to you on the $3,000. This concept is summarized in Exhibit 10–3.

Present value of an annuity *(P)*

The present value of an annuity is the value now (i.e., the present time) of a series of **equal amounts** (i.e., rents) to be received each period for some specified number of periods in the future. It can be said to be the inverse of the future value of an annuity explained immediately above. It involves compound **discounting** of each of the equal periodic amounts.

To illustrate, assume now is January 1, 19A, and that you are to receive $1,000 cash on each December 31, 19A, 19B, and 19C. How much would the sum of these three $1,000 future amounts be worth now, on January 1, 19A (i.e., the present value), assuming an interest rate of 10 percent per year? We could calculate laboriously the discounting on each rent as follows:

Year	Amount		Value from Table 10–2 $i = 10$ percent		Present value
1	$1,000	×	.9091 $(n = 1)$	=	$ 909.10
2	1,000	×	.8264 $(n = 2)$	=	826.40
3	1,000	×	.7513 $(n = 3)$	=	751.30
				Total present value	$2,486.80

---

[10] The equal amounts for each period in annuities often are referred to in the literature as "rents."

We can compute the present value more readily by referring to Table 10–4, **Present value of annuity of $1.** For $i = 10$ percent, $n = 3$ rents, we find the value 2.4869. Therefore, your three $1,000 amounts to be received in the future have a total present value of $1,000 \times 2.4869 = \$2,487$. The difference of $513 ($3,000 − $2,487) was due to the interest discount factor. This concept is summarized in Exhibit 10–3.

To conclude this section, observe that the preceding illustrations assumed annual interest rates and annual periods for compounding and discounting. While interest rates almost always are quoted on an annual basis, interest compounding periods often are less than one year (such as semiannually or quarterly). When interest periods are less than a year, the values of **n** and **i** must be restated to be consistent with the length of the interest period. To illustrate, 12 percent interest compounded annually for five years requires use of $n = 5$ and $i = 12$. If compounding is quarterly, the interest period is one quarter of a year (i.e., four periods per year), and the quarterly interest rate would be one quarter of the annual rate (i.e., 3 percent per quarter); therefore, 12 percent interest compounded quarterly for five years requires use of $n = 20$ and $i = 3$.

MEASUREMENT AND ACCOUNTING APPLICATIONS OF FV AND PV

There are numerous transactions where the concepts of future and present value are used for accounting measurements. Below are cited four different situations where these concepts must be employed.

Case A:

On January 1, 19A, Company A set aside $150,000 cash in a special building fund (an asset) to be used at the end of five years to construct a new building. The fund is expected to earn 10 percent interest per year, which will be added to the fund balance each year. On the date of deposit the company made the following entry:

January 1, 19A:

Special building fund	150,000	
Cash		150,000

Required:

1. What will be the balance of the fund at the end of the fifth year?
   Answer: This situation requires application of the future value of a single amount.

   Principal $\times$ Table 10–1 value ($i = 10\%$; $n = 5$) = Future value
   $150,000 \times 1.6105$ = $241,575

2. How much interest revenue was earned on the fund during the five years?
   Answer:

$$\$241{,}575 - \$150{,}000 = \$91{,}575$$

3. What entry would be made on December 31, 19A, to record the interest revenue for the first year?
   Answer: Interest for one year on the fund balance is added to the fund and recorded as follows:

December 31, 19A:

Special building fund	15,000	
Interest revenue ($150,000 × .10)		15,000

4. What entry would be made on December 31, 19B, to record interest revenue for the second year?
   Answer:

December 31, 19B:

Special building fund	16,500	
Interest revenue		16,500
($150,000 + $15,000) × .10 = $16,500.		

Case B:
On January 1, 19A, Company B purchased a new machine at a list price of $20,000, which was payable at the end of two years with no interim interest payments. The going rate of interest was 12 percent.

Required:

1. The company accountant is preparing the following journal entry:

January 1, 19A:

Machinery	$?	
Account payable (special)		$?

What amount should be recorded in this entry?
Answer: This situation requires application of the present value of a single amount. Under the cost principle, the cost of the machine is its current

cash equivalent price, which is the present value of the future payment. The present value of the $20,000 is computed as follows:

$$\text{Future amount} \times \text{Table 10-2 } (i = 12\%; n = 2) = \text{Present value}$$
$$\$20,000 \times .7972 \qquad\qquad = \$15,944$$

Therefore, the journal entry would be as follows:

January 1, 19A:

Machinery	15,944	
Account payable (special)		15,944

2. What journal entry would be made at the end of the first and second years for interest expense on the accounts payable?

   Answer: Interest expense for each year on the amount in the Account Payable account would be recorded by means of an adjusting entry, as follows:

December 31, 19A:

Interest expense	1,913	
Account payable (special)		1,913

$15,944 \times .12 = \$1,913$.

Note: The account payable would be reported on the 19A balance sheet at $15,944 + $1,913 = $17,857.

December 31, 19B:

Interest expense	2,143	
Account payable (special)		2,143

$(\$15,944 + \$1,913) \times .12 = \$2,143$.

The effect of these two entries is to increase the balance in Account Payable for the new accrued interest payable at maturity date. By maturity date, the balance will have been increased to the maturity amount, $20,000, which is the total amount payable at due date. Interest expense was $1,913 + $2,143 = $4,056, or alternatively, $20,000 − $15,944 = $4,056.

3. What journal entry would be made to record payment of the note on December 31, 19B (the maturity date)?

Answer: At this date the amount to be paid is the balance of Account Payable, which is the same as the maturity amount on the due date, that is, $15,944 + $1,913 + $2,143 = $20,000.[11]

The journal entry to record full payment of the debt would be:

December 31, 19B:

Account payable (special)	20,000	
Cash		20,000

Case C:

Company C decided to make five equal annual deposits of $30,000 with a financial institution to acccumulate a debt retirement fund. The deposits will be made each December 31, starting December 31, 19A. The fifth and last deposit will be made December 31, 19E. The financial institution will pay 8 percent annual compound interest, which will be added to the fund at the end of each year.

1. What entry should be made to record the first deposit?
    Answer:

December 31, 19A:

Debt retirement fund	30,000	
Cash		30,000

2. What will be the balance in the fund immediately after the fifth and last deposit (i.e., on December 31, 19E)?

---

[11] These entries also could be made as follows with the same results:

January 1, 19A:

Machinery	15,944	
Discount on account payable	4,056	
Account payable (special)		20,000

December 31, 19A:

Interest expense ($15,944 × .12)	1,913	
Discount on account payable		1,913

At the end of 19A, the liability would be reported at net as $20,000 − $2,143 = $17,857.

December 31, 19B:

Interest expense ($17,857 × .12)	2,143	
Account payable (special)	20,000	
Cash		20,000
Discount on account payable		2,143

Answer: This situation requires application of future value of an annuity.

$$\text{Rent} \quad \times \text{Table 10–3 } (i = 8\%; n = 5) = \text{Future value}$$
$$\$30,000 \times 5.8666 \qquad\qquad\qquad = \$175,998$$

3. What entries would be made at the end of 19B?
    Answer:
    a. Interest for one year on the fund balance would be added to the fund and recorded as follows:

    December 31, 19B:

Debt retirement fund	2,400	
Interest revenue ($30,000 × .08)		2,400

    b. The second deposit would be recorded as follows:

    December 31, 19B:

Debt retirement fund	30,000	
Cash		30,000

4. What would be the amount of interest revenue to be recorded at the end of the 19C?
    Answer: Interest would be computed on the increased fund balance as follows:

    $$(\$30,000 + \$2,400 + \$30,000) \times .08 = \$4,992$$

Case D:

On January 1, 19A, Company D purchased a new machine at a cash price of $40,000. The company was short of cash so arrangements were made to execute a $40,000 note payable to be paid off in three equal annual installments. Each installment includes principal plus interest on the unpaid balance at 11 percent per year. The equal annual installments are due on December 31, 19A, 19B, and 19C. The acquisition was recorded as follows:

January 1, 19A:

Machinery	40,000	
Note payable		40,000

Required:

1. What would be the amount of each equal annual installment?
    Answer: The $40,000 is the amount of the debt today; hence, $40,000 is the present value of the three future installment payments required. Therefore, $n = 3$, $i = 11$ percent, and the present value is $40,000. To compute the amount of each equal payment required, the present value of an annuity must be used as follows:

    Payment $\times$ Table 10–4 value ($i = 11\%$; $n = 3$) = Present value
    Substituting:
    Payment $\times$ 2.4437 = $40,000
    Payment = $40,000 $\div$ 2.4437
    $\qquad\qquad$ = $16,369 (amount of each annual payment)

2. What was the amount of interest expense in dollars?
    Answer:

    $$(\$16,369 \times 3) - \$40,000 = \$9,107$$

3. What journal entry should be made at the end of each year to record the payment on this $40,000 note payable?
    Answer:
    a. To record the first installment payment on the note:

    December 31, 19A:

Note payable	11,969	
Interest expense ($40,000 $\times$ .11)	4,400	
$\qquad$ Cash (computed above)		16,369

    b. To record the second installment payment on the note:

    December 31, 19B:

Note payable	13,285	
Interest expense ($40,000 − $11,969) $\times$ .11	3,084	
$\qquad$ Cash (computed above)		16,369

    c. To record final installment payment on the note:

    December 31, 19C:

Note payable	14,746	
Interest expense	1,623	
Cash (computed above)		16,369
Interest: ($40,000 − $11,969 − $13,285) × .11 = $1,623		
(rounded to accommodate rounding errors).		

4. Prepare a **debt payment schedule** that shows the effect on interest expense and the unpaid amount of principal each period.

Debt Payment Schedule

Date	Payment of cash (cr.)	Interest expense (dr.)	Reduction of principal (dr.)	Unpaid principal
1/1/A				40,000
12/31/A	16,369[a]	4,400[b]	11,969[c]	28,031[d]
12/31/B.......................................	16,369	3,084	13,285	14,746
12/31/C	16,369	1,623*	14,746	−0−
Total	49,107	9,107	40,000	

* To accommodate rounding error.
Sequential computations:
  [a] Annual payment: Computed above.
  [b] Interest expense: Unpaid principal, $40,000 × .11 = $4,400.
  [c] Reduction of principal: Annual payment, $16,369 − Interest, $4,400 = $11,969.
  [d] New unpaid balance: Prior Balance, $40,000 − Reduction, $11,969 = $28,031.

Observe in the debt payment schedule that of each successive payment an increasing amount is payment on principal and a decreasing amount is interest expense. This effect occurs because the interest each period is based on a lower amount of unpaid principal.

Although there are many other applications of the concept of the time value of money in the recording and reporting processes, the above examples are typical. The application of present value and future value concepts to capital budgeting is deferred to *Fundamentals of Management Accounting*.

PRESENT VALUE CONCEPTS AND LEASE LIABILITIES

A lease is a contract that specifies that a particular asset will be leased by the owner (i.e., the lessor) to another party (i.e., the lessee) under certain agreements. For accounting purposes, leases are classified as **operating leases** (usually short term) or **capital leases** (usually long term).

Significantly different accounting approaches are required for operating leases than for capital leases. Because of the importance of these differences, the FASB established four criteria to differentiate capital leases from operating leases. If **any one** of the four criteria is met by the lease contract, the lease **must** be accounted for as a **capital** lease; all other leases must be accounted for as **operating** leases. The four criteria for a **capital lease** may be summarized as follows: (1) the leased property transfers to the lessee by the end of the lease term, (2) the lessee can purchase the leased asset at a "bargain" price, (3) the lease term is at least 75 percent of the estimated useful life of the leased asset, and (4) the present value of the minimum lease payments is at least 90 percent of the market value of the leased asset on the date of the lease contract.

Basically, accounting for an **operating lease** requires a journal entry for each rental payment (i.e., for the lessee, debit Rent Expense and credit Cash). In contrast, accounting for a **capital lease** assumes that the **lessor sold** the leased asset and the **lessee purchased** it. This assumption means that when the lease contract is signed, the **lessee** will debit an asset and credit a long-term lease liability.

A typical operating and a typical capital lease are illustrated in Exhibit 10–4. On January 1, 19A, Daly Construction Company must acquire a heavy-duty machine ready to operate. The machine has a cash price of $100,000, and it has a five-year estimated useful life and no residual value. Daly's top management, in the face of a serious cash problem, is considering three alternative ways of acquiring the machine: *(a)* purchase by signing a note for the full purchase price, *(b)* lease the machine on an **operating** lease, and *(c)* lease the machine on a **capital** lease. The basic entries for each alternative are presented in Exhibit 10–4. Let's examine each alternative.

> **Alternative a.** Purchase the machine and sign a two-year interest-bearing note; 15 percent interest and principal payable each month-end (i.e., 24 equal payments). On January 1, 19A, Daly would record the purchase at cost and a liability as illustrated in Exhibit 10–4. Equal monthly payments of principal plus interest ($4,849) are to be made; the journal entry to record the first payment is illustrated in Exhibit 10–4. Under this alternative Daly would own the machine; therefore, Daly would record depreciation expense, and all other expenses incurred, such as maintenance, insurance, and taxes.

> **Alternative b.** Lease the machine on a month-to-month **operating lease** at a monthly rental of $6,000 (as determined by the lessor), payable at each month-end. Under this alternative Daly would not own the machine; therefore, the only journal entries to be recorded by Daly would be for the monthly rental payments as illustrated in Exhibit 10–4. Under this alternative Daly would have to continue lease payments as long as the machine is used and would never own the machine.

> **Alternative c.** Lease the machine on a three-year **capital lease.** The contract requires Daly to pay 36 month-end rentals of $3,321, computed by the **lessor** to earn 12 percent on the $100,000 cash equivalent price. In addition, Daly is required to pay most of the "ownership" costs, such as maintenance insurance and taxes. The lessee learned that the rental of $3,321 was based on 12 percent interest; therefore, the **lessee** computed the **present value** of the future lease rentals as follows:

$$\text{Present value} = \text{Rents (payments)} \times \text{Table 10–4} \ (i = 1\%; \ n = 36)$$
$$= \$3,321 \times 30.1075 \ \text{(given; Table 10–4}$$
$$\text{does not contain values for 36 periods)}$$
$$= \$100,000 \ \text{(rounded)}$$

EXHIBIT 10–4
Operating and capital leases illustrated

Situation:

Daly Construction Company intends to acquire a heavy-duty machine that will cost $100,000 cash equivalent price. Estimated useful life of the machine is five years and no residual value. Daly is considering three alternatives: *(a)* purchase by signing note, *(b)* rent on an operating lease, and *(c)* rent on a capital lease.

Alternative *a*:

On January 1, 19A, purchased the machine for $100,000 and signed a two-year 15 percent note that requires equal month-end payments (24) of $4,849.

Journal entries:

Purchase, January 1, 19A:

Machinery	100,000	
Note payable, long term		100,000

Payment on note, January 31, 19A:

Interest expense ($100,000 × 1¼ %)	1,250	
Note payable ($4,849 − $1,250)	3,599	
Cash (per note)		4,849

Alternative *b*:

Lease on a month-to-month **operating lease;** month-end rental payments of $6,000, as required by lessor.

Journal entries:

January 31, 19A:

Machinery rental expense	6,000	
Cash (per lease agreement)		6,000

Alternative *c*:

Lease on a **capital lease** that requires month-end payments of $3,321 for 36 months (the implied interest rate is 12 percent. Daly is required by the lease to pay all ownership costs.

Journal entries:

January 1, 19A—Inception date of the lease (record as a purchase):

Machinery (under capital lease)	100,000	
Liability, capital lease		100,000

    Computation:

      Present value = Payments × Table 10–4 ($i = 1\%$; $n = 36$)

          = $3,321 × 30.0175*

          = $100,000 (rounded)

January 31, 19A, first monthly rental payment:

Interest expense ($100,000 × 1%)	1,000	
Liability, capital lease ($3,321 − $1,000)	2,321	
Cash (per lease contract)		3,321

* This value is given for illustrative purposes. Table 10–4 does not contain values for 36 periods.

Because a **capital lease** is viewed in accounting as a sale of the asset by the lessor to the lessee, Daly (the lessee) would record a purchase of the machine on the date of the lease contract for $100,000 (its present value). On January 1, 19A, Daly would debit machinery and credit a lease liability for $100,000 as illustrated in Exhibit 10–4. Each of the 36 month-end lease payments would be recorded, in part as payment of principal and in part as payment of interest expense. Exhibit 10–4 illustrates entries at the inception of the lease (i.e., a "purchase" of the machine is recorded) and the first interest payment on January 31, 19A.

Because Daly is assumed to "own" the machine during the lease term, Daly will record depreciation expense and all other "ownership" expenses incurred, such as maintenance, insurance, and taxes. Under this alternative, Daly will own the machine after the last rental payment with no further obligations to the lessor.

The above example is not intended to suggest which alternative is the "best" for Daly. Such a determination would necessitate considerably more information than given. Rather, it is intended to differentiate between the required accounting approaches for an operating lease versus a financing lease. The basic difference requires the application of **present value** determination for **capital leases.**

PRESENT VALUE CONCEPTS AND NOTES PAYABLE

A note may be designated as either "interest bearing" or as "noninterest bearing." Nevertheless, all commercial notes involve interest, either explicitly or implicitly, because money loaned, or borrowed, has a time value that cannot be avoided.

An **interest-bearing note** is one that explicitly specifies (1) a stated rate of interest (such as 12 percent) on the note itself, and (2) that the interest is to be paid at maturity, or in future installments, **in addition to the face or principal amount** of the note. For example, a $30,000, 12 percent, one-year, **interest-bearing** note would (1) provide the borrower with $30,000 cash, (2) have a face or principal amount of $30,000, and (3) require the payment of the principal ($30,000) plus interest for one year ($3,600)—a total of $33,600.

In contrast, a **noninterest-bearing note** is one that has implicit interest; that is, it is a note that (1) does not specify a rate of interest on the note itself but (2) includes the interest in the face amount of the note. For example, a $33,600, one-year, noninterest-bearing note (assuming an implicit rate of interest of 12 percent) (1) would provide the borrower $30,000 cash (i.e., $33,600 − $3,600 implicit interest) and (2) would require the payment of only the face amount of the note at maturity date ($33,600). Observe that the implicit interest is included in the face amount of the note. In each case, the note is recorded at the present value of the future cash payments:

$$PV = \text{Future amount} \times \text{Table 10–2 } (i = 12\%; \, n = 1)$$
$$= \$33,600 \times .8929$$
$$= \$30,000 \text{ (rounded)}$$

The journal entries for the two different types of notes payable (cited above) are given in Exhibit 10–5.

The illustration in Exhibit 10–5 suggests the important concepts in the measurement of liabilities and interest expense. The concept of **present value** is important

EXHIBIT 10–5
Interest-bearing and noninterest-bearing notes illustrated

Transactions	Kind of note	
	Interest bearing	Noninterest bearing
a. November 1, 19A, date of note:		
Cash	30,000	30,000
Discount on note payable		3,600
Note payable, short term	30,000	33,600
(12% interest; term, one year).		
b. December 31, 19A, end of accounting period:		
Interest expense (two months)	600	600
Interest payable	600	
Discount on note payable		600
Adjusting entry for 2 months' accrued interest; $30,000 \times .12 \times 2/12 = \$600$.		
c. October 31, 19B, maturity date of note:*		
Note payable	30,000	33,600
Interest expense (10 months)	3,000	3,000
Interest payable	600	
Discount on note payable		3,000
Cash	33,600	33,600
Payment of note at maturity.		

* It would have simplified this entry if a **reversing entry** of the accrual of December 31, 19A, had been made on January 1, 19B.

in the measurement of liabilities. The present value of a note is the value today of its future cash flows. In the case of the interest-bearing note, the present value, the face amount, and the principal are the same at all dates, that is, $30,000 (at 12 percent). In the case of the noninterest-bearing note, the present value on the date of the note (November 1, 19A) is $30,000, the amount of cash received; however, the face amount is $33,600.

SUMMARY OF CHAPTER

This chapter discussed accounting for three types of obligations: current, long-term, and contingent liabilities. Accounting for bonds payable is discussed in Chapter 11. Liabilities are obligations of either a known or estimated amount. Detailed information concerning the liabilities of an entity is especially important to many decision makers, whether internal or external to the enterprise, because liabilities represent claims against the resources of an entity. Decision makers often may be unable to identify the kinds and amounts of liabilities without reliable financial statements. The existence and amount of liabilities sometimes are easy to conceal from outsiders. The accounting model and the verification by the independent CPA constitute the best assurance that all liabilities are disclosed.

Current liabilities are obligations that will be paid from the resources reported on the same balance sheet as current assets. Thus, they are short-term obligations that will be paid within the coming year or within the normal operating cycle of the business, whichever is longer. All other liabilities (except contingent liabilities) are reported as long-term liabilities. A contingent liability is not an effective liability; it is a potential claim due to some event or transaction that has happened already, but whether it will materialize as an effective liability is not certain because that depends upon some future event or transaction. Contingent liabilities must be disclosed fully on the financial statements. Disclosure usually is by a note to the financial statements.

SUPPLEMENT 10A—PAYROLL ACCOUNTING

Payroll accounting does not involve any new accounting concepts or principles, but payroll accounting deserves additional discussion because of the necessity to pay employees for their services promptly and correctly. In addition, detailed payroll accounting is necessary to fulfill legal requirements under federal and state laws with respect to withholding taxes, social security taxes, and unemployment taxes. Further, the management of an enterprise, for planning and control purposes, need detailed and accurate cost figures for wages and salaries. Frequently, salaries and wages constitute the largest category of expense in an enterprise. As a consequence of the large amount of detailed recordkeeping that is required, payroll accounting often is computerized, including the production of individual checks for the employees.

A detailed payroll record must be maintained for each employee. The payroll record varies with the circumstances in each company; however, it must include for each individual such data as social security number, number of dependents (for income tax withholding), rate of pay, a time record (for hourly paid employees), deductions from gross pay, and so on.

To understand payroll accounting, a distinction must be made between (1) payroll deductions and taxes that must be paid by the **employee** (i.e., deducted from the employee's gross earnings); and (2) payroll taxes that must be paid by the **employer.** Both types of payroll amounts must be transmitted to the governmental unit or other party to whom the amounts are owed. Payroll taxes and deductions apply only in situations where there is an employer-employee relationship. Independent contractors that are not under the direct supervision of the client, such as outside lawyers, independent accountants, consultants, and building contractors, are not employees; hence; amounts paid to them are not subject to payroll taxes and related deductions.

An employee usually receives take-home pay that is much less than the gross earnings for the period. This is due to two types of payroll deductions:

1. Required deductions for taxes that must be paid by the employee as specified by state and federal laws.
2. Optional deductions authorized by the employee for special purposes.

Required deductions

There are two categories of taxes that the employee must pay and thus must be deducted from the employee's gross earnings; they are income taxes and social security taxes. The employer must remit the total amount deducted to the appropriate government agency.

Employee income taxes. Practically every employee must prepare an annual federal income tax return. Wages and salaries earned during the year must be reported on the income tax return as income. Federal laws require the employer to deduct an appropriate amount of income tax each period from the gross earnings of each employee. The amount of the deduction for income tax is determined from a tax table (provided by the Internal Revenue Service) based upon the earnings and number of exemptions (for self and dependents) of the employee. The amount of income tax withheld from the employee's wages is recorded by the employer as a current liability between the date of deduction and the date the amount withheld is remitted to the government. The total amount withheld must be paid to the Internal Revenue Service within a specified short period of time. An especially designed form to accompany each remittance is provided by the Internal Revenue Service to identify the employees and the amounts withheld. Some states also require withholding for state income tax.

Employee FICA taxes. The social security taxes paid by the employee generally are called FICA taxes because they are required by the Federal Insurance Contributions Act. This act provides that persons who are **qualified** under the provisions of the act, upon reaching age 62, may retire and receive the minimum monthly benefits for life, plus certain medical benefits after age 65.[12] Retirement at age 65 provides maximum pension benefits. It also provides benefits for the family of a deceased person who was qualified.

The funds required by the government to provide the benefits under the Social Security Act are obtained by payroll taxes, which are imposed in equal amounts on **both the employee and the employer.** Effective January 1, 1983, the FICA rate was 6.7 percent on the first $35,700 paid to each employee during the year. Because FICA rates and the wage maximum change frequently, for convenience in calculations we will use a rounded rate of 6 percent for illustrative and problem purposes.

At the end of each year, the employer is required to provide each employee with a **Withholding Statement, Form W-2,** which reports to the employee (1) gross earnings for the year, (2) earnings subject to FICA taxes, (3) income taxes withheld, and (4) FICA taxes withheld. A copy of this form also is sent to the Internal Revenue Service.

Optional deductions

Many companies encourage programs of voluntary deductions from earnings by employees. Typical of these voluntary deductions are savings funds, insurance premiums, charitable contributions, supplementary retirement programs, repay-

---

[12] To qualify under the act for retirement and medical benefits, the employee must be in "covered" employment for a specified period of time. Covered employment requires payroll deductions for these taxes. The amount of benefits and the FICA tax deductions are frequently changed by the U.S. Congress.

ment of loans, stock purchase plans, and the purchase of U.S. savings bonds. The employer agrees to make these deductions, subject to employee authorization, as a matter of convenience to the employees. The amounts deducted are remitted in a short time to the organization or agency in whose behalf the deduction was authorized. Another type of deduction is for union dues as specified in the union contract. In some states, this deduction may not be voluntary on an individual basis. The employer is required to remit the deductions, along with the employee list, to the union each month.

Accounting for employee deductions

The employer must maintain detailed and accurate records of all deductions from the earnings of each employee. From the employer's viewpoint, the employee deductions are **current liabilities** from the date of the payroll deduction to the date of remittance to the government or other entity.

To illustrate the basic accounting entry to be made for the payment of a payroll and the accrual of liabilities for the **employee** deductions, assume that Real Company accumulated the following data in the detailed payroll records for the month of January 19B:

Gross earnings:
Salaries	$60,000
Wages (hourly paid employees)	40,000
Income taxes withheld	21,000
Union dues withheld	400
FICA taxes (assume no maximums were exceeded in January, $100,000 \times 6\%$)	6,000

The entry to record the payroll and employee deductions would be:

January 31, 19A:

Salaries expense	60,000	
Wages expense	40,000	
Liability for income taxes withheld—employees		21,000
Liability for union dues withheld—employees		400
FICA taxes payable—employees ($100,000 \times 6\%$)		6,000
Cash (take-home pay)		72,600
Payroll for January, including employee payroll deductions.		

Employer paid payroll taxes

Remember that the payroll taxes illustrated above are those levied on the **employees.** The employer simply serves as a tax collector with respect to them. Specific payroll taxes also are levied on the employer. These taxes represent **operating expenses** of the business. The liability for these taxes is extinguished when the taxes are remitted to the designated agencies of the state and federal governments. Usually, three different payroll taxes must be paid by the employer— FICA taxes, FUTA taxes, and state unemployment compensation taxes.

Employer FICA taxes. The employer must pay an additional FICA tax equal to the amount withheld from the employee's wages. Thus, the FICA tax paid by the employer is at the same rate as the FICA employee tax and on the same amount of wages (i.e., for 1983, 6.7 percent on the first $35,700 of gross earnings of each employee).

Employer FUTA taxes. The Social Security Act provides for another program known as unemployment compensation. This program derives its monetary support under the provisions of the Federal Unemployment Tax Act. The FUTA, or unemployment tax, is paid **only by the employer.** Currently, the federal tax amounts to 3.4 percent of the first $6,000 in wages paid to each employee during the year.

State unemployment compensation taxes. The unemployment program specified in the Federal Unemployment Tax Act is a joint federal-state program; consequently, each state participates in the program by sharing both in providing benefits and in funding the program through payroll taxes. Although state laws vary in some respects, 2.7 percent is payable to the state (of employment), and the remaining .7 percent is payable to the federal Treasury (i.e., the total of 3.4 percent on the first $6,000 wages paid). Most states have a merit-rating plan that provides for a reduction in the tax rate for employers that establish a record of stable employment over a period of time.

Accounting for employer payroll taxes

Payroll taxes paid by the employer are debited to an expense account and credited to a current liability when the payroll is paid each period. To illustrate, the January entry for the employer's payroll taxes for Real Company (data shown on page 486), assuming a 2.7 percent state unemployment tax rate, would be as follows:[13]

Payroll tax expense	9,400*	
FICA taxes payable—employer ($100,000 × 6% matching)		6,000
FUTA taxes payable—employer ($100,000 × .7%)		700
State unemployment taxes payable—employer		
($100,000 × 2.7%)		2,700
To record employer payroll taxes.		
* Total payroll expenses, $100,000 + $9,400 = $109,400.		

When the taxes are remitted to the government, the liability accounts are debited and Cash is credited.

SUPPLEMENT 10B—THE VOUCHER SYSTEM

The voucher system is designed to attain strict control over cash expenditures from the point an obligation is incurred (by means of purchase of merchandise

---

[13] In this and the preceding entries, it was assumed that none of the employees received remuneration above the $35,700 and $6,000 maximums for the year.

for resale, services, operational assets, investments, etc.) through the payment of cash. The incurrence of an obligation and the payment of cash to satisfy it are viewed as separate and independent transactions. When a voucher system is used, an account called **Vouchers Payable** replaces the account **Accounts Payable** in the ledger. Similarly, a **voucher register** and a **check register** replace the purchases journal and the cash disbursements journal, respectively (see Supplement 8B).

The basic document in the voucher system is the **voucher.** A voucher is a form, prepared and used within the business, on which a transaction is (1) summarized and supported adequately, (2) approved, (3) analyzed for recording, and (4) approved for payment. Thus, it is a comprehensive document that follows a transaction from the transaction date to the final cash payment. A voucher is prepared for **each** transaction involving the payment of cash, such as the purchase of assets, the use of services, the incurrence of expenses, and the payment of debt. The form of a voucher varies between companies because it should be designed to meet the specific internal requirements of the individual company. For control purposes, all voucher forms and checks should be numbered consecutively when printed.

Each voucher, after approval, is entered in the voucher register in order of number. The voucher register is designed to record the basic information from the voucher, including the accounts to be debited and credited.

To illustrate the mechanics of a voucher system, we will follow a purchase of merchandise for resale through the system from the **order date** to the final cash payment date. Each step in the sequence may be illustrated and explained as follows:

19A
Jan. 10   Merchandise ordered from Box Supply Company, cost $1,000; terms, n/15. A purchase order is prepared and approved.

12   Merchandise ordered from Box Supply Company on January 10 is received; invoice is received. Voucher No. 47 is drawn and the purchase order is attached (see Exhibit 10–6). Goods are checked for quantity and condition; a receiving report is prepared.

12   Receiving report and invoice sent to accounting department; they are attached to the voucher. Voucher is approved, and then recorded in the voucher register (see Exhibit 10–7).

26   Voucher is approved by designated manager for payment on January 27 and sent to disbursements department; Check No. 90 is prepared.

27   Check No. 90 is signed by treasurer and mailed.

28   The accounting department enters Check No. 90 in the check register (see Exhibit 10–8); enters payment notation in the voucher register (see Exhibit 10–7); and files the voucher in the **Vouchers Paid File.**

For illustrative purposes, two more transactions are recorded in the voucher register, one of which remains unpaid.

At the end of the month the voucher register and the check register are totaled and the equality of the debits and credits is verified. Posting to the ledger from

EXHIBIT 10–6
Voucher

Voucher No. _47_

MAY DEPARTMENT STORE
Boston, Mass.

Date of Voucher _Jan. 12, 19A_   Date Paid _Jan. 27, 19A_

Pay to: _Box Supply Company_   Check No. _90_

1119 Brown Street

Philadelphia, Pa.

For the following goods or services: (attach all supporting documents)

Date Incurred	Terms	Explanation of Details	Amount
Jan. 12	n/15	Merchandise, Dept. 8	1,000.00
		Invoice No. 17-8132	
		Receiving Report No. 123	
		Net payable	1,000.00

Approvals:

Voucher Approval: Date _1/12/A_   Signature _R. C. Roe_

Payment Approval: Date _1/26/A_   Signature _A. B. Doe_

Accounting Analysis:

Account Debited:	Acct. No.	Amount
Purchases	91	1,000.00
Office Supplies		
Sales Salaries		
Operational Assets		
Etc.		
Total, Voucher Payable Credit	41	1,000.00

EXHIBIT 10–7   **Voucher register**

Date	Vou. No.	Payee	Payment		Vouchers Payable (Credit)	Purchases (Debit)	Selling Expense Control			Adm. Expense Control			Other Accounts to Be Debited		
			Date	Check No.			Account Code	Folio	Amount (Debit)	Account Code	Folio	Amount (Debit)	Account Name	Folio No. P	Amount (Debited)
Jan.12	47	Box Supply Co.	1/27	90	1,000.00	1,000.00									
Jan.14	48	John Day—salary	1/15	89	600.00		64	✓	600.00						
Jan.31	98	Capital Nat'l Bank—note			2,160.00								Notes payable	44 ✓	2,000.00
													Interest expense	82 ✓	160.00
		Totals			27,605.00	14,875.00			7,410.00			3,160.00			2,160.00
		Posting notations			(41)	(91)			(60)			(70)			(✓)

these two special journals follows the same pattern explained in Supplement 8B, for the special journals illustrated there. Posting involves two separate phases:

1. Current posting—During the period, and perhaps daily, the details in the Voucher Register columns are posted to (a) the selling expense subsidiary ledger (under the selling expense control); (b) the administrative expense subsidiary ledger (under the administrative expense control); and (c) other accounts to be debited. No current posting is required from the check register as illustrated.

2. Monthly posting—The totals from the voucher register, except for the "Other Accounts to Be Debited" are posted at the end of each month. The account number to which each total is posted is entered below the amount. The column for "Other Accounts to Be Debited" was posted individually; hence, the total should not be posted. The totals from the check register are posted to the accounts at the end of each month as indicated by the account numbers entered below the total.

EXHIBIT 10–8
Check register

Date	Payee	Voucher No. Paid	Check No.	Vouchers Payable (Debit)*	Cash (Credit)*
Jan. 15	John Day	48	89	600.00	600.00
27	Box Supply Co.	47	90	1,000.00	1,000.00
31	Totals			18,751.00	18,751.00
	Posting notation			(41)	(11)

* These two columns could be combined.

The balance in the ledger account Vouchers Payable is reported on the balance sheet as a liability and is designated as Accounts Payable. The amount should be allocated and classified between current and long-term liabilities, depending on due dates.

The Vouchers Payable account is a control account, the balance of which represents all of the **unpaid** vouchers at any given time. The total of all vouchers in the **Unpaid Voucher File** must agree with the balance of the Vouchers Payable account; therefore, the Vouchers Payable account replaces the Accounts Payable control account in the ledger (see Supplement 6A).

In studying the mechanics of the voucher system, as illustrated above, you should not overlook its most important aspect—the high degree of **internal control** attained through formalization of the sequence of acquiring operational assets, services, and merchandise, and in making the cash payments. The internal control feature rests upon (1) clear-cut separation and designation of specific approval responsibilities, (2) a prescribed routine for carrying out these responsibilities, and (3) accounting for the results.

Although a manual approach was illustrated, these routines are adapted easily to the computer. A computer program can be designed to accomplish the same steps and procedures illustrated above. Most companies of any size have computerized the voucher system in order to attain a high degree of control over expenditures and to accelerate the processing of a large volume of transactions, including cash disbursements.

IMPORTANT TERMS DEFINED IN THIS CHAPTER

Terms (alphabetically)	Key words in definitions of important terms used in chapter	Page reference
Accrued expenses	Expenses that have been incurred but have not yet been paid or recorded at the end of the accounting period; a liability.	455
Annuity	A series of periodic cash receipts or payments that are equal in amount.	470
Capital lease	A lease that is viewed as a purchase/sale, for accounting purposes.	461
Contingent liability	Potential liability that has arisen as the result of a past event; not an effective liability.	464
Current liabilities	Short-term obligations that will be paid within the current operating cycle or one year, whichever is longer.	454
Deferred income tax	Difference between income tax expense and income tax liability, caused by timing differences.	461
Deferred revenues	Revenues that have been collected but not earned; a liability.	457
Future value	The sum to which an amount will increase as the result of compound interest.	468
Interest-bearing note	A note that explicitly specifies a stated rate of interest.	482
Liabilities	Probable future sacrifices of economic benefits that arise from past transactions.	452
Long-term liabilities	All obligations not properly classified as current liabilities.	458
Noninterest-bearing note	A note that does not explicitly state a rate of interest but has implicit interest; interest is included in the face amount of the note.	482

Terms (alphabetically)	Key words in definitions of important terms used in chapter	Page reference
Operating lease	A rental agreement between a lessor and lessee that is not viewed in accounting as a purchase/sale.	460
Permanent difference	An income tax difference that does not give rise to deferred taxes.	463
Present value	The value now of an amount to be received in the future.	470
Time value of money	Interest that is associated with the use of money over time.	459
Timing difference	An income tax difference that causes deferred taxes; will reverse or turn around in the future.	401
Working capital	The dollar difference between total current assets and total current liabilities.	454
Working capital ratio	The ratio of total current assets divided by total current liabilities; also known as the current ratio.	454

QUESTIONS FOR DISCUSSION

PART A

1. Define a liability and distinguish between a current liability and a long-term liability.

2. How can external parties be informed in respect to liabilities of an enterprise?

3. Liabilities are measured and reported at their current cash equivalent amount. Explain.

4. A liability is a known obligation of either a definite or estimated amount. Explain.

5. Define working capital. How is it computed?

6. What is the current ratio? What is another name for the current ratio? How is the current ratio related to the classification of liabilities?

7. Define an accrued liability. What kind of an entry usually reflects an accrued liability?

8. Define a deferred revenue and explain why it is a liability.

9. Define a note payable and distinguish between a secured and an unsecured note.

10. Distinguish between an interest-bearing note and a noninterest-bearing note.

11. Define deferred income tax. Explain why deferred income tax is said to reverse, or turn around, in subsequent periods.

12. What is a contingent liability? How is a contingent liability reported?

13. Briefly explain the primary purpose of a voucher system.

PART B

14. Briefly explain what is meant by the time value of money.

15. Explain the basic difference between future value and present value.

16. What is an annuity?

17. Complete the following schedule:

Concept	Symbol	Table Values		
		$n = 4; i = 5\%$	$n = 7; i = 10\%$	$n = 9; i = 15\%$
FV of $1 *PV* of $1 *FV* of annuity of $1 *PV* of annuity of $1				

18. What is a lease liability?

19. What is meant by a capital lease?

EXERCISES

PART A

E10–1. Banks Company is preparing its 19B balance sheet. The company records reflect the following related amounts:

Total current assets	$157,100
Total all remaining assets	665,000
Liabilities:	
Note payable (10%, due in 5 years)	22,000
Accounts payable.....................	60,000
Income tax payable	15,000
Liability for withholding taxes	4,000
Rent revenue collected in advance	3,000
Bonds payable (due in 15 years)	200,000
Wages payable	6,000
Property taxes payable	2,000
Note payable, 12% (due in 6 months)	5,000
Interest payable	100

Required:

a. Compute total owners's equity.
b. Compute (1) working capital in dollars and (2) the working capital ratio (show computations).
c. Compute the amount of interest expense for 19B on the 10 percent note assuming it was dated October 1, 19B.

E10–2. During 19B, the two transactions given below were completed by Post Company. The annual accounting period ends December 31.

1. Wages paid and recorded during 19B amounted to $70,000; however, at the end of December 19B, there were two days' wages unpaid and unrecorded because the weekly payroll will not be paid until January 6, 19C. Wages for the two days amounted to $700.
2. On December 10, 19B, Post Company collected rent revenue amounting to $600 on some office space that it rented to another party. The rent collected was for the month from December 10, 19B, to January 10, 19C, and was credited to Rent Revenue.

Required:

a. Give (1) the adjusting entry required on December 31, 19B, and (2) the January 6, 19C, journal entry for payment of any unpaid wages from December 19B.

b. Give (1) the journal entry for the collection of rent on December 10, 19B, and (2) the adjusting entry on December 31, 19B (compute rent to the nearest ten days).

c. Show how any liabilities related to the above transactions should be reported on the balance sheet at December 31, 19B.

E10–3. Corning Manufacturing Company has completed the payroll for January 19B, reflecting the following data:

Salaries and wages earned	$80,000
Employee income taxes withheld	11,000
Union dues withheld	1,100
FICA payroll taxes*	4,800
FUTA payroll taxes	560
State unemployment taxes	2,160

* Assessed on both employer and employee (i.e., $4,800 each).

Required:

a. Give the journal entry to record payment of the payroll and employee deductions.

b. Give the journal entry to record employer payroll taxes.

c. What was the amount of additional labor expense to the company due to tax laws? Explain. What was the employee take-home pay? Explain.

E10–4. On November 1, 19A, Quality Auto Parts Company borrowed $40,000 cash from the City Bank for working capital purposes and gave an interest-bearing note with a face amount of $40,000. The note was due in six months, and the interest rate was 12 percent per annum payable at maturity.

Required:

a. Give the journal entry to record the note on November 1.

b. Give the adjusting entry that would be required at the end of the annual accounting period, December 31, 19A.

c. Give the journal entry to record payment of the note and interest on the maturity date, April 30, 19B (disregard reversing entries).

E10–5. Trend Company sells a wide range of goods through two retail stores that are operated in adjoining cities. Most purchases of goods for resale are on invoices with credit terms of 2/10, n/30. Occasionally, a short-term note payable is executed to obtain cash for current use. The following transactions were selected from those occurring during 19B:

1. On January 10, 19B, purchased merchandise on credit, $14,000; terms, 2/10, n/30. Record at net (see Chapter 6); the company uses the periodic inventory system.

2. On March 1, 19B, borrowed $30,000 cash from City Bank and gave an interest-bearing note payable: face amount, $30,000; due at the end of six months, with an annual interest rate of 12 percent payable at maturity.

Required:

a. Give the journal entry for each of the above transactions. Record purchases and accounts payable at net.

b. Give the journal entry assuming the account payable of January 10, 19B, was paid within the discount period.

c. Give the journal entry assuming the account payable of January 10, 19B, was paid after the discount period.

d. Give the journal entry for the payment of the note payable plus interest on the maturity date.

E10–6. The comparative income statements of Telex Company at December 31, 19B, reflected the following data (summarized and excluding income taxes):

	Annual income statement for	
	19A	19B
Sales revenue	$50,000	$60,000
Expenses	40,000	48,000
Pretax income	$10,000	$12,000

Included on the 19B income statement given above was an expense amounting to $6,000 that was deductible on the income tax return in 19A rather than in 19B. Assume an average tax rate of 20 percent.

Required:

a. For each year compute (1) income tax expense, (2) income tax payable, and (3) any deferred tax.
b. Give the journal entry for each year to record income tax, including any deferred tax.
c. Show how the income tax liabilities would be shown on the balance sheet for each year assuming the tax is paid the following April.

E10–7. The comparative income statement for Blues Company for the years ended December 31, 19A, and 19B, reflected the following data (summarized and excluding income taxes):

	Annual income statement for	
	19A	19B
Revenues	$90,000	$94,000
Expenses	75,000	78,000
Pretax income	$15,000	$16,000

Included on the 19B income statement given above was a revenue item amounting to $5,000 that was included on the income tax return for 19A rather than in 19B. Assume an average income tax rate of 20 percent.

Required:

a. For each year, compute (1) income tax expense, (2) income tax payable, and (3) deferred income tax. (Hint: Deferred income tax will have a debit balance for 19A.)
b. Give the journal entry for each year to record income tax, including any deferred tax.
c. Show how income tax would be reported on the balance sheet each year assuming the tax is paid the following April.

E10–8. Green Corporation reported the following income statement data (summarized):

	Income statement for year ended December 31		
	19A	19B	19C
Revenues	$150,000	$150,000	$150,000
Expenses (including depreciation)	110,000	110,000	110,000
Pretax income	$ 40,000	$ 40,000	$ 40,000

Depreciation expense included on the income statement was computed as follows:

Machinery cost (acquired on January 1, 19A), $60,000; estimated useful life, three years, no residual value; annual depreciation (straight line) $60,000 ÷ 3 years = $20,000. The company uses sum-of-the-years'-digits depreciation on the income tax return and has an average income tax rate of 30 percent.

Required:

a. For each year, compute (1) income tax expense for the income statement and (2) income tax payable for the tax return (show computations).
b. Give the journal entry for each year to record income tax including any deferred income tax.
c. What kind of "tax difference" was involved? Explain.
d. What advantage was gained by using SYD depreciation on the tax return?

PART B

E10–9. On January 1, 19A, Hyper Company, completed the following transactions (assume on 12 percent annual interest rate):

1. Deposited $10,000 in a special fund (designated Fund A).
2. Decided to establish a special fund (designated Fund B) by making six equal annual deposits of $2,000 each.
3. Decided to establish a special fund (designated Fund C) by depositing a single amount that will increase to $50,000 by the end of Year 7.
4. Decided to deposit a single sum in a special fund (designated Fund D) that will provide 10 equal annual year-end payments of $10,000 to a retired employee (payments starting December 31, 19A.)

Required (show computations and round to the nearest dollar):

a. What will be the balance of Fund A at the end of Year 9?
b. What will be the balance of Fund B at the end of Year 6?
c. What single amount must be deposited in Fund C on January 1, 19A?
d. What single sum must be deposited in Fund D on January 1, 19A?

E10–10. On January 1, 19A, you deposited $5,000 in a savings account. The account will earn 9 percent annual compound interest, which will be added to the fund balance at the end of each year. You recorded the deposit as follows:

Savings account   5,000
   Cash   5,000

Required:

a. What will be the balance in the savings account at the end of 10 years (round to the nearest dollar)?
b. What is the time value of the money in dollars for the 10 years?
c. How much interest revenue did the fund earn in 19A? 19B?
d. Give the journal entry to record interest revenue at the end of 19A and 19B.

E10–11. On December 31, 19A, Parent decided to deposit an amount in a savings account that will provide $20,000 four years later to send Offspring to Super University. The savings account will earn 8 percent which will be added to the fund each year-end.

Required (show computations and round to the nearest dollar):

a. How much must Parent deposit on January 1, 19A?
b. Give the journal entry that Parent should make on January 1, 19A.
c. What is the time value of the money for the four years?
d. Give the journal entry Parent should make on (1) December 31, 19A, and (2) December 31, 19B.

E10–12. On each December 31, you plan to deposit $600 in a savings account. The account will earn 9 percent annual interest, which will be added to the fund balance at year-end. The first deposit will be made December 31, 19A.

Required (show computations and round to the nearest dollar):

a. Give the required journal entry on December 31, 19A.
b. What will be the balance in the savings account at the end of the 10th year (i.e., 10 deposits)?
c. What is the time value of money in dollars for the 10 deposits?
d. How much interest revenue did the fund earn in 19B? 19C?
e. Give all required journal entries at the ends of 19B and 19C.

E10–13. You have decided to take a trip around the world upon graduation, four years from now (January 1, 19A). Your grandfather desires to deposit sufficient funds for this purpose in a savings account for you. On the basis of a carefully drawn budget you estimate the trip now would cost $8,000. To be generous, your grandfather decided to deposit $2,200 in the fund at the end of each of the next four years. The savings account will earn 7 percent annual interest, which will be added to the savings account at each year-end.

Required (show computations and round to the nearest dollar):

a. Give the required journal entry on December 31, 19A, to record the first deposit.
b. What will be the balance in the fund at the end of Year 4 (i.e., four deposits)?
c. What is the time value of the money for the four years?
d. How much interest revenue would the fund earn in 19A, 19B, and 19C?
e. Give the journal entries at the end of 19B and 19C.

E10–14. You have an opportunity to purchase the royalty interest of a land owner in an oil well. Your best estimate is that the net royalty income will average $30,000 per year for five years. There will be no residual value at that time. Assume the cash inflow is at each year-end and that, considering the uncertainty in your estimates, you expect to earn 20 percent per year on the investment.

Required:

a. What should you be willing to pay for this investment on January 1, 19A? Show computations and round to nearest dollar.
b. Give the required journal entry (cash paid in full) on January 1, 19A.
c. Give the required journal entry on December 31, 19A, assuming the net cash received was 10 percent above your estimate.

E10–15. On November 1, 19A, Design Furniture Company borrowed $40,000 cash from the City Bank for working capital purposes and gave a noninterest-bearing note payable. The note was due in six months, and the face amount was $42,400. The going rate of interest was 12 percent per year.

Required:

a. Give the journal entry to record the note on November 1, 19A.
b. Give the adjusting entry that would be required at the end of the annual accounting period, December 31, 19A.
c. Show how the note should be reported on the December 31, 19A, balance sheet.
d. Give the journal entry to record payment of the note at maturity on April 30, 19B (disregard reversing entries).

E10–16. Assume you needed to borrow exactly $3,600 cash for one year. The City Bank charges 12 percent interest per annum on such loans. You are to respond to the following questions (show computations):

Required:

a. What would be the face amount of the note assuming the bank agreed to accept an interest-bearing note?
b. What would be the face amount of the note assuming the bank insisted on a noninterest-bearing note?
c. Give the journal entries to record the note in *(a)* and *(b)*. Set the entries in parallel columns.
d. Give the journal entries at date of maturity in *(a)* and *(b)*.

PROBLEMS/CASES

PART A

PC10–1. Webster Company completed the transactions listed below during 19B. The annual accounting period ends December 31, 19B.

Jan. 8 Purchased merchandise for resale at an invoice cost of $15,000; terms, 2/10, n/60. Record at net (see Chapter 6); assume a periodic inventory system.

    17 Paid invoice of January 8.

Apr. 1 Borrowed $20,000 from the National Bank for general use; executed a 12-month, 12 percent, interest-bearing note payable.

June 3 Purchased merchandise for resale at an invoice cost of $30,000; terms, 1/20, n/30; record at net.

July 5 Paid invoice of June 3.

Aug. 1 Rented two rooms in the building owned by Webster and collected six months' rent in advance amounting to $1,800. Record the collection in a way that will not require an adjusting entry at year-end.

Dec. 20 Received a $200 deposit from a customer as a guarantee to return a large trailer "borrowed" for 30 days.

    31 Wages earned but not paid on December 31 amounted to $4,000 (disregard payroll taxes).

Required:

a. Prepare journal entries for each of the above transactions.
b. Prepare all adjusting entries required on December 31, 19B.
c. Show how all of the liabilities arising from the above transactions would be reported on the balance sheet at December 31, 19B.

PC10–2.   Arbor Company completed the transactions listed below during 19A. The annual accounting period ends December 31.

May   1   Purchased an operational asset (fixtures) for $60,000; paid $20,000 cash and gave a 12-month, 12 percent, interest-bearing note payable for the balance.

June   5   Purchased an operational asset (machine) at an invoice cost of $10,000; terms, 3/10, n/60.

      14   Paid invoice of June 5.

Sept. 1   Collected rent revenue on some office space rented to another company; the rent of $6,000 was for the next six months. Record the collection so as to avoid an adjusting entry at the end of 19A.

Dec. 31   Received a tax bill for property tax for 19A in the amount of $900; the taxes are payable no later than March 1, 19B.

Required:

a.   Give the journal entries for each of the above transactions.
b.   Prepare any adjusting entries required on December 31, 19A (exclude depreciation).
c.   Show how all liabilities arising from the above transactions would be reported on the balance sheet at December 31, 19A.

PC10–3.   Hi-Fi Retailers sold a Super-set stereo to a customer for $2,000 cash on December 30, 19A. Hi-Fi gave the customer a one-year guarantee on the Super-set. Experience with this set by Hi-Fi indicates that to maintain the warranty would cost approximately 5 percent of the sales price.

    Assume a perpetual inventory system and that the Super-set cost Hi-Fi Retailers $900. Actual cash for warranty expenditures (parts and labor) to make good the warranty on the set during 19B amounted to $95.

Required:

a.   Give the journal entry or entries required on December 30, 19A. Explain the basis for your entries.
b.   Give the journal entry or entries required on December 31, 19A, end of the annual accounting period. Explain the basis for your responses. (Hint: Consider the liability for warranty work.)
c.   Show how the income statement and balance sheet for 19A would reflect the above data.
d.   Give the journal entry to record the repair made to the set in 19B. Discuss any issues that are evident.

PC10–4.   On April 1, 19A, Perduyn Company purchased equipment at a cost of $110,000. A cash down payment in the amount of $30,000 was made. An interest-bearing note (including a mortgage on the equipment) for $80,000 was given for the balance. The note specified 14 percent annual interest. Two payments on principal of $40,000 each plus interest on the unpaid balance on March 31, 19B, and March 31, 19C, are required. (Note: These will be unequal cash payments.)

Required:

a.   Give the journal entries on April 1, 19A, and December 31, 19A (end of the annual accounting period).

b. Show how the liabilities related to the purchase should be shown on the Perduyn balance sheet on December 31, 19A.

c. Give the journal entry on March 31, 19B.

PC10–5. Radney Company is in the process of preparing comparative statements at December 31, 19B. The records reflect the following summarized income statement data, exclusive of income tax expense:

	19A	19B
Revenues	$180,000	$190,000
Expenses	(110,000)	(129,000)
Extraordinary item	(10,000)	4,000
Income before income tax	$ 60,000	$ 65,000

Included in the 19B revenues of $190,000 is a revenue item amounting to $20,000 that was included on the income tax return for 19A rather than 19B. Also included in the 19B expenses of $129,000 was an expense item amounting to $6,000 that was deducted on the income tax return for 19A rather than 19B. Assume an average 20 percent income tax rate. Assume there were no deferred income taxes in the extraordinary items.

Required:

a. For each year, compute (1) income tax expense, (2) income tax liability, and (3) deferred income tax.

b. Give the journal entry for each year to record income tax expense, including any deferred income taxes.

c. Restate the above comparative income statement, including the appropriate presentation of income tax for each year. (Hint: Allocate income tax expense between operations and extraordinary items.)

d. What kind of "tax difference" was represented by the two items? Explain.

PC10–6. At December 31, 19A, the records of Laymon Corporation provided the following pretax information:

1. Revenues $150,000
2. Expenses (including $13,000 depreciation expense) 113,000
3. Depreciation expense was computed as follows for income statement purposes:
   Operational asset cost (acquired January 1, 19A) 52,000
   Four-year useful life (no residual value).
   Depreciation expense per year $52,000 ÷ 4 years 13,000
4. Extraordinary loss 10,000
5. The revenues given in 1 include $5,000 interest on tax-free municipal bonds.
6. Assume an average income tax rate of 20 percent on both ordinary income and extraordinary income.
7. Sum-of-the-years'-digits depreciation on the operational asset will be used on the income tax return and straight line on the income statement.

Required:

a. Compute income tax expense.

b. Compute income tax on the tax return.

c. Give the journal entry to record income tax including any deferred income tax.

d. Prepare a single-step income statement.

e. What kind of "tax differences" were involved? Explain the basis for your treatment of them.

PART B

PC10–7. On January 1, 19A, Illustrative Company completed the following transactions (assume a 10 percent annual interest rate):

1. Deposited $30,000 in a special debt retirement fund. Interest will be computed at six-month intervals and added to the fund at those times (i.e., semiannual compounding). (Hint: Think carefully about n and i.)

2. Decided to establish a plant addition fund of $150,000 to be available at the end of Year 5. A single sum will be deposited on January 1, 19A, that will grow to the $150,000.

3. Decided to establish a pension retirement fund of $400,000 by the end of Year 6 by making six equal annual deposits each at year-end, starting on December 31, 19A.

4. Decided to purchase a $100,000 machine on January 1, 19A, and pay cash, $25,000. A three-year note payable is signed for the balance. The note will be paid in three equal year-end payments starting on December 31, 19A.

Required (show computations and round to the nearest dollar):

a. In transaction 1 above, what will be the balance in the fund at the end of Year 4? What is the total amount of interest revenue earned?

b. In transaction 2 above, what single sum amount must the company deposit on January 1, 19A? What is the total amount of interest revenue earned?

c. In transaction 3 above, what is the required amount of each of the six equal annual deposits? What is the total amount of interest revenue earned?

d. In transaction 4 above, what is the amount of each of the equal annual payments that must be paid on the note? What is the total amount of interest expense?

PC10–8. Giant Company has decided to build another plant during 19C that they estimate will cost $800,000. At the present time, January 1, 19A, they have excess cash, some of which they may decide to set aside in a special savings account to defray $600,000 of the plant cost. The savings account would earn 10 percent annual interest which would be credited to the savings account each year-end.

Required (show computations and round to the nearest dollar):

a. What single amount would have to be deposited in the savings account on January 1, 19A, to create the desired amount by the end of 19C?

b. What will be the time value of the money by the end of 19C?

c. How much interest revenue will be earned each year?

d. Give the following journal entries:
   (1) Interest earned at each year-end.
   (2) Use of the fund to pay on the plant (completed December 31, 19C).

PC10–9. On January 1, 19A, Delta Construction Company signed a construction contract with Dawn Company. Delta Company was required to deposit with an independent trustee $50,000 cash as a performance guarantee on a construction project. The trustee agreed to pay 7 percent annual interest on the fund and to add it to the fund balance at each year-end. At the end of the third year, the construction project was completed satisfactorily and the trustee returned the balance of the fund to Delta Construction Company. The entry by Delta Construction Company to record the deposit was as follows:

Performance fund 50,000
    Cash 50,000

Required (show computations and round to the nearest dollar):

a. What was the balance of the fund at the end of the three years?
b. What was the time value of the money for the three years?
c. How much interest revenue did the fund earn each year?
d. Give the following journal entries for Delta Construction Company:
   (1) To record interest revenue at each year-end.
   (2) To record receipt of the fund balance at the end of 19C.

PC10–10. On January 1, 19A, the management of Flood Company agreed to set aside a special fund in order to provide sufficient cash to pay off the principal amount of a $55,000 long-term debt that will be due at the end of five years. The single deposit will be made with an independent party (a bank), which will pay 8 percent annual interest on the fund balance. The interest will be added to the fund balance at each year-end.

Required (show computations and round to the nearest dollar):

a. How much must be deposited as a single sum on January 1, 19A, to satisfy the agreement?
b. What was the time value of the money in dollars for the five years?
c. How much interest revenue would the fund earn in 19A? 19B?
d. Give the journal entries for Flood Company:
   (1) To record the deposit on January 1, 19A.
   (2) To record the interest revenue for 19A and 19B (separately).
   (3) To record payment of the maturing liability at the end of the fifth year.

PC10–11. On December 31, 19A, the management of Moe Company agreed to set aside, in a special fund, sufficient cash to pay the principal amount of a $50,000 debt which will be due on December 31, 19D. Moe Company will make four equal annual deposits on each December 31, 19A, 19B, 19C, and 19D. The fund balance will earn 10 percent annual interest, which will be added to the balance of the fund at each year-end. The fund trustee will pay the loan principal (to the creditor) upon receipt of the last fund deposit.

Required (show computations and round to the nearest dollar):

a. How much must be deposited each December 31? (Hint: Use Table 10–3 and divide instead of multiply.)
b. What will be the time value of the money in dollars for the fund?
c. How much interest revenue will the fund earn in 19A, 19B, 19C, and 19D?
d. Give the journal entries for the following for Moe Company:
   (1) For the first deposit on December 31, 19A.
   (2) For all amounts at the ends of 19B and 19C.
   (3) For payment of the debt on December 31, 19D.

PC10–12. On January 1, 19A, Big Company sold to Small Company a new machine for $40,000. A cash down payment of $10,000 was made by Small Company. A $30,000, 12 percent note was signed by Small Company for the balance due. The note is to be paid off in three equal installments due on December 31, 19A, 19B, and 19C. Each payment is to include principal plus interest on the unpaid balance. The purchase was recorded by Small as follows:

January 1, 19A:

Machine	40,000	
Cash		10,000
Note payable		30,000

Required (show computations and round to the nearest dollar):

a. What is the amount of the equal annual payment that must be made by Small Company? (Hint: Use Table 10–4 and divide instead of multiply.)
b. What was the time value of the money, in dollars, on the note?
c. Complete the following debt payment schedule:

Date	Cash Payment	Interest Expense	Reduction of Principal	Unpaid Principal
1/1/19A				
12/31/19A				
12/31/19B				
12/31/19C				
Total				

d. Give the journal entries for each of the three payments.
e. Explain why interest expense decreased in amount each year.

PC10–13. On January 1, 19A, you purchased a new Super-Whiz automobile for $15,000. You paid a $5,000 cash down payment and signed a $10,000 note, payable in four equal installments on each December 31, the first payment to be made on December 31, 19A. The interest rate is 14 percent per year on the unpaid balance. Each payment will include payment on principal plus the interest.

Required:

a. Compute the amount of the equal payments that you must make (Hint: Use Table 10–4.)
b. What is the time value of the money in dollars for the installment debt?
c. Complete a schedule using the format below.

DEBT PAYMENT SCHEDULE

Date	Cash Payment	Interest Expense	Reduction of Principal	Unpaid Principal
1/1/A				
12/31/A				
12/31/B				
12/31/C				
12/31/D				
Total				

    d. Explain why the amount of interest expense decreases each year.

    e. Give the journal entries on December 31, 19A, and 19B.

PC10–14. This problem was designed to illustrate and compare the accounting for *(a)* an interest-bearing note payable and *(b)* a noninterest-bearing note payable. The annual accounting period ends December 31 in both cases. Cove Company executed a note payable to American Bank for a loan of cash on April 1, 19A. The loan was for 12 months with a maturity date of March 31, 19B. The bank charges a 12 percent annual rate on loans of this type. The amount of cash borrowed was $20,000. We will assume:

    Case A—The note was interest bearing—that is, the principal plus the interest is payable at maturity. The face amount of note was $20,000.

    Case B—The note was noninterest bearing—that is, the interest was on the cash received and was included in the face amount of the note.

Required:

    a. Record the issuance of the note on April 1, 19A, under each of the two cases. Your solution can be simplified by setting up five columns: Account Titles; Case A (debit and credit), and Case B (debit and credit). Thus, the two cases can be presented in your solution in parallel columns.

    b. Give the journal entry to record the adjusting entry that would be required for each case on December 31, 19A.

    c. Give the journal entry to record payment of the note under each case at maturity, March 31, 19B; disregard any reversing entries.

    d. In respect to each case show the following:

        (1) Liabilities that would be reported on the balance sheet at December 31, 19A.

        (2) Interest expense that would be reported on the income statements for 19A and 19B (separately).

PC10–15. Several years ago, Rapid Service Company borrowed a large amount of money from First American Bank. At the time the loan was approved, Rapid Service agreed not to borrow any additional money from any other sources until the First American loan was repaid. As the result of continued growth, Rapid Service must acquire a large computer during the current year. Unfortunately, Rapid Service does not have sufficient cash to purchase the computer or to repay the loan to First American. You have been engaged as a consultant to Rapid Service. The president of Rapid Service, Allison Payne, described the problem during your first meeting:

    The computer can be purchased from Super Computer Company for $500,000, but we don't have the cash and the bank won't let us borrow any more money. However, the computer company has agreed to lease the computer to us on a 10-year lease which is the expected useful life of the computer with no residual value. Annual lease payments of $81,372 would be paid based on an interest rate of 10 percent. I think that this lease deal will solve our problem because we will not violate our agreement with First American as long as we don't report any additional debt on the balance sheet. But I have to admit that I don't understand accounting. What do you think?

    In order to help the president understand the required accounting treatment, the president could consider three alternative situations:

Alternative No. 1—Rapid Service could purchase the computer but would have to borrow $500,000 with a note payable to the computer company at 10 percent interest for 10 years. Annual year-end payments for principal and interest amount to $81,372.

Alternative No. 2—Rapid Service could rent the computer on a monthly lease basis. The terms of the lease cause it to be considered an operating lease. Annual rent payments would be $125,000 at each year-end.

Alternative No. 3—Rapid Service could acquire the computer on a long-term lease basis. At the expiration date of the lease, the computer would be returned to Super Computer Company. The terms of the lease cause it to be considered a capital lease. The lease payments would be $81,372.

Required:

a. Assume that the computer was acquired on January 1, 19D, which is the beginning of the accounting period. Prepare journal entries to record the acquisition of the computer by Rapid Service under each of the three alternatives.

b. Assume Rapid Service makes cash payments under each alternative on December 31 of each year. Prepare the required journal entries on December 31, 19D (include adjusting entries, if required). Rapid Service uses straight-line depreciation for all assets.

c. Would the capital lease alternative, described by the president, permit Rapid Service to acquire the computer and to conform to GAAP?

d. What are the primary problems of alternatives 1 and 2?

PC10–16. In recent years, it was possible to buy a U.S. Savings Bond for $18.75. When the bond was "cashed in" at the end of five years, the U.S. government would pay $25.

Required (show computations):

a. Determine the approximate annual interest rate that the government paid on the savings bonds (Hint: This is a present value problem where you are given the time to maturity, the future cash inflow [$25] and the present value [$18.75] but not the interest rate.)

b. If you want to earn 6 percent on your savings and the government agreed to pay you $25 at the end of five years if you purchase a savings bond, what price would you be willing to pay for the savings bond at the beginning of Year 1?

PC10–17. Walter Carrington, a home builder, published an advertisement that offered for sale "a $120,000 house with a zero interest rate mortgage." If the purchaser made monthly payments of $2,000 for five years ($120,000 ÷ 60 months), there would be no additional charge for interest. When the offer was made, mortgage interest rates were 12 percent. PV for n = 60, and i = 1% is 44.9550.

Required:

a. Did Walter Carrington actually provide a mortgage at zero interest?

b. Estimate the true price of the home that was advertised. Assume that the $2,000 monthly payment was based on an implicit interest rate of 12 percent.

PC10–18. (Based on Supplement 10A) Tappen Company has completed the salary and wage payroll for March 19A. Details provided by the payroll were:

Salaries and wages earned $200,000*
Employee income taxes withheld   42,000
Union dues withheld   2,000
Insurance premiums withheld   900
FICA tax rate, 6%.
FUTA tax rate, .7%.
State unemployment tax rate, 2.7% (based on same
   amount of wages as FUTA taxes).
   * Subject in full to payroll taxes.

Required:

a. Give the journal entry to record the payroll for March, including employee deductions. Show computations.
b. Give the journal entry to record the employer's payroll taxes.
c. Give a combined journal entry to reflect remittance of amounts owed to governmental agencies and other organizations.
d. What was the total labor cost for Tappen Company? Explain. What percent of the payroll was take-home pay? Explain.

PC10–19.   (Based on Supplement 10B)   Holt Company uses a voucher system to attain control of expenditures. The following transactions have been selected from December 19B for case purposes. The accounting year ends December 31.

You are to design a voucher register and a check register similar to those shown in Supplement 10B. The transactions that follow will be entered in these two special journals.

Dec. 2   Purchased merchandise from AB Wholesalers for resale, $2,000; terms, 2/10, n/30; record purchases at net and assume a periodic inventory system (see Chapter 6); Invoice No. 14; start with Voucher No. 11.
      7   Approved contract with Ace Plumbing Company for repair of plumbing, $450; account, Building Repairs, No. 77.
     11   Paid Voucher No. 11; start with Check No. 51.
     22   Purchased store supplies for future use from Crown Company; Invoice No. 21 for $90; account, Store Supplies Inventory, No. 16.
     23   Advertising for pre-Christmas sale $630; bill received from Daily Press and payment processed immediately; account, Advertising Expense, No. 54.
     31   Monthly payroll voucher, total $2,500; $1,500 was selling expense (Sales Salaries, No. 52) and $1,000 was administrative expense (Administrative Salaries, No. 62). The voucher was supported by the payroll record; therefore, one voucher was prepared for the entire payroll. The voucher was approved for immediate payment. Six checks with consecutive numbers were issed.

Required:

a. Enter the above transactions in the voucher register and the check register.
b. Total the special journals and check the equality of the debits and credits. Set up T-accounts and post both registers. Complete all posting notations. The following accounts may be needed:

Account titles	Account No.
Cash	01
Store supplies inventory	16
Vouchers payable	30
Purchases	40
Selling expense control	50
Subsidiary ledger:	
Sales salaries	52
Advertising expense	54
Administrative expense control	60
Subsidiary ledger:	
Administrative salaries	62
Building repairs	77

c. Reconcile the Vouchers Payable account balance with the Unpaid Vouchers File at the end of December.

C·H·A·P·T·E·R
11

Measuring and Reporting Bonds Payable

PURPOSE OF THIS CHAPTER

The issuance of bonds is a primary way to obtain resources for long-term growth and expansion by businesses, nonprofit organizations (such as colleges), and public subdivisions (such as municipalities and water districts). Bonds are long-term debt instruments. When bonds are issued (i.e., sold), they become an investment to the buyer and an obligation of the issuer. Accounting for bonds is complex because of the wide range of characteristics they possess. Both the issuing entity and the investor need to understand the characteristics of bonds and their varying economic effects. Accounting seeks to measure and report these economic effects.

Because of the special characteristics of bonds and the related accounting complexities, we give bonds separate consideration. The purposes of this chapter are to discuss the characteristics of bonds payable and to explain the accounting approaches used to measure, record, and report their economic impact on the entity. To provide flexibility the chapter is divided into two parts:

Part A—Fundamentals of measuring, recording, and reporting bonds payable

Part B—Some special problems in accounting for bonds payable

PART A—FUNDAMENTALS OF MEASURING, RECORDING, AND REPORTING BONDS PAYABLE

CHARACTERISTICS OF BONDS PAYABLE

Funds required for long-term purposes, such as the acquisition of high-cost machinery or the construction of a new plant, often are obtained by issuing long-term debt instruments, such as long-term notes payable (discussed in Chapter 10) or bonds payable. Bonds payable may be secured by a mortgage on specified assets, or the bonds may be unsecured. Bonds commonly are issued in denominations of $1,000 or $10,000 and, occasionally, in denominations of $100,000. They usually are negotiable (i.e., transferable by endorsement), and the bonds of most large companies are bought and sold daily by investors on the major stock exchanges.[1] A typical bond certificate is shown in Exhibit 11–1.

EXHIBIT 11–1   **Typical bond certificate**

---

[1] In addition to bonds that are issued by corporations, bonds also are issued by governmental units, such as federal and state governments, cities, counties, school districts, water districts, and by nonprofit institutions. The discussions in this chapter apply to both types, although we will focus mainly on those issued by corporations.

The **principal** of a bond is the amount payable at the maturity or due date as specified on the bond certificate. This amount also is called its **par value, maturity value,** or its **face amount.** Throughout the life of a bond, the issuing company makes periodic interest payments, usually semiannually, to the bondholders.

A company desiring to sell a bond issue must draw up a **bond indenture** (or bond contract) that specifies the legal provisions of the bonds, such as the maturity date, rate of interest to be paid, date of each interest payment, and any conversion privileges (explained later). When a bond is issued, the investor receives a **bond certificate** (i.e., a bond). All of the bond certificates for a single bond issue are identical. Specified on the face of each certificate are the same maturity dates, interest rate, interest dates, and other provisions. Usually when a company issues bonds, an **underwriter** is engaged to sell the bonds to the public. A third party, called the **trustee,** usually is appointed to represent the bondholders. The duties of an independent trustee are to ascertain whether the issuing company fulfills all of the provisions of the bond indenture.

SPECIAL CHARACTERISTICS OF BONDS

A particular bond issue will have a combination of characteristics that will be specified in the bond indenture. The issuing company often will add special characteristics to a bond issue in order to make the bond more attractive to potential investors. Bonds may be classified in a number of ways, depending upon their characteristics. Typical bond characteristics and their related classifications are presented in Exhibit 11–2.

ADVANTAGES OF ISSUING BONDS

The advantages of issuing bonds instead of capital stock stem from the fact that the bondholders are **creditors** and not owners (as are stockholders). A bondholder does not share in the management, the accumulated earnings, or the growth in assets, as does the stockholder. Payments to bondholders are limited to (1) the amount of interest specified on the bond and (2) the principal or face amount of the bond at maturity. Interest payments to bondholders are a tax-deductible expense, but dividend payments to owners are not tax deductible. This fact significantly reduces the net (i.e., aftertax) cost of funds acquired by issuing bonds.

Use of creditors' funds often increases the rate of return to owners' equity. This enhancement of the return to owners is called **financial leverage.** When leverage is positive, an important financial advantage to the stockholders occurs. Financial leverage is **positive** when the net aftertax interest rate on borrowed funds is **less** than the aftertax rate of return earned by the company on total assets.

To illustrate, assume Spicewood Corporation earned a 15 percent return (after income tax) on total assets (i.e., net income, $75,000 ÷ total assets, $500,000 = .15) and that the interest on total debt was 9.0 percent (i.e., interest expense, $18,000 ÷ total debt, $200,000 = .09). The income tax rate for Spicewood Corpora-

EXHIBIT 11–2
Bond characteristics and classifications

Bond Classification	Bond Characteristic
1. On the basis of collateral:	
a. Unsecured bonds (often called debentures).	a. Bonds that do **not** include a mortgage or pledge of specific assets as a guarantee of repayment at maturity.
b. Secured bonds (often designated on the basis of the type of asset pledged, such as a real estate mortgage).	b. Bonds that include the pledge of specific assets as a guarantee of repayment at maturity.
2. On the basis of repayment of principal:	
a. Ordinary or single-payment bonds.	a. The principal is payable in full at a single specified maturity date in the future.
b. Serial bonds.	b. The principal is payable in installments on a series of specified maturity dates in the future.
3. On the basis of early retirement:	
a. Callable bonds.	a. Bonds that may be called for early retirement at the option of the **issuer.**
b. Redeemable bonds.	b. Bonds that may be turned in for early retirement at the option of the **bondholder.**
c. Convertible bonds.	c. Bonds that may be converted to other securities of the issuer (usually common stock) at the option of the **bondholder.**
4. On the basis of the payment of interest:	
a. Registered bonds.	a. Payment of interest is made by check and mailed direct to the bondholder whose name must be on file (i.e., in the bond register).
b. Coupon bonds.	b. Bonds with a printed coupon attached for each interest payment. The bondholder "clips" the coupon on the interest date and deposits it in a bank like a check, or mails it to the issuing company which, in turn, mails the interest check direct to the person and address shown on the completed coupon. The interest rate on coupon bonds often is called the coupon rate.

tion is 40 percent. The $18,000 interest expense reduced both taxable income and Spicewood's tax liability. The **net interest cost** of the debt was the interest expense ($18,000) minus the tax savings associated with the interest expense ($18,000 $\times$ .40 = $7,200). Thus, Spicewoods' aftertax interest cost was $10,800 (i.e., $18,000 − $7,200). There was positive financial leverage in this situation because the creditors provided funds for 5.4 percent aftertax interest ($10,800 ÷ $200,000 = .054) and the company is earning 15 percent on those (and the other) assets. Because the only return paid to the creditors is 5.4 percent aftertax interest, the difference between 15 percent and 5.4 percent (of the $200,000) increases net income, which in turn accrues to the long-term benefit of the company and, therefore, to the stockholders. Exhibit 11–3 presents two comparative cases for Spicewood Corporation to illustrate the cause and economic effects of financial leverage. Case A assumes that the company has total assets of $500,000, which were provided in full by stockholders (i.e., it has no debt). In contrast, Case B assumes that of the total amount of assets, $300,000, was provided by stockholders and the remaining $200,000 was provided by creditors (i.e., debt). For illustrative purposes, the other variables are held constant in order to demonstrate the cause and economic effects of using debt to help finance a business.

Observe in Exhibit 11–3, Case A, that return on total assets and return on stockholders' equity are the same (15 percent) because there was no debt. There is no financial leverage because it is caused only by debt. In contrast, in Case B, the $200,000 of debt caused return on stockholders' equity (21 percent) to be higher than the return on total assets (15 percent); thus there was **positive financial leverage,** which is measured as the difference between the return on stockholders' equity and the return on total assets (i.e., 21% − 15% = 6%). This illustration demonstrates that financial leverage is caused by the existence of debt and that the economic effect of financial leverage can be measured. Finan-

**EXHIBIT 11–3
Effects of financial
leverage**

<table>
<tr><td colspan="5" align="center">Spicewood Corporation</td></tr>
<tr><td></td><td colspan="2">Case A: No debt</td><td colspan="2">Case B: Debt, $200,000 @ 9 Percent</td></tr>
<tr><td colspan="5">Balance sheet:</td></tr>
<tr><td>   Total assets . . . .</td><td>$ 500,000</td><td></td><td></td><td>$ 500,000</td></tr>
<tr><td>   Total debt (9% interest) . . . .</td><td>–0–</td><td></td><td></td><td>200,000</td></tr>
<tr><td>   Stockholders' equity,</td><td></td><td></td><td></td><td></td></tr>
<tr><td>   (10,000 shares) . . . .</td><td>$ 500,000</td><td>(6,000 shares) . . . .</td><td></td><td>$ 300,000</td></tr>
<tr><td colspan="5">Income statement:</td></tr>
<tr><td>   Revenues . . . .</td><td>$ 300,000</td><td></td><td></td><td>$ 300,000</td></tr>
<tr><td>   Operating expenses . . . .</td><td>(175,000)</td><td></td><td></td><td>(175,000)</td></tr>
<tr><td>   Income tax (40%) . . . .</td><td>(50,000)</td><td></td><td></td><td>(50,000)</td></tr>
<tr><td>   Interest expense</td><td></td><td>$200,000 × 9% = $18,000</td><td></td><td></td></tr>
<tr><td>   (net of income tax) . . . . . .</td><td>–0–</td><td>Less: $18,000 × 40%</td><td></td><td></td></tr>
<tr><td>   Net income . . . .</td><td>$ 75,000</td><td>   = ($7,200) . . .</td><td></td><td>(10,800)</td></tr>
<tr><td></td><td></td><td></td><td></td><td>$ 64,200</td></tr>
<tr><td colspan="5">Analysis:</td></tr>
<tr><td> a. Return on total assets</td><td></td><td>[($64,200 + $10,800)</td><td></td><td></td></tr>
<tr><td>   ($75,000 ÷ $500,000)</td><td>15%</td><td> ÷ $500,000]* . . . .</td><td></td><td>15%</td></tr>
<tr><td> b. Return on stockholders'</td><td></td><td></td><td></td><td></td></tr>
<tr><td>   equity ($75,000 ÷</td><td></td><td></td><td></td><td></td></tr>
<tr><td> $500,000) . . . .</td><td>15%</td><td>($64,200 ÷ $300,000) . . . .</td><td></td><td>21%</td></tr>
<tr><td> c. Financial leverage</td><td></td><td></td><td></td><td></td></tr>
<tr><td>   ([b] − [a])† . . . .</td><td>–0–</td><td></td><td></td><td>6%</td></tr>
<tr><td> d. EPS ($75,000 ÷ 10,000</td><td></td><td></td><td></td><td></td></tr>
<tr><td>   shares) . . . .</td><td>$7.50</td><td>($64,200 ÷ 6,000 shares) . . . . . .</td><td></td><td>$10.70</td></tr>
</table>

* Interest on debt, net of income tax, is added back to derive total return to all fund providers (also see Chapter 15).
† Also see discussion of financial leverage in Chapter 16.

cial leverage will be positive when the overall earnings rate of the company is more than the average aftertax interest rate on debt. **Negative financial leverage will exist if the overall earnings rate is less than the average aftertax interest rate on debt.** The significance of the economic effect of financial leverage depends upon (1) the difference between the aftertax interest rate and the earnings rate on total assets and (2) the relative amount of total assets provided by creditors.

Despite the advantages of financial leverage, sound financing of a large business requires a realistic **balance** between the amounts of debt (including bonds payable) and owners' equity (i.e., common and preferred stock and retained earnings). For example, in Case A, there was no debt, which is the most conservative position. In Case B, the $200,000 of debt was 40 percent of total assets employed (not an unusual situation). However, if Spicewood Corporation had $400,000 debt, the 80 percent debt to total assets would be considered too high in most situations. It would be considered too high because interest payments to bondholders are **fixed charges.** Interest payments legally must be paid each period, regardless of whether the corporation earns income or incurs a loss. In contrast, dividends usually are paid to stockholders only if earnings are satisfactory. Each year, some companies go bankrupt because of their inability to make required interest payments to creditors.

MEASURING BONDS PAYABLE AND BOND INTEREST EXPENSE

The accounting approach used to measure, record, and report bonds payable is based primarily on the **cost** and **matching principles.** When a bond is issued (i.e., sold), the proceeds include the net cash received, plus the market value of any noncash resources received. Under the cost principle, bonds payable are recorded at their **issue price,** which is their **current cash equivalent amount** (the present value of the future cash flows). Subsequent to the issuance of the bonds, the present value will change from period to period if the bond was issued at a discount or at a premium.

Bonds may be sold at **par;** that is, at the face or maturity amount (these are alternative terms for the same amount). If sold above par, bonds are said to have been issued at a **premium.** If sold below par, bonds are said to have been issued at a **discount.** To illustrate, if the issuing corporation received $1,000 cash for a bond with a $1,000 face, maturity, or par value, there would be no premium or discount. Alternatively, if the corporation received $967 for the bond, there would be a discount of $33; or if $1,035 cash were received, there would be a premium of $35. Typically, bond prices are quoted on the security exchanges as a **percent** of the par amount. A bond quoted at 100 sells at par; if quoted at 96.7, it sells at a discount of 3.3 percent below its par; if quoted at 103.5, it sells at a premium of 3.5 percent above its par.

Interest rates on bonds

A bond specifies an **annual** rate of interest based on the par value (face or maturity amount) of the bond. This rate is called variously **the stated, coupon, nominal,** or **contract rate.** Interest usually is paid on a semiannual basis; thus, an 8 percent bond of $1,000 par will pay semiannual **cash** interest of 4 percent

(8 percent ÷ 2 = 4 percent) or $40 (i.e., $1,000 × .04 = $40) each six months regardless of whether the bond sold at par, a discount, or a premium. The **stated rate** is set by the issuing company to approximate the market rate of interest when the bond issue is authorized. It is printed on each bond certificate and does not change over the term of the bond.

The stated rate establishes the fixed amount of cash interest that will be paid each interest period over the entire life of the bond regardless of the issuing price of the bond. However, bonds sell at a market rate of interest that often is different from the stated rate. Whether a bond sells at par, at a discount, or at a premium is determined by the forces of supply and demand in the capital markets. The **market rate** of interest on a bond is the rate that borrowers (issuers) are willing to pay and lenders (investors) are willing to accept on their money taking into consideration the perceived level of risk involved. Market rates tend to fluctuate from day to day, but the stated rate of interest is fixed by contract for the life of the bond. As a result, the market price of a bond will be affected by changes in the market rate of interest.

When the market and stated rates of interest are the **same,** a bond will sell at par. When the market rate for a bond is **higher** than the stated rate, the bond will sell at a discount; and when the market rate is **lower** than the stated rate, a bond will sell at a premium.

When a bond is issued at a **discount,** the issuer receives less cash than will be paid at maturity date. When a bond is issued at a **premium,** the issuer receives more cash than will be paid at maturity. The difference between the market and stated rates of interest on a bond causes a different cash flow on issue date than on maturity date. The specified cash flow for interest on each interest payment date is determined by the stated rate of interest times the par and is not changed by the issue price of the bond.

Each period bond interest is measured, recorded, and reported in conformance with the **matching principle.** Interest is incurred on the basis of passage of time. At the end of each period, the amount of interest unpaid must be accrued and reported as expense so that it will be matched with the revenues in the period in which it was incurred. The measurement and reporting of interest on bonds is similar to interest on notes receivable and notes payable. When bonds are issued at a premium or discount, however, an additional measurement problem arises because these affect both the price of the bond and the amount of **interest expense** (but not the periodic **cash** payment of interest).

Accounting for bonds and bond interest is illustrated in Exhibit 11–4 under three independent situations: (1) bonds issued at par, (2) bonds issued at a discount, and (3) bonds issued at a premium.

Bonds sold at par

Bonds sell at their par value when buyers (investors) are willing to invest in them at the stated interest rate on the bond. To illustrate, assume that on January 1, 19A, Mason Corporation issued $400,000 of the bonds payable and received $400,000 in cash for them. The bonds were dated to start interest on January 1, 19A. The entry by Mason Corporation to record the issuance of the bonds is given in Exhibit 11–4 (bonds issued at par).

Subsequent to the sale of the bonds, interest at 5 percent (i.e., 10% per year) on the face amount of the bonds must be paid each June 30 and December 31 until maturity. The entries to record the interest payments during 19A are given in Exhibit 11–4.

At the end of the accounting period, December 31, 19A, the financial statements would report bond interest expense and a long-term liability, as illustrated in Exhibit 11–4.

In this example, Mason Corporation received $1,000 cash for each $1,000 bond sold and will pay back $1,000, principal + ($50 × 20, semiannual interest payments) = $2,000. The $1,000 difference is the amount of interest expense for the 10 years; therefore, the interest cost was $100 per year and the yield or effective rate of interest was $100 ÷ $1,000 = 10 percent per year. The stated rate called for on the bond also was 10 percent.

The $1,000 cash that Mason Corporation received when each bond was sold is the present value of the future cash flows associated with the bond (refer to Chapter 10, Part B) computed as follows:

		Present value
a.	Principal: $1,000 × $p_{n=20;\ i=5\%}$ (Table 10–2, .3769) =	$ 377
b.	Interest: $50 × $P_{n=20;\ i=5\%}$ (Table 10–4, 12.4622) =	623
	Issue (sale) price of one Mason bond	$1,000

When the effective rate of interest is equal to the stated rate of interest, the present value of the future cash flows associated with a bond **always** will equal the bond's par amount.

Bonds sold at a discount

Bonds sell at a discount when the buyers (investors) are willing to invest in them only at a yield or market rate of interest that is **higher** than the stated interest rate on the bonds. To illustrate, assume the capital market established a 12 percent market rate of interest for the 10-year Mason bonds (Exhibit 11–4) stated rate 10 percent, payable semiannually, which means the bonds would sell at a **discount.** At a 12 percent market rate, how much cash would a $1,000 bond of Mason Company generate if sold on January 1, 19A? To compute the cash issue (sale) price of one bond requires computation of the present value, at the **market rate,** of the two future cash flows specified on the bond: (a) the principal (n = 20, i = 6%) and (b) the cash interest paid each semiannual interest period (n = 20, i = 6%). Thus, the cash issue (sale) price of one Mason bond would be computed as follows (refer to Chapter 10, Part B):

		Present value
a.	Principal: $1,000 × $p_{n=20;\ i=6\%}$ (Table 10–2, .3118) =	$312
b.	Interest: $50 × $P_{n=20;\ i=6\%}$ (Table 10–4, 11.4699) =	573
	Issue (sale) price of one Mason bond	$885*

* Thus, the issue price would be 88.5.

EXHIBIT 11–4   **Accounting for bonds payable illustrated**

Situation:

Mason Corporation approved the following bond issue on January 1, 19A: Bonds payable authorized, 500 bonds, $1,000 par per bond, 10 percent interest (payable semiannually each June 30 and December 31), maturity in 10 years on December 31, 19J.
Mason's accounting period ends December 31.

Bonds issued at par:

On January 1, 19A, Mason issued 400 of the bonds at par (i.e., an effective rate of 10 percent) and received $400,000 cash.

Entries throughout 19A:

January 1, 19A—To record issuance of the bonds at par:

Cash (400 bonds × $1,000) 400,000
    Bonds payable (400 bonds)   400,000

Interest payments during 19A:

	June 30, 19A	December 31, 19A
Bond interest expense	20,000	20,000
Cash ($400,000 × 5%)	20,000	20,000

Financial statement for 19A:

Income statement:
Bond interest expense .... $ 40,000

Balance sheet:
Long-term liabilities:
    Bonds payable, 10% (due December 31, 19J) 400,000

Bonds issued at a discount:

On January 1, 19A, Mason issued 400 ($400,000 par) of the bonds at an effective interest rate of 12 percent (i.e., at a price of 88.5) and received $354,000 cash.

Entries throughout 19A:

January 1, 19A—To record issuance of the bonds at a discount:
Cash (400 bonds × $885) 354,000
Discount on bonds payable [400 bonds × ($1,000 − $885)] 46,000*
    Bonds payable (400 bonds × $1,000) 400,000*
    * Note: In effect, the bonds are recorded at their **issue price** because the liability is reported on the balance sheet **net** of these two balances.

Interest payments during 19A:

	June 30, 19A	December 31, 19A
Bond interest expense	22,300	22,300
Discount on bonds payable, straight-line amortization		
($46,000 ÷ 20 periods)	2,300	2,300
Cash ($400,000 × .05)	20,000	20,000

EXHIBIT 11–4 *(concluded)*

Financial statements for 19A:

Income statement:
Bond interest expense ($22,300 × 2) .... $ 44,600

Balance sheet:
Long-term liabilities:
Bonds payable 10%, due December 31, 19J $400,000
Less unamortized discount 41,400* 358,600

Or, alternatively:

Bonds payable, 10%, due December 31, 19J
(maturity amount, $400,000, less unamortized discount)........................ 358,600†

* $46,000 − $2,300 − $2,300 = $41,400.
† This amount is called the net liability.

Bonds issued at a premium:

On January 1, 19A, Mason issued 400 ($400,000 par) of the bonds at an effective interest rate of 8½ percent (i.e., at a price of 110) and received $440,000 cash.

Entries throughout 19A:

Cash (400 bonds × $1,100) 440,000
Premium on bonds payable [400 bonds × ($1,100 − $1,000)] 40,000
Bonds payable (400 bonds × $1,000) 400,000

Interest payments during 19A:

	June 30, 19A	*December 31, 19A*
Bond interest expense	18,000	18,000
Premium on bonds payable, straight-line amortization ($40,000 ÷ 20 periods)	2,000	2,000
Cash ($400,000 × .05)...	20,000	20,000

Financial statements for 19A:

Income statement:
Bond interest expense ($18,000 × 2) .... $ 36,000

Balance sheet:
Long-term liabilities:
Bonds payable, 10% (due December 31, 19J) $400,000
Add unamortized premium .... $ 36,000* 436,000

Or, alternatively:

Bonds payable, 10%, due December 31, 19J
(maturity amount, $400,000, plus unamortized premium)........................ 436,000†

* $40,000 − $2,000 − $2,000 = $36,000.
† This amount is called the net liability.

Payment of principal (face) amount at maturity date (all three situations):

December 31, 19J:

Bonds payable 400,000
Cash 400,000

The cash issue price of the 400 bonds issued by Mason would be $354,000 (i.e., 400 bonds × $885).

When a bond is sold at a discount (i.e., $115 discount per bond in the above example), the Bonds Payable account is credited for the face or maturity amount and the discount is recorded as a debit to Discount on Bonds Payable. To illustrate, the issuance of 400 of the bonds of Mason Company at a cash sale price of $885 per bond (i.e., a 12 percent market rate) would be recorded as shown in Exhibit 11–4 (bonds issued at a discount).

The journal entry to record the issuance of the bonds (Exhibit 11–4) recorded the amount of the discount in a separate contra liability account (Discount on Bonds Payable) as a **debit.** The discount must be accorded special treatment on the income statement (in measuring interest expense) and on the balance sheet, which reports the bonds payable at their **carrying value** (maturity amount less any **unamortized** discount).

Measuring and recording interest expense (on bonds sold at a discount)

The computation and related entry given in Exhibit 11–4 indicate that each of the 10 percent Mason bonds issued at a 12 percent market rate commanded $885 cash and a discount of $115 (i.e., $1,000 − $885). During the 10-year term of the bonds, Mason must make 20 semiannual interest payments of $50 each (i.e., $50 × 20 = $1,000 total interest) and at maturity must pay back the $1,000 cash principal. Therefore, in addition to the cash interest of $1,000, $115 more cash per bond is paid back than was borrowed. This, $115 discount on each bond causes the yield or effective rate to be 12 percent (instead of the 10 percent stated on the bonds). The discount is an adjustment of the amount of interest expense that will be **reported** each accounting period on the income statement. Bond discount, in the economic sense, represents an **increase in bond interest expense.** To give accounting effect to bond discount in periods subsequent to issuance, the $46,000 debit to Discount on Bonds Payable (in Exhibit 11–4), must be apportioned to each semiannual interest period as an increase in bond interest expense from the date of issuance to maturity date. There are two different methods for doing this: (1) **straight-line amortization** and (2) **effective-interest amortization.** Straight-line amortization is easy to understand and compute; however, it is conceptually deficient. Effective-interest amortization requires use of the present value concepts (discussed in Part B of Chapter 10). The effective-interest method is required; however, it or the straight-line method may be used when the difference between the two results is not material in amount each year. Although the difference may appear material for Mason Company, we will introduce the subject with straight-line amortization because it is easy to follow. The more complex **effective-interest method** will be presented in Part B of this chapter.

Straight-line amortization. To amortize the $46,000 bond discount over the period from date of issuance to maturity date on a straight-line basis, an equal dollar amount is allocated to each interest period. Since there are 20 six-month interest periods, the computation would be: $46,000 ÷ 20 periods = $2,300 amortization on each semiannual interest date. Therefore, the payments of interest on the bonds during 19A would be recorded as shown in Exhibit 11–4 (bonds issued at a discount).[2]

In accordance with the thrust of *APB Opinion 21*, "Interest on Receivables and Payables," bonds payable should be measured and reported on the balance sheet at their **net liability amount,** that is, the maturity amount less any unamortized bond discount or plus any unamortized bond premium. Therefore, at the end of the accounting period, December 31, 19A, the financial statements would report interest expense and bonds payable as shown in Exhibit 11–4 (bond issued at a discount).

✳ Each succeeding year the unamortized discount will **decrease** by $4,600, and as a consequence, the net liability will **increase** each year by $4,600. At the maturity date of the bonds, the unamortized discount (i.e., the balance in the Discount on Bonds Payable account) will be **zero.** At that time the maturity or face amount of the bonds and the current net liability amount will be the same (i.e., $400,000).

Bonds sold at a premium

Bonds sell at a premium when the buyers (investors) are willing to invest in bonds at a market or yield rate of interest that is **lower** than the stated interest rate on the bonds. To illustrate, assume the capital market established an 8½ percent market rate of interest for the 10-year Mason bonds (Exhibit 11–4, stated rate, 10 percent, payable on semiannual basis), which means the bonds would sell at a **premium.** Computation of the cash issue (sale) price of one Mason bond would be as follows (refer to Chapter 10, Part B):

		Present value
a.	Principal: $1,000 $\times p_{n=20;\ i=41/4\%}$ (Table 10–2, .4350) =	$ 435
b.	Interest: $50 $\times P_{n=20;\ i=41/4\%}$ (Table 10–4, 13.2944) =	665
	Issue (sale) price of one Mason bond	$1,100

The cash issue price (110) of the 400 bonds issued by Mason would be $440,000 (i.e., 400 bonds $\times$ $1,100).

When a bond is sold at a premium ($100 premium per bond in the above example), the Bonds Payable account is credited for the par amount, and the premium is recorded as a credit to Premium on Bonds Payable. To illustrate,

---

[2] The amount of interest expense recorded each semiannual period may be confirmed as follows:

Cash to be paid out by the borrower:	
Par amount of the bonds—payable at maturity	$400,000
Interest payments ($20,000 $\times$ 20 semiannual payments)	$400,000
Total cash payments	800,000
Cash received by the borrower	354,000
Total interest expense over ten years	$446,000
Interest expense per semiannual period ($446,000 ÷ 20 periods)	$ 22,300

(Alternatively, $20,000 cash interest + $2,300 discount amortization = $22,300.)

the issuance of 400 of the bonds of Mason Company at a cash sale price of $1,100 each (i.e., at an 8½ percent market rate) would be recorded as shown in Exhibit 11–4 (bonds issued at a premium).

Measuring and recording interest expense (bonds sold at a premium)

The premium of $40,000 recorded by Mason must be apportioned to each of the 20 interest periods. The effective-interest method usually must be used to make the allocation; however, the straight-line method may be used if the results are not different materially from the other method. For illustrative purposes, the straight-line method is used because of its simplicity. The amortization of premium each semiannual interest period would be: $40,000 ÷ 20 periods = $2,000. Therefore, the payments of interest on the bonds during 19A would be recorded as shown in Exhibit 11–4 (bonds issued at a premium).[3]

In the journal entry to record the sale and issuance of the bonds by Mason, the premium was recorded in a separate account, Premium on Bonds Payable, as a **credit**. The premium has the effect of **decreasing** interest expense; therefore, in each period a portion of it is amortized to interest expense. Observe that in the illustration in Exhibit 11–4 (bonds issued at a premium), Bond Interest Expense was reduced by $2,000 each semiannual period because straight-line amortization was assumed. At the end of 19A, the financial statements of Mason Company would report interest expense and bonds payable as shown in Exhibit 11–4.

At maturity date, after the last interest payment, the bond premium of $40,000 will be amortized fully and the maturity or face amount of the bonds and the current net liability of the bonds will be the same (i.e., $400,000). At maturity, December 31, 19J, the bonds will be paid off in full, resulting in the same entry whether originally sold at par, a discount, or a premium, as illustrated at the bottom of Exhibit 11–4.

The effect of amortization of bond discount and bond premium on a $1,000 bond is shown graphically in Exhibit 11–5.

The preceding discussion has focused on the fundamental issues in measuring and reporting bonds payable. This discussion has provided the background essential to understanding the economic impact of bonds payable on the issuing company and its reporting on the periodic financial statements. The next part of the chapter discusses some complexities often encountered in accounting for bonds payable.

---

[3] The amount of interest expense recorded each semiannual period may be confirmed as follows:

Cash paid out by the borrower:	
Par amount of bonds at maturity	$400,000
Interest payments ($20,000 × 20 periods)	400,000
Total cash payments	800,000
Cash received by the borrower	440,000
Total interest expense over 10 years	$360,000
Interest expense per semiannual period ($360,000 ÷ 20 periods)	$ 18,000

(Alternatively, $20,000 cash interest − $2,000 premium amortization = $18,000.)

EXHIBIT 11–5
Graphic illustration of straight-line amortization of bond premium and discount

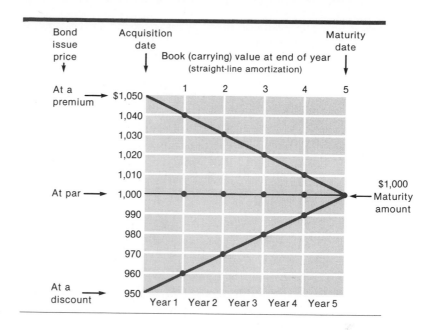

PART B—SOME SPECIAL PROBLEMS IN ACCOUNTING FOR BONDS PAYABLE

This part of the chapter focuses primarily on four special problems commonly encountered in accounting for bonds payable. These four problems are (1) accounting for bonds sold between interest dates, (2) adjusting entries for accrued bond interest, (3) bond sinking funds, and (4) effective-interest amortization.

ACCOUNTING FOR BONDS SOLD BETWEEN INTEREST DATES

The bond certificates specify the **date** and **amount** of each cash interest payment. Although bonds may be sold on an interest date, usually market factors cause them to be sold **between** interest dates. Nevertheless, the exact amount of interest specified on the bond certificate for each interest date will be paid, regardless of whether a bond is sold on an interest date or between interest dates. Therefore, when bonds are sold between two interest dates, the investor (i.e., the buyer) must pay the interest that has accrued **since the last interest date** in addition to the market price of the bond. The amount of the next interest payment will be for a **full** interest period; therefore, the accrued interest is effectively returned to the buyer. The net effect is that the investor will realize interest revenue only for the number of months the bonds were held from the date of sale. Similarly, the issuing corporation will incur interest expense for the same period. This situation presents two complexities in accounting for bonds: (1) the amount of accrued interest charged to the buyer must be included in the journal entry of the issuer to record the sale of bonds; and (2) any premium or discount

**EXHIBIT 11–6
Some special
problems in
accounting for
bonds payable
illustrated**

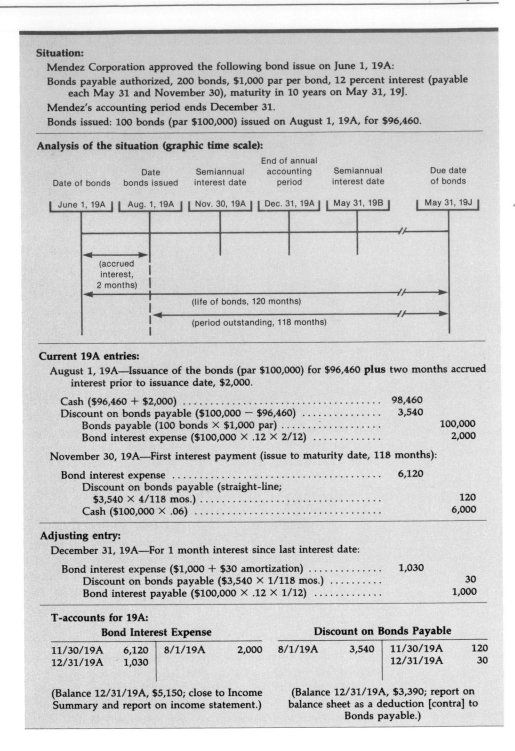

Situation:

Mendez Corporation approved the following bond issue on June 1, 19A:

Bonds payable authorized, 200 bonds, $1,000 par per bond, 12 percent interest (payable each May 31 and November 30), maturity in 10 years on May 31, 19J.

Mendez's accounting period ends December 31.

Bonds issued: 100 bonds (par $100,000) issued on August 1, 19A, for $96,460.

Analysis of the situation (graphic time scale):

Date of bonds	Date bonds issued	Semiannual interest date	End of annual accounting period	Semiannual interest date	Due date of bonds
June 1, 19A	Aug. 1, 19A	Nov. 30, 19A	Dec. 31, 19A	May 31, 19B	May 31, 19J

(accrued interest, 2 months)

(life of bonds, 120 months)

(period outstanding, 118 months)

Current 19A entries:

August 1, 19A—Issuance of the bonds (par $100,000) for $96,460 **plus** two months accrued interest prior to issuance date, $2,000.

Cash ($96,460 + $2,000)	98,460	
Discount on bonds payable ($100,000 − $96,460)	3,540	
Bonds payable (100 bonds × $1,000 par)		100,000
Bond interest expense ($100,000 × .12 × 2/12)		2,000

November 30, 19A—First interest payment (issue to maturity date, 118 months):

Bond interest expense	6,120	
Discount on bonds payable (straight-line; $3,540 × 4/118 mos.)		120
Cash ($100,000 × .06)		6,000

Adjusting entry:

December 31, 19A—For 1 month interest since last interest date:

Bond interest expense ($1,000 + $30 amortization)	1,030	
Discount on bonds payable ($3,540 × 1/118 mos.)		30
Bond interest payable ($100,000 × .12 × 1/12)		1,000

T-accounts for 19A:

Bond Interest Expense				Discount on Bonds Payable			
11/30/19A	6,120	8/1/19A	2,000	8/1/19A	3,540	11/30/19A	120
12/31/19A	1,030					12/31/19A	30

(Balance 12/31/19A, $5,150; close to Income Summary and report on income statement.)

(Balance 12/31/19A, $3,390; report on balance sheet as a deduction [contra] to Bonds payable.)

must be amortized by the issuer over the remaining period that the bonds will be outstanding, that is, the period from date of sale to date of maturity of the bonds.

In this section, we will illustrate the four special problems in accounting for bonds with data for Mendez Corporation, given at the top of Exhibit 11–6. Mendez Corporation issued bonds on August 1, 19A, which was two months after the date of the bonds (June 1, 19A). The time scale given in Exhibit 11–6 will be helpful in analyzing the effect of different dates on the accounting for the bond issue.

On August 1, 19A, date of the issuance of the 100 bonds, Mendez Corporation would receive cash for the sale price of the bonds, **plus** two months accrued interest (June 1, 19A to July 31, 19A), computed as follows (refer to the bond time scale, Exhibit 11–6):

Market price (for 100 bonds)	$96,460
Add accrued interest for 2 months (June and July):	
$100,000 × 12% × 2/12	2,000
Total cash received	$98,460

The bond investors must pay two months of accrued interest to Mendez because the bond indenture (contract) requires that Mendez pay a full six months of interest on the next interest date (i.e., November 30). On the first interest date, the bonds will have been outstanding for only four months (August 1 through November 30). Therefore, on November 30, 19A, the investors will have earned four months interest revenue and the issuer (Mendez) will have incurred four months interest expense. The payment of two months accrued interest when the bonds are purchased is an offset that causes interest to be adjusted to a four month basis for both the investor and the issuer.

The journal entry by the issuer, Mendez Corporation, to record the issuance of the 100 bonds payable is shown in Exhibit 11–6. In that entry, Bond Interest Expense was credited for $2,000 accrued interest collected because that amount will be refunded to the investor when the next interest payment is made. That interest payment will be recorded as a credit to Cash and a debit to Bond Interest Expense (Exhibit 11–6).

The $3,540 recorded in the Discount on Bonds Payable account is amortized over the **period outstanding** of 118 months; therefore, straight-line amortization would be $3,540 ÷ 118 months = $30 per month. The entry to record the first interest payment would include amortization of discount only for the four months that the bonds have been outstanding. Therefore, the first interest payment would be recorded as illustrated in Exhibit 11–6.

After journal entries are made to record the collection of accrued interest (August 1, 19A) and the payment of interest (November 30, 19A), the Bond Interest Expense account will reflect a debit balance of $4,120. This amount is equivalent to four months' interest (i.e., $100,000 × 12% × 4/12 = $4,000) plus four months'

amortization of discount (i.e. $30 \times 4 = \$120$). The Bond Interest Expense account
would appear as follows:

Bond Interest Expense

11/30/19A	6,120	8/1/19A	2,000

(Balance, 11/30/19A, $4,120)

✳ ADJUSTING ENTRY FOR ACCRUED BOND INTEREST

In Chapter 10, we discussed the **adjusting entry** that must be made for any
interest expense accrued since the last interest payment date for a note payable.
The same adjustment procedure must be applied to bonds payable. However,
in the case of bonds, the adjusting entry must include **both** the accrued interest
and amortization of any bond discount or premium. To illustrate, Mendez Corporation (Exhibit 11–6) recorded an interest payment on November 30, 19A; therefore, on December 31, 19A, there is accrued interest for one month. Bond discount
also must be amortized for one more month. The adjusting entry at December
31, 19A, is illustrated in Exhibit 11–6.

After the adjusting entry is posted on December 31, 19A, the Bond Interest
Expense account will reflect a debit balance of $5,150, which represents interest
expense for the five months that the bonds have been outstanding during 19A
(August 1 to December 31). The Bond Interest Expense account for 19A is illustrated at the bottom of Exhibit 11–6. The ending balance of $5,150 can be verified
as follows:

Interest: $100,000 $\times$ 12% $\times$ 5/12 . . . . $5,000
Add discount amortized: $30 $\times$ 5   150
Total interest expense for 19A $5,150

Bond Interest Expense is closed to Income Summary at the end of the accounting
period and is reported on the 19A income statement. The Bond Discount account
for 19A is reported on the balance sheet as follows:

Long-term liabilities:
Bonds payable $100,000
Less: Discount on Bonds payable   3,390
$96,610

BOND SINKING FUNDS

On the maturity date of bonds payable, the issuing company must have available a large amount of cash to pay off the bondholders. Such a demand for a
large amount of cash might place the issuing company in a severe financial strain.
In order to avoid this situation, some companies build up a separate **cash fund**

by making equal annual contributions over a period of time in advance of the bond maturity date. Such a separate cash fund customarily is called a **bond sinking fund.** A bond sinking fund is an asset that is invested pending the due date of the bonds; it is reported on the balance sheet under the caption "Investments and funds."

A bond sinking fund also adds a measure of security for the bondholders because it assures them that funds will be available for retirement of the bonds at their maturity date. Each cash contribution to the fund usually is deposited with an independent trustee (a designated third party such as bank or another financial institution). The trustee invests the funds received and adds the fund earnings to the fund balance each year. Interest earned on a sinking fund is recorded as an increase in the fund balance (a debit) and as interest revenue (a credit). Thus, a bond sinking fund typically has the characteristics of a regular savings account such as was illustrated in Chapter 10, Part B. At the maturity date of the bonds, the balance of the fund is used to pay the bondholders. Any excess cash is returned to the issuing corporation, or, in the case of a deficit, it must be made up by the issuer.

Exhibit 11–7 illustrates a bond sinking fund for Mendez Corporation. The fund will be built up over the last five years that the bonds are outstanding by making five equal annual deposits each May 31, starting in 19F. The sinking fund contributions will be deposited with City Bank, as trustee, which will pay 8 percent annual interest on the fund balance each May 31. The amount of each deposit required can be calculated using the time value of money concepts discussed and illustrated in Chapter 10, Part B. If the fund earned no interest, obviously each deposit would have to be $20,000 (i.e., $100,000 ÷ 5 contributions = $20,000). Instead of $20,000, the annual deposit required is less than $20,000 because the interest earned each year will be added to the fund balance. The required annual deposit was determined to be $17,046, as illustrated in Exhibit 11–7.

The journal entries for May 31, 19F, and 19G, for the sinking fund are illustrated in Exhibit 11–7.[4] Observe that the fund is increased by **both** the annual deposits and the accumulation of interest. Identical journal entries with different interest amounts would be made for each of the five years of the accumulation period. The interest amounts increase each year because of the increasing balance in the fund. At the maturity date of the bonds, payment will be made to the bondholders using the cash accumulated in the sinking fund. The journal entry to retire the bonds payable is illustrated in Exhibit 11–7.

Often it is useful to develop a fund accumulation schedule as shown in Exhibit 11–7. Observe that the schedule provides data for (1) the entry on each interest date and (2) the buildup of the fund to maturity date.

---

[4] In connection with such funds, a company also may restrict, or appropriate, an equivalent amount of retained earnings as a dividend restriction. The restriction of retained earnings by a corporation is discussed in Chapter 12.

EXHIBIT 11–7
Accounting for a bond sinking fund

Situation:

Mendez Corporation plans to accumulate a bond sinking fund sufficient to retire the $100,000 bond issue outstanding on maturity date, May 31, 19J (see Exhibit 11–6). Five equal annual deposits are to be made each May 31, starting in 19F. Expected earning rate on the fund is 8 percent.

Computation of periodic deposits ($n = 5$, years F through J; $i = 8\%$):

Computation (application of future value of annuity of $1):
Future value $=$ Periodic rent $\times F_{n=5;\, i=8\%}$
Substituting:
$100,000 =$? $\times 5.8666$ (Table 10–3)
Periodic rent $= \$100,000 \div 5.8666$
$= \$ \underline{\underline{17,046}}$

Entries—for first year of the fund and the second deposit):

May 31, 19F—To record the first deposit by Mendez:

Bond sinking fund	17,046	
Cash (computed above)		17,046

May 31, 19G—To record interest revenue for 1 year added to the fund:

Bond sinking fund (observe, not the cash account)	1,364	
Interest revenue ($17,046 \times .08$)		1,364

May 31, 19G—To record the second deposit by Mendez:

Bond sinking fund	17,046	
Cash (computed above)		17,046

Entry at maturity date, (May 31, 19J) to retire the bonds:

Bonds payable	100,000	
Bond sinking fund		100,000

Sinking fund accumulation schedule (Deposits, $17,046; $n = 5$; $i = 8\%$):

Date	Cash Deposit (Credit Cash)	Interest Revenue (Credit)	Fund Increase (Debit Fund)	Accumulated Fund Balance
5/31/19F	17,046 [a]		17,046	17,046
5/31/19G	17,046	$17,046 \times .08 =$ 1,364 [b]	18,410 [c]	35,456 [d]
5/31/19H	17,046	$35,456 \times .08 =$ 2,836	19,882	55,338
5/31/19I	17,046	$55,338 \times .08 =$ 4,427	21,473	76,811
5/31/19J	17,046	$76,811 \times .08 =$ 6,143*	23,189	100,000
Totals	85,230	14,770	100,000	

* Rounded $2 to accommodate prior rounding errors.
[a] Computed above.
[b] Interest earned on beginning balance in the fund each period at 8 percent.
[c] Period deposit ($17,046) plus interest earned ($1,364) = $18,410 (etc.).
[d] Prior balance ($17,046) plus increase in fund ($18,410) = $35,456 (etc.).
(Note: This is an ordinary annuity (i.e., end-of-period contributions.)

EFFECTIVE-INTEREST AMORTIZATION ON BONDS PAYABLE

Effective-interest amortization of bond discount or bond premium is the only conceptually sound method for measuring both (1) the effective-interest expense on bonds and (2) the carrying amount of the bonds (at the current net liability amount). This approach uses the concept of present value discussed in Chapter 10, Part B.

APB Opinion 21, "Interest on Receivables and Payables," requires effective-interest amortization of bond discounts or premiums. However, the straight-line approach is permitted when the difference in amortization results is not material in amount. Conceptually, the effective-interest method is similar to the debt repayment which was discussed in Chapter 10. Each equal payment made on the debt consists of two parts: (1) a payment of principal and (2) a payment of interest.

A simplified case is used to illustrate effective-interest amortization and the related journal entries. The facts for the example are presented in Exhibit 11–8.

The sale price of the West Corporation bonds is the present value of the future cash flows associated with the bonds. The difference between the total par value of the bonds ($10,000) and the present value of the bonds ($8,558) is the discount ($1,442) which must be amortized over the life of the bonds. The journal entry to record the issuance of the bonds is shown in Exhibit 11–8.

When the effective-interest amortization method is used, the amount of interest expense and the amount of discount or premium that is amortized **change** each interest period. The amount of cash interest paid does not change because it is based on the stated rate of interest that is specified by the bond contract. The amounts for each journal entry to record the payment of interest must be computed uniquely. An organized approach to this computation is based on the preparation of a **debt payment schedule.** The schedule provides the amortization and interest expense amounts that must be recorded each interest period, as illustrated in Exhibit 11–8. The journal entries to record periodic interest are based on the amounts contained in the debt payment schedule. The journal entries for West Corporation are illustrated in Exhibit 11–8.

The effective-interest amortization method is preferred conceptually because it measures the effective, or true, interest expense each period. To illustrate, West Corporation borrowed $8,558 on January 1, 19A, at a market interest rate of 12 percent. The interest expense for the first year should be $1,027 (i.e., 12% × $8,558 = $1,027) which is the amount recorded in the journal entry for 19A, in Exhibit 11–8. In contrast, if the straight-line method had been used, the amortization of the bond discount would have been $288 (i.e., $1,442 ÷ 5 = $288), and interest expense would have been $1,088 (i.e., $288 + $800 = $1,088). The straight-line method is acceptable only if its use results in amounts that are not materially different from effective-interest amounts.

The net liability measured and reported on the balance sheet under the effective-interest method is the present value of the remaining cash flows associated with the bond, which is the conceptually preferred amount. The straight-line method approximates this amount and is acceptable if there is not a material difference between the two amounts.

EXHIBIT 11–8
Effective-interest amortization on bonds payable

Situation: West company sold ten, $1,000 bonds as follows:

Bonds payable authorized (10 bonds at $1,000 par each)	$10,000
Date printed on each bond	January 1, 19A
Maturity date (five-year term)	December 31, 19E
Interest, **payable per annum** each December 31	8%
Issued (sold) all of the bonds	January 1, 19A
Market interest rate	12%
Sale price (at a discount)	$8,558*
End of the accounting period for West	December 31

* Issue price computed as follows:
$10,000 \times p_{n=5;\,i=12\%}$ (Table 10–2 = .5674) = $5,674
$800 \times p_{n=5;\,i=12\%}$ (Table 10–4 = 3.6048) = 2,884
$8,558

Entry: To record issuance (sale) of the bonds at a discount:

January 1, 19A:

Cash (computed above)	8,558	
Discount on bonds payable ($10,000 − $8,558)	1,442	
Bonds payable (10 bonds × $1,000 par)		10,000

Bond payment schedule, effective-interest amortization:

(a) Date	(b) Cash Interest Paid on Each Interest Date ($10,000 × 8%)	(c) Interest Expense (based on beginning unpaid liability at market rate of 12%)	(d) Effective-Interest Amortization (increase of liability)*	(e) Net Liability (unpaid balance)
1/1/19A				8,558
12/31/19A	800	8,558 × .12 = 1,027	227	8,785
12/31/19B	800	8,785 × .12 = 1,054	254	9,039
12/31/19C	800	9,039 × .12 = 1,085	285	9,324
12/31/19D	800	9,324 × .12 = 1,119	319	9,643
12/31/19E	800	9,643 × .12 = 1,157	357	10,000
Subtotal	4,000	5,442	1,442	
12/31/19E	10,000†		10,000	–0–

* Adjusts the net liability to the maturity amount.
† Payment of principal.

Periodic entries to record interest paid and discount amortization.

	19A	19B	19C	19D	19E
Bond interest expense	1,027	1,054	1,085	1,119	1,157
Discount on bonds payable	227	254	285	319	357
Cash	800	800	800	800	800

Financial statements:

	19A	19B	19C	19D	19E
Income statement:					
Bond interest expense	$1,027	$1,054	$1,085	$1,119	$1,157
Balance sheet:					
Bonds payable (maturity amount $10,000) minus unamortized discount	8,785	9,039	9,324	9,643	–0–

To summarize, effective-interest amortization conceptually is superior to straight-line amortization because, for each period, consistent with the issue price of the bonds, it measures (1) the true amount of interest expense each period on the income statement and (2) the true current net carrying amount of the bonds outstanding (net liability) on the balance sheet each period. Straight-line amortization provides approximations of these amounts and can be used only when the difference between the two methods is deemed not material (refer to exception principle, materiality). In such situations, straight-line amortization often is used because it is less complex.

DEMONSTRATION CASE

(Try to resolve the requirements before proceeding to the suggested solution that follows.)

In order to raise funds to construct a new plant, the management of Reed Company decided to issue bonds. Accordingly, a proposed bond indenture was submitted to the board of directors and approved. The provisions in the bond indenture and specified on the bond certificates were:

Par value of bonds to be issued ($1,000 bonds) $600,000
Date of bond issue—February 1, 19A, due in 10 years on January 31, 19K.
Interest—10% per annum, payable 5% on each July 31 and January 31.

The bonds were sold on June 1, 19A, at 102½ plus accrued interest. The annual accounting period for Reed Company ends on December 31.

Required:

a. How much cash was received by Reed Company from the sale of the bonds payable on June 1, 19A? Show computations.

b. What was the amount of premium on the bonds payable? Over how many months should it be amortized?

c. Compute the amount of amortization of premium per month and for each six-month interest period; use straight-line amortization. Round to the nearest dollar.

d. Give the journal entry on June 1, 19A, to record the sale and issuance of the bonds payable.

e. Give the journal entry for payment of interest and amortization of premium for the first interest payment on July 31, 19A.

f. Give the adjusting entry required on December 31, 19A, at the end of the accounting period.

g. Give the optional reversing entry that could be made on January 1, 19B.

h. Give the journal entry to record the second interest payment and the amortization of premium on January 31, 19B.

i. Show how bond interest expense and bonds payable would be reported on the financial statements at December 31, 19A.

Suggested solution

Requirement a:

Sales price of the bonds: ($600,000 × 102.5%)	$615,000
Add accrued interest for four months (February 1 to May 31) ($600,000 × 10% × 4/12)	20,000
Total cash received for the bonds	$635,000

Requirement b:

Premium on the bonds payable ($600,000 × 2.5%)	$ 15,000
Months amortized: From date of sale, June 1, 19A, to maturity date, January 31, 19K. 120 months − 4 months = ...	116 months

Requirement c:

Premium amortization: $15,000 ÷ 116 months = $129 per month, or $774 each six-month interest period (straight line).

Requirement d:

June 1, 19A:

Cash (per Requirement [a] above)	635,000	
Premium on bonds payable (per Requirement [b] above)		15,000
Interest expense (per Requirement [a] above)		20,000
Bonds payable		600,000
To record sale of bonds payable at 102½ plus accrued interest for four months, February 1 to May 31, 19A.		

Requirement e:

July 31, 19A:

Bond interest expense	29,742	
Premium on bonds payable ($129 × 2 months)	258	
Cash ($600,000 × 5%)		30,000
To record payment of semiannual interest and to amortize premium for two months, June 1 to July 31, 19A.		

Requirement f:

December 31, 19A:

Bond interest expense	24,355	
Premium on bonds payable ($129 × 5 months)	645	
Bond interest payable ($600,000 × 10% × 5/12)		25,000
Adjusting entry for five months' interest accrued plus amortization		
of premium, August 1 to December 31, 19A.		

Requirement g:

January 1, 19B:

Bond interest payable	25,000	
Premium on bonds payable		645
Bonds interest expense		24,355
Reversing entry; optional.		

Requirement h:

January 31, 19B (assuming reversing entry [g] was made):[5]

Bond interest expense	29,226	
Premium on bonds payable (per Requirement [c])	774	
Cash ($600,000 × 10% × 6/12)		30,000
To record payment of semiannual interest and to amortize premium		
for six months.		

Requirement i:

Interest expense to be reported on the 19A income statement should be for the period outstanding during the year (i.e., for seven months, June 1 through December 31). Interest expense, per the above entries, is $29,742 + $24,355 —

---

[5] If no reversing entry was made on January 1, 19B, this entry would be:

Bond interest payable	25,000	
Premium on bonds payable	129	
Bond interest expense	4,871	
Cash		30,000

$20,000 = \$34,097$; or, alternatively, ($600,000 \times 10\% \times 7/12 = \$35,000$) minus ($129 \times 7$ months $= \$903$) $= \$34,097$.

Income statement for 19A:

Interest expense .... $ 34,097

Balance sheet, December 31, 19A:

Long-term liabilities:

Bonds payable, 10% (due January 31, 19K)	$600,000	
Add unamortized premium*	14,097	614,097

* $15,000 - (\$258 + \$645) = \$14,097$.

SUMMARY OF CHAPTER

This chapter discussed bonds payable, which represent one of the primary ways to obtain funds to acquire long-term assets and to expand a business. An important advantage of bonds payable is that the **cost** of borrowing the funds— interest expense—is deductible for income tax purposes which reduces the interest cost to the business.

Bonds may be sold at their par (or face) amount; at a premium; or at a discount, depending upon the stated interest rate on the bonds compared with the market (or yield) rate of interest that the bond buyers demand and the issuer will accept. In each case, bonds are measured, recorded, and reported at their current cash equivalent amount. The price of a bond varies based on the relationship between the market and stated rates of interest. If the market rate is higher than the stated rate on the bond, the bonds will sell at a discount. Conversely, if the market rate is lower than the stated rate on the bond, the bonds will sell at a premium.

Discounts and premiums on bonds payable are adjustments of the cash interest payments made by the issuing company during the term of the bonds. As a consequence, discount or premium on bonds payable is amortized to interest expense over the time from issue date to maturity date.

To assure that funds are available to retire bonds payable at maturity, a company may set aside cash in advance by means of periodic contributions to a bond sinking fund. Such a fund is similar to a savings account. The bond sinking fund usually is administered by an independent third party, such as a bank (called the trustee). Interest earned on the fund balance is added to the fund each period. At the maturity date of the bonds, the fund is used to pay the bondholders. Such a fund is reported on the balance sheet under the caption "Investments and funds." Interest earned on the fund is reported on the income statement as "Interest revenue."

IMPORTANT TERMS DEFINED IN THIS CHAPTER

Terms (alphabetically)	Key words in definitions of important terms used in chapter	Page reference
Bond certificate	The physical bond document; an example is presented in Exhibit 11–1.	510
Bond discount	A bond that is sold for less than par is sold at a discount.	513

Bond premium	A bond that is sold for more than par is sold at a premium.	519
Bond principal	The amount payable at the maturity of the bond; face amount.	510
Bond sinking fund	A cash fund accumulated for repayment of a bond upon maturity.	525
Callable bond	Bond that may be called for early retirement at the option of the issuer.	511
Convertible bond	A bond that may be converted to other securities of the issuer (usually common stock).	511
Coupon rate of interest	Another name for the stated rate of interest; particularly on coupon bonds.	513
Debenture	An unsecured bond; no assets specifically pledged to guarantee repayment.	511
Effective-interest amortization	Theoretically preferred method to amortize a bond discount or premium.	527
Face amount	Another name for bond principal or principal amount.	510
Financial leverage	Use of creditors' funds to increase the rate of return on owners' equity; occurs when the interest rate on debt is lower than the earnings rate on total assets.	511
Indenture	Bond contract that specifies the legal provisions of the bond.	510
Net interest cost	Interest cost, less the tax savings associated with interest expense.	511
Par value	Another name for bond principal or maturity amount.	510
Redeemable bond	Bond that may be turned in for early retirement at the option of the bondholder.	511
Stated rate	The rate of cash interest per period specified in the bond contract.	513
Straight-line amortization	Simplified method to amortize a bond discount or premium.	518
Trustee	An independent party appointed to represent the bondholders.	510

QUESTIONS FOR DISCUSSION

PART A

1. What are the primary characteristics of a bond? For what purpose are bonds usually issued?

2. What is the difference between a bond indenture and a bond certificate?

3. Distinguish between secured and unsecured bonds.

4. Distinguish among callable, redeemable, and convertible bonds.

5. Distinguish between registered and coupon bonds.

6. From the perspective of the issuer, what are some advantages of issuing bonds, as compared with issuing capital stock?

7. As the tax rate increases, the net cost of borrowing money decreases. Explain.

8. Briefly explain financial leverage. Can financial leverage be negative?

9. At the date of issuance, bonds are recorded at their current cash equivalent amount. Explain.

10. What is the nature of the discount and premium on bonds payable?

11. What is the difference between the stated interest rate and the effective interest rate on a bond?

12. Distinguish between the stated and effective rates of interest on a bond *(a)* sold at par, *(b)* sold at a discount, and *(c)* sold at a premium.

PART B

13. Why are bond discounts and premiums amortized over the outstanding life of the related bonds payable rather than the period from the date of the bonds to their maturity date?

14. What is meant by the "current net liability" of a bond payable?

15. Why is the lender (i.e., the purchaser of a bond) charged for the accrued interest from the last interest date to the date of purchase of the bonds?

16. What is a bond sinking fund? How should a bond sinking fund be reported in the financial statements?

17. Explain the basic difference between straight-line amortization and effective-interest amortization of bond discount or premium. Explain when each method should, or may, be used.

EXERCISES

PART A

E11–1. On January 1, 19A, Orange Corporation borrowed $90,000 on a three-year note payable. The interest rate is 12 percent per annum, payable each year. The company computed its return on total assets [i.e., Net income ÷ (Liabilities + Owners' equity)] to be 20 percent. The average income tax rate for the company is 40 percent.

Required:

a. What amount of interest would be paid the first year?
b. Considering the effect of income tax, what would be the net interest cost and the net interest rate?
c. Would financial leverage be present in this situation? Explain.
d. List two primary advantages to Orange Corporation in favor of the note payable versus selling more of its unissued capital stock to obtain needed funds.

E11–2. London Corporation is planning to issue $100,000, five-year, 10 percent bonds. Interest is payable semiannually each June 30 and December 31. Assume all of the bonds will be sold on January 1, 19A, and that they will mature on December 31, 19E.

Required (round to the nearest dollar):

a. Compute the issue (sale) price on January 1, 19A, for each of the following three independent cases (show computations).

  Case A—The market (yield) rate is 10 percent.
  Case B—The market (yield) rate is 8 percent.
  Case C—The market (yield) rate is 12 percent.

b. Give the journal entry to record the issuance for each case.

E11–3. Jacob Corporation had $200,000, 10-year, coupon bonds outstanding on December 31, 19A (end of the accounting period). Interest is payable each June 30 and December 31.

The bonds were issued (sold) on January 1, 19A. The 19A annual financial statements reflected the following:

Income statement:
Bond interest expense (straight-line amortization) . . . . . $ 18,600
Balance sheet:
Bonds payable (net liability)   194,600

Required (show computations):

a. What was the issue price of the bonds?
b. What was the coupon rate on the bonds?
c. Prepare computations which will show that the above amounts of (1) interest expense and (2) bonds payable (net liability) are correct.

E11–4. The summarized information below was taken from the 19B annual financial statements of two competing companies in the same industry (assume 50,000 shares of common stock outstanding):

	Thousands of dollars	
	Company A	*Company B*
Balance sheet:		
Total assets	$900	$900
Total liabilities (10% interest)	400	600
Income statement:		
Total revenues	480	421
Total expenses (including income tax)	300	400
Tax rate	40%	20%

Required:

a. Complete a tabulation similar to the following (show computations):

Item	Company A	Company B
Earnings per share		
Return on stockholders' equity		
Return on total assets		
Financial leverage		

b. Interpret and compare the financial leverage figures for the two companies.

E11–5. Adams, Incorporated, sold a $150,000, 8 percent bond issue on January 1, 19A, for $140,372 (9 percent market rate). The bonds were dated January 1, 19A, and pay interest each December 31. The bonds mature 10 years from January 1, 19A.

Required:

a. Give the journal entry to record the issuance of the bonds.
b. Give the journal entry to record the interest payment on December 31, 19A. Assume straight-line amortization.
c. Show how the bond interest expense and the bonds payable should be reported on the December 31, 19A, annual financial statements.
d. Verify the sales price of $140,372 (show computations).

E11–6. Keller Corporation sold a $60,000, 14 percent bond issue on January 1, 19A, for $66,782 (at a market rate of 12 percent). The bonds were dated January 1, 19A, and interest is paid each December 31. The bonds mature 10 years from January 1, 19A.

Required:

a. Give the journal entry to record the issuance of the bonds.
b. Give the journal entry for the interest payment on December 31, 19A. Assume straight-line amortization.
c. Show how the bond interest expense and the bonds payable should be reported on the December 31, 19A, annual financial statements.
d. Verify the issue (sale) price of $66,782 (show computations).

E11–7. In order to obtain cash to purchase operational assets, Day Corporation, whose annual accounting period ends on December 31, issued the following bonds:

Date of bonds: January 1, 19A.
Maturity amount and date: $100,000, due in 10 years (December 31, 19J).
Interest: 11 percent per annum payable each December 31.
Date sold: January 1, 19A.

Required:

a. Give the journal entry to record the issuance and the first two interest payments under each of three different independent assumptions (assume straight-line amortization):
  (1) The bonds sold at par.
  (2) The bonds sold at 96.
  (3) The bonds sold at 104.
b. Provide the following amounts to be reported on the 19A financial statements:

	Assumption 1	Assumption 2	Assumption 3
1. Interest expense	$_____	$_____	$_____
2. Bonds payable	_____	_____	_____
3. Unamortized premium or discount	_____	_____	_____
4. Net liability	_____	_____	_____
5. Stated rate of interest	_____	_____	_____
6. Cash interest paid	_____	_____	_____

c. Explain why items 1 and 6 are different in Requirement *(b)*.

PART B

E11–8. Dymo Corporation authorized the issuance of $300,000, 9 percent, 10-year bonds. The date printed on the bond certificates was January 1, 19A, and the interest is payable each June 30 and December 31.

On September 1, 19A, the company issued (sold) $200,000 of the bonds at 96 plus any accrued interest.

Required:

a. How much cash did Dymo Corporation receive on September 1, 19A? Show computations.
b. Give the journal entry to record the issuance.
c. How much net cash interest did Dymo Corporation pay during 19A on the $200,000 issuance? Show computations.

E11–9. White Corporation issued the following bonds:

Bonds payable authorized	$60,000
Date on each bond	Jan. 1, 19A
Maturity date (10 years)	Dec. 31, 19J
Interest, 10% per year, payable each December 31.	

White sold all of the bonds on March 1, 19A, and received $62,180 cash which included the accrued interest.

Required:

a. What was the amount of discount or premium?
b. Over what period of time should the discount or premium be amortized?
c. What would be the amortization amount per month assuming straight-line amortization?
d. Give the journal entry to record the issuance.
e. Give the journal entry on first interest payment date.
f. What amount should be reported as interest expense for 19A?
g. What amount of net liability should be shown on the balance sheet at December 31, 19A?

E11–10. Dopuch Corporation issued $10,000, 9 percent bonds dated April 1, 19A. Interest is paid each March 31. The bonds mature in three years on March 31, 19D. The bonds were sold on June 1, 19A, for $9,660 plus accrued interest. The accounting period ends each December 31.

Required:

a. Give the journal entry to record the issuance on June 1, 19A.
b. Give the adjusting entry required on December 31, 19A; use straight-line amortization.
c. What amount of interest expense should be reported on the income statement for 19A?
d. Show how the bonds should be reported on the balance sheet at December 31, 19A?
e. Give the journal entry to record the first interest payment on March 31, 19B.

E11–11. Tower Corporation has a $100,000 bond issue outstanding that is due four years hence. It desires to set up a bond sinking fund for this amount by making five equal annual contributions. The first contribution will be made immediately and the last one on the due date (i.e., an ordinary annuity). The corporation will deposit the annual contributions with a trustee that will increase the fund at the end of each year for 8 percent on the fund balance that existed at the beginning of the year.

Required:

a. Compute the annual contribution (rent) to the fund.
b. Give the journal entry for the first and second contributions, including interest.
c. Show how the effects of the fund would be reported on the financial statements at the end of the second year.

E11–12. Small Company has a $90,000 debt that will be due at the end of three years. The management has decided to deposit three equal year-end amounts of $27,723 in a debt retirement fund (i.e., an ordinary annuity). The fund balance will earn 8 percent interest which will be added to the fund at each year-end.

Required:

a. Prepare a fund accumulation schedule similar to Exhibit 11–7. Round to the nearest dollar and show computations.
b. Give the journal entry(s) at the end of the second year to record the increase in the fund.
c. Show how the $27,723 was computed.
d. Did the earnings on the fund increase the balance of the company's cash account? Explain.

E11–13. Jolly Corporation issued a $1,000 bond on January 1, 19A. The bond specified an interest rate of 8 percent payable at the end of each year. The bond matures at the end of 19C. It was sold at a market rate of 9 percent per year. In respect to the issuance of the bond, the following schedule was completed:

Date	Cash	Interest	Amortization	Balance
Jan. 1, 19A (issuance)				$ 975
End of Year A	$80	$88	$8	983
End of Year B	80	88	8	991
End of Year C	80	89	9	1,000

Required:

Respond to the following questions:

a. What was the issue price of the bond?
b. Did the bond sell at a discount or a premium? How much?
c. What amount of cash was paid each year for bond interest?
d. What amount of interest expense should be shown each year on the income statement?
e. What amount(s) should be shown on the balance sheet for bonds payable at each year-end (for Year C, show the balance just before retirement of the bond)?
f. What method of amortization was used?
g. Show how the following amounts were computed for Year B: (1) $80, (2) $88, (3) $8, and (4) $983.
h. Is the method of amortization used preferable? Explain why.

E11–14. Butle Company issued a $10,000, 11 percent, three-year bond on January 1, 19A. The bond interest is paid each December 31. The bond was sold to yield 10 percent (issue price, $10,249).

Required:

a. Complete a bond payment schedule.
b. Give the interest and amortization entry at the end of 19B.
c. Show how the $10,249 issue price was computed.

PROBLEMS/CASES

PART A

PC11–1. The financial statements of Stickney Corporation for 19A reflected the following:

Income Statement

Revenues	$200,000
Expenses	(139,000)
Interest expense	(1,000)
Pretax income	60,000
Income taxes (40%)	(24,000)
Net income	$ 36,000

Balance Sheet

Assets	$150,000
Liabilities (average interest rate, 10%)	$ 10,000
Common stock, par $10	100,000
Retained earnings	40,000
	$150,000

To demonstrate financial leverage, assume that Stickney Corporation during 19A had $60,000 liabilities (instead of $10,000) and common stock of $50,000 (5,000 shares) instead of $100,000 (10,000 shares). That is, more debt was used to finance the buisness.

Required:

a. Complete a table similar to the following to demonstrate the economic effects of financial leverage.

Item	Actual results for 19A	Results assuming an increase in debt of $50,000
a. Total debt		
b. Total assets		
c. Total stockholders' equity		
d. Interest expense (total @ 10%)		
e. Net income		
f. Return on total assets		
g. Earnings available to stockholders:		
(1) Amount		
(2) Per share		
(3) Return on stockholders' equity		

b. Write an explanation of the advantages and disadvantages of higher debt financing (i.e., higher leverage) in this particular situation.

PC11–2. On January 1, 19A, Beckwith Corporation sold and issued $100,000, 8 percent, five-year bonds. The bond interest is payable annually each December 31. Assume the bonds were sold under three separate and independent cases: Case A, at par; Case B, at 95; and Case C, at 105.

Required:

a. Complete a tabulation similar to the following for each separate case assuming straight-line amortization of discount and premium. Disregard income tax.

	At Start of 19A	At End of 19A	At End 19B	At End of 19C	At End of 19D	At End of 19E Prior to Payment of Principal	At End of 19E Payment of Principal
Case A—Sold at par (100): Pretax cash inflow	$	$	$	$	$	$	$
Pretax cash outflow							
Interest expense on income statement							
Net liability on balance sheet							
Case B—Sold at a discount (95): Pretax cash inflow							
Pretax cash outflow							
Interest expense on income statement							
Net liability on balance sheet							
Case C—Sold at a premium (105): Pretax cash inflow							
Pretax cash outflow							
Interest expense on income statement							
Net liability on balance sheet							

b. For each separate case, calculate each of the following:
    (1) Total pretax cash outflow.
    (2) Total pretax cash inflow.
    (3) Difference—net pretax cash outflow.
    (4) Total pretax interest expense.
c. (1) Explain why the net pretax cash outflows differ among the three cases.
    (2) For each case, explain why the net pretax cash outflow is the same amount as total interest expense.

PC11–3. Southwick Corporation sold a $200,000, 8 percent bond issue on January 1, 19A. The bonds pay interest each December 31, and will mature 10 years from January 1, 19A. For comparative study and analysis, assume three separate cases (show computations, assume straight-line amortization, and disregard income tax unless specifically required):

Case A—The bonds sold at par.
Case B—The bonds sold at 97.
Case C—The bonds sold at 103.

	Case A	Case B	Case C
1. Cash inflow at issue (sale) date			
2. Total cash outflow through maturity date . . .			
3. Difference—total interest expense			
Income statement for 19A:			
4. Bond interest expense, pretax			
Balance sheet at December 31, 19A:			
Long-term liabilities:			
5. Bonds payable, 8%			
6. Unamortized discount			
7. Unamortized premium			
8. Net liability			
9. Stated interest rate			
10. Total interest expense, net of income tax (40% tax rate)			

Required:

a. Complete a schedule similar to the one outlined above.
b. Give the journal entries for each case on January 1, 19A, and December 31, 19A (excluding closing entries).
c. For each case, explain why items 3, 4, and 10 of Requirement *(a)* are the same, or different.

PC11–4. Ward Company issued bonds with the following provisions:

Maturity value: $300,000.
Interest: 11% per annum payable semiannually each June 30 and December 31.
Terms: Bonds dated January 1, 19A, due five years from that date.

The annual accounting period for Ward ends December 31. The bonds were sold on January 1, 19A, at a 10 percent market rate.

Required:

a. Compute the issue (sale) price of the bonds (show computations).
b. Give the journal entry to record issuance of the bonds.
c. Give the journal entries at the following dates (assume straight-line amortization): June 30, 19A; December 31, 19A; and June 30, 19B.
d. How much interest expense should be reported on the income statement for 19A? Show how the liability related to the bonds would be reported on the December 31, 19A, balance sheet.

PC11–5. Hi-Risk Company issued $75,000 bonds, due in five years, at 11 percent interest. The bonds were dated January 1, 19A, and interest is payable each June 30 and December 31.

The bonds were sold on January 1, 19A, to yield 12 percent interest. The annual accounting period ends December 31.

Required:

a. Compute the issue (sale) price of the bonds (show computations).

b. Give the journal entry to record the issuance of the bonds on January 1, 19A.

c. Give the journal entry to record the first interest payment and amortization of discount on June 30, 19A. Assume straight-line amortization.

d. Give the amounts that should be reported on the 19A financial statements for:
    Interest expense.
    Bonds payable.
    Unamortized discount or premium.
    Net liability.

e. What would be the aftertax net interest cost for 19A (dollars and percent) assuming a 30 percent tax rate? Show computations.

PART B

PC11–6.   Raynard Corporation authorized the following bond issue:

> Bonds payable authorized ($1,000 bonds) $100,000
> Date printed on each bond . . . .   Jan. 1, 19A
> Maturity date (10 years) . . . .   Dec. 31, 19J
> Interest, 9% per year, payable each June 30 and
>   December 31.

During 19A, Raynard Corporation issued (sold) the following bonds:

			Market price (does not include any accrued interest)
Date	*Issuance (sale)*		
Jan. 1, 19A	#1	10 bonds	100
May 1, 19A	#2	20 bonds	94
Sept. 1, 19A	#3	30 bonds	106

Required:

a. Complete a schedule for Raynard Corporation similar to the following (show computations, round to the nearest dollar, and disregard income tax):

	Cash received			Cash disbursed		
Date	*#1*	*#2*	*#3*	*#1*	*#2*	*#3*
Jan. 1, 19A						
May 1, 19A						
June 30, 19A						
Sept. 1, 19A						
Dec. 31, 19A						

b. Give a separate journal entry to record each of the three issuances.

c. How much net cash interest was paid during 19A to the investors in each of the three issuances? Show computations.

PC11–7. Cody Corporation authorized a $300,000, 10-year bond issue dated July 1, 19A. The bonds pay 8 percent interest each June 30. The accounting period ends December 31. Assume the bonds were sold on August 1, 19A, under three different assumptions as follows:

Case A—Sold at par.
Case B—Sold at 98.
Case C—Sold at 102.

Required:

Complete a schedule for Cody Corporation similar to the following assuming straight-line amortization. Show computations.

	Case A par	Case B 98	Case C 102
1. Cash received at issuance (sale) date	$ _____	$ _____	$ _____
2. Cash received for accrued interest at issuance date	_____	_____	_____
3. Amount of premium or discount at issuance date	_____	_____	_____
4. Stated rate of interest (annual)	_____ %	_____ %	_____ %
5. Net cash interest paid during 19A	$ _____	$ _____	$ _____
6. Interest expense reported for 19A	_____	_____	_____
7. Bonds payable reported at end of 19A	_____	_____	_____
8. Unamortized premium or discount reported at end of 19A	_____	_____	_____
9. Net liability reported at end of 19A	_____	_____	_____
10. Interest payable reported at end of 19A	_____	_____	_____

PC11–8. In order to expand to a new region, Goode Manufacturing Company decided to construct a new plant and warehouse. It was decided that approximately 60 percent of the resources required would be obtained through a $600,000 bond issue. Accordingly, the company developed and approved a bond indenture with the following provisions:

Date of bonds .... Mar. 1, 19A, due in 10 years
Amount authorized ..... $600,000 (par amount)
Interest .... 10% per annum, payable 5% each Feb. 28 and Aug. 31

The annual accounting period ends on December 31. The bonds were issued (sold) on May 1, 19A, at 102.36.

Required:

a. How much cash was received by Goode on May 1, 19A?
b. What was the amount of the premium? Over how many months will it be amortized?
c. Complete the following tabulation (use straight-line amortization):

	Per month
Interest payment	$ _____
Premium amortization	$ _____
Interest expense	$ _____

d. Give journal entries, if any, at each of the following dates: May 1, 19A; August 31, 19A; December 31, 19A; January 1, 19B; and February 28, 19B.
e. In respect to the financial statements for December 31, 19A:
   (1) How much interest expense should be reported on the income statement?
   (2) Show how the liabilities related to the bonds should be reported on the balance sheet.

PC11–9. On January 1, 1970, Boston Corporation issued $500,000, 6 percent bonds due at the end of 20 years (December 31, 1989). The bonds specified semiannual interest payments on each June 30 and December 31. The bonds originally sold at par. Additionally, the bond indenture called for the establishment of a bond sinking fund to be accumulated over the last five years by making five equal annual deposits on each December 31, starting in 1985. Interest on the fund balance at 8 percent is to be added to the fund at year-end.

Required:

a. Give the journal entry for issuance of the bonds on January 1, 1970.
b. Give the journal entry for the semiannual interest payment on the bonds on June 30, 1985.
c. Give the journal entry on December 31, 1985, for the first $85,228 contribution of cash to the sinking fund. Show how this amount was computed.
d. Give the sinking fund entry at the end of 1986.
e. Prepare a fund accumulation schedule.
f. Give the journal entry to record retirement of the bonds at maturity assuming the total bond sinking fund accumulation is $500,000.

PC11–10. To obtain funds to acquire additional long-term assets, National Company approved the following bond indenture:

Maturity value authorized: $600,000 (in $1,000 denominations).
Interest: 8% per annum, payable 4% each May 31 and November 30.
Maturity: Ten years from June 1, 19A.
Bond sinking fund: Starting on July 1 of the eighth bond year, deposit $150,000 annually (three deposits) into a bond sinking fund under the control of Trustee X. Interest earned by the fund will be deposited in the fund. The bond sinking fund will be used only to retire the bonds at maturity.

The annual accounting period for National Company ends on December 31. The bonds were sold on August 1, 19A; for $625,700, that included two months' accrued interest (June 1 to July 31).

Required:

a. Give the journal entry to record the issuance of the bonds on August 1, 19A.
b. Give the journal entries at the following dates (assume straight-line amoritization):
   (1) First interest date.
   (2) End of first annual accounting period (19A).
   (3) Beginning of second accounting period (19B).
   (4) Second interest date.
c. In respect to the 19A financial statements.
   (1) How much interest expense would be reported on the 19A income statement?
   (2) Show how the liabilities related to the bonds would be reported on the December 31, 19A, balance sheet.

  d. Give the journal entry to record:
   (1) The first contribution to the sinking fund.
   (2) Interest earned on the sinking fund by December 31, bond Year 8, $6,000 (net of fund expenses).
  e. Give the journal entry to retire the bond issue at the end of the 10th bond year assuming the bond sinking fund has a balance of $510,000. (Note: The fund earnings rate varied from year to year.)

PC11–11. Foster Corporation issued bonds and received cash in full for the issue price. The bonds were dated and issued on January 1, 19A. The stated interest rate was payable at the end of each year. The bonds mature at the end of four years. In respect to the issuance of the bonds, the following schedule has been completed:

Date	Cash	Interest	Amortization	Balance
Jan. 1, 19A				$5,173
End of Year 19A	$350	$310	$40	5,133
End of Year 19B	350	308	42	5,091
End of Year 19C	350	305	45	5,046
End of Year 19D	350	304	46	5,000

Required:

 Respond to the following questions:
 a. What was the maturity amount of the bonds?
 b. How much cash was received at date of issuance (sale) of the bonds?
 c. Was there a premium or a discount? If so, which and how much?
 d. How much cash will be disbursed for interest each period and in total for the full life of the bond issue?
 e. What method of amortization is being used? Explain.
 f. What is the stated rate of interest?
 g. What is the yield rate of interest?
 h. Show how the following amounts for 19C were computed: (1) $350, (2) $305, (3) $45, and (4) $5,046.
 i. What amount of interest expense should be reported on the income statement each year?
 j. Show how the bonds should be reported on the balance sheet at the end of each year (show the last year immediately before retirement of the bonds).
 k. Why is the method of amortization being used preferable to other methods? When must it be used?

PC11–12. On December 31, 19F, Steady Company had bonds outstanding of $120,000, par (8 percent annual interest payable each December 31). The bonds will mature at the end of 19J. Anticipating the maturity date, the maturity amount, and some possible miscellaneous related costs, Steady Company decided to accumulate a bond sinking fund of $122,102 so that cash will be available to pay the bonds on maturity date. Steady will make five equal annual deposits on December 31, 19F, G, H, I, and J. The trustee will handle the fund and will increase its balance by 10 percent at each year-end starting in 19G.

Required:

a. Compute the amount of each of the five equal deposits that Steady Company must make to accumulate $122,102.
b. Give the journal entry to record the first deposit by Steady Company (December 31, 19F).
c. Prepare a fund accumulation schedule for the five annual deposits.
d. Give the journal entry that Steady Company should make on December 31, 19G.
e. Assume it is December 31, 19J.
   (1) Give the journal entry that Steady Company should make to record the payment of the bond principal.
   (2) What balance remains in the bond sinking fund? What dispositon should Steady Company make of this amount?

PC11–13. Early in 1981, J. C. Penney Company issued "zero coupon" bonds with a face (maturity value) of $400,000 due in 1989 (8 years after issuance). At the time the bonds were sold to the public, similar bonds paid a 15 percent effective (true) interest. An article in *Forbes* magazine (May 25, 1981) discussed the J. C. Penney bonds and stated: "It's easy to see why corporations like to sell bonds that don't pay interest. But why would anybody want to buy that kind of paper (bond)?"

Required:

a. Explain why an investor would buy a J. C. Penney bond with a zero interest rate. If investors could earn 15 percent on similar investments, how much should they be willing to pay for a J. C. Penney bond with a par value of $1,000 (due eight years after issuance)?
b. Assume that J. C. Penney sold the $400,000 bond issue on May 1, 1981, the first day of the term (life) of the bond issue. Give the journal entry to record the sale of the bonds for cash.
c. Assume that the accounting period for J. C. Penney ends on December 31 each year. Give the journal entry required on December 31, 1981, to record accrued interest expense. If none is required, state why.

PC11–14. Tumbleweed Corporation manufactures electronic equipment. Tumbleweed authorized bonds on January 1, 19A, with the following terms:

Maturity (par) value: $500,000.
Interest: 9% per annum payable each December 31.
Maturity date: December 31, 19E.

The bonds were sold at an effective interest rate of 13 percent. Tumbleweed received $429,674 when the bonds were issued on January 1, 19A.

Required:

a. Show how the bond issue price of $429,674 was determined. Give the entry to record this bond issue.
b. Assume that Tumbleweed used the straight-line approach to amortize the discount on the bond issue. Compute the following amounts for each year (19A–19E):
   (1) Cash payment for bond interest.
   (2) Bond interest expense.

        (3)   Bond interest expense as a percent of the net liability of the bonds at the beginning of each year.

   c. Assume that Tumbleweed used the effective-interest method to amortize the discount on the bond. Compute the amounts listed in Requirement *(b),* above.

   d. Which method should be used by Tumbleweed to amortize the bond discount?

C·H·A·P·T·E·R
12

Measuring and Reporting Owners' Equity

PURPOSE OF THIS CHAPTER

Owners' equity is defined as the excess of total assets over total liabilities. It is a residual amount that represents the **book value** of the owners' interest in the business enterprise. Because of the **reporting principle** (Exhibit 2–6) and certain legal differences, owners' equity appears somewhat differently on the balance sheet (and in the accounts) of sole proprietorships, partnerships, and corporations. Given the same set of transactions, however, the **total amount** of owners' equity on a given date would be the same (except for income tax effects) regardless of the type of business organization. The accounting entries and financial reporting for the three types of business organizations essentially are the same in all situations, **except for those entries that directly affect owners' equity.** This commonality exists because the underlying fundamental accounting concepts apply equally to each of the three types of business organizations.

This chapter discusses the accounting for, and reporting of, owners' equity. It focuses primarily on corporations because they constitute the most prominent type of accounting entity.

To accomplish the above purposes, the chapter is divided into two parts:

Part A—Stockholders' equity

Part B—Accounting for dividends and retained earnings and for unincorporated businesses

Supplement 12A—Participating dividend preferences on preferred stock

Supplement 12B—Accounting for owners' equity for sole proprietorships and partnerships

PART A—STOCKHOLDERS' EQUITY

NATURE OF A CORPORATION

A corporation is a separate legal entity, authorized by law, with certain rights and duties as if it were a distinct individual, although it is owned by a number of persons and perhaps other entities. Ownership in the corporation is evidenced by shares of capital stock. The life of a corporation is unaffected by changes in the group of individuals, or other entities, that own it.

In terms of volume of business, the corporation is the dominant type of business organization in the United States because the corporate form has three important advantages over the sole proprietorship and the partnership. First, the corporate form facilitates the bringing together of large amounts of funds through the sale of ownership interests (capital stock) to the public. Second, it facilitates the transfer of separate ownership interests because the shares can be transferred easily to others. Third, it provides the investor or stockholder with limited liability.[1]

In contrast to a sole proprietorship or a partnership, a corporation is recognized in law as a separate legal entity. Legally, as a distinct entity, the corporation enjoys a continuous existence separate and apart from its owners. It may own assets, incur liabilities, expand and contract in size, sue others, be sued, and enter into contracts independently of the stockholder owners.

STRUCTURE OF A CORPORATION

Ownership of a corporation is evidenced by shares of **capital stock** that are freely transferable without affecting the corporation. The owners of a corporation are known as **stockholders** or **shareholders.**

Each state has laws that govern the organization and operation of corporations within their boundaries. The provisions of these laws vary considerably among the states. The laws of each state establish the requirements that must be met to organize a corporation. To form a corporation, an **application for a charter** must be submitted to the appropriate state official. The application must specify the name of the corporation, the purpose (type of business), kinds and amounts of capital stock **authorized,** and a certain minimum amount of capital (resources) that must be invested by the owners at the date of organization. Most states require a minimum of three stockholders initially. Upon approval of the application, the state issues a **charter** (sometimes called the **articles of incorporation).** The governing body of a corporation is the **board of directors,** which is elected by the stockholders.

When a person acquires shares of capital stock, a **stock certificate** is received as evidence of an ownership interest in the corporation. The certificate designates the name of the stockholder, date of purchase, type of stock, number of shares

---

[1] In case of insolvency of a corporation, the creditors have recourse for their claims only to the assets of the corporation. Thus, the stockholders stand to lose, as a maximum, only their equity in the corporation. In contrast, in the case of a partnership or sole proprietorship, creditors have recourse to the personal assets of the owners if the assets of the business are insufficient to meet the outstanding debts of the business.

EXHIBIT 12–1   **Common stock certificate**

represented, and description of the characteristics of the stock. Exhibit 12–1 shows a stock certificate for 50 shares of common stock. On the back of the certificate are instructions and sections to be completed when the shares are sold or transferred to another party.

Stockholders, in the absence of other agreements, have the following basic rights:

1. Vote in stockholders' meeting (or by proxy) on major issues in respect to management of the corporation.[2]
2. Participate proportionately with other stockholders in distribution of profits of the corporation.
3. Share proportionately with other stockholders in the distribution of entity assets upon liquidation.

---

[2] A voting proxy is a written authority given by a stockholder that gives another party the right to vote the stockholders' shares in the annual meeting of the stockholders. Typically, proxies are solicited by, and given to, the president of the corporation.

EXHIBIT 12–2
Typical organizational structure of a corporation

STOCKHOLDERS
(owners of voting shares)

Elects (proxies)

Board of Directors
Internal (managers) and External (nonmanagers)

Appoints

PRESIDENT

Employs

| Vice President (Production) | Vice President (Marketing) | Vice President (Finance) | Vice President (Controller) |

4. Purchase shares of any additional new issues on a pro rata basis in order to maintain their percentage of ownership.

Stockholders exercise their control of a corporation by voting in the annual meeting of the stockholders. The usual organizational structure of a corporation is shown in Exhibit 12–2.

AUTHORIZED, ISSUED, AND OUTSTANDING CAPITAL STOCK

Accounting for, and reporting of, capital stock involves the terms: authorized, issued, and outstanding shares of capital stock. The corporate charter specifies the maximum number of shares of capital stock the corporation can issue; this maximum is called the **authorized** number of **shares.** Subsequent to the granting of the charter, the number of shares issued, and the number of shares outstanding are determined by the stock transactions of the corporation. Exhibit 12–3 defines and illustrates the five terms usually used in respect to corporate shares.

Typically, the corporate charter provides for (authorizes) a larger number of shares than the corporation expects to issue in the near future after its organization. This strategy provides future flexibility for the issuance of additional shares without amending the charter.

TYPES OF CAPITAL STOCK

The capital stock of a corporation may consist of only one kind of stock, which would be known as **common stock;** or it may consist of two kinds of stock—common stock (which must be issued) and **preferred stock.** Common stock may be viewed conveniently as the "usual" or "normal" stock of the corporation. In contrast, preferred stock (if issued) is distinguished because it grants

EXHIBIT 12–3
Authorized, issued,
and outstanding
shares

Definition	Illustration
Authorized number of shares: The **maximum** number of shares that can be issued as specified in the **charter** of the corporation.	Charter of Tye Corporation specifies "authorized capital stock, **100,000 shares,** par value $1 per share."
Issued number of shares: The total cumulative number of shares that has been issued to date by the corporation.	To date, Tye Corporation sold and issued **30,000** shares of its capital stock.
Unissued number of shares: The number of authorized shares that have never been issued to date.	Authorized shares .... 100,000 Issued shares .... 30,000 Unissued shares **70,000**
Subscribed number of shares: Shares of authorized stock sold on credit and not yet issued.	Tye Corporation sold 1,000 shares on credit; the shares will be issued when the sale price is collected in full. Subscribed shares = **1,000.**
Outstanding number of shares: The number of shares currently owned by stockholders; that is, the total (maximum) number of shares authorized minus the total number of unissued shares.	Tye Corporation: Authorized shares .... 100,000 Unissued shares .... 70,000 Outstanding shares **30,000***

* Observe that outstanding shares and issued shares are the same (i.e., 30,000 shares) in this situation. **Treasury stock** (i.e., shares that have been issued then subsequently repurchased by the issuing corporation) will be presented later. When treasury stock is held, the number of shares issued and the number outstanding will differ by the number of shares of treasury stock held (treasury stock is included in "issued" but not in "outstanding").

certain **preferences** that the common stock does not have. These preferences usually specify, as a minimum, that the preferred stockholders must receive their dividends **before** any dividends can be declared or paid to the common stockholders. Because of the important differences between common and preferred stock, they are identified separately in accounting and reporting (and on the stock exchanges).

Common stock

When only one class of stock is issued, it must be common. It always has voting rights and often is called the **residual equity** because it ranks **after** the preferred stock for dividends and assets distributed upon dissolution or liquidation of the corporation. Because common stock does not have a dividend rate comparable with those associated with preferred, it has the possibility of higher dividends (after the preferred dividends are paid) and increases in market value. The two primary classifications of common stock are par value and nopar value.

Par value and nopar value stock.   Many years ago, all capital stock had to specify a par value. Par value is a **nominal** value per share established for the stock in the charter of the corporation and is printed on the face of each stock certificate. Stock that is sold by the corporation to investors above par value is said to sell at a **premium;** whereas, stock sold below par is said to sell at a **discount.** In recent years, the laws of all states have been changed to forbid the initial sale of stock by the corporation to investors below par value.[3] Originally, the concept of par value was established as a protection to creditors and investors by specifying a "cushion" of assets that could not be impaired. Par value has no relationship to market value, and the original idea that it represented a financial cushion was ill-conceived. Today, par value, when specified, only serves to identify the stated or **legal capital** of the corporation (otherwise, it has no particular significance).

The par value concept proved to be ineffective in protecting either creditors or stockholders. For that reason, many states enacted legislation permitting **nopar value** stock. Nopar value common stock does not have an amount per share specified in the charter; therefore, it may be issued at any price without involving a **discount or premium.** Nopar value stock avoids giving the impression of a market value. When nopar stock is used by a corporation, the legal, or stated, capital is as defined by the state law.

In recent years, when par value stock is used, the par value typically is set at a very low amount (such as $1 per share) and the issuing (asking) price is set much higher (such as $10 per share). This arrangement reduces significantly the possibility of a discount.

The term **legal capital** is defined by the law of the state of incorporation. It varies among states; however, legal capital usually is viewed as the par value of the stock outstanding (in the case of par value stock), or in the case of nopar value stock, the stated value set by the company or the amount for which the stock was sold originally. We shall see later that legal capital usually cannot be used as the basis for dividends. The stock certificate shown in Exhibit 12–1 represents common stock, par $1.

Preferred stock

When stock other than common stock is issued, the additional classes are called **preferred stock.** Preferred stock has some characteristics that make it different from the common stock. The usual characteristics of preferred stock are:

1. Dividend preferences.
2. Conversion privileges.
3. Asset preferences.
4. Nonvoting specifications.

Preferred stock has both favorable and unfavorable characteristics.[4] For example, the nonvoting characteristic is an unfavorable characteristic. Preferred stock

---

[3] The discussions throughout this chapter in respect to the sale of capital stock refer to the **initial** sale of the stock by the corporation rather than to later sales between investors as is the common situation in the day-to-day transactions of the stock markets. Because the sale of stock by a corporation at a discount no longer is legal, no further discussion of it is included. The sale of stock among **individuals** is not recorded in the accounts of the corporation.

[4] A majority of corporations issue only common stock. Large corporations tend to have both common and preferred in their financial structures. Some large companies also issue more than one class of preferred stock in addition to the common stock.

may be nopar value, although typically it has a par value. For example, the charter of Tye Corporation may have specified "Authorized capital stock: nonvoting, 6 percent **preferred stock,** 10,000 shares, par value $10 per share" in addition to the common stock. In this situation, the annual preferred dividend preference would be 6 percent of par, or $.60 per share. In contrast, if the preferred stock is nopar value, the preferred dividend preference would be specified as $.60 per share.

A corporation may choose to issue more than one class of stock to (1) obtain favorable control arrangements from its own point of view, (2) issue stock without voting privileges, and (3) appeal to a wide range of investors with the special provisions of the preferred stock.

The dividend preferences of preferred stock take precedence over the common stock, up to a specified limit. Dividend preferences will be discussed and illustrated later in Part B of the chapter. The other features of preferred stock are explained below.

Convertible preferred stock. **Convertible preferred stock** provides preferred stockholders the option to exchange their preferred shares in return for shares of **common** stock of the corporation. The terms of the conversion will specify dates and a conversion ratio. To illustrate, a charter could read: "Each share of preferred stock, at the option of the shareholder, can be converted to two shares of the nopar common stock anytime after January 1, 19A."

Asset preferences of preferred stock. Two **asset preferences** almost always are specified on preferred stock. One is a preference price that the corporation must pay to the stockholders if the preferred stock is **callable.** The timing of the call is determined by the corporation. The call price almost always is higher than the par value. Upon call of the preferred stock, the preferred stockholders would receive cash equal to, but no more than, the asset preference of their stock before any distributions could be made to the common stockholders. To illustrate, in the above example (Tye Corporation), the asset preference could have been specified at $15 per share. At this preference rate, a holder of the preferred stock would be entitled to receive $15 per share upon "call" by the corporation.

The other asset preference on the preferred stock occurs when the corporation **dissolves** (e.g., in case of termination of operations). Preferred stock almost always has a specified preference amount per share that must be paid upon dissolution to the preferred stockholders before any assets can be distributed to the common shareholders. Usually, the preference amount also is the maximum that would be paid to the preferred stockholders.

Nonvoting specifications on preferred stock. **Nonvoting** preferred stock is customary, despite the fact that the nonvoting features is undesirable to the investors. This feature denies the preferred stockholder the right to vote at stockholder meetings. It is one method for obtaining capital without diluting the control of the common stockholders.

In summary, preferred stock is advantageous to the investor because of dividend, conversion, and asset preferences (to the extent that they are specified), but suffers from the disadvantages of nonvoting and upper dividend limits. In contrast, common stock is not constrained on dividend limits, asset limits, and voting rights (compared to preferred stock). In prosperous times for the corporation, commom stock is more attractive to investors than preferred stock. Preferred stock usually may be viewed as less risky than common stock because of the dividend, conversion, and asset preferences.

ACCOUNTING FOR, AND REPORTING OF, CAPITAL STOCK

Accounting for and reporting stockholders' equity is based upon a **concept of sources.** Under this concept, the owners' equity from different sources is recorded in different accounts and reported separately in the stockholders' equity section of the balance sheet. The three basic sources of stockholders' equity usually identified are:

1. **Contributed capital (often called paid-in capital)**—the amount invested by stockholders through the purchase of shares of stock from the corporation. Contributed capital is comprised of two distinct components: (a) stated capital—par or stated amounts derived from the sale and issuance of capital stock; and (b) additional contributed capital—amounts derived from the sale of stock in excess of par. This often is referred as additional **paid-in capital.**
2. **Retained earnings**—the **cumulative** amount of net income earned since organization of the corporation less the cumulative amount of dividends paid by the corporation since organization.
3. **Unrealized capital** (discussed in Chapter 13).

Sale and issuance of par value capital stock

When par value stock is sold for cash and issued, three accounts are affected: (1) cash is debited, (2) an appropriately designated contributed capital account for each type of stock is credited, and (3) any difference between the sale price and the par value of the stock is credited to a separate additional contributed capital account entitled "Contributed Capital in Excess of Par." The par value is recorded in a separate account because it represents legal capital.

The sale and issuance of par value common and preferred stock is illustrated in Exhibit 12–4. Observe in the first journal entry that the preferred and common accounts were credited for the **par value** of the shares sold, and the differences between the sale prices and the par values were credited to two capital in excess of par accounts. Tye Corporation recognized **two** different sources of stockholders' equity—preferred and common stock—and each source was subdivided between the par value and the excess received over par.[5]

Capital stock sold and issued for noncash assets and/or services

Often **noncash** considerations, such as buildings, land, machinery, and services (e.g., attorney fees), are received in payment for capital stock issued. In these cases, the assets received (or expenses incurred in the case of services) should be recorded by the issuing corporation at the **market value** of the stock issued at the date of the transaction in accordance with the **cost principle.** Alternatively,

---

[5] Contributed capital in excess of par sometimes is called premium on capital stock or paid-in capital in excess of par.

EXHIBIT 12–4
Sale and issuance
of par value
capital stock

Situation of Tye Corporation:

Authorized:
Preferred stock, 6 percent par $10; 10,000 shares.
Common stock, par $1, 100,000 shares.

Sale and issuance for cash:

Preferred stock, 1,000 shares @ $12.
Common stock, 30,000 shares @ $5.

Cash (1,000× $12) + (30,000 × $5)	162,000	
Preferred stock (1,000 × par $10)		10,000
Common stock (30,000 × par $1)		30,000
Contributed capital in excess of par, preferred		
[1,000 × ($12 − $10)]		2,000
Contributed capital in excess of par, common		
[30,000 × ($5 − $1)]		120,000

Sale and issuance for services:

Issued 100 shares of preferred stock for legal services when the stock was selling at $12.

Legal expense	1,200	
Preferred stock (100 × par $10)		1,000
Contributed capital in excess of par, preferred		
[100 × ($12 − $10)]		200

Reporting on the financial statements:

Balance sheet—stockholders' equity:
Contributed capital:

Preferred stock, 6%, par $10; authorized 10,000 shares,		
issued and outstanding, 1,100 shares	$ 11,000	
Common stock, par $1; authorized 100,000 shares, issued		
and outstanding, 30,000 shares	30,000	
Contributed capital in excess of par:		
Preferred stock	2,200	
Common stock	120,000	
Total contributed capital		$163,200
Retained earnings (illustrated later)		

Income statement:

Legal expense	$1,200

if the market value of the stock issued cannot be determined, then the market value of the consideration received should be used. To illustrate, assume Tye Corporation issued 100 shares of preferred stock for legal services when the stock was selling at $12 per share. The second journal entry given in Exhibit 12–4 records this transaction.

Reporting stockholders' equity

The **reporting principle** (Exhibit 2–6) requires that the major classifications of stockholders' equity be reported separately, viz: contributed (or paid-in) capital, retained earnings, and unrealized capital (discussed later). Also, the subdivisions of each of these major classifications must be reported.

Exhibit 12–4 illustrates the typical reporting of **contributed capital** and its subdivisions. Observe the clear separation of each type of stock and of par values and amounts in excess of par. Also, notice that the number of **shares** of each kind of stock authorized, issued, and outstanding are reported.

Sales and issuance of nopar capital stock

Nopar stock does not have a specific dollar amount designated in the charter of the corporation. However, the laws of all states specify how legal capital must be determined. There are two typical specifications, depending upon the particular state that issued the charter, that affect the way the sale and issuance of nopar stock is recorded, viz:

1. The corporation, in its bylaws, must specify a **stated** value per share as legal capital. This stated value is a substitute for par value.
2. The corporation must record the **total** proceeds received from each sale and issuance of nopar stock as legal capital.

Recall that **legal** capital is credited to the capital stock account (e.g., common or preferred stock) and any excess of sale price over legal capital is credited to a separate account (e.g., Contributed Capital in Excess of Stated Value, Nopar Common, or Preferred, Stock).

Exhibit 12–5 illustrates the sale and issuance of nopar capital stock.

EXHIBIT 12–5
Sale and issuance of nopar capital stock

Situation of Sun Corporation:

Authorized capital stock—common stock, **nopar,** 200,000 shares.
Issued and sold—60,000 shares @ $6 per share (cash).

Sale and issuance:

Case A—The state law requires that the corporation set a **stated** value per share to represent legal capital for nopar stock. The company's charter specified a stated value of $.50 per share.

Cash (60,000 × $6)	360,000	
Common stock, nopar (with stated value of $.50)		
(60,000 × $.50)		30,000
Contributed capital in excess of stated value		
60,000 × ($6.00 − $.50)		330,000

Case B—The state law requires that the total proceeds received be recorded as legal capital.

Cash	360,000	
Common stock, nopar		360,000

TREASURY STOCK

Treasury stock is a corporation's own capital stock that was sold, issued, **reacquired** subsequently and still held by the corporation. Treasury stock frequently is purchased for sound business reasons, such as to obtain shares needed for employee bonus plans, to influence the market price of the stock, to increase the earnings per share amount, or to have shares on hand for use in the acquisition

EXHIBIT 12–6
Accounting for, and reporting of, treasury stock

Situation of May Corporation on January 1, 19B:

MAY CORPORATION
Summarized Balance Sheet
January 1, 19B

Assets		Stockholders' Equity	
Cash	$ 30,000	Contributed capital:	
Other assets	70,000	Common stock, par $10, authorized 10,000 shares, issued 8,000 shares	$ 80,000
		Retained earnings	20,000
Total assets	$100,000	Total stockholders' equity	$100,000

Purchase of treasury stock:

On January 2, 19B, May Corporation purchased 300 of its own outstanding shares of common stock at $12 per share.

Treasury stock, common (300 shares @ $12 per share)	3,600	
Cash		3,600

(Note: This transaction reduces both assets and stockholders' equity by $3,600.)

Sale of treasury stock:

On February 15, 19B, May sold one third of the treasury stock at $13 per share.

Cash (100 shares @ $13)	1,300	
Treasury stock, common (100 shares @ cost, $12)		1,200
Contributed capital, treasury stock transactions		100

(Note: This transaction increases both assets and stockholders' equity by $1,300.)

Reporting treasury stock:

MAY CORPORATION*
Summarized Balance Sheet
February 15, 19B

Assets		Stockholders' Equity	
Cash	$27,700	Contributed capital:	
Other assets	70,000	Common stock, par $10, authorized 10,000 shares, issued 8,000, of which 200 shares are held as treasury stock	$ 80,000
		Contributed capital, treasury stock transactions	100
		Total contributed capital	80,100
		Retained earnings	20,000
		Total	100,100
		Less cost of treasury stock held	2,400
Total assets	$97,700	Total stockholders' equity	$ 97,700

* Reflects the additional effects of the two transactions given above.

of other companies. Treasury stock, while held by the issuing corporation, has no voting, dividend, or other stockholder rights.[6]

When a corporation purchases its own capital stock, the assets (usually cash) of the corporation and the stockholders' equity are reduced by equal amounts. When treasury stock is sold, the opposite effects occur. Purchases of treasury stock are recorded by debiting its cost to a stockholders' equity account called Treasury Stock (by type of stock) and crediting Cash. Because the Treasury Stock account has a debit balance, it often is referred to as a **negative** (or contra) stockholders' equity account. When treasury stock is sold, the Treasury Stock account is credited at cost and Cash is debited. Usually the purchase and sale prices of treasury stock are different, necessitating recognition of the difference in an appropriately designated **contributed capital** account in the entry to record the sale.[7]

Accounting for, and reporting of, treasury stock are illustrated in Exhibit 12–6. Observe in the first journal entry that the **Treasury Stock** account is debited for the **cost** of the treasury stock purchased ($3,600). The second journal entry credits the Treasury Stock for the **cost** of the 100 shares of treasury stock sold. A corporation is not permitted by GAAP to increase its income or retained earning by buying or selling its own stock. Therefore, in Exhibit 12–6, upon resale of the 100 shares of treasury stock, **contributed capital** was increased by $100, which was the difference between cost and sales price of the treasury shares sold [i.e., 100 shares × ($13 − $12)]. Observe that this difference was **not** recorded as a gain as would be done for the sale of an asset (such as investments in marketable securities). The basic accounting concept is that "gains or losses" on transactions involving a corporation's own stock are balance sheet **(stockholders' equity)** items and not income statement items. Therefore, the balance sheet of May Corporation, presented at the bottom of Exhibit 12-6, reports "Contributed capital, treasury stock transactions" of $100.

The Treasury Stock account never has a credit balance, although owners' equity accounts normally carry a credit balance. The balance in the Treasury Stock account reflects a **contraction** of stockholders' equity; thus, it is a **negative** equity account. The debit balance in the Treasury Stock account represents the acquisition **cost** of the treasury stock still held at the date of the balance sheet. Observe this deduction on the balance sheet at the bottom of Exhibit 12-6.[8] That balance sheet reports the number of shares as:

---

[6] The laws of most states impose certain restrictions on the amount of treasury stock a corporation can hold at any one time because the purchase of treasury stock is an avenue for taking resources out of the corporation by the owners (stockholders), which may jeopardize the rights of creditors. The law in some states limits the cost of treasury stock that can be purchased to the balance reflected in the Retained Earnings account.

[7] Two alternative approaches are used to account for treasury stock—the cost method and the par value method. We will limit our discussions to the cost method because it is less complex and used more widely. The par value method is discussed in most accounting texts at the intermediate level.

[8] Some persons argue that the debit balance in the Treasury Stock account should be reported on the balance sheet as an asset rather than as a reduction in stockholders' equity. This position is supported by the argument that the treasury stock could be sold for cash just as readily as the shares of other corporations. The argument is fallacious; all **unissued** stock of the corporation presumably also could be sold for cash, yet unissued shares never are considered to be an asset.

Classification	*Shares*
Authorized	10,000
Unissued	(2,000)
*Issued	8,000
Treasury shares	—(200)
* Outstanding	7,800

* Different by the number of treasury shares held.

The purchase and/or resale of treasury stock does not affect the number of shares of **unissued** (or issued) stock; however, the number of shares of **outstanding** stock is affected. The only difference between treasury stock and unissued stock is that treasury stock has been sold at least once and recorded in the accounts.

To illustrate the **resale** of treasury stock at a price **less than cost,** assume that an additional 50 shares of the treasury stock were resold by May Corporation on April 1, 19B, at $11 per share; that is, $1 per share below cost. The resulting entry would be:

April 1, 19B:

Cash	550	
Contributed capital, treasury stock transactions	50	
Treasury stock, common (50 shares)		600
Sold 50 shares of treasury stock at $11 per share; cost, $12 per share.		

Note that the difference between sale price and cost was debited to the same contributed capital account to which the difference in the preceding journal entry (Exhibit 12–6) was credited. Retained Earnings would be debited for some or all of the amount of the difference only if there were an insufficient credit balance in the account Contributed Capital, Treasury Stock Transactions.

PART B—ACCOUNTING FOR DIVIDENDS AND RETAINED EARNINGS AND UNINCORPORATED BUSINESSES

DIVIDENDS DEFINED

A **dividend is a distribution of cash (or other assets) or capital stock to stockholders by a corporation.** Dividends must be approved by the board of directors of the corporation (i.e., a dividend declaration) **before** they can be paid. The term **dividend,** without a qualifier, usually is understood to mean a **cash** dividend, which is the most common type. A dividend distribution of the corporation's own stock is called a **stock dividend.** Dividends usually are stated in terms of dollars per share, or as a percent of par value.

The declaration and payment of a **cash dividend** reduces the assets (cash) and the stockholders' equity (retained earnings) by the total amount of the dividend. Exhibit 12–7 illustrates the declaration and payment of a cash dividend.

EXHIBIT 12–7
Declaration and payment of a cash dividend

Situation prior to cash dividend (Box Corporation):

Cash	$ 20,000	
Remaining assets	135,000	
Liabilities	(35,000)	$120,000
Stockholders' equity:		
Preferred stock, 6%, par $20, shares outstanding, 2,000	$ 40,000	
Common stock, par $10, shares outstanding, 5,000	50,000	
Retained earnings	30,000	$120,000

Dividend declaration:

"On December 1, 19E, the Board of Directors of Box Corporation hereby declares an annual cash dividend of $2 per share on the common stock and 6 percent per share on the preferred stock to the stockholders on date of record, December 10, 19E, payable on December 30, 19E."

Journal entries:*

December 1, 19E:

Retained earnings (or Dividends declared which is closed to Retained earnings)	12,400	
Dividends payable (a current liability)		12,400

    Declaration of a cash dividend:
        Preferred stock (2,000 shares × par $20 × rate 6%) = $ 2,400.
        Common stock (5,000 shares × $2)   = 10,000.

December 30, 19E:

Dividends payable	12,400	
Cash		12,400

    Payment of dividend liability.

Effects of the cash dividend on the balance sheet:

Cash	$ 7,600	
Remaining assets	135,000	
Liabilities	(35,000)	$107,600
Stockholders' equity:		
Preferred stock	$ 40,000	
Common stock	50,000	
Retained earnings	17,600	$107,600

* These two entries could be combined into one journal entry on the date of payment, as a debit to Retained Earnings and a credit to Cash of $12,400 because they were in the same accounting year.

Observe that assets and stockholders' equity **both** were reduced by the amount of the cash dividend ($12,400).

DIVIDENDS FROM THE PERSPECTIVES OF THE INVESTOR AND THE ISSUER

An **investor** pays cash (and perhaps incurs some debt) to acquire shares of stock as an investment. The incentive for buying the shares is to earn a future economic return on the investment, usually in future cash inflows. The investor's future cash inflows from the stock investment are expected to come from two sources: (1) periodic cash inflows in the form of dividends on the shares and (2) a cash inflow at the time the stock is sold. The investor anticipates that the sum of the present values of these two cash inflows will be greater than the original investment in the shares. Cash dividends are considered by the investor as revenue, that is, the return **on** the investment. The other cash inflow, a return **of** the investment (from sale of the shares), usually result in a **realized gain or loss,** depending on whether the investor sells the shares above or below their acquisition price. The amounts and frequency of dividends paid by a corporation have an effect on the market price of the stock.

The primary objective of the issuing corporation is to earn income on the resources provided by the stockholders and creditors. The ability to attract and retain resources from present and potential stockholders (and creditors), in the long run, depends in good measure upon the income record of the company. The earnings of a corporation may be retained in the business for corporate expansion or paid to the stockholders as dividends. One of the significant decisions faced by the board of directors of a corporation is how much of the earnings should be retained and how much should be distributed to the stockholders as dividends each year.

Exhibit 12–7 demonstrated that a cash dividend reduces both assets (cash) and stockholders' equity (retained earnings). This fact suggests that there are
* two fundamental requirements for the payment of a cash dividend, viz:

1. **Sufficient retained earnings**—The corporation must have accumulated a sufficient amount of retained earnings to cover the amount of the dividend. State laws usually place restrictions on cash dividends. For example, the state laws often limit cash dividends to the balance in retained earnings. As a matter of financial policy, and to meet growth objectives, corporations seldom disburse more than 40 to 60 percent of the average net income amount as dividends.

2. **Sufficient cash**—The corporation must have access to cash sufficient to pay the dividend and, in addition, adequate cash to meet the continuing operating needs of the business. The mere fact that there is a large **credit** in the Retained Earnings account does not indicate sufficient cash to support a cash dividend. The cash generated in the past by earnings represented in the Retained Earnings account may have been expended to acquire inventory, purchase operational assets, and/or pay liabilities. Consequently, there is no necessary relationship between the balance of retained earnings and the balance of cash on any particular date (simply, retained earnings is not cash).

Exhibit 12–7 indicated a cash balance of $20,000 and a balance in retained earnings of $30,000. In this typical example, it appears that cash may be the constraining factor on dividends. Some companies overcome this cash constraint (at least temporarily) by borrowing cash to pay cash dividends. The balance in retained earnings is a more inflexible constraint because retained earnings cannot be borrowed.

DIVIDENDS ON PREFERRED STOCK

Recall that preferred stock provides certain rights that have precedence over the rights of common stock. The primary distinguishing characteristics of preferred stock are dividend preferences. The **dividend preferences** may be classified as follows:[9]

1. Current dividend preference.
2. Cumulative dividend preference.
3. Participating dividend preference.

Preferred stock may have one or a combination of these three dividend preferences. The charter and the stock certificates of the corporation must state specifically the distinctive features of the preferred stock.

Current dividend preference on preferred stock

Preferred stock always carries a **current dividend preference.** This annual preference assures the **preferred shareholders** that if any **current dividends** are declared, the current preferred dividend must be declared and paid before any dividends can be declared and paid on the common stock. When the current dividend preference is met (and no other preference is operative), dividends then can be paid to the common stockholders. The current dividend preference on par value preferred stock is a specified percent of the par value of the preferred stock.

Declared dividends must be **allocated** between the preferred and common stock. First, the preferences of the preferred stock are met, then the remainder of the total dividend is allocated to the common stock. Exhibit 12–8, Case A, illustrates the allocation of the **current dividend** preference under four different assumptions concerning the **total** amount of dividends to be paid.

Cumulative dividend preference on preferred stock

If preferred stock has the **cumulative preference,** it is called cumulative preferred stock. This preference means that if all or a part of the specified current dividend preference (6 percent in Exhibit 12–8) is not paid in full during a given year, the unpaid amount becomes **dividends in arrears.** Thus, when the preferred stock is cumulative, the amount of any preferred dividends in arrears must be paid before any common dividends can be paid. In this situation, the preferred stock in any one year cannot receive total dividends in excess of the current year dividend preference plus all dividends in arrears. Of course, if the preferred stock is **noncumulative,** dividends never can be in arrears. Therefore any dividends passed (i.e., not declared) are lost permanently by the preferred stockholders. Because preferred stockholders are unwilling to accept this unfavorable feature, preferred stock usually is cumulative.

The allocation of dividends between **cumulative** preferred stock and common

---

[9] A dividend preference does not mean that dividends will be paid automatically. Dividends are paid only when **formally declared** by the corporation's board of directors. Thus, the declaration of a dividend is discretionary. A typical dividend problem involves the allocation of a total amount of dividends declared between the preferred stock and common stock as illustrated in the next section.

EXHIBIT 12–8
Dividends on
preferred stock

Case A—Current dividend preference only:

Preferred stock outstanding, 6%, par $20; 2,000 shares = $40,000 par.
Common stock outstanding, par $10; 5,000 shares   = 50,000 par.

Allocation of dividends between preferred and common stock assuming
current dividend preference only:

Assumptions	Total dividends paid	Amount of dividend paid to stockholders of	
		6% preferred stock (2,000 shares @ $20 par = $40,000)*	Common stock (5,000 shares @ $10 par = $50,000)
No. 1	$ 1,000	$1,000	–0–
No. 2	2,000	2,000	–0–
No. 3	3,000	2,400	$ 600
No. 4	18,000	2,400	15,600

* Preferred dividend preference, $40,000 × .06 = $2,400; or 2,000 shares × $1.20.

Case B—Cumulative dividend preference:

Preferred and common stock outstanding—same as above. Dividends in
arrears for the two preceding years.

Allocation of dividends between preferred and common stock assuming
cumulative preferred stock:

Assumptions (dividends in arrears, 2 years)	Total dividends paid	Amount of dividend paid to stockholders of	
		6% preferred stock (2,000 shares @ $20 par = $40,000)*	Common stock (5,000 shares @ $10 par = $50,000)
No. 1	$ 2,400	$2,400	–0–
No. 2	7,200	7,200	–0–
No. 3	8,000	7,200	$ 800
No. 4	30,000	7,200	22,800

* Current dividend preference, $40,000 × .06 = $2,400; dividends in arrears
preference, $2,400 × 2 years = $4,800; and current dividend preference plus dividends
in arrears = $7,200.

stock is illustrated in Exhibit 12–8, Case B, under four different assumptions concerning the **total** amount of dividends to be paid. Observe that the dividends in arrears are paid first, next the current dividend preference is paid, and, finally, the remainer is paid to the common shareholders. Participating preferred stock dividends are discussed in more detail in Supplement 12A.

STOCK DIVIDENDS

Instead of declaring and paying a cash dividend, the board of directors may vote to declare and issue a stock dividend. A **stock dividend is a distribution of additional shares of a corporation's own capital stock on a pro rata basis to its stockholders at no cost.** Stock dividends usually consist of common stock issued to the holders of common stock. **Pro rata basis** means that each stockholder receives additional shares equal to the percentage of shares already held by the stockholder. To illustrate, if a shareholder owns 10 percent of the outstanding shares, that stockholder would receive 10 percent of any additional shares issued as a stock dividend. Therefore, a stock dividend does not change the proportionate ownership of any stockholder; it does not involve the distribution of any assets (e.g., cash or other assets) of the corporation to the stockholder; and it does not increase the **total** stockholders' equity of the issuing corporation. To illustrate, assume King Corporation has outstanding 100,000 shares of common stock, par $5, originally sold at $8 per share. The board of directors voted to declare and issue a 10 percent common stock dividend (i.e., 10,000 shares) when the market value of the common stock was $11 per share. The entry by King Corporation to record the declaration and issue of this stock dividend would be:[10]

```
Retained earnings (10,000 shares × $11) ..........................   110,000
   Common stock, par $5 (10,000 shares × $5) ..................            50,000
   Contributed capital in excess of par, common stock
      10,000 shares × ($11 − $5) ..............................            60,000
   Common stock dividend of 10 percent distributed when the market
   value per share was $11.
```

Observe in the above entry that **retained earnings** was **decreased** by $110,000 and that **contributed capital** (i.e., common stock and contributed capital in excess of par) was increased by $110,000; assets and liabilities were unaffected. Therefore, the stock dividend did **not** change total stockholders' equity—it only changed some of the balances of the accounts that comprise stockholders' equity. This process of transferring an amount from retained earnings to contributed (i.e., permanent) capital often is referred to as **capitalizing earnings** because it reduces the amount of retained earnings subject to future dividends.

After a stock dividend, each **stockholder** has the same **proportionate** ownership of the corporation as before, and no additional assets are received by the stockholders (only more shares to represent the same total value previously held). Because more shares now represent the same "value," the **market** price per share of the stock should drop proportionately.

Observe in the above illustration that the amount (for the stock dividend) transferred from Retained Earnings to Contributed Capital was the **current market value** of the shares issued as a stock dividend. Market value amount is considered appropriate when the stock dividend is "small"; that is, when it is less than 25 percent of the previously outstanding shares. In those cases where a stock dividend is "large" (i.e., more than 25 percent), some accountants believe that the amount transferred should be the total par value of the shares issued. Par value is the absolute **minimum** because stock cannot be issued at a discount. Market value

---

[10] Some accountants prefer to debit an account called Stock Dividends Distributed, which is closed to Retained Earnings at the end of the period. The effect is precisely the same.

is preferred by many accountants in all situations (it is the maximum) primarily because (1) it is the amount that would be credited to Contributed Capital if the stock were sold at the current market price and (2) it is the amount that would be debited to Retained Earnings for all other types of dividends.

Reasons for stock dividends

Stock dividends often serve useful purposes both from the viewpoint of the corporation and the individual stockholder. The two primary purposes of a stock dividend are:

1. **To maintain dividend consistency**—Many corporations prefer to declare dividends each year. In the case of a cash shortage, the dividend record may be maintained by issuing a stock dividend. Stock dividends tend to satisfy the demands of stockholders for continuing dividends and yet avoid the demand on cash. Also, a stock dividend is not considered as revenue to the stockholder for income tax purposes. Stockholders view stock dividends as quite different from cash dividends.

2. **To capitalize retained earnings**—A stock dividend is used to transfer retained earnings to permanent capital and thus remove such earnings from cash dividend availability. When a corporation consistently retains a substantial percent of its earnings for growth, the related funds are, more or less, invested permanently in long-term assets such as plant and other property. Therefore, it is considered realistic to transfer those accumulated earnings to permanent capital. A stock dividend is a convenient approach to capitalize retained earnings. This may be the fundamental reason why stock dividends often are distributed by profitable corporations that are expanding rapidly.

STOCK SPLITS

Stock splits are **not** dividends. However, we will digress for the moment to consider **stock splits** because they are *(a)* similar in some respects to a stock dividend, *(b)* often confused with a stock dividend, and *(c)* quite different from a stock dividend as to their internal impact upon the stockholders' equity accounts of the issuing corporation. In a stock split, the **total** number of authorized shares is increased by a specified amount, such as a two-for-one split. In this instance, each share held is called in, and two new shares are issued in its place. Typically, a stock split is accomplished by **reducing the par or stated value** per share of all authorized shares so that the **total** par value (in dollars) of all authorized shares is unchanged. For example, assume 1,000 shares of $20 par value stock were outstanding before a two-for-one split. This stock split would involve reducing the par value of each new share to $10 and the issuance of 2,000 shares of $10 par value stock. In contrast to a stock dividend, a stock split does **not** result in a transfer of retained earnings to contributed capital. No transfer is needed because the reduction in the par value per share compensates for the increase in the number of shares. The primary reason for a stock split is to **reduce the market price per share,** which tends to increase the market activity of the stock. Sometimes a corporation desires to **reduce** the number of shares outstanding.

One way to do this is to implement a **reverse** stock split. A stock dividend requires a journal entry while **a stock split does not require a journal entry.**

In both a stock dividend and a stock split the investor (i.e., stockholder) receives more shares of stock and does not disburse any additional assets for those additional shares.

The **comparative effects** of a stock dividend versus a stock split may be summarized as follows:

	Stockholders' equity		
	Before a stock dividend or split	After a 100 percent stock dividend	After a two-for-one stock split
Contributed capital:			
Number of shares outstanding	30,000	60,000	60,000
Par value per share	$ 10	$ 10	$ 5
Total par value outstanding	300,000	600,000	300,000
Retained earnings	650,000	350,000	650,000
Total stockholders' equity	950,000	950,000	950,000

DIVIDEND DATES

The preceding discussions assumed that a dividend was paid immediately after its declaration by the board of directors. Almost always, by necessity, there is a time lag between declaration and payment. For example, a typical dividend declaration is as follows:

> On November 20, 19B, the Board of Directors of XY Corporation hereby declares a $.50 per share cash dividend on the 200,000 shares of nopar common stock outstanding. The dividend will be paid to stockholders of record at December 15, 19B, on January 15, 19C.

This declaration specifies **three important dates:**

1. **Declaration date—November 20, 19B:** This is the date on which the board of directors officially approved the dividend. As soon as a public announcement of the declaration is made, legally it is irrevocable; therefore, a **dividend liability** immediately is created. Accordingly, on this date the **declaration** by XY Corporation would be recorded as follows:

November 20, 19B:

```
Retained earnings (or Dividends declared) .................  100,000
    Dividends payable ....................................           100,000
  Cash dividend declared: 200,000 shares × $.50 = $100,000.
```

The December 31, 19B, balance sheet would report **Dividends Payable as a current liability.**

2. **Date of record—December 15, 19B:** This date follows the declaration date, usually by about one month, as specified in the declaration. It is the date on which the corporation prepares the list of individuals owning the outstanding shares based on the **stockholder records.** The dividend is payable only to those names listed on the record date. Thus, share transfers between buyers and sellers reported to the corporation before this date result in the dividend being paid to the new owner. Changes reported **after** this date result in the dividend being paid to the old owner; the new owner will receive all subsequent dividends. No journal entry would be made on this date.

3. **Date of payment—January 15, 19C:** This is the date on which the **cash** is disbursed to pay the dividend liability. It follows the date of record as specified in the dividend announcement. The entry to record the cash disbursement by XY Corporation would be as follows:

January 15, 19C:

Dividends payable	100,000	
Cash		100,000
To pay the liability for a cash dividend declared and recorded on November 20, 19B.		

For instructional purposes this time lag customarily is disregarded because it does not pose any substantive issues. Also, when all of the three dates fall in the same accounting period, a single entry on the date of payment may be made in practice for purely practical reasons.

STOCKHOLDER RECORDS

A corporation must maintain a record of each stockholder. The record includes at least the name and address of each stockholder, number of shares purchased of each type of stock, certificate numbers, dates acquired, and the number of shares currently owned. Such a record is known as the **stockholders' subsidiary ledger.** The Capital Stock account serves as the **control account** in the general ledger for this subsidiary ledger. Sales of shares by a stockholder to others must be reported to the corporation so that new stock certificates can be issued and the stockholders' subsidiary ledger can be changed accordingly. Dividends are sent only to the names and addresses shown in the stockholders' subsidiary ledger on the date of record. Large corporations with thousands of stockholders usually pay an independent **stock transfer agent** to handle the transfer of shares, to issue new stock certificates, and to maintain the equivalent of a stockholders' subsidiary ledger.

A particularly important record that must be maintained by all corporations is called the **minute book.** This is an official record of the actions taken at all meetings of the board of directors and of the stockholders. The independent auditor is required to inspect the minute book as a part of the audit program. Frequently, it is introduced as evidence in lawsuits and in income tax litigation.

REPORTING RETAINED EARNINGS

The preceding chapters emphasized that the income statement reports two income amounts: (1) income before extraordinary items and (2) net income (i.e., after extraordinary items). Net income is closed to the Income Summary account, and net income is reflected on the statement of retained earnings. **Extraordinary items** are reported on the income statement. APB Opinion 30 (dated June 1973) defines **extraordinary items** as those transactions and events that meet two criteria; that is, to be classified as extraordinary, a gain or loss must be both (1) **unusual in nature for the business** and (2) **infrequent in occurrence.** Extraordinary items are set out separately on the income statement to enable statement users to focus on the usual and frequent results; that is, income **before** extraordinary items because it is more reflective of future earnings and cash inflow than is net income (i.e., after extraordinary items).

In several prior chapters we discussed and illustrated the statement of retained earnings. Although not a required statement, it almost always is presented to conform with the **reporting principle** (Exhibit 2–6). Because retained earnings is one of two basic components of stockholders' equity, users of financial statements require sufficient disclosures to understand the causes of changes in the amount of retained earnings. A typical statement of retained earnings is shown in Exhibit 12–9.

The statement of retained earnings shown in Exhibit 12–9 reports two items that have not been discussed: (1) prior period adjustments and (2) restrictions on retained earnings.

EXHIBIT 12–9
Statement of retained earnings

FERRARI CORPORATION
Statement of Retained Earnings
For the Year Ended December 31, 19C

Retained earnings balance, January 1, 19C		$226,000
Prior period adjustment:		
Deduct adjustment for correction of prior		
accounting error (net of income tax)		10,000
Balance as restated		216,000
Net income for 19C		34,000
Total		250,000
Deduct dividends declared in 19C:		
On preferred stock	$ 6,000	
On common stock	12,000	18,000
Retained earnings balance, December 31, 19C (see Note 5)		$232,000

Note 5. Restrictions on retained earnings; total, $137,400:
    a. Treasury stock—The corporation has treasury stock that cost $37,400. The state law requires that retained earnings equal to the cost of all treasury stock held be restricted from dividend availability.
    b. Bonds payable—The indenture requires that retained earnings be restricted in accordance with an agreed schedule. The schedule amounts for 19B and 19C total $100,000.

Prior period adjustments

This category of events is defined in FASB Statement 16, as follows:

> Items of profit and loss related to the following shall be accounted for and reported as prior period adjustments and excluded from the determination of net income for the current period:
>
> a) Correction of an error in the financial statements of a prior period and
> b) Adjustments that result from realization of income tax benefits of preacquisition operating loss carryforwards of purchased subsidiaries.[11]

Prior period adjustments must be reported on the statement of retained earnings, as an **adjustment of the beginning balance of retained earnings,** (not on the income statement). Prior period adjustments should be recorded in specially designated gain and loss accounts, which are closed at the end of the period **directly** to the Retained Earnings account. Examples of prior period adjustments would be corrections of **accounting errors** made in a prior period such as in depreciation, revenues, operational assets, liabilities, and expenses. Exhibit 12–9 illustrates reporting of a prior period adjustment.[12] Observe that prior period adjustments are defined and reported quite differently than extraordinary items.

Restrictions on retained earnings

Corporations frequently have restrictions on retained earnings. Basically, such a **restriction temporarily removes the restricted amount of retained earnings from availability for dividends.** When the restriction is removed, the amount that was restricted is available for dividends and other "uses" of retained earnings. Restrictions on retained earnings may be voluntary or involuntary. For example, the two restrictions reported on Exhibit 12–9 are considered involuntary; one was imposed by **law** (i.e., the treasury stock restriction) and the other was imposed by **contract.** On occasion, the management or the board of directors may voluntarily establish a restriction on retained earnings for expansion of the business; this restriction reduces the amount of retained earnings subject to dividends. The amount of retained earnings restricted for this purpose often is called "Retained earnings appropriated for earnings invested in plant and equipment." Of course, this restriction can be removed at anytime by the management or board of directors.

The **reporting principle** (Exhibit 2–6) requires that restrictions on retained earnings be reported on the financial statements or in a separate note to the financial statements. The approach most widely used is by note as illustrated in Exhibit 12–9.

A practice used widely in past years, but now used infrequently, was to set up a special retained earnings account for each appropriation. Such accounts, somewhat illogically, often were called reserves. To illustrate, a journal entry to establish a "reserve" for the restriction of retained earnings by Ferrari Corporation (Exhibit 12–9) would be:

---

[11] FASB Statement 16, "Prior Period Adjustments" (Stanford, Conn., 1977), par. 11.

[12] Discussion of the second category of prior period adjustments, which relates to certain income tax benefits due to loss carryforwards, is deferred to more advanced accounting courses.

Retained earnings 137,400
    Reserve for cost of treasury stock*   37,400
    Reserve for bonds payable   100,000
    * A much more descriptive title would be preferable, such as "Retained earnings appropriated equal to the cost of treasury stock held."

In preparing the statement of retained earnings, Ferrari Corporation would list the two "reserve" accounts on the statement of retained earnings, and Note 5 would be unnecessary. When the restrictions are removed, the above entry is reversed.

An appropriation (or restriction) of retained earnings is **not cash.** Observe in the above entries that cash was not affected; the **only** effect was to remove a specific amount of retained earnings from dividend availability. To set aside cash for a special purpose, cash is credited and a **fund** account (e.g., building construction fund) is debited. Such fund accounts are assets similar to a savings account. Thus, there is no necessary relationship between appropriations of retained earnings and cash.

ACCOUNTING AND REPORTING FOR UNINCORPORATED BUSINESSES

There are three basic forms of organization for profit-making entities: **corporations** (i.e., shares of stock owned by a number of stockholders), **sole proprietorships** (i.e., one owner), and **partnerships** (i.e., two or more owners). The fundamentals of accounting and reporting for unincorporated businesses are the same as for a corporation except for **owners' equity.** Typical account structures for the three basic forms of business organizations are outlined in Exhibit 12–10.

Accounting for sole proprietorships and partnerships is discussed and illustrated in Supplement 12B.

DEMONSTRATION CASE

(Try to resolve the requirements before proceding to the suggested solution that follows.)

This case focuses on the organization and operations for the first year of Shelly Corporation, which was organized on January 1, 19A, the date on which the charter was granted by the state. The laws of the state specify that the legal capital for nopar stock is the full sale amount. The corporation was organized by 10 local entrepreneurs for the purpose of operating a business to sell various operating supplies to hotels. The charter **authorized** the following capital stock:

Common stock, nopar value, 20,000 shares.
Preferred stock, 5 percent, $100 par value, 5,000 shares (cumulative, nonparticipating, nonconvertible, and nonvoting; liquidation value, $110).

EXHIBIT 12–10
**Comparative
account structures
among types of
business entities**

TYPICAL ACCOUNT STRUCTURE		
Corporation (stockholders' equity)	**Sole Proprietorship** (proprietor's equity)	**Partnership** (partners' equity)
Capital stock Contributed capital in excess of par	Doe, capital	Able, capital Baker, capital
Retained earnings	Not used	Not used
Dividends paid	Doe, drawings	Able, drawings Baker, drawings
Income summary (closed to Retained Earnings)	Income summary (closed to Doe, Capital)	Income summary (closed to Able, Capital and Baker, Capital)
Revenues, expenses, gains, and losses	Same	Same
Assets and liabilities	Same	Same

The following summarized transactions, selected from 19A, were completed on the dates indicated:

1. Jan. Sold a total of 7,500 shares of nopar common stock to the 10 entrepreneurs for cash at $52 per share. Credit the Nopar Common Stock account for the total sales amount.

2. Feb. Sold 1,890 shares of preferred stock at $102 per share; cash collected in full.

3. Mar. Purchased land for a store site and made full payment by issuing 100 shares of preferred stock. Early construction of the store is planned. Debit Land (store site). The preferred stock is selling at $102 per share.

4. Apr. Paid $1,980 cash for organization costs. Debit an intangible asset account entitled "Organization Cost."

5. May Issued 10 shares of preferred stock to A. B. Cain in full payment of legal services rendered in connection with organization of the corporation. Assume the preferred stock is selling regularly at $102 per share. Debit Organization Cost.

6. June Sold 500 shares of nopar common stock for cash to C. B. Abel at $54 per share.

7. July Purchased 100 shares of preferred stock that had been sold and issued earlier. The stockholder was moving to another state and "needed the money." Shelly Corporation paid the stockholder $104 per share.

8. Aug.   Sold 20 shares of the preferred treasury stock at $105 per share.
9. Dec. 31   Purchased equipment at a cost of $600,000; paid cash. No deprecia-
               tion expense should be recorded in 19A.
10. Dec. 31   Borrowed $20,000 cash from the City Bank on a one-year, interest-
               bearing note. Interest is payable at a 12 percent rate at maturity.
11. Dec. 31   Gross revenues for the year amounted to $129,300; expenses, in-
               cluding corporation income tax but excluding amortization of orga-
               nization costs, amounted to $98,000. Assume, for simplicity, that
               these summarized revenue and expense transactions were paid in
               cash. Because the equipment and the bank-loan transactions were
               on December 31, no related adjusting entries at the end of 19A
               are needed.
12. Dec. 31   Shelly Corporation decided that a "reasonable" amortization period
               for organization costs, starting as of January 1, 19A, would be
               10 years. This intangible asset must be amortized to expense. Give
               the required adjusting entry for 19A.

Required:

a. Give appropriate journal entries, with a brief explanation for each of the
   above transactions.
b. Give appropriate closing entries at December 31, 19A.
c. Prepare a balance sheet for Shelly Corporation at December 31, 19A. Emphasize full disclosure of stockholders' equity.

Suggested solution

Requirement a. Journal entries:

1. January 19A:

Cash	390,000	
Nopar common stock (7,500 shares)		390,000
Sale of nopar common stock ($52 × 7,500 shares = $390,000).		

2. February 19A:

Cash	192,780	
Preferred stock, 5 percent, par $100 (1,890 shares)		189,000
Contributed capital in excess of par, preferred		
stock [1,890 shares × ($102 − $100)]		3,780
Sale of preferred stock ($102 × 1,890 shares = $192,780).		

3. March 19A:

```
Land (store site) .......................................   10,200
    Preferred stock, 5 percent, par $100 (100 shares) .........          10,000
    Contributed capital in excess of par, preferred stock......             200
Purchased land for future store site; paid in full by issuance
of 100 shares of preferred stock. The market value is, $102
× 100 shares = $10,200.
```

4. April 19A:

```
Organization cost .......................................    1,980
    Cash ................................................             1,980
Paid organization cost.
```

5. May 19A:

```
Organization cost .......................................    1,020
    Preferred stock, 5 percent, par $100 (10 shares) ..........           1,000
    Contributed capital in excess of par, preferred stock......              20
Organization cost (legal services) paid by issuance of 10 shares
of preferred stock. The implied market value is, $102 × 10
shares = $1,020.
```

6. June 19A:

```
Cash ...................................................   27,000
    Nopar common stock (500 shares) ....................            27,000
Sold 500 shares of the nopar common stock ($54 × 500 shares
= $27,000).
```

7. July 19A:

```
Treasury stock, preferred (100 shares at $104) ..............   10,400
    Cash ................................................            10,400
Purchased 100 shares of preferred treasury stock ($104 × 100
shares = $10,400).
```

8. August 19A:

```
Cash (20 shares at $105) ....................................  2,100
    Treasury stock, preferred (20 shares at $104) ...........        2,080
    Contributed capital from treasury stock transactions .....           20
Sold 20 shares of the preferred treasury stock at $105.
```

9. December 31, 19A:

```
Equipment ..............................................  600,000
    Cash ..............................................          600,000
Purchased equipment.
```

10. December 31, 19A:

```
Cash ...................................................  20,000
    Note payable ......................................          20,000
Borrowed on one-year, 12 percent, interest-bearing note.
```

11. December 31, 19A:

```
Cash ...................................................  129,300
    Revenues ..........................................          129,300

Expenses ..............................................  98,000
    Cash ..............................................           98,000
To record summarized revenues and expenses.
```

12. December 31, 19A:

```
Expenses ..............................................  300
    Organization cost .................................          300
Adjusting entry to amortize organization cost for one year
($1,980 + $1,020) ÷ 10 years = $300.
```

Requirement b. Closing entries:

13. December 31, 19A:

Revenues	129,300	
Income summary		129,300
Income summary	98,300	
Expenses ($98,000 + $300)		98,300
Income summary	31,000	
Retained earnings		31,000
($129,300 − $98,300 = $31,000).		

Requirement c:

SHELLY CORPORATION
Balance Sheet
At December 31, 19A

Assets

Current assets:		
Cash		$ 50,800
Tangible assets:		
Land	$ 10,200	
Equipment (no depreciation assumed in the problem)	600,000	610,200
Intangible assets:		
Organization cost (cost, $3,000 less amortization, $300)		2,700
Total assets		$663,700

Liabilities

Current liabilities:		
Note payable, 12%		$ 20,000

Stockholders' Equity

Contributed capital:		
Preferred stock, 5%, par value $100, authorized 5,000 shares, issued 2,000 shares of which 80 shares are held as treasury stock	$200,000	
Common stock, nopar value, authorized 20,000 shares, issued and outstanding 8,000 shares	417,000	
Contributed capital in excess of par, preferred stock	4,000	
Contributed capital from treasury stock transactions	20	
Total contributed capital	621,020	
Retained earnings	31,000	
Total	652,020	
Less cost of preferred treasury stock held (80 shares)	8,320	
Total stockholders' equity		643,700
Total liabilities and stockholders' equity		$663,700

SUMMARY OF CHAPTER

This chapter discussed accounting for and reporting of owners' equity for corporations. Sole proprietorships and partnerships are discussed in Supplement 12B. With the exception of owners' equity, the accounting and reporting basically is unaffected by the type of business organization. Accounting for owners' equity is based upon the concept of **source:** each specific source of owners' equity should be accounted for and reported separately. The two basic sources of owners' equity for a corporation are contributed capital and retained earnings. Separate accounts are maintained for each type of capital stock and contributed capital.

The earnings of a corporation that are not retained in the business for growth and expansion are distributed to the stockholders by means of dividends. Dividends are paid only when formally declared by the board of directors of the corporation. A cash dividend results in a decrease in assets (cash) and a commensurate decrease in stockholders' equity (retained earnings). In contrast, a stock dividend does not change assets, liabilities, or total stockholders' equity. A stock dividend results in a transfer of retained earnings to the permanent or contributed capital of the corporation by the amount of the stock dividend (a stock dividend affects only certain account balances within stockholders' equity). A stock split affects only the par value of the stock and the number of shares outstanding; the individual equity account balances are not changed. Frequently a corporation purchases its own stock in the marketplace. Such stock, previously sold and issued by the corporation and subsequently reacquired, is known as **treasury stock** as long as it is held by the issuing corporation. The purchase of treasury stock is viewed as a contraction of corporate capital, and the subsequent resale of the treasury stock is viewed as an expansion of corporate capital.

SUPPLEMENT 12A—PARTICIPATING DIVIDEND PREFERENCE ON PREFERRED STOCK

Preferred stock may be nonparticipating, fully participating, or partially participating. Participation relates to the dividends that can be paid on preferred stock **after** dividends in arrears and **after** the current dividend preference.

Most preferred stock is **nonparticipating,** as illustrated in Exhibit 12–8. Preferred stock that is **participating** may be either noncumulative or cumulative.

Fully participating and **noncumulative** preferred stock receives a first priority for the current dividend preference; then a matching proportionate amount is allocated to the common stock; and finally any remaining balance of the total dividend is allocated on a proportionate basis to the preferred and common stock as illustrated in Exhibit 12–11, Case A.

Fully participating and **cumulative** preferred stock receives a first priority on both dividends in **arrears** and the current dividend preference. After those preferences are satisfied, a proportionate amount is allocated to the common stock; and finally, any remaining balance of total dividends to be paid is allocated on a proportionate basis to the preferred and common stock as illustrated in Exhibit 12–11, Case B.

EXHIBIT 12–11   Dividends on participating preferred stock

Situation (Box Corporation; refer to Exhibit 12–7):

Preferred stock, 6 percent, par $20; shares outstanding, 2,000 = $40,000.
Common stock, par $10, shares outstanding, 5,000 = $50,000.
Dividends in arrears for the two previous years.

Allocation of dividends between preferred and common stock assuming fully participating:

	Amount of dividends paid		
Assumptions *(dividends in arrears,* *two years)*	*6 percent preferred* *stock* *(total par, $40,000)*	*Common stock* *(total par, $50,000)*	*Total dividends* *paid*
Case A—Preferred stock is fully participating and noncumulative (two years in arrears). Total dividends paid, $7,200:			
Current dividend ($40,000 × .06)	$ 2,400		$ 2,400
Equivalent amount to common ($50,000 × .06)		$3,000	3,000
Subtotal			5,400
Full participation—balance allocated in ratio of par values:			
($40,000/$90,000) × ($7,200 − $5,400)	800		800
($50,000/$90,000)× ($7,200 − $5,400)		1,000	1,000
Totals	$ 3,200	$4,000	$ 7,200
Case B—Preferred stock is fully participating and cumulative (two years in arrears). Total dividends paid, $16,500:			
Arrears ($2,400 × 2 years)	$ 4,800		$ 4,800
Current preference ($40,000 × .06)	2,400		2,400
Equivalent amount to common ($50,000 × .06)		$3,000	3,000
Subtotal			10,200
Full participation—balance allocated in ratio of par:			
($40,000/$90,000) × ($16,500 − $10,200)	2,800		2,800
($50,000/$90,000) × ($16,500 − $10,200)		3,500	3,500
Totals	$10,000	$6,500	$16,500

Partially participating preferred stock essentially is the same as fully participating, except that the participating preference above the current dividend rate is limited to a stated percent of par. For example, the corporate charter may read, "and partially participating only up to an additional two percent." Fully participating and partially participating preferred stock preferences are rare.[13]

SUPPLEMENT 12B—ACCOUNTING FOR OWNERS' EQUITY FOR SOLE PROPRIETORSHIPS AND PARTNERSHIPS

A sole proprietorship is an unincorporated business owned by one person. The only owner's equity accounts needed are (1) a capital account for the proprietor

---

[13] Textbooks for more advanced courses in accounting contain additional discussion and illustrations of the participating features and the payment of a dividend in assets other than cash, such as property and stock of other corporations being held as an investment.

(for example, J. Doe, Capital; or J. Doe, Owner's Equity), and (2) a drawing (or withdrawal) account for the proprietor (for example, J. Doe, Drawings; or J. Doe, Withdrawals). The **capital account** of a sole proprietorship is used to record investments by the owner and to accumulate the periodic income or loss. Thus, the **Income Summary** account is closed to the capital account at the end of each accounting period. The **drawing account** is used to record withdrawals of cash or other assets by the owner from the business. The drawing account is closed to the capital account at the end of each accounting period; thus, the capital account cumulatively reflects all investments by the owner, plus all earnings of the entity, less all withdrawals of resources from the entity by the owner. In most respects, the accounting for a sole proprietorship is the same as for a corporation.

Exhibit 12–12 presents the recording of selected transactions for 19A and the owner's equity section of the balance sheet of Doe Retail Store to illustrate the accounting for and reporting of **owner's equity** for a sole proprietorship.[14]

There are two additional differences between accounting for corporations and sole proprietorships. A sole proprietorship, as a business entity, does not pay income taxes. Therefore, the financial statements of a sole proprietorship will not reflect income tax expense or income taxes payable. The net income of a sole proprietorship must be included on the **personal** income tax return of the owner. Also, because an employer/employee contractual relationship cannot exist with only one party involved, a "salary" to the owner is not recognized as an expense of a sole proprietorship. The salary of the owner is accounted for as a distribution of profits (i.e., a withdrawal).

Owners' equity for a partnership

The Uniform Partnership Act, which has been adopted by most states, defines a partnership as "an association of two or more persons to carry on as co-owners of a business for profit." The partnership form of business is used by small businesses and professionals, such as accountants, doctors, and lawyers. A partnership is formed by two or more persons reaching mutual agreement as to the terms of the partnership. The law does not require an application for a charter as in the case of a corporation. The agreement between the partners constitutes a **partnership contract** that should be in writing. The partnership contract or agreement should specify such matters as division of periodic income, management responsibilities, transfer or sale of partnership interests, disposition of assets upon liquidation, and procedures to be followed in case of the death of a partner. If the partnership agreement does not specify on these matters, the laws of the resident state will be binding. The primary advantages of a partnerships are (1) ease of formation, (2) complete control by the partners, and (3) no income taxes on the business itself. The primary disadvantage is the unlimited liability of each partner for the liabilities of the partnership.

As with a sole proprietorship, accounting for a partnership follows the same underlying fundamentals of accounting as any other form of business organization,

[14] Alternatively, the balance sheet may reflect only "J. Doe, capital, December 31, 19A, $156,000," with a supplemental or supporting **statement of owner's equity** that would be the same as shown in the exhibit.

EXHIBIT 12–12
Accounting and
reporting of owner's
equity for a sole
proprietorship

Selected entries during 19A:

January 1, 19A:

J. Doe started a retail store by investing $150,000 of personal savings. The journal entry for the business would be as follows:

Cash	150,000	
J. Doe, capital		150,000
Investment by owner.		

During 19A:

Each month during the year, Doe withdrew $1,000 cash from the business for personal living costs. Accordingly, each month the following journal entry was made:

J. Doe, drawings	1,000	
Cash		1,000
Withdrawal of cash by owner for personal use.		

Note: At December 31, 19A, after the last withdrawal, the drawings account will reflect a debit balance of $12,000.

December 31, 19A:

Usual journal entries for the year, including adjusting and closing entries for the revenue and expense accounts, resulted in an $18,000 **credit balance** in the Income Summary account (i.e., $18,000 net income). The next closing entry will be:

Income summary	18,000	
J. Doe, capital		18,000
Closing entry to transfer net income for the year to the owner's equity account.		

December 31, 19A:

The journal entry required on this date to close the drawings account would be:

J. Doe, capital	12,000	
J. Doe, drawings		12,000
Closing entry to transfer drawings for the year to the capital account.		

Balance sheet December 31, 19A (partial):

Owner's Equity

J. Doe, capital, January 1, 19A	$150,000	
Add: Net income for 19A	18,000	
Total	168,000	
Less: Withdrawals for 19A	12,000	
J. Doe, capital December 31, 19A		$156,000

---

except for those entries that directly affect owners' equity. Accounting for partners' equity follows the same pattern as illustrated earlier for a sole proprietorship, except that separate partner capital and drawings accounts must be established for **each** partner. Investments by each partner are credited to separate capital accounts. Withdrawals of cash and other resources from the partnership by each partner are debited to the respective drawings accounts. The net income for a partnership is divided between the partners in the **profit ratio** specified in the partnership contract. The Income Summary account is closed to the respective partner capital accounts in accordance with the distribution of income. The respective drawings accounts also are closed to the partner capital accounts. Therefore, after the closing process, the capital account of each partner cumulatively reflects all investments of the individual partner, plus the partner's share of all partnership earnings, less all withdrawals by the partner.

Exhibit 12–13 presents selected 19A journal entries and partial financial statements of AB Partnership to illustrate the accounting for and reporting of the distribution of income and partners' equity.

The financial statements of a partnership follow the same format as for a corporation, except (1) the income statement includes an additional section entitled "Distribution of net income," (2) the partners' equity section of the balance sheet is detailed for each partner in conformity with the reporting principle, as illustrated

EXHIBIT 12–13
Accounting for and reporting of partners' equity

Selected entries during 19A:

January 1, 19A:

AB Partnership was organized by A. Able and B. Baker on this date. Able contributed $60,000 and Baker $40,000 cash in the partnership and agreed to divide net income (and net loss) 60 percent and 40 percent, respectively. The journal entry for the business to record the investment would be:

Cash	100,000	
A. Able, capital		60,000
B. Baker, capital		40,000
Investment to initiate a partnership.		

During 19A:

It was agreed that in lieu of salaries, Able would withdraw $1,000 and Baker $650 per month in cash. Accordingly, **each month** the following journal entry for the withdrawals was made:

A. Able, drawings	1,000	
B. Baker, drawings	650	
Cash		1,650
Withdrawal of cash by partners for personal use.		

December 31, 19A:

Assume the normal closing entries for the revenue and expense accounts resulted in a $30,000 **credit balance** in the Income Summary account (i.e., $30,000 net income). The next closing entry would be:

Income summary	30,000	
A. Able, capital		18,000
B. Baker, capital		12,000

Closing entry to transfer net income to the respective capital accounts. Net income divided as follows:

A. Able	$30,000 × .60 = $18,000
B. Baker	$30,000 × .40 = 12,000
Total	$30,000

EXHIBIT 12–13
(concluded)

December 31, 19A:

The journal entry required to close the drawings accounts would be:

A. Able, capital	12,000	
B. Baker, capital	7,800	
A. Able, drawings		12,000
B. Baker, drawings		7,800

Closing entry to transfer drawings for the year to the respective capital accounts.

After the closing entries the partners' accounts would reflect the following balances:

Income summary	–0–
A. Able, drawings	–0–
B. Baker, drawings.....	–0–
A. Able, capital	$66,000
B. Baker, capital	44,200

Reporting partners' distribution of net income and partners' equity:

Income statement for the year ended December 31, 19A:

Net income	$ 30,000

Distribution of net income:	
A. Able (60%)	$18,000
B. Baker (40%)	12,000
	$30,000

Balance sheet December 31, 19A:
Partners' Equity

A. Able, capital	$66,000	
B. Baker, capital	44,200	
Total partners' equity		$110,200

A separate statement of partners' capital similar to the following customarily is prepared to supplement the balance sheet:

AB PARTNERSHIP
Statement of Partners' Capital
For the Year Ended December 31, 19A

	A. Able	B. Baker	Total
Investment, January 1, 19A	$60,000	$40,000	$100,000
Add: Additional investments during the year	–0–	–0–	–0–
Net income for the year.............................	18,000	12,000	30,000
Totals..	78,000	52,000	130,000
Less: Drawings during the year	12,000	7,800	19,800
Partners' equity, December 31, 19A	$66,000	$44,200	$110,200

in Exhibit 12–13, and (3) partnerships, as an entity do not pay income taxes (each partner must report his or her share of the partnership profits on the individual tax return); therefore, income tax expense and income taxes payable will not be recorded, and (4) salaries paid to partners are not recorded as expense but are treated as a distribution of earnings (i.e., withdrawals).

IMPORTANT TERMS DEFINED IN THIS CHAPTER

Terms (alphabetically)	*Key words in definitions of important terms used in chapter*	*Page reference*
Authorized shares	Maximum number of shares of the corporation that can be issued as specified in the charter.	551
Charter of a corporation	The legal articles of incorporation by the state that creates a corporation; specifies purpose and capital.	549
Common stock	The basic, normal, voting stock issued by a corporation; not preferred stock; residual equity.	552
Convertible preferred stock	Preferred stock that is convertible, at the option of the holder, to common stock.	554
Cumulative dividend preference	Preferred stock preference that dividends not declared for a particular year cumulate as a subsequent preference.	563
Current dividend preference	The basic dividend preference on preferred stock for a particular year.	563
Dividend dates:		
Declaration	Date dividend declared; entry for cash dividend; dividends payable.	567
Record	Date on which the stockholders are individually indentified to receive a declared dividend.	568
Payment	Date on which a cash dividend is paid to the stockholders of record; cash is disbursed.	568
Dividends in arrears	Dividends on cumulative preferred stock that have not been declared in prior years.	563
Issued shares	Total shares of stock that have been issued; shares outstanding plus treasury shares held.	552
Legal or stated capital	Defined by state law; usually par value; provides a "cushion" for creditors; cannot be used for dividends.	553
Minute book	An official record of the actions of the board of directors of a corporation.	568
No par value stock	Shares of capital stock that have no par value specified in the corporate charter.	552
Outstanding shares	Shares of stock, in total, that are owned by stockholders on any particular date.	552
Par value	Nominal value per share of capital stock; specified in the charter; basis for legal capital.	552
Partnership	An unincorporated business owned by two or more persons.	571
Preferred stock	Shares of stock that have specified rights over the common stock.	553
Prior period adjustments	Amounts debited or credited directly to retained earnings resulting from correction of accounting errors.	570
Restrictions on retained earnings	Temporay removal of some or all of the balance of retained earnings from dividend availability.	570
Sole proprietorship	An unincorporated business owned by only one person (one owner).	571
Stock certificate	Evidence of the number of shares of stock held by an investor; ownership interest.	549
Stock dividends	Distribution of additional shares of stock to current stockholders on a proportional basis at no cost; decreases retained earnings.	564
Stock splits	The total number of authorized shares are increased by a specified ratio; issued at no cost; does not change proportional ownership of each stockholder; does not decrease retained earnings.	566

Terms (alphabetically)	Key words in definitions of important terms used in chapter	Page reference
Stock transfer agent	An individual or organization appointed by a corporation to transfer shares and maintain stockholders' records.	568
Stockholders' subsidiary ledger	A record, usually maintained by a stock transfer agent, of the names, addresses, and shares owned, of all of the stockholders.	568
Treasury stock	A corporation's own stock that has been issued, then reacquired and still held by that corporation.	557
Unissued shares	Shares of a corporation's stock that have never been issued.	552

QUESTIONS FOR DISCUSSION

PART A

1. Define a corporation and cite its primary advantages.

2. What is the charter of a corporation?

3. Briefly explain each of the following terms: *(a)* authorized capital stock, *(b)* issued capital stock, *(c)* unissued capital stock, and *(d)* outstanding capital stock.

4. Briefly distinguish between common stock and preferred stock.

5. Briefly explain the distinction between par value stock and nopar value capital stock.

6. What are the usual characteristics of preferred stock?

7. What are the two basic sources of stockholders' equity? Explain them briefly.

8. Owners' equity is accounted for by source. Explain what is meant by source.

9. Define treasury stock. Why do corporations acquire treasury stock?

10. How is treasury stock reported on the balance sheet? How is the "gain or loss" on treasury stock which has been sold reported on the financial statements?

PART B

11. What are the two basic requirements to support a cash dividend? What are the effects of a cash dividend on assets and stockholders' equity?

12. Distinguish between cumulative and noncumulative preferred stock.

13. Define a stock dividend. In what major respects does it differ from a cash dividend?

14. What are the primary purposes in issuing a stock dividend?

15. Identify and briefly explain the three important dates in respect to dividends.

16. Define retained earnings. What are the primary components of retained earnings at the end of each period?

17. Define prior period adjustments. How are they reported?

18. Explain what is meant by restrictions on retained earnings.

EXERCISES

PART A

E12–1. Fox Corporation was organized in 19A for the purpose of operating an engineering service business. The charter authorized the following capital stock: common stock, par value $5 per share, 10,000 shares. During the first year, the following selected transactions were completed:

1. Sold and issued 5,000 shares of common stock for cash at $25 cash per share.
2. Issued 500 shares of common stock for a piece of land that will be used for a facilities site; construction was started immediately. Assume the stock was selling at $27 per share at the date of issuance. Debit Land.
3. Sold and issued 1,000 shares of common stock for cash at $27 cash per share.
4. At year-end, the Income Summary account reflected a $7,000 loss. Because a loss was incurred, no income tax expense was recorded.

Required:

a. Give the journal entry required for each of the transactions listed above.
b. Assume it is the year-end and the financial statements must be prepared. Prepare the stockholders' equity section as it should be reported on the balance sheet.

E12–2. Davis Corporation was organized in January 19A by 10 stockholders to operate an air conditioning sales and service business. The charter issued by the state authorized the following capital stock:

Common stock, $1 par value, 50,000 shares.
Preferred stock, $10 par value, 7 percent, nonparticipating, noncumulative, 20,000 shares.

During January and February 19A, the following stock transactions were completed:

1. Collected $30,000 cash from each of the 10 organizers and issued 1,000 shares of common stock to each of them.
2. Sold 8,000 shares of preferred stock at $30 per share; collected the cash and immediately issued the stock.

Required:

a. Give the journal entries to record the above stock transactions.
b. Assume it is the end of the annual accounting period, December 31, 19A, and net income for the year was $35,000; also assume that cash dividends declared and paid at year-end amounted to $15,000. Prepare the stockholders' equity section of the balance sheet at December 31, 19A.

E12–3. Video Systems, Incorporated, was issued a charter on January 15, 19A, that authorized the following capital stock:

Common stock, nopar, 80,000 shares.
Preferred stock, 6 percent, par value $10 per share, 10,000 shares.

The board of directors established a stated value on the nopar common stock of $5 per share.

During 19A, the following selected transactions were completed in the order given:

1. Sold and issued 30,000 shares of the nopar common stock at $30 cash per share.
2. Sold and issued 4,000 shares of preferred stock at $21 cash per share.
3. At the end of 19A, the Income Summary account reflected a credit balance of $15,000.

Required:

a. Give the journal entry indicated for each of the above transactions.
b. Prepare the stockholders' equity section of the balance sheet at December 31, 19A.

E12–4. Garcia Corporation obtained a charter at the start of 19A that authorized 50,000 shares of nopar common stock and 5,000 shares of preferred stock, par value $10. The corporation was promoted and organized by five individuals who "reserved" 51 percent of the common stock shares for themselves. The remaining shares were to be sold to other individuals at $50 per share on a cash basis. During 19A, the following selected transactions occurred:

1. Collected $20 per share cash from four of the organizers and received two adjoining lots of land from the fifth organizer. Issued 3,000 shares of common stock to each of the five organizers and received title to the land.
2. Sold and issued 5,000 shares of common stock to an "outsider" at $50 cash per share.
3. Sold and issued 4,000 shares of preferred stock at $15 cash per share.
4. At the end of 19A, the Income Summary account, after income taxes, reflected a credit balance of $30,000.

Required:

a. Give the journal entries indicated for each of the transactions listed above.
b. Prepare the stockholders' equity section of the balance sheet at December 31, 19A.
c. Explain the basis that you used to determine the cost of the land.

E12–5. The stockholders' equity section on the December 31, 19D, balance sheet of Rice Corporation was:

Stockholders' Equity

Contributed capital:
Preferred stock, par value $30, authorized 8,000 shares;   ?   issued, of
   which 500 shares are held as treasury stock $165,000
Common stock, nopar, authorized 10,000 shares; issued and
   outstanding 7,000 shares 630,000
Contributed capital in excess of par, preferred 7,150
Contributed capital, treasury stock transactions 2,000
Retained earnings 40,000
Cost of treasury stock, preferred 16,000

Required:

Complete the following statements and show your computations.

a. The number of shares of preferred stock issued was _____ .
b. The number of shares of preferred stock outstanding was _____ .
c. The average sale price of the preferred stock when issued apparently was $ _____ per share.
d. Have the treasury stock transactions (1) increased corporate resources _____ ; or (2) decreased resources _____ ? By how much? $ _____ .
e. How much did the treasury stock transactions increase (decrease) stockholders' equity?
f. How much did the treasury stock held cost per share? $ _____ .

g. Total stockholders' equity is $ _____ .

h. What was the average issue price of the common stock?

i. Assuming one fourth of the treasury stock is sold at $30 per share, the remaining balance in the Treasury Stock account would be $ _____ .

E12–6. The balance sheet (summarized) of Pope Corporation reflected the information shown below at December 31, 19B:

POPE CORPORATION
Balance Sheet
At December 31, 19B

Assets		Liabilities	
Cash	$100,000	Current liabilities	$ 60,000
All other assets	412,000	Long-term liabilities	80,000
			140,000
		Stockholders' Equity	
		Contributed capital:	
		Common stock, par $20, authorized 20,000 shares; outstanding 12,000 shares	240,000
		Contributed capital in excess of par	72,000
		Retained earnings	60,000
	$512,000		$512,000

During the next year, 19C, the following selected transactions affecting stockholders' equity occurred:

Feb.   1   Purchased in the open market, 500 shares of Pope's own common stock at $40 cash per share.

July 15   Sold 100 of the shares purchased on February 1, 19C, at $41 cash per share.

Sept. 1   Sold 20 more of the shares purchased on February 1, 19C, at $38 cash per share.

Dec. 15   Sold an additional 80 of the treasury shares at $35 per share.

Dec. 31   The credit balance in the Income Summary account was $31,140.

Required:

a. Give the indicated journal entries for each of the five transactions.

b. Prepare the stockholders' equity section of the balance sheet at a December 31, 19C.

PART B

E12–7. The records of Stewart Supply Company reflected the following balances in the stockholders' equity accounts at December 31, 19H:

Common stock, par $5 per share, 30,000 shares outstanding.

Preferred stock, 6 percent, par $10 per share, 3,000 shares outstanding.

Retained earnings, $150,000.

On September 1, 19H, the board of directors was considering the distribution of a $42,000 cash dividend. No dividends were paid during 19F and 19G. You have been asked to determine the total and per share amounts that would be paid to the common stockholders and to the preferred stockholders under three independent assumptions (show computations):

a. The preferred stock is noncumulative and nonparticipating.
b. The preferred stock is cumulative and nonparticipating.
c. The preferred stock is cumulative and fully participating (solve this assumption only if Supplement 12A is assigned for study).
d. Give the journal entry to record dividends separately for preferred and common stock under each assumption.
e. Explain why the dividend per share of common stock was less for each assumption than for the preceding assumption.
f. What factor would cause a more favorable per share result to the common stockholders?

E12–8. Rye Corporation has the following capital stock outstanding at the end of 19B:

Preferred stock, 6 percent, par $20, outstanding shares, 6,000.

Common stock, par $5, outstanding shares, 20,000.

On October 1, 19B, the board of directors declared dividends as follows:

Preferred stock, the full cash preference amount; payable December 20, 19B.

Common stock, a 10 percent common stock dividend (i.e., one additional share for each 10 held), issuable December 20, 19B.

On December 20, 19B, the market prices were: Preferred stock, $50, and common stock, $15.

Required:

a. Give any required journal entry(s) to record the declaration and subsequent payment of the dividend on the preferred stock.
b. Give any required journal entry(s) to record the declaration and issuance of the stock dividend on the common stock.
c. Explain the comparative overall effect of each of the dividends on the assets, liabilities, and stockholders' equity of Rye Corporation.

E12–9. On December 31, 19E, the stockholders' equity section of the balance sheet of Hye Corporation reflected the following:

Common stock, par $10, shares authorized 50,000; shares outstanding 20,000	$200,000
Contributed capital in excess of par	15,000
Retained earnings	103,000

On February 1, 19F, the board of directors declared a 20 percent stock dividend to be issued April 30, 19F (that is, one additional share will be issued for each five shares now outstanding). The market value of the stock on February 1, 19F, was $16 per share. The market value will be capitalized.

Required:

a. Give any required journal entry(s) to record the declaration and issuance of the stock dividend.
b. For comparative purposes, prepare the stockholders' equity section of the balance sheet (1) immediately before the stock dividend and (2) immediately after the stock dividend. (Hint: Use two amount columns for this requirement.)

c. Explain the effects of this stock dividend on the assets, liabilities, and stockholders' equity.

E12–10. The following account balances were selected from the records of Tucker Corporation at December 31, 19E, after all adjusting entries were completed:

Common stock, par $5, authorized 200,000 shares; issued 120,000 shares, of
    which 500 shares are held as treasury stock $600,000
Contributed capital in excess of par 280,000
Bond sinking fund 70,000
Dividends declared and paid in 19E 24,000
Retained earnings, January 1, 19E 90,000
Correction of prior period accounting error (a debit, net of income tax) 10,000
Treasury stock at cost (500 shares) 3,000
Income summary for 19E (credit balance) 45,000
Restriction on retained earnings equal to the cost of treasury stock held is required
    by law in this state.

Required:

Based upon the above data, prepare (a) the statement of retained earnings for 19E and (b) the stockholders' equity section of the balance sheet at December 31, 19E. (Hint: Total stockholders' equity is $978,000.)

E12–11. The data given below were selected from the records of Stonewall Corporation at December 31, 19B.

Common stock, par $2, authorized 300,000 shares, issued 110,000 shares of which
    1,000 are held as treasury stock (purchased at $8 per share) $220,000
Preferred stock, 6%, par $10, authorized 20,000 shares, issued and outstanding
    15,000 shares 150,000
Contributed capital in excess of par:
    Common stock 230,000
    Preferred stock 120,000
Dividends declared and paid during 19B 24,000
Net income for 19B 64,000
Retained earnings balance, January 1, 19B 130,000
Prior period adjustment (gain, net of income tax) 10,000
Extraordinary loss (unusual and infrequent, net of income tax) 22,000

Required:

a. Prepare a statement of retained earnings for the year ended December 31, 19B.
b. Prepare the stockholders' equity section of the balance sheet dated December 31, 19B. (Hint: Total stockholders' equity is $892,000.)

E12–12. On July 1, 19B, Oregon Corporation had the following capital structure:

Common stock, par $2, authorized shares 100,000
Common stock, par $2, unissued shares 80,000
Contributed capital in excess of par, $60,000.
Retained earnings, $90,000.
Treasury stock, none.

Required:

a. The number of issued shares is _____ .
b. The number of outstanding shares is _____ .
c. Total stockholders' equity is $_____ .

d. Assume the board of directors declared and issued a 20 percent stock dividend (i.e., one new share for each five shares already owned) when the stock was selling at $11 per share. Give any required journal entry(s). If none is required, explain why.

e. Disregard the stock dividend in *(d)* above. Assume instead that the board of directors voted six-to-five stock split (i.e., a 20 percent increase in the number of shares). The market price prior to the split was $11 per share. Give any required journal entry(s). If none is required, explain why.

f. Complete the following comparative tabulation followed by comments on the comparative effects:

Items	Before Dividend and Split	After Stock Dividend	After Stock Split
Common stock account	$	$	$
Par per share	$2	$	$
Shares outstanding	#	#	#
Contributed capital in excess of par	$60,000	$	$
Retained earnings	$90,000	$	$
Total stockholders' equity	$	$	$

PROBLEMS/CASES

PART A

PC12–1. Caine Corporation received its charter during January 19A. The charter authorized the following capital stock:

Preferred stock, 7 percent, par $10, authorized 10,000 shares.
Common stock, par $2, authorized 150,000 shares.

During 19A, the following transactions occurred in the order given:

1. Issued a total of 60,000 shares of the common stock to the six organizers at $5 per share. Caine collected cash in full from five of the organizers, and a plot of land was received from the other organizer in full payment for the shares. The stock was issued immediately.

2. Sold 3,000 shares of the preferred stock at $22 per share. Collected the cash and issued the stock immediately (10,000 shares to each organizer).

3. Sold 2,000 shares of the common stock at $7 per share and 1,000 shares of the preferred stock at $30. Collected the cash and issued the stock immediately.

4. Total revenues for 19A, $206,000, and total expenses (including income tax), $160,000.

Required:

a. Give all of the journal entries required for the above items including closing entries.

b. Prepare the stockholders' equity section of the balance sheet at December 31, 19A.

c. What was the average issue price of the common stock?

d. Explain the basis you used to value the land in the first journal entry.

PC12–2.   Utah Corporation began operations in January 19A. The charter authorized the following capital stock:

> Preferred stock, 6 percent, $10 par, authorized 20,000 shares.
> Common stock, nopar, authorized 100,000 shares.
> The corporation, in conformance with state laws, established a stated value per share of $2 for the nopar common stock.

During 19A, the following transactions occurred in the order given:

1. Issued 20,000 shares of the nopar common stock to each of the three organizers. Collected $8 cash per share from two of the organizers, and received a plot of land, with a small building thereon, in full payment for the shares of the third organizer and issued the stock immediately. Assume that 20 percent of the noncash payment received applies to the building.
2. Sold 4,000 shares of the preferred stock at $15 per share. Collected the cash and issued the stock immediately.
3. Sold 200 shares of the preferred stock at $16 and 1,000 shares of the nopar common stock at $10 per share. Collected the cash and issued the stock immediately.
4. Operating results at the end of 19A, were reflected as follows:

> | | |
> |---|---|
> | Revenue accounts .... | $160,000 |
> | Expense accounts, including income taxes..... | 120,000 |

Required:

a. Give the journal entries indicated (including closing entries) for each of the above transactions.
b. Prepare the stockholders' equity section of the balance sheet at December 31, 19A.
c. Explain what you used to determine the cost of the land and the building in the first journal entry.

PC12–3.   Dyno Company was issued a charter in January 19A, which authorized 50,000 shares of common stock. During 19A, the following selected transactions occurred in the order given:

1. Sold 10,000 shares of the stock for cash at $70 per share. Collected the cash and issued the stock immediately.
2. Acquired land to be used as a future plant site; made payment in full by issuing 500 shares of stock. Assume a market value per share of $70.
3. At the end of 19A, the Income Summary account reflected a credit balance of $30,000.

Three independent cases are assumed as follows for comparative study purposes:

> Case A—Assume the common stock was $30 par value per share. The state law specifies that par value is legal capital.
> Case B—Assume the common stock was nopar and that the total sale price is credited to the Common Stock, Nopar account because the state law specifies this amount as legal capital.
> Case C—Assume the common stock is nopar with a stated value, specified by the board of directors, of $10 per share.

Required:

For each independent case:

a. Give the journal entries for each of the three transactions.
b. Prepare the stockholders' equity section·of the balance sheet at December 31, 19A.
c. Should total stockholders' equity be the same amount among the three independent cases? Explain why.
d. Should the noncash asset (land) be recorded at the same cost under each of the three independent cases? Explain why.

PC12–4. Mika Company obtained a charter from the state in January 19A, which authorized 100,000 shares of common stock, $1 par value. The stockholders comprised 20 local citizens. During the first year, the following selected transactions occurred in the order given:

1. Sold 80,000 shares of the common stock to the 20 shareholders at $5 per share. Collected the $400,000 cash and issued the stock.
2. During the year, one of the 20 stockholders needed cash and wanted to sell the stock back to Mika. Accordingly, the corporation purchased the investor's 5,000 shares at $5.50 cash per share.
3. Two months later, 1,000 of the shares of treasury stock (purchased in 2) were resold to another individual at $5.75 cash per share.
4. An additional 2,000 shares of the treasury stock were sold at $5.40 cash per share.
5. On December 31, 19A, the end of the first year of business, the Income Summary account reflected a credit balance of $28,550.

Required:

a. Give the indicated journal entry for each of the above items.
b. Prepare the stockholders' equity section of the balance sheet at December 31, 19A.
c. What dollar effect did the treasury stock transactions have on the assets, liabilities and stockholders' equity of Mika Corporation? Explain.

PC12–5. Doss Manufacturing Company was granted a charter that authorized the following capital stock:

Common stock, nopar, 50,000 shares. Assume the nopar stock is not assigned a stated value per share.
Preferred stock, 6 percent, par $10, 10,000 shares.

During the first year, 19A, the following selected transactions occurred in the order given:

1. Sold 20,000 shares of the nopar common stock at $30 cash per share and 3,000 shares of the preferred stock at $22 cash per share. Collected cash and issued the stock immediately. For the nopar stock, credit the full selling price to the common stock account.
2. Issued 1,000 shares of preferred stock as full payment for a plot of land to be used as a future plant site. Assume the stock was selling at $22.
3. Purchased 300 shares of the nopar common stock sold earlier; paid cash, $26 per share.
4. Sold all of the treasury stock (common) purchased in 3 above. The sale price was $28 per share.

5. Purchased 200 shares of the company's own preferred stock at $24 cash per share.
6. At December 31, 19A, the Income Summary account reflected a credit balance of $21,200.

Required:

a. Give the journal entries indicated for each of the above transactions.
b. Prepare the stockholders' equity section of the balance sheet at December 31, 19A, end of the annual accounting period.

PART B

PC12–6. Brown Equipment Company had the following stock outstanding and retained earnings at December 31, 19E:

Common stock, $10 par, outstanding 20,000 shares $200,000
Preferred stock, 6%, $20 par, outstanding 5,000 shares 100,000
Retained earnings 240,000

The board of directors is considering the distribution of a cash dividend to the two groups of stockholders. No dividends were declared during 19C or 19D. Three independent case situations are assumed:

Case A—The preferred stock is noncumulative and nonparticipating; the total amount of dividends is $36,000.

Case B—The preferred stock is cumulative and nonparticipating; the total amount of dividends is $18,000.

Case C—Same as Case B, except the amount is $58,000.

Required:

a. Compute the amount of dividends, in total and per share, that would be payable to each class of stockholders for each case. Show computations.
b. Give the journal entry to record the cash dividends declared and paid in 19E for Case C only. Assume for simplicity that the declaration and payment occurred simultaneously on December 31, 19E.
c. Give the required journal entry assuming, instead of a cash dividend, the declaration and issuance of a 10 percent common stock dividend on the outstanding common stock. Assume the market value per share of common stock was $22.
d. Complete the following comparative schedule including explanation of the comparative differences.

Item	Amount of Dollar Increase (Decrease)	
	Cash Dividend—Case C	Stock Dividend
Assets	$	$
Liabilities	$	$
Stockholders' equity	$	$

PC12–7. KAT Manufacturing Company has outstanding 50,000 shares of $5 par value common stock and 15,000 shares of $10 par value preferred stock (6 percent). On December 1, 19B, the board of directors voted a 6 percent cash dividend on the preferred stock and a 10 percent common stock dividend on the common stock (i.e., for each 10 shares of common stock held 1 additional share of common stock is to be issued as a stock dividend). At the date of declaration, the common stock was selling at $32 and the preferred at $20 per share. The dividends are to be paid, or issued on February 15, 19C. The annual accounting period ends December 31.

Required:

a. Give any journal entry(s) required to record the declaration and payment of the cash dividend.
b. Give any journal entry(s) required to record the declaration and issuance of the stock dividend.
c. Explain the comparative effects of the two dividends on the assets, liabilities, and stockholders' equity (1) through December 31, 19B, (2) on February 15, 19C, and (3) the overall effects from December 1, 19B, through February 15, 19C. A schedule similar to the following might be helpful:

Item	Comparative Effects Explained	
	Cash Dividend on Preferred	Stock Dividend on Common
1. Through December 31, 19B: Assets		
etc.		

PC12–8. The accounts of AFC Corporation reflected the following balances on January 1, 19C:

Preferred stock, 5%, $50 par value, cumulative, authorized 10,000 shares, issued and outstanding 2,000 shares	$100,000
Common stock, $10 par value, authorized 100,000 shares, outstanding 20,000 shares	200,000
Contributed capital in excess of par, preferred	5,000
Contributed capital in excess of par, common	10,000
Retained earnings	200,000
Total stockholders' equity	$515,000

The transactions during 19C relating to the stockholders' equity are listed below in order:

1. Purchased 200 shares of preferred treasury stock at $120 per share.
2. The board of directors declared and paid a cash dividend to the preferred stockholders only. No dividends were declared during 19A or 19B. The dividend was sufficient to pay the arrears plus the dividend for the current year.
3. The board of directors declared a 1-for-10 (i.e., 10 percent) common stock dividend on the outstanding common stock. Market value of $15 per share is to be capitalized.
4. Net income for the year was $50,000.

Required:

a. Give the journal entry for each of the above transactions, including the closing entries. Show computations.

b. Prepare a statement of retained earnings for 19B and the stockholders' equity section of the balance sheet at December 31, 19C. (Hint: Total stockholders' equity is $527,500.)

c. Explain the comparative effects on assets and stockholders' equity of the (1) cash dividend and (2) the stock dividend.

PC12–9. (Review)   At December 31, 19E, the records of Reedy Corporation provided the following selected and incomplete data:

> Common stock, par $5 (no changes during 19E):
> Shares authorized, 500,000.
> Shares issued ? issue price $12 per share; cash collected in full, $1,800,000.
> Shares held as treasury stock, 2,000 shares—cost $15 per share.
> Net income for 19E, $176,000.
> Dividends declared and paid during 19E, $74,000.
> Bond sinking fund balance, $20,000.
> Prior period adjustment—correction of 19B accounting error, $14,000 (a credit, net of income tax).
> Retained earnings balance, January 1, 19E, $180,000.
> State law places a restriction on retained earnings equal to the cost of treasury stock held. The treasury stock was acquired after the stock dividend was issued.
> Extraordinary gain (net of income tax), $16,000.

Required:

a. Complete the following tabulation:
   Shares authorized _____
   Shares issued _____
   Shares outstanding _____

b. The balance in the Contributed Capital in Excess of Par account appears to be $ _____   _____ .

c. EPS on net income is $ _____ .

d. Dividend paid per share of common stock is $ _____ .

e. The bond sinking fund should be reported on the balance sheet under the classification _____ .

f. Net income before extraordinary items was $ _____ .

g. The prior period adjustment should be reported on the _____   _____ _____ as an addition ___ or a deduction _____ .

h. Treasury stock should be reported on the balance sheet under the major caption _____ in the amount of $ _____ .

i. The amount of retained earnings available for dividends on January 1, 19E, was $ _____ .

j. Assume the board of directors voted a 100 percent stock split (the number of shares will double). After the stock split, the par value per share will be $ _____ and the number of outstanding shares will be _____ .

k. Assuming the stock split given in (j) above, give any journal entry that should be made. If none explain why.

l. Disregard the stock split (assumed in [j] and [k] above). Assume instead that a 10 percent stock dividend (i.e., one share for each 10 shares already held) was declared and issued when the market price of the common stock was $6. Give any journal entry that should be made.

PC12–10. Walker Company is in the process of completing its year-end accounting, including the preparation of the annual financial statements, at December 31, 19E. The stockholders' equity accounts reflected the following balances at the end of the year, 19E:

> Common stock, par $10, shares outstanding 50,000 .... $500,000
> Contributed capital in excess of par   50,000
> Retained earnings, January 1, 19E (credit) 300,000
> Cash dividends declared and paid during 19E (debit)   30,000
> Income summary account for 19E (credit balance; after tax)   60,000

The following selected transactions occurred near the end of 19E; they are not included in the above amounts:

1. During 19D, Walker Company was sued for $35,000, and it was clear that the suit would be lost. Therefore, in 19D, Walker should have debited a loss and credited a liability for this amount. This journal entry was not made, and the accounting error was found in 19E. (Hint: Credit Liability for Damages.) Disregard any income tax effects.
2. The board of directors voted a voluntary restriction on retained earnings of $100,000. It is to be designated as "Earnings appropriated for plant expansion" effective for the 19E financial statements.

Required:

a. Give the appropriate journal entries for the events listed immediately above. If no entry is given, explain why.
b. Prepare a statement of retained earnings for 19E and the stockholders' equity section of the balance sheet at December 31, 19E. (Hint: The ending balance of stockholders' equity is $845,000.)

PC12–11. Rye Company has completed all of the annual information processing at December 31, 19D, except for preparation of the financial statements. The following account balances were reflected at that date:

RYE COMPANY
Adjusted Trial Balance
December 31, 19D

	Debit	Credit
Cash	$ 57,000	
Accounts receivable (net)	58,000	
Merchandise inventory, December 31, 19D	120,000	
Long-term investment in Company Y	20,000	
Bond sinking fund	40,000	
Land	20,000	
Buildings and equipment (net)	738,000	
Other assets	29,200	
Accounts payable		$ 86,000
Income tax payable		18,000
Bonds payable, 7%, payable December 31		100,000
Preferred stock, par $10, authorized 50,000 shares.....		100,000
Common stock, par $5, authorized 200,000 shares		660,000
Contributed capital in excess of par, preferred		6,100
Contributed capital in excess of par, common		19,900
Treasury stock, preferred, 10 shares at cost	1,100	
Retained earnings, January 1, 19D		163,300
19D net income		40,000
19D cash dividends on preferred	26,000	
19D common stock dividends distributed (10,000 shares)	70,000	
19D, discovered an accounting error made in 19A in recording a purchase of land (the correction required a net credit to land of $14,000)	14,000	
	$1,193,300	$1,193,300

Note: Retained earnings is restricted in an amount equal to the bond sinking fund per the provisions of the bond indenture.

Required:

Prepare a statement of retained earnings for 19D and a classified balance sheet at December 31, 19D. (Hint: Total stockholders' equity is $878,200.)

PC12–12. This case is based upon the financial statements of Johnson & Johnson presented in Special Supplement B immediately preceding the Index. Use the 1982 data to respond to the following questions:

1. Complete the following tabulation about the capital stock for 1982:

Stock	Number of Shares				Par Value per Share
	Authorized	Issued	Treasury	Outstanding	
Common					
Preferred					

2. How much did retained earnings change during 1982? $ _____ . Explain what caused this change.

3. Give the amount of the 1982 ending balances in the following accounts and show proof of the total:

a. Preferred stock .... $ _____
b. Common stock ....   _____
c. Additional contributed capital ....   _____
d. Treasury stock ....   _____
e. Cumulative currency translation adjustments .....   _____
f. Retained earnings ....   _____
Proof:

4. Briefly explain the "cumulative current translation adjustments" of $163.5 million.

5. What position did the Independent Certified Public Accountants take in respect to the "currency adjustments"?

6. Complete the following tabulation:

Common Stock Information	1982	1981
Dividends paid per share		
Stockholders' equity per share		
Average shares outstanding (millions)		
Stockholders of record (thousands)		

PC12–13. (Review) The bookkeeper for Careless Company prepared the following balance sheet:

CARELESS COMPANY
Balance Sheet
For the Year 19W

Assets

Current assets	$ 45,000
Fixed assets (net of depreciation reserves, $70,000)	125,000
Other assets	50,000
Total debits	$220,000

Liabilities

Current liabilities	$ 32,000
Other debts	25,000

Capital

Stock, par $10, authorized 10,000 shares	60,000
Stock premium	30,000
Earned surplus	58,000
Treasury stock (500 shares)	(10,000)
Reserve for treasury stock (required by law)	10,000
Correction of prior year error (a credit, net)	7,000
Cash dividends paid during 19W	(12,000)
Net profit for 19W	20,000
Total credits	$220,000

Required:

a. List all of the deficiencies you can identify in the above statement. Assume the amounts given are correct.

b. Prepare a statement of retained earnings for 19W.

c. Recast the above balance sheet in good form; focus especially on stockholders' equity.

PC12–14. (Based on Supplement 12B)   Assume for each of the three independent cases below that the annual accounting period ends on December 31, 19W, and that the Income Summary account at that date reflected a debit balance of $30,000 (i.e., a loss).

> Case A—Assume that the company is a **sole proprietorship** owned by Proprietor A. Prior to the closing entries, the capital account reflected a credit balance of $70,000 and the drawings account a balance of $6,000.
>
> Case B—Assume that the company is a **partnership** owned by Partner A and Partner B. Prior to the closing entries, the owners' equity accounts reflected the following balances: A, Capital, $50,000; B, Capital, $45,000; A, Drawings, $7,000; and B, Drawings, $6,000. Profits and losses are divided equally.
>
> Case C—Assume that the company is a **corporation.** Prior to the closing entries, the stockholders' equity accounts showed the following: Capital Stock, par $20, authorized 20,000 shares, outstanding 4,000 shares; Contributed Capital in Excess of Par, $2,000; and Retained Earnings, $40,000.

Required:

a. Give all of the closing entries indicated at December 31, 19W, for each of the separate cases.
b. Show how the owners' equity section of the balance sheet would appear at December 31, 19W, for each case.

C·H·A·P·T·E·R
13

Measuring and Reporting Long-Term Investments

PURPOSE OF THIS CHAPTER[1]

One corporation may invest in another corporation by acquiring either **debt securities** (e.g., bonds) or **equity securities** (e.g., capital stock) of the other corporation. The objective of an investment in another corporation often is to earn a return on idle cash, or to obtain influence or control over the other corporation.

In Chapter 8, short-term investments (a current asset) were defined as those that meet two tests: (1) **ready marketability** and (2) **management intention** to convert them to cash in the short run. Those not meeting these two tests are classified as long-term investments (a noncurrent asset).

The purpose of this chapter is to discuss measuring and reporting of long-term investments, except for those situations in which **consolidated statements** must be prepared. Consolidated statements are discussed in Chapter 14. To accomplish this purpose, the chapter is subdivided into two parts:

Part A—Long-term investments in equity securities (stocks)

Part B—Long-term investments in debt securities (bonds)

---

[1] We suggest that you review the discussion of short-term investments in Chapter 8 prior to studying this chapter.

PART A—LONG-TERM INVESTMENTS IN EQUITY SECURITIES (STOCKS)

A company may invest in the equity securities (either common or preferred stock) of one or more corporations for various reasons such as to use idle cash, to exercise influence or control over the other company, to attain growth through sales of new products and new services, to gain access to new markets and new sources of supply, or to attain other economic purposes. Basically, one entity may acquire capital stock of a corporation by purchasing outstanding shares from other shareholders for cash (or other assets); or if the investor is a corporation, by exchanging some of its own capital stock for outstanding capital stock of the other corporation.

When one company purchases **outstanding** shares of stock of another company, the transaction is between the acquiring company and the **shareholders** of the other company (not the other company itself). Thus, the transaction affects the acquiring entity only. The accounting of the other company is unaffected.

The purchasing entity (i.e., the **investor**) may acquire **some or all** of either the preferred or the common stock **outstanding** of the other company (often called the **investee**). If the purpose of the investment is to gain influence or control, the investor typically will acquire **common stock** because it is the voting stock. The number of shares of outstanding stock of a corporation acquired by another entity usually depends upon the investment objectives of the investing company (i.e., the acquiring company). For measuring and reporting purposes, **three different levels of ownership** are recognized. Each of these levels calls for different measuring and reporting methods. The three levels usually are related to the percentage of shares of **voting** capital stock owned by the investing company in relation to the total number of such shares that are outstanding.

MEASURING LONG-TERM INVESTMENTS IN VOTING COMMON STOCK

Accounting for long-term investments in voting common stock involves measuring the investment amount that should be reported on the balance sheet and the periodic investment revenue that should be reported on the income statement. In accordance with the cost principle, long-term investments in the voting stock of another company are measured and recorded, at the dates of acquisition of the shares, as the total consideration given to acquire them. This total includes the market price, plus all commissions and other buying costs. Subsequent to acquisition, measurement of the investment amount and the investment revenue depends upon the relationship between the investor and the investee company. The relevant characteristic of the relationship is the extent to which the investing company can exercise **significant influence or control over the operating and financial policies** of the other company. Significant influence and control are related to the number of voting shares owned of the investee company in proportion to the total number of such shares outstanding.

For measuring and reporting long-term investments in the voting capital stock

EXHIBIT 13–1   Measuring and reporting long-term investments in voting stock of another company

Status of ownership	Method	Measurement at date of acquisition	Measurement after date of acquisition	
			Investment	*Revenue*
1. **Investor can exercise no significant influence or control.** Presumed if investor owns less than 20 percent of the outstanding voting stock of the investee company.	Cost method	Investor records the investment at cost. Cost is the total outlay made to acquire the shares.	Investor reports the investment on the balance sheet at LCM.	Investor recognizes revenue each period when dividends are declared by the investee company. A realized gain or loss is recognized when the investment is sold.
2. **Investor can exercise significant influence, but not control,** over the operating and financing policies of the investee company. Presumed if the investor owns at least 20 percent but not more than 50 percent of the outstanding voting stock of the investee company.	Equity method	Same as above.	Investor measures and reports the investment at cost **plus** the investor's share of the earnings (or less the losses) and **minus** the dividends received from (i.e., declared by) the other company. (Dividends received are not considered revenue. To recognize dividends as revenue, rather than as a reduction in the investment, would involve double counting.)	Investor recognizes as revenue each period the investor's proportionate share of the earnings (or losses) reported each period by the investee company.
3. **Investor can exercise control** over the operating and financing policies of the investee company. Control is presumed if the investor owns more than 50 percent of the outstanding voting stock of the investee company.	Consolidated financial statement method	Same as above.	Consolidated financial statements required each period. Discussed in Chapter 14.	

of another company, *APB Opinion 18* defines the two terms "significant influence" and "control" essentially as:

1. **Significant influence**—the ability of the investing company to have an important impact on the operating and financing policies of another company in which it owns shares of the voting stock. Significant influence may be indicated by *(a)* membership on the board of directors of the other company, *(b)* participation in the policy-making processes, *(c)* material transactions between the two companies, *(d)* interchange of management personnel, or *(e)* technological dependency. In the absence of a clear-cut distinction based upon these factors, **significant influence is presumed** if the investing company owns at least 20 percent but not more than 50 percent of the outstanding voting shares of the other company.

2. **Control**—the ability of the investing company to determine the operating and financing policies of another company in which it owns shares of the voting stock. For all practical purposes, **control is assumed** when the investing company owns more than 50 percent of the outstanding voting stock of the other company.

The three levels of ownership that relate to the measuring and reporting of long-term investments in voting capital stock are as follows:

Level of ownership	*Measuring and reporting approach*
1. Neither significant influence nor control	Cost method
2. Significant influence but not control	Equity method
3. Control	Consolidated statement method

Each of these approaches is outlined in Exhibit 13–1. The first two are discussed in this chapter, and the third is discussed in Chapter 14.

COST METHOD—NO SIGNIFICANT INFLUENCE

The **cost method** of accounting must be used when the investment by one entity in the **voting** capital stock of a corporation does not give the former the ability to exercise significant influence or control. Under the cost method of accounting, the investment is measured at the acquisition date in the accounts at cost in accordance with the cost principle. Subsequent to acquisition, the investment amount is measured at the **current lower of cost or market** (LCM), and this amount is reported on the balance sheet under "Investments and funds." Cash dividends declared by the investee corporation are reported by the investing entity as "Revenue from investments" in the period declared. The cost method is essentially the same as the accounting and reporting previously discussed and illustrated for short-term investments in Chapter 8.

FASB Statement 12 requires that long-term **equity** investments accounted for under the cost method be valued at LCM after acquisition. Thus, at the end of each accounting period, the **entire portfolio** of long-term equity investments, accounted for under the cost method, must be calculated at both total cost and

EXHIBIT 13–2
Cost method of
measuring and
reporting long-term
investments in
equity securities

Situation:

Able Corporation purchased the following long-term investments on February 1, 19A:

Baker Corporation common stock (nopar), 1,000 shares at $12 per share (represents 10 percent of the outstanding shares).

Cox Corporation, 5 percent preferred stock (par $20), nonvoting, 500 shares at $40 per share (represents 10 percent of the outstanding shares).

February 1, 19A, to record the acquisition:

Long-term investments	32,000	
Cash		32,000

Computations:
Baker common stock, 1,000 shares × $12 = $12,000
Cox preferred stock, 500 shares × $40 = 20,000
Total acquisition cost $32,000

November 30, 19A, cash dividends declared (payable in January 19B) as follows: Baker common stock, $1 per share; Cox preferred stock, 5 percent of par.

Dividends receivable...	1,500	
Revenue from investments		1,500

Computations:
Baker common stock, 1,000 shares × $1 = $1,000
Cox preferred stock, 500 shares × $20 × 5% = 500
Total dividends $1,500

December 31, 19A, end of the accounting period, quoted market prices: Baker common stock, $13; Cox preferred stock, $36.

Unrealized loss on long-term investments	1,000	
Allowance to reduce long-term investments to market		1,000

Computations:

	Shares	Market Dec. 31, 19A	Acquisition cost	Market Dec. 31, 19A
Baker common stock	1,000	$13	$12,000	$13,000
Cox preferred stock	500	36	20,000	18,000
			$32,000	$31,000

LCM: $32,000 − $31,000 = $1,000 (balance required in the allowance account).

January 15, 19B, received cash for the dividends of Baker and Cox Corporations (declared on November 30, 19A).

Cash	1,500	
Dividends receivable.......................................		1,500

June 15, 19B, sold 300 shares of the Cox preferred stock at $41.

Cash (300 shares × $41)	12,300	
Long-term investments (300 × $40)........................		12,000
Gain on sale of investment		300

November 30, 19B, cash dividends declared (payable December 30, 19B) as follows: Baker common stock, $.90 per share; Cox preferred stock, 5 percent of par.

Dividends receivable	1,100	
Revenue from investments		1,100

Computations:
Baker common stock, 1,000 shares × $.90 = $ 900
Cox preferred stock, 200 shares × $20 × 5% = 200
Total dividends $1,100

EXHIBIT 13–2
(concluded)

December 30, 19B, received cash for the dividends of Baker and Cox Corporations (declared on November 30, 19B).

Cash	1,100	
Dividends receivable		1,100

December 31, 19B, end of the accounting period, quoted market prices: Baker common stock, $11; Cox preferred stock, $43.

Allowance to reduce long-term investments to market	600	
Unrealized loss on long-term investments		600

Computations:

	Shares	Market Dec. 31, 19B	Acquisition cost	Market Dec. 31, 19B
Baker common stock	1,000	$11	$12,000	$11,000
Cox preferred stock .	200	43	8,000	8,600
			$20,000	$19,600

LCM: $20,000 − $19,600 = $400 (balance required in the allowance account). Reduction in the allowance account: $1,000 − $400 = $600.

December 31, 19A, and 19B, reporting on the **income statement** and **balance sheet** (partial):

	19A		19B	
Income statement:				
Revenue from investments		$ 1,500		$ 1,100
Gain on sale of investment				300
Balance sheet:				
Current assets:				
Dividends receivable		1,500		
Investments and funds:				
Investments in equity securities	$32,000		$20,000	
Less: Allowance to reduce long-term				
investments to market	1,000	31,000	400	19,600
Stockholders' equity:				
Unrealized loss on long-term investments		(1,000)		(400)

total market. If total market is less than total cost, the difference (an unrealized loss) must be recorded as a credit to a contra asset account called Allowance to Reduce Long-Term Investments to Market; the offsetting debit is to a contra owners' equity account called Unrealized Loss on Long-Term Investments. The recording of this unrealized loss does not affect the income statement. If, at the end of a subsequent period, market exceeds the LCM valuation reported the prior period, the portfolio is written up to the new market **not to exceed** the original acquisition cost of the securities portfolio. **Market** is measured as the number of shares owned multiplied by the actual market price per share at the balance sheet date.

When long-term securities are sold, the difference between the sale price and acquisition cost is recorded and reported as a **realized** gain or loss.

Application of the cost method is illustrated in Exhibit 13–2. The journal entry to record the acquisition of a long-term investment is in accordance with the **cost principle.** Observe that on November 30, 19A, dividend revenue was recorded on the date that cash dividends were **declared.**

In Exhibit 13–2, the portfolio is valued at LCM on December 31, 19A, the end of the accounting period. Observe that LCM is applied to the total cost and market amounts for the portfolio (instead of being applied to each individual security amount). The total portfolio was written down to LCM, from cost ($32,000) to market ($31,000), and an unrealized loss of $1,000 was recorded.

On June 15, 19B, 300 shares of Cox stock were sold. The journal entry to record the sale removes the shares sold from the investment account at the original cost and does not affect the allowance account. The difference between the original cost of the stock ($12,000) and the sale price ($12,300) is recorded as a **realized** gain of $300. The allowance account was unaffected in this entry because the account is adjusted **only** at the end of each accounting period to reflect the LCM valuation of the ending portfolio (as illustrated in the journal entry on December 31, 19B).

Exhibit 13–2 presents the reporting effects of the cost method on the income statement and the balance sheet. Observe that the unrealized loss on long-term investments does not affect the income statement in either year. The unrealized loss account is a **contra equity account,** reported on the balance sheet. The income statement is affected only by dividend revenue and gains on the sale of investments.

The journal entries given in Exhibit 13–2 reflect application of the cost principle at the date of acquisition and application of LCM subsequent to that time. The investment is carried continuously at LCM, and dividend revenue is recognized from the investment **only** in periods in which dividends are declared.

The fact that Able Corporation purchased 10 percent of the outstanding voting common shares of Baker Corporation and 10 percent of the outstanding preferred shares of Cox Corporation had absolutely no affect on the accounting and reporting by either Baker or Cox Corporations.

All **nonvoting** stock owned as a long-term investment, regardless of the level of ownership, is accounted for under the cost method as described above and illustrated in Exhibit 13–2.

EQUITY METHOD—SIGNIFICANT INFLUENCE EXISTS (BUT NOT CONTROL)

When significant influence can be exercised over the dividend policies of an investee corporation, the dividend income from the investee corporation can be obtained, almost at will, by the investor company. The equity method prevents the investor company from manipulating its income by affecting the dividend policy of the investee company. Under the equity method, each year the investor company recognizes its proportionate part of the net income (or net loss) of the investee corporation as investment revenue rather than awaiting the declaration of dividends. No cash is received at the time investment revenue is recorded under the equity method; the offsetting debit is to the investment account (an asset increase). Thus, under the equity method, both the **investment account** and **investment revenue account** of the investor company reflect the investor's proportionate share of the income (and losses) of the investee corporation. When dividends are received (i.e., declared), Dividends Receivable or Cash is debited, and the investment account is credited.[2] Thus, dividends declared reduce the investment account balance; they are **not** credited to Revenue from Investments. The revenue already was recognized by the investor in the prior period in which the investee corporation earned the income.

Application of the equity method is illustrated in Exhibit 13–3.[3] The illustration is based on the assumption that Crown Corporation (the investor company) purchased from other investors 3,000 shares of the outstanding common stock of Davis Corporation (the investee company) at a cash price of $120 per share. At the date of purchase, Davis Corporation had outstanding 10,000 shares of common stock (par $100 per share). The equity method must be used because Crown Corporation purchased 30 percent of the outstanding voting stock of Davis Corporation. The first journal entry in Exhibit 13–3 illustrates how the investment would be recorded by Crown Corporation.

After the acquisition date, each year when the investee corporation reports income (or loss), the investor company records its percentage share (i.e., equity) of the investment revenue. The second entry by Crown Corporation (the investor company) given in Exhibit 13–3 recognizes its proportionate share of the net income of Davis Corporation.

In Exhibit 13–3, the proportionate share of the net income of Davis Corporation was recorded by Crown Corporation as revenue and as an **increase** in the investment account. When a dividend is received, it is necessary to avoid double-counting the income from the investee company; therefore, the dividend from the investee company is recorded as a debit to Cash and as a **credit to the investment account.** This entry reflects the fact that a dividend represents the conversion of a part of the investment account balance to cash.

To recapitulate, under the equity method, the balance in the investment account initially starts at cost. Subsequently, the account balance is increased by the proportionate share of the earnings (or decreased by losses) of the investee company and decreased by the proportionate share of the dividends declared by the investee company. The investment and revenue accounts on the books of the investor company, Crown Corporation, are illustrated in Exhibit 13–3. The financial statements for Crown also are illustrated in Exhibit 13–3.

LCM is not used with long-term investments accounted for under the equity method because under the equity method, investments, after acquisition are accounted for and reported at equity, not cost.

Information in respect to the method of measuring the investment and the related investment revenue is important for interpretation and use of financial

---

[2] When a cash dividend is declared in one year and paid in the following year, the dividend is recognized by the investor when declared by debiting Dividends Receivable (a current asset) instead of Cash. Subsequently, when the cash is received, the Cash account is debited and Dividends Receivable is credited. In contrast, dividends declared and paid in the same year may be recorded by the investor on payment date as a debit to Cash and credit to Investment Revenue.

[3] This example assumes that the investment was purchased at "book value." The accounting and reporting procedures for other situations are more complex because they involve asset write-ups and write-downs and, perhaps, the recognition of "goodwill." This chapter presents the fundamentals devoid of this complexity. More advanced accounting courses devote considerable attention to these complexities.

EXHIBIT 13–3
Equity method of measuring and reporting long-term investments in equity securities

Situation:

Crown Corporation (the investor company) purchased 3,000 shares of the outstanding common stock of Davis Corporation (the investee company) on January 15, 19E, at a cash cost of $120 per share. At date of purchase, Davis Corporation had outstanding 10,000 shares of common stock (par $100 per share).

Analysis:

The equity method must be used by Crown Corporation because it now owns between 20 and 50 percent of the outstanding voting stock of the investee company.

January 15, 19E, to record the acquisition:

Investment in common stock, Davis Corporation (3,000 shares) ..	360,000	
Cash		360,000

Purchased 3,000 shares (30 percent) of the common stock of Davis Corporation at $120 per share.

December 31, 19E, end of the accounting period, Davis Corporation reported net income of $50,000. On this date, Crown Corporation recognized its proportionate share as follows:

Investment in common stock, Davis Corporation	15,000	
Revenue from investments		15,000

To record the proportionate share of 19E income reported by Davis Corporation ($50,000 × 30% = $15,000). The credit often is called Equity in Earnings of Partially Owned Company.

December 31, 19E, Davis Corporation declared and paid immediately a $10,000 cash dividend, of which 30 percent (i.e., $3,000) was received by the investor, Crown Corporation. Crown Corporation recorded its share of the dividend as follows:

Cash	3,000	
Investment in common stock, Davis Corporation		3,000

To record the receipt of a cash dividend from Davis Corporation ($10,000 × 30% = $3,000).

statements. The financial statements must disclose the method used. In addition, regardless of whether the cost or the equity method is used, the original cost, current market value, and carrying value of the investment should be disclosed; this disclosure was illustrated in Exhibits 13–2 and 13–3.

The cost and equity methods to measure the effects of long-term investments represent a compromise on the part of the accounting profession. Many accountants believe that all marketable securities should be measured and reported at their **market values** at each balance sheet date. Under this approach, which is not currently acceptable, both dividends received and changes in the market value of the stock since the last period would be reported as revenue (or loss) on the income statement. Accountants who support this approach believe that it meets most closely the objective of reporting the **economic consequences** of holding an investment in marketable securities. The **cost method** measures only the dividends received by the investor as revenue, but dividends may have absolutely no relationship to the earnings of the investee company for the period. The cost method does not indicate to the investor or statement user the earnings pattern of the investee company. The **equity method** tends to overcome this deficiency;

EXHIBIT 13–3
(concluded)

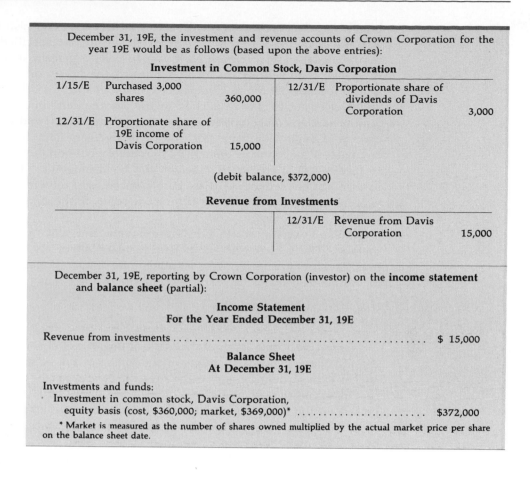

December 31, 19E, the investment and revenue accounts of Crown Corporation for the year 19E would be as follows (based upon the above entries):

Investment in Common Stock, Davis Corporation

1/15/E	Purchased 3,000 shares	360,000	12/31/E	Proportionate share of dividends of Davis Corporation	3,000
12/31/E	Proportionate share of 19E income of Davis Corporation	15,000			

(debit balance, $372,000)

Revenue from Investments

		12/31/E Revenue from Davis Corporation	15,000

December 31, 19E, reporting by Crown Corporation (investor) on the **income statement** and **balance sheet** (partial):

Income Statement
For the Year Ended December 31, 19E

Revenue from investments . . . . $ 15,000

Balance Sheet
At December 31, 19E

Investments and funds:
 Investment in common stock, Davis Corporation,
  equity basis (cost, $360,000; market, $369,000)* $372,000

 * Market is measured as the number of shares owned multiplied by the actual market price per share on the balance sheet date.

however, it does not reflect the economic impact on the investor of market changes in the investment shares held. The effect of such market changes is significant to the investor. After consideration of these and other factors, the accounting profession, for the present time, has accepted the three different measurement approaches for long-term investments in shares that are outlined in Exhibit 13–1.

PART B—LONG-TERM INVESTMENTS IN DEBT SECURITIES (BONDS)

In Chapter 11 we discussed measuring and reporting of bonds as long-term liabilities of the issuing corporation. This part of the chapter discusses bonds of another company held as a **long-term investment.** Bonds offer significantly different investment risks and returns than does capital stock. Bonds provide a stated rate of interest (which determines the dollar amount of interest that will be received on each interest date) and a specified maturity value (which will be received in cash at maturity date). For example, assume that Smith Company issued $100,000, 10 percent, 20-year bonds. At the specified maturity date, the investors in the bonds (i.e., the bondholders) will receive exactly $100,000 cash for the principal amount of the bonds. The 10 percent stated interest specified on the face of the bonds is received in cash each year (usually 5 percent semiannually, which is $5,000) regardless of the market price of the bonds or the earnings of the issuing company. If Smith Company experienced a net loss, the board of directors might elect not to pay dividends to the stockholders, but in such a situation Smith has a legal obligation to continue to pay interest to bondholders. In contrast, owners of Smith Company stock might receive very large increases in dividend payments if the company were highly profitable, but bondholders would continue to receive the interest rate stated in the bond indenture. The owner (i.e., the investor) of one or more of these bonds has no right to vote in the annual stockholders' meeting as would be the case if some of the common stock of Smith Company were owned.

Similar to capital stock, bonds are bought and sold in the regular security markets. The market price of bonds fluctuates **inversely** with changes in the **market rate** of interest because the **stated rate** of interest, paid on the face amount of the bonds, remains constant over the life of the bonds (see Chapter 11).

MEASURING AND REPORTING BOND INVESTMENTS

Investors may buy bonds at their date of issuance or at subsequent dates during the life of the bonds. Regardless of the timing of the bonds' acquisition, at the end of each accounting period the investor must measure the (1) cost, adjusted for the cumulative amount of discount or premium that has been amortized (reported on the balance sheet) and (2) interest revenue earned (reported on the income statement). An understanding of the measurement approaches used is helpful in interpreting and using financial statements.

At the date of acquisition, a bond investment is measured, recorded, and reported in accordance with the **cost principle.** The purchase cost, including all incidental acquisition costs (such as transfer fees and broker commissions), is debited to an investment account such as "Long-Term Investment, Bonds of Beta Corporation." The amount recorded under the cost principle is the **current cash equivalent amount;** and it may be the same as the maturity amount (if acquired at par), less than the maturity amount (if acquired at a discount), or more than the maturity amount (if acquired at a premium).[4] The premium or discount on a bond investment usually is not recorded in a separate account as is done for bonds payable (Chapter 11); rather, the investment account reflects the current book or carrying amount. However, the bond investment account can be debited at par and a separate discount or premium account can be used with precisely the same results.

On each date subsequent to acquisition, a bond investment is measured as the acquisition cost plus any amortized **discount** or minus any amortized **pre-**

---

[4] Fees, commissions, and other incidental costs decrease the discount, or increase the premium; therefore, they are amortized over the remaining period to maturity. Alternatively, such costs sometimes are recorded separately and amortized on the same basis as the discount or premium.

mium. If the bond investment was acquired at par (maturity value) the carrying value amount remains constant over the life of the investment because there is no premium or discount to be amortized. In this situation, revenue earned from the investment each period is measured as the amount of cash interest collected (or accrued).

When a bond investment is purchased at a discount or premium, measurement of the carrying value of the investment after date of acquisition necessitates adjustment of the investment account balance from acquisition cost to maturity amount each period over the life of the investment. This adjustment is the periodic amortization of the discount or premium. The periodic amortization is made as a debit or credit to the investment account, depending on whether there was a discount or premium at acquisition, so that the investment account at the end of each period reflects the **then current carrying amount.**

When a bond investment is acquired at a discount or premium, the revenue from interest each period is measured as the cash interest collected (or accrued) plus or minus the periodic amortization of discount or premium. As was illustrated in Chapter 11 for bonds payable, bond discount or premium may be amortized by using either the straight-line or effective-interest method. The former is simpler, whereas the latter conceptually is preferable. In the paragraphs to follow, we will assume straight-line amortization; effective-interest amortization is explained at the end of this part.

In contrast to long-term investments, discount or premium is not amortized on bonds held as a **short-term** investment because the bonds will be converted to cash (i.e., sold) within the coming year (or the operating cycle if longer) instead of being held to maturity.

The concepts of the carrying value of a $1,000 bond investment and amortization of a discount or premium may be portrayed graphically in the following manner:

When effective-interest amortization of a discount or premium is used, the carrying value lines will be curved instead of straight.

After the date of acquisition, interest revenue must be accrued (by means of an adjusting entry) for periods between the last date on which interest revenue

EXHIBIT 13–4
Bonds purchased at par

Situation:

On July 1, 19E, Roth Company purchased $10,000, 8 percent, 10-year bonds of Ellsworth Company for cash, $10,000 (i.e., at par). The bonds were issued originally on July 1, 19A, and mature June 30, 19J. Interest is paid each June 30. Roth's accounting period ends December 31.

July 1, 19E, to record purchase of bond investment at par (100):

Long-term investment, bonds of Ellsworth Company	10,000	
Cash		10,000

Purchased at par, $10,000 maturity value, 8 percent bonds of Ellsworth Company. (Note: Because the bonds were purchased on an interest date, there was no accrued interest.)

December 31, 19E, adjusting entry at end of the accounting period (and each year through maturity date):

Bond interest receivable	400	
Revenue from investments*		400

Adjusting entry to accrue six months interest revenue on Ellsworth Company bonds ($10,000 × .08 × 6/12 = $400).

   * Alternate titles are Interest Revenue and, sometimes, Interest Income.

June 30, 19F, to record annual interest (and each year until maturity):[a]

Cash ($10,000 × .08)	800	
Bond interest receivable (from December 31 entry)		400
Revenue from investments		400

Receipt of annual interest payment on the Ellsworth Company bonds.

June 30, 19J, maturity date of the bonds; to record cash received for face (maturity) amount of the bond investment:[b]

Cash	10,000	
Long-term investment, bonds of Ellsworth Company		10,000

Retirement of bonds at maturity date (assumes last interest receipt already recorded).

December 31, 19E, Roth Company's **income statement** and **balance sheet** (partial):

Income statement for the year ended December 31, 19E:

Revenue from investments	$	400

Balance sheet at December 31, 19E:

Current assets:

Bond interest receivable	$	400

Investments and funds:

Investment in bonds, at cost (market, $10,125)	10,000	

Notes: *a.* This entry presumes that there was no reversal on January 1, 19F, of the prior adjusting entry. A reversing entry is optional because it serves only to facilitate the subsequent entry (see Chapter 5).

      b. Because the bond investment was purchased at par, there was no premium or discount to be amortized.

was collected and the end of the accounting period. The procedure for accruing interest expense and interest revenue was discussed and illustrated in several prior chapters.

ACCOUNTING FOR BONDS ILLUSTRATED

To illustrate accounting and reporting for a long-term investment, we will assume that on July 1, 19E, Roth Company purchased $10,000, 8 percent, 10-year bonds in the open market. The bonds were issued originally on July 1, 19A, and mature on June 30, 19J. The 8 percent interest is paid each June 30.[5] Roth Company's annual accounting period ends December 31. The sequence of journal entries made by Roth Company during 19E are illustrated under three different purchase cost assumptions as follows:

Assumptions	*Exhibits*
1. Bond investment purchased at par (100)	13–4
2. Bond investment purchased at a discount (98)	13–5
3. Bond investment purchased at a premium (102)	13–6

BONDS PURCHASED AT PAR

When bond investors accept a rate of return (i.e., interest) on a bond investment that is the **same** as the stated rate of interest on the bonds, the bonds will sell at par (i.e., at 100). Bonds that sell at par will not cause a premium or discount. Exhibit 13–4 illustrates the recording and reporting of an **investment** in bonds purchased at par.

BONDS PURCHASED AT A DISCOUNT

When bond investors demand a rate of interest that is higher than the **stated rate,** bonds will sell in the market at a **discount.** When a bond investment is purchased at a discount, the investor receives back in cash the periodic interest payments stated on the bond plus the maturity value, which is a greater amount than the initial cash invested. A discount increases the interest revenue earned on a bond investment. To illustrate, assume that on July 1, 19E, Roth Company purchased a $10,000, 8 percent bond issued by Baker Company for $9,800 cash. The bond will mature in five years (in 19J). Interest of $10,000 × .08 = $800 will be collected annually.

Although $800 cash is collected each year, the annual revenue **earned** from the investment is $840; the additional $40 is due to amortization of the discount. Analysis of the interest revenue, assuming straight-line amortization, is as follows:

---

[5] Bonds usually pay interest semiannually. Annual interest is used in this illustration to reduce the number of repetitive entries. The concepts are applied the same way in either case.

Cash inflows from the investment:
 Annual interest collected, July 1, 19E, through
  June 30, 19J ($10,000 × .08 × 5 years) .... $ 4,000
  Collection of bond at maturity date, June 30, 19J 10,000 $14,000

Cash outflow for the investment:
 July 1, 19E—purchase of bond   9,800
  Difference—net increase in cash (the
   total interest earned) .... $ 4,200

Revenue from investment per year: $4,200 ÷ 5 years =
 $840 (assuming straight-line amortization).

Exhibit 13–5 illustrates the recording and reporting of a bond investment purchased at a discount.

When a bond is purchased, it is recorded at its current cash equivalent amount in accordance with the cost principle. Therefore, when a bond investment is

EXHIBIT 13–5
Bonds purchased at a discount

Situation:
 Exactly the situation given in Exhibit 13–4, except that on July 1, 19E, Roth Company purchased $10,000 of bonds of Baker Company for $9,800 (i.e., at 98), rather than at par.

July 1, 19E, to record purchase of bond investment at a discount (98):

Long-term investment, bonds of Baker Company (at cost)   9,800
 Cash   9,800
 Purchased $10,000 maturity value, 8 percent bonds of the Baker
 Company at 98.

 Note: This entry records the investment at its cost; that is, net of any discount or premium. Some accountants prefer to record it at **gross** as follows with the same end result:

Long-term investment   10,000
 Discount on long-term investment   200
 Cash   9,800

December 31, 19E, end of accounting year; to record adjusting entry for interest revenue and amortization of discount on bond investment (and each year until maturity):

Bond interest receivable ($10,000 × .08 × 6/12)   400
Long-term investment, bonds of Baker Company
 (amortization: $40 × 6/12)   20
 Revenue from investments   420
 Adjusting entry to (1) accrue interest revenue for six months and
 (2) amortize discount on the bond investment for six months (July
 1 to December 31); $200 ÷ 5 years = $40 amortization per year.

June 30, 19F, to record cash interest received and to amortize discount on bond investment (and each year until maturity):

Cash ($10,000 × .08)   800
Long-term investment, bonds of Baker Company
 (amortization: $40 × 6/12)   20
 Bond interest receivable (from December 31 entry)   400
 Revenue from investments   420
 Receipt of annual interest on Baker Company bonds and
 amortization of discount for six months (January 1 to June 30).

EXHIBIT 13–5
(concluded)

June 30, 19J, maturity date; to record cash maturity amount received:

Cash 10,000
        Long-term investment, bonds of Baker Company   10,000
        Retirement of bonds at maturity (assumes last interest receipt
        already recorded).

December 31, 19E, long-term investment account for 19E–19J:

Long-Term Investment, Bonds of Baker Company

July 1, 19E At acquisition	9,800	June 30, 19J Retirement	10,000
Yearly amortizations by:			
Dec. 31, 19E	20		
31, 19F	40		
31, 19G	40		
31, 19H	40		
31, 19I	40		
June 30, 19J	20		
	10,000		10,000

December 31, 19E, **income statement** and **balance sheet** for year 19E (partial)

Income statement for the year ended December 31, 19E:

Revenue from investments .... $ 420

Balance Sheet at December 31, 19E:

Current assets:
    Bond interest receivable .... $ 400

Investments and funds:
    Investment in bonds, at amortized cost (market, $10,125)..... 9,820

purchased at a discount, the investment account balance at the purchase date will be less than par or maturity value. Through **amortization** of the discount, the balance of the investment account must be **increased** each period so that the carrying value will be the same as the par amount on maturity date. Amortization of the discount each period over the **remaining life** of the bond also **increases** the amount of interest revenue earned. The amount of discount amortized each period is debited to the investment account and credited to Interest Revenue. The effects of this periodic amortization, over the life of the investment, are (1) to reflect in the investment account the current carrying amount of the bond at the end of each accounting period, and (2) to increase interest revenue earned each year by the amount of the amortization.

To illustrate these effects, in Exhibit 13–5, Roth Company each year must amortize a part of the discount ($10,000 − $9,800 = $200), so that the total discount ($200) will be amortized over the remaining life of the bond investment. Assuming straight-line amortization, the amount of discount amortized each full year will be $200 ÷ 5 years = $40 per year (as illustrated in Exhibit 13–5).

The increase in the balance of the long-term investment account from cost at date of purchase to par value at maturity date which results from the amortization of the bond discount is reflected in the investment ledger account in Roth's accounts shown in Exhibit 13–5.[6] Also shown in Exhibit 13–5 is 19E financial statement information for Roth Company.

BONDS PURCHASED AT A PREMIUM

When bond investors are willing to invest at a rate of interest that is **less** than the **stated rate** of interest on bonds, the bonds will sell at a **premium.** When bonds are purchased at a premium, the investment account is debited for an amount greater than the par or maturity value of the bonds. Therefore, the premium must be **amortized** over the **remaining life** of the bonds as a **decrease** in the balance of the investment account so that the investment account balance will be the par value on maturity date. The amortization parallels the procedure illustrated above for a discount, except that each period the investment account is credited and the premium amortization **decreases** interest revenue.

To illustrate the accounting and reporting where there is a premium, assume that in the preceding example, Roth Company purchased Garden Company bonds on July 1, 19E, for $10,200 cash. The bonds have an 8 percent interest rate and mature in five years from that date, on June 30, 19J. The cash outflow and inflows for this investment, assuming straight-line amortization, may be analyzed to illustrate the effect of the premium on interest revenue as follows:

Cash inflows from the investment:
  Annual interest collected, July 1, 19E, through
    June 30, 19J ($10,000 × .08 × 5 years) . . . . $ 4,000
    June 30, 19E, collection of bond at maturity 10,000 $14,000

Cash outflow for the investment:
  July 1, 19J—purchase of bond   10,200
    Difference—net increase in cash (the total
      interest revenue earned) $3,800

Revenue from investment, per year: $3,800 ÷ 5 years = $760

Exhibit 13–6 presents the journal entries and financial statements for the investor, Roth Company.

---

[6] Observe that the amortization of discount or premium on bond investments conceptually is the same as the amortization discussed and illustrated in Chapter 11 in the issuer's accounts. Here, we simply are looking at the other side of the transaction. A minor procedural difference may be noted. In Chapter 11, premium or discount was recorded in a separate account; in this chapter, the **net amount** (i.e., the cost) was recorded in the investment account. Either procedure can be used in either situation with the same results. Common practice follows the procedures illustrated in the respective chapters.

EXHIBIT 13–6
Bonds purchased at a premium

Situation:

Exactly the same situation given in Exhibit 13–4, except that on July 1, 19E, Roth Company purchased $10,000 of bonds of Garden Company for $10,200 (i.e., at 102), rather than at par.

July 1, 19E, to record purchase of bond investment at a premium (102):

Long-term investment, bonds of Garden Company (at cost)	10,200	
Cash		10,200

Purchased $10,000 maturity value, 8 percent bonds of Garden Company at 102.

December 31, 19E, end of accounting year; to record adjusting entry for interest revenue and amortization of premium on bond investment (and each year until maturity):

Bond interest receivable ($10,000 × .08 × 6/12)	400	
Long-term investment, bonds of Garden Company (amortization: $40 × 6/12)		20
Revenue from investments		380

Adjusting entry to (1) accrue interest revenue for six months and (2) amortize premium on the investment for six months (July 1 to December 31); $200 ÷ 5 years = $40 amortization per year.

June 30, 19F, to record cash interest received and to amortize premium on bond investment (and each year until maturity):

Cash ($10,000 × .08)	800	
Bond interest receivable (per December 31 entry)		400
Long-term investment, bonds of Garden Company (amortization: $40 × 6/12)		20
Revenue from investments		380

Receipt of annual interest revenue on Garden Company bonds and amortization of premium for six months (January 1 to June 30).

June 30, 19J, maturity date; to record cash maturity amount received:

Cash	10,000	
Long-term investment, bonds of Garden Company		10,000

Retirement of bonds at maturity (assuming the last interest receipt has been recorded).

December 31, 19E, **income statement** and **balance sheet** for year 19E (partial):

Income statement for year ended December 31, 19E:

Revenue from investments	$	380

Balance sheet at December 31, 19E:

Current assets:		
Bond interest receivable	$	400
Investments and funds:		
Investment in bonds, at amortized cost (market, $10,225)	10,180	

BONDS PURCHASED BETWEEN INTEREST DATES

Investors usually purchase bond investments between the interest dates specified on the bonds. In these situations, the investor must pay the amount of **interest accrued** since the last interest date in addition to the purchase price of the bond. The bond market operates in this fashion because the seller of the bond is entitled to interest from the last interest date to the date of the sale transaction; but on the next interest payment date, the new owner will receive interest for the full period between interest dates, regardless of the purchase date. To illustrate, assume Hays Company purchased a $1,000 bond, 12 percent interest, payable 6 percent each March 31 and September 30. The bond was purchased on June 1, 19F, at 100 plus any accrued interest. The purchase of this bond investment would be recorded by Hays Company as follows:

June 1, 19F:

```
Long-term investment, 12 percent bond ...........................   1,000
Revenue from investments ($1,000 × .12 × 2/12)* ...............          20
     Cash [$1,000 + ($1,000 × .12 × 2/12)] ......................              1,020
   Purchase of a $1,000, 12 percent bond as a long-term investment at 100
   plus accrued interest for two months, March 31, 19F (last interest date)
   to June 1, 19F (date of purchase).

   * Alternatively, an account, Bond Interest Receivable, could have been debited on June 1 for $20
   and then credited for that amount on September 30. The net effect would have been the same. When
   the end of the accounting period falls between the purchase date and the next interest date, such a
   procedure may be less complex.
```

In the journal entry recorded on June 1, 19F, the long-term investment account was debited for the cost of the investment, which **excludes** the accrued interest. The $20 accrued interest was paid in cash by the purchaser; however, it will be returned to the purchaser at the next interest date, September 30, 19F. At that time, the purchaser will receive the full amount of cash interest for six months, although the purchaser has owned the bond for only four months (i.e., June 1 to September 30, 19F).

The journal entry to record the first interest collection after the purchase would be:

September 30, 19F:

```
Cash.........................................................   60
     Revenue from investments................................        60
   Collected interest for six months on bond investment ($1,000 × .06 = $60).
```

After these two entries are posted, the Revenue from Investments account on the books of Hays Company will reflect $40 interest earned for the four months since purchase as follows:

Revenue from Investments			
6/1/19F	20	9/30/19F	60

(balance, $1,000 \times .12 \times 4/12 = \$40$ credit)

SALE OF A BOND INVESTMENT

When bonds are acquired as a long-term investment, they are accounted for with the expectation that they will be held to maturity. This expectation is the basis for amortizing any premium or discount over the period from the date of purchase to the maturity date. Nevertheless, a long-term bond investment may be sold prior to the maturity date. When an investor sells bonds prior to maturity, the difference between the sale price and the balance in the investment account (i.e., the book or carrying value) is recorded as a "Gain (or Loss) on the Sale of Investments."

To illustrate, assume Carson Corporation has two $1,000, 12 percent bonds of Drake Company that are being held as a long-term investment. Each bond was purchased at 104; therefore, the long-term investment account was debited for $2,080. Because of amortization of bond premium to January 1, 19F, the investment account balance is $2,040. On that date one of the bonds was sold at 100. The entry by Carson Company to record the sale would be as follows:

```
Cash .......................................................... 1,000
Loss on sale of investments .................................... 20
    Long-term investment, Drake Company bonds ...................        1,020
    Sale of long-term investment.
```

EFFECTIVE-INTEREST AMORTIZATION ON BOND INVESTMENTS

Effective-interest amortization of the discount or premium on a bond investment is similar to the procedures discussed for bonds payable in Chapter 11. This method of amortization is superior conceptually because it is based on the **effective-interest rate;** therefore, (1) interest revenue is measured correctly each period for income statement purposes, and (2) the carrying amount of the investment is measured correctly for balance sheet purposes at the end of each accounting period. Each interest revenue collection (in cash) is assumed to be part principal and part interest. To illustrate the effective-interest method, assume that on January 1, 19A, Farmer Company purchased a five-year, $10,000, 8 percent bond of Research Corporation as a long-term investment. The purchase price, based on a 12 percent effective-interest rate, was 85.58. Therefore, the cash paid was $8,558 (a $1,442 discount). The bonds carried a stated rate of interest of 8 percent per year, payable each December 31. The acquisition was recorded by Farmer Company as follows:[7]

January 1, 19A:

Long-term investment, Research Corporation bonds		
(maturity amount $10,000)	8,558	
Cash		8,558
Purchase of long-term investment.		

Farmer Company decided to use effective-interest amortization of the discount rather than straight line. The journal entries for a bond investment are the same regardless of the amortization method used, except for some of the **amounts** in the periodic interest entries.

Computation of effective-interest amortization is shown in Exhibit 13–7. Observe that the effective rate of interest of 12 percent, rather than the stated rate of 8 percent, is used to compute the interest revenue amounts.

EXHIBIT 13–7
Schedule of effective-interest amortization

Date	Cash Interest Received Each Interest Date	Interest Revenue (based on beginning balance of investment)	Amortization (increase investment)*	Net Investment
1/1/19A (acquisition)				8,558
12/31/19A	800	$8,558 \times .12 = 1,027$	227	8,785
12/31/19B	800	$8,785 \times .12 = 1,054$	254	9,039
12/31/19C	800	$9,039 \times .12 = 1,085$	285	9,324
12/31/19D	800	$9,324 \times .12 = 1,119$	319	9,643
12/31/19E	800	$9,643 \times .12 = 1,157$	357	10,000
Totals	4,000	5,442	1,442	

Note: This example is identical to the illustration of the issuer's situation shown in Exhibit 11–8. Computation of the sale price of the bonds at an effective rate of 12 percent is shown in footnote 7.
* Adjusts the net investment balance to the maturity amount.

The first amount column in Exhibit 13–7 reflects the cash inflow each period for interest (at the stated rate). The second column shows the interest revenue amount to be reported on the income statement each period (i.e., the effective rate on the net investment). The third column shows the amount of the discount

[7] Given the effective rate of 12 percent, the price of the bonds can be determined from a bond table or computed as follows:

$$\$10,000 \times p_{n=5, \, i=12\%} = \$10,000 \times .5674 \text{ (Table 10–2)} \quad \$5,674$$
$$\$800 \times P_{n=5, \, i=12\%} = \$800 \times 3.6048 \text{ (Table 10–4)} = 2,884$$
$$\text{Bond price } (PV \text{ of future cash flows}) \quad \underline{\$8,558}$$

that is amortized (which is the difference between the interest revenue earned and the amount of cash received). The last column shows the carrying value of the investment (i.e., the unamortized principal) that will be reported on the balance sheet at the end of each period under "Investments and funds." The entry for interest revenue each period can be taken directly from the schedule (Exhibit 13–7):

	Year 1	Year 2	Etc.
Cash	800	800	
Long-term investment	227	254	
Revenue from investments	1,027	1,054	

Conceptually, the effective-interest method derives the true interest revenue earned during each period and the correct carrying value of the investment at the end of each period. The straight-line approach provides only approximations of these amounts. When there is a material difference in the amortization amounts between the two methods, *APB Opinion 21* requires use of the effective-interest method. Straight-line amortization often is used because it is simple to apply and the different amounts of premium or discount amortized each period are not material. If the difference is not material, the departure from the conceptually superior method is justified by the exception (i.e., materiality) principle of accounting.

DEMONSTRATION CASE

(Try to resolve the requirements before proceeding to the suggested solution that follows.)

Howell Equipment Corporation has been in operation for 18 years. The company sells a major line of farm equipment. In recent years its service department has expanded significantly. Both sales and service operations have been quite profitable. At the beginning of 19S, the company had considerable excess cash. At that time, the management decided to invest in some securities of two of the manufacturers that supply most of the equipment purchased by Howell for resale. The annual accounting period ends on December 31.

This case focuses on the two long-term investments purchased in 19S. One investment was in equity securities, and the other in debt securities. The transactions follow:

19S

a. Jan. 1 Purchased 2,000 shares of common stock of Dear Company at $40 per share. This was 1 percent of the shares outstanding.

b. Aug. 1 Purchased $100,000, 9 percent bonds payable of the Massey Company at 102, plus any accrued interest. The bonds pay semiannual interest each May 31 and November 30. The bonds mature on May 31, 19X (i.e., five years from June 1, 19S). Brokerage fees amounted to $900.

c. Nov. 30   Received semiannual interest on Massey Company bonds. Use straight-line amortization.

d. Dec. 28   Received $4,000 cash dividend on the Dear Company stock.

e. Dec. 31   Adjusting entry for accrued interest on the Massey Company bonds.

f. Dec. 31   The current market price of the Dear stock is $39 and $103 for the Massey bonds.

g. Dec. 31   Closed Revenue from Investments to Income Summary.

Required:

a.   Give the journal entry for each of the above transactions.

b.   Show how the two investments, the accrued interest receivable and the related revenue, would be reported on the balance sheet and income statement at December 31, 19S.

Suggested solution

Requirement a.

a.   January 1, 19S:

Long-term investment, stock of Dear Company		
(2,000 shares)	80,000	
Cash		80,000
Purchased 2,000 shares Dear Company common stock at $40 per share.		

b.   August 1, 19S:

Long-term investment, bonds of Massey Company	102,900	
Revenue from investments ($100,000 × .09 × 2/12)	1,500	
Cash		104,400
Purchased $100,000 bonds of the Massey Company.		

Computations:
Cost ($100,000 × 1.02) + $900 = $102,900
Accrued interest for 2 months
$100,000 × .09 × 2/12   =   1,500
      Total cash paid $104,400

c. November 30, 19S:

Cash	4,500	
Long-term investment, bonds of Massey Company		200
Revenue from investments		4,300
Computations:		
Semiannual interest: $100,000 \times .045 = \$4,500$		
Amortization of premium:		
$\$2,900 \div 58$ months $= \$50^*$		
per month; $\$50 \times 4$ months $=$ 200		
Revenue from investments ... $\underline{\$4,300}$		
* August 1, 19S, to May 31, 19X $= 58$ months remaining life.		

d. December 28, 19S:

Cash	4,000	
Revenue from investments		4,000
Received dividend on Dear Company stock.		

e. December 31, 19S:

Interest receivable	750	
Long-term investment, bonds of Massey Company		50
Revenue from investments		700
Adjusting entry for accrued interest and premium amortization		
for one month on Massey Company bonds.		
Computations:		
Accrued interest receivable:		
$\$100,000 \times .09 \times 1/12$ $= \$750$		
Amortization of premium:		
$\$50 \times 1$ month $=$ 50		
Revenue from investments ..... $\underline{\$700}$		

f. December 31, 19S:

Unrealized loss on long-term equity investment	2,000	
Allowance to reduce long-term investment to LCM		2,000
To record LCM on Dear stock:		
2,000 shares $\times$ ($40 - $39) = $2,000.		

g. December 31, 19S:

> Revenue from investments 7,500
>   Income summary 7,500
>   Closing entry: ($4,300 − $1,500 + $4,000 + $700 = $7,500).

Requirement b.

HOWELL EQUIPMENT CORPORATION
Balance Sheet (partial)
At December 31, 19S

Current assets:
  Interest receivable .... $ 750

Investments and funds:
  Stock of Dear Company, at LCM, 2,000 shares
    (cost, $80,000) .... $ 78,000*
  Bonds of Massey Company, at amortized cost
    ($100,000 maturity value; market, $103,000) .... 102,650†   180,650

Stockholders' equity:
  Unrealized loss on long-term equity investments ..... (2,000)

    * Cost of equity securities 80,000
    Less: Allowance to reduce long-term
      equity investment to LCM 2,000

    Equity investment at LCM .... $ 78,000

    † Cost of debt securities $102,900
    Less: Amortization of premium
      ($200 + $50) 250
    Debt investment at amortized cost $102,650

HOWELL Equipment Corporation
Income Statement (partial)
For the Year Ending December 31, 19S

Revenue from investments .... $ 7,500

SUMMARY OF CHAPTER

This chapter discussed the measuring and reporting of two types of long-term investments: the capital stock (equity securities) and the bonds (debt securities) of another company. An entity (investor) may acquire a part or all of the outstanding capital stock of a corporation by **purchase** of its shares or, if the investor is a corporation, by **exchange** of its own stock for shares in the other company. The measuring and reporting of long-term investments in shares of capital stock of another company are determined by the percent of shares owned in relation to the total number of shares outstanding.

If the ownership level of **voting** shares is less than 20 percent, or if the ownership is of nonvoting stock, the **cost method** must be used. Under this method, the investment amount reported by the investor company is the lower of cost or market, and investment revenue is recognized on the basis of dividends declared by the investee corporation.

If the ownership is at least 20 percent but not more than 50 percent, the **equity method** must be used. Under this method, the investment is recorded at cost by the investor company at date of acquisition. Each period thereafter, the investment amount is increased (or decreased) by the proportionate interest in the income (or loss) reported by the investee corporation and decreased by the proportionate share of the dividends declared by the investee corporation. The LCM basis is not used with the equity method. Each period, the investor company recognizes as revenue its proportionate share of the income (or loss) reported by the investee company.

When there is a controlling interest—that is, more than 50 percent ownership of the outstanding voting stock is held by the investor—the financial statements of the affiliated companies (investor and investee) are **consolidated.** This subject is discussed in Chapter 14.

An entity may purchase the bonds (i.e., debt securities) of another entity as a long-term investment. In contrast to capital stock, bonds are a liability of the issuing company; therefore, bonds (1) have a specified maturity date and maturity amount, (2) require the payment of a stated rate of interest at regular specified interest dates, and (3) do not convey voting privileges. At the date of purchase, a long-term investment in bonds is recorded at cost, which may be at par, at a discount, or at a premium. When purchased at a premium or a discount, amortization of such premium or discount over the **remaining life** of the bonds is required. The periodic amortization adjusts (1) the investment amount to a carrying value which is reported on the balance sheet and (2) the interest revenue which is reported on the income statement.

IMPORTANT TERMS DEFINED IN THIS CHAPTER

Terms (alphabetically)	Key words in definitions of important terms used in chapter	Page reference
Control	The ability of an investor to determine the operating and financing policies of another company (the investee).	603
Cost method	Method used by investor if less than 20 percent of the voting stock of the investee company is owned by the investor.	603
Discount	A bond that is purchased for less than par value is purchased at a discount; the difference between cost and par of a bond.	613
Effective interest	The real or true rate of interest; also called the market rate of interest.	613
Equity method	Method used by investor if 20–50 percent of the voting stock of the investee company is owned by the investor.	606
Premium	A bond that is purchased for more than par value is purchased at a premium; the difference between cost and par of a bond.	616
Significant influence	The ability of an investor to have an important impact on the operating and financing policies of another company (the investee).	603
Stated interest rate	The annual rate of cash interest specified in the bond contract.	613

QUESTIONS FOR DISCUSSION

PART A

1. Explain the difference between a short-term investment and a long-term investment.

2. Match the following:

    Measurement method
    _____ Cost method.
    _____ Equity method.
    _____ Consolidation.

    Level of ownership of the voting capital stock
    a. More than 50 percent ownership.
    b. Less than 20 percent ownership.
    c. At least 20 percent but not more than 50 percent.

3. Explain the application of the cost principle to the purchase of shares of capital stock in another company.

4. Under the cost method, when and how is revenue measured by the investor company?

5. Under the equity method, why is revenue measured on a proportionate basis by the investor company when income is reported by the other company, rather than when dividends are declared?

6. Under the equity method, dividends received from the investee company are not recorded as revenue. To record dividends as revenue would involve double counting. Explain.

7. Match the following items that relate to the long-term investment amount reported on the balance sheet of the investor company:

    Measurement method
    _____ Cost method.
    _____ Equity method.

    Explanation of balance in the investment account
    a. LCM.
    b. Original cost plus proportionate part of the income of the investee, less proportionate part of the dividends declared by investee.

PART B

8. Explain the difference between an equity security and a debt security.

9. Explain why interest revenue must be accrued on a long-term investment in bonds but not on a long-term investment in capital stock.

10. Under what conditions will a bond sell at *(a)* par, *(b)* a discount, and *(c)* a premium?

11. Distinguish between a long-term investment in bonds and a long-term investment in the capital stock of another company.

12. Why is it necessary to amortize premium or discount that arises from the purchase of a long-term bond investment above or below par? Over what period should the premium or discount be amortized?

13. When a bond investment is purchased between interest dates, the purchaser must pay accrued interest plus the purchase price of the bond. Explain why the accrued interest must be paid.

EXERCISES

PART A

E13–1. Company P purchased a certain number of the outstanding voting shares of Company S at $15 per share as a long-term investment. Company S had outstanding 10,000 shares of $10 par value stock. On a separate sheet complete the following matrix relating to the measurement and reporting by Company P after acquisition of the shares of Company S stock.

Questions	Method of Measurement	
	Cost Method	Equity Method
a. What is the applicable level of ownership by Company P of Company S to apply the method?	Percent	Percent
For (b), (e), (f), and (g) that follow, assume: Number of shares acquired of Company S stock Net income reported by Company S in the first year Dividends declared by Company S in the first year Market price at end of first year, Company S stock, $13.50	1,000 $40,000 $10,000	3,000 $40,000 $10,000
b. At acquisition, the investment account on the books of Company P should be debited at what amount?	$	$
c. On what basis should Company P recognize revenue earned on the stock of Company S? Explanation required.		
d. After acquisition date, on what basis should Company P change the balance of investment account in respect to the stock of Company S owned (other than for disposal of the investment)? Explanation required.		
e. What would be the balance in the investment account on the books of Company P at the end of the first year?	$	$
f. What amount of revenue from the investment in Company S should Company P report at the end of the first year?	$	$
g. What amount of unrealized loss should Company P report at the end of the first year?	$	$

E13–2. During 19B, Adams Company acquired some of the 60,000 shares of the common stock, par $10, of Cox Corporation as a long-term investment. The accounting period for both companies ends December 31. The following transactions occurred:

19B
July 2 Purchased 6,000 shares of Cox common stock at $20 per share.
Dec. 31 Received a copy of the 19B annual financial statement of Cox Corporation that reflected net income of $40,000.
31 Cox Corporation declared and paid a cash dividend of $.50 per share.
31 Market price of Cox stock was $19 per share.

Required:

a. What accounting method should Adams Company use? Why?
b. Give the required journal entries by Adams Company for each transaction. If no entry is required, explain why.
c. Show how the long-term investment and the related revenue should be reported on the 19B financial statements of Adams Company.

E13–3. Black Company acquired some of the 40,000 shares of outstanding common stock (nopar) of Noe Corporation during 19E as a long-term investment. The annual accounting period for both companies ends December 31. The following transactions occurred during 19E:

19E
Jan. 10 Purchased 16,000 shares of Noe stock at $30 per share.
Dec. 31 Received the 19E financial statement of Noe Corporation which reported net income of $70,000.
      31 Noe Corporation, declared and paid a cash dividend of $1.25 per share.
      31 Market price of Noe stock was $28 per share.

Required:

a. What method of accounting should Black Company use? Why?
b. Give the journal entries by Black Company for each of the above transactions. State if no entry is required and explain why.
c. Show how the long-term investment and the related revenue should be reported on the 19E financial statements of Black Company.

E13–4. During 19H, Ross Company purchased some of the 100,000 shares of common stock, par $10, of Salt Marine, Inc., as a long-term investment. The annual accounting period for each company ends December 31. The following transactions occurred during 19H.

19H
Jan. 7 Purchased 15,000 shares of Salt stock at $15 per share.
Dec. 31 Received the 19H financial statement of Salt Marine, which reported net income of $70,000.
      31 Salt declared and paid a cash dividend of $1.10 per share.
      31 Market price of Salt stock was $17.50 per share.

Required:

a. What method of accounting should Ross Company use? Why?
b. Give the journal entries for Ross Company for each of the above transactions. State if no entry is required and explain why.
c. Show how the long-term investment and the related revenue should be reported on the 19H financial statements of Ross Company.

E13–5. You are to use the same situation for Ross Company and the data given in Exercise 13–4, **except** for the January 7, 19H, transaction. Assume it was as follows:

19H
Jan. 7 Purchased 30,000 shares of Salt stock at $15 per share.

(The data for December 31 are unchanged.)

Required:

a. What method of accounting should Ross Company use? Why?
b. Give the journal entries for Ross Company for each transaction (refer also to transactions given in Exercise 13–4). State if no entry is required and explain why.
c. Show how the long-term investment and the related revenue should be reported on the 19H financial statements of Ross Company.

PART B

E13–6. On July 1, 19A, AB Company purchased at par a $10,000, 9 percent, 20-year bond of CD Corporation as a long-term investment. The annual bond interest is payable each year on June 30. The accounting period for AB Company ends December 31. At the date of purchase, the bond had five years remaining before maturity.

Required:

Give the journal entries on the books of AB Company for the following transactions:

a. July 1, 19A, for acquisition.
b. December 31, 19A, adjusting entry at the end of the accounting period.
c. June 30, 19B, collection of first interest.
d. Maturity date of the bond, June 30, 19F.

E13–7. On April 1, 19A, Nash Company purchased at par eight $1,000, 9 percent, 10-year bonds of HI Corporation as a long-term investment. The bond interest is payable semiannually each March 31 and September 30. The accounting period for Nash Company ends on December 31. At the date of purchase, the bonds had six years remaining to maturity.

Required:

Give the journal entry for each of the following dates in the accounts of Nash Company in respect to the long-term investment: April 1, 19A; September 30, 19A; December 31, 19A; March 31, 19B; and the maturity date.

E13–8. On February 1, 19A, Ham Company purchased at par a $15,000, 10 percent, 20-year bond of Lam Corporation as a long-term investment. The bond interest is payable semiannually each January 31 and July 31. The accounting period for Ham Company ends December 31. At the date of purchase, the bonds had four years remaining to maturity.

Required:

Give all journal entries required in the accounts of Ham Company for the period February 1, 19A, through January 31, 19B, and on the maturity date.

E13–9. On July 1, 19B, Ray Company purchased three different bonds as long-term investments. Data with respect to the three bonds and the purchase prices were:

Bond designation	Par of bond	Annual interest	Payable semiannually	Remaining years to maturity	Market purchase price*
A	$1,000	10%	Dec. 31 and	5	$1,000
B	1,000	9	June 30	5	970
C	1,000	12	each year	5	1,020

* These amounts do not include any accrued interest.

Required:

a. Give the journal entries to record separately the purchase of each bond.
b. Give the journal entries to record separately collection of interest on the first interest date after purchase. Use straight-line amortization of any discount or premium.
c. Give the journal entries to record separately the maturity of each bond.

E13–10. On May 1, 19B, Delta Company purchased $9,000 maturity value bonds of Opel Corporation at 96.25 (plus any accrued interest) as a long-term investment. The bond interest rate is 12 percent per annum payable 6 percent each April 30 and October 31. The bonds mature in four years from May 1, 19B.

Required:

a. Give the journal entries for Delta Company on May 1, 19B; October 31, 19B; and December 31, 19B (adjusting entry for accrued interest). Use straight-line amortization and round all amounts to the nearest dollar.
b. Show how this long-term investment and the related revenue should be shown on the December 31, 19B, annual financial statements of Delta Company. (Hint: Include the investment, interest receivable, and any revenue.)

E13–11. On May 1, 19B, Kent Company purchased $10,000, 8 percent bonds of Cook Corporation, at 106 (plus any accrued interest) as a long-term investment. The bonds pay interest each April 30 and October 31. The bonds mature in five years on April 30, 19G.

Required:

a. Give the journal entries for Kent Company on May 1, 19B; October 31, 19B; and December 31, 19B (adjusting entry for accrued interest). Use straight-line amortization and round to the nearest dollar.
b. Show how this long-term investment should be shown on the December 31, 19B, annual financial statements of Kent Company.

E13–12. On March 1, 19B, Star Corporation purchased $6,000, 10 percent bonds of TU Corporation as a long-term investment. The bonds pay interest each June 30 and December 31. The bonds mature in 10 years on December 31, 19K. The purchase price was $6,236, plus any accrued interest.

Required:

a. Give the journal entry by Star Corporation to record the purchase on March 1, 19B.
b. Give the journal entry to record the interest received on June 30 and December 31, 19B. Use straight-line amortization.
c. What was the amount of interest revenue in 19B? At what amount should the bond investment be reported on the balance sheet at December 31, 19B?

E13–13. On January 1, 19A, Cotton Company purchased, as a long-term investment, a $3,000 bond of Devons Company for $2,922 (plus any accrued interest). The bond had a stated interest rate of 7 percent, payable each January 1. The bond matures in three years on December 31, 19C. Cotton Company uses effective-interest amortization. As a consequence, the amortization table given below was developed.

Date	Cash inflow	Interest revenue	Investment change	Investment balance
January 1, 19A				$2,922
End year 19A	$210	$234	$24	2,946
End year 19B	210	236	26	2,972
End year 19C	210	238	28	3,000

Required:

Respond to the following questions:

a. How much was the discount or premium?
b. What was the total cash outflow and the total cash inflow over the life of this investment? What does the difference represent? Explain.
c. How much interest revenue should be recognized on the income statement each year and in total?
d. What amounts should be reported on the balance sheet each year? For the last year give the amounts just prior to collection of the maturity amount.
e. What was the effective rate of interest per year? Show computations.
f. Show how the four different amounts that are listed on the line 19B were computed.
e. Show how the price of the bond of $2,922 was computed.

E13–14. On January 1, 19A, Indian Company purchased, as a long-term investment, a $10,000 par value, 12 percent bond issued by Jackson Corporation. The bond pays interest each year on December 31 and has five years' remaining life to maturity from January 1, 19A. The accounting period for Indian Corporation ends December 31.

The bond was purchased to yield a 10 percent effective rate of interest; therefore, the price of the bond was computed as follows:

$$\$10,000 \times p_{n=5; i=10\%} \ (.6209) = \$ \ 6,209$$
$$\$1,200 \times P_{n=5; i=10\%} \ (3.7908) = \quad 4,549$$
$$\text{Sales price} \ \ldots\ldots\ldots \quad \$10,758$$

Required:

a. Give the journal entry for Indian Company to record the purchase of the bond on January 1, 19A.
b. Prepare a schedule of effective-interest amortization similar to Exhibit 13–7.
c. Give the journal entries for the collection of interest on the bond investment during 19A and 19B.
d. Complete the following schedule (show computations):

	December 31	
	19A	19B
Income statement:		
Revenue from bond investment	$ _____	$ _____
Balance sheet:		
Bond interest receivable	_____	_____
Long-term investment, bond of Jackson Corporation	_____	_____

PROBLEMS/CASES

PART A

PC13–1. During January 19A, Seven Company purchased 10,000 shares of the 100,000 outstanding common shares (nopar value) of Eleven Corporation at $40 per share. This block of stock was purchased as a long-term investment. Assume the accounting period for each company ends December 31.

Subsequent to acquisition, the following data were available:

	19A	19B
Income reported by Eleven Corporation at December 31	$60,000	$70,000
Cash dividends declared and paid by Eleven Corporation during the year	20,000	30,000
Market price per share of Eleven common stock on December 31	37	38

Required:

a. What accounting method should be used by Seven Company? Why?
b. Give the journal entries required in the accounts of Seven Company for each year (use parallel columns) for the following (if none, explain why):
    (1) Acquisition of Eleven Corporation stock.
    (2) Net income reported by Eleven Corporation.
    (3) Dividends received from Eleven Corporation.
    (4) Market value effects at year-end.
c. Show how the following amounts should be reported on the financial statements for Seven Company for each year:
    (1) Long-term investment.
    (2) Stockholders' equity—unrealized loss.
    (3) Revenues.

PC13–2. During January 19A, Doe Corporation purchased the shares listed below as a long-term investment:

		Number of shares		
Corporation	Stock	Out-standing	Purchase	Cost per share
M	Common (nopar)	80,000	12,000	$10
N......	Preferred, nonvoting (par $10)	10,000	4,000	15

Assume the accounting period of each company ends on December 31. Subsequent to acquisition, the following data were available:

	19A	19B
Net income reported at December 31:		
Corporation M	$20,000	$22,000
Corporation N	30,000	31,000
Dividends declared and paid per share during the year:		
Corporation M common stock	$ 1.00	$ 1.10
Corporation N preferred stock	.20	.20
Market value per share at December 31:		
Corporation M common stock	8.00	9.00
Corporation N preferred stock	16.00	15.00

Required:

a. What accounting method should be used by Doe for the M common stock? N preferred stock? Why?
b. Give the journal entries for Doe Corporation for each year in parallel columns (if none, state why) for each of the following:
    (1) Purchase of the investments.
    (2) Income reported by Corporations M and N.
    (3) Dividends received from Corporations M and N.
    (4) Market value effects at year-end.

    c. For each year, show how the following amounts should be reported on the financial statements for 19A:

       (1) Long-term investment.

       (2) Stockholders' equity—unrealized loss.

       (3) Revenues.

PC13–3. Company S had outstanding 20,000 shares of common stock, par value $10 per share. On January 1, 19B, Company P purchased some of these shares at $20 per share. At the end of 19B, Company S reported the following: income, $40,000; and cash dividends declared and paid during the year, $10,000. The market value of Company S stock at the end of 19B was $15 per share.

Required:

    a. For each case given below (in the tabulation), identify the method of accounting that should be used by Company P. Explain why.

    b. Give the journal entries required of Company P at the dates indicated below for each of the two independent cases. If no entry is required, so indicate and explain. Use the following format:

Tabulation of items	Case A—2,000 shares purchased	Case B—8,000 shares purchased
1. Entry to record the acquisition at January 1, 19B.	_____	_____
2. Entry to recognize the income reported by Company S for 19B.	_____	_____
3. Entry to recognize the dividends declared and paid by Company S for 19B.	_____	_____
4. Entry to recognize market value effect at end of 19B.	_____	_____

    c. Complete the following schedule to show the separate amounts that should be reported on the 19B financial statements of Company P.

	Dollar amounts	
	Case A	Case B
Balance sheet:		
Investments and funds	_____	_____
Stockholders' equity	_____	_____
Income statement:		
Revenue from investments	_____	_____

    d. Explain why assets, stockholders' equity, and revenues are different between the two cases.

PC13–4. Fortner Company purchased, as a long-term investment, some of the 100,000 shares of the outstanding common stock of Towns Corporation. The annual accounting period for each company ends December 31. The following transactions occurred during 19E.

19E

Jan. 10   Purchased shares of common stock of Towns at $11 per share as follows:

      Case A—10,000 shares.

      Case B—30,000 shares.

Dec. 31   Received the 19E financial statements of Towns Corporation; the reported net income was $70,000.

    31   Received a cash dividend of $.30 per share from Towns Corporation.

    31   Market price of Towns stock, $8 per share.

Required:

a. For each case, what accounting method should be used by Fortner? Explain why.

b. Give the journal entries for Fortner Company for each case for the above transactions. State if no entry is required and explain why. (Hint: You can save time by using parallel columns for Case A and Case B.)

c. Give the amounts for each case that should be reported on the 19E financial statements of Fortner Corporation. Use the following format:

	Case A	Case B
Balance sheet (partial):		
Investments and funds:		
Investment in common stock, Towns Corporation.....	_____	_____
Stockholders' equity:		
Unrealized loss	_____	_____
Income statement (partial):		
Revenue from investments	_____	_____

PC13–5. Sub Corporation had outstanding 200,000 shares of nopar common stock. On January 10, 19B, Par Company purchased a block of these shares in the open market at $20 per share. At the end of 19B, Sub Corporation reported net income of $200,000 and cash dividends of $.30 per share. At December 31, 19B, the Sub stock was selling at $19.50 per share. This problem involves two separate cases:

Case A—Par Company purchased 30,000 shares of Sub common stock.

Case B—Par Company purchased 60,000 shares of Sub common stock.

Required:

a. For each case, what accounting method should be used by Par Company? Explain why.

b. For each case, give, in parallel columns, the journal entries of Par Company for each of the following (if no entry is required, explain why):
   (1) Acquisition.
   (2) Revenue recognition.
   (3) Dividends received.
   (4) Market value effects.

c. For each case, show how the following should be reported on the 19B financial statements of Par Company:
   (1) Long-term investments.
   (2) Market effects.
   (3) Revenues.

d. Explain why the amounts reported (in Requirement [c]) are different between the two cases.

PC13–6. On January 1, 19B, Emerson Company purchased 40 percent of the outstanding common stock of Reed Corporation at a total cost of $780,000. On December 31, 19B, the investment in Reed Corporation was reported by Emerson as $950,000, but Emerson did not purchase any additional Reed stock. Emerson Company received $120,000 in cash dividends from Reed. The dividends were declared and paid during 19B. Emerson used the equity method to account for its investment in Reed. The market price of Reed stock increased during 19B.

Required:

a. Explain why the investment account balance increased from $780,000 to $950,000 during 19B.

b. What amount of revenue from the Reed investment was reported by Emerson during 19B.

c. If Emerson used the cost method, what amount of revenue from the Reed investment should have been reported in 19B?

d. If Emerson used the cost method, what amount should be reported as the investment in Reed Corporation on the December 31, 19B, Emerson Company balance sheet?

PART B

PC13–7. On January 1, 19B, Ace Company purchased $60,000, 10 percent bonds of Bye Company as a long-term investment, at 100 (plus any accrued interest). Interest is payable annually on December 31. The bonds have six years to maturity from December 31, 19A. The annual accounting period for Ace Company ends December 31. In addition, on January 2, 19B, Ace Company purchased in the market 5 percent of the 10,000 shares of outstanding common stock of Bye Company at $30 per share.

Required:

a. Give the journal entry by Ace Company to record the purchase of the bonds on January 1, 19B.

b. Give the journal entry to record the purchase of the common stock on January 2, 19B.

c. Give the journal entry assuming a cash dividend of $2.50 per share was declared and received on the Bye stock on December 28, 19B.

d. Give the journal entry for the receipt of the interest on the Bye bonds on December 31, 19B.

e. Show how the long-term investments and the related revenues should be reported on the 19B annual financial statements of Ace Company. Market price of Bye stock was $31 at the end of 19B.

PC13–8. On May 1, 19B, Sun Company purchased $30,000, 8 percent bonds of Taylor Company, as a long-term investment. The interest is payable each April 30 and October 31. The bonds have four years to maturity from May 1, 19B. The bonds were purchased at 96 (plus any accrued interest). In addition, brokerage fees of $240 were paid by Sun Company.

Required:

a. Give the 19B journal entries of Sun Company on the following dates:

May 1 Purchase.
Oct. 31 First interest date. Use straight-line amortization.
Dec. 31 Adjusting entry for accrued interest at the end of the annual accounting period.

b. Show how the investment, interest receivable, and related revenue should be reported on the 19B annual financial statements of Sun Company.

c. Give the journal entry at the maturity date of the bonds.

PC13–9.   On June 1, 19B, Fry Company purchased $30,000, 12 percent bonds of Gray Company, as a long-term investment. The interest is payable each April 30 and October 31. The bonds have five years to maturity from the issue date, May 1, 19B. The bonds were purchased at 103 (plus any accrued interest). In addition, Fry Company paid brokerage fees of $280. The annual accounting period for Fry Company ends December 31.

Required:

a.   Give the journal entries for Fry Company on the following dates:

   June   1   Purchase plus any accrued interest.
   Oct.   31   First interest date. Use straight-line amortization.
   Dec.   31   Adjusting entry for accrued interest.

b.   Show how the investment, interest receivable, and related revenue should be reported on the 19B annual financial statements of Fry Company.
c.   Give the journal entry at the maturity date of the bonds, April 30, 19G.

PC13–10.   During 19A, Akers Company purchased the following bonds of Bounds Corporation as a long-term investment:

	Series A	Series B	Series C	Series D
Maturity amount	$10,000	$10,000	$10,000	$10,000
Date purchased	7/1/19A	7/1/19A	7/1/19A	9/1/19A
Interest per annum	8%	7%	9%	9%
Interest dates, annual	June 30	June 30	June 30	June 30
Maturity date	6/30/19F	6/30/19F	6/30/19F	6/30/19F
Purchase price*	100	95	106	100

   * Plus any accrued interest.

Required:

a.   Give the journal entries to record separately the purchase of the long-term investments.
b.   Give the adjusting entries of Akers Company for December 31, 19A, assuming this is the end of the accounting period. Give a separate journal entry for each series. Use straight-line amortization.
c.   Give the journal entry of Akers Company for each separate series that should be made on June 30, 19B, for collection of the first interest payment.
d.   Complete the following schedule to show the amounts that should be reported on the 19A financial statements (show each series separately):

   Income statement (19A):
   Revenue from investments .... $_____

   Balance sheet (at December 31, 19A):
   Long-term investment, bonds of Bounds Corporation ..... $_____

PC13–11.   On January 1, 19A, Evans Corporation purchased, as a long-term investment, a bond of Fable Corporation. The following schedule was prepared based on the investment (table captions have been omitted intentionally):

January 1, 19A				$10,339
End year 19A	$800	$724	$76	10,263
End year 19B	800	718	82	10,181
End year 19C	800	713	87	10,094
End year 19D	800	706	94	10,000

Required:

Respond to the following questions in respect to the investment by Evans Corporation:

a. What was the maturity amount of the bond?
b. What was the acquisition price of the investment?
c. Give the journal entry that Evans Corporation should make at acquisition date.
d. Was the bond acquired at a premium or discount? How much?
e. What was the stated rate of interest per year? Show computations.
f. What method of amortization apparently will be used? Explain.
g. What was the effective rate of interest?
h. What were the total cash inflow and total cash outflow on the investment? What does the difference represent? Explain.
i. How much interest revenue should be reported each period on the income statement? How does this amount relate to the difference in *(h)?*
j. What amount will be reported on the balance sheet at the end of each year? (Show the amount for year 19D just prior to collection of the maturity amount.)
k. How were the amounts in each of the four columns of the above schedule computed? Use year 19B to demonstrate the computations.
l. Why is the method of amortization being used conceptually preferable?

PC13–12. On January 1, 19A, Austin Corporation purchased $50,000, 9 percent bonds of Boston Company to yield an effective rate of 10 percent. The bonds pay the interest on June 30 and December 31 and will mature on December 31, 19C.

This long-term investment was recorded by Austin Corporation as follows:

January 1, 19A:

Long-term investment, Boston Company bonds	48,730	
Cash		48,730

Computations:

Principal—$50,000 × $p_{n=6;i=5\%}$ (.7462)	= $37,310
Interest—$2,250 × $P_{n=6;i=5\%}$ (5.0757)	= 11,420
Bond price	$48,730

Required:

a. What were the stated and effective rates of interest?
b. What was the amount of the discount or premium? What would be the amount of discount or premium amortization each interest period assuming straight-line amortization?
c. Prepare a schedule of effective-interest amortization similar to Exhibit 13–7.
d. Give the journal entries to record interest (including amortization) on June 30 and December 31, 19A, assuming (1) straight-line and (2) effective-interest amortization.
e. Explain when it is appropriate to use each method of amortization.

Consolidated Statements—Measuring and Reporting

PURPOSE OF THIS CHAPTER

The preceding chapter discussed long-term investments in equity securities when one company owns 50 percent or less of the outstanding voting stock of another corporation. This chapter discusses those situations in which there is a controlling interest evidenced by ownership of more than 50 percent of the outstanding voting stock of another corporation. Prior to studying this chapter you should review Chapter 13.

Basically, when a company has a controlling interest in another company, the financial statements for each company often will be combined into a single set of financial statements by an accounting process called **consolidation.** Those persons who do not plan to study accounting beyond the introductory level need a general background in order to understand and evaluate the economic and accounting implications of business combinations. In most business courses, financial statements are encountered in various situations, and most of them will be consolidated statements. Outside the classroom, you frequently will encounter consolidated statements. For those persons who plan to study accounting further, this background will help you understand the broad issues, measurement approaches, and underlying concepts of consolidated statements. This chapter has as its primary objective the presentation of the basic issues associated with consolidated financial statements.

This chapter discusses the preparation, interpretation, and use of consolidated financial statements. Measuring approaches and reporting on a consolidated basis are accorded primary attention. The important differences that result between two alternative approaches for accounting for a combination (pooling of interests and a combination by purchase) are identified and discussed.

To accomplish the broad purpose of this chapter, two parts and two supplements are presented:

Part A—Acquiring a controlling interest

Part B—Reporting consolidated operations after acquisition

Supplement 14A—Consolidation procedures—100 percent ownership

Supplement 14B—Consolidation procedures—less than 100 percent ownership

PART A—ACQUIRING A CONTROLLING INTEREST

CRITERIA FOR CONSOLIDATED FINANCIAL STATEMENTS

When an investor company owns more than 50 percent of the outstanding voting stock of another corporation, a **parent** and **subsidiary** relationship is said to exist. The investing corporation is known as the parent company, and the other corporation is called a subsidiary. Both corporations continue as **separate legal entities.** Each company has its own accounting system, and each prepares its own financial statements. However, because of their special relationship, they are viewed as a **single economic entity** for financial measuring and reporting purposes. Because the parent and subsidiary are viewed as a single economic entity, the parent company (but not the subsidiary) is required to prepare **consolidated financial statements.** The individual financial statements of the parent and each of its subsidiaries are combined by the parent company into one overall or consolidated set of financial statements, as if there were only one entity. The three required statements—balance sheet, income statement, and statement of changes in financial position—are consolidated by the parent company.

There are a number of operating, economic, and legal advantages to the parent-subsidiary relationship. As a consequence, most large corporations, and many medium-sized corporations, have a controlling interest in one or more other corporations.

Consolidated financial statements are prepared in situations in which two basic elements are present. The two basic elements are control and economic compatibility.

Control is presumed to exist when more than 50 percent of the outstanding voting stock of an entity is owned by one investor. The nonvoting stock is not included in the determination of control because it does not provide the investor with any ability to control the policies of the subsidiary. In special circumstances, effective control may not exist, even though more than 50 percent of the voting stock is owned. This situation may exist when the subsidiary is located in a foreign country where **governmental restrictions** prevent the parent company from exercising meaningful control regardless of the number of shares of voting stock owned by the parent company. In circumstances where control is lacking, consolidated statements are inappropriate.

Economic compatibility means that the operations of the affiliated companies are related so that one complements the other. For example, the operations of an automobile manufacturer (such as General Motors) would be economically compatible with the operations of a company that manufactures spark plugs. On the other hand, a manufacturing company and a bank lack economic compatibility and should not be consolidated.

Consolidated statements are not prepared when one company owns more than 50 percent of the voting stock of another company, but the company lacks either (a) meaningful control or (b) economic compatibility with the other company. In such situations, the investment in the subsidiary is reported as a long-term investment on the balance sheet of the parent as "Investment in unconsolidated subsidiary." The investment is accounted for under the **equity method** as discussed in Chapter 13 and is not consolidated.

Consolidated statements affect only the **reporting** by the parent company of the financial results of the parent and its subsidiaries. The accounting for each subsidiary company is unaffected. The fact that a parent company owns a controlling interest has no affect on the accounting and reporting by a subsidiary. At the end of the accounting period, the subsidiary prepares its own financial statements. Similarly, the parent company carries out the accounting for its own operations in the normal manner and prepares its own financial statements at the end of each period.

When consolidation is appropriate, the financial statements of the parent and the subsidiaries, prepared in the normal manner, are combined by the parent company on an **item-by-item basis** to develop the parent's consolidated financial statements. Thus, the consolidated statement concept does not affect the recording of transactions by the parent and the subsidiaries but affects only the **reporting phase** of the combined entity represented by the parent company and its subsidiaries.

METHODS OF ACQUIRING A CONTROLLING INTEREST

One corporation may acquire a controlling interest in another corporation either *(a)* by creating a new corporation and **retaining** more than 50 percent of the voting stock of the new entity or *(b)* by **acquiring** more than 50 percent of the outstanding voting stock of an existing corporation. Both approaches of acquiring a controlling interest are used widely. A parent company may acquire the voting capital stock of a subsidiary in either of two ways as follows:[1]

1. **Exchanging shares of parent company voting stock for more than 50 percent of the outstanding voting capital stock of the subsidiary (owned by the stockholders of the subsidiary)**—If certain additional criteria are met, this type of acquisition is called a **pooling of interests.** In this situation, the stockholders of the subsidiary give up their subsidiary shares and become stockholders only of the parent company.
2. **Purchasing by the parent, using cash, other assets, or debt, of more than 50 percent of the outstanding voting shares from the stockholders of the subsidiary**—This is known as a **combination by purchase.** In this situation, the stockholders of the subsidiary sell more than 50 percent of their voting shares and subsequently they are not stockholders of either the parent or the subsidiary.

The pooling and purchase methods have significantly different impacts on the consolidated income statement and balance sheet. The next few paragraphs discuss

---

[1] There is a basic distinction between a pure combination by pooling of interest and a pure purchase. However, a controlling interest may be acquired in part by a stock exchange and in part by a cash purchase. In these "nonpure" situations, a rigid list of criteria must be met to qualify as a pooling of interest (see footnote 2); otherwise, the combination must be accounted for as a combination by purchase.

EXHIBIT 14–1
Illustrative data for
consolidation

COMPANY P AND COMPANY S
Separate Balance Sheets
January 1, 19A, Immediately before Acquisition

	Company P		Company S	
Assets				
Cash		$205,000		$ 35,000
Accounts receivable (net)*		15,000		30,000
Receivable from Company S		10,000		
Inventories		170,000		70,000
Plant and equipment (net)*		100,000		45,000
Total assets		$500,000		$180,000
Liabilities and Stockholders' Equity				
Liabilities:				
Accounts payable		$ 60,000		$ 20,000
Payable to Company P				10,000
Stockholders' equity:				
Common stock, Company P (par $6)	$300,000			
Common stock, Company S (par $10)			$100,000	
Retained earnings	140,000	440,000	50,000	150,000
Total liabilities and stockholders' equity		$500,000		$180,000

* Accounts receivable, less the allowance for doubtful accounts; and plant and equipment, less accumulated depreciation. The net amounts are used to simplify the example. The end results will be the same as they would have been had the separate contra accounts been used.

these major impacts and the problems of measuring and reporting on the consolidated financial statements of the parent company.

Throughout the chapter we will use a continuing example to illustrate the measuring approaches involved with consolidated financial statements. We will use data for Company P (the parent) and Company S (the acquired subsidiary) shown in Exhibit 14–1.

POOLING OF INTERESTS METHOD

When one corporation acquires more than 50 percent of the voting stock of another corporation by **exchanging** stock, the stockholders of the two corporations have, in effect, pooled their ownership interests. This transaction often is not viewed as a purchase/sale transaction.[2] Because there is no purchase/sale transaction, the cost principle is **not** applied to pooling of interests acquisitions. As a

---

[2] AICPA, *APB Opinion No. 16,* "Business Combinations" (New York, August 1970), states precise conditions under which a business combination **must** be measured and reported as a pooling of interests. The *Opinion* states: "The combination of existing voting common stock interests by the exchange of stock is the essence of a business combination accounted for by the pooling of interests." The *Opinion* specifies a number of additional conditions that, if present, **require** use of the pooling of interests method. Because of these conditions, many stock exchanges (particularly if cash also is involved) do not qualify for the pooling of interests method. All combinations not meeting the specified conditions for pooling of interests must be accounted for by the purchase method. The usual, although not exclusive, mode of combination in these latter situations is by disbursement of cash or by incurrence of debt for the stock.

EXHIBIT 14–2
**Balance sheets
immediately after
acquisition (pooling
of interests method)**

COMPANY P AND COMPANY S
Separate Balance Sheets (pooling of interests method)
January 2, 19A, Immediately after Acquisition

	Company P	Company S
Assets		
Cash	$205,000	$ 35,000
Accounts receivable (net)	15,000	30,000
Receivable from Company S	10,000	
Inventories	170,000	70,000
Investment in Company S (100%)	150,000*	
Plant and equipment (net)	100,000	45,000
Total assets	$650,000	$180,000
Liabilities and Stockholders' Equity		
Accounts payable	$ 60,000	$ 20,000
Payable to Company P		10,000
Common stock, Company P	360,000*	
Common stock, Company S		100,000
Contributed capital from pooling of interests	90,000*	
Retained earnings, Company P	140,000	
Retained earnings, Company S		50,000
Total liabilities and stockholders' equity	$650,000	$180,000

* Amounts changed from preacquisition balance sheets given in Exhibit 14–1.

consequence, when the financial statements of the parent and subsidiary are combined by the parent company, the book values of each company, as shown on their respective financial statements, are added together with no consideration of the market values of the assets of the subsidiary on the date of the exchange.

To illustrate the consolidation process, we will combine the two separate balance sheets shown in Exhibit 14–2 into a single **consolidated balance sheet.** Basically, the process of consolidation by the parent company involves combining the balances in each account on the financial statements of the parent and subsidiary companies to produce consolidated financial statements that appear as if there were a **single entity.** Thus, when the parent company consolidates the balance sheets shown in Exhibit 14–2, the consolidated balance sheet will report a cash balance of $240,000 (i.e., $205,000 + $35,000). During the consolidation process, some accounts are **eliminated** (or adjusted) to avoid including amounts that would not be reported if only a single entity existed. For example, the balance sheet of Company P shows a receivable from Company S of $10,000, and the balance sheet of Company S shows a payable to Company P of $10,000. During consolidation, these accounts must be eliminated (which means that they will not be reported on the consolidated balance sheet). The consolidated balance sheet is prepared as if a single entity existed, and it would not be proper to report an amount that the entity owed to itself.

Two items must be eliminated when the balance sheets shown in Exhibit 14–2 are consolidated on the pooling of interests method:

a. The debit balance in the investment account of $150,000 shown in the accounts of Company P will be replaced on the consolidated balance sheet with the assets (less the liabilities) of Company S; therefore, to prevent double counting, the investment account must be eliminated (dropped out). The credit balance in the common stock account of $10,000 shown in the accounts of Company S is owned by Company P; therefore, it is an intercompany item that must be eliminated. Finally, the difference between the balances in the investment account and the common stock account of Company S ($150,000 − $100,000 = $50,000) must be eliminated from the account on Company P's books, Contributed Capital from Pooling of Interests. This elimination is necessary because it is an intercompany amount (refer to the acquisition entry). These three eliminations of intercompany items must be made by Company P to avoid double counting; they can be summarized as follows:[3]

		Eliminations
	Consolidated assets	Consolidated stockholders' equity
Investment account—decrease	−$150,000	
Common stock, Company S—decrease		−$100,000
Contributed capital from pooling of interests—decrease (for the difference)		− 50,000

b. The accounts of Company P show a receivable of $10,000 from Company S, and the accounts of Company S show this as a payable to Company P. This amount is called an **intercompany debt.** When the two balance sheets are combined into a single consolidated balance sheet, this intercompany debt must be eliminated because there is no external debt or receivable for the combined entity. Thus, the following elimination must be made when the two balance sheets are combined:

		Eliminations
	Consolidated assets	Consolidated liabilities
Receivable from Company S—decrease	−$10,000	
Payable to Company P—decrease		−$10,000

The balance sheets of Company P and Company S are shown separately in Exhibit 14–3 and in the last column are combined (aggregated) on a line-by-line basis, after deducting the "Eliminations," to develop the "Consolidated balance sheet." In an external consolidated financial statement, only the last column—the "Consolidated balance sheet" (and not the "Separate balance sheets")—would be reported by the parent company.

---

[3] This tabulation also can be viewed in the debit/credit format as follows:

Common stock, Company S	100,000	
Contributed capital from pooling of interests	50,000	
Investment in Company S		150,000

EXHIBIT 14–3
Preparation of
consolidated
balance sheet
(pooling of interests
method)

COMPANY P and Its Subsidiary, COMPANY S (100 percent owned)
Consolidated Balance Sheet (pooling of interests method)
At January 2, 19A, Immediately after Acquisition

	Separate balance sheets			Consolidated balance sheet
	Company P*	Company S*	Eliminations*	
Assets				
Cash	$205,000	$ 35,000		$240,000
Accounts receivable (net)	15,000	30,000		45,000
Receivable from Company S	10,000		(b) — 10,000	–0–
Inventories	170,000	70,000		240,000
Investment in Company S	150,000		(a) — 150,000	–0–
Plant and equipment (net)	100,000	45,000		145,000
Total assets	$650,000	$180,000		$670,000
Liabilities				
Accounts payable	$ 60,000	$ 20,000		$ 80,000
Payable to Company P		10,000	(b) — 10,000	–0–
Stockholders' Equity				
Common stock, Company P	360,000			360,000
Common stock, Company S		100,000	(a) — 100,000	–0–
Contributed capital from pooling	90,000		(a) — 50,000	40,000
Retained earnings, Company P	140,000			190,000
Retained earnings, Company S		50,000		
Total liabilities and stock- holders' equity	$650,000	$180,000		$670,000

  * Included for instructional purposes only. A worksheet usually is used to derive the consolidated amounts. See Supplements 14A and 14B.

In the "Consolidated balance sheet" by the pooling of interests method, as shown in the last column of Exhibit 14–3, the following measurement procedures are evident: (1) the amounts on each line for the consolidated assets, liabilities, and stockholders' equity are the **combined book values** of the parent and the subsidiary as were reflected on the separate balance sheets; (2) the intercompany amounts for investment, subsidiary common stock, a part of contributed capital from pooling, and the intercompany debt are eliminated; and (3) the **consolidated** retained earnings amount is the sum of the two separate retained earnings amounts ($140,000 + $50,000 = $190,000).[4]

The balance reflected in the capital stock account of Company S is eliminated because it is an intercompany item (all of the capital stock is owned by Company P). Retained earnings of Company S is not eliminated because it is not an intercompany item; the old stockholders of Company P plus the new stockholders of Company P (the former Company S stockholders) have dividend claims on the **total** of retained earnings for the combined unit.

---

[4] The pooling of interests method also requires that all comparative statements presented for prior years must be restated as if consolidated statements had been prepared.

PURCHASE METHOD

The preceding discussion considered the consolidation process for a pooling of interests (an exchange of stock). In contrast, when a corporation pays cash to acquire the stock of another corporation, a **purchase** transaction takes place.[5] As was the case in previous chapters, the purchase of assets must be recorded in conformity with the **cost principle.** Thus, on the acquisition date, the investment account on the books of the parent company must be measured at cost, which is the **market value of the shares at date of purchase** (i.e., the cash or cash equivalent paid).

To illustrate a combination by **purchase,** we will use the balance sheets of Companies P and S as given in Exhibit 14–1. Assume that on January 2, 19A, Company P **purchased** 100 percent of the 10,000 shares of outstanding voting stock of Company S, from Company S's stockholders, at $16.50 per share (i.e., for $165,000) and paid cash. On this date, Company P would make the following journal entry in its accounts:

January 2, 19A:

Investment in stock of Company S (10,000 shares, 100 percent)	165,000	
Cash		165,000
Acquisition by purchase.		

Note that Company P paid $165,000 cash for 100 percent of the owners' equity of Company S, although the **total book value** of the stockholders' equity of Company S that was purchased was only $150,000. Thus, Company P paid $15,000 more than "book value." In consolidating the two balance sheets, this $15,000 difference must be taken into account as explained below.

This purchase by Company P will have no effect on the accounting and reporting by the subsidiary Company S because the stock was sold (and cash was received) by the stockholders of Company S (and not by Company S itself).

After the above journal entry is posted to the accounts of Company P, the two separate balance sheets then would be changed as shown in the first two columns of Exhibit 14–4. You should compare these two columns with Exhibit 14–1 and observe that for (a) Company P cash decreased by $165,000 and the investment increased by the same amount and (b) Company S accounts are unchanged.

The consolidated balance sheet under the **purchase method** is shown in Exhibit 14–4. The two separate balance sheets for Companies P and S (given in Exhibit 14–4) were combined immediately after acquisition to develop the consolidated

---

[5] Refer to footnote 2. In some instances, stock exchanges do not qualify for the pooling method. In these instances, the purchase method must be used.

EXHIBIT 14–4
Preparation of a consolidated balance sheet (purchase method)

COMPANY P and Its Subsidiary, COMPANY S (100 percent owned)
Consolidated Balance Sheet (purchase method)
At January 2, 19A, Immediately after Acquisition

	Company P*	Company S*	Eliminations*	Consolidated balance sheet
Assets				
Cash	$ 40,000	$ 35,000		$ 75,000
Accounts receivable (net)	15,000	30,000		45,000
Receivable from Company S	10,000		(b) − 10,000	–0–
Inventories	170,000	70,000		240,000
Investment in Company S	165,000		(a) − 165,000	–0–
Plant and equipment (net)	100,000	45,000	(a) + 5,000	150,000
Goodwill†			(a) + 10,000	10,000
Total assets	$500,000	$180,000		$520,000
Liabilities				
Accounts payable	$ 60,000	$ 20,000		$ 80,000
Payable to Company P		10,000	(b) − 10,000	–0–
Stockholders' Equity				
Common stock, Company P	300,000			300,000
Common stock, Company S		100,000	(a) − 100,000	–0–
Retained earnings, Company P	140,000			140,000
Retained earnings, Company S		50,000	(a) − 50,000	–0–
Total liabilities and stockholders' equity	$500,000	$180,000		$520,000

*Separate balance sheets

* Included for instructional purposes only. A worksheet usually is used to derive the consolidated amounts. See Supplements 14A and 14B.

† A title preferred by most accountants is "Excess of purchase price over the current value of the net assets of the subsidiary" rather than "Goodwill." However, the length of this term causes the shorter term to be used extensively.

balance sheet of Company P. The consolidation process for a purchase is similar to consolidation for a pooling of interests (as illustrated in Exhibit 14–3). There are two intercompany items that require eliminations similar to those illustrated for the pooling of interests method; however, one differs significantly. The two eliminations are:

a. The investment account debit balance of $165,000, in the accounts of Company P, is at **market value** (i.e., at acquisition cost). It is eliminated against the stockholders' equity of the subsidiary, which is at **book value.** Company P paid $15,000 more than book value (i.e., $165,000 − $150,000) to acquire Company S for two reasons: (1) Company P determined that the plant and equipment owned by Company S had a market value of $50,000 at acquisition (compared with the book value of $45,000 reported by Company S), and (2) Company S had developed a good reputation with its customers which increased the overall value of Company S. The difference between the cost and the book value of the investment may be analyzed as follows:

Purchase price for 100% interest in Company S		$165,000
Net assets purchased, valued at market:		
Book value, $180,000 + market value increment		
of plant and equipment, $5,000 = ...	$185,000	
Less liabilities assumed	30,000	
Total market value purchased		155,000
Goodwill purchased		$ 10,000

Company P paid $165,000 cash for Company S, which had net assets (total assets minus liabilities) with a **market** value of $155,000; therefore, the goodwill of Company S cost $10,000. **Goodwill** is the amount that Company P actually paid for the good reputation, customer appeal, and general acceptance of the business that Company S had developed over the years. All successful companies enjoy a measure of goodwill. Its "value" is never known except when a business is purchased, as it was in this instance.

To eliminate the investment account on the books of Company P and the owner's equity accounts on the books of Company S, the following five steps must be completed:

1. Increase the plant and equipment of Company S from the book value of $45,000 to market value of $50,000; the increase is $5,000.
2. Recognize the $10,000 goodwill purchased as an asset.
3. Eliminate the investment account balance of $165,000.
4. Eliminate the Company S common stock balance of $100,000.
5. Eliminate the Company S retained earnings balance of $50,000.

These five steps are implemented as follows:[6]

		Eliminations
	Consolidated assets	Consolidated stockholders' equity
Plant and equipment—increase	⊦$ 5,000	
Goodwill—increase	+10,000	
Investment—decrease	−165,000	
Common stock Company S—decrease		−$100,000
Retained earnings, Company S—decrease		−50,000

b. The intercompany debt must be eliminated, viz:

---

[6] This tabulation also can be viewed in the debit-credit format as follows (see supplements):

Plant and equipment	5,000	
Goodwill	10,000	
Common stock, Company S	100,000	
Retained earnings, Company S	50,000	
Investment, Company S		165,000

		Eliminations	
		Consolidated assets	*Consolidated liabilities*
Receivable from Company S—decrease		−$10,000	
Payable to Company P—decrease			−$10,000

In contrast to the pooling of interests method, when the purchase method is used, the balance of Retained Earnings of the subsidiary at acquisition is eliminated. This elimination is made because the retained earnings of the subsidiary was in effect paid out to the former stockholders of Company S when they were reimbursed in cash for the market value of their shares (they are no longer stockholders of either company).

The accounts of Company S are not affected by a purchase because the transaction was between the parent company and the former stockholders of the subsidiary (and not the subsidiary itself).

The two "Separate balance sheets" are shown in Exhibit 14–4 and, using the eliminations, are combined on a line-by-line basis to develop the "Consolidated balance sheet" of Company P shown in the last column. In an external consolidated financial statement of Company P, only the "Consolidated balance sheet" shown in the last column (and not the "Separate balance sheets") would be reported.

To reemphasize the measurements for consolidation purposes when the purchased method is used, the **market values** at date of acquisition of the subsidiary's assets are added on an item-by-item basis to the **book values** of the parent, Company P.

COMPARISON OF THE EFFECTS ON THE BALANCE SHEET OF POOLING VERSUS PURCHASE METHODS

To gain some insight into the differences in measurement of balance sheet amounts that arise when the pooling of interests method is used versus the purchase method, we can compare several of the consolidated amounts shown in Exhibits 14–3 and 14–4 as follows:

		Acquisition method		
		Pooling method	*Purchase method*	*Difference*
1.	Cash	$240,000	$ 75,000	$(165,000)
2.	Plant and equipment (net)	145,000	150,000	5,000 *
3.	Goodwill		10,000	10,000 *
4.	Common stock Company P	360,000	300,000	(60,000)
5.	Contributed capital from pooling	40,000		(40,000)
6.	Retained earnings Company P	190,000	140,000	(50,000)*

* These three amounts reflect the basic differences between the two methods (see footnote 7).

The $165,000 difference in cash was the purchase price of the subsidiary (under the pooling method, only stock was exchanged). The $100,000 difference in the amount of common stock is due to the effect of issuing stock under pooling of interests rather than paying cash when the purchase method is elected.[7] The plant and equipment amount is higher when the purchase method is used than when pooling of interests is used, because the former requires application of the cost princple so that **market value** at date of acquisition rather than book value must be recognized for the assets of the subsidiary. Goodwill usually arises in purchase but does not in pooling of interests. These higher amounts for assets under the purchase method, of course, mean higher expenses will be reported on the income statements in the future periods; that is, depreciation expense and amortization expense for goodwill will be higher. Finally, under the pooling of interests method, the reported retained earnings amount is higher because the amount of retained earnings of the subsidiary must be added to that of the parent as shown in Exhibit 14–3.

Thus, when one compares the basic differences between the pooling of interests and purchase methods, three items usually stand out on the consolidated balance sheet, viz:

1. Operational assets almost always are higher in valuation under the purchase method because they are valued at market rather than at the subsidiary's book values.
2. Goodwill almost always is recorded under the purchase method but never is recorded under the pooling of interests method.
3. Retained earnings is lower under the purchase method because under this method only the parent company's retained earnings is reflected, while under the pooling of interests method consolidated retained earnings always is the sum of the parent and subsidiary retained earnings.

Part B will discuss and illustrate other significant effects that are reflected on the consolidated income statement of the parent company.

PART B—REPORTING CONSOLIDATED OPERATIONS AFTER ACQUISITION

The preceding discussions focused on the impact of the pooling of interests method and the purchase method on the consolidated balance sheet immediately after acquisition. The impact of the two methods on the income statement, for accounting periods following the date of acquisition, also is significant. Exhibit 14–5 presents the consolidated income statement and balance sheet for Company P and its subsidiary, Company S, after one year of operations (i.e., for the accounting year ended December 31, 19A). The underlying data and consolidation procedures

---

[7] In the example of the purchase method, the subsidiary stock was purchased by Company P for cash without borrowing or selling unissued stock. Had Company P borrowed the $165,000, the cash position would have been unaffected; however, there would have been an increase in debt by the same amount.

Alternatively, Company P could have sold the 10,000 shares of its common stock for $165,000 cash and then purchased the 10,000 shares of Company S stock with that cash. In this scenario, the cash position and the contributed capital accounts would have been the same under both methods.

EXHIBIT 14–5
Consolidated
financial statements
under the pooling
and purchase
methods one year
after acquisition

COMPANY P and Its Subsidiary, COMPANY S (100% Owned)
Consolidated Financial Statements
Pooling and Purchase Methods Compared
At December 31, 19A, One Year after Acquisition

Consolidated statements

	Pooling method	Purchase method
Income statement (for the year ended December 31, 19A):		
Sales revenue	$ 510,000	$ 510,000
Expenses:		
Cost of goods sold	(279,000)	(279,000)
Expenses (not detailed)	(156,500)	(156,500)
Depreciation expense	(14,500)	(15,000)
Amortization expense (goodwill)		(500)
Income tax expense	(26,000)	(26,000)
Net income (carried to retained earnings)	$ 34,000	$ 33,000
Balance sheet (at December 31, 19A):		
Assets		
Cash	$ 271,500	$ 106,500
Accounts receivable (net)	46,000	46,000
Inventories	250,000	250,000
Plant and equipment (net)	130,500	135,000
Goodwill		9,500
Total assets	$ 698,000	$ 547,000
Liabilities		
Accounts payable	$ 74,000	$ 74,000
Stockholders' Equity		
Common stock	400,000*	300,000
Retained earnings	190,000	140,000
Add: Net income (from above)	34,000	33,000
Total liabilities and stockholders' equity	$ 698,000	$ 547,000

* Includes contributed capital from pooling of interests, $40,000.

used to derive these two financial statements are shown in Supplement 14A, Exhibit 14–10, and Exhibit 14–11.

The objective in Part B is to provide an overview of the impact of the pooling of interests and purchase methods on reporting consolidated results after acquisition.

THE IMPACT OF THE POOLING AND PURCHASE METHODS ONE YEAR AFTER ACQUISITION

Recall that at the date of acquisition, the plant and equipment shown on the balance sheet of Company S had a market value of $5,000 in excess of book value. These assets are being depreciated over a remaining life of 10 years by

EXHIBIT 14–6
Comparison of pooling of interests and purchase methods one year after acquisition

		Acquisition approach		
		Pooling method	Purchase method	Difference
Income statement:				
1.	Depreciation expense	$ 14,500	$ 15,000	$ 500*
2.	Amortization expense (goodwill)		500	500*
3.	Net income	34,000	33,000	$ 1,000*
Balance sheet:				
4.	Cash	271,500	106,500	$165,000
5.	Plant and equipment (net)	130,500	135,000	(4,500)
6.	Goodwill		9,500	(9,500)
7.	Total	698,000	547,000	$151,000
8.	Common stock	360,000	300,000	$ 60,000
9.	Contributed capital from pooling of interests	40,000		40,000
10.	Retained earnings	224,000	173,000	51,000
11.	Total	698,000	547,000	$151,000

* Basic differences on the income statement.

Company S. Also, the acquisition of Company S resulted in the recognition of $10,000 goodwill when the purchase method was used. This goodwill will be amortized over the next 20 years.[8]

A comparison of the impact of the pooling method and the purchase method on the consolidated statements of Company P after one year of operations is shown in Exhibit 14–6.

The comparison in Exhibit 14–6 shows that 11 amounts were different between the two consolidation methods. Net income was $1,000 less under the purchase method because **additional** depreciation expense and amortization expense (goodwill) must be recognized in consolidation when the assets of the subsidiary are recognized at their acquisition market values. The causes of the $1,000 difference are:

		Items	Difference
a.	Depreciation expense on pooling of interests method (on parent and subsidiary assets at book value)	$14,500	
	Add depreciation on the increased asset amount of the subsidiary (to market value from book value, $5,000 ÷ 10 years)	500	$ 500
	Depreciation expense on purchase method (on parent assets at book value and subsidiary assets at market value)	$15,000	
b.	Amortization expense on the intangible asset, goodwill, of $10,000, which is to be amortized over the next 20 years ($10,000 ÷ 20 years)		500
	(There is no goodwill recognized under pooling of interests.)		
	Total of the differences		$1,000

---

[8] *APB Opinion No.* 17, "Accounting for Intangible Assets" (New York, August 1970) states: "The cost of each type of intangible asset [including goodwill] should be amortized on the basis of the estimated life of that specific asset. . . ." The Opinion limits the amortization to a maximum of 40 years.

The additional expenses that must be recognized on the consolidated income statement in future periods cause less net income to be reported when the purchase method is used. Businesses usually do not like this unfavorable impact of the purchase method.

The $151,000 difference in the balance sheet totals shown in Exhibit 14–6 is caused by the different way in which the stock was acquired (shares exchanged versus cash payment) and the accounting measurements implicit in each of the two methods. These differences may be explained as follows:

Cash—The $165,000 difference reflects the cash price paid for the stock of the subsidiary purchased under the purchase method as opposed to the exchange of shares under pooling of interests (see footnote 7).

Plant and equipment (net)—This difference reflects the effects of including the plant and equipment of the subsidiary at book value under the pooling of interests method compared with including them at **acquisition** market value under the purchase method. The $4,500 difference in plant and equipment may be explained as follows:

Difference between market value and book value of
   subsidiary assets at date of acquisition $5,000
Deduct depreciation on the difference for one year
   ($5,000 ÷ 10 years)   500
      Difference: Operational assets (higher under purchase method) $4,500

Goodwill—Goodwill often is recognized under the purchase method (and amortized over 40 years or less); it is not recognized under pooling of interests.

Common stock—The common stock of Company P is greater by $60,000 under a pooling of interests because of the issuance of shares in exchange for the shares of Company S. Note that this amount is the same as it was at acquisition.

Contributed capital from pooling of interests—This amount arises only under pooling of interests as a result of the exchange of shares. In consolidation, a part or all of it is eliminated.

Retained earnings—Retained earnings is $51,000 more under the pooling of interests method than under the purchase method. This difference is due to two factors, viz:

Amount of retained earnings eliminated:
   Under pooling of interests method . . . . $ –0–
   Under purchase method 50,000 $50,000
Amount of consolidated net income:
   Under pooling of interests method   34,000
   Under purchase method   33,000   1,000
      Difference: Retained earnings (higher under
      pooling of interests method) $51,000

The preceding discussion of the pooling of interests and purchase methods should make clear why pooling of interests usually is preferred by the acquiring company, and also why the accounting profession established specific criteria for limiting its use. The pooling of interests method usually is preferred because it (1) requires little or no disbursement of cash, other assets, or the creation of debt; (2) results in a higher net income reported on the consolidated income statement than does the purchase method; (3) reports higher retained earnings; and (4) is susceptible to manipulation, which was evidenced by numerous abuses prior to the issuance of *APB Opinion 16* (August 1970). The pooling of interests method usually is preferred by acquiring companies because of the "favorable" reporting impacts cited above. However, in the opinion of many persons, the opportunities for manipulation of net income are significant deficiencies of the pooling of interests method. Three fairly common manipulative practices of the past were:

1. **Instant earnings**—To illustrate, assume Company P acquired Company S through a pooling of interests. At acquisition date, Company S owned three separate plants, each of which had a relatively low book value of $100,000 and a high market value of $600,000. Following the pooling of interests method, the $100,000 book value of each plant was reported on the subsequent consolidated balance sheet as an asset. Assume that during the next year one of the plants was sold for the $600,000 market value. The result was a gain on the sale of operational assets of $500,000 (disregarding income taxes), which then was reported on the income statement. This came to be referred to, in a derogatory way, as making "instant earnings." The reported gain would significantly increase **net income** and EPS and often caused the price of the shares of Company P to rise. At the higher stock prices, shares were sold to the public and/or used for another round of mergers following the same pattern. Many persons believe that there was no economic gain because the cost of the plant, to the acquiring company, was the market value of the shares given in exchange (and that it should have been recorded at this amount), that is, $600,000. Under this view (i.e., it would be the purchase method) no gain would be reported when the plant was sold for $600,000.

2. **Escalating EPS**—This term refers to what was a common practice of seeking out smaller successful companies, usually near year-end, to acquire through a pooling of interests, so that their earnings could be **added** to those of the parent. Thus, by the simple expedient of year-end pooling acquisitions, at no cash cost, the acquiring company could escalate net income and EPS reported on a consolidated basis by the parent company. Many of the year-end acquisitions for this purpose were consummated **after** the end of the year but before publication of the financial statements, in which case they were allowed for inclusion in the consolidated statements of the past year. This action became a favorite way to "doctor" net income and EPS at year-end.

3. **Tricky mixes**—This situation represented the ultimate in misleading and illogical accounting. It was referred to as "part-purchase, part-pooling of interests accounting." A corporation, in acquiring another company by pooling, often found a number of stockholders of the other company who would not accept

shares in exchange; they wanted cash immediately. For example, it often worked out that, say, two thirds of the shares of the subsidiary would be acquired by exchange of shares and the remaining third would be purchased for cash. In order to derive some of the "reporting benefits" of pooling of interests accounting, two thirds of the acquisition would be accounted for on that basis and one third on the purchase basis—thus part-purchase, part-pooling accounting. This mixture of accounting approaches not only was theoretically untenable but also was misleading and not subject to any rational explanation; it was stopped by APB Opinion 16.

The "merger movement" in the 1960s came under considerable criticism because pooling of interests accounting often was used in situations that were, in substance, purchases. In response to extensive criticism, the APB issued *Opinions 16*, "Business Combinations," and *17*, "Intangible Assets," which tended to stop the abuses cited above. *Opinion 16* states 12 criteria that, if met, require use of the method. If any one of the criteria is not met, the purchase method must be used. It is interesting to note that a number of the members of the APB strongly believed, both for conceptual and practical reasons, that pooling of interests accounting should be disallowed completely. The conceptual argument against the pooling of interests method is that it ignores the market values on which the parties traded shares and substitutes, in violation of the cost principle, the book values carried in the accounts of the seller (i.e., the subsidiary). The practical argument against the pooling of interests method is that it leads to abuses of the kinds cited above.

The primary arguments in favor of the pooling of interests method of reporting are (1) it avoids the problems of measuring the market value of the different assets of the subsidiary at acquisition date; (2) it avoids the necessity of recognizing goodwill, then having to amortize it as an expense in future periods; and (3) the exchange of shares is not a purchase/sale transaction but, rather, is a joining of common interests and risks. Many accountants predict that the FASB eventually will eliminate the pooling of interests method altogether.

DEMONSTRATION CASE

This case is based on selected parts of the Johnson & Johnson financial statements given in Special Supplement B immediately preceding the Index.

Refer to Special Supplement B and respond to the following questions:

a. What was the amount of the short-term investments reported on the 1982 balance sheet? How were the short-term investments valued on the balance sheet?

b. What was the amount of the long-term investments reported on the 1982 balance sheet? How were the long-term investments valued on the balance sheet?

c. What amount of minority interest is reported on the 1982 balance sheet? Explain what this amount represents and the reason for its particular classification on the balance sheet.

    d. Explain how the 1982 income statement reflects revenue from consolidated subsidiaries.

    e. Determine the amount, if any, of intercompany debt (obligations between affiliated companies) reported on the 1982 balance sheet.

    f. Did Johnson & Johnson have any acquisitions of subsidiary companies under the pooling of interests method during 1982?

Suggested solution

    a. The short-term investment amount is $225,100,000 for 1982. The short-term investments are valued at cost which approximates market. If market had been less than cost, the investments would have been valued on the lower of cost or market basis.

    b. The long-term investment amount is $222,100,000 for 1982. The long-term investments are valued at cost which approximates market. If market had been less than cost, the investments would have been valued on the lower of cost or market basis. There were no investments accounted for under the equity method.

    c. At the end of 1982, the "Minority interest" in international subsidiaries was $9,700,000. This item means that the parent company, although it owned a controlling interest in the voting stock of one or more of the subsidiaries, did not own 100 percent. This amount represents the portion of the stockholders' equity of the subsidiary identified with the minority stockholders.

    d. Revenue from consolidated subsidiaries is not reported separately because it is added to the revenues of the parent.

    e. There is no intercompany debt reported on the consolidated balance sheet because intercompany debt must be eliminated during the consolidation process.

    f. The Consolidated Statement of Common Stock, Additional Capital and Treasury Stock reports that there were acquisitions by pooling of interests during 1982.

SUMMARY OF CHAPTER

This chapter discussed the use of consolidated financial statements that must be prepared in most situations when one corporation owns more than 50 percent of the outstanding voting stock of another corporation. The concept of consolidated statements is based upon the view that a parent company and its subsidiaries constitute one economic entity. Therefore, the separate income statements, balance sheets, and statements of changes in financial position should be combined each period on an item-by-item basis as a single set of financial statements for the parent company.

Ownership of a controlling interest (i.e., more than 50 percent of the outstanding voting stock) of another corporation may be accounted for and reported as either a pooling of interests or combination by purchase. The measurement of amounts reported on the consolidated financial statements of the parent company is influenced to a significant degree by these two quite different accounting methods.

The pooling of interests method usually is used when the parent company

EXHIBIT 14–7
Differences between the pooling of interests and purchase methods summarized

Item	Pooling of Interests	Purchase
1. Measuring and recording at date of acquisition by the parent company.	Acquisition is accomplished by exchanging shares of stock. A purchase/sale transaction is not assumed; therefore, the cost principle **is not** applied. The investment account is debited for the **book value** of the subsidiary stock acquired.	Acquisition usually is accomplished by purchasing the shares with cash and/or debt. A purchase/sale transaction is assumed; therefore, the cost principle **is** applied. On acquisition date the investment account is debited for the **market value** of the resources acquired.
2. Goodwill.	Goodwill is not recognized by the parent company.	Goodwill is recognized by the parent company to the extent that the purchase price exceeds the sum of acquisition market values of the assets (less the liabilities) of the subsidiary.
3. Method of aggregating or combining by the parent company to derive the consolidated balance sheet.	Assets and liabilities (less any eliminations) of the subsidiary are added, at **book value,** to the book values of the parent.	Assets and liabilities (less any eliminations) of the subsidiary are added, at their acquisition **market values,** to the book values of the assets and liabilities of the parent.
4. Method of aggregating or combining by the parent company to derive the consolidated income statement.	Revenues and expenses as reported by each company, less any eliminations, are aggregated.	Revenues as reported, less any eliminations, are aggregated. Expenses, plus additional depreciation and amortization of goodwill, less any eliminations, are aggregated.
5. Eliminations.	Eliminate all intercompany debts, revenues, and expenses. Eliminate investment account on parent's books and owners' equity of the subsidiary, excluding retained earnings.	Eliminate all intercompany debts, revenues, and expenses. Eliminate the investment account on parent's books and common stock and retained earnings of the subsidiary.
6. Usual comparative effects on the consolidated financial statements.	Expenses—lower Net income—higher EPS—higher Assets—higher cash Noncash assets—lower Liabilities—same Capital stock—higher Retained earnings—higher	Expenses—higher Net income—lower EPS—lower Assets—lower cash Noncash assets—higher Liabilities—same Capital stock—lower Retained earnings—lower

exchanges shares of its own voting stock for a controlling interest in the voting shares of the subsidiary. In this situation it usually is deemed that there was no purchase/sale (exchange) transaction. Rather, there was merely a joining of interests by exchanging stock certificates, and the cost principle is not applied. Therefore, in preparing consolidated statements under the pooling of interests method, the book values (i.e., those amounts reflected on the financial statements) of each related company are added together and acquisition market values are disregarded.

In a combination by purchase, the parent company usually pays cash and/or incurs debt for the voting shares of the subsidiary. In these circumstances, a purchase/sale transaction has been completed, and the acquisition is accounted for in conformance with the cost principle. Therefore, to prepare consolidated statements under the purchase method, the assets of the subsidiary must be measured at their acquisition market values when combined with the statements of the parent company (i.e., at book value).

Consolidation under the pooling of interests method versus the purchase method causes significant differences on the consolidated financial statements. The pooling of interests method in the past led to many abuses.

A large percentage of published financial statements of corporations are consolidated statements. It is important, therefore, that statement users understand the basic concept of consolidated statements and the measurement distinctions between the pooling method and the purchase method in reporting the results of business combinations.

The differences between the pooling of interests and purchase methods in measuring and reporting the results of business combinations may be generalized, as shown in Exhibit 14–7. The acquisition of a controlling interest **does not** affect the accounting and reporting of the subsidiary companies (the subsidiary companies do not prepare consolidated statements).

SUPPLEMENT 14A—CONSOLIDATION PROCEDURES— 100 PERCENT OWNERSHIP

This supplement discusses in more depth the measurement procedures used in preparing consolidated financial statements. To accomplish this objective, we use a **consolidation worksheet** because, through it, the underlying concepts and measurement procedures come into sharp focus. The worksheet should be viewed as a learning device and not something only to be mastered mechanically. At the outset we remind you that the worksheet and the entries made on it are **supplemental** to the ledger accounts of the parent company. **The worksheet entries are not recorded in the accounts under any circumstances because the worksheet is an analytical device only.** We will consider the various topics in the same order they were presented in the body of the chapter. The example for Company P and its subsidiary, Company S, given in Exhibit 14–1, will be continued for all of the illustrations in this supplement.

The consolidated balance sheets for Company P and its subsidiary, Company S, immediately after acquisition, were shown under the pooling of interests method in Exhibit 14–3 and under the purchase method in Exhibit 14–4. Those exhibits indicated in the first three columns the worksheet procedures essential to development of the statements. There is no need to repeat those discussions.

Developing consolidated statements for periods subsequent to acquisition

At the end of each accounting period after acquisition, a consolidated balance sheet, income statement, and statement of changes in financial position must be prepared by the parent company. We will discuss consolidation procedures for both a consolidated balance sheet and a consolidated income statement for accounting periods subsequent to acquisition. We will illustrate a single worksheet that will meet this dual need.

To illustrate the consolidation worksheet, we will continue the situation involving the acquisition of Company S stock by Company P. Recall that on January 2, 19A, Company P acquired 100 percent of the outstanding stock of Company S. To adapt the example, we will assume that it is now December 31, 19A, and after operating for a year, each company has just prepared its separate income statement and balance sheet as shown in Exhibit 14–8. Two sets of financial statements are shown for Company P; the first is based on the assumption that Company S was acquired through an exchange of stock, and the second is based on the assumption that Company S stock was acquired with cash.

EXHIBIT 14–8

Illustrative data for consolidated financial statements subsequent to acquisition (100 percent ownership)

COMPANY P AND COMPANY S
Separate Financial Statements for 19A (unclassified)

	At December 31, 19A		
	Company P		
	Exchange of stock	Purchase with cash	Company S
Income statement (for 19A):			
Sales revenue	$ 400,000	$ 400,000	$110,000
Revenue from investments (dividend from Company S)	10,000	10,000	
Cost of goods sold	(220,000)	(220,000)	(59,000)
Expenses (not detailed)	(130,000)	(130,000)	(26,500)
Depreciation expense	(10,000)	(10,000)	(4,500)
Income tax expense	(20,000)	(20,000)	(6,000)
Net income	$ 30,000	$ 30,000	$ 14,000
Balance sheet (at December 31, 19A):			
Cash	$ 226,000	$ 61,000	$ 45,500
Accounts receivable (net)	18,000	18,000	28,000
Receivable from Company S	6,000	6,000	
Inventories	185,000	185,000	65,000
Investment in Company S (by purchase, at cost)	150,000*	165,000*	
Plant and equipment (net)	90,000	90,000	40,500
	$ 675,000	$ 525,000	$179,000
Accounts payable	$ 55,000	$ 55,000	$ 19,000
Payable to Company P			6,000
Common stock, par $10	360,000	300,000	100,000
Contributed capital in excess of par	90,000		
Beginning retained earnings*	140,000	140,000	50,000
Dividends declared and paid during 19A			(10,000)
Net income for 19A (per above)	30,000	30,000	14,000
	$ 675,000	$ 525,000	$179,000

* Balance at date of acquisition.

At the end of 19A, the following data relating to intercompany eliminations were available to Company P:

a. The Investment in Company S balance of $165,000 was the same as at date of acquisition; the balance of Retained Earnings of Company S at acquisition was $50,000.

b. At date of purchase, January 2, 19A, the plant and equipment of Company S had an acquisition market value of $5,000 above book value and goodwill purchased amounted to $10,000.

c. Intercompany debt owed by Company S to Company P was $6,000 at the end of 19A.

d. The plant and equipment owned by Company S had a 10-year remaining life from January 1, 19A, for depreciation purposes. The company uses straight-line depreciation.

e. Goodwill is to be amortized from January 1, 19A, over 20 years on a straight-line basis.

f. During December 19A, Company S declared and paid a $10,000 cash dividend to Company P. Accordingly, each company made the following journal entry in its accounts:

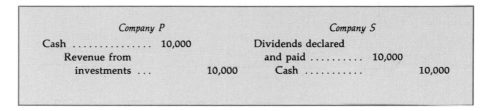

Company P		*Company S*	
Cash	10,000	Dividends declared	
Revenue from		and paid	10,000
investments ...	10,000	Cash	10,000

A consolidated income statement and balance sheet must be developed at the end of 19A. These statements were shown in Exhibit 14–5, assuming (1) pooling of interests method and (2) purchase method. A separate consolidation worksheet for each method will be discussed and illustrated.

Pooling of interests method—income statement and balance sheet. This worksheet (Exhibit 14–9) has side captions for each income statement and balance sheet account, and vertical columns for the parent company, the subsidiary company, eliminations, and the **"Consolidated Balances."** The amounts entered in the first two columns are taken directly from the separate financial statements of 19A prepared by the parent and the subsidiary (as given in Exhibit 14–8).

The worksheet is designed so that the eliminations are entered in debit and credit format. This provides an excellent check on the accuracy of the work. We remind you, however, that the elimination entries are **worksheet entries only;** they are never entered into the accounts of either the parent or the subsidiary. Consolidated statements represent a **reporting concept** that does not affect the accounts of either the parent or the subsidiaries.

To complete the worksheet, the elimination entries must be developed; then each line is accumulated horizontally to derive the consolidated amount in the last column for each item to be reported on the consolidated income statement

EXHIBIT 14–9
Consolidation
worksheet (pooling
of interests
methods; 100
percent ownership)

COMPANY P and Its Subsidiary, COMPANY S
Consolidation Worksheet (pooling of interests) for the Balance Sheet
and Income Statement December 31, 19A (100 percent ownership)

Items	Statements		Intercompany Eliminations		Consolidated Balances
	Company P	Company S	Debit	Credit	
Income statement:					
Sales revenue	400,000	110,000			510,000
Revenue from investments	10,000		(c) 10,000		
Cost of goods sold	(220,000)	(59,000)			(279,000)
Expenses (not detailed)	(130,000)	(26,500)			(156,500)
Depreciation expense	(10,000)	(4,500)			(14,500)
Income tax expense	(20,000)	(6,000)			(26,000)
Net income (carried down)	30,000	14,000			34,000
Balance sheet:					
Cash	226,000	45,500			271,500
Accounts receivable (net)	18,000	28,000			46,000
Receivable from Company S	6,000			(b) 6,000	
Inventories	185,000	65,000			250,000
Investment in Company S	150,000*			(a) 150,000	
Plant and equipment (net)	90,000	40,500			130,500
	675,000	179,000			698,000
Accounts payable	55,000	19,000			74,000
Payable to Company P		6,000	(b) 6,000		
Common stock, Company P	360,000*				360,000
Common stock, Company S		100,000	(a) 100,000		
Contributed capital from pooling	90,000*		(a) 50,000		40,000
Beginning retained earnings, Company P	140,000				140,000
Beginning retained earnings, Company S		50,000			50,000
Dividends declared and paid during 19A		(10,000)		(c) 10,000	
Net income, 19A (from above; not added across)	30,000†	14,000†			34,000†
	657,000	179,000	166,000	166,000	698,000

Explanation of eliminations:
  (a) To eliminate Investment in Company S against Common Stock of Company S and Contributed Capital from Pooling of Interests.
  (b) To eliminate the intercompany debt.
  (c) To eliminate the intercompany revenue and dividends (paid by the subsidiary to the parent).
   * These amounts are based upon the pooling of interests method. The parent would have made the following journal entry at acquisition date:

Investment in Company S 150,000
    Common stock, Company P 60,000
    Contributed capital from pooling of interests 90,000
  † Carried down from above.

and balance sheet. At the end of 19A, three elimination entries are reflected on the worksheet under the pooling of interests method. They are identified briefly at the bottom of the worksheet; however, we will elaborate on them as follows:

a. Eliminate the investment in Company S with offsets to the accounts for (1) Common Stock, Company S, and (2) Contributed Capital from Pooling (see page 643). These eliminations can be accomplished by means of the following intercompany elimination entry on the worksheet (which is illustrated in a journal entry format):

Common stock, Company S	100,000	
Contributed capital from pooling of interests	50,000	
Investment in Company S		150,000

b. Eliminate the intercompany debt of $6,000 owed by Company S to Company P. These two eliminations can be accomplished by means of the following intercompany elimination entry on the worksheet:

Payable to Company P	6,000	
Receivable from Company S		6,000

c. During the year, Company S declared and paid dividends amounting to $10,000. Because Company P owned 100 percent of the outstanding stock, all of the dividends were paid to Company P. This is another intercompany item that must be eliminated. The Revenue from Investments account of Company P is debited on the worksheet and the Dividends Declared and Paid account of the subsidiary credited for $10,000. Observe that separate lines are set up on the worksheet for dividends and net income. This is simply a matter of convenience and clarity. The worksheet entry to accomplish these two eliminations is:

Revenue from investments	10,000	
Dividends declared and paid (Retained earnings, Company S)		10,000

Purchase method—income statement and balance sheet. Under the purchase method, a few more eliminations are necessary because the acquisition market values for the subsidiary must be recognized when the consolidation is by purchase. The intercompany eliminations on Exhibit 14–10, purchase method,

EXHIBIT 14–10
Consolidation
worksheet
(purchase method;
100 percent
ownership)

COMPANY P and Its Subsidiary, COMPANY S
Consolidation Worksheet (by purchase) for the Balance Sheet
and Income Statement
December 31, 19A (100 percent ownership)

Items	Statements		Intercompany Eliminations		Consolidated Balances
	Company P	Company S	Debit	Credit	
Income statement:					
Sales revenue	400,000	110,000			510,000
Revenue from investments	10,000		(e) 10,000		
Cost of goods sold	(220,000)	(59,000)			(279,000)
Expenses (not detailed)	(130,000)	(26,500)			(156,500)
Depreciation expense	(10,000)	(4,500)	(c) 500		(15,000)
Amortization expense (goodwill)			(d) 500		(500)
Income tax expense	(20,000)	(6,000)			(26,000)
Net income (carried down)	30,000	14,000			33,000
Balance sheet:					
Cash	61,000	45,500			106,500
Accounts receivable (net)	18,000	28,000			46,000
Receivable from Company S	6,000			(b) 6,000	
Inventories	185,000	65,000			250,000
Investment in Company S (at cost)	165,000			(a) 165,000	
Plant and equipment (net)	90,000	40,500	(a) 5,000	(c) 500	135,000
Goodwill			(a) 10,000	(d) 500	9,500
	525,000	179,000			547,000
Accounts payable	55,000	19,000			74,000
Payable to Company P		6,000	(b) 6,000		
Common stock, Company P	300,000				300,000
Common stock, Company S		100,000	(a) 100,000		
Beginning retained earnings, Company P	140,000				140,000
Beginning retained earnings, Company S		50,000	(a) 50,000		
Dividends declared and paid during 19A		(10,000)		(e) 10,000	
Net income, 19A (from above; not added across)	30,000*	14,000*			33,000*
	525,000	179,000	182,000	182,000	547,000

* Carried down from above.
Explanation of eliminations:
  (a) To eliminate the investment account against the subsidiary stockholders' equity and to allocate the difference between purchase price and book value purchased to the appropriate accounts.
  (b) To eliminate the intercompany debt.
  (c) To record additional depreciation for one year on the asset increase resulting from the acquisition.
  (d) To record amortization for one year on the goodwill recognized.
  (e) To eliminate intercompany revenue and dividends (paid by the subsidiary to the parent).

are identified at the bottom of the worksheet; however, we will elaborate on them as follows:

a. Eliminate the investment account, reported on the parent's balance sheet, against the owners' equity accounts, reflected on the balance sheet of the subsidiary. This eliminating entry will be the same as at date of acquisition for each succeeding period because it is based upon the values recognized at the date of acquisition. The $15,000 difference between the purchase price and the book value must be allocated to the assets (including goodwill as shown in the analysis of the purchase transaction given on page 647).

The **worksheet** entry is as follows (illustrated in a journal entry format):

Common stock, Company S	100,000	
Retained earnings, Company S	50,000	
Plant and equipment	5,000	
Goodwill	10,000	
Investment in Company S		165,000

b. Eliminate the intercompany debt of $6,000 with the following entry on the worksheet:

Payable to Company P	6,000	
Receivable from Company S		6,000

c. Because the plant and equipment amount for Company S was increased to acquisition market value by $5,000, for consolidation purposes we must record additional depreciation on the $5,000 increment. The depreciation reflected on the statements of Company S does not include this $5,000 increase to market value. Accordingly, the worksheet entry must be:

Depreciation expense (Company S)	500	
Plant and equipment (Company S) (or accumulated depreciation)		500
$5,000 ÷ 10 years = $500.		

d. Goodwill is an intangible asset (see Chapter 9) that must be amortized over a realistic period not longer than 40 years (ABP Opinion 17). Company P decided to use a 20-year life. Because $10,000 goodwill was recognized in entry (a) above, for consolidated statement purposes it must be amortized on the worksheet. Therefore, the worksheet entry to accomplish this effect is:

```
Amortization expense (goodwill) ...........................     500
    Goodwill ............................................              500
  $10,000 ÷ 20 years = $500.
```

e. During the year, Company S declared and paid dividends amounting to
$10,000. Because Company P owned 100 percent of the outstanding stock,
all of the dividends were paid to Company P. This is an intercompany item
that must be eliminated. The Revenue from Investments account of Company
P must be debited on the worksheet and the Dividends Declared and Paid
account of the subsidiary credited for $10,000. Observe that separate lines
are set up on the worksheet for dividends and net income. This procedure
simply is for convenience and clarity. The worksheet entry to accomplish
these eliminations is:

```
Revenue from investments ................................    10,000
    Dividends declared and paid (retained earnings,
        Company S) ........................................            10,000
```

All of the intercompany eliminations have been entered on the worksheet.
The consolidated balances are determined by accumulating each line horizontally
to derive the balances in the last column. The consolidated balances taken directly
from the last column of the worksheet are classified in the normal manner in
preparing the consolidated income statement and balance sheet.

SUPPLEMENT 14B—CONSOLIDATION PROCEDURES—LESS THAN 100 PERCENT OWNERSHIP

When the parent company owns a controlling interest that is less than 100
percent, the consolidation procedures are identical, except that certain consolidation worksheet eliminations must be based upon the **proportionate** ownership
level. When there is less than 100 percent ownership, there will be a group of
stockholders of the subsidiary company known as the **minority stockholders.**
Their interest in the subsidiary is unaffected by the parent's interest; therefore,
the minority stockholders' interest must be accorded appropriate measurement
and reporting recognition. Less than 100 percent ownership causes a new kind
of owners' equity on the consolidated statements referred to as the **minority
interest.** It includes the minority stockholders' proportionate share of both the
earnings and the contributed capital of the subsidiary.

To illustrate the measurement of amounts for consolidated statements for a
controlling interest of less than 100 percent, we will adapt the data for Company
P and Company S given in Exhibit 14–1. Assume that on January 2, 19A, Company
P purchased 80 percent of the 10,000 shares of outstanding capital stock of Com-

pany S for $132,000 cash.[9] At acquisition date, Company P recorded the purchase of the 8,000 shares of capital stock as follows:

January 2, 19A:

Investment, stock of Company S (80 percent ownership)	132,000	
Cash		132,000
Acquisition of 8,000 shares (80 percent) of the capital stock of Company S at $16.50 per share.		

On the date of acquisition, the owners' equity accounts of Company S reflected the following amounts: Capital Stock, $100,000; and Retained Earnings, $50,000 (total owners' equity was $150,000). Company P paid $132,000 cash for 80 percent of the owners' equity of Company S. The book value of the investment was $120,000 ($150,000 × .80). Thus, Company P paid $12,000 more than the book value of Company S. Of this amount, $4,000 (i.e., $5,000 × 80 percent) was for the greater market value of the plant and equipment. The remaining amount, $8,000, was for **goodwill.** The analysis of the purchase transaction, at date of acquisition, follows:[10]

Purchase price for 80% interest in Company S	$132,000
Net assets purchased, valued at market:	
Book value, $150,000 + market value increment of	
plant and equipment, $5,000 × .80 = ...	124,000
Goodwill purchased	$ 8,000

Assume it is December 31, 19A, and both companies have completed one year's operations as affiliated companies. Each company has prepared the separate 19A financial statements as shown in Exhibit 14–11.

Additional data developed by Company P for the consolidation worksheet:

a. Investment account balance of $132,000 to be eliminated against 80 percent of stockholders' equity of subsidiary.

b. Plant and equipment of Company S to be increased by $4,000 to market value (i.e., the increment attributable to ownership by Company P). Goodwill will be recognized, $8,000 (see analysis of purchase transaction above).

c. Company S owed Company P $6,000 on December 31, 19A.

d. The plant and equipment is being depreciated on a straight-line basis over a remaining life of 10 years by Company S (no residual value).

e. Goodwill will be amortized over 20 years.

f. Company S declared and paid $10,000 cash dividends on December 15, 19A.

---

[9] Ownership interests of less than 100 percent usually are on the purchase basis because, APB Opinion 16 does not permit use of the pooling of interest basis when the ownership interest held by the parent company is less than 90 percent.

[10] Some accountants believe that the plant and equipment difference should be 100 percent (i.e., $5,000) rather than 80 percent (i.e., $4,000). This difference in opinion has not been resolved; however, it appears that most companies currently use the lower amount.

EXHIBIT 14–11
Illustrative data for
consolidation (less
than 100 percent
ownership)

COMPANY P AND COMPANY S
Separate Financial Statements for 19A

	Company P	Company S
Income statement (for 19A):		
Sales revenue	$ 400,000	$110,000
Revenue from investments (dividends from Company S)	8,000	
Cost of goods sold	(220,000)	(59,000)
Expenses (not detailed)	(130,000)	(26,500)
Depreciation expense	(10,000)	(4,500)
Income tax expense	(20,000)	(6,000)
Net income	$ 28,000	$ 14,000
Balance sheet (at December 31, 19A):		
Cash	$ 92,000	$ 45,500
Accounts receivable (net)	18,000	28,000
Receivable from Company S	6,000	
Inventories	185,000	65,000
Investment in Company S (80%, at cost)	132,000	
Plant and equipment	90,000	40,500
	$ 523,000	$179,000
Accounts payable	$ 55,000	$ 19,000
Payable to Company P		6,000
Common stock, par $10	300,000	100,000
Beginning retained earnings	140,000	50,000
Dividends declared and paid during 19A		(10,000)
Net income for 19A (from above)	28,000	14,000
	$ 523,000	$179,000

The consolidation worksheet, under the purchase method, is shown in Exhibit 14–12. It is the same as the worksheet shown in Exhibit 14–10 for 100 percent ownership, except for elimination entries *(a), (c), (d),* and *(e)*. These intercompany eliminations differ only as to **the amounts. They have been reduced to the 80 percent ownership level.**

EXHIBIT 14–12
Consolidation
worksheet
(purchase method;
less than 100
percent ownership)

COMPANY P and Its Subsidiary, COMPANY S
Consolidation Worksheet (by purchase) for the Balance Sheet and Income Statement
December 31, 19A (80 percent ownership)

Items	Statements		Intercompany Eliminations		Consolidated Balances
	Company P	Company S	Debit	Credit	
Income statement:					
Sales revenue	400,000	110,000			510,000
Revenue from investments	8,000		(e) 8,000		
Cost of goods sold	(220,000)	(59,000)			(279,000)
Expenses (not detailed)	(130,000)	(26,500)			(156,500)
Depreciation expense	(10,000)	(4,500)	(c) 400		(14,900)

EXHIBIT 14–12
(concluded)

Items	Statements Company P	Statements Company S	Intercompany Eliminations Debit	Intercompany Eliminations Credit	Consolidated Balances
Amortization expense (goodwill)			(d) 400		(400)
Income tax expense	(20,000)	(6,000)			(26,000)
Net income	28,000	14,000			33,200
Carried down:					
Minority interest ($14,000 × 20%)					2,800 M*
Parent interest income					30,400
Balance sheet:					
Cash	92,000	45,500			137,500
Accounts receivable (net)	18,000	28,000			46,000
Receivable from Company S	6,000			(b) 6,000	
Inventories	185,000	65,000			250,000
Investment in Company S (at cost)	132,000			(a) 132,000	
Plant and equipment (net)	90,000	40,500	(a) 4,000	(c) 400	134,100
Goodwill			(a) 8,000	(d) 400	7,600
	523,000	179,000			575,200
Accounts payable	55,000	19,000			74,000
Payable to Company P		6,000	(b) 6,000		
Common stock, Company P	300,000				300,000
Common stock, Company S		100,000	(a) 80,000		20,000 M
Beginning retained earnings, Company P	140,000				140,000
Beginning retained earnings, Company S		50,000	(a) 40,000		10,000 M
Dividends declared and paid during 19A		(10,000)		(e) 8,000	(2,000)M
Net income, 19A (from above; not added across)	28,000	14,000			2,800 M / 30,400
	523,000	179,000	146,800	146,800	575,200

M—Minority interest.
* The minority interest in the earnings of the subsidiary is unaffected by the consolidation procedures of the parent company. Thus, the minority interest in the earnings is $14,000 × 20% = $2,800. This amount is subtracted from consolidated income to derive the amount of consolidated income identifiable with the controlling interest. The two separate amounts then are carried down to the balance sheet section.
Explanation of eliminations:
  (a) To eliminate the investment account against 80 percent of the owners' equity of the subsidiary and to allocate the difference between purchase price and book value to the appropriate accounts.
  (b) To eliminate the intercompany debt.
  (c) To record depreciation for one year on the asset increase resulting from the acquisition.
  (d) To amortize goodwill recognized (one year).
  (e) To eliminate intercompany revenue arising from dividends declared and paid by the subsidiary.

EXHIBIT 14–13
Consolidated
financial statements
(with minority
interest)

COMPANY P and Its Subsidiary, COMPANY S
Consolidated Income Statement (purchase method)
For the Year Ended December 31, 19A

Sales revenue		$510,000
Cost of goods sold		279,000
Gross margin		231,000
Less:		
Expenses (not detailed)	$156,500	
Depreciation expense	14,900	
Amortization expense (goodwill)	400	
Income tax expense	26,000	197,800
Consolidated net income		33,200
Less: Minority interest in net income		2,800
Controlling interest in net income		$ 30,400

EPS of common stock ($33,200 ÷ 30,000 shares) = $1.107
(some accountants prefer to use $30,400 as the numerator).

COMPANY P and Its Subsidiary, COMPANY S
Consolidated Balance Sheet (purchase method)
At December 31, 19A

Assets

Current assets:		
Cash	$137,500	
Accounts receivable (net)	46,000	
Inventories	250,000	$433,500
Tangible operational assets:		
Plant and equipment (net)		134,100
Intangible operational assets:		
Goodwill (or excess of cost over market value of assets		
of subsidiary)		7,600
Total assets		$575,200

Liabilities

Current liabilities:		
Accounts payable		$ 74,000

Stockholders' Equity

Contributed capital:		
Common stock, par $10, 30,000 shares outstanding	$300,000	
Retained earnings	170,400	
Total	470,400	
Minority interest	30,800*	
Total stockholders' equity		501,200
Total liabilities and stockholders' equity		$575,200

* $20,000 + $10,000 + $2,800 − $2,000 = $30,800.

On the worksheet, the minority interest (20 percent) is designated with an
"M." In the income statement portion of the worksheet, 20 percent of the **subsidiary** net income (i.e., $2,800) is coded "M" and the remainder ($30,400) is identified
with the parent. On the worksheet, these income amounts are carried down to
the retained earnings section of the balance sheet. The 20 percent of subsidiary

stockholders' equity was not eliminated; therefore, it is carried across as minority interest and coded "M." Aside from these adaptations, the Consolidated Balances column is completed as previously explained.

The consolidated income statement and balance sheet, based on the data in the Consolidated Balances column of the worksheet, are shown in Exhibit 14–13. The **minority interest** share of net income is identified separately on the income statement. Similarly, the minority interest share of stockholders' equity is identified separately on the balance sheet. Alternatively, the minority interest share of stockholders' equity often is shown as a special caption between liabilities and stockholders' equity rather than as illustrated in Exhibit 14–13.

IMPORTANT TERMS DEFINED IN THIS CHAPTER

Terms (alphabetically)	Key words in definitions of important terms used in chapter	Page reference
Consolidation	The accounting process of combining financial statements from related companies into a single set of financial statements.	638
Control	Presumed to exist when more than 50 percent of the voting stock of an entity is owned by one investor.	639
Economic compatibility	The operations of affiliated companies complement each other.	639
Goodwill	The amount that was paid for the good reputation and customer appeal of an acquired company.	647
Minority interest	The proportionate share of both the earnings and the contributed capital of the subsidiary that is not "owned" by the parent.	664
Parent company	The company that has a significant investment in a subsidiary company.	639
Pooling of interests	An acquisition that is completed by exchanging parent company stock for subsidiary voting capital stock.	641
Purchase	An acquisition which is completed by purchasing subsidiary company voting capital stock for cash.	645
Subsidiary	The company that is owned by a parent company as evidenced by 50% or more of the voting capital stock.	639

QUESTIONS FOR DISCUSSION

PART A

1. Explain what is meant by a parent-subsidiary relationship.

2. Explain the basic concept underlying consolidated statements.

3. What two basic elements must be present before consolidated statements are appropriate?

4. The concept of consolidated statements relates only to reporting as opposed to preparing and posting journal entries in the accounts. Explain.

5. Explain briefly what is meant by pooling of interests.

6. Explain briefly what is meant by combination by purchase.

7. When one corporation acquires a controlling interest in another corporation, the acquiring corporation debits a long-term investment account. In the case of a pooling of interests, describe how to determine the amount that is debited to the investment account.

8. Explain what is meant by intercompany eliminations in consolidation procedures.

9. Explain why the investment account must be eliminated against stockholders' equity when consolidated statements are prepared.

10. Explain why the "book values" of the parent and subsidiary are aggregated on consolidated statements when there is a pooling of interests, but acquisition market values of the subsidiary assets are used when the combination is by purchase.

11. Why is goodwill not recognized in a pooling of interests? Why is it recognized in a combination by purchase?

PART B

12. Explain why additional depreciation expense usually must be recognized on consolidation when the combination was by purchase.

13. Explain what is meant by goodwill when the combination was by purchase.

14. Explain why pooling of interests was much more popular in the merger movement than combination by purchase.

15. Explain the basis for each of the following statements:
    a. Pooling of interests, given the same situation basically, reports a higher net income than does combination by purchase.
    b. The cash position, other things being equal, usually is better when the combination is by pooling of interests than when the combination is by purchase.
    c. Pooling of interests, other things being equal, reports a higher amount of retained earnings than does combination by purchase.

EXERCISES

PART A

E14–1. On January 2, 19A, Company P acquired all of the outstanding voting stock of Company S by exchanging, on a share-for-share basis, its own unissued stock for the stock of Company S. Immediately after the acquisition of Company S, the separate balance sheets showed the following:

| | Balances, January 2, 19A, immediately after acquisition | |
	Company P	Company S
Cash	$ 38,000	$12,000
Receivable from Company S	7,000	
Inventory	35,000	18,000
Investment in Company S (100%)	60,000	
Operational assets (net of accumulated depreciation)	80,000	50,000
Total	$220,000	$80,000
Liabilities	$ 25,000	$13,000
Payable to Company P		7,000
Common stock (Company P, par $5)		
(Company S, par $5)	140,000	40,000
Contributed capital from pooling of interests	20,000	
Retained earnings	35,000	20,000
Total	$220,000	$80,000

Required:

a. Is this a pooling of interests or a combination by purchase? Explain why.

b. Give the journal entry that was made by Company P to record the acquisition.

c. Prepare a consolidated balance sheet immediately after the acquisition.

d. Were the assets of the subsidiary added to those of the parent, in the consolidated balance sheet, at book value or at market value? Explain why.

e. What were the balances in the accounts of Company P immediately prior to the acquisition for (1) investment and (2) common stock? Were any other account balances for either Company P or Company S changed by the acquisition? Explain.

E14–2. On January 1, 19A, Company P acquired 100 percent of the outstanding common stock of Company S. At date of acquisition, the balance sheet of Company S reflected the following book values (summarized):

Total assets (market value, $220,000)*	$180,000
Total liabilities	30,000
Stockholders' equity:	
Common stock, par $10	100,000
Retained earnings	50,000

* One half subject to depreciation; 10-year remaining life and no residual value.

Two separate and independent cases are given below that indicate how Company P acquired 100 percent of the outstanding stock of Company S, viz:

Case A—Exchanged two shares of its own common stock (par $1) for each share of Company S stock.

Case B—Paid $20 per share for the stock of Company S.

Required:

For each case, answer the following:

a. Was this a combination by pooling of interests or by purchase? Explain.

b. Give the journal entry that Company P should make to record the acquisition. If none, explain why.

    c. Give the journal entry in the accounts of Company S to record the acquisition. If none, explain why.

    d. Analyze the transaction to determine the amount of goodwill purchased. If no goodwill was purchased, explain why.

    e. In preparing a consolidated balance sheet, should the subsidiary assets be included at book value or market value? Explain.

E14–3.   On January 1, 19A, Company P purchased 100 percent of the outstanding voting shares of Company S in the open market for $70,000 cash. On that date (prior to the acquisition) the separate balance sheets (summarized) of the two companies reported the following book values:

	Prior to acquisition	
	Company P	*Company S*
Cash	$ 80,000	$18,000
Receivable from Company P		2,000
Operational assets (net)	80,000	60,000
Total	$160,000	$80,000
Liabilities	$ 28,000	$20,000
Payable to Company S	2,000	
Common stock:		
Company P, nopar	100,000	
Company S, par $10		50,000
Retained earnings	30,000	10,000
Total	$160,000	$80,000

It was determined on date of acquisition that the market value of the operational assets of Company S was $66,000.

Required:

    a. Was this a combination by pooling of interests or by purchase? Explain why.

    b. Give the journal entry that should be made by Company P at date of acquisition. If none is required, explain why.

    c. Give the journal entry that should be made by Company S at date of acquisition. If none is required, explain why.

    d. Analyze the acquisition to determine the amount of goodwill purchased.

    e. Should the assets of Company S be included on the consolidated balance sheet at book value or market value? Explain.

    f. Prepare a consolidated balance sheet immediately after acquisition.

E14–4.   On January 4, 19A, Company P acquired all of the outstanding stock of Company S for $10 cash per share. At the date of acquisition, the balance sheet of Company S reflected the following:

Common stock, par $5	$50,000
Retained earnings	30,000

Immediately after the acquisition, the balance sheets reflected the following:

	Balances, Jan. 4, 19A, immediately after acquisition	
	Company P	Company S
Cash	$ 13,000	$17,000
Receivable from Company P		3,000
Investment in Company S (100%), at cost	100,000	
Operational assets (net)	122,000	70,000*
Total	$235,000	$90,000
Liabilities	$ 22,000	$10,000
Payable to Company S	3,000	
Common stock, par $5	150,000	50,000
Retained earnings	60,000	30,000
Total	$235,000	$90,000

* Determined by Company P to have a market value of $78,000 at date of acquisition.

Required:

a. Was this a combination by pooling of interests or by purchase? Explain why.
b. Give the journal entry that should be made by Company P to record the acquisition.
c. Analyze the acquisition to determine the amount of goodwill purchased.
d. Should the assets of Company S be included on the consolidated balance sheet at book value or market value? Explain.
e. Prepare a consolidated balance sheet immediately after acquisition.

PART B

E14–5. On January 1, 19A, Company P acquired all of the outstanding voting stock of Company S by exchanging one share of its own stock for each share of Company S stock. At the date of the exchange, the balance sheet of Company S showed the following:

Common stock, par $10	$40,000
Retained earnings	10,000

One year after acquisition the two companies prepared their separate financial statements as shown on the following worksheet:

COMPANY P and Its Subsidiary, COMPANY S (100 percent owned)
Consolidated Balance Sheet and Income Statement
December 31, 19A

Items	Separate Statements		Eliminations	Consolidated Statements
	Company P	Company S		
Income statement (for 19A):				
Sales revenue	96,000	42,000		
Revenue from investments	4,000			
Cost of goods sold	(60,000)	(25,000)		
Expenses (not detailed)	(17,000)	(10,000)		
Net income	23,000	7,000		
Balance sheet (at December 31, 19A):				
Cash	21,000	19,000		
Receivable from Company P		2,000		
Investment in Company S (100%)	50,000			
Operational assets (net)	59,000	47,000		
Total	130,000	68,000		
Liabilities	17,000	15,000		
Payable to Company S	2,000			
Common stock, Company P (par $10)	50,000			
Contributed capital from pooling of interests	10,000			
Common stock, Company S (par $10)		40,000		
Beginning retained earnings, Company P	28,000			
Beginning retained earnings, Company S		10,000		
Dividend declared and paid, 19A;				
Company S		(4,000)		
Net income, 19A (from above)	23,000	7,000		
Total	130,000	68,000		

Required:

a. Give the journal entry that was made by Company P to record the pooling of interests on January 1, 19A.

b. Complete the Eliminations column in the above worksheet, then combine the two sets of statements in the last column to develop the consolidated income statement and balance sheet. (Hint: Eliminate Revenue from Investments against Dividends Declared and Paid because this represents an intercompany transaction. The consolidated net income is $26,000.)

E14–6. (Analytical) On January 1, 19A, Company P purchased all of the outstanding voting stock of Company S at $2.50 per share. At that date the balance sheet of Company S reflected the following:

Common stock, par $1 . . . . . $20,000
Retained earnings   10,000

One year after acquisition each company prepared its own separate financial statements and Company P set up the following consolidation worksheet (partially completed):

Items	Separate Statements		Intercompany Eliminations		Consolidated Balances
	Company P	Company S	Debit	Credit	
Income statement (for 19A):					
Sales revenue	99,000	59,000			
Revenues from investments	6,000		(e) 6,000		
Expenses (not detailed)	(71,000)	(40,400)			
Depreciation expense	(9,000)	(3,600)	(c) 1,200		
Amortization expense (goodwill)			(d) 400		
Net income	25,000	15,000			
Balance sheet					
(at December 31, 19A):					
Cash	16,000	6,000			
Receivable from Co. P		4,000		(b) 4,000	
Investment in Co. S	50,000			(a) 50,000	
Operational assets (net)	90,000	40,000 *	(a) 12,000	(c) 1,200	140,800
Goodwill (amortize over 20 years)			(a) 8,000	(d) 400	
Totals	156,000	50,000			170,400
Liabilities	15,000	11,000			
Payable to Co. S	4,000		(b) 4,000		
Common stock, Co. P	80,000				
Common stock, Co. S		20,000	(a) 20,000		
Beginning retained earnings, Co. P	32,000				
Beginning retained earnings, Co. S		10,000	(a) 10,000		
Dividends declared and paid, Co. S, 19A.		(6,000)		(e) 6,000	
Net income, 19A (per above)	25,000 †	15,000 †			32,400†
Totals	156,000	50,000	81,600	81,600	

* Market value of the operational assets at acquisition was $12,000 above book value and their remaining useful life was 10 years.
† Carried down.

Required:

a. Give the journal entry made by Company P on January 1, 19A, to record the purchase of Company S stock.

b. Show how the $8,000 of goodwill was computed.

c. Complete the last column of the worksheet (note that under "Eliminations" debit/credit instead of +/− were used).

d. Give a brief explanation of eliminations (c), (d), and (e).

PROBLEMS/CASES

PART A

PC14–1. During January 19A, Company P acquired all of the outstanding voting shares of Company S by exchanging one share of its own unissued voting common stock for two shares of Company S stock. Immediately prior to the acquisition, the separate balance sheets of the two companies reflected the following:

	Balances immediately prior to acquisition	
	Company P	Company S
Cash	$200,000	$ 32,000
Receivable from Company P		3,000
Inventory	75,000	5,000
Operational assets (net of accumulated depreciation)	75,000	80,000
Total	$350,000	$120,000
Liabilities	$ 57,000	$ 30,000
Payable to Company S	3,000	
Common stock, Company P (par $4)	180,000	
Common stock, Company S (par $5)		50,000
Contributed capital from pooling		
Retained earnings.......................	110,000	40,000
Total	$350,000	$120,000

Additional data:

At the date of acquisition, Company S stock was quoted on the market at $16 per share; there was no established market for Company P stock.

The operational assets of Company S were appraised independently at the date of acquisition at $130,000.

Required:

a. Is this a purchase or a pooling of interests? Explain why.
b. What account balances would be changed by the exchange of shares on each of the above balance sheets? List each account and amount.
c. Give the journal entry that should be made by each company to record the exchange; if no entry is required, explain why.
d. How much goodwill should be recognized? Why?
e. Prepare a consolidated balance sheet immediately after the acquisition.
f. Did you use any market values in solving the above requirements? Explain why.

PC14–2.   Assume the same facts given in PC14–1 except that instead of an exchange of shares of stock, Company P purchased from the stockholders 100 percent of the outstanding voting shares of Company S at a cash price of $160,000.

Required:

a. Is this a purchase or a pooling of interests? Explain why..
b. What account balances would be changed by the purchase of the shares on each of the balance sheets? List each account and amount.
c. Give the journal entry that should be made by each company to record the exchange; if no entry is required, explain why.
d. How much goodwill should be recognized? Why?
e. Prepare a consolidated balance sheet immediately after acquisition.
f. Did you use any market values in solving the above requirements? Explain why.

PC14–3.   On January 1, 19A, the separate balance sheets of two corporations showed the following:

| | Balances, Jan. 1, 19A | |
	Company P	Company S
Cash	$ 21,000	$ 9,000
Receivable from Company P		4,000
Operational assets (net)	99,000	32,000
Total	$120,000	$45,000
Accounts payable	$ 16,000	$10,000
Payable to Company S	4,000	
Common stock, par $20	60,000	20,000
Retained earnings	40,000	15,000
Total	$120,000	$45,000

On January 3, 19A, Company P acquired all of the outstanding voting shares of Company S by exchanging one share of its own stock for two shares of Company S stock.

Required:

a. Was this a combination by pooling of interests or by purchase? Explain why.

b. Company P made the following journal entry on its books, at the date of acquisition, to record the investment:

January 3, 19A:

Investment in Co. S	35,000	
Common stock		10,000
Contributed capital from pooling of interests		25,000

Explain the basis for each of the three amounts in this entry.

c. Should any goodwill be recognized on the consolidated balance sheet? Explain why.

d. Prepare a consolidated balance sheet immediately after the acquisition.

PC14–4. On January 2, 19A, Company P acquired all of the outstanding stock of Company S by exchanging its own stock for the stock of Company S. One share of Company P stock was exchanged for two shares of Company S stock. Immediately after the acquisition was recorded by Company P, the balance sheets reflected the following:

| | Balances, Jan. 2, 19A, immediately after acquisition | |
	Company P	Company S
Cash	$ 38,000	$26,000
Receivable from Company S	6,000	
Inventory	30,000	10,000
Investment in Company S (100%)	70,000	
Operational assets (net)	90,000	50,000
Other assets	6,000	4,000
Total	$240,000	$90,000
Liabilities	$ 16,000	$14,000
Payable to Company P		6,000
Common stock, par $5	125,000	50,000
Contributed capital from pooling of interests	45,000	
Retained earnings	54,000	20,000
Total	$240,000	$90,000

Required:

a. Was this a combination by pooling of interests or by purchase? Explain why.
b. Give the journal entry that was made by Company P to record the acquisition on January 2, 19A. Explain the basis for each amount included in the entry.
c. Should the assets of Company S be included on the consolidated balance sheet at book value or market value? Explain.
d. Will any goodwill be recognized on the consolidated balance sheet? Explain why.
e. Prepare a consolidated balance sheet immediately after acquisition.

PC14–5.   On January 5, 19A, Company P purchased all of the outstanding stock of Company S for $100,000 cash. Immediately after the acquisition the separate balance sheets of the two companies reflected the following:

| | *Jan. 5, 19A,*
immediately
after acquisition | |
	Company P	Company S
Cash	$ 22,000	$ 9,000
Accounts receivable (net)	14,000	6,000
Receivable from Company S	4,000	
Inventory	50,000	25,000
Investment in Company S (at cost)	100,000	
Operational assets (net)	153,000	67,000
Other assets	7,000	3,000
Total	$350,000	$110,000
Accounts payable	$ 20,000	$ 16,000
Payable to Company P		4,000
Bonds payable.......................	90,000	
Common stock, par $5	180,000	60,000
Contributed capital in excess of par	8,000	
Retained earnings	52,000	30,000
Total	$350,000	$110,000

The operational assets of Company S were estimated to have a market value at date of acquisition of $71,000.

Required:

a. Was this a combination by pooling of interests or by purchase? Explain why.
b. Give the journal entry that Company P should make at the date of acquisition.
c. Analyze the acquisition to determine the amount of goodwill purchased.
d. Should the assets of Company S be included on the consolidated balance sheet at book value or market value? Explain.
e. Prepare a consolidated balance sheet immediately after acquisition.

PC14–6.   On January 4, 19A, Company P purchased 100 percent of the outstanding common stock of Company S for $240,000 cash. Immediately after the acquisition, the separate balance sheets for the two companies were prepared as shown in the worksheet below.

COMPANY P and Its Subsidiary, COMPANY S
Consolidated Balance Sheet
January 4, 19A, Immediately after Acquisition

| | Separate balance sheets | | | |
	Company P	Company S	Eliminations	Consolidated balance sheet
Assets				
Cash	$ 80,000	$ 40,000	_____	_____
Accounts receivable (net)	26,000	19,000	_____	_____
Receivable from Company P		8,000	_____	_____
Inventories	170,000	80,000	_____	_____
Long-term investment, bonds, Z Company........................	15,000		_____	_____
Long-term investment, Company S	240,000		_____	_____
Land	12,000	3,000	_____	_____
Plant and equipment (net)	157,000	130,000	_____	_____
Goodwill			_____	_____
Total assets	$700,000	$280,000	_____	_____
Liabilities				
Accounts payable	$ 22,000	$ 40,000	_____	_____
Payable to Company S	8,000		_____	_____
Bonds payable, 5%	100,000	30,000	_____	_____
Stockholders' Equity				
Common stock, Company P	500,000		_____	_____
Common stock, Company S (par $10)		150,000	_____	_____
Retained earnings, Company P	70,000		_____	_____
Retained earnings, Company S		60,000	_____	_____
Total liabilities and stockholders' equity	$700,000	$280,000	_____	_____

It was determined at the date of acquisition that on the basis of a comparison of market value and book value, the assets as reflected on the books of Company S should be adjusted as follows: (a) inventories should be reduced by $3,000, (b) plant and equipment should be increased to $148,000, and (c) land should be increased by $2,000.

Required:

a. Was this a combination by pooling of interests or by purchase? Explain why.
b. Give the journal entry that was made on the books of Company P to record the acquisition.
c. Analyze the acquisition transaction to determine the amount of goodwill purchased. Use data from the worksheet if needed.
d. At what amount will the assets of Company S be included on the consolidated balance sheet? Explain.
e. Complete the "Eliminations" column in the worksheet and then extend the amounts for the consolidated balance sheet.

PART B

PC14–7. (Analytical) On January 1, 19A, Company P acquired 100 percent of the outstanding stock of Company S for $106,000 cash. At the date of acquisition the balance sheet of Company S reflected the following:

Total assets (including operational assets*)	115,000
Total liabilities	25,000
Common stock, par $10	60,000
Retained earnings	30,000

* Book value, $42,000; market value, $48,000 (20-year remaining life).

One year after acquisition the two companies prepared their December 31, 19A, financial statements. Company P developed the following consolidation worksheet (partially completed):

COMPANY P AND ITS SUBSIDIARY, COMPANY S
Consolidation Worksheet
Income Statement and Balance Sheet, December 31, 19A (100% ownership)

Items	Separate Statements		Eliminations				Consolidated balances
	Company P	Company S	Debit		Credit		
Income statement:							
Sales revenue	80,000	47,000					
Revenue from investments	4,000		(e)	4,000			
Cost of goods sold	(45,000)	(25,000)					
Expenses (not detailed)	(15,000)	(10,000)					
Depreciation expense	(4,000)	(2,000)	(c)	300			
Amortization of goodwill			(d)	500			
Net income	20,000	10,000					
Balance sheet:							
Cash	15,000	10,000					
Accounts receivable (net)	19,000	9,000					
Receivable from Co. P		1,000			(b)	1,000	
Inventories	70,000	50,000					
Investment in Co. S (100%)	106,000				(a)	106,000	
Plant and equipment (net)	80,000	40,000	(a)	6,000	(c)	300	
Goodwill			(a)	10,000	(d)	500	
	290,000	110,000					
Accounts payable	26,000	14,000					
Payable to Co. S	1,000		(b)	1,000			
Common stock, Co. P	200,000						
Common stock, Co. S		60,000	(a)	60,000			
Beginning retained earnings, Co. P	50,000						
Beginning retained earnings, Co. S		30,000	(a)	30,000			
Dividends declared and paid during 19A, Co. P	(7,000)						
Dividends declared and paid during 19A, Co. S		(4,000)			(e)	4,000	
Net income (from above)	20,000	10,000					
	290,000	110,000		11,800		111,800	308,200

Required:

a. Was this a purchase or pooling? Explain.
b. Give the journal entry made by each company to record the acquisition.
c. Complete the last column of the worksheet to develop the consolidated income statement and balance sheet.
d. How much goodwill was recognized? How was it computed?
e. Briefly explain each of the eliminations shown on the worksheet. Note that debit and credit rather than plus and minus were used in the Eliminations column.

PC14–8. (Analytical) This problem presents the income statement and the balance sheet on a consolidated basis for Company P and its subsidiary, Company S, one year after acquisition, under two different assumptions: Case A—pooling of interests, and Case B—purchase. The two different assumptions are used so that we can compare and analyze the differences between the pooling and purchase methods.

On January 2, 19A, Company P acquired all of the outstanding common stock of Company S. At that date the stockholders' equity of Company S showed the following: common stock, par $10, $50,000; and retained earnings, $20,000. The journal entry made by Company P to record the acquisition under each case was as follows:

Case A—Pooling of interests method:

Investment in Co. S (5,000 shares, 100%)	70,000	
Common stock, par $8		40,000
Contributed capital from pooling		30,000

Case B—Purchase method:

Investment in Co. S (5,000 shares, 100%)	80,000	
Cash		80,000

On January 2, 19A, the acquisition by purchase (Case B) was analyzed to determine the goodwill as follows:

Purchase price paid for 100% interest in Company S		$80,000
Net assets purchased, valued at market:		
Book value of net assets ($50,000 + $20,000 = $70,000 + increase of $2,000 in operational assets to market value)		72,000
Goodwill purchased		$ 8,000

For consolidated statement purposes the operational assets are being depreciated over 10 years' remaining life and the goodwill will be amortized over 20 years.

One year after acquisition, the two companies prepared separate income statements and balance sheets (December 31, 19A). These separate statements have been consolidated under each case as reflected on page 682.

Required:

a. Prepare a schedule of amounts that shows what items are different between each statement for Case A, compared with Case B.
b. Explain the reasons why net income is different under pooling of interests versus purchase. Use amounts from the two statements in your explanation and tell why they are different.
c. Explain why the cash balance is different between the two cases.
d. What was the balance in the account "Investment in Company S" in each case prior to its elimination? Explain.

e. Explain why the operational asset (net) amounts are different between the two cases.

f. Why is there a difference in goodwill between the two cases? Provide computations.

g. How much was eliminated for inter-company debt? Why was it eliminated?

h. What amount of "Common stock, Company S," was eliminated? Why was it eliminated?

i. Why was only $20,000 of the $30,000 of contributed capital from pooling of interests eliminated?

j. Explain why the account "Contributed capital in excess of par, $10,000," was not eliminated.

k. Explain why "Beginning retained earnings, Company S, $20,000," is shown under Case A (pooling) but not under Case B (purchase).

COMPANY P and Its Subsidiary, COMPANY S (100% owned)
Consolidated Income Statement and Balance Sheet
December 31, 19A

	Consolidated statements December 31, 19A	
	Pooling method (Case A)	Purchase method (Case B)
Income statement (for the year ended December 31, 19A):		
Sales revenue	$ 236,000	$ 236,000
Revenue from investments ($4,000, eliminated)		
Cost of goods sold	(112,000)	(112,000)
Expenses (not detailed to simplify)	(75,500)	(75,500)
Depreciation expense	(12,500)	(12,700)
Amortization expense (goodwill)		(400)
Net income	$ 36,000	$ 35,400
Balance sheet (at December 31, 19A):		
Assets		
Cash	$ 128,000	$ 48,000
Accounts receivable (net)	53,000	53,000
Receivable from Company S ($5,000, eliminated)		
Inventory	37,000	37,000
Investment in Company S (eliminated)		
Operational assets (net)	125,000	126,800
Goodwill		7,600
Total	$ 343,000	$ 272,400
Liabilities		
Current liabilities	$ 30,000	$ 30,000
Payable to Company P (eliminated)		
Bonds payable	50,000	50,000
Stockholders' Equity		
Common stock, Company P	140,000	100,000
Common stock, Company S (eliminated)		
Contributed capital in excess of par	10,000	10,000
Contributed capital from pooling of interests ($20,000, eliminated)	10,000	
Beginning retained earnings, Company P	47,000	47,000
Beginning retained earnings, Company S	20,000	
Dividends declared and paid in 19A (eliminated)		
Net income, 19A (from income statement above)	36,000	35,400
Total	$ 343,000	$ 272,400

PC14–9. (Based on Supplement 14A) On January 1, 19A, Company P purchased 100 percent of the outstanding capital stock of Company S for $98,000 cash. At that date the stockholders' equity section of the balance sheet of Company S reflected the following:

Capital stock, $10 par, 5,000 shares outstanding $50,000
Retained earnings   30,000
$80,000

At the date of acquisition, it was determined that the market values of certain assets of Company S, in comparison with the book values of those assets as reflected on the balance sheet of Company S, should be reflected by *(a)* decreasing inventories by $2,000 and *(b)* increasing equipment by $8,000.

It is now one year after acquisition, December 31, 19A, and each company has prepared the following separate financial statements (summarized):

	Company P	Company S
Balance sheet (at December 31, 19A):		
Cash	$ 52,000	$ 30,000
Accounts receivable (net)	31,000	10,000
Receivable from Company P		3,000
Inventories	60,000	70,000
Investment in Company S (at cost)	98,000	
Equipment	80,000	20,000
Other assets	9,000	17,000
	$ 330,000	$ 150,000
Accounts payable	$ 42,000	$ 30,000
Payable to Company S	3,000	
Bonds payable, 10%	70,000	30,000
Capital stock, $10 par	140,000	50,000
Beginning retained earnings	50,000	30,000
Dividends declared and paid during 19A	(10,000)	(5,000)
Net income, 19A (from income statement)	35,000	15,000
	$ 330,000	$ 150,000
Income statement (for 19A):		
Sales revenue	$ 360,000	$ 140,000
Revenue from investments	5,000	
Cost of goods sold	(220,000)	(80,000)
Expenses (not detailed)	(106,000)	(44,000)
Depreciation expense	(4,000)	(1,000)
Net income	$ 35,000	$ 15,000

Additional data during 19A:

1. Near the end of 19A, Company S declared and paid a cash dividend amounting to $5,000.
2. The equipment is being depreciated on the basis of a 20-year remaining life (no residual value).
3. Goodwill is to be amortized over a 40-year period.

Required:

a. Give the journal entry that Company P should make to record the acquisition of the capital stock of Company S on January 1, 19A.

b. Analyze the acquisition of the stock to determine the purchased goodwill.

c. Prepare a consolidation worksheet (purchase method) for the year 19A as a basis for the 19A income statement and balance sheet. (Hint: Consolidated net income is $44,300.)

d. Prepare a consolidated income statement and balance sheet based on the data provided by the consolidation worksheet.

PC14–10. (Based on Supplement 14B) On January 1, 19A, Company P purchased 90 percent of the outstanding voting stock of Company S for $100,000 cash. At the date of acquisition, the stockholders' equity accounts of Company S reflected the following: Capital Stock (par $10), $60,000; Contributed Capital in Excess of Par, $10,000; and Retained Earnings, $20,000. At that date it was determined that the book value of the operational assets was $10,000 less than their market value.

It is now December 31, 19A, and each company has prepared the following separate financial statements (summarized):

	Company P	Company S
Balance sheet (at December 31, 19A):		
Cash	$ 23,000	$ 11,000
Accounts receivable (net)	57,000	13,000
Receivable from Company P		7,000
Inventories	110,000	24,000
Investment in Company S (at cost; 90% owned).....	100,000	
Operational assets (net)	120,000	50,000
Other assets	6,000	5,000
	$ 416,000	$ 110,000
Accounts payable...............................	$ 30,000	$ 8,000
Payable to Company S	7,000	
Bonds payable, 9%	80,000	10,000
Capital stock, $10 par	200,000	60,000
Contributed capital in excess of par	4,000	10,000
Beginning retained earnings	80,000	20,000
Dividends declared and paid, 19A	(15,000)	(8,000)
Net income (from income statement)	30,000	10,000
	$ 416,000	$ 110,000
Income statement (for 19A):		
Sales revenue	$ 195,000	$ 75,000
Revenue from investments	7,200	
Cost of goods sold	(115,000)	(43,000)
Expenses (not detailed)	(52,200)	(19,500)
Depreciation expense	(5,000)	(2,500)
	$ 30,000	$ 10,000

Required:

a. Give the journal entry that Company P should make to record the acquisition of the stock of Company S.

b. Analyze the stock purchase to determine the amount of goodwill purchased.

c. Prepare a consolidation worksheet (purchase method) for a balance sheet and income statement for 19A. Assume the operational assets of Company S have a 10-year remaining life and that any goodwill will be amortized over 20 years. (Hint: Consolidated net income is $31,400.)

d. Prepare an income statement and balance sheet for 19A based upon the data provided by the consolidation worksheet.

e. What is the minority interest claim to earnings and stockholders' equity at December 31, 19A?

C·H·A·P·T·E·R
15

The Statement of Changes in Financial Position

PURPOSE OF THIS CHAPTER

Three basic statements must be presented for **external** reporting purposes; they are the (1) income statement, (2) balance sheet, and (3) statement of changes in financial position.[1] The prior chapters did not discuss and illustrate preparation and use of the statement of changes in financial position (abbreviated SCFP). The purpose of this chapter is to present the concepts of the SCFP, illustrate how the SCFP is developed, and emphasize its importance to external financial statement users. Also, this chapter discusses two alternative concepts of the SCFP—the cash basis and the working capital basis.

This chapter is subdivided as follows:

Part A—Purpose and concept of the SCFP, cash basis

Part B—Purpose and concept of the SCFP, working capital basis

Supplement 15A—T-account preparation of the SCFP

---

[1] Other supporting schedules, such as a statement of cost of goods sold, statement of retained earnings, statement of changes in capital, and a schedule of lease commitments, are essential in certain circumstances to meet the requirements of the reporting principle (Exhibit 2–6).

PART A—PURPOSE AND CONCEPT OF THE SCFP, CASH BASIS

ACCRUAL BASIS REPORTING VERSUS CASH BASIS REPORTING

The income statement reports the entity's operating performance (revenues and expenses) for a period of time, and the balance sheet reports the financial position (assets, liabilities, and owners' equity) at a specific date. Both the income statement and the balance sheet are developed on the **accrual basis;** that is, the financial effects of transactions are measured and recorded in the accounting system when the various transactions occur rather than when the cash inflows and outflows resulting from those transactions occur. As a result, these two financial statements do not report the **timing, amounts,** and **causes** of the cash inflows and cash outflows during the reporting period. Therefore, they do not report the causes of the changes in the **liquidity** of the entity.

The accrual basis is used for most reporting purposes because it provides meaningful measurements of revenues, expenses, assets, and liabilities. For example, a sale transaction on credit should be recognized when the sale transaction was completed rather than as of the later date of the cash collection because the revenue is earned when the completed transaction takes place. Similarly, an expense on credit should be recognized when the expense transaction was incurred rather than as of the later date when the cash is paid because the benefit associated with the expense is received when the completed expense transaction occurs. These two examples indicate why the income statement must be based on the accrual basis (i.e., transactions are recorded when their initial economic effects occur). For the same basic reason the balance sheet must report assets, liabilities, and owners' equity on the accrual basis.

In addition to the accrual basis income statement and balance sheet, decision makers need information on the sources and uses of cash. The SCFP, cash basis, reports only cash inflow and cash outflow transactions (including direct exchanges discussed later). Therefore, the SCFP is strictly a cash basis report. For example, instead of reporting income on the accrual basis (as reported on the income statement), the SCFP reports income for the period on the cash basis (on the SCFP this amount may be called Net cash inflow from normal operations).

HOW THE SCFP, CASH BASIS, HELPS DECISION MAKERS

Although statement users need to know the accrual basis results reported on the income statement and balance sheet, they also need financial information on the **timing, amounts,** and **causes** of the cash inflows and cash outflows of the entity during the accounting period. Fundamentally, knowledge about the **liquidity** (i.e., cash inflows and outflows) of an entity is very important to statement users because ultimately the success of an entity is measured by the cumulative amount of net cash inflow that it provides. Investors (creditors and owners) are interested in the net cash inflow of an entity because it provides their cash returns (e.g., dividends or interest, and cash received upon disposition of their shares or maturity of the debt). Also, the very existence of an entity depends upon cash flows; sufficient cash must be received and be available monthly (even daily) to pay for such items as salaries, rent, interest and principal on debt, assets purchased, and cash dividends. The first symptom of an impending economic problem is a shortage of cash. It is no wonder, then, that financial statement users need current and understandable data about the timing, sources, and uses of cash by the entity during the period covered by the financial statements. The **statement of changes in financial position, cash basis,** is designed to provide cash flow (i.e., liquidity) information for the statement users.[2] The SCFP supplements, but does not replace, the income statement and balance sheet because the SCFP provides information that is not provided by the other two statements.[3]

As a complement to the income statement and balance sheet, the SCFP (cash basis) is designed to provide information that is particularly useful to external users of the financial statements in answering questions such as:

1. How much cash was provided by the **normal operations** of the entity?
2. What were the primary sources of cash from such activities as borrowing, issuance of capital stock, and sale of operational assets?
3. How much cash was derived from **nonrecurring** transactions?
4. How much cash was used to pay long-term debts?
5. How much cash was used to acquire operational assets?
6. Why were large borrowings necessary? What uses were made of the cash borrowed?
7. What are the causes of any persistent liquidity problems of the entity?
8. Does a critical cash flow problem appear imminent?
9. What was the financial effect of noncash exchanges (such as the settlement of a debt by issuing company shares)?
10. Does the company have idle cash? How does the company "use" its idle cash?
11. What is the potential ability of the company to generate cash in the long term?

The SCFP, cash basis, serves a very useful and significant purpose because it can assist external users of the financial statements in answering the above questions.

CONCEPT OF THE SCFP

The income statement and the SCFP often are called **change statements** because they "explain" the reasons why the **ending balance sheet** amounts for the accounting period are different from the **beginning balance sheet** amounts of that same period. As change statements, both the income statement and the SCFP are "dated" as For the year ended December 31, 19A. In contrast, the balance

---

[2] FASB, *Statement of Financial Accounting Concepts No. 1,* "Objectives of Financial Reporting by Business Enterprises" (Stamford, Conn., November 1978), states: "Since investors' and creditors' cash flows are related to enterprise cash flows, financial reporting should provide information to help investors, creditors, and others assess the amounts, timing, and uncertainty of prospective net cash inflows to the related enterprise."

[3] *APB Opinion 19* states: "The funds statement cannot supplant either the income statement or the balance sheet but is intended to provide information that the other statements either do not provide or provide only indirectly about the flow of funds and changes in financial position during the period."

sheet is dated as At December 31, 19A, because it is a **position** statement rather than a change statement.

The income statement "explains" the **changes** between the beginning and ending balance sheet amounts **caused by accrual basis** revenues, expenses, and extraordinary gains and losses. There are numerous **changes** in the beginning and ending balance sheet amounts (e.g., the purchase of an operational asset) that are not reported on the accrual basis income statement. In contrast to the income statement, the SCFP, cash basis, reports the **cash effects of all changes** between the beginning and ending balance sheets, including those reported on the income statement. Exhibit 15–1 presents a SCFP, cash basis, for Brownlee Service Corporation (designed for instructional purposes). Observe the two major captions "Sources (inflows) of cash" (four inflows are illustrated) and "Uses (outflows) of cash" (four outflows are illustrated). This SCFP indicates that the net increase in cash was $10,000 during the year. Most important, the SCFP reports how Brownlee Service Corporation obtained cash and specifically how that cash was used. This information is not reported on the accrual basis income statement and balance sheet. To illustrate another use of the SCFP, cash basis, assume you are interested in purchasing all of the outstanding capital stock of Brownlee Service Corporation. As a rational investor, you should be vitally concerned about the sources and uses of cash by that company during the last few years. The cash flow information should assist you in assessing the **future** cash flow problems and any advantages that you could expect as the owner.

Exhibit 15–2 presents an overview of the relationships between the beginning balance sheet, the SCFP, and the ending balance sheet. The SCFP given in Exhibit 15–1 is presented again in Exhibit 15–2 in a tabular format **between** the beginning and ending balance sheets (for instructional purposes only). Observe how the SCFP "explains" the changes in each balance sheet item in terms of the actual cash inflows and cash outflows and the **causes** of each of those changes.

FUNDS DEFINED

In business, the terms **funds, cash,** and **working capital** frequently are used interchangeably; however, clarity and precision are essential when they are used in accounting, especially with respect to the SCFP. **Cash** was defined in Chapter 8 as currency, balances on deposit in checking accounts, and negotiable instruments that a bank will accept for immediate deposit in a checking account. **Working capital** was defined in Chapter 2 as the **difference** between total current assets and total current liabilities.

With respect to the SCFP, *APB Opinion 19* specifies that the "funds" **may be measured as either:**[4]

1. **Cash basis**—Based on inflows and outflows of cash, as defined above.
2. **Working capital basis**—Based on inflows and outflows of working capital.

---

[4] The word *funds* also is used in other ways by accountants. It has been used to refer to assets, usually cash, set aside for a specific future use, such as a building fund or a bond sinking fund; and in governmental accounting, it has an entirely different meaning. This wide range of inconsistent usage of the term suggests the desirability of using more descriptive terms, such as **cash** and **working capital,** and the use of more descriptive titles, such as "statement of changes in financial position," rather than the older title, "funds flow statement."

EXHIBIT 15–1
Statement of
changes in financial
position, cash basis
(designed for
instructional
purposes only)

BROWNLEE SERVICE CORPORATION
Statement of Changes in Financial Position, Cash Basis
For the Year Ended December 31, 19B

Sources (inflows) of cash:
1. Net cash inflow from normal operations (based on the income
   statement; computed below) $64,000*
2. Cash sale of noncash assets (such as machinery and investments) 6,000
3. Cash borrowing (such as on notes and bonds payable) 30,000
4. Cash sale and issuance of Brownlee capital stock 20,000
      Total cash inflow during 19B $120,000

Uses (outflows) of cash:
1. Cash purchase of noncash assets (such as machinery and
   investments) 35,000
2. Cash payment on debts (such as notes and bonds payable) 50,000
3. Cash dividends declared and paid during 19B (such as on
   common or preferred stock) 10,000
4. Cash purchase of treasury stock 15,000
      Total cash outflow during 19B   110,000

Net increase in cash during 19B .... $ 10,000

* Income Statement Converted to Cash Basis
For the Year Ended December 31, 19B

Items	Accrual basis	Explanation of restatements to cash basis	Cash basis
Service revenues	$127,000	Service revenue not collected, $3,000	$124,000
Expenses			
Salary expense	38,000	Salaries payable, $2,000	36,000
Depreciation expense	18,000	A noncash expense, $18,000	–0–
Utilities	5,000	Paid in full	5,000
Remaining expenses	9,000	19C expense paid in advance, $3,000	12,000
Income tax expense	8,000	Income tax payable, $1,000	7,000
Total expenses	78,000		60,000
Net income	$ 49,000	Net cash inflow from normal operations	$ 64,000

Proof based on net income:
  Net income (accrual), $49,000 − $3,000 + $2,000 + $18,000 − $3,000 + $1,000 = $64,000 (cash inflow from
    normal operations).

Working capital always is defined as current assets minus current liabilities.
Current assets include cash, short-term investments, short-term receivables,
inventory, and prepaid expenses. The current liabilities are short-term debts
that are expected to be paid out of the current assets.

In contrast to cash, which can be touched, counted, and used to purchase goods
and services, to pay debts, and to invest, working capital is an **abstract** concept
because it is the arithmetical difference between the sum of the several current
assets and the sum of the several current liabilities. It is impossible to use the
difference called working capital to deposit, pay debts, invest, etc. (also, it cannot
be touched). Generally accepted accounting principles permit the SCFP to be
prepared on either a cash or working capital basis and require that the SCFP
disclose whether funds are measured as cash or as working capital. The discussions
in Part A of this chapter assume the cash basis SCFP. The SCFP, working capital
basis, is discussed in Part B.

EXHIBIT 15–2 Relationship between the SCFP (cash basis) and the balance sheet (SCFP data is from Exhibit 15–1)

Balance Sheet
At December 31, 19A

Cash	$ 20,000
Noncash assets	140,000
Total	$160,000
Liabilities	$ 50,000
Owners' equity:	
Common stock	100,000
Treasury stock	
Retained earnings	10,000
Total	$160,000
Net increase in cash; to check (first line above)	

Statement of Changes in Financial Position
For the Year Ended December 31, 19B

Sources of Cash		Uses of Cash	
Causes	*Amount*	*Causes*	*Amount*
Disposal (sold)	$ 6,000	Purchase	$ 35,000
Borrowing	30,000	Payment	50,000
Issuance (sold)	20,000	Purchase	15,000
Operations	64,000	Dividends	10,000
Total sources	120,000	Total uses	110,000
			10,000
	$120,000		$120,000

Balance Sheet
At December 31, 19B

Cash		$ 30,000
Noncash assets	=	169,000
Total		$199,000
Liabilities	=	$ 30,000
Owners' equity:		
Common stock	=	120,000
Treasury stock	=	(15,000)
Retained earnings	=	64,000
Total		$199,000

A change statement that explains the causes of the changes in the balance sheet accounts—assets, liabilities, and owners' equity. (Assumptions: Funds measured as cash and no direct exchanges.)

ALL-RESOURCES CONCEPT OF THE SCFP

The SCFP must be based on the **all-resources concept** which means that it must report all of the **financing and investing activities** of the entity, not just those that cause an inflow or outflow of **funds** (i.e., cash or working capital). **Financing activities** are those transactions that cause an increase (inflow) of funds into the business. In contrast, **investing activities** cause a decrease (outflow) of funds. Transactions that do not cause an inflow or outflow of funds are called **direct exchanges** because they involve the exchanges of **nonfund** assets, liabilities, or capital stock. An example of a direct exchange would be the purchase of an operational asset with full payment by transferring land owned by the purchaser. This transaction would not cause a cash outflow; nevertheless, this direct exchange must be reported on the SCFP because there was, in effect, a simultaneous **source** of funds (for the sale of the land) and **use** of funds (for the purchase of the operational asset). Two additional examples of direct exchanges follow.

Case A:

AB Company acquired a $6,000 machine by issuing 100 shares of its own common stock, par $50 per share. The stock was selling regularly at $60 per share; therefore, the company recorded the transaction in the accounts as follows:

Machine (100 shares × $60)	6,000	
Common stock, par $50 (100 shares × $50)		5,000
Contributed capital in excess of par (100 shares × $10)		1,000

The above journal entry does not reflect a debit or credit to any "fund" account because neither cash nor working capital was affected. However, the transaction involved both a financing activity (the issuance of the stock) and an investing activity (the acquisition of the machine). Consequently, the all-resources concept holds that there was an implied (though not explicit) and concurrent inflow and outflow of funds. In contrast, instead of the direct exchange, assume that the company sold the common stock for $6,000 cash and immediately purchased the machine with the $6,000 received from the sale. Under this assumption, the sale of the common stock was a financing activity and the debit to Cash of $6,000 reflected a source (inflow) of funds. On the other side, the purchase of the machine was an investing activity and the credit to Cash of $6,000 reflected a use (outflow) of funds. In order to report all of the financing and investing activities, the all-resources concept requires that direct exchanges be reported on the SCFP because there is no economic difference between a direct exchange and an actual concurrent inflow and outflow of funds. Therefore, in Case A the direct exchange of the common shares for the machine must be reported on the SCFP "as if" **two separate transactions** occurred concurrently. That is, in this example the SCFP must report (1) a **source** of cash and (2) a **use** of cash for the direct exchange. AB Company would report the following on the SCFP:

Sources of cash:
Sale and issuance of common stock (Note A) $6,000

Uses of cash:
Purchase of machine (Note A)   6,000

Note A: This was a direct exchange. A machine was acquired at a cost of $6,000; payment was made by issuing 100 shares of common stock, par $50 per share, that had a market value of $6,000.

Case B:

AB Company owed a $30,000 note payable that was paid off in full by issuing 500 of its own common shares, par $50, with a $60 market value per share. The company would record the direct exchange as follows:

Note payable	30,000	
Common stock, par $50 (500 shares × $50)		25,000
Contributed capital in excess of par (500 shares × $10)		5,000

In the above journal entry, no fund accounts (cash or working capital) were debited or credited (i.e., there was no inflow or outflow of funds), nevertheless, the SCFP would report the $30,000 as if it were (1) a source of funds and (2) a use of funds in a manner similar to the example in Case A.

CASH BASIS CONCEPT OF THE SCFP

The SCFP, cash basis, defines, measures, and reports the sources and uses of funds in terms of cash. For SCFP purposes, any short-term investments held almost always are added to cash because such investments are very near to cash and can be converted to cash easily at any time (this is permitted by *APB Opinion 19*). Fundamentally, cash is used as the measure of funds because investors, creditors, and other external statement users view current cash flows as relevant information that can help them **project the ability of the company to generate favorable net cash inflows in the future.** In addition, a basic objective of the SCFP is to report on the liquidity of the entity, and cash is the most liquid of all assets. Cash represents the funds that circulate through a business on a daily basis. A company deals in terms of cash, and it is generated and used continuously.

In contrast to working capital, cash is accounted for separately (in the Cash account), and it can be physically counted. Cash inflows and outflows are understood and communicated easily (via the SCFP). Compared with cash, working capital is an elusive concept to many persons, particularly because the measurement of working capital includes **all** of the individual current assets with an offset which includes **all** of the current liabilities. The difference, which is called working capital, is only an amount—not a specific asset. The SCFP, cash basis, reports all of the **sources of cash,** all of the **uses of cash,** and the **difference** between the total cash inflows and total cash outflows of the period. The **net increase or decrease in cash during the period** reported on the SCFP is the same amount as the change in Cash account balance between the two consecutive balance sheets (see Exhibit 15–2).

Preparation of the SCFP, cash basis, involves identification of *(a)* all cash inflows including the net cash inflow from operations (i.e., from the income statement); *(b)* all cash outflows; and *(c)* all direct exchanges. Calculation of the net cash flow from normal operations requires that the accrual basis income statement be converted to a cash basis.

PREPARING THE SCFP, CASH BASIS

Detailed knowledge of the technical procedures used to prepare a SCFP is not essential to be able to use it. However, as with the income statement and balance sheet, a general understanding of the procedures used to prepare the SCFP often is helpful in interpreting and using it more effectively.

Preparation of a SCFP, cash basis, requires identification and measurement of the amount of cash inflows from each source and the amount of cash outflows for each use. The primary **sources of cash** are *(a)* normal operations, *(b)* borrowing, *(c)* issuance of capital stock, and *(d)* sale of company assets. The primary **uses of cash** are *(a)* purchase of operational assets, *(b)* purchase of investments, *(c)* payment of debt, and *(d)* payment of cash dividends.

Measurement of the net cash inflow (or net outflow) from **normal operations** involves a careful analysis to **convert** the income statement from the accrual basis to the cash basis. This conversion involves conversion of each revenue and each expense from the accrual basis to the cash basis.

The SCFP, cash basis, can be prepared by using one of the following three analytical approaches:[5]

1. **Direct analysis**—This approach can be used efficiently only when the situation is very simple as illustrated in Exhibit 15–1. It involves careful analysis of the income statement, the beginning and ending balance sheets, and selected transactions for the current period. It has no built-in accuracy checks except that the **net increase (decrease) in cash** must agree with the net change in the Cash account during the period.

2. **Worksheet analysis**—This approach is widely used, especially in practical and complex situations, because it is very efficient and provides some built-in checks of accuracy. The worksheet approach is wholly consistent with the SCFP concept of "explaining" the changes between the beginning and ending balance sheet. For these reasons it is illustrated in Exhibit 15–4.

3. **T-account analysis**—This approach is similar to the worksheet approach except that a separate **T-account** is set up for each item for analysis purposes. It often is used for instructional purposes because students are familiar with

---

[5] The discussions of the worksheet and T-account analytical approaches that follow can be omitted without significantly impinging upon the remaining discussions.

T-account analyses of various sorts. The T-account approach is illustrated in Supplement 15A.

ILLUSTRATIVE CASE

Throughout the remainder of this chapter, the Fina Company case will be used as a basis for discussion and illustration. Assume it is December 31, 19B, the end of the annual accounting period, and that Fina Company has completed all of the year-end procedures, including the preparation of the income statement and the balance sheet. The remaining requirement is preparation of a SCFP for 19B.

Comparative balance sheets for the current and past year and the income statement for the current year are shown in Exhibit 15–3. The prior balance sheet, at December 31, 19A, is needed for analytical purposes regardless of the analysis approach used.

WORKSHEET ANALYSIS FOR PREPARING THE SCFP, CASH BASIS

Preparing a SCFP, cash basis, involves five procedural steps that are illustrated for Fina Company in Exhibits 15–4 (worksheet analysis), 15–5 (conversion of income statement from accrual to cash basis), and 15–6 (the formal SCFP). Preparing the SCFP requires data from the current income statement and the comparative balance sheets (Exhibit 15–3), and selected data about certain transactions. The preparation procedures, using either the worksheet or the T-account analysis, require an **analysis of all of the noncash balance sheet accounts.** The **net increase or decrease** in each of these noncash accounts, between the two consecutive balance sheets, must be analyzed to identify the cash inflows and cash outflows during the period. The results of this analysis are used to (1) identify and measure the amount of each cash source and each cash use and (2) determine the **causes** of the cash inflows and outflows (including all direct exchanges). Recall that these are the two purposes of the SCFP.

Four relatively simple procedural steps are involved in preparing the SCFP, cash basis; they are (1) data collection, (2) set up a worksheet, (3) complete the worksheet and (4) prepare the formal SCFP.

Step 1—**Data collection.** Obtain the current income statement and comparative balance sheets (see Exhibit 15–3).

Step 2—**Set up a worksheet** with five-column headings as shown in Exhibit 15–4. In Part A—analysis of balance sheet accounts—list each balance sheet account and its balance as reported on the comparative balance sheets. In Part B—SCFP outlined—set up the two major captions on the SCFP: "Sources of cash" and "Uses of cash." The sources of cash will be represented by **debits** in this special account and the uses of cash by **credits.** Provide for two "source" subcaptions, "From normal operations" and "From other sources." **"From normal operations"** is the section on the worksheet where net income (accrual basis) is converted to **net cash inflow from normal**

EXHIBIT 15–3
Comparative
balance sheets and
income statement,
Fina Company

FINA COMPANY
Balance Sheets
At December 31, 19B, and 19A

	December 31, 19B		December 31, 19A [a]	
Assets				
Current assets:				
Cash	$41,300		$31,000	
Accounts receivable (net) [b]	25,000		20,000	
Inventory (periodic)	20,000	$ 86,300	24,000	$ 75,000
Long-term investments:				
Common stock of X Corporation		1,000		6,000
Operational assets: [b]				
Equipment (net) [c]	59,000			
Patent (cost, $3,400 − amort., $200)	3,200	62,200		60,000
Total assets		$149,500		$141,000
Liabilities				
Current liabilities:				
Accounts payable	$22,000		$20,000	
Income tax payable	500		1,000	
Short-term note payable (nontrade)	10,000	$ 32,500	14,000	$ 35,000
Long-term liabilities:				
Long-term note payable	10,000			
Bonds payable	32,000	42,000		40,000
Stockholders' Equity				
Stockholders' equity:				
Common stock, par $10	60,000		50,000	
Contributed capital in excess of par	6,000		5,000	
Treasury stock (at cost)	(3,000)			
Retained earnings [d]	12,000	75,000	11,000	66,000
Total liabilities and stockholders' equity		$149,500		$141,000

[a] The ending balance sheet for the past period is the beginning balance sheet for the current period.

[b] In analyzing and reporting changes in financial position, accounts receivable and operational assets usually are shown **net** of the contra accounts as a matter of convenience.

[c] A machine that cost $5,000 was acquired on January 1, 19B, and payment in full was made by exchanging $5,000 of the investment in the common stock of X Corporation (the carrying value of these shares was the same as their current market value).

[d] Dividends declared and paid during 19B amounted to $7,000.

FINA COMPANY
Income Statement
For the Year Ended December 31, 19B

Sales revenue		$100,000
Cost of goods sold		60,000
Gross margin		40,000
Less expenses:		
Expenses (not detailed)	$23,800	
Depreciation expense	6,000	
Amortization expense (patent)	200	
Income tax expense	2,000	32,000
Net income		$ 8,000

operations" (also see Exhibit 15–1). All other **sources** of cash are identified under the subcaption "From other sources." Step 3 (complete the worksheet) is discussed below, and Step 4 (prepare the formal SCFP) is discussed starting on page 701.

The SCFP worksheet, cash basis (Exhibit 15–4), is designed to reflect all of the accounts reported on the comparative balance sheets in the upper portion (Part A) including the current year's **beginning** balances (i.e., the ending balances from the prior period) and the **ending** balances (i.e., the ending balances for the current period). The prior year's balances are entered in the first amount column, and the current year's balances are entered in the last (fourth) amount column. Two inner amount columns are used for the debits and credits of the **analytical entries. The amounts entered in the two inner amount columns represent only the analytical entries and must account fully for the difference on each line between the beginning (first column) and ending balances (last column).**

The bottom portion of the worksheet represents the SCFP; therefore, it is set up with the following side captions (leaving sufficient space under each caption to complete the analytical entries):

> **Sources of cash:**
> From normal operations
> From other sources
> **Uses of cash:**
>
> **Net increase (decrease) in cash**

Step 3—**Complete the worksheet.** The "Analysis of Interim Entries" provides for the worksheet analysis (in summary fashion) of all changes during the period in each **noncash** account entered on the worksheet. These changes are analyzed to determine those that (1) generated (increased) cash, (2) used (decreased) cash, and (3) those that did not affect cash. The analytical entries are entered directly on the worksheet in the normal debit-credit fashion; however, **instead of entering amounts in the Cash account, the debits to cash are entered in Part B, "Sources of cash" and the credits are entered as "Uses of cash."**

The final step in completing the worksheet is to record the **analytical entries** on the worksheet. The analytical entries are based upon data provided by the two balance sheets, the income statement, and other accounting records. The analytical entries on the worksheet for Fina Company (Exhibit 15–4) are entered as explained in Exhibit 15–7.[6]

After the analytical entries are made on the worksheet, a careful check should be made to ascertain whether the change between the beginning and ending balances on each line (i.e., each balance sheet account) is accounted for fully. This check indicates that the worksheet analysis is complete. At this point, the

---

[6] This same procedure, including the same analytical entries, are used in the T-account approach (presented in Supplement 15A, Exhibit 15–11).

EXHIBIT 15–4
Worksheet to
develop SCFP, cash
basis (Fina
Company for the
year ended
December 31, 19B)

Part A—Analysis of balance sheet accounts:

Items	Balances Dec. 31, 19A	Analysis of Interim Entries*		Ending Balances Dec. 31, 19B
		Debit	Credit	
Debits				
Cash account	31,000	(√) 10,300		41,300
Noncash accounts:				
Accounts receivable (net)	20,000	(d) 5,000		25,000
Inventory	24,000		(e) 4,000	20,000
LT investment, X Corp. stock†	6,000		(f-1) 5,000	1,000
Equipment (net)	60,000	(f-2) 5,000	(b) 6,000	59,000
Patent (net)		(g) 3,400	(c) 200	3,200
Total	141,000			149,500
Credits				
Accounts payable	20,000		(h) 2,000	22,000
Income tax payable	1,000	(i) 500		500
Short-term note payable (non-trade)	14,000	(j) 4,000		10,000
Long-term note payable			(k) 10,000	10,000
Bonds payable	40,000	(l) 8,000		32,000
Capital stock, par $10	50,000		(m) 10,000	60,000
Contributed capital in excess of par	5,000		(m) 1,000	6,000
Treasury stock		(n) 3,000		(3,000)
Retained earnings	11,000	(o) 7,000	(a) 8,000	12,000
Total	141,000	46,200	46,200	149,500

change in the Cash account during the period (as indicated on the first line) can be entered at the bottom of the worksheet and the debit and credit columns in the bottom portion of the worksheet may be summed to test for equality. This provides a partial check on the accuracy of the results.

Completion of the worksheet involves conversion of **accrual** net income to net cash inflow from the normal operations of the entity.

Net cash inflow from normal operations reflects the net cash effect of all of the revenue and expense transactions. Accrual revenues, accrual expenses, and accrual income must be converted to a **strictly current cash basis** for reporting on the SCFP, cash basis. Cash inflow from normal operations sometimes is referred to as "Net cash generated from normal operations." **Noncash revenues** must be excluded from this amount because they do not cause cash to increase during the period. The reporting principle **requires** that the conversion adjustments of accrual income to cash inflow or outflow from operations (shown in detail on the SCFP as reflected in Exhibit 15–6.

Normal operations (i.e., as illustrated by the income statement) usually are

EXHIBIT 15–4
(concluded)

Part B—SCFP outlined:

Items	Income and Additions	Income Deductions
Sources of cash:		
From normal operations:		
Net income	*(a)* 8,000	
Depreciation expense	*(b)* 6,000	
Amortization of patent	*(c)* 200	
Accounts receivable increase		*(d)* 5,000
Inventory decrease	*(e)* 4,000	
Accounts payable increase	*(h)* 2,000	
Income tax payable decrease		*(i)* 500
	Sources	Uses
From other sources:		
Exchange of investment for equip.	*(f*-1) 5,000	
LT note payable	*(k)* 10,000	
Sold and issued common stock	*(m)* 11,000	
Uses of cash:		
Exchange of investment for equip.		*(f*-2) 5,000
Purchase of patent		*(g)* 3,400
Payment on ST note		*(j)* 4,000
Payment on bonds payable		*(l)* 8,000
Purchase of treasury stock		*(n)* 3,000
Declared and paid cash dividend		*(o)* 7,000
Net increase in cash (per line 1, Part A)		(√) 10,300
	46,200	46,200

Net cash inflow from normal operations, $14,700; see Exhibits 15–5 and 15–6.

* These entries are keyed for ready reference to the text discussion; see Exhibit 15–7.
† Equipment was acquired in exchange for common stock of X Corporation, which was being held as a long-term investment.

the primary single source of cash for all businesses over the long term. Income reflects the effect of operations for the period on the **accrual basis.** As goods and services are sold during the period, there is an inflow of cash from **revenues** (i.e., from customers); however, the cash inflow from the revenues is affected by credit sales of the current and prior periods. To illustrate, assume a company sold goods during Year 1 amounting to $100,000, of which $5,000 remained uncollected at year-end. In this case, the cash inflow would be $95,000 (i.e., $100,000, minus the $5,000 in accounts receivable). Now, if sales for Year 2 totaled $120,000 and if accounts receivable decreased by $5,000, cash inflow during the period would be $125,000 (i.e., $120,000 plus the collection of $5,000 for credit sales that were reported in Year 1).

During an accounting period, **expenses** are incurred that cause a cash outflow; however, the cash outflow for expenses is affected by the amount of expenses incurred on credit in the current and prior periods. To illustrate, assume a company incurred expenses during Year 1 of $92,000, of which $2,000 was unpaid at year-end. In this case, the cash outflow would be $90,000 (i.e., $92,000, minus the $2,000 increase in accounts payable). Now, if expenses for Year 2 totaled $95,000 and at the same time accounts payable decreased by $2,000, cash outflow during the current period would be $97,000 (i.e., $95,000 plus the payment of $2,000 for expenses that were reported in Year 1).

Depreciation expense and amortization expense (e.g., patents) are **noncash expenses** of the current period that are deducted on the income statement to derive accrual income. Therefore, to measure cash flow from the income statement, such expenses must be added to the amount of accrual income. To illustrate, assume Company T sold goods for $100,000 cash, paid cash for all current expenses of $86,000, and reported depreciation expense of $6,000. Accrual income reported on the income statement would be $100,000 − $86,000 − $6,000 = $8,000. However, the cash inflow from the income statement (i.e., from operations) would be $14,000 (i.e., accrual income, $8,000 plus depreciation expense, $6,000).

Cost of goods sold is an expense; however, the cash outflow for this expense must be calculated by analyzing the changes in **two related accounts**—merchandise inventory and accounts payable (for purchases of merchandise). To convert accrual income to cash inflow from operations, a **decrease** in inventory during the period must be added to income because cash payments for purchases of inventory precede the sale or use of inventory. Similarly, an **increase** in inventory must be subtracted from income because a cash payment has been made for inventory that is not reflected in cost of goods sold. Relatedly, a decrease in accounts payable during the period must be subtracted from income because cash payments for accounts payable were more than the amount of purchases. Similarly, an increase in accounts payable must be added to income to convert it to the cash basis.[7]

Therefore, the amount of net cash inflow (or outflow) usually will be different from accrual income because of the effect of **noncash revenues and noncash expenses.**

To illustrate the income additions and deductions for the period to derive cash inflow (or cash outflow) from operations, refer to Fina Company. The income

---

[7] The adjustments to convert accrual income to cash flow from operations are quite varied. Although careful analysis is required, the following tabulation may be useful for checking purposes:

Item	*Plus and minus adjustments to convert income to net cash flow from operations*	
	When item increases	*When item decreases*
Accounts receivable (trade)	−	+
Accounts payable (trade)	+	−
Accrued liability and unearned revenue	+	−
Prepaid asset and accrued revenue	−	+
Inventory	−	+
Depreciation, depletion, and amortization	+	
Amortization of discount on bonds payable	+	
Amortization of premium on bonds payable	−	
Amortization of discount on bond investment	−	
Amortization of premium on bond investment	+	

statement shown in Exhibit 15–3 reported income of $8,000. On the basis of an **analysis** of each revenue and each expense, income was converted to net cash inflow from normal operations as illustrated in Exhibit 15–5.

Observe in Exhibit 15–5 that net cash inflow from normal operations (i.e., $14,700) was $6,700 more than accrual income (i.e., $8,000). In some cases, net cash inflow from normal operations will be less than accrual income.

EXHIBIT 15–5 Conversion of accrual net income to net cash inflow from normal operations	

Income (as reported on the income statement; accrual basis) .... $ 8,000
Add (deduct) adjustments to convert to cash basis:
    Accounts receivable increase .... (5,000)
    Depreciation expense 6,000
    Amortization expense 200
    *Merchandise inventory decrease 4,000
    *Accounts payable increase 2,000
    Income tax payable decrease .... (500)
Net cash inflow from normal operations during the period $14,700

* These two items may be combined as a conversion of cost of goods sold on the accrual basis to a cash basis as follows:

CGS—accrual basis (Exhibit 15–3)	$60,000
Inventory change—decrease (Exhibit 15–3)	(4,000)
Purchases—accrual basis	56,000
Accounts payable change—increase (Exhibit 15–3)	(2,000)
CGS—Cash basis	$54,000
Adjustment (add) for conversion of CGS to cash basis ($60,000 − $54,000) = ...	$ 6,000

The analytical entries follow the pattern of the regular journal entries and must be made to account for all of the net increases and net decreases in each account in Part A of the worksheet. The offsetting debits and credits to **Cash** are recorded in Part B of the worksheet.

When changes in each account in Part A of the worksheet are accounted for, the analysis is complete and Part B of the worksheet will reflect **each source and use of cash** during the period. One check of accuracy is indicated in Exhibit 15–4; that is, the balancing amount in Part B of the worksheet (i.e., $10,300) must agree with the net change in the Cash account during the period.

Step 4—**Prepare the formal SCFP.** All of the information needed to prepare the formal SCFP is reflected in Part B of the worksheet. The SCFP, cash basis, for Fina Company (Exhibit 15–6) was prepared directly from Exhibit 15–4. Some variations in terminology and classifications may be observed in actual practice.

For study purposes, the analytical entries entered on the worksheet (Exhibit 15–4) are repeated and explained in more detail in Exhibit 15–7.

EXHIBIT 15–6
Statement of changes in financial position, cash basis, Fina Company

FINA COMPANY
Statement of Changes in Financial Position, Cash Basis
For the Year Ended December 31, 19B [a]

Sources of cash: [b]

From normal operations:

Income	$ 8,000	
Add (deduct) adjustments to convert to cash basis:		
Accounts receivable increase	(5,000)	
Depreciation expense	6,000	
Amortization expense (patent)	200	
Merchandise inventory decrease	4,000	
Accounts payable increase	2,000	
Income tax payable decrease	(500)	
Net cash from normal operations		$14,700 [c]
From other sources:		
Borrowing on long-term note	10,000	
Sale of unissued common stock	11,000	
Disposal of long-term investment (Note A)	5,000	
Total cash from other sources		26,000
Total cash generated (inflow) during the period		40,700

Uses of cash: [b]

Cash dividend on common stock declared and paid during 19B	7,000	
Payment on bonds payable	8,000	
Payment on notes payable, short term (nontrade)	4,000	
Purchase of patent	3,400	
Purchase of treasury stock	3,000	
Acquisition of equipment (Note A)	5,000	
Total cash used (outflow) during the period		30,400
Net increase of cash during the period		**$10,300**

Note A: Equipment was acquired in exchange for common stock of X Corporation, which was being held as a long-term investment.

[a] Source of data. Exhibit 15–4.

[b] Sometimes referred to as "Cash generated" and "Cash applied," respectively.

[c] Some persons prefer to set the computations above this line to separate revenues from expenses, which has two distinct advantages: (1) separate computing and reporting of the cash inflows from revenues and the cash outflows for expenses and (2) no implication that depreciation and amortization expenses are sources of cash. To illustrate:

Revenues	$100,000	
Add (deduct) adjustments to convert to cash basis:		
Accounts receivable increase	(5,000)	
Cash generated from revenues		$95,000
Expenses ($60,000 + $32,000)	92,000	
Add (deduct) adjustments to convert to cash basis:		
Depreciation expense	(6,000)	
Amortization expense	(200)	
Merchandise inventory decrease	(4,000)	
Accounts payable increase	(2,000)	
Income tax payable decrease	500	
Cash disbursed for expenses		80,300
Net cash inflow from operations		$14,700

EXHIBIT 15-7
Analytical
worksheet entries,
with explanations
(refer to Exhibit
15-4)

Code	Data source	Analytical entry with explanation
(a)	Income statement (Exhibit 15–3)	Sources of cash (income) .... 8,000 Retained earnings .... 8,000 This analytical entry (1) in Part A of the worksheet partially accounts for the $1,000 net credit increase in retained earnings and (2) in Part B reflects income as a source of cash. Because net income of $8,000 is an **accrual basis** amount, additions and subtractions must be made in subsequent analytical entries to convert it to a **strictly current cash basis** (see entries [b], [c], [d], [e], [h], and [i]).
(b)	Income statement (Exhibit 15–3)	Sources of cash (income addition) .... 6,000 Equipment (or accumulated depreciation) .... 6,000 This analytical entry (1) in Part A accounts for the $6,000 credit increase in the equipment account and (2) in Part B adds the $6,000 to income because depreciation is a **noncash** expense that was deducted to derive accrual income.
(c)	Income statement (Exhibit 15–3)	Sources of cash (income addition) .... 200 Patent (or Accumulated amortization) 200 This analytical entry accomplishes the same effects as entry (b) except that it relates to an intangible asset account.
(d)	Balance sheet (Exhibit 15–3)	Accounts receivable (trade) .... 5,000 Sources of cash (income deduction) ... 5,000 This analytical entry (1) in Part A accounts for the $5,000 net debit increase in accounts receivable and (2) in Part B deducts the $5,000 from accrual income because credit sales were more than cash sales by this amount; it represents noncash sales for the period.
(e)	Balance sheet (Exhibit 15–3)	Sources of cash (income addition) .... 4,000 Merchandise inventory .... 4,000 This analytical entry (1) in Part A, accounts for the net credit decrease in inventory and (2) in Part B adds the $4,000 to income because that amount of goods was withdrawn from inventory in excess of purchases. Thus, it represents a noncash expense (cost of goods sold) for this period which was deducted to derive accrual net income.
(f)	Balance sheet (Exhibit 15–3 and related data about the direct exchange)	(f-1) Sources of cash (direct exchange) .. 5,000 LT investment, stock of X Corp. 5,000 (f-2) Machine .... 5,000 Uses of cash (direct exchange) . 5,000 This was a direct exchange; therefore two entries were required. Analytical entry (f-1) reflects the **financing activity;** the debit recognizes the implied "as if" source of cash and the credit accounts for the net credit decrease in the investment account. Analytical entry (f-2) reflects the **investing activity;** the credit recognizes the implied use of cash and the debit accounts for the increase in the asset account. This $5,000 debit increase and the $6,000 credit decrease for depreciation expense (entry [b]) account fully for the $1,000 net credit decrease in the equipment account.

EXHIBIT 15–7
(continued)

Code	Date source	Analytical entry with explanation
(g)	Balance sheet (Exhibit 15–3 and related data)	Patent .... 3,400 Uses of cash (purchase of patent) .... 3,400 This analytical entry (1) in Part A accounts for a $3,400 debit increase in the patent account (which was its cost) and (2) in Part B recognizes a use of cash. This $3,400 debit increase and the $200 credit decrease for amortization (entry [*c*]) account fully for the net credit increase of $3,200 in the patent account.
(h)	Balance sheet (Exhibit 15–3)	Sources of cash (income addition) .... 2,000 Accounts payable .... 2,000 This analytical entry (1) in Part A accounts for the $2,000 credit increase in accounts payable and (2) in Part B adds the $2,000 to income because the accrual expenses deducted to derive income amounted to $2,000 more than the cash currently paid; thus, this amount is recognized as a noncash expense for the period.
(i)	Balance sheet (Exhibit 15–3)	Income tax payable .... 500 Sources of cash (income deduction) ... 500 This analytical entry (1) in Part A accounts for the net debit increase in income tax payable and (2) in Part B deducts $500 from income because income tax expense deducted to derive accrual income was $500 less than the cash currently paid for income taxes; thus, this amount represented an additional **cash** expense for the current period.
(j)	Balance sheet (Exhibit 15–3)	ST note payable (nontrade) .... 4,000 Uses of cash (payment of debt) ...... 4,000 This analytical entry (1) in Part A accounts for the net debit decrease in note payable and (2) in Part B reflects a use of cash to pay debt.
(k)	Balance sheet (Exhibit 15–3)	Sources of cash (LT note) .... 10,000 LT note payable .... 10,000 This analytical entry (1) in Part A accounts for the $10,000 net credit increase in LT note payable and (2) in Part B reflects a source of cash.
(l)	Balance sheet (Exhibit 15–3)	Bonds payable .... 8,000 Uses of cash (payment on bonds) .... 8,000 This analytical entry (1) in Part A accounts for the $8,000 net debit decrease in bonds payable and (2) in Part B reflects a use of cash to pay debt.
(m)	Balance sheet (Exhibit 15–3)	Sources of cash (issued capital stock) ..... 11,000 Common stock, par $10 .... 10,000 Contributed capital in excess of par .. 1,000 This analytical entry (1) in Part A accounts for the credit increases in the two capital stock accounts and (2) in Part B reflects a cash source.

EXHIBIT 15–7
(concluded)

Code	Date source	Analytical entry with explanation	
(n)	Balance sheet (Exhibit 15–3)	Treasury stock .... 3,000 Uses of cash (purchase of treasury stock) .... 3,000 This analytical entry (1) in Part A accounts for the debit increase in the treasury stock account and (2) in Part B reflects a use of cash.	
(o)	Statement of retained earnings	Retained earnings .... 7,000 Uses of cash .... 7,000 This analytical entry for cash dividends declared and paid during 19B, (1) in Part A accounts for a $7,000 debit decrease in retained earnings and (2) in Part B reflects a use of cash. When this $7,000 debit decrease is combined with the $8,000 credit increase (entry [a]) the net credit increase in the retained earnings account is fully accounted for. Note: A cash dividend declared in 19A and paid in 19B would not decrease **cash** until 19B. However, the declaration would decrease **working capital** in 19A (because of the credit to dividends payable) but would have no effect on working capital in 19B.	

ANALYSIS OF DISPOSAL OF AN ASSET

The illustration of Fina Company does not include transactions involving the disposal of nonfund assets, such as the sale of an operational asset (e.g., equipment). Because of such disposals, net income (accrual basis) often includes a gain or loss on disposal. The total cash inflow from such should be reported on the SCFP, "From other sources." This requires that the gain or loss on the disposal be removed from the "Net income amount" as one of the conversion adjustments. To illustrate, assume that Fina Company sold an operational asset (say, equipment) that had a book (carrying) value of $2,000 for $3,000 cash. The conversion adjustment would deduct the $1,000 gain from net income and the $3,000 cash inflow would be reported under "From other sources." If the $1,000 gain is not subtracted from net income, the gain would be "double counted" as a source of cash from (1) normal operations and (2) from other sources. The **analytical entry** on the worksheet would be:

```
Sources of cash, from other sources .............................. 3,000
    Equipment (net)................................................      2,000
    Sources of cash (income deduction)............................      1,000
```

PART B—PURPOSE AND CONCEPT SCFP, WORKING CAPITAL BASIS

CONCEPT OF WORKING CAPITAL

The only difference between the SCFP prepared on a working capital basis and one prepared on a cash basis is the way in which "funds" are **measured.** This part of the chapter discusses the sources and uses of funds in terms of **working capital** instead of cash. Compared with cash, working capital is a much broader, and a significantly different, concept of funds because it involves an arithmetical difference—**total current assets minus total current liabilities.** Thus, working capital is an abstraction because it does not represent a single asset, or group of similar assets; rather it includes total current assets and an offset—total current liabilities. It cannot be counted, handled, or used to settle receivables and payables. Because of its abstract nature, working capital often is not fully understood by statement users. Although working capital is used widely as the SCFP measurement basis, a growing use of the cash basis is clearly evident.[8]

To understand and interpret properly the SCFP prepared on the working capital basis, one should understand clearly the concept of working capital as a measurement of **funds.** As a basis for discussion, observe in Exhibit 15–3, for Fina Company, that the comparative balance sheets reported working capital which may be tabulated as follows:

| | December 31 | | Working capital increase (decrease) |
	19B	19A	19A to 19B
Current assets:			
Cash	$41,300	$31,000	$10,300
Accounts receivable	25,000	20,000	5,000
Inventory	20,000	24,000	(4,000)
Total current assets	86,300	75,000	
Current liabilities:			
Accounts payable	22,000	20,000	(2,000)
Income tax payable	500	1,000	500
Short-term note payable (nontrade)	10,000	14,000	4,000
Total current liabilities	32,500	35,000	
Working capital (at year-end)	$53,800	$40,000	$13,800

Examination of the working capital tabulation given above reveals two fundamental relationships that relate directly to the SCFP, working capital basis:

1. Increases in current assets and/or decreases in current liabilities **increase working capital,** and decreases in current assets and/or increases in current liabilities **decrease working capital.**
2. A transaction that affects **only** working capital accounts during a given period does **not** change the amount of working capital for that period; therefore, the amount of working capital during a given period is changed only by transactions that affect one or more **noncurrent** (i.e., nonworking capital) accounts—noncurrent assets, noncurrent liabilities, and owners' equity accounts. This relationship may be demonstrated by using the basic accounting model (A = L + OE), assuming CA = current assets, NA = noncurrent assets, CL = current liabilities, NL = noncurrent liabilities, and OE = owners' equity:

---

[8] Refer to footnote 2.

$$a. \quad CA \; + \; NA \; = \; CL \; + \; NL \; + \; OE; \quad \text{transposing}$$

$$\underbrace{CA \; + \; NA}_{\text{Working capital}} \qquad \underbrace{CL \; + \; NL \; + \; OE}_{\text{Noncurrent accounts}}$$

$$b. \quad CA \; - \; CL \; = \qquad\qquad NL \; + \; OE \; - \; NA$$

Therefore, **changes in the noncurrent accounts** (i.e., NL, OE, NA) **represent sources and uses of working capital.** From this analysis we can develop the following summary of the effects of increases and decreases in the noncurrent accounts on the **uses and sources of working capital:**

Noncurrent (nonworking capital) accounts	Working capital Sources	Working capital Uses
Noncurrent assets—increase		x
—decrease	x	
Noncurrent liabilities—increase	x	
—decrease		x
Owner's equity—increase	x	
—decrease		x

Thus, an analysis of the **noncurrent** balance sheet accounts is used to develop a SCFP on the working capital basis (see Exhibits 15–8 and 15–9).

SOURCES OF WORKING CAPITAL

Transactions that **increase** working capital represent sources of working capital. Transactions of this type involve a debit to either a current asset or current liability account and a credit to one or more **nonworking capital accounts.** The four primary sources of working capital are:

1. **Current operations**—Income reflects the net results of operations. It is composed of **total revenues less total expenses** (accrual basis). As goods and services are sold during the period, there is an inflow of cash and/or accounts receivable (both working capital items). Also, during the period, as expenses are incurred, usually there is a decrease in working capital because of cash payments and/or the incurrence of current liabilities (both working capital items). Therefore, a reported income usually results in an increase (source) of working capital. In the case of a loss, working capital usually will decrease.

The increase in working capital from operations usually is somewhat more than the amount of income for the period. This result is due to the fact that the income statement usually includes some expenses that do not involve the use of working capital during the period, such as depreciation and depletion of tangible assets and amortization of intangible assets. For example, the income statement for Fina Company, Exhibit 15–3, shows that there was an inflow of working capital of $100,000 from sales revenue during the year. It also shows that there were outflows of working capital for cost of goods sold, $60,000; ex-

EXHIBIT 15–8
Worksheet to develop the SCFP, working capital basis (Fina Company for the year ended December 31, 19B)

Part A—Analysis of the noncurrent balance sheet accounts:

Items	Balances Dec. 31, 19A	Analysis of Interim Entries†		Ending Balances Dec. 31, 19B
		Debit	Credit	
Debits				
Working capital	40,000	(√) 13,800		53,800
Noncurrent accounts:				
LT investment, X Corp. stock	6,000		(f-1) 5,000	1,000
Equipment (net)	60,000	(f-2) 5,000	(b) 6,000	59,000
Patent (net)		(g) 3,400	(c) 200	3,200
Total	106,000			117,000
Credits				
LT note payable (nontrade)			(k) 10,000	10,000
Bonds payable	40,000	(l) 8,000		32,000
Common stock, par $10	50,000		(m) 10,000	60,000
Contributed capital in excess of par	5,000		(m) 1,000	6,000
Treasury stock		(n) 3,000		(3,000)
Retained earnings	11,000	(o) 7,000	(a) 8,000	12,000
Total	106,000	40,200	40,200	117,000

Part B—SCFP outlined:

Items	Income and Additions	Income Deductions	
Sources of working capital:			⎫ Net working
From normal operations:			capital inflow
Net income	(a) 8,000		from normal
Depreciation expense	(b) 6,000		operations, $14,200;
Amortization expense	(c) 200		⎭ see Exhibit 15–9.
	Sources	**Uses**	
From other sources:			
Exchange of investment for equipment*	(f-1) 5,000		
LT note payable	(k) 10,000		
Sold and issued common stock	(m) 11,000		
Uses of working capital:			
Exchange for investment for common stock*		(f-2) 5,000	
Purchased patent		(g) 3,400	
Payment on bonds payable		(l) 8,000	
Purchased treasury stock		(n) 3,000	
Declared and paid a cash dividend		(o) 7,000	
Increase in working capital (line 1)		(√) 13,800	
	40,200	40,200	

* Equipment acquired in exchange for common stock of X Corporation, which was being held as a long-term investment.

† These entries are keyed for ready references to the text discussions (see Exhibit 15–7). The analytical entries for working capital do not include all of the analytical entries that were required for the cash basis; therefore, some of the code letters are not reflected here.

EXHIBIT 15–9
Statement of changes in financial position, working capital basis, Fina Company

FINA COMPANY
Statement of Changes in Financial Position, Working Capital Basis
For the Year Ended December 31, 19B

Part A—Sources and uses of working capital during the period:

Sources of working capital:

From normal operations:

Income	$ 8,000	
Add (deduct) to convert to working capital basis:		
Depreciation expense	6,000	
Amortization expense (patent)	200	
Total working capital generated from normal operations		$14,200
From other sources:		
Borrowed on long-term note	10,000	
Sale of unissued common stock	11,000	
Disposal of long-term investment (Note A)	5,000	
Total working capital generated from other sources		26,000
Total working capital generated during the period		40,200

Uses of working capital:

Cash dividend on common stock declared and paid during 19B	7,000	
Payment on bonds payable	8,000	
Purchase of patent	3,400	
Purchase of treasury stock	3,000	
Acquisition of equipment (Note A)	5,000	
Total working capital used during the period		26,400
Net increase in working capital during the period		**$13,800***

Part B—Changes in working capital during the period:

Working capital accounts	Balances, December 31 19B	Balances, December 31 19A	Working capital increase (decrease)
Current assets:			
Cash	$41,300	$31,000	$10,300
Accounts receivable (net)	25,000	20,000	5,000
Merchandise inventory	20,000	24,000	(4,000)
Total current assets	86,300	75,000	
Current liabilities:			
Accounts payable	22,000	20,000	(2,000)
Income tax payable	500	1,000	500
Note payable, short term (nontrade)	10,000	14,000	4,000
Total current liabilities	32,500	35,000	
Working capital	$53,800	$40,000	$13,800*

Note A: Equipment was acquired in exchange for common stock of X Corporation, which was being held as a long-term investment.

Part A—source of data, Exhibit 15–8.
Part B—source of data, Exhibit 15–3.
* These two amounts must agree.

penses, $23,800; and income tax, $2,000 (resulting in a net working capital inflow of $14,200). In this computation, no deductions were made for depreciation expense of $6,000 and amortization expense of $200 because these two items were **nonworking** capital expenses. This latter point is evident if we recall the two expense entries:

Depreciation expense	6,000	
Accumulated depreciation		6,000
Amortization expense	200	
Patent		200

These journal entries neither increased nor decreased working capital because no working capital account was debited or credited; however, income was decreased. The **working capital increase from normal operations,** therefore, would be computed and reported as follows:*

Income	$ 8,000
Add (deduct) to convert to working capital basis:	
Depreciation expense	6,000
Amortization expense	200
Net working capital from normal operations	$14,200

    * See Exhibits 15–8 and 15–9.

This example illustrates that the conversion of income (accrual basis) to a working capital basis involves less computations than the conversion to net cash flow from normal operations.

    2. **Sale of capital stock for cash or short-term receivables**—A sale of capital stock is a source of working capital because cash or a short-term receivable flows in for the sale price of the stock.

    3. **Sale of noncurrent assets**—When a long-term investment, an operational asset, or an "other noncurrent asset" is sold, working capital is increased by the total amount of the cash and/or short-term receivable that results from its disposition (the increase is not the amount of the disposal gain or loss).

    4. **Long-term borrowing**—When a loan is obtained on a long-term basis, working capital (cash) is increased by the proceeds of the loan. In contrast, when a short-term loan is obtained, working capital is not increased because a working capital account (Cash) is increased and another working capital account (a current liability) is increased by the same amount. Because the two changes offset each other, working capital (current assets minus current liabilities) does not change. To illustrate, assume Fina Company borrowed $5,000 cash on a 90-day loan near the end of 19B. The working capital effect would be as follows:

	Before short-term loan	Effect of short-term loan	After short-term loan
Current assets	$ 86,300	+$5,000	$ 91,300
Current liabilities	(32,500)	(+ 5,000)	(37,500)
Working capital	$ 53,800	–0–*	$ 53,800

* Effect on working capital = (+$5,000) − (+$5,000) = 0.

USES OF WORKING CAPITAL

Transactions that **decrease** working capital represent uses of working capital. Transactions of this type involve a credit to a working capital account and a debit to a **nonworking capital account.** The three primary uses of working capital are:

1. **Purchase operational assets and other noncurrent assets for cash or short-term debt**—Transactions of this type usually require a payment of cash and, sometimes, the creation of a short-term debt. To the extent that cash is paid or short-term debt is incurred, working capital is reduced.
2. **Declare cash dividends**—This transaction causes the creation of a current liability; therefore, working capital is reduced (used) by that amount. However, the subsequent cash payment of the dividend already declared does not reduce working capital.[9]
3. **Pay a long-term liability**—Payments on long-term notes, bonds, and other long-term obligations involve an outflow of cash; therefore, they represent uses of working capital. In contrast, the payment of a **current liability does not change working capital** for the same reason explained above in respect to borrowing (source) on a short-term debt basis; that is, the two working capital effects offset one another.

To summarize, (1) working capital is not increased or decreased by any transaction that involves **only** debits and credits to working capital accounts, and (2) working capital is increased or decreased by each transaction that involves debits and/or credits to working capital accounts and **also** debits and/or credits to nonworking capital accounts.

SCFP FORMAT FOR SCFP, WORKING CAPITAL BASIS

The SCFP, working capital basis, for Fina Company is shown in Exhibit 15–9. The **standard format** for the SCFP, working capital basis, includes two distinct parts (in contrast to the SCFP, cash basis, which needs only the first part):

---

[9] When a dividend is declared, working capital is reduced by the amount of the dividend even though payment in cash is in a later period. In this situation, the dividend payable is recorded as a current liability on declaration date. The cash payment in the later period does not affect working capital at that time because equal debits and credits to working capital accounts will be made. This distinction is important only when declaration and payment dates fall in different accounting periods. The declaration and payment of a cash dividend in the same year reduces both cash and working capital for that year.

Part A—Sources and uses of working capital

Part B—Changes in the working capital during the period

Part A reports the financing activities (sources of working capital) and the investing activities (uses of working capital) during the period. Part A is the basic report because Part B simply lists each current asset and current liability, the resulting increases and decreases, and the net change in working capital during the period.[10] The format in Part A of the statement follows the cash basis format, except that it relates only to the sources and uses of **working capital.**

PREPARING THE SCFP, WORKING CAPITAL BASIS

Preparing the SCFP, working capital basis, essentially follows the cash basis approach discussed in Part A of this chapter. The four consecutive steps to prepare the SCFP worksheet are:

Step 1—**Collect data.** Obtain the current income statement and comparative balance sheets (see Exhibit 15–3).

Step 2—**Set up the worksheet format** as shown in Exhibit 15–8. In Part A of the worksheet, list each noncurrent (i.e., nonworking capital) account and its balances as reported on the comparative balance sheets. Use the first line for the working capital amounts (these are "balancing" amounts). Observe in Exhibit 15–8 how the accounts, beginning balances and ending balances, are entered on the worksheet.

Step 3—**Complete the worksheet.** The analytical entries are entered only on the worksheet; they follow the pattern of regular journal entries and must account for all of the net increases and decreases in the noncurrent accounts, in Part A of the worksheet. The offsetting debits and credits that represent increases and decreases of working capital are recorded in Part B of the worksheet (debits = sources and also credits = Uses).

Step 4—**Prepare the formal SCFP.** Part B of the worksheet completed in Step 3 provides all of the data needed to complete the "Sources and uses" part of the formal SCFP. The second part of the SCFP is copied directly from the comparative balance sheets. Exhibit 15–9 presents the formal SCFP, working capital basis.

The detailed discussions and illustrations provided in Part A of the chapter for the cash basis apply exactly the same for the working capital basis with two exceptions: (1) the working capital analysis is limited to only the nonworking capital asset, liability, and owners' equity accounts (therefore there are fewer analytical entries); and (2) the term **working capital** is used instead of **cash.**

Preparation of the SCFP, working capital basis, for Fina Company is illustrated in Exhibits 15–8 and 15–9. The analytical entry codes used in Exhibit 15–4 (cash

---

[10] Part B is copied directly from the related comparative balance sheets. For this reason, some accountants consider Part B to be redundant; however, it is required by *APB Opinion 19.* The two parts of the SCFP, working capital basis, are not called "Part A and Part B" in actual practice; this designation is used here only for instructional convenience.

basis) also were used in Exhibit 15–8 (working capital basis) to facilitate study and comparison. You should reread the explanations in Exhibit 15–7 for entries *(a)*, *(b)*, *(c)*, *(f)*, *(g)*, *(k)*, *(l)*, *(m)*, *(n)*, and *(o)* (i.e., the working capital analytical entries).

The T–Account analysis for preparation of the SCFP is illustrated in Supplement 15A.

DEMONSTRATION CASE

The 1982 statement of changes in Consolidated financial position of Dennison Manufacturing Company and Subsidiaries was taken from the annual report:

	(Thousands of Dollars)		
Years Ended December 31	**1982**	1981	1980
Cash Provided by Operations:			
Net earnings	**$20,637**	$30,074	$23,255
Non-cash items included in net earnings:			
Depreciation	**18,353**	15,432	13,826
Deferred income taxes	**521**	655	985
Other	**298**	591	476
	39,809	46,752	38,542
Increase (decrease) in cash caused by certain working capital items:			
Trade accounts receivable	**2,474**	(16,812)	(5,404)
Inventories	**(1,582)**	(15,933)	(1,300)
Prepaid expenses and other current assets	**306**	(13)	2,031
Accounts payable	**(52)**	8,183	3,839
Other current liabilities	**5,980**	3,297	2,266
Effect of exchange rate changes	**(181)**	(477)	
Net Cash Flow from Operations	**46,754**	24,997	39,974
Financing Activities:			
Issuance of long-term debt	**2,500**	27,000	
Payment of long-term debt	**(1,104)**	(3,785)	(2,222)
Increase in current notes payable to banks	**2,622**	1,799	6,313
Payments from Employee Stock Ownership Trust	**703**	1,267	1,289
Common Stock issued in connection with acquisition of a business		2,278	
Proceeds from the exercise of stock options	**24**	487	217
Other—net	**592**	(427)	591
	5,337	28,619	6,188
Net Cash Provided from All Sources	**52,091**	53,616	46,162
Cash Used For:			
Purchase of property, plant and equipment, net	**23,206**	29,001	24,885
Net non-current assets of businesses acquired	**5,724**	6,690	
Acquisition of minority interests		2,840	
Cash dividends to shareholders	**14,048**	12,551	11,004
	42,978	51,082	35,889
Net Increase in Cash and Marketable Securities	**9,113**	2,534	10,273
Cash and marketable Securities at Beginning of Year	**15,505**	12,971	2,698
Cash and Marketable Securities at End of Year	**$24,618**	$15,505	$12,971

Required:

a. What period does this statement cover? How does Dennison define "funds"?
b. Explain why (1) depreciation and (2) deferred income taxes are added to net earnings to determine cash inflow from operations.
c. Explain why (1) accounts receivable was added to and (2) inventories was deducted from net earnings to calculate cash inflow based on operations.
d. What was the amount of net cash flow from the income statement?
e. Explain why (1) the issuance of long-term debt was added and (2) the payment of long-term debt was deducted to determine net cash provided from all sources.
f. Assume the 1982 income statement and balance sheet are available. Explain how you could verify the overall accuracy of the SCFP.

Suggested solution

a. Period covered by the SCFP, **Year ended December 31** for each year (1980, 1981, and 1982). The SCFP uses the term **cash;** however, the last three lines indicate that the cash definition includes **cash and short-term marketable securities.**
b. On the SCFP, net earnings, **accrual** basis (i.e., $20,637), must be converted to the cash basis by making certain adjustments. **Depreciation** is added to convert net earnings to the cash basis because (1) it is a noncash expense and (2) was deducted to compute net earnings. **Deferred income taxes** is a liability; the related part of income tax expense is added to convert net earnings to the cash basis because (1) it is a noncash expense and (2) was deducted to compute net earnings.
c. During 1982, **accounts receivable decreased** by $2,474, which increased cash inflow (compared to accrual revenue); therefore, that amount was added to net earnings to convert it to the cash basis. **Inventories increased** during 1982 by $1,582, which caused cash of this amount to be paid (when purchased or when the related accounts payable is paid); therefore, this amount must be deducted from net earnings to convert it to the cash basis.
d. Net cash inflow from operations (i.e., the income statement) was $46,754.
e. Long-term debt of $2,500 was added because it is a source of cash borrowing. In contrast, long-term debt of $1,104 was deducted because this was the total payment on debts.
f. Overall accuracy of the SCFP can be verified by referring to the beginning and ending balances of the two "cash equivalent" accounts, viz:

	Beginning balance	*Ending balance*	*Net increase*
Cash	$	$	$
Short-term marketable securities			
Total	$15,505	$24,618	$9,113*

* Check figure for the SCFP.

SUMMARY OF CHAPTER

The annual financial statements of publicly held companies must include, as a minimum, a balance sheet, income statement, and statement of changes in financial position. The purpose of a SCFP is to provide investors, creditors, and other external statement users information not provided by the other two statements that will help them project the future cash flows of the entity. To accomplish this purpose, the SCFP reports on the **liquidity** of the company in terms of the **sources and uses of funds;** it also reports the **causes** of the inflows and outflows of funds. The SCFP may be prepared using **either** (1) cash or (2) working capital as the measure of funds. When prepared on a cash basis, the sources and uses of funds are measured in terms of a specific asset, cash. When prepared on a working capital basis, the sources and uses of funds are measured in abstract terms because working capital is the difference between the total current assets and total current liabilities.

The primary source of funds during the period is normal operations (i.e., the amount of funds based on the income statement). Other common sources of funds are borrowing, sale of operational assets, and the sale and issuance of capital stock. Typical uses of funds are payment on debt, purchase of operational assets, long-term investments, and payment of cash dividends.

Because *APB Opinion 19* permits the SCFP to be based on either cash or working capital, there is a question as to which approach better serves the typical external users of financial statements. The summary in Exhibit 15–10 may provide some insights into this issue.

SUPPLEMENT 15A—T-ACCOUNT ANALYSIS TO DEVELOP THE SCFP

Parts A and B of the chapter indicated that the SCFP, on either the cash or working capital basis, can be prepared using the (1) T-account analysis or (2) worksheet analysis. The T-account analysis traditionally has been used for instructional purposes, while the worksheet analysis is used almost exclusively in practice and in situations characterized by complexity and large amounts of data. The worksheet analysis is viewed by many persons as a more sophisticated and more efficient approach than the T-account analysis.

This supplement presents two T-account analyses—one illustrating the cash basis and the other the working capital basis. The illustrative case used in the chapter (Fina Company) also is used in this supplement. The T-account analysis presented in this supplement closely parallels the worksheet analysis in all respects except format. Each account is analyzed in a straightforward Debit = Credit manner, and the **analytical entries are identical** to those used in the worksheet approach. The worksheet has the distinct advantage of being designed so that the bottom portion may suffice for the formal SCFP in many problem and examination situations (see Exhibit 15–4).

T-account analysis for the SCFP, cash basis

The T-account analysis to develop the SCFP, cash basis, is started by setting up separate T-accounts for each **noncash** account reported on the comparative balance sheets and then entering in each account the net change (NC) in the

EXHIBIT 15–10   SCFP—Cash and working capital bases compared

Comparative Criteria	Evaluation		Comments
	Cash Basis	Working Capital Basis	
Choice of reporting entity	Low	High	Most companies elect to use working capital basis.
Relevance in projecting future cash flows by users	High	Low	Cash basis focuses only on cash sources and uses; working capital basis merges current assets and current liabilities into a difference. Working capital basis not accorded much attention in recent FASB statements of "concepts" and "objectives."
Measurement basis	Specific	Abstract	Because it is a broad measure, working capital basis tends to obscure the primary concern of users—cash flows.
Reports liquidity	Short term Long term	Long term	Working capital focuses primarily on the long-term assets and liabilities.
Complexity in preparing SCFP	Low	Low	Both methods involve use of either a worksheet or T-account format during preparation.
Extent of preparation analyses	More	Less	Because there are more noncash accounts than non-working capital accounts, the cash basis requires somewhat more analysis.
Understandability of SCFP	High	Low	External users (other than security analysts) tend to have problems with the abstract concept of working capital; most people understand cash.
Objectivity (and not subject to manipulation)	High	Low	Cash is easy to define, identify, and classify; it **excludes** all estimates, such as bad debt expense, depreciation, estimates of current assets (such as certain prepayments) and current liabilities (such as current portions of deferred tax, warranties, lease liabilities, pension liabilities, and accruals). Working capital often **includes** a number of these estimates; also, working capital is plagued with subjectivity in classification of many items (such as marketable securities).
Redundancies	None	High	The current asset and current liability sections on the comparative balance sheets are repeated item by item on the SCFP, working capital basis. There are no such redundancies on the cash basis statement.
Information content related to the kind of "funds" that circulate throughout a business entity	High	Low	It has been said that a properly prepared and detailed cash flow SCFP "bares the financial soul of a company." Working capital is said to combine too many diverse items and thereby not reveal many critical financing and investing activities. Potential failure of an entity almost always is first revealed in the cash flows.
Used by all industries	Permitted in **all** industries	Not permitted in some industries	The cash basis must be used in certain types of companies such as real estate development and financial institutions.

account balance from the beginning and ending balance sheets (this is equivalent to Part A of the worksheet). Also, two T-accounts are set up to account for sources and uses of cash. These T-accounts are labeled "From normal operations" and "From other." In these two accounts, Debits = Sources and Credits = Uses (this is equivalent to Part B of the worksheet). Next, the **analytical entries** are entered in the T-accounts; these entries are **identical** to those that would be entered on the worksheet analysis (Exhibit 15–4). Thus, the T-account analysis is identical to the worksheet analysis except for format. The T-account format for Fina Company is illustrated in Exhibit 15–11.

EXHIBIT 15–11
SCFP, cash basis;
T-account analysis

FINA COMPANY
T-Account Approach to Develop Sources and Uses of Cash
Noncash Balance Sheet Accounts

Accounts Receivable (net)				Inventory				LT Investment—Stock X Corporation		
NC	5,000					NC	4,000		NC	5,000
(d)	5,000					(e)	4,000		(f-1)	5,000

Equipment (net)				Patent (net)				Accounts Payable		
		NC	1,000	NC	3,200				NC	2,000
(f-2)Pur. 5,000		(b)	6,000	(g) Pur. 3,400		(c) Amort. 200			(h)	2,000

Income Tax Payable				ST Note Payable (nontrade)				LT Note Payable		
NC	500			NC	4,000				NC	10,000
(i)	500			(j)	4,000				(k)	10,000

Bonds Payable				Common Stock, Par $10				Contributed Capital in Excess of Par		
NC	8,000					NC	10,000		NC	1,000
(l)	8,000					(m)	10,000		(m)	1,000

Treasury Stock (cost)				Retained Earnings		
NC	3,000				NC	1,000
(n)	3,000			(o) Div. 7,000	(a) NI	8,000

NC = Net change from 19A to 19B.

EXHIBIT 15–11
(concluded)

Sources and Uses of Cash
From Normal Operations

	Sources			Uses	
	Income Plus Additions			*Income Reductions*	
(a)	Net income	8,000	(d)	Accounts receivable increase	5,000
(b)	Depreciation expense	6,000	(i)	Income tax payable decrease	500
(c)	Amortization of patent	200			
(e)	Inventory decrease	4,000			
(h)	Accounts payable increase	2,000			

From Other

	Sources			Uses	
(f-1)	Exchange of investment for equipment	5,000	(f-2)	Exchange of investment for equipment	5,000
(k)	LT note payable	10,000	(g)	Purchased patent	3,400
(m)	Sold and issued common stock	11,000	(j)	ST note payable (nontrade)	4,000
			(l)	Payment on bonds payable	8,000
			(n)	Purchased treasury stock	3,000
			(o)	Paid cash dividend	7,000
				Check: Change in Cash account ($41,300 − $31,000)	10,300
	Totals	46,200			46,200

T-account analysis for the SCFP, working capital basis

The T-account analysis is started by setting up separate T-accounts for each **nonworking capital** account reported on the comparative balance sheets and entering the net change (NC) in each account balance (this is equivalent to Part A of the worksheet). Also, two T-accounts are set up for sources and uses of working capital "From operations" and "From other" (this is equivalent to Part B on the worksheet). Next, the **analytical** entries are entered in the T-accounts; these analytical entries are identical to those entered on the worksheet (see Exhibit 15–8). The T-account format is illustrated in Exhibit 15–12.

EXHIBIT 15–12
**SCFP, working
capital basis; T-
account analysis**

FINA COMPANY
T-Account Approach to Develop Sources and Uses of Working Capital
Nonworking Capital Balance Sheet Accounts*

LT Investment— Stock X Corporation	
NC 5,000	
(f-1) 5,000	

Equipment (net)	
	NC 1,000
(f-2)Pur. 5,000	(b) 6,000

Patent (net)	
NC 3,200	
(g) Pur. 3,400	(c) Amort. 200

LT Note Payable	
	NC 10,000
	(k) 10,000

Bonds Payable	
NC 8,000	
(l) 8,000	

Common Stock, Par $10	
	NC 10,000
	(m) 10,000

Contributed Capital in Excess of Par	
	NC 1,000
	(m) 1,000

Treasury Stock	
NC 3,000	
(n) 3,000	

Retained Earnings	
	NC 1,000
(o) Div. 7,000	(a) NI 8,000

NC = Net change from 19A to 19B.

Sources and Use of Working Capital*
From Normal Operations

Sources		Uses	
Income Plus Additions		*Income Reductions*	
(a) Net income	8,000		
(b) Depreciation expense	6,000		
(c) Amortization of patent	200		

From Other

Sources		Uses	
(f-1) Exchange of invest. for equip.	5,000	(f-1) Exchange of investment for equip.	5,000
(k) LT note payable	10,000	(g) Purchased patent	3,400
(m) Sold and issued common stock	11,000	(l) Payment on bonds payable	8,000
		(n) Purchased treasury stock	3,000
		(o) Declared cash dividend	7,000
		Check: Change (increase) in working capital ($53,800 − $40,000)	13,800
Totals	40,200		40,200

*Analytical entry codes used are the same as in Exhibit 15–4 (cash basis) to facilitate comparison and study. Not all of the analytical entries for cash are used in working capital analysis.

IMPORTANT TERMS DEFINED IN THIS CHAPTER

Terms (alphabetically)	Key words in definitions of important terms used in chapter	Page reference
All-resources concept	SCFP must report **all** sources and uses of funds; this includes direct nonfund exchanges (direct swaps).	692
Analytical entries, SCFP	Entries used on a SCFP worksheet to reconcile the nonfund accounts and to develop the SCFP.	697
Change statements	Statements that explain why balance sheet accounts change during a period; Income Statement and SCFP.	688
Direct exchanges, SCFP	Transactions that involve the exchange of only nonfund assets, liabilities, or capital stock; direct swaps.	692
Financing activities	Transactions and activities that cause an increase in funds during the period (sources of funds).	692
Funds	A broad financial term; for the SCFP it means either *(a)* cash or *(b)* working capital.	689
Investing activities	Transactions and activities that cause a decrease in funds during the period (uses of funds).	692
Noncash expenses	Expenses reported on the income statement that did not require cash payments during the period; depreciation.	700
Noncash revenues	Revenues of a period reported on the income statement that did not cause funds to increase during that period.	698
SCFP, cash basis	SCFP that reports sources and uses of funds in terms of cash, or cash equivalents.	693
SCFP, working capital basis	SCFP that reports sources and uses of funds in terms of working capital.	705
Sources of cash	Activities and transactions that cause a cash inflow into a company; from operations, borrowing, etc.	694
Sources of working capital	Transactions that cause working capital to increase; debits to working capital accounts.	707
T-account approach, SCFP	Used to develop the SCFP; an organized approach used for instructional purposes; uses T-accounts.	694
Uses of cash	Transactions that increase cash; from normal operations, borrowing, issuing capital stock, etc.	694
Uses of working capital	Transactions that decrease working capital; credits to working capital accounts.	711
Working capital	Current assets minus current liabilities; one way to measure funds on the SCFP.	689
Worksheet approach, SCFP	Used to develop the SCFP; an organized and systematic approach; analyzes the nonfund accounts; used for either cash or working capital.	695

QUESTIONS FOR DISCUSSION

PART A

1. What are the basic statements that are required to be included in the annual financial statements? Fundamentally, what does each report?

2. What are the primary sources and uses of funds in a business?

3. What is the essential difference between a SCFP prepared on a *(a)* cash basis and *(b)* working capital basis?

4. Company X acquired a track of land in exchange for a $10,000 bond payable. How does this transaction relate to the SCFP all-resources concept?

5. What is a direct exchange? How does a direct exchange affect the SCFP?

6. Why is the SCFP called a change statement?

7. Explain what is meant by each of the following terms. Give two examples of each.
   a. Nonfund asset accounts.
   b. Nonfund liability accounts.

8. Explain why income (i.e., from normal operations) often is the primary source of funds in a business in the long term.

9. In developing "sources of funds, from operations (cash or working capital)," on the SCFP, explain why depreciation, amortization of intangible assets, and depletion are added back to net income.

10. What is the basic reason why the SCFP, cash basis, is particularly relevant to the average external statement user?

11. Explain why the SCFP, cash basis, requires the conversion of net income to another amount.

12. Assume you are completing a SCFP, cash basis, and have the data listed below. On a separate sheet, complete the blanks to the right.

Income (accrual basis)		$10,000
Increase in accounts receivable	$1,400	_____
Depreciation expense	1,500	_____
Amortization of patent	200	_____
Decrease in merchandise inventory	2,200	_____
Decrease in accounts payable	1,000	_____
Net cash inflow from normal operations for the period		$_____

13. Total sales revenue for 19B amounted to $300,000, of which one third was on credit. The balances in accounts receivable at year's end were 19B $15,000; and 19A, $23,000. The cash inflow from sales revenue during 19B was $_____ .

14. Total expenses for 19B amounted to $200,000, of which $10,000 was depreciation expense and $30,000 was on credit (accounts payable). The balances in accounts payable at year's end were 19A, $16,000; and 19B, $12,000. The cash outflow for expenses during 19B was $_____ .

15. Assume that you are preparing a SCFP, cash basis, and have the data listed below. On a separate sheet, complete the blanks to the right.

Income (accrual basis)		$20,000
Decrease in accounts receivable	$2,000	_____
Decrease in accounts payable	3,000	_____
Depreciation expense	8,000	_____
Gain on sale of operational asset (cash sale price, $3,000, book value, $2,000)	1,000	_____
Net cash inflow from normal operations		$_____

16. Company X is preparing the SCFP, cash basis, for 19B. During the year, the company acquired a tract of land and paid in full by issuing 1,000 shares of its own capital stock, par $10 per share (market value $15 per share). Show how this transaction should be reported on the SCFP. Explain. Would this transaction be reported in the same manner on the SCFP, working capital basis? Why?

PART B

17. Complete the following tabulation:

		Working capital	
Transactions		Source	Use
a. Collected on account receivable, $150		$	$
b. Sold land for $4,000, one half collected in cash and the balance on one-year note; gain, $500			
c. Paid a bond payable, $1,000			
d. Sold and issued common stock, $2,500 cash			
e. Paid short-term note payable, $1,300			

18. Complete the following tabulation:

Income, $32,000 (accrual basis)	$
Depreciation expense, $5,000	
Inventory increase, $10,000 (paid cash)	
Working capital from normal operations ...	$

19. Company T reported working capital at year-end of 19A, $90,000; and 19B, $75,000. During 19B, the company (a) paid a $5,000 short-term note and (b) paid a $15,000 long-term note. Disregarding interest, how much did each of these transactions change working capital during 19B? Explain.

20. Company S purchased a machine that cost $30,000; payment was made as follows: cash, $10,000; short-term note payable, $4,000; and long-term note payable, $16,000. How much did working capital change? Explain.

21. What are the two basic parts of a SCFP, working capital basis? Why is the second part considered by some people to be redundant?

22. As a statement user interested in the statement of changes in financial position, would you prefer the (a) cash basis or (b) working capital basis? Explain.

EXERCISES

PART A

E15–1. Below is listed a number of transactions of Rye Company during 19B. Enter a letter to the right which indicates whether the transaction usually is a source or use of funds measured as cash. Use S for source, U for use, and N for none of these. Assume cash unless otherwise stated.

	Transactions	Effect on funds measured on cash basis
a.	Income (accrual basis)	_____
b.	Write off of a bad debt (allowance method)	_____
c.	Purchased an operational asset	_____
d.	Depletion expense (on gravel pit)	_____
e.	Declared a cash dividend (cash to be paid later)	_____
f.	Depreciation expense	_____
g.	Collection on a long-term note	_____
h.	Issued a stock dividend	_____
i.	Sold a long-term investment	_____
j.	Borrowed cash on a long-term note	_____
k.	Sold an operational asset at a loss	_____
l.	Amortization of discount on bonds payable	_____
m.	Purchased treasury stock	_____
n.	Payment on bonds payable	_____
o.	A stock split	_____
p.	Extraordinary gain	_____
q.	Amortization of premium on bond investment	_____
r.	Purchased a long-term investment	_____
s.	Exchange of unissued stock for operational asset	_____
t.	Exchange of land for equipment	_____
u.	Sale of treasury stock	_____
v.	Payment of debt by issuance of company shares	_____
w.	Net loss	_____
x.	Amortization of patent...............................	_____
y.	Bad debt expense recorded	_____
z.	Declared and paid a property dividend.................	_____
zz.	Paid the dividend declared in (e) above	_____

E15–2. Tower Corporation has just completed its 19A income statement and balance sheet. The SCFP, cash basis, must be prepared. The following 19A data have been extracted from the income statement, balance sheet, and other company records:

a. Depreciation expense, $9,000.
b. Purchased treasury stock, $4,000 (cash).
c. Sold a long-term investment at book value, $6,000 (cash).
d. Declared and paid a $7,000 cash dividend during 19A.
e. Recorded but unpaid salaries on December 31, 19A, $1,000.
f. Income, accrual basis, $25,000.
g. Borrowed $10,000 on an interest-bearing note (15 percent interest).
h. Recorded but uncollected service revenue on December 31, 19A, $3,000.
i. Sold 200 shares of its own common stock, par $1, for $5 per share (cash).
j. Paid a $16,000 note payable.
k. Purchased operational assets, $30,000 (cash).

Required:

a. Prepare the 19A SCFP, cash basis, for Tower Corporation.
b. Reconcile the 19A income (accrual basis) of $25,000 with the "net increase (decrease) in cash during 19A."
c. Explain why "net cash inflow from normal operations" is different from "income, accrual basis." Use amounts to support your explanation.

E15–3. The 19D income statement of Coffey Company is summarized below. Additional 19D data taken from the 19C and 19D balance sheets are as follows:

a. Decrease in accounts receivable (for services rendered) during 19D, $14,000.
b. Purchased a small service machine, $6,000 (cash).
c. Increase in salaries payable during 19D, $8,000.
d. Decrease in service revenue collected in advance, during 19D, $5,000.
e. Decrease in income tax payable during 19D, $7,000.

Income Statement, 19D

Items	Accrual Basis	Cash Basis	
		Explanation	Amount
Service revenues	$ 60,000		
Expenses:			
Salaries	51,000		
Depreciation	11,000		
Depletion	200		
Utilities (cash)	4,000		
Remaining expenses (cash)	3,800		
Income tax	–0–		
Total expenses	70,000		
Net income (loss)	$(10,000)		

Required:

a. Complete the above income statement schedule to determine the "net cash inflow (outflow) from normal operations."
b. Because there is a net loss for 19D would you expect the net cash flow from normal operations to be negative (i.e., an outflow)? Explain why.
c. Present a proof of your answer to Requirement (a) by starting with the $10,000 loss.

E15–4. Stonewall Company has completed its income statement and balance sheet at December 31, 19B. The following data were taken from a worksheet (or T-account) analysis completed as a basis for the SCFP:

Net income (Revenues, $156,000 — Expenses, $128,000)	$28,000
Depreciation expense	4,000
Purchase of operational assets for cash	25,000
Sale of long-term investment (sold at book value for cash, $6,000)	6,000
Inventory increase during the period	3,000
Declared and paid cash dividends during 19B	8,000
Borrowed on short-term note	20,000
Accounts payable decrease	2,000
Payment of long-term note	30,000
Acquired land for future use; issued capital stock in payment	24,000

Required:

Prepare the SCFP, cash basis, properly classified. Use the direct analysis approach.

E15–5. The accounting department of Teddy Company assembled the following unclassified SCFP data at December 31, 19B, end of the accounting period, as a basis for preparing a SCFP, cash basis:

| | | Cash* | |
Transactions		Sources	Uses
Net income (Revenues, $204,000 − Expenses, $169,000)		$35,000	
Depreciation expense		7,000	
Purchase of operational assets for cash			$42,000
Wages payable increase		5,000	
Inventory decrease		5,000	
Accounts payable decrease			8,000
Declared and paid a cash dividend on common stock during 19B			20,000
Amortization of patent		1,000	
Payment on short-term note payable (nontrade)			40,000
Sale of common stock for cash		17,000	
Sale of operational assets for cash (sold at book value, $9,000)		9,000	
Accounts receivable increase			6,000
Long-term borrowing during the period		50,000	
Purchase of long-term investment, stock of X Co. (paid cash)			30,000

* Including income additions and deductions.

Required:

a. Use the above data to prepare a SCFP, cash basis, properly classified. Use the direct analysis approach.

b. Answer the following questions:

(1) What adjustment item(s) related to revenues, and what effect did the item(s) have on cash flow?

(2) What two adjustment items affected cost of goods sold (cash basis)? What cash flow effects did they have?

(3) What was the amount of the increase or decrease in cash as reported on the balance sheet?

(4) What was the effect of the increase in wages payable on cash flow for 19B?

(5) Would the declaration and issuance of a stock dividend be reported on the SCFP, cash basis? Explain.

E15–6. The following actual statement was taken from the annual financial statements of Lazy Corporation:

LAZY CORPORATION
Funds Statement
Year, December 31, 19B

Funds generated:

Sales and service revenue	$85,000	
Depreciation	6,000	
Accounts receivable decrease	700	
Merchandise decrease	3,000	
Borrowing (short-term note)	20,000	
Sale of unissued stock	15,000	
Total cash		$129,700

Funds applied:

Cost of sales	48,000	
Expenses (including depreciation and income tax)	20,000	
Accounts payable decrease	1,000	
Income tax payable decrease	300	
Payment on long-term mortgage	25,000	
Acquisition of operational asset	9,000	
Dividends (cash) declared and paid during 19B	7,000	
Total		110,300
Increase in funds		$ 19,400

Required:

a. Is this a cash basis or a working capital basis statement? Give the basis for your conclusion.

b. Did Lazy give adequate attention to the communication of financial information to stockholders?

c. What was the amount of net income (or loss) reported for 19B?

d. Recast the above statement in good form (and preferred terminology).

e. Did operations generate more or less cash than net income? Explain what caused the difference.

E15–7. The SCFP must be based on the all-resources concept. During 19B, West Corporation completed the two transactions given below on which they have asked your assistance:

1. A large machine was acquired that had a list price of $25,000. West was short of cash; therefore, it paid for the machine in full by giving a $10,000, 15 percent, interest-bearing note due at the end of two years and 200 shares of its capital stock, par $50 (market value $60).

2. A small machine was acquired (list price $9,995), and full payment was made by transferring a tract of land that had a market value of $9,500 (surprisingly, this was also its book value).

Required:

For each machine show what should be reported on the SCFP, cash basis, under *(a)* sources of cash and *(b)* uses of cash. Briefly, explain the basis for your responses.

E15–8. Brown Company prepared the tabulation given below at December 31, 19E. Provide an appropriate amount for each blank. Use parentheses for deductions and enter a zero if no adjustment is required.

Sources of cash	*SCFP, cash basis*
From normal operations:	
Net income (accrual basis)	$150,000
Add (deduct) adjustments to convert to cash basis:	
Depreciation expense, $2,000	_____
Increase in trade accounts receivable, $6,000.....	_____
Decrease in inventory, $11,000	_____
Amortization of patent, $1,000	_____
Decrease in rent revenue receivable, $1,500	_____
Increase in prepaid insurance, $4,000	_____
Decrease in trade accounts payable, $7,000	_____
Decrease in income tax payable, $2,500	_____
Gain on sale of operational asset $2,000	
(sold for cash, $8,000)	_____
Net cash generated from normal operations	$ _____

E15–9. Situation *(a)*—Ransom Corporation reported net income of $100,000. To compute cash generated from normal operations, the corporation added the recorded depreciation expense ($20,000, on the straight-line basis) to net income deriving a cash basis amount of $120,000 because "depreciation is one of the largest sources of cash in our company." Assume the company could have used accelerated depreciation instead of straight-line depreciation and reported $30,000 depreciation expense. Would this change increase the cash inflow (disregarding any income tax considerations)? Explain and illustrate your response.

Situation *(b)*—Ransom Corporation sold a machine (an operational asset) for $28,000 cash. At date of sale the accounting records reflected the following:

Machine No. 12 (cost)	$30,000
Accumulated depreciation (Machine No. 12)	10,000

At year-end the income statement (summarized) reported the following:

Revenues (all cash)	$ 900,000
Expenses (all cash except depreciation expense of $60,000)	(796,000)
Gain on sale of operational asset	8,000
Net income	$ 100,000

Explain and illustrate how the disposal (sale) of the machine and depreciation expense should be reflected on the SCFP, cash basis.

PART B

E15–10. Below is a tabulation that gives information relating to both cash and working capital for Ross Company.

Transactions	(a) Cash basis	(b) Working capital basis
Net income reported (accrual basis)	$17,000	$17,000
Depreciation expense, $2,700		
Increase in wages payable, $500		
Decrease in trade accounts receivable, $6,800		
Increase in merchandise inventory, $9,300		
Amortization of patents, $300		
Increase in bonds payable, $10,000		
Decrease in trade accounts payable, $7,400		
Sale of unissued common stock, $5,000		
Total cash generated from operations	$	
Total working capital generated from operations		$20,000

Required:

a. Provide appropriate amounts for each of the blanks in the above tabulation; if none, enter a zero.
b. Briefly compare the total of cash with the total of working capital and explain why they are different.
c. Which result do you think would be of most use to statement users? Why?

E15–11. The following "Funds Statement" was taken from the annual financial statements of Fisher
Corporation:

FISHER CORPORATION
Funds Statement
December 31, 19B

Funds generated:

Net profit (plus $10,000 depreciation)	$18,000
Common stock	9,000
Long-term debt	10,000
Total	$37,000

Funds applied:

Equipment	$15,000
Dividend	8,000
Debt	12,000
Change	2,000
Total	$37,000

Working capital:

	19B	Change
Cash	$ 3,200	$ 6,500
Receivables	7,500	5,000*
Inventory	30,000	13,500*
Payables (trade)	(4,800)	2,500*
Notes	(12,000)	7,500*
Total	$23,900	$ 2,000*

* Increase.

Required:

a. What was the amount of 19B income?
b. Is this a working capital or cash basis statement? Explain the basis for your response.
c. Did working capital increase or did it decrease? By how much?
d. Did "operations" generate more or less working capital than income? Explain why.
e. Explain why the amount of the change in working capital was different than income.
f. Assess the soundness of the cash dividend.
g. Can you spot any potential future problems for Fisher Corporation? Explain why.
h. Did Fisher Corporation give adequate attention to communication of financial information to stockholders? Explain the basis for your response.
i. Was the dividend paid or only declared? Explain.
j. Compare and explain the amounts of change in working capital versus cash.
k. Was the equipment purchased on credit? Explain.
l. Recast the above statement in good form consistent with your comments in Requirement (h).

E15–12. The following statement has just been prepared by Slow Company:

SLOW COMPANY
Statement of Changes in Financial Position, Working Capital Basis
For the Year Ended December 31, 19B

Sources of working capital:

From operations:

Net income	$ 2,000	
Add expenses not requiring working capital:		
Depreciation expense	4,000	
Patent amortization expense	1,000	
Total working capital generated by operations		$ 7,000
From other sources:		
Sale of unissued stock	10,000	
Long-term loan	33,000	
Sale of land (at cost)	5,000	
Total working capital from other sources		48,000
Total working capital generated during the period		55,000

Uses of working capital:

Acquisition of machinery	22,000	
Payment of mortgage	20,000	
Cash dividend declared and paid	12,000	
Total working capital applied during the period		54,000

Net increase in working capital during the period .... $ 1,000

Changes in working capital accounts:

	Balances at December 31 19B	Balances at December 31 19A	Working capital increase (decrease)
Current assets:			
Cash	$ 1,000	$ 9,000	$(8,000)
Accounts receivable	31,000	24,000	7,000
Inventory	38,000	21,000	17,000
Total current assets	70,000	54,000	
Current liabilities:			
Accounts payable	18,000	15,000	(3,000)
Short-term notes payable	22,000	10,000	(12,000)
Total current liabilities	40,000	25,000	
Working capital	$30,000	$29,000	$ 1,000

Required:

a. Was there an increase or decrease in working capital? How much? What were the primary source and the major use of working capital?

b. Explain how working capital of $55,000 was generated when income was only $2,000.

c. Explain the fact that while working capital increased $1,000 cash decreased $8,000.

d. How much cash was generated and how much was used? How much cash was generated by normal operations?

e. What current asset increased the most? What current liability increased the most? How were these two changes related to cash?

f. Assess the soundness of the cash dividend.

g. Can you identify a potential problem in respect to liabilities? Explain.

h. Evaluate the cash and working capital positions at the end of 19B.

E15–13. Busby Company has completed the income statement and the comparative balance sheet at year-end, December 31, 19B. A statement of changes in financial position must be developed. The following data are available:

	Balances at Dec. 31	
	19A	19B
From balance sheet:		
Current assets:		
Cash	$ 8,000	$15,000
Accounts receivable (net)	17,000	12,000
Inventory	15,000	18,000
Current liabilities:		
Accounts payable	10,000	12,000
Notes payable, short term	18,000	13,000
From income statement:		
Net income		$20,000
Depreciation expense...		6,000
From other records:		
Purchase of long-term investment		15,000
Payment of long-term note		5,000
Sale of unissued capital stock		10,000
Declaration and payment of cash dividend during 19B		8,000
Purchased land for future plant site, issued		
capital stock as payment in full		25,000

Required:

Prepare a SCFP, working capital basis. (Hint: Unless instructed otherwise, try a direct analysis [instead of a worksheet or T-account analysis].)

E15–14. Cullen Company has never prepared a SCFP. At the end of 19B, the company bookkeeper assembled the data given below (which have been determined to be correct) for such a statement:

	Balances at Dec. 31	
	19A	19B
From the balance sheet:		
Current assets:		
Cash	$ 15,000	$ 20,000
Accounts receivable (net)...	24,000	17,000
Merchandise inventory	30,000	27,000
Current liabilities:		
Accounts payable	(19,000)	(15,000)
Notes payable, short term	(10,000)	(12,000)
Working capital...	$ 40,000	$ 37,000

	Balances at Dec. 31
	19B
From the income statement and other sources:	
Net income..	$ 21,000
Depreciation expense	4,500
Amortization of patent	500
Purchase of operational assets	(6,000)
Sale of operational assets (at book value) for cash	2,000
Payment of long-term note payable	(40,000)
Issuance of bonds payable for cash	30,000
Sale and issuance of common stock for cash	10,000
Declaration and payment of a cash dividend on common stock	
during 19B	(25,000)
Difference	$ (3,000)

Required:

Use the above data to prepare a SCFP, working capital basis, for 19B. Because the information is simplified, unless instructed otherwise, you may use a direct analysis (instead of a worksheet or T-account analysis).

E15–15. Lakeland Company is developing its annual financial statements at December 31, 19B. The income statement and balance sheet have been completed, and the SCFP, working capital basis, is to be developed. The income statement and comparative balance sheets are summarized below:

	19A	*19B*
Balance sheet at December 31:		
Cash	$12,800	$10,800
Accounts receivable (net)	9,000	10,500
Merchandise inventory	6,600	5,000
Operational assets (net)	40,000	43,000
Patent	3,000	2,700
	$71,400	$72,000
Accounts payable	$11,000	$ 9,000
Income tax payable	400	500
Notes payable, long term	10,000	5,000
Capital stock (nopar)	42,000	45,000
Retained earnings	8,000	12,500
	$71,400	$72,000
Income statement for 19B:		
Sales revenue		$60,000
Cost of goods sold		35,000
Gross margin		25,000
Expenses (including depreciation, $4,000, and patent amortization, $300)		18,000
Net income		$ 7,000

Additional data for 19B:
Purchased operational assets for cash, $7,000.
Paid $5,000 on long-term note payable.
Sold and issued capital stock for $3,000 cash.
Declared and paid a $2,500 cash dividend on capital stock during 19B.

Required:

a. Based upon the above data, prepare a worksheet or T-account analysis to develop the SCFP, working capital basis.
b. Prepare the formal SCFP, working capital basis.

PROBLEMS/CASES

PART A

PC15–1. Below is a list of 19B transactions that involve sources and uses of funds. Some of the transactions relate only to sources and uses of cash; others relate to sources and uses of both cash and working capital. You are to analyze each transaction and enter its 19B dollar effect in the spaces to the right. Assume cash transactions unless stated otherwise.

| | Cash | | Working capital | |
	Sources	Uses	Sources	Uses
Transactions during 19B				
a. Sold a short-term investment for cash $500.	$_____	$_____	$_____	$_____
b. Sold an operational asset and received a short-term note, $600.	_____	_____	_____	_____
c. Prepaid a one-year insurance premium, $200.	_____	_____	_____	_____
d. Purchased a small machine (an operational asset) and gave a short-term note, $150.	_____	_____	_____	_____
e. Sold a patent for $700 cash (book value, $500; gain, $200).	_____	_____	_____	_____
f. Purchased land, $9,900 cash.	_____	_____	_____	_____
g. Sold a long-term investment, $9,000; collected cash, $1,000, short-term note, $3,000, and long-term note, $5,000.	_____	_____	_____	_____
h. Purchased an operational asset, $9,000; paid cash, $4,000 short-term note, $3,000, and long-term note, $2,000.	_____	_____	_____	_____
i. Declared and paid a preferred stock cash dividend, $3,000 during 19B.	_____	_____	_____	_____
j. Declared a common stock cash dividend, $4,000 during 19B and payable during 19C.	_____	_____	_____	_____

PC15–2. This case emphasizes the effect on working capital of increases and decreases of the components of working capital.

a. Provide the missing amounts in the schedule of working capital effects given below.

Schedule of Working Capital Effects

Current (Working Capital) Accounts	December 31 19B	December 31 19A	Working Capital Increase (Decrease)
1. Cash	$?	$30,000	$(29,000)
2. Short-term investment in securities	5,000	20,000	?
3. Accounts receivable (net)	70,000	?	30,000
4. Inventory	95,000	70,000	?
5. Prepaid expense (e.g., insurance)	?	2,000	1,000
6. Accounts payable	74,000	?	(4,000)
7. Income tax payable	4,000	6,000	?
8. Revenue collected in advance (unearned)	?	1,000	(1,000)
9. Product warranty liability (estimated)	3,000	4,000	?
10. Working capital	?	?	10,000

b. This case emphasizes the difference between the SCFP, cash basis, versus the SCFP, working capital basis. Provide the appropriate dollar amounts in the blank spaces to the right on the following schedule of SCFP sources and uses. Assume cash transactions unless otherwise stated.

Schedule of SCFP Sources and Uses

Transaction	Cash Basis		Working Capital Basis	
	Sources	Uses	Sources	Uses
1. Sold and issued capital stock, $5,000 cash.	$	$	$	$
2. Declared and paid a cash dividend, $3,000.				
3. Sold a short-term investment, $2,000 cash.				
4. Borrowed on a long-term note, $8,000.				
5. Sold an operational asset, $7,500 cash.				
6. Purchased an operational asset; gave a one-year interest-bearing note, $6,000.				
7. Declared a cash dividend (payable next year), $1,500.				
8. Paid a short-term note, $2,500.				
9. Collected a short-term note, $1,800.				
10. Collected a long-term note, $7,000.				
11. An operational asset was sold at a gain on disposal of $500; it originally cost $10,000 and was 75 percent depreciated (straight line). Cash was collected for the sale price.				
12. Sales revenue during 19B amounted to $100,000; the balances in Accounts Receivable at year's end were 19A, $20,000; and 19B, $14,000.				
13. Sold and issued 1,000 shares of common stock, par $10; credited Contributed Capital in Excess of Par in the amount of $5,500. Cash was collected for half of the issue price and the balance is due at the end of one year.				

PC15–3. The following statement has just been prepared by Careless Corporation:

CARELESS CORPORATION
Funds Flow Statement
Year, December 31, 19E

Funds earned:

Sales and other incomes	$ 90,000
Accounts receivable decrease	4,200
Expenses (including depreciation and income tax)	(70,000)
Depreciation	2,000
Inventory increase	(3,000)
Accounts payable increase	1,000
Prepaid insurance increase	(100)
Income tax payable decrease	(100)
Capital stock	5,000
Total funds earned	29,000

Funds spent:

Equipment	(7,000)
Bonds payable	(30,000)
Dividends declared and paid	(2,000)
Total funds spent	$ 10,000

Required:

a. Is the above statement based on a working capital or on a cash basis? How did you determine the basis on which the statement was prepared?

b. List the format and terminology deficiencies on the statement.

c. Recast the above statement using preferred format and terminology.

PC15–4. The income statement of Josey Corporation is given below. Provide the appropriate cash flow amounts for the blanks given to the right. Use parentheses to indicate cash deductions and enter a zero for no change. Prove the results starting with accrual net income of $40,000.

JOSEY CORPORATION
Income Statement for the Year Ended December 31, 19C
Accrual Basis

			Cash flow
Sales revenue (one third on credit; accounts receivable year's end—19A, $11,000; 19B, $15,000)		$3,000	$ _____
Cost of goods sold (one fourth on credit; accounts payable year's end—19A, $9,000; 19B, $8,000 (net); inventory at year's end—19A, $50,000; 19B, $45,000)		180,000	_____
Gross margin on sales		120,000	
Expenses:			
Salaries and wages (including accrued wages payable at year's end—19A, $500; 19B, $300)	$44,000		
Depreciation expense..........................	8,000		
Rent expense (no accruals)	6,000		_____
Bad debt expense	300		_____
Remaining expenses (no accruals)	11,700		_____
Income tax expense (income tax payable at year's end—19A, $2,000; 19B, $3,000)	10,000		_____
Total expenses		80,000	
Net income		$ 40,000	
Cash generated from normal operations			$ _____
Proof of results:			
Net income (accrual basis)_____			$40,000
Add (deduct) adjustments to convert to cash basis:			
_____			_____
_____			_____
_____			_____
_____			_____
_____			_____
_____			_____
_____			_____
Cash generated from normal operations_____			$ _____

Note: This problem depicts two somewhat different approaches to derive cash inflow from operations; the proof of results approach above is the one usually used because it is more direct.

PC15–5.   The following statement has just been prepared by Young Corporation:

YOUNG CORPORATION
Statement of Changes in Financial Position, Cash Basis
For the Year Ended December 31, 19B

Sources of cash:		
From normal operations:		
Net loss	$(10,000)	
Add (deduct) adjustments to convert to cash basis:		
Accounts receivable decrease	2,000	
Depreciation expense	3,000	
Amortization expense........................	300	
Inventory increase	(1,500)	
Accounts payable decrease	(1,000)	
Prepaid insurance decrease	200	
Cash generated from (used in) operations		$ (7,000)
From other sources:		
Sale of capital stock	10,000	
Long-term note payable	30,000	
Land (exchanged for machinery)	7,000	
Cash from other sources		47,000
Total cash generated during the period.....		40,000
Uses of cash:		
Machinery (acquired in exchange for land)	7,000	
Payment on mortgage	6,000	
Cash dividends declared and paid	12,000	
Total cash expended during the period		25,000
Net increase in cash during the period		$15,000

Required:

a.   Explain why the net loss was $3,000 more than the cash "used" in operations.

b.   Explain how the company showed a net increase in cash of $25,000 more than the net loss.

c.   Explain the land transaction. Why is it reported under two different captions on the above SCFP?

d.   Explain why the decrease in accounts receivable is "added" as an adjustment to the net loss.

e.   Explain why both the inventory increase and the accounts payable decrease are "deducted" as an adjustment to the net loss.

f.   Explain how the amount "Net increase in cash during the period, $15,000" can be verified independent of the SCFP computations.

PC15–6.   The following statement was prepared by Old Corporation:

OLD CORPORATION
Funds Statement
December 31, 19X

Where got:

Revenues	$ 180,000	
Accounts receivable decrease	15,000	
Expenses (including depreciation and income tax)	(160,000)	
Depreciation	14,000	
Inventory increase	(6,000)	
Accounts payable increase	7,000	
Income tax payable decrease	(3,000)	
Total		$ 47,000
Sale of permanent assets (at book value)		17,000
Issuance of common stock for land		25,000
Borrowing—short-term note		40,000
Total cash received		$129,000

Where gone:

Dividends	20,000	
Payment on long-term mortgage	80,000	
Machinery	15,000	
Land (5,000 shares of stock)	25,000	
Funds (decrease)	(11,000)	
Total		$12,000

Required:

a. Is this a cash basis or a working capital basis statement? Explain the reason for your answer.

b. What was the amount of net income reported for 19X?

c. Did cash increase or decrease? Explain. How can this amount be verified independent of the SCFP?

d. Did the company give adequate attention to communication of financial information to the stockholders? Explain the basis for your response.

e. Recast the above statement using preferred format and terminology.

f. What was the amount of the difference between net income and cash generated from normal operations? Why were they different?

g. Do you suspect any potential problems for this company? Explain the reason for your response.

PC15–7. Hamilton Company is developing the 19B annual report. A SCFP, cash basis, is being developed. The following worksheet has been set up to develop the statement:

HAMILTON COMPANY
Worksheet to Develop Statement of Changes in Financial Position, Cash Basis
For the Year Ended December 31, 19B

Items	Ending Balance, Dec. 31, 19A	Analysis of Interim Entries		Ending Balances, Dec. 31, 19B
		Debit	Credit	
Debits				
Cash account	24,000			32,200
Noncash accounts:				
Accounts receivable (net)	26,000			30,000
Inventory	30,000			28,000
Prepaid insurance	1,200			800
Investments, long term	10,800			8,000
Operational assets (net)	30,000			39,000
Patent (net)	3,000			2,700
	125,000			140,700
Credits				
Accounts payable	21,000			18,000
Wages payable	3,000			2,000
Income tax payable	1,000			1,200
Note payable, long term	25,000			20,000
Capital stock par $10	60,000			70,000
Contributed capital in excess of par	1,000			3,000
Retained earnings	14,000			26,500
	125,000			140,700
Sources of cash:				
Uses of cash				
Change in cash				

Additional data for 19B:

a. Revenues, $120,000; expenses, $100,000; and net income, $20,000.
b. Depreciation expense, $3,000.
c. Amortization of patent, $300.
d. Sale of long-term investment $2,800 cash, which was equal to its book value.
e. Purchased operational assets, and issued 1,000 shares of capital stock as full payment (market value, $12 per share).
f. Declared and paid cash dividend, $7,500.
g. Increase in accounts receivable balance during the period.
h. Decrease in inventory during the period.
i. Decrease in prepaid insurance balance during the period.
j. Decrease in accounts payable balance during the period.
k. Decrease in wages payable balance during the period.
l. Increase in income tax payable balance during the period.

Required:

Complete the above worksheet on a cash basis. Also, show on the worksheet "Net cash inflow from normal operations."

PC15–8. Mason Company is developing the annual financial statements at December 31, 19B. The statements are complete except for the SCFP, cash basis. The completed comparative balance sheets and income statement are summarized below:

	19A	19B
Balance sheet at December 31:		
Cash	$ 20,000	$ 31,500
Accounts receivable (net)	26,000	25,000
Merchandise inventory	40,000	38,000
Operational assets (net)	64,000	67,000
	$150,000	$161,500
Accounts payable	$ 24,000	$ 27,000
Wages payable	500	400
Notes payable, long term	35,000	30,000
Capital stock, nopar	70,000	80,000
Retained earnings	20,500	24,100
	$150,000	$161,500
Income statement for 19B:		
Sales		$ 90,000
Cost of goods sold		(52,000)
Expenses (including depreciation expense, $4,000)		(32,000)
		$ 6,000

Required:

a. Set up either a worksheet analysis or a T-account analysis to develop the SCFP, cash basis. Analytical entries should be made for the following:
   a. Net income—from income statement.
   b. Depreciation expense from income statement.
   c. Purchased operational assets for cash, $7,000.
   d. Paid $5,000 on the long-term note payable.
   e. Sold unissued common stock for $10,000 cash.
   f. Declared and paid a $2,400 cash dividend.
   g. Accounts receivable decrease from balance sheets.
   h. Merchandise inventory decrease—from balance sheets.
   i. Accounts payable increase—from balance sheets.
   j. Wages payable decrease—from balance sheets.
b. Based upon the analysis completed in Requirement (a), prepare the formal SCFP, cash basis.

PC15–9. Texmo Company is preparing its 19B financial statements, which include the following information:

	Comparative	
	19A	*19B*
Balance sheet:		
Cash	$ 40,000	$ 52,000
Inventory	30,000	37,000
Accounts receivable (net)	20,000	17,000
Long-term investment, stock Co. A	10,000	3,000
Machinery and equipment (net)	80,000	75,000
	$180,000	$184,000
Accounts payable	$ 15,000	$ 11,000
Income tax payable	4,000	6,000
Note payable, long term	20,000	10,000
Bonds payable...........................	30,000	10,000
Capital stock, par $10	100,000	110,000
Contributed capital in excess of par	8,000	11,000
Retained earnings	3,000	26,000
	$180,000	$184,000
Income statement:		
Revenue		$140,000
Cost of goods sold		(65,000)
Depreciation expense		(8,000)
Patent expense		(600)
Remaining operating expenses		(28,400)
Income tax expense		(9,000)
Gain on disposal of machine (net of tax).....		1,000
Net income		$ 30,000

Additional data for 19B:

1. Machinery that had a book value of $10,000 was sold for $11,000 cash.
2. Long-term investment (shares of Company A stock) was sold for $7,000 cash, which had a carrying value of $7,000.
3. Equipment was acquired and payment in full was made by issuing 1,000 shares of capital stock which had a market value of $13 per share.
4. Payments on debt: long-term note, $10,000; bonds payable, $20,000.
5. Declared and paid a cash dividend, $7,000.

Required:

a. Prepare either a worksheet analysis or a T-account analysis to develop a SCFP, cash basis.
b. Prepare the formal SCFP, cash basis.

PC15–10.   Sureshot Oil Company prepared the following income statement:

**Income Statement
For the Year Ended December 31, 1984**

		Millions	
a.	Revenue from sale of crude oil and natural gas		$40
b.	Depletion of crude oil and natural gas reserves	$ 5	
c.	Depreciation of production equipment	1	
d.	Salaries and wages	4	
e.	Remaining expenses	20	30
f.	Net income		$10

Additional information for 1984:

a.   Accounts receivable balance at year's end: 1983, $.5; and 1984, $2.5.

b.   Sureshot uses cost depletion which is based on an old and low "finding cost" incurred in 1957. It is expected that the production will cease at the end of 1990 because the remaining reserves will be uneconomical to produce. The company is involved in the risky and high cost activities of searching for new reserves.

c.   Depreciation is computed using the straight-line method. The equipment is very old and inefficient.

d.   Salaries and wages unpaid (in millions) at year's end: 1983, $1.5; and 1984, $.5.

e.   All items on the income statement, other than items *(a), (b),* and *(c)* above, were on the cash basis (including income tax).

f.   The board of directors is considering declaring and paying immediately a $5 million cash dividend which the company president opposes.

Required:

a.   Prepare a SCFP, cash basis (for normal operations only). You should be able to prepare the SCFP using the direct-analysis approach.

b.   Compare the income statement and the SCFP results. Which statement best indicates the ability of the company (1) to pay the dividend, (2) search for new reserves, and (3) replace the equipment? Give the primary arguments for and against the dividend.

Suppose $11 million should be spent in 1984–85 for new equipment and well workover projects.

PC15–11.   This case is based upon the 1982 financial statements of Johnson & Johnson given in Special Supplement B immediately preceding the Index. You are to use the 1982 data to respond to the following requirements:

a.   What period does the SCFP cover?

b.   How does the company measure "funds" on the SCFP?

c.   How much did funds increase, or decrease?

d.   Recast the SCFP presented by Johnson & Johnson to a format similar to the illustration in Exhibit 15–6 and the Demonstration Case.

e.   Reconcile the SCFP with the balance sheet.

PART B

PC15–12.   The following actual SCFP was extracted from the published annual financial statements of Laird Corporation:

LAIRD CORPORATION
Statement of Working Capital
December 31, 19B

Working capital provided:

Net income	$14,000	
Add: Depreciation	15,000	
Patent amortization	1,000	
Total	30,000	
Bonds	50,000	
Common stock (for equipment)	15,000	
Total working capital provided		$95,000

Working capital applied:

Mortgage	60,000	
Equipment	15,000	
Dividends	10,000	
Total working capital applied		85,000
Working capital increase		$10,000

Working capital changes:

	19B	Change
Cash	$ 7,400	$(12,400)
Accounts receivable	9,000	6,000
Inventory	24,900	19,900
Accounts payable	(7,000)	(4,000)
Other short-term debt	(1,400)	500
Total	$32,900	$ 10,000

Required:

a. Compare, and explain the significance of, the change in cash with the change in working capital.
b. Explain why the amount of the change in working capital was different from the amount of net income.
c. What were the largest source and use of working capital?
d. Is the working capital position sound? Explain the basis for your decision.
e. Compare the cash position with the working capital position.
f. List all of the communication deficiencies in the above format.
g. Recast the above statement to correct it for the deficiencies you listed in Requirement *(f)*.

PC15–13. The following statement was prepared by Clay Corporation:

CLAY CORPORATION
Funds Statement
December 31, 19E

Funds provided:

Net income	$ 40,000
Adjustments:	
Depreciation	12,000
Patent amortization	1,000
Goodwill amortization	3,000
Total	56,000
Other:	
Bonds payable, maturity value $100,000 . . .	98,000
Sale of land (at cost)	25,000
Common stock (issued for plant site)	40,000
Total funds provided	219,000

Funds applied:

Mortgage	20,000
Plant	150,000
Plant machinery	20,000
Plant site	40,000
Dividends	6,000
Total funds applied	236,000
Decrease in working capital	$ 17,000

Working capital changes:

Current items	Balances Dec. 31, 19E	Working capital increase (decrease)
Cash	$ 6,000	$(27,000)
Accounts receivable	13,000	4,000
Inventory	52,000	12,000
Accounts payable	(8,000)	5,000
Short-term notes	(16,000)	(11,000)
Working capital	$47,000	$(17,000)

Required:

a. Compare, and explain the significance of, the change in cash with the change in working capital.
b. What was the primary source of working capital?
c. What was the primary use of working capital?
d. Explain the transaction involving the common stock. Did it directly affect working capital? Why is it reported on the statement?
e. Explain why working capital decreased although there was a net income for the period.
f. Assess the soundness of the declaration and payment of the cash dividend.
g. Assess the cash position compared with the working capital position.
h. Can you spot any potential problems with respect to the future? Explain.
i. List all of the format, caption, and terminology deficiencies that you can identify.
j. Prepare a formal SCFP, working capital basis, to correct the deficiencies that you identified.

PC15–14. Riverside Company is completing its 19B financial statements. The following information is provided by the just completed 19B comparative balance sheet and income statement:

	19A	19B
Balance sheet:		
Cash	$ 10,000	$ 2,000
Accounts receivable (net)	16,600	21,000
Inventory	17,000	25,000
Prepaid expenses	1,400	400
Operational assets (net)	59,000	68,000
Plant site		20,000
Long-term investment	16,000	7,000
	$120,000	$143,400
Accounts payable........................	$ 8,000	$ 12,000
Wages payable	1,000	1,500
ST note payable (interest, December 31).....	6,000	3,000
LT note payable (interest, December 31).....	10,000	4,000
Bonds payable (interest, December 31)	30,000	50,000
Capital stock, par $10	60,000	60,500
Contributed capital in excess of par	3,000	3,400
Retained earnings	2,000	9,000
	$120,000	$143,400
Income statement:		
Revenues...............................		$135,000
Depreciation expense		(15,000)
Remaining expenses		(95,000)
Loss on sale of long-term investment		(3,000)
Net income		$ 22,000

Additional data:

1. Purchased operational asset for cash $24,000.
2. Sold long-term investment for $6,000 cash; carrying value $9,000.
3. Sold 50 shares of capital stock at $18 cash per share.
4. Declared and paid a cash dividend of $15,000.
5. Payment on short-term note, $3,000.
6. Payment on long-term note, $6,000.
7. Acquired plant site and issued bonds, $20,000, for full purchase price (the bonds were selling at par).

Required:

a. Prepare a worksheet or T-account analysis for SCFP, working capital basis.
b. Prepare the formal SCFP, Working Capital Basis.

PC15–15. Green Acres Company is preparing the 19B annual financial statements. The 19B comparative balance sheet and income statement reports the following information:

	19A	19B
Balance sheet:		
Cash	$ 10,000	$ 1,000
Accounts receivable (net)...............	30,000	48,500
Inventory	20,000	21,400
Short-term investments	7,000	
Long-term investments	5,000	
Operational assets (net)	50,000	57,000
Patent (net)	4,000	3,600
Land		7,500
	$126,000	$139,000
Accounts payable	$ 43,500	$ 40,000
Income tax payable....................	500	
Wages payable........................	2,000	3,000
Bonds payable	15,000	10,000
Capital stock, par $1	40,000	54,000
Contributed capital in excess of par		3,500
Retained earnings	25,000	28,500
	$126,000	$139,000
Income statement:		
Revenue		$ 80,000
Depreciation expense		(2,000)
Amortization expense..................		(400)
Remaining expenses		(73,600)
Gain on sale of long-term investment.....		3,000
Net income...........................		$ 7,000

Additional data for 19B:

1. Sold long-term investment that cost $5,000 for $8,000 cash.
2. Annual payment on bond principal, $5,000.
3. Sold and issued 8,000 shares of capital stock at $1.25 per share (cash).
4. Declared and paid a cash dividend of $3,500.
5. Purchased an operational asset for $9,000 cash.
6. Acquired land for future use and paid in full by issuing 6,000 shares of capital stock, market value $1.25 per share.

Required:

a. Prepare a worksheet or T-account analysis to develop the SCFP, working capital basis.
b. Prepare the formal SCFP, working capital basis.

PC15–16.   All-Steel Company is preparing the annual financial statements, including a SCFP, working capital basis, at December 31, 19B. The 19B comparative balance sheet and the income statement and some additional data are summarized below:

	19B	19A
Balance sheet at December 31:		
Cash	$ 21,500	$ 15,000
Accounts receivable (net)	23,000	20,000
Merchandise inventory	27,000	22,000
Prepaid insurance	300	600
Investments, long term (S Corp. stock)	12,000	
Operational assets (net)	220,000	134,000
Patent (net)	16,000	
	$319,800	$191,600
Accounts payable	$ 18,000	$ 12,000
Note payable, short term (nontrade)	10,000	18,000
Wages payable	800	1,000
Income tax payable	1,000	600
Note payable, long term	10,000	30,000
Bonds payable	100,000	
Capital stock, par $10	140,000	100,000
Contributed capital in excess of par	6,000	5,000
Retained earnings	34,000	25,000
	$319,800	$191,600

Income statement for 19B:		
Sales revenue		$200,000
Cost of goods sold		126,000
Gross margin on sales		74,000
Expenses (not detailed)	$39,000	
Depreciation expense	14,000	
Amortization of patent	1,000	
Income tax expense	7,000	61,000
Net income		$ 13,000

Additional data for 19B:

1. Purchased patent on January 1, 19B, for $17,000 cash.
2. Purchased stock of S Corporation as a long-term investment for $12,000 cash.
3. Paid $20,000 on the long-term note payable.
4. Sold and issued 4,000 shares of capital stock for $41,000 cash.
5. Declared and paid a $4,000 cash dividend.
6. Acquired a building (an operational asset) and paid in full for it by issuing $100,000 bonds payable at par to the former owner—date of transaction was December 30, 19B.

Required:

a. Based upon the above data, prepare a worksheet analysis to develop the SCFP, working capital basis.

b. Based upon the completed worksheet, prepare a formal SCFP, working capital basis.

C·H·A·P·T·E·R
16

Using and Interpreting Financial Statements

PURPOSE OF THIS CHAPTER

Throughout the preceding chapters, we emphasized the rationale and conceptual basis that support the accounting process. The fundamental concepts that underlie financial accounting and reporting are summarized in Exhibit 2–6. We have emphasized the conceptual foundation of accounting for two reasons: (1) an understanding of financial accounting concepts makes your understanding of accounting procedures more complete, and (2) effective analysis and interpretation of financial statements depend on an understanding of the underlying concepts. A good understanding of accounting concepts and procedures enables a decision maker to appreciate the advantages and limitations of financial statements.

The purpose of this chapter is to discuss the evaluation and interpretation of external financial statements by decision makers and some analytical techniques that are used widely to interpret financial statements.

FINANCIAL REPORTS IN THE DECISION-MAKING PROCESS

The basic objective of financial statements is to help the users make better economic decisions. Decision makers who use financial statements constitute two broad groups. One group is the management of the business (i.e., internal decision makers) who rely on accounting data in making important management decisions. This aspect of accounting is considered in *Fundamentals of Management Accounting.*

The second broad group that uses financial reports is referred to as "external" decision makers. This group consists primarily of investors (both present and potential owners), investment analysts, creditors, government, labor organizations, and the public at large. Financial accounting and the external financial reports discussed in the preceding chapters are oriented toward serving this diverse group of decision makers.

There are three primary types of measurements that decision makers use in making decisions:

1. **Measurement of past performance**—The decision maker needs to know how the business has performed in the past. For example, information concerning such items as income, sales volume, extraordinary items, cash and working capital flows, and return earned on the investment helps assess the success of the business and the effectiveness of the management. Such information also helps the decision maker compare one entity with others.

2. **Measurement of the present condition of a business**—The decision maker must have data on how the entity stands today in order to answer questions such as: What types of assets are owned? How much debt does the business owe, and when is it due? What is the cash position? How much of the earnings have been retained in the business? What are the EPS, return-on-investment, and debt/equity ratios? What is the inventory position? Answers to these and similar economic questions help the decision maker assess the successes and failures of the past; but, more importantly, they provide useful information in assessing the cash flow and profit potentials of the business.

3. **Prediction of the future performance of the business**—Statement users typically make decisions by selecting from among several alternative courses of action. Each course of action will cause different conditions to exist **in the future.** In decision making, one is faced with the problem of predicting the probable future results of the alternatives under consideration. All decisions are future oriented because they do not (and cannot) affect the past. However, in predicting the probable future impact of a decision, reliable measurements of what has happened in the recent past are valuable. These measurements are particularly relevant when the decision relates to a business entity. For example the recent sales and earnings trends of a business are good indicators of what might be expected reasonably in the future. The primary value in measuring past performance and the present condition of a business is to aid in predicting the future cash flows of the business.

Thus, decision makers must rely substantially on the past data presented in financial reports in making assessments and predictions of probable future performance. Usually, this is the most important use of financial statements by decision makers.

Some decisions are made intuitively and without much supporting data. In such cases there is no systematic attempt to collect measurable data, which makes it practically impossible to array, measure, and evaluate the advantages and disadvantages of each alternative. Numerous reasons exist for intuitive decision making. Time and cost of collecting the data may prevent a careful analysis. Sometimes the decision maker is unsophisticated and consequently does not understand the systematic approach to decision making and is not aware of all of the basic factors that should be considered in making the decision. Unsophisticated decision makers tend to oversimplify the decision-making process, disregard basic information, and quite frequently overlook the financial impacts.

In contrast, a sophisticated decision maker will make a systematic analysis of each alternative. Information regarding each alternative will be collected and evaluated. In decisions relating to a business, the financial statements usually provide critical financial data relevant to the decision. We must emphasize, however, that the financial result is only one of several important factors that should be evaluated in most decisions.

To use financial information effectively, one must understand what was measured and how it was measured. With a reasonable level of understanding of the fundamentals of the accounting process, you are able to evaluate effectively the strengths and limitations of the financial data presented in the financial reports of a business. One of the objectives of the preceding chapters was to enable you to appreciate and evaluate these aspects of accounting.

The three basic financial statements—income statement, balance sheet, and statement of changes in financial position (SCFP)—and the related disclosure notes have evolved primarily to meet the special needs of external decision makers. Because of the varied needs of these users, special and supplementary financial data and analyses frequently are needed.

INVESTORS

Investors constitute a primary group to which external financial statements are addressed. This group includes present owners, potential owners, and investment analysts (because they advise investors). Investors include individuals, other businesses, and institutions, such as your college or university.

When purchasing shares of stock of a corporation, most investors do not seek a controlling interest. Instead, they do so in the anticipation of earning a return on their investment. This return is made up of two components: (1) revenue in the form of dividends during the investment period and (2) subsequent increases in the market value of the shares over the amount invested. Thus, when considering an investment of this type, the investor is faced with the problem of predicting the future **income** and **growth** of the enterprise. Investors are interested in enterprise income because it is the "source" of future dividends. They are interested in enterprise growth because it tends to cause the market value of the shares to increase. In making these predictions, the investor should consider three types of general factors:

1. **Economy-wide factors**—The overall health of the economy often will have a direct impact on the performance of an individual enterprise. The investor should consider such data as the gross national product, productivity, unemployment rate, general inflation rate, and changes in interest rates.

2. **Industry factors**—Certain events have a major impact on each company within an industry, but have only a minor impact on other companies. For example, policy changes by OPEC (the oil cartel) have a major impact on the oil industry.

3. **Individual company factors**—These factors may be either financial or nonfinancial in nature. Nonfinancial factors would include the introduction of a new product, a lawsuit, and changes in key personnel. Data pertaining to financial factors are presented in the basic financial statements. The income statement provides significant information for the investor, such as revenue from products and services, extraordinary items, income tax impacts, net income, and earnings per share. Other relationships, such as gross margin, profit margin, and expense relationships, can be computed. Similarly, the balance sheet, the statement of changes in financial position, and the notes to the financial statements provide measurements of past profit performance, funds flow, and current financial position. These data constitute an important base from which predictions of future income and growth can be made. These data are particularly valuable when compared with recent past periods as illustrated in Exhibit 16–1.

CREDITORS

Financial institutions, as well as other parties, grant long-term and short-term credit to businesses. Creditors lend money in order to earn a return, that is, interest revenue. Creditors expect to collect periodic interest during the credit period and the principal at maturity. As a consequence, in granting credit to a business, the creditor is concerned basically about items such as the following:

1. Profit potential of the business because a profitable entity is much more likely to meet its maturing obligations.

2. Ability of the business to generate cash consistently from recurring operations because it will be in a more favorable position to pay its debts.

3. Financial position (assets owned and debts owed) of the business because the assets comprise security for the debts and the debts indicate the future demand for cash at debt maturity dates.

Credit grantors almost always look to the financial reports for information. To enhance the credibility of these reports, creditors often require that the reports be audited by an independent CPA. In addition to the financial statements, the disclosure notes and the "auditors' opinion" convey important information because they often provide detailed quantified facts to support the reported amounts and other nonquantified explanations such as certain future contingencies (e.g., major lawsuits pending).

EXHIBIT 16–1
Illustration of
comparative
financial statements

PACKARD COMPANY
Comparative Income Statements (simplified for illustration)
For the Years Ended December 31, 19B, and 19A

	Year ended Dec. 31		Increase (decrease) 19B over 19A	
	19B	19A*	Amount	Percent
Sales revenue	$120,000	$100,000	$20,000	20.0
Cost of goods sold	72,600	60,000	12,600	21.0
Gross margin on sales	47,400	40,000	7,400	18.5
Operating expenses:				
Distribution expenses	22,630	15,000	7,630	50.9
Administrative expenses	11,870	13,300	(1,430)	(10.8)
Interest expense	1,500	1,700	(200)	(11.8)
Total expenses	36,000	30,000	6,000	20.0
Pretax income	11,400	10,000	1,400	14.0
Income taxes	2,600	2,000	600	30.0
Net income	$ 8,800	$ 8,000	$ 800	10.0

* Base year for computing percents.

PACKARD COMPANY
Comparative Balance Sheets (simplified for illustration)
At December 31, 19B, and 19A

	At December 31		Increase (decrease) 19B over 19A	
	19B	19A*	Amount	Percent
Assets				
Current assets:				
Cash	$ 13,000	$ 9,000	$ 4,000	44.4
Accounts receivable (net)	8,400	7,000	1,400	20.0
Merchandise inventory	54,000	60,000	(6,000)	(10.0)
Prepaid expenses	2,000	4,000	(2,000)	(50.0)
Total current assets	77,400	80,000	(2,600)	3.3
Investments:				
Real estate	8,000	8,000		
Operational assets:				
Equipment and furniture	82,500	75,000	7,500	10.0
Less accumulated depreciation	(23,250)	(15,000)	8,250	55.0
Total operational assets	59,250	60,000	(750)	(1.3)
Other assets	1,900	2,000	(100)	(5.0)
Total assets	$146,550	$150,000	$(3,450)	(2.3)
Liabilities				
Current liabilities:				
Accounts payable	$ 13,200	$ 12,000	$ 1,200	10.0
Notes payable, short term	15,000	20,000	(5,000)	(25.0)
Accrued wages payable	7,200	8,000	(800)	(10.0)
Total current liabilities	35,400	40,000	(4,600)	(11.5)
Long-term liabilities:				
Notes payable, long term	7,150	10,000	(2,850)	(28.5)
Total liabilities	42,550	50,000	(7,450)	(14.9)
Stockholders' Equity				
Common stock, par $10	85,000	85,000		
Retained earnings	19,000	15,000	4,000	26.7
Total stockholders' equity	104,000	100,000	4,000	4.0
Total liabilities and stockholders' equity	$146,550	$150,000	$(3,450)	(2.3)

* Base year for computing percents.

ANALYSIS OF FINANCIAL STATEMENTS

Financial statements include a large volume of quantitative data supplemented by disclosure notes. The notes are intended to be particularly helpful to users in interpreting the statements; therefore, they are viewed as an integral part of the financial statements. Notes elaborate on accounting policies, major financial effects and events, and certain nonquantifiable events that may contribute to the success or failure of the firm.

In respect to the quantitative data presented in the financial statements, four techniques used widely to assist decision makers in understanding and interpreting the external financial statements are: (1) comparative statements, (2) long-term summaries, (3) graphic presentations, and (4) ratio analyses.

COMPARATIVE FINANCIAL STATEMENTS

The accounting profession requires the presentation of **comparative financial statements** covering, as a minimum, the current year and the immediately prior year.

Practically all financial statements present, side by side, the results for the current and the preceding years (similar to the statements shown in Exhibit 16–1). Analysis of comparative statements is facilitated if two additional columns are added for (1) the **amount** of change for each item and (2) the **percent** of change. These additional variance columns (amount and percent) are illustrated in Exhibit 16–1. Frequently the percent of change from the prior period is more helpful for interpretative purposes than the absolute dollar amount of change. Observe that the percents are determined independently on each line by dividing the amount of the change by the amount for the preceding year. For example, in Exhibit 16–1, the percentage on the Cash line was computed as $4,000 ÷ $9,000 = 44.4 percent. Thus, the amount from the earlier year was used as the base amount.

LONG-TERM SUMMARIES

In the interest of full disclosure, many annual reports contain 5-, 10-, and even 20-year summaries of basic data, such as sales revenue, net income, total assets, total liabilities, total owners' equity, and selected ratios (a good 10-year summary is shown in Special Supplement B preceding the Index). Data for a series of years are particularly important in interpreting the financial statements for the current period. There is considerable likelihood of misinterpretation and unwarranted conclusions when the statement user limits consideration to only the last one or two periods. The vagaries of business transactions, economic events, and accounting techniques are such that the financial reports for a single time period usually do not provide a sound basis for assessing the long-term potentials of an enterprise. Sophisticated financial analysts typically use data covering a number of periods so that significant trends may be identified and interpreted.

However, care must be exercised in interpreting long-term summaries because data for a period in the distant past may not be comparable, or even useful, because of changes in the company, industry, and environment. For example, Exxon is a very different company now than it was when a gallon of gasoline sold for 25 cents.

In interpreting comparative data, the items showing significant increases and decreases should receive special attention. Care should be exercised to identify evidence of significant **turning points,** either upward or downward, in trends for important items such as net income and cash flow. The turning points often provide indication of significant future trends. Fundamental to the interpretation is the need to determine the **underlying causes** for significant changes in either direction (favorable or unfavorable).

RATIO AND PERCENTAGE ANALYSIS

Some amounts on financial statements, such as net income, are highly significant in and of themselves; however, the significance of many amounts is highlighted by their relationships to other amounts. These significant relationships can be examined through the use of an analytical tool known as **ratio** or **percentage analysis.** A ratio or percent simply expresses the proportionate relationship between two different amounts. A ratio or percent is computed by dividing one quantity by another quantity. For example, the fact that a company earned net income of $500,000 assumes greater significance when net income is compared with the stockholders' investment in the company. Assuming that stockholders' equity is $5,000,000, the relationship of earnings to shareholder investment would be $500,000 ÷ $5,000,000 = .1, or 10 percent. Clearly, this ratio indicates a different level of performance than would be the case if stockholders' equity had been $50,000,000. Thus, ratio analysis enables decision makers to compare companies more realistically than does the income amount alone.

Fundamentally, there are two aspects of ratio analysis: (1) relationships **within one period** and (2) relationships **between periods.** In addition, ratios may be computed between amounts within one statement, such as the income statement, or between statements, such as the income statement and the balance sheet. In Exhibit 16–1, the percents of change represent a percentage analysis between periods within each statement.

There is not a particular list of ratios or percentages that can be identified as appropriate to all situations. Each analytical situation may require the calculation of several ratios. There are a number of ratios or percentages that usually are used because they are appropriate to many situations. The next paragraphs will discuss and illustrate the ratios and percentages that are used often by decision makers.

COMPONENT PERCENTAGES

Component percentages are used to express each item on a particular statement as a percentage of a single **base amount** (i.e., the denominator of the ratio). Exhibit 16–2 presents a component analysis for the 19A and 19B income statements

EXHIBIT 16–2
Illustration of component percentages

PACKARD COMPANY
Income Statements (simplified for illustration)
For the Years Ended December 31, 19B, and 19A

	For the year ended			
	Dec. 31, 19B		Dec. 31, 19A	
	Amount	Percent	Amount	Percent
Sales revenue (net)*	$120,000	100.0	$100,000	100.0
Cost of goods sold	72,600	60.5	60,000	60.0
Gross margin on sales	47,400	39.5	40,000	40.0
Operating expenses:				
Distribution expenses	22,630	18.9	15,000	15.0
Administrative expenses	11,870	9.9	13,300	13.3
Interest expense	1,500	1.2	1,700	1.7
Total expenses	36,000	30.0	30,000	30.0
Pretax income	11,400	9.5	10,000	10.0
Income taxes	2,600	2.2	2,000	2.0
Net income	$ 8,800	7.3	$ 8,000	8.0

*Base amount.

PACKARD COMPANY
Balance Sheets (simplified for illustration)
At December 31, 19B, and 19A

	At			
	Dec. 31, 19B		Dec. 31, 19A	
	Amount	Percent	Amount	Percent
Assets				
Current assets:				
Cash	$ 13,000	8.9	$ 9,000	6.0
Accounts receivable (net)	8,400	5.7	7,000	4.6
Merchandise inventory	54,000	36.8	60,000	40.0
Prepaid expenses	2,000	1.4	4,000	2.7
Total current assets	77,400	52.8	80,000	53.3
Investments.				
Real Estate	8,000	5.5	8,000	5.3
Operational assets:				
Equipment and furniture	82,500	56.3	75,000	50.0
Less accumulated depreciation	(23,250)	(15.9)	(15,000)	(10.0)
Total operational assets	59,250	40.4	60,000	40.0
Other assets	1,900	1.3	2,000	1.4
Total assets*	$146,550	100.0	$150,000	100.0
Liabilities				
Current liabilities:				
Accounts payable	$ 13,200	9.0	$ 12,000	8.0
Notes payable, short term	15,000	10.2	20,000	13.3
Accrued wages payable	7,200	4.9	8,000	5.3
Total current liabilities	35,400	24.1	40,000	26.6
Long-term liabilities:				
Notes payable, long term	7,150	4.9	10,000	6.7
Total liabilities	42,550	29.0	50,000	33.3
Stockholders' Equity				
Common stock, par $10	85,000	58.0	85,000	56.7
Retained earnings	19,000	13.0	15,000	10.0
Total stockholders' equity	104,000	71.0	100,000	66.7
Total liabilities and stockholders' equity*	$146,550	100.0	$150,000	100.0

* Base amount.

and balance sheets for Packard Company. To compute component percentages for the income statement, the base amount is **net sales revenue.** Thus, each expense is expressed as a proportionate part of net sales revenue. On the balance sheet, the base amount is **total assets.** The percents are derived by dividing the amount on each line by total assets.

Component percentages often are useful in interpreting and evaluating the reported financial data because they reveal important proportional relationships. For example, on the income statement in Exhibit 16–2, observe that distribution expenses were 18.9 percent of sales revenue in 19B, compared with 15 percent in 19A. On the balance sheet we note that at the end of 19B, merchandise inventory was 36.8 percent of total assets, compared with 40 percent for 19A. These changes in important relationships often suggest the need for further inquiry because they tend to indicate problems and opportunities for corrective action and increased profitability.

SOME WIDELY USED RATIOS

Numerous ratios and percentages can be computed from a single set of financial statements; however, only a selected number may be useful in a given situation. Thus, a common approach is to compute certain widely used ratios and then decide which additional ratios are relevant to the particular type of decisions contemplated. Because balance sheet amounts relate to one instant in time, while income statement amounts relate to a period of time, care must be exercised in calculating ratios that use amounts from both statements. Thus, when an income statement amount is compared with a balance sheet amount, a balance sheet **average amount** often is used to compensate for the difference in time periods. In the examples to follow, the selected balance sheet amount usually is computed as the average of the amounts shown on the beginning and ending balance sheets. When additional information is available, such as monthly or quarterly data, an average of the additional data often is more representative.

Commonly used financial ratios can be grouped into the five categories shown in Exhibit 16–3.

TESTS OF PROFITABILITY

Continuing profitability is a primary measure of the overall success of a company; it is a necessary condition for survival. Investors and creditors would prefer a **single measure** of profitability that would be meaningful in all situations. Unfortunately, no single measure can be devised to meet this comprehensive need. Tests of profitability focus on measuring the adequacy of income by comparing it with one or more primary activities or factors that are measured in the financial statements. Five different tests of profitability are explained below.

1. Return on owners' investment (ROI$_o$).   This ratio is regarded as a fundamental test of profitability. It relates income to the investment that was committed by the owners to earn the income. To measure the profitability of any investment, whether for a company, a project, or for an individual investment, the amount of income must be compared to the amount invested. Investors commit their

EXHIBIT 16–3		
Widely used accounting ratios	*Ratio*	*Basic computation*

Tests of profitability:

1. *Return on owners' investment (ROI$_o$).

$$\frac{\text{Income}}{\text{Average owners' equity}}$$

2. Return on total investment (ROI$_t$).

$$\frac{\text{Income} + \text{Interest expense (net of tax)}}{\text{Average total assets}}$$

3. Financial leverage (ROI$_o$ − ROI$_t$).

$$\text{Return on owners' investment} - \text{Return on total investment}$$

4. Earnings per share.

$$\frac{\text{Income}}{\text{Average number of shares of common stock outstanding}}$$

5. Profit margin.

$$\frac{\text{Income (before extraordinary items)}}{\text{Net sales revenue}}$$

Tests of liquidity:

6. Working capital ratio.

$$\frac{\text{Current assets}}{\text{Current liabilities}}$$

7. Quick ratio.

$$\frac{\text{Quick assets}}{\text{Current liabilities}}$$

8. Receivable turnover.

$$\frac{\text{Net credit sales}}{\text{Average net trade receivables}}$$

9. Inventory turnover.

$$\frac{\text{Cost of goods sold}}{\text{Average inventory}}$$

Test of solvency and equity position:

10. Debt/equity ratio.

$$\frac{\text{Total liabilities}}{\text{Owners' equity}}$$

Market tests:

11. Price/earnings ratio.

$$\frac{\text{Current market price per share}}{\text{Earnings per share}}$$

12. Dividend yield ratio.

$$\frac{\text{Dividends per share}}{\text{Market price per share}}$$

Miscellaneous ratio:

13. Book value per share.

$$\frac{\text{Common stock equity}}{\text{Number of shares of common stock outstanding}}$$

* The numbers to the left are maintained in the subsequent discussions to facilitate reference.

funds to an enterprise because they expect to earn a return (i.e., a profit) on those funds. Fundamentally, the return on owners' investment ratio is computed as follows:

$$\textbf{Return on owners' investment} = \frac{\textbf{Income*}}{\textbf{Average owners' equity†}}$$

$$\textbf{Packard Company, 19B} = \frac{\$8,800^*}{\$102,000†} = 8.6\%$$

Based on Exhibit 16–2.
 * Income **before** extraordinary items should be used.
 † Average owners' equity is preferable when available; that is ($100,000 + $104,000) ÷ 2 = $102,000.

Thus, Packard Company earned 8.6 percent, after income taxes, on the investment provided by the **owners.** Return on owners' investment is a particularly useful measure of profitability from the **viewpoint of the owners** because it relates the two fundamental factors in any investment situation—the amount of the owners' investment and the return earned for the owners on that investment.

2. Return on total investment (ROI$_t$). Another view of the return on investment concept <u>relates income to **total assets**</u> (i.e., total investment) rather than to owners' investment only. Under this broader concept, return on total investment would be computed as follows:

$$\text{Return on total investment} = \frac{\text{Income}^* + \text{Interest expense (net of tax)}}{\text{Average total assets}\dagger}$$

$$\text{Packard Company 19B} = \frac{\$8,800^* + (\$1,500 \times .77)}{\$148,275\dagger} = 6.7\%$$

Based on Exhibit 16–2.
* Income before extraordinary items should be used. This illustration assumes an average income tax rate of 23 percent.
† Average total assets should be used; that is ($150,000 + $146,550) ÷ 2 = $148,275.

Packard Company earned 6.7 percent on the **total resources it employed** during the year. This concept views **investment** as the amount of resources provided by both owners and creditors. Return is viewed as the return to both owners and creditors. Thus, to compute return on **total** investment, interest expense (net of income tax) must be added back to income because it is the return on the creditors' investment and was previously deducted to derive income. The denominator represents **total** investment; therefore, interest expense must be added back to raise the numerator (income) to a **total** return basis. Interest net of income tax is used because it represents the net cost to the corporation of the funds provided by creditors.

Return on total investment reflects the combined effect of both the operating and the financing activities of a company as illustrated in Exhibit 16–4 (remember that total assets always equals total liabilities plus total owners' equity).

Most analysts compute return-on-investment ratios for both total investment and owners' equity as illustrated above. Return on total investment is viewed as the preferable measure of **management performance** in using all of the resources available to the company. The return on owners' equity is viewed as particularly relevant to the owners because it measures the return that has "accrued" to them.

3. Financial leverage. Financial leverage is the advantage, or disadvantage, which derives from earning a return on owners' investment that is different from the return earned on total investment (i.e., $\text{ROI}_o - \text{ROI}_t$). Most companies earn a higher rate on owners' equity than on total investment and thus enjoy positive leverage. <u>Positive leverage occurs when the average net (aftertax) interest rate on borrowed funds is less than the company's earnings rate on its total investment.</u>

**EXHIBIT 16-4
Components of
return on total
investment**

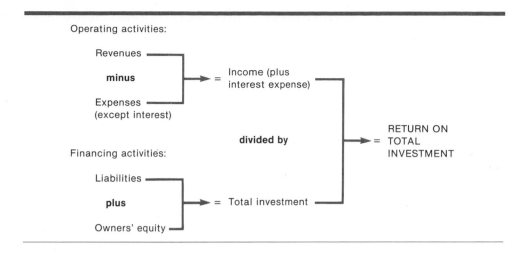

Financial leverage can be measured by comparing the two return-on-investment ratios as follows:

$$\text{Financial leverage} = \frac{\text{Return on}}{\text{owners' investment}} - \frac{\text{Return on}}{\text{total investment}}$$

Packard Company, 19B = 8.6% − 6.7% = 1.9% (positive leverage)

When a company can borrow funds at an aftertax (i.e, net) interest rate and invest those funds to earn a higher aftertax rate of return, the difference "accrues" to the benefit of the owners. Of course, this is the primary reason that most companies adopt a strategy of obtaining a significant amount of needed resources from creditors rather than obtaining outside resources only from the sale of their capital stock.

4. Earnings per share (EPS). This test evaluates profitability strictly from the common stockholders' point of view. Rather than being based on the dollar amount of the investment, it is based on the number of shares of common stock outstanding. It provides a measure of profitability that can be adjusted readily for the number of shares outstanding. Basically, EPS on common stock is computed as follows:

$$\text{Earnings per share} = \frac{\text{Income}}{\text{Average number of shares of common stock outstanding}}$$

$$\text{Packard Company, 19B} = \frac{\$8,800}{8,500} = \$1.04 \text{ per share}$$

EPS usually is computed on three amounts if extraordinary items are reported on the income statement: (1) income before extraordinary items (required), (2) extraordinary items (optional), and (3) net income (required). Of the three EPS amounts, the first one usually is considered the most relevant.

5. *Profit margin.* This percent is based on two income statement amounts. It is computed as follows:

$$\text{Profit margin} = \frac{\text{Income (before extraordinary items)}}{\text{Net sales}}$$

$$\text{Packard Company, 19B} = \frac{\$8,800}{\$120,000} = 7.3\%$$

This profitability test simply is the percent of each sales dollar, on the average, that represents profit. For Packard Company it may be interpreted as follows:

a. Income was 7.3 percent of net sales.
b. $.073 of each $1 of sales was income.

Profit margin also is reflected in the component percentages illustrated in Exhibit 16–2. Care must be exercised in analyzing the profit margin because it does not take into account the amount of resources employed (i.e., total investment) to produce the income. For example, the income statements of Company A and Company B may reflect the following:

		Company A	Company B
a.	Sales revenue	$100,000	$150,000
b.	Income	$ 5,000	$ 7,500
c.	Profit margin *(b)* ÷ *(a)*	5%	5%
d.	Total investment	$ 50,000	$125,000
e.	Return on total investment* *(b)* ÷ *(d)*	10%	6%

* Assuming no interest expense.

In this example, both companies reported the same profit margin (5 percent). Company A, however, appears to be performing much better because it is earning a 10 percent return on the total investment versus the 6 percent earned by Company B. The profit margin percents do not reflect the effect of the $50,000 total investment in Company A compared to the $125,000 total investment in Company B. The effect of the different amounts of investment in each company is reflected in the return on investment (ROI) percents. Thus, the profit margin ratio omits one of the two important factors that should be used in evaluating return on the investment.

TESTS OF LIQUIDITY

Short-term liquidity refers to a company's ability to meet its currently maturing obligations; therefore, tests of liquidity focus on the relationship between current assets and current liabilities. The ability of a company to meet its current liabilities is an important factor in evaluating short-term financial strength. For example, a company that does not have cash available to pay for purchases on a timely basis will lose its cash discounts and run the risk of discontinued credit by vendors. Recall that working capital is measured as the difference between total current assets and total current liabilities. There are two ratios that are used to measure short-term liquidity; they are the working capital (or current) ratio and the quick (or acid-test) ratio.

6. Working capital ratio.   This ratio measures the relationship between total current assets and total current liabilities at a specific date. It is computed as follows:

$$\text{Working capital ratio} = \frac{\text{Current assets}}{\text{Current liabilities}}$$

$$\text{Packard Company, 19B} = \frac{\$77,400}{\$35,400} = 2.2 \text{ times or 2.2 to 1}$$

The working capital ratio tends to measure the adequacy of working capital as well as liquidity. For Packard company it can be said that at year-end current assets were 2.2 times current liabilities or, alternatively, that for each $1 of current liabilities there were $2.20 of current assets. Thus, the working capital ratio measures the cushion of working capital maintained in order to allow for the inevitable unevenness in the flow of "funds" through the working capital accounts.[1]

7. Quick ratio.   This ratio is similar to the working capital ratio except that it is a much more stringent test of short-term liquidity. It is computed as follows:

$$\text{Quick ratio} = \frac{\text{Quick assets}}{\text{Current liabilities}}$$

$$\text{Packard Company, 19B} = \frac{\$21,400}{\$35,400} = .60 \text{ times or .60 to 1}$$

Quick assets are assets that are readily convertible into cash at approximately their stated amounts. Quick assets include cash, short-term investments, and accounts receivable (net of the allowance for doubtful accounts). Inventories usually are omitted from quick assets because of the uncertainty of when cash will be received from the sale of inventory in the future. However, if the inventory will turn to cash very quickly, it should be included. In contrast, prepaid expenses do not "convert" to cash; rather their prepayment means that there will be no related cash outflow in the future; therefore, they are excluded from quick assets. Thus, the quick or acid-test ratio is a much more severe test of liquidity than is the working capital ratio.

8. Receivable turnover.   Short-term liquidity is related to the specific items of working capital. Nearness to cash of some current assets often is measured in terms of **turnover.** There are two ratios, in addition to the two illustrated above, that measure nearness to cash: the receivable turnover and the inventory turnover.

Receivable turnover is computed as follows:

---

[1] Occasionally, "working capital" is taken to mean total current assets which is confusing and unnecessary because "total current assets" is more descriptive. Sometimes the term **net working capital** is used to describe the difference between current assets and current liabilities. Throughout this book, we have followed the more general use of working capital to mean the difference between current assets and current liabilities.

$$\text{Receivable turnover} = \frac{\text{Net credit sales*}}{\text{Average net trade receivables}}$$

$$\begin{array}{l}\text{Packard Company, 19B}\\\text{(net credit sales assumed}\\\text{to be \$77,000 for 19B)}\end{array} = \frac{\$77,000}{(\$7,000 + \$8,400) \div 2} = 10 \text{ times}$$

* When the amount of credit sales is not known, total sales may be used as a rough approximation.

This ratio is called a turnover ratio because it reflects how many times the trade receivables "turn over" (i.e., were recorded, collected, then recorded again during the period). Receivable turnover expresses the relationship of the average balance in Accounts Receivable (including Trade Notes Receivable) to the transactions that generated those receivables—credit sales. This ratio tends to measure the effectiveness of the credit-granting and collection activities of the company. A high receivable turnover ratio suggests effective collection activities. Granting credit to poor credit risks and ineffective collection efforts will cause this ratio to be low. The receivable turnover ratio often is converted to a time basis known as the average age of receivables. The computation is as follows:

$$\text{Average age of trade receivables} = \frac{\text{Days in year}}{\text{Receivable turnover}}$$

$$\text{Packard Company, 19B} = \frac{365}{10} = 36.5 \text{ average days to collect}$$

The effectiveness of credit and collection activities sometimes is judged by a "rule of thumb" that the **average days to collect** should not exceed 1½ times the credit terms. For example, if the credit terms are 2/10, n/30, the average days to collect should not exceed 45 days (i.e., not more than 15 days past due). Like all rules of thumb, this one is rough and has many exceptions. However, an increase or decrease in the receivable turnover or average days to collect, from one period to the next, would suggest changes in the implementation of credit policies and/or changes in collection efficiency. An increase in the average age of trade receivables would indicate an increasing time lag between credit sales and cash collection.

9. Inventory turnover. Inventory turnover tends to measure the liquidity (i.e., nearness to cash) of the inventory. It reflects the relationship of the inventory to the volume of goods sold during the period. The computation is as follows:

$$\text{Inventory turnover} = \frac{\text{Cost of goods sold}}{\text{Average inventory}}$$

$$\text{Packard Company, 19B} = \frac{\$72,600}{(\$60,000 + \$54,000) \div 2} = 1.3 \text{ times}$$

The inventory "turned over" 1.3 times on the average during the year because cost of goods sold was 1.3 times the average inventory level. Because profit normally is realized each time the inventory is sold (i.e., turned over), an increase in the ratio is favorable, up to a point. If the ratio is too high, sales may be lost because of items that are out of stock. The turnover ratio often is converted to a time-basis expression called the **average days' supply in inventory.** The computation would be:

$$\text{Average days' supply in inventory} = \frac{\text{Days in year}}{\text{Inventory turnover}}$$

$$\text{Packard Company, 19B} = \frac{365}{1.3}$$

$$= \frac{281 \text{ average days' supply in}}{\text{inventory}}$$

Turnover ratios are used extensively because they are easy to understand. Normal (or average) inventory turnover ratios vary significantly by industry classification. Companies in the food industry (grocery stores and restaurants) have high inventory turnover ratios while companies that sell expensive merchandise (jewelry stores and automobile dealers) have a much lower ratio.

TESTS OF SOLVENCY AND EQUITY POSITION

We noted above that short-term liquidity refers to the relationship between current assets and current liabilities. In contrast, **solvency** refers to the ability of a company to meet its **long-term obligations** on a continuing basis. Certain critical relationships can be identified by analyzing how a company has financed its assets and activities. The relative amount of resources provided by creditors and owners is known as a company's **equity position.** The debt/equity ratio is used to reflect the equity position of a company.

10. Debt/equity ratio. This ratio expresses the direct proportion between debt and owners' equity.[2] It is computed as follows:

$$\text{Debt/equity ratio} = \frac{\text{Total liabilities (i.e., creditors' equity)}}{\text{Owners' equity}}$$

$$\text{Packard Company, 19B} = \frac{\$42,550}{\$104,000} = .41 \text{ (or } 41\%)$$

---

[2] The relationship between debt and owners' equity alternatively may be calculated with the following two ratios:

$$\text{Owners' equity to total equities} = \frac{\text{Owners' equity}}{\text{Total equities}}$$

$$\text{Packard Company, 19B} = \frac{\$104,000}{\$146,500} = 71\%$$

$$\text{Creditors' equity to total equities} = \frac{\text{Creditors' equity}}{\text{Total equities}}$$

$$\text{Packard Company, 19B} = \frac{\$42,500}{\$146,550} = 29\%$$

In effect, this ratio states that for each $1 of owners' equity, there was $.41 of liabilities.

Debt capital is risky for a company because there are *(a)* specific maturity dates for the principal amounts and *(b)* specific interest payments that must be made. Debt obligations are enforceable by law and do not depend upon the earning of income by the company. In contrast, resources supplied by owners do not give rise to similar obligations; that is, owners' equity is not fixed as to amounts and dates of principal and dividend payments. Thus, equity capital usually is viewed as much less risky than debt capital for a company.

In the long run, the rate of return on stockholders' equity usually will be higher than interest rates paid to creditors. Despite the element of risk associated with debt, it may be advantageous to the stockholders if the company derives significant amounts of resources through borrowing (because of positive financial leverage). For example, assume a company is earning 15 percent return on total investment, while its borrowing rate on debt is 7 percent (net of income tax) on the average. The difference between the earnings rate on total resources (15 percent) and the interest paid to the creditors (7 percent) "accrues" to the benefit of the stockholders.[3] In the long run, the stockholders benefit by the 15 percent earned on the resources provided by them, plus the difference between the 15 percent return and the 7 percent interest rate paid on the resources provided by the creditors. A company with a high proportion of debt is said to be **highly levered.** The debt/equity ratio indicates the balance that the management has attained between the resources provided by creditors and the resources provided by owners.

MARKET TESTS

Several ratios have been developed to measure the "market worth" of a share of stock. Basically, these market tests attempt to relate the current market price of a share of stock to some indicator of the gain or loss that might accrue to an investor. The tests focus on the **current market price** of the stock because that is the amount the buyer would invest. Two market test ratios quoted widely by analysts, stockbrokers, investors, and others are the price/earnings ratio and the dividend yield ratio.

11. Price/earnings ratio (P/E). This ratio measures the relationship between the current market price of the stock and its earnings per share. Assuming a current market price of $15.60 per share for Packard Company common stock in 19B and earnings per share of $1.04, the P/E ratio is computed as follows:

$$\text{Price/earnings ratio} = \frac{\text{Current market price per share}}{\text{Earnings per share}}$$

$$\text{Packard Company, 19B} = \frac{\$15.60}{\$1.04} = 15 \text{ (or 15 to 1)}$$

---

[3] Interest expense on debt is a deductible expense on the income tax return; in contrast, dividend payments to stockholders are not deductible. Thus, in addition to the lower stated rate for debt, funds obtained by means of debt tend to be less costly because of the income tax saving. The real cost of debt in the above example depends upon the income tax rate.

Thus, Packard stock was selling at 15 times the EPS. The P/E ratio frequently is referred to as the **multiple.** The P/E ratio is used widely as an indicator of the future performance of the stock. It changes with each change in the current market price per share and with each earnings report.

Sometimes the components of this ratio are inverted, giving what is referred to as the **capitalization rate.** This is said to be the rate at which the stock market apparently is capitalizing the current earnings. For example, computation of the capitalization rate on current earnings per share would be $1.04 \div $15.60 = 6.67$ percent.

12. Dividend yield ratio.   This yield ratio measures the relationship between the dividends per share paid in the past and the current market price of the stock. Assuming dividends paid by Packard Company of $.75 per share for 19B, and a current market price per share of $15.60, the ratio is computed as follows:

$$\text{Dividend yield ratio} = \frac{\text{Dividend per share}}{\text{Market price per share}}$$

$$\text{Packard Company, 19B} = \frac{\$.75}{\$15.60} = 4.81\%$$

This ratio measures the current dividend yield to the investor, based upon the dividends declared per share (which is revenue to the investor), against the cost of the investment as indicated by the current market price per share. Like the P/E ratio, it is a volatile measure because the price of stock may change materially over short periods of time, and each change in market price or dividend payment changes the ratio.

MISCELLANEOUS RATIO

13. Book value per share.   The book value per share of stock measures the owners' equity in terms of each share of common stock outstanding. In the case of a simple capital structure, with **only** common stock outstanding, the computation of book value per share is not difficult. To illustrate, assume Day Corporation had total owners' equity of $250,000 and 10,000 outstanding shares of common stock, par $10. The computation of book value per share would be as follows:

Book value per share of common stock:

$$\begin{array}{l}\text{Book value per} \\ \text{common share}\end{array} = \frac{\begin{array}{c}\text{Total owners' equity} \\ \text{(applicable to common shares)}\end{array}}{\text{Common shares outstanding}}$$

$$= \frac{\$250,000}{10,000 \text{ shares}} = \$25$$

Computation of book value per share is more difficult if both common and preferred shares are outstanding. In this situation, total owners' equity must be allocated between common and preferred stock. This allocation is accomplished by assigning an amount to preferred stock, based on its preferences, and, then, assigning the remaining amount of owners' equity to common stock. To illustrate, assume Bye Corporation had total owners' equity of $273,000; 1,000 shares outstanding of its 5 percent preferred stock, par $20, cumulative (no dividends in arrears for past years), and liquidation value of $22 per share; and 10,000 outstanding shares of common stock, par $10.

```
Allocation:
  Total owners' equity  ...................................          $273,000
  Less equity allocated to preferred stock:
    Liquidation value (1,000 shares × $22) .................  $22,000
    Cumulative dividend preference for the current year
      (1,000 shares × $20 × 5%) ..........................     1,000
  Amount allocated to preferred stock ....................                23,000
  Remainder allocated to common stock ...................            $250,000

Book value per share:
  Preferred, $23,000 ÷ 1,000 shares = $23
  Common, $250,000 ÷ 10,000 shares = $25
```

Book value per share has limited significance because it has no necessary relationship to market value. Because it is a low conservative amount (historical cost basis), some persons consider a market value below book value to imply underpriced shares.

INTERPRETING RATIOS

When using ratios computed by others, it is important to remember that the computation of a particular ratio is not standardized. Neither the accounting profession nor security analysts have prescribed the manner in which a ratio must be computed (except for earnings per share). Thus, users of financial statements should compute the various ratios in accordance with their decision objectives. As a consequence, before relying on a ratio or a series of ratios, the user should be informed as to the basic computational approach used. The discussions and illustrations in this section follow the approaches commonly used.

Ratio analysis is a useful technique; however, ratios pose significant interpretative problems to the user. To evaluate a ratio, it must be compared with some standard that represents an optimal or desirable level. For example, the return-on-investment ratio may be compared with a long-range objective expressed in this manner. Some ratios, by their characteristics, are unfavorable if they are **either** too high or too low. For example, analysis may indicate that a working capital ratio of approximately 2:1 may be considered optimal for a given company. In this situation, a ratio of 1:1 would tend to indicate a danger of being unable to meet maturing obligations, whereas, a ratio of 3:1 may indicate that excess funds are being left idle rather than being employed profitably. Furthermore, an optimal ratio for one company frequently will not be an optimal ratio for another company. Thus, comparisons of ratios among companies frequently are of questionable validity, particularly when there are important differences among the companies, such as industry and nature of operations.

Another limitation is that most ratios represent **averages** and, therefore, ratios may tend to obscure the underlying causative factors of large variations above and below the average. To illustrate, a working capital ratio of $2:1$ was considered optimal in the example above. But even an optimal working capital ratio may obscure a short-term liquidity problem if the company has a very large amount of inventory and a minimal amount of cash with which to pay obligations as they mature.

Despite certain limitations, ratio analysis is a useful analytical tool. Financial ratios have been shown to be particularly effective in predicting bankruptcy. Exhibit 16–5 presents the working capital ratio and the debt/equity ratio for Braniff International Corporation. Observe the deterioration of these ratios each year. In 1981, the independent auditor issued a qualified audit opinion and noted, "there are conditions which indicate that the company may be unable to continue as a going concern." In the spring of 1982, Braniff filed for bankruptcy. Analysts who studied the financial ratios each year probably were not surprised by the bankruptcy of Braniff.

EXHIBIT 16–5
Selected financial ratios for Braniff International

	1977	1978	1979	1980	1981
Working capital ratio	1.20	.91	.74	.60	.49
Debt/equity ratio	2.03	2.45	4.88	15.67	N/A*

* In 1981, Braniff reported negative owners' equity as the result of a large net loss that produced a negative balance in retained earnings. Creditors' equity exceeded **total** equities.

Financial analysts often use four types of "standards" against which ratios and percents are compared:

1. **Comparison of the ratios for the current year with the historical ratios for the same company**—Particular attention is given to the **trend** of each ratio over time.

2. **Comparison of the ratios for the current year with ratios of other companies for the same year**—These comparisons include the use of ratios and percents from other similar companies and from industry averages. Industry averages are published by many trade associations, governmental agencies, and others. For example, a variety of ratios can be found in the publications of Dun & Bradstreet, Inc., Moody's *Manual of Investments,* and Standard and Poor's *Corporation Records.*

3. **Experience of the analyst who has a subjective feel for the "right" relationships in a given situation**—These subjective judgments of an experienced and competent observer tend to be more reliable than purely mechanical comparisons.

4. **Comparison of the ratios for the current year with planned goals and objectives expressed as ratios**—Many companies prepare comprehensive profit plans (i.e., budgets) on a continuing basis that incorporate realistic plans for the future. These plans usually incorporate planned goals for significant ratios, such as profit margin, return on investment, and EPS. These internally developed standards clearly have less inherent difficulties than any of the other comparisons; however, they seldom are available to external parties.

SUMMARY OF CHAPTER

Interpretation of amounts reported on financial statements may be enhanced by expressing certain relationships as ratios or percents. Although many ratios can be calculated, a few usually will suffice for a given decision. Having selected the relevant ratios, the analyst has the central problem of evaluating the results. This evaluation involves the task of selecting one or more realistic standards with which to compare the results. Four types of standards frequently are used: (1) historical standards, (2) external standards, (3) experience, and (4) planned standards. Experience and competence are particularly important. The interpretation of ratios often may suggest strengths and weaknesses in the operations and/or the financial position of the company that should be accorded in-depth investigation and evaluation if significant decisions are contemplated.

IMPORTANT TERMS DEFINED IN THIS CHAPTER

Terms (alphabetically)	Key words in definitions of important terms used in chapter	Page references
Common ratios	Selected ratios that are used widely. Exhibit 16–3 presents a list of 13 commonly used accounting ratios.	757
Comparative statements	Financial statements for several years, amounts are presented side by side for comparative purposes.	753
Component percentages	A percentage that expresses each item on a particular financial statement as a percent of a single base amount.	754
Long-term summaries	Summaries of basic accounting data for many years (typically 10 years).	753
Market tests	Ratios that tend to measure the "market worth" of a share of stock.	764
Ratio analysis	An analytical tool designed to identify significant relationships; measures proportional relationship between two financial statement amounts.	754
Tests of liquidity	Ratios that measure a company's ability to meet its currently maturing obligations.	760
Tests of solvency	Ratios that measure a company's ability to meet its long-term obligations.	763

QUESTIONS FOR DISCUSSION

1. What are the three fundamental uses of external financial statements by decision makers?

2. What are some of the primary items on financial statements about which creditors usually are concerned?

3. Explain why the notes to the financial statements are particularly important to decision makers.

4. What is the primary purpose of comparative financial statements?

5. Why are statement users especially interested in financial summaries covering several years? What is the primary limitation of long-term summaries?

6. What is ratio analysis? Why is ratio analysis useful?

7. What are component percentages? Why are component percentages useful?

8. Explain the two concepts of return on investment.

9. What is financial leverage? How is financial leverage measured?

10. Is profit margin a useful measure of profitability? Explain.

11. Compare the working capital ratio with the quick ratio.

12. What does the debt/equity ratio reflect?

13. Explain what is meant by "market tests."

14. What are the primary problems when using ratios?

EXERCISES

E16–1. The comparative financial statements prepared at December 31, 19B, for Doan Company reflected the following summarized data:

	19B	19A
Income statement:		
Sales revenue	$150,000*	$140,000*
Cost of goods sold	90,000	85,000
Gross margin	60,000	55,000
Operating expenses and interest expense	43,000	40,500
Pretax income	17,000	14,500
Income tax	5,000	4,500
Net income	$ 12,000	$ 10,000
Balance sheet:		
Cash	$ 8,000	$ 11,000
Accounts receivable (net)	12,000	14,000
Inventory	30,000	28,000
Operational assets (net)	50,000	43,000
	$100,000	$ 96,000
Current liabilities (no interest)	$ 15,000	$ 17,000
Long-term liabilities (10% interest)	35,000	35,000
Common stock (par $10)	40,000	40,000
Retained earnings†	10,000	4,000
	$100,000	$ 96,000

* One third were credit sales.
† During 19B, cash dividends amounting to $6,000 were declared and paid.

Required:

a. Complete the following columns for each item in the above comparative financial statements:

Increase (decrease)	
19B over 19A	
Amount	*Percent*

b. Respond to the following questions:
   (1) Compute the percentage increases in sales revenue, net income, cash, inventory, liabilities, and owners' equity.

(2) By what amount did working capital change?
(3) What was the percentage change in the average income tax rate?
(4) What was the amount of cash inflow from revenues for 19B?
(5) By what percent did the average markup realized on goods sold change?
(6) By how much did the book value per share change?

E16–2. Use the data given in Exercise 16–1 for Doan Company.

Required:

a. Present component percentages for 19B only.
b. Respond to the following questions for 19B:
    (1) What was the average percentage markup on sales?
    (2) What was the average income tax rate?
    (3) Compute the profit margin. Was it a good or poor indicator of performance? Explain.
    (4) What percent of total resources was invested in operational assets?
    (5) Compute the debt/equity ratio. Does it look good or bad? Explain.
    (6) What was the return on owners' investment?
    (7) What was the return on total investment?
    (8) Compute the financial leverage percent. Was it positive or negative? Explain.
    (9) What was the book value per share of common stock?

E16–3. Use the data given in Exercise 16–1 for Doan Company. Use a separate sheet and complete the following tabulation for 19B only (assume a common stock price of $33 per share); compute the ratios that usually are included under each category:

Name and Computation of the Ratio (show computations)	Brief Explanation of the Ratio

A. **Tests of profitability:**
   1. Return on owners' investment
   2. Etc.	

B. **Tests of liquidity:**
   1. Working capital ratio
   2. Etc.	

C. **Tests of solvency and equity position:**
   1. Debt/equity ratio
   2. Etc.	

D. **Market tests:**
   1. Price/earnings ratio
   2. Etc.	

E. **Miscellaneous ratio:** 1. Book value per share	

E16–4. Match the following by entering the appropriate letters in the blanks.

Ratio or percent	Computation
1. _____ Profit margin	A. Income (before extraordinary items) ÷ Net sales.
2. _____ Inventory turnover ratio	B. Days in year ÷ Receivable turnover.
3. _____ Average collection period	C. Income ÷ Average owners' equity.
4. _____ Creditors' equity to total equities	D. Income ÷ Average number of shares of common stock outstanding.
5. _____ Dividend yield ratio	E. Return on owners' investment − Return on total investment.
6. _____ Return on owners' investment	F. Quick assets ÷ Current liabilities.
7. _____ Working capital ratio	G. Current assets ÷ Current liabilities.
8. _____ Debt/equity ratio	H. Cost of goods sold ÷ Average inventory.
9. _____ Price/earnings ratio	I. Net credit sales ÷ Average net trade receivables.
10. _____ Financial leverage	J. Creditors' equity (debt) ÷ Total equities.
11. _____ Receivable turnover ratio	K. Days in year ÷ Inventory turnover.
12. _____ Average days' supply of inventory	L. Total liabilities ÷ Owners' equity.
13. _____ Owners' equity to total equities	M. Dividends per share ÷ Market price per share.
14. _____ Earnings per share	N. Owners' equity ÷ Total equities.
15. _____ Return on total investment	O. Current market price per share ÷ Earnings per share.
16. _____ Quick ratio	P. Owners' equity ÷ Shares outstanding.
17. _____ Book value per share	Q. Income + Interest expense (net of tax) ÷ Total assets.

E16–5. Situation A—Current assets totaled to $60,000, and the working capital ratio was 2.00. Assume the following transactions were completed: (1) purchased merchandise for $3,000 of which one third was on short-term credit; and (2) purchased a delivery truck for $8,000, paid $2,000 cash and signed a two-year interest-bearing note for the balance. Compute the cumulative working capital ratio after each transaction.

Situation B—Sales for the year amounted to $600,000 of which one half was on credit. The average gross margin rate was 40 percent on sales. Account balances were:

	Beginning	Ending
Accounts receivable (net)	$30,000	$20,000
Inventory	20,000	16,000

Compute the turnover for the accounts receivable and inventory, the average age of the receivables and the average days' supply of inventory.

Situation C—The financial statements reported the following at year-end:

Total assets	$100,000
Total debt (10% interest)	60,000
Net income (average tax rate 20%).....	12,000

Compute the financial leverage and indicate whether it was positive or negative.

E16–6. Ryan Retail Company has just prepared the comparative annual financial statements for 19B given below:

RYAN RETAIL COMPANY
Income Statement
For the Years Ended December 31, 19B, and 19A

		For the year ended	
		19B	19A
Sales revenue (one half on credit)		$100,000	$ 95,000
Cost of goods sold		48,000	46,000
Gross margin		52,000	49,000
Expenses (including $3,000 interest expense each year)		34,000	33,000
Pretax income		18,000	16,000
Income tax on operations (22%)		3,960	3,520
Income before extraordinary items		14,040	12,480
Extraordinary loss.........................	$3,000		
Less income tax saved	660	2,340	
Extraordinary gain			$1,000
Applicable income tax			220	780
Net income		$ 11,700	$ 13,260

RYAN RETAIL COMPANY
Balance Sheet
At December 31, 19B, and 19A

	19B	19A
Assets		
Cash	$ 47,200	$ 20,000
Accounts receivable (net) (terms 1/10, n/30)	35,000	30,000
Inventory	30,000	40,000
Operational assets (net)	90,000	100,000
Total assets	$202,200	$190,000
Liabilities		
Accounts payable	$ 60,000	$ 50,000
Income tax payable.......................................	1,500	1,000
Note payable, long term	25,000	25,000
Stockholders' Equity		
Capital stock, par $10	80,000	80,000
Retained earnings	35,700	34,000
Total liabilities and stockholders' equity	$202,200	$190,000

Required (round percents and ratios to two places):

a. Compute for 19B the tests of (1) profitability, (2) liquidity, (3) solvency, and (4) market. Assume the quoted price of the stock was $26.50 for 19B. Dividends declared and paid during 19B amounted to $10,000.

b. Respond to the following for 19B:

(1) Compute the percentage changes in sales, income before extraordinary items, net income, cash, inventory, and debt.

(2) What appears to be the pretax interest rate on the note payable?

c. Identify at least two problems facing the company that are suggested by your responses to (a) and (b).

PROBLEMS/CASES

PC16–1. Peterson Corporation has just completed its comparative statements for the year ended December 31, 19B. At this point, certain analytical and interpretative procedures are to be undertaken. The completed statements (summarized) are as follows:

	19B	19A
Income statement:		
Sales revenue	$400,000*	$390,000*
Cost of goods sold	220,000	218,000
Gross margin	180,000	172,000
Operating expenses (including interest on bonds)	147,000	148,000
Pretax income	33,000	24,000
Income tax	9,000	7,000
Net income	$ 24,000	$ 17,000
Balance sheet:		
Cash	$ 5,400	$ 2,700
Accounts receivable (net)	44,000	30,000
Merchandise inventory	30,000	24,000
Prepaid expenses	600	500
Operational assets (net)	120,000	130,000
	$200,000	$187,200
Accounts payable	$ 19,000	$ 20,000
Income tax payable	1,000	1,200
Bonds payable (10% interest rate)	50,000	50,000
Common stock, par $10	100,000†	100,000
Retained earnings	30,000‡	16,000
	$200,000	$187,200

* Twenty-five percent were credit sales.
† The market price of the stock at the end of 19B was $24 per share.
‡ During 19B, the company declared and paid a cash dividend of $10,000.

Required:

a. Complete a tabulation similar to the following (show computations, round percents and ratios to two places):

Name and Computation of the 19B Ratio	Brief Explanation of the Ratio
Tests of profitability: 1. Return on owners' investment. 2. Etc.	
Tests of liquidity: 1. Working capital ratio. 2. Etc.	
Tests of solvency and equity position: 1. Debt/equity ratio. 2. Etc.	
Market tests: 1. Price/earnings ratio. 2. Etc.	

b. Respond to the following questions for 19B:
   (1) Evaluate the financial leverage amount and explain what it means by using the computed amount(s).
   (2) Evaluate the profit margin amount and explain how a stockholder might use it.
   (3) Explain to a stockholder why the working capital ratio and the quick ratio are different. Do you observe any liquidity problems? Explain.
   (4) Assuming credit terms are 1/10, n/30, do you perceive an unfavorable situation for the company related to credit sales? Explain.

PC16–2. The following information was contained in the annual financial statements of Taterwood Company, that started business January 1, 19A (assume account balances only in Cash and Capital Stock on this date; all amounts are in thousands of dollars).

	19A	19B	19C	19D
Accounts receivable (net) (terms, n/30).....	$ 8	$10	$ 16	$ 22
Merchandise inventory..................	10	12	20	25
Net sales (¾ on credit)	40	60	100	120
Cost of goods sold	26	36	64	80
Net income (loss).......................	(10)	6	14	10

Required (show computations and round to two decimal places):

a. Complete the tabulation given below.
b. Evaluate the results of the three related ratios 1, 2, and 3, to identify the favorable or unfavorable factors. Give your recommendations to improve Taterwood's operations.
c. Evaluate the results of the last four ratios (4, 5, 6, and 7) and identify any favorable or unfavorable factors. Give your recommendations to improve Taterwood's operations.

Items	19A	19B	19C	19D
1. Profit margin—percent.				
2. Gross margin—ratio.				
3. Expenses as a percent of sales, excluding cost of goods sold.				
4. Inventory turnover.				
5. Days' supply in inventory.				
6. Receivable turnover.				
7. Average days to collect.				

PC16–3. The 19B financial statements for Able and Baker companies are summarized below:

	Able Company	Baker Company
Balance sheet:		
Cash	$ 25,000	$ 11,000
Accounts receivable, net	30,000	17,000
Inventory	80,000	20,000
Operational assets, net	125,000	300,000
Other assets	40,000	252,000
Total assets	$300,000	$600,000
Current liabilities	$ 90,000	$ 40,000
Long-term debt (10%)	50,000	60,000
Capital stock, par $10	120,000	400,000
Contributed capital in excess of par	10,000	60,000
Retained earnings	30,000	40,000
Total liabilities and stockholders' equity	$300,000	$600,000
Income statement:		
Sales revenue (on credit) .... ($\frac{1}{3}$)	$600,000 ($\frac{1}{9}$)	$900,000
Cost of goods sold	(350,000)	(450,000)
Expenses (including interest and income tax)	(205,000)	(360,000)
Net income	$ 45,000	$ 90,000
Selected data from the 19A statements:		
Accounts receivable, net	$ 25,000	$ 19,000
Inventory	70,000	24,000
Long-term debt	50,000	60,000
Other data:		
Per share price at end of 19B (offering price)	$ 30	$ 18
Average income tax rate	30%	30%
Dividends declared and paid in 19B	$ 25,800	$150,400

Able and Baker companies are in the same line of business and are direct competitors in a large metropolitan area. They have been in business approximately 10 years, and each has experienced a relatively steady growth. The two managements have essentially different viewpoints in many respects; however, Baker is considered to be the more conservative and, as the president said, "We avoid what we consider to be undue risks." Neither company is publicly held. Able Company has an annual audit by a CPA but Baker Company does not.

Required:

a. Complete a schedule that reflects a ratio analysis of each company. As a minimum, compute the 13 ratios discussed in the chapter.

b. Assume a client of yours has the opportunity to purchase 10 percent of the shares in one or the other company at the per share prices given above. Your client has decided to invest in one of the companies. Based on the data given, prepare a comparative evaluation of the ratio analyses (and any other available information) and give your recommended choice with the supporting explanation.

PC16–4. The 19B financial statements for Doe and Roe companies are summarized below:

	Doe Company	Roe Company
Balance sheet:		
Cash	$ 20,000	$ 40,000
Accounts receivable, net	60,000	10,000
Inventory	120,000	30,000
Operational assets, net	500,000	150,000
Other assets	155,000	54,000
Total	$855,000	$284,000
Current liabilities	$100,000	$ 20,000
Long-term debt (10%)	200,000	50,000
Capital stock, par $10	500,000	200,000
Contributed capital in excess of par	25,000	2,000
Retained earnings	30,000	12,000
Total	$855,000	$284,000
Income statement:		
Sales revenue (on credit)	(½) $900,000	(⅓) $300,000
Cost of goods sold	(522,000)	(180,000)
Expenses (including interest and income tax)	(288,000)	(84,000)
Net income	$ 90,000	$ 36,000
Selected data from the 19A statements:		
Accounts receivable, net	$ 40,000	$ 14,000
Long-term debt (10% interest)	200,000	50,000
Inventory	100,000	40,000
Other data:		
Per share price at end of 19B	$ 12.75	$ 10.50
Average income tax rate	30%	20%
Dividends declared and paid in 19B	$ 40,000	$ 10,000

These two companies are in the same line of business and in the same state but in different cities. Each company has been in existence for approximately 10 years. Doe Company is audited by one of the "Big-8" accounting firms and Roe Company is audited by a local accounting firm. Both companies received an unqualified opinion (i.e., the independent auditors found nothing wrong) on the financial statements. Doe Company wants to borrow $75,000 cash, and Roe Company needs $30,000. The loans will be for a two-year period and are needed for "working capital purposes."

Required:

a. Complete a schedule that reflects a ratio analysis of each company. As a minimum compute the ratios discussed in the chapter.

b. Assume you work in the loan department of a local bank. You have been asked to analyze the situation and recommend which loan is preferable. Based on the data given, your analysis prepared in *(a),* and any other information, give your choice and the supporting explanation.

PC16–5. Refer to the financial statements of Johnson & Johnson, given in Special Supplement B immediately preceding the Index.

Required:

a. Compute each of the 13 accounting ratios (for 1982) listed in Exhibit 16–3. If you are unable to compute a particular ratio, explain why. Assume the current stock price is $45 per share.

b. Evaluate the ratios and identify any potential problems that you think exist. Comment on any suggestions you may have for management.

PC16–6. The following information was contained in the actual financial statements of a large manufacturing company which currently is listed on The New York Stock Exchange:

Balance Sheet

	December 31 (millions of dollars)	
	19B	*19A*
Assets		
Current Assets		
Cash	$ 188.2	$ 123.2
Time deposits	120.8	248.8
Marketable securities	165.3	150.8
Accounts receivable (less allowance for doubtful accounts: 19B—$34.9 million; 19A—$16.7 million)	610.3	848.0
Inventories—at the lower of cost (substantially FIFO) or market	1,873.8	1,980.8
Prepaid insurance, taxes and other expenses	162.3	210.2
Total Current Assets	3,120.7	3,561.8
Total Investments and Other Assets	1,183.5	1,396.5
Property, Plant and Equipment		
Land, buildings, machinery, and equipment	3,733.1	3,391.3
Less accumulated depreciation	2,097.1	1,963.9
	1,636.0	1,427.4
Special tools	712.9	595.5
Net Property, Plant and Equipment	2,348.9	2,022.9
Total Assets	$ 6,653.1	$ 6,981.2
Liabilities and Stockholders' Investment		
Current Liabilities		
Accounts payable	$ 1,530.4	$ 1,725.0
Accrued expenses	807.9	698.0
Short-term debt	600.9	49.2
Payments due within one year on long-term debt	275.6	12.4
Taxes on income	16.8	1.2
Total Current Liabilities	3,231.6	2,485.8
Total Long-term Debt and Other Liabilities	1,559.1	1,564.1
Minority interest in consolidated subsidiaries	38.3	4.8
Preferred stock—nopar value	218.7	217.0
Common stock—par value $6.25 per share	416.9	397.7
Additional paid-in capital	692.2	683.1
Net earnings retained	496.3	1,628.7
Total Liabilities and Stockholders' Investment	$ 6,653.1	$ 6,981.2

Income Statement

| | Year Ended December 31 (In millions of dollars) | |
	19B	19A
Net sales	$12,004.3	$13,669.8
Cost of goods sold	11,631.5	12,640.1
Depreciation of plant and equipment	180.6	154.0
Amortization of special tools	220.0	198.2
Selling and administrative expenses	598.5	572.1
Pension plans	260.6	262.3
Interest expense	215.4	128.9
	13,106.6	13,955.6
Loss Before Taxes on Income	(1,102.3)	(285.8)
Taxes on income (credit)	(5.0)	(81.2)
Net Loss	$ (1,097.3)	$ (204.6)

Required:

a. Calculate the following ratios:
   (1) Return on owners' investment.
   (2) Return on total investment.
       (For purposes of this case, assume that the interest expense reported on the income statement is net of income taxes.)
   (3) Financial leverage.
   (4) Earnings per share.
   (5) Working capital ratio.
   (6) Quick ratio.
   (7) Inventory turnover.
   (8) Debt/equity ratio.

b. Based on your analysis of the ratios that you calculated in Requirement *(a),* do you think that this company will be able to continue in existence? Explain. Would you be willing to invest in this company? Explain.

PC16–7. Aggressive Company uses the FIFO method to cost inventory and Conservative Company uses the LIFO method. The two companies are exactly alike except for the difference in inventory costing methods. Costs of inventory items for both companies have been rising steadily in recent years and each company has increased its inventory each year. Each company has paid its tax liability in full for the current year (and all previous years), and each company uses the same accounting methods for both financial reporting and income tax reporting. Identify which company will report the higher amount for each of the following ratios. If it is not possible, explain why.

a. Working capital ratio.
b. Quick ratio.
c. Debt/equity ratio.
d. Return on owners' investment.
e. Earnings per share.

PC16–8. Fast Company uses the sum-of-years'-digits method to depreciate its property, plant, and equipment and Slow Company uses the straight-line method. Both companies use 175 percent declining balance depreciation for income tax purposes. The two companies are exactly alike except for the difference in depreciation methods.

Required:

a. Identify the financial ratios discussed in Chapter 16 that are **likely** to be affected by the difference in depreciation methods.

b. Which company will report the higher amount for each ratio that you have identified? If you cannot be certain, explain why.

PC16–9. Nearly Broke Company requested a sizable loan from Second City National Bank in order to acquire a large tract of land for future expansion. Nearly Broke reported current assets of $1,750,000 ($475,000 in cash) and current liabilities of $975,000. Second City denied the loan request for a number of reasons including the fact that the working capital ratio was below two to one. When Nearly Broke was informed of the loan denial, the comptroller of the company immediately paid $470,000 that was owed to several trade creditors. The comptroller then asked Second City to reconsider the loan application. Based on these abbreviated facts, would you recommend that Second City approve the loan request? Why?

Financial Reporting and Changing Prices

PURPOSE OF THIS CHAPTER

In recent years the economy of the United States (and practically all other countries) has been affected significantly by increasing prices of most commodities and services. This fact has important, and often adverse, effects on most people because the price increases are not uniform among different goods, services, and individuals. Therefore, some groups suffer more from inflation than other groups. Also, measurements of economic events in terms of the monetary unit (dollars in the United States) become distorted. For example, from 1967 to 1982, the dollar declined in **purchasing power** (i.e., its command over real goods and services) by approximately 185 percent; that is, in 1982, it required almost three dollars to purchase what one dollar would have purchased in 1967.

The rapid and continuing increase in prices has caused most users of financial statements to question the dollar measurements of assets, liabilities, revenues, and expenses reported in the traditional historical cost (HC) financial statements. In periods of inflation, HC financial statements typically aggregate amounts that include dollars of different purchasing power. This aggregation of "apples and oranges" tends to produce unrealistic measurements of accounting values.

For financial accounting purposes two distinctly different kinds of price changes usually are identified, viz:

1. **General price level changes**—These price level changes occur when the **average** level of the prices of commodities and services changes; that is, the purchasing power (i.e., the command over goods and services) of the monetary unit changes. Such changes are called **inflation** when the general price level increases (i.e., the purchasing power of the monetary unit decreases) and **deflation** when the general price level decreases (i.e., the purchasing power of the monetary unit increases). Part A discusses general price level (GPL) changes.
2. **Specific price level changes**—These price level changes occur when the price of a **specific** commodity or service changes. Such changes cause **real value changes** if the rate of specific price level change is different than the rate of general price level changes. Part B of this chapter discusses current cost (CC), which involves the reporting of real value changes.

To discuss these issues, this chapter is divided as follows:

Part A—Reporting the effects of general price level (GPL) changes

Part B—Reporting the effects of current cost (CC) changes

PART A—REPORTING THE EFFECTS OF GENERAL PRICE LEVEL (GPL) CHANGES

The impact of inflation upon HC financial statements is difficult to assess by statement users, particularly when the related price change information is not reported. Accountants, economists, and persons in business and government are not in agreement as to what should be done to make the financial statements more useful under conditions of significant price changes.

First, we will consider general price level changes. Reporting the effects of general price level (GPL) changes on financial statements requires that the traditional historical cost (HC) financial statements be **restated** from the HC basis to the latest GPL dollars, usually called **constant dollars.** This restatement requires use of general price level (GPL) index numbers.[1] The resulting financial statements are known as **constant dollar** (CD) financial statements.

USING PRICE LEVEL INDEX NUMBERS

Price level index numbers may be used to restate HC financial statement amounts for price changes. A **price level index** is a statistical value that expresses the relative price level of each of a series of periods. To construct a price level index, the prices of one specific item, or a group of items, for a number of periods are expressed in relative terms as a series of index numbers. A base year is selected and assigned the base index value of 100. Subsequent changes in prices are expressed in relation to this base. Two kinds of indexes are used widely:

1. **General price level (GPL) index**—A GPL price index is computed on the basis of an **average** "market basket" of commodities and services.[2] An average index is computed by collecting the prices of each of the many items that make up the average market basket. Each period the average price of the basket is computed and then related to the base year index of 100. A GPL index is intended to measure **general inflation** (cheaper dollars) and **general deflation** (more expensive dollars). A GPL index is used in accounting to measure the effects of general price level (GPL) changes and to restate the HC financial statements to the latest (constant dollar) (CD) basis. To illustrate, assume a tract of land was purchased in 1967 at a cost of $10,000 when the GPL index was 100. Assume that at the end of the current year, the land is still owned, and the GPL index is 280. The $10,000 cost of the land would be reported on a CD restated balance sheet at $10,000 × 280/100 = $28,000. The GPL increase was $18,000 (i.e., $28,000 − $10,000).

---

[1] Throughout this chapter the descriptive term **restated** is used because the HC basis amounts simply are restated to current GPL or constant dollars. Alternatively, the term **adjusted** sometimes is used. It is less descriptive and suggests the notion of "adjusting" entries, which is based on a completely different concept.

[2] The two GPL series usually used are the Gross National Product Deflator (which is published quarterly) and the Consumer Price Index for all Urban Consumers (CPI-U) which is published monthly). Both indexes are published by the U.S. Department of Labor. The CPI-U index is the more widely used index in accounting.

2. **Specific price level index**—A specific price level index is computed in the same manner as a GPL index except that it is related to a **single** item (or small group of homogeneous items). Specific price index values often are used to estimate the current replacement cost of **specific** commodities or services. To illustrate, assume the land example given in 1 above (HC, $10,000) had a specific price index of 120 when acquired in 1967 and has a specific price index of 240 at the end of the current year. The estimated current replacement cost of the land could be computed as $10,000 × 240/120 = $20,000. This computation indicates that the specific value of the land increased by $10,000, which was less than the GPL increase of $18,000. A specific price index does **not** measure **general** inflation; rather, it measures the change in price of the specific item to which it relates. Use of specific index numbers is illustrated in Part B of this chapter.

The pervasiveness of **general inflation** (i.e., as measured by a GPL index) in recent years is reflected in the index values from the Consumer Price Index for all Urban Consumers (CPI-U) presented in Exhibit 17–1.

EXHIBIT 17–1
Selected consumer price index values

	CPI-U index*	
Year	Average for the year	At year-end
1967 (base year)	100.0	101.6
1970	116.3	119.1
1971	121.3	123.1
1972	125.3	127.3
1973	133.1	138.5
1974	147.7	155.4
1975	161.2	166.3
1976	170.5	174.3
1977	181.5	186.1
1978	195.4	202.9
1979	217.4	229.9
1980	246.8	258.4
1981	272.4	281.5
1982	289.1	292.4

* Source: Economic Indicators Joint Economic Committee, U.S. Government Printing Office (monthly).

Another application of a GPL index may be illustrated by indicating the effect of general inflation on the cost of attending college. To illustrate, assume that in 1967 the average cost of attending "State University" for two semesters was $4,000 per student. Using the CPI-U index amounts given above, general inflation has increased the total cost as follows:

Year	CPI-U index (average)	Restatement computation	Average cost per student
1967	100.0		$4,000
1970	116.3	$4,000 × 116.3/100.0 =	4,652
1975	161.2	$4,000 × 161.2/100.0 =	6,448
1979	217.4	$4,000 × 217.4/100.0 =	8,696

THE STABLE MONETARY UNIT ASSUMPTION

One of the underlying assumptions of GAAP is the **unit-of-measure assumption** (Exhibit 2–6), which states that with many diverse items and transactions to be accounted for, it is necessary that a single unit of measure be adopted. Accounting assumes the U.S. monetary unit—the dollar—as the common denominator in the measurement process. Implicit in this assumption is that the dollar has a constant value, which is an important measurement characteristic (a "meter-stick" is always one meter long!). However, during a period of inflation or deflation, the constant value assumption is not valid; the monetary unit literally becomes a "rubber" measuring unit (it stretches and contracts) as the GPL changes.

The dollar is the common denominator used for accounting measurements because it is used by the society as a measure of value. That is, the dollar will command a certain amount of real goods and services in the marketplace at a given time. Unfortunately, the dollar (or any other currency) does not maintain a stable value in terms of the real goods and services it can command.

Over time, a single dollar will command fewer goods and services in the case of inflation or, alternatively, more goods and services in the case of deflation; that is, its purchasing power changes. As a result of using the historical cost principle, transactions are recorded in the accounts and reported subsequently on the financial statements in historical cost (HC) basis dollars. Some of those dollar amounts (such as the cost of an old operational asset) remain in the accounts and are reported in the financial statements over many years. Thus, over a period of time, the accounting system accumulates and reports dollars that have different purchasing power, given inflation or deflation. Under historical cost (HC) accounting, dollars having different real values are **aggregated** on the balance sheet and **matched** on the income statement. Thus, during periods of significant inflation or deflation, the accounting amounts are apt to reflect considerable distortion from current dollars because of the effects of the changing value of the monetary unit.

To illustrate this distortion, consider a company that purchased a building for $200,000 when the GPL index was 100. Assuming straight-line depreciation, no residual value, and a 40-year life, the annual depreciation would be $5,000 per year. Let's assume that the current year is Year 30 (since acquisition) and that the current GPL index is 300. At the end of Year 30, the financial statements would show the following amounts, based on historical cost (HC) as recorded in the accounting system:

Balance sheet:
Operational assets:
Building (at cost).............................. $200,000
Accumulated depreciation ($5,000 × 30 years)..... 150,000
Carrying value $50,000

Income statement:
Depreciation expense 5,000

All of the amounts shown above represent dollars "valued" at acquisition date (30 years earlier). Those dollars had a purchasing power equivalent of 100 (the

GPL index). With the current GPL index at 300, these amounts are aggregated with other dollar amounts that have different purchasing power equivalents. On the income statement, depreciation expense, expressed in dollars with one purchasing power (index 100) is matched with revenue, which is in current dollars with another purchasing power (index 300). The current GPL index of 300 means that each current dollar will command (buy) only one third (i.e., 100/300) as much **real** goods and services as when the index was 100. One could **restate** the above amounts to constant dollars for the GPL change (inflation in this case). The restatement can be accomplished by multiplying the HC amount by a CD index ratio in the following manner:

$$\text{Historical cost (HC) amount} \times \frac{\text{Current period GPL index}}{\text{Transaction date GPL index}} = \text{CD restated amount}$$

The calculations and the resulting CD restated amounts for the data given above would be as follows:

Item	HC basis	CD restatement computation		CD restated amount
Balance sheet amounts:				
Operational assets:				
Building	$200,000	× 300/100	=	$600,000
Accumulated depreciation	150,000	× 300/100	=	450,000
Carrying value	$ 50,000	× 300/100	=	$150,000
Income statement amount:				
Depreciation expense	$ 5,000	× 300/100	=	$ 15,000

CONCEPTS UNDERLYING CD RESTATEMENT OF FINANCIAL STATEMENTS

Constant dollar (CD) restatement of financial statements does not involve the recording of journal entries, rather it is a **supplementary reporting approach.** The traditional HC financial statements are prepared each period in accordance with GAAP. The HC statements continue as the basic periodic reports of the entity. When CD restatement is used, the HC basis financial statements simply are restated in current end-of-period dollars (i.e., in constant dollars). Thus, the CD restated financial statements continue to be cost basis statements except that all dollar amounts are in **constant dollars,** that is, dollars of constant purchasing power. The CD restatement computations are simple and straightforward; they involve the following three steps:

Step 1: Classify all accounts on the financial statements as either monetary or nonmonetary (defined later in the chapter). **Monetary** items are **not** restated on the CD financial statements while the **nonmonetary** items **are** restated. Exhibit 17–2 presents the classification of several accounts.

EXHIBIT 17–2
Classification of monetary and nonmonetary items

	Monetary	Nonmonetary
Assets		
Cash	X	
Marketable securities:		
Most common stock		X
Most bonds	X	
Accounts and notes receivable	X	
Allowance for doubtful accounts	X	
Inventories		X
Prepaid expense:		
Claims to future services		X
Prepayments that are deposits or advance payments	X	
Long-term receivables	X	
Property, plant, and equipment		X
Accumulated depreciation		X
Patents and trademarks		X
Goodwill		X
Liabilities		
Accounts and notes payable	X	
Accrued expenses	X	
Cash dividends payable	X	
Bonds payable and other long-term debt	X	
Premium or discount on bonds payable	X	
Deferred income taxes	X	
Owners' equity		
Preferred stock (nonmonetary if not carried at a fixed redemption price)	X	
Common stock		X
Retained earnings		
This amount usually is restated as a plug or balancing amount		X

Source: Adapted from *FASB Statement 33*, "Financial Reporting and Changing Prices," (Stamford, Conn., September, 1979).

Step 2: Restate each **nonmonetary** item by multiplying its HC amount by the appropriate restatement ratio (i.e., the current period GPL index divided by the GPL index that existed at the date on which the transaction was recorded).

Step 3: Calculate the purchasing power gain or loss on monetary items. This gain or loss is measured as the difference between the HC amount and the CD restated amount for each monetary item. Each of these basic steps is discussed and illustrated in the remainder of this part of the chapter.

CD RESTATEMENT—ILLUSTRATIVE CASE

A simplified situation is used as the basis for discussing and illustrating the computations used to develop CD restated financial statements.

Assume ACE Corporation was organized December 31, 19A, when the GPL index was 120. The accounting period ends December 31, and the company prepares HC financial statements. Restatement of the HC financial statements of ACE Corporation to a CD restated basis is discussed and illustrated in the paragraphs to follow. Exhibit 17–3 presents the following data for ACE Corporation:

1. All transactions completed during 19A and 19B (summarized) and the GPL index at the date of each transaction.
2. Balance sheet at December 31, 19B (HC basis).
3. Income statement for the year ended December 31, 19B (HC basis).
4. Statement of retained earnings at December 31, 19B (HC basis).
5. Selected GPL index data.

Step 1—Identify monetary and nonmonetary items

Restatement of HC financial statements to a CD restated basis requires that a careful distinction be maintained between two distinctly different types of items on the financial statements. These two types are known as **monetary items** and **nonmonetary items.** They cause significantly different economic effects on their holder (owner) when the real value of the monetary unit (the dollar) changes (i.e., inflation or deflation occurs).

A **monetary item** is an item that by its nature or as the result of a contract is stated in a **fixed** number of dollars and the fixed number of dollars does not change in response to changes in price levels. Thus, monetary items include cash, payables, and receivables but would not include revenues or expenses. Because inflation does not affect the amount of cash or the number of dollars to be paid or received for monetary items, these items are **not restated** on CD financial statements.

While monetary items are not restated on CD financial statements, the **purchasing power** of monetary items is affected by inflation. Consider what would happen if you left $1,000 in your wallet during a year in which the inflation rate was 20 percent. At the end of the year, you could buy less real goods and services with the $1,000 than you could have purchased at the beginning of the year. Your loss of purchasing power on this **asset** amounted to $200 [i.e., $1,000 − ($1,000 × 120/100)]. This $200 loss is called a purchasing power loss on monetary items.

In contrast, if you held monetary **liabilities** during a period of inflation, you would experience a purchasing power gain on monetary items because the liabilities will be paid in dollars that have less purchasing power than the dollars that were borrowed. In other words, a dollar owed through a period of inflation is still a dollar owed, although it will command fewer real goods at the end of the period.

In summary, monetary items (i.e., monetary assets and monetary liabilities) are not restated on the CD financial statements but their existence can cause the holder (or debtor) to incur a real gain or loss during each period of inflation. A purchasing power **gain** on net monetary items is reported (on the CD financial statements) if the purchasing power gain on monetary liabilities is more than the purchasing power loss on monetary assets. Alternatively, a purchasing power

EXHIBIT 17–3
Historical cost and GPL data of ACE Corporation

Summary of transactions:
Year 19A:
 a. December 31, 19A: Sold and issued capital stock (nopar) for $80,000 cash (GPL index, 120).
 b. December 31, 19A: Borrowed $40,000 cash from a local bank; signed a $40,000 interest-bearing note due December 31, 19C (GPL index, 120).
 c. December 31, 19A: Purchased equipment for use in the business at a cash cost of $60,000 (GPL index, 120).

Year 19B:
 d. March 19B: Purchased land for use in the business at a cash cost of $6,350 (GPL index, 127).
 e. During 19B: Purchased merchandise (evenly throughout the year) at a cash cost of $121,500 (average GPL index for 19B, 135). Assume a perpetual inventory system (average costing), cost of goods sold, $108,000, and an ending inventory of $13,500 (i.e., total, $121,500).
 f. During 19B: Sales revenue, $162,000, sold evenly throughout the year (average GPL index for 19B, 135). Assume total cash collections on sales of $129,600 and accounts receivable at year-end of $32,400 (i.e., total, $162,000).
 g. During 19B: Expenses paid in cash $27,000, which included interest expense and income tax expense, but excluded depreciation expense (average GPL index for 19B, 135).
 h. July 1, 19B: Declared and paid a cash dividend, $2,700 (GPL average index, 135).
 i. December 31, 19B: Depreciation expense on equipment (estimated five-year life and no residual value), $60,000 ÷ 5 years = $12,000.

Balance sheet, at December 31, 19B (HC basis amounts):

Assets		Liabilities	
Cash	$32,050	Note payable, long term	$ 40,000
Accounts receivable (net)	32,400		
Inventory	13,500	**Stockholders' Equity**	
Equipment	60,000	Capital stock (nopar)	80,000
Accumulated depreciation	(12,000)	Retained earnings	12,300
Land	6,350		
Total	$132,300	Total	$132,300

Income statement, for the year ended December 31, 19B (HC basis amounts):

Sales revenue	$ 162,000
Cost of goods sold	(108,000)
Depreciation expense	(12,000)
Remaining expenses	(27,000)
Net income	$ 15,000

Statement of retained earnings, at December 31, 19B (HC basis amounts):

Beginning balance, January 1, 19B	$ –0–
Add: Net income of 19B	15,000
Deduct: Dividends of 19B	(2,700)
Ending balance, December 31, 19B	$12,300

GPL index data

December 31, 19A	120
January 1, 19B	120
Average during 19B	135
December 31, 19B	150

loss is reported if the purchasing power loss on monetary assets is more than the purchasing power gain on monetary liabilities.

Observe in Exhibit 17–4 that the three monetary items (cash, accounts receivable, and note payable) are not restated in the CD financial statements. However, a purchasing power loss on monetary items of $5,050 is reported on the CD income statement (this loss is computed in Exhibit 17–5).

EXHIBIT 17–4
CD restatement of financial statements, ACE Corporation, year end 19B

Items	HC Basis	CD Restatement Computations	CD Restated Basis
Balance sheet, at December 31, 19B: **Assets**			
Cash	$ 32,050	Monetary, not restated	$ 32,050
Accounts receivable (net)	32,400	Monetary, not restated	32,400
Inventory	13,500	Nonmonetary, $13,500 × 150/135	15,000
Equipment	60,000	Nonmonetary, $60,000 × 150/120	75,000
Accumulated depreciation (credit)	(12,000)	Nonmonetary, $12,000 × 150/120	(15,000)
Land	6,350	Nonmonetary, $6,350 × 150/127	7,500
Total	$ 132,300		$ 146,950
Liabilities			
Note Payable, long term	$ 40,000	Monetary, not restated	$ 40,000
Stockholders' Equity			
Capital stock, nopar	80,000	Nonmonetary, $80,000 × 150/120	100,000
Retained earnings	12,300	Nonmonetary, plug, $146,950 − $40,000 − $100,000	6,950
Total	$ 132,300		$ 146,950
Income statement, for the year ended December 31, 19B:			
Sales revenue	$ 162,000	Nonmonetary, $162,000 × 150/135	$ 180,000
Deduct:			
Cost of goods sold	(108,000)	Nonmonetary, $108,000 × 150/135	(120,000)
Depreciation expense	(12,000)	Nonmonetary, $12,000 × 150/120	(15,000)
Remaining expenses	(27,000)	Nonmonetary, $27,000 × 150/135	(30,000)
Income from normal operations	$ 15,000		$ 15,000
Purchasing power gain (loss) on monetary items		Computed, per Exhibit 17–5	(5,050)
Income, CD restated (common dollar)		Carry to statement of retained earnings	$ 9,950
Statement of retained earnings, at December 31, 19B			
Beginning balance, January 1, 19B	$ –0–	Nonmonetary	$ –0–
Add: Income of 19B	15,000	Nonmonetary, from restated income statement	9,950
Deduct: Dividends of 19B (debit)	(2,700)	Nonmonetary, $2,700 × 150/135	(3,000)
Ending balance, December 31, 19B	$ 12,300	Proof: check per balance sheet plug amount	$ 6,950

EXHIBIT 17–5
Computation of the purchasing power gain (loss) on net monetary items,—ACE Corporation, year end 19B

Items	HC Basis	CD Restatement Computations	CD Restated Basis	Purchasing Power Gain (Loss) on Net Monetary Items
Cash: [a]				
Beginning balance	$ 60,000	$ 60,000 × 150/120	$ 75,000	
Debits:				
Sales and accounts receivable	129,600	129,600 × 150/135	144,000	
Credits:				
Purchase of land	(6,350)	6,350 × 150/127	(7,500)	
Merchandise, expenses, and dividends ($121,500 + $27,000 + $2,700)	(151,200)	151,200 × 150/135	(168,000)	
Ending balance	$ 32,050		$ 43,500	$(11,450)
Accounts receivable: [b]				
Ending balance	$ 32,400	32,400 × 150/135	$ 36,000	(3,600)
Note payable: [c]				
Beginning balance	$ 40,000	40,000 × 150/120	$ 50,000	10,000
Purchasing power net gain (loss) on net monetary items (to income statement)				$ (5,050)

Explanation:
[a] Restatement of an account that has several changes during the period at **different** GPL ratios requires restatement of each increase and decrease separately. Thus, the beginning balance and each change (grouped by GPL index numbers) are restated.

[b] Accounts receivable can be restated in this case on the basis of the ending balance because (1) there was no beginning balance and (2) the increases and decreases during the year were at the average GPL index (135).

[c] Note payable can be restated in this case on the basis of the beginning balance because there were no increases or decreases in the account during the year (the beginning balance was recorded on December 31, 19A, when the GPL index was 120).

Nonmonetary items include all items on the financial statement except for the monetary assets and liabilities. The basic characteristic of nonmonetary items is that they have dollar amounts that are **not** fixed in the future by their nature or by contract. The value of nonmonetary items in the market place tend to move up and down with inflation and deflation. For example, a tract of land purchased for $6,350 (see Exhibit 17–3) when the GPL index was 127 would **tend** to increase in market value to $7,500 as a result of an increase of the GPL price index to 150 (i.e., $6,350 × 150/127 = $7,500). If this happened, the owner would not experience a real gain on this nonmonetary asset due to general inflation. The owner would not experience a real gain because, if the land that cost $6,350 could be sold for $7,500, the $7,500 would purchase (at the date of sale of the land) the same quantity of real goods and services that the $6,350 would have bought when the owner originally purchased the land. Of course, the land may have changed in "dollar value" more or less than the GPL, in which case there would have been a real value change (this situation is discussed later). Examples of nonmonetary items are inventories, investments in common stock, operational assets, patents, revenues, expenses, and the common stock accounts.[3]

In summary, nonmonetary items are restated on the CD financial statements, and they do not cause the holder to incur a real gain or loss as a result of changes only in the GPL.

Step 2—CD restatement of HC financial statements.

Now, let's return to our illustration of ACE Corporation and the three HC basis financial statements given in Exhibit 17–3. CD restatement of each HC financial statement in terms of the current GPL index of 150 is shown in Exhibit 17–4.

Restatement of the balance sheet. The ACE Corporation balance sheet reflects three monetary items: cash, accounts receivable, and the note payable. As explained above, these three **monetary items** were not restated because each has a fixed monetary amount in the future that is not affected by inflation or deflation. Therefore, the three monetary HC amounts were extended across on the balance sheet to the CD restatement column. In contrast, the four nonmonetary asset amounts on the balance sheet were CD restated because their market prices are free to change as a result of changes in the general price level.

Observe in Exhibit 17–4 that 10 **nonmonetary items** are restated on the CD balance sheet and income statement. Also, observe that any real gain or loss on the **nonmonetary** items is not reported on the CD financial statements (see Part B of this chapter).

Exhibit 17–4 presents the CD restatement computation for each nonmonetary item. For example, the Land account was restated as follows:

$$\begin{array}{c}\text{Historical cost}\\\text{(HC) basis}\\\text{amount}\end{array} \times \frac{\text{Current period GPL index}}{\text{Transaction date GPL index}} = \begin{array}{c}\text{CD}\\\text{restated}\\\text{amount}\end{array}$$

$$\text{Land, \$6,350} \times \frac{150}{127} = \$7,500$$

Restatement of the income statement. All items on the income statement are **nonmonetary;** therefore, each item is restated. The numerator of the GPL restatement ratio is the ending GPL index, and the denominator usually is the average GPL index for the current period because it is assumed often that price changes and business transactions occurred evenly throughout the period. Observe that depreciation expense always is restated by using the same GPL index amounts

---

[3] Preferred stock usually is classified as a monetary item because it usually has a fixed redeemable value. In contrast, receivables and liabilities which can be settled with goods and services (rather than cash) are classified as nonmonetary items.

used to restate the related asset (150/120 in the illustration). The only unique feature of the income statement is inclusion of the "Purchasing power gain (loss) on monetary items." This **gain or loss** must be computed separately on the monetary assets and monetary liabilities as illustrated in Step 3 (Exhibit 17–5).

Step 3—
Computation of
the purchasing
power gain or
loss on net
monetary items

Computation of the purchasing power gain or loss requires restatement of each monetary asset and each monetary liability. Often this is the most tedious phase of CD restatement. Monetary items that have identical numerator indexes and identical denominator indexes can be grouped for computation purposes with the same results.

Computation of the purchasing power gain (loss) on the monetary items for ACE Corporation is illustrated in Exhibit 17–5. Observe in this exhibit that the HC amount of each monetary item (first money column) is CD restated by using the appropriate numerator and denominator indexes. The net gain or loss on each monetary item simply is the difference between its **ending** actual HC basis amount and its **ending** CD restated amount (i.e., for cash, $32,050 − $43,500 = $11,450 loss).

The restatement of monetary items is tedious because the beginning balance of the account as well as each transaction that affects the account must be restated with the appropriate GPL indexes. We reemphasize that **monetary** items are restated **only** for purposes of calculating the purchasing power gain or loss on net monetary items; they are **not** restated on the balance sheet.

The total purchasing power gain (loss) on monetary items ($5,050) is the algebraic sum of the purchasing power **losses on monetary assets** and the purchasing power **gains on monetary liabilities.** In the illustration, the $5,050 is a loss during a period of inflation because the monetary assets exceeded the monetary liabilities (in the opposite case, there would have been a gain). This amount is carried to the income statement (as illustrated in Exhibit 17–4) because it represents an economic (purchasing power) gain or loss.

In summary, CD restated financial statements are prepared by restating the **nonmonetary** HC-items on the balance sheet, income statement, and statement of retained earnings. The monetary items are included in the CD financial statements at their HC basis amounts. However, the **monetary** assets and liabilities are restated separately to compute the purchasing power gain or loss on monetary items, which is reported on the income statement. The CD restated net income is carried to the CD statement of retained earnings, and the CD restated ending balance of retained earnings is reported on the CD balance sheet.[4]

---

[4] In view of CD restatement on the balance sheet of only the nonmonetary items (not the monetary items), the question always arises as to why a CD balance sheet "balances." Technically, the reason is that the monetary assets and monetary liabilities are not restated on the balance sheet, but total **owners' equity** is restated. Therefore, the residual, owners' equity $(A - L = OE)$ **includes** a restatement amount for **both** the nonmonetary and monetary items. Inclusion of the purchasing power gain (loss) on monetary items on the income statement (and hence in retained earnings on the balance sheet) provides the mathematically necessary amount to bring the equation $A - L = OE$ into balance on the CD restated balance sheet.

OVERVIEW OF CD EFFECTS

A comparison of the two balance sheets presented in Exhibit 17–4 shows that the CD restatement increased total assets from $132,300 to $146,950 which was an 11.1 percent increase. In contrast, the income statement reflected a decrease in reported income of $15,000 to $9,950 which was a 34 percent decrease. When there is an inflationary trend, and the relationship between monetary assets and monetary liabilities remains essentially constant, **CD restated income** usually will be lower than the cost basis amount, primarily because of higher restated assets and correspondingly higher restated depreciation expense.

Having presented the concept and related procedures to derive CD restated financial statements, let's examine them in overall perspective. The HC basis financial statements rest on the unit-of-measure assumption (Chapter 2), which holds that each transaction should be measured in those dollars that "existed" at the date of each transaction. In the case of GPL changes (i.e., inflation or deflation), the HC financial statements comingle dollars that have different amounts of purchasing power. In contrast, the concept of CD restated financial statements retains the HC amounts except that they are restated in constant dollars. That is, the HC amounts are restated for the effects of changes in the purchasing power of the monetary unit (inflation or deflation) that have occurred since each transaction was recorded. This means that all nonmonetary HC dollar amounts (but not the monetary amounts) reflected in the HC statements are restated to constant (current) dollars, each having equivalent purchasing power. The CD restated income statement reports a new type of gain or loss: purchasing power gain or loss on monetary items.

Those who advocate the concept of CD restatement contend that two sets of financial statements should be presented: (1) one set prepared on the traditional HC basis, and (2) another set prepared on the CD restated basis. The primary **arguments for** presenting CD restated financial statements are (1) during periods of significant inflation or deflation, HC basis statements contain serious measurement distortions that are not presented; (2) the CD restated amounts, including the purchasing power gain or loss on monetary items, are relevant to the users of financial statements; and (3) the HC approach essentially is retained with all amounts stated in terms of dollars of the same purchasing power. In contrast, the primary **arguments against** CD restated statements are (1) two sets of financial statements (restated and not restated) potentially can confuse statement users, (2) it is difficult to justify a particular GPL price index to use for restatement purposes, (3) statement users do not find the restated amounts to be particularly useful, and (4) GPL effects and real value changes on **nonmonetary** items are not revealed separately (discussed in Part B).

The Financial Accounting Standards Board (FASB) issued *Statement of Financial Accounting Standards No. 33*, "Financial Reporting and Changing Prices," in September 1979. This **Statement,** which applied only to very large companies, states that

> for fiscal years ended on or after December 25, 1979, enterprises are required to report:

    a. Income from continuing operations adjusted for the effects of general inflation.

    b. The purchasing power gain or loss on monetary items.[5]

These minimum requirements usually are met by including the two required amounts in the notes to the financial statements. *FASB Statement 33* does not require a complete set of CD restated financial statements, although complete and comprehensive CD reporting (as illustrated on Exhibit 17–4) is to be encouraged.

PART B—REPORTING CURRENT COST CHANGES

Accounting academicians and professional accountants long have discussed the concept of reporting **current values** rather than HC basis amounts on the financial statements. The primary argument in favor of reporting current values is that statement users (investors, creditors, and others) are more interested in the "worth" of the assets at the date of the financial statements than in the HC amounts now reported under GAAP. The acceptance of current value accounting has been slow because opinions vary as to exactly what current value means and how it should be measured. Two basic implementation approaches are under consideration:

1. Report **current value** amounts in the financial statements instead of HC amounts. This view is that current value would be a substitute for, and not be supplementary information to, the traditional HC statements. A second view, which prevails currently, is that two different sets of financial statements should be presented each period: *(a)* one set on the traditional HC basis and *(b)* another set on the current value basis.
2. Report both current value and constant dollar in **combination.** In effect, under this approach, current values are restated so that both current value and GPL effects are reported.

In the discussions to follow, the **combination reporting approach** is assumed because it provides considerable information on both current value and GPL effects. This reporting approach usually is called the current cost/constant dollar (CC/CD) approach.

DEFINITION OF CURRENT VALUE IN FINANCIAL REPORTING

The term **current value,** as used in financial reporting, is a general term that encompasses three different concepts of value; that is the:

1. **Present value**—This value represents the present value of the expected net future cash inflow attributable to an **asset** (such as inventories, equipment, and land). This concept of the valuation of an asset was discussed briefly in Part B of Chapter 10. The expected net future cash inflows are discounted to the present at an appropriate interest rate. Conceptually, this approach is

---

[5] *FASB Statement 33,* "Financial Reporting and Changing Prices" (Stamford, Conn., September 1979).

superior to HC or CD; however, it is not used widely to determine "current value" in financial statements because of uncertainty in *(a)* projecting the future net cash inflow by period, and *(b)* selecting an appropriate discount rate.

2. **Net realizable value**—The net realizable value of an asset is the expected price at which the asset could be sold in its present condition, less all disposal costs. This concept of valuing an asset was discussed in Part B of Chapter 7 in respect to inventories. This method of asset valuation is used in circumstances in which current cost cannot be determined reasonably by other approaches.[6]

3. **Current cost (CC)**—The current replacement cost of an asset at the current balance sheet date is the cost of replacing the asset in its present operating condition with an identical asset. Estimating the CC of some assets (such as a plant, because there seldom is an established market for a one-of-a-kind plant) is a complex problem. For operational assets current cost often is defined as the resources required to acquire the same "service potential" as the old asset. In contrast, CC may be estimated reasonably for some assets, such as merchandise inventory, because there is an established market. For inventory, CC is defined as the resources that currently would be required to purchase or produce the goods held. Primary sources for estimating CC are current price lists, prices in established markets for used items, specific price indexes, and professional appraisals.

CONCEPTS UNDERLYING CC/CD FINANCIAL REPORTING

CC/CD financial reporting does **not** require the recording of CC/CD valuations in the accounts, although many accountants view it as a full-blown accounting and reporting method to replace the current GAAP historical cost valuation model. The discussions and illustrations that follow assume that HC basis financial statements will be reported and that CC/CD financial statements will be prepared for supplementary reporting purposes without entering the CC/CD values in the accounts.

When CC/CD financial statements are prepared, the HC amounts are converted to CC/CD amounts. Primarily, CC/CD reporting involves changes in the **nonmonetary** asset and income statement amounts. For **monetary items,** the HC carrying amounts and CC/CD carrying amounts usually will be the same. Preparation of CC/CD financial statements involves the following steps:

Step 1. At the end of each accounting period a **CC valuation** is derived for each nonmonetary financial statement amount by using current price lists, prices for comparable used assets, specific price indexes, and professional appraisals.

Step 2. On the CC/CD balance sheet, the **monetary** items are not changed from the HC amounts. The **nonmonetary** amounts are changed from the

---

[6] *FASB Statement 33* specifies that current cost cannot exceed net realizable value for financial statement reporting purposes.

HC to CC amounts and are reported on the CC/CD balance sheet in constant dollars.

Step 3. On the CC/CD income statement, revenues are reported at their HC amounts restated for the GPL change that occurred during the year. Expenses are reported at their CC amounts expressed in constant dollars.

Step 4. A new item, "CC/CD real holding gain (loss) on **nonmonetary** items," is computed and reported on the income statement. This holding gain (loss), on nonmonetary items, is the difference between the CD restated HC amounts and the CC amounts (on both the balance sheet and income statement). Thus, it is the total amount that the items changed because CC at the end of the period was different from the CD restated HC amounts. These gains and losses usually are aggregated and then reported on the income statement as a single amount.[7] CC/CD reporting restates those CC amounts that are not already in constant end-of-period dollars. This combination approach has the distinct advantage of reporting both CC and GPL effects; therefore, it is discussed and illustrated in the next section.[8]

CC/CD FINANCIAL REPORTING—ILLUSTRATIVE CASE

The simplified situation of ACE Corporation used in Part A will be continued for the CC/CD illustrations and discussions in this part of the chapter. The HC financial statements were shown in Exhibit 17–3.

Step 1— Determine current cost data

The first step in developing CC/CD financial statements is to determine current cost data for each **nonmonetary** item. CC amounts for ACE Corporation are given in Exhibit 17–6.

Step 2— Determine balance sheet changes

Exhibit 17–7 presents the *(a)* HC financial statements (as illustrated previously in Exhibit 17–3) and *(b)* converted CC/CD financial statements. The basis used to determine each CC amount also is shown in Exhibit 17–7. In particular, note the following: (1) the difference between the CC treatment of monetary and nonmonetary items, (2) the several approaches used to determine the CC values of the nonmonetary items (e.g., specific indexes and appraisals), and (3) restatement of all items in year-end constant dollars (e.g., capital stock, revenue, and expenses).

In Exhibit 17–7, the monetary assets (cash and accounts receivable) were reported at their HC carrying values because HC and CC are the same (they already are expressed in constant dollars). Inventory, equipment, and accumulated depreciation were CC valued (in constant dollars) by using specific price indexes at year-end; and land was CC valued by year-end appraisal (in constant dollars). The monetary liabilities were reported at their HC carrying values, which are the same as CC (they already are expressed in constant dollars). The capital

---

[7] This amount can be separated into two amounts: (1) unrealized, which relates to assets still owned, and (2) realized, which relates to assets sold during the period.

[8] Another variation of CC reporting does not include the CD feature.

EXHIBIT 17–6
Current cost/
constant dollar data
for ACE
Corporation

Item	Current Cost Determination*	CC Valuation Amount (in Constant Dollars at Dec. 31, 19B)
Ending inventory, December 31, 19B	The specific price index at year's end of the inventory, based on CC, was 120 percent of HC. $13,500 × 1.20 =	16,200
Equipment	The specific price index at year's end of the equipment, based on estimated current cost in present condition, was 130 percent of HC. $60,000 × 1.30 =	78,000
Accumulated depreciation, equipment	The equipment has a five-year useful life, no residual value, and is being depreciated on a straight-line basis. At the end of 19B, CC accumulated depreciation is one fifth of the CC amount for equipment: $78,000 × $\frac{1}{5}$ =	15,600
Depreciation expense	The CC amount for this expense is determined by applying the depreciation rate (one fifth) to the **average** CC amount for equipment during the year 19B and restating the result to end-of-period constant dollars: $\left(\frac{\$60,000 + \$78,000}{2}\right) \times \frac{1}{5} \times \frac{150}{135} =$	15,330
Land	Professionally appraised at year's end	6,985
Cost of goods sold	The average specific price index, based on the current cost when the goods were sold, was 108 percent of HC. $108,000 × 1.08 × 150/135	129,600
Remaining expenses	HC average and CC average were the same for the year. $27,000 × 150/135 =	30,000

* For GPL data, refer to Exhibits 17–3 and 17–4.

stock account at HC is the same as CC, but it must be CD restated to express it in constant dollars.

Step 3—
Determine
income
statement
changes

On the CC/CD income statement, HC sales revenue is CD restated to express it in constant dollars at year-end. CC/CD cost of goods sold was determined by using the average CC specific price index (108) when the goods were sold; the CC then is expressed in year-end constant dollars by using the ending GPL index of 150 and the average GPL index of 135. CC/CD depreciation expense was determined by multiplying the CC of equipment by the depreciation rate and then restating the result in year-end constant dollars.

EXHIBIT 17–7   **Current cost (in constant dollars) financial statements, ACE Corporation, end of Year 19B**

Items	HC Basis	CC/CD Basis of Determination	CC/CD Amount
Balance sheet, at December 31, 19B:			
Assets			
Cash	$ 32,050	Monetary—HC and CC are the same	$ 32,050
Accounts receivable (net)	32,400	Monetary—HC is net realizable value	32,400
Inventory	13,500	× specific price index (at year's end), 1.20	16,200
Equipment	60,000	× specific price index (at year's end), 1.30	78,000
Accumulated depreciation (credit)	(12,000)	× specific price index (at year's end), 1.30	(15,600)
Land	5,350	Per professional appraisal (in constant dollars)	6,985
Total	$132,300		$150,035
Liabilities			
Note payable, long term	$ 40,000	Monetary—HC and CC are the same	$ 40,000
Stockholders' Equity			
Capital stock (nopar)	80,000	× GPL index, 150/120 (to restate in constant dollars)	100,000
Retained earnings	12,300	To balance (plug) $150,035 − $40,000 − $100,000	10,035
Total	$132,300		$150,035
Income statement, for the year ended December 31, 19B:			
Sales revenue (credit)	$162,000	× GPL index, 150/135 (to restate in constant dollars)	$180,000
Deduct:			
Cost of goods sold (debit)	(108,000)	× specific price index, 1.08 × 150/135 (to restate in constant dollars)	(129,600)
Depreciation expense (debit)	(12,000)	Calculated by applying depreciation rate to average CC of equipment $$\frac{\$60,000 + \$78,000}{2} \times \frac{1}{5} \times \frac{150}{135}$$	(15,330)*
Remaining expenses (debit)	(27,000)	× GPL index, 150/135 (to restate in constant dollars)	(30,000)
Income from operations	$ 15,000		5,070
Purchasing power gain (loss) on net monetary items (Exhibit 17–5)			(5,050)
CC real holding gain (loss) on non-monetary items (Exhibit 17–8)			13,015
CC/CD income			$13,035
Statement of retained earnings, at December 31, 19B:			
Beginning balance	$ –0–		$ –0–
Add: Income of 19B	15,000	Per income statement	13,035
Deduct: Dividends of 19B	(2,700)	× GPL index, 150/135 (to restate in constant dollars)	(3,000)
Ending balance, December 31, 19B	$ 12,300	Carried to balance sheet	$ 10,035

* This solution follows FASB 33. Note that accumulated depreciation and depreciation expense for this first year are different by $270. We believe a conceptually preferable approach would reflect the same amount for the increase in accumulated depreciation and depreciation expense. This approach would increase the CC real holding gain on nonmonetary items by $270.

**Step 4—
Determine real
holding gain
(loss) on
nonmonetary
items**

The CC/CD income statement, after "Income from operations," is completed by entering the two different **real gains or losses;** one is based on the **monetary items** and the other is based on **nonmonetary items,** viz:

1. Purchasing power gain (loss) on monetary items, ($5,050)—this real gain or loss occurs when monetary items are held during a period of inflation or deflation. It is the same calculation that was discussed and illustrated in Part A (Exhibit 17–5).
2. CC real holding gain (loss) on nonmonetary items, $13,015—this real gain or loss occurs when nonmonetary assets that are still owned at the end of the period and expenses of the period change in dollar value at a rate more or less than the inflation rate. Computation of this amount is illustrated in Exhibit 17–8.

Computation of CC **real holding** gains and losses on **nonmonetary** items (Exhibit 17–8) is based on the conceptual differences between **GPL fictional changes** and **CC real value changes,** viz:

1. **GPL fictional changes on nonmonetary items** are differences between the HC amounts and the CD amounts. These differences are **not real value changes** because they represent only the number of dollars required to exactly keep even with general inflation (GPL).
2. **CC real holding gains (losses) on nonmonetary items** are differences between CC amounts and the related CD restated amounts. These differences represent **real value changes** because they measure the extent to which CC changed more (or less) than the general inflation rate.

To illustrate these concepts, the 19B ending inventory in Exhibit 17–6 was reported as follows: HC, $13,500; and CC, $16,200. The total price difference between these two amounts, $2,700, represents the effects of two different kinds of price changes:

1. GPL fictional change:
    CD, restated, $15,000 − HC, $13,500 = $1,500 GPL fictional gain
2. CC real holding gain:
    CC, $16,200 − CD restated, $15,000 = $\underline{1,200}$ CC real holding gain
    Total price change .... $\underline{\underline{\$2,700}}$

The above analysis may be presented graphically as follows:

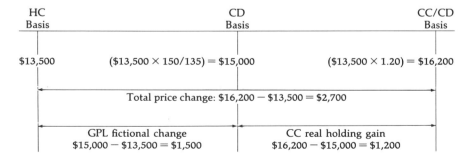

(Check: $1,500 + $1,200 = $2,700)

EXHIBIT 17-8　　Computation of CC real holding gains (losses) on nonmonetary items, ACE Corporation

	HC Basis	CD Restated Basis (See Exhibit 17-2)		CC/CD Basis		Total Change HC to CC	GPL Fiction Change Gain (Loss)	CC Real Holding Gain (Loss)
	A	B		C		C − A	B − A	C − B
Nonmonetary assets:								
Inventory	$ 13,500	A × 150/135	$ 15,000	A × 1.20	$ 16,200	$ 2,700	$ 1,500	$ 1,200
Equipment	60,000	A × 150/120	75,000	A × 1.30	78,000	18,000	15,000	3,000
Accumulated depreciation (credit)	(12,000)	A × 150/120	(15,000)	A × 1.30	(15,600)	(3,600)	(3,000)	(600)
Land	6,350	A × 150/127	7,500	Appraisal	6,985	635	1,150	(515)
Operations:								
Sales revenue (credit)	(162,000)	A × 150/135	(180,000)	A × 150/135*	(180,000)	(18,000)	(18,000)	-0-
Deduct:								
Cost of goods sold	108,000	A × 150/135	120,000	A × 1.08 × 150/135†	129,600	21,600	12,000	9,600
Depreciation expense	12,000	A × 150/120	15,000	From Exhibit 17-7	15,330	3,330	3,000	330
Remaining expenses	27,000	A × 150/135	30,000	A × 150/135*	30,000	3,000	3,000	-0-
Totals	$ 52,850		$ 67,500		$ 80,515	$27,665	$14,650	$13,015

* No CC change specified in the problem; to convert to constant dollars.

† Observe that the related assets (e.g., inventory and equipment) are "CC valued" at the year's end specific index, while the expenses (i.e., cost of goods sold, depreciation expense, etc.) are "CC valued" at the average specific index when incurred and then are CD restated to year-end.

While the computation of the CC real holding gain or loss on **nonmonetary** items (Exhibit 17–8) looks complicated, remember that it is based on the simple concept presented in the graph on page 798. In Exhibit 17–8, the nonmonetary items are listed at their HC amounts in Column A. Following the concepts diagrammed on page 798, the CD restated HC amounts are computed in Column B and the CC/CD amounts are computed in Column C.

The remaining columns in Exhibit 17–8 reflect the differences caused by the price changes of each item—total change, GPL fictional, and CC real holding gains and losses. In particular, observe that the **CC real holding gain (loss) on nonmonetary items** (the last column) is the difference between the CC/CD amounts and the CD restated HC amounts. The CC real holding gain (loss) on nonmonetary items is reported on the CC/CD income statement (Exhibit 17–7). The GPL fictional gain (loss) (the fifth column) is not reported separately on the CC/CD financial statements because the GPL effects are included in the various nonmonetary CC amounts. Therefore, the fourth and fifth columns in Exhibit 17–8 (i.e., the total and fictional changes) do not have to be computed to develop the CC/CD financial statements (however, preparing a the last three columns provides a valuable check of the last column).

OVERVIEW OF CC/CD EFFECTS

Now that you understand the "content" of the three different sets of financial statements—HC, CD restated, and CC/CD—it is appropriate to view them in the perspective of the needs of investors, creditors, and other users of such statements, given the expectation of continuation of the current inflationary trend.

HC financial statements often are distorted during periods of significant inflation because the measuring unit (the dollar in our case) declines in purchasing power. Large changes in purchasing power result in aggregating dollars with different values (in terms of purchasing power) in the financial statements. This "adding of apples and oranges" is not very meaningful for measuring financial results. Simply stated, **HC reporting disregards both GPL and CC effects.** On the other hand, HC reporting is quite **objective** because the HC dollars recorded are those established by transactions between two or more parties with different economic interests (i.e., the buyer is motivated to buy low while the seller is motivated to sell high, and they strike a bargain).

CD restated financial statements (in contrast to HC statements) attempt to report the effects of inflation and deflation by restating the HC amounts in terms of the current GPL (i.e., in constant dollars). CD restatement retains the HC model; however, it adds two features that the HC model does not incorporate: (1) restatement of the HC amounts to constant dollars and (2) measurement of the real purchasing power gains and losses on monetary items held during periods of inflation and deflation. Thus, it fulfills its objective to resolve one of the deficiencies of HC reporting (i.e., the changing value of the measurement unit). However, it does not report CC effects. Also, some people argue that CD restated financial statements necessitate two separate sets of financial statements (e.g.,

HC and CD, restated). The basic argument against the two sets of financial statements is that the decision makers would be confused by an "information overload."

CC/CD financial statements attempt to correct the two basic deficiencies of HC financial statements—the GPL and CC effects. CC/CD financial statements attempt to do this by (1) reporting all amounts at their current CC values and (2) expressing the CC values in terms of constant dollars.[9] The conceptual objective of CC/CD reporting is simple: to tell decision makers the current "worth" of each item reported. This objective is important because decision makers necessarily base their decisions on (1) the current situation and (2) their predictions about the future. For example, a person considering the purchase of a 20-year-old office building would be concerned primarily about (1) its value today and (2) its potential to generate net cash inflows during the expected holding period. The fact that it cost a certain amount 20 years earlier, or that its current HC book value is another amount, should be of little, or no, concern to the potential buyer.

Although CC/CD conceptually is an ideal financial reporting model, it has a significant implementation problem; that is, attaining objectivity and accuracy in determining the CC of each item at the end of each accounting period. This burden of attaining objective measurement of CC values is not easy to resolve. Of course, it may be relatively easy in some situations but extremely difficult in others. If it can be resolved so that CC values are reasonably accurate and believable, the CC/CD model should replace both HC and CD restated financial statements.

REPORTING THE EFFECTS OF CHANGING PRICES

Recent financial statements of most large companies have reported the effects of changing prices in a manner similar to the discussions and illustrations in this chapter. Exhibit 17–9 presents an example of the supplemental disclosure required by *FASB Statement 33*. Observe that balance sheet and income statement data are presented under the three different approaches discussed in the chapter: (1) historical cost, (2) constant dollar, and (3) current cost.

The supplemental disclosure presented in Exhibit 17–9 provides decision makers with important insights concerning how a company is affected by inflation. Analysts often calculate the accounting ratios discussed in Chapter 16 under each accounting approach shown in Exhibit 17–9.

---

[9] *FASB Statement 33* specifies that the GPL (constant dollars) may be expressed as (1) at year-end or (2) the average for the year.

EXHIBIT 17–9   Reporting the effects of changing prices,—Gulf & Western Industries

Note O—Supplemental Information on the Effects of Inflation and Changing Prices (Unaudited)

In a limited attempt to portray the effects of inflation, the Statement of Financial Accounting Standards No. 33 requires that companies give selected information under two different measurement approaches in addition to the information in the Company's financial statements, which statements are based on historical cost. These two approaches are referred to as (1) "Constant Dollar" and (2) "Current Cost."

Constant Dollar—This method adjusts inventories and property, plant and equipment and their related expenses, cost of goods sold and depreciation and depletion, upward by the amount of the increases in the rate of general inflation, as measured by the U.S. Consumer Price Index, subsequent to the dates of acquisition by the Company of these assets.

Current Cost—This method adjusts the same assets and their related expenses, cost of goods sold and depreciation and depletion, upward based on the estimated cost of assets at the latest balance sheet date. This method is based on use of current vendor quotations, production costs, appraisals and/or price indexes applicable to the Company's specific industries. Theatrical and television production inventories and related cost of sales, as well as the cost and related depletion of mineral resource assets have been adjusted using the Constant Dollar method only, and the resulting amounts have been included in both the Constant Dollar and Current Cost computations.

Under both methods, the adjusted amounts are stated in average dollars of purchasing power for the most recent year.

Both methods are experimental and neither method measures fully all of the complex effects of inflation. Therefore, the results shown under these supplemental computations are at best imprecise measurements of the effects of inflation and are not necessarily indicative of the present or future economic condition of the Company.

Adjusted "Constant Dollar" earnings from continuing operations of $42 million and adjusted "Current Cost" earnings from continuing operations of $28 million compare to reported earnings from continuing operations of $199 million, reflecting the increased cost of replacing assets during inflationary periods. This hypothetical decrease in net earnings from continuing operations is due to higher depreciation and depletion expense on property, plant and equipment and higher costs of inventories sold. Depreciation and depletion expense under both methods was based on the same methods and depreciable lives as used in the "As Reported" financial statements. Although these computations result in lower earnings from continuing operations before income taxes, the provision for income taxes was not adjusted since income taxes are based on historical costs. As a result, income tax expense increases, as a percent of earnings before income taxes, pointing out the higher real tax burden during times of inflation.

This decrease in earnings from continuing operations is substantially offset in the case of the Company by the gain from decline in purchasing power of net monetary items (primarily cash, receivables and payables). See below for discussion of the effect of inflation on monetary items.

Consolidated balance sheet information:

July 31, 1982	Historical Cost (As Reported)	Adjusted for	
		General Inflation (Constant Dollar)	Specific Cost Changes (Current Cost)
Monetary assets	$1,116	$1,083	$1,083
Inventories	1,309	1,367	1,388
Property, plant and equipment—net	1,316	2,227	2,752
Other non-monetary assets, less non-monetary liabilities	1,883	1,883	1,883
Monetary liabilities	(3,447)	(3,344)	(3,344)
Net assets (convertible preferred and common stockholders' equity)	$2,177	$3,216	$3,762
Net assets (convertible preferred and common stockholders' equity) per common share	$28.18	$42.22	$49.62

(Millions, Except Per Share)

As shown above, inflation generally causes an understatement of net asset values in the balance sheet based on historical costs. When prices are increasing, monetary assets lose purchasing power since a given number of dollars buys less at the end of a period, conversely, monetary liabilities gain purchasing power since dollars of a lesser value are used to pay them; and inventories and property, plant and equipment cost more to replace. Thus the net assets (convertible preferred and common stockholders' equity), in inflationary times, is understated in terms of current dollars.

During the 1982 fiscal year, inventories and property, plant and equipment held by the Company increased under the Constant Dollar method by approximately $110 million while the increase under the Current Cost method was approximately $104 million.

EXHIBIT 17–9 *(continued)*

Consolidated statement of earnings information:

Year Ended July 31, 1982	Historical Cost (As Reported)	General Inflation (Constant Dollar)	Specific Cost Changes (Current Cost)
		(Millions, Except Per Share) Adjusted for	
Total income	$5,498	$5,498	$5,498
Expenses:			
Cost of goods sold (excluding depreciation and depletion)	$3,933	$4,016	$4,019
Selling, administrative and general expenses (excluding depreciation and depletion)	936	936	936
Depreciation and depletion	112	186	197
Interest expense—net	247	247	247
Minority interest	(4)	(4)	(4)
Provision for income taxes	75	75	75
	$5,299	$5,456	$5,470
Earnings from continuing operations	$ 199	$ 42	$ 28
Gain from decline in purchasing power		153	153
	$ 199	$ 195	$ 181
Earnings from continuing operations per share:			
Primary	$ 2.57	$ .47	$ .28
Fully diluted	2.43	.47	.28
Earnings from continuing operations per share (including gain from decline in purchasing power):			
Primary	$ 2.57	$ 2.52	$ 2.33
Fully diluted	2.43	2.38	2.20

Five Year Comparison of Selected Supplementary Financial Data Adjusted for Effects of Changing Prices:

In Average 1982 Dollars (except as reported amounts) Year Ended or at July 31	1982	1981	1980	1979	1978
As Reported:					
Net sales and other revenues	$5,331	$5,478	$5,126	$4,662	$3,780
Earnings from continuing operations	199	253	214	173	155
Earnings from continuing operations per share—fully diluted	2.43	3.01	2.63	2.06	1.85
Net assets (convertible preferred and common stockholders' equity)	2,177	2,179	1,666	1,479	1,341
Constant Dollar Information:					
Net sales and other revenues	5,311	5,933	6,184	6,381	5,675
Earnings from continuing operations (including gain from decline in purchasing power)	195	323	374		
Earnings from continuing operations per share (including gain from decline in purchasing power)	2.38	3.85	4.52		
Net assets (convertible preferred and common stockholders' equity)	3,216	3,737	3,022		

EXHIBIT 17–9 *(concluded)*

Five Year Comparison of Selected Supplementary Financial Data Adjusted for Effects of Changing Prices:

In Average 1982 Dollars (except as reported amounts)		(Dollars in Millions, Except Per Share)			
Year Ended or at July 31	1982	1981	1980	1979	1978
Current Cost Information:					
Earnings from continuing operations (including gain from decline in purchasing power)	181	307	343		
Earnings from continuing operations per share (including gain from decline in purchasing power)	2.20	3.66	4.15		
Net assets (convertible preferred and common stockholders' equity)	3,762	4,136	3,628		
Increase in general price level over (under) increase in the specific cost changes (current cost) of inventories and property, plant and equipment held during the year	6	39	(82)		
Other Information Adjusted for General Inflation:					
Gain from decline in purchasing power of net monetary items	153	273	361		
Cash dividends paid per common share:					
As reported	.75	.75	.638	.58	.536
In average 1982 constant dollars	.75	.81	.770	.79	.805
Market price per common share at year-end:					
As reported	11.50	18.75	17.50	13.00	11.30
In average 1982 constant dollars	11.15	19.37	20.02	16.83	16.28
Average consumer price index	283	262	235	207	189

IMPORTANT TERMS DEFINED IN THIS CHAPTER

Terms *(alphabetically)*	Key words in definitions of important terms used in chapter	Page reference
CD restatement	Restatement of financial statements to reflect general price level changes.	784
Constant dollars	Dollars with constant (or equal) purchasing power.	784
CPI-U	Consumer Price Index for All Urban Consumers; a measure of general inflation.	782
Current cost	The cost of replacing an asset in its present operating condition.	774
GPL index	Any price index which measures general inflation.	781
Monetary items	Cash or the obligation to pay or receive a fixed number of dollars (Exhibit 17–2).	786
Nonmonetary items	All items which are not properly classified as monetary items (Exhibit 17–2).	789
Purchasing power gain (or loss)	The gain or loss in purchasing power that results from holding monetary items during a period of inflation (or deflation).	791
Specific price index	Similar to a general price level index except that it is related to a single item (or a small group of homogeneous items).	782

QUESTIONS FOR DISCUSSION

PART A

1. Explain the difference between general price level changes and specific price level changes.

2. What is a price level index? Explain the difference between a general price level index and a specific price level index.

3. What happens to the "value" of a dollar during a period of inflation, and alternatively, during a period of deflation?

4. A tract of land was acquired for $15,000 when the GPL index was 150. Five years later the GPL index was 270. At what price would the land have to sell for the owner to keep up exactly with inflation? Explain.

5. Define monetary items and nonmonetary items. Give some examples of each. Explain why a careful distinction between monetary and nonmonetary items is essential when financial statements are restated on a CD basis.

6. At the beginning of the current period, the Land account reflected a balance of $18,000 (GPL index at acquisition date, 100), and the Note Payable account reflected no beginning balance but had an ending balance of $30,000 (GPL index at transaction date, 150). The GPL index at the end of the current period was 200. Compute the purchasing power gain (loss) on monetary items. Explain the nature of this gain or loss.

7. Items on the balance sheet may be either monetary or nonmonetary, while all items on the income statement are nonmonetary. Is this statement true or is it false? Explain why.

PART B

8. Briefly define each of the following concepts of "current value": (a) present value, (b) net realizable value, and (c) current cost (CC).

9. Are CC amounts usually entered into the journal and ledger? Explain.

10. Explain the nature and composition of the item "CC real holding gain (loss) on nonmonetary items." Contrast it with the "purchasing power gain (loss) on monetary items."

11. Contrast "GPL fictional changes" with "CC real value changes."

12. A tract of land was purchased at a cost of $10,000 when the GPL was 100. At the end of Year 5, the GPL was 240 and the appraised value of the land was $27,000. Prepare a diagram that exhibits the price change effects.

EXERCISES

PART A

E17–1. During 1967, a Quality Stereo set sold at $200. Assume that each year this particular set increased in price exactly the same as the changes in the GPL index.
However, in 1983 it sold at $495.

Required:

    a. What was the selling price in 1970, 1975, and 1978? Use the average CPI-U index values given in the chapter and round to the nearest dollar. Show computations.

    b. Analyze the change in price during 1983. Assume that the CPI-U for 1983 was 290.

E17–2. In 1964, Norwood Company purchased a plant site for $23,100. Immediately thereafter, construction of a plant building was started. The building was completed in January 1965, at a cost of $336,000. The building is being depreciated on a straight-line basis assuming an estimated useful life of 30 years and no residual value.

    Assume the GPL index in 1964 was 110, in 1965 it was 112, and at the end of 1984 it was 290.

Required:

    a. Complete a schedule similar to the following:

	Amount to be reported assuming	
	HC basis	*CD restated*
Balance sheet at December 31, 1984:		
Operational assets:		
Land		
Building		
Less accumulated depreciation (20 years)		
Income statement for 1984:		
Depreciation expense		

    Show your computations.

    b. Would the CD restatement affect income tax expense for the company? Explain. Do you think it should? Explain.

E17–3. The balance sheet for Fargo Company, prepared on the HC basis at December 31, 19F, has been completed. Supplemental statements are to be developed on a "CD restated basis." The following four items were selected from the balance sheet:

Items	HC basis (when acquired)	GPL index (when acquired or incurred)
Receivables	$69,000	115
Investment, common stock	42,000	105
Land, plant site	15,000	100
Payables	99,000	110

The GPL at the end of 19F was 120.

Required:

    a. Indicate which items are monetary and which are nonmonetary.

    b. Set up a schedule to derive the amount "CD restated basis" that should be shown on the supplementary CD balance sheet for each item. Show computations.

    c. Compute the purchasing power gain (loss) on monetary items that should be reported on the CD income statement. Show computations.

    d. Explain why certain items were omitted from your computation in *(c)*.

E17–4. The items listed below were taken from the December 31, 19A, balance sheet of Environmental Systems Company (HC basis). This date is the end of the first year of operations. The GPL index at January 1, 19A, was 200, and at December 31, 19A, it was 220.

	Debits	Credits	GPL index transaction date
Cash	$ 21,000		210†
Accounts receivable (net)	45,000		210†
Investments, common stock	12,000		215
Land	15,000		205
Equipment	100,000		200
Accumulated depreciation		$ 8,000	
Accounts payable		18,000	210†
Notes payable		43,000	200
Capital stock (nopar)		110,000	200
Retained earnings*		14,000	
	$193,000	$193,000	

* Cash dividends declared and paid on December 31, 19A, amounted to $5,000.
† Average.

Required:

a. Prepare a CD restated balance sheet. Use a format similar to Exhibit 17–4 and round all amounts to the nearest dollar.
b. What was the amount of CD restated income for 19A? Explain.
c. Compute the amount of CD restated income from normal operations assuming the purchasing power gain on monetary items is $2,014. Show how this gain was computed.

E17–5. At the end of 19A (the first year of operations), Strong Company prepared the summarized HC basis income statement shown below. At January 1, 19A, the GPL index was 220; and at December 31, 19A, it was 260.

STRONG COMPANY
Income Statement
For the Year Ended December 31, 19A

	Amount	GPL index at average transaction date
Sales revenue	$ 330,000	234
Cost of goods sold	(165,000)	234
Depreciation expense*	(11,000)	
Remaining expenses	(94,000)	230
Pretax income	60,000	
Income tax expense	(18,000)	260
Net income	$ 42,000	

* The related asset was acquired when the GPL index was 220.

Required:

a. Prepare a CD restated income statement. Use a format similar to Exhibit 17–4. The monetary items and their GPL indexes at transaction dates were: receivables, $32,000 (index 234), and liabilities, $16,000 (index 220). Round all amounts to the nearest dollar.
b. Prepare a CD restated statement of retained earnings assuming cash dividends of $4,000 were declared but not paid on December 31, 19A.

E17–6. This exercise illustrates computation of the purchasing power gains and losses on two monetary items in situations that involve numerous transactions during the period. At December 31, 19D, the following summary data were taken from the ledger:

	GPL at transaction date	Cash	Payable
Beginning balance	118	$ 30,000	$18,000
Purchased land	125		+12,000
Sales revenue	130	+150,000	
Borrowing on note	120	+60,000	+60,000
Payment	122	−15,000	−15,000
Payment	132	−42,000	−42,000
Expenses paid	130	−90,000	
Dividends paid	132	−10,000	
Equipment purchased	120	−80,000	
Payment	125		−13,000
Ending balance		$ 3,000	$20,000

Note: GPL index numbers: January 1, 19D, 118; December 31, 19D, 132.

Required:

Compute the purchasing power gain or loss on monetary items for each account (cash and payable) separately. Round all amounts to the nearest dollar.

PART B

E17–7. On January 1, 19A, Southwest Gas Company acquired a tract of land that cost $120,000 when the GPL was 120. Payment was made in cash, $50,000, plus a $70,000 three-year, interest-bearing note. One year later the note was still outstanding, and the GPL index was 150. The specific index, related to the land, was 100 at the beginning of 19A and was 140 at the end of 19A. The land and the note will be included on the December 31, 19A, CC/CD financial statements.

Required (show computations and round to the nearest dollar):

a. The CC/CD value for the land that should be reported on the 19A CC/CD balance sheet is $ _____ .
b. The purchasing power gain (loss) on the monetary liability which should be reported on the 19A CC/CD income statement is $ _____ .
c. The CC real holding gain (loss) on the nonmonetary asset that should be reported on the 19A CC/CD income statement is $ _____ .
d. The amount of the GPL fictional change on the land was $ _____ .
e. Diagram the above responses in respect to the land (not the note payable).

E17–8. On January 1, 19A, Davis Company purchased a machine (an operational asset) that cost $15,000. Cash paid was $10,000 and a $5,000, three-year, interest-bearing note was given to the seller. On January 1, 19A, the GPL index was 100. At the end of 19A, the Accumulated Depreciation account reflected $1,500 (i.e., straight-line depreciation; estimated life 10 years and no residual value). During 19A, the average GPL index was 115 and at the end of 19A the GPL index was 120. The specific price index for the machine was 110 at the beginning of 19A and 143 at the end of 19A. The machine, accumulated depreciation, and note payable will be reported on the 19A CC/CD financial statements.

Required (show computations and round to the nearest dollar):

a. Complete the following tabulation of the amounts that should be reported on the 19A financial statements:

Item	HC basis	CC/CD basis
Balance sheet:		
Machine		
Accumulated depreciation		
Note payable		
Income statement:		
Depreciation expense		

b. The purchasing power gain (loss) on monetary items that should be reported on the CC/CD income statement is $ _____ .

c. The CC real holding gain (loss) on nonmonetary items that should be reported on the income statement is $ _____ .

d. The amounts of the GPL fictional changes were:
   (1) Machinery, net, $ _____ .
   (2) Depreciation expense, $ _____ .

E17–9. Rose Company purchased merchandise for resale during 19A (the first year of operations) that cost $76,000. Payment was in cash except for an $11,400 ending balance in Accounts Payable. The purchases, and payments on accounts payable, occurred evenly throughout the year. The average GPL index for 19A was 190 and at the end of 19A it was 200.

The ending inventory was $15,200; therefore, cost of goods sold was $60,800. Current cost of the ending inventory was $17,000 and $68,000 for cost of goods sold (the CC cost of goods sold is based on the average cost during the year). Accounts payable, inventory, and cost of goods sold will be reported on the 19A CC/CD financial statements.

Required (show computations and round to the nearest dollar):

a. Complete the following tabulation of amounts that should be reported at the end of 19A:

Item	HC basis	CC/CD basis
Balance sheet:		
Inventory		
Accounts payable		
Income statement:		
Cost of goods sold		

b. The purchasing power gain (loss) on monetary items that should be reported on the CC/CD income statement is $ _____ .

c. The CC real holding gain (loss) on the nonmonetary items that should be reported on the CC/CD income statement is $ _____ .

d. The amounts of the GPL fictional changes were:
   (1) Inventory, $ _____ .
   (2) Cost of goods sold, $ _____ .

PROBLEMS/CASES

PART A

PC17–1. Gerald Company has prepared the annual HC basis financial statements at December 31, 19F. The company is considering the development of supplemental statements on the "CD restated basis." The following seven items were selected from the balance sheet:

Items	HC basis (when acquired)	GPL index (when acquired or incurred)
1. Cash:		
Beginning balance	$ 20,000	141.5
Debits	38,800	146*
Credits	(44,600)	147*
2. Merchandise inventory (average cost)	58,000	145
3. Accounts receivable, net	28,800	144*
4. Land (no changes during 19F)	12,000	100
5. Building, net (no changes during 19F)	157,500	105
6. Accounts payable	42,000	140*
7. Bonds payable (no changes during 19F)	88,000	110

At the end of 19F the price-level index was 150.
* Average GPL index for these items.

Required:

a. Group the above items into two categories: monetary and nonmonetary.
b. Set up a schedule and compute the amount "CD restated basis" that should be shown on the CD balance sheet for each of the items. Show calculations. Round to the nearest $100 in the restatement.
c. Set up a schedule and compute the purchasing power gain or loss on monetary items that will be shown on the CD restated income statement. Show calculations and round to the nearest $100.
d. Explain why some of the seven items were omitted from your computations in *(c)*.

PC17–2.   At the end of the first year of operations, DE Company prepared the following balance sheet and income statement (HC basis):

DE COMPANY
Balance Sheet
At December 31, 19A

Assets

Cash	$ 3,330
Accounts receivable (net)	5,650
Inventory	46,000
Operational assets (net)	55,000
Total	$109,980

Liabilities

Accounts payable	$ 3,480
Bonds payable	23,000

Stockholders' Equity

Capital stock (nopar)	66,000
Retained earnings	17,500
Total	$109,980

Income Statement
For the Year Ended December 31, 19A

Revenues	$ 69,000
Expenses (not detailed)	(46,000)
Depreciation expense	(5,500)
Net income	$ 17,500

	GPL (when acquired or incurred)
Items	
GPL at start of year—110	
GPL at end of year—120	
Cash (no beginning balance)	111*
Accounts receivable	113*
Inventory	115
Operational assets	110
Accounts payable	116
Bonds payable	115
Revenues	115*
Expenses	115*
Depreciation expense	110
Capital stock (nopar)	110

* Average GPL index for all items in the account.

Required:

a. Restate the income statement and balance sheet; use the following headings: (1) HC Basis, (2) Restatement Computations, and (3) CD Restated Basis. Round amounts to the nearest $10.

b. Explain why net income is different between the two statements; identify amounts.

c. Why were the nonmonetary items, but not the monetary, restated on the balance sheet?

d. Does the CD income statement better match expenses with revenues? Explain.

PC17–3. After operating for one year, DO Company completed the following income statement and balance sheet:

DO COMPANY
Balance Sheet
At December 31, 19A

Assets

Cash	$42,300*
Accounts receivable (net)	29,580
Long-term investment, common stock	7,400
Land	11,200
Plant	154,000
Accumulated depreciation	(14,000)
Total	$230,480

Liabilities

Accounts payable	$ 5,880
Bonds payable	28,000

Stockholders' Equity

Capital stock (nopar)	182,000
Retained earnings	14,600
Total	$230,480

Income Statement
For the Year Ended December 31, 19A

Revenues	$ 87,000
Expenses (not detailed)	(58,400)
Depreciation expense†	(14,000)
Net income	$ 14,600

* Beginning balance, $58,800 (GPL index, 140); debits $49,600 (GPL index, 148) credits, $66,100 (GPL index, 145.3).

† Depreciation is recorded on a straight-line basis; estimated life of the plant is 11 years and no residual value.

	Items	GPL (when acquired or incurred)

GPL index at start of year—140
GPL index at end of year—150
GPL index average for 19A—145
Cash .... * above
Accounts receivable .... 141†
Long-term investment purchased, common stock 148
Land purchased 140
Plant acquired 140
Accounts payable .... 147†
Bonds payable 140
Capital stock (nopar) 140
Revenues... 145†
Expenses .... 146†
Depreciation expense 140

† Average GPL for these amounts.

Required:

a. Restate the income statement and balance sheet with the following headings: (1) HC Basis, (2) Restatement Computations, and (3) CD Restated Basis. Round amounts to the nearest $10.
b. Explain why net income is different between the two statements; identify amounts.
c. Why were the nonmonetary items, but not the monetary, restated on the balance sheet?
d. Does the CD restated income statement better match expenses with revenues? Explain.

PC17–4. The transactions summarized below were completed by Sullins Company during its first year of operations. The accounting period ends December 31. The GPL index on January 1, 19A, was 100, on December 31, 19A, it was 144, and the average for the year was 120.

January 1, 19A: Issued 10,000 shares of capital stock (nopar) for $60,000 cash and borrowed $36,000 cash on a two-year, interest-bearing note (GPL index, 100).
February 1, 19A: Purchased equipment for use in the business, $75,000 cash (GPL index, 105).
During 19A: Purchased merchandise on credit (evenly throughout the year), $180,000 (GPL average index, 120).
During 19A: Sales revenue (evenly throughout the year), $300,000, all cash (GPL average index, 120).
During 19A: Paid expenses (evenly throughout the year), $80,000 (GPL average index, 120); includes all expenses except depreciation expense.
During 19A: Paid accounts payable, $161,200 (GPL average index on payments, 124).
December 1, 19A: Declared and paid a cash dividend of $6,900 (GPL index, 138).
December 31, 19A: Depreciation on equipment based on estimated life of 10 years and a $5,000 residual value.
December 31, 19A: Cost of goods sold, $170,000 (GPL average index for cost of goods sold and ending inventory, 120).

The above entries resulted in the following preclosing HC account balances at December 31, 19A (the 19A adjusting entries already have been completed).

Debits

Cash	$ 72,900
Inventory	10,000
Equipment	75,000
Cost of goods sold	170,000
Expenses	80,000
Depreciation expense	7,000
Retained earnings (dividend declared and paid)	6,900
Total	$421,800

Credits

Accumulated depreciation	$ 7,000
Accounts payable	18,800
Note payable	36,000
Capital stock (nopar)	60,000
Revenues	300,000
Total	$421,800

Required:

a. Set up a format similar to Exhibit 17–4 to derive CD restated financial statements. Enter thereon the HC basis amounts for each statement.

b. Restate each item on each statement on a CD basis. Prepare a separate schedule similar to Exhibit 17–5 to compute the purchasing power gain or loss on monetary items. Round all amounts to the nearest dollar. (Hint: There was a $32,083 loss on cash.)

PC17–5. Small Company was organized on January 1, 19A, at which time the GPL index was 150. The accounting period ends December 31. The transactions completed during 19A were:

a. January 1, 19A: Sold and issued 10,000 shares of capital stock (par $10) for $150,000 cash (GPL index, 150).

b. January 1, 19A: Purchased merchandise on credit for resale, $60,000 (GPL index, 150).

c. February 1, 19A: Purchased equipment for use in the business; paid cash, $31,000, and gave a $46,500, interest-bearing note due December 31, 19C (GPL index, 155).

d. During 19A: Sales revenue, $180,000 (sold evenly throughout the year); one third was on credit (GPL average index, 165).

e. During February–December 19A: Purchased merchandise on credit (evenly throughout the year) for resale, $44,000 (GPL index, 165).

f. During 19A: Collected accounts receivable, $50,000 (average GPL index for collections, 170).

g. During 19A: Paid accounts payable, $84,000 (average GPL index for payments, 160).

h. During 19A: Paid expenses in cash (evenly throughout the year), $61,000 (average GPL index, 165), which included interest, income tax, and all other expenses except depreciation expense.

i. July 1, 19A: Invested $96,000 cash for common stock of X Corporation (GPL index, 160).

j. December 31, 19A: Declared and paid a dividend of $10,000 (GPL index, 180).

k. December 31, 19A: Depreciation expense on equipment, $14,000.

l. December 31, 19A: Cost of goods sold, $84,000 (average GPL index for cost of goods sold and ending inventory, 156).

The above transactions resulted in the following preclosing HC account balances (adjusting entries already have been made):

Debits

Cash		$ 38,000
Accounts receivable (net)		10,000
Inventory		20,000
Investment, common stock		96,000
Equipment		77,500
Cost of goods sold		84,000
Expenses		61,000
Depreciation expense		14,000
Retained earnings (dividend)		10,000
		$410,500

Credits

Accumulated depreciation		$ 14,000
Accounts payable		20,000
Note payable		46,500
Capital stock (par $10)		100,000
Contributed capital in excess of par		50,000
Revenues		180,000
		$410,500

Required:

a. Set up a format similar to Exhibit 17–4 to derive CD restated financial statements. Enter thereon the historical cost basis amounts for each statement. The GPL index at December 31, 19A, was 180.

b. Restate each item on each statement on a CD basis. Prepare a separate schedule similar to Exhibit 17–5 to compute the purchasing power gain or loss on monetary items. (Hint: there was a $10,805 loss on cash). Round all amounts to the nearest dollar.

PART B

PC17–6. This problem is based on the data given in PC17–3 (DO Company). The balance sheet and income statement (HC basis) and the GPL index numbers are not changed. Current cost (CC) information is as follows:

Item	Current cost (CC) data, December 31, 19A	
Long-term investment, common stock	Based on stock market quotation	$ 8,500
Land	Per professional appraisal	14,000
Plant (net)	Specific index, 1.10 of carrying value.	
Expenses (not detailed)	HC average and CC average the same.	
(GPL index data given in Problem 17–3)		

Required (show computations and round all amounts to the nearest $10):

a. Set up a schedule similar to Exhibit 17–7 to develop a CC/CD balance sheet and income statement at December 31, 19A. Enter the HC data and complete the CC/CD amounts through "Income from operations." The purchasing power loss on monetary items was $2,500.

b. Compute the CC real holding gains (losses) on nonmonetary items.

c. Use the amounts computed in *(b)* to complete the CC/CD income statement. (Hint: The CC/CD balance sheet totals are, $248,380.)

PC17–7.   Thu Company began operations on January 1, 19A, at which time the GPL index was 130. The 19A balance sheet and income statement, along with relevant GPL index numbers and CC information, are given below. The 19A average GPL index was 143, and it was 156 at December 31, 19A.

	HC basis	GPL Index at transaction date	CC valuations (which are different from HC) at December 31, 19A
Balance sheet:			
Assets:			
Cash	$ 14,300	143	
Accounts receivable	28,600	143	
Inventory (average)	57,200	143	Specific index, 165/143 of HC
Equipment	78,000	130	Specific index, 1.282 of HC
Accumulated depreciation	(7,800)	130	Specific index, 1.282 of HC
Other assets	19,500	130	Specific index, 160/130 of HC
Total	$189,800		
Liabilities:			
Accounts payable	$ 14,300	143	
Note payable...............	39,000	130	
Stockholders' equity:			
Capital stock	130,000	136.84	
Retained earnings	6,500		
Total	$189,800		
Income statement:			
Revenue	$114,400	143	
Cost of goods sold	(71,500)	143	Average specific price index, 1.0577 of HC
Depreciation expense*	(7,800)	143	Based on average CC of equipment during 19A
Remaining expenses	(28,600)	143	HC and CC averages are the same
Net income	$ 6,500		

* Straight-line depreciation, 10-year estimated life and no residual value (Cost, $78,000 ÷ 10 years = $7,800).

Required:

Based on the above data, the company desires to construct a CC/CD balance sheet and income statement at December 31, 19A. Show all computations and round to the nearest $10.

a.   Set up a schedule similar to Exhibit 17–7 to develop CC/CD statements. Enter the HC data given above and complete the CC/CD amounts through "Income from operations."

b.   The purchasing power gain on monetary items was $5,200. Show how this was computed (refer to Exhibit 17–5).

c.   Compute the CC real holding gain (loss) on nonmonetary items (refer to Exhibit 17–8).

d.   Use the amounts computed in *(b)* and *(c)* to complete the CC/CD income statement. (Hint: The CC/CD balance sheet totals are $222,900.)

PC17–8.   (Comprehensive problem—Chapters 16 and 17)   The following information was contained in the annual report of Standard Oil Company (Indiana):

	1981	1980	1979	1978	1977
Total revenues					
—as reported	$31,729	$27,832	$20,197	$16,350	$14,263
—constant dollars	31,729	30,719	25,307	22,793	21,407
Net income from operations					
—as reported	$ 1,922	$ 1,915	$ 1,507	$ 1,076	$ 1,032
—constant dollars	1,254	1,522	1,385	1,055	1,179
—current costs	960	1,043	977	744	909
Net income from operations per share					
—as reported	$ 6.56	$ 6.54	$ 5.12	$ 3.68	$ 3.52
—constant dollars	4.28	5.20	4.70	3.61	4.02
—current costs	3.28	3.56	3.32	2.54	3.10
Cash dividends per share					
—as reported	$ 2.60	$ 2.00	$ 1.50	$ 1.40	$ 1.30
—constant dollars	2.60	2.21	1.88	1.95	1.95
Net assets at year end					
—as reported	$10,665	$ 9,385	$ 8,369	$ 7,146	$ 6,475
—constant dollars	16,340	15,424	14,847	13,954	13,265
—current costs	21,273	21,444	20,413	17,810	17,143
Excess of increase in specific prices over increase due to general inflation	$ 71	$ 656	$ 965	$ 74	$ (29)
Unrealized gain from decline in purchasing power of net amounts owed	$ 490	$ 574	$ 537	$ 349	$ 279

Required:

a. Calculate the following:
   (1) Return on net assets for 1981: *(a)* as reported, *(b)* constant dollars; and *(c)* current costs (state as a percent).
   (2) Growth in revenues from 1980 to 1981: *(a)* as reported; and *(b)* constant dollars (state as a percent).
   (3) Growth in net income from operations from 1980 to 1981: *(a)* as reported; *(b)* constant dollars; and *(c)* current costs (state as a percent).
   (4) Profit margin for 1981: *(a)* as reported; *(b)* constant dollars; *(c)* current costs (state as a percent).
b. What do your calculations in Requirement *(a)* tell you about the impact of inflation on Standard Oil Company (Indiana)?
c. By studying the data presented by Standard Oil, it is possible to determine whether the constant dollar information is presented in average dollars for 1981 or year-end dollars for 1981. Did Standard Oil use average dollars or year-end dollars?
d. Which amount is larger for Standard Oil: total monetary assets or total monetary liabilities?

PC17–9. Frank Smith, president of Delta Corporation, has asked that you help him understand inflation accounting. During a meeting, Mr. Smith made the following comments:

I have been told that it is possible to make money by borrowing money during a period of inflation. I plan to recommend that Delta borrow $10 million, at 18 percent interest, on January 1, 19D, and deposit the money in Delta's checking account (which does not pay interest). One year later, we will repay the money. The average inflation rate during 19D is expected to be 12 percent, consequently Delta should have a purchasing power gain on the debt. Delta will be able to use the cash from the purchasing power gain to pay a dividend to the stockholders of the company. The only thing I don't understand is why bankers are willing to lend money during a period of inflation. If we can make money by borrowing, don't the bankers lose money by lending money?

Required:

a. Determine the amount of the purchasing power gain that Mr. Smith *expects* Delta to earn by borrowing $10 million. Will Delta actually earn the purchasing power gain that Mr. Smith expects? Explain why. Would your answer be different if the $10 million were invested in a tract of land during the year? Why?

b. Evaluate Mr. Smith's plan to use cash from a purchasing power gain on monetary items to pay a cash dividend to the stockholders.

c. Prepare a response to Mr. Smith's question concerning why bankers are willing to lend money during a period of inflation.

Special Supplement A
Overview of Income Taxes

PURPOSE OF THIS SUPPLEMENT

Income taxes are complex and pervasive; they affect most persons and businesses. Each individual and manager should consider the income tax implications when making economic decisions. A general knowledge of income taxes enables the decision maker to *(a)* recognize the importance of various income tax implications, *(b)* know when to seek professional assistance, and *(c)* carry on tax planning to minimize income taxes.

Federal, state, and local governments not only assess income taxes but also property taxes (i.e., on real property), sales taxes (i.e., on the sale of goods and services), and excise taxes (i.e., on gasoline). Because income taxes are levied by the federal government and most states, the total amount exceeds any other tax, and as a result, it exerts a pervasive effect on many business decisions. Basically there are three major groups of taxpayers: individuals, corporations, and fiduciaries (that is, trusts and estates).

The purpose of this supplement is to present an overview of **federal income taxes** applicable to **individuals** and **corporations.** This overview is designed to *(a)* enhance your general knowledge of the primary federal income tax provisions, *(b)* give you a basic understanding of income tax returns, and *(c)* provide an overview of the relationship between **accounting income** (reported on the income statement) and **taxable income** (reported on the income tax return).[1] The discussion in this supplement is based upon current income tax information. By the time you read this supplement, certain tax provisions may be out of date. However, the discussion will be relevant because it deals with key concepts and terminology rather than with the numerous exceptions and detailed rules. We reemphasize that our objective is to provide a broad overview of income tax provisions rather than a highly technical view. The examples given are intended to illustrate key concepts and terminology. Congress may change the tax rates or specific tax law which may make certain illustrations out of date but our educational objective will remain intact. For exam-

---

[1] It appears that the first U.S. federal income tax was proposed in 1815. Later during the Civil War, a federal income tax law was enacted and income taxes were collected; however, this law was repealed shortly thereafter. During 1894, another income tax law was passed, which was soon held to be unconstitutional. At the outset of World War I, the 16th Amendment to the Constitution was passed that made income taxes constitutionally allowable. Our present federal income tax law dates from measures passed by the U.S. Congress in 1913.

ple, a change in the individual income tax rates will not affect the method used to calculate the tax obligation.

To accomplish this purpose, this supplement is subdivided as follows:

Part A—Income taxes paid by individuals

Part B—Income taxes paid by corporations

PART A—INCOME TAXES PAID BY INDIVIDUALS

Current income tax law (as set forth in the Internal Revenue Code) states the legal provisions for all taxpayers, including individuals and corporations. Due to the complexity of the tax law, the Treasury Department issues **regulations** that state the government's position on that law and provides guidelines for implementing it. Much of the Code and the regulations apply to both individual and corporate taxpayers; however, there are certain provisions that apply only to individuals and not to corporations, and vice versa. For example, different tax rates apply to each. This part of the supplement will present an overview of the income tax provisions that specifically apply to **individual** taxpayers, along with a sample tax return.

INCOME TAX FILING REQUIREMENTS

An individual must file a tax return annually on a *(a)* calendar-year basis (ending December 31), or *(b)* fiscal-year basis (ending on the last day of a month other than December). The tax return must be filed on or before the 15th day of the fourth month following the taxable year-end (i.e., April 15 for the calendar year basis). Most individual taxpayers file the standardized form entitled "Form 1040, U.S. Individual Income Tax Return" (Exhibit A–3) which is submitted to the appropriate regional service center of the Internal Revenue Service, Department of the Treasury.

A return must be filed if the **gross income** of a taxpayer under age 65 is equal to or more than *(a)* $3,300 if single or head of a household; *(b)* $4,400 if a surviving spouse; *(c)* $5,400 if married, filing jointly; or *(d)* $400 of self-employed income. If a taxpayer is 65 years of age or older, or if blind, these amounts increase by $1,000 for each such incidence.

Basically, computation of the income tax is accomplished by multiplying an amount called taxable income by the appropriate income tax rate for the individual taxpayer. A discussion of the determination of **taxable income** follows.

GROSS INCOME

Computation of **taxable income** starts with determination of gross income. For an individual taxpayer, **gross income,** for income tax purposes, is broadly defined as income from whatever source derived. Gross income by the individual taxpayer may be measured on what usually is called the *(a)* cash basis or *(b)* accrual basis.[2] Exhibit A–1 lists 12 different income items that may be included in **gross income.** Of these the most typical items are wages and salaries, rental income, investment income, and business income.

With respect to income, most individual taxpayers will receive a W-2 or a 1099 form from each source of income; these forms are required by tax law and provide some of the requisite income data needed to complete the individual tax return. Exhibit A–2 provides examples of these two forms for the Doe family. Observe on these standardized forms that the amounts of *(a)* total earnings and *(b)* income taxes withheld (i.e., prepayments of income tax) are reported for the tax year. In addition, the individual taxpayer usually will need to refer to tax law and the regulations to determine whether a particular receipt or payment will affect the amount of taxable income.

Some receipts are excluded in full, or in part, from gross income for tax purposes. Typical examples are: interest on state and municipal bonds (called tax-free bonds), most life insurance proceeds, gifts, inheritances, most workmen's compensation, most social security benefits, disability pensions to veterans, GI benefits, compensation for damages, and $100 of dividend income per taxpayer.

Frequently, an individual taxpayer owns a small business or an interest in a partnership. In either case, these two types of business entities do not pay income taxes; rather, each owner must include his individual share of the net income or loss from the business on his own individual income tax return (see Exhibit A–3, lines 12 and 18). If the individual taxpayer derives business income from a sole proprietorship, "Schedule C, Profit (Loss) from Business or Profession" must be attached to the income tax return. A typical Schedule C is shown in Exhibit A–4.

DEDUCTIONS FROM GROSS INCOME

The overview given in Exhibit A–1 lists 16 different **deductions** from gross income. Generally, these deductions are of two kinds: (1) expenses incurred in the production of income (e.g., depreciation on rental property) and expenses in operating a business, or (2) personal deductions (e.g., alimony paid). The operating expenses of a sole proprietorship are reported as a direct reduction of the income from the business on Schedule C, Profit or Loss from Business or Profession (see Exhibit A–4). The **personal deductions** are reported directly on Form 1040, lines 23–30 (see Exhibit A–3).[3]

In 1982, tax legislation created a new deduction for married couples filing a joint return in situations when each spouse earned income (Form 1040, line 29). The amount of the deduction is 10 percent (5 percent in 1982 only) times the

---

[2] Other options, which are modifications of these two bases, are available. Discussion of these options is beyond the scope of this supplement. Most individual taxpayers elect the cash basis because *(a)* it does not require the taxpayer to maintain a formal set of books and *(b)* it provides the taxpayer opportunities to time cash receipts and payments to effect tax savings.

[3] Note that these personal deductions are not the same as "itemized deductions" which are discussed in a later section of this supplement.

EXHIBIT A–1
Overview of Form
1040, Individual
Income Tax Return

Major captions	Specific items included

1982 Individual Return, Form 1040, Simplified

```
                  ┌─────────────┐     ⎧ Gains on Sales or Exchanges (¶ 901)
                  │             │     │ Wages, Salaries (¶ 717)
                  │             │     │ Annuities, Pensions (¶ 722, 815)
                  │   GROSS     │     │ Gross Business Profits (¶ 701)
                  │   INCOME    │─────┤ Farm Income (¶ 771)
                  │             │     │ Dividends Received (¶ 737, 745)
                  │             │     │ Interest Received (¶ 727, 745)
                  └─────────────┘     │ Commissions, Bonuses, Tips (¶ 717, 721)
                         │            │ Rents and Royalties (¶ 767, 768)
                         ▼            │ Prizes (¶ 782)
                                      │ Alimony Received (¶ 774)
                       minus          ⎩ Unemployment Compensation (¶ 726)
```

Gross Income specific items:
- Gains on Sales or Exchanges (¶ 901)
- Wages, Salaries (¶ 717)
- Annuities, Pensions (¶ 722, 815)
- Gross Business Profits (¶ 701)
- Farm Income (¶ 771)
- Dividends Received (¶ 737, 745)
- Interest Received (¶ 727, 745)
- Commissions, Bonuses, Tips (¶ 717, 721)
- Rents and Royalties (¶ 767, 768)
- Prizes (¶ 782)
- Alimony Received (¶ 774)
- Unemployment Compensation (¶ 726)

minus

DEDUCTIONS FROM GROSS INCOME specific items:
- Trade or Business Expenses (¶ 1003, 1040)
- Travel Expenses (¶ 1020-1026A)
- Transportation Costs (¶ 1020, 1027)
- Outside Salesmen's Expenses (¶ 1016)
- Employee's Reimbursed Expenses (¶ 1015)
- Depreciation Allowable (¶ 1151)
- Losses from Sales or Exchanges (¶ 1006)
- Net Operating Loss Deduction (¶ 1119)
- Alimony Paid (¶ 774)
- IRA or H. R. 10 Plan Payments (¶ 555, 575)
- Moving Expenses (¶ 1037)
- Two-Earner Deduction (¶ 1008)
- Interest Forfeited on Premature Withdrawals from Time Savings Accounts (¶ 1002)
- Disability Income Exclusion (¶ 842)
- Supplemental Unemployment Compensation Benefit Repayments (1974 Trade Act) (¶ 1002)
- Reforestation Amortization (¶ 1159A)
- (See also Check List XII at ¶ 66)

equals

ADJUSTED GROSS INCOME

minus

EXCESS OF ITEMIZED DEDUCTIONS [OR PLUS UNUSED ZERO BRACKET AMOUNT] specific items:
- Charitable Contributions (¶ 1138)
- Nonitemizers' Charitable Deduction (¶ 1007)
- Taxes Paid (¶ 1078)
- Interest Paid (¶ 1071)
- Nonbusiness Casualty Losses (¶ 1097)
- Medical Expenses (¶ 1131)
- Investor's Expenses (¶ 1129)
- Union Dues and Employee Expenses Not Listed Above (¶ 1035)
- Qualifying Adoption Expenses (¶ 1130A)

and minus

EXEMPTIONS specific items:
- Taxpayer (¶ 151), Spouse (¶ 151), Dependents (¶ 154), Blind (¶ 153), 65-or-Over (¶ 152)

equals

TAXABLE INCOME

EXHIBIT A–2

Forms used to report income earned and taxes withheld (W-2 and 1099)

1 Control number	22222	For Official Use Only OMB No. 1545-0008		
2 Employer's name, address, and ZIP code		3 Employer's identification number 74-2333444	4 Employer's State number	
University of Texas at Austin		5 Stat. employee / Deceased / Pension plan / Legal rep. ☐ ☐ ☐ ☐	942 emp. / Sub-total / Cor-rection / Void ☐ ☐ ☐ ☐	
Austin, Texas 78712		6 *	7 Advance EIC payment	
8 Employee's social security number 123-45-6789	9 Federal income tax withheld 6,800.00	10 Wages, tips, other compensation 50,000.00	11 FICA tax withheld 2,170.80	
12 Employee's name (first, middle, last) John J. Doe		13 FICA wages 32,400.00	14 FICA tips	
1770 Mountain Drive Austin, Texas 78703		16 Employer's use		
		For Paperwork Reduction Act Notice, see back of Copy D.		
15 Employee's address and ZIP code				

Form **W-2 Wage and Tax Statement 1982**   Copy A For Social Security Administration   * See Instructions for Forms W-2 and W-2P   Department of the Treasury Internal Revenue Service

Do NOT CUT or Separate Forms on This Page

For Official Use Only		OMB No. 1545-0112 Statement for Recipients of **1982**
TYE Savings and Loan Assoc. P.O. Box 9877 Austin, Texas 78701 74-1667889	Type or print PAYER'S name, address, ZIP code, and Federal identifying number.	**Interest Income** Copy A For Internal Revenue Service Center
92 ☐ Recipient's identifying number 123-45-6789	1 Earnings from savings and loan associations, credit unions, etc. $ 1,250.00	2 Other interest on bank deposits, etc. (Do not include amounts from box 1)	3 Amount of forfeiture
Name ► Type or print RECIPIENT'S name, address, and ZIP code below (Name must align with arrow). John J. Doe 1770 Mountain Drive Austin, Texas 78703		4 Foreign tax paid (If eligible for foreign tax credit)	5 Foreign country or U.S. possession
		For Paperwork Reduction Act Notice and instructions on completing this form, see Instructions for Form 1096.	

Form **1099–INT**   ☆ U.S. GOVERNMENT PRINTING OFFICE 1981—343-105   13-134-8-50   Department of the Treasury—Internal Revenue Service

amount of qualified earned income (limited to $30,000) of the spouse with the lower amount of earned income. Therefore, for years 1983 and later, the maximum deduction allowable is $3,000 (or, 10 percent times $30,000 of earned income).

ADJUSTED GROSS INCOME

Gross income **less** the deductions from gross income results in an amount that is called **Adjusted Gross Income** (AGI). This amount is significant because the actual amount of certain **itemized deductions** is based on it. For example, the 1982 deduction for medical expenses is limited to 3 percent of adjusted gross income (5 percent after 1982). A more detailed discussion of itemized deductions follows.

Itemized deductions

Broadly defined, itemized deductions are certain personal expenditures paid by the taxpayer that are specifically provided for by the tax law. Exhibit A–1 lists nine itemized deductions. These deductions reduce adjusted gross income (see Exhibit A–3, Form 1040, line 32). The individual taxpayer may either (1) itemize the personal deductions by using "Schedule A—Itemized Deductions" (presented in Exhibit A–5) or (2) use a standard amount called the zero bracket amount. The zero bracket amount (ZBA) is $2,300 for single individuals, $3,400 for married individuals filing jointly, and $1,700 for married individuals filing separately. These zero bracket amounts have been built into the tax rate schedules (see Exhibit A–6). Therefore, if the total **itemized** deductions are equal to, or less than the ZBA, no amount for itemized deductions is entered on the tax return (Form 1040, line 34b). However, if the total amount of the itemized deductions **exceeds** the ZBA, then this excess is entered on the tax return (Form 1040, line 34b). To illustrate, John and Jane Doe reported total itemized deductions of $11,536 (see Exhibit A–5, line 28). However, on Form 1040, line 34a (see Exhibit A–3), $8,136 was reported (i.e., $11,536 − $3,400, the zero bracket amount).

Exemptions

In addition to itemized deductions, personal and dependency exemptions from adjusted gross income are permitted. Exemptions of $1,000 each are allowed for the taxpayer, the taxpayer's spouse, the taxpayer and/or spouse who is blind, the taxpayer and/or spouse 65 years of age or older, and dependents. In general, a dependent is *(a)* a close relative of the taxpayer *(b)* with gross income of less than $1,000 for the tax year and *(c)* with over half of the dependent's support being furnished by the taxpayer. The exemptions are entered directly on the income tax return, Form 1040, lines 6a through 6e (see Exhibit A–3). The total deduction then is taken on Form 1040, line 36 (see Exhibit A–3).

TAXABLE INCOME

Now that all of the components used to compute **taxable income** have been discussed, we can once again focus on the overall computation of taxable income outlined in Exhibit A–1:

$$\frac{\text{Gross}}{\text{income}} - \text{Deductions} - \frac{\text{Excess itemized}}{\text{deductions}} - \text{Exemptions} = \frac{\text{Taxable}}{\text{income}}$$

The individual taxpayer uses taxable income, usually computed in this manner, to figure his or her income tax liability for the year.

COMPUTATION OF INCOME TAX LIABILITY

Basically, the amount of income taxes payable is computed by multiplying **taxable income** by the appropriate income tax rates. The income tax rates frequently are changed by legislation. Current rates are different for individual taxpayers than they are for corporate taxpayers. Exhibit A–6 presents the **four** 1982–83 Income Tax Rate Schedules for individual taxpayers. Note the different tax rates for each group of taxpayers.

To calculate the income tax liability, the taxpayer must use the rate schedule that corresponds to his or her tax filing status. To illustrate, assume taxpayer Smith is a single individual with taxable income of $14,000. The 1982 rate schedule

EXHIBIT A–3   **Individual Income Tax Return**

Form **1040** Department of the Treasury—Internal Revenue Service
U.S. Individual Income Tax Return **1982** (O)

For the year January 1–December 31, 1982, or other tax year beginning   1982, ending   , 19 . OMB No. 1545-0074

Use IRS label. Other-wise, please print or type.	Your first name and initial (if joint return, also give spouse's name and initial)	Last name	Your social security number
	John J. and Jane A.	Doe	123 : 45 : 6789
	Present home address (Number and street, including apartment number, or rural route)		Spouse's social security no.
	1770 Mountain Drive		789 : 56 : 1234
	City, town or post office, State and ZIP code	Your occupation ► College Professor	
	Austin, Texas 78703	Spouse's occupation ► Housewife	

Presidential Election Campaign ►
Do you want $1 to go to this fund? . . . .   Yes X No
If joint return, does your spouse want $1 to go to this fund? . . .   Yes X No
Note: Checking "Yes" will not increase your tax or reduce your refund.

Filing Status
Check only one box.

1 ☐ Single
2 ☒ Married filing joint return (even if only one had income)
3 ☐ Married filing separate return. Enter spouse's social security no. above and full name here ►
4 ☐ Head of household (with qualifying person). (See page 6 of Instructions.) If the qualifying person is your unmarried child but not your dependent, enter child's name ►
5 ☐ Qualifying widow(er) with dependent child (Year spouse died ► 19). (See page 6 of Instructions.)

For Privacy Act and Paperwork Reduction Act Notice, see Instructions.

Exemptions
Always check the box labeled Yourself. Check other boxes if they apply.

6a ☒ Yourself ☐ 65 or over ☐ Blind
b ☒ Spouse ☐ 65 or over ☐ Blind
    Enter number of boxes checked on 6a and b ► **2**
c First names of your dependent children who lived with you ► John Jr. (son), Joyce (daughter)
    Enter number of children listed on 6c ► **2**

d Other dependents: (1) Name	(2) Relationship	(3) Number of months lived in your home	(4) Did dependent have income of $1,000 or more?	(5) Did you provide more than one-half of dependent's support?	
					Enter number of other dependents ►

Add numbers entered in boxes above ► **4**

e Total number of exemptions claimed . . . .

Income

Please attach Copy B of your Forms W–2 here.

If you do not have a W–2, see page 5 of Instructions.

Please attach check or money order here.

7	Wages, salaries, tips, etc.	7	50,000	00
8	Interest income *(attach Schedule B if over $400 or you have any All-Savers interest)*	8	2,650	00
9a	Dividends *(attach Schedule B if over $400)* 1,200 :00, 9b Exclusion 200 :00			
c	Subtract line 9b from line 9a . . .	9c	1,000	00
10	Refunds of State and local income taxes *(do not enter an amount unless you deducted those taxes in an earlier year—see page 9 of Instructions)*	10		
11	Alimony received	11		
12	Business income or (loss) *(attach Schedule C)* . . . . ►	12	4,900	00
13	Capital gain or (loss) *(attach Schedule D)*	13	40	00
14	40% capital gain distributions not reported on line 13 (See page 9 of Instructions)	14		
15	Supplemental gains or (losses) *(attach Form 4797)*	15		
16	Fully taxable pensions, IRA distributions, and annuities not reported on line 17 . .	16		
17a	Other pensions and annuities. Total received 17a			
b	Taxable amount, if any, from worksheet on page 10 of Instructions	17b		
18	Rents, royalties, partnerships, estates, trusts, etc. *(attach Schedule E)*	18		
19	Farm income or (loss) *(attach Schedule F)* . . . . ►	19		
20a	Unemployment compensation (insurance). Total received 20a			
b	Taxable amount, if any, from worksheet on page 10 of Instructions	20b		
21	Other income (state nature and source—see page 10 of Instructions) ►	21		
22	**Total income.** Add amounts in column for lines 7 through 21 . . . . ►	22	58,590	00

Adjustments to Income

(See Instructions on page 11)

23	Moving expense *(attach Form 3903 or 3903F)* . . .	23		
24	Employee business expenses *(attach Form 2106)* . .	24		
25	Payments to an IRA. You **must** enter code from page 11 (........)	25		
26	Payments to a Keogh (H.R. 10) retirement plan . . .	26		
27	Penalty on early withdrawal of savings	27		
28	Alimony paid	28		
29	Deduction for a married couple when both work (attach Schedule W)	29		
30	Disability income exclusion *(attach Form 2440)* . . .	30		
31	**Total adjustments.** Add lines 23 through 30. . . . . ►	31		

Adjusted Gross Income

32	**Adjusted gross income.** Subtract line 31 from line 22. If this line is less than $10,000, see "Earned Income Credit" (line 62) on page 15 of Instructions. If you want IRS to figure your tax, see page 3 of Instructions . . . . ►	32	58,590	00

☆ U.S. GOVERNMENT PRINTING OFFICE 1982—O—363-302 48-0627165

EXHIBIT A–3 *(concluded)*

Form 1040 (1982)	John J. and Jane A. Doe	S.S.No. 123-45-6789	Page 2

Tax Computation
(See Instructions on page 12)

33	Amount from line 32 *(adjusted gross income)*	33	58,590 00
34a	If you itemize, complete Schedule A (Form 1040) and enter the amount from Schedule A, line 30	34a	8,136 00

Caution: If you have unearned income and can be claimed as a dependent on your parent's return, check here ▶ ☐ and see page 12 of the Instructions. Also see page 12 of the Instructions if:
- You are married filing a separate return and your spouse itemizes deductions, OR
- You file Form 4563, OR   ● You are a dual-status alien.

34b	If you do not itemize, complete the worksheet on page 13. Then enter the allowable part of your charitable contributions here	34b	
35	Subtract line 34a or 34b, whichever applies, from line 33	35	50,454 00
36	Multiply $1,000 by the total number of exemptions claimed on Form 1040, line 6e . .	36	4,000 00
37	Taxable Income. Subtract line 36 from line 35	37	46,454 00
38	Tax. Enter tax here and check if from ☒ Tax Table, ☐ Tax Rate Schedule X, Y, or Z, or ☐ Schedule G	38	11,745 00
39	Additional Taxes. (See page 13 of Instructions.) Enter here and check if from ☐ Form 4970, ☐ Form 4972, ☐ Form 5544, or ☐ section 72 penalty taxes	39	
40	**Total.** Add lines 38 and 39 . . . . ▶	40	11,745 00

Credits
(See Instructions on page 13)

41	Credit for the elderly *(attach Schedules R&RP)*	41		
42	Foreign tax credit *(attach Form 1116)*	42		
43	Investment credit *(attach Form 3468)*	43		
44	Partial credit for political contributions	44		
45	Credit for child and dependent care expenses *(attach Form 2441)*.	45		
46	Jobs credit *(attach Form 5884)*	46		
47	Residential energy credit *(attach Form 5695)*	47		
48	Other credits—see page 14 ▶	48		
49	Total credits. Add lines 41 through 48		49	
50	**Balance.** Subtract line 49 from line 40 and enter difference (but not less than zero) . ▶		50	11,745 00

Other Taxes
(Including Advance EIC Payments)

06

51	Self-employment tax *(attach Schedule SE)*	51	
52	Minimum tax *(attach Form 4625)*	52	
53	Alternative minimum tax *(attach Form 6251)*	53	
54	Tax from recapture of investment credit *(attach Form 4255)*	54	
55	Social security (FICA) tax on tip income not reported to employer *(attach Form 4137)* .	55	
56	Uncollected employee FICA and RRTA tax on tips *(from Form W–2)*	56	
57	Tax on an IRA *(attach Form 5329)*	57	
58	Advance earned income credit (EIC) payments received *(from Form W–2)*	58	
59	**Total tax.** Add lines 50 through 58 . . . . ▶ ■	59	11,745 00

Payments
Attach Forms W–2, W–2G, and W–2P to front.

60	Total Federal income tax withheld	60	6,800 00	
61	1982 estimated tax payments and amount applied from 1981 return	61	4,000 00	
62	Earned income credit. If line 33 is under $10,000, see page 15 of Instructions	62		
63	Amount paid with Form 4868	63		
64	Excess FICA and RRTA tax withheld (two or more employers) .	64		
65	Credit for Federal tax on special fuels and oils *(attach Form 4136)*	65		
66	Regulated Investment Company credit *(attach Form 2439)*	66		
67	**Total.** Add lines 60 through 66 . . . . ▶		67	10,800 00

Refund or Amount You Owe

68	If line 67 is larger than line 59, enter amount **OVERPAID** . . . . ▶	68	
69	Amount of line 68 to be **REFUNDED TO YOU** . . . . ▶	69	
70	Amount of line 68 to be applied to your 1983 estimated tax . . . ▶ 70		
71	If line 59 is larger than line 67, enter **AMOUNT YOU OWE.** Attach check or money order for full amount payable to Internal Revenue Service. Write your social security number and "1982 Form 1040" on it. ▶ (Check ▶ ☐ if Form 2210 (2210F) is attached. See page 16 of Instructions.) ▶ $	71	945 00

Please Sign Here

Under penalties of perjury, I declare that I have examined this return, including accompanying schedules and statements, and to the best of my knowledge and belief, it is true, correct, and complete. Declaration of preparer (other than taxpayer) is based on all information of which preparer has any knowledge.

▶ Your signature   Date   ▶ Spouse's signature (if filing jointly, BOTH must sign)

Paid Preparer's Use Only

Preparer's signature ▶	Date	Check if self-employed ▶ ☒	Preparer's social security no. 477 82 5555
Firm's name (or yours, if self-employed) and address ▶	Jones & Jones, CPA 1400 First Street	E.I. No. ▶	74 2225555
	Austin, Texas	ZIP code ▶	78701

EXHIBIT A–4   Schedule C, Profit or (Loss) from Business or Profession

| SCHEDULE C
(Form 1040)
Department of the Treasury
Internal Revenue Service (0) | **Profit or (Loss) From Business or Profession**
(Sole Proprietorship)
Partnerships, Joint Ventures, etc., Must File Form 1065.
▶ Attach to Form 1040 or Form 1041.   ▶ See Instructions for Schedule C (Form 1040). | OMB. No. 1545–0074
19**82**
08 |

Name of proprietor: John J. Doe   Social security number of proprietor: 123 45 6789

A Main business activity (see Instructions) ▶ Retail Sales   ; product ▶ Antiques

B Business name ▶ Doe's Antiques   C Employer identification number

D Business address (number and street) ▶ 10800 Industrial Blvd.
City, State and ZIP Code ▶ Austin, Texas 78746

E Accounting method: (1) X Cash   (2) ☐ Accrual   (3) ☐ Other (specify) ▶ _____

F Method(s) used to value closing inventory:
(1) X Cost   (2) ☐ Lower of cost or market   (3) ☐ Other (if other, attach explanation)

	Yes	No
G Was there any major change in determining quantities, costs, or valuations between opening and closing inventory? . . If "Yes," attach explanation.		X
H Did you deduct expenses for an office in your home?		X
I Did you operate this business at the end of 1982?	X	

J How many months in 1982 did you actively operate this business? ▶   12

Part I   Income

1 a Gross receipts or sales	1a	13,100 00	
b Returns and allowances	1b	1,100 00	
c Balance (subtract line 1b from line 1a)	1c	12,000 00
2 Cost of goods sold and/or operations (Schedule C–1, line 8)	2	3,000 00
3 Gross profit (subtract line 2 from line 1c)	3	9,000 00
4 a Windfall Profit Tax Credit or Refund received in 1982 (see Instructions)	4a	
b Other income	4b	
5 Total income (add lines 3, 4a, and 4b) . . . . ▶	5	9,000 00

Part II   Deductions

6 Advertising	100 00	25 Taxes (Do not include Windfall Profit Tax here. See line 29.) . .	160 00
7 Bad debts from sales or services (Cash method taxpayers, see Instructions)		26 Travel and entertainment . .	
8 Bank service charges	20 00	27 Utilities and telephone . . .	450 00
9 Car and truck expenses		28 a Wages . . 1,500 00	
10 Commissions		b Jobs credit	
11 Depletion		c Subtract line 28b from 28a .	1,500 00
12 Depreciation, including Section 179 expense deduction (from Form 4562)		29 Windfall Profit Tax withheld in 1982	
13 Dues and publications	30 00	30 Other expenses (specify):	
14 Employee benefit programs . .		a _____	
15 Freight (not included on Schedule C–1) .		b _____	
16 Insurance	150 00	c _____	
17 Interest on business indebtedness .		d _____	
18 Laundry and cleaning		e _____	
19 Legal and professional services .	300 00	f _____	
20 Office supplies and postage . . .	40 00	g _____	
21 Pension and profit-sharing plans .		h _____	
22 Rent on business property . . .	600 00	i _____	
23 Repairs	400 00	j _____	
24 Supplies (not included on Schedule C–1) .	350 00	k _____	
		l _____	
		m _____	

31 Total deductions (add amounts in columns for lines 6 through 30m) . . . . ▶	31	4,100 00
32 Net profit or (loss) (subtract line 31 from line 5). If a profit, enter on Form 1040, line 12, and on Schedule SE, Part I, line 2 (or Form 1041, line 6). If a loss, go on to line 33	32	4,900 00

33 If you have a loss, do you have amounts for which you are not "at risk" in this business (see Instructions)? . . ☐ Yes   X No
If you checked "No," enter the loss on Form 1040, line 12, and on Schedule SE, Part I, line 2 (or Form 1041, line 6).

For Paperwork Reduction Act Notice, see Form 1040 Instructions.

EXHIBIT A–5   Schedule A—Itemized Deductions

Schedules A&B (Form 1040)
Department of the Treasury
Internal Revenue Service (O)

Schedule A—Itemized Deductions
(Schedule B is on back)
▶ Attach to Form 1040.   ▶ See Instructions for Schedules A and B (Form 1040).

OMB No. 1545–0074

1982
07

Name(s) as shown on Form 1040
John J. and Jane A. Doe

Your social security number
123 45 6789

Medical and Dental Expenses (Do not include expenses reimbursed or paid by others.) (See page 17 of Instructions.)	**1** Medicines and drugs	**1**	600	00	
	2 Write 1% of Form 1040, line 33	**2**	586	00	
	3 Subtract line 2 from line 1. If line 2 is more than line 1, write zero	**3**	14	00	
	4 Total insurance premiums you paid for medical and dental care	**4**	1,200	00	
	5 Other medical and dental expenses:				
	a Doctors, dentists, nurses, hospitals, etc.	**5a**	1,650	00	
	b Transportation	**5b**	50	00	
	c Other (list—include hearing aids, dentures, eyeglasses, etc.) ▶				
		5c			
	6 Add lines 3 through 5c	**6**	2,914	00	
	7 Multiply amount on Form 1040, line 33, by 3% (.03)	**7**	1,758	00	
	8 Subtract line 7 from line 6. If line 7 is more than line 6, write zero	**8**	1,156	00	
	9 Write one-half of amount on line 4, but not more than $150	**9**	150	00	
	10 COMPARE amounts on line 8 and line 9, and write the **LARGER** amount here ▶	**10**	1,156	00	
Taxes (See page 18 of Instructions.)	**11** State and local income	**11**			
	12 Real estate	**12**	1,200	00	
	13 a General sales (see sales tax tables)	**13a**	360	00	
	b General sales on motor vehicles	**13b**			
	14 Other (list—include personal property) ▶	**14**			
	15 Add lines 11 through 14. Write your answer here ▶	**15**	1,560	00	
Interest Expense (See page 19 of Instructions.)	**16 a** Home mortgage interest paid to financial institutions	**16a**	5,500	00	
	b Home mortgage interest paid to individuals (show that person's name and address) ▶	**16b**			
	17 Credit cards and charge accounts	**17**	80	00	
	18 Other (list) ▶ Univ. of Texas Credit Union	**18**	240	00	
	19 Add lines 16a through 18. Write your answer here ▶	**19**	5,820	00	
Contributions (See page 19 of Instructions.)	**20 a** Cash contributions. (If you gave $3,000 or more to any one organization, report those contributions on line 20b.)	**20a**	2,500	00	
	b Cash contributions totaling $3,000 or more to any one organization. (Show to whom you gave and how much you gave.) ▶	**20b**			
	21 Other than cash (see page 19 of Instructions for required statement)	**21**			
	22 Carryover from prior years	**22**			
	23 Add lines 20a through 22. Write your answer here ▶	**23**	2,500	00	
Casualty and Theft Losses and Miscellaneous Deductions (See page 20 of Instructions.)	**24** Total casualty or theft loss(es) (attach Form 4684)	**24**	150	00	
	25 a Union and professional dues	**25a**	100	00	
	b Tax return preparation fee	**25b**	250	00	**A**
	26 Other (list) ▶	**26**			
	27 Add lines 24 through 26. Write your answer here ▶	**27**	500	00	
Summary of Itemized Deductions (See page 20 of Instructions.)	**28** Add lines 10, 15, 19, 23, and 27	**28**	11,536	00	
	29 If you checked Form 1040, Filing Status box { 2 or 5, write $3,400 . 1 or 4, write $2,300 . 3, write $1,700 . }	**29**	3,400	00	
	30 Subtract line 29 from line 28. Write your answer here and on Form 1040, line 34a. (If line 29 is more than line 28, see the Instructions for line 30 on page 20.) ▶	**30**	8,136	00	

For Paperwork Reduction Act Notice, see Form 1040 Instructions.

for this taxpayer (Exhibit A–6) shows $12,900 with a corresponding tax liability of $1,847 **plus** 23 percent of the $1,100 excess of $14,000 over $12,900 (an additional $253), giving a total tax liability of $2,100 (i.e., $1,847 + $253). Although the **marginal tax rate** (i.e., the tax rate on the next dollar of taxable income) is 23 percent, the **average** tax rate is only 15 percent (i.e., $2,100 ÷ $14,000). Additional examples are:

Individual	Taxable income	Computation of total income tax	Computed average tax rate
Smith	$ 14,000	$ 1,847 + ($ 1,100 × 23%) = $ 2,100	15.0
Jones	30,000	$ 6,692 + ($ 1,200 × 40%) = $ 7,172	23.9
Brown ...	70,000	$21,318 + ($10,000 × 50%) = $26,318	37.6
Wilson ...	150,000	$41,318 + ($50,000 × 50%) = $66,318	44.2

COMPLETION OF THE INDIVIDUAL INCOME TAX RETURN ILLUSTRATED

The preceding discussions and illustrations included an income tax return for John and Jane Doe. At this point you should review the following steps used to complete Form 1040, U.S. Individual Income Tax Return (Exhibit A–3), viz:

Step	Activity	Source of information
1	Enter name, address, and other required taxpayer information—top portion of Form 1040	Taxpayer
2	Enter filing status of taxpayer, lines 1–5	Taxpayer
3	Enter exemptions, lines 6a through 6e	Taxpayer
4	Enter amount of exemptions, line 36 (exemptions multiplied by $1,000)	Line 6e and tax code
5	Enter gross income, lines 7–22	
	Line 7, wages and salaries	W-2
	Line 8, interest income	1099
	Line 9, dividend income	1099
	Line 12, business income (loss)	Schedule C
	Line 13, capital gain (loss)	Schedule D
	Line 22, total	Summation
6	Adjustments to income, lines 23–30	Taxpayer records
7	Compute adjusted gross income, line 32	Line 22 minus line 31
8	Compute income tax, lines 33 through 40	
	Line 33, adjusted gross income	Line 32
	Line 34a, itemized deductions	Schedule A
	Line 37, taxable income	Line 35 minus line 36
	Line 40	Summation
9	Tax credits, lines 41–49	Taxpayer records
10	Other taxes, lines 51–58	Taxpayer records
11	Compute total tax, add lines 50 through 58	Summation
12	Compute tax payments (already made), lines 60–67	
	Line 60, income taxes withheld	W-2 and 1099
	Line 61, estimated income tax paid	Taxpayer records
	Line 67	Summation
	Compute refund due or amount owed	Line 59 compared with line 67

EXHIBIT A–6 Income tax rate schedules for individuals

SINGLE INDIVIDUALS

Taxable Income Over	Not Over	1982 Pay	% on Excess	1983 Pay	% on Excess
$ 0–$	2,300	$ 0	0	$ 0	0
2,300–	3,400	0	12	0	11
3,400–	4,400	132	14	121	13
4,400–	6,500	272	16	251	15
6,500–	8,500	608	17	566	15
8,500–	10,800	948	19	866	17
10,800–	12,900	1,385	22	1,257	19
12,900–	15,000	1,847	23	1,656	21
15,000–	18,200	2,330	27	2,097	24
18,200–	23,500	3,194	31	2,865	28
23,500–	28,800	4,837	35	4,349	32
28,800–	34,100	6,692	40	6,045	36
34,100–	41,500	8,812	44	7,953	40
41,500–	55,300	12,068	50	10,913	45
55,300–	60,000	18,968	50	17,123	50
60,000–	70,000	21,318	50	19,473	50
70,000–	80,000	26,318	50	24,473	50
80,000–	90,000	31,318	50	29,473	50
90,000–	100,000	36,318	50	34,473	50
100,000 and over		43,318	50	39,473	50

HEADS OF HOUSEHOLDS

Taxable Income Over	Not Over	1982 Pay	% on Excess	1982 Pay	% on Excess
$ 0–$	2,300	$ 0	0	$ 0	0
2,300–	4,400	0	12	0	11
4,400–	6,500	252	14	231	13
6,500–	8,700	546	16	504	15
8,700–	11,800	898	20	834	18
11,800–	15,000	1,518	22	1,392	19
15,000–	18,200	2,222	23	2,000	21
18,200–	23,500	2,958	28	2,672	25
23,500–	28,800	4,442	32	3,997	29
28,800–	34,100	6,138	38	5,534	34
34,100–	44,700	8,152	41	7,336	37
44,700–	60,600	12,498	49	11,258	44
60,600–	81,800	20,289	50	18,254	48
81,800–	110,000	30,889	50	28,430	50
110,000–	120,000	44,989	50	42,530	50
120,000–	150,000	49,989	50	47,530	50
150,000–	200,000	64,989	50	62,530	50
200,000 and over		89,989	50	87,530	50

SEPARATE RETURNS—MARRIED PERSONS

Taxable Income Over	Not Over	1982 Pay	% on Excess	1983 Pay	% on Excess
$ 0–$	1,700	$ 0	0	$ 0	0
1,700–	2,750	0	12	0	11
2,750–	3,800	126	14	115	13
3,800–	5,950	273	16	252	15
5,950–	8,000	617	19	574	17
8,000–	10,100	1,006.50	22	923	19
10,100–	12,300	1,468.50	25	1,322	23
12,300–	14,950	2,018.50	29	1,828	26
14,950–	17,600	2,787	33	2,517	30
17,600–	22,900	3,661.50	39	3,312	35
22,900–	30,000	5,728.50	44	5,167	40
30,000–	42,800	8,852.50	49	8,007	44
42,800–	54,700	15,124.50	50	13,639	48
54,700–	70,000	21,074.50	50	19,351	50
70,000–	100,000	28,724.50	50	27,001	50
100,000 and over		43,724.50	50	42,001	50

MARRIED INDIVIDUALS JOINT RETURNS AND SURVIVING SPOUSES

Taxable Income Over	Not Over	1982 Pay	% on Excess	1983 Pay	% on Excess
$ 0–$	3,400	$ 0	0	$ 0	0
3,400–	5,500	0	12	0	11
5,500–	7,600	252	14	231	13
7,600–	11,900	546	16	504	15
11,900–	16,000	1,234	19	1,149	17
16,000–	20,200	2,013	22	1,846	19
20,200–	24,600	2,937	25	2,644	23
24,600–	29,900	4,037	29	3,656	26
29,900–	35,200	5,574	33	5,034	30
35,200–	45,800	7,323	39	6,624	35
45,800–	60,000	11,457	44	10,334	40
60,000–	85,600	17,705	49	16,014	44
85,600–	109,400	30,249	50	27,278	48
109,400–	120,000	42,149	50	38,702	50
120,000–	150,000	47,449	50	44,002	50
150,000–	200,000	62,449	50	59,002	50
200,000 and over		87,449	50	84,002	50

CAPITAL GAINS AND LOSSES (FOR INDIVIDUAL TAXPAYERS)

For income tax purposes a capital gain or loss results from the sale or exchange of a capital asset. A **capital asset** includes any item of property owned **except** merchandise inventories, depreciable property, and three other types of special assets (e.g., copyrights). For example, the personal residence, furnishings, and autos of an individual taxpayer would be capital assets.

A capital gain or loss may be either long term or short term. A **long-term** capital gain or loss results from the sale or exchange of a capital asset after being held for more than one year; a **short-term** capital gain or loss results if the asset has been held for one year or less. This distinction between long-term and short-term capital gains and losses is important for income tax purposes.

A capital gain or loss is **measured,** for income tax purposes, as the difference between the "amount realized" and its "adjusted basis" at the date of disposal. A **net short-term capital gain** results when the short-term capital gains **exceed** the short-term capital losses for the tax year. Basically, short-term capital gains are taxed at ordinary tax rates, whereas long-term capital gains are accorded favorable tax treatment (i.e., only 40 percent of long-term capital gains are taxed). A **net short-term capital loss** results when the short-term capital losses exceed short-term capital gains for the tax year.[4]

Because taxpayers are creative and aggressive in having (1) long-term capital gains rather than short-term capital gains and (2) long-term losses to offset short-term gains during the tax year, complex tax regulations of capital gains and losses have been developed by the Treasury Department to constrain these taxpayer strategies. Detailed discussion of the complexities of capital gains and losses is beyond the scope of this overview of income taxes.

TAX PLANNING FOR THE INDIVIDUAL TAXPAYER

Individual taxpayers should plan, in order to minimize their income tax liabilities, within the provisions of the tax law. Basically, there are two ways to accomplish this objective: (1) timing and/or structural strategies and (2) tax return strategies. Some suggested strategies that should be discussed with a competent tax adviser are as follows:[5]

---

[4] Casualty and theft losses (i.e., involuntary losses) usually are not capital losses; they are deducted in full (see Exhibit A–5, Schedule A—Itemized Deductions). The deduction for a personal casualty loss is limited to the amount of each loss in excess of $100. For years after 1982, a taxpayers' aggregate personal casualty and theft losses, less the $100 floor for each separate loss are deductible only to the extent that the total exceeds 10 percent of adjusted gross income.

[5] Tax planning should not be confused with tax evasion. Tax evasion involves illegal activities to reduce the tax liability, such as not reporting cash receipts from a source other than recorded income (e.g., tips). Severe penalties are proscribed for tax evasion activities.

Timing and/or structural strategies	Tax return preparation strategies
1. Investments in equity securities versus debt securities.	1. Whether to itemize deductions or to use the zero bracket amount.
2. Investments in tax-free municipal bonds.	2. Use of credit cards; an expenditure when charged for a "cash basis" return.
3. Individual Retirement Accounts (IRAs).	3. Choice of depreciation method used for income producing property.
4. Long-term versus short-term capital gains and losses.	4. Control of cash payments near year-end.
5. Income tax shelters (risk).	5. Deductions for sales taxes, property taxes, and licenses.
6. Ownership and operation of incorporated businesses.	6. Interest expense (prepaid interest).
7. Investment tax credits (recapture provisions).	7. Casualty and theft losses, and related insurance recovery.
8. Sale of personal residence.	8. Child care, job-seeking costs, medical costs, education costs.
9. Energy savings credits and pollution controls.	9. Short-term and long-term capital gains and losses (carryforwards).
10. Gifts, contributions, trusts, estate planning.	10. Avoidance of interest and penalties for incorrect and late tax return and tax payments (estimated.)

PART B—INCOME TAXES PAID BY CORPORATIONS

A business may be organized as a sole proprietorship, partnership, or corporation. Sole (or single) proprietorships and partnerships are not required to pay income taxes.[6] In Part A we explained that the earnings (or losses) of sole proprietorships and partnerships must be included on the individual income tax return(s) of the owner(s). In contrast, a **corporation,** as a separate taxable entity, is required to file an annual income tax return and to pay any income taxes based upon its taxable income. The **stockholders** of a corporation pay income taxes on the corporation's earnings only when, and to the extent that, they receive dividends (out of corporate "earnings and profits").[7]

INCOME TAX RATES FOR CORPORATIONS

Corporate income tax rates are as shown below along with an illustration of their application.

---

[6] Federal income tax law views sole proprietorships and partnerships as conduits for earnings to flow through to the owners. Partnerships must file an information return showing the determination of net income and the share of that income allocated to each partner. Distribution of assets to partners are not considered as partnership expenses for income tax purposes.

[7] Some people criticize this tax structure on the basis that the earnings of a corporation are subject to double taxation—once when earned and again when those earnings are distributed to stockholders as cash dividends.

Corporate income tax		*Illustration assuming*
Rate	*Bracket*	*taxable income of $150,000*
16%*	on first $25,000	16% × $25,000 = $ 4,000
19%*	on next 25,000	19% × $25,000 = 4,750
30%	on next 25,000	30% × $25,000 = 7,500
40%	on next 25,000	40% × $25,000 = 10,000
46%	on remaining income	
	over $100,000	46% × $50,000 = 23,000
		Total income tax $49,250

* After 1982, 15 percent and 18 percent, respectively.

Both individual and corporate income taxpayers may have to estimate their income tax liability. Corporations may have to make quarterly installment payments thereon during the year. Individual taxpayers have their taxes withheld by their employers; however, when they have taxable income that is not subject to withholding, they also may have to make quarterly payments.

SPECIAL INCOME TAX PROVISIONS FOR CORPORATIONS

Taxable income for a corporation is determined in much the same manner as it is for individual taxpayers. However, there are some differences in the income tax provisions for corporations including the following:

1. The required tax forms—Form 1120, U.S. Corporation Income Tax Return, is significantly different from Form 1040, U.S. Individual Income Tax Return (compare Exhibits A–3 and A–8).
2. Currently, a corporation may elect to use either the cash or accrual basis for measuring **taxable income;** however, when the production, purchase, or sale of goods is a significant activity of the corporation, the accrual basis must be used.
3. There is no category "itemized deductions" or a "zero bracket amount" for corporations; also, corporations cannot have personal deductions.
4. A corporation may exclude from taxable income 85 percent of any **dividend** revenue received from taxable domestic corporations (it is 100 percent under specified conditions).
5. A corporation may deduct **organization** expenditures and amortize them over a five-year period or longer.
6. Corporations can deduct charitable contributions up to 10 percent of income before the contribution deduction. Any contribution in excess of this limit may be carried forward to five successive years provided that the 10 percent limit is not exceeded in any of those years.
7. Corporations may deduct, as expense, salaries paid to stockholders (i.e., owners) to the extent that the amount paid is reasonably related to the services performed.

8. A corporation must present beginning and ending balance sheets with the annual tax return.

9. The annual tax return of a corporation must include a reconciliation of the ending balance of retained earnings with the income data presented on the tax return.

10. A corporation has the option of using a 28 percent tax rate on its capital gains.

COMPUTATION OF CORPORATE INCOME TAX

Taxable income of a corporation basically is computed as GROSS INCOME minus ORDINARY DEDUCTIONS minus SPECIAL DEDUCTIONS. Exhibit A–7 presents an overview of the corporate tax return and lists the specific items that are included in gross income, ordinary deductions, and special deductions. This overview of "Form 1120, U.S. Corporation Income Tax Return" is presented to help you understand the basic components of the corporate income tax return. Exhibit A–8 presents a copy of the 1982 **corporation** income tax return; the basic tax return (Form 1120) has the following **nine** attached schedules to support it:

Schedule designation	Schedule title
A	Cost of goods sold
C	Dividends and special deductions
E	Compensation of officers
F	Bad debts, reserve method
J	Tax computation
—	Additional information
L	Balance sheets
M–1	Reconciliation of income per books with income per tax return
M–2	Analysis of unappropriated retained earnings per books

(Other special schedules are available and used as needed.)

The corporate income tax form is presented in Exhibit A–8 for the sole purpose of giving you an idea of the nature and complexity of a corporation tax return. You may wish to compare it with the individual tax return (given in Exhibit A–3).

ACCOUNTING INCOME VERSUS TAXABLE INCOME

Accounting income is reported on the income statement; it measures the income or loss of a business on the accrual basis in accordance with generally accepted accounting principles (GAAP). In contrast, **taxable income** is reported on the income tax return; it is determined in accordance with tax law and the regulations. The U.S. Congress identifies the objectives and specifies in general terms the manner of computing taxable income. These objectives usually are different than the objectives of financial reporting (per GAAP). The objectives of the income

EXHIBIT A–7
**Overview of form
1120, U.S.
corporation income
tax return**

Major captions	Specific items included

1982 Corporation Return, Form 1120, Simplified
[¶ 200]

The chart below is provided as an aid to visualizing the integration of the income tax law with corporation Form 1120. It is intended for corporations in general, and not for special classes of corporations, such as Subchapter S corporations (¶ 244), life insurance companies (¶ 286), regulated investment companies (¶ 273), etc.

GROSS INCOME

Gross Profit:
  Gross Sales (¶ 702)
  Gross Receipts from Services (¶ 701, 702)
Dividends 100% Includible in Gross Income (¶ 737)
Interest (¶ 727)
Rents and Royalties (¶ 767, 768)
Capital Gain Net Income (¶ 962)
Net Gain (or Loss) on Sales or Exchanges (¶ 901, 902)
Other Income

minus

ORDINARY DEDUCTIONS FROM GROSS INCOME

Compensation of Officers (¶ 1043)
Salaries and Wages (¶ 1043)
Repairs (¶ 1041)
Bad Debts (¶ 1111)
Rents (¶ 1054)
Taxes (¶ 1003, 1078)
Interest (¶ 1071)
Contributions (¶ 1147)
Amortization, Depreciation and Depletion (¶ 1151-1199)
Advertising (¶ 1059)
Pension and Profit-Sharing Plans; Employee Benefit Programs (¶ 540)
Other; including Casualty Losses (¶ 1097) and Research and Experimental Costs (¶ 1048)

and minus

SPECIAL DEDUCTIONS

Net Operating Loss Deduction (¶ 1119)
85% Dividends Received Deduction (100% Election in Case of Certain Corporate Groups) (¶ 233, 234)
Organizational Expense Amortization, Elective (¶ 237)

equals

TAXABLE INCOME

To which rates are applied:
  Rates range from 16% to 40% on taxable income of up to and including $100,000 and 46% on taxable income in excess of $100,000 (¶ 213).
And from Total Tax There Are Deducted 1982 Estimated Tax Payments, Any Investment Tax Credit (¶ 1179), Any Foreign Tax Credit (¶ 1351), Any Targeted Jobs Tax Credit (¶ 175F), Any Employee Stock Ownership Credit (¶ 1178), Any Nonconventional Source Fuel Credit (¶ 1190), Any Incremental Research Credit (¶ 175H), Any Alcohol Fuels Credit (¶ 1191), and Any Credit for Federal Excise Tax on Gasoline, Special Fuels, and Lubricating Oil Used for Nontaxable Purposes (¶ 173)
And There Are Added Any Personal Holding Company Tax (¶ 261), Any Tax from Recomputating a Prior Year Investment Credit (¶ 1183) and Any Minimum Tax on Tax Preferences (¶ 238)

EXHIBIT A–8
U.S. corporation income tax return

U.S. Corporation Income Tax Return

For calendar year 1982 or other tax year beginning ...., 1982, ending ...., 19........
▶For Paperwork Reduction Act Notice, see page 1 of the Instructions

OMB No. 1545–0123

1982

Check if a—

A. Consolidated return ☐
B. Personal Holding Co. ☐
C. Business Code No. (See page 9 of Instructions)

Use IRS label. Otherwise please print or type.	Name	
	Number and street	
	City or town, State, and ZIP code	

D. Employer identification number

E. Date incorporated

F. Total assets (see Specific Instructions)
$

Gross Income

1 (a) Gross receipts or sales $ .... (b) Less returns and allowances $ .... Balance ▶	1(c)	
2 Cost of goods sold (Schedule A) and/or operations (attach schedule)	2	
3 Gross profit (subtract line 2 from line 1(c))	3	
4 Dividends (Schedule C)	4	
5 Interest	5	
6 Gross rents	6	
7 Gross royalties	7	
8 Capital gain net income (attach separate Schedule D)	8	
9 Net gain or (loss) from Form 4797, line 11(a), Part II (attach Form 4797)	9	
10 Other income (see instructions—attach schedule)	10	
11 TOTAL income—Add lines 3 through 10	11	

Deductions

12 Compensation of officers (Schedule E)	12	
13 (a) Salaries and wages .... 13(b) Less jobs credit .... Balance ▶	13(c)	
14 Repairs (see instructions)	14	
15 Bad debts (Schedule F if reserve method is used)	15	
16 Rents	16	
17 Taxes	17	
18 Interest	18	
19 Contributions (not over 10% of line 30 adjusted per instructions)	19	
20 Depreciation (attach Form 4562) 20		
21 Less depreciation claimed in Schedule A and elsewhere on return . . 21(a) ( )	21(b)	
22 Depletion	22	
23 Advertising	23	
24 Pension, profit-sharing, etc. plans (see instructions)	24	
25 Employee benefit programs (see instructions)	25	
26 Other deductions (attach schedule)	26	
27 TOTAL deductions—Add lines 12 through 26	27	
28 Taxable income before net operating loss deduction and special deductions (subtract line 27 from line 11) .	28	
29 Less: (a) Net operating loss deduction (see instructions—attach schedule) . . 29(a)		
(b) Special deductions (Schedule C) . . . . 29(b)	29	
30 Taxable income (subtract line 29 from line 28)	30	

Tax

31 TOTAL TAX (Schedule J)	31	
32 Credits: (a) Overpayment from 1981 allowed as a credit . .		
(b) 1982 estimated tax payments		
(c) Less refund of 1982 estimated tax applied for on Form 4466 . ( )		
(d) Tax deposited: Form 7004 Form 7005 (attach) Total ▶		
(e) Credit from regulated investment companies (attach Form 2439)		
(f) Federal tax on special fuels and oils (attach Form 4136)	32	
33 TAX DUE (subtract line 32 from line 31—If line 32 is greater than line 31, skip line 33 and go to line 34). See instruction C3 for depositary method of payment	33	
(Check ▶ ☐ if Form 2220 is attached. See instruction D.) ▶ $		
34 OVERPAYMENT (subtract line 31 from line 32)	34	
35 Enter amount of line 34 you want: Credited to 1983 estimated tax ▶ .... Refunded ▶	35	

Please Sign Here

Under penalties of perjury, I declare that I have examined this return, including accompanying schedules and statements, and to the best of my knowledge and belief, it is true, correct, and complete. Declaration of preparer (other than taxpayer) is based on all information of which preparer has any knowledge.

▶		
Signature of officer	Date	▶ Title

Paid Preparer's Use Only

Preparer's signature ▶	Date	Check if self-employed ▶ ☐	Preparer's social security no.
Firm's name (or yours, if self-employed) and address ▶		E.I. No. ▶	
		ZIP code ▶	

tax system include *(a)* providing revenue to meet the expenditures of the federal government and *(b)* implementing certain public policy decisions (such as defense, social programs, education, and foreign aid). Therefore, it is no surprise that in a given year accounting income and taxable income of a particular corporation may differ significantly. To illustrate, consider six of the major areas of difference: (1) cash versus accrual basis of accounting, (2) the modified accrual basis used for tax is different from the strict accrual basis used for accounting purposes, (3) special tax provisions for recognizing certain revenues and expenses, (4) capital gains and losses, (5) tax-exempt income, and (6) use of different accounting methods for some items, such as depreciation. To illustrate, we discuss three major areas: (1) revenue and expense recognition, (2) modifications of the "cash" and "accrual" bases, and (3) use of different accounting methods.

REVENUE AND EXPENSE RECOGNITION FOR INCOME TAX PURPOSES

Many, but not all, of the income tax provisions are designed to prevent both individual and corporate taxpayers from manipulating the timing and structuring of transactions to shift income (or loss) among periods simply to take advantage of more favorable tax policy and tax rates. There is a never ending "battle" between the taxing authorities and the taxpayers (who become very creative). As a consequence, tax provisions dealing with revenue and expense recognition often cause major differences between accounting income and taxable income. Some of the more common examples are:

1. Interest revenue on state and municipal bonds is excluded from taxable income, although it is included in accounting income.
2. Amortization of purchased goodwill is not deducted in computing taxable income, although it is deducted in computing accounting income.
3. Statutory depletion, rather than depletion based on cost, sometimes may be used to compute taxable income, but cannot be used to compute accounting income.
4. Rent revenue collected in advance is included in taxable income when collected, but it is included in accounting income on the accrual basis.

MODIFIED CASH BASIS AND MODIFIED ACCRUAL BASIS USED FOR MEASURING TAXABLE INCOME

As discussed throughout this book, accounting income must be measured using a pure accrual basis. Under this basis, **recognition** occurs when revenues are realized (i.e., when the earnings process is essentially completed) and when expenses are incurred, regardless of the timing of the related cash flows. GAAP prohibits use of cash basis accounting because it does not appropriately measure income.

In contrast, for income tax purposes either a (1) modified accrual basis or (2) a modified cash basis may be used. The **modified accrual basis** excludes certain revenues (such as interest on tax-free bonds, capital gains and losses). In respect to expenses, the timing of recognition may be different (e.g., depreciation expense), and some expenses are entirely excluded for income tax purposes (e.g., amortization of goodwill). The **modified cash basis** used to measure taxable income is not strictly cash receipts minus cash payments. Cash receipts are measured as taxable revenue when the cash has been **constructively received** (this term is essentially defined as: although not yet in possession, but so much within the control of the taxpayer that possession is reasonably assured). In respect to expenses, cash payments cannot include cash paid to purchase **depreciable property** that has an estimated useful life of more than one year. Under the cash basis for computing taxable income, such a purchase is an acquisition of an asset, and that asset then must be depreciated for tax purposes. Thus, you see that the cash basis treats such property as if the accrual basis is being used.

Use of different accounting methods

Tax law and the regulations permit use of accounting methods for computing taxable income that differ from those permitted for determining accounting income. For example, a company may use the straight-line method of depreciation for computing accounting income, but use an accelerated depreciation method to compute taxable income. Four other common examples relate to depletion, profit on long-term construction contracts, capital gains and losses, and gross margin or profit on installment sales.[8]

TAX PLANNING BY BUSINESS MANAGERS

Because income tax rates are high and the related income tax law and regulations are complex, tax planning is an important consideration in many of the business decisions made by the management of any business. The basic objective of tax planning is to minimize income taxes within the framework of tax law and the regulations prescribed by the Treasury Department. Tax planning focuses on anticipated tax consequences of future transactions. To provide an overview of tax planning we will discuss three of the major areas that affect most business entities: (1) selecting the type of business organization, (2) financing the business, and (3) structuring transactions before they occur.

Selecting the type of business organization

Sole proprietorships, partnerships, and corporations have different income tax implications for owners and managers. When starting a new business, selecting the type of business organization poses several substantive issues, one of which has the long-term income tax implications. The tax obligation related to the operations of a sole proprietorship depends upon the marginal income tax rate of the individual owner, and for a partnership it depends upon the marginal tax rates of each partner. Marginal tax rates are applied to the annual earnings of the business whether they are withdrawn by the owners or not. In contrast, the tax obligation on corporate earnings depends upon *(a)* the tax rates of the corporation (when the earnings are realized) and *(b)* the marginal tax rates of the stockholders when the corporation pays dividends out of those earnings. The relevant

---

[8] The installment method of income recognition permits taxpayers to defer income recognition until cash is collected, and therefore the taxpayer has the funds to pay the tax.

income tax provisions for these issues are beyond the scope of this overview; however, keep in mind that they have significant impact at date of organization, over the life of the business, and eventually upon dissolution of the business.

Financing a business

Basically, a business obtains funds (e.g., cash) from three sources: (1) investments by owners, (2) borrowing, and (3) earnings of the business. Often when new or additional funds are needed (e.g., for operations and expansion), the management of the company must decide between equity and debt (or some combination) as the source(s) of funds. Such decisions have important income tax implications, particularly for a corporation, because interest on debt is a fully deductible expense in computing taxable income; in comparison dividends paid to shareholders (of common and preferred stock) are not deductible. To illustrate, assume Tye Corporation needs $500,000 cash to acquire a new productive facility. The management is considering two alternatives as follows:

Alternative A—Borrow the needed funds at 12 percent interest; the marginal income tax for the company is 46 percent.

Alternative B—Issue for cash, 50,000 shares of the company's cumulative 8 percent, preferred stock, at $10 par value per share.

The two financing alternatives can be analyzed as follows:

Alternative A, borrowing:

$$\$500,000 \times 12\% \times (1.00 - .46) = \$32,400 \text{ aftertax cost per year}$$
$$\text{Net interest rate: } \$32,400 \div \$500,000 = \underline{6.48\%}$$

Alternative B, issue capital stock:

$$\$500,000 \times 8\% = \$40,000 \text{ aftertax cost per year}$$
$$\text{Net interest rate: } \$40,000 \div \$500,000 = \underline{8.0\%}$$

The borrowing alternative is less costly because the interest expense expense is deducted from taxable income at the 46 percent marginal tax rate. However, a number of other factors should be considered in making this decision. For instance, the company is legally required to make the fixed interest payments of $60,000 per year and to repay the $500,000 principal amount on maturity date, regardless of whether the company earned income or incurred a loss. In contrast, by choosing to issue capital stock, these fixed payments may be avoided; dividends can be paid only if there are accumulated earnings (i.e., a positive balance in retained earnings); also, there is no payment on a maturity date for the shares issued. It may be helpful at this point to review the sections in Chapters 11 and 12 on *(a)* return on owners' equity, *(b)* return on total assets, and *(c)* financial leverage.

Structuring and timing transactions to minimize income taxes

Business transactions often can be structured and/or timed in ways to maximize their favorable, or minimize their unfavorable, income tax consequences. It is important to realize that such structuring and timing must be accomplished prior to, and not after, the transaction has been completed. Some typical transactions that can be structured or timed for this purpose are:

1. Leasing versus purchase of operating assets.
2. Installment sale of real estate.
3. Valuation of several "used" assets purchased at a lump-sum price (i.e., land and the building thereon).
4. Valuation of assets and liabilities of a purchased business.
5. Allocation of the lump-sum purchase price of depreciable versus nondepreciable assets.
6. Recognition of investment tax credit (deferral versus flow through).
7. Accelerated depreciation (change in mid-life).
8. Energy credits and pollution control costs.
9. Tax-free exchanges of certain types of assets.
10. Capital gains and losses (short term versus long term).
11. The wide range of approved "tax shelters."
12. Purchase of merchandise for inventory (related to the inventory flow method, such as LIFO).

DEMONSTRATION CASE

(To illustrate, for instructional purposes only, computation of income tax without using the required standardized forms.)

The accounting records of Dow Corporation (no subsidiaries) provided the following 19D data:

Sales revenue	$700,000	Cash dividends received	$ 8,000
Interest revenue	3,000	Compensation of officers	125,000
Bad debt expense	1,800	Advertising expense	7,000
Taxes (excluding income tax)	5,000	Interest expense	15,000
Depreciation expense	20,000	Repair expense	1,200
Charitable contributions		Salaries and wages	121,000
(net allowable)	4,000	Special deductions	9,000
19D estimated income tax		Employee benefit programs	40,000
payments (total paid)	30,000		
Cost of goods sold	242,000		

Required:

Prepare a schedule to compute the 19D income tax for Dow Corporation. To compute total tax, assume there are no additional complications not given above, such as investment tax credit, jobs credit, personal holding company, minimum tax, etc. Set up the major captions listed in Exhibit A–8. Use terminology and identifying lines from Form 1120. Assume that 1982 income tax rates apply.

Suggested solution

Line	Item	Amount	
	Gross income:		
1	Sales revenue	$ 700,000	
2	Cost of goods sold	(242,000)	
3	Gross profit	458,000	
4	Dividends	8,000	
5	Interest	3,000	
11	Total income		$469,000
	Ordinary deductions:		
12	Compensation of officers	125,000	
13	Salaries and wages	121,000	
14	Repairs	1,200	
15	Bad debts	1,800	
17	Taxes	5,000	
18	Interest	15,000	
19	Contributions	4,000	
20	Depreciation	20,000	
23	Advertising	7,000	
25	Employee benefit programs	40,000	
27	Total deductions		340,000
28	Taxable income before special deductions		129,000
	Special deductions:		
29b	Special deduction		(9,000)
30	Taxable income		$120,000
	Tax:		
31	Total tax	35,450	
32	Credits:		
	(b) 19D estimated tax payments	(30,000)	
33	Tax due		$ 5,450

* Computation:
(16% $\times$ $25,000) + (19% $\times$ $25,000) + (30% $\times$ $25,000) + (40% $\times$ $25,000) + (46% $\times$ $20,000) = $35,450.

QUESTIONS FOR DISCUSSION

PART A

1. *(a)* What is the form number and title of the individual income tax return? *(b)* When and where must the return be filed? *(c)* What are the minimum gross income amounts that make the filing of an individual income tax return required?

2. Why do most individual taxpayers elect the cash basis to measure taxable income?

3. Give the formula for determining taxable income for an individual taxpayer.

4. The files of Dr. Joe Rock, an optometrist, showed that $60,000 cash was collected from patients during 19X. At the beginning of 19X, total receivables from patients amounted to $12,000, and at the end of 19X the amount was $8,500. What amount of gross income should be included in the computation of taxable income assuming the *(a)* cash basis $_____ and *(b)* the accrual basis $_____ ?

5. John P. Jones is regularly employed by CT Company as personnel director. His monthly salary during 19G (before any deductions) was $3,000. During 19G, Jones collected $7,500

cash from another source for independently contracted consulting services. List the two forms that Jones should receive relating to his earnings and indicate basically what each form should report.

6. Explain the income tax treatment of interest received on state and municipal bonds.

7. What is a capital asset for tax purposes? What are the two kinds of gains or losses that usually arise when capital assets are sold?

PART B

8. Indicate whether each of the following types of business organizations is required to file a separate income tax return: (a) sole proprietorship, (b) partnership, and (c) corporation. Explain the basis for each answer.

9. Complete the following tabulation based on the 1982 corporate tax rates:

Case	Taxable income	Amount of income tax
A	$ 25,000	_____
B	56,000	_____
C	110,000	_____

10. Give the formula for determining taxable income for a corporation.

11. Form 1120, U.S. Corporation Income Tax Return, is a one-page standardized form; however, attached to it are nine subschedules. What is the primary purpose of these nine sub-schedules?

12. List and briefly explain three areas in which there are differences between corporate accounting income and taxable income.

13. If a corporate taxpayer uses the cash basis to measure taxable income, it must depreciate (not expense as one amount) property having a useful life of more than one year (as is done in accrual accounting). Is this statement true or false? Explain.

14. Explain why a corporation often prefers to obtain needed cash (e.g., for expansion) by selling bonds rather than by issuing shares of its own capital stock.

EXERCISES

PART A

EA–1. Assume you are a CPA in public practice and have agreed to speak on the subject of income taxes. You have decided to use transparencies with data on some of your typical clients. Two of the transparencies will be organized as shown below.

Required:

Complete the following transparencies:

a. Clients A, B, C, and D each have taxable income of $40,000. Use 1982 tax rates.

Cliental Filing Status	Taxable Income	Income Tax		Average Tax Rate
		Computation	Amount	
A. Single	$40,000			
B. Head of household	40,000			
C. Married, separate	40,000			
D. Married joint	40,000			

What primary point on this transparency would you emphasize?

b. Clients E, F, and G, each married, will file jointly with the indicated income.

Client	Taxable Income	Income Tax		Average Tax Rate
		Computation	Amount	
E	$ 12,000			
F	50,000			
G	130,000			

What primary point on this transparency would you emphasize?

EA–2. On Form 1040, U.S. Individual Income Tax Return, Line 6e, is entitled "Total number of exemptions claimed." Assume you are preparing income tax returns for eight different clients.

Required:

a. Based on the data given below, determine the number of exemptions to which each taxpayer is entitled and complete the last column of the following schedule:

Client	Filing Status	Age	Number of Dependents	Blind	Form 1040, Line 6e Exemptions Claimed
A	Single	22	0	No	
B	Married, separately	33*	2	No	
C	Married, jointly	41*	9	No	
D	Head of household	65	1	No	
E	Single	66	0	Yes	
F	Married, separately	67*	1	No	
G	Married, jointly	75*	0	Yes	
H	Head of household	65	2	No	

* Age of spouse:
  Client B, 28; Client C, 37: Client F, 43; and Client G, 72 and blind.

b. Assume that the amount for each one of the above taxpayers on Form 1040, line 35, is $30,000. Compute taxable income (line 37).

EA–3. Assume you are a CPA in public practice and that the amounts given below are the total itemized deductions for six of your clients.

Client and Filing Status	Total Itemized Deductions	Zero Bracket Amount	Amount that Should Be Entered on Form 1040, Line 34a
A. Single	$5,000		
B. Single	2,000		
C. Single	3,300		
D. Married, jointly	2,000		
E. Married, jointly	7,000		
F. Married, jointly	3,400		

Required:

a. Complete the above schedule.

b. Explain the basis for each amount that you entered in the last column.

EA–4.   Two of your clients, Samuel and Sue Smith, have engaged you to prepare their 19C, U.S. individual income tax return. They have four children and will file a joint return (cash basis). Sam and Sue are 36 and 34, respectively. They have provided you with the following information:

Salary (W-2)	$75,000
Income taxes withheld (W-2)	14,000
Business income, consulting (net of applicable expenses)	5,000
Interest revenue (including $2,000 on tax-free bonds)	10,000
Rental revenue (per Schedule F)	6,000
Casualty loss theft, from residence (net of $100 deduction)	1,800
Interest paid (on residence)	23,000
Medical deductions	None
Property taxes paid (on residence)	2,100
Sales taxes paid (including $200 on vehicles).....	2,000
Payments to Keogh (HR10) retirement plan......	7,000
Residential energy credit (from Form 5695)	500
Estimated payments on 19C income tax	3,000

Required:

Set up an abbreviated schedule in a manner similar to the demonstration case (instead of using Form 1040) and compute the amount of the required income tax payment (or refund) on April 15, 19D. Use the major captions shown in Exhibit A–1 and show all computations. Use terminology and identifying lines from Form 1040. Use 1982 rates.

PART B

EA–5.   Doss Corporation is preparing its 19G federal income tax return. Taxable income has been computed as $115,000 (accrual basis). An overpayment of income tax for 19F of $9,000 was carried over and will be applied to the 19G income tax liability. Also, the company remitted 19G total estimated income tax payments of $18,000.

Required:

Refer to Exhibit A–8 and complete lines 30–35 of the corporate tax return. Show computations.

EA–6.   Below is a list of 20 items, each of which may or may not be related to taxable income (either as an increase or decrease). For each item, enter a check mark under either "Yes" or "No" to indicate whether that item should be included in measuring taxable income. Assume the individual taxpayer does not own a sole proprietorship or an interest in a partnership.

Item	Included in Computation of Taxable Income			
	Individual*		Corporation	
	Yes	No	Yes	No
1. Interest revenue on tax-exempt municipal bonds				
2. Cost of traveling from home to place of employment (by owner[s])				
3. Fee paid to CPA for preparing tax return				
4. Interest paid on debt on residence of owner(s)				
5. Storm damage to personal auto				
6. Contributions to charity				
7. IRS penalty for late tax return				
8. Income taxes withheld (reported on W-2)				
9. State income taxes				
10. Medical expenses				
11. Insurance on residence of owner(s)				
12. Depreciation expense				
13. Amortization of organization expenditures				
14. Exemptions (personal)				
15. Depletion expense (oil and gas)				
16. Union dues paid				
17. Presidential election campaign (deduction)				
18. Bad debts				
19. Casualty insurance on residence of owner(s)				
20. Zero bracket amount				

* With no separate sole proprietorship or partnership interest.

EA–7.   Reneau Corporation's 19W income statement reported pretax items as follows:

Sales revenue	$1,033,000
Interest revenue (including $4,000 on interest-free municipal bonds)	9,000
Salaries and wages paid	102,000
Repairs	7,000
Bad debts (Schedule F)	2,000
Cost of goods sold (Schedule A)	460,000
Gross rent received	7,200
Compensation of officers (Schedule E)	130,000
Gross royalties received	4,800
Rents paid	8,000
19W estimated income tax payments	60,000
Special deduction (Schedule C)	15,000
Depreciation (Form 4562)	18,000
Advertising	20,000
Interest paid and accrued	30,000
Contributions	4,000
Overpayment of 19V income tax (applicable to 19W)	6,000
Taxes paid (on property)	24,000

Required:

Prepare a schedule to compute the income tax due when the tax return is filed. Assume there are no complications other than those presented above. Set up the major captions given in Exhibit A–7. Use terminology and identifying lines from Form 1120. Use 1982 tax rates.

PROBLEMS/CASES

PART A

PCA–1.   The following information has been provided to you by your client, Gene Horton:

Salary	$55,000
Charitable contributions, cash (allowable)	5,000
Interest on home mortgage	2,300
Interest on Visa charge card	78
Interest on school loan	149
Federal income taxes withheld (Form W-2) ...	20,000
Property taxes	780
Sales tax	164
Rental income	1,800
Professional dues (AICPA)	50
Interest income	200
Penalty on early withdrawal of savings	54
Residential energy credit	150
Contribution to IRA	1,000

Gene is a single, 44-year-old, cash basis, calendar-year taxpayer. Assume that 1982 rates apply.

Required:

Using the demonstration case in the chapter as a model, set up an abbreviated schedule to compute the amount of income tax due or the refund for this year. Show computations, and use terminology from Form 1040.

PCA–2. Two of your clients, Raymond and Sherry Stewart, engaged you to prepare their 19C individual income tax return. They want to file the return in a manner that will minimize their tax liability. Raymond and Sherry have asked you to evaluate whether it would be more beneficial to them to file a joint return or to file separately (using the tax tables for married filing separately). Assume that 1982 income tax rates apply.

Salary from Raymond's W-2	$27,000
Salary from Sherry's W-2	25,000
Sherry's consulting revenue (net of applicable expenses)	18,250
There are no other sources of income and their total deductions do not exceed the zero bracket amount.	

Required:

a. What would you recommend with respect to their tax return(s)? Show calculations to support your recommendations.

b. What would you recommend assuming Raymond did not earn a salary in 19C?

PART B

PCA–3. John Springer, a single individual, age 31, wants to incorporate his small business. As a primary job, John works as an engineer for TPX Corporation and receives a yearly salary of $41,000 ($12,000 was withheld from his paycheck for 19C). Two years ago John started a small business which has been operated as a sole proprietorship. Gross revenues from the business average about $12,000 per year, with the following expenses:

Advertising	$500
Supplies	700
Interest	800
Depreciation	450
Travel	910
Telephone	360
Legal and professional fees	240

John expects his income from TPX to remain approximately the same for the next several years, but foresees considerable growth potential in his own consulting business. Assume 1982 rates apply in all situations.

Required:

a. Compute John's total income tax obligation based on the assumption that his consulting business is continued as a sole proprietorship. Alternatively, what would the income tax be if he incorporated his own consulting business and withdraw all of its earnings as dividends?

b. Would your answer to requirement *a* be different if the **taxable income** (Schedule C) from John's own consulting business was $100,000? Support your response with calculations.

PCA–4. XYZ Corporation is considering financing alternatives to expand its current facilities at a cost of $300,000. The president of XYZ suggests issuing 30,000 shares of its 10 percent preferred stock, cumulative, par $10 to finance the expansion. The controller recommends that XYZ sell 300 bonds with a stated rate of 10 percent paid annually (yield rate 10 percent) to get the funds. Each bond has a par value of $1,000 and matures in 10 years. Assume 1982 tax rates apply.

Required:

a. Assume taxable income, before interest expense, of $150,000. What effect does each alternative have on income taxes?
b. Evaluate the two alternatives in terms of cash flows now and in future years.
c. What alternative would you recommend? Explain the basis for your recommendation.

Special Supplement B
1982 Financial Statements of Johnson & Johnson

Johnson & Johnson and Subsidiaries   Consolidated Balance Sheet

At January 2, 1983 and January 3, 1982 (Dollars in Millions Except Per Share Figures)	1982	1981
Assets		
Current assets		
Cash and cash items	$ 140.4	101.2
Marketable securities, at cost, which approximates market value	225.1	325.8
Accounts receivable, trade, less allowances $24.8 (1981, $22.2)	758.1	705.9
Inventories (Notes 1 and 6)	957.5	900.1
Prepaid expenses and other receivables	172.0	169.2
Total current assets	2,253.1	2,202.2
Marketable securities, non-current, at cost, which approximates market value	222.1	193.5
Property, plant and equipment, at cost (Note 1)		
Land and land improvements	142.2	123.9
Buildings and building equipment	924.7	772.9
Machinery and equipment	1,005.9	899.1
Construction in progress	238.6	217.7
	2,311.4	2,013.6
Less accumulated depreciation and amortization	733.5	678.0
	1,577.9	1,335.6
Other assets	156.5	89.1
Total assets	$4,209.6	3,820.4
Liabilities and Stockholders' Equity		
Current liabilities		
Loans and notes payable (Note 7)	$ 213.9	195.4
Accounts payable, trade	266.6	247.0
Miscellaneous accounts payable	45.5	50.0
Taxes on income	1.3	90.8
Salaries, wages and commissions	75.0	70.9
Miscellaneous taxes	53.6	50.2
Miscellaneous accrued liabilities	244.3	176.9
Total current liabilities	900.2	881.2
Long-term debt (Note 7)	142.2	91.7
Certificates of extra compensation (Note 11)	42.9	38.3
Deferred investment tax credits	35.3	30.1
Other liabilities and deferrals	279.8	239.6
Minority interests in international subsidiaries	9.7	11.6
Stockholders' equity		
Preferred stock—without par value (authorized and unissued 2,000,000 shares)	—	—
Common stock—par value $1.00 per share (authorized 270,000,000 shares; issued 189,361,000 and 187,297,000 shares)	189.4	187.3
Additional capital	234.5	178.2
Cumulative currency translation adjustments (Note 4)	(163.5)	(85.7)
Retained earnings	2,540.1	2,249.1
	2,800.5	2,528.9
Less common stock held in treasury, at cost (234,000 and 235,000 shares)	1.0	1.0
Total stockholders' equity	2,799.5	2,527.9
Total liabilities and stockholders' equity	$4,209.6	3,820.4

See Notes to Consolidated Financial Statements

Johnson & Johnson and Subsidiaries   Consolidated Statement of Earnings and Retained Earnings

Dollars in Millions Except Per Share Figures (Note 1)	1982	1981 *	1980 *
Revenues			
Sales to customers	**$5,760.9**	5,399.0	4,837.4
Other revenues			
Interest income	**88.9**	78.8	50.0
Royalties and miscellaneous	**49.3**	28.6	26.4
	138.2	107.4	76.4
Total revenues	**5,899.1**	5,506.4	4,913.8
Costs and expenses			
Cost of products sold	**2,450.9**	2,368.4	2,194.3
Selling, distribution and administrative expenses	**2,248.8**	2,030.6	1,794.2
Research expense	**363.2**	282.9	232.8
Interest expense	**74.4**	60.7	37.0
Interest expense capitalized	**(46.3)**	(43.5)	(32.7)
Other expenses	**20.9**	23.4	12.9
Total costs and expenses	**5,111.9**	4,722.5	4,238.5
Earnings before provision for taxes on income and extraordinary charge	**787.2**	783.9	675.3
Provision for taxes on income (Note 3)	**263.8**	316.3	274.6
Earnings before extraordinary charge	**523.4**	467.6	400.7
Extraordinary charge—withdrawal of TYLENOL capsules (net of $50.0 taxes) (Note 2)	**(50.0)**	—	—
Net earnings	**473.4**	467.6	400.7
Retained earnings at beginning of period	**2,249.1**	1,940.1	1,676.3
Cash dividends paid (per share: 1982, $.97; 1981, $.85; 1980, $.74)	**(182.4)**	(158.6)	(136.9)
Retained earnings at end of period	**$2,540.1**	2,249.1	1,940.1
Per share of common stock			
Earnings before extraordinary charge	**$ 2.79**	2.51	2.17
Extraordinary charge	**(.27)**	—	—
Net earnings per share	**$ 2.52**	2.51	2.17

Consolidated Statement of Common Stock, Additional Capital and Treasury Stock

Dollars in Millions, Shares in Thousands (Note 1)	Common Stock Issued		Additional Capital	Treasury Stock	
	Shares	Amount	Amount	Shares	Amount
Balance, December 30, 1979	183,871	$183.9	$127.4	235	$ .9
Employee compensation and stock option plans	648	.6	16.2	(1)	—
Acquisitions by pooling of interests	1,128	1.1	.7	—	—
Balance, December 28, 1980	185,647	185.6	144.3	234	.9
Employee compensation and stock option plans	1,161	1.2	33.0	1	.1
Acquisitions by pooling of interests	489	.5	.9	—	—
Balance, January 3, 1982	187,297	187.3	178.2	235	1.0
Employee compensation and stock option plans	1,893	1.9	55.2	(1)	—
Acquisitions by pooling of interests	171	.2	1.1	—	—
Balance, January 2, 1983	189,361	$189.4	$234.5	234	$1.0

* Reclassified to conform to 1982 presentation.

See Notes to Consolidated Financial Statements

Johnson & Johnson and Subsidiaries   **Consolidated Statement of Changes in Financial Position**

Dollars in Millions (Note 1)	1982	1981°	1980°
Funds from operations before extraordinary charge			
Earnings before extraordinary charge	**$523.4**	467.6	400.7
Expenses not requiring outlay of cash or marketable securities			
Depreciation and amortization	**176.2**	152.4	138.7
Other, principally other liabilities and deferrals	**68.5**	103.0	47.1
Total funds provided from operations before extraordinary charge	**768.1**	723.0	586.5
Extraordinary charge	**(50.0)**	—	—
Total funds provided from operations	**718.1**	723.0	586.5
Funds invested in operations			
Accounts receivable, trade	**52.2**	62.1	102.1
Inventories	**57.4**	51.3	103.3
Additions to property, plant and equipment	**470.2**	388.5	364.0
Additions to patents	**44.5**	6.4	2.0
Change in current payables and prepaid expenses	**2.3**	(29.4)	(74.4)
Other items	**28.2**	31.5	(18.9)
Total funds invested in operations	**654.8****	510.4°°	478.1
Net funds from operations	**63.3**	212.6	108.4
Dividends to stockholders	**(182.4)**	(158.6)	(136.9)
Net funds (used) provided	**(119.1)**	54.0	(28.5)
Funds provided by (used in) financing activities			
Loans and notes payable and long-term debt	**69.0**	50.0	71.2
Proceeds from the exercise of stock options	**35.4**	18.2	4.4
Other items	**(18.2)**	(4.7)	(.1)
Total funds provided by financing activities	**86.2**	63.5	75.5
(Decrease) increase in cash and marketable securities, including non-current	**(32.9)**	117.5	47.0
(Increase) decrease in marketable securities, non-current	**(28.6)**	(49.6)	.8
(Decrease) increase in cash and current marketable securities	**$(61.5)**	67.9	47.8

° Reclassified to conform to 1982 presentation
** Net of translation adjustments charged to the separate component of stockholders' equity of $77.8 million in 1982 and $85.7 million in 1981 relating primarily to inventories and property, plant and equipment (see Note 4)

See Notes to Consolidated Financial Statements

Johnson & Johnson and Subsidiaries   Notes to Consolidated Financial Statements

Note 1. Summary of Significant Accounting Policies

Principles of Consolidation

The consolidated statements include the accounts of Johnson & Johnson and subsidiaries. All significant intercompany accounts and transactions are eliminated.

Inventories

While cost is determined principally by the first-in, first-out (FIFO) method, the majority of domestic inventories are valued using the last-in, first-out (LIFO) method. Inventories are valued at the lower of cost or market.

Depreciation and Amortization

Charges to earnings for depreciation and amortization of property, plant and equipment are generally determined using an accelerated method over the estimated useful lives of domestic assets and the straight-line method over the estimated useful lives of international assets.

Income Taxes

Domestic investment tax credits and certain international tax incentives are deferred. The deferred amount is amortized over the estimated useful lives of the related assets.

The Company intends to continue to reinvest its undistributed international earnings to expand its international operations. Therefore no tax has been provided to cover the repatriation of such undistributed earnings. At January 2, 1983, the cumulative amount of undistributed international earnings for which the Company has not provided United States income taxes was approximately $445 million.

Earnings Per Share

Earnings per share are calculated using the average number of shares outstanding during each year. Shares issuable under stock option and compensation plans would not materially reduce earnings per share.

Annual Closing Date

The Company follows the concept of a fiscal year which ends on the Sunday nearest to the end of the calendar month of December. Normally each fiscal year consists of 52 weeks, but every five or six years, as was the case in 1981, the fiscal year consists of 53 weeks.

Note 2. Extraordinary Charge

As a result of the criminal tampering with TYLENOL Extra-Strength Capsules in the Chicago area during the third quarter of 1982, the Company withdrew all TYLENOL capsule products from the market. The withdrawal costs, including disposal, handling, couponing and other associated costs resulted in an extraordinary after-tax charge in 1982 of $50 million or $.27 per share.

Note 3. Income Taxes

Income tax expense before extraordinary charge consists of:

Year 1982 (Dollars in Millions)	U.S.	International	Total
Federal and international			
Currently payable	$ 57.2	177.7	234.9
Net tax effect—timing differences	(5.3)	12.0	6.7
Investment tax credits	14.1	—	14.1
Investment tax credits amortization	(8.9)	—	(8.9)
Domestic state and local	17.0	—	17.0
	$ 74.1	189.7	263.8
Effective tax rate	20.6%	44.4%	33.5%

Year 1981 (Dollars in Millions)	U.S.	International	Total
Federal and international			
Currently payable	$106.7	166.9	273.6
Net tax effect—timing differences	(9.2)	18.7	9.5
Investment tax credits	12.3	—	12.3
Investment tax credits amortization	(5.9)	—	(5.9)
Domestic state and local	26.8	—	26.8
	$130.7	185.6	316.3
Effective tax rate	33.3%	47.5%	40.3%

Year 1980 (Dollars in Millions)	U.S.	International	Total
Federal and international			
Currently payable	$ 77.7	167.0	244.7
Net tax effect—timing differences	(1.7)	9.9	8.2
Investment tax credits	8.2	—	8.2
Investment tax credits amortization	(5.1)	—	(5.1)
Domestic state and local	18.6	—	18.6
	$ 97.7	176.9	274.6
Effective tax rate	34.6%	45.0%	40.7%

Earnings before provision for taxes on income and before extraordinary charge were:

(Dollars in Millions)	U.S.	International	Total
Year 1982	$359.9	427.3	787.2
Year 1981	392.9	391.0	783.9
Year 1980	282.4	392.9	675.3

Note 3. Income Taxes (continued)

A comparison of the federal statutory rate of 46% to the Company's effective tax rate is as follows:

Percent of pre-tax income	1982	1981	1980
Statutory tax rate	46.0%	46.0%	46.0%
Puerto Rico operations	(6.8)	(5.7)	(4.9)
Research tax credits	(1.9)	(.7)	—
Difference in effective tax rate of international subsidiaries	(.9)	.7	(.6)
Domestic state and local income taxes	1.2	1.8	1.5
All other	(4.1)	(1.8)	(1.3)
Effective tax rate	33.5%	40.3%	40.7%

The Company has domestic subsidiaries operating in Puerto Rico under grants providing for tax relief expiring at various dates between 1985 and 1997. The estimated tax savings of these subsidiaries compared to the federal statutory rate was $53.3 million in 1982, $44.4 million in 1981 and $33.0 million in 1980. Beginning in 1983 the United States Tax Equity and Fiscal Responsibility Act modifies the computation of profits allocatable to subsidiaries in Puerto Rico. Management believes that the newly enacted legislation will not have a material adverse effect on its operations or financial position.

Note 4. Foreign Currency Translation

In 1981, the Company adopted FAS No. 52, Foreign Currency Translation, which replaced FAS No. 8. The financial statements for 1980 have not been restated for the change as the effect of FAS No. 52 in that year was immaterial. Under FAS No. 8, net earnings would have been reduced by $58.6 million or $.32 per share in 1981. Net currency transaction gains and losses included in net earnings were a gain of $4.6 million in 1982 and losses of $.7 million and $.1 million in 1981 and 1980.

Under FAS No. 52, balance sheet currency effects are recorded in a separate component of stockholders' equity. This equity account includes the results of translating all balance sheet assets and liabilities at current exchange rates except for those located in highly inflationary economies, principally Argentina, Brazil, Colombia and Mexico.

An analysis of the changes during 1982 and 1981 in the separate component of stockholders' equity for cumulative currency translation adjustments follows:

(Dollars in Millions)	1982	1981
Beginning of year	$ (85.7)	(5.0)
Translation adjustments	(76.8)	(78.6)
Income taxes allocated to translation adjustments	(1.0)	(2.1)
End of year	$(163.5)	(85.7)

Translation adjustments relate primarily to inventories and property, plant and equipment and do not exist in terms of functional currency cash flows. FAS No. 52 provides that these translation adjustments should not be reported as part of operating results since realization is remote unless such international businesses were sold or liquidated.

Note 5. International Subsidiaries

The following amounts are included in the consolidated financial statements for international subsidiaries:

(Dollars in Millions)	1982	1981
Current assets	$964.0	981.4
Current liabilities	519.5	513.6
Net property, plant and equipment	698.8	626.2
Parent company equity in net assets	916.9	844.8
Excess of parent company equity over investments	735.5	687.9

International sales to customers were $2,456.9, $2,373.1 and $2,203.8 million for 1982, 1981 and 1980, respectively. After elimination of minority interests, international net earnings for the same years were $237.6, $205.4 and $216.1 million, respectively.

Note 6. Inventories

At the end of 1982 and 1981, inventories comprised:

(Dollars in Millions)	1982	1981
Raw materials and supplies	$301.8	304.1
Goods in process	223.2	204.7
Finished goods	432.5	391.3
	$957.5	900.1

If all inventories were valued on the FIFO basis, total inventories would have been $1,098.0 million and $1,023.8 million at January 2, 1983 and January 3, 1982, respectively.

Note 7. Borrowings

Loans and notes payable generally result from bank borrowings of international subsidiaries. Aggregate maturities of long-term debt obligations for each of the next five years are $17.8, $13.3, $13.6, $34.2 and $10.7 million. The interest rates on long-term debt obligations vary from 5%–58% according to local conditions. The Company has access to sources of funds at numerous banks worldwide. While the total amount of credit available is not readily quantifiable, international subsidiaries' unused lines of credit approximate $250 million. Total credit available is deemed sufficient to meet the needs of the Company.

Note 8. Rental Expense and Lease Commitments

Rentals of space, vehicles and office and data processing equipment under operating leases amounted to approximately $122.9 million in 1982, $100.7 million in 1981 and $88.0 million in 1980. The approximate minimum rental payments required under operating leases that have initial or remaining noncancellable lease terms in excess of one year at January 2, 1983 are:

(Dollars in Millions)

1983	1984	1985	1986	1987	After 1987	Total
$40.7	37.4	28.2	16.7	9.6	46.5	179.1

Commitments under capital leases are not significant.

Note 9. Stock Option and Stock Compensation Plans

The Company has stock option plans which provide for the granting of options to certain officers and employees to purchase shares of its common stock within prescribed periods at prices equal to the fair market value on the date of grant. Activity during 1982 and 1981 under the Company's stock option plans is summarized below in shares:

(Shares in Thousands)	1982	1981
Held at beginning of year by 3,091 employees (1981—2,826)	14,158	11,367
Granted to 543 employees (1981—1,704)	948	3,992
	15,106	15,359
Exercised (1980—225)	(1,427)	(739)
Cancelled or expired	(668)	(462)
Held at end of year by 3,003 employees (1981—3,091)	13,011	14,158

The price range per share of options exercised during 1982, including those assumed through acquisitions, was $3.75 to $30.29 (1981—$3.75 to $32.08, 1980—$3.75 to $29.27). The price range per share of options held at the end of the year was $16.95 to $48.88 (1981—$3.75 to $44.27). The number of shares (in thousands) exercisable at the end of each year were: 1982—4,278; 1981—4,069; 1980—3,481. Shares available for future grants at the end of each year were: 1982—7,344; 1981—7,966; 1980—8,921.

At year-end, the Company was obligated to deliver, over a period of not more than two years, 455 thousand shares of common stock (1981—431) in performance of outstanding stock compensation agreements with 5,596 employees (1981—5,205).

Note 10. Retirement and Pension Plans

The Company has various retirement and pension plans which cover substantially all employees of its domestic operations. Most international subsidiaries also have retirement plans. Pension expense is primarily determined by the aggregate level funding method which allocates costs related to both prior and future service on a level basis over the remaining future service lives of plan members.

In general, the amounts are paid into trusts and approximate annual pension expense. Total pension expense related to these plans amounted to $64.5 million in 1982, $74.8 million in 1981 and $55.8 million in 1980. For certain domestic plans, the weighted average assumed rate of return on investment used in determining funding requirements was changed in 1981 and 1980. The assumed rate of return for 1982 was 7.5% while ranges of rates for the previous two years were: 1981, 7.0–7.5%; 1980, 6.0–6.5%. The effect of these changes resulted in no reduction in the 1982 expense; however, the 1981 expense was reduced by $7.5 million. Domestic amendments which resulted in improved benefits increased pension expense for 1982 and 1981 by $1.3 million and $8.3 million. International pension expense increased significantly by $13.2 million in 1981, primarily due to revisions to a number of plans.

A comparison of accumulated plan benefits and plan net assets for the Company's domestic defined benefit pension plans is presented below:

Actuarial present value of accumulated plan benefits

(Dollars in Millions)	January 1, 1982	January 1, 1981
Vested	$249.1	217.7
Nonvested	24.3	20.2
Total	$273.4	237.9
Net assets available for benefits	$364.2	333.6

The Company's objective in funding its pension plans is to accumulate funds sufficient to provide for all accrued pension benefits and to maintain a relatively stable contribution level in the future. The excess of assets over the present value of accumulated benefits is not the result of the plans being funded on an overly conservative basis. Rather, company contributions are based on a projected benefit actuarial cost method which recognizes future benefit increases expected to result from future increases in members' salaries. In accordance with FAS No. 35, the present value of accumulated benefits does not reflect these future increases. The weighted average assumed rate of return used in determining the actuarial present value of accumulated plan benefits was 7.5% for 1982 and 1981.

International subsidiaries are not required to determine the actuarial value of accumulated benefits or net assets available for benefits as calculated and disclosed above. Accordingly, such information is not readily available. As of the latest valuation date for those plans, the value of vested benefits was fully funded.

Effective June 1, 1982, the Company established a voluntary savings plan for eligible domestic employees. The plan is designed to enhance the existing retirement program of eligible employees and to assist them in strengthening their financial security by providing an incentive to save and invest regularly. Company contributions to the savings plan in 1982 amounted to $6.0 million.

Note 11. Certificates of Extra Compensation

The Company has a deferred compensation program for senior management and other key personnel. The value of units awarded under the program is related to the asset value and historical earning power of the Company's common stock. Amounts earned under the program are payable only after employment with the Company has ended.

Note 12. Pending Legal Proceedings

The Company is involved in numerous product liability cases in the United States, a majority of which concern contraceptive products. The Company cannot predict what liability may be imposed on it in connection with such suits. It believes the liability, if any, resulting from such suits will be substantially covered by insurance and that any uninsured liability resulting from such cases will not have a material adverse effect on its operations or financial position.

In July, 1981, a jury in the Minneapolis Federal District Court decided in favor of three individuals who brought an action against the Company in connection with the acquisition of their business, Stimulation Technology, Inc., in 1974. Judgment was filed against the Company in the amount of approximately $170 million. The Company is currently appealing the judgment and believes it will be overturned.

In October, 1982, the Company announced an extraordinary before tax charge of $100 million in connection with the withdrawal of TYLENOL capsule products following the criminal tampering with Extra-Strength TYLENOL Capsules. The Company's McNeil subsidiary responsible for the manufacture of TYLENOL products has filed an action in Federal District Court in Newark, New Jersey against several insurance companies claiming coverage under various excess and umbrella liability policies for approximately $80 million of its withdrawal expenses, and claiming maximum coverage under a $50 million all-risk policy for lost profits resulting from interruption of McNeil's business. It is not possible to predict what amount, if any, McNeil will recover in such action.

Representatives of the estates of four of the seven victims of the criminal tampering have brought wrongful death actions against the Company and McNeil. The Company believes that such actions will not result in liability. Also, a class action against the Company and McNeil has been filed in state court in Chicago seeking a refund on behalf of consumers who had TYLENOL products in their possession when the criminal tampering occurred. The Company believes that such action will not result in liability.

In addition, the Company is involved in a number of patent, trademark, private antitrust and other law suits incidental to its business. The Company believes that such proceedings in the aggregate will not have a material adverse effect on its operations or financial position.

Note 13. Segments of Business and Geographic Areas

See pages 46 and 47 for information on segments of business and geographic areas.

Note 14. Selected Quarterly Financial Data (Unaudited)

Selected unaudited quarterly financial data for the years 1982 and 1981 were:

(Dollars in Millions Except Per Share Figures)

Year 1982	1st Quarter	2nd Quarter	3rd Quarter	4th Quarter	Total Year
Sales to customers	$1,451.9	1,450.4	1,476.8	1,381.8	5,760.9
Gross margin	857.9	849.2	857.6	745.3	3,310.0
Earnings before provision for taxes on income and extraordinary charge	260.6	232.4	225.7	68.5	787.2
Earnings before extraordinary charge					
—domestic	89.4	80.2	82.5	33.7	285.8
—international	66.3	61.6	64.0	45.7	237.6
—worldwide	155.7	141.8	146.5	79.4	523.4
Extraordinary charge (net of taxes)	—	—	(50.0)	—	(50.0)
Net earnings—worldwide	$ 155.7	141.8	96.5	79.4	473.4
Per share of common stock					
Earnings before extraordinary charge	$ .83	.76	.78	.42	2.79
Extraordinary charge	—	—	(.27)	—	(.27)
Net earnings per share	$ .83	.76	.51	.42	2.52

Year 1981	1st Quarter	2nd Quarter	3rd Quarter	4th Quarter	Total Year
Sales to customers	$1,336.0	1,334.2	1,338.0	1,390.8	5,399.0
Gross margin*	742.0	758.4	762.8	767.4	3,030.6
Earnings before provision for taxes on income	208.1	214.8	219.5	141.5	783.9
Net earnings—domestic	$ 62.5	66.6	73.6	59.5	262.2
Net earnings—international	58.8	61.1	56.3	29.2	205.4
Net earnings—worldwide	$ 121.3	127.7	129.9	88.7	467.6
Net earnings per share	$ .65	.69	.69	.48	2.51

*The 1981 gross margin has been restated to conform with the 1982 presentation.

Report of Certified Public Accountants

To the Stockholders and Board of Directors of Johnson & Johnson:

We have examined the consolidated balance sheet of Johnson & Johnson and subsidiaries as of January 2, 1983 and January 3, 1982, and the related consolidated statements of earnings and retained earnings, common stock, additional capital and treasury stock, and changes in financial position for each of the three years in the period ended January 2, 1983. Our examinations were made in accordance with generally accepted auditing standards and, accordingly, included such tests of the accounting records and such other auditing procedures as we considered necessary in the circumstances.

In our opinion, the financial statements referred to above present fairly the financial position of Johnson & Johnson and subsidiaries at January 2, 1983 and January 3, 1982, and the results of their operations and the changes in their financial position for each of the three years in the period ended January 2, 1983, in conformity with generally accepted accounting principles applied on a consistent basis, after giving effect to the adoption in 1981, with which we concur, of FAS No. 52, Foreign Currency Translation, as described in Note 4. The financial statements for 1980 have not been restated because the effect of the change is not material.

New York, New York
February 16, 1983   Coopers & Lybrand

Common Stock
Listed New York
Stock Exchange
Stock Symbol JNJ

Transfer Agent
Morgan Guaranty Trust
Company of New York
30 West Broadway,
New York,
New York 10015

Registrar
Morgan Guaranty Trust
Company of New York
30 West Broadway,
New York,
New York 10015

Segments of Business

(Dollars in Millions)	1982	1981	1980	1979	1978
Sales to customers (2)					
Consumer—Domestic	**$1,304.3**	1,238.1	1,133.9	1,004.4	874.6
International	**1,172.7**	1,124.7	990.8	823.0	677.3
Total	**2,477.0**	2,362.8	2,124.7	1,827.4	1,551.9
Professional—Domestic	**1,311.2**	1,127.6	953.6	861.4	639.2
International	**620.3**	606.8	586.9	486.1	385.8
Total	**1,931.5**	1,734.4	1,540.5	1,347.5	1,025.0
Pharmaceutical—Domestic	**598.5**	511.2	392.2	309.1	279.9
International	**520.1**	496.9	476.6	393.1	328.4
Total	**1,118.6**	1,008.1	868.8	702.2	608.3
Industrial—Domestic	**90.0**	149.0	153.9	197.2	197.6
International	**143.8**	144.7	149.5	137.3	114.5
Total	**233.8**	293.7	303.4	334.5	312.1
Worldwide total	**$5,760.9**	5,399.0	4,837.4	4,211.6	3,497.3
Operating profit (3)					
Consumer	**$ 362.4**	338.4	263.7	241.3	176.6
Professional	**152.6**	177.9	191.5	177.0	184.1
Pharmaceutical	**314.7**	288.5	228.2	183.2	148.5
Industrial	**23.9**	32.9	29.5	32.3	37.1
Segments total	**853.6**	837.7	712.9	633.8	546.3
Expense not allocated to segments (4)	**(66.4)**	(53.8)	(37.6)	(42.1)	(32.1)
Earnings before taxes on income (3)	**$ 787.2**	783.9	675.3	591.7	514.2
Identifiable assets at year-end					
Consumer	**$1,371.7**	1,308.5	1,157.6	989.6	876.5
Professional	**1,490.7**	1,274.3	1,121.1	986.3	715.3
Pharmaceutical	**911.1**	815.9	702.0	549.0	495.4
Industrial	**234.4**	281.1	277.5	285.5	261.5
Segments total	**4,007.9**	3,679.8	3,258.2	2,810.4	2,348.7
General corporate	**201.7**	140.6	84.3	63.6	33.7
Worldwide total	**$4,209.6**	3,820.4	3,342.5	2,874.0	2,382.4
Additions to property, plant and equipment					
Consumer	**$ 158.2**	137.0	127.6	114.8	94.1
Professional	**131.3**	108.9	77.2	63.0	49.4
Pharmaceutical	**94.5**	71.1	77.9	52.3	34.9
Industrial	**33.9**	31.0	44.5	31.3	38.0
Segments total	**417.9**	348.0	327.2	261.4	216.4
General corporate	**52.3**	40.5	36.8	11.9	12.1
Worldwide total	**$ 470.2**	388.5	364.0	273.3	228.5
Depreciation and amortization					
Consumer	**$ 67.1**	59.0	57.0	51.1	43.1
Professional	**55.6**	43.0	36.9	33.5	26.7
Pharmaceutical	**26.4**	24.9	22.6	15.4	15.2
Industrial	**22.4**	20.4	18.3	18.9	16.1
Segments total	**171.5**	147.3	134.8	118.9	101.1
General corporate	**4.7**	5.1	3.9	2.3	2.0
Worldwide total	**$ 176.2**	152.4	138.7	121.2	103.1

Geographic Areas

(Dollars in Millions)	1982	1981	1980	1979	1978
Sales to customers (2)					
United States	$3,304.0	3,025.9	2,633.6	2,372.1	1,991.3
Europe	1,182.2	1,153.8	1,201.9	1,023.9	817.0
Western Hemisphere excluding U.S.A.	816.2	790.3	641.3	525.0	421.6
Africa, Asia and Pacific	458.5	429.0	360.6	290.6	267.4
Worldwide total	$5,760.9	5,399.0	4,837.4	4,211.6	3,497.3
Operating profit (3)					
United States	$ 407.3	432.0	316.3	305.8	261.0
Europe	258.9	221.7	250.6	217.6	189.4
Western Hemisphere excluding U.S.A.	131.4	125.6	95.5	77.5	55.9
Africa, Asia and Pacific	56.0	58.4	50.5	32.9	40.0
Segments total	853.6	837.7	712.9	633.8	546.3
Expense not allocated to segments (4)	(66.4)	(53.8)	(37.6)	(42.1)	(32.1)
Earnings before taxes on income (3)	$ 787.2	783.9	675.3	591.7	514.2
Identifiable assets at year-end					
United States	$2,298.1	2,044.6	1,733.2	1,557.6	1,276.7
Europe	819.8	803.5	831.8	717.5	587.8
Western Hemisphere excluding U.S.A.	578.3	533.5	420.1	324.7	279.0
Africa, Asia and Pacific	311.7	298.2	273.1	210.6	205.2
Segments total	4,007.9	3,679.8	3,258.2	2,810.4	2,348.7
General corporate	201.7	140.6	84.3	63.6	33.7
Worldwide total	$4,209.6	3,820.4	3,342.5	2,874.0	2,382.4

(1) See Management's Discussion and Analysis, pages 30 and 31, for a description of the segments in which the Company does business.
(2) Export sales and intersegment sales are not significant. No single customer represents 10% or more of total sales.
(3) Excludes in 1982 an extraordinary charge of $100 million associated with the withdrawal of TYLENOL capsules.
(4) Expense not allocated to segments includes interest expense, minority interests and general corporate income and expense.
(5) In 1981, the Company adopted FAS No. 52, Foreign Currency Translation. FAS No. 8 would have lowered segment operating profit in 1981 as follows: Consumer—$12.4 million, Professional—$21.3 million, Pharmaceutical—$17.1 million and Industrial—$5.7 million.

Supplementary Information on the Effects of Changing Prices

Introduction

Financial Accounting Standard (FAS) No. 33 as amended by FAS No. 70 requires the disclosure of supplementary income calculations based on two methods of accounting: constant dollar accounting, which adjusts inventory and property, plant and equipment for general inflation using the U.S. Consumer Price Index for all Urban Consumers, and current cost accounting, which adjusts for specific price changes of inventories and property, plant and equipment.

FAS No. 70, however, exempts the presentation of the constant dollar method when a significant part of a company's operations is measured in functional currencies other than the U.S. dollar. Since this is the case for the Company, constant dollar data has been omitted.

The current cost information which is presented has been calculated by the translate-restate option available under FAS No. 70, which requires the translation of the foreign currency data in accordance with FAS No. 52 and restatement of the current cost data based on the U.S. Consumer Price Index for all Urban Consumers.

This method is essentially the same as the original requirements of FAS No. 33 concerning the disclosure of the current cost information, except that the translation adjustment is now disclosed as a separate item in the Five Year Selected Financial Data Adjusted for Changing Prices. Such disclosure is a result of the adoption of FAS No. 52 which requires that translation adjustments be recorded as a separate component of stockholders' equity rather than in the determination of income from continuing operations.

Summary Results

The adjustments to cost of products sold for current costs are not significant because of frequent inventory turnover, use of LIFO inventory valuation and current exchange rates that reflect a strong U.S. dollar, all of which reduce the effects of inflation on reported earnings. The accelerated methods of depreciation used in the primary financial statements partially allow for expected price changes. For this reason, the current cost adjustment was computed using the straight-line method. This difference in method has the effect of reducing the amount of the adjustment. Also, FAS No. 33 specifically prohibits the restatement of income tax expense, thus illustrating that effective tax rates increase as inflation erodes earnings.

The Five Year Selected Financial Data Adjusted for Changing Prices presents current cost information adjusted to average 1982 dollars to make the years comparable.

This supplementary data on changing prices is informative but requires prudent analysis before conclusions can be reached. The current cost information gives an approximation of the amount of distributable income available for dividends and reinvestment after maintenance of existing capacity.

Management also believes that the current cost method is not a good predictor of future cash flows. Johnson & Johnson is a growth-oriented company and future cash flows are substantially affected by management's strategy in pursuing new markets, further developing technology and increasing productivity. Future cash flows, therefore, cannot be properly assessed solely by evaluating existing assets.

Statement of Earnings Adjusted for Changing Prices

For the Year Ended January 2, 1983 In Average 1982 Dollars (Dollars in Millions)	As Reported in the Primary Statements	Adjusted for Specific Costs (Current Costs)	Amount Increase (Decrease)
Sales to customers and other revenues	$5,899	5,899	—
Cost of products sold (excluding depreciation)	2,332	2,365	33
Depreciation and amortization	176	223	47
Other operating expenses (excluding depreciation)	2,604	2,604	—
Provision for taxes on income	264	264	—
Earnings before extraordinary charge	$ 523	443	(80)

Five Year Selected Financial Data Adjusted for Changing Prices

Current Cost Data in Average 1982 Dollars (Dollars in Millions Except Per Share Figures)	1982	1981	1980	1979	1978
Sales and other revenues—as reported	$5,899	5,506	4,914	4,278	3,543
—in average 1982 dollars	5,899	5,842	5,756	5,687	5,240
Earnings before extraordinary charge—as reported	523	468	401	352	299
—in current costs	443	393	377	384	
Earnings per share before					
extraordinary charge—as reported	2.79	2.51	2.17	1.92	1.67
—in current costs	2.36	2.11	2.04	2.09	
Dividends per share—as reported	.97	.85	.74	.67	.57
—in average 1982 dollars	.97	.90	.87	.89	.84
Net assets at year-end—as reported	2,800	2,528	2,269	1,987	1,701
—in current costs	3,572	3,404	3,449	3,449	
Translation adjustment—in current costs	(187)	(213)			
(Loss) from decline in general purchasing power of net monetary assets held	(12)	(30)	(47)	(57)	
Current cost increases of inventories and net property, plant and equipment greater (less) than the increase in general price level (CPI)	98	(64)	(144)	(99)	
Market price per share					
at year-end—as reported	49.63	37.13	33.38	26.63	24.63
—in average 1982 dollars	49.08	38.13	37.27	33.47	35.02
Average consumer price index (1967 = 100)	289.1	272.4	246.8	217.4	195.4
Annual percent increase in average CPI	6.1	10.4	13.5	11.3	7.7

(1) The current cost of net property, plant and equipment at the end of 1982 was $2,237 million and was established based on several methods, including indexing and unit pricing. Potential technological improvements and efficiencies which might be associated with actual replacement of assets have not been reflected.
(2) At the end of 1982, the current cost of inventories was $1,110 million estimated on the FIFO or actual cost method.
(3) Cost of goods sold for current costs approximates a LIFO basis.
(4) Depreciation and amortization was computed using the straight-line method. In the primary financial statements, accelerated methods are generally used for domestic assets and the straight-line method for international assets.
(5) Unreported 1978 data not required by FAS No. 33 as it would be impractical to provide on a retrospective basis.
(6) The current cost data for years prior to 1981 have not been restated for FAS No. 70.
(7) The increase in the general price level of inventories and net property, plant and equipment for 1982 was $115 million. The effect of increases in current costs for those assets was $213 million.
(8) 1980–1978 market price per common share data is adjusted for the 1981 three-for-one stock split.

Ten Year Summary of Operations and Statistical Data

(Dollars in Millions Except Per Share Figures)	1982	1981
Earnings data		
Sales to customers		
Domestic	$3,304.0	3,025.9
International	2,456.9	2,373.1
Total sales	5,760.9	5,399.0
Interest income	88.9	78.8
Royalties and miscellaneous	49.3	28.6
Total revenues	5,899.1	5,506.4
Cost of products sold (1)	2,450.9	2,368.4
Selling, distribution and administrative expenses	2,248.8	2,030.6
Research expense (1)	363.2	282.9
Interest expense	74.4	60.7
Interest expense capitalized	(46.3)	(43.5)
Other expenses	20.9	23.4
Total costs and expenses	5,111.9	4,722.5
Earnings before provision for taxes on income (2)	787.2	783.9
Provision for taxes on income	263.8	316.3
Earnings before extraordinary charge	$ 523.4	467.6
Percent of sales to customers (2)	9.1	8.7
Domestic earnings (2)	$ 285.8	262.2
International earnings	$ 237.6	205.4
Per share of common stock (2) (3)	$ 2.79	2.51
Percent return on average stockholders' equity (2)	19.6	19.5
Percent increase over previous year		
Sales to customers	6.7	11.6
Earnings per share (2)	11.2	15.7
Supplementary expense data		
Cost of materials and services	$3,078.1	2,843.4
Total employment costs	1,821.7	1,693.6
Depreciation and amortization	° 176.2	152.4
Maintenance and repairs (4)	123.6	126.2
Total tax expense (5)	436.3	477.0
Total tax expense per share (3) (5)	2.32	2.56
Supplementary balance sheet data		
Property, plant and equipment—net investment	$1,577.9	1,335.6
Additions to property, plant and equipment	470.2	388.5
Total assets	4,209.6	3,820.4
Long-term debt	142.2	91.7
Common stock information		
Dividends paid per share (3)	$ .97	.85
Stockholders' equity per share (3)	$ 14.80	13.51
Average shares outstanding (millions) (3)	188.0	186.4
Stockholders of record (thousands)	43.0	38.2
Employees (thousands)	79.7	77.1

(1) Reclassified to conform to 1982 presentation.
(2) Excludes in 1982 an extraordinary charge of $100 million ($50 million after taxes or $.27 per share) associated with the withdrawal of TYLENOL capsules.
(3) After giving effect for the 1981 three-for-one common stock split.

1980	1979	1978	1977	1976	1975	1974	1973
2,633.6	2,372.1	1,991.3	1,713.6	1,493.2	1,268.0	1,138.1	975.7
2,203.8	1,839.5	1,506.0	1,200.5	1,029.3	956.7	799.1	636.1
4,837.4	4,211.6	3,497.3	2,914.1	2,522.5	2,224.7	1,937.2	1,611.8
50.0	43.3	28.7	18.9	19.3	11.8	14.8	15.2
26.4	23.1	17.2	16.8	16.7	15.6	15.9	13.6
4,913.8	4,278.0	3,543.2	2,949.8	2,558.5	2,252.1	1,967.9	1,640.6
2,194.3	1,950.2	1,580.3	1,368.0	1,222.9	1,071.7	960.8	758.4
1,794.2	1,505.3	1,258.9	1,002.3	847.9	746.6	626.1	515.0
232.8	192.7	163.6	131.8	112.5	97.8	83.6	70.9
37.0	21.9	13.5	8.5	6.3	8.8	7.7	5.4
(32.7)	—	—	—	—	—	—	—
12.9	16.2	12.7	7.0	7.4	8.4	2.3	2.8
4,238.5	3,686.3	3,029.0	2,517.6	2,197.0	1,933.3	1,680.5	1,352.5
675.3	591.7	514.2	432.2	361.5	318.8	287.4	288.1
274.6	239.6	215.1	184.9	156.1	135.0	125.8	139.7
400.7	352.1	299.1	247.3	205.4	183.8	161.6 (6)	148.4
8.3	8.4	8.6	8.5	8.1	8.3	8.3	9.2
184.6	172.4	144.4	129.3	107.5	90.5	80.1 (6)	80.3
216.1	179.7	154.7	118.0	97.9	93.3	81.5	68.1
2.17	1.92	1.67	1.41	1.18	1.06	.93	.86
18.8	19.1	18.8	17.8	16.7	17.1	17.3	18.5
14.9	20.4	20.0	15.5	13.4	14.8	20.2	22.3
12.8	15.2	18.2	19.8	11.0	13.6	8.1	20.5
2,532.4	2,200.1	1,803.0	1,494.5	1,294.4	1,151.0	989.7	790.6
1,535.2	1,337.4	1,101.6	892.0	785.1	682.9	603.4	491.4
138.7	121.2	103.1	86.5	77.5	68.6	59.9	49.0
116.1	118.2	102.0	89.1	74.8	61.9	55.5	44.8
425.3	373.2	323.0	274.9	231.1	203.7	183.4	184.9
2.30	2.04	1.80	1.57	1.32	1.17	1.06	1.07
1,161.9	947.8	788.2	652.4	568.5	528.3	467.0	365.1
364.0	273.3	228.5	171.7	119.2	136.0	157.6	102.5
3,342.5	2,874.0	2,382.4	2,019.8	1,730.7	1,537.1	1,393.6	1,189.1
70.1	69.5	52.1	37.1	26.7	39.4	43.9	40.6
.74	.67	.57	.47	.35	.28	.24	.18
12.24	10.82	9.47	8.43	7.45	6.61	5.76	5.03
184.8	183.3	179.4	175.2	174.6	173.7	173.1	172.2
35.6	35.6	31.9	31.2	31.1	31.0	29.7	29.5
74.3	71.8	67.0	60.5	57.9	53.8	54.3	49.1

(4) Also included in cost of materials and services category.
(5) Includes taxes on income, payroll, property and other business taxes. Excludes in 1982 tax
  benefit of $50 million ($.27 per share) on the extraordinary charge.
(6) After giving effect for the adoption of LIFO in 1974.

Index

A

AAA, 15
Accelerated depreciation, 408
Accounting
    accrual basis, 66, 102, 687, 699
    defined, 3
    entity, 6
    environment, 4
    income, 834
    information processing cycle, 102, 109, 116, 197
    information processing system, 68
    model, 96, 100, 101, 109
    objectives, 3
    practices and procedures, 66
    principles, 65
    process, 97
Accounting Principles Board (APB), 14
Accounting Research Bulletins (ARBs), 14
Accounting Review, The, 15
Accounting Series Releases (ASR), 15
Accounts payable, 454
Accounts receivable, see also Receivable
    aging, 270
    defined, 19, 53
    factoring, 360
Accrual basis
    accounting, 66, 102, 687, 699
    modified, 836
Accrued, 157
Adjusted trial balance, 199
Adjusting entries
    defined, 154
    recording, 167
Aging accounts receivable, 270
AICPA, 14
All-resources concept (SCFP), 692
Allowance for doubtful accounts, 53
American Accounting Association (AAA), 15
American Institute of Certified Public Accountants (AICPA), 14
Amortization
    bond premium and discount, 518, 520, 527
    defined, 402, 421
    expense, 403

Analysis

Analysis
    financial statement, 753
    proportional, 62
Annuity, 459, 467
APB, 14
APB Opinions, 14
ARBs, 14
Articulation, 149
ASR, 15
Assets
    additions to, 419
    capital, 830
    current, 53
    defined, 22, 65
    fixed, 55, 404
    intangible, 22, 56
    liquid, 342
    noncurrent, 54
    operational, 55, 396
        disposal of, 425
        intangible, 397, 420
        tangible, 397, 404
    other, 56
    tangible, 22
    trading in, 430
Assumptions
    continuity, 64, 405
    separate-entity, 6, 64
    time-period, 64, 150
    unit-of-measure, 5, 64, 783
Audit function, 11
Audit trail, 111, 114
Auditor's opinion (Auditor's Report), 12
    opinion paragraph, 71
    qualified, 72
    scope paragraph, 71
Average age of trade receivables, 762
Average days' supply in inventory, 763

B

Bad debts
    aging accounts receivable, 270
    allowance method, 239
    measuring, 239
    writing off, 241
Balance sheet, 70, 149
    account format, 53
    accounting model, 21, 53
    accounts, 203

Balance sheet—Cont.
    captions, 21
    heading, 21
    purpose, 21
    report format, 53
Bank reconciliation, 347
Bank service charges, 345
Bank statement, 345
Base amount, 62, 754
Basket purchases (of assets), 399
Beginning inventory, 243; see also Inventory
Benefit-cost analysis, 17
Board of directors, 6, 549
Bond
    certificate, 510
    discount, 513, 515, 518, 613
    indenture, 510
    interest rates, 513
    investments, 609
    par value, 510
    premium, 513, 519, 616
    purchased between interest dates, 618
    sinking funds, 524
    sold between interest dates, 521
Bonds payable, 508
Book of final entry, 114; see also Ledger
Book of original entry, 111; see also Journal
Book value, 55, 163, 403, 548, 642, 644, 645, 646, 648, 765; see also Carrying value
Book value per share, 765
Bookkeeping, 67
Boot, 430
Breakeven, 20

C

Callable bonds, 511
Capital expenditures, 417
Capital stock, 549
    reporting, 555
    types, 551
Capitalization of interest, 399
Capitalization rate, 765
Capitalizing earnings, 565
Carrying value, 55; see also Book value
Cash
    accounts in ledger, 346

This book has been set Video Comp, in 10 and 9 point Compano, leaded 2 points. Chapter numbers are 36 pt. Compano semibold and Chapter titles are 18 pt. Compano semibold. The size of the type page is 38 by 48 picas.